WEST ACADEMIC PUBLISHING'S LAW SCHOOL ADVISORY BOARD

PRINCIPLES OF CONSTITUTIONAL STRUCTURE

Dan T. Coenen
University Professor, Josiah Meigs Distinguished Teaching Professor & Harmon W. Caldwell Chair in Constitutional Law, University of Georgia School of Law

Michael Coenen
Professor of Law, Seton Hall University School of Law

CONCISE HORNBOOK SERIES™

WEST ACADEMIC PUBLISHING

444 Cedar Street, Suite 700
St. Paul, MN 55101
1-877-888-1330

Printed in the United States of America

ISBN: 978-1-64708-296-3

For Sally, Amy, and Claire, with love, thanks, and deep admiration—DTC

For Anna (with gratitude for your patience and support), Alice (with admiration for your joie de vivre), and Lola (with excitement for the years to come)—MC

Preface

The origins of this book lie in an earlier work, *Constitutional Law: The Commerce Clause* (Foundation Press Turning Point Series; 2004), that one of us authored nearly two decades ago. A starting-point goal of this project has been to update that book's treatment of Commerce Clause law in light of the many significant rulings on that subject issued by the Supreme Court in the intervening years. The much more important objective, however, has been to produce a book with a far broader reach—that is, a work that deals in an across-the-board way with federalism, the separation of powers, and related matters of "constitutional structure."

Our book takes a two-track approach to addressing this subject. First, its text provides an overview of the most relevant constitutional provisions and Supreme Court case law—a treatment designed to be general, but also non-superficial, in laying out key doctrinal principles. Second, for the reader who wants to dig deeper, the footnotes provide more specialized information, often by citing lower-court rulings or secondary materials that address more nuanced, yet invariably important and oftentimes contested, features of the law. Within this single volume, we cannot offer anything approaching a comprehensive treatment of every topic we discuss. But many of the works we cite will, if consulted, lead the reader to other materials that provide much more elaborate treatments of matters we only touch on here.

Fellow travelers in the legal academy offered valuable feedback on drafts of various portions of the book, and these friends and colleagues have our enduring thanks. This group includes Diane Amann, Kent Barnett, Randy Beck, Anya Bernstein, Harlan Cohen, Jenny-Brooke Condon, Seth Davis, Brannon Denning, Jonathan Hafetz, Edward Hartnett, Paul Heald, Thomas Healy, Walter Hellerstein, Brian Kalt, Michael Klarman, Paul M. Kurtz, Brian Lea, Gerard Magliocca, Merritt McAlister, Ndjuoh MehChu, David Opderbeck, Lori Ringhand, Jon Romberg, David Shipley, Scott Sullivan, Justin Weinstein-Tull, and Michael Wells. We are especially grateful to these scholars for pointing out errors, omissions, oversimplifications, and the like in what we had previously written. For all problems that remain, we alone take responsibility, while encouraging readers to let us know of any slip-ups they encounter in the pages that follow.

Many outstanding students also provided us with help along the way. Especially significant in this regard has been the exceptional assistance offered by Gregory O'Connell, Zachary Lundgren, and Jacob Swanstrom of the University of Georgia Law School. Other students who have made significant contributions include Mark Bailey, Mary Frances Dennis, Wes Giglio, Graham Goldberg, Roby Jernigan, Christian Jones, Cameron Keen, Taylor Lear, Anna Malcolm, Sarah Nelson, Noah Nix, Jack Pease, Anne Reynolds, George Shepherd, David Stewart, Brianna Taylor, Antonio Vayas, Ellen Williams, and Miranda Bidinger Worthington. We are very thankful to each of these students as well as to T.J. Striepe, Stephen Wolfson, and other members of the UGA Law Library staff who offered various forms of support along the way. Finally, we express our gratitude to Michele Bassett, Louis Higgins, Laura Holle, Allison Larson, Greg Olson, Mac Soto, and others at West Academic for their careful and generous assistance in preparing this book for publication.

Our efforts in pursuing this project have impressed upon us the extraordinary complexity and fluidity of the body of doctrine with which this book engages. Our hope is that it proves helpful to students, lawyers, judges, and others who likewise find themselves working to comprehend more fully the principles of constitutional structure.

DTC and MC

January 2022

Summary of Contents

Table of Contents

PRINCIPLES OF CONSTITUTIONAL STRUCTURE

AN INTRODUCTION TO THE LAW OF CONSTITUTIONAL STRUCTURE

Analysis

A. THE FOCUS OF THIS BOOK

A key feature of the U.S. Constitution is its dispersal of governing authority across a multiplicity of governmental institutions. Broadly speaking, this allocation of power proceeds along two dimensions. First, the Constitution allocates power vertically by establishing a system of *federalism*, through which a centralized, national government shares sovereignty with the governments of the fifty states. Second, at the national level, the Constitution divides up governing authority horizontally by establishing a *separation of powers* across a federal legislative branch (made up of the House of Representatives and the Senate), a federal executive branch (overseen by the President), and a federal judicial branch (headed by the Supreme Court of the United States). The aim of this book is to examine in detail the body of federal constitutional rules that define, mediate, and give effect to these two fundamental power-sharing arrangements—a body of rules often referred to as the law of "constitutional structure."

Much of the material covered in the ensuing chapters is associated with introductory law-school courses that focus on U.S. constitutional doctrine. But the book also touches on material associated with such related fields as administrative law, federal-courts law, state-and-local taxation, federal Indian law, and foreign-affairs law, among other subjects. This is the case in part because constitutional law, due to its foundational nature, inevitably bears on every field of public law. But it is also the case because, in our view, one cannot fully grasp the structural aspects of the U.S. constitutional system without attending to materials that often receive little or no treatment in introductory constitutional-law courses.

At the same time, this book does not purport to offer a comprehensive overview of all aspects of U.S. constitutional law.

Most important, the chapters that follow give no serious attention to the Constitution's many safeguards of individual rights, including the First Amendment's guarantees of free speech and religious liberty, the substantive and procedural components of the Fifth and Fourteenth Amendments' Due Process Clauses, the anti-discrimination protections of the Equal Protection Clause, and other provisions of the federal-power-limiting Bill of Rights and the state-power-limiting Reconstruction Amendments. To be sure, one cannot altogether disaggregate the law of constitutional rights from the law of constitutional structure,[1] and the book for that reason does sometimes touch upon rights-based matters in the course of outlining broader structural principles.[2] At the same time, most questions related to the judicially enforceable *substance* of individual constitutional rights—what distinguishes "protected" from "unprotected" speech?, what rights qualify as "fundamental"?, what constitutes a "suspect classification" for equal-protection purposes?, etc.—do not in themselves engage with matters of constitutional structure, and the book accordingly does not address them in any meaningful way.

Four other points about the book's scope and approach merit mention at the outset. First, the primary objective of the book is to offer a *descriptive overview* rather than *normative assessment* of structural constitutional doctrine. In other words, we seek to set forth as clearly and accurately as we can an account of the operative rules, principles, and frameworks that apply within this area of law without delving deeply into questions about their legal soundness or overall desirability. This is not to say that evaluative questions lie entirely

---

1 For one thing, rights-based protections influence the overall structural arrangement in the straightforward sense that they impose limits on the powers of the governments against which they apply. In addition, the special role of the federal judiciary in enforcing individual rights has the effect of enhancing that branch's authority both vis-à-vis the other branches of the federal government and vis-à-vis the state governments. Perhaps most important, the Constitution's drafters and ratifiers saw the power-dividing government structure they established—particularly in its aspiration to ensure that no single person or group could amass excessive power—as designed at bottom to protect individual interests in autonomy and equality of treatment, *see, e.g.*, DAN T. COENEN, THE STORY OF THE FEDERALIST: HOW HAMILTON AND MADISON RECONCEIVED AMERICA 107–11, 173–74 (2007) (highlighting the centrality of this idea in the thinking of the Framers), and the Court has often adverted to this idea in defending its structurally-focused decisions, *see, e.g.*, Bond v. United States, 564 U.S. 211, 220–24 (2011).

2 One aspect of rights-related law that we do consider in detail has to do with the Enforcement Clauses of the Reconstruction Amendments, which empower Congress to "enforce" those amendments' guarantees "by appropriate legislation," *see* U.S. CONST. amend. XIII, § 2; *id.* amend. XIV, § 5; *id.* amend XV, § 2, thus rendering the breadth of federal legislative power at least somewhat dependent on the scope of the rights that those amendments confer. *See infra* Chapter 11 (discussing the Fourteenth and Fifteenth Amendment enforcement powers); *infra* Chapter 12 (discussing the Thirteenth Amendment enforcement power).

outside this book's purview; on occasion, we do highlight points of scholarly and judicial disagreement about matters of constitutional structure, and we also sometimes offer analytical observations of our own. In general, however, the discussion attends to the task of describing what the law is rather than advocating for what the law ought to be.

Second, the book's emphasis lies with the law as it stands *in the present* rather than as it stood *in the past*: What we offer, in other words, is more of a snapshot of modern-day governing principles than a chronological recounting of how those principles came to be. Here too, however, the distinction is not entirely clear-cut. For one thing, much of the law as it currently stands hinges on the meaning and application of cases decided long ago, and one therefore must (as we do here) grapple with key centuries-old precedents (*e.g.*, *Marbury v. Madison*, *McCulloch v. Maryland*, *Worcester v. Georgia*) in order to understand the doctrinal principles and debates of today. In addition, we sometimes discuss some now-overruled (or at least marginalized) precedents that, in our view, remain relevant because they provide important background context for understanding now-governing case law.[3] On the whole, however, we avoid discussions of history for its own sake, and to the extent we delve into no-longer-operative principles of constitutional structure, it is for the purpose of helping to facilitate comprehension of and facility with the law in its present-day form.

Third, the book trains most of its attention on *judicial decisions* about structural questions, particularly decisions rendered by the Supreme Court of the United States. That the federal judiciary enjoys a robust power of "judicial review" is itself an important, non-inevitable, and controversial aspect of the law of constitutional structure—one that, in effect, channels to a body of unelected and all-but-life-tenured officials the authority to undo the decisions of democratically elected officials—and a later chapter of the book explores that doctrine's structural implications in detail.[4] Outside that chapter, however, the existence and legitimacy of the federal judicial review power is largely taken as a given, and the book thus treats relevant judicial decisions about constitutional structure as setting forth, for better or for worse, the controlling rules of the road.

Finally, in attempting to explicate and synthesize the Supreme Court's (and other courts') decisions about constitutional structure,

---

3 For example, we trace in some detail several pre-New Deal Supreme Court decisions concerning congressional power under the Commerce Clause, because those decisions—though no longer "good law" in a formal sense—remain highly relevant to arguments, analogies, and points of caution that lawyers can and do rely upon when litigating modern-day commerce-power disputes. *See infra* Chapter 2.

4 *See infra* Chapter 34.

we develop an account of the underlying case law that is predominantly *internalist,* rather than *externalist,* in orientation—that is, an account that engages directly with the doctrinal concepts, principles, and arguments that judges have publicly invoked as opposed to the various non-legal forces (*e.g.*, politics, economics, ideology, human psychology, intra-court dynamics, etc.) that might actually have motivated (at least in part) the outcomes of their decisions.[5] This choice might strike some readers as naive, particularly with regard to areas of structural constitutional doctrine as to which: (a) the indeterminacy of the background legal materials leaves wide room for the exercise of interpretive discretion; and (b) the issues to be decided carry an obviously political, ideological, and/or economic salience. We should therefore emphasize at the outset that, in focusing on the internalist aspects of the law of constitutional structure, we do not mean to deny the significance of these externalist forces, much less to suggest that the Justices are somehow "above," and thus immune to, their influence.[6] Rather, the internalist focus of the book derives from the more practical proposition that a firm grasp of the law of constitutional structure on its own terms—whether or not helpful, for example, in predicting the outcome of discrete, politically-charged Supreme Court cases—is essential for anyone who seeks to "speak" the "language" of this body of law. Put differently, our treatment of this subject engages with judicial opinions on their own terms not because we believe that those opinions offer an invariably complete set of causal explanations for the decisions that the Court has reached. Rather, we do so because these opinions furnish a critical body of source material with which practicing lawyers must engage as they do their day-to-day work.

B. A BRIEF OUTLINE

We have organized this book into three parts, the first two of which generally address issues of vertical federalism and the third of which focuses specifically on the horizontal separation of powers. In particular, Part I of this book considers federalism-based limits on

---

[5] On the internalist/externalist distinction more generally, see H.L.A. HART, THE CONCEPT OF LAW 89–91 (3d ed. 2012).

[6] Indeed, familiarity with the internalist practices, conventions, and norms of constitutional reasoning may well provide aid in evaluating the overall strength of the justifications publicly given by the Justices for the results that they reach and thus, by extension, in gauging the extent to which those results are ones for which externalist forces predominated in motivating the underlying decision. *See, e.g.*, Michael J. Klarman, Bush v. Gore *Through the Lens of Constitutional History*, 89 CAL. L. REV. 1724, 1724–1748, 1727 (2001) (concluding, in part on the basis of a sustained doctrinal critique of the Court's decision in *Bush v. Gore*, 531 U.S. 98 (2000), which had the effect of resolving the 2000 presidential election in favor of the Republican nominee, George W. Bush, that the result of the case "can be explained only in terms of the conservative majority's partisan political preferences").

the powers of the national government (and of Congress in particular), Part II considers federalism-based limits on the powers of state governments (and other nonfederal entities), and Part III considers the internal allocations of authority across the federal government's three branches.

1. Part I: The Lawmaking Powers of the National Government

The lawmaking powers of the national government are primarily set forth in Article I, section 8 of the Constitution, though other provisions establish additional powers as well. Chapter 1 offers an introductory overview of this topic, highlighting two Marshall Court decisions—*McCulloch v. Maryland* and *Gibbons v. Ogden*—that lay the foundation for much of the Court's work in defining the scope of congressional authority. The next several chapters (Chapters 2 through 5) discuss Congress's highly consequential (and thus hotly contested) power to regulate "Commerce . . . among the several States," including by canvassing in detail limits that the modern Court has imposed on its exercise. Having surveyed the Commerce Clause, the discussion moves next to other sources of congressional authority. Chapter 6 considers the power-enhancing effects of Article I, section 8, clause 18's stipulation that Congress can "make all Laws which shall be necessary and proper for carrying into Execution" its own enumerated powers as well as other powers of the federal government. Chapters 7 and 8 address Congress's respective powers to raise federal revenue through taxation and to use that revenue to support federal spending programs. And Chapter 9 looks at Congress's power to regulate federal elections, while Chapter 10 deals with a hodgepodge of other Article I powers (including Congress's powers to regulate federal property, establish copyrights and patents, implement treaties, and legislate with respect to war and military affairs).

Our treatment of congressional power next turns to Congress's ability to enforce the rights-based guarantees of the Thirteenth, Fourteenth, and Fifteenth Amendments. More specifically, Chapters 11 and 12 grapple with the complex body of decisions delineating the scope of these powers, while Chapter 13 considers the extent to which various "external constraints" traditionally associated with the commerce power might also apply to Congress's exercise of the Reconstruction Amendment enforcement powers and other non-commerce-related powers as well. Chapter 14 concludes our treatment of federal legislative authority by considering the powers of each House of Congress to manage its own internal affairs.

2. Part II: Structural Constitutional Limits on the Powers of States and Other Nonfederal Entities

Part II shifts attention away from the federal government, focusing instead on structural rules that limit the ability of state governments to make and enforce their own laws in light of the value of national unification. Chapter 15 highlights several explicit constitutional limits on state authority (such as Article I, section 10's restrictions on the making of interstate compacts and state taxation of imports and exports), as well as limits on the states' ability to tax and regulate instrumentalities of the federal government itself. Chapters 16 through 21 then explore the consequential, complicated, and frequently litigated "dormant Commerce Clause" doctrine, which stems from the longstanding (though still-disputed) idea that the Constitution's express grant to Congress of the power to regulate interstate commerce carries with it an implied restriction on state-based measures that discriminate against or unduly interfere with cross-state commercial activities. Chapter 22 considers the extent to which similar state-power-limiting principles attach to Congress's powers to regulate "Commerce with foreign nations."

The remainder of this part moves beyond the regulation of commerce to consider additional structural matters related to the powers of state and other nonfederal entities. Chapter 23 directs attention to the protections that states must afford to nonresident visitors pursuant to the Privileges and Immunities Clause of Article IV. Chapter 24 then explores the Supremacy Clause-based duty of states to honor federal legal commands, as articulated by federal "preemption" law. Part II concludes with Chapter 25's treatment of the intricate constitutional principles that apply to nonfederal entities other than the states, with that discussion focusing on Native nations, federal territories, and the District of Columbia.

3. Part III: The Allocation of Power Within the Federal Government

The final part of the book addresses both the sharing and the separation of *national powers* among the three coordinate branches of the federal government. Chapter 26 begins that examination by addressing the basic theory underlying the horizontal separation of powers, while also offering a brief overview of the President's distinct role within the scheme put in place by the Framers. The next two chapters consider in greater detail the balance of authority between the executive and legislative branches in relation to matters concerning both international affairs (Chapter 27) and military affairs (Chapter 28). Chapter 29 shifts attention to the nature and function of the federal administrative agencies that assist the

President in enforcing federal law, including by exploring Congress's role in establishing these agencies and overseeing their work. The next two chapters target more specifically the relationship between Congress and the President in the *appointment* of officials to lead these agencies (Chapter 30) and the *removal* of these individuals from office (Chapter 31).

The next two chapters turn to constitutional rules that deal with the misconduct of federal officials and other related matters. Chapter 32 focuses on the Article I impeachment process, the Twenty-fifth Amendment's mechanism for sidelining a President "unable" to discharge the duties of office, and section 3 of the Fourteenth Amendment, which addresses the ineligibility for federal (and state) office of persons involved in insurrection against the United States. Chapter 33 goes on to address the extent to which the President and other federal officials enjoy specialized protections from legal process, including in the form of subpoenas to provide information, actions for civil damages, and criminal indictment and prosecution.

The final two chapters of Part III take a closer look at the role of the federal courts in the overall constitutional scheme. Chapter 34 considers the development, scope, and nature of the federal judiciary's long-asserted authority to review the constitutionality of federal and state enactments and other governmental actions as well. Chapter 35 then investigates the constraints imposed on the judicial branch by Article III's "case or controversy" requirement, which has long been understood to limit the range of requests for legal rulings that the federal courts may entertain.

* * *

As this summary overview illustrates, not every line of doctrine bearing on the law of constitutional structure receives attention in the pages that follow. No treatment is given, for example, to important topics within civil-procedure and federal-courts law (*e.g.*, federal-question jurisdiction, personal jurisdiction, abstention rules, and the *Erie* doctrine), administrative law (*e.g.*, the *Chevron* doctrine, finality and exhaustion requirements, and due-process-based limits on administrative adjudication), foreign affairs law (*e.g.*, the act-of-state doctrine, foreign sovereign immunity, and limits on the extraterritorial application of U.S. law), and various other structure-related doctrines with constitutional or quasi-constitutional roots. In sum, we do not purport to offer anything approaching a comprehensive restatement of all the rules that bear on inter- and intra-governmental relationships within the U.S. constitutional system. Nonetheless, we hope that what follows provides a useful frame of reference for understanding, evaluating, and arguing about the enduring complexities to which these relationships give rise.

Part I

THE LAWMAKING POWERS OF THE NATIONAL GOVERNMENT

Chapter 1

THE BUILDING BLOCKS OF CONSTITUTIONAL FEDERALISM

Analysis

Sec.

From the beginning, American constitutional thought has focused on, perhaps more than any other subject, the proper division of powers between the federal government and the states.[1] Struggles over this subject pre-dated ratification. Indeed, the Philadelphia Convention of 1787 was called to address one overarching problem—the shared sense that the then-governing Articles of Confederation rendered the federal government too weak, and the states too strong, particularly with respect to the powers of money-raising and the regulation of interstate and foreign commerce. At the Constitutional Convention itself, and in the state ratification conventions that followed it, differing views about how to deal with these and other problems spurred deliberation, conflict, and compromise. The result was the adoption of a new charter of government that fundamentally reshaped the relationship between the federal government and the states.

In a critical move, the Framers of the Constitution vested the central government with greatly expanded powers, while leaving to the states their preexisting powers to the extent they were not assigned exclusively to federal decision-makers. Most prominent among those federal decision-makers was the newly constructed Congress of the United States, and the Framers laid out its core powers in Article I, section 8. Many of the powers set forth in that text—such as the powers to "establish Post Offices," to "fix the Standard of Weights and Measures," to "Provide for the Punishment

---

[1] *See* ROBERT G. MCCLOSKEY, THE AMERICAN SUPREME COURT 17 (2d ed. 1994) (revised by Sanford Levinson) (describing "the nation-state relationship" as the "greatest of all the questions left unresolved by the founders").

of counterfeiting," and to "grant Letters of Marque and Reprisal"[2]—have stirred little debate over the years. But other powers—such as the powers to "lay and collect Taxes," to "regulate Commerce . . . among the several States," and to "make all laws which shall be necessary and proper for carrying into Execution the foregoing powers"[3]—have proven to be enormously controversial. By way of example, the Commerce Clause as supplemented by the Necessary and Proper Clause has given rise to congressional claims of authority to regulate many local matters, historically overseen by state governments, on the theory that those matters have a meaningful relationship to interstate commercial activity. But how far does this authority go? May Congress impose minimum-wage requirements on operators of coal mines? How about bans on discrimination directed at hotels, big-box stores, or the operators of a local café? May Congress criminalize the possession of heroin? Machine guns? The disruption of access to local abortion clinics? May Congress control hunting or fishing within a state, or the filling of small ponds, or the destruction of a rare localized plant species? We return in due course to these and many other questions about the scope of congressional authority. Properly thinking about these questions, however, requires a sense of why the Constitution both grants and limits congressional power, and why it sometimes restricts the exercise of state powers as well.

A. WHY AND HOW THE CONSTITUTION DIVIDES UP LAWMAKING POWER

As the delegates to the Constitutional Convention gathered in 1787, questions about how to allocate state and federal lawmaking power crowded their thoughts and conversations.[4] One option was to

---

2 U.S. CONST. art. I, § 8.

3 *Id.*

4 As noted above, one point of central importance concerned the regulation of commerce, and another had to do with revenue-raising by the federal government. Two other subjects, each tied closely to the allocation of federal and state power, also factored prominently in the delegates' deliberations. The first had to do with the Articles' failure to prevent states from enacting debtor-relief and paper-money laws—laws that often posed a threat to the financial interests of creditors and other economic elites. There is no doubt that the Framers intended for the new Constitution to restrict these practices, *see id.* art. I, § 10 (prohibiting states from, among other things, "coin[ing] money," "emit[ting] Bills of Credit, and "impair[ing] the obligation of Contracts"), but historians have long disagreed on the question of how great a role this objective played in motivating the Framers' efforts at Philadelphia and in shaping the ensuing ratification debates. *See* MICHAEL J. KLARMAN, THE FRAMERS' COUP: THE MAKING OF THE UNITED STATES CONSTITUTION 376–80 (2016) (offering an overview of this debate, while also noting that debtor-versus-creditor status operated as one of a "few factors" that was key in "explain[ing] why some people became Federalists and others Antifederalists"). Also weighing on the minds of the Framers was the issue of slavery. Although "slavery had nothing to do with the calling of the convention, it played an enormous role in the proceedings," *id.* at 264, as virulently proslavery

leave in place the existing Articles of Confederation. Under the Articles, however, things had gone badly for nearly a decade.[5] The Articles created a federal Congress, but that body lacked the power to impose taxes or to regulate interstate commerce. Although in theory the national legislature could deal with war-related matters and foreign affairs, even in these areas it lacked a practical effectiveness because its authority to raise funds was extremely limited and because no federal executive or judiciary was in place to carry out congressional mandates. The result was that individual states operated much like independent countries, bound together by a loose-knit alliance that depended on the continuing goodwill of its members. "Congress, in short, had responsibility without power. It could recommend endlessly but no one either inside or outside the United States paid much attention to what it recommended."[6]

---

delegates from the deep south pushed for the addition of several slavery-promoting measures as a condition of securing their signatures. These measures included: (1) the Three-Fifths Clause of Article I, section 2, which accorded outsized federal influence to states with large populations of enslaved persons, *see* U.S. CONST. art. I, § 2 (allocating representation in the House of Representatives—and by extension the Electoral College—based on "the whole Number of free Persons . . . excluding Indians not taxed" plus "three fifths of all other Persons"); *see also* AKHIL REED AMAR, AMERICA'S CONSTITUTION: A BIOGRAPHY 87–100, 97 (2009) (noting that "[t]he radical vice of Article I as drafted and ratified was that it gave slaveholding regions extra clout in every election as far as the eye could see"); (2) the Fugitive Slave Clause of Article IV, section 2, which empowered slaveholders nationwide to demand from any state the return of any "person held to Service or Labour in one State" who had fled into another state's territory, *see* U.S. CONST. art. IV, § 2; *see also* Prigg v. Pennsylvania, 41 U.S. (16 Pet.) 539, 613 (1842) (upholding, by reference to the Fugitive Slave Clause, the federal Fugitive Slave Act of 1793, which prohibited free states from enforcing anti-kidnapping laws against out-of-state slaveholders who engaged in the forcible "seizure and recaption" of alleged fugitives within their boundaries); and (3) the Slave Trade Clause of Article I, section 9, which disabled Congress from prohibiting "[t]he Migration or Importation of Such Persons as any of the States now existing shall think proper to admit" until 1808 at the earliest, U.S. CONST. art. I, § 9; *see also* art. V (declaring this provision of the Constitution, along with the provision guaranteeing equal-state representation in the Senate, to be unamendable); *cf.* KLARMAN, *supra*, at 291–92 (noting that while Congress would move to prohibit the foreign slave trade in 1808, that prohibition did little to slow slavery's expansion, particularly within the southern states). Thus, what emerged from the Convention was in many ways a proslavery document—one that, over the ensuing decades, would end up accelerating slavery's entrenchment in the south and its subsequent westward expansion into new federal territories and states. Indeed, it was only with the post-Civil War ratification of the Reconstruction Amendments that the Constitution came to include an explicit repudiation of slavery and an explicit recognition of rights-based and structural guarantees aimed at realizing the "new birth of freedom" for which the war had been fought. Abraham Lincoln, Address Delivered at the Dedication of the Cemetery at Gettysburg (Nov. 19, 1863), *available at* https://avalon.law.yale.edu/19th_century/gettyb.asp (last visited Nov. 8, 2021); *see infra* Chapters 11–12 (discussing the new congressional powers conferred by the Reconstruction Amendments).

5 For a useful overview of the many defects apparent in the Articles regime, see KLARMAN, *supra* note 4, at 11–72.

6 JOHN M. BLUM ET AL., THE NATIONAL EXPERIENCE 122 (1963).

To make matters worse, the spirit of collaboration that marked the days of the American Revolution had eroded—at least when it came to commercial relations—during the pre-Constitution period. Individual states erected tariffs and imposed duties on goods that moved across their territory at the expense of outsider exporters and importers in other states.[7] These strategies, in turn, "engendered rival, conflicting and angry regulations."[8] As Joseph Story observed, "thus a state of affairs disorderly and unnatural grew up, the necessary tendency of which was to destroy the Union itself."[9] Leaders who had endured the snows of Valley Forge viewed with horror the prospect that internecine conflicts might abort the American experiment. As conditions grew worse, the leadership of Virginia proposed a gathering of representatives from all the states "to take into consideration the trade of the United States; to examine the relative situations and trade of the said States; to consider how far a uniform system in their commercial regulations may be necessary to their common interest and their permanent harmony."[10] This overture resulted in the Annapolis Convention of 1786, which in turn made the call for the Philadelphia Convention of 1787, which ultimately put to paper the Constitution of the United States.[11]

The delegates to the Constitutional Convention might have addressed rising fears of a fragmented and dispute-riven union by trying to create a single nation, ruled by a unitary government, unencumbered by any state boundaries at all. But the leaders gathered in Philadelphia knew that this path was not open to them. As Chief Justice John Marshall would later write: "No political dreamer was ever wild enough to think of breaking down the lines which separate the states, and of compounding the American people into one common mass."[12] The Framers thus steered a middle course between leaving matters as they stood and obliterating state boundaries altogether. They dealt with the worst flaws of the Articles

---

[7] *See generally* H.P. Hood & Sons v. Du Mond, 336 U.S. 525, 531–34 (1949) (detailing this history).

[8] *Id.* at 534 (quoting James Madison in 3 THE RECORDS OF THE FEDERAL CONVENTION OF 1787, at 547 (Max Farrand, ed. 1937) [hereinafter FARRAND'S RECORDS]).

[9] 2 JOSEPH STORY, COMMENTARIES ON THE CONSTITUTION OF THE UNITED STATES § 1062 (Carolina Academic Press 1987) (1833). As Professors Rotunda and Nowak have noted, "Joseph Story lived at an ideal time and under ideal circumstances to reflect upon the nature of our constitutional system," including because of his service as an Associate Justice of the Supreme Court from 1811 to 1845. Ronald D. Rotunda & John E. Nowak, Introduction to STORY, *supra*, at v.

[10] Resolution of the General Assembly of Virginia (Jan. 21, 1786), *available at* https://avalon.law.yale.edu/18th_century/const03.asp, *quoted in Hood*, 336 U.S. at 533.

[11] *See Hood*, 336 U.S. at 533.

[12] McCulloch v. Maryland, 17 U.S. (4 Wheat.) 316, 403 (1819).

of Confederation by fashioning a much-energized federal government, including by assigning to Congress dramatically expanded lawmaking powers.[13] Using three main strategies, however, they also took steps to ensure that the new federal authority would not overwhelm the already-existing state governments.

First, the Framers devised a system that, simply put, made it difficult for the central government to legislate at all. Enactment of any law required the concurrent action of two very different chambers of the legislative branch: the Senate (made up of two representatives from each state, with members chosen for staggered six-year terms)[14] and the House of Representatives (made up of differing numbers of representatives from each state based on state population, with all members elected to brief and identical two-year terms).[15] In addition, all enacted bills were subject to presidential veto, which in turn could be overridden only by the concurrent action of two-thirds of the Senate and two-thirds of the House.[16]

Second, the Framers built into the processes for selecting federal officers vital roles for the states. Under the original Constitution, state legislatures chose senators.[17] Even under the modern Constitution, all Senators and Representatives come from and represent particular states, and each state is equally represented in the Senate regardless of its population. In addition, under Article II of the Constitution, presidential electors are selected from within each state in a manner established by the state legislature, rather than by federal authorities.[18] In short, the Framers protected the repositories of local authority from being swallowed up by the federal government in part by crafting the structure of the central government in a way that took account of state boundaries, state institutions, and state interests.[19]

---

[13] *See* U.S. CONST. art. I, § 8.

[14] *Id.* art. I, § 3, cl. 1.

[15] *Id.* art. I, § 2, cl. 1.

[16] *Id.* art. I, § 7, cl. 2.

[17] In 1913, the provision for state legislators' election of Senators was displaced by the Seventeenth Amendment, which provided that Senators must be "elected by the people" of the states. U.S. CONST. amend. XVII.

[18] U.S. CONST. art. II, § 1, cl. 2.

[19] For the canonical scholarly treatment of these mechanisms, see Herbert Wechsler, *The Political Safeguards of Federalism: The Role of the States in the Composition and Selection of the National Government*, 54 COLUM. L. REV. 543 (1954). For a more recent treatment of the "political safeguards" thesis, which focuses more on the workings of political parties than representative federal bodies, see Larry D. Kramer, *Putting the Politics Back into the Political Safeguards of Federalism*, 100 COLUM. L. REV. 215 (2000). *But see* David Schleicher, *The Seventeenth Amendment and Federalism in an Age of National Political Parties*, 65 HASTINGS L.J. 1043, 1048 (2014) (contesting Kramer's thesis and instead contending that "[t]he failures of party

Third, the Framers—even while declaring that federal law took priority over incompatible state law[20]—insisted that the federal government could legislate only in specified fields. Most important, the Framers refused to give the federal government a general police power to pass laws concerning the health, safety, and morals of the national community. They also rejected proposals made early in the Convention to vest in Congress a vaguely defined power "to legislate in all Cases for the general Interests of the Union, and also in those Cases to which the States are separately incompetent."[21] Instead the Framers took a "laundry list" approach by setting forth in Article I, section 8, seventeen separate purposes that Congress could pursue with legislative enactments, as well as several additional powers laid down elsewhere in the Constitution.[22] The Framers also supplemented these grants of authority with the additional power to "make all Laws which shall be necessary and proper for carrying into Execution the foregoing Powers, and all other Powers vested by this Constitution in the Government of the United States."[23] The critical point—that Congress could do very much, albeit not everything it might wish to do—was later reaffirmed in the Tenth Amendment, which provides that: "The powers not delegated to the United States by the Constitution, nor prohibited by it to the States, are reserved to the States respectively, or to the people."[24]

These constitutional provisions, while laying down the essential architecture of American federalism, gave rise to large questions that surface time and again in this book: How far do Congress's powers reach? What limits, if any, do the Tenth Amendment and non-textual postulates of state autonomy place on federal authority? What limits based on the need for federal cohesiveness does the Constitution place on the powers of state officials? In particular, to what extent do the grant of the commerce power and the vision of a national common market that it reflects inhibit state action that interferes with free-flowing interstate trade? In wrestling with these questions, the

---

democracy at the state level are an important limitation on the functioning of American federalism").

20 *See* U.S. CONST. art. VI, cl. 2.

21 2 FARRAND'S RECORDS, *supra* note 8, at 131.

22 U.S. CONST. art. I, § 8, cl. 1–17; *see also, e.g., id.* art. IV, §§ 1, 3, 4. Article I, section 8 vests in Congress powers, in addition to those involving taxation and commerce, to enact (among other things) "uniform Laws on the subject of Bankruptcies," to "coin Money," to pass laws concerning patents and copyrights, to "constitute Tribunals inferior to the supreme Court," to "raise and support Armies," to "provide and maintain a Navy," and "[t]o declare War." *Id.* art. I, § 8. Among the powers granted to Congress by Article IV are those that permit it to admit new states to the union and to "make all needful Rules and Regulations respecting the Territory or other Property belonging to the United States." *Id.* art. IV, § 3.

23 *Id.* art. I, § 8, cl. 18.

24 *Id.* amend. X.

Supreme Court has both defined the essential features of the U.S. constitutional system and played a key role in addressing many of the most contentious political battles of the American past, battles that date back to the earliest days of the republic.

B. *McCULLOCH V. MARYLAND*

In the spring of 1789, the first Congress assembled, and George Washington took his constitutional oath as President of the United States. With the birth of the nation, questions quickly began to arise about how far the powers of Congress reached. Taking the lead in this debate were President Washington's nationally minded Secretary of the Treasury, Alexander Hamilton, and his more state-autonomy-oriented Secretary of State, Thomas Jefferson. Early disagreements concerned such questions as whether Congress could or should assume state war debts, aid domestic manufacturers, and undertake to build canals, bridges, and roads. But a particularly contentious debate focused on whether Congress had the power to charter a national bank.

Hamilton contended that the Necessary and Proper Clause authorized a National Bank Act because a proper construction of that provision permitted enactment of any law "incidental, useful, or conducive to" the exercise of Congress's more specifically enumerated powers.[25] In his view, this principle supported creation of a national bank because it "has a relation, more or less direct, to the power of collecting taxes, to that of borrowing money, to that of regulating trade between the States, and to those of raising and maintaining fleets and armies."[26] Jefferson responded that Congress could not create a bank because the Constitution's laundry list of powers did not authorize in express terms the chartering of corporations and the Necessary and Proper Clause was properly read to permit the enactment of only those laws "without which the [specific grants] of power would be nugatory."[27] He insisted, in particular, that recognizing a federal power to charter a bank would require such an energetic interpretation of the Necessary and Proper Clause that it soon "would swallow up all the delegated powers" and authorize congressional interference with even "the most ancient and fundamental laws of the several States; such as . . . rules of

---

[25] Alexander Hamilton, *Opinion as to the Constitutionality of the Bank of the United States* (Feb. 23, 1791), *available at* https://avalon.law.yale.edu/18th_century/bank-ah.asp (last visited Nov. 8, 2021).

[26] *Id.*

[27] Thomas Jefferson, *Opinion on the Constitutionality of a National Bank* (Feb. 15, 1791), *available at* https://avalon.law.yale.edu/18th_century/bank-tj.asp (last visited Nov. 8, 2021).

descent."[28] In the end, President Washington acceded to the pleas of his Secretary of the Treasury, and dismissed those of his Secretary of State, signing into law in 1791 a bill that established the first Bank of the United States.

That bank's charter lapsed in 1811, before any challenge to its constitutionality found its way to the Supreme Court. In 1816, however, Congress passed a statute that created the second Bank of the United States, and President Madison (although a career-long ally of Jefferson and an ardent opponent of the first national bank as a then-member of the House of Representatives) signed it into law during the "period of nationalistic optimism that followed the end of the War of 1812."[29] The constitutionality of this act came before the Supreme Court in *McCulloch v. Maryland*.[30]

In essence, the act of 1816 created a federally chartered and federally regulated bank that competed directly with existing banks licensed to operate by the individual states. Many local leaders had opposed adoption of that law. Thus, when Congress passed it anyway, some states struck back. Among the most aggressive was Maryland, which enacted legislation imposing a charge of $15,000 per year on any bank not chartered by it unless that bank bought stamps from the state for each note that it issued. One feature of the Maryland law exposed individual officers of the Bank of the United States to penalties for failing to pay these charges, and the *McCulloch* case was initiated as a suit to collect such a penalty from the cashier of the Baltimore branch of the Bank. After the state courts ruled against the defendant, the case came before the Supreme Court, which invalidated the Maryland statute.[31]

In his opinion for a unanimous Court, Chief Justice Marshall identified the first question in the case as whether Congress had the constitutional power to create a national bank. Endorsing the Hamiltonian position, he concluded that it did. The Chief Justice began his analysis by contrasting the language of the Constitution with the language of the Articles of Confederation, under which the federal Congress possessed only those powers "expressly" delegated

---

[28] *Id.*

[29] GERALD GUNTHER, CONSTITUTIONAL LAW 81 (12th ed. 1991).

[30] 17 U.S. (4 Wheat.) 316 (1819).

[31] A recent symposium devoted to *McCulloch*—and in particular Professor David S. Schwartz's book-length treatment of the case—elicited a cornucopia of treatments by important academic scholars. *See Scholarship in Review: A Response to David Schwartz's* The Spirit of the Constitution: *John Marshall and the 200-Year Odyssey of* McCulloch v. Maryland, 73 ARK. L. REV. 69 *et seq.* (2020) (collecting the work of Professors Schwartz, Sanford Levinson, Richard Primus, Mark Graber, Franita Tolson, and Kurt Lash); *see also* DAVID S. SCHWARTZ, THE SPIRIT OF THE CONSTITUTION: JOHN MARSHALL AND THE 200-YEAR ODYSSEY OF *MCCULLOCH V. MARYLAND* (2019).

to it.[32] He observed that the Framers "had experienced the embarrassments resulting from the insertion of this word in the articles"[33] and he added that, if a Constitution were "to contain an accurate detail of . . . all the means by which [the government's enumerated powers] may be carried into execution," it "would partake of the prolixity of a legal code."[34] As a result, only the Constitution's "great outlines should be marked, its important objects designated, and the minor ingredients which compose those objects, be deduced from the nature of the objects themselves."[35] "[W]e must never forget," Chief Justice Marshall famously declared, "that it is a *constitution* we are expounding."[36]

The Chief Justice, however, did not stop there. He also argued that (1) the Constitution vested the war-making and other "great powers" in the federal Congress; (2) "a government, intrusted with such ample powers, on the due execution of which the happiness and prosperity of the nation so vitally depends, must also be intrusted with ample means for their execution";[37] and (3) this conclusion was all the more compelled in construing a document "intended to endure for ages to come"[38] and to provide for a "vast republic."[39] In short, Chief Justice Marshall relied on "general reasoning" from the history, structure, and purposes of the Constitution, as well as on common sense, to conclude that broad "incidental" powers followed from the assignment of critically important enumerated powers to the federal Congress.[40]

There was, however, a fly in the ointment. The problem, according to the Jeffersonians, was that the text of the Constitution rendered the Chief Justice's appeal to the "dictates of reason" beside

---

32 *McCulloch*, 17 U.S. at 406.

33 *Id.*

34 *Id.* at 407.

35 *Id.*

36 *Id.* (emphasis in original). Marshall added that his commodious view of "deduced" powers found support in other features of the constitutional text as well. For example, no enumerated power even obliquely indicates that Congress has the power to grant titles of nobility; thus, the express prohibition on the grant of such titles in Article I, section 9 suggested that the Framers' understanding of the authority to grant these titles was deducible as a means "necessary and proper" to carry Congress's enumerated powers into execution. After all, if such a power were not deducible in this way, it would not exist at all; thus, there would be no need separately to prohibit its exercise. And such a power was plainly not, as Jefferson had suggested, needed to avoid rendering any enumerated power nugatory. *See id.*

37 *Id.* at 408.

38 *Id.* at 415.

39 *Id.* at 408. Particularly in this context, the Chief Justice observed, Congress had to have broad flexibility to fashion practical approaches to deal with the "various" and often-unforeseeable "*crises* of human affairs." *Id.* at 415 (emphasis in original).

40 *See id.* at 386, 388, 411.

the point.[41] The Constitution, they argued, specifically treats the subject of incidental powers, and it stipulates that Congress has only those powers "necessary and proper" for carrying into execution its otherwise enumerated grants of authority. On any fair interpretation, the Jeffersonians claimed, establishment of a national bank was not "necessary" for spending federal money, collecting federal taxes, raising armies, or regulating interstate commerce. Instead, the federal government could use the existing state banks for all of these purposes.

Chief Justice Marshall, however, found this textual argument unpersuasive. In his view, two interpretations of the word "necessary" were available: (1) the Jeffersonian interpretation, under which the term meant "indispensable"; and (2) the Hamiltonian interpretation, under which the term meant "convenient, or useful, or essential."[42] In endorsing the second and more expansive of these two definitions, Chief Justice Marshall began by relying on "common usage," asserting that "in the common affairs of the world" a means "necessary" to an end "is generally understood" to denote "any means calculated to produce the end," rather than being confined to "those single means, without which the end would be entirely unattainable."[43] This common-meaning argument found support in the linguistic reality that the critical term admitted "of all degrees of comparison" because "a thing may be necessary, very necessary, absolutely or indispensably necessary."[44]

The Chief Justice added to this linguistic exegesis two additional, and no less significant, points. First, he argued that endorsement of the Jeffersonian interpretation would wreak havoc on the operation of the federal government. Existing federal law, for example, prohibited robbing the mail, yet such a prohibition was not "indispensably necessary" to carrying out Congress's enumerated

---

41 *Id.* at 409.

42 *Id.* at 413, 418.

43 *Id.* at 413–14.

44 *Id.* at 414. Any doubt in this regard, Chief Justice Marshall added, was negated by the Constitution itself, which in Article I, section 10 authorizes state imposition of duties on imports and exports only to the extent they are "*absolutely* necessary for executing its inspection laws." *Id.* (emphasis in original). In other words, according to Marshall, the Framers knew how to use the term "absolutely necessary" when they meant "absolutely necessary," and they had not included the term "absolutely necessary" in the Necessary and Proper Clause of Article I. *Id.* In addition, the Framers' use of the word "proper" in that clause carried significance for the Court because, "[i]f the word 'necessary' was used in that strict and rigorous sense for which the counsel for the State of Maryland contend," the full clause would require either the "extraordinary" conclusion that some indispensable means for carrying out the enumerated powers were improper or the alternative conclusion that the word "proper" had no effect whatsoever. *Id.* at 418–19. For this reason, the very "necessary and proper" language on which Maryland based its argument cut, in Chief Justice Marshall's view, against and not in favor of Maryland's constitutional position.

power to "establish post-offices and post-roads."[45] Likewise, outlawing perjury was "conducive" to pursuing the due administration of justice in federal courts, but it was not indispensable to "constitut[ing] tribunals inferior to the supreme court."[46] By way of these examples, Chief Justice Marshall constructed the sort of "parade-of-horribles" argument that would recur in constitutional discourse from his day to this one, particularly in debates about the scope of congressional power under the Commerce Clause.

Second, Chief Justice Marshall defended his interpretive stance against the Jeffersonians' argument that the convenience-based Hamiltonian view of the Necessary and Proper Clause would produce a federal lawmaking power subject to no meaningful limits. In keeping with his broad view of federal power, the Chief Justice decreed that "where the law . . . is really calculated to effect any of the objects intrusted to the government, to undertake here to inquire into the degree of its necessity, would be to pass the line which circumscribes the judicial department, and to tread on legislative ground."[47] In another passage, however, he emphasized that the Constitution does place some judicially enforceable limits on the scope of congressional authority. As he wrote: "Should congress, in the execution of its powers, adopt measures which are prohibited by the constitution; or should congress, under the pretext of executing its powers, pass laws for the accomplishment of objects not intrusted to the government; it would become the painful duty of this tribunal . . . to say, that such an act was not the law of the land."[48] Chief Justice Marshall did not explain just how the Court would determine whether any given congressional action constituted an impermissible "pretext." With this passage, however, he left the door open for later judicial declarations that some congressional enactments reached beyond Congress's delegated powers.[49]

The Court's decision that Congress had the authority to charter a national bank did not in itself resolve the *McCulloch* case because the Court had to answer yet another question: Even if Congress could create a national bank, did the Constitution require invalidation of the tax that Maryland had imposed on its operations? The Chief Justice began his analysis of this second issue by conceding there was "no express provision" in the Constitution that rendered the

---

45 *Id.* at 417.

46 *Id.* at 381, 417.

47 *Id.* at 423.

48 *Id.*

49 *See infra* Section 2.A (discussing the Court's reliance on pretext-based reasoning in connection with several of its pre-1937 commerce-power decisions).

Maryland statute invalid.[50] He went on, however, to speak of "a principle which so entirely pervades the Constitution" and is "so interwoven with its web, so blended with its texture, as to be incapable of being separated from it."[51] This principle, which emanated from the Constitution's express recognition of the primacy of federal law, mandated that states lacked the power to "defeat the legitimate operations of a supreme government."[52] And because "the power to tax involves the power to destroy,"[53] a "fair construction" of this principle required invalidation of Maryland's effort to impose its tax on the national bank.[54]

The Court found further support for this ruling in a "just theory" of government taxation.[55] According to the Chief Justice, the "only security against . . . abuse" of the taxing power lay in the fact that "the legislature acts upon its constituents"—a fact that ordinarily provides "a sufficient security against erroneous and oppressive" imposition of government levies on citizen-taxpayers.[56] "But when a state taxes the operations of the government of the United States, it acts upon institutions created, not by their own constituents, but by people over whom they claim no control."[57] The intolerable nature of this sort of "action of a part on the whole"[58] was so patent that the Chief Justice detected "a total failure" of the claimed right of the state "to tax the means employed by the government of the Union."[59]

Chief Justice Marshall's opinion in *McCulloch* is not immune to criticism. For example, it might be said that, in endorsing Congress's use of the Necessary and Proper Clause, the Chief Justice expended most of his energy attacking a "straw man."[60] In particular, he gave

---

50 *McCulloch*, 17 U.S. at 426.

51 *Id.*

52 *Id.* at 427.

53 *Id.* at 431.

54 *Id.* at 427. The Court added that settled principles of governmental autonomy in the field of interstate relations helped to support this conclusion. It reasoned that just as surely as it would be intolerable for one state to suffer controls placed on its operations by other states, it was intolerable for a state to hinder the operations of a duly enacted federal program. *Id.* at 429–31. In making this observation, however, the Court did not advert to the potentially salient fact that the Bank of the United States was (unlike state-chartered banks operating in other jurisdictions) conducting business operations within the territorial limits of Maryland.

55 *Id.* at 430.

56 *Id.* at 428.

57 *Id.* at 435.

58 *Id.* at 436.

59 *Id.* at 430.

60 *See, e.g.*, David Currie, *The Constitution in the Supreme Court: State and Congressional Powers, 1801–1835*, 49 U. CHI. L. REV. 887, 933–34 (1982) (contending that Marshall "devoted most of his effort" on this score "to demolishing the straw man

almost no attention to the possibility that the word "necessary" might have some meaning short of "indispensable"—such as "substantially related" or "highly important"—that would have departed from the most extreme version of the Jeffersonian position but still cast doubt on Congress's power to establish the bank. Likewise, in railing against the Maryland tax, Chief Justice Marshall never acknowledged that Congress could have protected the national interests at stake in the case by simply enacting a law that explicitly preempted programs such as the one adopted by Maryland.[61]

Even so, *McCulloch* remains "perhaps the greatest of our constitutional cases."[62] The decision embodied styles of analysis—centered on text, history, and structure—that would come to pervade constitutional decisionmaking throughout American history. Of no less importance, *McCulloch* launched the two central themes that have echoed through the Court's efforts to mark the proper balance of state and federal power. First, the ruling left no doubt that federal lawmaking authority, though limited in some nebulous way, was both expansive and largely beyond the power of the judiciary to constrain. Second, *McCulloch* recognized the possibility of implying from the "web" and "texture" of the Constitution judicially enforceable constraints on state power and also, at least possibly, on federal power as well.

C. *GIBBONS V. OGDEN*

As we have seen, a key move made by the Framers was to vest the federal Congress with a new power "[t]o regulate Commerce with foreign Nations, and among the several States, and with the Indian Tribes."[63] The chapters that follow will reveal how this single clause has dominated judicial work with the law of constitutional federalism. And that story begins with the Court's 1824 ruling in *Gibbons v. Ogden*[64]—a case, like *McCulloch*, of such foundational significance that it warrants an extensive stand-alone treatment.[65]

---

of indispensable necessity and slid over the real question of the propriety of the Bank itself").

61 *See, e.g.*, Nelson Lund, *The Destructive Legacy of* McCulloch v. Maryland, *in* *MCCULLOCH V. MARYLAND* AT 200: DEBATING JOHN MARSHALL'S JURISPRUDENCE 19, 28 (Gary J. Schmitt & Rebecca Burgess, eds., 2019) (asserting that "[t]he practical effect of *McCulloch* was to create, through judicial fiat, a law that Congress had not enacted and possibly would have refused to enact").

62 CHARLES L. BLACK, JR., STRUCTURE AND RELATIONSHIP IN CONSTITUTIONAL LAW 5 (1969).

63 U.S. CONST. art. I, § 8, cl. 3.

64 22 U.S. (9 Wheat.) 1 (1824).

65 For focused treatments of *Gibbons*, reflecting on (among other things) its seminal importance, see Norman R. Williams, *The Dormant Commerce Clause: Why*

In the early 1800s, Aaron Ogden took over operation of a steamboat ferry service that enjoyed, under New York state law, an exclusive right to transport passengers between New York City and Elizabethtown, New Jersey. Thereafter, Thomas Gibbons, a former partner of Ogden's, obtained a license under a federal statute to engage in "the coasting trade" and began to operate a competing ferry service. Ogden brought suit to enjoin the operation of Gibbons's service, to the extent it made use of New York waters, on the ground it was barred by New York law. One argument that Gibbons offered in response was that the federal statute under which he held his license preempted that state's monopoly grant. Ogden countered by claiming that the federal statute, to the extent it authorized Gibbons's competing activities, reached beyond Congress's power to "regulate Commerce . . . among the several states." In essence, Ogden argued that neither he nor Gibbons was a constitutionally proper target of federal regulation under that clause because the term "commerce" was rightly limited to "buying and selling, or the interchange of commodities," as opposed to (among other things) operating ferries.[66]

Just as in *McCulloch*, however, Chief Justice Marshall, rejected this circumscribed view of a key constitutional power-granting term. Addressing the immediate issue presented by the case, the Chief Justice made short shrift of Ogden's core contention, declaring instead that "all America understands, and has uniformly understood, the word 'commerce,' to comprehend navigation."[67] Even more important, the Chief Justice took the occasion to define the terms "regulate Commerce" and "among the states" in ways that accorded the Commerce Clause an expansive reach. "Commerce," he wrote, "is traffic, but it is something more: it is intercourse," and regulating commerce entails "prescribing rules for carrying on that intercourse."[68] As for the meaning of "among the states," the Chief

---

Gibbons v. Ogden *Should Be Restored to the Canon*, 49 ST. LOUIS UNIV. L. J. 817 (2005), and Norman R. Williams, Gibbons, 79 N.Y.U. L. REV. 1398 (2004).

66 *Gibbons*, 22 U.S. at 189.

67 *Id.* at 190.

68 *Id.* at 189–90. Debate over the meaning of the word "commerce" hardly ended with the Court's musings in *Gibbons*. Indeed, it has persisted to the present day. An elaborate treatment supportive of an expansive reading of the term has come from Professor Jack Balkin. *See* Jack M. Balkin, *Commerce*, 109 MICH. L. REV. 1, 15–16, 19 (2010) (arguing in detail, in part based on *Gibbons*, that the original meaning of "Commerce" embraced human "interactions, exchanges, interrelated activities, and movements back and forth, including, for example, travel, social connection, or conversation" and that "[e]conomic transactions were only a special case of social intercourse"). For a leading critique of Professor Balkin's thesis, see Randy E. Barnett, *Jack Balkin's Interaction Theory of "Commerce,"* 2012 U. ILL. L. REV. 623; *see also* United States v. Lopez, 514 U.S. 549, 585–86 (Thomas, J., concurring) (viewing commerce as limited to the purchase or exchange of goods "as well as transporting for these purposes"; adding that the Framers "used trade (in its selling/bartering sense)

Justice emphasized that Congress could not reach trade that "is carried on between man and man in a State, or between different parts of the same State, and which does not extend to or affect other States."[69] This assertion, while suggesting that the commerce power was subject to limits, held out the tantalizing prospect that Congress could regulate wholly intrastate activities on the theory that they do "affect other States," whether or not those activities directly concerned the sort of border-crossing movements involved in *Gibbons* itself.[70]

Finally, Chief Justice Marshall laid out two ideas that have continued to play prominent roles in supporting a capacious conception of the commerce power. First, he described that power as "plenary" as to the "objects" within its reach, adding that it "may be exercised to its utmost extent, and acknowledges no limitations, other than are prescribed in the constitution."[71] Second, he observed that, as long as Congress acts pursuant to this power, protection of the people from the risk of its abuse should come not from the judiciary but from "[t]he wisdom and the discretion of Congress, their identity with the people, and the influence which their constituents possess at elections."[72] In sum, the Court in *Gibbons*, like the Court in *McCulloch*, recognized the existence of limits on federal power but offered up a rhetoric available for later use to support a sweeping conception of how far that power might reach.

D. THE VALUES OF CENTRALIZATION AND DECENTRALIZATION

McCulloch and *Gibbons* introduced themes that have dominated constitutional discourse about the proper scope of congressional authority to the present day. Drawing on the open-textured language of the Constitution, they endorsed the view that a broad conception of federal power would wisely facilitate congressional flexibility and an ability to adapt to new conditions over time. At an even deeper

---

and commerce interchangeably"). For a few of the many additional treatments of the subject, *see* Robert G. Natelson, *The Legal Meaning Of "Commerce" in the Commerce Clause*, 80 ST. JOHN'S L. REV. 789 (2006); and Grant S. Nelson & Robert J. Pushaw, Jr., *Rethinking the Commerce Clause: Applying First Principles to Uphold Federal Commercial Regulations but Preserve State Control Over Social Issues*, 85 IOWA L. REV. 1 (1999).

[69] *Gibbons*, 22 U.S. at 194.

[70] *Id.*

[71] *Id.* at 196–97. Early in the nation's history, some observers took a very different view, going so far as to suggest the Commerce Clause was meant to vest Congress with only a power to preempt state laws and not a power to regulate private parties directly. The Court, however, has long rejected this restrictive interpretive stance. *See* BORIS I. BITTKER, BITTKER ON THE REGULATION OF INTERSTATE AND FOREIGN COMMERCE § 2.02 (1999) (recounting the emergence of this theory and its ensuing rejection).

[72] *Gibbons*, 22 U.S. at 197.

level, the Marshall Court's commitment to expansive congressional authority squared with a key element of James Madison's ratification-era defense of the overall constitutional design. In Madison's view, the greatest danger presented by democratic self-rule lay in the risk that a "powerful faction" would capture the processes of government rooted in majority rule and then use those processes to oppress "the weaker party."[73] This problem, as Madison saw it, grew as the size of the self-governing group diminished, because

> [t]he smaller the society, the fewer probably will be the distinct parties and interests composing it; the fewer the distinct parties and interests, the more frequently will a majority be found of the same party; and the smaller the number of individuals composing a majority, and the smaller the compass within which they are placed, the more easily will they concert and execute their plans of oppression.[74]

Madison thus argued for a broad empowerment of the federal government, and a reciprocal disempowerment of the states, on the theory that a great "advantage . . . in controlling the effects of faction . . . is enjoyed by the Union over the States composing it."[75]

Neither Madison nor Marshall, however, envisioned such an enlargement of federal power that it would do away with a constitutional system built around the existence of "two distinct governments,"[76] including state governments that retained "numerous and indefinite" powers.[77] It was for this reason that the Court in *McCulloch* recognized that both "the letter and spirit of the constitution" comport with placing some limits on congressional authority.[78] These limits, in turn, reflect the benefits that have long been understood to flow from vesting geographically defined subunits of government with control over significant public policy matters. A strong system of state and local lawmaking, for example, might help to encourage citizen participation and governmental responsiveness

---

[73] THE FEDERALIST NO. 10 (Madison).

[74] *Id.*

[75] *Id.* Although neither Madison in *The Federalist* nor Marshall in *McCulloch* discussed the point explicitly, another potential benefit to a strongly centralized national government lies in its ability to deal with externalities, spillover problems, coordination difficulties, redundancies, and other practical issues likely to emerge from the piecemeal regulation by multiple states of activities whose effects are felt beyond state boundaries. For a catalogue of these different problems—and of the ways in which a centralized national government can address them—see generally DAVID L. SHAPIRO, FEDERALISM: A DIALOGUE 34–50 (1995).

[76] THE FEDERALIST NO. 51 (Madison).

[77] THE FEDERALIST NO. 45 (Madison).

[78] *McCulloch*, 17 U.S. at 421.

by keeping political decisionmakers near at hand.[79] The dispersion of power within a federal system, it has been said, enables each state to "serve as a laboratory . . . and try novel social and economic experiments without risk to the rest of the country."[80] The existence of different self-governing polities also might facilitate the development of different policies responsive to distinct local conditions and preferences—for example, no marijuana in some states, only medicinal marijuana in other states, and marijuana for all purposes in still others—thus serving to maximize satisfaction among diverse citizen groups who gather together in diverse locales.[81] In addition, the emergence of different legal regimes in different states creates opportunities for members of the national polity to "vote with their feet" by moving to states whose legal regimes best align with their own values.[82] Perhaps most important, the Court has pointed to the "vertical" division of government authority as a mechanism designed to protect "our fundamental liberties" by helping to ensure that tyrannical power is not too readily seized by any single group of public officials at either the national or the state level.[83]

---

[79] *Cf.* Erwin Chemerinsky, *The Values of Federalism*, 47 FLA. L. REV. 499, 524–33 (1995) (evaluating the traditionally stated values of federal systems, including their role in enhancing governmental responsiveness).

[80] Reeves, Inc. v. Stake, 447 U.S. 429, 441 (1980) (quoting New State Ice Co. v. Liebmann, 285 U.S. 262, 311 (1932) (Brandeis, J., dissenting)).

[81] *See* Kramer, *supra* note 19, at 22 ("The whole point of federalism (or at least the best reason to care about it) is that, because preferences for governmental policy are unevenly distributed among the states and regions of the nation, more people can be satisfied by decentralized decisionmaking."); Michael W. McConnell, *Federalism: Evaluating the Founders' Design*, 54 U. CHI. L. REV. 1484, 1494 (1987) (reviewing RAOUL BERGER, FEDERALISM: THE FOUNDERS' DESIGN (1987)) (illustrating the same point by way of an example that assumes the existence of a nation of two states, each with population of 100, where 70% of the residents of State A and 40% of residents of State B "wish to outlaw smoking in public buildings"; observing that a nationwide majority rule would please only 110 individuals, but that two statewide majority rules would please 130 (and even more than 130 if smokers move from State A to State B and vice versa)); *see also* Alan P. Hamlin, *Decentralization, Competition and the Efficiency of Federalism*, 67 ECON. REC. 193, 194–99 (1991) (discussing the choice-enhancing effects of decentralization).

[82] *See* Ilya Somin, *Foot Voting, Federalism, and Political Freedom*, 55 NOMOS 83, 83 (2014) ("The idea of 'voting with your feet' has been an important element in debates over federalism for several decades. Economists, legal scholars, and others have analyzed its efficiency and equity. But foot voting is still underrated as a tool for enhancing political freedom: the ability of the people to choose the political regime under which they wish to live." (internal footnote omitted)).

[83] Gregory v. Ashcroft, 501 U.S. 452, 458 (1991) (quoting Atascadero State Hosp. v. Scanlon, 473 U.S. 234, 242 (1985)); *see also id.* (observing that "[j]ust as the separation and independence of the coordinate branches of the Federal Government serve to prevent the accumulation of excessive power in any one branch, a healthy balance of power between the States and the Federal Government will reduce the risk of tyranny and abuse from either front").

The Court in *McCulloch* and *Gibbons* recognized that sorting through competing claims of federal and state power would require a fair accommodation of competing constitutional values in the context of expounding a vague constitutional text. Those decisions also hinted at three sets of considerations that would play a prominent role in later judicial decision-making concerning the scope of the congressional power: (1) that, on the one hand, a variety of considerations—including the existence of process-centered protections for the states built into the Constitution's structuring of federal lawmaking institutions—counseled against a strong judicial role in protecting state-autonomy interests; (2) that, on the other hand, allowing Congress to regulate any local activity (including on the theory that it somehow, no matter how obliquely, affects interstate commerce) would violate the Framers' basic plan of limited federal power; and (3) that, in any event, the Court must accord the Constitution's grants of legislative authority a practical and adaptive reading, so as to give Congress the ability to deal effectively with "exigencies . . . best provided for as they occur" as not only years, but "ages," pass.[84] Against this complex backdrop, the Supreme Court has issued hundreds of rulings that, during different stages of the nation's history, have reflected different views of the scope of Congress's lawmaking authority.

---

[84] *McCulloch*, 17 U.S. at 415. One other force that inevitably comes to bear in congressional-power adjudication emanates from the reality that disputes over state and federal power never arise in a vacuum. Rather, each such structural dispute invariably involves an underlying controversy about substantive rights and interests. Aaron Ogden, for example, did not sue Thomas Gibbons (or at least he did not do so primarily) because of an abstract commitment to limited federal power. Rather, Ogden sued because he wanted to protect his monopoly and the economic advantages it afforded him. Moreover, as the Court considered Ogden's contention, there lurked in the background deeply held libertarian, fairness, and efficiency-based concerns about the soundness of governmental monopoly grants as a general matter—concerns that had everything to do with monopolies and nothing to do with the vertical allocation of lawmaking power. The interaction of the law of federalism and underlying substantive values is extremely complex. Observers of constitutional law, however, must be prepared to consider how that interaction has played itself out in the work of the Supreme Court, as well as in their own views of the law of constitutional federalism.

Chapter 2

THE COMMERCE POWER THROUGH 1936: THE QUEST FOR LIMITING PRINCIPLES

Analysis

Sec.

In the period prior to 1937, the Court forged the basic structure of commerce-power doctrine. In particular, it suggested that Congress can justify its invocation of the commerce power on any one of three alternative grounds.[1] First, Congress can regulate the *channels and instrumentalities of interstate commerce*, including by prohibiting the cross-border movement of specified goods or persons—that is, through use of the "commerce-prohibiting" technique.[2] Second, Congress can regulate even wholly intrastate activities on the theory that they are *in commerce*—that is, to put the same point more metaphorically, within the stream of commerce as it flows across state lines. Third, Congress can regulate intrastate

---

1 The Court also carried forward the spirit of *Gibbons* by continuing to define "commerce" broadly. *See, e.g.*, Thornton v. United States, 271 U.S. 414, 425 (1926) (characterizing the ranging of cattle across state lines as interstate commerce even if those cattle are not driven or transported); *see also* United States v. Simpson, 252 U.S. 465, 468 (1920) (Clarke, J., dissenting) (describing and criticizing the view taken by the eight-Justice majority to the effect that interstate commerce includes "isolated movements of small amounts of private property, by private persons for their personal use" across state lines).

2 It is worth noting that the Court has not been entirely clear in identifying the distinction (if any) between "channels" and "instrumentalities" of commerce. One might, for instance, posit that the former term focuses on corridors of movement and trade (sea routes, air routes, highways, rail and communications lines, electrical wires, pipelines, etc.), whereas the latter term focuses on vehicles and other tools used in exploiting those corridors (planes, trains, ships, etc.), but that distinction (or any other like it) has never been explicitly spelled out in the doctrine. The key point, however, is that the Court's cases suggest a specialized and broad power in Congress to regulate: (a) such channels and instrumentalities (however each term might be defined) that stands apart from (b) its separate power to regulate the persons or things that move in commerce by way of such channels and instrumentalities and (c) its further power to regulate local activities that affect interstate commerce.

activities by establishing that they *affect interstate commerce* in a substantial way. Although this three-part conception of the commerce power has been much refined since 1936, it continues to provide the core framework for analyzing commerce-power questions in the present day.

A. THE CHANNELS/INSTRUMENTALITIES THEORY AND THE COMMERCE-PROHIBITING TECHNIQUE THROUGH 1936

Gibbons in effect held that the Commerce Clause authorizes Congress to remove obstructions to interstate commerce—there, in the form of eliminating local impediments to transporting people across state borders by way of ship.[3] In *The Daniel Ball*,[4] the Court expanded on this aspect of *Gibbons* by upholding federal licensing and inspection requirements for a steamboat that operated entirely within a single state on a river that emptied into Lake Michigan. According to the Court, the congressional power extended to this case because the river was part of "a continued highway for commerce, both with other States and with foreign countries," and the boat "was employed as an instrument of that commerce."[5] Later decisions built on this ruling by establishing that the Commerce Clause reaches instrumentalities and channels of shipment by land as well as by water.[6] These cases laid the basis for recognizing a comprehensive federal power over the infrastructure of interstate movement, including in due time an expansive authority over railways, aircraft, and the facilities of telephone and telegraph communications.[7]

---

[3] *See supra* Section 1.C.

[4] 77 U.S. 557 (1870).

[5] *Id.* at 564–65. Another early ship-related commerce-power case is *United States v. Coombs*, 37 U.S. (12 Pet.) 72 (1838), in which the Court upheld on commerce-power grounds a federal criminal prohibition on theft of shipwrecked cargo from land above the high-water mark. According to Justice Story, this statute was "perfectly within the constitutional authority of Congress" because "[a]ny offense which . . . interferes with, obstructs, or prevents [foreign or interstate] commerce and navigation . . . may be punished by congress, under its general authority to make all laws necessary and proper to execute their delegated constitutional powers." *Id.* at 78. The opinion, however, does not clearly indicate whether the goods in the case were destined for interstate (as opposed to intrastate) delivery and whether that fact mattered to the Court in assessing the constitutionality of the challenged statute.

[6] *See, e.g.*, *In re* State Freight Tax, 82 U.S. 232, 275 (1873).

[7] *See, e.g.*, Fischer's Blend Station, Inc. v. State Tax Comm'n, 297 U.S. 650, 654–55 (1936) (concluding that "the transmission of information interstate is a form of 'intercourse,' which is commerce"). *See generally In re* Debs, 158 U.S. 564, 591, 599 (1895) (recognizing the federal power "to remove all obstructions upon highways, natural or artificial, to the passage of interstate commerce" and that this power "operates today upon modes of interstate commerce unknown to the fathers, and it will operate with equal force upon any new modes of such commerce which the future may develop"); Pensacola Tel. Co. v. W. Union Tel. Co., 96 U.S. 1, 9 (1878) (observing that powers under the Commerce Clause "are not confined to the instrumentalities of

Cases such as *Gibbons* and *The Daniel Ball* established that Congress had ample power to facilitate the conducting of commerce across state lines. Those cases, however, did not address another question: Could Congress invoke its authority over the channels of commerce to block interstate movements of goods or people to achieve "police power" objectives of protecting the general well-being of the citizenry? The legitimacy of this "commerce-prohibiting" technique first came before the Supreme Court in the *Lottery Case* (*Champion v. Ames*),[8] which involved an attack on a federal law that prohibited interstate shipments of lottery tickets. The challengers of the law argued that it violated the Constitution for both textual and historical reasons. As to the text, they asserted that the law did not "regulate" interstate commerce in lottery tickets; rather it "prohibit[ed]" such commerce.[9] As to history, they argued that the law lacked any connection with the Framers' underlying concerns about removing impediments to free interstate trade.[10]

A five-Justice majority of the Supreme Court saw things differently. As to the challengers' textual argument, Justice John Marshall Harlan reasoned that a prohibition is a form of government regulation (as an earlier decision sustaining congressional power to block interstate movements of diseased cows had indicated).[11] As to the challengers' historical argument, Justice Harlan emphasized the Court's insistence in *Gibbons* that the congressional power to regulate commerce among the states "may be exercised to its *utmost extent*."[12] In other words, because a prohibition on moving lottery tickets across state lines was in its very nature a regulation of interstate commerce, further inquiry into constitutional history or congressional motives was beside the point.

Writing for four dissenters, Chief Justice Fuller first attacked the majority's attempt to characterize the lottery-ticket prohibition as a "regulation" of interstate commerce. He reasoned that the exclusion of diseased animals from trains and steamboats—unlike the exclusion of lottery tickets—made commerce-regulating sense because diseased animals were "in themselves injurious to the transaction of interstate commerce."[13] More fundamentally, Chief Justice Fuller worried that the Court had laid the groundwork for the

commerce . . . known or in use when the Constitution was adopted, but they keep pace with the progress of the country").

8 188 U.S. 321 (1903).

9 *Id.* at 354.

10 *Id.* at 357.

11 *Id.* at 358–59. The quarantined-cow case was *Reid v. Colorado*, 187 U.S. 137 (1902).

12 *The Lottery Case*, 188 U.S. at 374 (emphasis in original).

13 *Id.* at 374 (Fuller, C.J., dissenting).

establishment of a *de facto* federal police power, thus taking a "long step in the direction of wiping out all traces of state lines, and the creation of a centralized government."[14] Indeed, according to the Chief Justice, the Lottery Act embodied just the sort of "pretext"-based exercise of congressional power anticipated and condemned in *McCulloch* because it involved an invocation of the commerce power to regulate matters of morality reserved for state control by the Tenth Amendment.[15]

The Court in the *Lottery Case* took care to limit its holding to the facts presented.[16] Before a decade had passed, however, the Court signaled that Congress could use the commerce-prohibiting technique to block the cross-border transportation of most anything it chose to target. A significant move in this direction came in *Hoke v. United States*,[17] which involved the constitutionality of a federal prohibition on transporting women across state lines for "immoral purposes."[18] Writing for a unanimous Court, Justice McKenna reasoned that "if the facility of interstate transportation can be taken away from the demoralization of lotteries, the debasement of obscene literature, the contagion of diseased cattle or persons, the impurity of food and drugs, the like facility can be taken away from the systematic enticement to and the enslavement in prostitution and debauchery of women . . . ."[19] Four years later, in *Caminetti v. United States*,[20] the Court relied on *Hoke* to sustain the conviction of a man for taking a woman across state lines to make her "his mistress and concubine," even in the absence of any plan of "commercialized vice."[21]

In *Hipolite Egg Co. v. United States*,[22] the Court turned its attention to the interaction of the commerce-prohibiting technique and Congress's authority under the Necessary and Proper Clause. At issue in the case was the legality of the confiscation by federal

---

14 *Id.* at 371.

15 *Id.* at 372.

16 *See id.* at 357 (majority opinion) (emphasizing the particular importance of "guarding the people of the United States against the widespread pestilence of lotteries" (internal quotations omitted)).

17 227 U.S. 308 (1913).

18 *Id.* at 308 (quoting 36 Stat. 825 (1910)).

19 *Id.* at 322.

20 242 U.S. 470 (1917).

21 *Id.* at 483–84. Justice Day, writing for the majority, assumed arguendo "that Congress has no power to punish one who travels in interstate commerce merely because he has the intention of committing an illegal or immoral act at the conclusion of the journey." *Id.* at 491. This case was different, however, because it involved the "transportation of passengers in interstate commerce." *Id.* Notwithstanding this qualification, Justice McKenna and two other Justices dissented. *Id.* at 496 (McKenna, dissenting).

22 220 U.S. 45 (1911).

authorities of "preserved whole eggs" that had been unlawfully shipped across state lines because their labels did not conform with federally established standards.[23] The defendant argued that the seizure violated the Constitution because the eggs "had passed out of interstate commerce" when they were commingled with other items at the place they were received.[24] The Court, however, declined to engage in a metaphysical inquiry about whether the eggs were "in" or "out" of interstate commerce at the time of the seizure.[25] Instead, with a tip of the hat to *McCulloch*, the Court reasoned that the power to confiscate mislabeled eggs, whether or not they remained in interstate commerce, was "an appropriate means to [the] end"[26] of preventing "trade in them between the states."[27]

The Court's reasoning in *Hipolite Egg* raised questions about Congress's ability to "boot-strap" its commerce-prohibiting power to justify regulation of intrastate activities. For example, could Congress prohibit all printing of lottery tickets, all production of preserved eggs, or all sexual acts between unmarried persons on the theory that laws of this kind would help to effectuate the bans on cross-border transit involved in the *Lottery Case*, *Hipolite Egg*, and *Hoke*? On this score, the Court's rhetoric seemed far-reaching. "The principle," the Court declared in *Caminetti*, "is the simple one . . . that Congress has power over transportation 'among the several states' . . . and that Congress, as an incident to it, may adopt not only means necessary but convenient to its exercise, and the means may have the quality of police regulations."[28]

Within eighteen months of making this pronouncement, however, the Court moved to cabin the scope of this commerce-prohibiting power. *Hammer v. Dagenhart*[29] was a case that grew out of the complex societal changes that marked the opening decades of the twentieth century. The late 1800s had seen sharp increases in immigration, industrialization, and urbanization in the United States, along with the emergence of crowded and unsanitary living environments and the exposure of countless laborers to unsafe, if not barbaric, working conditions. In response came entreaties for reform. As novelists, sociologists, and muckraking journalists decried the human costs of laissez faire capitalism, political movements that favored ameliorative legislation (loosely collected under the label of

---

[23] *Id.* at 49.

[24] *Id.* at 50.

[25] *See generally infra* Section 2.B (discussing the separate "in-commerce" theory of the commerce power).

[26] *Hipolite Egg*, 242 U.S. at 50.

[27] *Id.* at 58.

[28] *Caminetti*, 242 U.S. at 492 (quoting *Hoke*, 227 U.S. at 323).

[29] 247 U.S. 251 (1918).

"progressivism" and most famously personified in the form of President Theodore Roosevelt) began to take hold at both the state and federal levels. Reformers made important inroads when some state legislatures enacted protective measures such as minimum wage and maximum hour laws. It stood to reason, however, that the adoption of such measures might well cause employers to flee to states that touted more "pro-industry" legal regimes. There was, in part for this reason, a case to be made for federal intervention, and advocates of worker-protection laws made that case by calling on Congress to deploy the commerce-prohibiting technique.

A breakthrough came with Congress's adoption of the Child Labor Act of 1916. Built squarely on the commerce-prohibiting theory of federal power, the Act barred the interstate transportation of goods produced in factories that employed children under the age of 14 or that employed children between the ages of 14 and 16 at night, more than eight hours per day, or more than six days per week.[30] When the law was challenged, however, a five-Justice majority found a constitutional violation.[31] Writing for the Court, Justice Day reasoned that all the commerce-prohibiting precedents involved items that were intrinsically "harmful."[32] Here, in contrast, "[t]he goods shipped are of themselves harmless,"[33] and upholding the law would improperly bring "all manufacture intended for interstate shipment . . . under federal control to the practical exclusion of the authority of the states."[34]

The Court's opinion in *Hammer* spurred one of the most famous opinions of the "great dissenter," Oliver Wendell Holmes, Jr. Invoking the *Lottery Case* and its progeny, Justice Holmes insisted that the power of "prohibiting the carriage of certain goods in interstate or foreign commerce" was given to Congress "in unqualified terms."[35] He continued: "The notion that prohibition is any less prohibition when applied to things now thought evil I do not understand. But if there is any matter upon which civilized countries have agreed . . . it is the evil of premature and excessive child labor."[36] For Justice Holmes it was singularly wrong-headed to say

---

30 *See id.* at 268 n.1.

31 *Id.* at 276.

32 *Id.* at 271.

33 *Id.* at 272.

34 *Id.* Notably, Justice Day advanced this distinction after resurrecting the prohibition-is-not-regulation argument that had not been a winner in the *Lottery Case*. The commerce power, he explained, "is one to control the means by which commerce is carried on, which is directly the contrary of the assumed right to forbid commerce from moving." *Id.* at 269–70.

35 *Id.* at 277 (Holmes, J., dissenting).

36 *Id.* at 280.

that a prohibition on cross-border transit "is permissible as against strong drink but not as against the product of ruined lives."[37] In 1918, however, even Justice Holmes's eloquence could not save the Child Labor Act from his colleagues' fears that an unchecked congressional ability to employ the commerce-prohibiting technique would swallow up the states' police powers.[38]

B. THE IN-COMMERCE THEORY THROUGH 1936

After *Hammer* the commerce-prohibiting technique held little promise for justifying most federal laws that dealt with working conditions. It followed that, if such laws were going to take hold, lawyers would have to devise another strategy for defending them against federalism-based attack. The seeds of such a strategy lay in Justice Holmes's 1905 opinion for the Court in *Swift & Co. v. United States*,[39] which concerned an injunction under the Sherman Antitrust Act against meatpacking firms that conspired to hold down cattle prices in midwestern stockyards. In sustaining the federal action, Justice Holmes explained:

> When cattle are sent for sale from a place in one state, with the expectation that they will end their transit, after purchase, in another, and when in effect they do so, with only the interruption necessary to find a purchaser at the stock yards, and when this is a typical, constantly recurring course, the current thus existing is a current of commerce among the states, and the purchase of the cattle is a part and incident of such commerce.[40]

Four years after *Hammer*, in *Stafford v. Wallace*,[41] the Court again invoked this current-of-commerce theory in upholding the unfair-trade-practice prohibition of the Packers and Stockyards Act of 1921. As stated by Chief Justice Taft: "The stockyards are but a throat through which the current flows, and the transactions which occur

---

37 *Id.*

38 Even so, in keeping with the rationale of *Hammer* the Court continued to uphold exercises of the commerce-prohibiting technique as to goods that were seen as threatening "the spread of any evil or harm." Brooks v. United States, 267 U.S. 432, 436 (1925) (stolen cars). *See, e.g.*, *Simpson*, 252 U.S. at 467 (holding that "Congress could . . . control" the "introduction of intoxicating liquor" from one state into another).

39 196 U.S. 375 (1905).

40 *Id.* at 398–99. It was also in this case that Justice Holmes coined the oft-quoted passage that "commerce among the states is not a technical legal conception, but a practical one, drawn from the course of business." *Id.* at 398.

41 258 U.S. 495 (1922).

therein are only incident to this current from the West to the East, and from one state to another."[42]

Swift and *Stafford*, however, left many questions unanswered. Could Congress, for example, invoke the in-commerce theory to regulate activity—including child labor, wages, and working hours—that did not concern, at least directly, prices or product-marketing practices? Could Congress use this theory to regulate activities at the beginning or the end, rather than in the middle, of a product-distribution process? In short, just how long, wide, and deep was this "stream of commerce" that the Court had empowered Congress to regulate?[43]

Telling answers to these questions came in the Supreme Court's then-seminal decisions in *A.L.A. Schechter Poultry Corp. v. United States*[44] and *Carter v. Carter Coal Co.*[45] Each of these cases grew out of events stirred by the stock market collapse of 1929. As the Great Depression gripped the nation—with joblessness, mortgage foreclosures, and business failures reaching unprecedented proportions—the Republican-controlled government under the leadership of President Herbert Hoover responded with only minimal federal intervention. One consequence of this choice was a sweeping Democratic victory in the election of 1932, which placed President Franklin D. Roosevelt in office with a mandate for reform. And President Roosevelt did not hesitate to act. Sweeping new programs, brought into law under his leadership, engaged the federal government in regulating securities markets, overseeing welfare programs, and supervising labor conditions.

Schechter Poultry involved a challenge to one such initiative, the National Industrial Recovery Act of 1933 (NIRA), which delegated authority to the President to promulgate "codes of fair competition" that regulated, among other things, minimum pay and maximum hours in marketplaces throughout much of the nation. The case arose from the prosecution of two operators of a small wholesale poultry market in Brooklyn for violating wage and hour rules (as well as inspection, licensing, and disclosure rules) imposed by a code of fair

---

[42] *Id.* at 516.

[43] Addressing one aspect of this question, the Court made it clear in *Chicago Board of Trade v. Olsen*, 262 U.S. 1 (1923), that the principle of *Swift* and *Stafford* was not limited to cases involving cattle. Relying squarely on those cases, the Court upheld price-related regulations applicable to grain "stored on its way from the West to the East as it is being sold on the exchange." *Id.* at 36.

[44] 295 U.S. 495 (1935).

[45] 298 U.S. 238 (1936). In addition to raising questions about the scope of Congress's power under the Commerce Clause, both *Schechter Poultry* and *Carter Coal* raised questions about whether Congress had violated the "nondelegation" doctrine by conferring too much rulemaking authority on nonlegislative actors. For further discussion of these issues, see *infra* Section 29.B.

competition, promulgated under the NIRA, for the poultry industry in metropolitan New York City. The operators predictably argued that application of the NIRA to their localized business exceeded the reach of the commerce power. Lawyers for the government predictably responded that the market was part of the "stream" of interstate commerce because 96% of poultry purchased for resale in New York (and thus passed along by wholesalers like the defendants) had come from other states.[46] Writing for the Court, Chief Justice Hughes concluded that the current of commerce recognized and relied on in *Swift* and *Stafford* did not flow this far. Rather, as he explained, "[w]hen defendants had made their purchases, whether at the West Washington Market in New York City or at the railroad terminals serving the city . . . for local disposition . . . [t]he interstate transactions in relation to that poultry then ended."[47] Thus, "decisions which deal with a stream of interstate commerce—where goods come to rest within a state temporarily and are later to go forward in interstate commerce—and with the regulations of transactions involved in that practical continuity of movement, are not applicable here."[48]

What *Schechter Poultry* did to the mouth of the stream of commerce, *Carter Coal* did to its source. At issue in that case was the constitutionality of the wage and hour provisions of the Bituminous Coal Conservation Act of 1935. More specifically, the case presented the question whether Congress could regulate the underlying causes of labor discord within the coal industry on the theory that the industry provided the well-spring of a great stream of commerce that carried essential fuel to every metropolis and hamlet of the nation. The answer was "no." In *Swift* and *Stafford*, Justice Sutherland explained, "[i]t was nowhere suggested . . . that the interstate commerce power extended to the growth or production of the things which, after production, entered the flow."[49] And any lingering doubt about whether "*Swift* and kindred cases" reached beyond this "restricted field" had been removed by *Schechter Poultry*.[50]

In short, the in-commerce theory was not destined to sustain the boldest expressions of New Deal regulatory energies so long as the Supreme Court remained unshaped by the guiding hand of President Roosevelt. Advocates of federal power, however, had one last arrow in their quiver. Citing *Gibbons*, they argued that Congress could pass

---

[46] *Schechter Poultry*, 295 U.S. at 519.

[47] *Id.* at 542–43.

[48] *Id.* at 543.

[49] *Carter Coal*, 298 U.S. at 305.

[50] *Id.* at 306 ("In the Schechter case the flow had ceased. Here it had not begun. The difference is not one of substance. The applicable principle is the same.").

laws, including the laws at issue in *Schechter Poultry* and *Carter Coal*, on the theory that they dealt with matters that "affected" interstate commerce.

C. THE AFFECTING-COMMERCE THEORY THROUGH 1936

Even though the Court in *Gibbons* had suggested that the commerce power authorizes regulation of intrastate activities that "affect other states,"[51] Congress seldom invoked this theory of the Commerce Clause to enact federal legislation during the 1800s. As the century neared its close, however, the proliferation of railroads and other large business enterprises triggered enactment of two major federal laws based in large part on the affecting-commerce theory: the Interstate Commerce Act of 1887 and the Sherman Antitrust Act of 1890.

As soon as the Sherman Act's ban on monopolization landed in the law books, federal authorities began to put it to work. An early civil action targeted acquisitions that gave a single corporation control of 98% of the nation's sugar refining business. In response to the government's demand for divestiture, the firm argued that the commerce power did not permit Congress to outlaw a monopoly in manufacture, and the Court agreed in *United States v. E. C. Knight Co.*[52] The problem with the government's position, according to Chief Justice Fuller, was that "[c]ommerce succeeds to manufacture, and is not a part of it"[53] because commerce involves "buying and selling and the transportation incidental thereto."[54] The Chief Justice acknowledged that "the power to control the manufacture of a given thing involves, in a certain sense, the control of its disposition."[55] He added, however, that controlling the manufacture of an item "affects [commerce] only incidentally and indirectly" or in "a secondary, and not the primary, sense."[56] In short, Congress could not control the production of refined sugar, including by busting a trust in that industry. Otherwise "congress would be invested, to the exclusion of the states, with the power to regulate, not only manufactures, but also agriculture, horticulture, stock-raising, domestic fisheries, mining; in short, every branch of human industry."[57]

---

[51] 22 U.S. (9 Wheat.) 1, 195 (1824).

[52] 156 U.S. 1 (1895).

[53] *Id.* at 12.

[54] *Id.* at 14.

[55] *Id.* at 11.

[56] *Id.*

[57] *Id.* at 14. This thought was not an original one. It reached back at least as far as the events that led to the nullification crisis of 1832, when South Carolina proclaimed its constitutional authority to ignore federal tariffs on imported cotton

Conveniently omitted from the Court's exegesis (though not from Justice Harlan's lone but prescient dissent) was any reference to *McCulloch*'s endorsement of a capacious congressional authority to choose among different potential means for carrying its enumerated powers into effect. In particular, a Court guided by *McCulloch* might well have concluded that the congressional effort to counteract monopoly pricing was "conducive" to facilitating interstate commerce in sugar and thus fell squarely within the authority granted to Congress by the conjoined operation of the Commerce and Necessary and Proper Clauses. Instead, the Court embraced an entirely different style of analysis. Relying on a parade-of-horribles argument, it forged a categorical rule designed to keep the affecting-commerce prong of the congressional power within meaningful, judicially discernable bounds. The rule was simple: Manufacturing (and other forms of production) were in and of themselves beyond the reach of congressional regulation even in the face of powerful arguments that those activities did have a profound real-world effect on interstate commerce. But just how far did this principle extend?[58]

The Court began to answer that question, while simultaneously salvaging the federal antitrust laws, in *Addyston Pipe & Steel Co. v. United States*[59] and *Northern Securities Co. v. United States*.[60] In the former case, it was enough to establish a "direct, immediate and intended relation"[61] to interstate commerce that the pipe-manufacturer defendants had entered into a conspiracy for the purpose of fixing prices for "the future disposition of the

---

goods. Even this purported use of the federal taxing authority, theorists such as John C. Calhoun declared, was an unconstitutional attempt to promote domestic manufacture. *See* DANIEL A. FARBER, LINCOLN'S CONSTITUTION 59 (2003). Notably, Joseph Story criticized this view in his treatise on constitutional law. 2 JOSEPH STORY, COMMENTARIES ON THE CONSTITUTION §§ 1073–1090 (1833).

[58] It bears emphasis that the Court in *E.C. Knight* did not address whether the monopolist's action took place "in" interstate commerce—perhaps because the Court deemed it apparent (as a successor Court would later declare in *Carter Coal*, *see infra* notes 81–84 and accompanying text) that the production of goods necessarily occurs before the stream of commerce in those goods begins to flow. Put another way, it is critical to see that the in-commerce theory and the affecting-commerce theory of the commerce power provide entirely different doctrinal touchstones for assessing the constitutionality of any claimed exercise of the commerce power. Thus, the preceding discussion of the in-commerce theory (including with regard to the production-related federal law at issue in *Carter Coal*) is not relevant, at least in a direct way, to the discussion here of the entirely separate affecting-commerce theory. As we soon will see, however, the treatment of the affecting-commerce theory in *E.C. Knight* did bear heavily on the Court's treatment of that same affecting-commerce theory (as opposed to the government's alternative in-commerce theory) in assessing the constitutionality of the law at issue in *Carter Coal*.

[59] 175 U.S. 211 (1899).

[60] 193 U.S. 197 (1904).

[61] *Addyston Pipe & Steel Co.*, 175 U.S. at 243.

manufactured article."[62] In the latter case, the Court concluded that Congress could outlaw an acquisition of corporate securities that threatened to decrease competition in interstate train rates because the transaction directly affected interstate commerce.[63] A cohort of four dissenters stood ready to fence off securities transfers altogether from the reach of the federal commerce power, advocating in effect a categorical rule of non-regulability akin to the rule applied to manufacturing in *E. C. Knight*.[64] Emphasizing fact over form, however, the Court's majority refused to distinguish a competition-squelching consolidation by way of share transfers from a conspiracy of independent operators effected by way of contractual arrangement.

Any doubt about the freestanding significance of the affecting-commerce prong of the commerce power fell away with the Court's decision in the *Shreveport Rate Case* (*Houston, East & West Texas Railway Co. v. United States*).[65] At issue was an order promulgated pursuant to the Interstate Commerce Act that in effect set rates charged by railroad companies for the intrastate transport of goods in an effort to counter discrimination against interstate shipments.[66] A seven-Justice majority upheld this order, reasoning that Congress's regulatory authority over "instruments of interstate commerce" extended to intrastate "matters having such a close and substantial relation to interstate traffic that the control is essential or appropriate to the . . . maintenance of conditions under which interstate commerce may be conducted upon fair terms."[67] The Court noted that it had previously upheld federal regulation of the equipment used on intrastate trains because of the "close relation" that the safety of intrastate traffic bore to the effective operation of rail cars moving across state lines.[68] Here too, the Court reasoned, federal regulatory authority could be "exerted to prevent the intrastate operations of such carriers from being made a means of injury to that which has been confided to Federal care."[69]

---

62 *Id.* at 240 (emphasis added).

63 *No. Secs. Co.*, 193 U.S. at 344.

64 *Id.* at 402–03 (Holmes, J., dissenting).

65 234 U.S. 342 (1914).

66 For example, prior to issuance of the order, "[t]he rate on furniture from Dallas to Longview, Texas, 124 miles, was 24.8 cents, and that from Shreveport [in Louisiana] to Longview, 65.7 miles was 35 cents." *Id.* at 346.

67 *Id.* at 351.

68 The key case was *Southern Railway Co. v. United States*, 222 U.S. 20, 27 (1911) (upholding the application of a federal rule requiring the use of safe coupling devices to railroad cars employed only in intrastate journeys, albeit on tracks that covered interstate routes, because "trains on the same railroad are . . . interdependent; for whatever brings delay or disaster to one, or results in disabling one of its operatives, is calculated to impede the progress and imperil the safety of other trains").

69 *Shreveport Rate Case*, 234 U.S. at 351; *see also id.* at 353 ("This is not to say that Congress possesses the authority to regulate the internal commerce of a state, as

As President Roosevelt crafted his New Deal program, these precedents loomed large. "Cases such as *Shreveport* were encouraging; yet cases like *Knight* looked the other way."[70] It remained for the Court to say how far Congress could go in regulating local matters on the theory that they "affected" interstate commerce, and the first test came in *Railroad Retirement Board v. Alton R. Co.*[71] The issue in *Alton Railroad* was whether Congress could force interstate railroad carriers to adopt pension plans for their employees. The basic argument for constitutionality was simple: Sound retirement structures would help build employee loyalty and morale, thus "promot[ing] . . . efficiency and safety in interstate transportation."[72] A five-Justice majority, however, found this argument unavailing. Justice Roberts recognized (as he had to in light of past decisions) that rules that limited railroad workers' hours and that assured them fair compensation for injuries "have a direct and intimate connection with the actual operation of the railroads."[73] Marshaling empirical and intuition-based arguments, however, he declared that any connection between governmentally mandated pensions and efficient interstate train service was too tenuous to sustain the legislation as a regulation of "commerce . . . among the several states."[74] To this thought he added the now-familiar parade-of-horribles flourish. If the challenged retirement-payment scheme were sustained, he observed, federal mandates requiring employers to provide "for free medical attendance and nursing, for clothing, for food, for housing, for the education of children, and a hundred other matters, might with equal propriety be proposed as tending to relieve

---

such, but that it does possess the power to foster and protect interstate commerce, and to take all measures necessary or appropriate to that end, although intrastate transactions of interstate carriers may thereby be controlled."). For a later case employing similar logic in a different setting, *see United States v. Ferger*, 250 U.S. 199, 203–05 (1919) (upholding a federal prohibition on the forgery of bills of lading; relying in part on the assertion that such bills "are instrumentalities of . . . commerce" but also citing the "effect" on the regulated behavior and the danger that "the credit and confidence which sustains interstate commerce would . . . be impaired or weakened by the unrestrained right to fabricate and circulate spurious bills").

70 KATHLEEN M. SULLIVAN & GERALD GUNTHER, CONSTITUTIONAL LAW 130 (14th ed. 2001).

71 295 U.S. 330 (1935).

72 *Id.* at 364.

73 *Id.* at 369. Justice Roberts did not discuss these cases in great detail, but he did offer some comments on why other railroad-employee laws were, or might be, constitutional. A law governing labor relations in the railroad industry, for example, was constitutional because facilitating "the amicable settlement of disputes which threatened the service of the necessary agencies of interstate transportation tended to prevent interruptions of service." *Id.* at 367. And a worker's compensation program for railroad workers was more readily sustainable than the challenged retirement law in part because "the very certainty that compensation must be paid for every injury . . . promotes and encourages precaution on the part of the employer against accident and tends to make transportation safer and more efficient." *Id.* at 370.

74 *Id.* at 351.

the employee of mental strain and worry."[75] Without citing the pretext language of *McCulloch*, Justice Roberts in effect invoked its principle: "Is it not apparent that [such laws] are really and essentially related solely to the social welfare of the worker, and therefore remote from any regulation of commerce as such? We think the answer is plain. These matters obviously lie outside the orbit of congressional power."[76]

The precedential significance of *Alton Railroad* was unclear from the start. The Railroad Retirement Act had been clumsily drawn, the Court's reliance on federalism principles to invalidate it came in an alternative holding, and the Court carefully distinguished a compulsory retirement program from maximum-hour and collective-bargaining laws applicable to the railroad industry. Nonetheless, the pretext reasoning of *Alton Railroad* hung like the sword of Damocles over other New Deal initiatives that had been enacted on an affecting-commerce theory. Would the sword fall? The answer came—as it had with regard to the scope of the in-commerce principle—in *Schechter Poultry* and *Carter Coal*.

In *Schechter Poultry*, government lawyers had not relied solely on the in-commerce theory. They also advanced an affecting-commerce rationale in defense of federal minimum-wage laws that targeted localized work forces. "Maintaining wage distributions," the government asserted, "would provide the necessary stimulus in starting 'the cumulative forces making for expanding commercial activity,' " which in turn would revitalize the entire border-crossing economy of the United States.[77] The Court responded to this effects-based argument by insisting that "[e]xtraordinary conditions do not create or enlarge constitutional power,"[78] that already-operative precedents required attention to "the well-established distinction between direct and indirect effects,"[79] and that the hours and wages of Schechter Poultry's employees had "no direct relation to interstate commerce" because they concerned only "the details of defendants' management of their local business."[80]

---

75 *Id.* at 368.

76 *Id.*

77 *Schechter Poultry*, 295 U.S. at 550.

78 *Id.* at 528.

79 *Id.* at 546.

80 *Id.* at 548. Seeking to tie its affecting-commerce defense of the statute more directly to interstate commerce in poultry, the government also argued that low wages contributed to lower charges for chickens and "that the cutting of prices brings about a demoralization of the price structure," which generally inhibits commerce in poultry products. *Id.* at 548–49. Once again moved by a parade-of-horribles counterattack, however, the Court responded that this argument "proves too much." *Id.* at 549. If the federal government could control wages because of their effect on prices, then on the

Shortly thereafter, in *Carter Coal*, the Court completed the circle by holding that Congress could not justify application of wage-and-hour rules to the nation's coal mines on an affecting-commerce rationale. In reaching this conclusion, the Court invoked both *E. C. Knight* and *Hammer v. Dagenhart* for the proposition that production involved "a purely local activity," which in its nature had only an "indirect" effect on interstate commerce.[81] In a critical passage, Justice Sutherland explained:

> The distinction between a direct and an indirect effect turns, not upon the magnitude of either the cause or the effect, but entirely upon the manner in which the effect has been brought about. If the production by one man of a single ton of coal intended for interstate sale and shipment, and actually so sold and shipped, affects interstate commerce indirectly, the effect does not become direct by multiplying the tonnage, or increasing the number of men employed, or adding to the expense or complexities of the business, or by all combined. It is quite true that rules of law are sometimes qualified by considerations of degree, as the government argues. But the matter of degree has no bearing upon the question here, since that question is not—What is the extent of the local activity or condition, or the extent of the effect produced upon interstate commerce? but—What is the relation between the activity or condition and the effect?[82]

Put another way, it might well be that struggles over "wages, working conditions, the right of collective bargaining, etc." invite strikes and work stoppages that "greatly" affect coal prices and the resulting vibrancy of interstate commerce.[83] "But . . . the conclusive answer is that the evils are all local," and "[s]uch effect as they may have upon commerce, however extensive it may be, is secondary and indirect."[84]

Carter Coal did not resolve all questions concerning the constitutionality of New Deal reforms. The Court, for example, was careful to sidestep the simmering question whether Congress could establish federal price controls for coal sales (as opposed to wage-and-hour controls for coal workers) on an affecting-commerce theory.[85]

---

same theory it could "control . . . the number of employees, rents, advertising, methods of doing business, etc." *Id.*

[81] *Carter Coal*, 298 U.S. at 304.

[82] *Id.* at 308.

[83] *Id.* at 304.

[84] *Id.* at 304, 309.

[85] The majority invalidated price-control regulations made applicable to coal sales on the theory that these regulations—whether or not constitutional under the Commerce Clause in and of themselves—were not severable from the invalidated

From President Roosevelt's perspective, however, the *Schechter Poultry* and *Carter Coal* decisions were nothing short of catastrophic. Decrying them as usurpations, the President declared to the nation that "we must take action to save the Constitution from the Court and the Court from itself."[86] Follow-up action came in the form of the President's effort to "pack" the Court with additional Justices of his own choosing. This gambit ultimately failed,[87] but the Court itself soon gave the President just what he had sought to secure—namely, a substantially reworked (and far more capacious) judicial understanding of Congress's power to regulate interstate commerce.

---

wage-and-hour regulations. *Id.* at 316–17. In a dissenting opinion joined by Justices Brandeis and Stone, Justice Cardozo reached the question whether the price rules were constitutional and found no Commerce Clause problem. He reasoned that "[t]o regulate the price for [coal sold in interstate transactions] is to regulate commerce itself," and that "prices for intrastate sales of coal have so inescapable a relation to those for interstate sales that a system of regulation for transactions of the one class is necessary to give adequate protection to the system of regulation adopted for the other." *Id.* at 326 (Cardozo, J., dissenting). Notably, Justice Cardozo's position in time carried the day. *See* Sunshine Anthracite Coal Co. v. Adkins, 310 U.S. 381 (1940).

[86] Franklin D. Roosevelt, *Fireside Chat on Reorganization of the Judiciary* (March 9, 1937), *available at* http://docs.fdrlibrary.marist.edu/030937.html.

[87] For further discussion of the court-packing plan, see *infra* Section 34.B.1.c.

Chapter 3

THE COMMERCE POWER FROM 1937 THROUGH 1994: THE ROOSEVELT-ERA REVOLUTION AND BEYOND

Analysis

In March of 1937, the Court handed President Roosevelt a major victory when it upheld the National Labor Relations Act's protections of union activity, including in the manufacturing sector, in *NLRB v. Jones & Laughlin Steel Corp.*[1] This action was followed by a string of rulings hospitable to the President's New Deal program. In each case, the four outliers in *Alton Railroad* and *Carter Coal* (Chief Justice Hughes and Justices Brandeis, Stone, and Cardozo) found a new ally in Justice Roberts, who had joined the majority opinion in the latter case and written passionately for the Court in the former.[2] The judicial revolution touched off in 1937 had profound implications for each of the three prongs of the congressional commerce power. Within five short years, the limiting approaches of *Hammer*, *Schechter Poultry*, and *Carter Coal* would be things of the past. In coming decades, a Court dominated by disciples of the New Deal would uphold sweeping federal legislation concerning labor relations, civil

---

1 301 U.S. 1 (1937).

2 In this set of decisions, the Court not only moved away from the direct/indirect distinction of its earlier commerce-power jurisprudence, but also abandoned previous "freedom of contract" rulings about individual rights that threatened minimum-wage and other business-regulating efforts under both state and federal law. *See generally* ROBERT G. MCCLOSKEY, THE AMERICAN SUPREME COURT 117–20 (2d ed. 1994) (revised by Sanford Levinson). Most significantly, during the same term that produced *Carter Coal*, *see supra* Section 2.B, the Court in *Morehead v. New York ex rel. Tipaldo*, 298 U.S. 587 (1936), had invalidated New York's minimum wage for female employees by a five-to-four vote. Yet, in *West Coast Hotel v. Parrish*, 300 U.S. 379 (1937), decided two weeks before *Jones & Laughlin Steel*, the Court again by a five-to-four vote upheld a Washington statute that likewise established a minimum wage for women. Once again, it was Justice Roberts who joined the majority in both cases.

rights, environmental protection, and local crime, relying primarily on a much-broadened affecting-commerce theory. Indeed, the spirit of judicial restraint became so pronounced that, for a period of nearly 60 years, the Court did not identify a single federal law that exceeded the commerce power.

A. THE CHANNELS/INSTRUMENTALITIES THEORY AND THE COMMERCE-PROHIBITING TECHNIQUE FROM 1937 THROUGH 1994

In the period following 1936, the Court built on its earlier rulings that endorsed Congress's power to regulate the "channels" and "instrumentalities" of interstate commerce.[3] As new technologies proliferated, so did the Court's willingness to sustain congressional measures concerning such things as airplanes, telecommunications facilities, and natural gas pipelines.[4] These laws and rulings served to keep the avenues of interstate commerce open and well-functioning. But the Court also strengthened Congress's ability to block interstate trade by lending new energy to the commerce-prohibiting technique. The Court's key post-1936 encounter with the theory came in *United States v. Darby*,[5] and the Court's decision in that case left no doubt that a new day for the commerce power had dawned.

Following the Court's validation of the National Labor Relations Act (NLRA) in 1937,[6] Congress quickly erected another major pillar of modern labor law, the Fair Labor Standards Act of 1938 (FLSA). The question of that act's constitutionality came before the Court in *Darby*, which involved a prosecution under each of the statute's two principal sections. The first provision, section 15(a)(1), barred transportation across any state line of goods manufactured by workers who were not paid a specified minimum wage or who were required to work more than a specified maximum number of hours. The Court recognized that this attempted use of the commerce-prohibiting technique could not stand under the authority of *Hammer v. Dagenhart*[7] because goods made by underpaid and

---

3 Perez v. United States, 402 U.S. 146, 150 (1971) (referencing this line of cases); *see, e.g.*, Oklahoma *ex rel.* Phillips v. Guy F. Atkinson Co., 313 U.S. 508, 523 (1941) (noting, among other things, that "Congress may exercise its control over the non-navigable stretches of a river in order to preserve or promote commerce on the navigable portions").

4 *See, e.g.*, Consolidated Edison Co. v. NLRB, 305 U.S. 197, 213 (1938) (lumping telegraph, telephone, radio, and airport operations together with railroads and shipping in discussing the mechanisms of "interstate and foreign commerce").

5 312 U.S. 100 (1941).

6 *See Jones & Laughlin Steel*, 301 U.S. 1; *see infra* Section 3.C.1 (discussing this decision in greater detail).

7 247 U.S. 251 (1918) (discussed *supra* Section 2.A).

overworked laborers, no less than goods made by underaged laborers, failed to qualify as condemnable "of themselves."[8] The Court dealt with this difficulty by declaring that *Hammer* "should be and now is overruled."[9] Tracking the "powerful and now classic dissent of Mr. Justice Holmes,"[10] the Court declared that exercises of the commerce-prohibiting technique would be constitutional, from that day forward, whatever the underlying motive of Congress and whether or not the transported goods were intrinsically "harmful or deleterious."[11]

The second provision at issue in *Darby*, section 15(a)(2), required employers to comply with federal wage-and-hour rules for all employees engaged in making goods for shipment across state lines. The commerce-prohibiting technique, standing alone, could not sustain this provision because it did not target interstate movements per se; rather, it directed its prohibition at the employers of workers involved in the production of goods prior to their shipment. Even so, the Court sustained the provision by relying on two separate affecting-commerce-related rationales, one of which was intimately connected to the congressional ban on cross-border movements.[12] In

---

8 *Id.* at 272.

9 *Darby*, 312 U.S. at 117. Citing the *Lottery Case* and its progeny, the Court explained that *Hammer* "was a departure from the principles which have prevailed in the interpretation of the commerce clause both before and since the decision." *Id.* at 116–117. Particularly important among the post-*Hammer* precedents was *Kentucky Whip & Collar Co. v. Illinois Cent. R.R. Co.*, 299 U.S. 334 (1937). There the Court had distinguished *Hammer* on the ground that the challenged law reflected not just an attempt to achieve favored federal objectives, but a genuine effort "to prevent [interstate] commerce from being used to impede the carrying out of the state policy." *Id.* at 351. For a general discussion of how the commerce-prohibiting technique developed in the pre-1937 period, see *supra* Section 2.A.

10 *Darby*, 312 U.S. at 115.

11 *Id.* at 116. The Court, moreover, has been true to its word. *See, e.g.*, Cleveland v. United States, 329 U.S. 14, 19 (1946) (upholding a ban on interstate transport of women for "immoral purpose[s]" as applied to men who transported women across state lines for purposes of involving them in polygamous marriages); United States v. Carolene Prods. Co., 304 U.S. 144 (1938) (upholding a prohibition on interstate shipment of "filled" milk).

12 The Court's alternative affecting-commerce rationale focused on "the evils . . . of substandard labor conditions" and the "dislocation of the commerce" they brought about, *Darby*, 312 U.S. at 122, including by, as the Court would later put it in *Maryland v. Wirtz*, 392 U.S. 183 (1968), "driving down labor conditions in [other] states." *Id.* at 189. In addition, "substandard labor conditions tended to lead to labor disputes and strikes" and those conditions inevitably threatened "the flow of goods in commerce" across state lines. *Wirtz*, 392 U.S. at 191 (discussing *Darby*'s ratio decidendi). Notably, in *Wirtz*, the Court made clear that this rationale applied not only to suppliers but also to purchasers of goods in interstate commerce. *See id.*; *see also* Overnight Motor Transp. Co. v. Missel, 316 U.S. 572, 576 (1942) (noting, in upholding the FLSA as applied to a transit company employee, that "undue extension of hours, . . . by inducing labor discontent [is] apt to lead to interference with commerce through interruption of work"; also adverting to the problem of unfair competition and resulting "friction between production areas with different length workweeks"). Notably, by the time of *Darby*, the Court's decisions in the NLRA cases had retreated enough from the manufacturing-is-not-commerce principle that the Court could apply

particular, this line of analysis hinged on the Court's willingness to let Congress adopt "appropriate aids" to effectuating the prohibition on cross-border shipments imposed by section 15(a)(1).[13] As the Court explained: "Congress, having by the present Act adopted the policy of excluding from interstate commerce all goods produced for the commerce which do not conform to the specified labor standards . . . may choose the means reasonably adapted to the attainment of the permitted end, even though they involve control of intrastate activities."[14] Although this rationale harkened back to *Hipolite Egg*'s approval of post-delivery seizures of improperly shipped goods based on an invocation of the Necessary and Proper Clause,[15] it made clear that the governing principle had an even longer reach. Now the Court stood ready to countenance bans not only on post-shipment activities concerning goods that had already unlawfully moved across state lines, but also on pre-shipment activities that might facilitate violations of channels-of-commerce-type restrictions.[16]

Professor Gerald Gunther famously detected in this latter rationale a "superbootstrap suggestion" that raised questions about just how far Congress could go in leveraging the commerce-prohibiting technique to regulate intrastate behavior.[17] Could Congress ban intrastate production-related activities by all workers paid less than a specified wage (including, for example, employees in a local bakery or sandwich shop) to effectuate the federal prohibition on the interstate transport of goods made in violation of federal wage standards? Could Congress bar the interstate movement of persons in polygamous relationships and then impose a nationwide ban on

---

this broadened affecting-commerce rationale to the lumber producer involved in the case. *See infra* Section 3.C.1.

[13] *Darby*, 312 U.S. at 120.

[14] *Id.* at 121.

[15] *See supra* Chapter 2.

[16] As the Court noted in *Darby*, this sort of means-to-the-end justification for regulating pre-shipment local activity had surfaced in the pre-1937 period. For example, in *Thornton v. United States*, 271 U.S. 414 (1926), the Court held that "Congress may require inspection and preventive treatment of all cattle in a disease infected area in order to prevent shipment in interstate commerce of some of the cattle without the treatment." *Darby*, 312 U.S. at 121 (citing *Thornton*). Not surprisingly, however, the Court in *Thornton* had emphasized the distinctly national nature of the problem posed by "the spread of disease from one state to another by [infected] cattle." *Thornton*, 271 U.S. at 425. The Court in *Thornton* also had pointed out that the indictment at issue in the case concerned activity in a county "on the line between Georgia and Florida" and that "cattle ranged between one state and the other in that region." *Id.* at 421; *see also Kentucky Whip & Collar Co.*, 299 U.S. at 352–53 (reasoning that Congress could pass laws "reasonable and appropriate" for effectuating its ban on interstate shipments of "convict-made goods" into states where possession of such goods was unlawful and concluding that this authority authorized a congressional ban on interstate shipment of all such goods not labeled in conformance with federal standards "regardless of the law of the State of destination").

[17] GERALD GUNTHER, CONSTITUTIONAL LAW 143–44 (11th ed 1985).

such relationships, even if they were permissible under governing state law, to make sure that no such interstate movements occur?[18] The answers to these questions, insofar as they concern the commerce power, remain unclear to this day.[19] In the post-1936 period, however, the Court continued to uphold regulations of intrastate activities on the ground that they helped to block the occurrence of federally outlawed cross-border movements.[20]

In *United States v. Sullivan*,[21] for example, the Court held that Congress could prohibit the movement of drugs labeled in violation of federal standards and, so as to effectuate that prohibition, could also bar any post-shipment relabeling of drugs in violation of those standards. In addition, the Court held that Congress could apply this ban on intrastate relabeling even to a pharmacist who (1) had not been involved at all in the drugs' interstate shipment; (2) had obtained the drugs in a purely intrastate purchase six months after their arrival in the state; and (3) had violated the law not by removing the label from any container shipped across state lines but instead by failing to re-affix the federally required label to separate smaller containers used in repackaging the drugs for retail

---

[18] *Cf.* Cleveland v. United States, 329 U.S. 14, 19 (1946) (noting that "[t]he fact that the regulation of marriage is a state matter does not, of course, make the Mann Act . . . unconstitutional" and that the commerce-prohibiting power "may be used to defeat what are deemed to be immoral practices" even if the means used "have 'the quality of police regulations' " (quoting Hoke v. United States, 227 U.S. 308, 323 (1913)).

[19] This statement is qualified with the words "insofar as they concern the commerce power" because exercises of that commerce power may be trumped by freestanding constitutional restraints, such as those imposed by the Bill of Rights. For example, a constitutional right of free interstate travel or a right of intimate association might override congressional efforts to inhibit the interstate movement (either directly or indirectly) of persons in polygamous relationships.

[20] *See, e.g.*, United States v. Walsh, 331 U.S. 432, 437–38 (1947) (sustaining a prohibition on the making of false guaranties that drugs are properly labeled to "one engaged wholly or partly in an interstate business" as a proper means to block interstate shipments of mislabeled drugs because, absent the prohibition, the purchaser is "more likely to engage in interstate distribution without making an independent check of the product"; upholding application of this law even though the wrongful sale occurred intrastate and there was no showing of the purchaser's intention to resell the particular drugs out of state); Oklahoma Press Publ'g Co. v. Walling, 327 U.S. 186, 192 (1946) (upholding congressional authority to permit the administrator of the U.S. Department of Labor's Wage and Hour Division to issue subpoenas under the FLSA designed to get information about whether firms are subject to the act or have violated it); Kirschbaum v. Walling, 316 U.S. 517, 526 (1942) (finding no constitutional problem in applying the FLSA to elevator operators and other employees of the lessor of work space used by lessees in the production of goods for interstate shipment under a statutory provision extending it to any person engaged in an "occupation necessary to [such] production"); Cloverleaf Butter Co. v. Patterson, 315 U.S. 148, 154–55 (1942) (vindicating federal authority over "manufacturing processes" of "renovated butter," including by preempting state rules regarding pre-shipment seizures, as part of the "appropriate means" Congress could use in connection with its ban on cross-border movements of this product).

[21] 332 U.S. 689 (1948).

transfer.[22] Given the separate ban on cross-border shipments of mislabeled drugs, the majority deemed it sufficient that the law dealt with "the branding of articles that have completed an interstate shipment and are being held for future sales."[23]

The implications of *Sullivan* for future "super-bootstrapping" efforts, particularly in regulating pre-shipment conduct, remain unclear. After all, the Court in *Sullivan*, like the Court in *Hipolite Egg*, dealt with post-shipment, rather than pre-shipment, behavior. No less important, *Darby* itself is susceptible to a reading that does not authorize prohibitions on all forms of local activity by way of a "superbootstrap" theory. In particular, the wage-and-hour rules made applicable to local workers by section 15(a)(2) did not extend to employees engaged in any and all production activities, but only those particular employees who were involved in "the production of goods for interstate commerce."[24] The bottom line is that neither *Darby* nor its progeny unequivocally gave to Congress an unbounded ability to pass any law governing any intrastate activity on the theory that it effectuates to any extent a statutory ban on the movement of particular items or persons across state lines.[25]

---

[22] *Id.* at 691–92, 696.

[23] *Id.* at 698. The Court relied on *McDermott v. Wisconsin*, 228 U.S. 115 (1913), in which it had upheld a federal statute that required the proper labeling of foods shipped in interstate commerce and that barred the post-shipment intrastate relabeling of such foods as long as they remained "unsold." *Id.* at 131. Citing *McCulloch* and *Hipolite Egg*, the Court found this ban on relabeling a "means appropriate" to keeping "the channels of [interstate] commerce free from the transportation of illicit or harmful articles," *id.* at 128, because the "opportunity for inspection en route may be very inadequate" and because the "real opportunity" for effective inspection might well exist only after delivery and prior to resale, *id.* at 136. In *Sullivan*, the Court found *McDermott* controlling notwithstanding asserted distinctions based on the defendant's intrastate repurchasing of the items and his repackaging of them prior to sale.

[24] *Darby*, 312 U.S. at 117. *See also* N. Am. Co. v. SEC, 327 U.S. 686 (1946) (observing that the Commerce Clause "permits Congress to attack an evil directly at its source, provided that the evil bears a substantial relationship to interstate commerce").

[25] In *United States v. Five Gambling Devices*, 346 U.S. 441, 445–48 (1953), the Court confronted a law in which Congress (1) outlawed cross-border shipments of gambling machines into states that had not specifically exempted themselves from the act's coverage; and (2) in an effort to effectuate this prohibition, also required all sellers of gambling devices to file monthly reports with federal authorities detailing each sale of a device. One issue presented by the case was whether the reporting requirement extended to purely intrastate sales. In considering this question, four Justices were prepared to say that the reporting provision did apply to intrastate sales and that, as so applied, it was constitutional because it helped "make effective and enforceable the interstate shipment ban" by complicating efforts to evade that ban through "straw-man transactions . . . and the like." *Id.* at 459 (Clark, J., dissenting). Three Justices, however, argued that application of the law to purely intrastate transfers raised "serious constitutional questions" and accordingly interpreted the reporting requirement to apply only to interstate transfers. *Id.* at 446–48 (opinion of Jackson, J.). (The other two Justices did not speak to commerce-power issues because they focused instead on constitutional vagueness problems.) How would *Five Gambling*

In one respect, however, the post-1936 cases have significantly expanded the reach of the commerce-prohibiting technique and its "superbootstrapping" corollary by endorsing the view—or at least assuming—that, as one scholar has put it, "Congress may regulate behavior involving any object that has previously crossed a state line."[26] The well-spring of this theory is *United States v. Bass*,[27] in which the Court construed a federal statute that outlaws receipt of a gun by persons with a prior felony conviction as applicable whenever the "the Government . . . demonstrates that the firearm received has previously traveled in interstate commerce."[28] Similarly, in *Scarborough v. United States*,[29] the Court held that the same statute applies to any case in which the prosecution establishes "the minimal nexus that the firearm ha[s] been, at some time, in interstate commerce."[30] Although as a technical matter both *Bass* and *Scarborough* presented only questions of statutory interpretation, it seems clear that the Court in each case assumed that the statute, as interpreted, constituted a constitutional exercise of the commerce power.[31] Yet the sort of regulations sanctioned by *Bass* and

---

Devices come out today if the constitutional issue were squarely presented? It is likely that the modern Court would uphold the law, even as applied to intrastate activity, because sales transactions, whether interstate or intrastate in nature, plainly constitute "economic activity." *See infra* Chapter 4 (discussing the *Lopez* and *Morrison* cases); *see also* Robert L. Stern, *The Commerce Clause Revisited—The Federalization of Intrastate Crime*, 15 ARIZ. L. REV. 272, 275–76 (1973) (arguing that "[i]n retrospect, the *Gambling Devices* case would seem to have presented a pretty simple constitutional question" because "requiring all manufacturers and dealers to register and file reports as to their sales would facilitate the determination of which devices were transported interstate").

26 Donald H. Regan, *How to Think About the Federal Commerce Power and Incidentally Rewrite* United States v. Lopez, 94 MICH. L. REV. 554, 561 (1995). This conception of the commerce power apparently made its first appearance in *Five Gambling Devices* (discussed *supra* note 25). There, Justice Clark, writing for the only four Justices who reached a definitive conclusion on the commerce power issue, found it "clearly established" that "activities local in nature may be regulated . . . if local goods . . . were previously in interstate commerce." *Id.* at 460 (Clark, J., dissenting). Notably, this assertion came in dicta because the challenged prohibition on intrastate possession of unreported gambling machines was tethered to a federal ban on interstate shipments of unreported machines. In addition, Justice Clark cited to no authority for this broad assertion other than cases such as *Sullivan*, which similarly involved an intrastate possession ban directly linked to an exercise of the commerce-prohibiting power.

27 404 U.S. 336 (1971).

28 *Id.* at 350.

29 431 U.S. 563 (1977).

30 *Id.* at 575; *see also* Barrett v. United States, 423 U.S. 212, 215 (1976) (permitting application of a similar statute so long as "the firearm at some time in its past had traveled in interstate commerce").

31 *See* LAURENCE H. TRIBE, AMERICAN CONSTITUTIONAL LAW § 5–5, at 830 (3d ed. 2000). In *Bass*, for example, the Court fully recognized that its approach reflected "not the narrowest possible reading of the statute" but nonetheless deemed that reading "consistent with our regard for the sensitive relation between federal and state criminal jurisdiction" because it "preserves as an element of all the offenses a

Scarborough went well beyond even the broad regulation of intrastate activities previously sustained in *Sullivan*. In particular, those regulations did not, from all appearances, find their justification in any congressional effort to help effectuate a ban on specified cross-border movements; rather, the prior state-line-crossing movement of the gun was, without more, enough to justify congressional regulation of its later possession. In practical effect, *Bass* and *Scarborough*—in keeping with the theme of broad congressional power that marked the post-1936 period—thus suggested a willingness to recognize an entirely new prong of the commerce power. Gesturing towards what might be called the super-channels-of-commerce theory, the Court did not question Congress's power to regulate intrastate activities on the ground that they concerned an item that had "at some time" moved across a state line, regardless of whether that item thereafter remained "in" interstate commerce or was in any way connected to a separate ban on cross-border movements.[32]

B. THE IN-COMMERCE THEORY FROM 1937 THROUGH 1994

In the years immediately following the judicial revolution of 1937, the Court took steps to reinvigorate the in-commerce prong of the commerce power, just as surely as it had moved to resuscitate the commerce-prohibiting technique in *Darby*. Most important, in *Currin v. Wallace*,[33] the Court invoked the in-commerce theory to uphold a federal statute that barred the sale of tobacco from auction houses, at which farmers customarily sold products destined for interstate commerce, unless the tobacco first was inspected and graded by federal authorities. This regulatory scheme had been developed to address recurring problems, including sharp practices by sophisticated buyers and "an unusual degree of uncertainty in . . . prices," that resulted from a lack of information about product quality at the time of auctioning.[34] The Court first concluded that it was "idle to contend" that the case did not concern "sales in interstate or foreign commerce" because "[w]here goods are purchased in one State for transportation to another the commerce includes the purchase

requirement suited to federal criminal jurisdiction alone." 404 U.S. at 351. Indeed, in neither *Bass* nor *Scarborough* did the Court even note the possibility that federal regulation of gun receipt or possession premised on the gun's past movement across a state line presented a debatable constitutional point. For more on the implications of *Bass* and *Scarborough*, see *infra* Section 4.B.3.

[32] For more on the in-commerce theory, see *supra* Section 2.B and *infra* Sections 3.B, 4.C.

[33] 306 U.S. 1 (1939).

[34] *Id.* at 8.

quite as much as it does the transportation."[35] The Court added that practical considerations permitted Congress to apply its program even to tobacco destined solely for intrastate uses. As the Court explained, "the transactions on the tobacco market were conducted indiscriminately at virtually the same time, and in a manner which made it necessary, if the congressional rule were to be applied, to make it govern all the tobacco thus offered for sale."[36] In short, just as *Darby* signaled that Congress could reach intrastate production activities to render effective its exercise of the commerce-prohibiting theory, *Currin* showed that Congress could place safeguards on post-production intrastate sales activities as part of a broader scheme focused on targeting conduct taking place "in" interstate commerce.[37]

Most of the Court's post-1936 in-commerce cases have focused on questions of statutory interpretation.[38] Such cases arise because Congress has passed a number of laws that, by their terms, apply only if the defendant has engaged "in" interstate commerce.[39] Not surprisingly, these cases carry forward the idea, well established in the pre-1937 context, that some local activities lie outside the stream of commerce. In *United States v. Yellow Cab Co.*,[40] for example, the Court held that intrastate taxi trips that immediately precede or follow interstate train travel are "too unrelated to interstate

---

[35] *Id.* at 10; *see also id.* at 12 (adding that it made no difference that the required "inspection and grading of the tobacco take place before the auction" because "it is obvious that the inspection and grading have immediate relation to the sales in interstate and foreign commerce").

[36] *Id.* at 32.

[37] In *Mulford v. Smith*, 307 U.S. 38 (1939), the Court relied on a similar theory to sustain federally imposed limits on the quantities of tobacco properly sold at market, reasoning that the rule reaches interstate commerce "at the throat where tobacco enters the stream of commerce,—the marketing warehouse." *Id.* at 47. Citing *Currin*, the Court added that: "In markets where tobacco is sold to both interstate and intrastate purchasers it is not known, when the grower places his tobacco on the warehouse floor for sale, whether it is destined for interstate or intrastate commerce. Regulation, to be effective, must, and therefore may constitutionally, apply to all sales." *Id.* (internal footnote omitted). Notably, the Court went on to supplement its in-commerce defense of the statute with an invocation of the commerce-prohibiting theory, reasoning that a congressional power to prohibit all cross-border movements of a product extended "a fortiori to limitation of the amount of a given commodity which may be transported in such commerce." *Id.* at 48; *see also* United States v. Rock Royal Co-op., 307 U.S. 533, 568–69 (1939) (relying on *Currin* and *Mulford*, among other cases, to uphold price regulations for both intrastate and interstate sales of milk as applied to defendants whose product "reaches the [regulated] marketing area through the channels of interstate commerce").

[38] *See, e.g.*, Mitchell v. C.W. Vollmer & Co., 349 U.S. 427, 429–30 (1955) (holding that workers were "engaged 'in commerce' " for FLSA purposes when building a lock on the Gulf Intercoastal Waterway).

[39] *See, e.g.*, FTC v. Bunte Bros., 312 U.S. 349, 355 (1941) (construing the Federal Trade Commission Act to cover only activity in interstate commerce and thus excluding intrastate retail candy sales from its reach).

[40] 332 U.S. 218 (1947).

commerce to constitute a part thereof within the meaning of the Sherman Act" even though the stream of commerce does reach taxi rides that take passengers from one train station to another in the middle of an interstate journey.[41] Notwithstanding cases such as *Yellow Cab*, the Court has insisted that the in-commerce theory must be viewed "in a practical sense."[42] In *Goldfarb v. Virginia State Bar*,[43] for example, the issue was whether local lawyers who conducted residential title searches operated "in commerce" for purposes of the Sherman Act. Without dissent, the Court concluded that they did. Because funds for home purchases "frequently" come from outside the state and title examinations are a "practical necessity" to the securing of financing, "a title examination is an integral part of an interstate transaction."[44] The regulated lawyers, in other words, had acted "in commerce" even though they had not handled any of the funds that gave the transaction its interstate character and had provided services only with respect to the title search and not with respect to the broader sale or financing transaction itself. By thus extending the in-commerce theory to persons on the edge of an interstate transaction, the Court created space to argue that Congress may regulate large numbers of persons caught up in local activities that facilitate or disrupt cross-border commercial activity.[45]

Despite the post-1936 reinvigoration of the in-commerce theory, the Court has invoked it infrequently in the post-New Deal period. This state of affairs has resulted, more than anything else, from the Court's endorsement of a sufficiently expansive view of the affecting-commerce theory that, at least until 1995, provided a ready mechanism for sustaining almost any law that bears on the flow of interstate trade. We turn now to an examination of the development of the affecting-commerce theory in the 1936–1994 period.

---

41 *Id.* at 230.

42 Goldfarb v. Virginia State Bar, 421 U.S. 773, 784 (1975).

43 *Id.*

44 *Id.* at 783–85.

45 *But cf.* McLain v. Real Estate Bd. of New Orleans, Inc., 444 U.S. 232, 244–45 (1980) (considering application of Sherman Act to alleged price fixing by realtors on an affecting-commerce, rather than an in-commerce, theory; noting along the way, albeit without endorsing the point, the lower court's distinction of *Goldfarb*, with respect to the in-commerce theory, based on the fact that lawyers were "necessary" for conducting title searches, whereas residential real estate sales often occur with no involvement of realtors at all).

C. THE AFFECTING-COMMERCE THEORY FROM 1937 THROUGH 1994

1. The National Labor Relations Act Cases

Schechter Poultry and *Carter Coal* embodied efforts by the Supreme Court to put judicially enforceable restrictions on the affecting-commerce component (as well as the in-commerce component) of Congress's Article I powers.[46] The Court's work with the affecting-commerce theory, however, dramatically changed course following the election of 1936, and the first sign of a transformation came in *NLRB v. Jones & Laughlin Steel Corp.*[47] That case brought before the Court the constitutionality of the NLRA as applied to an attempt to impede unionizing efforts at a plant operated by one of the nation's largest steel companies. Citing *Carter Coal*, the lower court found this application of the act unconstitutional because it concerned only manufacturing activity. But in an opinion written by Chief Justice Hughes for a five-Justice majority now including Justice Roberts, the Court reversed this ruling, reasoning that the regulated activities, though "intrastate in character," had "such a close and substantial relation to interstate commerce that their control is essential or appropriate to protect that commerce from burdens and obstructions."[48] In reaching this conclusion, the Court swept away the principle laid down 32 years earlier in *E. C. Knight* and reaffirmed just one year before in *Carter Coal*. "[T]he fact that the employees here concerned were engaged in production," Chief Justice Hughes declared, "is not determinative."[49] What mattered instead was the fact that the "stoppage of [the steel company's] operations by industrial strife would have a most serious effect upon interstate commerce."[50]

How could the Court issue such a ruling in light of *Carter Coal*? That case, the Chief Justice wrote, did not control because "the Court was of the opinion that the provisions of the statute relating to production were invalid upon several grounds."[51] Chief Justice Hughes did not explain why, even assuming that alternative holdings had supported the Court's decision in *Carter Coal*, its categorical rule of excluding production from the regulatory reach of Congress should now be abandoned. On behalf of the four dissenters, Justice McReynolds could only shake his head in disbelief. "Every

---

46 *See supra* Chapter 2.

47 301 U.S. 1 (1937).

48 *Id.* at 37.

49 *Id.* at 40.

50 *Id.* at 41.

51 *Id.*

consideration brought forward to uphold the Act before us," he remarked, "was applicable [in *Carter Coal* and *Schechter Poultry*]."[52] He then added the now-predictable parade-of-horribles warning: "Whatever effect any cause of [labor] discontent may ultimately have upon commerce is far too indirect to justify Congressional regulation. Almost anything—marriage, birth, or death—may in some fashion affect commerce."[53]

Non-New-Dealers rightly saw in *Jones & Laughlin Steel* a harbinger of wholesale retreat from the interventionist spirit of *Schechter Poultry* and *Carter Coal*. Chief Justice Hughes's opinion, however, offered glimmers of hope to those who disapproved of the Democrats' most far-reaching programs. Of greatest importance, some passages of the opinion suggested that the principle of the case might extend only to "far-flung" enterprises that "organize themselves on a national scale."[54] In a companion case, however, the Court revealed that it was not about to limit the principle of *Jones & Laughlin Steel* in this way. *NLRB v. Friedman-Harry Marks Clothing*,[55] like *Jones & Laughlin Steel*, involved an effort to enforce the NLRA for purposes of remedying the retaliatory discharge of union organizers. Unlike in *Jones & Laughlin Steel*, however, the enforcement action targeted what Professor David Currie would later describe as a "small clothing manufacturer with a minuscule share of the interstate market."[56] As Justice McReynolds suggested in dissent, this fact made the case tough to distinguish not only from *Carter Coal* but from *Schechter Poultry* as well.[57] The Court's new five-Justice juggernaut, however, was not to be denied. Offering no additional legal analysis, it declared that "for the reasons" set forth

---

52 *Id.* at 77 (McReynolds, J., dissenting).

53 *Id.* at 99.

54 *Id.* at 41 (majority opinion). In particular, before declaring that labor strife at Jones & Laughlin Steel's Aliquippa plant would in fact have a "direct" effect on commerce, the Chief Justice emphasized the expansive, multi-faceted character of the steel company's overall business activities. Thus, with operations that extended from "mines in Michigan and Minnesota" to "steamships on the Great Lakes" to "warehouses in Chicago, Detroit, Cincinnati and Memphis" to fabricating shops in "Long Island City, New York, and in New Orleans," this employer was a nationwide operation, with production mills "that might be likened to the heart of a self-contained, highly integrated body." *Id.* at 27 (internal quotations omitted). On the basis of this rhetoric, the principle of the case might have been confined to firms, such as Jones & Laughlin Steel, which "transform . . . materials and then pump them out to all parts of the nation through [a] vast mechanism." *Id.*

55 301 U.S. 58 (1937).

56 DAVID P. CURRIE, THE CONSTITUTION IN THE SUPREME COURT: THE SECOND CENTURY, 1888–1986 at 237 (1990).

57 *Friedman-Harry Marks Clothing*, 301 U.S. at 77 (McReynolds, J., dissenting).

in *Jones & Laughlin Steel*, any constitutional challenge to the Labor Board's intervention was "without merit."[58]

2. *Wickard v. Filburn* and the Aggregation Technique

The other shoe dropped in *Wickard v. Filburn*.[59] At issue in the case was the application of the Agricultural Adjustment Act of 1938 to Roscoe C. Filburn, an Ohio dairy farmer, who grew 462 bushels of wheat on his land, including for his family's and his livestock's consumption. Sued by the Secretary of Agriculture for exceeding a federally imposed production limit, Filburn argued that this exercise of the commerce power offended both common sense and the Constitution. The case came before the Court in 1942, by which time President Roosevelt had replaced all four dissenters in *Jones & Laughlin Steel* with tried-and-true New Dealers. And this Court, without a single dissenting vote, upheld this application of the act.

Justice Jackson began his opinion for the majority with a statement of principles that captured recent shifts in the law. He declared that "[t]he Court's recognition of the relevance of . . . economic effects . . . has made the mechanical application of legal formulas no longer feasible."[60] Thus "questions of federal power cannot be decided simply by finding the activity in question to be 'production' nor can consideration of its economic effects be foreclosed by calling them 'indirect.' "[61] Citing *Gibbons*, Justice Jackson instead invoked Chief Justice Marshall's "warning that effective restraints on [the commerce power's] exercise must proceed from political rather than from judicial processes."[62] Because in this instance Congress had regulated activities that had a "substantial effect" on interstate commerce, it had not exceeded its constitutional authority.[63]

---

58 *Id.* at 75.

59 317 U.S. 111 (1942).

60 *Id.* at 123–24.

61 *Id.* at 124.

62 *Id.* at 120.

63 Two years after *Filburn* sealed the demise of the categorical exclusion of production from regulation under the Commerce Clause, the Court rejected another similarly categorical exclusion in *United States v. South-Eastern Underwriters Ass'n*, 322 U.S. 533 (1944). In a series of decisions dating back to 1869 the Court had held that "contracts of insurance are not commerce at all" and thus could not be regulated under the commerce power. New York Life Ins. Co. v. Deer Lodge County, 231 U.S. 495, 510 (1913). Relying largely on *Filburn*, the Court overruled these cases in *South-Eastern Underwriters*, reasoning that "past decisions of this Court emphasize that legal formulae devised to uphold state power cannot uncritically be accepted as trustworthy guides to determine Congressional power under the Commerce Clause." 322 U.S. at 545. Because the term "commerce" has always embraced "businesses in which persons bought and sold, bargained and contracted," *id.* at 539, and the business

But how could it be that the growing of wheat on a patch of land for one family's needs created such a "substantial" impact? The answer was that, in wielding the commerce power, Congress could regulate each individual member of a group—even assuming each individual's effect on commerce was itself *de minimis*—so long as the activity of that individual, "taken together with that of many others similarly situated, is far from trivial."[64] In other words, for Commerce Clause purposes, the activities of Roscoe Filburn did not stand alone. He and all "similarly situated" wheat growers, viewed in the aggregate, posed a substantial danger to the interstate wheat market, susceptible to a congressional corrective, because unregulated production threatened such problems as the industry-wrecking suppression of wheat prices and a proliferation of "tied up railroad cars."[65]

Lurking quietly in the background of *Filburn* was a question that recurs in judicial decisions that deploy this sort of aggregation approach: Who precisely gets aggregated with whom? In *Filburn*, for example, the case for finding a substantial effect on interstate commerce would be easy if Congress had authority to view together the activities of all wheat growers of all sorts. The Court, however, also had the option of saying that Congress could look in the aggregate only at those persons who grew wheat for home consumption, thus significantly narrowing the universe of actors whose actions would be assessed in the aggregate in gauging relevant commerce-altering effects. This latter course might in theory have led to invalidation of the statute as applied in *Filburn*. After all, if very few farmers grow wheat for home use, then unlimited production by such growers, even in the aggregate, might well not have a "substantial" effect on interstate commerce.[66] In *Filburn* the Court in fact dealt with this frame-of-reference problem by looking only at home-use wheat growers. It then determined, however, that

of insurance had come to include "a continuous and indivisible stream of intercourse among the states composed of collections of premiums, payments of policy obligations, and . . . countless documents and communications," *id.* at 541—and because "Congress can regulate traffic though it consist of intangibles," *id.* at 546—the "exception of the business of insurance" from the commerce power could no longer stand, *id.* at 553.

64 *Filburn*, 317 U.S. at 128.

65 *Id.* at 125.

66 Nor is this point only theoretical in nature. In the early 1940s, for example, Congress had no need to regulate home-use tobacco and cotton precisely because farmers "brought nearly all [of these products] to the tobacco warehouse or the cotton gin for marketing" in the ordinary course of events. Robert L. Stern, *The Commerce Clause and the National Economy, 1933–1946 (Part Two)*, 59 HARV. L. REV. 883, 902 (1946). Had Congress sought to regulate tobacco or cotton grown for home use, it is possible, if not likely, that the Court would have deemed this effort unconstitutional on the ground that aggregate home use of each such crop did not substantially affect interstate pricing and product movements. At the least, the Court would have had to expand on the rationale it employed in *Filburn* to uphold such a law.

the activities of this thus-narrowed group of wheat growers did, in the aggregate, have the requisite "substantial" effect. That effect existed, the Court explained, because many growers produced home-use wheat, and that activity in the aggregate influenced prices in interstate markets by affecting both supply and demand. On the supply side, such wheat "overhangs the market and if induced by rising prices tends to flow into the market and check price increases."[67] On the demand side, such wheat "supplies a need of the man who grew it which would otherwise be reflected by purchases in the open market."[68] In sum, the Court reported: "This record leaves us in no doubt that Congress may properly have considered that wheat consumed on the farm where grown if wholly outside the scheme of regulation would have a substantial effect in defeating and obstructing its purpose to stimulate trade therein at increased prices."[69]

The Court's abandonment of *Carter Coal* and its embrace of aggregation analysis left no doubt that the affecting-commerce prong of the commerce power had a long reach—so long, in fact, that the Court would find no law beyond its grasp for the next half-century.[70] In early post-*Jones & Laughlin Steel* cases, for example, the Court upheld laws that regulated intrastate activities in an effort to ensure the effective movement of natural gas across state lines[71] and to protect cross-border commerce in milk.[72] In addition, the Court had

---

67 *Filburn,* 317 U.S. at 128.

68 *Id.*

69 *Id.* at 128–29.

70 *See, e.g.*, Mandeville Island Farms v. Am. Crystal Sugar Co., 334 U.S. 219, 236 (1948) (repudiating *E. C. Knight* and its production-versus-commerce distinction in an antitrust action involving an alleged conspiracy among three local sugar-beet processors; reasoning that "the individual activity when multiplied into a general practice is subject to federal control"). Extensive consideration of the precedents of this period is provided by PAUL R. BENSON, JR., THE SUPREME COURT AND THE COMMERCE CLAUSE, 1937–1970 (1970); Robert L. Stern, *The Commerce Clause and the National Economy, 1933–1946 (Part One)*, 59 HARV. L. REV. 645 (1946); and Stern, *supra* note 66, among other sources.

71 Illinois Nat. Gas Co. v. Central Ill. Pub. Serv., 314 U.S. 498, 509 (1942) (eschewing an "in commerce" analysis, and reasoning instead that intrastate "extension of appellant's facilities . . . would so affect . . . distribution among the states as to be within the Congressional power to regulate those matters which materially affect interstate commerce").

72 United States v. Wrightwood Dairy Co., 315 U.S. 110, 118, 120 (1942) (upholding extension of price controls for interstate milk sales to competing intrastate milk sales lest "the effective sanction of the order will wither before the force of competition, the morale of the market will disintegrate, and this attempt at solution of the problem by the National Government will fail"; adding that "[t]he injury, and hence the power, does not depend upon the fortuitous circumstance that the particular person conducting the intrastate activities is, or is not, also engaged in interstate commerce" and that "[i]t is the effect upon the interstate commerce or its regulation, regardless of the particular form which the competition may take, which is the test of federal power").

no difficulty sustaining the application of federal labor laws to large numbers of intrastate employment relationships.[73]

3. The Commerce Power and the Civil Rights Act of 1964

When Lyndon Johnson stepped into the presidency in 1963, following the assassination of President John F. Kennedy, racial discrimination—including in the form of outright segregation—pervaded the workplace, the restaurant and hotel industries, housing rentals and sales, and government operations in much of the United States. President Johnson responded to these conditions by throwing his support (and substantial political skills) behind proposals for broad civil-rights reforms. A bitter legislative struggle followed as Senators and Representatives, particularly from the deep south, attacked both the substance and the constitutionality of the proposed statute. In response, some proponents of this legislation sought to justify it as a proper exercise of Congress's power to "enforce by appropriate legislation" the guarantee of "equal protection of the laws" embodied in section 1 of the Fourteenth Amendment. Invoking supportive Supreme Court precedent, critics responded that the Fourteenth Amendment guarded against only state action and not the sort of purely private discrimination targeted by the administration's proposal.[74] In the end, Congress chose to rely primarily on its commerce power, rather than its Fourteenth Amendment enforcement power, in enacting what might well be the most significant piece of anti-discrimination legislation in American history, the Civil Rights Act of 1964.[75]

Title II of the act broadly prohibited discrimination on the basis of race, color, religion, or national origin in any "place of public accommodation . . . if its operations affect commerce."[76] Facilities covered by the act included hotels and motels, as well as any eating establishment that "offers to serve interstate travelers" or as to which "a substantial portion of the food [it sells has] moved in commerce."[77]

---

[73] *See, e.g.*, Polish Nat'l All. v. NLRB, 322 U.S. 643, 645–46, 648–50 (1944) (insurance company; reasoning that the exercise of "practical judgment," concerning effects on interstate commerce, "the Constitution entrusts primarily and very largely to the Congress, subject to the latter's control by the electorate"); NLRB v. Fainblatt, 306 U.S. 601 (1939) (upholding application of the act to a relatively small, cloth-processor employer); *Consolidated Edison Co.*, 305 U.S. at 221–22 (permitting regulation of an intrastate electric-power utility that supplied electricity to, for example, railroad facilities and a broadcaster).

[74] *See The Civil Rights Cases*, 109 U.S. 3, 11 (1883) (stating that "[i]ndividual invasion of individual rights is not the subject-matter of the [fourteenth] amendment"); *see generally infra* Section 11.C.

[75] Pub. L. 88–352, 78 Stat. 241.

[76] *See* 42 U.S.C. § 2000a(b).

[77] *See id.* §§ 2000a(b), 2000a(c).

In *Heart of Atlanta Motel v. United States*,[78] the Court upheld the application of Title II to a motel located in downtown Atlanta, emphasizing that extensive evidence before Congress established that "discrimination by hotels and motels impedes interstate travel."[79] It did not matter to the Court that this particular business could be characterized as having a "purely local character"[80] because "if it is interstate commerce that feels the pinch, it does not matter how local the operation which applies the squeeze."[81] Nor was it of consequence that a "moral" purpose had propelled enactment of the law.[82] As the Court explained, "that fact does not detract from the overwhelming evidence of the disruptive effect that racial discrimination has had on commercial intercourse."[83]

The Court's validation of the Civil Rights Act's application to a bustling motel did not answer the question whether Congress could regulate local restaurants on the theory that they sold food that had moved across state lines. In *Katzenbach v. McClung*,[84] however, the Court drew on its affecting-commerce precedents to uphold this feature of Title II as well.[85] The case involved Ollie's Barbecue, a 220-seat family restaurant in Birmingham, Alabama, which during the previous year had bought $69,683 worth of meat (constituting 46% of its total food purchases) from a local dealer who had obtained it from outside Alabama.[86] Making "no claim that interstate travelers frequented the restaurant,"[87] the Justice Department argued that the restaurant's practice of relegating Black customers to a take-out counter was subject to federal regulation because it affected interstate commerce. The restaurant's owners responded—as had Roscoe Filburn—that application of the Act to their small-time operation exceeded constitutional limits. A unanimous Court,

[78] 379 U.S. 241 (1964).

[79] *Id.* at 253.

[80] *Id.* at 258.

[81] *Id.* (quoting United States v. Women's Sportswear Mfg. Ass'n, 336 U.S. 460, 464 (1949)) (internal alterations omitted).

[82] *Id.* at 257.

[83] *Id.*

[84] 379 U.S. 294 (1964).

[85] *McClung* pre-dated cases such as *Bass* and *Scarborough*, *see supra* notes 27–32 and accompanying text, and the Court did not consider whether a restaurant's serving of food that previously had crossed a state line in itself justified application of the statutory ban on discrimination. Questions about the scope of the "jurisdictional nexus" theory of regulation, and whether it supports the constitutionality of the sort of law involved in *McClung*, would, however, clearly be in the picture if the case, or one like it, were to arise today. *See infra* Section 4.B.3.

[86] *McClung*, 379 U.S. at 296.

[87] *Id.* at 298.

however, found that the commerce power fully supported this application of the act's public-accommodations provision.

Drawing upon *Darby* and *Filburn*, the Court began by articulating a deferential standard of review: So long as "the legislators, in light of the facts and testimony before them, have a *rational basis* for finding a chosen regulatory scheme necessary to the protection of commerce, [judicial] investigation is at an end."[88] It did not matter in this regard that Congress had not made "specific findings which were embodied" in the statute itself.[89] Nor, given the now-settled aggregation principle, was the operation of Ollie's Barbecue to be "viewed in isolation."[90] Rather, it sufficed that the legislative record was "replete with testimony of the burdens placed on interstate commerce by racial discrimination in restaurants."[91] Studies showed reduced spending in restaurants among Black citizens even "after discounting income differences, in areas where discrimination is widely practiced," and it was obvious that "[t]he fewer customers a restaurant enjoys the less food it sells and consequently the less it buys."[92] Still other evidence revealed that race discrimination had caused "wide unrest" that had "a depressant effect on general business conditions"; that discrimination by restaurants "had a direct and highly restrictive effect upon interstate travel" by Black citizens; and that "discrimination deterred professional, as well as skilled, people from moving into areas where such practices occurred and thereby caused industry to be reluctant to establish there."[93] To be sure, there was no "direct evidence" that linked discriminatory restaurant service to an overall reduction in the "flow of interstate food."[94] (After all, anyone denied or discouraged from seeking meals in a segregated restaurant would still end up spending money on food elsewhere.) That fact, however, was not "a crucial matter" in light of the demonstrated "effect of such practices on other aspects of commerce."[95]

The Ollie's Barbecue case raised interesting questions about the affecting-commerce prong of the commerce power. Was it enough that race discrimination cut down on interstate shipments of restaurant food even if it did not cut down on interstate shipments of food as a

---

88 *Id.* at 303–04 (emphasis added).

89 *Id.* at 304.

90 *Id.* at 300.

91 *Id.* at 299.

92 *Id.*

93 *Id.* at 300.

94 *Id.* at 304.

95 *Id.* at 305.

whole?[96] Could Congress have directed its regulation at a broadened group of local operators—for example, all restaurants, whether or not they received goods in interstate commerce,[97] or all business establishments,[98] or all business and non-business establishments that served food, including social clubs[99]—on the theory that, in the aggregate, their discriminatory activities blocked interstate food shipments, interstate travel, and/or interstate business relocation? Could Congress constitutionally aggregate religious discrimination with racial discrimination in regulating the restaurant industry? What if the latter practice but not the former was extensive?[100]

The Court's opinion also raised interesting questions about the Justices' methods and purposes. Was the Court saying, in effect, that, because Congress had an aggregation-based power to regulate *all* restaurants, it could accordingly wield the lesser power to regulate those restaurants that received food that moved in interstate commerce?[101] Was the Court—while highlighting the destructive

---

96 *Cf. Perez*, 402 U.S. at 153 (noting that the Court in *McClung* had considered "the effect on the flow of food in commerce to restaurants").

97 *See* Stern, *supra* note 25, at 272 (suggesting that the most "easily defensible" justification for the result in *McClung* may be that Congress has the power to regulate "all restaurants," whether or not they serve interstate travelers, "because of the inevitable uncertainty as to which [restaurants] interstate travelers might choose to patronize and the fact that the discrimination in itself would discourage interstate travel"). *But cf. Heart of Atlanta Motel*, 379 U.S. at 275 (Black, J., concurring) (speculating that an "isolated and remote lunchroom" might be beyond the reach of Congress under the Commerce Clause); Daniel v. Paul, 395 U.S. 298, 315 (1969) (Black, J., dissenting) (objecting to Congress's use of the commerce power to reach a snack bar at "country people's recreation center . . . miles away from any interstate highway").

98 *See, e.g.*, GUNTHER, *supra* note 17, at 162 (reprinting the statement of Bruce Bromley, a prominent New York attorney, who testified at a Senate committee hearing that the proposed Civil Rights Act could not constitutionally be applied to a local barber shop).

99 *See, e.g.*, *id.* at 160 (quoting from Senate hearings in which Attorney General Robert F. Kennedy suggested that applying the proposed Civil Rights Act to a "personal or social relationship" would exceed the reach of the Commerce Clause).

100 Another set of questions that lurked in the background in *McClung* concerned the super-bootstrap and in-commerce theories touched on earlier: Could Congress regulate the local service to local customers in a local restaurant because (regardless of all else) the food being served had previously crossed state lines and/or because it remained "in" interstate commerce at the time it was sold to restaurant customers? *See* Stern, *supra* note 25, at 271–72 (suggesting that the Civil Rights Act provision involved in *McClung* was "perhaps" sustainable on the theory "that a restaurant which obtained goods from outside the state was thereby subject to federal regulation of all its practices"; adding that the Court itself seemed to endorse this theory, thus "suggesting that the slightest interstate connection can provide an adequate basis even for a federal statute which serves a noneconomic national purpose").

101 It is worth noting in this regard that the aggregation technique invites criticism because it suggests that the more sweeping a congressional program is the more likely it is to be constitutional. In other words (and ironically), the more broadly a federal program intrudes on federalism concerns by sweeping across fields previously regulated by states, the more likely it is to survive federalism-based attack. One response to this argument is that it ignores the key point that powerful built-in checks

effects of pervasive race discrimination on the vibrancy of the national economy—intentionally writing in an oblique style to leave itself room to put limits on the commerce power in later cases involving other subjects?[102] Or was the Court in effect declaring that all elements of the national economy had by 1964 become so interwoven that Congress in effect could now regulate under an affecting-commerce theory any activity that was in any way connected up with business operations? Whatever the answers to these questions might be, the drift of *McClung* was clearly in the direction of permitting Congress to decide for itself whether the "total incidence" of the regulated behavior unduly impedes interstate commerce.[103]

4. Local Crimes, Local Lands, and the Rejection of New Categorical Limits from 1937 Through 1994

Notwithstanding the broad rhetoric and reach of *Heart of Atlanta Motel* and *McClung*, litigants continued to push for judicial recognition of limits on the congressional commerce power. *Hodel v. Virginia Surface Mining & Reclamation Association*,[104] for example, involved a challenge to federal strip-mining restrictions founded on the view that Congress could not regulate "the use of private lands within the borders of the States."[105] A unanimous Court made short shrift of this attempt to engraft a new categorical limit on the Court's post-*Carter Coal* jurisprudence. As Justice Thurgood Marshall explained, it was enough to support Congress's action that "many surface mining operations result in disturbances . . . that burden and adversely affect commerce . . . by destroying or diminishing the utility of land for commercial, industrial, residential, recreational, agricultural, and forestry purposes, by causing erosion and landslides, by contributing to floods, by polluting the water, [and] by destroying fish and wildlife habitats."[106]

---

exist on sweeping (and especially gratuitous) exercises of federal power. *See infra* Section 5.A (discussing this point in connection with the Court's decision in *Garcia v. San Antonio Metropolitan Transit Authority*, 469 U.S. 528 (1985)). Another response is that, as noted earlier, judges may well choose to break broad regulatory programs into functional sub-units for aggregation-analysis purposes. *See supra* Section 3.C.2 (discussing this point in connection with *Filburn*).

[102] *See generally* CASS R. SUNSTEIN, ONE CASE AT A TIME: JUDICIAL MINIMALISM ON THE SUPREME COURT (1999) (exploring, albeit without a specific focus on *McClung*, the practice (and desirability) of deciding cases on narrow and undertheorized grounds so as to retain flexibility in the handling of later cases).

[103] *McClung*, 379 U.S. at 301 (internal quotation omitted).

[104] 452 U.S. 264 (1981).

[105] *Id.* at 275.

[106] *Id.* at 277 (quoting 30 U.S.C. § 1201(c)). Speaking more generally about the burgeoning field of federal environmental controls, the Court added that "the power

In *Perez v. United States*,[107] the Court rebuffed another invitation to recognize a specialized restriction on the affecting-commerce theory. That case involved the prosecution, under a federal statute that broadly criminalized "extortionate credit transactions," of a local loan shark who threatened to break the legs of a neighborhood butcher if he did not promptly repay a $1,000 loan.[108] In dissent, Justice Stewart seized on these facts to argue that Congress could not, consistent with the Tenth Amendment, use the affecting-commerce theory to regulate "local, intrastate crime" unless it showed that the outlawed category of behavior had "interstate attributes that distinguish it in some substantial respect from other local crime."[109] But all of his colleagues on the Court disagreed. They deemed it determinative that "the loan shark racket provides organized crime with its second most lucrative source of revenue, exacts millions from the pockets of people, coerces its victims into the commission of crimes against property, and causes the takeover by racketeers of legitimate businesses."[110] Moreover, even though nothing indicated that the local loansharking activity involved in the *Perez* case itself had any connection to organized crime, "a class of activities [is] properly regulated by Congress without proof that the particular intrastate activity against which a sanction was laid had an effect on commerce."[111]

So where did the congressional commerce power stand in light of these post-New Deal precedents? Taken as whole, the Court's rulings signaled that "Congress' power under the Commerce Clause is very broad,"[112] and many observers found reason to conclude that, as a practical matter, Congress could justify on Commerce Clause grounds any law it wished to enact. Yet even as the Court was handing down decisions like *Filburn*, *McClung*, and *Perez* it continued to insist that the Constitution placed some limits on the commerce power.[113] It was against this backdrop that Chief Justice

---

conferred by the Commerce Clause [is] broad enough to permit congressional regulation of activities causing air or water pollution, or other environmental hazards that may have effects in more than one State." *Id.* at 282.

107 402 U.S. 146 (1971).

108 *Id.* at 146–47.

109 *Id.* at 157–58 (Stewart, J., dissenting).

110 *Id.* at 156 (majority opinion).

111 *Id.* at 152 (citing *Darby*, 312 U.S. at 120–21).

112 Fry v. United States, 421 U.S. 542, 547 (1975) (upholding an application of federal wage controls to state employers; reasoning that the law "could well result" in increased interstate commerce because "raises to state employees could inject millions of dollars of purchasing power into the economy and might exert pressure on other segments of the work force to demand comparable increases").

113 In *Wirtz*, for instance, the Court, even while upholding an expansion of the FLSA, suggested that Congress could not "use a relatively trivial impact on commerce

Burger announced his retirement, and President Ronald Reagan received the chance to alter the membership and jurisprudential direction of the Supreme Court.

as an excuse for broad general regulation of state or private activities." 392 U.S. at 196 n.27.

Chapter 4

THE COMMERCE POWER AFTER 1994: THE REHNQUIST AND ROBERTS COURTS' REVIVAL OF CONSTITUTIONAL LIMITS

Analysis

In 1986, William H. Rehnquist became the Chief Justice of the United States, and Antonin Scalia assumed his position as an Associate Justice. In 1991, another key shift in the Court's membership occurred when Justice Clarence Thomas filled the vacancy created by the retirement of Justice Thurgood Marshall. These changes meant that the Court now included five members—Chief Justice Rehnquist and Justices O'Connor, Scalia, Kennedy, and Thomas—who stood ready to subject challenged congressional enactments to energized forms of federalism-based judicial review. In later years, additional shifts in the membership of the Court occurred—most notably with the appointment of John G. Roberts, Jr., as Chief Justice in 2005—without significantly diminishing the Court's reenergized commitment to checking perceived congressional overzealousness in regulating matters said to intrude on state autonomy.[1] In keeping with this commitment, the Court over the past

[1] Some observers might contend that the Roberts Court retreated from this heightened attention to federalism concerns in *NFIB v. Sebelius* 567 U.S. 519 (2012), when it upheld the "individual mandate" of the Affordable Care Act as a valid exercise of Congress's taxing power. *See infra* Section 7.A.2 (discussing the Court's taxing-power analysis). But several other aspects of the *NFIB* decision cut in the other direction, including the Court's refusal to view the mandate as justified by the commerce power, *see infra* Section 5.E.1, or by the Necessary and Proper Clause, *see infra* Section 6.B.2, and the Court's separate determination that the expansion of

three decades has narrowed the Fourteenth and Fifteenth Amendment enforcement powers,[2] restricted Congress's authority to implement conditional spending programs,[3] and recognized a broadened set of "external" restraints on federal lawmaking under the state-sovereign-immunity and "anticommandeering" doctrines.[4] At the heart of the work of the Rehnquist and Roberts Courts, however, has been a reappraisal of the scope of the commerce power itself. Resulting invigorations of the "internal" limits on that power, most prominently exemplified by the Court's landmark rulings in *United States v. Lopez*,[5] *United States v. Morrison*,[6] and *NFIB v. Sebelius*[7] have brought to the fore a new set of issues in the law of constitutional federalism.[8]

Medicaid coverage called for by the act exceeded the scope of Congress's spending power, *see infra* Section 8.D. Other rulings of the Roberts Court also support the conclusion that its jurisprudence reflects more of a continuation of than a retreat from the federalism-related work of the Rehnquist Court. *See* Ilya Somin, *Federalism and the Roberts Court*, 46 PUBLIUS: THE JOURNAL OF FEDERALISM 441, 441 (2016) ("In some crucial respects, the Roberts Court has gone beyond the 'Federalism Revolution' that began in the Rehnquist Court era.").

2 *See infra* Chapter 11.

3 *See infra* Chapter 8.

4 *See infra* Chapter 5.

5 514 U.S. 549 (1995).

6 529 U.S. 598 (2000).

7 567 U.S. 519 (2012).

8 Here, as elsewhere, the focus is on detailing the Court's elaboration of these principles, as opposed to assessing the merits and demerits of the Court's rulings. There exists, however, an expansive literature on the soundness of the Court's commerce-power jurisprudence that comes at the topic from many different points of view. Some analysts argue that the Court should decline altogether to second-guess congressional decisions about the reach of the power. *See, e.g.*, Jesse H. Choper, *The Scope of National Power Vis-à-Vis the States: The Dispensability of Judicial Review*, 86 YALE L.J. 1552 (1977) (advocating for the abandonment of substantive judicial review of challenges based on claimed overreaches of congressional power due to the existence of structural protections of the states in the lawmaking process). Other observers have argued on originalist grounds that the commerce power should have a more limited reach than the Court has accorded to it in past cases—in part on the theory that the Constitution's drafters and ratifiers sharply distinguished between (1) the (impermissible) regulation of activities involved in the production of goods and (2) the (permissible) regulation of subsequent acts of cross-border buying and selling of those goods, coupled with transportation in connection with those transactions. *See, e.g.*, Randy E. Barnett, *The Original Meaning of the Commerce Clause*, 68 U. CHI. L. REV. 101, 146–47 (2001) (arguing that "[t]he most persuasive evidence," including that provided by *The Federalist Papers* and "statements made during the drafting and ratification of the Constitution," supports a narrower view of Congress's commerce power than the Court has embraced). Others perceive the originally intended scope of the power to be neither so clearly established nor so narrowly drawn. Among other things, they rely on: (1) the need to read the Commerce Clause in connection with the Necessary and Proper Clause, which channels supplementary authority to Congress beyond the power to regulate interstate commerce in and of itself, *see infra* Chapter 6; (2) indications that the Framers understood the word "commerce" itself to be far-reaching in its scope, *see, e.g.*, Jack M. Balkin, *Commerce*, 109 MICH. L. REV. 1 (2010); and (3) the suggestion of the Court, in the early days of the Republic, that the commerce power authorizes Congress to deal with matters that "affect" interstate

A. THE *LOPEZ* AND *MORRISON* DECISIONS

On March 10, 1992, Alfonso Lopez, a twelfth grader in San Antonio, Texas, carried a concealed handgun into Edison High School. This episode led to the conviction of Lopez under 18 U.S.C. § 922(q), a law that, as amended by the Gun Free School Zones Act of 1990 (GFSZA), made it a federal crime "for any individual knowingly to possess a firearm at a place that the individual knows, or has reasonable cause to believe, is a school zone."[9] Mr. Lopez appealed, relying squarely on federalism concerns in challenging the constitutionality of the GFSZA as applied to his highly localized conduct. In response, the Court—for the first time since its 1936 decision in *Carter Coal*—ruled that Congress had exceeded the internal limits established by the Commerce Clause.

The opinion of the Court, written for a five-Justice majority by Chief Justice Rehnquist, began by canvassing key post-1936 precedents. This review led the Chief Justice to conclude that the Commerce Clause enabled Congress to regulate "three broad categories of activity."

> First, Congress may regulate the use of the channels of interstate commerce. Second, Congress is empowered to regulate and protect the instrumentalities of interstate commerce, or persons or things in interstate commerce, even though the threat may come only from intrastate

---

trade and transit, *see* Wickard v. Filburn, 317 U.S. 111, 120 (1942) (describing the Marshall Court's observations on this point in *Gibbons v. Ogden*, 22 U.S. 1 (1824), as defining the commerce power "with a breadth never yet exceeded"). *But see Lopez*, 514 U.S. at 585–87 (Thomas, J., concurring) (arguing that the Court has greatly overread *Gibbons* because "[a]t the time the original Constitution was ratified, 'commerce' consisted of selling, buying, and bartering, as well as transporting for these purposes . . . rather than business generally"). Greatly complicating matters is the fact that the Court has had to discern the meaning of the Commerce Clause as applied to modern conditions—built around routine cross-border travel and trade; daily mass movements of goods, services, and capital; satellite and internet communication; and on and on—that could not differ in more unimaginable ways from those of the (literally) horse-and-buggy world of the late eighteenth century. Against this backdrop, some observers have suggested that the Court has both blithely and wrongly disregarded the Framers' intentions in defining the scope of the commerce power. But another account is that the Court has found itself with no choice but to do its best in translating across time the original design of the Framers to invigorate greatly the federal legislative power. To be sure, some critics believe that the Court has wrongly diluted the powers of state governments in this process of judicial decisionmaking. But most of the Justices of the post-New Deal era—including the current Justices—might well respond by observing that the doctrine steers a middle course between the Framers' own counterpoised purposes by (as we shall see) subjecting to broad congressional oversight the national populace's engagement in interstate commercial activity while (as we also shall see) simultaneously placing guardrails on the use of commerce power that help to ensure that the states remain key players in the overall structure of American government.

[9] The act defined a "school zone" to include any location within 1000 feet of a school building. *See* 18 U.S.C. § 921(a)(25).

> activities. Finally, Congress' commerce authority includes the power to regulate those activities having a substantial relation to interstate commerce, *i.e.*, those activities that substantially affect interstate commerce.[10]

Because the first two categories plainly did not cover a restriction placed on simple gun possession, the case presented a single question: Did the challenged statute pass muster under the third component of the commerce power—namely, the affecting-commerce theory?

The Chief Justice acknowledged that Congress possessed wide-ranging authority to regulate matters that affect interstate commerce. Even so, he concluded that none of the Court's post-New Deal precedents controlled the *Lopez* case because each of them had involved a regulation of "economic activity."[11] As the Chief Justice explained:

> Even *Wickard*, which is perhaps the most far reaching example of Commerce Clause authority over intrastate activity, involved economic activity in a way that the possession of a gun in a school zone does not. . . . Section 922(q) is a criminal statute that by its terms has nothing to do with "commerce" or any sort of economic enterprise, however broadly one might define those terms. Section 922(q) is not an essential part of a larger regulation of economic activity, in which the regulatory scheme could be undercut unless the intrastate activity were regulated. It cannot, therefore, be sustained under our cases upholding regulations of activities that arise out of or are connected with a commercial transaction, which viewed in the aggregate, substantially affects interstate commerce.[12]

Building on this analysis, the Chief Justice indicated that a different analysis more favorable to Congress might have applied if the challenged law had included an "express jurisdictional element which might limit its reach to a discrete set of firearm possessions that additionally have an explicit connection with or effect on interstate commerce."[13] But "[s]ection 922(q) contains no jurisdictional element which would ensure, through case-by-case inquiry, that the firearm possession in question affects interstate commerce."[14] The Chief Justice also went on to note that the pre-

---

10 *Lopez*, 514 U.S. at 558–59 (internal citations omitted).

11 *Id.* at 560.

12 *Id.* at 560–61 (internal footnote omitted).

13 *Id.* at 562.

14 *Id.* at 561.

enactment legislative record contained no evidence that linked guns near schools to the vitality of cross-border trade. He continued:

> We agree with the Government that Congress normally is not required to make formal findings as to the substantial burdens that an activity has on interstate commerce. But to the extent that congressional findings would enable us to evaluate the legislative judgment that the activity in question substantially affected interstate commerce, even though no such substantial effect was visible to the naked eye, they are lacking here.[15]

In the end, it was not enough that the presence of guns near schools could result in violent crimes that deter travel or generate monetary costs spread through the nation by way of "the mechanism of insurance."[16] Nor was it sufficient that guns in schools create disruptions of student learning that "result in a less productive citizenry," which in turn undercuts "the Nation's economic well-being."[17] The implications of these effect-on-commerce arguments were simply too much for the majority to bear. Under the government's chain-reaction logic, Chief Justice Rehnquist observed, Congress could regulate even "family law (including marriage, divorce, and child custody)" and "areas such as criminal law enforcement or education where States historically have been sovereign."[18] In the view of the majority, however, it could not be the case, for example, that "Congress could mandate a federal curriculum for local elementary and secondary schools" on the theory that better instruction fosters a more energized national economy.[19]

The dissenters' responses were predictable. Justice Souter decried what he saw as the majority's disregard of the "chastening experiences" endured by the Court following its ill-fated decisions in *Hammer*, *Schechter Poultry*, and *Carter Coal*.[20] In particular, he fretted that the majority's newly minted "noneconomic activity" test would resuscitate just the type of sorting process—built on woodenly excluding specified categories of activity from congressional control under the commerce power—that the Court had wisely abandoned beginning in 1937.[21] In a separate dissent, Justice Breyer added that, even accepting the soundness of the majority's methodology, the

---

15 *Id.* at 562–63 (internal citations omitted).

16 *Id.* at 565.

17 *Id.*

18 *Id.*

19 *Id.*

20 *Id.* at 604 (Souter, J., dissenting). *See supra* Section 2.C (discussing these decisions).

21 *Id.* at 608.

operation of schools should qualify as an "economic activity" because it entails the provision of valuable educational services at a cost of billions of dollars per year.[22] To the latter point, the majority offered the now-familiar it-proves-too-much response. If schooling were to constitute an economic activity, Chief Justice Rehnquist observed, so too would "child rearing" because it likewise entails the provision of "a 'valuable service—namely, to equip [children] with the skills they need to survive in life and, more specifically, in the workplace.' "[23]

In a concurring opinion joined by Justice O'Connor, Justice Kennedy cautioned that past experience "counsels great restraint" when the Court confronts challenges to congressional invocations of the commerce power.[24] Nonetheless, he insisted that the maintenance of "two governments . . . with distinct and discernible lines of political accountability"[25] remained "vital . . . in securing freedom."[26] According to Justice Kennedy, "[w]ere the Federal Government to take over the regulation of entire areas of traditional state concern, areas having nothing to do with the regulation of commercial activities, the boundaries between the spheres of federal and state authority would blur and political responsibility would become illusory."[27] Thus, while the concurring Justices went out of their way to emphasize the limited scope of the *Lopez* holding, their joining in the majority opinion sufficed, for the first time in 59 years, to take down a federal statute because it was not authorized, even with the Necessary and Proper Clause in view, by Congress's power to "regulate Commerce . . . among the several States."[28]

In the wake of *Lopez*, some commentators predicted that the Court's five-to-four decision might prove to be little more than a symbolic nod to the Framers' rejection of unlimited federal lawmaking authority.[29] The Court's decision in *United States v.*

---

22 *Id.* at 629 (Breyer, J., dissenting).

23 *Id.* at 565 (quoting *id.* at 629 (Breyer, J., dissenting)).

24 *Id.* at 568 (Kennedy, J., concurring).

25 *Id.* at 576.

26 *Id.* at 578.

27 *Id.* at 577.

28 U.S. CONST. art. I, § 8, cl. 3. For further discussion of the interactions between the Commerce Clause and the Necessary and Proper Clause, see *infra* Section 6.A.1.

29 *See, e.g.*, Jesse H. Choper, *Taming Congress's Power Under the Commerce Clause: What Does the Near Future Portend?*, 55 ARK. L. REV. 731, 732 & n.9 (2003) (collecting authorities suggesting that *Lopez* would or might well be an "aberration"); Michael C. Dorf, *No Federalists Here: Anti-Federalism and Nationalism on the Rehnquist Court*, 31 RUTGERS L.J. 741, 744 (2000) (noting that *Lopez* creates the appearance that "some areas of traditional state activity are completely immune from federal regulation" but predicting that "the appearance will prove false"); Robert F. Nagel, *The Future of Federalism*, 46 CASE W. RES. L. REV. 643, 659–61 (1996) (opining that the complex "political and cultural forces" working toward the centralization of government authority will cause *Lopez* to "recede into relative insignificance"); *see also*

Morrison[30] revealed, however, that *Lopez* was not an isolated event. *Morrison* addressed whether Congress could grant to the plaintiff-victim of gender-motivated violence a federal cause of action against the defendant-attacker. Once again writing for a five-Justice majority, Chief Justice Rehnquist acknowledged that, unlike in *Lopez*, Congress had made elaborate findings about the law under review—findings that specifically addressed the effects of gender-based violence on interstate commerce. Indeed, four years of legislative investigation had revealed that rape, spousal abuse, and similar forms of gender-motivated brutalization burdened the American economy with lost work time, forgone travel and business transactions, and increased medical costs.[31] For the majority, however, neither these sobering realities nor Congress's documented reliance on them were enough to overcome constitutional federalism concerns. As in *Lopez*, the commerce power failed to support a statute that addressed only noneconomic activity and was grounded in only a generalized "costs of crime" rationale.[32] As in *Lopez*, the majority saw no proper stopping point to the government's argument because its underlying logic would allow Congress even "to regulate murder or any other type of violence."[33] And as in *Lopez*, the law's lack of a "jurisdictional element"—that is, a provision that might "lend support" to its constitutionality by limiting the cause of action to acts involving "the use of channels of interstate commerce"—further undercut the case for its constitutionality.[34]

Writing for four dissenters, Justice Souter again declared that "categorical exclusions" had no place in the commerce-power field because history revealed them to be "as unworkable in practice as they are unsupportable in theory."[35] He saw in the majority's approach—now firmly tethered to the economic/noneconomic-activity dividing line—an ill-conceived return to the "earlier and nearly disastrous experiment" that reached its crest in the years before *Jones & Laughlin Steel*.[36] In a separate dissent, Justice Breyer added that, "in a Nation knit together by two centuries of scientific,

Deborah Jones Merritt, *Commerce!*, 94 MICH. L. REV. 674, 677–82, 750 (1995) (suggesting that *Lopez* involved "prun[ing] an excessive and unnecessary piece of congressional meddling while leaving prior Commerce Clause decisions untouched"; adding that the Court sought to confirm that "the Commerce Clause confers a limited grant of authority on Congress . . . that the courts will enforce . . . through deferential, but authentic, review").

30 529 U.S. 598 (2000).

31 *Id.* at 629–31 (Souter, J., dissenting).

32 *Id.* at 612–13 (majority opinion); *see id.* at 615–16.

33 *Id.* at 615.

34 *Id.* at 613–14 & n.5 (internal quotation omitted).

35 *Id.* at 640 (Souter, J., dissenting).

36 *Id.* at 642–43.

technological, commercial, and environmental change,"[37] it was wrongheaded for the Court, and harmful for the country, to "depriv[e] Congress of the power to regulate activities that have a genuine and important effect upon interstate commerce."[38] The dissenters seemed ready to limit the significance of *Lopez* to cases in which Congress had failed to make findings demonstrating a connection between the operative enactment and the vitality of interstate trade. In the view of the majority, however, the noneconomic-activity principle properly focused on the substance of—as opposed to the quality of the deliberative processes that produced—the challenged congressional intrusion on state decisionmaking authority.

To be sure, the dissenters' pleas for judicial restraint did not go entirely unheeded. In *Morrison*, as in *Lopez*, the Court gave no hint that it was abandoning any of its post-1936/pre-1995 substantial-effects precedents or that it was interfering in any way with Congress's ability to invoke the separate in-commerce or instrumentalities-and-channels prongs of its commerce power. Even so, the Congress-limiting spirit of *Lopez* and *Morrison* was unmistakable. These rulings thus raised both hopes and fears that the Justices would recognize additional restrictions on the reach of the commerce power. And in important rulings handed down in the wake of *Lopez* and *Morrison*—most notably, *National Federation of Independent Business v. Sebelius*[39]—the Court continued to build out the Commerce Clause's internal limits.[40]

B. THE CHANNELS/INSTRUMENTALITIES THEORY AND THE COMMERCE-PROHIBITING TECHNIQUE AFTER 1994

1. Regulating the Channels and Instrumentalities of Interstate Commerce

Even as the Court in *Lopez* and *Morrison* trimmed the sails of the affecting-commerce theory of congressional power, it reaffirmed the federal government's broad authority to regulate the "instrumentalities" and the "channels" of interstate activity.[41] No less important, the Court's post-*Morrison* decision in *Pierce County v. Guillen*[42] confirmed that the instrumentalities-and-channels-based theories of the commerce power continue to have a powerful

---

37 *Id.* at 660 (Breyer, J., dissenting).

38 *Id.*

39 567 U.S. 519 (2012).

40 *See infra* Section 4.E.1 (detailing the Court's treatment of the commerce power in *NFIB*).

41 *Lopez,* 514 U.S. at 558.

42 537 U.S. 129 (2003).

independent significance. That case concerned the constitutionality of a federal statute that prohibited state and federal courts from permitting the discovery, and admission into evidence, of certain data collected by state authorities concerning unsafe highway conditions. In upholding this measure, a unanimous Court reasoned that the evidentiary privilege this law put in place heightens accuracy in the reporting of highway hazards, which in turn facilitates road-safety enhancements. It followed, according to Justice Thomas, that the challenged statute was constitutional because it both "improv[es] safety in the channels of commerce and increas[es] protection for the instrumentalities of interstate commerce."[43]

The logic of *Pierce County* seems to confirm the validity of a wide range of other federal laws concerning the pathways and mechanisms of interstate movement. Consider, in this respect, 18 U.S.C. § 2119, the federal law that makes it a crime to carjack any automobile that has moved in interstate commerce. One might well defend this law as a valid exercise of the commerce power by pointing out that the behavior it targets (1) involves interference with an instrumentality of commerce in the form of the stolen car, and (2) impairs the channels of commerce by discouraging travel and slowing down drivers confronted with pulled-over vehicles, gawking bystanders, high-speed police chases, and the like. Critics of the statute might respond that carjackings (which, among other things, sometimes occur on private property) pose no direct threat to the roadways that facilitate cross-border movement. They might also claim that automobiles do not qualify as "instrumentalities of commerce" because drivers most often use them for noncommercial and purely local transit.[44] The lower courts, however, have chosen not to travel these analytical routes. Instead, they have upheld the federal carjacking ban by relying largely on the instrumentalities-of-commerce and channels-of-commerce theories.[45]

---

[43] *Id.* at 147.

[44] *Cf.* Perez v. United States, 402 U.S. 146, 150 (1971) (indicating that Congress could outlaw the intrastate destruction of airplanes because they qualify as instrumentalities of commerce).

[45] *See, e.g.*, United States v. Bishop, 66 F.3d 569, 590 (3d Cir. 1995) (upholding a challenged law in part on the basis "that motor vehicles are instrumentalities of interstate commerce"); United States v. Runyon, 707 F.3d 475, 489 (4th Cir. 2013) (same); United States v. Rivera-Figueroa, 149 F.3d 1, 3 (1st Cir. 1998) (finding that "Congress's effort to extend protection to the very instruments of interstate and foreign commerce [such as the use of motor vehicles] is reasonable on its face and amply supported by precedent"); United States v. Cortes, 299 F.3d 1030, 1033–34 (9th Cir. 2002) (collecting additional authorities); *see also* United States v. Small, 988 F.3d 241, 251–52 (6th Cir. 2021) (upholding the defendant's conviction under a federal kidnapping statute because his use of a rental car involved an instrumentality of interstate commerce), *cert. denied*, 142 S. Ct. 191 (2021); United States v. Marek, 238 F.3d 310, 318–19 (5th Cir. 2001) (en banc) (acknowledging, in the course of upholding an application of the federal murder-for-hire statute, that "automobiles" are a means

Assessment of the constitutionality of the federal carjacking law hinges in large part on how broad of a scope courts should give to the terms "instrumentalities of commerce" and "channels of commerce." Paradigms provide guidance. Major highways and railroad corridors, for example, fit comfortably into the "channels" category,[46] while airplanes, trains, and big-rig trucks readily qualify as "instrumentalities."[47] Modern-era courts, responding to modern-era conditions, have found that these constitutional categories embrace many other phenomena as well—including, for example, the many financial institutions through which border-crossing streams of capital flow.[48] One federal statute, long upheld by the courts, outlaws wire fraud, thus allowing federal authorities to prosecute highly localized acts of deception on the theory that the connective tissues of interstate communication, including telephone lines, constitute channels and/or instrumentalities of commerce.[49] Drawing on these

---

of interstate commerce that may create "a criminal federal jurisdictional nexus during intrastate use"). In *Garcia v. Vanguard Car Rental USA, Inc.*, 540 F.3d 1242 (11th Cir. 2008), however, the Eleventh Circuit balked at endorsing the view that all automobiles are, without more, instrumentalities of interstate commerce in light of concerns that doing so would subject "quintessentially state law matters" to congressional control. *Id.* at 1250; *see id.* at 1252 (suggesting in particular that rental cars are "frequently," but not always, instrumentalities of interstate commerce). Notably, the Court in *Garcia* went on to uphold the challenged statute, which protects the owners of rented vehicles from various forms of liability for damages caused by the vehicle during the vehicle's rental period, under a substantial-effects aggregation analysis, thus highlighting the independent significance of each separate prong of the commerce power. *See id.* (emphasizing the "size and national scope" of the rental car industry). This aspect of *Garcia* reveals how the federal carjacking statute might likewise be upheld on the basis of a substantial-effects aggregation-driven analysis—so long as one views theft as an "economic activity"—even if automobiles were not to qualify as instrumentalities of commerce. *See Bishop*, 66 F.3d. at 581 (characterizing forcible takings as an economic activity and reasoning that when carjackings are "[r]eplicated 15,000 or 20,000 times per year, the economic effects are indeed profound"). *See generally infra* note 107.

[46] *See, e.g.*, United States v. Ballinger, 395 F.3d 1218, 1225–26 (11th Cir. 2005) (en banc) (asserting that the "[c]hannels of commerce are the interstate transportation routes through which persons and goods move" and thus include "highways, railroads, navigable waters, and airspace" (internal quotations, footnotes, and citations omitted)).

[47] *See, e.g.*, *id.* at 1226 ("Instrumentalities of interstate commerce . . . are the people and things themselves moving in commerce, including automobiles, airplanes, boats, and shipments of goods."); *see also supra* note 44 (noting the Court's characterization in *Perez* of airplanes as instrumentalities of commerce).

[48] *See* United States v. Watts, 256 F.3d 630, 633–34 (7th Cir. 2001) (reasoning that Congress may outlaw robbery from financial institutions insured by the Federal Deposit Insurance Corporation on the theory that they "are instrumentalities and channels of interstate commerce"). *Accord, e.g.*, United States v. Spinello, 265 F.3d 150, 158 (3d Cir. 2001) (adding that banks are "integral to the web of interstate commercial activity"); United States v. Robinson, 389 F.3d 582, 594 (6th Cir. 2004) (likewise upholding the federal bank-robbery statute and collecting supportive rulings from multiple courts).

[49] *See, e.g.*, Choper, *supra* note 29, at 761.

authorities, lower courts have concluded that the internet likewise fits into the channels-and-instrumentalities category.[50]

Professor Jesse Choper, among others, has noted that *Lopez* and *Morrison* raised new questions about Congress's ability to invoke this aspect of the commerce power. As he wondered not long after *Morrison* came down:

> Could Congress add other crimes apart from fraud to the mail and wire statutes: conspiracy to commit murder, robbery, assault, and so on? Seemingly, all it would take is one phone call in the course of planning to rob or attack a victim to make something a federal crime. Further, could Congress make it a federal offense to use the interstate highways, or any road connected to a federal road, in the commission of any unlawful act? Could Congress make it a federal crime to use the Internet, or a computer network attached to the Internet, to engage in designated misconduct?[51]

The Court may ultimately derive from the logic of *Lopez* and *Morrison* a restriction on Congress's authority to adopt some or all of the laws posited by Professor Choper, at least when they concern such traditionally state-regulated subjects as murder, rape, and other violent crimes.[52] For now, however, it is important to see that the *Lopez/Morrison* principle does not itself require—or even come close to requiring—the invalidation of any of these hypothesized laws. This is the case because these laws concern congressional invocation of the "channels" and "instrumentalities" theories of the commerce power, as opposed to the affecting-commerce theory that was the only theory in the picture in *Lopez* and *Morrison* themselves.

---

50 *See, e.g.*, United States v. Le, 902 F.3d 104, 119 (2d Cir. 2018); *see also* Katherine Parker, Note, *Expanding the Regulation of Online Speech through the Commerce Clause to Reduce Cyber Harassment*, 47 HASTINGS CONST. L.Q. 475, 481, 492–93 (2020) (arguing that Congress can outlaw cyber-harassment, to the extent it is not protected by the First Amendment, because "the Internet [is] an instrumentality of commerce" in that "[l]ike motels, the Internet is used to facilitate interstate commerce" (citing United States v. Panfil, 338 F.3d 1299, 1300 (11th Cir. 2003), and Hillis v. Equifax Consumer Servs., 237 F.R.D. 491, 511 (N.D. Ga. 2006))).

51 Choper, *supra* note 29, at 762 (internal footnote omitted).

52 With regard to the question raised by Professor Choper as to violent offenses committed on federal highways, see *infra* note 76 (discussing prosecutions under federal hate-crime legislation). On another point, it is noteworthy that Professor Choper lumps robbery together with murder and assault as though they obviously fall into the same category. Perhaps he is right to do so. But because robbery involves the transfer, albeit the forcible transfer, of property from one person to another, it may well qualify as "economic activity" and thus not be subject to the same limits on congressional authority applicable to person-on-person physical attacks. *See infra* note 107 (discussing this issue).

2. The Commerce-Prohibiting Technique

Another set of questions brought into focus by *Lopez* and *Morrison* involves Congress's ability to control the "channels" of interstate commerce through use of the commerce-prohibiting technique. Because Chief Justice Rehnquist's opinions in those cases did not question this long-recognized source of federal power, it seems clear that Congress may continue to (1) impose prohibitions on cross-border movements of goods or persons it deems objectionable and (2) limit intrastate behavior, to a substantial extent, to effectuate such prohibitions.[53] New questions have arisen, however, about how far Congress can push this latter "super-bootstrapping" strategy in the post-*Lopez* world. Assume, for example, that Congress had responded to *Lopez* itself by enacting (1) Statute Alpha, which outlaws the carrying of any gun across a state line with the intent of possessing it within 1000 feet of a school; and (2) Statute Beta, which outlaws the possession of any gun within 1000 feet of a school. There can be little doubt that, even after *Lopez*, Statute Alpha would fall within Congress's lawmaking authority under the Commerce Clause as a straightforward exercise of the commerce-prohibiting technique.[54] In addition, government lawyers would argue that Statute Beta is "reasonably adapted" to effectuating Statute Alpha because Statute Beta will help to catch Statute Alpha violators who might otherwise escape prosecution in light of the difficulty of proving the defendant's (1) past cross-border carrying of a gun and (2) engagement in that conduct with the then-existing (and extremely hard-to-establish) *mens rea* of intending to possess the weapon in or near a school. Statute Beta's defenders also can argue that the law will help to carry Statute Alpha into execution by tending to ensure that—given the looming prospect of prosecution under Statute Beta—violations of Statute Alpha do not occur in the first place.[55]

---

[53] *See supra* Section 3.A.

[54] *See, e.g.*, United States v. Lankford, 196 F.3d 563 (5th Cir. 1999) (upholding a federal statute criminalizing movement across a state line with the intent to injure a spouse or intimate partner); *see generally* United States v. Ballinger, 312 F.3d 1264, 1273 n.8 (11th Cir. 2002) (collecting examples of statutory interstate-travel prohibitions of this kind), *vacated en banc on other grounds*, 395 F.3d 1218 (11th Cir. 2005). For a case validating another sort of law that allows interstate movement only under certain conditions, see *United States v. Whaley*, 577 F.3d 254, 258 (5th Cir. 2009) (upholding a federal ban on "failing to register . . . after traveling in interstate commerce" by designated categories of sex offenders). Questions related to the scope of the commerce power, which are addressed here, differ from questions related to whether such a law might violate any individual rights, including perhaps rights under the Second Amendment.

[55] *See* United States v. Darby, 312 U.S. 100, 121 (1941) (observing that, once Congress has legislated a ban on interstate movement of certain items, "it may choose the means reasonably adapted to the attainment of the permitted end, even though

Even so, many lawyers will sense that coupling Statute Beta with Statute Alpha will not save Statute Beta from judicial condemnation. After all, Statute Beta is *identical* to the statute the Court struck down in *Lopez*.[56] In addition, while the existence of Statute Alpha provides a conceivable basis for rendering *Lopez* a distinguishable case, the real-world linkage between Statute Alpha and Statute Beta is extremely weak because almost all Statute Beta violators will never have run afoul of Statute Alpha. These points help to illustrate why strong pressures long have pushed courts to limit Congress's ability to make use of the super-bootstrapping theory. They direct attention to another point, too: The state-protective philosophy reflected in *Lopez* and *Morrison* may inspire some judges to look with heightened skepticism on particular uses of that theory and perhaps even to rethink the soundness of the commerce-prohibiting technique itself.[57] To be sure, it seems unlikely that the Court will tinker with its now-unquestioned-for-decades commerce-prohibiting doctrine, especially because that doctrine brings to this legal field both a strong textual foundation and the advantages of a bright-line sorting mechanism. With regard to the super-bootstrap theory, however, much remains to be seen. Courts have continued to uphold congressional enactments on super-bootstrap grounds in post-*Lopez* rulings, and understandably so in light of its long-accepted textual anchorage in the Necessary and Proper Clause.[58] The Necessary and Proper Clause, however, is

they involve control of intrastate activities"). For additional earlier treatments of this "super-bootstrap" technique, see *supra* Sections 2.A & 3.A.

56 Highlighting this point, challengers would argue forcefully that lawmakers may not achieve "indirect[ly]" what the Constitution "directly" forecloses them from doing. *See* U.S. Term Limits, Inc. v. Thornton, 514 U.S. 779, 829 (1995). *See generally* Brannon P. Denning & Michael B. Kent, *Anti-Anti-Evasion in Constitutional Law*, 41 FLA. ST. U. L. REV. 397 (2014).

57 *See, e.g.*, Donald H. Regan, *How to Think About the Federal Commerce Power and Incidentally Rewrite* United States v. Lopez, 94 MICH. L. REV. 554, 576–78 (1995) (challenging the federal "toll-gate power" vindicated in the Court's commerce-prohibiting-technique cases); Grant S. Nelson, *A Commerce Clause Standard for the New Millennium: "Yes" to Broad Congressional Control Over Commercial Transactions, "No" to Federal Legislation on Social and Cultural Issues*, 55 ARK. L. REV. 1213, 1221–24 (2003) (arguing that some, though not all, past uses by the Court of the commerce-prohibiting technique were inappropriate).

58 An example is provided by the provisions of the federal Sex Offender Registration and Notification Act (SORNA). This act contains two separate rules directed at covered individuals. One essentially requires each such person to register as a sex offender in the jurisdiction of the offender's residence, employment, and schooling regardless of any interstate movement. The second rule makes it a federal crime for any covered individual to fail to register as a sex offender after that person has moved in interstate or foreign commerce under specified conditions, including by changing that person's residence or place of employment or schooling. The first rule is said to effectuate the second rule in part because, if everyone must register, then, necessarily, interstate travelers will register. In addition, pre-interstate-movement registration provides a record of the registrant's starting-point location, thus facilitating determinations of whether alleged interstate relocations unaccompanied

subject to limitations of its own,[59] and (as noted earlier) even the Court's seminal super-bootstrap ruling in *United States v. Darby* is susceptible to a more confined reading than it sometimes receives.[60] At the least, one thing is clear: Should Congress use the super-bootstrap technique to enact a law with no tighter of a linkage to a commerce-prohibiting measure than Statute Beta has to Statute Alpha, constitutional combatants are sure to launch attacks against it under the battle flags of *Lopez* and *Morrison*.

3. The Jurisdictional-Nexus Theory

Another set of conundrums tied to the channels-and-instrumentalities prong of the commerce power stems from the Court's post-1936 endorsement of federal restrictions on possessing or using objects that previously moved across a state line.[61] Most notably, in *United States v. Bass*[62] and *Scarborough v. United States*,[63] the Court read a statute that targeted gun possession by persons with a prior felony conviction to require "[no] more than the minimal nexus that the firearm have been, at some time, in interstate commerce."[64] (Indeed, *Scarborough* itself involved the defendant's conviction based on his possession of a firearm that "was manufactured in France in the 19th century and was somehow later brought into Virginia."[65]) Picking up on this point, the Court in *Lopez* stressed that the GFSZA did not include an "express jurisdictional element which might limit its reach to a discrete set of firearm

---

by required registration have in fact occurred. Several circuit courts have upheld applications of the first rule on the theory that it is reasonably adapted "to the goal [reflected in the second statute] of ensuring that sex offenders register and update previous registrations when moving among jurisdictions." *Whaley*, 577 F.3d at 261 (footnotes omitted; collecting earlier cases); *accord* United States v. Guzman, 591 F.3d 83, 90–91 (2d Cir. 2010); *see also* United States v. Vasquez, 611 F.3d 325, 329–30 (7th Cir. 2010) (rejecting the argument that the "failure to require a connection between the jurisdictional element of travel and the criminal act of failing to register" is fatal to the Act). It is noteworthy, however, that at least two district court judges have relied on *Lopez* to invalidate the first rule, albeit without clearly assessing the applicability in this context of the super-bootstrap theory. *See* United States v. Waybright, 561 F. Supp. 2d 1154, 1164 (D. Mont. 2008), *disapproved of in* United States v. George, 625 F.3d 1124 (9th Cir. 2010), *opinion vacated on other grounds*, 672 F.3d 1126 (9th Cir. 2012); United States v. Guzman, 582 F. Supp. 2d 305, 312 (N.D.N.Y. 2008), *rev'd in part*, United States v. Guzman, 591 F.3d 83 (2d Cir. 2010).

59 *See infra* Section 6.B.

60 *See supra* Section 3.A.

61 *See generally supra* Section 3.B.

62 404 U.S. 336 (1971).

63 431 U.S. 563 (1977).

64 *Id.* at 575.

65 *Id.* at 565 n.2; *see also* LAURENCE H. TRIBE, AMERICAN CONSTITUTIONAL LAW § 5–5, at 830 (3d ed. 2000) (noting that although "the issue squarely presented in *Scarborough* concerned only the interpretation of the statute," the Court's reasoning indicated its belief that the statute, thus construed, fell within Congress's "full Commerce Clause power").

possessions."[66] Savvy lawmakers were quick to recognize the possibilities this passage created. Drawing on it, Congress promptly reenacted the same guns-near-schools ban invalidated in *Lopez* with the sole modification that the possessed gun had to have "moved in or . . . otherwise affect[ed] interstate or foreign commerce."[67] Does this retooled version of the GFSZA satisfy Commerce Clause requirements? Lower courts have said "yes," invoking the super-channels-of-commerce rationale supported by *Bass* and *Scarborough*.[68] In other post-*Lopez* cases, courts likewise have rejected challenges to possession laws that contain jurisdictional hooks tied to the past interstate movement of targeted items of personalty.[69]

As part of his broadside assault on the Court's commerce-power jurisprudence, Justice Thomas has called for abandonment of the jurisdictional-hook principle that underlies these rulings.[70] The

---

[66] *Lopez*, 514 U.S. at 562.

[67] Pub. L. No. 104–208 § 101(f), 110 Stat. 3009, codified as amended at 18 U.S.C. § 922(q)(2)(A).

[68] *See* United States v. Dorsey, 418 F.3d 1038, 1045–47 (9th Cir. 2005); United States v. Danks, 221 F.3d 1037, 1038–39 (8th Cir. 1999).

[69] Particularly plentiful are post-*Lopez* decisions that reaffirm the constitutionality of the felon-in-possession law involved in *Bass* and *Scarborough* themselves. *See, e.g.*, United States v. Lemons, 302 F.3d 769, 771–73 (7th Cir. 2002) (indicating that the nexus requirement discussed in *Scarborough* applies in the post-*Lopez* context); United States v. Singletary, 268 F.3d 196, 199–205 (3d Cir. 2001) (reevaluating the law of the circuit in light of *Lopez* and *Morrison* and finding *Scarborough* still applicable to uphold the statute); *see generally* Choper, *supra* note 29, at 759 n.137 (collecting circuit-court cases). Other post-*Lopez* decisions have relied on the principle of *Bass* and *Scarborough* to uphold convictions involving regulated items other than firearms. *See, e.g.*, United States v. Patton, 451 F.3d 615, 634–35 (10th Cir. 2006) (upholding the federal felon-in-possession-of-body-armor statute); United States v. Cook, 488 Fed. App'x 643, 646 (3d Cir. 2012) (same). Notably, courts have recognized that a statutory "jurisdictional element" need not always involve the prior interstate movement of a person or property to satisfy commerce-power standards. *See, e.g.*, United States v. Faasse, 265 F.3d 475, 490 (6th Cir. 2001) (finding an "explicit jurisdictional nexus" present in the federal child-support-nonpayment statute because it reaches only the non-custodial parent's obligations to pay for children located in another state). Indeed, in *United States v. Hill*, 927 F.3d 188, 204 (4th Cir. 2019), *cert. denied sub nom.* Hill v. United States, 141 S. Ct. 272 (2020), the court went so far as to declare that it could not find a case in which "a federal criminal statute including an interstate commerce jurisdictional element has been held to exceed Congress's authority under the Commerce Clause." *But cf. infra* notes 73–74 (discussing United States v. McCoy, 323 F.3d 1114 (9th Cir. 2003)).

[70] *See* Alderman v. United States, 562 U.S. 1163, 1166–67 (2011) (Thomas, J., dissenting from denial of certiorari) (urging that lower courts' practice of upholding a law merely because it has a jurisdictional hook similar to the one in *Scarborough* "cannot be reconciled with *Lopez*," threatens to "remove any limit on the commerce power," and invites congressional usurpation of the states' police power); *see also* Brent E. Newton, *Felons, Firearms, and Federalism: Reconsidering* Scarborough *in Light of* Lopez, 3 J. APP. PRAC. & PROCESS 671, 683–84 (2001) (asserting that the rule of *Scarborough* "cannot logically survive the Court's recent shift in its Commerce Clause jurisprudence"). In *Cortes*, 299 F.3d 1030, the court (rightly) noted that the continuing "vitality of *Scarborough* engenders significant debate" but also (and no less rightly)

present-day legal landscape, however, suggests that this proposed retrenchment is unlikely to occur, especially in light of the Court's pointed effort to distinguish the "jurisdictional element" line of cases in *Lopez* itself. At the same time, the Court might in time find support in *Lopez* and *Morrison* for reining in the jurisdictional-element concept as a source of congressional power.[71] Indeed, already-existing case law suggests at least three possibilities along these lines.

First, it is one thing to uphold federal regulation of a problematic item (such as a handgun in the possession of a convicted felon) on the ground that the item previously moved from one state to another; but it is another thing to uphold federal regulation of a problematic item on the ground that some raw material incorporated into that item (such as steel or plastic) or used in that item's production (such as a die cast or welding torch) once moved across a state border. In due course, the Justices might distinguish between these two types of prohibitions, citing along the way a passing reference in *Lopez* itself to the absence of any "*concrete* tie" between interstate commerce and the firearm involved in that case.[72] Indeed, the Ninth Circuit endorsed precisely this approach in *United States v. McCoy*,[73] holding that the cross-border transit of a camera and film used in making photographs failed to support a federal prosecution for possession of child pornography that itself was both created and possessed exclusively within one state.[74]

---

observed that lower courts must "follow *Scarborough* unwaveringly" until "the Supreme Court tells us otherwise." *Id.* at 1037 n.2; *see also Patton*, 451 F.3d at 634–35 (canvassing earlier circuit-court rulings that have continued to apply *Scarborough* notwithstanding the Court's ruling in *Lopez*).

[71] *See, e.g.*, United States v. Wilson, 73 F.3d 675, 685 (7th Cir. 1995) (noting that "[i]n discussing the lack of a jurisdictional element in *Lopez*, the Court simply did not state or imply . . . that all statutes with such an element would be constitutional"); United States v. Rodia, 194 F.3d 465, 472–73 (3d Cir. 1999) (rejecting any "hard and fast rule that the presence of a jurisdictional element automatically ensures the constitutionality of a statute").

[72] *Lopez*, 514 U.S. at 567 (emphasis added).

[73] 323 F.3d 1114.

[74] More specifically, the court held unconstitutional a federal ban on the possession of child pornography, the production of which involved materials that had moved in interstate commerce, as applied to a photograph that had not itself moved across state lines (and was held solely for personal, rather than commercial, purposes with no plans for interstate shipment). In so doing, the court reasoned that the government's theory of the jurisdictional-hook concept could not save the statute, as applied in this case, because relying on the *Bass/Scarborough* principle in these circumstances would cause it to "encompass[ ] virtually *every* case imaginable" involving a possessory crime. *Id.* at 1124 (emphasis in original). *See also* United States v. Maxwell, 386 F.3d 1042, 1062–63 (11th Cir. 2004) (overturning on constitutional grounds a federal conviction for possessing child pornography based on a showing that images were placed on computer disks that had moved in interstate commerce; expressing worry about federal invasion of state police powers based on "pretextual incantations evoking the phantasm of commerce," including by raising the specter of allowing a federal prosecution for murder because "the defendant ate a cheeseburger

Second, the Court might choose to require some temporal connection between the cross-border movement of the regulated item and the *actus reus* of the federal offense.[75] To be sure, a rule requiring that the relevant border crossing must have occurred within a limited time before the key events giving rise to the federal offense could create line-drawing problems viewed as sufficiently intractable to persuade the Court to abandon the project altogether. The Court, however, could at least choose to hold that Congress itself has to spell out in its statutes, at least for purposes of cases not obviously unproblematic on time-related grounds, some defined temporal connection between the regulated behavior and the cross-border movement to which that behavior is jurisdictionally hooked.

Finally, the Court might develop special rules regarding jurisdictional elements that target the movement of the defendant who is subject to prosecution, as opposed to the movement of a problematic physical object that comes into a defendant's possession. It seems farfetched to believe, for example, that the Justices would have upheld the statute struck down in *Morrison* had it required nothing more than a showing that the defendant at some point earlier in life had crossed a state line.[76] Indeed, this conclusion finds support

---

that traveled in interstate commerce"), *rev'd following remand on other grounds*, 446 F.3d 1210 (11th Cir. 2006); United States v. Holston, 343 F.3d 83, 89 (2d Cir. 2003) (questioning the constitutional efficacy of Congress's use of a jurisdictional hook when "the interstate component underpinning the jurisdictional element, for example, the shipment of a video camera, is attenuated from the criminal conduct—the production of child pornography—which occurs entirely locally"). Notably, there is a significant body of authority supportive of the conclusion—albeit one not based on the jurisdictional-element theory—that the Court's later decision in *Gonzales v. Raich*, 545 U.S. 1 (2005) (discussed *infra* Section 5.D.2.a) effectively overruled *McCoy*. *See, e.g.*, United States v. Overton, No. CR 07–28–BU-DWM, 2007 WL 2815986 at *2, *3 (D. Mont. Sept. 26, 2007) (citing multiple post-*Raich* cases, including the Eleventh Circuit's post-*Raich* ruling following remand in *Maxwell*, in support of this view; reasoning in part that, if Congress can regulate "home-grown marijuana produced for purely personal use . . . as part of a larger scheme to control the interstate market for controlled substances, then Congress can regulate so-called home-grown child pornography produced for purely personal use in an effort to control the interstate marketing of child pornography"), *aff'd*, 573 F.3d 679 (9th Cir. 2009); *see also* United States v. McCalla, 545 F.3d 750, 756 (9th Cir. 2008) (noting that "to the extent the reasoning employed in *McCoy* relied on the local nature of the activity, it has been overruled by the Supreme Court's decision in *Raich*").

[75] *See, e.g.*, United States v. Pappadopoulos, 64 F.3d 522, 527 (9th Cir. 1995) (asserting that "Congress's power to regulate articles or goods in commerce may not permit it to regulate an item for eternity simply because it has once passed state lines"); *Patton*, 451 F.3d at 633 ("[S]ection 931's requirement that the body armor must once have traveled in interstate commerce is so sweeping as to be unhelpful in determining whether the activities regulated by the statute have a substantial and non-attenuated effect on interstate commerce."); *see also* United States v. Coleman, 675 F.3d 615, 620–21 (6th Cir. 2012) (considering, but rejecting, an argument based on a claimed time-attenuated linkage problem in applying the federal sex-offender-registration statute).

[76] *See* Anthony J. Colangelo, *The Foreign Commerce Clause*, 96 VA. L. REV. 949, 999 (2010) (noting that "jurisdictional hook statutes . . . traditionally apply to things—

in *Lopez* itself because the Court in that case specifically flagged the absence of evidence indicating that the defendant had "*recently* moved in interstate commerce."[77]

The underlying problem in cases of this kind is not hard to miss: Judicial acquiescence in the face of machinations of statutory draftsmanship could undermine the core principle that drove the

not persons—traveling in commerce, for the reason [that otherwise] anything done by anyone who has ever traveled interstate would . . . be subject to congressional regulation, thus erasing the distinction between federal and state authority" (internal footnote omitted)); *see also* Carr v. United States, 560 U.S. 438, 470 (2010) (Alito, J., dissenting) (appearing to raise questions about whether Congress would have "exceeded its authority under the Commerce Clause" by relying on past interstate travel by the defendant as a jurisdictional nexus for criminalizing behavior not otherwise subject to federal control). Two types of statutes are less problematic and thus readily distinguishable. First, as noted in the text, a statute such as the new GFSZA, *see supra* note 67 and accompanying text, falls into a different category because its jurisdictional element focuses on the movement of a commonly regulated *object*—namely a gun—the possession of which is the gravamen of the criminal offense. Second, there should be no problem in upholding laws marked by a jurisdictional element that targets border crossing by an individual when that border crossing has a demonstrable relation to the targeted wrongful conduct—for example, the crossing of a state line with the intent to murder a police officer. *See, e.g., Ballinger*, 395 F.3d at 1225–31 (finding constitutional a defendant's conviction based on local church burnings purposefully facilitated by his earlier interstate travel). *But see id.* at 1257 (Hill, J., dissenting) ("I cannot think of any local activity that Congress could not regulate, nor any crime that Congress could not federalize under such an expansive interpretation of the commerce power."). A case connected up with the latter point is *United States v. Jenkins*, 909 F. Supp. 2d 758 (E.D. Ky. 2012), in which the court sustained a conviction under the Hate Crimes Prevention Act (HCPA), in the face of an argument that the law exceeded Congress's commerce power. The court in that case acknowledged that the statute's prohibition of "bias-motivated violence," just like the prohibition struck down in *Morrison*, did not target an economic activity. *Id.* at 768. Even so, the court found that the law's jurisdictional element alleviated constitutional concerns because it limited the law's application to acts of violence—here an assault intentionally directed at a gay man—related to interstate commerce. (In *Jenkins* itself, the government had established the requisite jurisdictional nexus by proving that the prosecuted act of violence involved the use of a vehicle on an interstate highway. *Id.* at 770–71.) One way to think about such a law is to view it, on the facts presented, as embodying a proper federal regulation of the channels and/or instrumentalities of interstate commerce. Viewed another way, the case illustrates that a jurisdictional element need not always take the form a state-border-crossing event. Here, the use of a car on an artery of commerce, not at some random point in time, but instead in the very course of perpetrating the crime, sufficed to sustain application of the statute as a proper exercise of the commerce power. Related to the question presented in cases such as *Jenkins* is another issue: Can Congress utilize the super-bootstrapping technique to enact possession laws that are otherwise not salvageable through inclusion of a moved-in-commerce jurisdictional element standing alone? For example, 18 U.S.C. § 922(g)(1) prohibits a felon from receiving a gun by way of an interstate shipment, "which certainly involves congressional regulation of the channels of interstate commerce." Brannon P. Denning & Glenn H. Reynolds, *Rulings and Resistance: The New Commerce Clause Jurisprudence Encounters the Lower Courts*, 55 ARK. L. REV. 1253, 1272 (2003). The question thus arises: Given the presence of this prohibition in the U.S. Code, may Congress ban all possession of all guns by all felons to ensure that this ban operates effectively? Put more generally, how do the jurisdictional-element, the commerce-prohibiting, and the super-bootstrapping aspects of the commerce power fit together in the post-*Lopez* environment?

[77] *Lopez*, 514 U.S. at 567 (emphasis added).

result in *Lopez*—namely, that the commerce power is rightly subject to meaningful limits.[78] Put another way, the desideratum of avoiding absurd results suggests the need to place some boundaries on the power of Congress to use jurisdictional hooks to support the enactment of federal legislation. Otherwise, Congress would be able, for example, to pass a federal murder law made applicable to anyone who had worn any article of clothing in any place at any time so long as either the garment or anything in it—be it button, thread, or dye—had at some point crossed a state line.[79] It merits emphasis, however, that avoiding outcomes as extreme as this one does not require abandoning the jurisdictional-nexus concept in hook-line-and-sinker fashion. Rather, by supplementing this source of authority with the sort of component-part, time-tethered, and individual-travel-based limits suggested here, the Court can guard against legislative overreaches while continuing to honor a well-settled feature of commerce-power law on which Congress has relied in enacting many statutes over many years.

C. THE IN-COMMERCE THEORY AFTER 1994

Drawing on the legacy of the early stockyard-regulation cases,[80] the Court in *Lopez* reaffirmed that Congress may regulate "persons or things in interstate commerce," whether or not it can target the same activity under the affecting-commerce theory. This "in commerce" concept—as we saw earlier—has both a long history and a murky quality.[81] Even so, the Court's recent decisions confirm the persisting and freestanding significance of the in-commerce prong of the commerce power.

---

[78] *See* TRIBE, *supra* note 65, § 5–5, at 831 n.29 (providing additional problematic examples, including by hypothesizing a federal school-curriculum statute applied to any school made with any building materials that crossed a state line; noting that such cases "could well trigger further doctrinal developments in this area—such as a 'sham' exception, or 'proportionality' and 'nexus' requirements").

[79] *See* Denning & Reynolds, *supra* note 76, at 1273 (worrying about Congress's potential ability to "evade" constitutional difficulties with the federal arson statute as applied to a private residence merely by requiring that "some portion of the building materials used in [its] construction had moved in interstate commerce in the past"). To be clear, the concern expressed here is not applicable to most jurisdictional-hook statutes that Congress has thus far put in place. Even the retooled GFSZA, for example, is readily distinguishable from the border-crossing-clothes-component hypothetical discussed in the text because that statute's jurisdictional element focuses squarely on a specific object—namely, a gun—the possession of which is itself the gravamen of the criminal offense.

[80] *See supra* Section 2.B (discussing, for example, *Swift & Co. v. United States*, 196 U.S. 375 (1905)).

[81] *See supra* Section 3.B (discussing, for example, *United States v. Yellow Cab. Co.*, 332 U.S. 218 (1947)).

Telling in this regard is *Reno v. Condon*,[82] in which the Court demonstrated a willingness to take an accommodating view of this theory even in the wake of *Lopez*. In *Condon*, a unanimous Court held that Congress could forbid the transfer of personal data collected by states in the process of issuing motor vehicle licenses because that information "is a 'thing in interstate commerce.' "[83] As explained by Chief Justice Rehnquist, it made sense to attach the in-commerce label to the challenged statute because the "information which the States have historically sold is used by insurers, manufacturers, direct marketers, and others engaged in interstate commerce to contact drivers with customized solicitations."[84] In other words, "[b]ecause drivers' information is, in this context, an article of commerce, its sale or release into the interstate stream of business [was] sufficient to support congressional regulation," whether or not that distribution warranted the law's validation under the "substantial effects" test.[85]

One might wonder why the Court in *Condon* found it necessary to make use of the in-commerce rubric. The statute, after all, focused on the "economic activity" of selling commercially valuable data, thus seemingly rendering *Lopez* no obstacle to engaging in substantial-effects analysis. Perhaps the Court opted for the in-commerce rationale because doing so removed the need to explore whether the regulated activity, in the aggregate, had the requisite "substantial" impact on interstate trade.[86] Or perhaps this reasoning provided the only way to generate a unanimous ruling in the case.[87] In any event, *Condon* illustrates one important role that in-commerce analysis can play: It offers, in some instances, an analytical shortcut for use in validating a challenged law if a court is disinclined to explore the limits of the noneconomic activity principle and other problems posed by the *Lopez*/*Morrison* rule.[88]

---

82 528 U.S. 141 (2000).

83 *Id.* at 148 (quoting *Lopez*, 514 U.S. at 558–59) (internal alteration omitted).

84 *Id.*

85 *Id.* at 148–49.

86 In addition, the statutory language made reference to "disclos[ing] or otherwise mak[ing] available" such data, apparently whether for profit or not. *Condon*, 528 U.S. at 144. Thus, it might be that the Court gravitated to its in-commerce *ratio decidendi* because some Justices had qualms about characterizing a statute that covered all forms of distribution as targeting an "economic activity" under *Lopez*.

87 In particular, this may have been the case in light of Justice Thomas's earlier expressions of general disquietude with the Court's substantial-effects jurisprudence. *See infra* note 195.

88 *See* Denning & Reynolds, *supra* note 76, at 1288 (noting the potential "advantage" to courts of relying on Commerce Clause theories that permit courts "to avoid the more complicated 'affecting commerce' analysis of *Lopez*"). Similar thinking might also have influenced the Court's decision in *United States v. Robertson*, 514 U.S. 669 (1995), which involved a prosecution under the Racketeer Influenced and Corrupt

Condon also shines a light on a sometimes-overlooked feature of present-day in-commerce analysis. In *Lopez*, the Court adverted to the power "to regulate and protect . . . persons or things in interstate commerce, even though the threat may come only from intrastate activities."[89] In *Condon*, however, the Court did not uphold an effort by Congress to remove a "threat" to the interstate movement of drivers' license data. Rather, the Court in effect declared that, if an item qualifies as a "thing in interstate commerce," Congress may make it a thing *not* in interstate commerce by cutting off trade in it altogether.[90] No less important, the Court upheld Congress's use of

---

Organizations Act (RICO). The government in that case undertook to show that the defendant had invested proceeds earned from criminal drug activities in an Alaskan gold mine that, as required by the language of the statute, was "engaged in or affect[ed] . . . interstate or foreign commerce." *Id.* at 670. The Court sidestepped the affecting-commerce argument by sustaining the conviction on the theory that the mining business had "engaged in . . . interstate or foreign commerce" by purchasing equipment in California, hiring seven workers from out of state, and sending $30,000 in gold outside Alaska. *Id.* at 671–72. The *Robertson* case may reflect nothing more than a fact-specific ruling on a matter of statutory interpretation. Viewed through a constitutional lens, however, *Robertson* suggests that Congress has broad authority to regulate intrastate activity connected up with a business's operations (there, in the form of making use of ill-gotten drug money) based on a showing that other elements of its business operations (there, in the form of buying equipment, hiring workers, and shipping goods) have an interstate character. *See generally* Merritt, *supra* note 29, at 732–33 (claiming that the Court must have considered the constitutional implications of *Robertson* and that it did not focus on any interstate elements of Mr. Robertson's drug-proceeds-investment-related activities themselves). What if, for example, Congress made it a crime for persons working at a business engaged in interstate commerce to maintain possession of a gun near a school? Could the courts constitutionally apply that law to the defendant in *Robertson* if his gold-mine office sat next door to a schoolhouse and he kept a gun in his desk? Analytical difficulties arise in evaluating this sort of case because the Court in *Robertson* ended its analysis once it found that the gold mining business had engaged in interstate commerce and thus never explained what relationship, if any, the regulated conduct must have with the interstate elements of the business. For this reason, the extent to which Congress may rely on the in-commerce theory to regulate the intrastate activities of businesses that engage in interstate commerce remains unclear. Nonetheless, *Robertson* supplies a basis for arguing that many business-related activities (even if not all of them) lie in the stream of interstate commerce. In particular, it supports the claim that the in-commerce theory extends to businesses involved in producing goods and services (like Mr. Robertson's gold-mining company) that bring in workers or equipment from other states and/or send products across state lines. *See, e.g.*, United States v. Dinwiddie, 76 F.3d 913, 919 (8th Cir. 1996) (upholding a conviction under the Freedom of Access to Clinic Entrances Act by reference to the fact that the Planned Parenthood facility in question had a "number of patients and staff" who did not reside in the state where the clinic was located); *cf.* United States v. Bird, 124 F.3d 667, 674–75 (5th Cir. 1997) (declining to uphold, on an in-commerce theory, an application of the federal prohibition on obstructing access to abortion clinics because "there is no allegation or showing that, in the present case, [the clinic] ever employed physicians, treated patients, or used supplies" that had "traveled interstate").

89 *Lopez*, 514 U.S. at 558 (going on to highlight the federal prohibition on thefts from interstate shipments as a paradigmatic exercise of this power).

90 Applying something like the flipside of this principle, lower courts have relied on the in-commerce theory to uphold federal criminalization of the failure to pay court-ordered child support for a child who resides in another state. *E.g.*, *Faasse*, 265 F.3d at 481, 485 (noting that nine circuits have reached the same conclusion; relying on

its commerce power in this way to achieve the essentially non-commercial purpose of protecting the privacy interests of motor-vehicle owners. Finally, in keeping with the principle of *Currin v. Wallace*,[91] the Court did not question Congress's decision to proscribe all transfers of driver's license data, whether interstate or intrastate in nature, apparently on the theory that data destined for intrastate exploitation was functionally inseparable from the great bulk of data destined for use in transactions that would cross state lines.

This discussion of the in-commerce prong of congressional power reveals its continuing "obscurity" in the sense that its precise contours are not easy to mark.[92] In most modern cases, however, courts should not have to speculate about where streams of commerce begin and end. To be sure, in cases such as *Schechter Poultry* and *Carter Coal*, these sorts of judicial inquiries were of critical significance. That was true, however, only because constitutional principles of the time barred Congress from regulating the localized mining and wholesaling activities involved in those cases under the affecting-commerce theory.[93] Nothing in *Lopez*, however, even remotely suggests that the Court today would hesitate to uphold federal regulation of those activities on an affecting-commerce rationale in light of their "economic" character.[94] Nonetheless, the in-commerce theory remains important. This is so, in part, because some federal statutes require a showing that the defendant has acted "in" interstate commerce.[95] No less important, the practical

---

Lopez's recognition of power "to regulate things in interstate commerce," here child support payments, "be they commercial or not"). *But see id.* at 500 (Batchelder, J., dissenting) (arguing that Congress should not be able to use the in-commerce theory to "regulate the passive failure of individuals to engage in interstate commerce").

[91] 306 U.S. 1 (1939); *see also supra* Section 3.B (discussing this case).

[92] Regan, *supra* note 57, at 561 n.23.

[93] *See supra* Section 2.C.

[94] *See infra* Section 4.D.1. For this reason, under modern-day law, the Court would probably never reach the in-commerce issues presented in *Carter Coal, Schechter Poultry*, and other early cases. If the Court were to address those issues, however, intervening decisions might well dictate a different result than the Court of the New Deal era reached. For example, the Court in *United States v. American Building Maintenance Industries*, 422 U.S. 271 (1975), asserted that the "flow of commerce" embraces "the practical, economic continuity in the *generation of goods and services* for interstate markets and their transport and *distribution to the consumer.*" *Id.* at 276 (emphasis added). Notwithstanding this broad language, the Court went on to conclude that a local janitorial business was not operating "in" commerce for purposes of the Clayton Act simply because it made local purchases of supplies that had been produced outside the state. *Id.* at 284–85. That case, however, did not involve either the "generation" of goods by the regulated party for potential export (as did *Carter Coal*) or the local "distribution" of non-locally-made goods for resale (as did *Schechter Poultry*).

[95] *E.g.*, 18 U.S.C. § 247(b) (criminalizing the act of damaging religious property where the offender engages in or affects interstate commerce to commit the crime); 18 U.S.C. § 1962(a) (prohibiting income obtained from racketeering to be used in "any

significance of the in-commerce theory may wax or wane depending on the Court's future elaborations of the principle of *Lopez* and *Morrison*. More specifically, to the extent that the Court continues to rein in the affecting-commerce theory, arguments based on an in-commerce rationale will assume increasing importance.

D. THE AFFECTING-COMMERCE THEORY AFTER 1994 AND THE NONECONOMIC-ACTIVITY RULE

As we have seen, *Lopez* and *Morrison* left in place large reservoirs of congressional power to regulate the channels and instrumentalities of interstate commerce, as well as persons and things in interstate commerce. Of no less importance, the Court's recent Commerce Clause cases—notwithstanding the limitations endorsed in *Lopez* and *Morrison*—confirm that Congress retains far-reaching authority to regulate intrastate conduct on the theory that it *affects* cross-border commercial activity.

To see why, it is useful to recall the core components of the Court's pre-*Lopez* affecting-commerce jurisprudence. Perhaps most important, that body of law clarified that the affecting-commerce power was not limited to countering a particular category of distinctly national problems, such as "races to the bottom" among states worried about enacting labor laws or environmental controls that might cause in-state businesses to relocate their operations elsewhere. Rather, those cases suggested that (as one commentator put it) "Congress may regulate any behavior that affects the quantity or identity of goods or people moving across state lines."[96] The Court breathed life into this general proposition by recognizing an important set of sub-rules that invigorated this regulatory power. For example:

1. The Court would not intervene as long as Congress had a "rational basis" for finding that the activity it regulated had a substantial effect on interstate commerce.[97]

2. In calculating the existence of a substantial effect, Congress could consider the aggregate impact of entire classes of activity, regardless of whether the impact of

---

enterprise which is engaged in . . . interstate or foreign commerce"); *see also Ballinger*, 395 F.3d at 1229 (collecting additional statutes).

[96] Regan, *supra* note 57, at 561.

[97] Katzenbach v. McClung, 379 U.S. 294, 304 (1964) (discussed *supra* Section 3.C.3).

any individual instance of the regulated activity was only "trivial."[98]

3. Congress had the power to act in effective ways to achieve its goals in dealing with interstate economic activity, including, as one commentator described it, by regulating even "local acts which in themselves have no interstate nexus or effect if as a practical matter it is difficult to distinguish such transactions from others which may have some relation to interstate commerce."[99]

4. The Court would not second-guess congressional judgments about whether preexisting federal or state legislation already dealt adequately with the problem that its exercise of the commerce power purported to target.[100]

5. Congress, if otherwise permitted to act pursuant to its affecting-commerce power, could do so based on noneconomic (including moral) considerations.[101]

6. There were—at least the Court's dicta suggested—no categorical limits on the aggregation-based affecting-commerce power akin to the no-regulation-of-production limit recognized in *Carter Coal*. Rather, as the Court declared in *Wickard v. Filburn*: "[E]ven if [a person's] activity be local and though it may not be regarded as commerce, it may still, whatever its nature, be reached by Congress if it exerts a substantial economic effect on interstate commerce and this irrespective of whether such effect is what might at some earlier time have been defined as 'direct' or 'indirect.' "[102]

For three key reasons, *Lopez* and *Morrison* have had, at least so far, only a limited impact on the Court's post-1936 affecting-commerce jurisprudence. First, those two decisions cut back on only

---

98 Wickard v. Filburn, 317 U.S. 111, 127–28 (1942) (discussed *supra* Section 3.C.2).

99 Robert L. Stern, *The Commerce Clause Revisited: The Federalization of Intrastate Crime*, 15 ARIZ. L. REV. 271, 280 (1973).

100 *E.g.*, Hodel v. Va. Surface Min. and Reclamation Ass'n, Inc., 452 U.S. 264, 283 (1981) (rejecting a challenge to a federal law that was based on an assertion that the means it established for dealing with strip mining were "redundant or unnecessary"; emphasizing that the "effectiveness of existing laws . . . is ordinarily a matter committed to legislative judgment").

101 *See* Heart of Atlanta Motel v. United States, 379 U.S. 241, 257 (1964) (discussed *supra* Section 3.C.3).

102 *Filburn*, 317 U.S. at 125.

the last of these six separate sub-rules. Second, those two decisions cut back on that sub-rule in only one way—namely, by establishing that a specialized constraint applies to, but only applies to, congressional regulation of noneconomic activity.[103] Third, this newfangled "non-economic activity" limitation on the affecting-commerce power appears to be subject to important limitations of its own.[104] Most important, the Court in *Morrison* went out of its way to declare that "we need not adopt a categorical rule against aggregating the effects of any noneconomic activity in order to decide these cases."[105] In short, the Court's rulings in *Lopez* and *Morrison* reflect something less—indeed, far less—than a sea change in the Court's affecting-commerce jurisprudence. Nonetheless, they have

---

[103] For a post-*Lopez/Morrison* reaffirmation of Congress's broad authority to regulate local economic transactions on an aggregation-based affecting-commerce theory, see *The Citizens Bank v. Alafabco, Inc.*, 539 U.S. 52 (2003) (per curiam). There, the Court upheld application of the Federal Arbitration Act to a dispute concerning a local commercial-loan transaction entered into in part for the purpose of raising funds for out-of-state uses and secured in part by "goods assembled from out-of-state parts and raw materials." *Id.* at 57. Emphasizing Congress's ability to focus on a "general practice," rather than "individual . . . transactions, taken alone," the Court declared that *Lopez* did not "purport to announce a new rule governing Congress' Commerce Clause power over concededly economic activity such as the debt-restructuring agreements before us now." *Id.* at 56–58.

[104] Throughout his opinion in *Morrison*, for example, Chief Justice Rehnquist emphasized that the challenged statute targeted "noneconomic, violent conduct," thus providing an opening for future arguments designed to focus the operation of the "non-economic activity" principle itself on violent behavior or violence-connected behavior, such as gun possession. *Morrison*, 529 U.S. at 617; *see, e.g.*, *id.* at 615 (noting that the countering of violent crime "has always been the prime object of the States' police power"). The *Morrison* majority also left room for litigants to claim that proper legislative findings might support federal regulation of at least some noneconomic activity when it noted that the presence of findings "is not sufficient, *by itself*, to sustain . . . Commerce Clause legislation." *Id.* at 614 (emphasis added). In keeping with this rhetoric (as well as the Court's attentiveness to the absence of supportive legislative findings in *Lopez*) lower courts have sometimes made mention of the presence or absence of congressional findings in addressing commerce-power issues. *See, e.g.*, *McCoy*, 323 F.3d at 1127–29 (relying in part on the absence of supportive pre-enactment findings in deeming invalid the challenged application of a federal ban on possession of child pornography).

[105] 529 U.S. at 613. It also bears mention that the decisions in *Lopez* and *Morrison* do not foreclose all affecting-commerce-based regulation of noneconomic activity because some such activity—possessing weapons of mass destruction, for example—might entail a substantial effect on interstate commerce in and of itself, even in the absence of aggregation. *See, e.g.*, United States v. Wang, 222 F.3d 234, 239 (6th Cir. 2000) (suggesting that "extortion demand of $1,540,000" might justify federal regulation on this theory (citing United States v. Farrell, 877 F.2d 870, 875–76 (11th Cir. 1989))). In *Farrell*, the court considered the argument that the appellants' convictions for conspiracy and attempted extortion should be overturned because the kidnapping, the ransom demand, and the follow-up bank lending in the case all occurred within a single state. The court, however, rejected this contention in part on the theory that the sheer size of the extortion demand ($1,540,000) indicated that "the utilization of the funds by [appellants] would have affected interstate commerce to a legally cognizable degree." 877 F.2d at 875–76.

effected a change, and that change centers on the analytical touchstone of "economic activity."

1. The Economic-Activity Test

The most basic question raised by *Lopez* and *Morrison* concerns what types of activities do and do not qualify as "economic" in character. As lawyers grapple with this question in the context of handling concrete cases, there may be a temptation to focus on the economic *consequences* of the relevant regulated behavior. That move, however, reflects a category error. The essential point of the "economic activity" test is, after all, to require an assessment of the *nature of the activity* that Congress has regulated, as opposed to the *effects on commerce* that the regulated activity might have. That is why the Court in *Morrison*, for example, rejected Congress's effort to regulate sex-based violence despite the presentation of massive evidence that such violence profoundly affects in negative ways commerce among the states.

Oftentimes, characterization questions regarding the economic or noneconomic nature of the activity that Congress has regulated are easy to answer. Sports gambling laws, for example, plainly target an economic activity because wagering involves a consensual back-and-forth exchange.[106] But what about robbery?[107] Or murder for

---

[106] *See* United States v. Wall, 92 F.3d 1444, 1451 (6th Cir. 1996) (upholding a federal statute regulating gambling businesses because it "punished commercial activity"). Taking a similar view, the Fourth Circuit found that a federal law prohibiting animal fighting for "purposes of sport, wagering, or entertainment" regulated economic activity. United States v. Gibert, 677 F.3d 613, 619–21 (4th Cir. 2012). The court reasoned that "sport," "wagering," and "entertainment" are each "closely aligned in our culture with economics and elements of commerce," while also emphasizing the existence of congressional findings that linked animal-fighting ventures to interstate commerce via industries focused on breeding animals for fighting and the gambling that typically accompanies these fights. *Id.* at 624–26; *see also* United States v. Ho, 311 F.3d 589, 602 (5th Cir. 2002) (concluding that "asbestos removal[ ] is very much a commercial activity in today's economy").

[107] *Compare* United States v. Gray, 260 F.3d 1267, 1274 (11th Cir. 2001) (finding that the federal Hobbs Act "undeniably regulates economic activity" because "[r]obbery, even though accompanied by actual or threatened physical harm, is undeniably an *economic* crime that involves the involuntary transfer of economically valuable assets" (emphasis in original)), *and* United States v. Crowe, 614 F. App'x 303, 309 (6th Cir. 2015) (holding that a statute prohibiting robberies of controlled substances regulated economic activity because "the thief . . . makes an economic gain and the victim sustains an economic loss"), *with* United States v. McFarland, 311 F.3d 376, 396–97 (5th Cir. 2002) (Garwood, J., dissenting from the ruling of an equally divided *en banc* court) (reasoning that "economic activity" is properly equated with "commercial activity" and that robbery is not "commercial"), *and id.* at 421 (Jones, J., dissenting) ("Of course, robbery should not be considered an 'economic activity' " because "[t]he dictionary defines 'economic' as 'relating to, or concerned with the production, distribution and consumption of commodities' " (internal citation omitted)). In *United States v. Lynch*, 282 F.3d 1049 (9th Cir. 2001), the court appeared to steer its way between a "yes" and a "no" in answering to this question. There, the court observed that, although robbery has an "economic component" because it

hire?[108] What about committing a hate-crime-prohibited battery of a fellow employee at work in packaging goods for interstate delivery?[109]

---

involves "the forced transfer of currency or of goods," it also is an archetypal state-law crime at least when the victim is an individual. *Id.* at 1052–53. The court then weighed these competing considerations in assessing whether federal authorities could prosecute the defendant under the robbery-related provision of the Hobbs Act, which the court viewed as designed to reach as far as the Constitution would permit. The accommodation the court settled on was to adopt the test of susceptibility to prosecution initially set forth in *United States v. Collins*, 40 F.3d 95 (5th Cir. 1994), and later applied in other circuits. *But see* United States v. Lynch, 437 F.3d 902, 907 (9th Cir. 2006) (en banc) (subsequently clarifying that, for purposes of Ninth Circuit doctrine, the *Collins* test applies only "where the defendant's conduct had no *direct* effect upon interstate commerce, but only an *indirect* effect" (internal quotation omitted)). Under the *Collins* test, a federal robbery prosecution can proceed only if the defendant (1) stole property from a person "directly and customarily engaged in interstate commerce"; (2) created a likelihood that the assets of an entity engaged in interstate commerce would be depleted; or (3) victimized a sufficiently large number of individuals or took property so valuable that the effect on commerce was substantial. *See Lynch*, 282 F.3d at 1052–53 (internal quotations omitted). The Supreme Court itself touched on—albeit only indirectly—the "is robbery an economic activity?" question in *Taylor v. United States*, 579 U.S. 301 (2016). There, Justice Alito (writing for himself and seven of his colleagues) reasoned that the sale of marijuana was "unquestionably an economic activity" based on the fact that it "is a moneymaking endeavor" even if it is illegal. *Id.* at 306–07. Building on this proposition, the Court also concluded, in light of its earlier ruling in *Gonzalez v. Raich*, 545 U.S. 1 (2016), *see infra* Section 4.D.2.a, that Congress could invoke the commerce power to outlaw a robbery that specifically "targeted a marijuana dealer's drugs or illegal proceeds" whether or not that particular theft itself had anything to do with interstate commerce. *Taylor*, 579 U.S. at 308; *see also id.* at 309 (adding that "[a]ll that is needed is proof that the defendant's conduct fell within a category of conduct that, in the aggregate," affects interstate commerce and that "it makes no difference . . . that any actual or threatened effect on commerce in a particular case is minimal"). In a dissenting opinion, Justice Thomas argued that the commerce power does not allow Congress to criminalize "a local robbery" at least in the absence of proof, for example, that it disrupts the interstate movement of a truck being driven by the victim. *Id.* at 315 (Thomas, J. dissenting) (reasoning that "[a]llowing the Federal Government to reach a simple home robbery" would "encroach on States' traditional police powers to define the criminal law" and "subvert basic principles of federalism" (internal quotations and alterations omitted)). Justice Thomas, however, wrote only for himself. The majority neither needed to nor did address this question in light of its focus on the intentional targeting of a drug-merchant victim and the drug-context-specific implications of *Raich*.

[108] *See* Nelson, *supra* note 57, at 1233 (arguing that "Congress may . . . criminalize all murder for hire" because it "is a voluntary commercial transaction" and "the cumulative impact of murder for hire arrangements has an impact on commercial enterprises in other states such as life insurance companies").

[109] In *United States v. Hill*, 182 F. Supp. 3d 546, 555–56 (E.D. Va. 2016), *rev'd and remanded*, 700 F. App'x 235 (4th Cir. 2017), the court confronted this issue. The relevant statute prohibited causing injury to an individual because of that individual's religion, national origin, gender, sexual orientation, gender identity, or disability, so long as the injury-causing act related to interstate commerce in one of five specified ways, including because it interfered with commercial or economic activity carried out by the victim at the time of the offense. *Id.* at 549, 554. The government indicted the defendant under the statute for assaulting his co-worker, an Amazon employee, while they were both on the job, *id.* at 548, reasoning that the victim—who was targeted because of his sexual orientation—was engaged in economic activity insofar as he was preparing packages for interstate shipment and the assault interfered with interstate commerce because there was a delay in sending out packages because the victim had to leave work to receive treatment for his injuries. *Id.* at 554–55. The district court,

What about possessing drugs with an intent to distribute?[110] Does it matter, in such a case, whether the intended distribution is to occur by gift, rather than by sale?[111] What about female genital mutilation if done by a medical professional?[112] What about the consumption of

---

however, rejected this argument, holding that the act was unconstitutional as applied to these facts because the connection of the assault to interstate commerce was too remote. *Id.* at 555–56. The court reasoned that the government's "argument would effectively federalize commercial property and allow Congress to regulate conduct occurring on commercial premises, even when the conduct—here, violence based on discriminatory animus—has no connection to the commercial nature of the premises." *Id* at 555. The court also observed that the government's reasoning skated close to the reasoning rejected in *Lopez* and *Morrison*—namely, that Congress can regulate, without more, activities that decrease national productivity. *Id.* The Fourth Circuit reversed and remanded the case, stating it was premature to determine the constitutional issues until further development of the factual record occurred. United States v. Hill, 700 F. App'x 235, 237 (4th Cir. 2017). On remand, a jury found the defendant guilty, but the district court judge granted the defendant's motion for judgment of acquittal, ruling once again that the assault lacked a sufficient connection to interstate commerce to support a prosecution under federal law. The court of appeals, however, reversed this ruling, declaring that the challenged law was constitutional as applied to this defendant. *Hill*, 927 F.3d at 195, 198. The court relied on the statute's jurisdictional element, which requires that the conduct "interferes with commercial or other economic activity in which the victim is engaged at the time of the conduct." *Id.* at 196. It reasoned that Congress can "proscribe violent conduct when such conduct interferes with or otherwise affects commerce over which Congress has jurisdiction," *id.* at 199, and that here the "interstate commerce element ensures that the statute regulates only *economic*, violent criminal conduct." *Id.* at 203–04 (emphasis in original). For a critical assessment of the Fourth Circuit's ruling, see Drew Bencie, *Hate, Interstate: The Fourth Circuit, Hate Crimes, and the Commerce Clause in* United States v. Hill, 98 N.C. L. REV. 1447, 1454–55 (2020).

[110] *See, e.g.*, United States v. Kim, 94 F.3d 1247, 1250 (9th Cir. 1996) (upholding a federal prohibition on this behavior); United States v. Lerebours, 87 F.3d 582, 584–85 (1st Cir. 1996) (same). Not surprisingly, the courts have consistently rejected commerce-power challenges to convictions for actually selling or conspiring to sell illegal drugs. *See, e.g.*, United States v. Genao, 79 F.3d 1333, 1336–37 (2d Cir. 1996); *see also supra* note 107 (discussing *Taylor*, 579 U.S. 301).

[111] *See* Nelson, *supra* note 57, at 1227 (suggesting that the federal anti-possession statute would be unconstitutional as applied to a possessor who has an intent to distribute only by way of a gift). This hypothetical case starkly presents the question whether the Court in *Lopez* and *Morrison* meant to equate "economic activities" with commercial activities in the form of buying, selling, bartering, and transporting items as part of those transactions. Because "gifting" is not an "economic activity" according to this pared-down definition, gift-making would require the same treatment as gun possession for purposes of affecting-commerce analysis. Prior cases holding that robbery is an economic activity, *see supra* note 107, suggest, however, that this definition of "economic activity" may be too narrow.

[112] In *United States v. Nagarwala*, 350 F. Supp. 3d 613 (E.D. Mich. 2018), *appeal dismissed*, No. 19-1015, 2019 WL 7425389 (6th Cir. 2019), the court held that a federal statute criminalizing female genital mutilation (FGM) was not sustainable under the Commerce Clause. *Id.* at 627–30. The government argued that such procedures constitute "economic activity" in the form of "illegal . . . healthcare," in part because, in the case at hand, they took place at a medical clinic, were performed by a licensed physician, and required the use of commercial tools and medical supplies. *Id.* at 628. The court, however, rejected this argument as "unsuitable" on the ground that FGM is more properly characterized as "another form of gender-related violence"—indeed, "a form of physical assault"—directly analogous to the brutalization of women at issue in *Morrison*. *Id.* at 628–29. The government also claimed that there was an interstate market for FGM because several victims were brought to Michigan from neighboring

a hallucinogenic mushroom, including if it is found by chance on one's own property.[113]

Some post-*Lopez* cases raise questions about whether courts must split into two separate parts a single activity that, at least arguably, involves both economic and noneconomic elements. The Court's landmark ruling in *Katzenbach v. McClung*,[114] upholding the Civil Rights Act of 1964 as applied to a local restaurant, suggests that regulated persons may well encounter obstacles when they urge judges to disaggregate unitary business- or work-related activities in this way.[115] In that case, the Court might have said that race discrimination is not an economic activity, even if running a business (as to which the choice is made to engage in such discrimination) is an economic activity. The Court, however, had no difficulty applying aggregation-based substantial-effects analysis to uphold the outlawing of race discrimination in *McClung*, and the majority in *Lopez* found that the decision to do so posed no problem under its newly minted economic-activity test. Building on this idea, lower courts have rejected in a variety of cases regulated parties' efforts to dodge the operation of federal laws to the extent that those laws apply to business operations. It is far from clear, for example, that the picking of a rare flower species by an individual hiker qualifies as the sort of conduct that Congress can outlaw on the ground that it is an economic activity.[116] A number of lower courts, however, have

---

states in order to undergo the outlawed procedure. *Id.* at 627. Given the small number of FGM procedures that had occurred in the past, however, the court questioned whether any "market" for those procedures existed at all, *id.* at 627–29, and it did not in any event see these facts as altering the key point that "no evidence" demonstrated the regulated activity itself was "a commercial activity." *Id.* at 629.

[113] A possible argument in favor of viewing the ingestion of a mushroom as economic in nature stems from *Gonzalez v. Raich*, 545 U.S. 1 (2005), in which the Court suggested that the "consumption of commodities"—no less than the "production" and "distribution" of commodities—constitutes an economic activity. *Id.* at 25–26. *See infra* note 130 (discussing this view of the reasoning of *Raich*). This rhetoric also raises questions about what qualifies as "consumption," particularly as to forms of use apart from ingesting a food or a drug. What about, for example, hunting animals not for eating but for display? What about simply displaying taxidermied animals (such as bald eagles) as trophies, thus using them for visual enjoyment, even if they were killed many decades ago? On this subject, *see Patton*, 451 F.3d. at 625 (concluding that "possession of firearms or body armor cannot be described as 'consumption' " because "[c]onsumption is the 'act of destroying a thing by using it; the use of a thing in a way that thereby exhausts it' " (quoting BLACK'S LAW DICTIONARY (8th ed. 2004), in defining "consumption")). With regard to the status of production as an economic activity, see, e.g., *Overton*, 2007 WL 2815986 at *2 ("Production of child pornography is far more likely to be 'economic' in nature than 'mere possession.' ").

[114] 379 U.S. 294 (1964).

[115] *See supra* Section 3.C.3 (discussing *McClung*).

[116] *See, e.g.*, Gibbs v. Babbitt, 214 F.3d 483, 507 (4th Cir. 2000) (Luttig, J., dissenting) (asserting that "[t]he killing of even all 41 of the estimated red wolves that live on private property in North Carolina would not constitute an economic activity"); Nat'l Ass'n of Home Builders v. Babbitt, 130 F.3d 1041, 1064 (D.C. Cir. 1997) (Sentelle, J., dissenting) (asserting that "[n]either killing flies nor controlling weeds nor digging

upheld the Endangered Species Act (ESA)—which prohibits conduct that threatens nearly extinct animal and plant species—in its application to persons whose prohibited actions occur in the course of

---

holes is either inherently or fundamentally commercial" in nature and that, as in *Lopez*, "the challenged section of the ESA 'by its terms has nothing to do with "commerce" or any sort of economic enterprise, however broadly one might define those terms' " (quoting *Lopez*, 514 U.S. at 561)); People for the Ethical Treatment of Prop. Owners v. U.S. Fish & Wildlife Serv., 57 F. Supp. 3d 1337, 1346 (D. Utah 2014) (invalidating an application of the ESA aimed at protecting the Utah prairie dog because the law applies to all "takes" of the animal whether or not in connection with an economic activity), *rev'd*, 852 F.3d 990 (10th Cir. 2017). In support of the idea that the taking of rare species, regardless of the circumstances, might qualify as "economic" in character, see *Gibbs*, 214 F.3d at 506 (upholding the Endangered Species Act, albeit as applied to the operator of a farming business, while observing, albeit as part of much more elaborate discussion, that "[o]f course natural resource conservation is economic and commercial"); *see also id.* at 492 (reasoning that "[b]ecause the taking of red wolves can be seen as economic activity in the sense considered by *Lopez* and *Morrison*, the individual takings may be aggregated for the purpose of Commerce Clause analysis"). Consider in this regard, a hypothetical federal law that prohibits the implosion of currently unused, but still-potentially-exploitable, underground precious-metal mines enacted in response to concerns about future metal shortages as applied to a private homeowner whose residential property includes such a mine. It seems hard to say that this mine-preservation law targets only a "noneconomic activity" when its essential purpose is to preserve the economic value of the metals that those once-used mines might still hold. *Cf.* Preseault v. ICC, 494 U.S. 1, 19 (1990) (determining that Congress could rely on the commerce power to promote the conversion of no-longer-operated railroad lines into public trails because it "apparently believed that every line is a potentially valuable national asset that merits preservation even if no future rail use for it is currently foreseeable"). And if that is so, perhaps a federal species-preservation law should be sustainable, even as applied to flower pickers, on much the same theory. To be sure, one might distinguish the mine statute on the ground that the structures it subjects to mandatory preservation once were actively engaged in economic production. That distinction is questionable, however, precisely because the economic activity that the no-longer-utilized mine's operators once pursued is no longer occurring. One might also argue that upholding an across-the-board species preservation law would prove too much—for example, by logically requiring the upholding of an across-the-board federal murder law founded on the theory that it "preserves" human beings who are potentially valuable components of economic production. At the same time, there may be—as the court in *Gibbs* suggested, *see* 214 F.3d at 496–97—special reason for characterizing the conservation of biological species as distinctly "economic" in character, at least when the very survival of those species hangs in the balance, given their foundational character as, among other things, irreplaceable building blocks of scientific investigation, follow-on discoveries, and the resulting production of medical and other products of potentially immeasurable commercial significance. *See id.* at 496 (quoting H.R. Rep. No. 93–412, at 4 (1973), in describing "[t]he value of this genetic heritage" as "quite literally, incalculable"). *See generally* Bradford C. Mank, *After* Gonzales v. Raich: *Is the Endangered Species Act Constitutional Under the Commerce Clause?* 78 U. COLO. L. REV. 375, 447 (2007); Robin Kundis Craig, *Constitutional Environmental Law, or, the Constitutional Consequences of Insisting that the Environment is Everybody's Business*, 49 ENV'T L. 703, 711–12 (2019) (exploring the ways in which "*Lopez* inspired new constitutional challenges to many federal environmental statutes, especially those statutes, like the [ESA] and CERCLA, that can interfere with commercial development and land use" (internal footnotes omitted)).

commercial development, farming operations, and comparable business ventures.[117]

In similar fashion, courts have found that commerce-disrupting conduct that may not qualify as "economic" in and of itself is subject to congressional regulation under the substantial-effects principle so long as it targets business- or work-related activity. Many lower courts, for example, have upheld the Freedom of Access to Clinic Entrances Act, which outlaws the "intimidat[ion] of . . . persons . . . obtaining or providing reproductive health services."[118] This result, according to rulings such as *Cheffer v. Reno*,[119] is reconcilable with the principle of *Lopez* because "the Access Act does regulate commercial activity" in the form of transactions involving professional medical treatment.[120] Along the same lines, courts have

---

117 *See* Rancho Viejo, LLC v. Norton, 323 F.3d 1062, 1072 (D.C. Cir. 2003) (reasoning that "there is no question but that [the regulated activity] is economic in nature" because "the prohibited taking is accomplished by commercial construction"); *Gibbs*, 214 F.3d at 495 ("The regulation here targets takings that are economically motivated—farmers take wolves to protect valuable livestock and crops."); *In re* Delta Smelt Consol. Cases, 663 F. Supp. 2d 922, 946 (E.D. Cal. 2009) (noting that "the regulated activity is the operation of the [water project], not the listing, or even the take, of individual species"), *aff'd sub nom.* San Luis & Delta-Mendota Water Auth. v. Salazar, 638 F.3d 1163 (9th Cir. 2011); John Copeland Nagle, *The Commerce Clause Meets the Delhi Sands Flower-Loving Fly*, 97 MICH. L. REV. 174, 210 (1998) (suggesting that "[t]he application of the ESA to the construction of a hospital or a housing development in [an endangered species] habitat" is permissible); *see also Hodel*, 452 U.S. at 277 (upholding a federal ban on local land use in the form of strip mining in part because it "destroy[ed] fish and wildlife habitats" (internal quotation omitted)); *cf.* GDF Realty Invs., Ltd. v. Norton, 326 F.3d 622, 634, 639 (5th Cir. 2003) (initially indicating that that Congress may not "regulate activity (here, Cave Species takes) solely because [it results from] non-regulated conduct (here, commercial development) by the actor engaged in the regulated activity" but thereafter indicating that the destruction of species involved in the case was an economic activity in part because "the Cave Species takes would occur as a result of plaintiffs' planned commercial development"). *But see* GDF Realty Invs., Ltd. v. Norton, 362 F.3d 286, 291, 293 (5th Cir. 2004) (Jones, J., dissenting from denial of rehearing en banc) (describing this feature of the panel opinion in *GDF Realty* as "confusing and self-contradictory" in the course of contending that the principle of *Lopez* should have precluded operation of the ESA on the facts of the case; also suggesting, however, that "many ESA-prohibited takings of endangered species may be regulated . . . because they involve commercial or commercially-related activities like hunting, tourism and scientific research"); Rancho Viejo, LLC v. Norton, 334 F.3d 1158, 1160 (D.C. Cir. 2003) (Roberts, J., dissenting from denial of rehearing en banc) (questioning the panel's upholding of the ESA's application on the theory that "Rancho Viejo's commercial development constitutes interstate commerce . . . [and] not because the incidental taking of arroyo toads can be said to be interstate commerce," while also raising the question whether "alternative grounds for sustaining application of the Act . . . more consistent with Supreme Court precedent" might be available).

118 8 U.S.C. § 248.

119 55 F.3d 1517 (11th Cir. 1995).

120 *Id.* at 1520. *Accord, e.g.*, Norton v. Ashcroft, 298 F.3d 549, 556 (6th Cir. 2002) (noting that "[a]ll eight circuits to address the issue have held that Congress validly enacted the Act pursuant to its Commerce Clause authority"). *But see* United States v. Gregg, 226 F.3d 253, 270, 272 (3d Cir. 2000) (Weis, J., dissenting) (arguing that earlier decisions gave undue weight to congressional findings in light of *Morrison* and

sustained against Tenth Amendment attack the federal arson statute as applied to buildings used for business purposes, even though that statute has been construed not to cover the burning of privately owned and occupied homes.[121] Under the principle of these cases, can Congress constitutionally criminalize arson of a church on the theory that a place of worship is more akin to a place of business than to a homeowner's residence?[122] If so, can Congress criminalize arson of a school? At least if the arsonist targets a private school that charges tuition? And if such an application of the federal arson law is sustainable, might Congress, notwithstanding *Lopez*, likewise be able to prohibit gun possession in private schools run by private businesses?[123]

---

that "[t]he fact that criminal conduct may also have financial effects does not transform that activity into one commercial in nature"). For another suggestion that interference with a commercial entity involves economic activity, see *Spinello*, 265 F.3d at 156 (noting that "robbery of a bank . . . is an 'economic' activity almost by definition").

121 *See, e.g.*, United States v. Chowdhury, 118 F.3d 742, 745 (11th Cir. 1997) (asserting that "[f]ederal protection of commercial property [against arson] is easily sustained under 'cases upholding regulations of activities that arise out of or are connected with a commercial transaction, which viewed in the aggregate, substantially affects interstate commerce' " (quoting *Lopez*, 514 U.S. at 561)); United States v. Sherlin, 67 F.3d 1208, 1212–14 (6th Cir. 1995) (upholding a conviction for arson of a college dormitory); *see generally* Jones v. United States, 529 U.S. 848, 857–58 (2000) (concluding that privately owned houses, in contrast to commercial buildings, are not "used in" commerce, as required by the statute, in part to avoid "grave and doubtful constitutional questions" that otherwise would arise because the regulated area "was one of traditional state concern" and "neither the actors nor their conduct had a commercial character"; distinguishing, however, the Court's earlier ruling in *Russell v. United States*, 471 U.S. 858 (1985), that the federal arson statute applied to an income-generating dwelling-rental property (internal quotations omitted)).

122 *Compare* United States v. Odom, 252 F.3d 1289, 1297 (11th Cir. 2001) (reversing a federal conviction for church arson on the ground that the underlying conduct was insufficiently related to interstate commerce, even though the congregation's leaders purchased bibles from outside the state, received contributions from two out-of-state donors, and sent money out of state for philanthropic purposes), *with* United States v. Rayborn, 312 F.3d 229, 234–36 (6th Cir. 2002) (concluding that an act of church arson was validly prosecuted as a federal crime where, among other things, the church engaged in radio broadcasts, including from and into neighboring states, and, thanks to its location near a state boundary, regularly "drew members from Tennessee, Arkansas, and Mississippi"). Addressing a related question, the court in *Jingrong v. Chinese Anti-Cult World Alliance*, 314 F. Supp. 3d 420 (E.D.N.Y. 2018), *rev'd in part on other grounds*, 16 F. 4th 47 (2d Cir. 2021), rejected a Commerce Clause challenge to a federal ban on violence occurring in places of worship, reasoning that such places are economic in nature because they produce over "$74.5 billion in annual revenue" and "account[ ] for 1% of gross national product in the United States." *Id.* at 439–40.

123 *See Lopez*, 514 U.S. at 629 (Breyer, J., dissenting) ("Does it matter if the school is public or private, nonprofit or profit seeking? Does it matter if a city or State adopts a voucher plan that pays private firms to run a school?"). Another set of cases involving the economic-activity question concerns a federal statute that exempts certain entities from having to pay state and local taxes connected up with the transfer of real property. For some of the many rulings upholding this statute for a variety of reasons, see, e.g., *Bd. of Comm'rs of Montgomery County v. Federal Housing Finance Agency*,

A final set of unitary-activity cases involves criminal laws that enhance punishments for economic-activity crimes based on the defendant's engagement in otherwise non-regulable noneconomic activity. Can Congress, for example, make it a crime to carry a firearm while selling heroin? What if Congress outlaws a sweeping variety of economic activities, including heroin sales, and in an entirely separate section of the criminal code authorizes more severe punishments if a convicted defendant has carried a gun in the commission of any federal crime? Defendants have challenged laws of this sort. Lower courts, however, have generally agreed that the limiting principle of *Lopez* has no role to play in such cases because at bottom they involve economic activity as opposed to gun possession standing alone.[124]

2. Exceptions to the Noneconomic-Activity Rule

As the foregoing discussion shows, significant complexities lurk in deciding whether certain activities qualify as "economic" in character for purposes of applying the substantial-effects test. Even so, the linear mind may find comfort in the thought that, once we determine that congressionally regulated conduct falls on the noneconomic-activity side of the legal dividing line, the government has lost its case. That assumption, however, turns out to miss the mark because the Court's rulings leave room to argue that Congress can sometimes rely on the substantial-effects theory to regulate even concededly noneconomic behavior.

a. The "Comprehensive Regulatory Scheme" Exception

Chief Justice Rehnquist's majority opinion in *Lopez* itself set the stage for recognizing one significant limit on the noneconomic-activity rule. The Chief Justice gestured toward this limit as he wrestled with how the Court's invalidation of the GFSZA was reconcilable with its validation of the wheat-production restriction at

---

758 F.3d 706, 712–13 (6th Cir. 2014) (upholding the tax exemption based primarily on an "affecting-commerce" theory because "the transfer tax exemptions are connected to the sale of mortgages across state lines on the secondary mortgage market, and these sales, when viewed in the aggregate, substantially affect interstate commerce"), and *Delaware County v. Federal Housing Finance Agency*, 747 F.3d 215, 227–28 (3d Cir. 2014) (rejecting a challenge premised on the idea "that the collection of taxes is not economic activity but rather '[t]he sovereign right of the states' " in the process of upholding the tax exemption under the "affecting-commerce" theory).

[124] *See, e.g.*, United States v. Bell, 90 F.3d 318, 320–21 (8th Cir. 1996) (upholding 18 U.S.C. § 924(c)(1), which outlaws carrying a firearm "during . . . any . . . drug trafficking crime," on the theory that this statute "is tied to interstate commerce" in the form of the underlying drug trafficking crime); *see also* United States v. Zorrilla, 93 F.3d 7, 8 (1st Cir. 1996) (rejecting a challenge to a school-location-related law that is "nothing more than a sentence-enhancer applicable to certain proscribed drug trafficking activities," which are "clearly commercial in character").

issue in *Wickard v. Filburn*.[125] That case, he reasoned, differed from *Lopez* because Congress's treatment of homegrown wheat was "an essential part of a larger regulation of economic activity, in which the regulatory scheme could be undercut unless the intrastate activity were regulated."[126] Put another way, the Court seemed to be saying this: Even if one were to view the growing of wheat for home use as a noneconomic activity, Congress had authority to regulate that activity, by way of the statute challenged in *Filburn*, as "an essential part" of a "larger . . . regulatory scheme" aimed at controlling interstate grain movements.

The Court's treatment of *Filburn* in *Lopez* in effect gave rise to an exception to the noneconomic-activity rule, and lower courts quickly went to work in exploring that exception's contours.[127] But the seminal treatment of this comprehensive-regulatory-scheme principle came ten years after *Lopez* when the Supreme Court itself handed down its ruling in *Gonzalez v. Raich*.[128] That case concerned the constitutionality of a provision of the Controlled Substances Act (CSA), which in effect makes it a federal crime to grow, possess, or use marijuana. As applied in *Raich*, this prohibition operated to prohibit such activities even if: (1) they occurred entirely within the home; (2) they were undertaken solely for medical purposes; and (3) they were authorized by state law.[129] The Court in *Raich* had to decide whether the application of the CSA under these circumstances ran afoul of the principle of *Lopez*.

Looming in the background of the case were interesting questions about whether either growing marijuana or using marijuana in one's own home constitutes "economic activity."[130] At

---

125 *See supra* Section 3.C.2 (discussing *Filburn*).

126 *Lopez*, 514 U.S. at 561.

127 *See, e.g.*, *infra* notes 154–55 and accompanying text (noting lower-court rulings on whether the ESA was sustainable on the comprehensive-scheme theory).

128 545 U.S. 1 (2005).

129 *Id.* at 5–8.

130 In particular, Justice O'Connor, writing in dissent, suggested that none of the activities at issue in the case qualified as "economic" in nature. According to her, "*Lopez* and *Morrison* . . . suggested that economic activity usually relates directly to commercial activity" and "homegrown cultivation and personal possession and use of marijuana for medicinal purposes has no apparent commercial character." *Id.* at 50 (O'Connor, J., dissenting). In contrast, Justice Stevens, writing for the majority, pointed to the CSA's targeting of the "production, distribution, and consumption of commodities for which there is an established, and lucrative, interstate market" as demonstrating that the regulated behavior involved "quintessentially economic" activities. *Id.* at 25–26. One can read this passage in different ways. One possibility is that it indicates that the "consumption" of a substance—in contrast to mere possession—qualifies as an "economic activity" for purposes of the *Lopez* rule. According to this view, as Professor David Driesen has explained, "*Raich* suggests that commercial activity constitutes a subset of economic activity, with the latter [term also] encompassing . . . consumption . . . of commodities." David M. Driesen, *The*

the least, however, *Lopez* left behind no serious doubt that the act of *possessing* home-grown marijuana for medicinal purposes fell within this doctrinal category.[131] Nonetheless, Justice Stevens, writing for five Justices of a six-Justice majority, found the CSA valid in all of its challenged applications, and he did so by relying on the comprehensive-regulatory-scheme logic laid down in *Lopez*. After quoting the key language from the opinion in that case,[132] Justice Stevens observed that *Filburn*, as confirmed by *Lopez*, "establishes that Congress can regulate purely intrastate activity that is not itself 'commercial,' in that [the relevant commodity] is not produced for sale, if it concludes that failure to regulate that class of activity would undercut the regulation of the interstate market in that commodity."[133] For Justice Stevens, it was "pivotal" that *Lopez* and *Morrison* presented no opportunity to apply this principle because those cases concerned attacks on federal prohibitions that targeted noneconomic activity standing alone.[134] In contrast, the CSA was "a lengthy and detailed statute creating a comprehensive framework for regulating the production, distribution, and possession of five classes of 'controlled substances.' "[135] Put simply, *Raich* fit the mold of *Filburn*. Just like the wheat-targeting program upheld in that earlier case, the CSA embodied a "concededly valid statutory scheme" that as a whole regulates "quintessentially economic" activities in the "interstate market."[136]

In addition, the Court detailed why Congress's restriction of home-based marijuana-related activity played an important role in

---

Economic/Noneconomic Activity Distinction Under the Commerce Clause, 67 CASE W. RES. L. REV. 337, 352 (2016). As a result, he adds, "[t]he Court . . . seems to accept production and consumption as economic activities, even when production and consumption do not lead to commercial transactions." *Id.* at 359; *see also id.* at 360 (adding that this result, in his view, comports with *Lopez* even though that case "seems to reflect some ambivalence about accepting home consumption as an economic activity"). For a brief discussion of what activities qualify as "consumption," see *supra* note 113.

131 *See Raich*, 545 U.S. at 50 (O'Connor, J., dissenting) ("*Lopez* makes clear that possession is not itself commercial activity.").

132 *Id.* at 24 (majority opinion) (citing *Lopez*, 514 U.S. at 561).

133 *Id.* at 18.

134 *Id.* at 23–25.

135 *Id.* at 24; *see id.* at 26 (emphasizing the broad statutory scheme embodied in the CSA); *see also* United States v. Leshuk, 65 F.3d 1105, 1112 (4th Cir. 1995) (reasoning, in the pre-*Raich* context, that "the intrastate drug activities regulated in the [Comprehensive Drug Abuse Prevention and Control Act of 1970] are clearly tied to interstate commerce" and adding that "where a general regulatory statute bears a substantial relation to commerce, the *de minimis* character of individual instances arising under that statute is of no consequence" (emphasis in original) (quoting *Lopez*, 514 U.S. at 558)).

136 545 U.S. at 23, 25–26; *see also id.* at 26 (explaining that, in contrast to the laws at issue in *Lopez* and *Morrison*, the CSA as a whole "directly regulates economic, commercial activity").

fostering the success of the CSA's overall commerce-regulating program. The essential point was that "production of the commodity meant for home consumption, be it wheat or marijuana, has a substantial effect on supply and demand in the national market for that commodity," and "[p]rohibiting the intrastate possession . . . of an article of commerce is a rational (and commonly utilized) means of regulating commerce in that product."[137] Particularly important in this respect was the fungibility of marijuana, which facilitated its ready "diversion into illicit channels" and gave rise to "enforcement difficulties that attend distinguishing between marijuana cultivated locally and marijuana grown elsewhere."[138] In sum, just like in *Filburn*, it made no difference that Congress's "broader" regulatory program "ensnares some purely intrastate activity."[139] What mattered was that federal lawmakers "had a rational basis for concluding that leaving home-consumed marijuana outside federal control would . . . affect price and market conditions" with regard to marijuana in interstate commerce.[140]

Justice Scalia, while agreeing with the result in the case, did not join the majority opinion. His analysis centered on the assertion that that the correct "doctrinal foundation" for upholding this application of the CSA lay in the joint operation of the Commerce Clause and the Necessary and Proper Clause. The latter provision of Article I, he reasoned, permits Congress to "regulate even noneconomic local activity if that regulation is a necessary part of a more general regulation of interstate commerce."[141] And, for him, the proper application of this principle in *Raich* was "straightforward."[142] The Commerce Clause, after all, "unquestionably permits" Congress to "extinguish the interstate market" in CSA "Schedule I" substances, such as marijuana.[143] Accordingly, as a "necessary part of [the] larger regulation," Congress could prohibit "almost all intrastate activities related to Schedule I substances—both economic activities (manufacture, distribution, possession with the intent to distribute) and noneconomic activities (simple possession)."[144]

---

137 *Id.* at 19, 26.

138 *Id.* at 22.

139 *Id.* at 19.

140 *Id.* at 22.

141 *Id.* at 37 (Scalia, J., concurring in the judgment).

142 *Id.* at 39.

143 *Id.*

144 *Id.* at 40. Justice O'Connor wrote the major dissenting opinion in the case, which was joined by Chief Justice Rehnquist and Justice Thomas. In it, among other things, she faulted the majority for thwarting valuable state-by-state experimentation. *Id.* at 43 (O'Connor, J., dissenting). At the same time, she did not seem to rule out any and all uses of the comprehensive-regulatory-scheme principle (and, in particular, did not question the ruling in *Filburn* itself or the Court's treatment of that case in *Lopez*).

Lower courts have made similar use of the comprehensive-scheme limitation on the noneconomic-activity principle. In *United States v. Rambo*,[145] for example, the Ninth Circuit upheld a federal statute that outlawed (1) distributing machine guns and (2) possessing a machine gun so long as the defendant first obtained it following the date of the distribution law's enactment. Reasoning that the time-limited scope of the latter provision served to ensure that anyone it covered had to have participated in unlawful distribution as a machine-gun transferee, the court upheld the possession ban on the ground that it effectuated the prohibition on distribution.[146] Plainly, the two-part statute at issue in *Rambo* differs in significant ways from the elaborate, multi-layered drug-control scheme characterized as "comprehensive" in *Raich*. But it also seems doubtful that this difference should matter. On the reasoning of Justice Scalia, for example, Congress "unquestionably" can invoke its commerce power to "extinguish the interstate market" in machine guns.[147] Thus, Congress should also be able outlaw "all intrastate activities"—including machine-gun possession despite its "noneconomic" character—if doing so is useful in achieving that broader, commerce-stifling aim.[148] Other courts have endorsed the

---

She did, however, express concern about the down-the-road consequences that the Court's application of that principle in *Raich* might bring. As she observed: "If the Court is right, then *Lopez* stands for nothing more than a drafting guide: Congress should have described the relevant crime as 'transfer or possession of a firearm anywhere in the nation' " or simply have incorporated the GFSZA into a "pre-existing comprehensive (or even not-so-comprehensive) scheme" of federal gun control. *Id.* at 46. This particular criticism of the majority's analysis, however, merits some criticism of its own. This is the case because Congress's decision to enact the GFSZA as a targeted, freestanding measure was obviously not due to a slip-up in legislative "drafting." Given a social landscape in which concerns about gun rights had (and still have) distinctly high visibility, political volatility, and practical importance, Congress never could have enacted a law prohibiting "transfer or possession of a firearm anywhere in the nation" and then made the GFSZA an "essential part" of that broader regulatory scheme. *See, e.g.*, Ann Althouse, *Why Not Heighten the Scrutiny of Congressional Power When the States Undertake Policy Experiments?*, 9 LEWIS & CLARK L. REV. 779, 789 (2005) (noting that, in enacting the GFSZA, Congress "resorted to a brief single-subject statute because that was all it had the political support to do"). To put the point mildly, passing *any* federal law is difficult because of the many checks and balances that constrain legislative action, and this is especially true when Congress considers enacting sweeping, multifaceted legislation that deals with localized behavior traditionally overseen by the states. In addition, while passing such a law is always difficult, it is even more difficult when it comes to the passion-laden subject of gun control. In sum, there may be grounds for challenging the comprehensive-scheme rationale put to work in *Raich*. But it is strained to view Justice O'Connor's "drafting guide" critique, at least as framed in her *Raich* dissent, as one of them.

[145] 74 F.3d 948 (9th Cir. 1996).

[146] *Id.* at 952.

[147] *Raich*, 545 U.S. at 39 (Scalia, J., concurring in the judgment).

[148] *See id.* To be clear, the machine-gun law might conceivably raise a separate external-constraint question concerning the operation of the Second Amendment. But here we deal only with the internal constraints built into the Commerce Clause itself.

result in and reasoning of *Rambo*.[149] The consequence is that, notwithstanding *Lopez*, at least one important prohibition on gun possession continues to operate as part of the federal criminal code.

Nor is the underlying principle of *Rambo* limited to machine-gun laws. Congress, for example, might draw on that principle to enact dual distribution and possession bans that target other sorts of weaponry, bombs, body armor, burglary tools, or fighting animals,

---

[149] *Accord, e.g.*, United States v. Franklyn, 157 F.3d 90, 94 (2d Cir. 1998) (deeming the machine-gun-possession ban to be "integral to a larger federal scheme for the regulation of trafficking in firearms"); United States v. Beuckelaere, 91 F.3d 781, 786 (6th Cir. 1996) (distinguishing *Lopez* largely on "essential part" grounds). *But see* United States v. Kirk, 105 F.3d 997, 1013–16 (5th Cir. 1997) (en banc) (Jones, J., dissenting) (advocating invalidation of the machine-gun-possession law and attacking the "essential part" defense of it; distinguishing *Filburn*, albeit prior to the Court's ruling in *Raich*, on the ground that it involved a federal effort to support the wheat market, while the machine-gun law reflected an effort to "extirpate" a market). For more recent authorities, see *Taylor*, 579 U.S. at 307 ("Under *Raich*, the market for marijuana, including its intrastate aspects, is 'commerce over which the United States has jurisdiction.' It therefore follows as a simple matter of logic that a robber who affects or attempts to affect even the intrastate sale of marijuana grown within the State affects or attempts to affect commerce over which the United States has jurisdiction."); *Le*, 902 F.3d at 118–19 (refusing to overturn a conviction under the Biological Weapons Act for purchasing ricin over the internet because the defendant's argument that "the development, production, stockpiling, transfer, acquisition, retention, or possession of biological weapons . . . are not inherently economic in nature" is "defeated by [*Raich*]"; emphasizing that there the ban on intrastate possession of an article of commerce was viewed as a " 'rational (and commonly utilized) means of regulating commerce in that product' " (quoting *Raich*, 545 U.S. at 26)); and *United States v. Bowers*, 594 F.3d 522, 528 (6th Cir. 2010) (upholding a conviction for making and possessing child pornography because "Congress has a legitimate basis for attempting to regulate the interstate market in child pornography and . . . the statutes [the defendant] challenges are part of a larger comprehensive scheme to regulate that illicit interstate market"). In *United States v. Safehouse*, 985 F.3d 225 (3d Cir. 2021), *cert. denied sub nom.* Safehouse v. Dep't of Justice, 142 S. Ct. 345 (2021), the Third Circuit considered a part of the Controlled Substances Act that criminalizes opening up a property for the unlawful use of drugs by others. Relying primarily on *Raich*, the Court found the statute to be within Congress' commerce power even though the relevant drug use was entirely local. The court emphasized that the statutory provision at issue was a key part of the comprehensive CSA regulatory scheme because it "plug[ged] a 'gaping hole' in the Act that made it harder to stop drug use and dealing at crack houses and the like." *Id.* at 241–42. The consequence of the court's ruling was that a non-profit corporation could not open a "safe-injection site" as a public health response to drug addiction. As the court observed, "[b]ecause [the statute] is part of the Act's comprehensive regulatory scheme, Congress has the power to ban even local, noneconomic activity that would undercut that scheme." *Id.* at 242. For a case in which the government's invocation of the comprehensive-regulatory-scheme theory did not succeed, see *Nagarwala*, 350 F. Supp. 3d at 627–30, in which the court held that a ban on female genital mutilation was not sustainable under the commerce power. The court in *Nagarwala* emphasized that the Court in *Raich* confronted a statute that was genuinely "comprehensive" because, among other things, it "classifies a long list of drugs in one of five schedules" and "sets 'strict requirements regarding registration, labeling and packaging, production quotas, drug security, and recordkeeping.' " *Id.* at 628 (quoting *Raich*, 545 U.S. at 14). The case at hand, in contrast, involved no "comparable 'regulatory regime' "; instead, the challenged genital-mutilation law was "simply a ban on the practice." *Id.*; *see also supra* note 112 (discussing this case in further detail).

even though the possession of these items (or at least most of them) historically has been the subject of state regulation.[150] Lower courts also have invoked the comprehensive-scheme principle in cases involving nonpossessory offenses.[151] In *Gibbs v. Babbitt*,[152] for example, the Fourth Circuit upheld an agency ban on hunting and trapping 41 endangered red wolves, relying in part on the rationale that the ESA, pursuant to which the challenged rule was promulgated, constitutes "a comprehensive and far-reaching piece of legislation that aims to conserve the health of our national environment."[153] This result maps onto *Raich* and *Rambo* in that the ESA also includes a prohibition on the purchase and sale of endangered species, which the ban on hunting and trapping would presumably help to effectuate.[154] Other circuit courts have also

---

150 Notably, a refinement of the *Rambo* principle might lead to the validation of some of these possession bans, but not others. It could be, for example, that burglary tools may be and often are fabricated by their possessor from materials purchased in violation of no law that targets unlawful sales or distributions. In contrast, individuals almost never build their own machine guns, which means that such weaponry must be obtained from another person. Perhaps, based on this distinction, courts that adhere to the ruling in *Rambo* would nonetheless invalidate a burglary-tool possession ban, reasoning that machine guns—but not necessarily burglary tools—bear an almost inevitable connection to the quintessentially commercial purchase-and-sale transaction of a contraband item.

151 *See, e.g., Cortes*, 299 F.3d at 1035 (relying on an "essential part" rationale in sustaining the federal carjacking statute; reasoning that "[i]n addition to making carjacking a federal crime, the Act increased penalties for importing and exporting stolen cars; criminalized the operation of chop shops; provided federal funds for anti-car theft organizations; developed a national system for combating title fraud; and increased inspection at border checkpoints").

152 214 F.3d 483.

153 *Id.* at 497 (alternative holding). *Accord, e.g., People for Ethical Treatment of Prop. Owners*, 852 F.3d at 1002 (applying the comprehensive-regulatory-scheme principle to uphold a bar on takings of the Utah prairie dog).

154 *See Nat'l Ass'n of Home Builders*, 130 F.3d at 1047 (finding the ESA's ban on the taking of endangered species in this respect "analogous to the prohibition against transfer and possession of machine guns (including purely intrastate possession)" upheld in such cases as *Rambo*); *see also Patton*, 451 F.3d at 627 (pointing to cases holding that "Congress has authority under the Commerce Clause to prohibit mere possession of child pornography, on the rationale that prohibiting possession was an essential part of a comprehensive scheme to destroy the market for this pernicious commodity"; also asserting that that, "the federal government may elect to prohibit the possession of eagle feathers as a practical means of drying up the market for them, and thus protecting against the killing of eagles"; citing Andrus v. Allard, 444 U.S. 51, 58 (1979), in which the Court did not question Congress's authority to enact a prohibition on possessing parts of eagles to implement a ban on the purchase and sale of such items adopted to preserve these species). One might argue in response that Congress prohibited the killing of endangered species not nearly so much to thwart trading in them as simply to ensure their survival. Even so, as in *Raich*, there in fact exists a substantial interstate (and international) market in endangered species and their parts, which the ban on taking such species helps to extirpate. *See, e.g., In re Delta Smelt*, 663 F. Supp. 2d at 940 (highlighting a recent finding that "the illegal component of the worldwide trade in wildlife generates $5 billion to $8 billion in proceeds annually"). In addition, one might argue that even a comprehensive-regulatory-scheme-based defense of the ESA would not support the act's prohibition

invoked the comprehensive-regulatory-scheme rule in upholding the ESA's companion ban on habitat destruction[155]—a result sure to strike some observers as more controversial because habitat destruction, unlike killing and capture, may have no meaningful connection to the transfer of endangered animals or plants and their parts.[156] Whatever one thinks of the court's analysis in these cases, however, they drive home a broader point: In the wake of *Lopez* and *Morrison*, as refined by *Raich*, lower courts have hesitated to apply the noneconomic-activity principle to invalidate congressional enactments.[157]

b. *The "Tail of the Dog" Exception*

The Court often has suggested that Congress can include within its regulation of activities that have a demonstrable connection to interstate commerce other activities that do not have that same

---

on the taking of those many endangered species as to which no purchase-and-sale market of any kind exists. This argument, however, runs up against the Court's past willingness to permit Congress to frame broad and practical solutions to problems it is empowered to address, as well as the possibility that purchase-and-sale markets for now-untraded species might emerge in the future. *See, e.g., id.* at 945–46 (indicating that Congress can outlaw destruction of all endangered species, even species as to which there is no current market, as part of a "comprehensive scheme"); *see also* Alabama-Tombigbee Rivers Coal. v. Kempthorne, 477 F.3d 1250, 1273 (11th Cir. 2007) ("If the process of listing endangered species is 'an essential part of a larger regulation of economic activity,' then whether that process 'ensnares some purely intrastate activity is of no moment.' . . . The [ESA] prohibits all interstate and foreign commerce in endangered species." (quoting *Raich*, 545 U.S. at 24)).

155 *See, e.g., San Luis & Delta-Mendota Water Auth.*, 638 F.3d at 1177.

156 *Nat'l Ass'n of Home Builders*, 130 F.3d at 1063 n.29 (Sentelle, J., dissenting) ("While prohibiting the local possession and exchange of flies might arguably be necessary to preventing interstate transportation or exchange of flies, prohibiting destruction of fly habitat is not."). Perhaps with this problem in view, one court has asserted that: "The Supreme Court has never required that a statute be a . . . 'comprehensive regulatory scheme *for economic activity*' in order to pass muster under the Commerce Clause. . . . The only requirement—which was expressly detailed in *Raich*—is that the 'comprehensive regulatory scheme' have a 'substantial relation to commerce.'" *San Luis & Delta-Mendota Water Auth.*, 638 F.3d at 1177 (quoting *Raich*, 545 U.S. at 17). While this passage can be read in different ways, its most legislation-friendly translation—which would endorse comprehensive schemes that do not include any regulation of any economic activity—is not easy to square with *Raich*'s reliance on *Lopez*, which alluded only to upholding "an essential part of a larger regulation *of economic activity*." *Lopez*, 514 U.S. at 561 (emphasis added); *see also supra* text accompanying note 133 and accompanying text (noting that *Raich* tied the comprehensive-regulatory-scheme principle to Congress's "regulation of the interstate market in that commodity").

157 *See, e.g.*, Dan A. Akenhead, *Federal Regulation of Noncommercial, Intrastate Species Under the ESA After* Alabama-Tombigbee Rivers Coalition v. Kempthorne *and* Stewart & Jasper Orchards et al. v. Salazar, 53 NAT. RES. J. 325, 327 (2013) (observing that past rulings suggest that "future courts will likely apply the comprehensive scheme rationale within the context of federal regulation of intrastate species under the ESA"); *see generally* Denning & Reynolds, *supra* note 76, at 1256 (collecting "evidence from the lower courts' opinions that they are still reluctant to take *Lopez* seriously, even after *Morrison*'s clarifying opinion").

connection.[158] The underlying idea is that Congress, as it deals with conduct it is empowered to regulate, can paint with a broadened brush if doing so helps executive-branch officials administer programs and removes case-complicating line-drawing problems for the courts. Congress, in other words, can include in its regulation of activity that directly concerns interstate commerce other activity of the same genus even though it has little, if anything, to do with interstate affairs.[159] In *Perez v. United States*,[160] for example, the Court dealt with a statute that outlawed loansharking on the theory that this activity helps to bankroll the interstate operations of organized-crime networks. The case at hand, however, involved a single threat made by a local moneylender who had no demonstrable connection to organized crime or any interstate business operation. Even so, an eight-member majority of the Court upheld the defendant's conviction. In doing so, it relied on Congress's power to regulate activities that in the aggregate affect interstate commerce, coupled with Justice Holmes's earlier observation that "when it is necessary in order to prevent an evil to make the law embrace more than the precise thing to be prevented it may do so."[161] Put another way, along with Congress's power to crate the dog may come the power to crate its tail. But just how far does this dog-and-tail theory go? In particular, how does it interact with the noneconomic-activity principle launched in *Lopez* and reaffirmed in *Morrison*?[162]

---

[158] *See, e.g.*, Hodel v. Indiana, 452 U.S. 314, 329 n.17 (1981) ("A complex regulatory program . . . can survive a Commerce Clause challenge without a showing that every single facet of the program is independently and directly related to a valid congressional goal. It is enough that the challenged provisions are an integral part of the regulatory program and that the regulatory scheme when considered as a whole satisfies this test."); *see also supra* Section 3.B (discussing, for example, *Currin v. Wallace*, 306 U.S. 1 (1939), and *Mulford v. Smith*, 307 U.S. 38 (1939)).

[159] *See, e.g.*, *Guzman*, 591 F.3d at 90 (collecting cases upholding the constitutionality of SORNA even though it contains a provision that regulates wholly intrastate noneconomic activity because it is necessary to ensure adequate enforceability of another provision that is an appropriate regulation of interstate commerce).

[160] 402 U.S. 146 (1971).

[161] *Id.* at 154 (quoting Westfall v. United States, 274 U.S. 256, 259 (1927)) (internal alterations omitted).

[162] One question to be asked is whether this tail-of-the-dog theory differs in any way from the comprehensive-regulatory scheme theory addressed in the immediately preceding discussion. The answer is "yes" because the two rules, though both focused on the existence of a broader legislative package that contains the challenged subset of congressional controls, operate in different ways. In particular, the comprehensive-regulatory-scheme theory permits Congress to regulate one type of activity (in *Raich*, for example, possession of marijuana) because of its power to regulate *an entirely different type of activity* (in *Raich*, the purchase and sale of marijuana). In contrast, the tail-of-the-dog theory permits Congress to regulate activity, even if it is not subject to regulation when undertaken in certain circumstances (for example, noneconomic-activity-based pond fillings), because it is the *same type of activity* that Congress has

Consider again the Endangered Species Act. As noted earlier, the Court might uphold this law in all its applications on the theory that either: (1) species destruction is itself an economic activity; or (2) species destruction, even if not an economic activity, is permissibly regulated under the ESA as part of a comprehensive regulatory scheme.[163] Assume, however, that the Court rejects both arguments. Is there any other theory on which the ESA might be upheld in its most controversial applications? The answer is "yes." To begin with, courts generally have held that the *Lopez-Morrison* rule poses no problem for congressional action that prohibits persons engaged in economic activity from threatening the survival of endangered species in the course of that activity, thus rendering the ESA constitutional in most of its applications.[164] In other words, the noneconomic-activity principle would not seem to bar Congress from directing the ESA's prohibitions at acts of species destruction that occur in the course of engaging in real-estate development, farming operations, dam-building, and kindred forms of financially-driven undertakings. In addition, it seems clear as a factual matter that most applications of the ESA involve these sorts of commercial ventures. And if that is so, another question arises: Can Congress include within the act's coverage, not only such "economic" acts of species destruction, but also and equally "noneconomic" acts of such destruction on the same tail-of-the-dog rationale that operates—as cases such as *Perez* illustrate—in other areas of commerce-power doctrine?[165]

Some analysts would not hesitate to say "yes."[166] Indeed, in *Solid Waste Agency v. United States Army Corps of Engineers*,[167] four Justices banded together in an opinion built directly on this line of analysis. There, a landowner argued that a federal agency violated the principle of *Lopez* and *Morrison* in promulgating a regulation that impeded the filling of small bodies of water frequented by

---

chosen to regulate (for example, economic-activity-based pond fillings). *See infra* notes 166–170 and accompanying text.

[163] As to the former line of analysis, see *supra* note 116 and accompanying text. As to the latter line of analysis, see *supra* notes 152–156 and accompanying text.

[164] *See supra* note 117 and accompanying text.

[165] *Cf.* Choper, *supra* note 29, at 740–42 (inquiring whether a landowner who builds his own house on his own land, that is the habitat of an endangered species, may be properly included in the ESA prohibition because, even though there is no commercial contract in such a case, the "economic impact" of the conduct at issue "appears to be sufficiently similar" to that of the regulable conduct "to justify Commerce Clause coverage").

[166] Indeed, the case for applying this tail-of-the-dog reasoning can be seen as particularly compelling in this setting because of the glaring indistinguishability of the relevant economic and (presumably) noneconomic activities in terms of their commerce-affecting functional effects. *See infra* notes 178–81 and accompanying text.

[167] 531 U.S. 159 (2001).

migratory birds. A five-Justice majority skirted the constitutional challenge by declaring that this "Migratory Bird Rule" exceeded the agency's statutorily delegated powers insofar as it applied to, for example, the non-navigable water-filled sand-and-gravel pit at issue in the case. But what would have happened if the Court had decided to address the underlying commerce-power issue with regard to the rule as written?

In a dissenting opinion joined by three colleagues, Justice Stevens found that, contrary to the majority's key pronouncement in the case, Congress had delegated authority to the agency to apply its Migratory Bird Rule to such localized ponds. Accordingly, he turned to the question whether that rule comported with the principle of *Lopez* and *Morrison*. After first finding that "the discharge of fill material into the Nation's waters is almost always undertaken for economic reasons,"[168] Justice Stevens added that "[t]he fact that petitioner can conceive of some people who may discharge fill for noneconomic reasons does not weaken the legitimacy of the Corps' jurisdictional claims" because "[a]s we observed in *Perez* . . ., '[w]here the *class of activities* is regulated and that class is within the reach of federal power, the courts have no power to excise, as trivial, individual instances of the class.' "[169] Put another way, Justice Stevens and his fellow dissenters stood ready to uphold application of the Migratory Bird Rule to noneconomic, as well as economic, pond-fillings pursuant to a tail-of-the dog rationale, thus foreclosing any as-applied challenge based on a claim that the particular litigant's own activities were noneconomic in character.[170]

---

168 *Id.* at 193 (Stevens, J., dissenting).

169 *Id.* at 194 n.15 (quoting *Perez*, 402 U.S. at 154) (emphasis in original).

170 This was the case because the dissenters saw the major part of the "class of activities" roped in by the rule (that is, the "dog") to involve economic activity, thus causing the rule's companion coverage of a relatively "trivial" amount of noneconomic activity (that is, the "tail") to be permissible. Of course, determining whether a subset of statutory coverage qualifies as "trivial" can present its own (quite nontrivial) complexities. One question involves whether such a determination should focus on the *actual number* of covered events or on the *proportion* of the covered events that are said to fall into the supposedly tail-of-the-dog subset of regulated behavior. In any event, lines of some kind must be drawn. For example, the case for sustaining a universal application of the Migratory Bird Rule would weaken considerably if noneconomic-activity pond-filling constituted 30%, 40%, or 50% of the total amount of activity the challenged rule targeted. Indeed, at some point, especially as this "tail" number grows larger, the court might go so far as to invalidate the rule *in toto* (1) on the ground that its promulgators improperly aggregated regulable and non-regulable behavior in finding the requisite "substantial effect" and/or (2) on the ground that there is no basis for concluding that Congress would have chosen to pass the law in the first place if it had foreseen the constitutionally limited range of its coverage. It is noteworthy in this regard that, as it turns out, Alfonso Lopez's possession of a gun in a school zone appeared to qualify as an economic activity in that he "was being paid for acting as a courier and delivering the gun to somebody else." Regan, *supra* note 57, at 564 n.46. The economic character of Mr. Lopez's possessory act, however, did not

For a variety of reasons, it is far from certain that the Court as a whole would make use of Justice Stevens's tail-of-the-dog rationale in a future case. For one thing, a majority of the Justices might find that the Congress-accommodating approach of the dissenters in *Solid Waste Agency* clashes with the state-protective attitude reflected in *Lopez*, *Morrison*, and other post-1994 federalism cases.[171] Members of the Court also might fear the slippery-slope implications of applying the sort of analysis advanced by the dissenters in *Solid Waste Agency*.[172] Finally, some Justices might draw on general principles of severability law to conclude that the unconstitutional portion of the challenged statute must be cut away so as to leave it intact only to the extent that it targets economic (and not non-economic) behavior.[173] In keeping with these considerations, some

---

save his conviction under a statute that, on its face, assigned that fact no significance and applied as a real-world matter overwhelmingly to noneconomic instances of simple gun possession. Confronted with this situation, the Court in *Lopez*, from all appearances, had no difficulty in invalidating the GFSZA on its face in light of the noneconomic-activity rule even though the case at hand turned out to involve economic activity.

[171] Indeed, in *Solid Waste Agency* itself, the majority—in giving a constrained reading to the federal statutory authorization of agency rulemaking—relied in part on the proposition that giving the statute a broader reading would raise an issue of grave constitutional difficulty. 531 U.S. at 172–74 (majority opinion). Such a position, however, stands in some tension with Justice Stevens's seeming ease in applying the tail-of-the-dog rationale to the rule that had been issued pursuant to that statute.

[172] Professor Regan, for example, has outlined an argument that would allow Congress to pass exactly the same statute struck down in *Lopez* pursuant to a tail-of-the-dog rationale. On this theory, Congress (1) could (as it did in the immediate aftermath of *Lopez*) pass a law that prohibited near-school possession of guns that previously had moved in interstate commerce and (2) then also pass exactly the same law invalidated in *Lopez* coupled with findings that almost all guns have previously moved in interstate commerce so that this enactment should pass muster on a tail-of-the-dog theory. *See* Regan, *supra* note 57, at 567–68. To say the least, those members of the Court who support the *Lopez* decision are not likely to look with favor on this sort of congressional gamesmanship. And for this reason, they might well hesitate to apply the tail-of-the-dog theory to uphold *in toto* statutes that cover both economic and noneconomic activity. It merits emphasis, however, that Professor Regan's school-zones gun law and the Migratory Bird Rule at issue in *Solid Waste Agency* are marked by a significant functional difference. Why? Because the former statute involves a particularly troublesome fusion of *both* the jurisdictional-hook workaround of the economic-activity limit *and* the tail-with-the-dog-principle for regulating otherwise non-regulable activities. The Migratory Bird Rule, in contrast, does not involve any jurisdictional-element workaround at all. Rather, it targets almost entirely true economic activities while expanding the circle of coverage only to a small degree to cover some, but not many, noneconomic activities in light of practical concerns.

[173] Indeed, a severability-driven view of the problem might even lead the Court to refuse to apply a statute that replicated the Migratory Bird Rule in any setting whatsoever, including in cases in which the pond-filling occurs as part of an activity that is unquestionably "economic" in nature. Such an outcome would result if the court, having decided that the relevant question is one of severability, also determined that the statute was nonseverable. For analyses that touch on this point, see *Ballinger*, 312 F.3d at 1274 (refusing to apply the federal church-defacement statute to a case involving interstate travel to engage in that behavior because "[i]f Congress wants the statute to prohibit travel in the channels of interstate commerce to commit arson, then it may say so, just as it has done in [other] statutes," and here "this is not what the

courts and commentators have signaled a seeming hesitance to support Justice Stevens's approach by indicating that litigants can freely mount "as applied" challenges to federal laws based on the *Lopez/Morrison* principle.[174] Others, however, have indicated that they may be open to tail-of-the-dog-type reasoning, thus suggesting

---

statute says"), *vacated*, 395 F.3d 1218 (11th Cir. 2005) (en banc), and Nelson, *supra* note 57, at 1237 (arguing that the Hobbs Act may not be constitutionally applied even to otherwise properly-regulated thefts from business establishments because Congress must more carefully "identify the type of commercial activity or business being safeguarded" than it has in the present statute). Along the same lines, some analysts have suggested that any constitutional challenge to a law founded on an argument that it exceeds the commerce power must be viewed (in keeping, so it has been suggested, with the approach taken in *Lopez* and *Morrison*) as "facial" in nature. *See, e.g.*, Nicholas Quinn Rosenkranz, *The Subjects of the Constitution*, 62 STAN. L. REV. 1209, 1273–79, 1290 (2010) (going on to suggest, in keeping with this theory, that the proper enactment of laws pursuant to the substantial-effects prong of the commerce power might require an express statement in the statute that it targets commerce-related activity and thus implying the statues such as ESA may present commerce-power problems in all their applications); *see also McCoy*, 323 F.3d at 1141 (Trott, J., dissenting) (reasoning that the majority's holding that a particular application of the federal ban on possessing child pornography exceeds the commerce power should logically require it to invalidate the statute on its face). *But see, e.g., Rancho Viejo*, 323 F.3d at 1077–79 (concluding that, even if the ESA is unconstitutional in its application to certain noneconomic activities, it remains applicable at least to economic activities, so that "Plaintiff's 'overbreadth' argument [against the act] is unavailing"); Brian Charles Lea, *The Merits of Third-Party Standing*, 24 WM. & MARY BILL RTS. J. 315–23 (2015) (critiquing the so-called "valid-rule" approach to severability). *See generally* Gillian E. Metzger, *Facial Challenges and Federalism*, 105 COLUM L. REV. 873, 887–88 (2005) (discussing the relationship between severability and the facial invalidation of statutes).

[174] *See, e.g., Pappadopoulos*, 64 F.3d at 527–28 (reversing a conviction under the federal arson statute because the statute was unconstitutionally applied to a defendant charged with burning down a private residence as opposed to a commercial building); *Wang*, 222 F.3d at 238–40 (sustaining a challenge to the Hobbs Act in its application to robberies from individuals rather than from "a business entity"); *McCoy*, 323 F.3d at 1132, 1139 (invalidating an application of the federal child-pornography-possession law where a parent took a pornographic photo of a child for a family photo album and thus "was not the typical offender feared by Congress"; rejecting the argument that this holding in effect required wholesale invalidation of statute (quoting United States v. Corp, 236 F.3d 325, 333 (6th Cir. 2001))); *Faasse*, 265 F.3d at 487 (recognizing the possibility of an "as applied" challenge to a federal law criminalizing nonpayment of child-support for a nonresident child in the "unlikely" case in which the custodial parent lives in same state as the payor, although the child does not); *Rancho Viejo*, 323 F.3d at 1080 (Ginsburg, C.J., concurring) (indicating that, while the ESA has many permissible applications, there exists a "logical stopping point" to its permissible operation because "the lone hiker in the woods, or the homeowner who moves dirt in order to landscape his property, though he takes the toad, does not affect interstate commerce"); Nelson, *supra* note 57, at 1231 (suggesting that the Migratory Bird Rule would be constitutional as applied to commercial, but not noncommercial, fillings): *see generally* United States v. Stewart, 348 F.3d 1132, 1141 (9th Cir. 2003) (asserting that the Supreme Court has "always entertained as-applied challenges under the Commerce Clause"), *vacated on other grounds*, 545 U.S. 1112 (2005); Denning & Reynolds, *supra* note 76, at 1262 & n.62 (citing successful "as applied" challenges of this kind).

that it might in some cases support congressional regulation of noneconomic activity.[175]

c. *A Power to Regulate Freestanding Noneconomic Activities?*

Both the (actual) comprehensive-regulatory-scheme limit and the (possible) tail-of-the-dog limit on the noneconomic-activity principle come into play only if Congress has passed a broader statute that directly regulates economic activity. What if, however, no such broader statute is on the scene, or that broader statute fails to provide a sturdy enough fulcrum to support the entirety of Congress's effort to leverage its substantial-effects-based commerce power? Might there nonetheless be some types of noneconomic activity that, notwithstanding *Lopez* and *Morrison*, Congress remains able to regulate because of their impact on interstate commerce? The prospect of a positive answer to this question stems from the Court's observation in *Morrison* that "we need not adopt a categorical rule against aggregating the effects of any noneconomic activity in order to decide these cases."[176] With this language, the Court left open the possibility that it might, in narrow circumstances, permit Congress to treat in the aggregate certain types of noneconomic activities pursuant to the substantial-effects prong of the commerce power.

Perhaps the most promising candidates for judicial acceptance of such exercises of noneconomic-activity-regulating authority are statutes enacted to protect the environment. After all, when it comes to shared natural resources, such as air and water, it is hard to deny that "we are all in this together." Put another way, there may be something special about the environment, tied up with its inescapably interstate nature, that leads the Court to support a special role for federal oversight.[177] Professor Regan captured this idea when he wrote: "[I]t is easy to think up cases in which Congress's power to regulate noncommercial local behavior under the Commerce Clause should be obvious. Surely Congress can regulate . . . backyard

---

[175] *See, e.g.*, *Rancho Viejo*, 323 F.3d at 1077 (suggesting the possibility of endorsing this analysis to the ESA in observing that, under cases such as *Hodel*, 452 U.S. at 329 n.17, "it may well be that the [noneconomic-activity-based] hiker hypothetical proffered by the plaintiff is of no consequence to the statute's constitutionality" (internal quotations omitted)); *McCoy*, 323 F.3d at 1141 (Trott, J., dissenting) (reasoning that the statute should be upheld, including as applied, because Congress could regulate the child-pornography industry and "the factual non-commercial nature of a single item of the commodity is immaterial"); *see also supra* notes 91, 99.

[176] 529 U.S. at 613.

[177] *See, e.g.*, Nat'l League of Cities v. Usery, 426 U.S. 833, 856 (1976) (Blackmun, J., concurring) (recognizing, even while joining the majority to invalidate a federal wage-and-hour law on state-autonomy grounds, *see infra* Section 5.A.1, that federal regulation of states themselves would remain necessary "in areas such as environmental protection, where the federal interest is demonstrably greater").

incinerators if they are found to emit some airborne toxic chemical that is deposited hundreds of miles from the site of incineration."[178] Put another way, if "backyard incinerators" are emitting "some . . . toxic chemical" into the air that all of us—wherever we are located—have no choice but to breathe, why should it make any difference in defining federal regulatory power whether those emissions are the product of economic or noneconomic burning activities? The key point would seem to be that the relevant activities, whether economic or noneconomic in nature, contribute in exactly the same way to exactly the same commerce-undermining problem we all share—that is, the nationwide distribution of illness-generating airborne poisons.

Along these lines, the Supreme Court itself has noted that the ESA responds to, among other things, "the unforeseeable place [endangered] creatures may have in the chain of life on this planet," including with regard to the continued well-being of ecosystems that include now-unendangered species and the harms that will come to everyone from the loss of currently "unknown uses" to which threatened animals and plants, if they are able to survive, might someday be put.[179] Lower courts likewise have observed, particularly in light of race-to-the-bottom problems that the alternative of state-by-state regulation would invite, that "[p]rotection of endangered species is not a matter that can be handled in the absence of coherent national and international policies."[180] Against this backdrop, it is fair to wonder whether courts "should read *Lopez* as hamstringing Congress in . . . a regulatory area of such important economic, scientific and environmental dimensions."[181]

This is not to say that all activities that create environmental harms should be regulated at the federal level.[182] But few doubt that

---

[178] Regan, *supra* note 57, at 564.

[179] TVA v. Hill, 437 U.S. 153, 178–79 (1978) (emphasis omitted).

[180] *Gibbs*, 214 F.3d at 502 (quoting H.R. Rep No. 93–412, at 7 (1973)); *accord, e.g.*, *Rancho Viejo*, 323 F.3d at 1079. Race-to-the bottom difficulties arise because of the danger that, as states compete to attract business activity, they will collectively under-protect endangered animals and plants whose habitat-retention, and survival, might well stand in the way of local development projects.

[181] Bldg. Ind. Ass'n of Superior Cal. v. Babbitt, 979 F. Supp. 893, 908 (D.D.C. 1997).

[182] *See* Jonathan H. Adler, *Uncooperative Environmental Federalism 2.0*, 71 HASTINGS L.J. 1101, 1107 (2020) (arguing for a restructuring of environmental law that would decentralize governmental decisionmaking authority while allowing the federal government to better focus the use of its resources; contending that this approach makes sense because currently "many policy decisions that are more appropriately dealt with at the state or local level are made in Washington, D.C." while "the federal government has failed to address those sorts of environmental problems for which federal involvement is most need[ed] and most appropriate"); Sarah Fox, *Localizing Environmental Federalism*, 54 U.C. DAVIS L. REV. 133, 189 (2020) (arguing for reforms in the law of environmental federalism that take account of, among other

at least some such activities need to be made subject to federal control. And when they are—as Professor Regan posits—there is much to be said for the proposition that their susceptibility to centralized oversight should not hinge on whether courts find themselves legally authorized to attach to them the "economic activity" label.

3. The No-Substantial-Effect Limit on Congress's Power to Regulate Economic Activities

The foregoing discussion shows that Congress has some room to maneuver, even after *Lopez* and *Morrison*, in regulating local, noneconomic activities. But it is equally true—and no less important—that the noneconomic-activity principle does not operate as the only internal limit on Congress's ability to invoke the substantial-effects prong of the commerce power. In particular, even when Congress moves to regulate activity that is unquestionably economic in nature, it can do so only if the degree of the impact of the thus-targeted activity on interstate commerce suffices to warrant federal superintendence. In *Lopez*, Chief Justice Rehnquist (writing for a five-Justice majority) and Justice Breyer (writing for the four dissenters) skirmished over whether the Constitution requires the government to demonstrate a "substantial" effect or a "significant" effect on such commerce. The debate over which of these two adjectives to enshrine in the doctrinal rhetoric of commerce-power law might seem to mark the ultimate exercise in judicial hair-splitting. From the resolution of that debate in the Chief Justice's favor, however, there may be a deeper message to glean—namely, that new opportunities exist in the post-*Lopez* world for litigants to win on arguments that the regulated economic activities do not, even in the aggregate, rise to a level that surmounts the now-operative affecting-commerce threshold.

In her dissenting opinion in *Raich*, Justice O'Connor picked up this idea and ran with it.[183] Five Justices in that case had no difficulty concluding that the challenged law targeted activities that had, in the aggregate, a substantial effect on cross-border movements of marijuana. But Justice O'Connor, in so many words, responded "Not so fast!" As she wrote: "Even assuming that economic activity is at issue in this case, the Government has made no showing in fact that the possession and use of homegrown marijuana for medical

---

things, "when and whether local governments are well-suited to act on environmental issues").

[183] *See supra* Section 4.D.2.a (discussing *Raich*).

purposes, in California or elsewhere, has a substantial effect on interstate commerce."[184]

Lying just beneath the surface in *Raich* was an analytical conundrum that often goes unnoticed in judicial work with the substantial-effects test. The relevant question is this: On what portion of the activities subjected to regulatory control should a court focus as it determines whether a substantial effect on interstate commerce exists?[185] In *Raich* itself, Justice O'Connor opted to consider only the "personal cultivation, possession, and use of medical marijuana."[186] But other possibilities were also at hand. She might have focused, for example, on the cumulative effects of (1) all controlled substances, (2) all Schedule I drugs, (3) all marijuana, (4) all marijuana used in the home regardless of source or purpose, or (5) all marijuana used in the home for medical purposes, regardless of source. But she instead ultimately chose to focus on (6) all (but only) medical marijuana grown on-site exclusively for in-home use.[187] Fixing her gaze solely on this smallest circle of activity, Justice O'Connor concluded that there "is simply no evidence that homegrown medicinal marijuana users constitute, in the aggregate, a sizable enough class to have a discernable, let alone substantial, impact on the national illicit drug market—or otherwise to threaten the CSA regime."[188] "[C]ommon sense," she added, supported this conclusion because "medical marijuana users may be limited in number" and state legislation "may well isolate activities relating to medical marijuana from the illicit market."[189] Notably—and this is the matter of decisive significance here—these observations would have been beside the point if the operative category of regulated activities reached beyond those involving in-the-home, grown-on-site medical-marijuana use. Moreover, there existed a powerful justification for defining the scope of aggregate-able activities at a much higher level of generality—for example, as based on all controlled substances, all Schedule I drugs, or at least all marijuana, since those were the operative legal categories set forth in federal

---

[184] *Raich*, 545 U.S. at 51 (O'Connor, J., dissenting).

[185] For a general overview of this problem in the commerce-power context, see Michael Coenen, *Characterizing Constitutional Inputs*, 67 DUKE L.J. 743, 774–79 (2018).

[186] *Raich*, 545 U.S. at 48 (O'Connor, J., dissenting).

[187] *See also* Susan R. Klein, *Independent-Norm Federalism in Criminal Law*, 90 CAL. L. REV. 1541, 1590 (2002) (raising questions about whether medicinal marijuana growers and users may be aggregated with "the entire illegal-marijuana market" and whether that market may be aggregated with "the entire illicit-drug market").

[188] *Raich*, 545 U.S. at 53 (O'Connor, J., dissenting); *id* at 54 (adding that the majority's finding of a substantial effect was made "without any supporting evidence—descriptive, statistical, or otherwise").

[189] *Id.* at 53.

law, which drew no distinction between homegrown and non-homegrown (or medical and non-medical) marijuana.[190]

These points might lead a wise-guy critic of the *Raich* dissenters to ask: What were *they* smoking as they came up with that theory of properly aggregated marijuana-related behavior? But such a smug and simple-minded view of things fails to take account of important considerations that did support Justice O'Connor's approach. In fact, home-used medical marijuana is a relevant concept in modern culture, in doctors' treatment decisions, and in state law. And for these reasons, that same concept might sensibly inform application of the substantial-effects commerce-power test.[191] The broader point is that courts called on to engage in aggregation analysis can draw the boundaries that surround properly aggregated activities in different (and result-oriented) ways. No less important, at least for now, courts must draw those boundaries with the benefit of little guidance about how to do so from the Supreme Court.

Does this discussion concern only a "tempest in a teapot"? The argument that it does arises because the Court has not yet struck down a single federal statute on the ground that it targeted less than a "substantial" amount of economic activity. On this point, however, it may turn out that the past is not prologue to the future.[192] This is

---

190 Put differently, there was an element of strangeness in defining the scope of activities properly regulated by a *federal* law according to legal concept—that is, in-home medical marijuana use—that had legal significance solely as a matter of *state* law. Notably, however, the majority in *Raich* seemed (at least at points in its opinion) also to drift away from using the operative categories of regulated activity set forth in the CSA itself. At one point, for example, the majority analogized the activities at issue in *Raich* to those at issue in *Filburn*, thus suggesting that it was evaluating all uses of *homegrown* marijuana. *See id.* at 19 (referencing "production of the commodity meant for home consumption"). Elsewhere, however, the majority focused more generally on "marijuana cultivated locally," "home-consumed marijuana," and "intrastate activity" concerning marijuana. *Id.* at 18–19, 22, 24–25. Most important, the majority seemed to fault the lower court for viewing the range of regulated activities too narrowly. *See Raich*, 545 U.S. at 8–9, 27–28, 32–33 (2005) (challenging the lower court's holding that found intrastate, noncommercial cultivation and possession of marijuana for medical purposes as recommended by a physician to be a "separate and distinct class of activities" properly segregated from participation in the broader illicit drug market; indicating that this move "arbitrarily narrow[ed] the relevant class" because Congress itself treated "marijuana as contraband for *any* purpose" and Congress "could have rationally concluded that the aggregate impact on the national market of all" such uses "is unquestionably substantial" (emphasis in original)); *see also* Coenen, *supra* note 185, at 776–77.

191 *See also supra* Section 3.B.2 (explaining that the Court focused not on wheat growing in general, but only on wheat growing for home use in *Filburn*).

192 *See, e.g., Gibbs*, 214 F.3d at 507–08 (Luttig, J., dissenting) (reasoning that, even if the taking of 41 red wolves is economic activity, "it certainly is not an activity that has a substantial effect on interstate commerce" in part because "we are confronted here with an administrative agency regulation of an activity that implicates but a handful of animals"); *see also* Nagle, *supra* note 117, at 196-97 (raising the question whether Congress can protect all endangered plants and animals on the theory that their extinction, in the aggregate, threatens interstate commerce or whether Congress

true in part because one can readily come up with cases—as Justice O'Connor did in *Raich* itself—that do raise contestable substantial-effects questions. What if, for example, the President sends federal officers into a single city, pursuant to congressional authorization, to deal with "sit-in" protestors who, by blocking traffic, are disrupting would-be store users in a way said to stifle interstate commerce? What if Congress outlaws a harmful medical procedure that, precisely because it is harmful, is performed very infrequently?[193] What if Congress passes a law that imposes green-space preservation rules on neighborhoods in ten or twenty or thirty different cities? Could it be that the thus-regulated activities in those neighborhoods do not substantially affect interstate commerce, at least if the case-deciding court aggregates those activities on a neighborhood-by-neighborhood, rather than an all-these-neighborhoods-together, basis? And what if Congress regulates any number of localized activities—such as ingesting an unusual hallucinogenic mushroom or killing a troublesome but rare set of mice—without seriously considering whether the thereby-inhibited activity, even when viewed in the aggregate, affects interstate commerce? In particular, might the Court at least insist that federal legislators offer more than "abstract, unsubstantiated, generalized findings" in support of their exertion of power in cases of this kind?[194]

The dueling opinions in *Raich* illustrate the takeaway point: The plasticity of existing doctrine regarding how to assess whether a regulated activity has a substantial effect on interstate trade holds the potential of placing in the hands of judges new tools with which to chisel away at the commerce power.[195]

---

must instead aggregate on a species-by-species or some other basis). *But see People for the Ethical Treatment of Prop. Owners*, 852 F.3d at 1007 n.11 ("The relevant question is not whether the inability to regulate take of the Utah prairie dog alone would undermine the ESA but whether the inability to regulate take of intrastate species more generally would undermine the ESA."); *GDF Realty Invs.*, 326 F.3d at 640 (concluding that "Cave Species takes may be aggregated with all other ESA takes" because otherwise the purposes of ESA would be undermined, especially given "the interdependence of species [that] compels the conclusion that regulated takes under ESA do affect interstate commerce").

[193] In *Nagarwala* (which is discussed *supra* note 112), for instance, the court, while deciding the case on other grounds, suggested an openness to finding an absence of a substantial effect on interstate commerce in these circumstances. 350 F. Supp. 3d. at 627–28 (noting, in invalidating the federal FGM law, that there was only a "small number of alleged victims" so that the regulated activity contrasted sharply from the "multi-billion-dollar interstate markets for marijuana and pornography").

[194] *Raich*, 545 U.S. at 55 (O'Connor, J., dissenting).

[195] Another way in which the Court could narrow the commerce power would be to abandon the substantial-effects prong of that power altogether, as Justice Thomas has urged it to do for many years. Justice Thomas's core critique of the substantial-effects theory is that "much if not all of Art. I, § 8 . . . would be surplusage if Congress had been given authority over matters that substantially affect interstate commerce" and "[a]n interpretation of cl. 3 that makes the rest of § 8 superfluous simply cannot be

E. THE ANTI-MANDATE LIMIT ON THE COMMERCE POWER

1. *NFIB v. Sebelius*

The foregoing discussion reveals the existence of internal limits on Congress's ability to leverage each prong of the commerce power. In particular, it highlights the noneconomic-activity rule, as well as the requirement that use of the affecting-commerce theory, even in its application to economic activity, depends on a showing of a "substantial effect." Are there other internal limits on the commerce power, perhaps including limits that have an impact on more than only its substantial-effects component? In *NFIB v. Sebelius*,[196] the

correct." *Lopez*, 514 U.S. at 588–89 (Thomas, J., concurring). This mere-surplusage critique has not been endorsed by other members of the Court, and the argument seems questionable in light of the independent significance of the many other Article I, section 8 power grants, particularly insofar as they (1) clarify (as in the Declare War Clause) the primacy of legislative, over executive, authority in certain areas; (2) spell out (as in the Militia Clauses) the division of authority on an important subject matter among the Congress, the President, and the states; (3) settle (as in the Inferior Tribunals Clause) a controversial and specialized question about allocating state and federal decisionmaking power, including with regard to the operation of the nation's courts; (4) establish (as in the Taxing and the Bankruptcy Clauses) special text-based rules of uniformity that do not appear in the Commerce Clause; (5) set forth limits on congressional authority (as in the Intellectual Property Clause) that control by implication how far the commerce power reaches, including with regard to use of the substantial-effects theory; and (6) vest in Congress (as in the Federal District and Federal Enclaves Clauses) a full measure of the police power, thus giving it authority within particular locales that reaches unmistakably beyond the commerce power. *See generally infra* Chapter 10 (developing in greater detail many of these points as to the independent significance of the various Article I, section 8 clauses). In addition, whatever force Justice Thomas's argument might have had when it was initially advanced has been significantly diminished by the Court's recognition of additional restraints on the commerce power in and after *Lopez*. *See supra* Sections 4.D.1 & 4.E and *infra* Chapters 5, 10 & 11. Finally, Justice Thomas's mere-surplusage argument fails to account for the principle that Congress cannot invoke the Necessary and Proper Clause to wield any "great substantive and independent power." *See infra* Section 6.B.2. This is the case because, to the extent that the substantial-effects power is seen as stemming, at least in important respects, from the Necessary and Proper Clause, *see, e.g.*, *supra* notes 141–144 and accompanying text, it follows that Congress cannot make use of that clause to wield any such "great substantive and independent" power when invoking the substantial-effects theory. Yet many of the powers granted by Article I, section 8—to tax, to spend, to borrow, to coin money, to raise armies and navies, to declare war—obviously fall within the "great substantive and independent power" category. And *all* the powers enumerated in Article I, section 8 are, at a minimum, strong candidates for meriting this designation based on the very fact that they are expressly set forth in the original Constitution. The textual enumeration of these powers thus serves a vital purpose by making it clear that Congress can wield them, at least in many instances, even though it could *not* wield them (so it would seem) if the Necessary and Proper Clause and Commerce Clause were the lone occupants of Article I, section 8. In sum, there are many reasons for concluding that the Court's endorsement of the substantial-effects prong of the commerce power does not—even remotely—result in "an interpretation of cl. 3 that makes the rest of § 8 superfluous." *Lopez*, 514 U.S., at 588 (Thomas, J., concurring).

[196] 567 U.S. 519 (2012).

Court answered this question in the affirmative by recognizing an anti-mandate limit on the commerce power's use.[197]

NFIB addressed the constitutionality of key portions of the Affordable Care Act (ACA), which Congress enacted in 2010 to address problems in the nation's health care system. Those problems were far-reaching. To begin with, prior to passage of the ACA, many individuals lacked health insurance because they were either unable or unwilling to buy it. In addition, even for persons who secured insurance, the level of coverage provided by some policies was limited, and oftentimes extremely so. This situation arose in large part because insurance companies balked at covering individuals who suffered from "preexisting conditions"—that is, current medical problems that were likely to produce costly future claims. As a result, insurers often exempted these conditions from coverage, charged much-increased rates in light of their existence, or simply refused to deal with individuals who confronted medical problems of this kind. All of this led to a situation in which those individuals most in need of health insurance often were least able to obtain it. Further complicating matters was the fact that legal duties and professional standards commonly required hospitals and similar medical providers to offer emergency care to patients even when they could not to pay for services. The costs incurred in treating uninsured individuals thus had to be passed along to fee-paying patients, causing an escalation in medical-service charges which in turn drove up insurance costs for everyone.[198] Related to these problems was

---

[197] Two preliminary points about the anti-mandate principle merit mention. First, some observers might ask whether this limit on congressional power embodies an external, as opposed to an internal, restraint on the commerce power, particularly because it emanates, at least in part, from the word "proper" in the Necessary and Proper Clause. *See infra* notes 214–221 and accompanying text; *see generally infra* Chapter 5 (discussing the characteristics of "external," as opposed to "internal," limits on congressional powers). The limit is treated as an "internal" one here because the Court in *NFIB* directly tied it, including insofar as it stems from the Necessary and Proper Clause, to the text of the Commerce Clause itself. *See infra* notes 209 & 222, and accompanying text (noting the Justices' focus on the idea that the use of the word "regulate" in Article I, section 8, clause 3 cuts against recognition of a power to "create" commerce). Second, in *NFIB* itself, the Court applied the anti-mandate principle only in the context of assessing Congress's enactment of a law (there, involving the compulsory purchase of health insurance) under an affecting-commerce theory. The case thus leaves behind questions about how the anti-mandate principle intersects with the channels-and-instrumentalities and in-commerce prongs of the commerce power. What if, for example, Congress passed a law requiring all persons to buy cars and then sought to justify the law not on the affecting-commerce theory, but instead on the theory that cars are instrumentalities of commerce? The intuition that a car-purchase mandate is no more likely to come within the commerce power than an insurance-purchase mandate illustrates how the anti-mandate principle has potential implications that reach beyond cases that involve only the substantial-effects theory. Ultimately, however, the Court in *NFIB* itself neither needed to nor did specifically consider questions of this kind.

[198] *See generally id.* at 589–94 (Ginsburg, J., concurring in part, concurring in the judgment, and dissenting in part) (explaining the factual backdrop that led Congress

another problem, too—namely, that individual states faced strong disincentives to enact remedial legislation. In particular, if a state were to step forward to ban discrimination by insurers against persons with preexisting conditions, the risk arose that persons with those conditions would move to that state, purchase insurance, and then overwhelm the system with claims.[199]

Congress responded to these difficulties by enacting the ACA, which placed two new duties on private insurers throughout the nation. First, no insurer could any longer deny coverage to applicants who had preexisting conditions.[200] And second, no insurer could, as the Chief Justice described it, "charg[e] unhealthy individuals higher premiums than healthy individuals."[201] These strictures, however, gave rise to the new concern that insurers would have to raise rates far beyond previous levels to cover added claims-related costs. To deal with this issue, Congress wove into the ACA yet another provision, commonly referred to as the "individual mandate," which generally required individuals who failed to maintain health insurance to pay a monetary exaction into the federal treasury.[202] This requirement aided insurers by bringing into the coverage pool a large group of lower-risk and previously "self-insured" customers whose premium payments would help offset new costs triggered by the ACA, thereby allowing insurers to hold down policy prices in general.[203] In addition, the individual mandate removed any incentive for individuals to delay paying for coverage until they contracted a serious illness, at which point under the ACA the insurer no longer could refuse to issue a policy based on that illness's preexisting nature.[204]

In *NFIB*, a five-to-four majority of the Court upheld the individual mandate as a permissible exercise of the federal taxing

---

to enact the ACA and emphasizing that Congress found "[t]he large number of individuals without health insurance . . . heavily burdens the national health-care market" largely through health-care providers' "passing along the cost of uncompensated care to those who do pay reliably"—namely, "the government and private insurance companies").

[199] *See id.* at 594–95.

[200] *See id.* at 548 (opinion of Roberts, C.J.).

[201] *See id.*

[202] *See id.* at 538–39; *see also id.* at 539 (noting, in light of certain statutory exemptions, that the "mandate does not apply to some individuals").

[203] *See id.* at 596–98 (Ginsburg, J., concurring in part, concurring in the judgment, and dissenting in part) (discussing how the "individual mandate" sought to counteract "skyrocketing insurance premium costs").

[204] *See id.* at 598 (noting the concern that "[w]hen insurance companies are required to insure the sick at affordable prices, individuals can wait until they become ill to buy insurance"). For one of the many articles discussing the goals and operation of the ACA, see Brietta Clark, *A Moral Mandate & the Meaning of Choice: Conceiving the Affordable Care Act after* NFIB, 6 ST. LOUIS U. J. HEALTH L. & POL'Y 267 (2013).

power.[205] A different five-to-four majority, however, rejected the government's alternative argument that the provision was sustainable under the Commerce Clause, including insofar as that constitutional provision operated in tandem with the Necessary and Proper Clause. More specifically, Justices Ginsburg, Breyer, Kagan, and Sotomayor viewed the challenged provision as independently sustainable under both the taxing power and the commerce power.[206] Justices Scalia, Kennedy, Thomas, and Alito, by contrast, issued a "joint dissent" that deemed the individual mandate to be unconstitutional because it was not sustainable under either of those two powers.[207] The decisive vote came from Chief Justice Roberts, who—while finding that the individual mandate was a sustainable exercise of the taxing power—concluded that the Commerce Clause failed to support it.[208] Although the Chief Justice wrote separately and only for himself on this issue, both he and the joint dissenters agreed that this congressional mandate of economic activity—in contrast to permissible prohibitions of or restrictions on economic activity—fell beyond the reach of the commerce power.

The argument in support of this position started with the constitutional text. According to the Chief Justice, the power to "regulate" commerce was inherently incompatible with a power to "create" it.[209] This was the case, he asserted, because the power to "regulate commerce" bespoke a grant of federal lawmaking authority directed at "some preexisting activity."[210] In reaching this conclusion, the Chief Justice emphasized that *The Federalist No. 45* described the new power set forth in the Commerce Clause as one "from which no apprehensions are entertained."[211] Surely, the Chief Justice reasoned, citizens of 1778 would have had "apprehensions"—indeed, massive apprehensions—about a Commerce Clause power that allowed Congress to "compel individuals not engaged in commerce to purchase an unwanted product."[212] In sum, he concluded that the federal government could no more invoke the commerce power to mandate the purchase of insurance than it could invoke that power to force "everyone to buy vegetables."[213]

---

[205] *NFIB*, 567 U.S. at 588 (opinion of Roberts, C.J.). The Court's treatment of the taxing-power issue is discussed in Chapter 7.

[206] *Id.* at 603, 618, 623 (Ginsburg, J., concurring in part, concurring in the judgment, and dissenting in part).

[207] *Id.* at 646 (Scalia, Kennedy, Thomas, and Alito, JJ., dissenting).

[208] *Id.* at 588 (opinion of Roberts, C.J.).

[209] *Id.* at 550.

[210] *Id.* at 560.

[211] *Id.* at 554.

[212] *Id.* at 549.

[213] *Id.* at 554.

Chief Justice Roberts also found that that these problems persisted even when the Commerce Clause was read together with the Necessary and Proper Clause.[214] In effect, the Chief Justice conceded that, under the expansive view of the latter provision endorsed in *McCulloch v. Maryland*,[215] the individual mandate might well be "necessary" in the relevant sense that it was "convenient," or "useful," in rendering workable the constitutionally unassailable nondiscrimination and baseline-coverage provisions of the ACA.[216] The difficulty, he concluded, was that the individual mandate failed to qualify as "proper" within the meaning of the clause.[217] On this point, he explained that the Court in *McCulloch* had distinguished between laws that qualify as merely "incidental to" an enumerated power and laws that embody "the exercise of [a] 'great substantive and independent power,' " thus offending "the . . . spirit of the constitution."[218] In the Chief Justice's view, the individual mandate fell into the latter category because it was not "narrow in scope" and "reach[ed] beyond the natural limit of [Congress's] authority" by affording to it "the extraordinary ability to create the necessary predicate to the exercise of [the commerce] power."[219] The bottom line was that, with or without the Necessary and Proper Clause, Congress was, at least in this setting, "limited to regulating under the Commerce Clause those who by some preexisting activity bring themselves within the sphere of federal regulation."[220] Put another way, Congress had exceeded the commerce power in enacting the individual mandate by laying its regulatory hand on someone who was "doing nothing."[221]

The four Justices who, in the joint dissent, agreed with the Chief Justice's assessment of the commerce-power issue embraced much the same line of analysis. A pre-1800 dictionary, they noted, indicated that the power to "regulate commerce" did not include efforts to "direct[ ] the creation of commerce."[222] Post-ratification history supported the same conclusion in light of the "unprecedented" character of a congressional mandate to purchase an unwanted product.[223] The four joint dissenters also argued that endorsement of the federal government's position would set in motion a parade of

---

214 *Id.* at 537, 559–60.

215 17 U.S. (4 Wheat.) 316, 412 (1819).

216 *NFIB*, 567 U.S. at 559–61 (opinion of Roberts, C.J.).

217 *Id.* at 560.

218 *Id.* at 559–60 (internal quotation marks omitted).

219 *Id.* at 560.

220 *Id.*

221 *Id.* at 552.

222 *Id.* at 649–50 (Scalia, Kennedy, Thomas, and Alito, JJ., dissenting).

223 *Id.* at 654.

horribles. In their view, and contrary to the government's argument, the inevitability that individuals would seek health care at some point, and oftentimes very soon, did not provide any special justification for upholding a mandate to secure health insurance. After all, the joint dissenters reasoned, "[a]ll of us consume food," but "the mere fact that we . . . are thus, sooner or later, participants in the 'market' for food, does not empower the Government to say when and what we will buy."[224] Nor did the Necessary and Proper Clause save what Congress had done because, if it did, Congress could control "a field so limitless" that it would possess "a general authority to direct the economy."[225] In sum, "it must be *activity* affecting commerce that is regulated, and not merely the failure to engage in commerce."[226]

2. The Limits of the Anti-Mandate Rule

The bottom line is that a majority of the Justices in *NFIB* embraced a new anti-mandate principle. That same majority, however, recognized two important limits on that legislative-power-limiting rule. First, it applies only to the commerce power. The Court, for example, did not question the federal government's power to impose the mandate embodied in draft laws because those laws are rooted not in the Commerce Clause, but instead in Congress's separate military-related powers.[227] Second, many statutes enacted pursuant to the commerce power remain unobjectionable even though one might characterize them as imposing mandates. Federal law, for example, requires certain manufacturing firms to install pollution-abatement equipment. In such cases, however, the "mandate" the law imposes presents no constitutional difficulty because Congress is not dealing with someone who is "doing nothing"; rather, it is imposing a duty on a firm that does engage in commerce-related activity by producing goods for sale.[228]

Consistent with this proposition, lower courts have rejected a variety of challenges to the federal Sex Offender Registration and Notification Act (SORNA) premised on the anti-mandate principle. In *United States v. Howell*,[229] for example, the Eighth Circuit upheld a provision of the SORNA that requires convicted sex offenders to inform federal authorities of a change of address upon moving from one residence to another within the same state. The court reasoned that the duty to re-register was triggered by "the movement of sex

224 *Id.* at 657.

225 *Id.* at 654.

226 *Id.* at 658 (emphasis in original).

227 *See id.* at 549 n.3 (opinion of Roberts, C.J.).

228 *Id.* at 552, 560.

229 552 F.3d 709 (8th Cir. 2009).

offenders" as opposed to their taking of no action at all.[230] Moreover, while moving within a state did not qualify as interstate commerce, the court deemed application of the re-registration requirement in these circumstances to be a necessary and proper means of carrying into effect the law's separate prohibition on unreported interstate relocation.[231] More specifically, the court reasoned that the re-registration requirement is a "reasonable means to track [interstate] offenders" even if the requirement only affected the "wholly intrastate" movements of offenders because the government needs to know "where the offender has moved and where the offender originated" in order to monitor whether or not the offender has moved across a state line.[232] In *United States v. Anderson*,[233] the Eighth Circuit added an explanation as to why reporting requirements of this kind qualify—unlike the purchase mandate at issue in *NFIB*—as "proper" for purposes of the Necessary and Proper Clause. The ACA's individual mandate, the court observed, was so unusual and burdensome that five Justices could not bring themselves to view it as merely " 'incidental' to the exercise of the commerce power."[234] The sex offender registration requirements, however, were so "narrow" that they did qualify as merely "incidental" to the "constitutional power Congress has to punish [non-registering] sex offenders who cross state lines."[235]

Howell, *Anderson*, and kindred cases suggest that lower courts have thus far hesitated to give *NFIB*'s anti-mandate principle a long reach.[236] Even so, many questions linger. At oral argument in the

---

230 *Id.* at 716.

231 *See id.* at 717.

232 *Id.* The registration requirement upheld in *Howell* has survived renewed challenges to its constitutionality in the wake of *NFIB*. *See* United States v. Anderson, 771 F.3d 1064, 1070 (8th Cir. 2014) (reasoning that the registration requirement differs from the mandate in *NFIB* because it "only applies to 'those who by some preexisting activity bring themselves within the sphere of federal regulation' " (citations omitted)); United States v. White, 782 F.3d 1118, 1125–26 (10th Cir. 2015) (likewise rejecting a challenge to the law's sex-offender registration requirements based on *NFIB*'s anti-mandate principle). For a different line of reasoning, applicable at least to persons whose sex-related offenses post-date the enactment of SORNA, see *United States v. Robbins*, 729 F.3d 131, 136 (2d Cir. 2013) (noting that, "unlike the uninsured in *NFIB*, the sex offenders who are subjected to SORNA's requirements have all, in a sense, 'opted in' to the regulated group through their prior criminal activity" (citations omitted)). For a discussion of the application of such limits imposed by legislation enacted after the relevant wrongdoing, see Dan T. Coenen, *The Commerce Power and Congressional Mandates*, 82 GEO. WASH. L. REV. 1052, 1109–10 (2014). For another discussion of the future impact of *NFIB*, see Gillian E. Metzger, *To Tax, To Spend, To Regulate*, 126 HARV. L. REV. 83, 112–16 (2012).

233 771 F.3d at 1064.

234 *Id* at 1069 (citations omitted).

235 *Id.* at 1070.

236 *See also* Senne v. Vill. of Palatine, 695 F.3d 617, 620 (7th Cir. 2012) (noting that a prohibition on disclosing driver information does not implicate *NFIB* because

health care case, for example, counsel for the challengers of the individual mandate argued that the federal government could not compel individuals to secure vaccinations even in the time of a deadly pandemic.[237] But what if the government defended such a law based on the need to ensure military preparedness, rather than as a necessary means to save the national economy from collapse?[238] With regard to the commerce power itself, might the Court distinguish *NFIB* on the ground that the hypothesized vaccination case would not involve anything akin to an endorsement of Congress's creation of a "command economy"?[239] Would courts view such a vaccination law as a permissible regulation of "action," rather than "inaction," if it applied only to individuals who acted in such a way that they earn at least $13,000 per year? The facts of *NFIB* itself suggest such a drafting tweak probably would not remove it from the reach of the

"[h]ere, there is no instance of the federal government forcing a state or an individual to participate in an interstate market"); United States v. Sterling Centrecorp Inc., 960 F. Supp. 2d 1025, 1053 (E.D. Cal. 2013) (seeming to conclude that no anti-mandate problem arose where penalties were triggered under CERCLA by a decision to "ignore the continuous discharges of contaminated water into the environment, or to allow the timber dam to deteriorate to the point of failure" because a government rule with respect to these choices did not involve compelling someone "to purchase an unwanted product" (internal quotation marks omitted)); United States v. Roszkowski, 700 F.3d 50, 58 (1st Cir. 2012) ("In stark contrast to the individual mandate in *Sebelius*, [felon in possession] statutes do not 'compel[ ] individuals to become active in commerce'; rather, they prohibit affirmative conduct that has an undeniable connection to interstate commerce." (internal citation omitted)).

[237] *See* Coenen, *supra* note 232, at 1073–75 (2014) (noting and discussing this line of argument); *see also* David Schultz, *INSIGHT: State, Federal Police Quarantine Powers Raise Due Process Issue*, BLOOMBERG LAW, (March 23, 2020, 4:01AM), https://news.bloomberglaw.com/us-law-week/insight-state-federal-police-quarantine-powers-raise-due-process-issues (noting, in midst of the COVID-19 pandemic, that "[i]t is unlikely [that] there is federal authority to mandate vaccines or a quarantine").

[238] *See supra* note 227 and accompanying text.

[239] One of us elsewhere has suggested that such a distinction would be hard (if not impossible) to justify since it would oddly, if not anomalously, allow Congress, under the Commerce Clause, to impose mandates more freely with regard to non-commercial matters than commercial matters. *See* Coenen, *supra* note 232, at 1073–75. On the other hand, it might be argued that the vaccination program would be sustainable under the Necessary and Proper Clause on the ground that, unlike in *NFIB*, it would be merely one component of, rather than a "necessary predicate" for, a sweeping national crisis-addressing program and thus more readily reconcilable with "the . . . spirit of the Constitution." *See supra* notes 214–21, 224 and accompanying text. This point helps to highlight both the opaqueness and the controversial character of the Court's treatment of the Necessary and Proper Clause issue in *NFIB*, particularly in light of Congress's prior determination that the ACA was directed at addressing a commerce-related "crisis" in the American health care system. *See NFIB*, 567 U.S. at 622 (Ginsburg, J., concurring in part, concurring in the judgment, and dissenting in part); *see also* Celestine Richards McConville, *The (Not So Dire) Future of the Necessary and Proper Power after* National Federation of Independent Business v. Sebelius, 24 WM. & MARY BILL OF RTS. J. 369, 373–76 (2015) (discussing the "new and stringent limits" that *NFIB* imposed on use of the Necessary and Proper Clause and discussing how the Court might work with that clause in future cases).

anti-mandate principle.[240] But what if the duty to obtain a vaccination applied only to those individuals who chose to work at least 40 hours per week in a public setting?[241] Or ten hours per week in any setting? Or to only those persons, but all those persons, who chose at any to point to leave their homes?[242] In this last case, might a court say that the law did not *mandate* vaccination, but instead *prohibited* leaving the home unless a vaccination were obtained?[243] What if Congress enacted a program that every 21-year-old engage in a form of government-designated service for one year?[244] That they must do so unless they are currently enrolled in school?[245]

These questions, and others like them, show that courts may well find themselves distinguishing between impermissible and permissible forms of congressional action under *NFIB*'s anti-mandate principle. As *Howell* and *Anderson* illustrate, existing rulings signal some reluctance among lower courts to push the principle's reach far beyond the sort of purchase mandate involved in *NFIB* itself. Much of the Court's reasoning in *NFIB*—particularly with regard to the tell-tale "novelty" of the individual mandate—suggests the appropriateness of this cautionary stance.[246] So, too, does the fact that the Court's treatment of the commerce power in that case remains controversial, not only under the Court's post-New Deal jurisprudence, but also as a matter of originalist analysis.[247]

---

[240] *See* Coenen, *supra* note 232, at 1058–62 (noting that the "mandate" at issue in *NFIB* applied only to individuals whose income exceeded a particular level).

[241] *See id.* at 1095–1100 (discussing the constitutionality of mandates targeting specialized groups of workers and those targeting workers in general).

[242] This hypothetical brings into focus the sort of considerations that courts might bring to bear in dealing with close-call anti-mandate cases. One of us has described such factors in terms of "escapability," "relatedness," "invasiveness," and "policy sensitivity." *See id.* at 1072–76. In the case of conditioning the duty to secure a vaccination on the choice of individuals to leave their homes, for example, the escapability factor cuts in favor of invalidation, since it is extremely difficult to go through life without ever going outside. On the other hand, the relatedness factor might cut the other way because connecting up the duty to secure a vaccination with the choice to leave the home makes sense insofar as risks of contagion rise with levels of public exposure.

[243] *See supra* note 232 and accompanying text (noting cases distinguishing between mandates and prohibitions in other contexts).

[244] *See* Coenen, *supra* note 232, at 1072 (discussing how such a law would present a serious escapability problem in that "aging is an inevitable part of living").

[245] Such a law, so the argument against it would go, differs from laws that condition a duty to undertake certain conduct on the previous making of other independent choices to act in a particular way (such as an earlier choice to run a manufacturing plant); in contrast, the challenger would claim that such a law imposes an outright mandate—that is, a mandate to engage in either Activity A (performing service) or Activity B (attending college).

[246] *NFIB*, 567 U.S. at 549.

[247] *See generally* Dan T. Coenen, *Originalism and the "Individual Mandate": Rounding Out the Government's Case for Constitutionality*, 107 NW. U. L. REV. COLLOQUY 55 (2012). A key point in this regard is that a number of originalist

F. CONGRESSIONAL POWER OVER INDIAN COMMERCE AND FOREIGN COMMERCE

As the foregoing discussion suggests, the vast bulk of judicial work with Article I, section 8, clause 3 has involved an exploration of Congress's authority to "regulate Commerce . . . among the several States." That same clause, however, also empowers Congress to "regulate commerce with foreign Nations . . . and with the Indian Tribes." A question thus arises: What additional powers do these companion grants of authority channel to federal lawmakers?

1. The Indian Commerce Power

From early in the nation's history, the Court has viewed congressional power over Native nations as far-reaching.[248] To be sure, there is debate about whether this authority stems only from the Commerce Clause or whether it springs, at least in part, from structural postulates concerning the specialized federal role in dealing with separate sovereigns.[249] In either event, two doctrinal points illustrate the capaciousness of the power. First, federal authority concerning Native nations stretches well beyond those subjects that concern "commerce," at least as that term is typically used in modern parlance.[250] Second, as to all such matters, congressional power is so sweepingly "plenary" in nature that (putting to one side external constraints on federal lawmaking authority) "the Court has never found a challenged enactment to

---

arguments supportive of the individual mandate were neither aired nor addressed in the *NFIB* litigation. *See id.* at 61–63 (citing, for example, passages from *The Federalist* indicating that the nature of legislative tools available to Congress under the Necessary and Proper Clause should match the tools available to state governments to wield their reserved powers and that the scope of congressional means available to support the power to regulate commerce should not differ from the means available to support the exercise of military powers). A related line of argument posits that the Court focused its attention on the wrong issue in *NFIB*. On this view, the concerns underlying Chief Justice Roberts's (and the dissenters') commerce-power analysis implicated values less related to federalism and Article I than to individual freedom and the Bill of Rights. *See generally* Michael C. Dorf, *Commerce, Death Panels, and Broccoli: Or Why the Activity/Inactivity Distinction in the Healthcare Case was Really About the Right to Bodily Integrity*, 29 GA. ST. U. L. REV. 897, 899–900 (2013) (arguing that the "activity/inactivity distinction was a libertarian principle masquerading as a principle of federalism").

248 *See* Matthew L. M. Fletcher, *Tribal Consent*, 8 STANFORD J. CIV. RTS. & CIV. LIBERTIES 45, 75–78 (2012).

249 For a broader overview of the law within this area, see Section 25.A.

250 For one recent treatment of the subject, see *Brackeen v. Haaland*, 994 F.3d 249, 269, 299-309 (5th Cir. 2021) (en banc), *cert. granted*, 142 S. Ct. 1205 (2022). For contrasting views of the scope of Indian commerce power, rooted largely in different understandings of the original meaning of the word "commerce," compare Balkin, *supra* note 8, at 25–26, with Robert G. Natelson, *The Original Understanding of the Indian Commerce Clause*, 85 DENV. U. L. REV. 210 (2007).

exceed the federal power over Indian affairs."[251] A later chapter considers these matters in greater detail.[252]

2. The Foreign Commerce Power

In general, congressional exertions of the commerce power extend to foreign commerce in ways so clearly analogous or complementary to the regulation of interstate commerce that no serious questions of constitutional authority arise.[253] From time to time, however, edges are pushed, and specialized questions about the scope of the foreign-commerce power come into view.[254] Courts, in turn, have had to address those problems with the benefit of very little guidance in the existing case law.[255]

---

[251] TRIBE, *supra* note 65, § 5–4, at 807–08 n.1. *See generally* Nell Jessup Newton, *Federal Power over Indians: Its Sources, Scope, and Limitations*, 132 U. PA. L. REV. 195 (1984).

[252] *See infra* Section 25.A.3.

[253] The key difference is that exertions of the foreign commerce power, in contrast (at least in general) to exertions of the powers to regulate either interstate or Indian commerce, create opportunities to regulate activities that occur entirely on foreign soil. To be sure, a strong presumption against the extraterritorial operation of federal laws often pretermits constitutional arguments about the scope of congressional power by leading courts to decline to apply federal statutes in such circumstances. *See, e.g.*, F. Hoffman-La Roche Ltd. v. Empagran S.A., 542 U.S. 155, 164 (2004); Kiobel v. Royal Dutch Petroleum Co., 569 U.S. 108, 124 (2013) (declining to endorse an application of the Alien Tort Statute, despite its broad language, to "violations of the law of nations occurring outside the United States"); EEOC v. Arabian Am. Oil Co., 499 U.S. 244, 248 (1991) (refusing to construe Title VII as applying extraterritorially to the employment practices of U.S. business operations abroad). At the same time, there is no doubt that, in appropriate cases, such extraterritorial regulation is permissible. *See, e.g.*, Hartford Fire Ins. Co. v. California, 509 U.S. 764, 813–14 (1993) (Scalia, J., dissenting) ("Congress has broad power under [the Foreign Commerce Clause], and this Court has repeatedly upheld its power to make laws applicable to persons or activities beyond our territorial boundaries where United States interests are affected."); *see generally* GARY B. BORN & PETER B. RUTLEDGE, INTERNATIONAL CIVIL LITIGATION IN UNITED STATES COURTS 606 (5th ed. 2011) ("A fairly natural component of [the Foreign Commerce Clause] is the power to regulate conduct that occurs outside of U.S. territory."). For scholarly treatments of the Foreign Commerce Clause, see Colangelo, *supra* note 76, at 951 (noting the "new and complex constitutional puzzles" the Foreign Commerce Clause has created), and Saikrishna Prakash, *Our Three Commerce Clauses and the Presumption of Intrasentence Uniformity*, 55 ARK. L. REV. 1149, 1165–72 (2003). For a treatment of the dormant Foreign Commerce Clause, see *infra* Chapter 22.

[254] *See, e.g.*, United States v. Yunis, 681 F. Supp. 896, 907 & n.24 (D.D.C. 1988) (recognizing limits on Congress's ability to impose extraterritorial restrictions on "global air commerce" under the Foreign Commerce Clause in part because "[u]nlike the states, foreign nations have never submitted to the sovereignty of the United States government"), *aff'd*, 924 F.2d 1086 (D.C. Cir. 1991).

[255] *See* United States v. Clark, 435 F.3d 1100, 1102 (9th Cir. 2006) (noting the absence of significant case-law guidance in this field); Naomi Harlin Goodno, *When the Commerce Clause Goes International: A Proposed Legal Framework for the Foreign Commerce Clause*, 65 FLA. L. REV. 1139, 1148–49 (2013) (noting that the "Court has not yet articulated the extent" of this power).

Illustrative is the Eleventh Circuit's ruling in *United States v. Baston*.[256] That case arose out of the actions of Damion St. Patrick Baston, an international sex trafficker who at all relevant times was living unlawfully in the United States. One of Baston's victims was an Australian citizen whom Baston coerced to work as a prostitute through the use of threats and violence.[257] A few of the woman's acts of prostitution occurred in the United States.[258] Most, however, took place in Australia, from which monies paid to her would be wired to Baston's bank account in Miami.[259] Following the victim's escape from the clutches of Baston, federal authorities brought charges against him under the William Wilberforce Trafficking Victims Protection Reauthorization Act.[260] The constitutional problem arose because the act gives the United States "extra-territorial jurisdiction" to prosecute international sex trafficking if, among other things, "the alleged offender is present in the United States, irrespective of the nationality of the alleged offender."[261] Of particular importance in Baston's case was a component of the statute that required any defendant convicted under the act to reimburse the victim for the "gross income or value to the defendant of the victim's services or labor," wherever the coerced services have occurred.[262] Confronted with this mix of fact and law, the district court excluded from the statutory restitution award payable to the victim the $400,000 in payments that she had generated while engaging in prostitution in Australia. The court reasoned that the Foreign Commerce Clause did not support the compelled turning over of these monies because the acts that supported their transfer occurred exclusively outside the United States.[263]

The Eleventh Circuit reversed.[264] It first observed that Congress's power under the Foreign Commerce Clause, insofar as it supports the regulation of activity outside the nation's borders, is "plenary" in nature in part because, "like the Indian Commerce Clause," it "does not pose the federalism concerns that limit the scope of the Interstate Commerce Clause."[265] This conclusion, the court

---

256 818 F.3d 651 (11th Cir. 2016).

257 *Id.* at 657–58.

258 *Id.*

259 *Id.*at 657.

260 18 U.S.C. § 1591(a)(1).

261 18 U.S.C. § 1596(a)(2).

262 18 U.S.C. §§ 1593(b)(1) & (3).

263 *Baston*, 818 F.3d at 660.

264 *Id.* at 668.

265 *Id.* For a very different take on this matter, see Colangelo, *supra* note 76, at 955–57 (asserting that, at least in certain respects, the power over foreign commerce should be viewed as narrower than the power over interstate commerce because "foreign nations have never ceded a portion of their sovereignty to the federal

reasoned, also found support in earlier Supreme Court rulings that had taken a distinctly broad view of the dormant Commerce Clause when applied to foreign trade.[266] In light of these considerations, the court found that the challenged statute embodied a permissible regulation of sex trafficking, including insofar as it had an "extraterritorial effect" in requiring a payment of the full measure of restitution by Baston.[267] The court emphasized that it did not "need [to] demarcate the outer bounds of the Foreign Commerce Clause in this opinion."[268] But it had no doubt that the contested $400,000 paid for this victim's coerced sex acts was owed to her because "Congress had a rational basis to conclude that such conduct—even when it occurs exclusively overseas—is part of an economic class of activities that have a substantial effect on commerce between the United States and other countries."[269]

In a dissent from the denial of certiorari, Justice Thomas expressed misgivings about the Eleventh Circuit's ruling.[270] The difficulty, he explained, was that the lower court's substantial-effects rationale, if read for all it was worth, would support congressional regulation of broad swaths of conduct that occur entirely within the geographic confines of a foreign nation.[271] For Justice Thomas, it reached too far to say that courts must sustain any congressional regulation of "any economic activity anywhere in the world, so long as Congress had a rational basis to conclude that the activity has a substantial effect on commerce between this Nation and any other."[272] He worried in particular that, if Congress could "criminalize prostitution in Australia," it could also "regulate

---

government" and are "unprotected from federal encroachment by political mechanisms inherent in the federal law-making process"; thus concluding that lower courts "have turned [the distinction between the two clauses] completely on its head").

[266] *Baston*, 818 F.3d at 668. A leading case is *Japan Line, Ltd. v. Los Angeles County*, 441 U.S. 434, 448 (1979) (pointing to "evidence that the Founders intended the scope of the foreign commerce power to be . . . greater" than Congress's power over interstate commerce); *see also* Atlantic Cleaners & Dyers, Inc. v. United States, 286 U.S. 427, 434 (1932) (stating that the commerce power "when exercised in respect of foreign commerce may be broader than when exercised as to interstate commerce"). In *United States v. Bollinger*, 798 F.3d 201, 213, 215–16 (4th Cir. 2015), the court drew on earlier Supreme Court rulings to hold that "the Foreign Commerce Clause allows Congress to regulate activities that demonstrably affect such commerce," rather than "substantially affect" it, because applying the latter standard in the foreign-commerce context would be "unduly demanding." *But see* United States v. Al-Maliki, 787 F.3d 784, 793 (6th Cir. 2015) (taking a "skeptical" view of the proposition that Congress's power to regulate foreign commerce is more expansive than its power to regulate interstate commerce).

[267] *Baston*, 818 F.3d at 668.

[268] *Id.*

[269] *Id.* at 668–69 (internal quotations and citations omitted).

[270] 137 S. Ct. 850 (2017) (Thomas, J., dissenting from the denial of certiorari).

[271] *Id.* at 851.

[272] *Id.*at 853.

working conditions in factories in China, pollution from powerplants in India, or agricultural methods on farms in France."[273]

As Justice Thomas also observed, however, "[t]he few decisions from this Court addressing the scope of the clause have generally been confined to laws regulating conduct with a significant connection to the United States."[274] In addition, while Justice Thomas correctly pointed to the possibility that certain passages in the Eleventh Circuit's opinion might support some highly ambitious uses of the Foreign Commerce Clause, that court itself had noted that Baston's connections with the United States, including in interacting with his Australian victim, were nothing less than "legion."[275] Among other things, Baston had "trafficked [his victim] in both the United States and Australia, and when he trafficked her in Australia, he wired the proceeds back to Miami," all while he used "this country as a home base."[276] It was against the backdrop of these facts that the Eleventh Circuit concluded that Baston should have to submit to the burdens imposed by American law just as surely as he had enjoyed the benefits of that law while living in and operating from the United States.

In short, the Eleventh Circuit in *Baston* did not purport to endorse a reading of the Foreign Commerce Clause so sweeping as to allow Congress to "regulate economic activity anywhere in the world" on an affecting-commerce theory. To be sure, the boundaries of the foreign-commerce power remain uncertain. *Baston*, however, serves to illustrate the context in which that power is most likely to be sustained—namely, when the regulated behavior has a demonstrable case-specific connection with the United States above and beyond

---

[273] *Id.*

[274] *Id.* at 851.

[275] *Baston*, 818 F.3d at 669 (noting this point in rejecting the defendant's separate extraterritoriality-based due-process challenge).

[276] *Id.* at 670.

merely affecting, on an aggregation-based logic, cross-border trade in a generalized way.[277]

[277] *See, e.g.*, United States v. Cumming, 281 F.3d 1046, 1049 (9th Cir. 2002) (upholding application of a federal law prohibiting the retention of a child kidnapped from the United States in a foreign nation in light of the previous movement of the crime victim through the channels of commerce from the United States); *see also* United States v. Davila-Mendoza, 972 F.3d 1264, 1274–77 (11th Cir. 2020) (declining to find as authorized by the Foreign Commerce Clause an application of a federal statute to conduct outside of the United States, while distinguishing *Baston* as a case in which "the defendant's activities were so thoroughly intertwined with the United States's commerce with foreign nations that the issue was not a close call"). For an illuminating treatment of this subject, see Colangelo, *supra* note 76, at 954, 970–71 (concluding that the Foreign Commerce Clause imposes a "nexus" requirement because its text, by speaking of commerce "with" foreign nations, implicitly requires that the regulated commerce be "with" the United States as well); *id* at 991–1003, 1000, 1029–40 (invoking this theory to endorse some lower-court rulings, but also to criticize others, that apply the Prosecutorial Remedies and Other Tools to End the Exploitation of Children Today Act; rejecting in particular a generalized jurisdictional-hook theory for criminalizing any child-victim sex act committed after the defendant travels abroad without a purpose to engage in that act because that "would mean that any time a U.S. citizen or permanent resident travels in foreign commerce, every subsequent act by that individual"—such as smoking marijuana after arriving in the Netherlands—"is within Congress's regulatory authority").

Chapter 5

FEDERALISM-BASED EXTERNAL CONSTRAINTS ON THE COMMERCE POWER

Analysis

Lopez, *Morrison*, and *NFIB* recognize "internal" limits on the commerce power. They establish, in other words, that some activities are so loosely linked to interstate commercial behavior, that Congress cannot deal with them under its power to regulate "Commerce . . . among the several States," even as supplemented by the Necessary and Proper Clause. Other constraints on the commerce power work in a different way. These "external" limits trump otherwise-permissible exercises of the commerce power based on principles rooted in the Framers' expectation that states would continue to operate as freestanding centers of government authority under the new constitutional system.[1] Thus, as the Court explained in *Hodel v. Virginia Surface Mining & Reclamation Assn., Inc.*,[2] some federal laws fail to surmount a state-autonomy-based "constitutional barrier" even though they are "undoubtedly within the scope of the Commerce Clause."[3]

---

[1] One marker of this recognition lies in the Tenth Amendment, which states: "The powers not delegated to the United States by the Constitution, nor prohibited by it to the States, are reserved to the States respectively, or to the people." U.S. CONST. amend. X. For a suggestion that the external constraints considered in this chapter arise not from the Tenth Amendment but instead from background principles that that amendment only helps to evidence, see *infra* note 3.

[2] 452 U.S. 264 (1981).

[3] *Id.* at 286 (quoting National League of Cities v. Usery, 426 U.S. 833, 841 (1976)). *See* Richard Primus, *The Limits of Enumeration*, 124 YALE L.J. 576, 578 (2014) ("External limits . . . are affirmative prohibitions that prevent Congress from doing things that would otherwise be permissible exercises of its powers." (emphasis omitted)). Four overarching points about the nature of these external constraints merit mention. First, there are important external constraints on Congress's invocation of

Most, if not all, decisions applying these external constraints involve federal laws "directed, not to private citizens, but to the States as States."[4] In *Coyle v. Smith*,[5] for example, the Court confronted an effort by Congress to dictate the location of Oklahoma's capital upon that state's admission to the Union. In response, the Court declared that, whatever the otherwise-operative scope of Congress's authority under the Constitution might be, "[t]he power to locate [a state's] own seat of government" fell within those "essentially and peculiarly state powers" exempt from congressional tampering.[6] The scope of the *Coyle* principle remains uncertain.[7]

---

the commerce power—particularly external constraints rooted in the Bill of Rights—that focus on the protection of individual rights, rather than state autonomy. The operation of these rights-based external constraints lies beyond the scope of this book. Second, the external constraints that are explored here sometimes operate to trump not only Congress's power under the Commerce Clause, but other powers as well. As it turns out, however, the interaction of these external constraints with other powers is a complex subject—so much so that the subject receives its own extended treatment in Chapter 13. Third, analysts sometimes find the source of these external restraints in the text of the Tenth Amendment. There is, however, a significant problem with this attempt to find in that amendment a textual basis for these constraints because that amendment by its terms goes no further than to block Congress from wielding "powers not delegated to the United States." And the commerce power in *all* its applications *is* delegated to the United States. *See also infra* notes 10–12 and accompanying text. Finally, some analysts might prefer to characterize the limits discussed in this chapter as "internal" in that those limits (or at least some of them) might be seen as supported by restrictions on the grant of legislative power made within Article I itself by the Necessary and Proper Clause. *See infra* note 74 (noting the Court's description of a law found to violate the anticommandeering rule as failing to qualify as "proper" under that clause); *see also supra* Section 4.E.2 n.197 (noting the possibility of characterizing the anti-mandate principle as either an internal or an external constraint in light of the Court's reliance on the term "proper" in the Necessary and Proper Clause, and not only on the Commerce Clause itself, in applying that principle to invalidate the so-called individual mandate in *NFIB v. Sebelius*). In the end, however, differences of opinion on this matter of labeling are of little, if any, practical consequence. The important point is that the legal rules discussed in this chapter operate to limit Congress's otherwise-operative commerce power. And because they are commonly, if not routinely, characterized as "external" in nature, they are described in that way here.

4 *Hodel*, 452 U.S. at 286 (quoting *National League of Cities*, 426 U.S. at 845).

5 221 U.S. 559 (1911).

6 *Id.* at 565; *see also id.* at 580 (adding that states are "endowed with all the functions essential to separate and independent existence").

7 Might Congress, for example, require that state capitol buildings, along with other buildings, meet minimum design standards with respect to safety, access for persons with disabilities, or environmental quality? Might Congress extend statutes related to the workplace—for example, mandatory retirement laws—to key state employees, such as governors, their principal advisors, or state judges? *See* Gregory v. Ashcroft, 501 U.S. 452, 464 (1991) (noting that "the authority of the people of the States to determine the qualifications of their government officials may be inviolate" and thus trump the commerce power; interpreting a federal prohibition on age discrimination as inapplicable to state judges subject to mandatory retirement under state law in part for this reason, so as to "avoid a potential constitutional problem"). Might Congress authorize federal agents to seize and detain immigrants while they are present in state courthouses contrary to the wishes of state authorities? *See* New York v. U.S. Immigr. & Customs Enf't, 466 F. Supp. 3d 439, 441, 444 n.12 (S.D.N.Y.

Indeed, there exists some question (though probably not much of one) about whether that principle operates in any way to limit the commerce power in the wake of the Court's subsequent holding in *Garcia v. San Antonio Metropolitan Transit Authority*, which is discussed further below.[8] Well-supported by key decisions of the Rehnquist and Roberts Courts, however, are three distinct federalism-driven sets of external constraints on the commerce power: (1) limits that account for defects in the operation of national political processes; (2) prohibitions on congressional commandeering of state legislative and executive officials to implement federal programs; and (3) restrictions on congressional authority to expose states to monetary liability in the face of claims of sovereign

---

2020) (declining to address whether "ICE's policy [of arresting immigrants at courthouses] unconstitutionally infring[ed] on New York's state sovereignty, in violation of the Tenth Amendment," but noting that ICE's activities constituted "disruptions and intimidations . . . in violation of long-standing privileges and fundamental principles of federalism").

8 469 U.S. 528 (1985). *See id.* at 556 (citing *Coyle* in noting that the Court need not fully define "what affirmative limits the constitutional structure might impose on federal action" but also suggesting that such limits should relate to defects in the federal lawmaking process). Uncertainty as to *Coyle*'s continued vigor exists in part because (with the exception of *National League of Cities*, which was overruled in *Garcia*, as discussed below) the Court has repeatedly rejected *Coyle*-like challenges to federal enactments. *See, e.g.*, United States v. California, 297 U.S. 175, 185 (1936) (rejecting a constitutional challenge to an application of the Federal Safety Appliance Act to a state-owned railroad; reasoning in part that a "state can no more deny the [commerce] power if its exercise has been authorized by Congress than can an individual"); Oklahoma *ex rel.* Phillips v. Guy F. Atkinson Co., 313 U.S. 508, 534 (1941) (holding that "the fact that land is owned by a state is no barrier to its condemnation by the United States"); New York v. United States, 326 U.S. 572 (1946) (rejecting a challenge to the extension of a generally applicable federal tax on bottled water to New York's sale of bottled water extracted from state-owned springs); Maryland v. Wirtz, 392 U.S. 183, 195–96 (1968) (citing Sanitary Dist. v. United States, 266 U.S. 405 (1925), as having "put to rest the contention that state concerns might constitutionally 'outweigh' the importance of an otherwise valid federal statute regulating commerce"). It is noteworthy, however, that two Justices in the New York bottled-water case found an impermissible interference with the state's "exercise of its power of sovereignty," 326 U.S. at 591 (Douglas, J., dissenting), and that four others were "not prepared to say" that "an income tax laid upon citizens and States alike could be constitutionally applied to the State's capitol, its State-house, its public school houses, public parks, or its revenues from taxes or school lands." *Id.* at 586–88 (Stone, C.J., concurring). The reservations expressed in the opinions of Justice Douglas and Chief Justice Stone had roots in a principle recognized in much-earlier cases—namely, cases that indicated that the same principle of intergovernmental immunity found to protect federal instrumentalities from state taxation in *McCulloch v. Maryland*, *see supra* Section 1.B, should operate in symmetrical fashion to safeguard state institutions from federal taxation. *See* Collector v. Day, 78 U.S. (11 Wall.) 113, 127 (1870) (reasoning that "in this respect . . . the State is as sovereign and independent as the general government"). Both *Garcia* and other more recent cases—most notably *South Carolina v. Baker*, 485 U.S. 505 (1988)—suggest, however, that the state-protective prong of the intergovernmental tax immunity doctrine has lost much of its earlier sheen. Thus, the Court in the latter case, while not rejecting the notion of state tax immunity altogether, observed that "at least some nondiscriminatory federal taxes can be collected directly from the States even though a parallel state tax could not be collected directly from the Federal Government." *Id.* at 523.

immunity.[9] In addition, the Court has sought to protect states against congressional overreaching by narrowly construing federal statutes that threaten to invade areas of traditional local control.

A. *GARCIA V. SAN ANTONIO METROPOLITAN TRANSIT AUTHORITY* AND THE DEFECTIVE-PROCESS PRINCIPLE

1. The Rise and Fall of the "Traditional Government Functions" Rule

In *United States v. Darby*,[10] the Court left no doubt that trading money for labor was an activity that the Commerce Clause, especially when coupled with the Necessary and Proper Clause, broadly authorizes Congress to regulate. On its way to establishing this principle, the Court declared in a famous and important passage that the Tenth Amendment "states but a truism."[11] In other words, that amendment reaffirmed that the original Constitution granted to Congress all, but only, the limited powers established by Article I and elsewhere in the document, while reserving to the states such other powers as they previously had possessed. This vision of the Tenth Amendment signaled that its sole role was to confirm in clear terms "the relationship between the national and state governments as . . . established by the Constitution" in its pre-amendment form.[12] It followed that the Tenth Amendment did not create any new limitations on federal legislative power.

Even so, in *National League of Cities v. Usery*,[13] the Court drew in part on the Tenth Amendment to hold that a state-protective external limit, not otherwise set forth in the Constitution itself, inhibited congressional action. This limit, the Court held, precluded

---

9 Several still-operative federalism-related external constraints on the commerce power find expression in the express terms of the Constitution. *See, e.g.*, U.S. CONST. art. I, § 9, cls. 5 & 6 (barring congressional preference of "the Ports of one state over those of another," as well as federal taxation of "Articles exported from any state"); *see infra* Section 7.B (discussing the operation of these provisions). Another text-based, federalism-driven external limit appears in section 2 of the Twenty-first Amendment, which states: "The transportation or importation into any State . . . for delivery or use therein of intoxicating liquors, in violation of the laws thereof, is hereby prohibited." U.S. CONST. amend. XXI § 2. As this text indicates, there is a field of liquor regulation that the Congress cannot enter in light of distinct and countervailing state regulatory interests, including pursuant to its otherwise-operative power under the Commerce Clause. Most, if not all, judicial treatments of section 2, however, have come in cases involving the dormant Commerce Clause, rather than cases involving affirmative exercises of the commerce power. For a discussion of those cases, see *infra* Section 20.F.

10 312 U.S. 100 (1941); *see also* Section 3.A (discussing this case).

11 *Id.* at 124.

12 *Id.*

13 426 U.S. 833 (1976).

federal lawmakers from extending federal minimum-wage protections to police officers, firefighters, and other key employees of the states and their subdivisions.[14] The Court grounded this ruling in a more general principle—namely, that Congress may not enact laws that "directly displace the States' freedom to structure integral operations in areas of traditional governmental functions."[15] The Court, however, never again invalidated any federal law pursuant to this limiting principle,[16] and nine years later it overruled *National League of Cities* in *Garcia v. San Antonio Metropolitan Transit Authority*.[17]

In scuttling the *National League of Cities* rule, the five-Justice majority in *Garcia* first claimed that intervening cases had proven the integral-operations test to be "unworkable."[18] The Court also derided the principle as being more destructive than protective of federalism values because it forced an "unelected federal judiciary" to rank the centrality of state programmatic choices.[19] Most

---

[14] In reaching this conclusion, the Court overruled *Wirtz*, 392 U.S. 183, which it had handed down only eight years earlier. A stepping-stone decision on the journey from *Wirtz* to *National League of Cities* was *Fry v. United States*, 421 U.S. 542 (1975). There the Court reaffirmed *Wirtz* but also observed in a footnote that the Tenth Amendment "expressly declares the constitutional policy that Congress may not exercise power in a fashion that impairs the States' integrity or their ability to function effectively in a federal system." *Id.* at 547 n.7.

[15] 426 U.S. at 852. In *Hodel*, the Court further refined the *National League of Cities* rule by declaring that it applied only when Congress (1) subjected "States as States" (as opposed to private parties) (2) to rules that "address matters that are indisputably 'attribute[s] of state sovereignty' " (3) in a way that "would directly impair their ability 'to structure integral operations in areas of traditional governmental functions.' " 452 U.S. at 287–88 (quoting *National League of Cities*, 426 U.S. at 854, 845, 852). The Court found no violation of this standard in *Hodel* itself primarily because the application of federal rules regarding strip-mining operations that were challenged in that case targeted private mining businesses, rather than public entities.

[16] *See* EEOC v. Wyoming, 460 U.S. 226 (1983) (upholding a federal age-discrimination ban as applied to state employees; distinguishing *National League of Cities* on the grounds that (1) the Fair Labor Standards Act—unlike the age-discrimination law—had disrupted state budgeting by imposing direct financial burdens on states, and (2) application of the age-discrimination law threatened non-financial state interests only modestly because public employers remained free to pursue the underlying job-qualification-related goals of mandatory retirement rules through individualized assessments of employee competence); FERC v. Mississippi, 456 U.S. 742, 758–70 (1982) (rejecting a challenge to a federal law that required state agencies, if in place, to consider adoption of federally specified approaches to electric-utility regulation and ratemaking; reasoning that this law did not mandate state adoption of federal rules and that this purely process-based requirement of consideration was less intrusive than the treasury-burdening wage-payment requirement struck down in *National League of Cities*); United Transp. Union v. Long Island R.R. Co., 455 U.S. 678, 684–85 (1982) (upholding application of federal labor regulations to a state-owned railroad because its operation did not involve "integral" state activity).

[17] 469 U.S. 528 (1985).

[18] *Id.* at 531.

[19] *Id.* at 546.

important of all, the Court reasoned that the state-autonomy values that *National League of Cities* sought to promote were already adequately safeguarded by the Constitution's structuring of the federal government. Articles I and II, for example, vest state officials with extensive control over the qualifications of voters in federal elections and give state legislatures exclusive authority over the manner of selecting presidential electors. In addition, the Constitution accords the states a particularly "direct influence in the Senate, where each State received equal representation."[20] These and other state-protective features woven into the fabric of the federal government negated, in the majority's view, any need for an active judicial role in monitoring supposed congressional infringements of state autonomy. In sum, *Garcia*'s five-Justice majority concluded that the Court in *National League of Cities* had "underestimated . . . the solicitude of the national political process for the continued vitality of the States" because that "political process ensures that laws that unduly burden the States will not be promulgated."[21]

2. Defective-Process Constraints After *Garcia*

While *Garcia* marked a dramatic retreat in the judiciary's safeguarding of state-autonomy interests, the Court did not go so far as to abandon all federalism-based external limits on federal legislative authority. Rather, in keeping with the underlying rationale of the decision, the Court indicated that any future judicial role in checking congressional excesses would need to be "tailored to compensate for possible failings in the national political process."[22] The Court left the nature of any such process-centered external restraint deeply ill-defined, and since *Garcia* the Justices have gauged its reach on only one occasion, in *South Carolina v. Baker*.[23] In that case, the Court confronted a constitutional challenge to a federal statute that removed tax-exempt status for income generated by "bearer bonds" (as opposed to more readily traceable "registered bonds") issued by state and local governments. In rejecting an attack on the law mounted by South Carolina, Justice Brennan wrote for a six-Justice majority:

> South Carolina has not even alleged that it was deprived of any right to participate in the national political process or that it was singled out in a way that left it politically

---

[20] *Id.* at 551. *See generally* THE FEDERALIST NO. 62 (Madison) ("[T]he equal vote allowed to each State is at once a constitutional recognition of the portion of sovereignty remaining in the individual States, and an instrument for preserving that residuary sovereignty.").

[21] *Id.* at 556–57.

[22] *Id.* at 554.

[23] 485 U.S. 505 (1988).

> isolated and powerless. Rather, South Carolina argues that the political process failed here because [the law] was "imposed by a vote of an uninformed Congress relying upon incomplete information." But nothing in *Garcia* or the Tenth Amendment authorizes courts to second-guess the substantive basis for congressional legislation. Where, as here, the national political *process* did not operate in a defective manner, the Tenth Amendment is not implicated.[24]

In *Baker*, the Court again offered few clues about when any political-process limit on federal lawmaking might take hold.[25] Even so, other rulings of the Court suggest that two separate process-related restraints might operate in some cases to constrain federal legislative authority—namely, when (1) Congress subjects states to restrictions not made applicable to private entities, and (2) Congress passes laws that discriminate among the states.

a. Singling out States for Disadvantageous Treatment

Special state-autonomy-related problems can arise when Congress singles out states and their subdivisions for burdens not imposed on similarly situated private entities. This idea gains support from the Court's 1946 ruling in *New York v. United States*,[26] in which several Justices, while voting to uphold the enforcement against a state of a federal tax made applicable in equal fashion to both public and private bottled-water sellers, also suggested that a tax *only* on state purveyors of bottled water,[27] even to the extent it targeted a nontraditional government function, would not survive a constitutional challenge.[28] It seems fair to say that one problem such

---

[24] *Id.* at 512–13 (citations omitted).

[25] For an unsuccessful effort by litigants to work around the principle of *Baker* in the context of a revised treatment of state and local taxation in the imposition of federal income-tax levies, see *New York v. Mnuchin*, 408 F. Supp. 3d 399, 415–18 (S.D.N.Y. 2019) (rejecting recognition of an external constraint on Congress's power to tax income already used to pay state and local taxes notwithstanding the state's argument that the "historical novelty" of such levies rendered them vulnerable to constitutional attack; relying on the "plenary" nature of the federal taxing power, Congress's recognized ability to revise taxing rules, and the principles set forth in *Garcia* and *Baker*), *aff'd sub nom.* New York v. Yellen, 15 F.4th 569, 580–82 (2d Cir. 2021).

[26] 326 U.S. 572 (1946).

[27] In *Reno v. Condon*, 528 U.S. 141 (2000), one question was whether a federal ban on selling drivers' license data was, as a functional matter, a law that similarly imposed special disadvantages on the states. The Court concluded it was not because the prohibition extended not only to state sellers but to private resellers as well. *Id.* at 151. For further discussion of *Condon*, see *infra* Section 5.B.3.

[28] In particular, in the *New York* bottled-water case, Justice Frankfurter wrote for a plurality that there exists "no restriction upon Congress to include the States in levying a tax *exacted equally from private persons* upon the same subject matter." *New York*, 326 U.S. at 584 (opinion of Frankfurter, J.) (emphasis added). Justice Rutledge,

a tax would present stems from political-process concerns. In particular, as Professor Tribe has observed, congressional action that places regulatory burdens only on states "would deprive the states of their natural non-governmental allies in the legislative process, and thus would weaken the political check upon Congress to the point that judicial intervention could perhaps be justified even under *Garcia*."[29]

---

who joined the Frankfurter opinion but also wrote separately for himself, proclaimed with even greater specificity that "state functions may not be singled out for taxation when others performing them are not taxed." *Id.* at 584–85 (Rutledge, J., concurring). Concurring only in the result, meanwhile, Chief Justice Stone, writing for himself and three others, asserted along these same lines that "a general *non-discriminatory* real estate tax . . . or an income tax *laid upon citizens and States alike* could be constitutionally applied," albeit subject to some further state-protective limits. *Id.* at 587–88 (Stone, C.J., concurring) (emphasis added). Finally, Justice Douglas, who dissented in the case, was prepared to go even further, by insisting that states should enjoy protections from federal taxation even when the challenged exaction applies in in equal fashion to public and private entities. *See id.* at 591.

[29] *See* LAURENCE H. TRIBE, AMERICAN CONSTITUTIONAL LAW § 5–12, at 915 (3d ed. 2000). The flipside of this principle is that laws that apply equally to both public and private entities are (at least ordinarily) not susceptible to federalism-based attack. Indeed, it was on this very basis that the Court in a 1992 ruling, also under the caption of *New York v. United States*, 505 U.S. 144 (1992), distinguished *Garcia* (which involved application of federal minimum-wage/maximum-hour laws to both private and public employers) on its way to invalidating a law under the anti-commandeering principle. *Id.* at 160. *See infra* Section 5.B; *see also supra* note 27 (discussing *Condon*'s treatment of a similar issue). In some instances, however, federalism-based as-applied challenges will remain available to litigants prepared to take on facially neutral laws. First, and most obviously, principles of state sovereign immunity remain fully operative even as to federal laws that apply in equal terms to state and private defendants in civil actions. *See infra* Section 5.C. Second, state claims of tax or regulatory immunity are likely to win out in some instances, even when (at least at first glance) public and private entities receive equal treatment. Consider, for example, a hypothetical federal tax imposed on "revenues received by any entity in excess of $100,000,000" as applied to a state's tax revenues. The federal government might seek to escape the problematic-singling-out principle on the ground that this big-time-revenue tax applies equally to states and mega-corporations such as Google or Amazon. A case-deciding judge, however, might respond that no sensible person would equate private-firm revenues with state tax collections, precisely because those collections are made by states for public, rather than profit-making, purposes. Alternatively, the judge might declare that, even if the law qualifies as generally applicable, it still impairs state autonomy too much. *See supra* note 8 (discussing some Justices' reflections on federal taxation of state-collected taxes). Along these same lines, it is certainly true that *Garcia*—which involved the federal minimum-wage law—signaled with clarity that generally applicable employment-related laws normally can operate against states even in their performance of "integral" functions. But that does not mean that generally applicable employment laws will *never* offend constitutional restrictions on federal interference with state autonomy, at least when they concern core republican decision-making structures. It seems improbable, for example, that Congress could disqualify a fully eligible and duly elected state governor from serving in office pursuant to an otherwise valid federal law that mandated retirement of all employees at age of sixty-five. This notion stems from the twin postulates "that the Constitution does indeed presuppose the existence of the states as entities independent of the national government," TRIBE, *supra*, § 5–12, at 907, and that "the authority to decide, consistent with equal protection of the laws, *how* one's people will represent themselves and take part in their own governance—seems the very essence of all self-government." *Id.* at 908–09. Along these lines, the Court

b. *Discriminating Among the States*

A second political-process problem might arise when Congress discriminates not against states, but among states, in formulating federal legislation. More specifically, the question exists whether the Constitution limits the ability of a large number of states, acting through their federal representatives, to "gang up" on a single state or a small number of states as Congress doles out benefits and burdens. In the *Coyle* state-capital-location case, the Court gave a nod in this direction by suggesting that Congress could not place Oklahoma "on a plane of inequality with its sister States."[30] In *South Carolina v. Katzenbach*,[31] however, the Court declared that any such principle of equal treatment applied only to the state-admission power.[32] Accordingly, Congress could, as it did, subject some jurisdictions, but not others, to the "preclearance" obligations imposed by the Voting Rights Act of 1965, which Congress had enacted under its separately enumerated powers to enforce the

---

suggested in *Gregory v. Ashcroft*, 501 U.S. 452 (1991), that "the people of the state" have "authority . . . to determine the qualifications of their most important government officials." *Id.* at 463. To be sure, the Court in that case sidestepped the question whether this principle blocked Congress from extending the federal Age Discrimination in Employment Act to Missouri's judges, notwithstanding that state's choice to impose mandatory-retirement rules on judicial officials, by interpreting the act narrowly to avoid constitutional difficulties. *Gregory* nonetheless supports the idea that the federal government cannot "undermine ultimate popular control," wielded solely by the state's own citizenry, "over certain state officials, their qualifications, and the lawmaking process." TRIBE, *supra*, § 5–12, at 909. Indeed, such a conclusion would seem to follow, perhaps even *a fortiori*, from the Court's indication in *Coyle*, 221 U.S. 559, that a state has a federally untouchable authority to determine the location of its own capital city. *See supra* notes 5–7 and accompanying text. Notably, Professor Tribe seems ready to argue that this anti-tampering principle has roots in Article IV, section 4, which states that "[t]he United States shall guarantee to every State in this Union a Republican Form of Government." U.S. CONST. art. IV, § 4. On this view, that text supports recognition of "a *protection* from exercises of federal power" that would in effect "render non-republican" a state's choice of a particular structure for government" that otherwise would be permissible under the Article IV clause. TRIBE, *supra*, § 5–12, at 909 (drawing in large part on the analysis offered in Deborah Jones Merritt, *The Guaranty Clause and State Autonomy Federalism for a Third Century*, 88 COLUM. L. REV. 1 (1988)). Whatever one might think of this textual extrapolation (or its applicability to our hypothetical well-aged-governor case), it seems hard to dispute the overarching point—namely, that Congress (absent a valid federal need to target equal-protection or other rights-based problems, *see infra* Chapter 11) has no power to tinker with the fundamental architecture of a state's governing institutions so long as those institutions surmount the low bar of qualifying as "republican" in nature.

30 *Coyle*, 221 U.S. at 565 (discussed *supra* notes 5–7 and accompanying text). For another early case in which the Court considered the equal-sovereignty concept in the admission-of-new-states context, see *United States v. Sandoval*, 231 U.S. 28, 48–49 (1913) (finding no violation of the "principle of equality among the states" in Congress's incorporation into legislation regarding New Mexico's admission to the union of a ban on the introduction of liquor into Santa Clara Pueblo lands within the state).

31 383 U.S. 301 (1966).

32 *South Carolina*, 383 U.S. at 328–29 (limiting the *Coyle* doctrine of "equality of states" to the "terms upon which States are admitted to the Union, and not to the remedies for local evils which have subsequently appeared").

rights-based guarantees of the Fourteenth and Fifteenth Amendment.[33] Four decades later, however, a different set of Justices retreated from this pronouncement. In *Shelby County v. Holder*,[34] the Court held that the Voting Rights Act preclearance scheme no longer was constitutionally sustainable, largely because its jurisdiction-specific coverage formula conflicted with "the fundamental principle of equal sovereignty" among the states.[35]

A question thus arises: With the equal-sovereignty principle now cut loose from its anchorage in Congress's little-used authority to admit new states, does it follow that the principle should apply to constrain as a general matter Congress's lawmaking powers? In other words, is the principle's expanded operation limited to the Fourteenth and Fifteenth Amendment enforcement powers, or does it now apply to all (or at least most) of Congress's powers, beginning with the commerce power?[36] One might assume that the external constraint recognized in *Shelby County* must operate to constrain legislation based on the commerce power. In other settings, after all, the Court has applied external limits on federal lawmaking powers far more aggressively to legislation based on the commerce power than to legislation based on the Fourteenth and Fifteenth Amendment enforcement powers.[37] It thus might seem to follow *a fortiori* that the equal-sovereignty limit on federal legislative power must apply full-bore to commerce-power enactments.[38]

In the wake of *Shelby County*, however, lower courts have taken a different view of the relationship between the commerce power and the equal-sovereignty principle. The leading case is *NCAA v. Governor of New Jersey*.[39] There, New Jersey argued that the Professional and Amateur Sports Protection Act (PASPA) abridged the equal-sovereignty rule because the law generally exempted Nevada from the sports-gambling-related restrictions it placed on

---

33 *Id.*

34 570 U.S. 529 (2013).

35 *Id.* at 544. For a detailed treatment of the *South Carolina* and *Shelby County* cases, see *infra* Section 11.B.

36 For a brief treatment of scholarly works that reflect on the soundness and implications of this aspect of *Shelby County*, see *infra* Section 11.B.5.

37 *See infra* Chapter 13 (discussing the non-applicability to the enforcement powers of the sovereign-immunity and anti-commandeering principles that limit congressional use of the commerce power).

38 *See, e.g.*, Michael Welsh, Note, *Betting on State Equality: How the Expanded Equal Sovereignty Doctrine Applies to the Commerce Clause and Signals the Demise of the Professional and Amateur Sports Protection Act*, 55 B.C. L. REV. 1009, 1027–29 (2014) (concluding, based largely on this rationale, that "courts should apply the equal sovereignty doctrine to all legislation that discriminates among states, including economic legislation passed under the Commerce Clause").

39 730 F.3d 208 (3d Cir. 2013).

other states.[40] A unanimous panel of the Third Circuit, however, rejected this argument. According to the court, there was "nothing in *Shelby County* to indicate that the equal sovereignty principle is meant to apply with the same force outside the context of 'sensitive areas of state and local policymaking,' " such as state and local voting law.[41] The court noted that *Shelby County* had emphasized that "the Framers of the Constitution intended the States to keep for themselves . . . the power to regulate elections," thus suggesting that the franchise-related preclearance provision was "an uncommon exercise of congressional power."[42] "[T]he regulation of gambling via the Commerce Clause," the Court continued, "is . . . not of the same nature as the regulation of elections pursuant to the Reconstruction Amendments."[43]

Two additional considerations pushed along the court's conclusion that the equal-sovereignty principle should not restrict congressional use of the commerce power. First, some power-granting provisions of Article I— the Taxing, Naturalization, and Bankruptcy Clauses—set forth in express terms a requirement of geographic uniformity.[44] But the contemporaneously adopted Commerce Clause includes no such limitation. For this reason, the panel explained, a powerful text-based argument from negative implication supported its refusal to overlay on the commerce power a high-octane mandate of equal state treatment.[45] Second, the panel saw its approach as making good sense as a matter of constitutional policy. Wielding the

---

[40] *Id.* at 214. The relevant provisions of that statute were subsequently invalidated by the Court on different grounds. *See infra* Section 5.B.3 (discussing the Court's decision in *Murphy v. NCAA*, 138 S. Ct. 1461 (2018)).

[41] *Id.* at 239 (quoting *Shelby County*, 570 U.S. at 545). *Accord* Mayhew v. Burwell, 772 F.3d 80, 95 (1st Cir. 2014) (quoting this passage from *NCAA* in declining to apply the equal-sovereignty principle in evaluating Maine's challenge to Congress's spending-power-based issuance of Medicaid-eligibility rules put in place by the Affordable Care Act).

[42] *NCAA*, 730 F.3d at 238 (alteration in original) (quoting *Shelby County*, 570 U.S. at 543, 545).

[43] *Id.* at 238; *see also id.* (adding that, in light of these considerations, "the VRA is fundamentally different from PASPA").

[44] U.S. CONST., art. I, § 8, cls. 1, 4.

[45] *NCAA*, 730 F.3d at 238 (noting that "the Commerce Clause, '[u]nlike other powers of [C]ongress . . . does not require geographic uniformity' " (quoting Morgan v. Virginia, 328 U.S. 373, 388 (1946) (Frankfurter, J., concurring))); Currin v. Wallace, 306 U.S. 1, 14 (1939) ("There is no requirement of uniformity in connection with the commerce power such as there is with respect to the power to lay duties, imposts and excises." (citation omitted)); Ry. Labor Execs.' Ass'n v. Gibbons, 455 U.S. 457, 468 (1982) ("Such uniformity in the applicability of legislation is not required by the Commerce Clause."). *But see* Thomas B. Colby, *Revitalizing the Forgotten Uniformity Constraint on the Commerce Power*, 91 VA. L. REV. 249, 266–88 (2005) (arguing, on originalist grounds, that the Constitution does impose a geographic-uniformity requirement with regard to commerce-power legislation, thus restricting Congress's ability to intentionally discriminate among the states while not affecting its ability to impose differential burdens by way of incidental effects).

commerce power, the court explained, often requires Congress to take account of local and regional variations that inevitably crop up within a populous, expansive, and richly diverse nation.[46] Indeed, the case at hand illustrated this point well. Nevada, after all, had long authorized sports gambling, thus bringing into existence a now-well-established wagering industry of extraordinary importance to that state's economy. Thus, when Congress moved "to stop the spread of state-sanctioned sports gambling," it acted wisely, fairly, and in keeping with federalism-based geographic-diversity values in choosing not to disrupt the practices of a state "in which sports-wagering already existed."[47]

It remains to be seen whether the Supreme Court will agree that the equal-sovereignty doctrine of *Shelby County* is inapplicable in the Commerce Clause context.[48] It also remains to be seen how the Court, even if it declines to apply that doctrine in all-out fashion to laws based on the commerce power, will respond to federal laws if and when they discriminate among the states in particularly problematic

---

[46] *See NCAA*, 730 F.3d at 238 (reasoning that "Congress' exercises of Commerce Clause authority are aimed at matters of national concern and finding national solutions will necessarily affect states differently," thus rendering the "one-size-fits-all test for equal sovereignty analysis . . . a perilous proposition" in the commerce-power context).

[47] *Id.* at 239 (emphasis omitted). To be sure, one might respond that geographic distinctions also can make good sense when Congress wields its Reconstruction Amendment enforcement powers. Indeed, the Court itself has recognized this point by endorsing the appropriateness, in some circumstances, of directing enforcement-power legislation only at "wrongdoer" jurisdictions rightly subjected to distinct remedial intervention. *See infra* Section 11.B. One potential response to this point is that there is reason to believe that Congress needs the highest measure of flexibility to deal in non-uniform ways with a sprawling and richly diverse national commerce marked by countless location-specific variations. Another potential response is that the Court in *Shelby County*—much like the Third Circuit in *NCAA*—placed emphasis on the idea that enforcement-power laws direct their sting at distinctly "sensitive" features of state-government operations themselves. *Shelby County*, 570 U.S. at 545. The concerns raised by such laws, so *Shelby County* can be read to suggest, do not readily carry over to Congress's oversight of private actors in the marketplace pursuant to the commerce power. *But see* Leah M. Litman, *Inventing Equal Sovereignty*, 114 MICH. L. REV. 1207, 1272 (2016) (challenging "the idea that the Reconstruction Amendments uniquely limit Congress's ability to distinguish among the states" by emphasizing that it runs counter to the idea "that the Reconstruction Amendments authorize *greater* intrusions into state sovereignty than Article I does" (emphasis added)).

[48] Also in the picture are questions about how the principle of *Shelby County* interacts with other Article I powers. With regard to the spending power, see *Mayhew*, 772 F.3d at 95 (rejecting Maine's argument, regarding the spending power, that Congress's conditioning of Medicaid money based on a state's continued maintenance of its eligibility standards for children followed in only some states ran afoul of the "equal sovereignty" principle). With regard to the taxing power, see *Mnuchin*, 408 F. Supp. 3d at 420 (stating that "nothing in *Shelby County* suggests that the equal sovereignty principle bars Congress from using its tax powers to incentivize state-level policy changes simply because it knows that some states will feel those incentives more forcefully than others").

ways.[49] Until the Court turns to these matters, the ruling in *NCAA* will provide a key starting point for lower courts called on to deal with problems of this kind, and for now those courts seem inclined to agree that the principle of *Shelby County* does not carry over to federal enactments based on the commerce power.[50]

---

[49] Put another way, even if the Court declines to extend the *Shelby County* principle to commerce-power legislation as a general matter, it will not follow that *all* laws that discriminate, no matter how nefariously, against one state or a few of them will automatically escape constitutional challenge. Thus, the Court might still find that some form of anti-ganging-up doctrine operates in this context, albeit with less energy than the *Shelby County* equal-sovereignty principle. *See, e.g.*, Dan T. Coenen, *A Constitution of Collaboration: Protecting Fundamental Values with Second-Look Rules of Interbranch Dialogue*, 42 WM. & MARY L. REV. 1575, 1696 (2001) (raising questions about what might happen if "a traditionally favored group of states puts in place a procedural structure that ensures their favored position will persist" in a particular area of federal lawmaking, such as highway funding). In similar fashion, if the Court *does* apply the equal-sovereignty principle in the commerce-power context, many questions will arise about how the doctrine should operate in concrete cases. In *NCAA*, for example, the court (albeit without quite saying so) offered an alternative holding for the result it reached. It did so by sharply distinguishing PASPA from the VRA on the ground that the former law, unlike the latter, did not single out a minority of states for imposition of any federally imposed *burden*: instead, it singled out a one state to receive the *benefit* of a full-scale legislative exemption. *See NCAA*, 730 F.3d at 239 (emphasizing a statutory "feature that distinguishes PASPA from the VRA—that far from singling out a handful of states for disfavored treatment, PASPA treats *more favorably* a *single* state" (emphasis in original)). This distinction has much to be said for it because in "benefit" cases, unlike "burden" cases, there is no basis for concern that a majority of states are wrongfully "ganging up" on a minority of states when the whole point of the law is to treat the targeted jurisdictions *better* than the majority. *NCAA* also illustrates a point sure to surface in other cases involving the differential treatment of states in federal laws, just as surely as it surfaces in other areas of constitutional litigation—that is, the critical role played by the manner in which a court characterizes the relevant legislative purpose. In particular, when the court in *NCAA* chose to characterize Congress's purpose in enacting PASPA not as restricting state-sanctioned sports gambling, but instead as "stop[ping] the *spread* of *state-sanctioned* sports gambling," it naturally followed that Congress's treatment of Nevada was not only sensible, but "*precisely tailored*" to achieving the relevant congressional aim. *Id.* at 239 (emphasis in original). Put another way, in light of this alignment of the "Nevada grandfathering provision" with the thus-characterized federal anti-"spread" purpose, PASPA almost surely would have satisfied even a strict application of *Shelby County*'s equal-sovereignty principle. *Id.*; *see Shelby County*, 570 U.S. at 542, 551 (allowing differential treatment of states so long as the resulting law is "sufficiently related to the problem that it targets" (internal quotation and citation omitted)). Finally, courts are likely to uphold some laws challenged under the equal-sovereignty principle because they do not directly favor some states over others, but instead merely turn out to have differential incidental effects from one jurisdiction to another. *See* Welsh, *supra* note 38, at 1024 (highlighting this distinction).

[50] In *United States v. Taylor*, No. 1:14–CR–67, 2014 WL 12676320 (W.D. Mich. Aug. 8, 2014), for example, the court declined to hold that the equal-sovereignty principle justified dismissal of a prosecution for violating a federal marijuana law founded on the commerce power because "a fundamental aspect of state sovereignty [is not] at issue here." *Id.* at *5. *Taylor* is one of many cases in which a defendant charged with violating marijuana-related restrictions imposed by the commerce-power-based Controlled Substances Act sought to invoke the equal-sovereignty principle. The claim made in these cases was that federal prosecutors had backed away from pursuing such cases in some states—in particular, those states that had legalized marijuana use—while continuing to enforce applicable federal laws in other

A different, but related, political-process-based problem might rear its head in some unusual cases that do not, like *Shelby County* and *NCAA*, involve the drawing of explicit distinctions between some states and others. While facially neutral laws with incidentally discriminatory effects will seldom run afoul of a rule designed to guard against the efforts of a majority of states to disadvantage a minority, special problems might arise in rare instances. Assume, for example, that Congress passes a generally applicable law that prohibits what it sees as the cruel treatment of animals in specified commercial settings. Assume also that this law has strong support across the nation as a whole. As it turns out, however, the statute's practical effect is to limit private citizens in only one or a very small number of states from engaging in a practice uniquely connected to local values and traditions. Might those private citizens claim that Congress has abridged a *Garcia*-based political-process principle? Could they assert, in particular, that such a law—even though nondiscriminatory on its face—at bottom reflects a *de facto* national conspiracy against, or at least an intolerable insensitivity to, a geographically defined minority group, thus generating a result intolerably destructive of the value of regional diversity that lies at the root of the federal system?[51] Laws that work this way will not surface often, and that fact in and of itself may cut against recognizing an external constraint on Congress's regulatory authority that operates in such cases.[52] At the least, however,

---

jurisdictions. *See generally* Memorandum from James M. Cole, Deputy Att'y Gen., to U.S. Att'ys, Guidance Regarding Marijuana Enforcement (Aug. 29, 2013). The courts, however, have consistently rejected these claims, including in some instances with a tip of the hat (as in *Taylor*) to the idea that the equal-sovereignty principle is inapplicable (at least ordinarily) in the commerce-power context. *See* United States v. Brecker, No. 4:14CR250 CDP (TIA), 2015 WL 1565355, at *5 (E.D. Mo. Apr. 8, 2015) (relying on *NCAA*); United States v. Heying, No. 14–30 (1) (JRT/SER), 2014 WL 5286155, at *5 (D. Minn. Oct. 15, 2014) (distinguishing *Shelby County* as "focused on the 'sensitive areas of state and local policymaking,' whereas Congress's regulation of drugs through federal criminal laws involves Congress's broad authority to 'creat[e] . . . federal crimes' " (quoting *Shelby County*, 570 U.S. at 545, and then quoting United States v. Comstock, 560 U.S. 126, 136–37 (2010)) (alterations in original)); United States v. Wilde, 74 F. Supp. 3d 1092, 1099–1100 (N.D. Cal. 2014) (summarily rejecting a *Shelby County* argument in a marijuana prosecution). For a case considering application of the doctrine in another context, see *In re Border Infrastructure Environmental Litigation*, 284 F. Supp. 3d 1092, 1144–46 (S.D. Cal. 2018) (rejecting California's *Shelby County*-based challenge to statutory waiver determinations issued by the U.S. Department of Homeland Security in connection with the federal government's construction of a "border wall" within the state).

[51] Consider, for example, an effort by the federal Congress to outlaw horse racing notwithstanding the objections of Kentucky and a small number of other states.

[52] Another problem with applying such a rule—and one that counsels, at the least, against its liberal use—involves the challenge of separating the mine run of clearly permissible enactments from measures fairly characterized as compromising distinctly foundational and deep-seated local values. *See, e.g.*, United States v. Mills, 393 F. Supp. 3d 650, 669 (E.D. Mich. 2019) (rejecting a Tenth Amendment challenge to the application of federal death-penalty sentencing in a state that disallows capital

ruminations along these lines illustrate the potential of the political-process-centered reasoning of *Garcia* to support not-yet-recognized limits on the commerce power.

B. THE ANTI-COMMANDEERING PRINCIPLE

1. *New York v. United States*

In its 1992 ruling in *New York v. United States*,[53] the Court addressed the constitutionality of a complex federal law that targeted the ever-growing problems posed by low-level radioactive waste. The portion of the statute that most troubled the Court—the so-called "take title" provision—gave each state two options for dealing with waste of this kind generated within its borders. The state could either (1) regulate the disposal of the waste in accordance with congressionally established rules, or (2) take possession of the waste and thereby become liable for all damages caused by the thus-state-controlled material.[54] In addressing the constitutionality of this statute, a six-Justice majority first endorsed a specialized federalism-based limit on federal legislative authority. Congress, the Court declared, may not "commandee[r] the legislative processes of the States by directly compelling them to enact and enforce a federal regulatory program."[55] The Court then explained why the overall choice given to the states by the challenged law amounted to just such a form of impermissible commandeering. The problem was that the forced taking of possession of this material amounted "in principle" to "a congressionally compelled subsidy from state governments to radioactive waste producers," while the forced regulation of waste disposal pursuant to federal standards amounted to a "command to state governments to implement legislation enacted by Congress."[56] And because a "choice between two unconstitutionally coercive regulatory techniques [was] no choice at all," the take-title provision ran afoul of the anti-commandeering doctrine.[57]

The Court devoted the lion's share of its opinion to attempting to show why the newly declared anti-commandeering principle found

---

punishment; reasoning that, although the law could, for example, negatively affect "the psychological well-being of Michigan citizens when they are questioned during voir dire about their ability to serve in a death-eligible case," governing authority did not permit application of the "interest-balancing test" that undergirded this line of state-autonomy-based constitutional challenge); United States v. O'Reilly, No. 05–80025, 2007 WL 2421378, at *4 (E.D. Mich. Aug. 23, 2007) (rejecting a similar line of argument).

[53] 505 U.S. 144 (1992).

[54] *Id.* at 154–55.

[55] *Id.* at 161 (quoting *Hodel*, 452 U.S. at 288).

[56] *Id.*

[57] *Id.* at 176.

support in both constitutional history and key policies that underlie the federal system. With regard to history, the Court pointed to Alexander Hamilton's *Federalist No. 15*, and other framing-era materials, as indicating that the founders chose to create a federal government that would "exercise legislative authority directly upon individuals, without employing the States as intermediaries."[58] With regard to policy, the Court worried that federal compulsion of state legislation would inevitably lead to problems of voter confusion. More specifically, if the challenged law were allowed to stand, "it may be [that] state officials . . . will bear the brunt of public disapproval [for enacting that regulatory program], while the federal officials who devised the regulatory program may remain insulated from the electoral ramifications of their decision."[59] Adherence to the anti-commandeering principle, the Court continued, would keep choices of responsible officials "in full view of the public," thus ensuring that the proper set of lawmakers—whether state or federal—would "suffer the consequences if the decision turns out to be detrimental or unpopular."[60]

The Court also concluded that the anti-commandeering principle did not mark a break from past constitutional rulings, most notably *Garcia* and *Testa v. Katt*.[61] *Garcia* was distinguishable as "a case in which Congress . . . subjected a State to the same legislation applicable to private parties" in that the FLSA applied equally to both public and private employers.[62] Here, in contrast, the challenged law failed to qualify as a "generally applicable" law because it imposed legal duties only on state governments. To be sure, the Court in *Testa* had held that Congress may require state judicial officials to carry out the enforcement of federal laws.[63] According to the Court in *New York*, however, the challenged statute's imposition of duties on state legislatures differed qualitatively from the assignment of

---

[58] *Id.* at 163–64.

[59] *Id.* at 169.

[60] *Id.* at 168. The Court also noted that accountability concerns operated even when, as in this case, state governments had fully supported the federal legislation. In particular, the Court noted that it would almost always be in the interest of both federal and state lawmakers to seek to evade responsibility for siting radioactive waste-disposal facilities because of voters' "not in my backyard" objections. Moreover, the law at issue in *New York* might well, albeit unwisely, advance this political objective by blurring the source of responsibility for governmental decisions about such waste disposal. Keeping political officials properly "accountable to the voters" supported a system in which both (1) federal legislators could not evade responsibility for their own policy choice by forcing state legislators to adopt a genuinely federal regulatory scheme and (2) state legislators could not evade responsibility for a largely unpopular program they see fit to support by seeking cover in a congressional measure that compels them to act. *Id.* at 182–83.

[61] 330 U.S. 386 (1947).

[62] *New York*, 505 U.S. at 160.

[63] *See Testa*, 330 U.S. at 393–94.

federal-law-implementation duties to state courts. Of particular importance, the Court observed, the text of the Supremacy Clause[64]—which stipulates that "Judges in every State shall be bound" by "the Laws of the United States"—authorized "federal direction of state judges" without likewise permitting Congress to mandate that state legislatures comply with federal regulatory commands.[65]

Finally, the Court emphasized that its ruling would not unduly frustrate Congress's efforts to promote sound policy. To begin with, federal lawmakers were free to regulate radioactive waste producers directly and to preempt disfavored state rules in that process.[66] No less important, Congress could encourage adoption of congressionally favored regulatory programs by the states themselves in either of two ways. First, it could occupy a field with its own regulatory program unless and until the state legislature passed a state law (such as the provision at issue in *New York*) that Congress wanted to have on the books.[67] Second, Congress could encourage the states' adoption of a federally favored regulatory program by conditioning their access to federal funds on putting that program in place.[68] In the Court's view, congressional use of these tools of "conditional preemption" or "conditional spending" differed fundamentally from the issuance of an outright federal mandate, such as the one at issue in *New York*. As Justice O'Connor explained for the Court: "Where Congress encourages state regulation rather than compelling it, state governments remain responsive to the local electorate's preferences."[69] In other words, so long as a "choice remains . . . with the residents of the State," the vice of federal commandeering is not present.[70]

2. *Printz v. United States*

The Court in *New York* held that Congress could not force state *legislatures* to enact federally favored programs, while it held in *Testa* that Congress could require state *courts* to give effect to federal laws. One last question about the propriety of federal commandeering thus remained: Could Congress use its commerce power to compel state *executive* officials, such as police officers and agency members, to implement federal-law commands? The Court

---

64 U.S. CONST. art. VI, § 2, cl. 2.

65 *New York*, 505 U.S. at 180 (internal quotations omitted).

66 *Id.* at 178.

67 *Id.* at 167–68.

68 *Id.* at 167. For a more thorough discussion of the conditional-spending power, see *infra* Chapter 8.

69 *Id.* at 168.

70 *Id.* at 174.

said "no" in *Printz v. United States*.[71] That case concerned a provision of the Brady Handgun Violence Prevention Act that required handgun dealers to give to a local law enforcement officer (that is, an agent of the state rather than federal government) prior notice of any handgun transfer to a would-be buyer. The local law enforcement officer then had to "make a reasonable effort" to determine whether the transfer to that buyer would be lawful, including by conducting "research in whatever State and local recordkeeping systems are available and in a national system designated by the Attorney General."[72] The Court had little difficulty concluding that the Act entailed federal commandeering of state authorities. Put simply, it "pressed into federal service" local law enforcement officers by "compelling [them] to execute federal laws."[73] It took 81 pages of the United States Reports, however, to sort through the majority's and the dissenters' conflicting arguments about whether such a mandate offended governing principles of constitutional federalism.

In an opinion written for a five-Justice majority, Justice Scalia acknowledged that "there is no constitutional text speaking to this precise question," so that "the answer . . . must be sought in historical understanding and practice, in the structure of the Constitution, and in the jurisprudence of this Court."[74] As to historical understanding, Justice Scalia laid weight on the "absence of executive-commandeering statutes in the early Congresses [and] in our later history as well, at least until very recent years."[75] As to the structure of the Constitution, he emphasized two points. First, upholding laws of this kind would impinge on state-autonomy values by permitting Congress "to impress into its service—and at no cost to itself—the police officers of the 50 States."[76] Second, the challenged statute raised tensions with the Constitution's directive that the President—not local law enforcement officers—"shall take Care that the Laws be

---

71 521 U.S. 898 (1997).

72 *Id.* at 903. The act imposed further obligations on local law-enforcement officers if they chose to share with handgun dealers the results of the required investigation. *Id.*

73 *Id.* at 905.

74 *Id.* Justice Scalia did, however, direct attention to the text in rebuffing the dissenters' suggestion that the challenged law was sustainable under the Necessary and Proper Clause. According to him, that provision did not support the challenged enactment because "a 'La[w] . . . for carrying into Execution' the Commerce Clause" is not "proper" within the meaning of the Necessary and Proper Clause if it "violates the principle of state sovereignty" recognized by the majority in the *Printz* case. *Id.* at 923–24 (citing Gary Lawson & Patricia B. Granger, *The "Proper" Scope of Federal Power: A Jurisdictional Interpretation of the Sweeping Clause*, 43 DUKE L.J. 267, 297–326, 330–333 (1993)).

75 *Id.* at 916.

76 *Id.* at 922.

faithfully executed."[77] Finally, with respect to past judicial authority, Justice Scalia reasoned that *New York v. United States* all but disposed of the *Printz* case. Of particular importance, Justice Scalia saw the earlier ruling's voter-accountability logic as applying with full force to the commandeering of state executive authorities. He was especially concerned that "by forcing state governments to absorb the financial burden of implementing a federal regulatory program, Members of Congress can take credit for 'solving' problems without having to ask their constituents to pay for the solutions with higher federal taxes."[78]

The dissenters sought to counter these arguments by pointing to Hamilton's statement in *The Federalist No. 27* that the federal government could "employ" the states "in the execution of its laws," as well as assertions made by James Madison and others at the ratifying conventions that state officials would collect federal taxes.[79] In addition, the dissenters contended, the majority's reliance on a lack of similar earlier enactments proved too much because such a demand for founding-era analogues to constitutionally challenged legislation would, if consistently applied, "undermine most of our post-New Deal Commerce Clause jurisprudence."[80] The dissenters also worried that the Court's ruling would endanger, rather than promote, state autonomy values. The problem, they asserted, was that the rule laid down in *Printz* would incentivize Congress to "create vast national bureaucracies to implement its policies" with no state participation at all.[81] Finally, the dissenters in *Printz*—like the dissenters in *New York*—faulted the majority for ignoring *Garcia*'s admonition that state-autonomy interests found adequate protection in the state-protective constitutional architecture of federal political

[77] *Id.* (quoting U.S. CONST. art. II, § 3).

[78] *Id.* at 930 (noting further that "even when the States are not forced to absorb the costs of implementing a federal program, they are still put in the position of taking the blame for its burdensomeness and for its defects").

[79] *See id.* at 945 (Stevens, J., dissenting) (quoting THE FEDERALIST NO. 27 (Hamilton)). The dissenters added that: "The Court's response to this powerful historical evidence is weak. The majority suggests that 'none of these statements necessarily implies [that] Congress could impose these responsibilities without the consent of the States.' No fair reading of these materials can justify such an interpretation." *Id.* at 947 (citation omitted). In a history-based critique that might well also apply to the *New York* ruling, the dissenters added that it made little sense to devise new state-autonomy-based limits on congressional authority that did not operate under even the state-favoring Articles of Confederation. *See id.* at 945–46.

[80] *Id.* at 949. In the post-1936 period, after all, the Court had sustained numerous statutes that lacked any parallels in the prior work of the federal legislative branch. *Id.*

[81] *Id.* at 959. The dissenters added that, in their view, the majority's accountability logic was shaky because state officials forced to implement bad federal policy would be certain to proclaim "to their constituents where the source of the misfortune lies." *Id.* at 957 n.18.

institutions.[82] By 1997, however, arguments based on *Garcia* were carrying little water with the same five-Justice majority that, two years earlier, had handed down *Lopez*.[83]

3. Refining the Anti-Commandeering Principle: *Reno v. Condon* and *Murphy v. NCAA*

While *New York* and *Printz* established the foundations of the anti-commandeering principle, two more recent decisions of the Court have further developed its contours. First, in *Reno v. Condon*,[84] the Court upheld against anti-commandeering attack a federal law that restricted sales by the states of personal data gathered from automobile-license applications. This law, Chief Justice Rehnquist concluded, did not run afoul of the *Printz* prohibition. Instead, it was functionally indistinguishable from the federal law withdrawing tax-exempt status for state-issued bearer bonds, which the Court had sustained in *South Carolina v. Baker*.[85] To be sure, the statute challenged in *Condon* did "regulate[ ] state activities."[86] But it did not (as in *New York* and in *Printz*) "control or influence the manner in which States regulate private parties."[87] Nor was the law in *Condon* objectionable on the proposed alternative ground that Congress goes too far whenever "it regulates the States exclusively."[88] To this argument, Chief Justice Rehnquist responded that it was unnecessary to "address the question whether general applicability is a constitutional requirement for federal regulation of the States" because the statute was in fact generally applicable.[89] This characterization fit the challenged law, he continued, because it "regulates the universe of entities that participate as suppliers to the market for motor vehicle information—the States as initial suppliers

[82] *See id.* at 957.

[83] For a discussion of *United States v. Lopez*, 514 U.S. 549 (1995), see *supra* Section 4.A. Notably, the Court's decision in *Printz* came only a year after its significant expansion of the scope of state-sovereign-immunity protections in *Seminole Tribe of Florida v. Florida*, 517 U.S. 44 (1996). *See infra* Section 5.C. As noted by Professor Henry Monaghan and others, the Court in that case could have relied on the anti-commandeering principle to invalidate the challenged federal law, which required state authorities to engage in negotiations with the leaders of Native nations. Henry Paul Monaghan, Comment, *The Sovereign Immunity "Exception,"* 110 HARV. L. REV. 102, 119–20 (1996). It may be, however, that the Court chose not to go that route precisely because, as of the time that *Seminole Tribe* was decided, the Court had not yet extended, as it did in *Printz*, the principle of *New York v. United States* to encompass federal commandeering of state executive officials.

[84] 528 U.S. 141 (2000).

[85] *See supra* notes 23–25 and accompanying text.

[86] *Baker*, 485 U.S. at 512 (internal quotations omitted).

[87] *Condon*, 528 U.S. at 150 (quoting *Baker*, 485 U.S. at 514–15).

[88] *Id.* at 151. For a more detailed elaboration of this theory, at least in its application to particularly problematic federal laws, see *supra* Section 5.2.A.

[89] *Condon*, 528 U.S., at 151.

of the information in interstate commerce and private resellers or redisclosers of that information in commerce."[90]

The Court again considered the scope of the anti-commandeering principle in *Murphy v. NCAA*,[91] and this time, unlike in *Condon*, the Justices found that Congress had gone too far. *Murphy* arose after the NCAA asserted that legislation enacted by New Jersey conflicted with a federal statute generally prohibiting states from "authoriz[ing]" or "licens[ing]" a sports-gambling operation.[92] New Jersey in fact had previously enacted its own ban on sports gambling as a general matter. Following passage of the federal prohibition, however, the state repealed major portions of its prior law, thus permitting certain firms (for example, firms located in Atlantic City) to undertake sports-gambling operations.[93] The NCAA argued that the case was one of straightforward federal preemption premised on a statute, enacted pursuant to the commerce power, that directly prohibited exactly what New Jersey had done.[94] In an opinion by Justice Alito, however, a seven-Justice majority disagreed, concluding that the purportedly preemptive federal law itself was unconstitutional because it contravened the anti-commandeering principle.[95]

The critical point, according to Justice Alito, was that "Congress cannot issue direct orders to state legislatures," whether those orders involve an "affirmative" command or—as in this case—a "prohibition" on repealing an existing state law.[96] As he explained: "Suppose Congress ordered States with legalized sports betting to take the affirmative step of criminalizing that activity and ordered the remaining States to retain their laws prohibiting sports betting. There is no good reason why the former would intrude more deeply on state sovereignty than the latter."[97] In addition, Justice Alito

---

90 *Id.*

91 138 S. Ct. 1461 (2018).

92 *Id.* at 1472; *see also supra* Section 5.A.2.b (discussing earlier lower-court litigation concerning this same statute's validity under the equal-sovereignty principle).

93 *Id.* at 1471.

94 *Id.* at 1473.

95 *Id.* at 1481. In a dissenting opinion in *Murphy*, Justice Ginsburg, joined by Justice Sotomayor, disagreed with the majority's separate conclusion that other important features of the federal law were inseverable from the invalidated ban on state authorization, while only "[a]ssuming[ ] arguendo" that the majority's anti-commandeering analysis was correct. *Id.* at 1489 (Ginsburg, J., dissenting). Justice Breyer agreed with Justice's Ginsburg's position on the severability issue but joined those portions of Justice Alito's opinion that explained why a violation of the anti-commandeering rule had occurred. *See id.* at 1488 (Breyer, J., concurring in part and dissenting in part).

96 *Id.* at 1478 (majority opinion).

97 *Id.*

maintained that the Court's preemption jurisprudence lent no support to Congress's effort to shape New Jersey's gambling-law regime by way of the challenged prohibition. The Supremacy Clause, he emphasized, "is not an independent grant of legislative power to Congress."[98] Moreover, the federal statute at issue in the case was not sustainable as a proper exercise of the commerce power precisely because it ran afoul of the anti-commandeering principle.[99] Without question, he acknowledged, Congress possesses the authority to displace state laws with preemptive legislation adopted as part of a federal program that itself regulates private actors.[100] Put another way, Congress can invoke its enumerated powers in fixing the rights and duties of private persons, while also specifying that those persons are "free from any other [state] requirements" apart from those Congress chooses to leave in place.[101] In this case, however, the challenged federal law did not either "confer any federal rights on private actors interested in conducting sports gambling operations" or "impose any federal restrictions on private actors."[102] There was, accordingly, "no way to understand the provision prohibiting state authorization as anything other than a direct command to the States," so that ordinary principles of preemption were beside the point.[103]

As the Court in *Murphy* took with one hand, however, it also gave with the other. It did so by highlighting three ways in which Congress can pressure states to act in keeping with federal goals. First, citing *Condon*, the Court reaffirmed that the "[t]he anticommandeering doctrine does not apply when Congress evenhandedly regulates an activity in which both States and private actors engage."[104] Second, citing *South Carolina v. Baker*,[105] the Court acknowledged that Congress could continue to impose duties on non-state actors that have "the indirect effect of pressuring states" to abandon preexisting policy choices,[106] as it had validly done when

---

98 *Id.* at 1479.

99 *See id.* at 1478.

100 *Id.* at 1481.

101 *Id.*

102 *Id.*

103 *Id.* For a detailed effort to distinguish preemption from commandeering based on the framework laid down in *Murphy*, see Edward A. Hartnett, *Distinguishing Permissible Preemption from Unconstitutional Commandeering*, 96 NOTRE DAME L. REV. 351, 361 (2020) (explaining that "[i]f the national government directly regulates the people, and requires a state to stand aside, that is permissible preemption" but that "if the national government attempts to require a state to govern according to Congress's instructions by using a state against its will to regulate its people, that is impermissible commandeering").

104 *Murphy*, 138 S. Ct. at 1478.

105 485 U.S. 505 (1988).

106 *Murphy*, 138 S. Ct. at 1478.

it stripped away favorable federal income-tax treatment previously given to private persons for interest paid on unregistered state bonds.[107] Third, the Court made clear that Congress remained able to adopt conditional-preemption schemes under which states have the "choice of 'either implement[ing]' the federal program 'or else yield[ing] to a federally administered regulatory program.' "[108] As a result, *Murphy* did not undo the holding of *Hodel v. Virginia Surface Mining & Reclamation Assn., Inc.*,[109] in which the Court had sustained a federal law that gave states the option of regulating coal mining pursuant to federal standards or having their own coal-mining laws displaced by rules administered entirely by federal authorities.[110]

---

107 *Baker*, 485 U.S. at 514–15 (discussed *supra* notes 23–25 and accompanying text); *see Murphy*, 138 S. Ct. at 1478 (noting that no anti-commandeering problem inhered in the federal bearer-bond statute because it "did not order the States to enact or maintain any existing laws").

108 *Id.* at 1479 (quoting *Hodel*, 452 U.S. at 289).

109 452 U.S. 264 (1981).

110 *Murphy* also gave no indication that Congress could not continue to make use of conditional-spending programs to induce states to implement federal programs. *See infra* Chapter 8. For a case in which the Court used logic rooted in the Court's spending-power jurisprudence to reject an anti-commandeering challenge directed at a federal taxing measure, see *Mnuchin*, 408 F. Supp. 3d at 418–22 (upholding a cap on the federal income-tax deduction for taxes paid to state and local government and thus rejecting the argument that the law impermissibly arm-twists states to reduce their taxing levels; reasoning that, under cases such as *South Dakota v. Dole*, 483 U.S. 203 (1987), purposeful congressional efforts to reshape state laws do not ipso facto run afoul of the "gun to the head" principle of *NFIB v. Sebelius*, 567 U.S. 519 (2012), discussed *infra* Section 8.C, and that here there was no impermissible "coercion" because the challenged law's "implications are difficult to predict" at most and, in any event, did not portend "budgetary catastrophe," as in *NFIB* (internal quotations omitted)). For additional lower-court cases, in some of which the courts found at least potential anti-commandeering problems notwithstanding these limitations, see *City of Chicago v. Barr*, 961 F.3d 882, 898 (7th Cir. 2020) (declining to address a challenge to limits established by a federal grant program for state and local law enforcement agencies based on an application of the principle of constitutional avoidance, but first mentioning the district court's determination that the challenged statute "was unconstitutional under the anticommandeering doctrine of the Tenth Amendment" because "a state's ability to control its offices and employees is at the heart of state sovereignty"; noting that the lower court concluded that the challenged law commandeered state action by "eliminat[ing] the ability of a locality such as Chicago to control its employees' communications with federal immigration authorities" and preventing that locality from "extricating itself from federal immigration enforcement"), and *City of Philadelphia v. Sessions*, 309 F. Supp. 3d 271 (E.D. Pa. 2018) (holding that the city plausibly pleaded violations of the anti-commandeering principle). *See generally infra* Section 8.C (discussing cases presenting challenges to conditional-spending programs founded on claims that their excessive coerciveness caused them to run afoul of the anti-commandeering rule). For a fractured ruling in which different judges took different views of how the anti-commandeering principle applies to five separate provisions of the Indian Child Welfare Act, see *Brackeen v. Haaland*, 994 F.3d 249. 268–69 (5th Cir. 2021) (en banc), *cert granted*, 142 S. Ct. 1205 (2022).

4. The Future of the Anti-Commandeering Principle

Murphy has raised a cluster of questions about the future of the anti-commandeering doctrine. Consider, for instance, the Court's treatment in *Murphy* of *FERC v. Mississippi*,[111] in which it upheld a federal law that required state utility regulators to consider imposing—but did not require them to impose—regulations developed by federal authorities to cut back on the use of oil and natural gas. In *Murphy*, the Court could and did distinguish *FERC* on the ground that it involved only a "modest requirement" that did nothing more than "require states to *consider* Congress's preference."[112] But will this distinction hold up in the future? The Court in *Murphy* observed in the process of distinguishing *FERC* that the federal law challenged in that case "issued no command to a state legislature."[113] But the law in fact did issue a "command" by requiring state decisionmakers to consider adoption of federal proposals. To be sure, that command targeted state agencies rather than the state legislatures. But that fact seems doctrinally inconsequential in light of the Court's undiminished application of the anti-commandeering principle to state executive officials in *Printz*.[114]

Also posing problems for the continued efficacy of *FERC* (and other pre-*Murphy* precedents) was Justice Alito's striking suggestion that the anti-commandeering principle derived from the fact that a congressional power to commandeer state governments was "conspicuously absent from the list of powers given to Congress" by Article I.[115] At least in the absence of further elaboration, this not-expressly-enumerated rationale is subject to serious criticism.[116]

---

[111] 456 U.S. 742 (1982).

[112] *Murphy*, 138 S. Ct. at 1479 (emphasis in original).

[113] *Id.*

[114] *See supra* Section 5.B. *Printz* also casts a shadow over would-be efforts to exempt the *FERC* rule from the anti-commandeering doctrine on the theory that the rule involved only a "modest requirement." *Murphy*, 138 S. Ct. at 1479. Indeed, in invalidating the federal gun-background-check law, the Court in *Printz* specifically rejected an effort to defend that measure on the ground it imposed "a minimal and only temporary burden upon state officers." *Printz*, 521 U.S. at 932.

[115] *Murphy*, 138 S. Ct. at 1476.

[116] Among other things, the majority's view of the text seems to overlook the critical difference between the enumeration of "objects" that Congress may pursue and the non-enumeration of "means" (presumably including laws directed at states) that Congress may put to use in pursuing those objects. *See* THE FEDERALIST NO. 10 (Madison). Thus (to use Justice Alito's own words), "conspicuously absent from the list of powers given to Congress" in Article I are powers to pass criminal laws (except in unusual instances), to impose criminal sentences (including even the death sentence), to establish federal agencies, and to impose a military draft. But there is no doubt that Congress can act in all of these ways under the Necessary and Proper Clause to carry into execution the enumerated powers it possesses. It is telling in this regard that the Court in *Printz* clearly, and properly, eschewed the text-based failure-to-enumerate

Even so, at least for now, it lurks in an opinion joined by seven members of the Court. And if the relevant principle dictates that Congress may not "issue direct orders to the government of States," because no words in the Constitution affirmatively authorize such action, it is hard to see how even *FERC*-like "direct orders" to consider adoption of a federally endorsed program (of which the constitutional text also makes no mention) could escape an anti-commandeering attack.

It is true that the Court in *Murphy* grouped its treatment of *FERC* with its treatment of *Condon*, *Baker*, and *Hodel*, reasoning that none of the four cases involved "a federal statute that commanded state legislatures to *enact or refrain from enacting* state law."[117] And if a proper articulation of the post-*Murphy* anti-commandeering principle does in fact focus on the forced "enacting," or retention, of state laws, rules such as the one upheld in *FERC* should survive. There is also the matter of *stare decisis*, which may lead the Court to stick with *FERC*, despite its tension with *Murphy*, particularly in light of the concededly "modest" burden that just-think-about-this-idea congressional dictates impose.[118] On the other hand, the Court in *Murphy* went out of its way to note that *FERC* "was decided well before our decisions in *New York* and *Printz*,"[119] and constitutional prognosticators might well detect in this passage an ominous message about the future of *FERC*. At the least, it is clear that the rule of that case—in contrast to the rules of *Condon*, *Baker*, and *Hodel*—now lies in a constitutional danger zone.

Another question about the scope of the post-*Murphy* anti-commandeering rule stems from Justice O'Connor's earlier concurring opinion in *Printz*.[120] The Court, she wrote in that case, was not passing on the constitutionality of "purely ministerial reporting requirements imposed by Congress on state and local authorities," including requirements that those authorities identify "cases of missing children to the Department of Justice."[121] A strong supporter of the anti-commandeering principle might well argue that *Murphy* renders such requirements unconstitutional because (to use the language of that case) they "issue direct orders to the governments of the States"—namely, "direct orders" to turn over

line of argument that the Court seemed to embrace in *Murphy*, by acknowledging without hesitation that "there is no constitutional text speaking to this precise question." *Printz*, 521 U.S. at 905.

117 *Murphy*, 138 S. Ct. at 1478 (emphasis added).

118 *Id.* at 1479.

119 *Id.*

120 521 U.S. at 935–36 (O'Connor, J., concurring).

121 *Id.* at 936.

federally specified information.[122] Supporting that conclusion, such an analyst might add, are the policy concerns flagged in *Murphy* (as well as *Printz*) about Congress's "shifting the costs of regulation to the states."[123] Compiling and transmitting state-held information to federal authorities, after all, will saddle states with costs they may prefer not to bear.[124]

---

[122] *Murphy*, 138 S. Ct. at 1476.

[123] *Id.* at 1477.

[124] Notably, some post-*Murphy* lower-court rulings have struck down rules that address the subject of information-sharing. Specifically, several lower courts have held that 8 U.S.C. § 1373, which in effect requires state and local governments to provide to federal authorities certain information about noncitizens, "does just what *Murphy* proscribes: it tells States they may not prohibit . . . the sharing of information regarding immigration status with the INS or other government entities." City & Cty. of San Francisco v. Sessions, 349 F. Supp. 3d 924, 952 (N.D. Cal. 2018) (quoting United States v. California 314 F. Supp. 3d 1077, 1099 (E.D. Cal. 2018)), *aff'd on other grounds sub nom.* City & Cty. of San Francisco v. Barr, 965 F.3d 753 (9th Cir. 2020). (In so holding, these courts have also necessarily rejected the suggestion that Congress's immigration-related powers might be subject to a more lenient set of commandeering-based constraints. For more on this possibility, see *infra* Section 10.E.2.) Among other things, these courts have reasoned that section 1373 does not act as a mere "ministerial information-sharing statute" but that it "takes control over [a] State's ability to command its own law enforcement" officers. *City & Cty. of San Francisco*, 349 F. Supp. 3d at 953. Some of these courts have further reasoned that section 1373 "goes beyond information-sharing" by "requir[ing] local policymakers to stand aside and allow the federal government to conscript the time and cooperation of local employees" in support of federal regulatory objectives. *Id.* (quoting City of Chicago v. Sessions, 321 F. Supp. 3d 855, 873 (N.D. Ill. 2018)); *see also* United States v. California, 921 F. 3d 865, 891 (9th Cir. 2019) (emphasizing, with respect to section 1373, that "the federal government was free to *expect* as much as it wanted, but it could not *require* California's cooperation without running afoul of the Tenth Amendment" (emphasis in original)); *City of Chicago v. Sessions*, 321 F. Supp. 3d at 869 (holding section 1373 invalid because it commandeers states by preventing them from "limiting the amount of paid time [their] employees use to communicate with INS"), *aff'd on other grounds sub nom.* City of Chicago v. Barr, 961 F. 3d 882 (7th Cir. 2020); *cf.* Colorado v. U.S. Dep't of Justice, 455 F. Supp. 3d 1034, 1060 (D. Colo. 2020) (discussing, but not ruling on, the question whether section 1373 and a related requirement violate the anti-commandeering doctrine, while characterizing them as "more than just[ ] information-sharing provision[s]" that may "impermissibly intrude upon the functioning of state and local governments" (alterations in original; quoting *City of Chicago*, 321 F. Supp. 3d at 872)). In *Oregon v. Trump*, 406 F. Supp. 3d 940 (D. Or. 2019), the court explicitly rejected the notion that there is an "information-sharing carveout to the anti-commandeering doctrine." *Id.* at 973. But it also noted that, even if some such exception exists, section 1373 is more problematic than the information-sharing statutes described in the *Printz* concurrence because its form of conscripting the services of state and local officials involves much more than the imposition of a "purely ministerial" reporting requirement. *Id.* Supporting this proposition is a functional notion that aligns with the basic policies that underlie the federal system. On this view, it is one thing—indeed, a thing fairly characterized as "ministerial"—to have states report missing-children information to federal authorities whose resulting collaboration may be critically helpful (and well-understood by the state itself to be critically helpful) to the states as they discharge their own core police powers in an uncontroversial, needful, and humane way. But it is a different thing for Congress to commandeer states to assist national law-enforcement authorities in discharging their distinctly federal responsibility over immigration in a manner that directly contravenes state or local choices, and especially choices concerning deeply held views of policy, morality, proper resource use, and even what persons are viewed as members

There is reason to conclude, however, that the federal missing-children-report law is unlikely to fall victim to the anti-commandeering rule. To begin with, it seems fair to say that this measure does not operate to "regulate the States' sovereign authority to 'regulate their own citizens.' "[125] Such a law, after all, does not require state officers to monitor or otherwise interact with private persons in rooting out or punishing conduct made wrongful by federal law or even (as in *FERC*) require state officials to take the time to consider whether they should regulate private persons in a new and federally favored way.[126] Instead, the law simply calls on states to send along information that they already have gathered in the ordinary course of their operations,[127] much as federal tax law requires taxpaying corporations to submit information that those corporations have gathered in the ordinary course of their business

---

of the self-governing polity's own community as determined by that polity itself. *See City & County of San Francisco*, 349 F. Supp. 3d at 953 (noting the careful nature of state and local choices not to comply with federal requests based on underlying views about "the decidedly negative impact that entanglement with federal immigration enforcement has on community trust and reducing crime"). Post-*Murphy* decisions also have rejected the argument that section 1373 should escape challenge because it applies equally to private and public actors—not surprisingly, because "by [its] terms, Section 1373 . . . affect[s] only state and local government 'entit[ies] and official[s].' " *Oregon*, 406 F. Supp. 3d at 972 (citations omitted); *see City of Chicago*, 321 F. Supp. 3d at 868 ("Who but a government actor can restrict the activities of a government entity or official?"). At least one circuit court, however, has questioned the notion that section 1373 on its face violates the anti-commandeering doctrine. *See* New York v. U.S. Dep't of Justice, 951 F.3d 84, 113–14 (2d Cir. 2020) (rejecting a lower court's finding of facial unconstitutionality and noting that lower courts could not find a violation without identifying "what reserved power States have to enact laws or policies seemingly foreclosed by [section 1373]"). For a more detailed look at the constitutionality of Section 1373 and the question whether any information-sharing exception to the anti-commandeering doctrine exists, see Ilya Somin, *Making Federalism Great Again: How the Trump Administration's Attack on Sanctuary Cities Unintentionally Strengthened Judicial Protection for State Autonomy*, 97 TEX. L. REV. 1247, 1282–84 (2019). *See also* Toni M. Massaro & Shefali Milczarek-Desai, *Constitutional Cities: Sanctuary Jurisdictions, Local Voice, and Individual Liberty*, 50 COLUM. HUM. RTS. L. REV. 1, 39–51 (2018) (arguing that *Murphy* casts doubt on the constitutionality of section 1373); Josh Blackman, *Improper Commandeering*, 21 U. PA. J. CONST. L. 959, 983–89 (2019) (arguing that section 1373 is not a "proper" means under the Necessary and Proper Clause for carrying into effect Congress's power over either commerce or immigration).

[125] *Murphy*, 138 S. Ct. at 1479 (citations omitted). Justice O'Connor made much the same point in *Printz*. *See* 521 U.S. at 936 (O'Connor, J., concurring).

[126] A very different case would be presented, for example, if Congress compelled states to make available their machinery used to inflict the death penalty to help in carrying out capital sentences imposed on federal defendants convicted of federal crimes. Death-penalty opponents have directed challenges along these lines at the Federal Death Penalty Act. At least so far, however, courts have sidestepped these challenges by invoking the doctrine of ripeness. *See, e.g., Mills*, 393 F. Supp. 3d at 668 (noting other cases reaching the same result). *See generally infra* Section 35.B (discussing ripeness principles).

[127] *See* 34 U.S.C. § 41307 ("Each Federal, State, and local law enforcement agency shall report each case of a missing child . . . reported to such agency to the National Crime Information Center of the Department of Justice.").

operations. To be sure, the missing-children-report law imposes a duty only on state officials, but that seems sensible in this context because only state officials are in a position to have the relevant data.[128] And it is hard to imagine a state's people recoiling, based on some meaningful localized value choice, at the idea of helping the federal government find missing children who are residents of the state and may have been wrongfully taken elsewhere.[129]

A final question raised by the anti-commandeering cases concerns the extent to which the principle applies to congressional action not based on the commerce power. This subject gets closer attention in a later chapter.[130] For now, however, cases involving the federal Motor Voter Law[131] serve to illustrate the key point. That law

---

[128] For this same reason, it seems that a key argument offered in *Murphy* for the anti-commandeering rule—namely, that the rule "promotes political accountability"—carries little, if any, force in the missing-children-report context. 138 S. Ct. at 1477. Perhaps supporters of the anti-commandeering doctrine will claim that voters will inaccurately condemn state officials, rather than federal officials, when those state officials incur costs involved in complying with a federally required information-sharing program. But that possibility seems far more theoretical than real, at least in the absence of a specific demonstration that the costs of complying with such a federal requirement impose a meaningful burden on the state. In any event, the danger that "responsibility is blurred" in this setting is dramatically less than when "a State imposes regulations" that directly concern the behavior of private citizens as a result of federal (as opposed to its own) policy choices. *Id.* To be sure, it may be that some information-sharing mandates raise serious questions rooted in principles of federalism because they trigger high-stakes conflicts between deeply significant and competing value choices. In particular, one can imagine particular cases in which federal directives aimed at state officials, including as to sharing information, raise concerns about compromising serious state-based autonomy interests. *See supra* note 124 (discussing information-sharing mandates regarding undocumented immigrants). Constitutional problems would leap into view, for example, if federal information-sharing laws required the disclosure of information (*e.g.*, about religious beliefs or mental illness) that state or local decision-makers had decided not to share with others due to personal privacy concerns. It is not easy to conclude, however, that a duty to share information about missing children presents any problem of this sort.

[129] A point of practical importance also overhangs this subject: Even if courts were to strike down the present-day federal missing-children reporting law, it might be that workarounds would be available to federal lawmakers. Congress could, for example, apply missing-children-reporting rules both to the states and to similarly situated private entities, thus bringing those rules within the generally-applicable-law principle invoked in *Condon* and reaffirmed in *Murphy*. A counterargument would be that permitting such a work-around would glorify form over substance because the resulting burden would be borne for all practical purposes overwhelmingly by the states. A similar argument, however, was surely available in *Condon* itself, since the federal rule regarding *state* driver's license data obviously had its primary impact on the *states* themselves. (Indeed, at least going into the future, the law could be expected to have no effect on private purveyors of such data, precisely because that data could be obtained, if at all, only from state-transferors.) In addition, it might turn out that a generally applicable mandate to provide reports about missing children would not only apply to the states as a practical matter. One can imagine, for example, that nonprofit entities focused on child welfare would, to the extent possible, gather information of this kind.

[130] *See infra* Section 13.B.

[131] 52 U.S.C. §§ 20501–20511 (2018).

compels state officials to follow federally imposed dictates as to voter registration as local residents apply for drivers' licenses. Even though the law thus commandeers state regulatory behavior, lower courts have consistently upheld it on the ground that it comports with Congress's Article I, section 4 power to override state laws concerning the "Times, Places and Manner of holding Elections for Senators and Representatives."[132] More specifically, these courts have reasoned that Congress's authority to control "the Manner" of federal elections carries with it the authority to establish regulatory controls regarding registration with which state officials must comply.[133] The Motor Voter Law cases provide a powerful reminder of a basic point: External limits on congressional authority might well vary in their effects from one enumerated congressional power to the next.

C. STATE SOVEREIGN IMMUNITY AND THE ANTI-LIABILITY PRINCIPLE

1. State Sovereign Immunity: A Brief Introduction

Another external constraint on congressional authority stems from the law of sovereign immunity, which generally operates to insulate state governments from lawsuits brought against them without their consent. The underlying idea has its roots in the English common law, which long ago endorsed the view that the sovereign monarch "could do no wrong" and therefore was not amenable to suit.[134] The states of the Confederation-era regime asserted an analogous immunity on their own behalf,[135] but Article III's creation of an independent federal judiciary—and its explicit recognition that "the judicial Power [of the United States] shall extend to . . . Controversies . . . between a state and citizens of another state"[136]—raised questions about the continued viability of

---

[132] U.S. CONST. art. I, § 4, cl. 1. *See, e.g.*, Voting Rights Coalition v. Wilson, 60 F.3d 1411, 1415 (9th Cir. 1995); Ass'n of Cmty. Orgs. For Reform Now (ACORN) v. Edgar, 56 F.3d 791, 792–97 (7th Cir. 1995).

[133] As Judge Posner observed, the distinctive terms of the Elections Clause support this result because, under it, "Congress can . . . regulate federal elections *and* force the state to bear the expense of the regulation." *ACORN*, 56 F.3d at 795 (emphasis in original); *see also infra* Section 9.A (noting more generally the nonapplicability of the anti-commandeering doctrine to Congress's power to regulate federal elections).

[134] Nevada v. Hall, 440 U.S. 410, 414–15 (1979) (citing 1 BLACKSTONE'S COMMENTARIES *256), *overruled on other grounds by* Franchise Tax Bd. of Cal. v. Hyatt, 139 S. Ct. 1485 (2019).

[135] *See* Caleb Nelson, *Sovereign Immunity as a Doctrine of Personal Jurisdiction*, 115 HARV. L. REV. 1559, 1577 (2002) (noting that, during this time period, "people of widely varying perspectives agreed that unconsenting states were not amenable to suit by individuals").

[136] U.S. CONST. art. III, § 2.

that principle in the post-ratification constitutional world.[137] The Court addressed the key issue in its 1793 decision in *Chisholm v. Georgia*,[138] with four of the then-sitting five Justices endorsing the proposition that the Article III grant of "diversity" jurisdiction over suits between states and citizens of other states did indeed preclude the states from asserting sovereign immunity in such cases.[139] But that decision sparked a public outcry, leading to the almost-immediate ratification of the Eleventh Amendment. That provision stipulates that "[t]he Judicial power of the United States shall not be construed to extend to any suit in law or equity, commenced or prosecuted against one of the United States by Citizens of another State, or by Citizens or Subjects of any Foreign State."[140]

The Eleventh Amendment's ratification left no doubt that the Constitution's grant of federal-court jurisdiction over state-defendant diversity actions no longer negated the sovereign-immunity defense in suits of that kind. But a point of uncertainty remained: Did the amendment apply *only* to those state-noncitizen cases (such as *Chisholm*) that fell exclusively within the federal courts' diversity jurisdiction, or did it also cover other state-noncitizen cases, particularly federal-question cases, that were independently authorized by another jurisdictional provision of Article III?[141]

---

137 *Compare, e.g.*, 3 JONATHAN ELLIOT, DEBATES IN THE SEVERAL STATE CONVENTIONS ON THE ADOPTION OF THE FEDERAL CONSTITUTION 573 (1836) (statement of Edmund Randolph) (contending, at Virginia's ratification convention, that Article III would "render valid and effective existing claims" against the states), *with id.* at 555–56 (statement of John Marshall) (maintaining, with respect to the Article III grant of jurisdiction over suits between states and noncitizens, that "[t]he intent is, to enable states to recover claims of individuals residing in other states" and that "I hope that no gentleman will think that a state will be called at the bar of the federal court"); *id.* at 533 (statement of James Madison) (contending that, under Article III, "[i]t is not in the power of individuals to call any state into court").

138 2 U.S. (2 Dall.) 419 (1793).

139 *See* Seminole Tribe v. Florida, 517 U.S. 44, 106 (1996) (Souter, J., dissenting) (noting that "[t]he 4–1 majority [in *Chisholm*] adopted the reasonable (although not compelled) interpretation that the first of the two Citizen-State Diversity Clauses abrogated for purposes of federal jurisdiction any immunity the States might have enjoyed in their own courts"). The suit involved a common-law action brought by the estate of a South Carolina merchant seeking to recover on a debt owed by Georgia for purchases made during the Revolutionary War. *See* William A. Fletcher, *A Historical Interpretation of the Eleventh Amendment: A Narrow Construction of an Affirmative Grant of Jurisdiction Rather Than a Prohibition Against Jurisdiction*, 35 STAN. L. REV. 1033, 1054–56 (1983).

140 U.S. CONST. amend. XI.

141 *See Id.* art. III, § 2 (providing that "the judicial power shall extend to all cases, in law and equity, arising under this Constitution, the laws of the United States, and treaties made, or which shall be made, under their authority"). Scholars have long voiced competing views on this question. For a defense of the first, "literalist" view, see, e.g., William Baude & Stephen E. Sachs, *The Misunderstood Eleventh Amendment*, 169 U. PA. L. REV. 609, 614 (2021) (contending that the amendment's limits "apply across-the-board, whatever the head of federal jurisdiction"), and Lawrence C. Marshall, *Fighting the Words of the Eleventh Amendment*, 102 HARV. L.

Surprisingly, the Court in *Hans v. Louisiana*[142] would respond to that question by embracing neither position,[143] concluding instead that state-sovereign-immunity protections apply not only to all suits brought by noncitizens against a state but also to all suits brought against a state by *its own citizens* as well.[144] The ruling in that case

---

REV. 1342, 1346 (1986) ("[T]he amendment precludes federal jurisdiction over 'any suit in law or equity commenced or prosecuted against one of the United States by Citizens of another State, or by Citizens or Subjects of any Foreign State.' Thus, even if an out-of-state citizen brings the case under the federal question head of jurisdiction, the suit is barred."). For endorsements of the second, "diversity view," see, e.g., Akhil Reed Amar, *Of Sovereignty and Federalism*, 96 YALE L.J. 1425, 1474–75 (1987) (contending that the "jurisdictional repeal" occasioned by the Eleventh Amendment "was not designed as a barrier cutting across the other jurisdictional grants of Article III" and that it therefore "would not *oust* jurisdiction that was independently grounded—for example, in federal question or admiralty cases" (emphasis in original)), and William A. Fletcher, *The Diversity Explanation of the Eleventh Amendment: A Reply to Critics*, 56 U. CHI. L. REV. 1261, 1264 (1989) ("[T]he Eleventh Amendment was not intended to eliminate or restrict other heads of jurisdiction. If jurisdiction existed over a suit against a state under the admiralty jurisdiction or the federal question jurisdiction before the passage of the amendment, such jurisdiction continued to exist after its passage."). *But cf. id.* at 1292 (noting the possibility that the adopters of the Amendment did not decisively resolve the question of sovereign immunity in federal-question cases but "were simply postponing it").

142 134 U.S. 1 (1890).

143 More specifically, Justice Joseph Bradley reasoned for the majority: (a) that the drafters and ratifiers of the Eleventh Amendment sought to give full effect to Justice Iredell's *Chisholm* dissent, *see id.* at 12; *but see* John F. Manning, *The Eleventh Amendment and the Reading of Precise Constitutional Texts*, 113 YALE L.J. 1663, 1670 (2004) (criticizing this position in light of the "precise rule-like terms" of the Eleventh Amendment's text); (b) that the Iredell dissent endorsed the no-holds-barred view that private parties could never sue a state in federal court without its consent, *see Hans*, 134 U.S. at 12; *but see* John V. Orth, *The Truth About Justice Iredell's Dissent in* Chisholm v. Georgia *(1793)*, 73 N.C. L. REV. 255, 263 (1994) (asserting that Justice Iredell's dissent did not address the constitutional issue but instead "rested solely . . . on his interpretation of the Federal Judiciary Act of 1789," which he understood as not authorizing the Court to hear "an action of assumpsit" against a State (quoting *Chisholm*, 2 U.S. at 430 (Iredell, J., dissenting))); and therefore (c) that the amendment had a "force and meaning" that far exceeded the dictates of its text. *Hans*, 134 U.S. at 12. Not surprisingly, this reasoning has triggered an avalanche of scholarly criticism. *See generally* James E. Pfander, *History and State Suability: An "Explanatory" Account of the Eleventh Amendment*, 83 CORNELL L. REV. 1269, 1272 (1998) (noting that proponents of both the "so-called diversity and literal explanations of the Eleventh Amendment . . . believe that the *Hans* Court erred"). *But see* Alfred Hill, *In Defense of our Law of Sovereign Immunity*, 42 B.C. L. REV. 485, 517–20 (2001) (offering a defense of *Hans*).

144 Many commentators have suggested that the Court's decision in *Hans* was politically motivated. Hans's suit was one of many that had been brought on behalf of creditors seeking to recover on Civil War-related debts owed to them by the southern states. With the fall of Reconstruction, however, these states had been recaptured by white supremacist "redeemer" governments, whose officials and constituencies refused to pay war debts because they were viewed as "symbols of 'Yankee domination,' social radicalism, and the alleged corruption that had characterized the era of 'black rule.' " Edward A. Purcell, Jr., *The Particularly Dubious Case of* Hans v. Louisiana: *An Essay on Law, Race, History, and "Federal Courts,"* 81 N.C. L. REV. 1927, 1946 (2003) (citing ERIC FONER, RECONSTRUCTION: AMERICA'S UNFINISHED REVOLUTION, 1863–1877, at 382–88 (1988)). Then-operative Contract Clause doctrine supported the idea that the states were constitutionally barred from repudiating their debts in this fashion. But

also established a more general point of law that the Court has since repeatedly reaffirmed: The protections of state sovereign immunity extend well beyond those cases referenced by the text of the Eleventh Amendment itself.[145]

At the same time, several important limits on sovereign immunity continue to permit federal-court adjudication of some types of suits against states and affiliated parties. Most important, the Court in *Ex parte Young*[146] famously deemed sovereign immunity inapplicable in suits in which plaintiffs do not seek monetary relief from the state for past violations of federal law, but instead seek *injunctive* relief against *state officials* for *ongoing* violations of federal law.[147] The Court also has concluded that sovereign immunity does

---

the Justices, who, like the rest of the federal government at this time, had "turned their backs on the goals and policies of Reconstruction," had no interest in policing the states' obligation to pay. Purcell, *supra*, at 1946. An expanded sovereign-immunity doctrine thus enabled the federal judiciary to avoid any direct clash with the southern states without having "to abandon its general position guaranteeing the worth of government bonds." *Id.*; *see also Seminole Tribe*, 517 U.S. at 118 (Souter, J., dissenting) (suggesting that the Court decided *Hans* in the way it did because the case presented it with " 'a draconian choice between repudiation of some of its most inviolable constitutional doctrines and the humiliation of seeing its political authority compromised as its judgments met the resistance of hostile state governments' " (quoting John J. Gibbons, *The Eleventh Amendment and State Sovereign Immunity: A Reinterpretation*, 83 COLUM. L. REV. 1889, 1974 (1983))).

145 *See, e.g.*, Principality of Monaco v. Mississippi, 292 U.S. 313, 332 (1934) (rejecting the idea that "the letter of the Eleventh Amendment exhausts the restrictions upon suits against non-consenting States").

146 209 U.S. 123 (1908).

147 *See id.* at 159–60. The Court in *Young* relied on the legal fiction that a law-violating official is "stripped of his official or representative character" and thus can no longer invoke sovereign immunity on the state's behalf. *Id.* at 125. While this "stripping theory" has long been subject to criticism, *see, e.g.*, Florida Dept. of State v. Treasure Salvors, Inc., 458 U.S. 670, 685 (1982) (opinion of Stevens. J.) (noting the "irony" under *Young* that "unconstitutional conduct by a state officer may be 'state action' for purposes of the Fourteenth Amendment yet not attributable to the State for purposes of the Eleventh"), its practical importance cannot be gainsaid. Absent *Young*, after all, sovereign immunity rules would very often frustrate efforts to obtain federal-court review of state laws and practices alleged to violate federal law. Oftentimes, in particular, the only route open to the federal rightsholder would require (1) violating an allegedly unconstitutional state law; (2) awaiting a criminal prosecution (or some other government enforcement action) in state court; (3) asserting the federal-law claim as a defense in that proceeding; and (4) if unsuccessful in state court, pursuing the long-shot chance of securing successful review by the Supreme Court itself. Worse yet, the claimant would have to run this gauntlet while knowing that an adverse constitutional ruling would likely lead to criminal or civil punishment for violating the law that precipitated the state-court proceeding. With *Young* on the books, however, rightsholders have a comparatively risk-free route to judicial relief: Without having to put anything other than litigation costs on the line, they may seek an injunction in federal district court that bars the relevant official(s) tasked with implementing the challenged state law or policy from continuing to do so. *See* Edelman v. Jordan, 415 U.S. 651, 673 (1974) (noting that *Young* "has permitted the Civil War Amendments . . . to serve as a sword, rather than merely as a shield, for those whom they were designed to protect"); *see also* Michael E. Solimine, *Congress*, Ex Parte Young, *and the Fate of the Three-Judge District Court*, 70 U. PITT. L. REV. 101, 103 (2008) (noting that

not bar plaintiffs from recovering money damages from state officers in their personal (rather than official) capacity,[148] or from seeking any kind of relief against cities or city-like subunits of the states.[149] In addition, it has long been held that the sovereign-immunity principle does not bar state-party suits, whether at law or in equity, that are initiated either by another state[150] or by the federal government itself.[151] The Court has made it clear as well that states may waive their sovereign immunity and thereby consent to suits that courts would otherwise not be permitted to hear.[152]

Meanwhile, a separate question regarding the reach of state sovereign immunity would, following *Hans*, steadily grow in practical

---

absent the "sword" of the *Ex parte Young* action, "it appears that many of the iconic federal court decisions of th[e civil rights] era would not have been heard in federal court" and that "the issues of federal law would [instead] often have had to have been raised as shields to coercive actions by state authorities in state court"). To be sure, the *Young* rule is subject to important exceptions that in some respects limit its reach. *See, e.g.*, *Edelman*, 415 U.S. at 666 (holding that *Young* does not authorize nominally equitable suits against officers in which the sought-after remedy too "closely . . . resemble[s] a money judgment payable out of the state treasury"); Pennhurst State School & Hospital v. Halderman, 465 U.S. 89, 105–06 (1984) (holding that *Young* does not apply to federal-court cases in which plaintiffs seek injunctive relief against state officials alleged to have violated *state*, rather than *federal*, law). Even so, the overall effect of the decision has been to ensure a form of meaningful federal-court monitoring of state officials for violations of federal law—a form of monitoring that *Hans* itself might otherwise have rendered unavailable.

[148] *See Alden*, 527 U.S. at 757 (noting that sovereign immunity does not bar suit "so long as the relief is sought not from the state treasury but from the officer personally"). *But see infra* Section 33.B (noting the availability of various "official immunity" doctrines that officers may often invoke in such suits).

[149] *See, e.g.*, Monell v. Dept. of Soc. Servs., 436 U.S. 658, 690 n.54 (1978) (holding that municipal governments do not generally qualify as "part of the State for Eleventh Amendment purposes"); Northern Ins. Co. of New York v. Chatham Cty., 547 U.S. 189, 193 (2006) ("[T]his Court has repeatedly refused to extend sovereign immunity to counties."); Jinks v. Richland Cty., 538 U.S. 456, 466 (2003) (holding that "municipalities, unlike States, do not enjoy a constitutionally protected immunity from suit"); Mt. Healthy City Sch. Dist. Bd. of Educ. v. Doyle, 429 U.S. 274 (1977) (same). *But see* Fred Smith, *Local Sovereign Immunity*, 116 COLUM. L. REV. 409, 416 (2016) (suggesting that other limits on federal-law suits against local governmental entities have so stringently operated to insulate local governments against damages awards for the unlawful actions of their employees as to create a *de facto* form of "local sovereign immunity," which, as "a descriptive matter . . . shares core ideological and methodological features with state sovereignty doctrines" and which, "as a functional matter . . . render[s] specific classes of governmental defendants insusceptible to suit").

[150] *E.g.*, South Dakota v. North Carolina, 192 U.S. 286, 315–21 (1904). *But see Principality of Monaco*, 292 U.S. at 330 (refusing to apply this principle to suits brought against states by foreign nations); Blatchford v. Native Village of Noatak, 501 U.S. 775, 781–82 (1991) (similarly refusing to recognize a "surrender of immunity" in relation to suits brought against states by Native nations).

[151] *E.g.*, United States v. Mississippi, 380 U.S. 128, 140–41 (1965).

[152] *See* Atascadero State Hospital v. Scanlon, 473 U.S. 234, 238 (1985) (noting that "if a State waives its immunity and consents to suit in federal court, the Eleventh Amendment does not bar the action"). For a state waiver to be operative, however, it must be "unequivocally expressed." Sossamon v. Texas, 563 U.S. 277, 288 (2011) (internal quotations omitted)).

importance: To what extent may Congress abrogate the sovereign-immunity rule by enacting laws, including laws based on the commerce power, that authorize private-party damage suits against state governments?[153] Put another way, did *Hans* merely establish a common-law-like rule that Congress could override with statutory abrogations of its own, or did *Hans* instead set forth a constitutional prohibition that limited congressional power just as forcefully as it limited the powers of the federal courts? This question would remain unsettled for many years.[154]

2. State Sovereign Immunity and the Commerce Power

In the 1960s, Congress began to increase the federal regulatory role in fields such as civil rights, health care, and environmental protection. As it did so, new laws creating federal rights of action for monetary relief found their way into the U.S. Code. Many of these enactments raised no sovereign-immunity questions because they targeted only the behavior of private businesses and individuals. Some of these laws, however, applied in equal fashion to the states, thus raising questions about whether Congress could subject the states to statutorily created damage remedies notwithstanding otherwise applicable sovereign-immunity rules.[155]

An early encounter with this set of issues came in *Fitzpatrick v. Bitzer*,[156] which concerned a state's assertion of sovereign immunity in a money-damages action for sex discrimination brought against it pursuant to a 1972 amendment to the Civil Rights Act of 1964. The Court upheld Congress's abrogation of sovereign immunity in this setting, emphasizing that the 1972 amendment reflected a proper exercise of the Fourteenth Amendment power to "enforce by appropriate legislation" the guaranty of "equal protection of the laws."[157] The Fourteenth Amendment enforcement power, however,

---

[153] *See, e.g.*, Richard H. Fallon, Jr., *The "Conservative" Paths of the Rehnquist Court's Federalism Decisions*, 69 U. CHI. L. REV. 429, 481–82 (2002) (noting *Hans*'s ambiguity on this point).

[154] Although the foregoing section has focused only on the ability of *states* to invoke sovereign immunity, similar (though not identical) rules apply with respect to suits against the federal government, *see generally* Gregory C. Sisk, *A Primer on the Doctrine of Federal Sovereign Immunity*, 58 OKLA. L. REV. 439 (2005), and with respect to suits against Native nations, *see infra* Section 25.A.2 n.47 and accompanying text.

[155] Of particular significance, as the ensuing discussion will show, was Congress's extension of the Fair Labor Standards Act to many state and local employers in 1966. *See Wirtz*, 392 U.S. at 186–87.

[156] 427 U.S. 445 (1976).

[157] *Id.* at 453 (quoting U.S. CONST. amend. XIV). In reaching this conclusion, the Court emphasized that the Framers of the Fourteenth Amendment, which postdated the Eleventh Amendment by seven decades, had effected a critical "shift in the federal-state balance" by placing new and expansive "limitations on state authority." *Id.* at 455–56. At the same time, however, the Court has sought to safeguard the state

could not provide a constitutional basis for the great mass of federal legislation that concerned such matters as environmental safeguards, consumer protection, intellectual property, worker safety, unionization, and similar matters. *Fitzpatrick* thus left unresolved the extent of Congress's authority to abrogate state sovereign immunity pursuant to its *Article I* powers, including its power to regulate interstate commerce.

In its 1989 ruling in *Pennsylvania v. Union Gas Co.*,[158] a fractured Court appeared to resolve this issue in Congress's favor, with five Justices—albeit in two separate opinions—agreeing that the Eleventh Amendment did not inhibit congressional action, otherwise proper under the commerce power, that exposed states to monetary remedies.[159] In 1996, however, the same five Justices who had come together one year earlier in *United States v. Lopez*,[160] and who would again come together one year later in *Printz v. United States*,[161] proclaimed in *Seminole Tribe v. Florida*[162] that the Court in *Union Gas* had misstepped—thus establishing that Congress could *not* abrogate state sovereign immunity in federal civil actions by invoking the commerce power. Then, three years later, in *Alden v. Maine*,[163] the Court pushed the state-protective principle of *Seminole Tribe* even further when it held that Congress lacked the power to abrogate sovereign-immunity protections in *state-court* actions as well.

Claiming a violation of the Fair Labor Standards Act (FLSA), John H. Alden and other plaintiffs initially sued their employer, the state of Maine, in federal court. Soon thereafter, however, the Court decided *Seminole Tribe*, and the district court judge properly invoked that case to dismiss the pending suit. The plaintiffs then refiled the action in state court, and their argument for having access to that

---

interests that underlie the sovereign-immunity rule by insisting that it may be abrogated, including pursuant to the Reconstruction Amendments' enforcement powers, only if Congress makes this intention "unmistakably clear." *Atascadero State Hosp.*, 473 U.S. at 242–43. For a more detailed treatment of the interaction of the Fourteenth Amendment enforcement power and sovereign-immunity principles, see *infra* Section 11.B.4.

158 491 U.S. 1 (1989).

159 *Id.* The lead opinion setting forth this default-rule approach was written by Justice Brennan, who was joined by Justices Marshall, Blackmun, and Stevens. Justice White wrote separately to say, without further explanation, that "I agree with the conclusion . . . that Congress has the authority under Article I to abrogate the Eleventh Amendment immunity of the States, although I do not agree with much of [Justice Brennan's] reasoning." *Id.* at 57 (White, J., concurring in part and dissenting in part).

160 *See supra* Section 4.A.

161 *See supra* Section 5.B.2.

162 517 U.S. 44 (1996).

163 527 U.S. 706 (1999).

tribunal proceeded in three easy steps: (1) the Eleventh Amendment by its terms limits only the "Judicial power of the United States"; (2) *Testa v. Katt* held that Congress could force state courts to hear federal claims;[164] and (3) *Garcia v. San Antonio Metropolitan Transit Authority* left no doubt that the FLSA fully applies to state, as well as private, employers.[165] The same five Justices who came together in *Seminole Tribe*, however, found themselves unmoved by this line of logic. They declared that the sovereign-immunity principles set forth in *Hans* and *Seminole Tribe* applied no less in state-court litigation than in federal-court litigation, even in the face of a crystal-clear congressional pronouncement that the immunity should be inoperative in FLSA actions.

The majority opinion, written by Justice Kennedy, defended this position by relying on "structural" reasoning and the Tenth Amendment.[166] Also animating the decision were concerns about anomalous results, as Justice Kennedy maintained that it made no sense to hold that the Constitution permits "the National Government [to] wield greater power in the state courts than in its own judicial instrumentalities,"[167] thus "turn[ing] the State against itself."[168] At the same time, Justice Kennedy emphasized that the Court's holding did not "bar all judicial review of state compliance with the Constitution and valid federal law."[169] Why was that? Because individual victims could still seek injunctions against state officials under the principle of *Ex parte Young*;[170] because the United States remained able to bring suits against unconsenting states;[171] and because *Fitzpatrick* permitted Congress to authorize some state-defendant suits pursuant to the Fourteenth Amendment enforcement power.[172] It also mattered to the majority that the "good faith of the States" provided an "important assurance" that federal-law violations—even though not remediable in private damages actions—would not occur.[173] The dissenters, however, were unimpressed by these efforts to downplay the impact of the *Alden* decision. In their view, the majority had not only flouted the text of the Eleventh Amendment; it also had endorsed an approach that

---

164 *See supra* notes 61–65 and accompanying text.

165 *See supra* notes 17–21 and accompanying text.

166 *Alden*, 527 U.S. at 713, 731–33.

167 *Id.* at 752.

168 *Id.* at 749.

169 *Id.* at 757.

170 *See id.*; *see also supra* notes 146–47 and accompanying text.

171 *Id.*

172 *Id.*

173 *Id.* at 755.

"comes perilously close to legitimizing political defiance of valid federal law."[174]

The Court's rulings in *Seminole Tribe* and *Alden* have left behind important questions.[175] For example, does the United-States-as-plaintiff exception to the Eleventh Amendment[176] permit the pursuit of statutorily authorized "*qui tam*" damages actions, brought by private parties in the name of the United States, for injuries inflicted by state officials on the national government itself?[177] Does that same exception mean (as *Alden* might be read to indicate) that Congress may authorize suits by the United States to recover compensatory damages for the benefit of individuals injured by state statutory violations, including under the FLSA?[178] And if Congress may allow such suits by the United States, may it also broadly deputize private parties' lawyers to pursue such actions on behalf of the federal government?[179]

---

[174] *Id.* at 803 n.36 (Souter, J., dissenting).

[175] For an expansive treatment of these questions in the immediate wake of *Alden*, see generally Symposium, *Federalism After* Alden, 31 RUTGERS L.J. 631 (2000).

[176] *See supra* note 151 and accompanying text.

[177] *Compare* Vt. Agency of Nat. Res. v. United States *ex rel.* Stevens, 529 U.S. 765, 787 (2000) (declining to reach this question in light of the Court's resolution of a dispositive question of statutory interpretation but expressing "a serious doubt on that score" (internal quotation marks and citation omitted)), *with id.* at 802 (Souter, J., dissenting) (arguing that "even if one accepts *Seminole Tribe* as controlling, the State's immunity claim would still fail" in part because the *qui tam* plaintiff "is, in effect, suing as an assignee of the United States").

[178] *See Alden*, 527 U.S. at 759–60 (suggesting an affirmative answer by distinguishing cases in which a private party initiates the action from cases brought by the United States itself in light of the need for a determination of federal authorities that the case is of "sufficient importance to take action against the State"). *See generally* Sarah Louise House, Note, Alden v. Maine: *Protecting the States at the Expense of the People*, 62 LA. L. REV. 275, 296 (2001) (noting that a "potential remedy to the lapse of enforcement of federal law over states created by *Alden* would require suits to be brought by the Justice Department on behalf of large numbers of individuals adversely affected by non-compliant states," but also detailing problems inherent in this approach).

[179] For rhetoric that might cut against at least some forms of such a deputization, see *Vt. Agency of Nat. Res.*, 529 U.S. at 802 (Souter, J., dissenting) (finding no Eleventh Amendment problem with *qui tam* actions prosecuted by private parties on behalf of the United States, but relying in part in doing so on the fact that "the Attorney General retains significant control over a relator's action"). A related question concerns the federal government's ability to transfer to private parties its power of eminent domain to the extent that the power is directed at state landowners. In addressing this question, the Third Circuit held that the federal government could not thus delegate its "exemption from state sovereign immunity" to private parties, in part because private parties are not "accountable" to the electorate in the same way as are officers of the federal government. *In re* PennEast Pipeline Co., 938 F.3d 96, 105 (3d Cir. 2019). In an opinion for a five-Justice majority, however, Chief Justice Roberts rejected this position. He reasoned, in essence, that "[t]he eminent domain power may be exercised—whether by the Government or its delegatees—. . . against state property" because "the States consented to the exercise of that power—in its entirety—in the plan of the Convention." PennEast Pipeline Co. v. New Jersey, 141 S. Ct. 2244, 2257

Whatever the answers to these questions, the impact of *Seminole Tribe* and *Alden* has been profound, and to understand why it is useful to compare the effect of the rule of those cases to the rule of *National League of Cities*, which the Court later repudiated in *Garcia*.[180] To be sure, *Seminole Tribe* and *Alden* do not afford states as much protection as did *National League of Cities* in some respects. The rule of the latter case, after all, wholly barred any state and local employee in the pre-*Garcia* world from seeking any remedy of any kind under the FLSA from any public-employer defendant, so long as the law obstructed the operation of "integral" state or local government operations. In other words, to the extent that *National League of Cities* applied, it imposed a sweeping substantive restriction on employee access to any judicial relief, as opposed to simply blocking money-damages actions, and its operation applied fully to municipal governments, as well as to the states themselves. Even so, in important respects, the rule of *Seminole Tribe* and *Alden* protects states more broadly—indeed, far more broadly—than did the since-abandoned rule of *National League of Cities*. The key point is that *Seminole Tribe* and *Alden* do not shelter states only from lawsuits under federal statutes that "directly impair their ability to structure integral operations in areas of traditional governmental functions."[181] Instead, those rulings safeguard states from having to pay damages in *any* suit by *any* person for *any* injury caused by *any* state conduct—be it pollution, discrimination, workplace safety, or whatever—made actionable by Congress pursuant to its commerce

(2021). Accordingly, "[t]he States . . . have no immunity left to waive or abrogate when it comes to condemnation suits by the Federal Government and its delegatees." *Id.* No less important, because the assignment of the eminent domain power thus is intrinsically different from a congressional abrogation of state sovereign immunity, there is no need for an assignment of that power to be made with the same "unmistakable clarity" required to support sovereign-immunity abrogations. *See id.* at 2262.

[180] *See supra* Section 5.A.1.

[181] *Hodel*, 452 U.S. at 287–88 (internal quotations omitted). Notably, Justice Blackmun had made it clear in his critical concurrence in *National League of Cities* that the rule of that case would not preclude actions brought pursuant to some laws, even when enacted under the commerce power, such as those designed to guard members of the public from environmental harms. *See* 426 U.S. at 856 (Blackmun, J., concurring). The *Seminole Tribe/Alden* rule, however, plainly *does* preclude Congress from authorizing damages actions against states for violations of federal environmental-protection laws, as well as all other federal laws enacted under the commerce power. This consequence follows in part from the Court's later overruling of *Parden v. Terminal Ry. of Ala. State Docks Dep't*, 377 U.S. 184 (1964), which had recognized that states might at least sometimes "constructively" waive the Eleventh Amendment immunity when they enter a "field traditionally occupied by private persons." Coll. Sav. Bank v. Fla. Prepaid Postsecondary Educ. Expense Bd., 527 U.S. 666, 679–680 (1999) (overruling *Parden* and thus affirming the dismissal, on sovereign-immunity grounds, of a suit for alleged trademark infringement brought against a state agency).

power and most of its other Article I powers as well.[182] Thus even with respect to the operation of the FLSA, the principle of *Seminole Tribe* and *Alden* forecloses suit by a far larger range of workers than those workers whose federal statutory rights were cut off from federal protection by the integral-operations principle of *National League of Cities*.[183] No gauge exists for assessing whether, on balance, the sovereign-immunity rule of *Seminole Tribe* and *Alden* affords more protection to states than did the regulatory-immunity rule of *National League of Cities*. Plainly, however, the sovereign-immunity cases—which at first blush might seem to concern only a technical jurisdictional or remedial question—at least move a long distance in that direction.

In the wake of *Seminole Tribe* and *Alden*, plaintiffs' lawyers turned their attention to finding ways to dodge the federal-action-squelching effect of those rulings. Their main hope lay in arguing that congressional abrogations of state sovereign immunity, even if not sustainable under the Commerce Clause, qualified as proper exercises of the Fourteenth Amendment enforcement power, thus triggering the immunity-defeating rule of *Fitzpatrick v. Bitzer*.[184] In some cases, the Court found these arguments persuasive. More often, however, it did not.[185] Of particular note was the Court's ruling in *Kimel v. Florida Board of Regents*[186] that the Fourteenth Amendment power did not support Congress's attempt to expose states to money-damages suits in actions brought under the Age Discrimination in Employment Act (ADEA). Even during the heyday of *National League of Cities*, after all, the Court had held that its "directly impair integral operations" principle did not strip state employees, including law enforcement officers, of the ability to bring ADEA actions.[187] Thus, with the ruling in *Kimel*, the impact of *Seminole Tribe* and *Alden* has come into clear view. By denying relief to ADEA plaintiffs who would have faced no obstacle to securing

---

[182] *See, e.g.*, Fla. Prepaid Postsecondary Educ. Expense Bd. v. Coll. Sav. Bank, 527 U.S. 627, 635–36 (1999) (refusing to enforce a congressional abrogation of sovereign immunity for state patent infringement enacted pursuant to the Intellectual Property Clause); Allen v. Cooper, 140 S. Ct. 994 (2020) (holding that *Florida Prepaid* required invalidation of the Copyright Remedy Clarification Act of 1990 insofar as it abrogates state sovereign immunity in copyright-infringement suits). *But see* Central Va. Cmty. College v. Katz, 546 U.S. 356, 359 (2006) (holding that Congress may abrogate sovereign immunity when acting pursuant to its Article I power to enact "uniform Laws on the subject of Bankruptcies throughout the United States" (quoting U.S. CONST. art. I, § 8, cl. 4)). For a more detailed canvassing of this subject, see *infra* Section 13.A.

[183] 426 U.S. at 852.

[184] *See supra* notes 156–57 and accompanying text.

[185] For a treatment of the relevant cases, see *infra* Section 11.B.4.

[186] 528 U.S. 62 (2000).

[187] *See supra* note 16 (discussing *EEOC v. Wyoming*, 460 U.S. 226 (1983)).

monetary relief even under the pre-*Garcia* constraint imposed by *National League of Cities*, the Court signaled just how far, in the post-1994 period, the pendulum of federalism had swung.

D. FEDERALISM VALUES AND STATUTORY INTERPRETATION

As we have seen, the Rehnquist and Roberts Courts have reinvigorated limits on the commerce power by way of: (1) the *Lopez/Morrison* non-economic-activity principle; (2) the *NFIB* anti-mandate rule; (3) the *New York/Printz/Murphy* anti-commandeering doctrine; and (4) the *Seminole Tribe/Alden* damages-immunity rule. There is, however, another and a subtler way in which the Court has protected federalism values in commerce-power cases. It has done so by employing state-protective tools of statutory interpretation.

This story begins in the pre-Rehnquist Court era with decisions such as *United States v. Bass*.[188] That case involved a federal statute, 18 U.S.C. § 1202(a), which subjected to criminal punishment any person previously convicted of a felony "who receives, possesses, or transports in commerce or affecting commerce . . . any firearm."[189] Emphasizing the disjunctive phrasing of the provision, the government argued that the statutory ban on receiving or possessing a gun (as opposed to the ban on transporting one) applied regardless of the gun's connection to interstate commerce.[190] The Court, however, rejected this argument, relying on two statutory-interpretation rules. First, the Court cited the canon that "ambiguity concerning the ambit of criminal statutes should be resolved in favor of lenity" so as to foster values of fair warning and humane treatment.[191] Second, and more important for present purposes, the Court declared that "unless Congress conveys its purpose clearly, it will not be deemed to have significantly changed the federal-state balance."[192] The Court went on to justify this principle of statutory construction by suggesting that it would enhance the proper functioning of federal lawmaking processes. Thus, "[i]n traditionally sensitive areas, such as legislation affecting the federal balance, the requirement of clear statement assures that the legislature has in

---

[188] 404 U.S. 336 (1971).

[189] *Id.* at 337. A modified version of that provision is now codified at 18 U.S.C. § 922(g)(1).

[190] *Bass*, 404 U.S. at 340 n.6. In other words, the government argued that the limiting prepositional phrase "in or affecting commerce" modified only the verb "transports" and not the statute's two other verbs, "receives" and "possesses."

[191] *Id.* at 347–49.

[192] *Id.* at 349.

fact faced, and intended to bring into issue, the critical matters involved in the judicial decision."[193]

Commentators rightly noted that the *Bass*-based rule of narrow construction dovetailed with the Court's then-flourishing tendency to give broad scope to Congress's use of the commerce power. In particular, by requiring a heightened level of explicitness, the *Bass* rule pushed Congress in the direction of acting with heightened care when it contemplated legislating in fields deemed to be "traditionally sensitive" because historically subject to state control. In other words, *Bass* focused judicial attention on how carefully Congress had acted, thus anticipating the core idea that would later give rise to the ruling in *Garcia*—namely, that state-autonomy interests are best protected by fostering the operation of well-structured political processes as opposed to cordoning off, perhaps artificially, particular areas of substantive state lawmaking from federal control.[194]

As the foregoing discussion indicates, however, the Court in more recent years has moved away from the hands-off style of decisionmaking, rooted in political-process-centered thinking, that reached its highwater mark in *Garcia*. A question thus arises: Given the Rehnquist and Roberts Courts' resuscitation of significant substantive protections of federalism values, should the Court now move away from *Bass*'s pro-federalism rule of statutory interpretation on the ground that it took hold as a doctrinal corollary of the Court's now-flagging process-oriented Commerce Clause jurisprudence? However one might answer this question in the abstract, the Rehnquist and Roberts Courts have shown little interest in abandoning *Bass*'s federalism-friendly canon of construction.[195] Indeed, the Justices have invigorated that canon by

---

193 *Id.*

194 *See, e.g.*, TRIBE, *supra* note 29, § 5–12.

195 An illustrative case, focused on the particular problem posed by applying federal statutes to state government officials is *Kelly v. United States*, 140 S. Ct. 1565 (2020). That case involved a prosecution under fraud statutes (including the wire-fraud statute) that criminalize, according to binding case law, "schemes to deprive [the victim of] money or property." *Id.* at 1571 (alteration in original) (quoting McNally v. United States, 483 U.S. 350, 356 (1987)). Convicted at trial were participants in the "Bridgegate" scandal, which involved actions, accompanied by deception, undertaken by Republican state officials in New Jersey to embarrass the Democratic mayor of Fort Lee by suddenly closing lanes at the toll plaza for the George Washington Bridge, thus producing massive traffic jams for New York City-area commuters. The Court overturned the convictions in an opinion by Justice Kagan, who concluded that the statutes did not support this prosecution because no statutorily required deprivation of government "property" had resulted from the temporary closure of two traffic lanes. *Id.* at 1573. The Court emphasized that "not every corrupt act by state or local officials is a federal crime" and expressed concern that allowing U.S. Attorneys to prosecute every lie told in the process of making a regulatory decision would entail "a sweeping expansion of federal criminal jurisdiction." *Id.* at 1574 (citing Cleveland v. United States, 531 U.S. 12, 24 (2000)). More specifically, Justice Kagan explained, "[t]o rule otherwise would undercut this Court's oft-repeated instruction: Federal prosecutors

applying it not only to criminal statutes but to civil statutes as well.[196] In effect, then, the Rehnquist and Roberts Courts have shifted from a single-barreled to a double-barreled approach in protecting state-autonomy values. As a result, litigants seeking to escape the operation of federal laws can now rely not just on the "true" constitutional rules of *Lopez, Morrison, NFIB, New York, Printz, Seminole Tribe*, and *Alden*, but also on "quasi-constitutional" principles of statutory construction rooted in the values of constitutional federalism.[197]

---

may not use property fraud statutes to 'set standards of disclosure and good government for local and state officials.' " *Id.* (quoting *McNally*, 483 U.S. at 355) (alterations omitted).

[196] *See, e.g.*, Solid Waste Agency of N. Cook Cty. v. U.S. Army Corps of Eng'rs, 531 U.S. 159, 172–73 (2001) (refusing to read the Clean Water Act as authorizing an agency rule that precluded the filling of localized non-navigable ponds); *Vt. Agency of Nat. Res.*, 529 U.S. at 787 (refusing to construe the False Claims Act to apply to state defendants); *Gregory*, 501 U.S. at 460–61 (refusing to read the ADEA as applicable to state judges in light of their vital role in administering the state judicial system); *see also* Gonzaga Univ. v. Doe, 536 U.S. 273, 287 & n.5 (2002) (refusing to read 42 U.S.C. § 1983 to permit an action seeking redress for a school's disclosure of information protected by the Family Educational Rights and Privacy Act of 1974; relying in part on "a tradition of deference to state and local school officials"). *See generally* Dan T. Coenen, *The Rehnquist Court, Structural Due Process and Semisubstantive Constitutional Review*, 75 S. CAL. L. REV. 1281, 1295–1303 (2002) (collecting and discussing relevant cases).

[197] *See* William N. Eskridge, Jr. & Philip P. Frickey, *Quasi-Constitutional Law: Clear Statement Rules as Constitutional Lawmaking*, 45 VAND. L. REV. 593 (1992).

Chapter 6

THE NECESSARY AND PROPER CLAUSE

Analysis

The Necessary and Proper Clause occupies a curious place in constitutional law. It does no work on its own. Instead, it provides a source of authority that can operate only in connection with another grant of federal power. As stated in Article I, section 8, clause 18, Congress can "make all Laws which shall be necessary and proper for carrying into Execution the foregoing Powers, and all other Powers vested by this Constitution in the government of the United States, or in any Department or Officer thereof."[1] In *McCulloch v. Maryland*,[2] the Court rejected the argument that the Framers' choice of the word "necessary" put a short leash on Congress's ability to make use of the clause, declaring instead that laws passed under it need only be "conducive," "convenient," or "appropriate" to the "beneficial" exercise of a more specifically granted power.[3] Pursuant to this test, the federal law chartering the Bank of United States qualified as "necessary" because it served a "useful" role in carrying into execution Congress's enumerated powers to collect taxes, to spend money, to regulate interstate and foreign commerce, to support armies, and to maintain a navy.[4] This ruling set the stage for an energetic use of the Necessary and Proper Clause over the course of American history.[5] In fact, countless federal statutes, as well as

---

1 U.S. CONST. art. I, § 8, cl. 18.

2 17 U.S. (4 Wheat.) 316 (1819).

3 *Id.* at 413, 418.

4 *Id.* at 408–10, 413. *See generally supra* Section 1.B (discussing these aspects of the case in greater detail).

5 The Court, for example, has authorized the federal chartering of businesses other than banks. *See* Luxton v. North River Bridge, Co., 153 U.S. 525, 529 (1894) (noting that Congress "may create corporations as appropriate means of executing the powers of government"). Along these same lines, the Court has long recognized that Congress can use its necessary-and-proper power to condemn property through

agency rules promulgated pursuant to federal statutes, have their genesis in this provision, which observers have often and appropriately referred to as the "Sweeping Clause" or the "Elastic Clause."[6]

---

eminent domain proceedings. *See generally* William Baude, *Rethinking the Federal Eminent Domain Power*, 122 YALE L.J. 1738, 1804–05 (2013). For an early ruling upholding an invocation of the necessary-and-proper power in the bankruptcy context, see *United States v. Fox*, 95 U.S. 670, 672 (1877) (permitting Congress to legislate regarding the distribution of an insolvent individual's property pursuant to the Bankruptcy Clause and the resulting power to enact such laws as are useful to creating a "complete and effective bankrupt[cy] system").

[6] The literature on the Necessary and Proper Clause is expansive. For example, extensive treatments of the clause's linkage to pre-ratification administrative law, trust law, and corporate law appear in GARY LAWSON, GEOFFREY P. MILLER, ROBERT G. NATELSON & GUY I. SEIDMAN, THE ORIGINS OF THE NECESSARY AND PROPER CLAUSE (2010). Professors Lawson and Seidman argue that the clause imposes requirements of impartiality, relatedness, proportionality, and rights protection. *Id.* at 139–43. Professor Natelson emphasizes the conjunctive character of the terms "necessary" and "proper," urging that the latter term imposes fiduciary-like duties on Congress. *Id.* at 77, 119. Professor Miller sees pre-ratification corporate law as suggestive of (though not necessarily mandating) a reading that both (1) requires a significant connection between means and ends (described by him in terms of being "reasonably closely adapted") and (2) bans certain forms of regulatory discrimination. *Id.* at 171, 174. A thoughtful review of the book has been offered by Professor Harrison. John C. Harrison, *Enumerated Federal Power and the Necessary and Proper Clause*, 78 U. CHI L. REV. 1101 (2011). For related treatments, see Robert G. Natelsen, *The Agency Law Origins of the Necessary and Proper Clause*, 55 CASE W. RES. L. REV. 243 (2004), and Gary Lawson & Patricia B. Granger, *The Proper Scope of Federal Power: A Jurisdictional Interpretation of the Sweeping Clause*, 43 DUKE L.J. 267 (1993). A rights-protective view of the clause is offered in Randy E. Barnett, *The Original Meaning of the Necessary and Proper Clause*, 6 U. PA. J. CONST. L. 183 (2003), and Randy E. Barnett, *Necessary and Proper Unenumerated Rights*, 44 UCLA L. REV. 745 (1997). For treatments that challenge this view, see J. Randy Beck, *The New Jurisprudence of the Necessary and Proper Clause*, 2002 U. ILL. L. REV. 581, 642 (suggesting that the clause focuses on non-pretextual means-ends relationships, including by requiring that any congressional invocation of the clause must be "consistent with the nature of the power from which the constitutional end derives"), and Thomas B. McAffee, *Federalism and the Protection of Rights: The Modern Ninth Amendment's Spreading Confusion*, 1996 BYU L. REV. 351, 369 (rejecting the position that the clause protects unenumerated rights). A more recent, text-centered treatment—and one that aligns closely with *McCulloch*'s deferential tone—is John F. Manning, *The Means of Constitutional Power*, 128 HARV. L. REV. 1, 5, 78 (2014) (advocating "an approach . . . that defers, within broad bounds, to congressional authority to determine how to implement constitutional power," so as to allow judicial intervention only if Congress has not "reasonably interpreted its delegated power or, conversely, made a clear mistake"); *see also* John F. Manning, *The Necessary and Proper Clause and Its Legal Antecedents*, 92 B.U. L. REV. 1349, 1372 (2012); SOTIRIOS A. BARBER, THE FALLACIES OF STATES' RIGHTS (2013) (also endorsing a broad view of the necessary-and-proper power). For a response to Professor Manning, see William Baude, *Sharing the Necessary and Proper Clause*, 128 HARV. L. REV. F. 39 (2014). An earlier work by Professor Baude offers an originalist account that supports congressional use of the clause to exercise "incidental," but not "great," powers. *See* Baude, *supra* note 5, at 1749–61. Among other recent treatments of the necessary-and-proper power are John Mikhail, *The Necessary and Proper Clauses*, 102 GEO. L.J. 1045, 1048 (2014) (urging that the clause also references inherent powers vested in the federal government that Congress accordingly can carry into execution); David Louden, *When Do the Ends Justify the Means?: The Role of the Necessary and Proper Clause in the Commerce Clause Analysis*, 10 U. MASS. L. REV. 294, 336–37 (2015)

By way of example, one of the "foregoing Powers" cross-referenced by the clause is Congress's power to "lay and collect taxes."[7] That provision, however, includes not one word about establishing the IRS, fixing April 15 as a filing deadline, creating tax-related forms, requiring use of tax-identification numbers, constituting non-Article III tax courts, criminalizing tax fraud, or setting up a federal prison system to house (among others) persons who commit tax-related offenses. Nonetheless, Congress can pass laws that do all these things even though these laws do not themselves "lay" or "collect" taxes. It can enact these measures because they are "necessary and proper for carrying into Execution" the Article I taxing power.[8] In similar fashion, the Article I, section 8 text that vests Congress with the power to "constitute Tribunals inferior to the supreme Court" does not itself make mention of outlawing perjury in federal-court proceedings, issuing subpoenas to witnesses, staffing court chambers and clerks' offices, or providing for the promulgation of the Federal Rules of Civil Procedure.[9] But laws that accomplish these objectives fall comfortably within Congress's purview under the Necessary and Proper Clause because they are aimed at helping to make the federal court system operate effectively.[10]

(advocating for "intermediate scrutiny" of means-ends relationships" under the clause, so that courts can uphold "reasonable means" but not those that reflect "the remotest of connections"); Celestine McConville, *The (Not So Dire) Future of the Necessary and Proper Power After* National Federation of Independent Business v. Sebelius, 24 WM. & MARY BILL RTS. J. 369, 376 (2015) (suggesting that the Court's recent placement of limitations on use of the clause has emanated from particular concerns about the commerce power, as opposed to other powers); Robert Reinstein, *The Great Power of the Necessary and Proper Clause* (unpublished manuscript) (Sept. 8, 2015), *available at* https://ssrn/abstract=2644326 (criticizing on historical grounds the "great powers" limitation on the clause's scope); Robert J. Reinstein, *The Limits of Congressional Power*, 89 TEMP. L. REV. 1, 4, 6, 74–75, 92 (2016) [hereinafter Reinstein, *Limits*] (arguing that *McCulloch* reflected mainstream Federalist thinking and advocating for broad deference to Congress, at least if it spells out its means-end logic in legislative findings); and John T. Valauri, *Originalism and the Necessary and Proper Clause*, 39 OHIO N.U. L. REV. 773 (2013) (emphasizing the opaqueness of the clause's text as well as ambiguities in *McCulloch*).

7 U.S. CONST. art. I, § 8, cl. 18; *see also infra* Chapter 7 (discussing the taxing power).

8 It is worth noting that judges, lawyers, and commentators often describe the Necessary and Proper Clause as giving rise to "implied powers." This rhetoric has a misleading quality, however, because the Necessary and Proper Clause is itself an express term of the Constitution. Thus, as the Court explained in *United States v. Comstock*, 560 U.S. 126 (2010), "[t]he powers 'delegated to the United States by the Constitution' include those specifically enumerated powers listed in Article I along with the implementation authority granted by the Necessary and Proper Clause." *Id.* at 144.

9 *See* U.S. CONST. art. I, § 8, cl. 9.

10 *See, e.g., supra* Section 1.B (noting the Court's recognition in *McCulloch* of an implied power to outlaw perjury so as to support the administration of justice in the federal courts).

These illustrations reveal how Congress routinely relies on the Necessary and Proper Clause to enact legislation that effectuates its own enumerated powers. The clause, however, also does something more: It authorizes Congress to pass laws that are necessary and proper for carrying into execution "all *other Powers* vested by this Constitution in the government of the United States, or in any Department or Officer thereof."[11] In the discussion that follows, we focus primarily on the former (and legally predominant) congressional-power-implementing use of the Necessary and Proper Clause. But we also touch on some possibilities that the clause creates for the enactment of laws that build upon—and potentially limit—the powers of the executive and judicial branches.

A. USING THE NECESSARY AND PROPER CLAUSE TO IMPLEMENT ENUMERATED CONGRESSIONAL POWERS

Most judicial decisions regarding the Necessary and Proper Clause have come in cases, like *McCulloch*, that involve the leveraging of Congress's own Article I authority. These cases fall into two main categories: (1) cases involving *power-specific* applications of the Necessary and Proper Clause in connection with a single enumerated power of Congress or a small handful of such powers; and (2) cases involving *generalized* applications of the Necessary and Proper Clause in connection with all or most of Congress's enumerated powers.

1. Power-Specific Applications

Many statutes founded on the Necessary and Proper Clause work in tandem with a particular power, as illustrated by the previously itemized examples that build on the Taxing Clause and the Inferior Tribunals Clause. For additional examples, consider the following:

- In *United States v. Kebodeaux*,[12] the Court upheld Congress's application of the newly enacted federal Sex Offender Registration and Notification Act (SORNA) to former military personnel who, having previously been convicted of sex offenses pursuant to the Uniform Code of Military Justice, had served their sentences and already been released. Writing for the majority, Justice Breyer reasoned that, as applied to such persons, the statute reflected a permissible exercise of Congress's power under the Necessary and Proper Clause

---

[11] U.S. CONST. art. I, § 8, cl. 18 (emphasis added).

[12] 570 U.S. 387 (2013).

together with Congress's enumerated power to "make Rules for the . . . Regulation of the land and naval Forces."[13]

- In *Veazie Bank v. Fenno*,[14] the Court held that Congress can act to restrain the circulation of money-like negotiable instruments not issued pursuant to its own authority. Pointing to the Coinage Clause,[15] it reasoned that "[h]aving thus, in the exercise of undisputed constitutional powers, undertaken to provide a currency for the whole country, it cannot be questioned that Congress may, constitutionally, secure

[13] U.S. CONST. art. I, § 8, cl. 14. Important to the Court's conclusion were the facts that: (1) the challenger of the law was already subject to another statute known as the Wetterling Act at the time of his original conviction; (2) that statute "imposed . . . registration requirements very similar to those that SORNA later mandated"; and (3) "[n]o one here claims [that the Wetterling Act fell] outside the scope of the Necessary and Proper Clause" as applied to the defendant. *Id.* at 393–94. Pointing to this combination of circumstances, Justice Breyer, who wrote for the majority, observed: "Congress could promulgate the Uniform Code of Military Justice. It could specify that the sex offense of which Kebodeaux was convicted was a military crime under that Code. It could punish that crime through imprisonment and by placing conditions upon Kebodeaux's release. And it could make the civil registration requirement at issue here a consequence of Kebodeaux's offense and conviction." *Id.* at 395. More specifically, he reasoned that Congress had not acted impermissibly in subjecting the defendant to some new duties under SORNA that had not existed under the Wetterling Act because the defendant and others like him were already in a "special relationship" with the federal government and because Congress could invoke the Necessary and Proper Clause to implement these "few changes" to help make the registration program operate in a better and more uniform way. *Id.* at 397–98 (internal quotation omitted). In a separate opinion concurring only in the judgment, Chief Justice Roberts likewise emphasized these same points but distanced himself from any suggestion that the Court's ruling found support in the law's "[p]ublic safety benefits" because, he argued, Congress has no power to "alleviate public safety concerns" as a general matter. *Id.* at 401 (Roberts, C.J., concurring in the judgment) (internal quotation omitted). In another concurrence in the judgment, Justice Alito emphasized the complications that marked the application of *state* sex-offender registration systems to former *federal* service members—complications that threatened to create a "gap in the laws" absent a continuing federal role in cases of this kind. *Id.* at 405 (Alito, J., concurring in the judgment); *see also id.* at 406 (concluding that "[w]hen Congress, in validly exercising a power expressly conferred by the Constitution, creates or exacerbates a dangerous situation (here, the possibility that a convicted sex offender may escape registration), Congress has the power to try to eliminate or at least diminish that danger"). Justice Thomas, joined in part by Justice Scalia, dissented, reasoning that SORNA was "aimed at protecting society from sex offenders" and thus was unconstitutional because Congress had no such power. *Id.* at 412 (Thomas, J., dissenting). This description of SORNA, he added, made especially good sense in the case at hand because Congress had adopted SORNA, and thus directed its strictures at the defendant, only after federal authorities had released him from custody. *Id.* at 417–18. For a discussion of *Kebodeaux*, see Alison LaCroix, *The Shadow Powers of Article I*, 123 YALE L.J. 2044, 2074–77 (2014) (noting the role of the case, despite the result reached in it, in helping to establish a new and "subtle doctrinal hurdle to congressional regulation").

[14] 75 U.S. 533 (1869).

[15] U.S. CONST. art. I, § 8, cl. 5.

the benefit of it to the people by appropriate legislation."[16]

- Likely relying on the Article I power to "raise and support armies,"[17] the Court in *Wissner v. Wissner*[18] recognized Congress's authority (1) to provide soldiers and veterans with a "uniform and comprehensive system of life insurance," and (2) to establish rules regarding beneficiary designation structured to "enhance the morale of the serviceman" even if inconsistent with state community-property law.[19]
- Expanding on *McCulloch*, the Court in *First National Bank v. Union Trust Co.*[20] held that Congress could authorize the Federal Reserve Board to permit federally chartered banks to engage in trust operations. It reasoned that, among other things, granting this authority to these institutions would allow them to compete more effectively with state-chartered banks by creating a level playing field in the services that all banks could offer their customers.[21]

Lower courts have followed the lead of these cases, sometimes by relying on seldom-invoked grants of federal power. In *United States v. Alarcon Sanchez*,[22] for example, the Second Circuit upheld a conviction under the Maritime Drug Law Enforcement Act (MDLEA) of a defendant whose allegedly criminal conduct occurred outside of U.S. territory. The prosecution was permissibly authorized by Congress, according to the court, because Article I, section 8, clause 10 empowers Congress "[t]o define and punish Piracies and Felonies committed on the high Seas."[23] Here, the court explained, even though the defendant himself had engaged in the allegedly criminal conduct while on land, he had also conspired with others to transport drugs by boat on the Pacific Ocean. And because targeting all participants in the plan was useful in countering the occurrence of drug crimes committed on ocean waters, Congress could subject even non-seafarer conspirators to federal prosecution.[24]

---

16 *Veazie Bank*, 75 U.S. at 549.

17 U.S. CONST. art. I, § 8, cl. 12.

18 338 U.S. 655 (1950).

19 *Id.* at 658, 660–61 (citing *McCulloch*, 17 U.S. at 421).

20 244 U.S. 416 (1917).

21 *Id.* at 425–26.

22 972 F.3d 156 (2d Cir. 2020).

23 U.S. CONST. art. I, § 8, cl. 10.

24 *Alarcon Sanchez*, 972 F.3d at 167 (reasoning that "prosecuting MDLEA conspirators who are not on the high seas is a means that is rationally related to the

Other single-power-implementing uses of the necessary-and-proper power involve Congress's leveraging of the Commerce Clause. In applying the principles developed under this grant of authority, the Court seldom pauses to assess precisely how the Commerce Clause and the Necessary and Proper Clause interact. But very often they do operate together. Indeed, there is good reason to conclude that much, if not all, of the "substantial effects" prong of the commerce power emanates not from the Commerce Clause working alone, but rather from the collaborative interaction of the Article I, section 8, clause 3 power grant and the supplementary authority vested by the Necessary and Proper Clause.[25]

2. Generalized Applications

The Necessary and Proper Clause sometimes interacts not just with a separate single grant (or a few grants) of lawmaking authority, but instead with most, if not all, of the constitutional provisions that vest legislative powers in Congress. Establishment of the federal prison system, for example, relates to each (or nearly each) of the Constitution's delegations of federal lawmaking authority because the U.S. Code is full of criminal laws rooted not only in the commerce power, but in the taxing power, the counterfeiting power, the bankruptcy power, the postal power, and on and on. But how far does Congress's ability to make rules regarding the federal prison system go? Addressing this question in *United States v. Comstock*,[26] the Court reaffirmed the centrality of *McCulloch* in guiding judicial work with the Necessary and Proper Clause.

At issue in *Comstock* was a law that targets individuals held in federal prisons whose terms of confinement are about to expire. Under the statute, continued *civil* confinement of any such individual is permitted if a district court finds by clear and convincing evidence that that person (1) previously engaged in an act of sexual violence and (2) "would have serious difficulty in refraining from sexually violent conduct or child molestation if released" because that person

---

legitimate end of prosecuting MDLEA conspirators who are on the high seas," especially because "the conspirators most likely to control, direct, finance, and profit from such drug trafficking are more apt to remain on land").

[25] *See, e.g.*, United States v. Wrightwood Dairy Co., 315 U.S. 110, 119 (1942) (citing *McCulloch* in deeming Congress's regulation of intrastate commerce in milk as "necessary and appropriate" to effectuating the imposition of controls on interstate activity in rebuffing a challenge to the regulation as exceeding the commerce power); *see also* Stephen Gardbaum, *Rethinking Constitutional Federalism*, 74 TEX. L. REV. 795, 807–11 (1996); *see generally supra* Section 3.C (noting the Court's treatment of this subject in recognizing Congress's ability to regulate intrastate activity in cases such as *United States v. Darby*, 312 U.S., 100 (1941)); *supra* Section 4.D.2.a (noting Justice Scalia's endorsement of the affecting-commerce prong of the commerce power on this basis in *Gonzales v. Raich*, 545 U.S. 1 (2005)).

[26] 560 U.S. 126 (2010).

suffers from a serious mental illness.[27] Before seeking this form of continued detention, federal officers must "make all reasonable efforts to cause" the inmate's state of domicile (or the state in which the inmate was originally tried) to "assume responsibility" for that person's "custody, care, and treatment."[28] Discharge of the inmate from federal control can occur, however, only if state authorities do take on this responsibility, either initially or later in time, or if improvements in the individual's mental health result in discontinuance of the dangerous condition.[29]

Persons subjected to commitment proceedings under this statute argued that it reached beyond Congress's enumerated powers, even as amplified by the Necessary and Proper Clause. Seven Justices, however, rejected this argument, with five of them coming together in an opinion authored by Justice Breyer. Not surprisingly, the Court made no claim that Congress had a text-based power to deal in a general way with the punishment, civil commitment, or treatment of sex offenders.[30] Even so, Justice Breyer declared that this particular program bore a close enough linkage to Congress's enumerated powers to qualify as a permissible exercise of the necessary-and-proper power. This conclusion had its grounding in *McCulloch*'s foundational teaching that Congress can "enact laws that are 'convenient, or useful' or 'conducive' " to promoting the "beneficial exercise" of Congress's Article I authority.[31] Later cases, Justice Breyer explained, had built out this principle to clarify that it required only that the challenged measure be "*rationally related* to the implementation of a constitutionally enumerated power."[32]

Against this doctrinal backdrop, there was no doubt that Congress could establish a prison system to incarcerate individuals who commit federal crimes.[33] The question thus became whether

---

[27] 18 U.S.C. § 4248.

[28] *Id.*

[29] *Id.*

[30] *See, e.g.*, United States v. Morrison, 529 U.S. 598 (2000) (rejecting, as a rule, federal control over localized violent conduct under the Commerce Clause).

[31] *Comstock*, 560 U.S. at 133–34 (quoting *McCulloch*, 17 U.S. at 413, 418).

[32] *Id.* at 134 (emphasis added) (citing Sabri v. United States, 541 U.S, 600, 605 (2004), which described the requisite relationship in terms of "means-ends rationality"). Concern about the level of deference suggested by this standard found expression not only in the dissenting opinion of Justice Thomas, *see id.* at 158 (Thomas, J., dissenting), but also in the concurring opinions of Justice Kennedy and Justice Alito, *see id.* at 151 (Kennedy, J., concurring in the judgment); *id.* at 155 (Alito, J., concurring in the judgment). The rhetoric of "rational basis," however, has deep roots in the Court's jurisprudence of congressional power, particularly (but not only) in the commerce-power context. *See supra* Section 3.C.2.

[33] As Justice Breyer explained: "Congress routinely exercises its authority to enact criminal laws in furtherance of, for example, its enumerated powers to regulate interstate and foreign commerce, to enforce civil rights, to spend funds for the general welfare, to establish federal courts, to establish post offices, to regulate bankruptcy, to

Congress could put in place the challenged program on the ground that it was a "necessary" component of that system even though the program operated on persons whose judicially fixed terms of confinement had passed. Two dissenters argued that the Elastic Clause was not elastic enough to stretch this far.[34] Justice Breyer, however, reached the opposite conclusion by relying on five considerations, the first of which centered on the "broad" power given to Congress by the Necessary and Proper Clause.[35] In addition, he pointed to four specific features of the program that both supported the need for the challenged statute in soundly operating the federal prison system and minimized the degree to which the program's operation compromised state authority.[36] First, "the civil-commitment statute . . . constitutes a modest addition to a set of federal prison-related mental-health statutes that have existed for many decades."[37] Indeed, he noted, federal law had since 1949 provided for continued federal control of "insane criminals upon the expiration of their terms of confinement" so long as they remain dangerous.[38] Second, to the extent the challenged law placed additional constraints on sex offenders, it carried forward the federal government's role, as "custodian of its prisoners," to "protect nearby (and other) communities from the danger federal prisoners may pose."[39] Put differently, just as Congress might require prison authorities to delay the release of someone who had served a full

---

regulate naturalization, and so forth." *Id.* at 136 (citing to various statutes illustrative of the point and cases upholding such exercises of congressional power). The creation of these laws, in turn, supported creation of the federal prison system to ensure their effective enforcement. And "having established a prison system," Congress "can enact laws that seek to ensure that system's safe and responsible administration," including by protecting "the safety of the prisoners, prison workers and visitors, and those in surrounding communities by, for example, creating further criminal laws governing entry, exit, and smuggling." *Id.* at 136–37.

34 *Id.* at 166–67 (Thomas, J., dissenting).

35 *See id.* at 135 (majority opinion) ("The Constitution leaves to Congress a large discretion as to the means that may be employed in executing a given power." (quoting Champion v. Ames (*The Lottery Case*), 188 U.S. 321, 355 (1903) (internal alterations omitted))).

36 In his dissenting opinion, Justice Thomas voiced displeasure with this multi-factor approach, emphasizing that courts would now face uncertainty in dealing with cases in which (for example) only two or three of the considerations flagged by the majority were implicated by a challenged statute. *Id.* at 166 (Thomas, J., dissenting).

37 *Id.* at 137 (majority opinion).

38 The original statute (which was passed pursuant to the recommendation of a panel of judges) specified that continued detention of an individual was permissible if, upon release, "he will probably endanger the safety of the officers, the property, or other interests of the United States." *Id.* at 140. Later judicial rulings made clear that this language was meant to cover "the safety of persons, property or the public interest in general—not merely the interests peculiar to the United States as such." *Id.* at 140–41. In any event, Congress amended the law in 1984 in a way that provided clear support for the thus-broadened operation of the preexisting statute. *Id.* at 141.

39 *Id.* at 142.

sentence but was infected with a serious communicable disease, it could logically provide for continued detention of "an individual whose mental illness threatens others to the same degree."[40] Of particular importance in this regard, Congress could have "reasonably concluded" that the persons on whom the statute operates pose "an especially high danger to the public if released," while state governments might well fail to address this danger "because the Federal Government itself severed [those persons'] claim to 'legal residence in any State' by incarcerating them in remote federal prisons."[41]

Third, "the statute properly account[ed] for State interests"[42] by compelling federal authorities to "inform the State in which the federal prisoner 'is domiciled or was tried' that [federal prison administrators are] detaining someone with respect to whom those States may wish to assert their authority."[43] In fact, the statute went so far as to require federal officers to "encourage those States to assume custody of the individual" and to "immediately 'release' that person 'to the appropriate official of' [the] State 'if such State will assume such responsibility.' "[44] Finally, Justice Breyer emphasized

---

[40] *Id.* at 142–43.

[41] *Id.* at 143 (quoting Jinks v. Richland Cnty., 538 U.S. 456, 462 (2003), for the proposition that "a statute is authorized by the Necessary and Proper Clause when it 'provides an alternative to [otherwise] unsatisfactory options' that are 'obviously inefficient' "). In his separate opinion concurring in the judgment, Justice Alito—even while expressing misgivings "about the breadth of the Court's language"—relied heavily on this same point in finding the law to be constitutional. *Id.* at 155 (Alito, J., concurring in the judgment). He reasoned in part that "[j]ust as it is necessary and proper for Congress to provide for the apprehension of escaped federal prisoners, it is necessary and proper for Congress to provide for the civil commitment of dangerous federal prisoners who would otherwise escape civil commitment as a result of federal imprisonment." *Id.* at 157.

[42] *Id.* at 143 (majority opinion).

[43] *Id.* at 144.

[44] *Id.* at 144–45 (internal alteration omitted). Justice Breyer deemed *Greenwood v. United States*, 350 U.S. 366, 373 (1956)—which validated the federal government's pretrial commitment of mentally ill criminal defendants—to be especially supportive of the significance of this factor. There the Court upheld the 1949 statute, *see supra* note 38 and accompanying text, even as applied to a prisoner subject to "likely indefinite" detention. *Comstock*, 560 U.S. at 146. The statute in *Greenwood*, the Court concluded, "was *less* protective of state interests" than the current statute, in that it put stricter limits on federal authorities' ability to turn over detainees to local officials. *Id.* at 145–46 (emphasis in original). Thus, Justice Breyer declared, "if the statute at issue in *Greenwood* did not invade state interests, then, *a fortiori*, neither does § 4248." *Id.* at 145–46. In his dissenting opinion, Justice Thomas argued that *Greenwood* was distinguishable on the ground that it did not deal at all with the *continued* detention of anyone who had already served a full prison term. Instead, the law at issue in *Greenwood* concerned commitment of an individual who had been assigned no sentence at all because that individual was deemed mentally unable to stand trial. *Id.* at 170–71 (Thomas, J., dissenting). Thus, Justice Thomas reasoned, in *Greenwood* (unlike in *Comstock*) the challenged statute's " 'end' reasonably could be interpreted as preserving the Government's power to enforce a criminal law against the accused." *Id.* at 171.

that the law at issue in *Comstock* was not "too sweeping in its scope."[45] Rather, it "applied to only a small fraction of federal prisoners,"[46] all of whom had to remain in federal custody at the time of the issuance of the civil-commitment decision.[47]

The Court's ruling in *Comstock* triggered a wide range of scholarly reactions.[48] But four points about the Court's ruling stand out. First, *Comstock* reflects a strong recommitment to *McCulloch*'s endorsement of a capacious judicial willingness to sustain congressional invocations of the Necessary and Proper Clause. Second, the case confirms that the power vested by the clause nonetheless has limits. Indeed, the majority's painstaking treatment of the issue presented in *Comstock* indicates that most, if not all, the Justices saw the case as raising at least a debatable question as to the constitutionality of the challenged statute.[49] Third, the reasoning of *Comstock* suggests that, in applying the clause, courts should focus primarily on the proper allocation of state and federal authority, as opposed to the protection of individual rights.[50] (The Court, after all, did not weigh in the decisional balance the extreme deprivation of

---

45 *Id.* at 146 (majority opinion).

46 *Id.* at 148.

47 *Id.*

48 For commentary on *Comstock*, see, e.g., Robert J. Pushaw, *The Paradox of the Obamacare Decision: How Can the Federal Government Have Limited Unlimited Power?*, 65 FLA. L. REV. 1993, 2008 (2013) (explaining that the open-ended approach of the majority in the case "fuels suspicion" that future decisions can and will "reflect politics rather than law"); Reinstein, *Limits*, *supra* note 6, at 17 (noting that the law challenged in *Comstock* was "four steps removed from any express power," but nonetheless a proper exercise of the necessary-and-proper power in light of the strength of the relevant connection between the law and Congress's enumerated powers); and Ilya Shapiro & Trevor Burrus, *Not Necessarily Proper:* Comstock*'s Errors and Limitations*, 61 SYRACUSE L. REV. 413, 419 (2011) (sharply criticizing the majority opinion in *Comstock* on the ground it relies on a "jumble" of reasons, thus establishing a "vague test that 'raises more questions than it answers' " (quoting *Comstock*, 460 U.S. at 166 (Thomas, J., dissenting))).

49 *See* H. Jefferson Powell, *The Regrettable Clause:* United States v. Comstock *and the Powers of Congress*, 48 SAN DIEGO L. REV. 713, 715–17 (2011) (describing the result reached in *Comstock* as "obvious" while asserting that "[i]t is the Court's reluctant, half-uncomprehending stance toward Congress's powers under the Necessary and Proper Clause, not the majority's correct decision that the clause authorizes § 4248, that is truly regrettable").

50 For scholarly work that both advocates and challenges a rights-based approach to the clause, see *supra* note 6. While this debate is laden with complexity, the power-allocating focus suggested by *Comstock* would seem to find support in (1) the Framers' placement of the clause within Article I's enumeration of powers and (2) the location of specific protections of individual rights elsewhere in the constitutional text. *But see* Michael Coenen, *Combining Constitutional Clauses*, 164 U. PA. L. REV. 1067, 1082–86 (2016) (highlighting occasional instances in which the Court has adverted to rights-based concerns in holding that a federal law exceeded the scope of Congress's powers under Article I). Also, in the picture is Chief Justice Marshall's insistence in *McCulloch* that the clause was inserted in the Constitution to expand, not contract, congressional authority. *See supra* Section 1.B.

liberty experienced by persons subjected to continuing, post-sentence confinement pursuant to the challenged law.)

Finally, in assessing whether the law at issue in *Comstock* transgressed constitutional bounds, the Court focused heavily on Congress's effort to accommodate state interests. Thus, as Justice Breyer emphasized, the statutory scheme at issue in *Comstock* welcomed the exertion of state control over persons subjected to continued detention. No less important, the law addressed an unusual type of collective-action problem—rooted in the *de facto* statelessness of persons held in long-term federal custody—that greatly complicated state-by-state treatment of an underlying policy concern widely shared by the states themselves. In the end, the Court in *Comstock* struck a balance that led it to conclude that Congress had not gone too far in its invocation of the Sweeping Clause. But it left open important questions about what limits on that power remain subject to judicial vindication.

B. LIMITS ON THE NECESSARY-AND-PROPER POWER

The text of the Necessary and Proper Clause points to two separate limits on the power that it bestows. The first is that laws enacted under it must be "necessary" to carry an enumerated power into execution. The second is that those laws must be "proper."

1. The "Necessary" Limit on the Necessary-and-Proper Power

Without question, it is uncommon for courts to strike down federal statutes on the ground that they are not "necessary" under Article I, section 8, clause 18. Even so, courts sometimes find a way to invalidate laws on this basis. Indeed, the Court took up the *Comstock* case itself only after the Fourth Circuit had held in effect that the challenged sex-offender statute was not a "necessary" measure within the meaning of the Necessary and Proper Clause.[51] In the wake of *Comstock*, courts have continued to uphold federal laws in the face of arguments that they reach beyond the power that

[51] *See* United States v. Comstock, 551 F.3d 274 (4th Cir. 2009), *rev'd and remanded*, 560 U.S. 126 (2010). For an early ruling of the Supreme Court that in effect determined that a law was not "necessary" under the Necessary and Proper Clause, see *United States v. Dewitt*, 76 U.S. 41, 44–45 (1869) (invalidating a ban on the sale of certain illuminating oils as a supposedly "appropriate" means to facilitate collection of a federal tax on competing illuminating oils, which were said to be less likely to be sold and thus taxed unless the challenged ban were in place, at least where Congress had left the ban in operation even after repealing the tax, thus leading the Court to conclude that the ban was nothing more than a "police regulation").

the clause bestows.[52] In a few cases, however, challenges of this kind have met with success.[53]

Illustrative is the Eleventh Circuit's ruling in *United States v. Davila-Mendoza*.[54] That case involved a prosecution under the MDLEA based on the defendants' shipment of drugs on the waters of a foreign nation. The government sought to defend the statute's application to the facts of the case as reflecting a necessary and proper measure for carrying into execution the treaty power, relying in particular on the Convention Against Illicit Traffic Treaty and the Jamaica Bilateral Agreement. The Court, however, found this defense of the act to be unavailing because Congress had enacted the MDLEA *before* the United States entered into these treaties. In effect, the court found that a law could not qualify as "necessary and proper for carrying into Execution" the treaty power if "it was not *enacted* . . . to *effectuate* those international agreements" that it purportedly carries into execution.[55] The Court emphasized that "nothing in the legislative history of MDLEA mentions a treaty or intimates that the legislation is in compliance with treaty obligations."[56] Nor could the government point to "any case in which legislation has been upheld as necessary and proper for carrying into execution a treaty which did not yet exist at the time the legislation was enacted."[57] Thus, while the court never explicitly invoked the clause's "necessity" requirement, its logic signaled that the law as applied to the defendants failed to qualify as "necessary" means of implementing what was, at the time of its enactment, a non-existent treaty.

---

[52] *See, e.g.*, United States v. Aquart, 912 F.3d 1, 57–61 (2d Cir. 2018) (rejecting a Necessary-and-Proper-Clause-based challenge to an application of federal death-penalty legislation), *cert. denied*, 140 S. Ct. 511 (2019); United States v. Baumgartner, 581 F. App'x 522, 529 (6th Cir. 2014) (upholding under the "rationally related" test a challenged federal law regarding concealment of federal offenses because the law "aids federal law-enforcement efforts by making it easier for the government to discover felonies and catch felons").

[53] *See, e.g., infra* Section 10.C (discussing a case in which a federal district court relied on *Comstock* in rejecting the government's effort to defend a federal ban on female genital mutilation as a necessary means of carrying into execution the treaty power).

[54] 972 F.3d 1264 (11th Cir. 2020).

[55] *Id.* at 1277 (emphasis in original). The Court further held that the statute's application could not be justified by reference to Congress's enumerated power to punish "[f]elonies committed on the high seas" because the underlying crime was committed within the territory of a foreign nation, rather than on international waters. *See id.* at 1268–69.

[56] *Id.* at 1277 (quoting United States v. Cardales-Luna, 632 F.3d 731, 749 (1st Cir. 2011) (Torruella, J., dissenting)).

[57] *Id.*

2. The "Proper" Limit on the Necessary-and-Proper Power

In *Comstock,* Justice Thomas authored a dissent, joined by Justice Scalia, that directed attention to *McCulloch*'s opaque suggestion that federal laws enacted under the Necessary and Proper Clause must comport not only with the "letter" of the Constitution, but also with its "spirit."[58] Did Justice Thomas mean to suggest, in penning this passage, that the challenged law in *Comstock* might not be "proper," even if it qualified as "necessary"—that is, as "appropriate" or "useful"—for carrying Congress's Article I powers into execution? No Justice in *Comstock* addressed this question in a focused way. Indeed, putting to one side a promptly overruled precedent handed down in 1869, the Court, from all appearances, had persistently declined throughout the nation's history to suggest that a "necessary" federal statute that regulates private citizens might fail to qualify as "proper" under Article I, section 8, clause 18.[59]

In *National Federation of Independent Business v. Sebelius* (*NFIB*),[60] however, this longstanding practice of judicial quiescence came to a screeching halt. As detailed in Chapter 4, a key question presented in that case was whether a law that required most

---

[58] *Comstock,* 560 U.S. at 160–61 (Thomas, J., dissenting). He invoked this passage from *McCulloch* for the purpose of criticizing the majority's suggestion that the challenged statute's "right of first refusal" provision—giving states the option to take custody of persons subject to the law—helped to cause it not to "upset the balance of federalism." *Id.* at 178. That provision, Justice Thomas reasoned, was "mere window dressing" and "altogether hollow" because (as was acknowledged at oral argument) it "is not the usual course that the State does take responsibility" for persons covered by the act. *Id.* Justice Breyer responded, at least indirectly, by observing that (1) any such passivity on the part of the states reflected their own voluntary choice, and (2) the federal statute took care to restrict the ability of federal authorities to meddle with state decisions regarding the detention of their own citizens by indicating that (as was also acknowledged at oral argument) " 'the Federal Government would have no appropriate role' with respect to an individual covered by the statute once 'the transfer to State responsibility and State control has occurred.' " *Id.* at 145 (majority opinion).

[59] In *Hepburn v. Griswold,* 75 U.S. 603 (1869), the Court (albeit in what seemed to be an alternative holding) did indicate that a federal law that required creditors to accept newly issued federal currency, in satisfaction of debts incurred prior to the law's enactment, violated the "spirit of the Constitution" because that law was rightly viewed as inconsistent with "the establishment of justice." *Id.* at 622. Only two years later, however, *Hepburn* was overruled in the *Legal Tender Cases,* 79 U.S. 457 (1871); *see also* Juilliard v. Greenman, 110 U.S. 421, 444–45 (1884) (relying heavily on *McCulloch* in following the *Legal Tender Cases* to endorse Congress's authority to establish a paper currency). In a more recent case involving a commandeering-based challenge to a federal law that imposed duties on *public* officials, the Court did advert, albeit only briefly, to the "proper" language in the Necessary and Proper Clause. *See* Printz v. United States, 521 U.S. 898, 899–900, 924 (1997) (invalidating federal duties placed on state officials to help in conducting gun-buyer background checks pursuant to the anti-commandeering principle; reasoning that if "a law violates the state sovereignty principle, it is not a law 'proper for carrying into Execution' delegated powers within the Necessary and Proper Clause's meaning").

[60] 567 U.S. 519 (2012).

individuals to secure health insurance constituted a permissible means of carrying into execution Congress's power to regulate interstate commerce.[61] In addressing this question, all members of the Court appeared to proceed from the premise that this "individual mandate" was "necessary" for purposes of the Necessary and Proper Clause because it helped to effectuate Congress's effort to facilitate interstate transactions (especially for persons with preexisting conditions) in the health insurance market.[62] Five members of the Court, however, concluded that the mandate was not "proper." On their way to reaching this conclusion, these Justices highlighted what they saw as the "extraordinary" and "unprecedented" nature of the challenged statute[63] in concluding that it violated the "spirit of the Constitution."[64] Chief Justice Roberts, who wrote the tie-breaking opinion on this point, reasoned that the mandate went too far because it embodied the exercise of a "great substantive and independent power."[65] Under the teaching of *McCulloch*, he reasoned, Congress could not wield such a power because the Necessary and Proper Clause permits Congress to pass only laws that are "incidental" to its enumerated powers.[66] Put another way, a majority of the Court saw Congress's enactment of the individual mandate as such a big deal—insofar as it compelled individuals to engage in unwanted market transactions—that Congress could not enact that law, even it though it may have been "necessary," because it was not "proper."

NFIB raises new questions about federal legislative authority. Consider, for example, the power of eminent domain. Nowhere does the Constitution expressly grant this power to Congress. Thus, federal lawmakers can invoke it, so it seems, only pursuant to the Necessary and Proper Clause. In *NFIB*, however, the Court held that it is not "proper" for Congress to compel individuals to engage in purchase transactions for purposes of effectuating its powers under the Commerce Clause. And if it is not proper to compel individuals to engage in purchase transactions, should it follow that Congress also cannot compel individuals to engage in sales transactions of their lands as well? In short, does the Court's invalidation of the mandate at issue in *NFIB*, on the ground it was not "proper" under the Necessary and Proper Clause, require invalidation of the mandates

---

[61] *See supra* Section 4.E.

[62] *See NFIB*, 567 U.S. at 548, 559 (opinion of Roberts, C.J.).

[63] *Id.* at 560 ("extraordinary"); *id.* at 655 (Scalia, Kennedy, Thomas & Alito, JJ., dissenting) ("unprecedented").

[64] *Id.* at 559–60 (opinion of Roberts, C.J.); *id.* at 654 (Scalia, Kennedy, Thomas & Alito, JJ., dissenting).

[65] *Id.* at 559 (opinion of Roberts, C.J.) (quoting *McCulloch*, 17 U.S. at 411).

[66] *Id.* (quoting *McCulloch*, 17 U.S. at 418).

that federal authorities effectively impose when they invoke the commerce power to compel the transfer of privately owned property by way of eminent domain?[67]

In a compendious treatment of this subject, Professor William Baude has argued that the Framers understood the power of eminent domain to be a "great power" that Congress accordingly could not exercise pursuant to the Necessary and Proper Clause.[68] The Court itself, however, has rejected this position for nearly 150 years, and it has not shown any signs in the aftermath of *NFIB* that it is eager to revisit the issue.[69] In any event, three considerations suggest that the case for placing the eminent-domain power in the "great substantive and independent power" category is significantly weaker than was the case for applying that label to the "individual mandate" at issue in *NFIB*. First, a specialized text-based case exists for concluding that the Framers viewed eminent domain as a means available to Congress for carrying into execution its enumerated powers. Why? Because the Fifth Amendment proceeds from the premise that Congress *can*, if it pays just compensation, take "private property . . . for public use."[70] Second, in contrast to the imposition of a direct

---

[67] One possible answer is that the question is beside the point because Congress can always exercise the eminent domain power pursuant to the Spending and/or Property Clauses. It is far from self-evident, however, that the Framers' vesting in Congress the powers to spend its own money and to regulate its own property carries along with it a companion power to force private landowners to transfer their property to the federal government. At the least, the following question looms over the subject: If the power to compel the sale of property is (like the power to compel a purchase transaction) a "great substantive and independent power" when linked up with the commerce power, why should it not qualify as a "great substantive and independent power" when linked up with the spending or property powers? To be sure, the Chief Justice left open the possibility that the imposition of an individual mandate that is not "proper" when tied to the commerce power might well be "proper" if tied to another power. *Cf. NFIB*, 567 U.S. at 549 n.3 (opinion of Roberts, C.J.) (deeming permissible a variety of other mandates "based on constitutional provisions other than the Commerce Clause"). But it also is true that a law that is not "proper" based on its connection to the Commerce Clause may also not be proper based on its connection to other clauses. (For example, the Court in *NFIB* found that specialized difficulties arose from the Framers' use of the word "regulate" in the Commerce Clause. Thus, it may well be that the same difficulties ought to flow from the Framers' use of that very same word in the Article IV Property Clause.)

[68] *See* Baude, *supra* note 5.

[69] *See* Kohl v. United States, 91 U.S. 367, 372 (1875) (allowing the federal use of the eminent-domain power "so far as is necessary to the enjoyment of the powers conferred upon it by the Constitution"); *accord Luxton*, 153 U.S. at 529; United States v. Gettysburg Elec. Ry. Co., 160 U.S. 668, 681 (1896) (same); Oklahoma *ex rel.* Phillips v. Guy F. Atkinson Co., 313 U.S. 508, 534 (1941) (holding even that "the fact that land is owned by a state is no barrier to its condemnation by the United States"). *See generally* Baude, *supra* note 8, at 1741–42 (acknowledging that modern scholars assume that use of eminent domain is authorized by the Necessary and Proper Clause). With regard to post-NFIB developments, see *infra* note 70 (referencing the *PennEast Pipeline* case).

[70] This is the case because that amendment specifies that "private property [shall not] be taken for public use, without just compensation." *See* U.S. CONST. amend. V.

purchase mandate, invocations of the power of eminent domain have long been part and parcel of the operation of governments, thus distinguishing such actions from the "extraordinary" and "unprecedented" action taken by Congress in the run-up to *NFIB*.[71] Finally, the eminent-domain power parallels in a significant way the authority to incorporate businesses, which the Court in *McCulloch* viewed as not constituting a "great substantive and independent power." This is the case because the power to condemn property, like the power to incorporate a business, "is never used for its own sake" but instead is used "for the purpose of effecting something else," such as building a road or establishing an army base.[72] Thus, according to

---

In contesting this point, Professor Baude argues that the Fifth Amendment limit took aim only at takings of property in the District of Columbia and the federal territories, because those takings (but only those takings) were authorized under the distinctly broad grants of power concerning those areas. *See* Baude, *supra* note 8, at 1761–91 (marshaling historical evidence supportive of this idea). The Takings Clause, however, finds its lodging in the middle of some twenty other Bill of Rights protections, each of which affords nationwide coverage, thus providing textual support for viewing that clause as signaling an intended operation not subject to extreme geographical limitations. Important features of the Fifth Amendment may also reinforce the conclusion that the eminent-domain power is not "great," "substantive," or "independent" in nature. Specifically, congressional deployment of the power is explicitly made subject to built-in brakes on both its unjustifiable exercise and its real-world severity because (1) federal decisionmakers can condemn property only for "public use" (rather than private use) and (2) invocation of the power always requires the government to pay "just compensation" out of the federal treasury, thus rendering any exercise of it inherently costly to the government itself. Particularly in light of these points, it is not surprising that the Court itself has found that the text of the Fifth Amendment supports the existence of a broadly applicable federal eminent-domain power. *See Kohl*, 91 U.S. at 372–73. Of particular importance, the four joint opinion writers in *NFIB* specifically distinguished the individual mandate at issue in that case from exercises of the eminent domain power based on the inclusion of the Fifth Amendment in the Constitution. *See NFIB*, 567 U.S. at 659 n.3 (Scalia, Kennedy, Thomas and Alito, JJ., dissenting) ("As its name suggests, the condemnation power does not 'compel' anyone to do anything. It acts *in rem*, against the property that is condemned, and is effective with or without a transfer of title from the former owner. More important, the power to condemn for public use is a separate sovereign power, explicitly acknowledged in the Fifth Amendment, which provides that 'private property [shall not] be taken for public use, without just compensation.' "). For the Court's most recent treatment of these matters, which tracks its earlier rulings on the federal government's eminent-domain authority, see *PennEast Pipeline Co. v. New Jersey*, 141 S. Ct. 2244, 2255–56 (2021).

71 *See supra* note 65 and accompanying text (quoting the opinions of Chief Justice Roberts and the four dissenters, with whom he agreed on this point). With regard to the long-recognized character of the eminent-domain power, see *Kohl*, 91 U.S. at 371–72 (noting that the power was "well known when the Constitution was adopted" and that it is a logical extension of Congress's recognized powers to build post-offices, forts, and lighthouses, while also noting that "[s]uch an authority is essential to [the federal government's] independent existence" and, for all governments, "inseparable from sovereignty").

72 *McCulloch*, 17 U.S. at 411. In contrast, while the purchase mandate at issue in *NFIB* did help effectuate the broader plan to facilitate the purchase of health-insurance policies by others in the market, it also simultaneously advanced the government's overarching plan of broadening insurance coverage as a general matter. Viewed in this light, the coverage mandate could be seen—and clearly more readily so

the reasoning of *McCulloch*, it seems entirely plausible to view the eminent domain power "as incidental to those powers which are expressly given."[73]

* * *

This abbreviated discussion of Congress's ability to invoke the Necessary and Proper Clause to implement its own enumerated powers shines a light on three key points. First, after *Comstock*, courts are likely to view with skepticism claims that federal statutes are not "necessary" within the meaning of the clause. Second, the majority's focus in *NFIB* on what it saw as the highly unusual character of the insurance-purchase mandate suggests that the Court's ruling in that case is unlikely to create a wide opening for future claims that federal laws fail to qualify as "proper," at least when those laws regulate individual (as opposed to state) conduct.[74] Finally, and nonetheless, both *Comstock* and *NFIB* set forth first-of-their-kind constitutional approaches that create new "opportunities for creative litigation" based on arguments that federal laws are not "necessary" or are not "proper" under the Sweeping Clause.[75]

C. THE NECESSARY AND PROPER CLAUSE AND NON-CONGRESSIONAL POWERS

In the *Federalist Papers*, James Madison asserted that the Constitution would have given Congress the power described by the Necessary and Proper Clause even if the Framers had not bothered to include that clause in the document.[76] Chief Justice Marshall endorsed the same view in *McCulloch*, indicating that, if Congress has "a right to do an act," then "the dictates of reason" establish that "it may . . . select any appropriate means . . . of effecting the object."[77] In one important respect, however, the Sweeping Clause sweeps beyond simply confirming that Congress has the authority to wield with effectiveness its own enumerated powers. This is the case because the clause gives Congress the authority to make laws "for carrying into Execution" not only its own powers, but also "all other powers vested by this Constitution in the Government of the United

---

than exercises of the power of eminent domain—as enacted "for its own sake" and not for "effecting something else." *Id.*

73 *Id.*

74 *See supra* note 59.

75 LaCroix, *supra* note 13, at 2050; *see also* United States v. DeLeon, No. CR 15-4268 JB, 2020 WL 353856, at *72 (D.N.M. Jan. 21, 2020) (noting that, with *NFIB*, "the Supreme Court has begun to take seriously the notion that laws—no matter how necessary—are improper if they undermine the nation's constitutional structure").

76 THE FEDERALIST NO. 44 (Madison).

77 *McCulloch*, 17 U.S. at 409–10. *See generally* Akhil Reed Amar, *Constitutional Redundancies and Clarifying Clauses*, 33 VAL. U. L. REV. 1, 7–10 (1998).

States, or in any Department or Officer thereof."[78] The extent to which Congress can pass laws in tandem with grants of the executive and the judicial powers has gained little attention over the years. From time to time, however, intimations of the potential robustness of this authority come into view.[79]

Illustrative of the point is the War Powers Act of 1973 (WPA), which Congress enacted in the wake of the Vietnam War to limit the President's ability to send troops into combat in the absence of express congressional authorization, including by imposing on the President notice-to-Congress and time-tied troop-withdrawal rules.[80] Congress based this enactment in part on its authority to "carry into execution" its own powers, particularly its power to declare war. In the preambular text of the WPA, however, Congress also pointed out that "[u]nder article I, section 8, of the Constitution, it is specifically provided that the Congress shall have the power to make all laws necessary and proper for carrying into execution, not only its own powers but also all other powers vested by the Constitution in the Government of the United States, or in any department or officer thereof."[81] This passage, read together with the House Report offered in support of the act, suggests that Congress viewed the grave decision to initiate military hostilities as one that rightly called for the "collective judgment of both the Congress and the President."[82] In other words, Congress saw itself as empowered to require this

---

[78] U.S. CONST. art. I, § 8, cl. 18.

[79] One example of the workings of this aspect of Article I, section 8, clause 18 lies in Congress's treatment of admiralty law. Article I does not speak, at least directly, about Congress's role in this field. Instead, Article III, section 2 empowers the federal courts to hear "all cases of admiralty and maritime jurisdiction." Building on this text, the Court has recognized a congressional power under the Necessary and Proper Clause to pass legislation concerning this subject. Supportive of this view is *The Thomas Barlum*, 293 U.S. 21 (1934), in which the Court observed: "The framers of the Constitution did not contemplate that the maritime law should remain unalterable. The purpose was to place the entire subject, including its substantive as well as its procedural features, under national control. From the beginning the grant was regarded as implicitly investing legislative power for that purpose in the United States. When the Constitution was adopted, the existing maritime law became the law of the United States subject to power in Congress to alter, qualify or supplement it as experience or changing conditions might require." *Id.* at 38, 43 (internal quotations omitted). The tale of the development of this power—in terms of the division of both federal/state authority and congressional/judicial authority is a complex one, and the present-day scope of congressional (and judicial) authority to fashion admiralty and maritime law is beyond the scope of this book. For a comprehensive treatment, see THOMAS J. SCHOENBAUM, ADMIRALTY AND MARITIME LAW (6th ed. 2019). For a short-form treatment, see 1 LAURENCE H. TRIBE, AMERICAN CONSTITUTIONAL LAW § 5–3, 805 n.16 (3d ed. 2000).

[80] The War Powers Act, which is often referred to as the War Powers Resolution, is set forth at 50 U.S.C. §§ 1541–48 (1973). For more on this statute, see *infra* Section 28.A.2.

[81] *Id.* at § 1541(b).

[82] *Id.* at § 1541(a); H.R. REP. NO. 93–287, at 2349 (1973).

"collective judgment" because doing so was "necessary"—in that it was "appropriate" or "useful"—in carrying into execution in a "beneficial" way the President's exercise of authority as Commander in Chief.[83]

Is such a theory of the Necessary and Proper Clause sound? And if so, how far does it reach? Special considerations may militate in favor of the WPA's validity because the dividing line between congressional and presidential power in this field of constitutional responsibility is distinctly murky. At least in cases of this kind, as Professor John Manning has suggested, the Necessary and Proper Clause indicates that the Constitution "counsels that the Court give priority to the . . . reasonable . . . judgments of Congress."[84] To be

---

[83] Indeed, to the extent that the President invokes implied powers to act, including in using military forces, an argument exists that—at least sometimes—the Necessary and Proper Clause of its own force might operate to block such actions even if Congress has not acted to inhibit them. *See* William Van Alstyne, *The Role of Congress in Determining Incidental Powers of the President and of the Federal Courts: A Comment on the Horizontal Effect of "the Sweeping Clause,"* 36 OHIO ST. L.J. 788, 793 (1975) ("Put briefly, I think that there is a reasonable basis for questioning the very permissive view the executive has assumed in respect to the proper source and scope of incidental executive power. A fair case may be made that this power may be, constitutionally, far more dependent upon a requirement of congressional determination than has been commonly supposed. A textual source of this dependency may rest in the relatively unexamined second half of the very best known clause in the Constitution—the necessary and proper clause."). Others have reflected at greater length on issues of this kind. *See, e.g.*, David J. Barron & Martin S. Lederman, *The Commander in Chief at the Lowest Ebb—Framing the Problem, Doctrine, and Original Understanding*, 121 HARV. L. REV. 689, 735 (2008) ("On the now-common understanding of the Necessary and Proper Clause, Congress may 'exercise its best judgment in the selection of measures to carry into execution the constitutional powers of the government' as a whole, including the powers that the Constitution vests in the President (or in the federal judiciary)—at least so long as the means chosen are 'plainly adapted' to a permissible end. Thus, Congress may use its Necessary and Proper authority not only to create federal agencies and instrumentalities (such as the National Security Agency), but also to define the scope of those agencies' authorizations and the conditions under which they shall operate." (quoting *McCulloch*, 17 U.S. at 420–21)); Jules Lobel, *Conflicts Between the Commander in Chief and Congress: Concurrent Power over the Conduct of War*, 69 OHIO ST. L.J. 391, 395 (2008) (noting the role of the Necessary and Proper Clause in defining the admixture of presidential and congressional power).

[84] Manning, *supra* note 8, at 78. Other important treatments of the subject can be seen as expressing similar views. *See, e.g.*, Martin S. Flaherty, *The Most Dangerous Branch*, 105 YALE L.J. 1725, 1800 (1996) ("By granting Congress the power 'to make all laws for carrying into execution' the enumerated powers assigned to any of the branches, the text on its own terms contemplates that Congress will determine how these powers are best exercised. The Clause does not say that Congress can regulate the execution of federal power only so long as the President undertakes the execution."); Lawrence Lessig & Cass R. Sunstein, *The President and the Administration*, 94 COLUM. L. REV. 1, 67 (1994) (discussing prior recognition of the "unqualified nature of Congress' power"; going on to observe that "for our purposes, what is far more crucial is the second half of the clause[,] the horizontal dimension to the Necessary and Proper Clause," which "[i]n as clear a textual commitment as possible" gives Congress "the power to determine the means for specifying how powers—and again, all powers—in the federal government are to be exercised"); Harold J. Krent, *The Lamentable Notion of Indefeasible Presidential Powers: A Reply*

sure, Presidents might assert that the notice requirements and time restrictions imposed by the WPA violate constitutional separation-of-powers requirements.[85] There can be little doubt, however, that Professor Manning (and others, too) would disagree with this assessment in light of "the broad zone of discretion" he sees the Necessary and Proper Clause as vesting in Congress.[86] Stated otherwise, at least in hard-to-call separation-of-powers cases,[87] there is reason to believe that the Necessary and Proper Clause should and does serve to channel decisionmaking power to Congress and thus away from the President.[88]

Tricky problems exist, however, about how far this conception of congressional power under the Necessary and Proper Clause reaches. Consider, for example, a hypothetical federal statute that puts in place a one-year moratorium on the issuance of presidential pardons in response to a scandal involving a self-interested President's misuse of this executive power. Such a case presents a special problem because it involves Congress's *blocking* of the exercise of a granted executive power, even if for a limited time, as opposed to (at least so the President will argue) a legislative effort that involves "carrying [that power] into Execution."[89] Assuming the existence of such an anti-obstruction limit on the necessary-and-proper power, to what extent should it apply to congressional prerogatives? Consider next a statute that requires the President to engage in some form of notice-and-comment process before issuing a pardon to any specified

---

to Professor Prakash, 91 CORNELL L. REV. 1383, 1388–89 (2006) (arguing that "the Court's struggles [in resolving conflicts between executive and legislative power] should not militate for adoption of a strong default rule in favor of the President"; noting rather that "[j]ust as congressional regulation of information may trench on presidential privilege, Congress through the Necessary and Proper Clause may regulate in a way that implicates other presidential powers under Article II"; also observing that this "is precisely what the Supreme Court has attempted to do in the cases it has adjudicated that involve an overlap of congressional and executive powers").

85 *See infra* Section 28.A.2.

86 Manning, *supra* note 8, at 65; *see id.* at 65 n.381 (asserting that "the inclusion in the Necessary and Proper Clause of the powers of the coordinate branches signals that, as long as Congress acts within constitutional margins, its implemental statutes can displace the implemental preferences of the coordinate branches").

87 *See, e.g.*, Youngstown Sheet & Tube Co. v. Sawyer, 343 U.S. 579 (1952) (discussed *infra* Section 26.B.1.a).

88 Manning, *supra* note 8, at 81 n.463 (noting the connection of his view of the Necessary and Proper Clause to Justice Jackson's approach to the *Youngstown* case); Krent, *supra* note 84, at 1389 (same).

89 *See* Saikrishna B. Prakash & Michael D. Ramsey, *The Executive Power over Foreign Affairs*, 111 YALE L.J. 231, 256 (2001) (contending that "since [the congressional power] is derivative of the President's power, it must be exercised in coordination with, and not in opposition to, the President").

person.[90] On the view of some analysts, such a law would not permissibly carry the President's powers into execution because it would stand "in opposition[ ]to the President"[91] if the President would prefer not to honor it. A defender of the law, however, might assert that it does not *block* the exercise of the pardon power; instead, the law seeks to *channel* the use of that power, by coupling it with often-used procedural safeguards, in an effort to foster care, accountability, and the achievement of sound results. More to the point, if Congress can invoke the Necessary and Proper Clause to fashion rules of procedure governing the exercise of the federal judicial power,[92] why should it not be able to fashion rules of procedure for the exercise of the executive power as well? Under the logic of *McCulloch*, Congress might well determine that a notice-and-comment procedure would serve a "useful" role in promoting the "beneficial" exercise of the pardon power.[93] And it would be difficult for a court to rule that Congress could not "rationally" reach that conclusion.[94]

---

90 The reference to "a pardon for any specified person" is included in this sentence because the Framers seem to have envisioned that in some instances, particularly those involving rebellion-related amnesties, the President should be able to issue pardons to large numbers of persons without delay. *See* THE FEDERALIST NO. 74 (Hamilton) (adverting to the disadvantages of a "dilatory process" in the face of "often critical moments" during "seasons of insurrection or rebellion" when "a well timed offer of pardon to the insurgents or rebels may restore the tranquility of the commonwealth"). The broader point is that all attempted exercises of the Necessary and Proper Clause in connection with presidential powers are not created equal, and some such exercises—albeit not all of them—will trench on those powers too much. On the other hand, the Court in *Myers v. United States*, 272 U.S. 52 (1926), stated that it was open to Congress to establish qualifications for offices to be filled by Presidents pursuant to their textually granted appointment power, at least if such eligibility limits do not "so trench upon executive choice as to be in effect legislative designation." *Id.* at 128. And if Congress can impose such substantive "blocking" limits on the President's exercise of the Article II appointment power, the question arises why Congress should not similarly be able to impose some substantive "blocking" limits on the pardon power (and other presidential powers) as well. *But see* Note, *Congressional Restrictions on the President's Appointment Power and the Role of Longstanding Practice in Constitutional Interpretation*, 120 HARV. L. REV. 1914, 1920 (2007) (suggesting that Congress's specialized power to limit eligibility for executive offices might derive from the idea, not applicable in the pardon-power context, that "certain types of qualification are simply part of the definition of [the] given office" that Congress has validly chosen to create). For additional commentary on Congress's power to create statutory qualifications for executive-branch officeholders, see, e.g., Andrew Kent, *Congress and the Independence of Federal Law Enforcement*, 52 U.C. DAVIS L. REV. 1927, 1967–73 (2019).

91 *See* Prakash & Ramsey, *supra* note 89, at 256.

92 *See, e.g.*, Wayman v. Southard, 23 U.S. (10 Wheat.) 1, 43 (1825) (recognizing such a power).

93 *McCulloch*, 17 U.S. at 325, 356.

94 *See supra* note 32 and accompanying text. *But cf.* Krent, *supra* note 84, at 1385 (concluding that "almost all congressional efforts to regulate the President's pardon power should be rejected"). Kindred questions involving both other powers and more consequential matters are not hard to spot. For example, might Congress require that the President postpone any launch of nuclear weapons until consulting with the

The types of congressional enactments discussed in the preceding paragraphs are loaded with constitutional difficulty, in part because most observers would agree that there exist some areas of presidential authority that Congress cannot enter, whatever the Necessary and Proper Clause might say.[95] One difficulty in applying the clause thus lies in deciphering what those no-fly zones of presidential power might be. A separate difficulty lies in deciding how far Congress can go when it enters an area of executive decisionmaking in which some measure of legislative meddling is allowed.[96] The closing passage of the Necessary and Proper Clause leaves no doubt that, notwithstanding these difficulties, Congress has some power to enact laws that it otherwise could not enact, on the theory that those laws play a useful role in carrying into execution the powers of the other branches. But this power remains, at least for now, largely unused in practice, uncertain in scope, and untested in the courts.

Secretary of Defense and the Chair of the Joint Chiefs of Staff? Or with the full Cabinet or senior members of Congress? Might Congress go a long step farther by requiring formal approval of such a launch by the Defense Secretary and the Chair of the Joint Chiefs? What if these restrictions—or more severe restrictions—were made applicable only if the nation were not already subject to actual or imminent attack, with "imminent" defined very narrowly?

[95] With regard to pardons, for example, the Court, in a five-to-four post-Civil War ruling, stated that the pardon power is "unlimited" and "not subject to legislative control." *Ex parte* Garland, 71 U.S. (4. Wall.) 333, 380 (1867); *see also infra* Section 26.B.2.c. In doing so, however, the Court did not mention, far less consider in a serious way, the effect in the pardon context of the Necessary and Proper Clause. Moreover, even if *Garland*—which focused on the Bill of Attainder and Ex Post Facto Clauses—states a still-governing principle regarding pardon-power law, it remains open to question how far that principle extends. It is possible, for example, that a court might read the case as foreclosing only congressional action that limits as a *substantive* matter the issuance or the effect of pardons, particularly since *Garland* itself involved such a restriction—namely, the disbarment of attorneys in federal court based on their commission of crimes thereafter made the subject of a pardon. Interestingly, the four dissenters in *Garland* did point to the Necessary and Proper Clause in finding that Congress had authority to enact the challenged law, including insofar as it applied in that case. *Id.* at 383 (Miller, J., dissenting). In doing so, however, the dissenters relied on only Congress's own enumerated power to establish lower federal courts and the Article III provision that vests the judicial power both in those lower federal courts and the Supreme Court. *Id.* In sum, no Justice in the case considered the interaction of the Necessary and Proper Clause and the Pardon Clause itself.

[96] *See, e.g.*, Krent, *supra* note 84, at 1388 (viewing the constitutional text as necessarily repudiating the view that "Congress has no business regulating presidential powers," so that resolving these issues "must instead turn on how to accommodate a legitimate exercise of congressional power under the Necessary and Proper Clause when presidential powers thereby are implicated").

Chapter 7

THE TAXING POWER

Analysis

Sec.

Article I, section 8, clause 1 empowers Congress "[t]o lay and collect Taxes, Duties, Imposts and Excises, to pay the Debts and provide for the common Defence and general Welfare of the United States."[1] Some delegates to the Philadelphia Convention and the state ratification conventions argued that any new taxing power vested in the Constitution's refashioned federal Congress should reach no further than to permit it to place levies on imported goods. Nationally minded leaders, however, defeated efforts to constrain congressional prerogatives in this way by arguing that a broad and flexible taxing authority was key to ensuring effective national governance. As Alexander Hamilton explained in *Federalist No. 30*, a "general power of taxation, in one shape or another" was critical to support a wide range of federal functions, including "raising troops," "building and equipping fleets," and "the payment of national debts contracted."[2] Hamilton also argued that a federal power to tax only imports would not "suffice for . . . present necessities,"[3] far less provide the level of funds "essential" for successfully conducting military operations in which the nation might, even in the near future, find itself engaged.[4] James Madison was no less adamant in promoting these views. He emphasized that the Framers had to shape the taxing power with an awareness of "all the possible changes which futurity may produce,"[5] including the "revolutions" in both public and private activities that would occur over long spans of time.[6]

---

1 U.S. CONST. art. I, § 8, cl. 1.

2 THE FEDERALIST NO. 30 (Hamilton).

3 *Id.*

4 *Id.*

5 THE FEDERALIST NO. 44 (Madison).

6 THE FEDERALIST NO. 41 (Madison).

Building on these ideas, the Framers forged a power that permits the imposition of federal taxes reaching far beyond duties on imports,[7] and Congress has drawn on this power to enact taxing laws of many different kinds. At the same time, the Framers attached several important restrictions to the taxing power, the most prominent of which has greatly complicated congressional efforts to enact "direct taxes," such as head taxes or poll taxes.[8] This restriction gave rise to high-stakes legal battles in the late-nineteenth-century over whether Congress could enact a federal income tax.[9] This litigation came to a close with the adoption in 1913 of the Sixteenth Amendment, which authorized establishment of the income-based taxing system that now provides the principal source of federal revenue.[10] Over the years, however, Congress has incorporated constitutionally controversial rules into its income-tax laws and passed other tax-related measures that raise constitutional problems of their own. Taken as a whole, these problems can be grouped into two basic categories. The first involves questions related to the principle, long recognized by the Court, that the Taxing Clause does not authorize Congress to impose "penalties" on disfavored conduct. The second involves questions related to the five major textual restrictions placed by the Framers on the taxing power, including the restriction on the enactment of direct taxes.

A. THE TAX-PENALTY DISTINCTION

1. The Basic Idea

The core concept that underlies the tax-penalty distinction crops up often in constitutional law—namely, that the substance of a law should take precedence over its form. Thus: "If [an exaction is] in reality a penalty it cannot be converted into a tax by so naming it, and we must ascribe to it the character disclosed by its purpose and operation, regardless of name."[11] This limiting principle reflects two overarching notions. First, the Constitution vests Congress with only limited authority to impose monetary fines for wrongful conduct under the Commerce Clause and other non-tax-related grants of authority. Second, the purpose of the taxing power is to generate

---

[7] *See* New York v. Mnuchin, 408 F. Supp. 3d 399, 416 (S.D.N.Y. 2019) (noting that Congress's taxing authority "is exhaustive and embraces every conceivable power of taxation" (internal quotations omitted)), *aff'd sub nom.* New York v. Yellen, 15 F.4th 569 (2d Cir. 2021).

[8] *See infra* Section 7.B.5.

[9] *See, e.g.*, Pollock v. Farmers' Loan & Tr. Co., 157 U.S. 429 (1895) [hereinafter *Pollock I*], *opinion vacated on reargument*, 158 U.S. 601 (1895) [hereinafter *Pollock II*].

[10] U.S. CONST. amend. XVI.

[11] United States v. Constantine, 296 U.S. 287, 294 (1935) (internal footnote omitted).

revenue, not to impose fines. From these two propositions, the Court has derived the key constitutional corollary: Congress cannot enact what is functionally a regulatory penalty by formally calling it a tax. Put another way, Congress cannot defeat the intended division of state and federal authority by wrapping a regulatory sanction, not otherwise sustainable under Article I, in the "verbal cellophane" of the taxing power.[12]

The highwater mark of the Court's work with these concepts came in the *Child Labor Tax Case*.[13] In *Hammer v. Dagenhart*,[14] the Court had stymied a congressional effort to establish nationwide federal child-labor restrictions pursuant to the commerce power.[15] Within months of the *Hammer* decision, however, a persistent Congress struck again, relying on its power to "lay and collect Taxes" to impose an exaction amounting to 10% of the net annual profits of any business that used child labor in a manner incompatible with federal standards. In the *Child Labor Tax Case*, the Court held that Congress could not substitute this taxing-power goose for the commerce-power gander it had just shot down in the *Hammer* case. The problem, the Court declared, was that one "must be blind not to see" that the challenged law's true purpose was to impose a "penalty" on the employment of children.[16] Because the law thus imposed a *de facto* regulation, rather than a bona fide tax, it ran afoul of the anti-pretext principle of *McCulloch v. Maryland*.[17]

The Court pointed to several features of the would-be child-labor "tax" as indicative of its impermissible status as a penalty. In particular: (1) the law imposed a charge that (unlike most true excises) targeted "a detailed and specified course of conduct" in business;[18] (2) the law laid an unusually "heavy exaction" on employers who engaged in such conduct;[19] (3) in contravention of ordinary taxing norms, the law imposed this charge in blunderbuss fashion, regardless of the extent to which the employer actually engaged in the "taxed" behavior during the tax year;[20] (4) the law established a duty to pay only for the "knowing" employment of children, thus marking the statute with a scienter requirement more

---

12 United States v. Kahriger, 345 U.S. 22, 38 (1953) (Frankfurter, J., dissenting).

13 259 U.S. 20 (1922). The formal name of the proceeding was *Bailey v. Drexel Furniture Co. See id.* at 20.

14 247 U.S. 251 (1918).

15 *See supra* Section 2.A.

16 *The Child Labor Tax Case*, 259 U.S. at 37.

17 *Id.* at 40. *See generally supra* Section 1.B (discussing this feature of *McCulloch*).

18 *The Child Labor Tax Case*, 259 U.S. at 36.

19 *Id.*

20 *Id.*

familiar to criminal laws than to the imposition of taxes;[21] (5) the law involved not only the Internal Revenue Service, but also the Labor Department, in collection efforts;[22] and (6) the law did all these things pursuant to congressional action taken in the immediate aftermath of the *Hammer* decision.[23]

This distinctive matrix of facts may have doomed the child-labor tax, but it also enabled the Court to apply the anti-penalty principle with circumspection in later cases. In fact, the Court has declined to invalidate a single federal tax as an impermissible penalty in the post-1936 period,[24] upholding as permissible exercises of the taxing power a range of exactions targeting firearm dealers,[25] marijuana transfers,[26] and gambling,[27] among other things.[28] No less important than the outcome of these cases has been the Court's consistently deferential tone. In *United States v. Kahriger*,[29] for example, the Court emphasized that an underlying "intent to curtail and hinder, as well as tax," does not itself render a measure a penalty, pointing with approval to Congress's routine reliance on tax laws to pursue non-revenue-raising goals.[30] Nor, the Court held, does a federal levy qualify as a penalty simply because "the revenue obtained [from it] is negligible."[31] The Justices in *Kahriger* accordingly upheld the challenged measure in that case because, "regardless of its regulatory effect, the wagering tax produces revenue."[32]

Even so, the tax-penalty distinction cannot be ignored. What if, for example, immediately following the Court's decision in *United States v. Lopez*,[33] Congress had passed a law, included in the Internal Revenue Code, that imposed a levy of $10,000 for every instance of gun possession within 1,000 feet of a schoolyard. The odds are high

---

21 *Id.* at 36–37.

22 *Id.* at 37.

23 *Id.* at 39.

24 For another pre-1937 case in which the Court invalidated a would-be tax on the theory that "the sum it exacts [is] a penalty," see *Constantine*, 296 U.S. at 295–96 (addressing a federal "tax" that targeted only those malt liquor dealers who operated in violation of state law).

25 *See* Sonzinsky v. United States, 300 U.S. 506 (1937).

26 *See* United States v. Sanchez, 340 U.S. 42 (1950).

27 *See* United States v. Kahriger, 345 U.S. 22 (1953).

28 *See also infra* Section 7.A.2 (discussing the Court's holding in *NFIB v. Sebelius*, 567 U.S. 519 (2012)).

29 345 U.S. at 22.

30 *Id.* at 27.

31 *Id.* at 28.

32 *Id.*; *see also Sonzinsky*, 300 U.S. at 514 (suggesting that when a tax "is productive of some revenue" the Court is "not free to speculate as to the motives which moved Congress to impose it, or as to the extent to which it may operate to restrict the activities taxed").

33 *See supra* Section 4.A.

that the Court would have declared that this congressionally denominated "tax" constituted a real-world "penalty," reasoning that the exaction looked so exotic as a matter of taxing tradition that it differed in a qualitative way from the more orthodox excises upheld in the earlier firearms, marijuana, and wagering cases. The Court probably would have added that the school-zones-only feature of the law reflected congressional tampering with a "detailed and specified course of conduct," just like in the *Child Labor Tax Case*.[34] And it also may have highlighted the parallel to that earlier case in light of Congress's enactment of the guns-near-schools "tax" close on the heels of the invalidation of a purely regulatory measure targeting exactly the same behavior. In short, this combination of facts would likely have led the Court to find that the challenged "tax" was in actuality a "penalty" because its "regulatory effect and purpose" was "palpable."[35] And this recharacterization would have meant, in turn, that (1) the law was not sustainable under the taxing power because it was not a tax, and (2) the law was also not sustainable under the commerce power because Congress cannot invoke that power to impose a penalty (at least in cases such as this one) on conduct that that is "noneconomic" in character.[36]

2. *NFIB v. Sebelius* and Follow-On Cases

This hypothetical school-gun tax directs attention to a deeper question concerning the law of constitutional federalism: To what extent might the Court's Congress-limiting commerce-power precedents (and the federalist spirit underlying them) bleed into judicial work with the taxing power?[37] Consider *NFIB v. Sebelius*,[38] which concerned the constitutionality of the "individual mandate" put in place by the Affordable Care Act (ACA). That measure required most individuals to make a "shared responsibility payment" to the federal treasury, as part of their federal income-tax remittance, unless they maintained health-insurance coverage during the operative tax year. As we have seen, five Justices in *NFIB* refused to uphold the law as an exercise of the powers vested in Congress by the Commerce Clause and the Necessary and Proper

34 *The Child Labor Tax Case*, 259 U.S. at 36.

35 *Id.* at 37.

36 *See supra* Section 4.D.1.

37 *Cf. also* Dep't of Revenue v. Kurth Ranch, 511 U.S. 767, 778–90 (1994) (relying on the Court's characterization of a challenged taxing measure as a penalty in *Constantine*, discussed *supra* note 24, in concluding that the imposition of a state marijuana tax on persons who were arrested for unlawful possession constituted a punishment for double-jeopardy purposes).

38 567 U.S. 519 (2012).

Clause.[39] This ruling, however, required the Court to answer the separate question whether the individual mandate was independently justified by Congress's power to tax.[40] More specifically did the shared responsibility payment constitute a permissible tax or an impermissible penalty?[41]

On this decisive question, the Chief Justice—joined by Justices Ginsburg, Breyer, Sotomayor, and Kagan—concluded that the payment did constitute a "tax," thus rendering the individual mandate a permissible exercise of congressional power.[42] In writing for the majority, the Chief Justice emphasized three key distinctions between the exaction imposed by the ACA and the "penalty" invalidated in the *Child Labor Tax Case*. First, whereas the child-labor tax had "imposed an exceedingly heavy burden—10 percent of a company's net income—on those who employed children, no matter how small their infraction,"[43] the ACA imposed a non-"prohibitory" payment obligation because "for most Americans the amount due will be far less than the price of insurance, and, by statute, it can never be more."[44] Second, whereas the child-labor tax involved the sort of *scienter* requirement that was "typical of punitive statutes," the ACA's shared responsibility payment applied, in a less culpability-focused fashion, to even those persons who had unknowingly failed to obtain health insurance.[45] Third, whereas the exaction at issue in the *Child Labor Tax Case* had been enforced by the Labor Department, the ACA's levy was "collected solely by the IRS through the normal means of taxation."[46] Other distinctions, too, might also have been noted. The Court could have observed, for instance, that in contrast to the child-labor tax, the ACA targeted neither a highly detailed set of workplace-related practices nor a form of behavior broadly condemned as inherently immoral. Nor had Congress swiftly

---

[39] *See supra* Section 4.E (Commerce Clause); *supra* Section 6.B.2 (Necessary and Proper Clause).

[40] *NFIB*, 567 U.S. at 547.

[41] *Id.* at 561.

[42] *Id.* at 566–74. Another provision of the ACA—that is, the so-called "employer mandate"—places a duty on certain employers to pay money to the IRS if they fail to meet conditions concerning the provision of insurance to their employees. In *Liberty University, Inc. v. Lew*, 733 F.3d 72 (4th Cir. 2013), the Fourth Circuit rejected a taxing-power-based challenge to this law, holding that the employer mandate, like the individual mandate upheld in *NFIB*, put in place a permissible tax rather than an impermissible penalty.

[43] *NFIB*, 567 U.S. at 565–66.

[44] *Id.* at 566; *see also id.* at 566 n.8 (estimating that a qualifying insurance policy would cost $400 per month, while an insurance-forgoing person whose annual income is $100,000 would likely be required to pay approximately $200 per month under the ACA's shared-responsibility-payment rules).

[45] *Id.* at 566; *cf. id.* at 567–68 (noting that the ACA "need not be read to declare that failing to [purchase health insurance] is unlawful").

[46] *Id.*

substituted a "tax" obligation for a just-invalidated criminal prohibition, as it had done in 1919.

The majority in *NFIB* acknowledged that Congress meant for the challenged ACA exaction "to affect individual conduct."[47] But this fact was beside the point in light of both settled precedent[48] and the routine use of taxes to shape individual behavior while simultaneously raising revenue—a point powerfully exemplified by modern-day levies directed at the purchase of cigarettes.[49] The majority also explained why the Constitution permits Congress to target a broader scope of conduct when it imposes taxes than when it regulates commerce. The reason is that the commerce power, in contrast to the taxing power, permits "the Federal Government [to] bring its full weight to bear," including by directly imposing sanctions of imprisonment.[50]

In response to these points, the dissenters emphasized that the text of the ACA repeatedly referred to the shared responsibility payment as a "penalty," thus affixing to the challenged exaction the very label found determinative of unconstitutionality in the *Child Labor Tax Case*.[51] These four Justices also reasoned that permitting Congress to impose a tax, while refusing to call it a tax, raised serious risks of diluting congressional accountability. The problem, they observed, was that federal lawmakers could now dodge the distinctly negative responses that they often receive when they threaten voters openly—rather than surreptitiously—with the prospect of imposing tax increases.[52] For the majority, however, these arguments did not carry the day. In effect, Chief Justice Roberts reasoned that the same substance-over-form principle that gave rise to judicial recognition of the tax-penalty distinction also must guide the courts' work in applying that distinction.[53] Thus, the mere labeling by Congress of the shared responsibility payment as a "penalty" was far less

---

[47] *Id.* at 567.

[48] *See supra* note 32 and accompanying text (noting the development of this point in *Kahriger* and *Sonzinsky*).

[49] *NFIB*, 567 U.S. at 567.

[50] *Id.* at 573.

[51] *Id.* at 662–63 (Scalia, Kennedy, Thomas, and Alito, JJ., dissenting) (citing *The Child Labor Tax Case*, 259 U.S. at 38). For a pre-*NFIB* case that likewise emphasized the point, see *Florida* ex rel. *McCollum v. U.S. Dep't of Health and Human Servs.*, 716 F. Supp. 2d 1120, 1130–41 (N.D. Fla. 2010) (holding that the penalty imposed by the ACA was not a permissible tax); *see also* Thomas More Law Ctr. v. Obama, 651 F.3d 529, 550–54 (6th Cir. 2011) (Sutton, J., concurring in part) (reaching a similar conclusion with respect to the taxing power, while ultimately determining that the mandate reflected a valid exercise of the commerce power).

[52] *NFIB*, 567 U.S. at 678 (Scalia, Kennedy, Thomas, and Alito, JJ., dissenting).

[53] *See id.* at 565 (majority opinion) (applying a "functional approach" that involves "[d]isregarding the designation of the exaction, and viewing its substance and application" (alteration in original) (quoting *Constantine*, 296 U.S. at 294)).

important than how the shared responsibility payment operated in the real world. And on that score, the substantive features of the challenged law—particularly its non-prohibitory character, its lack of a scienter requirement, and its implementation solely by the IRS—dictated that it "may reasonably be characterized as a tax."[54]

The decision in *NFIB* has left behind a new set of tax-penalty questions.[55] In *Texas v. United States*,[56] for example, the Fifth Circuit considered how to deal with a revamped version of the individual mandate, which Congress had effectively (but not formally) repealed in 2017 by adjusting the "shared responsibility payment" amount down to $0.00. This change, the court concluded (albeit in a decision that the Supreme Court subsequently vacated on other grounds), sufficed to render the thus-revised statute no longer justifiable as a "tax" because it no longer functioned to raise any revenue.[57]

---

54 *Id.* at 574. In effect, this same conclusion undergirded the majority's ruling, found deeply mysterious by some analysts, that the individual mandate embodied a tax for constitutional purposes even though it did not constitute a tax for purposes of the federal Tax Injunction Act, thus allowing the Court to bypass an otherwise applicable statutory bar on assessing the law's constitutionality in the context of a pre-enforcement challenge. *Id.* at 546. The key point, according to the Chief Justice, was that Congress has plenary control over the reach of its own statutes, and here the evidence was strong that it had not intended for the Tax Injunction Act to block review of laws such as the individual mandate. *Id. at* 543–46. On the other hand, "Congress cannot change whether an exaction is a tax or a penalty for *constitutional* purposes simply by describing it as one or the other." *Id.* at 544 (emphasis in original). In sum, statutory interpretation and constitutional exegesis involve fundamentally different forms of judicial work, and all the more so in light of the principle, applicable only in the latter context, that "every reasonable construction must be resorted to, in order to save a statute from unconstitutionality." *Id.* at 521 (opinion of Roberts, C.J.) (quoting Hooper v. California, 155 U.S. 648, 657 (1895)).

55 Scholars, not surprisingly, have weighed in on the impact of *NFIB*'s treatment of the taxing power. *See, e.g.*, Bret N. Bogenschneider, *The Taxing Power After* Sebelius, 51 WAKE FOREST L. REV. 941, 954 (2016) (arguing that *NFIB* "effectively rendered [the Constitution] a blank slate when it comes to . . . the taxing power"); Barry Cushman, NFIB v. Sebelius *and the Transformation of the Taxing Power*, 89 NOTRE DAME L. REV. 133, 188–94 (2013) (exploring whether, in light of earlier understandings of the *Child Labor Tax Case*, the Court in *NFIB* effectively overruled that case); Mark Klock, *The Taxing Power of the Federal Government and the General Welfare: What Are the Limits in the Wake of* NFIB v. Sebelius*?*, 76 U. PITT. L. REV. 325, 372–76 (2015) (criticizing the Court's reasoning in *NFIB* on the ground that its logic effectively gives Congress virtually unlimited power to pursue regulatory aims by way of levies collected by the IRS).

56 945 F.3d 355 (5th Cir. 2019) , *vacated and remanded on other grounds*, California v. Texas, 141 S. Ct. 2104 (2021).

57 *Id.* at 390. One might ask why anyone would go to court to attack a legal command that carries with it no sanction. The answer is that the challengers wanted the court to treat the remainder of the ACA as inseverable from the zeroed-out individual mandate, meaning that the entire ACA would have to fall if the retooled version of the individual mandate was no longer sustainable under the taxing power. *But see* Abbe R. Gluck, *Reading the ACA's Findings: Textualism, Severability, and the ACA's Return to the Court*, 130 YALE L.J. FORUM 132, 134 (2020) (emphasizing that the case presented a "simple and straightforward" severability question: "the 2017 Congress itself eliminated the penalty but left the rest of the ACA intact—leaving an explicitly enacted, text-based congressional indication for the rest of the statute to

Considering a very different tax-penalty question, the Tenth Circuit in *United States v. Cox*[58] refused to invalidate a recently revamped version of the tax placed on gun importers, dealers, and manufacturers by the National Firearms Act (NFA). In *Sonzinsky v. United States*,[59] the Court had upheld this levy. Thereafter, however, Congress had effectively reassigned responsibility for ensuring compliance with the act from the Internal Revenue Service to the Department of Justice.[60] This "shift in oversight," the challengers argued, caused the thus-revised NFA to lose its constitutional character because it now "resemble[d] the regulatory scheme struck down in the *Child Labor Tax Case*."[61] The Tenth Circuit, however, rejected this contention, emphasizing that in the *Child Labor Tax Case* it was the joint operation of multiple considerations that had "convinced the Court that the so-called tax was really a penalty,"[62] whereas the change in enforcement responsibilities had not "so alter[ed]" the law's operation "as to unmoor today's NFA from the statute deemed constitutional in *Sonzinsky*."[63]

B. LIMITS ON THE TAXING POWER BEYOND THE TAX-PENALTY PRINCIPLE

The tax-penalty distinction arises out of Article I, section 8's textual grant of congressional power to impose, but to impose only,

---

survive, expressed as clearly as it possibly could be by the continued existence of the ACA"). In *California v. Texas*, 141 S. Ct. 2104 (2021), however, the Court sidestepped a ruling on the merits of both the taxing-power question and the severability question by finding that no litigant in the case had standing to raise these claims.

58 906 F.3d 1170 (10th Cir. 2018).

59 300 U.S. 506 (1937).

60 *Cox*, 906 F.3d at 1180.

61 *Id.*

62 *Id.*

63 *Id.* at 1181. Notably, the court was also unmoved by the challenger's claim that the tax, as presently administered, generates no "net" revenue because total enforcement costs exceeded total tax collections. *Id.* at 1181–83. On this point, the court viewed controlling Supreme Court precedent as requiring the generation of only gross, as opposed to net, tax revenues. It reasoned in part that, "as the government pragmatically puts it, 'If the focus were on net revenue, then the Executive Branch could negate the constitutionality of a tax imposed by Congress simply through spendthrift enforcement.' " *Id.* at 1183 (citation omitted). For other cases upholding the present-day components of the firearms tax, see *United States v. Bolatete*, 977 F.3d 1022, 1033 (11th Cir. 2020), *cert. denied*, 141 S. Ct. 1754 (2021); *United States v. Lim*, 444 F.3d 910, 912–914 (7th Cir. 2006); and United States v. White, No. 13–0440–01–CR-W-SRB, 2017 WL 11528245, at *2 (W.D. Mo. Oct. 13, 2017). The court in *Bolatete* left open the separate question whether the NFA presented Second Amendment problems. *See* 977 F.3d at 1035. *But see* Bezet v. United States, 276 F. Supp. 3d 576 (E.D. La. 2017) (holding that NFA taxing provisions do not impinge on core Second Amendment rights), *aff'd*, 714 Fed. App'x 335 (5th Cir. 2017); *Cox*, 906 F.3d at 1184–85 (rejecting Second Amendment-based challenges to an NFA-based tax associated with short-barreled rifles and silencers on the ground that the possession of such weaponry falls outside the scope of the amendment's protections).

"Taxes, Duties, Imposts and Excises."[64] Other limits on the taxing power stem from other features of the constitutional text. To begin with, the Constitution places some limits on all of Congress's lawmaking powers, including most prominently through the operation of the Bill of Rights.[65] It follows, for example, that Congress could not, consistent with the First Amendment, impose an otherwise permissible federal tax only on newspaper publishers.[66] Apart from the protections provided by the Bill of Rights, moreover, there exist five tax-specific limits set forth in the original Constitution, each of which is discussed below.[67]

1. The Uniformity Requirement

First, Article I, section 8, clause 1 dictates that "all Duties, Imposts and Excises shall be *uniform throughout the United States*."[68] This mandate does not require Congress to treat all

---

[64] U.S. CONST. art. I, § 8, cl. 1.

[65] *See, e.g.*, *supra* note 63 (noting cases involving challenges to tax laws under the Second Amendments).

[66] *See, e.g.*, Minn. Star & Tribune Co. v. Minn. Comm'r of Revenue, 460 U.S. 575 (1983).

[67] Also on the menu of federalism-based limits on the taxing power are principles of intergovernmental immunity that restrict to some degree Congress's ability to tax states themselves and (at least if problematic discrimination is present) persons associated with states. *See supra* Section 5.A. Particularly in light of the earlier treatment of the tax-penalty distinction, however, one point about these intergovernmental-immunity limits merits mention here: The courts have resisted one significant set of entreaties to apply the substance-over-form principle in fleshing out the intergovernmental-tax-immunity doctrine. More specifically, long-governing rules establish that the application of the doctrine does not hinge on who, as a practical matter, bears the impact of the tax—for example, in the many instances where a state passes along the cost of the tax to a private party or where a private party passes along the cost of the tax to the state. Instead, courts give determinative effect to the "legal incidence" of the tax, and "[l]egal incidence is determined by the 'clear wording of the statute,' not 'by who is responsible for payment . . . of the exaction.' " State v. Rettig, 987 F.3d 518, 536 (5th Cir. 2021) (quoting United States v. State Tax Comm'n, 421 U.S. 599, 607–08 (1975)).

[68] U.S. CONST. art. I, § 8, cl. 1 (emphasis added). A curiosity regarding this choice of phrasing merits notice: The Taxing Clause of Article I, section 8, clause 1 (1) speaks generally of a power to impose "Taxes, Duties, Imposts and Excises," but (2) by its terms applies the uniformity requirement only to "Duties, Imposts and Excises." Meanwhile, Article I, section 9, clause 4 indicates that "[n]o capitation, or other Direct, Tax" is subject to the uniformity requirement because direct taxes must be imposed according to state-population numbers regardless of the base of taxation. *See infra* Section 7.B.5. A question thus arises as to whether there might be *indirect* "Taxes" that do not constitute "Duties, Imposts, and Excises" and, if so, what courts should do with them in terms of the uniformity requirement. Fortunately, the question (which probably exists only because of a drafting error) has proven to be of only academic interest due to the problem-dodging work of the Court in dealing with these clauses. *See, e.g.*, Flint v. Stone Tracy Co., 220 U.S. 107, 151 (1911) ("[T]he terms duties, imposts, and excises are generally treated as embracing the indirect forms of taxation contemplated by the Constitution."); *Pollock I*, 157 U.S. at 557 ("[A]lthough there have been, from time to time, intimations that there might be some tax which was not a

taxpayers equally in all respects—thus, for example, Congress can tax high-wage earners at rates that exceed those applied to low-wage earners[69]—but only that Congress impose "Duties, Imposts and Excises" without *geographic* variation throughout the nation.[70] At the same time, the Court has held that even this geographically-focused requirement does not contemplate uniformity in the strictest sense. Consider in this respect *United States v. Ptasynski*,[71] in which the Court upheld an exemption from a crude-oil windfall-profits tax even though the exemption applied, according to the statute's express terms, only to Alaskan petroleum. The Court reasoned that Congress's action was permissible because Alaskan oil operations involved features that were genuinely distinctive—indeed, so distinctive that Congress could have, if it had taken the time to do so, referenced those features in the statute in such a way as to direct the exemption to only and all Alaskan oil without ever mentioning Alaska at all.[72] While it is unclear how far the Court might take the principle of *Ptasynski* in the future, the case sets forth the starting point for analysis in the following terms: "Where Congress defines the subject of a tax in nongeographic terms, the Uniformity Clause is satisfied . . . . But where Congress does choose to frame a tax in geographic terms, we will examine the classification closely to see if there is actual geographic discrimination."[73]

2. The Origination Clause

A second textual limit on the taxing power finds expression in the Origination Clause of Article I, section 7, which provides that "[a]ll Bills for raising Revenue shall originate in the House of Representatives; but the Senate may propose or concur with amendments as on other Bills."[74] The Framers viewed this clause as installing an important structural guardrail on excessive federal taxation by channeling primary responsibility for revenue raising to

---

direct tax, nor included under the words 'duties, imports, and excises,' such a tax, for more than 100 years of national existence, has as yet remained undiscovered . . . .").

69 *See, e.g.*, Knowlton v. Moore, 178 U.S. 41, 86 (1900) (clarifying that "uniformity" references only geographic uniformity; "[t]he tax is uniform when it operates with the same force and effect in every place where the subject of it is found" (quoting Edye v. Robertson, 112 U.S. 580, 594 (1884)); *see also* MILAN N. BALL, CONG. RSCH. SERV., R46551, THE FEDERAL TAXING POWER: A PRIMER 11 (Sept. 28, 2020) (noting that the rule of uniformity is a geographical one, which applies only to indirect taxes).

70 *See* La Belle Iron Works v. United States, 256 U.S. 377, 392 (1921) ("[T]he only rule of uniformity prescribed with respect to duties, imposts, and excises laid by Congress is the territorial uniformity required by [Article] 1, § 8."). *See generally* BALL, *supra* note 69, at 10–12.

71 462 U.S. 74 (1983).

72 *Id.* at 85.

73 *Id.*

74 U.S. CONST. art. I, § 8, cl. 1.

"the immediate representatives of the people" elected to the House.[75] For three reasons, however, this differentiation of House and Senate responsibilities has turned out to have little real-world importance. First, even if the Origination Clause did not exist, the House would remain fully involved in the tax-imposing process because no tax bill can become law without the House's approval. Second, the Origination Clause does nothing to prevent Senators from asking House allies to propose the enactment of a tax bill on their behalf. Third, the Origination Clause's specific allowance of Senate involvement in the amendment process removes any special measure of House control that might exist under a system pursuant to which the lower chamber could send bills to the Senate on a take-it-or-leave-it basis.[76] To be sure, the courts might still strike down tax laws that, due to slip-ups or otherwise, are initially passed in the upper chamber.[77] It says much about the limited significance of the Origination Clause, however, that the Supreme Court has never, even once, struck down an act of Congress due to a failure to adhere to the requirement that it imposes.[78]

3. The Export Clause

A third restriction on the taxing power appears in Article I, section 9, which specifies that "no Tax or Duty shall be laid on Articles exported from any State."[79] In *Dooley v. United States*[80] the Court held back the reach of this restriction by reading it to apply only to shipments to foreign countries, as opposed to unincorporated

---

75 THE FEDERALIST NO. 58 (Madison). It bears recalling on this point that, under the original Constitution and prior to ratification of the Seventeenth Amendment in 1913, state legislators chose the members of the Senate.

76 *See also Flint*, 220 U.S. at 142–44 (declining to treat the Senate amendment power with respect to tax statutes as subject to rigorous constitutional limits).

77 *See* United States v. Munoz-Flores, 495 U.S. 385, 389–96 (1990) (rejecting the assertion that the political-question doctrine bars suits claiming a violation of the Origination Clause).

78 Erik M. Jensen, *The Origination Clause and the Validity of Taxing Statutes*, 36 J. TAX'N INV. 61, 74 (2019) (noting that "the Supreme Court has decided several cases in which Origination Clause issues were raised, but in no case has the Court invalidated a piece of legislation because of Congress's failure to satisfy Origination Clause requirements"). For one lower court's treatment of an Origination Clause challenge to the ACA, see *Sissel v. U.S. Dep't of Health and Human Servs.*, 951 F. Supp. 2d 159, 167–68 (D.D.C. 2013) (holding that the individual mandate, although a constitutional exercise of Congress's taxing power, was not subject to the Origination Clause's requirements because the ACA as a whole was not itself a "Bill[ ] for raising Revenue" and because the Origination Clause does not apply to " 'bills for other purposes which may incidentally create revenue' " (quoting Twin City Nat'l Bank of New Brighton v. Nebecker, 167 U.S. 196, 202 (1897))), *aff'd*, 760 F.3d 1 (D.C. Cir. 2014). For a discussion of the distinctive way in which the Origination Clause intersects with the treaty power, see *infra* Section 10.C.

79 U.S. CONST. art. I, § 9.

80 183 U.S. 151 (1901).

territories of the United States.[81] On the other hand, in *Fairbank v. United States*,[82] the Court rejected the proposition that this limit, when applied in the context of exportation to foreign nations, should operate only to preclude targeted taxation of exported items themselves.[83] The Export Clause, the Court explained, requires "not simply an omission of a tax upon the articles exported, but also a freedom from any tax which directly burdens the exportation."[84] In both pre- and post-*Fairbank* rulings, however, the Court has declined to give this principle as broad a reach as its enthusiastic expression in that case might support.[85] Of particular significance, the Court has rejected *Fairbank*-inspired efforts to secure an exemption from the general income tax for income derived from export-related activities.[86]

4. The Ports Preference Clause

A fourth limit on Congress's taxing power finds expression in the Article 1, section 9 stipulation that "no Preference shall be given by any Regulation of Commerce or Revenue to the Ports of one state over those of another; nor shall Vessels bound to, or from, one State, be obliged to enter, clear, or pay duties in another."[87] One purpose of this clause is to foreclose Congress's favoring of some state ports over others. Another is to shelter shipping operations from efficiency-hampering impediments to free movement on navigable waters. As the opening words of the clause indicate, it takes aim at obligations imposed by Congress, including in the form of monetary exactions, under either the Taxing Clause or the Commerce Clause, thus (among other things) rendering the tax-penalty distinction inconsequential in this context.[88] The provision's closing words (set forth following the semicolon), while also limiting the adoption of both tax and non-tax rules, do give rise to one tax-specific question—namely, what forms of payments constitute "duties" within the meaning of the clause? In *Cooley v. Board of Wardens*,[89] the Court

---

81 *Id.* at 153–54; *see also infra* Section 25.B.2 (discussing the distinction between incorporated and unincorporated territories).

82 181 U.S. 283 (1901).

83 *Id.* at 293. The Court held that the tax at issue, a stamp tax imposed on a foreign bill of lading, was in effect "a tax on the articles included in that bill of lading, and therefore a tax or duty on exports" prohibited by Article I, section 9.

84 *Id.* at 293.

85 For a pre-*Fairbank* case, see *Turpin v. Burgess*, 117 U.S. 504, 507 (1886) (concluding that a nondiscriminatory tax placed on goods intended for export, but still in the factory, fell outside the constitutional prohibition).

86 *See* William E. Peck & Co. v. Lowe, 247 U.S. 165, 174–75 (1918).

87 U.S. CONST. art. I, § 9.

88 *See* Gibbons v. Ogden, 22 U.S. (9 Wheat.) 1, 191 (1824).

89 53 U.S. (12 How.) 299 (1851).

spoke to this question in the curious context of a case involving a charge imposed under state, rather than federal, law. Having chosen to address the issue, however, the Court held, with much justification, that a charge for the services provided by harbor pilots who steered vessels through a busy port was not the sort of "dut[y]" that the Framers had in mind when they crafted Article I, section 9.[90] Instead, the charge fell outside the provision because it was a permissible user fee.[91]

5. The Direct-Tax Apportionment Requirement

Finally (and as noted earlier), Article I, section 2 creates a special rule for congressional imposition of "direct taxes"—specifically, that those taxes "shall be apportioned among the several States which may be included within this Union, according to their respective numbers."[92] What does it mean for a tax to be "apportioned among the states . . . according to their respective numbers"? It means that if Congress imposes a tax properly characterized as direct—for example, a tax on land—it must do so in a state-population-based way that differs greatly from how such taxes ordinarily operate. Assume, for example, that States Alpha and Zeta each have the same amount, and the same assessed value, of taxable acreage. Alpha, however, has a total population of ten million persons and Zeta has a total population of twenty million persons. It follows that, because Zeta has twice the population as Alpha, the taxpayers of Zeta will have to make twice the amount of land-tax payments as their Alpha-based neighbors, and this is so even though the assessed value of the land in each state is exactly the same. In other words, the owner of one acre of land worth $10,000 in Zeta will have to pay twice as much tax as the owner of one acre of land worth $10,000 in Alpha, notwithstanding the obvious unfairness of that outcome and the extraordinary practical difficulties of applying such a tax to citizens with countless forms of landholdings across fifty different states with wildly varying total land acreages, total land values, and total human populations.[93]

---

[90] *Id.* at 314–15 (explaining that "pilotage-fees are not duties within the meaning of the Constitution").

[91] For a treatment of user fees under the dormant Commerce Clause, see *infra* Section 21.E.

[92] U.S. CONST. art. I, § 2, cl. 3. Doubling down on the same point, Article I, section 9 adds that "[n]o Capitation, or other direct, Tax shall be laid, unless in Proportion to the Census or Enumeration herein before directed to be taken." *Id.* art. I, § 8, cl. 1.

[93] *See* Neil S. Siegel & Steven J. Willis, *Direct and Indirect Taxes*, INTERACTIVE CONSTITUTION, NATIONAL CONSTITUTION CENTER, https://constitutioncenter.org/interactive-constitution/interpretation/article-i/clauses/757 (last visited Nov. 15, 2021) (noting, along similar lines, that a federal $1-per-acre tax would violate the apportionment requirement because it would not be calibrated based on the differing populations of the states).

Not surprisingly, Congress has steered away from enacting direct taxes because of the political and practical difficulties caused by the apportionment requirement. Indeed, these difficulties have proven so consequential as a practical matter that the Constitution might as well prohibit the imposition of direct taxes altogether.[94] A critical question thus arises: How do courts distinguish between the mutually exclusive categories of "direct" and "indirect" tax levies.[95]

On this point, the records of the framing period are notoriously obscure.[96] The Court accordingly had little to go on when it first considered the question in *Hylton v. United States*.[97] In that case, disgruntled horse-drawn buggy owners challenged a recently adopted federal tax on carriages, arguing that Congress had taken a wrong turn by failing to apportion it.[98] In a brief filed with the Court, Secretary of the Treasury Alexander Hamilton defended the tax against this line of attack,[99] defining direct taxes to encompass only "[c]apitation or poll taxes," "[t]axes on land and buildings," and "[g]eneral assessments, whether on the whole property of

---

[94] *See generally* Calvin H. Johnson, *Apportionment of Direct Taxes: The Foul-Up in the Core of the Constitution*, 7 WM. & MARY BILL RTS. J. 1, 3 (1998) (noting that the apportionment requirement renders direct taxes "impossible, in practice, to use").

[95] As to the mutually exclusive nature of "direct' and "indirect" taxes for federal constitutional purposes, see Erik M. Jensen, *The Apportionment of "Direct Taxes": Are Consumption Taxes Constitutional?*, 97 COLUM. L. REV. 2334, 2341 (1997) ("[T]he two rules are set up to be mutually exclusive: taxes other than direct taxes are not subject to the apportionment requirement, and the uniformity rule cannot apply to apportioned direct taxes."). For one explanation of how these requirements work in practice, see Joseph M. Dodge, *What Federal Taxes Are Subject to the Rule of Apportionment Under the Constitution?*, 11 U. PA. J. CONST. L. 839, 843–45 (2009).

[96] According to James Madison's notes from the Constitutional Convention, one delegate "asked what was the precise meaning of direct taxation," and no one answered. Jensen, *supra* note 95, at 2377 (quoting 2 THE RECORDS OF THE FEDERAL CONVENTION OF 1787, at 350 (Max Farrand, ed., rev. ed. 1966) (noting discussion of Aug. 20, 1787)). In *The Federalist*, Alexander Hamilton stated that a direct tax "principally relate[s] to land and buildings." THE FEDERALIST NO. 21 (Hamilton). *See also NFIB*, 567 U.S. at 570 ("Even when the Direct Tax Clause was written it was unclear what else, other than a capitation . . ., might be a direct tax." (citing Springer v. United States, 102 U.S. 586, 596–98 (1881))). To be sure, many historians agree that the state-population-tied power of Congress to impose direct taxes came as part of a trade-off involving the infamous Three-Fifths Clause, which dictated that each enslaved person would count as three-fifths of a person for purposes of determining state representation in the House of Representatives. *See, e.g.*, Calvin H. Johnson, *Fixing the Constitutional Absurdity of the Apportionment of Direct Tax*, 21 CONST. COMMENT. 295, 297 (2004). In the end, however, the Constitution's treatment of direct taxation, and later-developed understandings of the subject, rendered any original plan to offset a representation-related benefit for the southern states with a tax-related burden ineffective as a practical matter. *See, e.g.*, Bruce Ackerman, *Taxation and the Constitution*, 99 COLUM. L. REV. 1, 10 (1999) (arguing that, because the use of direct taxes was intended to be very limited, "the South could get its extra representation without paying for it").

[97] 3 U.S. (3 Dall.) 171 (1796).

[98] *See id.* at 172–73.

[99] *See* Jensen, *supra* note 96, at 2351, 2357.

individuals, or on their whole real or personal estate."[100] In the end, the Court determined that the carriage tax was "indirect" and thus permissible, with each of the participating Justices writing separately in support of that result.[101] The opinion that would later gain the most attention came from Justice Samuel Chase. He emphasized that taxing "any specific article by the rule of apportionment . . . would evidently create great inequality and injustice,"[102] and that the "direct" label therefore should not attach to a tax placed on a "consumeable commodity," such as a carriage.[103] Albeit in dicta,[104] Justice Chase also took the opportunity to offer his own definition of "direct" taxes. According to him: "[T]he direct taxes contemplated by the Constitution, are only two, to wit, a capitation, or poll tax, simply, without regard to property, profession, or any other circumstance; and a tax on LAND."[105]

Debates about the nature of "direct" taxation again took center stage a century later as the Court fielded challenges to the newly enacted—and unapportioned—federal income tax.[106] The first key decision came in *Pollock v. Farmers' Loan & Trust Co.* (*Pollock I*),[107] in which the Court ruled that a tax on "the income or rents of real estate" qualified as "direct," thus requiring population-based apportionment.[108] The Court reasoned that, at the time of

---

100 *Id.* at 2358 (quoting Brief for the United States, *Hylton*, 3 U.S. at 171, *reprinted in* 8 ALEXANDER HAMILTON, THE WORKS OF ALEXANDER HAMILTON 382 (Henry Cabot Lodge ed., Fed. ed. 1904)).

101 For a review of the Court's unusual handling of the case and a summary of the views of the participating Justices, see Joel Alicea & Donald L. Drakeman, *The Limits of New Originalism*, 15 U. PA. J. CONST. L. 1161, 1170–86 (2013).

102 *Hylton*, 3 U.S. at 174–75. With regard to this point, the essential difficulty is that a fair carriage tax would apply equally to everyone required to pay it. Requiring apportionment of such a tax according to state population would thus produce a result under which (much like the landowners subject to hypothetical acreage tax discussed *supra* notes 92–93 and accompanying text) carriage owners would be taxed at different rates—and, indeed, different rates of potentially enormous magnitude—depending solely on the happenstance of their state of residence.

103 *Id.* at 175 (opinion of Chase, J.).

104 *Id.* (noting his intention of "not giv[ing] a judicial opinion" on the subject).

105 *Id.* (emphasis in original). Thus, while Justice Chase agreed with Hamilton that capitation taxes and taxes on land were direct taxes, he "doubt[ed] whether a tax, by a general assessment of personal property, within the United States, [was] included within the term direct tax." *Id.*

106 The Court initially upheld one form of the federal income tax in *Springer v. United States*, 102 U.S. 586 (1880), in the face of a claim that it constituted an impermissibly unapportioned direct tax. *Id.* at 597–98. The Court's ruling stemmed from its view that the challenged exaction was not "a tax on the 'whole . . . personal estate' of the individual, but only on his income, gains, and profits." *Id.* at 598.

107 157 U.S. 429, *opinion vacated on reargument*, 158 U.S. 601 (1895).

108 *Id.* at 555. Lawyers for the plaintiffs characterized the tax as being "communistic" and "socialistic." Jensen, *supra* note 95, at 2366 (citing excerpts from the argument in *Pollock I*, 157 U.S. at 532). A lawyer defending the tax "conceded that

ratification, "all taxes on real estate . . . or the rents or income thereof were regarded as direct taxes."[109] The Court then went a long step further, declaring "that logically, if taxes on the rents, issues, and profits of real estate are equivalent to taxes on real estate, . . . taxes on the income of personal property as such are equivalent to taxes on such property, and therefore direct taxes."[110] The Court, however, declined to rule definitively on this second point, thus creating far-reaching confusion about the permissible reach of the federal income tax.[111] In response to a resulting clamor for clarification, the Court reheard the case later in the same year.[112] In its ensuing *Pollock II* ruling,[113] the Court squarely held that taxes on tangible personal property, and on income derived from such property, constitute direct taxes subject to apportionment.[114] Along the way, the Court also implied that taxes on intangible property, such as stock and bonds, enjoyed full-fledged membership on the direct-tax team.[115] The Court nonetheless declined to overrule *Hylton*, describing it as "badly reported"[116] and as holding only that "a tax on carriages was an excise."[117]

The immediate effects of *Pollock I* and *Pollock II*, in invalidating the federal income tax, were profound to say the least. The Court, however, reined in the reach of those rulings when it upheld the federal estate tax in *Knowlton v. Moore*.[118] Buoyed up by the *Pollock* decisions, the challengers of this law had argued that it imposed an impermissibly unapportioned "direct" levy on the ownership of property.[119] The Court, however, distinguished those earlier rulings by reasoning that direct taxes target the "ownership and possession" of real and personal property,[120] while estate taxes were "universally

---

the tax was 'class legislation in [a] sense.' " Jensen, *supra* note 95, at 2366 (citing *Pollock I*, 157 U.S. at 518).

109 *Pollock I*, 157 U.S. at 573–74.

110 *Id.* at 579.

111 *Id.* at 586. Because the Justices were divided, the Court declined to express an opinion on "[w]hether as to the income from personal property, as such, the act is unconstitutional, as laying direct taxes." *Id.* The *Pollock I* Court distinguished *Springer* on the ground that the income at issue in that case "was not derived in any degree from real estate, but [came] in part [from the taxpayer's work as an] attorney at law, and the rest [from] interest on United States bonds." *Id.* at 578–79.

112 *See* Jensen, *supra* note 95, at 2369. The Court had also declined to address practically important severability issues in *Pollock I*. *See* 157 U.S. at 586.

113 158 U.S. 601 (1895).

114 *Id.* at 637.

115 *See id.* at 618.

116 *Id.* at 626.

117 *Id.* at 627.

118 178 U.S. 41 (1900).

119 *Id.* at 45–46.

120 *Id.* at 47.

deemed to relate, not to property . . ., but to its *passage* by will."[121] The challenged tax was thus "indirect," rather than "direct," because it targeted the "transmission" of property "from the dead to the living."[122]

The ratification of the Sixteenth Amendment in 1913 scuttled the Court's undoing of the federal income tax in the twin *Pollock* decisions of 1895.[123] That amendment, however, did not alter the underlying principles regarding the nature of direct taxation. As a result, the *Pollock* rulings left behind the possibility that some newfangled non-income-tax levy might run afoul of constitutional apportionment requirements. As fate would have it, the latter-day tax that triggered such a challenge turned out to be the same "shared responsibility payment" that implicated the tax/penalty distinction in *NFIB*.[124]

The Court in *NFIB* had to deal with the subject of direct taxation because the challengers of the shared responsibility payment argued not only (and unsuccessfully, as we have seen) that it was a penalty rather than a tax, but also that, even if the exaction escaped characterization as a penalty, it constituted a direct tax that was impermissibly unapportioned.[125] The "direct tax" shoe fit, according to this argument, because the exaction functioned in practical effect as a levy "on the *retention* of one's 'general ownership of property,' "—that is, as a tax "for not having used some of [that property] to purchase insurance."[126] Put differently, so the argument went, the shared responsibility payment constituted a direct tax on "an individual's wealth, simply because the individual chooses to keep that wealth rather than spend it to purchase insurance."[127]

In the end, a five-Justice majority rejected this contention.[128] "A tax on going without health insurance," the Chief Justice reasoned, "does not fall within" either of the two "recognized categor[ies] of

---

121 *Id.* at 47 (emphasis added).

122 *Id.* at 56.

123 The amendment provides: "The Congress shall have power to lay and collect taxes on incomes, from whatever source derived, without apportionment among the several States, and without regard to any census or enumeration." U.S. CONST. amend. XVI.

124 *See supra* Section 7.A.2.

125 *NFIB*, 567 U.S. at 570.

126 Brief for Private Respondents on the Individual Mandate at 66, *NFIB*, 567 U.S. 519 (emphasis in original) (citing Bromley v. McCaughn, 280 U.S. 124, 136 (1929); *Pollock II*, 158 U.S. at 627–29).

127 Brief for State Respondents on the Minimum Coverage Provision at 62, *NFIB*, 567 U.S. 519 (citing Steven J. Willis & Nakku Chung, Special Report, *Constitutional Decapitation and Healthcare*, 128 TAX NOTES 169 (2010)).

128 *See NFIB*, 567 U.S. at 571.

direct tax."[129] First, "[t]he payment [was] plainly not a tax on the ownership of land or personal property."[130] Second, the payment was not a "capitation"—that is, a tax "paid by every person, 'without regard to property, profession, or *any other circumstance*' "[131]—because the duty to make it was "triggered by [the] specific circumstances" involved in choosing not to obtain health insurance.[132] In short, the Court in *NFIB* was unwilling to push the direct-tax concept any further than the *Pollock* decisions had done, and the consequence was that the shared responsibility payment survived this line of constitutional attack.

The four joint dissenters in *NFIB* took a different tack. In their view, the majority's terse treatment of the "direct tax" issue was unsatisfying because that term's meaning remains "famously unclear."[133] Indeed, the dissenters faulted the majority for even considering the direct-tax question given the scant attention it had received in the course of the *NFIB* litigation.[134] Under the circumstances, they contended, the better course would have been to order further proceedings focused squarely on the direct-tax issue. In other words, they argued, the Court should have required "more than fly-by-night briefing and argument before deciding a difficult constitutional question of first impression."[135]

Even for experts, the arcane subject of direct taxation can have a mind-numbing quality. As the *Pollock* cases show, however, this constitutional restriction, however obscure it might be, sometimes produces show-stopping legal rulings. Moreover, another such ruling could soon find its way into the U.S. Reports. The reason why is that, in recent years, some members of Congress have advocated for imposition of a "wealth tax" on the nation's richest citizens.[136] To be sure, Congress may never pass such a law. But if it does, the

---

129 *Id.* at 571.

130 *Id.* (citing *Pollock II*, 158 U.S. at 618).

131 *Id.* (citing *Hylton*, 3 U.S. at 175) (emphasis in original).

132 *Id.* at 571.

133 *Id.* at 669 (Scalia, Kennedy, Thomas, and Alito, JJ., dissenting).

134 The joint dissenters observed in particular that the direct-tax limitation had received only abbreviated treatment in the briefs and oral arguments presented to the Supreme Court in part because "no [lower] federal court [had] accepted the . . . argument that [the shared responsibility payment was] an exercise of the tax power." *Id.*

135 *Id.*

136 *See, e.g.*, Thomas Kaplan, *Bernie Sanders Proposes a Wealth Tax: 'I Don't Think That Billionaires Should Exist,'* N.Y. TIMES (Sept. 24, 2019), https://www.nytimes.com/2019/09/24/us/politics/bernie-sanders-wealth-tax.html.

enactment's constitutional fate will hinge on the Court's elaboration of the difference between direct and indirect taxation.[137]

[137] The central line of attack on such a law would draw on the reasoning of the *Pollock* cases coupled with the assertion that any tax on net worth necessarily lays its hand on the value of real and personal property. Professors Daniel Hemel and Rebecca Kysar have observed, for example, that "[t]he proposed wealth taxes would apply to real property, which would seem to make them 'direct taxes'" so that non-apportionment "would be a deal breaker." Daniel Hemel & Rebecca Kysar, Opinion, *The Big Problem with Wealth Taxes*, N.Y. TIMES (Nov. 7, 2019), https://www.nytimes.com/2019/11/07/opinion/wealth-tax-constitution.html (estimating that "[t]o match revenue fractions to population percentages, as the Constitution's direct tax clauses demand," the "wealth tax rate in West Virginia—the poorest state per capita—would need to be roughly 10 times the rate in more affluent California and more than 20 times the rate in prosperous Connecticut"); *see also* Dawn Johnsen & Walter Dellinger, *The Constitutionality of a National Wealth Tax*, 93 IND. L.J. 111, 132 (2018) (noting, among other things, that the citation to the *Pollock* rulings in *NFIB* places "a constitutional cloud over Congress's authority to tax wealth").

Chapter 8

THE SPENDING POWER

Analysis

Article I, section 8, clause 1 permits Congress to spend federal monies "for the common Defence and general Welfare of the United States."[1] As the modern-day proliferation of conditional-spending programs reveals, Congress often uses this power for regulatory purposes, much as it uses the taxing power in pursuit of similar ends.[2] To date, the Court has generally afforded Congress substantial leeway to use its spending power in this manner, although more recent doctrinal developments suggest that a narrowing of this authority might be in the works.

A. KEY EARLY DECISIONS: *UNITED STATES V. BUTLER*, THE SOCIAL SECURITY CASES, AND *OKLAHOMA V. CIVIL SERVICE COMMISSION*

In *United States v. Butler*,[3] the Court confronted a New Deal program that conditioned federal subsidy payments to farmers on their compliance with rules designed to limit the growing of certain crops. Under the Court's then-prevailing commerce-power jurisprudence, Congress could not use the stick of direct penalties to force farmers to comply with federally imposed production restrictions.[4] *Butler* presented the question whether Congress could pursue that same objective with the carrot of conditional outlays.

---

1 U.S. CONST. art. I, § 8, cl. 1.

2 *See supra* Chapter 7.

3 297 U.S. 1 (1936).

4 *See supra* Chapter 2.

Relying on the *Child Labor Tax Case*[5] and the pretext principle of *McCulloch*,[6] the Court in *Butler* invalidated this spending program.[7] Justice Owen Roberts's majority opinion sounded the same parade-of-horribles theme that marked *Carter Coal* and other commerce-power cases of the time,[8] insisting that validation of the law would support congressional "regulation of all industry throughout the United States . . . by similar exercises of the same power."[9] In a dissenting opinion joined by Justices Brandeis and Cardozo, Justice Stone responded that any "suggestion that [the spending power] must now be curtailed by judicial fiat because it may be abused by unwise use hardly rises to the dignity of argument."[10] The majority, however, was unmoved by the dissenters' protestations. The production-limiting subsidy program had to go because it entailed, albeit "indirectly," regulation of "a field in which the United States has no power to intermeddle."[11]

Butler's restrictive view of the spending power did not last for long. In a pair of 1937 decisions—handed down within months of the Court's transformative Commerce Clause ruling in *Jones & Laughlin Steel*[12]—the Court upheld then-controversial features of the Social Security Act of 1935 (SSA).[13] In doing so, the Court did not purport to retreat from *Butler*'s earlier repudiation of the federal crop-limit spending program.[14] But in these decisions, Justice Cardozo (writing

---

5 *See supra* Section 7.A.1.

6 *See supra* Section 1.B.

7 Notably, the Court issued its decision in *Butler* in 1936, the same year in which it handed down its Congress-limiting commerce-power ruling in *Carter v. Carter Coal Co.*, 298 U.S. 238 (1936); *see also supra* Section 2.B (discussing the *Carter Coal* decision).

8 *See id.*

9 *Butler*, 297 U.S. at 75.

10 *Id.* at 87 (Stone, J., dissenting).

11 *Id.* at 73 (majority opinion). Somewhat ironically, the majority's ruling was coupled with a holding (in keeping with the views of Alexander Hamilton and Joseph Story and in contrast to those of James Madison) that Congress's authority to spend was not limited to pursuit of "the other powers enumerated in the subsequent clauses" of the Constitution. *Id.* at 65. Thus, Congress could spend federal monies to promote "the general welfare of the United States" in ways not supported by the power to regulate interstate commerce, establish post offices, raise an army and a navy, and the like. But however far that added authority under the Spending Clause might reach, Congress could not use it "to purchase a compliance which the Congress is powerless to command" in light of overarching federalism-driven constraints. *Id.* at 68–70. Put another way, the Court in *Butler* viewed the statute at issue in *Butler* as an impermissible *de facto* "regulation" in much the same way the Court in the *Child Labor Tax Case* saw the challenged "tax" as an impermissible *de facto* "penalty." *Id.*

12 *See supra* Section 3.C.1.

13 *See* Charles C. Steward Mach. Co. v. Davis, 301 U.S. 548 (1937); Helvering v. Davis, 301 U.S. 619 (1937).

14 In particular, the law at issue in *Steward Machine* conditioned employer entitlements to federal largess, in the form of tax relief, on state enactment of an unemployment compensation program that conformed to federal standards. The Court

in one case for five Justices and in the other for seven) struck a much different tone than was sounded by the majority in *Butler*. According to him: "When money is spent to promote the general welfare, the concept . . . is shaped by Congress"; thus, so long as "the concept be not arbitrary, the locality must yield."[15]

For a near-century following its 1937 rulings, the Court unwaveringly upheld federal conditional-spending programs.[16] In *Oklahoma v. United States Civil Service Commission*,[17] for example, the Court sustained a law that doled out money, used in part to pay certain state workers, on the condition that the state prohibit those workers from engaging in political campaigning. Invoking the logic of *Butler*, Oklahoma argued that this program offended the Tenth Amendment because it effectively regulated local elections and structured that state's relationships with its own employees. The

---

distinguished *Butler* on the grounds that: "(a) The proceeds of the tax in controversy are not earmarked for a special group. (b) The unemployment compensation law which is a condition of the credit has had the approval of the state and could not be a law without it. (c) The condition is not linked to an irrevocable agreement, for the state at its pleasure may repeal its unemployment law, terminate the credit, and place itself where it was before the credit was accepted. (d) The condition is not directed to the attainment of an unlawful end, but to an end, the relief of unemployment, for which nation and state may lawfully cooperate." *Id.* at 592–93 (internal citation omitted). In *Helvering*, the Court likewise upheld against a Tenth Amendment attack a direct, as opposed to a conditional, spending program—namely, that aspect of the SSA that provides for federal payments, to be funded by federal taxes, to persons who have reached a designated retirement-related age.

[15] *Helvering*, 301 U.S. at 645. He also observed: "Nor is the concept of the general welfare static. Needs that were narrow or parochial a century ago may be interwoven in our day with the well-being of the Nation." *Id.* at 641.

[16] *See, e.g.*, Fullilove v. Klutznick, 448 U.S. 448, 474 (1980) (opinion of Burger, C.J.) (noting that "[t]his Court has repeatedly upheld against constitutional challenge the use of this [conditional-spending] technique to induce governments and private parties to cooperate voluntarily with federal policy"; upholding a statute that conditioned state access to public-works funds on using at least 10% of those funds on contracts to support minority-owned businesses); Lau v. Nichols, 414 U.S. 563, 569 (1974) (upholding a nondiscrimination requirement directed at recipients of federal aid as applied to a local school district that failed to provide English-language instruction to non-English-speaking children of Chinese ancestry); King v. Smith, 392 U.S. 309, 333 n.34 (1968) (noting, in giving effect to a federal aid-for-dependent-children rule, that "[t]here is of course no question that the Federal Government, unless barred by some controlling constitutional prohibition, may impose the terms and conditions upon which its money allotments to the States shall be disbursed"); *see also* Pennhurst State Sch. & Hosp. v. Halderman, 451 U.S. 1, 17 (1981) (noting that precedent broadly supports upholding conditional-spending programs and analogizing resulting conditions to contractual agreements made between the federal government and the grant recipient). For illustrative cases involving Bill of Rights-based challenges to spending programs, see *Buckley v. Valeo*, 424 U.S. 1 (1976) (considering, among other things, First Amendment restrictions on campaign expenditure limits imposed as a condition on receipt of federal campaign finance funding), and *Flemming v. Nestor*, 363 U.S. 603 (1960) (upholding against several rights-based challenges to a provision that terminated Social Security benefits otherwise payable to noncitizens after their removal from the United States).

[17] 330 U.S. 127 (1947).

Court, however, dismissed this argument without even mentioning *Butler*, emphasizing instead that complaints about undue federal intervention were overblown because the state could "adopt[ ] the 'simple expedient' of not yielding" to the program's financial inducements.[18]

B. *SOUTH DAKOTA V. DOLE* AND THE FOUR-PRONG TEST

The *Oklahoma* case, unlike *Butler*, involved a federal statute that conditionally offered funds to states themselves, as opposed to private individuals or firms. Focusing on these state-payee cases, the Court in *South Dakota v. Dole*[19] laid down a four-pronged test for assessing whether conditional spending programs exceed constitutional spending-power limits.[20] At issue in *Dole* was a federal statute that withheld five-to-ten-percent of federal highway funds from any state that permitted the purchase or public possession of alcoholic beverages by persons younger than twenty-one.[21] Even while assuming for purposes of argument that Congress could not "legislate directly a national minimum drinking age,"[22] the Court upheld this law as a proper exercise of the spending power. According to Chief Justice Rehnquist, who wrote for a seven-Justice majority, the measure passed muster because it satisfied each of four separate constitutional requisites that, the Court now held, any conditional spending program had to meet. First, by promoting highway safety, the law advanced the "general welfare," a subject on which "courts should defer substantially to the judgment of Congress."[23] Second,

---

[18] *Id.* at 143.

[19] 483 U.S. 203 (1987).

[20] As many observers have noted, "[t]he size and range of [such] programs have increased vastly in the post-New Deal United States, and detailed federal conditions have proliferated." NOAH R. FELDMAN & KATHLEEN M. SULLIVAN, CONSTITUTIONAL LAW 207 (20th ed. 2019). So too have scholarly treatments of the subject. For a sampling, see, e.g., Lynn A. Baker, *Conditional Federal Spending After* Lopez, 95 COLUM. L. REV. 1911, 1939–51 (1995); Lynn A. Baker & Mitchell Berman, *Getting off the Dole: Why the Court Should Abandon its Spending Doctrine, and How a Too-Clever Congress Could Provoke It to Do So*, 78 IND L.J. 459 (2003); Richard A. Epstein, *Foreword: Unconstitutional Conditions, State Power, and the Limits of Consent*, 102 HARV. L. REV. 4 (1988); and Thomas R. McCoy & Barry Friedman, *Conditional Spending: Federalism's Trojan Horse*, 1988 SUP. CT. REV. 85, 100–01.

[21] The law withheld 5% of funds in the first year following its enactment and 10% thereafter. *See* 23 U.S.C. § 148 (1982 ed., Supp. III).

[22] 483 U.S. at 206.

[23] *Id.* at 207. In general, courts have steered away from enforcing this potential limit on conditional (and other) federal spending programs. *See* Lynn A. Baker, *Rethinking the Senate*, 44 HARV. J. L. & PUB. POL'Y 39, 41 (2021) (viewing the Court as "rendering essentially meaningless or nonjusticiable [the phrase] 'general welfare' that could provide constraints on congressional power"); Lynn A. Baker, *Constitutional Ambiguities and Originalism: Lessons from the Spending Power*, 103 NW. U. L. REV. 495, 518–19 (2009) (adding that the Court's refusal to enforce the General Welfare

Congress had acted "unambiguously" in imposing the condition, thus facilitating the ability of states to "exercise their choice knowingly, cognizant of the consequences of their participation" in the federal program.[24] Third, despite South Dakota's argument to the contrary, the Twenty-first Amendment did not impose "an 'independent constitutional bar'" that precluded enactment of this federal legislation.[25] According to the Court, the *Oklahoma* case established that this independent-bar limit required merely that the spending

---

Clause enables small states to use their disproportionate power to their advantage). For a rare case that presented a disputed "general welfare" question, see *Stop H-3 Ass'n v. Dole*, 870 F.2d 1419, 1427–29 (9th Cir. 1989). There, the plaintiffs argued that the challenged federal program did not implicate the "*general* welfare" because it involved a "proposed highway . . . contained entirely within the state of Hawaii," which accordingly was "of 'local' rather than 'national' importance." *Id.* at 1427–28 (emphasis added). The Ninth Circuit rejected this argument, observing along the way that the planned highway "is a part of an interstate highway system which serves important defense functions." *Id.* at 1428; *cf.* Arbogast v. Kansas, Dep't of Labor, 789 F.3d 1174, 1187 (10th Cir. 2015) (citing *Dole*, 483 U.S. at 208, in suggesting that, to satisfy this requirement, Congress must pursue "a valid objective furthering the general welfare" and "the means Congress employs to achieve that objective" must "be 'reasonably calculated' to do so"); Hodges v. Shalala, 121 F. Supp. 2d 854, 873 (D.S.C. 2000) (rejecting a challenge to a federal spending program on the theory that it imposed conditions that were "not consistent with the nation's welfare"), *aff'd sub nom.* Hodges v. Thompson, 311 F.3d 316 (4th Cir. 2002).

[24] *Dole*, 483 U.S. at 207 (quoting *Pennhurst State Sch. & Hosp.*, 451 U.S. at 17). For one condition-limiting example of the application of this rule, see *T.W. v. New York State Bd. of Law Exam'rs*, 996 F.3d 87, 98 (2d Cir. 2021) (determining that, under even the broad terms of the federal Rehabilitation Act, the state's "entire judiciary is not subject to the [Act's abrogation of sovereign immunity] because several specialty courts receive financial aid"; relying in part on the Court's instruction in *College Savings Bank v. Florida Prepaid Postsecondary Education Expense Board*, 527 U.S. 666, 682 (1999), in emphasizing that courts should approach such questions with "every reasonable presumption against waiver" of sovereign immunity based on a state's acceptance of federal funds). An important question presented by this clear-statement requirement is whether it forecloses the federal government from adding post-fund-acceptance conditions, pursuant to a pre-fund-acceptance reservation of the discretionary ability to take such action. According to the Second Circuit, there is no problem with requiring states to adhere to such newly imposed conditions, at least so long as Congress made clear at the outset that it retained authority to put them in place. *See* Counsel v. Dow, 849 F.2d 731, 735–37 (2d Cir. 1988) (rejecting the defendants' argument that the clear-statement rule precluded an award of attorney's fees "because Congress made clear its intent to allow attorney's fees retroactively"); *but cf.* City and Cty. of San Francisco v. Sessions, 349 F. Supp. 3d 924, 957–58 (N.D. Cal. 2018) (finding that conditions placed by the Department of Justice on access to "Byrne grants" were unconstitutional because they "cannot have been unambiguously authorized by Congress if they were never statutorily authorized" (quoting City of Philadelphia v. Sessions, 280 F. Supp. 3d 579, 646 (E.D. Penn. 2017))), *aff'd in part and vacated in part on other grounds sub nom.* City and County of San Francisco v. Barr, 965 F.3d 753 (2020).

[25] *Dole*, 483 U.S. at 209 (quoting Lawrence Cty. v. Lead-Deadwood Sch. Dist. No. 40–1, 469 U.S. 256, 270 (1985)). Section 2 of the Twenty-first Amendment specifies that: "The transportation or importation into any state . . . for delivery or use therein of intoxicating liquors, in violation of the laws thereof, is hereby prohibited." U.S. CONST. amend. XXI. For a discussion of the extent to which this unusual constitutional endorsement of specialized state authority constricts congressional power under the Commerce Clause or otherwise, see *infra* Section 5.A.1 n.9.

power "not be used to induce the States to engage in activities that would themselves be unconstitutional."[26] This limit thus prohibited Congress from conditioning access to federal money, for example, on a state's willingness to censor speech in violation of First Amendment-based free-expression rights or to impose cruel and unusual punishments in violation of the Eighth Amendment guarantee. Here, however, the states had undisputed authority to enact minimum-drinking-age laws on their own, and thus the challenged condition on access to federal funds did not implicate the independent-bar limitation.[27]

Fourth, the Court concluded that the challenged condition was "reasonably calculated" to advance "the federal interest" that gave rise to the highway-spending program.[28] Justice O'Connor, in dissent, argued that the program abridged this " 'germaneness' or 'relatedness' " standard[29] because Congress had leveraged its funds to induce the state's adoption of a freestanding limitation on private conduct, as opposed to specifying only "how the money should be spent."[30] In the majority's view, however, the germaneness rule required only (1) identification of the purpose of the underlying spending program and (2) a determination that the challenged condition was sufficiently "relevant" with respect to achieving that purpose.[31] Here, the Court concluded that, because a key goal of Congress in establishing the highway spending program was to promote "safe interstate travel,"[32] the germaneness requirement was readily met. After all, the minimum-drinking-age condition fostered a salutary uniformity in state laws that cut down on dangerous driving by eighteen-, nineteen-, and twenty-year-olds who might otherwise venture across state borders to places where they could legally imbibe intoxicants before drunkenly driving home.[33]

Dole's treatment of the germaneness requirement left behind many questions. It remains unclear, for example, how close the

---

26 *Dole*, 483 U.S. at 210.

27 Put another way, Congress could not, for example, condition access to federal highway money on a state's criminalizing of all citizen complaints about federal highways because such a condition would call upon the state to violate the First Amendment as incorporated into the Fourteenth Amendment. But neither the Fourteenth Amendment nor any other constitutional provision bars states from passing minimum-drinking-age laws. *Dole* thus presented no independent-bar problem.

28 *Id.* at 208–09.

29 *Id.* at 208 n.3.

30 *Id.* at 216 (O'Connor, J., dissenting) (quoting Brief of the National Conference of State Legislatures, et. al. as Amici Curiae in Support of Petitioner at 20).

31 *Id.* at 208 (majority opinion) (internal quotation omitted).

32 *Id.*

33 *Id.* at 209.

relationship between the condition imposed by Congress and the spending program's purpose must be. In a footnote, for example, the Court declined to determine whether the condition must be "directly related" to the congressional purpose because it found that the test was met on the facts in any event.[34] Even harder questions concern application of the "germaneness" standard to specific conditions and programs. What if, for example, Congress conditioned entitlement to five percent of federal highway funds on the state's employment of dog catchers in all counties traversed by federal highways? Perhaps it would suffice to satisfy the germaneness standard that, on the face of things, dog catchers might keep traffic corridors clear of wandering animals otherwise destined to cause car crashes. Perhaps the Court would insist on empirical proof that dog-catcher employment actually enhances, perhaps significantly, safe interstate highway travel. It might even be that the Court would find *Dole* wholly inapposite because a dog-catcher condition would not remove any problem distinctly tied to interstate non-uniformity and the resulting danger of unsafe cross-border movements.[35]

C. A FIFTH PRONG OF THE *DOLE* TEST: *NFIB* AND THE ANTI-COERCION RULE

A final question lay between the lines of the Court's opinion in *Dole*: Would it have mattered if Congress had conditioned access to 100% of federal highway funds, rather than only five to ten percent,

---

[34] *Id.* at 208 n.3. In a later case, the Court described the "relatedness" limitation as requiring that any conditions on federal funding "bear *some* relationship to the purpose of the federal spending." New York v. United States, 505 U.S. 144, 167 (1992) (emphasis added). Circuit courts, too, have developed their own articulations of the "germaneness" requirement. *See, e.g.*, Gruver v. Louisiana Bd. of Supervisors for the La. State Univ. Agric. & Mech. Coll., 959 F.3d 178, 182 (5th Cir. 2020) (declaring that a condition must be "reasonably related to the purpose of the federal grant"), *cert. denied*, 141 S. Ct. 901 (2020); United States v. Felts, 674 F.3d 599, 608 (6th Cir. 2012) (finding the "germaneness" test satisfied if "the condition is rationally related to the purpose of the federal interest, program, or funding"); Koslow v. Pennsylvania, 302 F.3d 161, 175 (3d Cir. 2002) (requiring a "discernible relationship"); California v. United States, 104 F.3d 1086, 1092 (9th Cir. 1997) (specifying that "the conditions imposed are reasonably related to the federal interest in the particular program"); Kansas v. United States, 214 F.3d 1196, 1199 (10th Cir. 2000) (citing *New York*, 505 U.S. at 167, in declaring that "[t]he required degree of this relationship is one of reasonableness or minimum rationality"); Benning v. Georgia, 391 F.3d 1299, 1308 (11th Cir. 2004) (opining that *Dole* and *New York* "establish a minimal standard of rationality").

[35] For a real-world germaneness case, consider *Koslow*. There, the Third Circuit held that the conditioning of federal funds, made available by the Rehabilitation Act, on the recipient's waiver of sovereign immunity for claims based on violations of that act, did satisfy the "germaneness" requirement. 302 F.3d at 175–76. In the court's view, because the sovereign-immunity waiver tended to ensure adherence to the rules imposed by the statute that the federal funding was put in place to support, the requisite "discernible relationship" existed. *Id.* at 175. The Tenth Circuit, citing *Koslow*, followed much the same line of reasoning in *Arbogast v. Kansas Dep't of Labor*, 789 F.3d 1174, 1187 (10th Cir. 2015).

on state compliance with the minimum-drinking-age condition? In the closing section of his opinion, Chief Justice Rehnquist observed that, in some instances, a "financial inducement offered by Congress" might become "so coercive as to pass the point at which 'pressure turns into compulsion.' "[36] He also concluded, however, that Congress had not crossed this line because the challenged program involved only "a relatively small percentage" of only "certain federal highway funds."[37] With this talk of "compulsion," however, the Chief Justice laid the basis for recognizing a fifth limit on conditional spending programs—namely, a requirement that Congress may not structure its program in such a way that states, as a practical matter, cannot resist the inducement to participate.[38]

In *NFIB v. Sebelius*,[39] the Court picked up on this idea in finding that one key component of the Affordable Care Act (ACA) reached beyond constitutional limits. Among the various reforms implemented by that act was a change in governing eligibility rules under the federal Medicaid program, which has long provided government-funded health insurance to low-income individuals. While the Medicaid program is administered by state governments, most funding for its operation comes from federal grants made to states that comply with congressionally established conditions. Some of these conditions on access to federal Medicaid payouts took hold with the launch of the program in 1965, while others—including the one at issue in *NFIB*—were added in later years.

By way of the ACA, Congress made two major changes to the Medicaid program. First, it gave states the chance to receive a much-increased amount of federal Medicaid money. Second, it imposed a

---

36 *Dole*, 483 US. at 211 (quoting *Steward Machine*, 301 U.S. at 590).

37 *Id.*

38 In *Virginia Department of Education v. Riley*, 106 F.3d 559 (4th Cir. 1997), a majority of the Fourth Circuit sitting *en banc* invoked this aspect of Chief Justice Rehnquist's *Dole* opinion. *See id.* (adopting the opinion of Luttig, J., filed as a dissent from the earlier panel ruling). There, Judge Luttig, writing for a majority of the court, took aim at an agency rule that resulted in a state's loss of "100% of an annual special education grant" for what he characterized as an "insubstantial" departure from program rules. *Id.* at 569–70. Such a result, he reasoned was so much "more pernicious" than the would-be fund forfeiture at issue in *Dole* that it at least began "to resemble impermissible coercion, . . . if not forbidden regulation in the guise of a Spending Clause condition." *Id.* Notwithstanding *Virginia Department of Education*, Professors Lynn Baker and Mitchell Berman could report in 2003, after canvassing the full range of prior cases, that lower courts "have consistently failed to find impermissible coercion," even when the "amount or percentage of federal money at stake is so large that [the state] has 'no choice but to accept the [federal legislation's] many requirements.' " Baker & Berman, *supra* note 20 at 468–69 (quoting *Kansas*, 214 F.3d at 120). Accordingly, they observed, "[i]t is not surprising that the lower courts have increasingly questioned whether 'there is any viability left in the coercion theory.' " *Id.* at 468–69 (quoting *California*, 104 F.3d at 1092).

39 567 U.S. 519 (2012).

new condition on state access to Medicaid funding. This new condition required states to expand eligibility for Medicaid benefits in a major way by providing coverage to all claimants whose incomes fell below 133% of the government-established poverty line. Congress made the "carrot" it extended to states especially appealing by providing that federal grants, at least in the near term, would cover virtually all resulting increases in program costs. But Congress also put in place a "stick" that, if wielded, would inflict acute pain on noncooperating states. Specifically, a failure to expand Medicaid coverage in keeping with the new congressional condition would result not just in the state's inability to receive the additional increment of federal funding made available by the ACA, but also in the forfeiture of *all* preexisting Medicaid funding, regardless of how long and how otherwise-collaboratively the state had participated in the Medicaid program in past years.

While many states rushed to cash in on the chance provided by the ACA to secure more Medicaid money, twenty-six states brought legal actions claiming that this new law exceeded Congress's power under the Spending Clause. In *NFIB*, a seven-Justice majority agreed, albeit by way of two separately issued plurality opinions. The decisive treatment of the issue came from the pen of Chief Justice Roberts, who was joined by Justices Breyer and Kagan. A separate opinion—formally styled a dissent but referred to here as the "joint opinion"—was coauthored by Justices Scalia, Kennedy, Thomas, and Alito.[40] Both opinions focused on the difference between congressional "inducement" and congressional "compulsion."[41] In keeping with *South Dakota v. Dole*, spending program *inducements* presented no constitutional problem. The presence of *compulsion*, however, rendered conditional spending programs impermissible under the rule of *New York v. United States*,[42] which prohibits

40 As for the "narrower," and thus "binding," character of the Chief Justice's opinion on the conditional-spending issue, see, e.g., *Gruver*, 959 F.3d at 183 n.5.

41 *NFIB*, 567 U.S. at 577–79 (opinion of Roberts, C.J.); *id.* at 632–44 (Scalia, Kennedy, Thomas, and Alito, JJ., dissenting). While the four Justices who issued the joint opinion agreed with the Chief Justice that the Medicaid expansion exceeded the scope of the spending power, they disagreed with his separate conclusion that the constitutional violation could be remedied by stipulating that states declining to pursue the Medicaid expansion would forfeit only the *additional* Medicaid funding made available by the ACA. *Compare id.* at 585–88 (opinion of Roberts, C.J.), *with id.* at 689–91 (Scalia, Kennedy, Thomas, and Alito, JJ., dissenting) ("We should not accept the Government's invitation to attempt to solve a constitutional problem by rewriting the Medicaid Expansion so as to allow States that reject it to retain their pre-existing Medicaid funds.").

42 505 U.S. 144 (1992).

Congress from "compel[ling] the states to enact or administer a federal regulatory program."[43]

Turning to the application of this anti-coercion principle, Chief Justice Roberts concluded that the ACA's Medicaid spending rule reached too far because the pressure it exerted amounted to "economic dragooning" and, indeed, "a gun to the head."[44] He recognized that Congress had broad authority to fashion federal funding programs, especially when the conditions they impose require states to do no more than "comply[ ] with restrictions on the use of [program] funds."[45] In this instance, however, Congress had foisted on the states a condition that governed not only their access to new program pay-outs but also their continued access to "significant independent grants" put in place pursuant to pre-ACA law.[46] To be sure, the Court in *Dole* had upheld a condition that went beyond directing how federal monies were themselves to be used. In that case, however, the pressure placed on states by the challenged program amounted to only "relatively mild encouragement" because the threatened loss of financial support faced by states amounted to only five to ten percent of federal highway funds.[47] Here, in contrast, each state stood "to lose not merely 'a relatively small percentage' of its existing Medicaid funding, but *all* of it."[48] And that was the case even though Medicaid payments accounted "for over 20 percent of the average State's total budget, with federal funds covering 50 to 83 percent of those costs."[49]

The separate joint opinion of Justices Scalia, Kennedy, Thomas, and Alito likewise emphasized the large contribution made to overall state budgets by the federal Medicaid program.[50] These Justices added that:

> A state forced out of the program would not only lose this huge sum but would almost certainly find it necessary to increase its own health care expenditures substantially, requiring either a drastic reduction in funding for other programs or a large increase in state taxes. And these new taxes would come on top of the federal taxes already paid

---

[43] *Id.* at 188; *see supra* Section 5.B (discussing this anti-commandeering principle).

[44] *NFIB*, 567 U.S. at 523, 581 (opinion of Roberts, C.J.).

[45] *Id.* at 580.

[46] *Id.*

[47] *Dole*, 483 U.S. at 204, 211.

[48] *NFIB*, 567 U.S. at 581 (quoting *Dole*, 483 U.S. at 211) (emphasis in original).

[49] *Id.*

[50] *See id.* at 672 (Scalia, Kennedy, Thomas, and Alito, JJ., dissenting).

> by the State's citizens to fund the Medicaid program in other States.[51]

For the joint opinion writers, it also was significant that Medicaid grants accounted for some 40% of all federal money taken in by the states, which accordingly were "far less reliant on federal funding for any other program."[52] In addition, these Justices contended that both "the goal and structure of the ACA" made it clear that "the offer of the Medicaid Expansion was one that Congress understood no state could refuse."[53] All of this convinced the four joint opinion writers that, as a matter of "reality,"[54] the "States . . . have no choice other than to accept the package."[55]

In a partial dissent joined by Justice Sotomayor, Justice Ginsburg faulted the majority for characterizing the federal government's approach to Medicaid funding as involving two separate spending programs.[56] Rather, she asserted, the federal government had established "a single program with a constant aim—to enable poor persons to receive basic health care when they need it."[57] No less important, the ACA "simply requir[ed] States to do what States have long been required to do to receive Medicaid funding: comply with the conditions Congress prescribes for participation."[58] Indeed, Justice Ginsburg reasoned, it was especially appropriate to uphold the ACA's newly imposed condition because federal lawmakers had previously alerted the states—indeed, alerted them from the very outset of the Medicaid program—that "[t]he right to alter, amend, or repeal any provision of [the program] is hereby reserved to the Congress."[59] Put differently, the terms of the deal that states had accepted let them know from day one that Congress could freely revise the conditions on access to Medicaid funds, just as it had done in adopting the ACA. Finally, Justice Ginsburg questioned the workability of the distinction between inducement and compulsion now endorsed by seven of her colleagues. As she wrote:

> [I]n the wake of today's decision, how will litigants and judges assess whether "a State has a legitimate choice whether to accept the federal conditions in exchange for the federal funds"? Are courts to measure the number of dollars

---

[51] *Id.*

[52] *Id.* at 683.

[53] *Id.* at 689.

[54] *Id.* at 689.

[55] *Id.* at 679–80.

[56] *Id.* at 625 (Ginsburg, J., dissenting in part).

[57] *Id.*

[58] *Id.* at 626.

[59] *Id.* at 639 (quoting 42 U.S.C. § 1304).

> the Federal Government might withhold for noncompliance? The portion of the State's budget at stake? And which State's—or States'—budget is determinative: the lead plaintiff, all challenging States (26 in this litigation, many with quite different fiscal situations), or some national median? Does it matter that Florida, unlike most States, imposes no state income tax, and therefore might be able to replace foregone federal funds with new state revenue? . . . The coercion inquiry . . . appears to involve political judgments that defy judicial calculation.[60]

Responding to these points, the Chief Justice acknowledged that "[a] State confronted with statutory language reserving the right to 'alter' or 'amend' the pertinent provisions of the Social Security Act might reasonably assume that Congress was entitled to make adjustments to the Medicaid program as it developed."[61] But he nonetheless maintained that "[a] State could hardly anticipate that Congress's reservation of the right to 'alter' or 'amend' the Medicaid program included the power to transform it so dramatically" as Congress had done in the ACA.[62] Support for this conclusion came not only from the far-reaching financial consequences of the ACA reforms, but also from what the Chief Justice saw as Congress's sharp departure in that act from the historic mission of the Medicaid program. That mission, in his view, focused on directing aid to "four particular categories of the needy: the disabled, the blind, the elderly, and needy families with dependent children."[63] The Medicaid-related provisions of the ACA, however, addressed the "health care needs of the entire nonelderly population with income below 133 percent of the poverty level" as part of "a comprehensive national plan to provide universal health insurance coverage."[64] For all of these reasons, the changes wrought by the ACA did not, for Chief Justice Roberts, embody "a mere alteration of existing Medicaid"; instead, they involved the creation of a "new health care program"[65] that reflected "a shift in kind, not merely degree."[66]

---

60 *Id.* at 643–44 (Ginsburg, J., dissenting in part).

61 *Id.* at 583 (opinion of Roberts, C.J.).

62 *Id.* at 584.

63 *Id.* at 583.

64 *Id.* Significant, too, was the fact that the ACA's conditional spending program had structural features that disconnected it from the already-in-place Medicaid program. Of particular importance, the ACA both (1) offered the states a higher percentage of funding reimbursement for individuals made newly eligible by the Act and (2) allowed states to provide these newly eligible individuals with a lower level of coverage than pre-existing program participants could secure. *Id.* at 583–84.

65 *Id.* at 584.

66 *Id.* at 583.

Nor were the Justices supportive of striking down the Medicaid expansion moved by the dissenters' protestations about doctrinal unworkability. On this point, the authors of the joint opinion acknowledged that "[w]hether federal spending legislation crosses the line from enticement to coercion is often difficult to determine."[67] Even so, bedrock constitutional considerations of state autonomy—and, more specifically, the anti-commandeering rule of *New York v. United States*[68]—left the Court with no choice but to distinguish between permissible inducement and impermissible compulsion. The joint opinion writers added that one proper way to address concerns about judicial overreaching is to insist that "courts should not conclude that legislation is unconstitutional . . . unless the coercive nature of an offer is unmistakably clear."[69] Even under the aegis of this deferential standard, however, these four Justices had "no doubt" that the ACA's conditional spending program was unconstitutional. For them, "[i]f the anticoercion rule does not apply in this case, then there is no such rule."[70]

D. CONDITIONAL SPENDING IN THE AFTERMATH OF *NFIB*

How far might judges go in applying the *NFIB* anti-coercion rule in future cases? One clue came in the joint opinion filed by Justices Scalia, Kennedy, Thomas, and Alito. The Spending Clause, they suggested, would not permit Congress to interfere with the states' "traditional authority in the field of education" by broadly funding local educational programs only so long as state officials acceded to federal conditions concerning "curriculum, the hiring and tenure of teachers, the drawing of school districts, the length and hours of the school day, the school calendar, a dress code for students, and rules for student discipline."[71] It is far from certain that there would have been five votes for this position among the Justices who decided *NFIB*. The Chief Justice, after all, emphasized that past rulings had consistently "upheld Congress's authority to condition the receipt of funds on the States' complying with restrictions *on the use of those funds*."[72] And the law hypothesized by the joint opinion writers would seem to fit this description in that it would tie local authorities' access to federal money to their spending of that very money in program

---

[67] *Id.* at 681 (Scalia, Kennedy, Thomas, and Alito, JJ., dissenting).

[68] 505 U.S. 144 (1992); *see generally supra* Section 5.B.1.

[69] *NFIB*, 567 U.S. at 681 (Scalia, Kennedy, Thomas, and Alito, JJ., dissenting).

[70] *Id.* The Chief Justice took the same view of things, declaring that "wherever [the constitutional] line may be, this statute is surely beyond it." *Id.* at 585 (opinion of Roberts, C.J.).

[71] *Id.* at 680–81 (Scalia, Kennedy, Thomas, and Alito, JJ., dissenting).

[72] *Id.* at 580 (opinion of Roberts, C.J.) (emphasis added).

operations that comport with conditions imposed by Congress. Indeed, even Justice O'Connor's solo dissent in *Dole*, arguing for a much-narrowed interpretation of the spending power than was endorsed by the majority in that case, acknowledged that "Congress may only condition grants in ways . . . related to *the expenditure* of federal funds."[73] In sum, the four joint opinion writers staked out a view of the conditional spending power that might give rise to a new (and sixth) limit on the conditional spending power that operates in cases involving "traditional" state authority.

There were, however, only four votes for this view, and some analysts, including Professor Samuel Bagenstos, have advocated for a narrower reading of *NFIB*. According to this understanding of the Court's ruling, *NFIB* directly supports a finding of impermissible coercion "[w]hen Congress takes [1] an entrenched federal program that [2] provides large sums to the states and [3] tells states that they can continue to participate in that program only if they *also* agree to participate in a separate and independent program."[74] As Bagenstos has acknowledged, however, Chief Justice Roberts's opinion might instead be "read broadly," in which case it "would seriously threaten the constitutionality of a broad swath of federal spending legislation,"[75] with potential casualties including longstanding conditional spending programs related to education (including the Individuals with Disabilities Education Act and the No Child Left Behind Act), the safeguarding of civil rights (including portions of the Civil Rights Act of 1964 and other federal programs that condition federal funding on the avoidance of race-based or sex-based discrimination), and environmental protection (including significant provisions of the Clean Air Act).[76]

Some analysts believe that courts will hesitate to apply *NFIB* to invalidate conditional spending programs of this ilk.[77] Others are not so sure.[78] In the end, it remains to be seen just how the chips will

---

[73] *Dole*, 483 U.S. at 217 (O'Connor, J., dissenting) (emphasis added).

[74] Samuel R. Bagenstos, *The Anti-Leveraging Principle and the Spending Clause After NFIB*, 101 GEO. L.J. 861, 866 (2013) (emphasis in original).

[75] *Id.* at 864.

[76] *Id.* at 906–20.

[77] *See, e.g.*, Eloise Pasachoff, *Conditional Spending After* NFIB v. Sebelius: *The Example of Federal Education Law*, 62 AM. U. L. REV. 577, 651–52 (2013) (suggesting that *NFIB* "is unlikely to affect many other existing federal-state programs if states were to challenge them on coercion grounds in court").

[78] *See* Jonathan H. Adler & Nathaniel Stewart, *Is the Clean Air Act Unconstitutional? Coercion, Cooperative Federalism, and Conditional Spending After* NFIB v. Sebelius, 43 ECOLOGY L.Q. 671, 721 (2016) (opining that "the Court's willingness to find coercion within the [ACA's] choice architecture [in *NFIB*] opens the door to coercion arguments in other contexts"); Andrew Coan, *Commandeering, Coercion, and the Deep Structure of American Federalism*, 95 B.U. L. REV. 1, 3 (2015) (concluding that the Court's ruling in *NFIB* indicates that "coercive exercises of the

fall.[79] But at least for now, the lower courts' post-*NFIB* applications of the anti-coercion principle suggest that the ruling in that case might end up having more bark than bite. Consider in particular the following rulings:

- In *Gruver v. Louisiana Board of Supervisors*,[80] the Fifth Circuit rejected Louisiana's argument that *NFIB* mandated invalidation of its waiver of sovereign immunity for violating Title IX of the Civil Rights Act of 1964, after the state made that waiver to comply with a condition on access to federal education funds. Louisiana first argued that, after *NFIB*, this condition was unlawful because it did not "govern the use of the funds" made available by Congress.[81] The court, however, disagreed. It observed that, while this program feature justified subjecting the condition to a heightened measure of scrutiny, it did not—contrary to Louisiana's argument—automatically render the condition invalid.[82] The state also argued that Congress had, as with the ACA, improperly installed the challenged sovereign-immunity waiver as a new funding condition long after the state first chose to accept federal education dollars. The court, however, found no problem with later-added conditions as a general matter because "Congress make[s] changes to

---

conditional spending power and commandeering amount to the same thing" and expressing concern that "[t]he extension of this logic to the conditional spending power is important because it calls into question an enormous quantity of federal legislation"); *see also* Bradley W. Joondeph, *The* Health Care Cases *and the New Meaning of Commandeering*, 91 N.C. L. REV. 811, 815–16, 834 (2013) (arguing that the Court's holding in *NFIB* carries the "implicit premise" that "federal laws can constitute commands even when they do not legally require the states to act," thus requiring a rethinking of what compulsion means "as a practical matter").

[79] *See* Lynn A. Baker, *The Spending Power After* NFIB v. Sebelius, 37 HARV. J.L. & PUB. POL'Y 71, 72 (2014) ("Simply put, the problem for modern spending power doctrine is this: How can the courts distinguish and invalidate those conditional offers of federal funds to the States that threaten to render meaningless the Tenth Amendment and its notion of a federal government of limited powers, while at the same time affording Congress a power to spend for the general welfare that is greater than its power to directly regulate the States?"); *id.* at 81 (adding that, in her view, *Dole* no longer provides the "governing doctrine," but that it is "far from clear" what its replacement might be and how the Court will gauge the effects of *NFIB* in the future); Elizabeth G. Patterson, *The Spending Power after* NFIB: *New Direction, or Medicaid Exception?*, 68 SMU L. REV. 385, 425 (2015) (expressing concern about the "current weak voluntariness inquiry" and "overly constricting *Dole* analysis," while recognizing that, "although the *NFIB* opinions signal a new, more careful approach to Spending Clause analysis," their effects—including with regard to generating a new analytical methodology—remain uncertain).

[80] 959 F.3d 178.

[81] *Id.* at 183.

[82] *Id.* at 183–84.

federal spending programs all the time."[83] In addition, while the ACA had thrust upon the states "a brand-new legislative program," this case involved only the addition of one additional condition to a longstanding and unitary set of Title IX funding rules.[84] Finally, the court concluded, "[t]he threat of LSU losing what amounts to just under 10% of its funding is more like the 'relative mild encouragement' of a state losing 5% of its highway funding (less than 0.5% of South Dakota's budget)" than confronting the "gun to the head" aimed at the states by the ACA.[85]

- In similar fashion, Tennessee met defeat in attacking Congress's conditioning of continued access to Medicaid funds on the state's agreement to provide coverage to large numbers of resident noncitizen refugees.[86] The court distinguished *NFIB* on the ground that the provision at issue in the Tennessee case was not part of an "entirely new program"[87]; in fact, despite some changes in the federal government's treatment of refugees over the years, the state had afforded Medicaid coverage to this very set of individuals since the 1970s and, indeed, had done so without reimbursement since 1991.[88] In addition, the most recent change in federal law had narrowed, rather than expanded, the number of refugees for whom coverage was required.[89] The state argued that these program features did not matter because the number of refugees—and the resulting costliness of covering them—had grown to unexpected levels in recent years. In the court's view, however, the existence of "periodic international humanitarian crises accompanied by refugees seeking to resettle in the United States has always been foreseeable."[90] The court also observed that "[w]hile Tennessee could potentially lose all of its federal Medicaid funds," it was open to the federal government to "withhold only part of the State's federal Medicaid funding" if Tennessee failed to honor

---

[83] *Id.* at 184 (quoting Bagenstos, *supra* note 74, at 888).

[84] *Id.*

[85] *Id.* (internal quotation marks omitted).

[86] Tennessee v. U.S. Dep't of State, 329 F. Supp. 3d 597 (W.D. Tenn. 2018), *aff'd on other grounds*, 931 F.3d 499 (6th Cir. 2019).

[87] *Id.* at 627.

[88] *Id.* at 627–28.

[89] *Id.* at 627.

[90] *Id.* at 628.

the refugee-coverage rule.[91] In any event, "the amount of the loss of funding is only one element of the coercion test," and the key point here was that Congress, unlike in the ACA, was not "using [the] program's funding as leverage to force the states to accept [a] new condition."[92]

- In *Mayhew v. Burwell*,[93] Maine asserted that federal authorities had impermissibly moved from inducement to compulsion when they threatened to cut off all Medicaid funding unless the state provided coverage for eighteen- to twenty-year-olds in keeping with ACA standards. More specifically, the ACA required Maine not to discontinue the coverage it previously had provided to members of this age group, thus in effect locking in as a condition to federal funding for the foreseeable future a practice that Maine had undertaken on only a voluntary basis in the past. Even though this condition was new and its operation threatened Maine with a total loss of federal Medicaid money, the court concluded that it did not run afoul of *NFIB* because it reflected a shift only "in . . . degree" rather than "in kind."[94] Indeed, in the court's view, this condition embodied nothing more than "an unexceptional 'alter[ation]' . . . [of] the boundaries' of categories of individuals covered under the old Medicaid program, completely analogous to the many past alterations of the program that *NFIB* expressly found

---

[91] *Id.* at 629.

[92] *Id.* For a similar line of reasoning, see *Mississippi Commission on Environmental Quality v. EPA*, 790 F.3d 138 (D.C. Cir. 2015). That case involved a post-*NFIB* challenge to a federal law that conditioned access to some (but not all) federal highway money on compliance with pollution-control standards imposed under the Clean Air Act. This program, however, had been in place without any relevant alteration since 1977. In these circumstances, the Court concluded, the state "was not suddenly surprised by dramatically new conditions retroactively imposed after a long period in which the State had accepted and relied upon unconditional federal funding—as was the case in *NFIB*." *Id.* at 179. The court also reasoned that "the threatened loss of federal highway funding"—which would not exceed 4% of the state's budget and probably would total far less than that—"does not even approach" the fund forfeiture originally threatened by the ACA. *Id.* at 178. As stated by the court: "[I]t is clear that Texas does not risk losing anywhere near the percentage of its federal funding—either for the program at issue or of its overall budget—that the Court found fatal in *NFIB*. Precisely how much less, we do not know. But the burden of establishing unconstitutionality is on the challenger, and Texas has failed to provide the necessary information." *Id.*

[93] 772 F.3d 80 (1st Cir. 2014).

[94] *Id.* at 90 (alteration in original) (quoting *NFIB*, 567 U.S. at 583).

to be constitutional."[95] The court emphasized that the Medicaid program had always focused on supplying medical care to needy children, including some persons in the eighteen-to-twenty-year-old category. Thus, in sharp contrast to the "basic change" made to Medicaid by the ACA, the imposition of this single new eligibility rule did not "create a new program" and fell "comfortably within Congress's express reservation of power to 'alter' or 'amend' the terms of the Medicaid statute."[96]

- In *New York v. Department of Justice*,[97] the Second Circuit found no constitutional problem in the federal government's conditioning of access to "Byrne program" law-enforcement funding on the agreement of state and local governments to assist federal authorities in their efforts to identify undocumented immigrants.[98] Even though noncomplying jurisdictions faced the loss of 100% of Byrne program funds, the court viewed the case as "much more akin to *Dole* than to *NFIB*" because a "real choice" existed about whether to accept the proffered federal largesse. Illustrative was the situation of New York, which faced a total loss of "less than 0.1% of the State's annual $152.3 billion budget, a smaller percentage loss even than that in *Dole*."[99] According to the court, "[t]he funding loss associated with most grant conditions . . . does not raise . . . coercion concerns."[100]

---

[95] *Id.* at 89 (alterations in original) (quoting *NFIB*, 567 U.S. at 583); *see id.* at 92 (analogizing the program change to an earlier expansion of Medicaid to cover pregnant women, which "*NFIB* approved" as only "a shift in degree"). For this reason, the court flatly rejected, as inconsistent with *NFIB*, the state's contention that "Congress cannot threaten to withdraw all Medicaid funds from a State for failing or refusing to cover categories of adults for whom Medicaid has never previously mandated coverage." *Id.* at 91–92 (internal quotations omitted).

[96] *Id.* at 91; *see also* California v. United States, 104 F.3d 1086, 1092 (9th Cir. 1997) (rejecting the argument that, due to the evolution of the Medicaid program, the state "now has no choice but to remain in the program in order to prevent a collapse of its medical system" when new conditions on program participation are imposed).

[97] 951 F.3d 84 (2d Cir. 2020).

[98] *Id.* More specifically, states and localities were required: (1) to do away with any rules that precluded their officers from communicating with federal authorities about the alienage status of individuals; (2) to respond to inquiries by federal authorities about the release dates of incarcerated undocumented persons; and (3) to give federal authorities access to those individuals during the period of their incarceration. *Id.* at 90.

[99] *Id.* at 116.

[100] *Id.* at 115. Notably, an entirely separate question presented in the "Byrne program" cases—which has arisen in other conditional-spending cases as well—was whether the condition-imposing administrative body had congressional authority to put the challenged condition in place. In *New York* itself, the court found that the

> Emphasizing the choice afforded to the state-plaintiff complainants by the Byrne program (and quoting from the Chief Justice's plurality opinion in *NFIB*), the court declared: " 'The States are separate and independent sovereigns. Sometimes they have to act like it.' "[101]

As this review of recent rulings indicates, lower courts have proceeded with caution in dealing with post-*NFIB* attacks on conditional spending programs. But the rulings also illustrate the rich mix of settings within which *NFIB*'s anti-coercion principle can, does, and will continue to come into play.

Department of Justice did have the condition-imposing authority it claimed, even though its ruling on this point conflicted directly with the rulings of three other circuits. *See New York*, 951 U.S. at 100–04, 116–23. For a detailed account and analysis of spending-power litigation related to Byrne program funds, see Douglas M. Spencer, *Sanctuary Cities and the Power of the Purse: An Executive* Dole *Test*, 106 IOWA L. REV. 1209 (2021).

[101] *Id.* (quoting *NFIB*, 567 U.S. at 579). Along the same lines, in *NYC C.L.A.S.H., Inc. v. Carson*, 442 F. Supp. 3d 200 (D.D.C. 2020), the court held that the challenged "Smoke Free Rule" did not give rise to impermissible compulsion because a state can "choose[ ] not to accept the federal government's public housing funding" and thus is not "required to comply with" that rule. *Id.* at 212–13.

Chapter 9

CONGRESSIONAL POWER OVER FEDERAL ELECTIONS

Analysis

Sec.

This chapter canvasses a range of issues related to Congress's regulatory powers over federal elections.[1] We begin with Congress's core powers in relation to congressional elections, which derive from the Elections Clause of Article I, section 4. We then turn to Congress's powers to regulate presidential elections—powers that, though not expressly codified in the constitutional text, have nonetheless found support in an implied federal authority "to preserve the departments and institutions of the general government from impairment or destruction."[2]

A. CONGRESS'S POWER TO REGULATE CONGRESSIONAL ELECTIONS

1. The Elections Clause

Article I, section 4 provides that "[t]he Times, Places and Manner of holding Elections for Senators and Representatives, shall be prescribed in each State by the Legislature thereof; but the Congress may at any time by Law make or alter such Regulations, except as to the Places of chusing Senators."[3] The Elections Clause is

---

[1] The Constitution does not in explicit terms empower Congress to regulate elections for state office, but Congress may rely on its powers to enforce the Reconstruction Amendments to ensure that such elections (along with elections for federal office) are carried out in a manner that does not run afoul of those Amendments' rights-based guarantees. Of central importance in this respect are the statutory prohibitions on state-based discriminatory voting measures set forth in the Voting Rights Act of 1965 (VRA). For a discussion of the VRA and its constitutional underpinnings, *see infra* Section 11.B.

[2] Burroughs v. United States, 290 U.S. 534 (1934).

[3] U.S. CONST. art. I, § 4. The final clause regarding "the places" for selecting Senators was inserted because the original Constitution provided for the selection of Senators by state legislatures. It is a curiosity that this provision was unaltered upon adoption of the Seventeenth Amendment, which mandated direct senatorial elections. *See* U.S. CONST. amend. XVII. This omission is not one of practical importance,

thus "a default provision," which "invests the States with responsibility for the mechanics of congressional elections, but only so far as Congress declines to preempt state legislative choices."[4] Indeed, notwithstanding the applicability of the anti-commandeering principle to other federal legislative powers,[5] the Elections Clause allows Congress to direct state officers to conduct elections for House and Senate members in compliance with federal requirements.[6] By

---

however, particularly in light of the modern-day practice of simultaneous voting at designated polling stations for both Senate and House members.

4 Foster v. Love, 522 U.S. 67, 69 (1997) (citing Storer v. Brown, 415 U.S. 724, 730 (1974), and Roudebush v. Hartke, 405 U.S. 15, 24 (1972)). The Elections Clause is unusual insofar as it specifically vests the states with a particular form of authority, and it does so in two separate ways. First, the clause specifies that federal election rules are initially to be set by state (as opposed to federal) authorities. *See* U.S. Term Limits, Inc. v. Thornton, 514 U.S. 779, 804–05 (1995) (noting that "the context of federal elections provides one of the few areas in which the Constitution expressly requires action by the States, namely that 'the Times, Places and Manner of holding Elections for Senators and Representatives, shall be prescribed in each State by the Legislature thereof' " (internal alterations omitted)). According to the prevailing view, it logically follows from this proposition that states have the more basic duty to hold elections for these federal offices. *See* ACORN v. Edgar, 56 F.3d 791, 795 (7th Cir. 1995) (noting that the Elections Clause "first . . . requires the states to create and operate such a system and . . . second authorizes Congress to alter the state's system—but it is still the state's system, manned by state officers and hence paid for by the state"); *see also* Arizona v. Inter Tribal Council of Ariz. Inc., 570 U.S 1, 8 (2013) ("Upon the States [the Elections Clause] imposes the duty ('shall be prescribed') to prescribe the time, place, and manner of electing Representatives and Senators. . . ."). Second, the Elections Clause clarifies that these election-related state-law rules must be established by state *legislative* officials, as opposed to executive or judicial officials. The Court has interpreted action "by the Legislature thereof" to include action by way of the initiative process in states with constitutions that authorize the use of this form of lawmaking. *See, e.g.*, Ariz. State Legis. v. Ariz. Indep. Redistricting Comm'n, 576 U.S. 787 (2015) (applying this rule to uphold establishment of voting district lines by an independent redistricting commission put in place through the initiative process). For more on the scope and significance of the Election Clause's reference to state legislatures, see *infra* note 37.

5 *See supra* Section 5.B (commerce power) and *infra* Section 13.B (other powers).

6 *See* Voting Rights Coalition v. Wilson, 60 F.3d 1411, 1415 (9th Cir. 1995) ("Congress may conscript state agencies to carry out voter registration for the election of Representatives and Senators."); ACORN v. Miller, 129 F.3d 833, 836 (6th Cir. 1997) (finding that the anti-commandeering limit does not apply in the federal elections setting, within which Congress has the power "both to *make and alter* laws affecting the states" (emphasis in original)); Evan H. Caminker, *State Sovereignty and Subordinacy: May Congress Commandeer State Officers to Implement Federal Law?*, 95 COLUM. L. REV. 1001, 1032 n.122 (1995) ("[S]tates are originally responsible for designing federal election systems and implementing them through state elections officers. [Article 1,] Section Four specifies that Congress may choose to 'alter' those state-specified systems. A fair reading of this text suggests that Congress may still expect the same state elections officers to implement the altered systems, unless Congress chooses instead to replace them by authorizing the appointment of federal elections officials."); *see also* Franita Tolson, *Election Law "Federalism" and the Limits of the Antidiscrimination Framework*, 59 WM. & MARY L. REV. 2211, 2220 (2018) (asserting that the Elections Clause allows Congress "to legislate irrespective of state sovereignty"). On a related point, the Court has held that ordinary, state-protective principles of preemption, *see infra* Chapter 24, do not apply with regard to federal laws enacted under the Elections Clause. *See Inter Tribal Council*, 570 U.S. at 13–15 (holding that the presumption against preemption that applies broadly in other

way of example, Congress has invoked the clause to require state officials to conduct general elections for the federal offices on a nationally uniform date, which is fixed as the "Tuesday next after the 1st Monday in November."[7]

The Elections Clause sparked little controversy at the Constitutional Convention, but it became a lightning rod of debate during the ratification process.[8] In response to declamations about federal interference with state-run electoral processes, defenders of the Constitution argued that the provision was needed to thwart states from blocking altogether the selection of House and Senate members, thus precluding even the occurrence of House and Senate sessions.[9] The terms of the Elections Clause, however, reach far beyond providing a curative for wholesale state shutdowns of balloting for federal legislative seats.[10] Indeed, in keeping with the plain meaning of the provision's text, the Court has declared that it authorizes "comprehensive" congressional control of federal electoral processes.[11]

---

contexts does not apply to federal Elections Clause legislation because of that Clause's explicit vesting of state-limiting congressional authority in this context).

[7] 2 U.S.C. §§ 1, 7. For a case involving an application of this statutory provision, see *Foster*, 522 U.S. at 71–73 (finding that Louisiana's "open primary" statute, which treated some pre-November primary results as final for purposes of the general election, was preempted by the federal election-timing requirement).

[8] *See* DAN T. COENEN, THE STORY OF THE FEDERALIST: HOW HAMILTON AND MADISON RECONCEIVED AMERICA 77 (2007) ("Antifederalists trembled at the thought that House members could advantage themselves by abusing the power to regulate the time, place, and manner of their own elections.").

[9] *E.g., Inter Tribal Council*, 570 U.S. at 8 (noting this point, including by reference to the discussion of it in *The Federalist Papers* (quoting THE FEDERALIST NO. 59 (Hamilton))). *Accord, e.g.*, Paul E. McGreal, *Unconstitutional Politics*, 76 NOTRE DAME L. REV. 519, 575 (2001) ("[T]he Framers allocated Congress the power of self-preservation—final say on the times, places, and manner of electing its members. . . . If the States were unable or unwilling to hold federal elections, Congress could provide for such elections and ensure at least a quorum."); Robert A. Kengle, *To Accept or to Reject:* Arizona v. Inter Tribal Council of Arizona, *the Elections Clause, and the National Voter Registration Act of 1993*, 57 HOW. L.J. 759, 793–94 (2014).

[10] Indeed, reflecting worry about the breadth of the clause, several of the original states proposed amending section 4 to limit its application to remedying states' refusal to hold federal elections. *See Inter Tribal Council*, 570 U.S. at 33 (Thomas, J., dissenting) (collecting proposals of this kind); *see generally* Robert G. Natelson, *The Original Scope of the Congressional Power to Regulate Elections*, 13 U. PA. J. CONST. L. 1, 38–40 (2010).

[11] Smiley v. Holm, 285 U.S. 355, 366–67 (1932) (adding that the "times, places, and manner" language creates federal legislative "authority to provide a complete code for congressional elections," including as to "notices, registration, supervision of voting, protection of voters, prevention of fraud and corrupt practices, counting of votes, duties of inspectors and canvassers, and making and publication of election returns"). *Accord* Cook v. Gralike, 531 U.S. 510, 523–24 (2001) (quoting *Smiley*'s broad description of the Elections Clause power); *Inter Tribal Council*, 570 U.S at 8–9 (noting that the power conferred by section 4 is "broad" because of its " 'comprehensive words', which 'embrace authority to provide a complete code for congressional elections' " (quoting *Smiley*, 285 U.S. at 366)); *Foster*, 522 U.S. at 69, 71 n.2 (highlighting

Congress's initial use of the times-places-and-manner power involved mandating the selection of House members on a district-by-district basis, thus overriding the then-existing practice of some states to vote for these officeholders in statewide elections.[12] Thereafter, in an effort to safeguard the integrity of post-Civil War elections in the south, Congress again invoked the power in adopting the Enforcement Act of 1870.[13] This legislation outlawed fraudulent conduct in connection with registration and voting, bribery, the making of false returns by state officers, the neglect of other duties by those officers (including duties imposed by state law), and the interference by private individuals with the proper conduct of

---

Congress's "power to impose 'the numerous requirements as to procedure and safeguards which experience shows are necessary in order to enforce the fundamental right involved' " (quoting *Smiley*, 285 U.S. at 366)); *Ex parte* Siebold, 100 U.S. 371, 387 (1879) (adverting to Congress's "general supervisory power over the whole subject" of federal electoral processes). Notably, the Court has also found a measure of additional congressional authority to superintend federal elections in Article I, section 2, which specifies that "electors in each State shall have the Qualifications requisite for Electors of the most numerous Branch of the State Legislature." *See also* U.S. CONST. amend. XVII (replicating this rule for the election of senators). In particular, the Court has read this text to vest individuals eligible to vote in federal elections with an individual constitutional right to cast a ballot and have it fairly counted, and it also has endorsed the existence of congressional authority to legislate in a way that safeguards this right. *See* United States v. Mosley, 238 U.S. 383, 388 (1915) (recognizing that the "right to have one's vote counted is as open to protection by Congress as the right to put a ballot in a box"); United States v. Classic, 313 U.S. 299, 314–15 (1941) (pointing to Article I, section 2 as helping to establish "the right to vote for representatives in Congress" and a corresponding congressional power to protect that right against interference); *Ex parte* Yarbrough, 110 U.S. 651 (1884) (referencing the constitutionally guaranteed "right to vote for a member of the Congress of the United States"); Wiley v. Sinkler, 179 U.S. 58, 62 (1900) (holding that "[t]he right to vote for members of the Congress of the United States is not derived merely from the Constitution and laws of the state in which they are chosen, but has its foundation in the Constitution of the United States"); Swafford v. Templeton, 185 U.S. 487, 492 (1902) (quoting *Yarbrough* in support of the view that the right to vote in federal elections is "fundamentally based upon the Constitution of the United States, which created the office of member of Congress, and declared it should be elective, and pointed to the means of ascertaining who should be electors" (internal alterations omitted)). Not surprisingly, the Court has also made it clear that Congress can punish federal-government officials for interfering with individual rights to vote in elections for federal office. *See* United States v. Wurzbach, 280 U.S. 396, 398–99 (1930) ("It hardly needs argument to show that Congress may provide that its officers and employees neither shall exercise nor be subjected to pressure for money for political purposes, upon or by others of their kind, while they retain their office or employment.").

[12] *See* Natelson, *supra* note 10, at 5 (discussing the Apportionment Act of 1842, ch. 47, 5 Stat. 491).

[13] Enforcement Act of 1870, ch. 114, 16 Stat. 140 (imposing penalties for infringement of voting rights and allowing use of military forces to enforce the law). Many of the statute's provisions targeted race discrimination in connection with voting and thus found direct authorization in the Enforcement Clause of the Fifteenth Amendment. Other provisions, however, were aimed more broadly at "establish[ing] a federal regime for protecting the right to vote" and "[f]or that reason, the Act's constitutionality rests in large part on the Elections Clause." Eliza Sweren-Becker & Michael Waldman, *The Meaning, History, and Importance of the Elections Clause*, 56 WASH. L. REV. 997, 1040–41 (2021).

elections.[14] The act also provided for the appointment of federal election monitors to ensure compliance with these statutory commands.[15]

Congress repealed most of the Enforcement Act in 1894, as the once vigorous federal Reconstruction program crumbled in the face of white resistance.[16] In the meantime, however, federal courts had upheld many of its key provisions as proper exercises of the power conferred by the Elections Clause.[17] Building on this history, the Court in more recent years has emphasized the sweeping scope of the times-places-and-manner power,[18] particularly when wielded in conjunction with the supplementary authority granted by the Necessary and Proper Clause.[19] Four aspects of these rulings illustrate the power's overall breadth. First, "Congressional authority extends not only to general elections, but also to any 'primary election which involves a necessary step in the choice of candidates for election as representatives in Congress.' "[20] Second, as to both general elections and primaries, Congress's authority reaches beyond the regulation of elections themselves to deal with pre-election registration.[21] Third, Congress has authority to attack

---

[14] *See Siebold,* 100 U.S. at 382.

[15] *See id.* at 397–98 (rejecting a challenge to the 1870 Act's empowerment of circuit courts to appoint election supervisors); *see also* Michael T. Morley, *The Enforcement Act of 1870, Federal Jurisdiction Over Election Contests, and the Political Question Doctrine,* 72 FLA. L. REV. 1153, 1161 (2020).

[16] The sweeping and tragic character of the federal retreat from the Reconstruction-era effort to address the oppression of recently emancipated Black citizens can be seen in the House Report concerning the 1894 repeal act. As that report stated: "Let every trace of the reconstruction measures be wiped from the statute books; let the States of this great Union understand that the elections are in their own hands." H.R. REP. NO. 53–18, at 7, *quoted in Classic,* 313 U.S. at 335 (Douglas, J., dissenting).

[17] *See Siebold,* 100 U.S. at 387–88 (holding constitutional under the Elections Clause sections of the Enforcement Acts that penalized state election officials for violations of state or federal election laws); *Ex parte* Clarke, 100 U.S. 399 (1879) (rejecting a separate challenge to the Enforcement Act): United States v. Gale, 109 U.S. 65, 67 (1883) (same). *But see* Morley, *supra* note 15, at 1160 (noting that the Court struck down some provisions of the act, related to state elections, as exceeding the scope of Congress's power to enforce the Reconstruction Amendments (citing United States v. Reese, 92 U.S. 214 (1876)); *see also* United States v. Cruikshank, 92 U.S. 542 (1876).

[18] *See supra* note 11 (collecting authorities).

[19] *See Classic,* 313 U.S. at 315, 320 (noting the significance of the Necessary and Proper Clause in defining the scope of Congress's power under the Elections Clause); *see also* Kevin K. Green, Note, *A Vote Properly Cast—The Constitutionality of the National Voter Registration Act of 1933,* 22 J. LEGIS. 45, 83 (1996) ("To the extent such commandeering [of state officials pursuant to federal legislation] is not legitimated by the text of Article I, Section 4 itself, this authority alternatively arises out of the Necessary and Proper Clause.").

[20] *Foster,* 522 U.S. at 71 n.2 (quoting *Classic,* 313 U.S. at 320).

[21] Of particular importance, the Court in *Inter Tribal Council* upheld legislation that established a standard form for state use in conducting registration for federal

abuses that postdate the collection of votes, such as the stuffing of ballot boxes and other comparable mischief in the tallying of results.[22] Finally, Congress may regulate not only *official conduct* related to the states' implementation and administration of federal elections, but also *private-party conduct* that threatens the integrity of those elections.[23]

---

elections. *See* 570 U.S. at 15. This mandate was part of the National Voter Registration Act of 1993, widely known as the federal "Motor Voter Law," which also imposed a variety of additional duties on the states. Not surprisingly, in light of the broad scope of the times-places-and-manner power, this statute's provisions have been upheld in a variety of cases. *See, e.g., ACORN,* 56 F.3d at 795 (citing *Siebold* and *Smiley* in upholding the act based on Congress's "general supervisory power" under the Elections Clause); *Voting Rights Coalition*, 60 F.3d at 1413 (noting that the registration of voters by the states is within "the reach of the power of Congress, provided by Article I, section 4"); *see also* League of Women Voters v. Newby, 838 F.3d 1, 4 (D.C. Cir. 2016) (ordering the district court to enjoin the federal Election Assistance Commission from granting several states' requests to modify Motor Voter Law forms to require proof of citizenship); Georgia State Conference NAACP v. Georgia, No. 1:17–CV–1397–TCB, 2017 WL 9435558 (N.D. Ga. May 4, 2017) (finding that the plaintiffs were likely to succeed on their claim that, regardless of the dictates of the Georgia Constitution, the Motor Voter Law validly required Georgia to extend voter registration for a runoff election); *see generally* Green, *supra* note 19, at 63. The Court applied the Motor Voter Law (without in any way questioning its constitutionality) in *Husted v. A Philip Randolph Institute,* 138 S. Ct. 1833 (2018), finding that Ohio's particular approach to removing persons from the voting rolls did not run afoul of the statute's restrictions.

[22] *See* United States v. Saylor, 322 U.S. 385, 386–87 (1944) (highlighting Congress's ability to criminalize ballot box stuffing and the failure to count lawful votes); *Mosley,* 238 U.S. at 386 (similar); *see also Roudebush,* 405 U.S. at 24–26 (suggesting that Congress's power under the Elections Clause extends to regulation of recounts for federal elections, while at the same time holding that a state could permissibly establish its own recount procedures in the absence of congressional legislation).

[23] Thus, for instance, Congress can prohibit individuals from physically obstructing access to federal polling places, bribing voters in federal elections, and interfering with state officials as they do federal election-related work. *See, e.g., Yarbrough,* 110 U.S. at 658 (broadly recognizing, albeit without specific reference to the Elections Clause itself, the federal government's "power to protect the elections on which its existence depends, from violence and corruption" and to ensure that federal officeholders are "the free and uncorrupted choice of those who have the right to take part in that choice"). In addition, the Court has held that the Elections Clause authorizes Congress to enact various campaign-finance measures, including limits on the amount of money that private individuals may contribute to candidates for federal office. *See, e.g.,* Buckley v. Valeo, 424 U.S. 1, 13 n.16 (1976) (citing the Elections Clause as the basis of Congress's authority to limit the amount of money that an individual or entity can give to candidates for federal office and its related authority to require such candidates to disclose their donations and expenditures). *But cf.* Citizens United v. FEC, 558 U.S. 310 (2010) (holding that a federal campaign-finance prohibition on independent expenditures by corporations and unions violates the First Amendment); *Buckley,* 424 U.S. at 44–54 (holding that campaign-finance restrictions on independent expenditures by political candidates violate the free-speech guarantee). Notably, Congress in proper instances can find support for regulating private action connected to federal elections not only in the Elections Clause (and its companion provision in Article I, section 2, *see supra* note 11), but also in the Enforcement Clauses of the Reconstruction Amendments. *See infra* Chapter 12 (considering the extent to which Congress's power to enforce the Thirteenth Amendment permits regulation of private-party conduct as necessary to eliminate the "badges and incidents of slavery") and *infra* Section 11.C (addressing the scope of Congress's power to regulate private action

At the same time, the Elections Clause is subject to important restraints. Suppose, for instance, that Congress were to pass a statute that required states to permit all middle-school graduates, regardless of age, to vote in House and Senate elections. Such a law would fall outside Congress's time-places-and-manner power because it concerns the *substantive* matter of voter eligibility, as opposed to the *procedural* aspects of federal elections.[24] Notably, in *Oregon v. Mitchell*,[25] Justice Black concluded that Article I *did* empower Congress, prior to adoption of the Twenty-sixth Amendment, to mandate the nationwide enfranchisement of 18-to 21-year-old voters for federal (but not state) elections.[26] In reaching this conclusion, however, Justice Black wrote only for himself, and five Justices in three separate opinions contended that he was wrong.[27] Even more important, in *Arizona v. Inter Tribal Council of Arizona, Inc.*,[28] the Court officially rejected his position.[29] As Justice Scalia explained for a seven-member majority: "Prescribing voting qualifications . . . 'forms no part of the power to be conferred upon the national government' by the Elections Clause, which is 'expressly restricted to the regulation of the times, the places, and the manner of elections.' "[30]

---

under Enforcement Clauses of the Fourteenth and Fifteenth Amendments). Noteworthy in this regard are cases in which the Court held that the actions of purportedly private political parties in conducting outcome-determinative primary elections, from which Black voters were excluded, qualified as state action under, and therefore directly violated, the Fourteenth Amendment's Equal Protection Clause. *See, e.g.*, Smith v. Allwright, 321 U.S. 649 (1944). From these rulings, it follows *a fortiori* that Congress can enact enforcement-power legislation that targets such constitutional wrongdoing as well as other forms of conduct by private parties held to constitute state action that itself violates the substantive protections put in place by the Fourteenth and Fifteenth Amendments.

24 Indeed, wholly apart from reaching beyond regulation of the "Manner" of elections, this law would raise textual problems in light of the command of Article I, section 2 that eligibility to vote in federal elections is to mirror "the Qualifications requisite for Electors of the most numerous branch of the State Legislature." U.S. CONST. art. I, § 2; *see also Inter Tribal Council*, 570 U.S. at 26–31 (Thomas, J., dissenting) (emphasizing the constitutionally rooted authority of states "to determine the qualifications of voters in federal elections").

25 400 U.S. 112 (1970).

26 *Id.* at 130.

27 *See id.* at 143 (opinion of Douglas, J.); *id.* at 210 (opinion of Harlan, J.); *id.* at 288 (opinion of Stewart, J., joined by Burger, C.J., and Blackmun, J.). The remaining Justices (who agreed with Justice Black that this legislation passed muster as applied to federal elections but who based that decision only on Congress's Fourteenth Amendment enforcement power) did not address the Article I issue. *Id.* at 231 (opinion of Brennan, White & Marshall, JJ.).

28 570 U.S. 1 (2013).

29 *Id.* at 16 n.8. *See generally* Kengle, *supra* note 9, at 799.

30 *Inter Tribal Council*, 570 U.S. at 17. In *Inter Tribal Council*, the Court touched on, but did not flesh out, the extent to which the states' authority to establish voter qualifications carries with it some limit on congressional lawmaking power (particularly regarding registration processes) on the theory that some exercises of

2. Congress's Power to Judge Elections, Returns, and Qualifications

Article I, section 5, clause 1 creates an additional set of legislative powers related to House and Senate elections by stipulating that each chamber is to "be the Judge of the Elections,

---

that power might impermissibly interfere with state efforts to ensure that prospective voters meet the applicable qualification standards that the state itself has rightfully established. The case involved a state's claim that a requirement that voters submit documentary proof of citizenship was unconstitutionally displaced by a federal law requiring use of a uniform federal registration form that required only a sworn statement that the prospective voter was a United States citizen. Justices Thomas and Alito concluded that the challenged federal law impermissibly abridged the state's authority not only to create, but to police, voter-qualification rules—in this case, the qualification rule that requires voters to be citizens. *See* 570 U.S. at 23 (Thomas, J., dissenting); *id.* at 38–39 (Alito, J., dissenting). The majority expressed some receptiveness to the principle relied on by the dissenters, stating that: "Since the power to establish voting requirements is of little value without the power to enforce those requirements, Arizona is correct that it would raise serious constitutional doubts if a federal statute precluded a State from obtaining the information necessary to enforce its voter qualifications." *Id.* at 17 (majority opinion). The majority also concluded, however, that this principle had no application to the *Inter Tribal Council* case. The reason why lay in the details of the federal statutory scheme, which in effect addressed the problem by permitting states to secure federal authorization to use supplementary information-gathering techniques if needed to ensure effective enforcement of local voting-qualification rules. *See id.* at 19. The Court's ruling in *Inter Tribal Council* also comports with its indication in *U.S. Term Limits v. Thornton*, albeit in the context of a discussion about *candidate* eligibility requirements, that the Elections Clause does not empower Congress to deal with matters of substance, as opposed to promulgating "procedural regulations." *See* 514 U.S. at 833; *accord Cook*, 531 at 523–24. And that ruling, in turn, finds support in the framing history. *See* THE FEDERALIST NO. 60 (Hamilton) (indicating that ratification critics' concerns that Congress could use Article I, section 4 to reformulate state voter qualification rules—for example, by establishing property-ownership requirements—were misplaced because doing so would not fit within establishing the "times, the places, the manner of elections"). Building on this principle, the Court also has ruled that substance-over-form principles limit state efforts to impose *de facto* qualifications for holding federal legislative office, apart from the exclusive list set forth in the Constitution itself, through the use of purported "manner" restrictions concerning the content of electoral ballots. *See U.S. Term Limits*, 514 U.S. at 804–05 (rejecting a state-based effort to effectively block election of long-term-incumbent candidates by way of a supposed "manner" rule that excluded their names from the ballot while, in theory, permitting them to compete by way of write-in voting). *See generally infra* Section 15.B.3 (further discussing this principle). It merits emphasis that Congress's inability to require states to regulate voter (and candidate) qualifications under the Elections Clause does not mean that federal lawmakers lack all authority to legislate on these matters. To the contrary, the Enforcement Clauses of the Fourteenth and Fifteenth Amendments provide a separate basis for Congress to legislate on these topics, but only to remediate in a proper way substantive violations of the prohibitions those amendments impose on the states. *See, e.g.*, Katzenbach v. Morgan, 384 U.S. 641 (1966) (upholding a provision of the Voting Rights Act that was aimed at ensuring the full enfranchisement of certain non-English-speaking New Yorkers previously educated in Puerto Rico, in both state and federal elections, so as to counteract state discrimination against such persons implicating the protections of the Equal Protection Clause). *See generally infra* Chapter 11 (discussing the scope of the Fourteenth and Fifteenth Amendment enforcement powers).

Returns and Qualifications of its own Members."[31] This provision, by referring to "Elections" and "Returns," empowers the House to resolve contested House elections and the Senate to resolve contested Senate elections, in each instance by way of majority vote.[32] In similar fashion, each chamber has the power to determine, again by the vote of a simple majority, whether would-be Senators and Representatives satisfy the "Qualifications" for membership. This grant of authority is of little practical importance, however, because elected individuals can be deemed to lack those qualifications only if they fail to satisfy the basic qualifications set forth in the Constitution itself, including the citizenship, residence, and age requirements established in express terms by Article I, section 2.[33] As a result, neither House of Congress can exclude an electoral victor based on a posited lack of "Qualifications" even if, for example, that individual recently committed murder or another serious crime.[34] Instead, the chamber must seat the malefactor and then consider whether to order that member's expulsion by way of a two-thirds vote as required by Article I, section 5, clause 2.[35]

B. CONGRESSIONAL REGULATION OF PRESIDENTIAL ELECTIONS

As the foregoing discussion reveals, Article I, section 4 grants Congress sweeping power to regulate the "Times, Places and Manner" of House and Senate elections. The Constitution, however, contains no comparable provision regarding presidential elections; instead, it specifies only that "Congress may determine the Time of chusing the Electors [for President and Vice President], and the day on which they shall give their votes."[36] In addition, Article II, section 1, clause 2 states that "Each State shall appoint, in such Manner as the Legislature thereof may direct, a Number of Electors, equal to the whole Number of Senators and Representatives to which the

---

[31] U.S. CONST. art. I, § 5, cl. 1. For further discussion of this power, see *infra* Section 14.B.

[32] *See id.*

[33] *See* Powell v. McCormack, 395 U.S. 486, 533 (1969); *see also infra* Section 35.E (discussing this decision in connection with the political-question doctrine).

[34] *Id.* at 509 (relying on both historical evidence and basic democratic principles in finding a lack of power to supplement the enumerated qualifications set forth in the Constitution). *But see id.* at 521 n.41 (raising the possibility that a would-be member could be validly excluded from Congress for engaging in insurrectionist activity within the meaning of section 3 of the Fourteenth Amendment, which is discussed *infra* Section 32.C).

[35] U.S. CONST. art. I, § 5, cl. 2. For a further discussion of this subject, see *infra* Section 14.B.

[36] *Id.* art. II, § 1, cl. 5.

State may be entitled in the Congress."[37] Putting to one side rights-based constitutional constraints (such as the one-person-one-vote rule[38]) and federal statutory limits stemming from Congress's exercises of its powers to enforce the Thirteenth, Fourteenth, and Fifteenth Amendments,[39] Article I, section 3 conveys "the broadest power of determination" to each state to fix its own method of choosing its own Electoral College members, unconstrained by congressional tinkering.[40] The thus-chosen method might take many forms, ranging from legislative appointment to interbranch designation to electoral systems that involve (among other things) the proportionate designation of electors based on statewide vote tallies,[41] district-by-district election,[42] or (as is now the all-but-universal practice) winner-take-all systems under which a single statewide vote is cast for competing slates of electors pledged to support particular presidential candidates. Pursuant to the authority vested in them by Article II, section 1, states can also limit the pool of persons who are eligible to serve as electors.[43] This authority

---

[37] *Id.* art. II, § 1, cl. 3. This Clause's specific reference to state "Legislature[s]," along with the Election Clause's own reference to "the Legislature" of "each State," has led some members of the Court to assert for the federal judiciary a robust power to review state-court decisions about the content of state election law—notwithstanding the general and well-established practice of treating state courts' rulings on the content of state law as definitive in federal court. *See, e.g.*, Bush v. Gore, 531 U.S. 98, 111–22 (2000) (Rehnquist, C.J., concurring); *see also* Republican Party of Pa. v. Boockvar, 141 S. Ct. 1, 2 (2020) (statement of Alito. J., concurring in denial of a motion to expedite consideration of petition for certiorari) (maintaining that federal courts must review state-court judgments about state election law in order to ensure that a state court does not "override the rules adopted by the legislature"). For a sharp scholarly criticism of this idea, see Vikram D. Amar & Akhil Amar, *Eradicating* Bush-*League Arguments Root and Branch: The Independent-State-Legislature Notion and Related Rubbish*, 2021 SUP. CT. REV. ___(forthcoming 2022) (urging that "[a]ll sensible constitutionalists—whether on the Court or off it, whether originalists or precedentialists, whether left or right of center—should bury" this idea and that emphasizing that "[t]he recent efforts to revive and rehabilitate *Bush*'s reputation are thus genuine cause for jurisprudential concern—even alarm"), *available at* https://papers.ssrn.com/sol3/papers.cfm?abstract_id=3731755.

[38] *See, e.g.*, Wesberry v. Sanders, 376 U.S. 1, 27 (1964).

[39] *See infra* Chapters 11–12.

[40] McPherson v. Blacker, 146 U.S. 1, 27, 35 (1892) (noting that the power to choose the method for appointing electors "is conferred upon the legislatures of the states by the constitution of the United States, and cannot be taken from them"); *accord* Chiafalo v. Washington, 140 S. Ct. 2316, 2324 (2020) (recognizing each state's power to appoint presidential electors "in whatever way it likes").

[41] *See, e.g.*, Ky Fullerton, Comment, *Bush, Gore, and the 2000 Presidential Election: Time for the Electoral College to Go?*, 80 OR. L. REV. 717, 735–36 (2001).

[42] Today, only two states, Maine and Nebraska, elect members of the Electoral College not on a state-wide, winner-take-all basis, but instead by way of schemes that take account of the preferences of intrastate congressional districts.

[43] *See* Ray v. Blair, 343 U.S. 214, 227 (1952) (recognizing "the state's right to appoint electors in such manner, subject to possible constitutional limitations, as it may choose"); *Chiafalo*, 140 S. Ct. at 2324 (noting state authority to impose, for example, residency and voter-eligibility requirements).

reaches far enough to allow states to subject to criminal penalties so-called "faithless electors"—that is, electors who are chosen to vote only for a particular presidential ticket, but then refuse to do so.[44]

Against the backdrop of these state-empowering constitutional rules looms the question whether Congress can enact legislation to ensure the fair operation of state-created mechanisms for selecting Presidents. Might, for example, Congress enact a law that requires states to meet basic, nationally operative standards of clarity and evenhandedness in formulating ballots for presidential elections (that is, technically, for elections of members of the Electoral College)? On one view, the answer should be "no." According to this line of thought, any recognition of a congressional power to supervise the manner of presidential elections would clash with (1) the textual grant of power to Congress to establish only the "Time" of presidential elections,[45] (2) the contrasting grant of power to Congress to regulate the "Times, Places and Manner" of House and Senate elections,[46] and (3) the specification that a state's electors are to be appointed "in such Manner as the Legislature thereof may direct."[47] This argument from negative implication, however, is marked by a number of difficulties.[48] Even more important, the

---

[44] *Id.* at 2328.

[45] *See* U.S. CONST. art. II, § 1, cl. 5.

[46] *See id.* art. I, § 4.

[47] *See infra* note 48 and accompanying text. For a closer examination of arguments rooted in these textual passages, see Zachary Newkirk, *An Untapped "Arsenal of Power:" The Elections Clause, a Federal Election Administration Agency, and Federal Election Oversight*, 47 FLA. ST. U. L. REV. 143, 171–73 (2019).

[48] Consider, for example, the argument that Article II's assignment to the states of the power to appoint electors "in such Manner as the Legislature [of the state] may direct" bars federal regulation of the "Manner" of electing such electors. The difficulty with this argument is that it overlooks the specialized use of the word "Manner" in Article II, section 1. In particular, that provision's reference to the "Manner" of "appoint[ing]" electors was designed to permit state legislators to choose among various possible modes of selection, including modes of selection that, at least potentially, do not involve any election at all. To be sure, Congress may not be able to prohibit a state from selecting its "Manner" of presidential-elector appointment in this overarching mode-of-selection sense. But it does not follow from this proposition that Congress cannot pass rules that help ensure the fair operation of whatever mode of selection the state chooses to employ. Notably, Justice Thomas' concurring opinion in *Chiafalo* lends support to this view by emphasizing the Framers' focus in Article II on allowing each state to choose its own methodology of appointing electors—as opposed to foreclosing regulation of problematic behavior that occurs in carrying out whatever methodology the state employs. *See* 140 S. Ct. at 2330 (Thomas, J., concurring) (noting that "Article II requires state legislatures merely to set the approach for selecting Presidential electors"); *id.* ("Historical evidence from the founding . . . suggests that the 'Manner' of appointment refers to the method for selecting electors. . . ."); *id.* ("In context, it is clear that the Framers understood "Manner" in Article II, § 1, to refer to the mode of appointing electors. . ."). There is likewise a serious problem with drawing any negative implication from Article I's treatment of the "Times, Places and Manner of holding Elections for Senators and Representatives" with regard to Congress's supposed inability to regulate elections of Electoral College members. The difficulty is that Article I addresses the "Elections" of federal legislative officials pursuant to

Supreme Court, in rulings handed down by widely different groups of Justices, consistently has held that Congress does indeed have a role to play in policing presidential election processes.[49]

Just where does this authority come from? In *Burroughs v. United States*,[50] the Court pointed to an implied principle that "Congress, undoubtedly possesses . . . every . . . power . . . essential to preserve the departments and institutions of the general government from impairment or destruction, whether threatened by force or by corruption."[51] Relatedly, one might maintain that Congress's power to safeguard presidential elections stems from the joint operation of its Twelfth-Amendment-based responsibility to "count" the ballots of presidential electors[52] and its supplementary power under the Necessary and Proper Clause to ensure the "appropriate" and "beneficial" exercise of every legislative power.[53] On another theory, the uncorrupted election of the leader of the nation is so important to the sound exercise of all federal powers that, again under the Necessary and Proper Clause, Congress can adopt laws that ensure the fairness and accuracy of the selection of Electoral College members.[54] Whatever its precise source, the congressional power over presidential elections is, according to the general view, sufficiently expansive that it mirrors in its scope the congressional power to regulate the "Times, Places and Manner" of

---

electoral processes endorsed by the Constitution, whereas the Constitution's treatment of the appointment of presidential electors under Article II does not by its terms require states to conduct any "Elections" at all. *See also Inter Tribal Council*, 570 U.S. at 33 (Thomas, J., dissenting) (highlighting the specialized meaning of the term "Manner of Elections" in pre-constitutional law and in the view of the Framers).

[49] *See generally* Dan T. Coenen & Edward J. Larson, *Congressional Power Over Presidential Elections: Lessons from the Past and Reforms for the Future*, 43 WM. & MARY L. REV. 851, 888, 900 (2002) (reviewing these authorities).

[50] 290 U.S. 534 (1934).

[51] *Id.* at 545; *see also Yarbrough*, 110 U.S at 658, 662 (citing the congressional "power to protect the elections on which [the federal government] depends, from violence or corruption" and its "duty" to safeguard "the free and uncorrupted choice of those who have the right to take part in that choice"); Coenen & Larson, *supra* note 49, at 887–88 (noting that "the Court in *Burroughs* . . . invoked the federal government's inherent 'power of self protection' " to uphold a congressional campaign-finance restriction for presidential elections (internal citation omitted)).

[52] U.S. CONST. amend. XII (stating that "the votes shall then be counted").

[53] *See supra* Chapter 6 (discussing the Necessary and Proper Clause). More specifically, so the argument goes, Congress's duty to count these ballots includes a power to count the ballots which, in turn, carries with it the authority to help ensure that the process that generates those ballots operates in an objectively fair and accurate way. *See* Coenen & Larson, *supra* note 49, at 866–70.

[54] All three of these theories involve the recognition of congressional powers that are tethered only loosely, if at all, to express textual grants of authority. *See infra* Section 10.E (discussing the subject of "inherent" congressional powers); *see also* Vikram D. Amar, *The Case for Reforming Presidential Elections by Sub-Constitutional Means: The Electoral College, the National Popular Vote Compact and Congressional Power*, 100 GEO. L.J. 237, 255–56 (2011).

House and Senate races.[55] And whether or not a perfect parity of these powers exists, the cases establish that Congress's authority over the procedural aspects of presidential elections reaches well beyond outlawing only the most nefarious state and private practices related to those elections. In *Burroughs*, for example, eight Justices agreed that this power reaches far enough to support the imposition of disclosure requirements on organizations that collect funds and make expenditures in connection with presidential campaigns.[56] That such a law, according to Justice Sutherland, "discourage[d] the making and use of contributions for purposes of corruption" sufficed to render it a permissible exercise of the recognized congressional power.[57]

Whatever the rules might be with regard to Congress's *ex ante* authority over the processes of conducting presidential elections, the Twelfth Amendment—which stipulates that "the President of the Senate shall, in the presence of the Senate and House of Representatives, open all the certificates and the votes shall then be counted"[58]—also gives Congress a measure of *ex post* authority over the selection of the nation's chief executive. Congress's duty to count electoral votes took center stage as the body struggled to deal with the crisis presented by the Hayes-Tilden election of 1876, when competing groups of electors submitted different slates of votes on behalf of their respective states.[59] In the wake of that crisis, Congress invoked its electoral vote counting authority, coupled with the Necessary and Proper Clause, to enact the Electoral Count Act of

---

[55] In *Mitchell*, for example, Justice Black stated that "[i]t cannot be seriously contended that Congress has less power over the conduct of presidential elections than it has over congressional elections." 400 U.S. at 124 (opinion of Black, J.). *Accord, e.g.*, Michael T. Morley, *The New Elections Clause*, 91 NOTRE DAME L. REV. ONLINE 79, 96 n.101 (2016) (citing to both *Burroughs* and Justice Black's opinion in *Mitchell* for the proposition that the Elections Clause of Article I and the Presidential Electors Clause of Article II "are typically read *in pari materia*").

[56] *See* Coenen and Larson, *supra* note 49, at 887–89.

[57] *Burroughs*, 290 U.S at 548.

[58] U.S. CONST. amend. XII.

[59] Following the election, Samuel Tilden was in the lead by more than 260,000 popular votes and appeared to be on the verge of winning an Electoral College majority. However, 19 electoral votes from three states—Florida, Louisiana, and South Carolina—were challenged, as was one of Oregon's three electoral votes assigned to Tilden. When it became apparent that, if Rutherford Hayes received these disputed votes he would defeat Tilden by the scant margin of 185 to 184, both candidates claimed the disputed electoral votes, with Republican leaders contending in particular that white Democrats had unlawfully prevented Black Republicans from voting across the south. After a period of near-chaos, threats of violence, and partisan deadlock, Congress put in place an Electoral Commission to resolve the dispute, and—pursuant to the recommendation of that Commission and the accompanying "Corrupt Bargain" of 1877, which led to the withdrawal of federal troops from the south and the effective end of Reconstruction—Hayes was declared the winner. *See* Coenen & Larson, *supra* note 49, at 862–64.

1887, which in turn took on a starring role in the Supreme Court's resolution of the Bush-Gore election dispute of 2000.[60] Twenty years later, the act again came into play amidst the ultimately unsuccessful effort of former-President Trump to overturn the result of the 2020 election.[61] In sum, the Twelfth Amendment holds the potential to put Congress in the position to resolve—albeit subject to pre-existing statutory mandates and fundamental constitutional limits—genuine conflicts involving the appointment of and votes submitted by Electoral College members. Moreover, as the Electoral Count Act itself illustrates, that same clause has been relied on in the past to support congressional enactment of some overarching rules

---

[60] Specifically, the act created a "safe harbor" rule that purports to guarantee the congressional counting of a state's electoral votes if, but only if, they are submitted by a particular date. A majority of the Court relied on this provision in disallowing any further recounts in Florida, whose electoral votes were decisive in the contest, thus effectively awarding the election to President Bush. It reasoned (controversially, to say the least) that Florida had previously signaled its desire to take advantage of the safe-harbor provision, that any further vote-counting would make doing so impossible, and that the Florida Secretary of State's then-existing certification of the result, which favored soon-to-be-President Bush, accordingly was dispositive. *See Bush v. Gore*, 531 U.S. at 111.

[61] After unsuccessfully pressuring state officials to overturn the results of their own states' elections, then-President Trump sought to pressure congressional Republicans to file objections to the certified votes under the terms of the Electoral Count Act. *See* Nicholas Fandos & Michael S. Schmidt, *Trump Allies Eye Long-Shot Election Reversal in Congress, Testing Pence*, N.Y. TIMES (Dec. 13, 2020), https://www.nytimes.com/2020/12/13/us/politics/trump-allies-election-overturn-congress-pence.html. It soon became apparent, however, that the President lacked the requisite congressional support to prevail with this maneuver, at which point he turned to pressuring Vice President Pence—who, pursuant to the Twelfth Amendment and the Electoral Count Act, was to preside over the special session of Congress called for the purpose of counting the electoral votes and certifying the final result—to unilaterally exclude pro-Biden electoral votes from the official count. The Vice President refused to accede to the President's demands, but a violent mob of Trump supporters—following an inflammatory speech by the President, decrying the result dictated by the soon-to-be-counted certified electoral votes—breached the Capitol and shut down the special session for several hours before security was restored and the count was officially completed. Needless to say, this was an extraordinarily dangerous assault on American democracy, fueled by a combination of wildly inaccurate factual assertions and meritless legal claims. The episode also underscores the existence of serious vulnerabilities and opportunities for exploitation created by the Electoral Count Act and other rules governing the presidential-selection process. For a thoughtful set of proposals for reform aimed at mitigating the risk of a future attempt to subvert democracy, see Richard L. Hasen, *Identifying and Minimizing the Risk of Election Subversion and Stolen Elections in the Contemporary United States*, 135 HARV. L. REV. F. 265 (2022); *see also* J. Michael Luttig, *The Conservative Case for Avoiding a Repeat of Jan. 6*, N.Y. TIMES (Feb. 14, 2022), https://www.nytimes.com/2022/02/14/opinion/electoral-count-act.html (advocating for reforms to the Electoral Count Act).

governing the manner in which electoral votes are submitted and reviewed.[62]

[62] Another form of authority regarding presidential selection created by the Constitution lies in the power vested in the House to decide, on a one-vote-per-state basis, the holder of the presidential office when no candidate garners a majority of electoral votes. U.S. CONST. art. II, § 1, cl. 3. This power came into play during the election of 1800, when one party's presidential candidate, Thomas Jefferson, and his own vice-presidential candidate, Aaron Burr, received exactly the same number of votes from electors who were charged with casting two votes in a single balloting process. *See* EDWARD J. LARSON, A MAGNIFICENT CATASTROPHE: THE TUMULTUOUS ELECTION OF 1800, AMERICA'S FIRST PRESIDENTIAL CAMPAIGN (2007). The resulting crisis gave rise to the Twelfth Amendment and its dictate that members of the Electoral College must cast separate votes for the President and for the Vice President.

Chapter 10

OTHER GRANTS OF CONGRESSIONAL POWER UNDER THE ORIGINAL CONSTITUTION

Analysis

Sec.

Some observers have criticized the Court's commerce-power jurisprudence as reaching so far as to render Congress's other granted powers essentially meaningless. We have already suggested that this claim has never been particularly persuasive and that recent developments in commerce-power doctrine have rendered it even more untenable.[1] To take an obvious example, the Affordable Care Act case established—in a highly consequential ruling—that, while the commerce power did not support enactment of the "individual mandate," the taxing power did.[2] In like fashion, the spending power permits Congress to induce states to implement regulatory and enforcement programs that Congress cannot compel them to implement through the use of its commerce power.[3] Congress also can override state sovereign immunity principles when acting pursuant to the Fourteenth and Fifteenth Amendment enforcement powers even though it cannot do so in enacting legislation under the Commerce Clause.[4] And the Thirteenth Amendment's Enforcement Clause might well enable Congress to regulate acts of violence engaged in by private parties that it cannot reach in wielding the

---

1 *See supra* Section 4.D.3 n.195 (discussing and challenging Justice Thomas's argument to this effect in *United States v. Lopez*, 514 U.S. 549, 588–89 (1995) (Thomas, J., concurring)).

2 *See supra* Section 7.A.2.

3 *See supra* Section 5.B.

4 *See supra* Section 5.C.

commerce power by virtue of the *Lopez/Morrison* noneconomic-activity principle.[5]

Other enumerated congressional powers also have had important effects in past times and continue to have independent significance in the present day. The Coinage Clause, for example, allows the federal government to create money—an activity of at least debatable justifiability under the Commerce Clause due to the principle that bars Congress, at least as a general matter, from invoking that clause to "create" commerce in order to regulate it.[6] At first blush, the bankruptcy power might seem to add nothing to the commerce power because bankruptcies necessarily deal with economic matters. But a closer look reveals that the Bankruptcy Clause has its own individualized legal significance, in part because it permits Congress to abrogate state sovereign immunity, notwithstanding the now-settled rule that Congress can never

---

5 *See infra* Chapter 12.

6 NFIB v. Sebelius, 567 U.S. 519, 550 (2012) (opinion of Roberts, C.J.). Along the same lines, Congress can, for example, rely on the Coinage Clause and the Counterfeiting Clause, coupled with the Necessary and Proper Clause, to outlaw the possession of machines that might be used to produce counterfeit coins. *See* U.S. CONST. art. I, § 8, cl. 6 (authorizing Congress to "provide for the Punishment of counterfeiting the Securities and current Coin of the United States"); *see also* Baender v. Barnett, 255 U.S. 224, 227 (1921) ("It hardly needs statement that in the exertion of this power the conscious and willing possession, without lawful authority, of a die in the likeness or similitude of one used or designated for making genuine coin of the United States may be made a criminal offense. If this be not a necessary, it is at least an appropriate, step in effectively suppressing and preventing the making and use of illegitimate coin."). At least as a rule, however, Congress cannot establish possessory crimes under the Commerce Clause because possession, even of an object readily subject to misuse, does not of itself constitute an "economic activity." *See Lopez*, 514 U.S. at 567 (indicating that that the mere possession of a handgun failed to qualify as "economic activity" properly subject to regulation under the Commerce Clause). In similar fashion, the Court has made clear that Congress cannot issue "individual mandates" pursuant to the commerce power. *See supra* Section 4.E (discussing this limiting principle, as laid down in *NFIB*). But the Court has relied on the specialized treatment of coinage in Article I in justifying Congress's mandate that persons must surrender gold coins and gold certificates in exchange for federally issued currency. *See* Nortz v. United States, 294 U.S. 317, 328 (1935) (concluding that Congress's authority "to compel all residents of this country to deliver unto the Government all gold bullion, gold coins and gold certificates in their possession" pursuant to the coinage power could "not be successfully challenged" (internal quotations omitted; citing Norman v. Baltimore & O. R. Co., 294 U.S. 240, 303 (1935))). Along the same lines, the Court has upheld Congress's abrogation, including on a retroactive basis, of contractual pay-in-gold clauses, reasoning that "[e]very contract for the payment of money, simply, is necessarily subject to the *constitutional power of the government over the currency*, whatever that power may be, and the obligations of the parties is, therefore, assumed *with reference to that power*." Knox v. Lee, 79 U.S. (12 Wall.) 457, 549 (1870) (emphasis added); *accord Norman*, 294 U.S. at 304–05 (reaffirming this principle); *see also* United States v. Marigold, 50 U.S. (9 How.) 560, 568 (1850) ("We trace both the offence and the authority to punish it to the power given by the Constitution to coin money, and to the correspondent and necessary power and obligation to protect and to preserve in its purity this constitutional currency for the benefit of the nation.").

abrogate that immunity pursuant to the commerce power.[7] The Naturalization Clause, which rests right alongside the Bankruptcy Clause in Article I, section 8, clause 4,[8] likewise gives Congress authority to deal with matters not necessarily regulable under Article I, section 8, clause 3.[9]

---

[7] *See supra* Section 5.C.2 and *infra* Section 13.A. In addition, the specialized text of the Bankruptcy Clause imposes a requirement of "uniformity" that (among other things) negates any power Congress otherwise might have to establish non-uniform regulations regarding the treatment of insolvent debtors under the Commerce Clause. *See* U.S. CONST. art. I, § 8, cl. 4 (authorizing Congress to make "uniform laws on the subject of bankruptcies throughout the United States"); *see also infra* Section 5.A.2.b (discussing the general view that specialized uniformity rules do not apply to commerce-power legislation). The seminal case with regard to the uniformity constraint is *Railway Labor Executives' Association v. Gibbons*, 455 U.S. 457 (1982). There, the Court considered a federal statute enacted to prevent the liquidation in bankruptcy proceedings of one and only one specific railroad. The Court held that Congress could not use the commerce power to enact a bankruptcy-related statute that was impermissible under the Bankruptcy Clause, thus putting a limit on the operation of the Commerce Clause that would not have existed were the Bankruptcy Clause not in the Constitution. *Id.* at 468–69. To be sure, the uniformity requirement imposed by the Bankruptcy Clause puts only limited constraints on Congress because it requires nothing more than *geographic* uniformity, *see id.* at 469–70, so that Congress remains able, notwithstanding the uniformity requirement, to "define classes of debtors" and "structure relief accordingly." *Id.* at 473. *See, e.g.*, Blanchette v. Conn. Gen. Ins. Corps., 419 U.S. 102, 158–60 (1974) (upholding congressional establishment of special bankruptcy proceedings for certain insolvent railroads, including under conditions in which all affected railroads were located in "a single statutorily defined region" because there was "[n]o railroad reorganization proceeding . . . pending outside that defined region on the effective date of the Act" so that the law "in fact operate[d] uniformly upon all bankrupt railroads . . . and uniformly with respect to all creditors of each of these railroads"); *see also* Stellwagen v. Clum, 245 U.S. 605, 613–14 (1918) (holding that Congress also remains able to make use in bankruptcy proceedings of state law principles that shape the scope of relevant property interests, even though state rules are in their nature not geographically uniform).

[8] *See* U.S. CONST. art. I, § 8, cl. 4 (authorizing Congress to "establish an uniform Rule of Naturalization").

[9] In particular, this might be the case because the granting of citizenship does not appear to involve the regulation of an economic activity. *See supra* Section 4.D.1. In addition, the Naturalization Clause has an independent significance because it illustrates how the grant of a power can carry with it, when exercised, the vesting of an individual right, including a right that accordingly cannot be diminished by way of the use of another power, such as the commerce power. Why? Because "[a] naturalized citizen . . . becomes a member of the society, possessing *all the rights of a native citizen*, and standing, in the view of the constitution, on the footing of a native." Osborn v. Bank of United States, 22 U.S. (9 Wheat.) 738, 827 (1824) (emphasis added). Put another way, while "naturalization is a privilege, to be given, qualified, or withheld as Congress may determine, and which the alien may claim as of right only upon compliance with the terms which Congress imposes," once Congress grants citizenship to an individual, the thus-naturalized citizen enjoys the same rights and privileges as a person who acquired citizenship at birth. United States v. Macintosh, 283 U.S. 605, 615 (1931). It follows that: "The constitution does not authorize Congress to enlarge or abridge those rights. The simple power of the national Legislature, is to prescribe a uniform rule of naturalization, and the exercise of this power exhausts it, so far as respects the individual." *Osborn*, 22 U.S. at 827. In sum, the naturalized citizen cannot, consistent with the Naturalization Clause, be subjected to burdens not imposed on other citizens because such a result would contravene the no-second-class-citizens principle that inheres in the word "Naturalization." *See* Knauer v. United

The Post Office Clause[10] has an independent power-granting significance in part because Congress has long used it to regulate activities whether or not they qualify as "economic" in nature despite the centrality of that activity-sorting label in measuring the reach of the commerce power.[11] The Full Faith and Credit Clause of Article IV—which empowers Congress "to prescribe the manner in which" one state must afford "Full Faith and Credit" to the "public Acts, Records, and judicial Proceedings of every other State"[12]—likewise deals with both economic and noneconomic matters and thus reaches beyond the power merely to "regulate Commerce . . . among the several States."[13] The same is true of other powers as well, including the powers to admit new states to the union,[14] to ensure the operation

States, 328 U.S. 654, 658 (1946). And this is so even if Congress otherwise could discriminate against naturalized citizens in wielding its commerce power—for example, by subjecting naturalized citizens, or certain classes of naturalized citizens, to specialized limitations in conducting foreign or interstate business activity.

10 U.S. CONST. art. I, § 8, cl. 7.

11 For example, it is not clear that robbery constitutes an economic activity for commerce-power purposes, *see supra* Section 4.D.1 n.107, but Congress has long (and without controversy) outlawed the robbery of mail. *Cf. supra* Section 1.B (noting the endorsement of a federal ban on mail robbery in *McCulloch v. Maryland*, 17 U.S. (4 Wheat.) 316 (1819)). Even more fundamentally, there exists a serious question about whether Congress could establish a postal system at all—far less a government-run system with monopoly characteristics—under the Commerce Clause standing alone, given the Court's indication in *NFIB* that that clause does not support actions by Congress that "create" commerce, as opposed to regulating commerce that already exists. *See supra* note 6. Finally, although the question ranges far beyond the subject of this book, it may be that specialized power-granting provisions such as the Post Office Clause sometimes interact with rights-protecting clauses of the Constitution in ways that influence the formulation of rights in ways that would not occur if the Commerce Clause stood alone as a power-granting provision in Article I. *Cf., e.g.*, Hannegan v. Esquire, Inc., 327 U.S. 146, 155 (1946) (assuming, while finding that the Postmaster General exceeded his authority in excluding lewd and vulgar material from the second-class mailing privilege, "that Congress has a broad power of classification and need not open second-class mail to publications of all types").

12 U.S. CONST. art. IV, § 1.

13 *Id.* art. I, § 8, cl. 3. In particular, the Court has signaled that significant limits may apply to Congress's authority to regulate "family law" matters under the Commerce Clause. *See Lopez*, 514 U.S. at 565; *see also* United States v. Morrison, 529 U.S. 598, 613 (2000). There can be no doubt, however, that the power granted to Congress by the Full Faith and Credit Clause extends to "public Acts, Records, and Judicial Proceedings" directly concerning family-law matters. *See, e.g.*, V.L. v. E.L., 577 U.S. 404, 410 (2016) (reversing the Alabama Supreme Court's refusal to recognize an adoption by a woman in Georgia of the child of her same-sex partner because that court "erred in refusing to grant that judgment full faith and credit"); *see also infra* Section 13.B n.31 (noting the Court's indication in *Printz* that the commandeering of state authorities under the Full Faith and Credit Clause is permissible even though such commandeering is not supportable under the Commerce Clause).

14 U.S. CONST. art. IV, § 3, cl. 1. In particular, the grant of the power by the clause to admit new states reaches beyond the commerce power by establishing that the new nation was not set in stone as an amalgam of only its originally-existing thirteen members. The State Admission Clause also establishes the companion proposition that the extraordinary act of creating a new state is do-able by way of ordinary legislation—as opposed, for example, to requiring adherence to an implied rule of unanimous state consent. In addition, as previously noted, *NFIB* puts limits on Congress's power under

within each state of a republican form of government,[15] and to regulate the times, places and manner of federal elections.[16] Building on its power to establish federal courts, Congress can pass many measures—concerning, for example, rules of procedure and evidence and the issuance of injunctive relief—whether or not those rules concern the sort of economic activity subject to aggregation under the substantial-effects prong of the commerce power.[17] Similarly, the grants of congressional authority over the District of Columbia[18] and the federal territories, such as Puerto Rico and Guam,[19] are so comprehensive that they permit Congress, with regard to these geographical subunits, to wield the full measure of the police power that the Tenth Amendment otherwise insistently reserves to state authorities.[20]

There is a broader point, too—one that stems from the fact that the most far-reaching features of Congress's power under the Commerce Clause have their source in that clause's interaction with the Necessary and Proper Clause of Article I, section 1, clause 18.[21] The Court in *NFIB* indicated (by way of the decisive opinion of Chief

---

the Commerce Clause to do more than regulate already-existing commerce, *see supra* note 11, and any attempt to create a new state solely under the commerce power might well be seen as abridging that limitation. At the very least, admitting a new state might involve the exercise of a self-evidently "great substantive and independent" power so that, under the logic of *NFIB*, Congress could not admit a new state as a "necessary and proper" means of carrying its commerce power (or any other power) into execution. Finally, even if Congress somehow could admit a new state pursuant to its commerce power, it is not at all clear that the exercise of that power would give rise to the same "equal footing" doctrine that the Court has applied to the admission of new states under the State Admission Clause itself. *See supra* Section 5.A.2.b.

15 U.S. CONST. art. IV, § 4. *See generally infra* Section 15.A n.45 (discussing this power grant).

16 *Id.* art. I, § 4. *See supra* Section 9.A.1 (noting, for example, that the anti-commandeering principle applicable to the commerce power does not apply to legislation enacted under the Elections Clause). The Court's work with the Elections Clause also illustrates how different power grants can and do have consequences that distinguish them from the commerce power insofar as they bear upon the Court's formulation of subconstitutional law. *See id.* (noting the Court's endorsement of a different, and less state-supportive, approach to statutory preemption for laws enacted under the Elections Clause than for laws enacted under the Commerce Clause).

17 For example, regardless of any effects on interstate commerce, Congress can authorize the removal to federal court of various types of cases brought against federal officers acting in a federal capacity. *See, e.g.*, Tennessee v. Davis, 100 U.S. 257, 263 (1879). It also can enact all sorts of laws relating to the execution of federal court judgments, regardless of whether those judgments concern commercial matters. *See, e.g.*, Bank of United States v. Halstead, 23 U.S. (10 Wheat.) 51, 53 (1825) ("It cannot certainly be contended, with the least colour of plausibility, that Congress does not possess the uncontrolled power to legislate with respect both to the form and effect of executions issued upon judgments recovered in the Courts of the United States.").

18 U.S. CONST. art. I, § 8, cl. 17.

19 U.S. CONST. art. IV, § 3, cl. 2.

20 *See infra* Sections 25.B, 25.C.

21 *See supra* Section 6.A.1.

Justice Roberts) that Congress cannot rely on the Necessary and Proper Clause to pass laws—no matter how useful they might be in carrying its enumerated powers into execution—if those laws reflect the exercise of a "great substantive and independent" power.[22] It follows from this principle that the original Constitution's treatment of congressional powers apart from the commerce power—ranging from the coinage power, to the weights-and-measures power, to the letters-of-marque-and-reprisal power, and on and on—marks them, at least presumptively, as qualifying as "great substantive and independent" in nature. After all, each of these powers appears within a textual structure that locates them right alongside the taxing, spending, and commerce powers, while offering no suggestion that, for some reason, only this latter set of textually granted powers merits the "great substantive and independent" label. The resulting point is one of key significance. The Framers' enumeration of *all* the powers expressly set forth in Article I and elsewhere in the Constitution negates the Congress-constraining argument that would have existed absent their enumeration—namely, the argument that Congress could not invoke the Necessary and Proper Clause to wield any of those powers, in connection with the Commerce Clause or otherwise, because of their "great" character. Stated otherwise, any suggestion that modern Commerce Clause doctrine has rendered meaningless the Framers' listing of these other powers appears to overlook a core limiting principle regarding the Necessary and Proper Clause found determinative in *NFIB*—a principle that, according to the Chief Justice in that case, was so central to the constitutional plan that the Court endorsed it more than two centuries ago.[23]

Further treatment of the potpourri of powers canvassed in the foregoing paragraphs must be left to the more focused efforts of others. But four enumerated powers, in addition to those explored in earlier chapters, deserve a closer look because they surface with some frequency in modern-day litigation. Attention thus now shifts to (1) the Property Clause of Article IV; (2) the Intellectual Property Clause of Article I, section 8, clause 8; (3) the treaty power vested in the President and the Senate by Article II, section 2, clause 2; and (4) the multiple powers laid out in Article I regarding military affairs and

---

22 *NFIB*, 567 U.S. at 559 (opinion of Roberts, C.J.) ("Although the Clause gives Congress authority to 'legislate on that vast mass of incidental powers which must be involved in the constitution,' it does not license the exercise of any 'great substantive and independent power[s]' beyond those specifically enumerated." (quoting *McCulloch*, 17 U.S. at 411, 421)); *see also id.* at 653 (Scalia, Kennedy, Thomas & Alito, JJ., dissenting) (finding the individual mandate to be "not 'consist[ent] with the letter and spirit of the Constitution' " (quoting *McCulloch*, 17 U.S. at 421)). *See generally supra* Section 6.B.2.

23 *See NFIB*, 567 U.S. at 559 (opinion of Roberts, C.J.).

national defense. Also receiving separate consideration is a mixed bag of other congressional powers that the Court has described as "inherent" in the constitutional plan.

A. THE PROPERTY CLAUSE

Article IV, section 3 authorizes Congress to "make all needful Rules and Regulations respecting the . . . Property belonging to the United States."[24] This clause thus gives Congress a power that ranges well beyond the authority channeled to it by the Commerce Clause.[25] For example, Congress cannot generally prohibit homicide under its commerce power.[26] But Congress can outlaw homicide in federal office buildings, parks, training facilities, and the like—even though they lie within state boundaries—pursuant to its generalized

---

[24] The clause also empowers Congress to make "all needful Rules and Regulations" for federal territories. For a treatment of the latter subject, see *infra* Section 25.B.

[25] The nature of federal authority over federal property is complicated by the separate stipulation in Article I, section 8 that Congress may "exercise exclusive Legislation in all Cases whatsoever . . . over all Places purchased by the Consent of the Legislature of the State in which the Same shall be, for the Erection of Forts, Magazines, Arsenals, dock-Yards, and other needful Buildings." U.S. CONST. art. I, § 8, cl. 17. Importantly, the Court has held that this grant of authority does not preclude Congress from acquiring property for uses other than the "Erection of Forts, Magazines, Arsenals, dock-yard, and other needful buildings"—for example, to create national parks. *See* Collins v. Yosemite Park & Curry Co., 304 U.S. 518, 529–30 (1938). In similar fashion, this grant of authority as to "Places purchased by the Consent of the Legislature of the State" does not mean that federal authorities cannot acquire property without state consent. Indeed, the federal government can acquire land within a state not only by way of contract but also by way of eminent domain, and it may do so even in the face of a state's objections. *See, e.g., Kohl*, 91 U.S. at 371; James v. Dravo Contracting Co., 302 U.S. 134, 147 (1937) ("The right of eminent domain inheres in the federal government by virtue of its sovereignty, and thus it may, regardless of the wishes either of the owners or of the states, acquire the lands which it needs within their borders."). In the end, the key role of the "all Places purchased" clause in Article I, section 8, clause 17, when coupled with the separate Property Clause of Article IV, is to create a regime of differing default rules that gather around two ideas: (1) as for federal properties acquired "by the consent of the Legislature of the State"—which are generally referred to as "federal enclaves"—activity that occurs within those areas is entirely immune from state regulatory control (at least absent contrary federal legislation or a contrary agreement or perhaps during the post-transfer time period before Congress establishes its own regulatory regime); and (2) as for other federal property, activity that occurs on it generally is subject to state regulatory control absent the enactment of preemptive federal legislation. *See* California Coastal Comm'n v. Granite Rock Co., 480 U.S. 572, 593 (1987) ("[T]he Property Clause gives Congress plenary power over the federal land at issue; however, even within the sphere of the Property Clause, state law is pre-empted only when it conflicts with the operation or objectives of federal law, or 'when Congress evidences an intent to occupy a given field.' "). *See generally* LAURENCE H. TRIBE, AMERICAN CONSTITUTIONAL LAW § 5–8 (3d ed. 2000). The overarching result is that, as to both types of property, Congress in effect has the last word as to what police-power-type regulations will govern, and "[t]he presence or absence of state consent . . . does not affect the quantum or character of [that] congressional power." *Id.* at 849; *see also infra* note 34 (discussing the work of Professor Appel).

[26] *See Morrison*, 529 U.S. at 615.

power to make rules respecting federal property.[27] It is also at least open to question, in light of the still-protean nature of *NFIB*'s anti-mandate principle, whether Congress could invoke the commerce power to require individuals to wear face-coverings to promote public health, and thus the economy, in the midst of a pandemic.[28] Relying on congressional exercises of power under the Property Clause, however, federal authorities have required the wearing of masks within federal facilities.[29]

The Property Clause also permits Congress to regulate some activities (including noneconomic activities) that occur *outside* the boundaries of federal lands.[30] Thus, in *Kleppe v. New Mexico*,[31] the Court relied on Congress's Article IV authority to sustain restrictions on private interference with wild burros, including when they roam off federal ranges onto neighboring private property, as "needful" to "regulate and protect the wildlife living [on public land]."[32] In sum, an "expansive reading" of the Property Clause[33] permits Congress to apply any and all sorts of regulations to activities that occur on

---

[27] *See Kleppe*, 426 U.S. 529, 539 (1976) ("[E]ven over public land within the States, '(t)he general government doubtless has a power over its own property analogous to the police power of the several states . . . .' " (quoting Camfield v. United States, 167 U.S. 518, 525 (1897))). In *Benson v. United States*, 146 U.S. 325, 331 (1892), for example, the Court upheld a federal prosecution for a murder that occurred on federal land even though the transfer of the land to it was for military purposes and the murder was said to have occurred on a portion of land then being used only for farming. Notably, *Benson* involved land transferred with state consent, and the case was therefore governed by Article I, section 8, clause 17. As previously noted, however, Congress has the same power to apply its own rules to murder or other activities that occur on property not acquired with state consent pursuant to its Article IV property power. *See supra* note 25. For cases illustrating the federal government's extension of police-power controls to its own properties, see *United States v. Unzeuta*, 281 U.S. 138, 142 (1930) (upholding the federal court's exercise of jurisdiction over a prosecution for a murder committed on a freight car on the right of way of a railroad located on the Fort Robinson Military Reservation), and *Battle v. United States*, 209 U.S. 36 (1908) (affirming a federal conviction for murder because "[t]he crime was committed upon land bought by the United States in the city of Macon, on which it was building a post office and courthouse, and over which the state of Georgia had ceded jurisdiction.").

[28] *See supra* Section 4.E.

[29] *See, e.g.*, Exec. Order No. 13,991, 86 Fed. Reg. 7045 (Jan. 25, 2021) (instructing executive-branch agency officials, to the extent authorized by statutory delegations of authority, to require the wearing of masks in federal buildings).

[30] For early cases endorsing this principle, see *United States v. Alford*, 274 U.S. 264, 267 (1927) (upholding a federal statute that criminalized the failure to extinguish a fire built "near" any "public domain" and emphasizing that "Congress may prohibit the doing of acts upon privately owned lands that imperil the publicly owned forests"), and *Camfield*, 167 U.S. at 528 (holding that Congress properly "exercised its constitutional right of protecting the public lands from nuisances erected upon adjoining property" by prohibiting the installation of fences on private property that "inclosed" federal lands).

[31] 426 U.S. 529 (1976).

[32] *Id.* at 541.

[33] *Id.* at 539.

federal lands and not infrequently to activities that occur on other lands as well.[34]

B. THE INTELLECTUAL PROPERTY CLAUSE

1. A General Overview

Among the powers vested in Congress by Article I, section 8 is one of special salience in the information age: "To promote the Progress of Science and useful Arts, by securing for limited Times to Authors and Inventors the exclusive Right to their respective Writings and Discoveries."[35] This provision has played two key roles in the field of constitutional federalism. First, it has channeled to Congress the lion's share of authority to establish and protect copyrights and patents, notwithstanding the continuing dominance of the states in overseeing most aspects of general property law.[36] In

---

[34] For an in-depth discussion of *Kleppe* and related matters, see Peter A. Appel, *The Power of Congress "Without Limitation": The Property Clause and Federal Regulation of Private Property*, 86 MINN. L. REV. 1, 101 (2001) (discussing the history of the Property Clause and its implications for federal land management in light of the principle that, while "Congress may lack a general police power . . . it fully possesses a police power over its own lands"). *See also* Peter A. Appel, *The Power of Congress "Without Limitation" in the Twenty-First Century*, 24 PUB. LAND & RESOURCES L. REV. 25, 38 (2004). For an argument that the Court's broad interpretation of the Property Clause is incorrect and problematic from a policy perspective, see Jeffrey M. Schmitt, *Limiting the Property Clause*, 20 NEV. L.J. 145 (2019).

[35] U.S. CONST. art. I, § 8, cl. 8.

[36] One point here is subtle, but significant: It might be that modern Commerce Clause law would permit federal lawmakers to displace state authority across wide swaths of general property law, particularly with regard to "economic activity" in the form of property transfers. But congressional efforts to move in this direction would, understandably, raise objections from state and local authorities who traditionally have handled the legal aspects of local property interests, particularly as to real estate. Sweeping federal control over copyrights and patents, in contrast, is uncontroversial precisely because the Constitution speaks to the federal government's power over that matter in no uncertain terms. A related point is that the explicit grant of authority made by the Intellectual Property Clause sweeps off the table, with regard to patents and copyrights, a broad array of "edge issues"—for example, regarding the need for and consequences of recording ownership interests—that might arise in other contexts if Congress were, however unexpectedly, to federalize most or all features of general property law. Put another way, the Intellectual Property Clause addresses with clarity Congress's power to regulate copyrights and patents, as opposed to other kinds of property, and this fact has propelled a longstanding division of power between the states and the nation of critical significance to the law of constitutional federalism. Notably, Congress has ventured into areas of intellectual property law concerning matters that reach beyond patents and copyrights, particularly with regard to trademarks and trade secrets. As for trademark law, the key legislative goal is to guard against marketplace confusion. *See* Paul J. Heald & Suzanna Sherry, *Implied Limits on the Legislative Power: The Intellectual Property Clause as an Absolute Constraint on Congress*, 2000 U. ILL. L. REV. 1119, 1161. As for trade-secret law, the legislative purpose centers on countering the theft of valuable information, often by employees or in ways that violate fiduciary obligations. *See* David S. Levine & Christopher B. Seaman, *The DTSA at One: An Empirical Study of the First Year of Litigation Under the Defend Trade Secrets Act*, 53 WAKE FOREST L. REV. 105, 114 (2018). It follows, according to the general view, that federal laws that deal with these

particular, this power permits Congress to confer on private persons specialized intellectual-property interests, even where the creation (as opposed to the regulation of the transfer) of such interests might not be supported by the Commerce Clause.[37]

Second, the Intellectual Property Clause does more than create a freestanding federal power because it also constrains the reach of other federal powers, including the power to regulate interstate commerce. This limiting effect stems from the Framers' purposeful choice to use the Intellectual Property Clause to strike a balance between the encouragement of new creations through the grant of monopoly privileges and the facilitation of broad access to those creations through their eventual placement in the public domain.[38] The cornerstone of this plan lies in the clause's specification that copyrights and patents can operate only for "limited Times."[39] It

---

subjects do not implicate (and thus do not run afoul of) the Intellectual Property Clause because they do not concern the creation and eventual sharing of "Writings" and "Discoveries." Consequently, the basis for federal laws regarding trademarks and trade secrets primarily lies, as with most business regulation, in the Commerce Clause. *See* 1 ANNE GILSON LALONDE, GILSON ON TRADEMARKS § 1.04 (Matthew Bender ed. 2021).

[37] It might be, in particular, that courts would balk at the idea that Congress can rely on the commerce power to "create" intellectual property rights by way of the issuance of copyrights and patents on the theory that doing so would not involve regulating "commerce" that is already in existence. *See supra* Section 4.E (discussing the Court's drawing of a sharp distinction between creating commerce and regulating commerce in its seminal ruling in *NFIB*). In addition, with regard to legislation under the Commerce Clause standing alone, it might be that there exist some rights-based limits on the congressional creation of monopolies; the Intellectual Property Clause, however, specifically authorizes Congress to create monopolies, albeit only for "limited Times."

[38] *See, e.g.*, Heald & Sherry, *supra* note 36, at 1162–64.

[39] *See* Edward C. Walterscheid, *Defining the Patent and Copyright Term: Term Limits and the Intellectual Property Clause*, 7 J. INTELL. PROP. L. 315, 363 (2000) (stating that the purpose of the limited-times requirement is to ensure that "the subject matter of the grant go[es] into the public domain at some defined time," while enabling the author or inventor to obtain "a good rate of return on his time and investment"). Under current law, most patents last 20 years, while copyrights (for works created after 1978) generally operate for the lifespan of the author plus 70 years. 35 U.S.C. § 154; 17 U.S.C. § 302. In *Eldred v. Ashcroft*, 537 U.S. 186 (2003), a seven-Justice majority concluded that Congress did not violate the "limited Times" rule when it extended the length of already-granted and still-operative copyrights. *Id.* at 201 (relying largely on post-grant extensions of patent terms by early Congresses). *But see id.* at 243, 267 (Breyer, J., dissenting) (asserting that the 20-year extension made copyright protection "virtually perpetual" in violation of "the scope of legislative power that the Copyright Clause, read in light of the First Amendment, grants to Congress"). In addition, the Court in *Golan v. Holder*, 565 U.S. 302 (2012), upheld against a "limited Times"-based attack a portion of the Uruguay Round Agreements Act that, unlike the statute at issue in *Eldred*, granted copyright protection to certain foreign works that were already in the public domain because they had fallen outside U.S. copyright protection at the time they came into being in light of their creation in certain foreign countries. The challengers in *Golan* argued that the Intellectual Property Clause dictated that any relevant "limited time had already passed for works in the public domain." *Id.* at 319. The Court, however, rejected this contention in part because it entailed the untenable conclusion that certain types of works (such as those

almost certainly follows from that stipulation that federal lawmakers may not circumvent this constraint by invoking the commerce power to afford never-ending protection for "Writings and Discoveries," even if such a protection deals with "economic activity" that, in the aggregate, has substantial effects on interstate commerce.[40]

---

at issue in the case) would have had a limited term of "zero" (as they were never previously covered by any copyright at all in the United States). *See id.* at 320 (adding that the Court's conclusion made sense because "a 'limited time' of exclusivity must begin before it may end"). In sum, *Eldred* establishes that the "limited Times" language does not automatically preclude Congress from extending the duration of an existing copyright, and *Golan* establishes that Congress may at least sometimes confer federal copyright protection on works that were at no earlier point in time subject to such protection. It remains an open question whether Congress can resurrect copyright protection for a work (unlike the one at issue in *Golan*) that once enjoyed monopoly protection but as to which the lifespan of that earlier monopoly grant has come and gone. *See* Graham v. John Deere Co., 383 U.S. 1, 6 (1966) (suggesting, albeit with respect to patents, that resurrection of protection after expiration of the original term of protection is impermissible); *see also* David E. Shipley, *Congressional Authority over Intellectual Property Policy After* Eldred v. Ashcroft: *Deference, Empty Limitations, and Risks to the Public Domain*, 70 ALB. L. REV. 1255, 1293 (2007) ("Recapturing a work from the public domain is not the same as extending the life of an existing copyright, and the Supreme Court has made many statements about the importance of the public domain and that 'the Constitution forbids grants of exclusive rights in that which is already in the public domain.' " (quoting Pamela Samuelson, *The Constitutional Law of Intellectual Property After* Eldred v. Ashcroft, 50 J. COPYRIGHT SOC'Y U.S.A. 547, 563 (2003))). *But cf.* Howard B. Abrams, Eldred, Golan *and Their Aftermath*, 60 J. COPYRIGHT SOC'Y U.S.A. 491, 523 (2013) ("[T]he majority opinion [in *Golan*] strongly suggests Congress has a nearly unlimited right to remove works from the public domain. While it is extremely doubtful the majority would accept wholesale or unprincipled removal of works from the public domain, the language of *Golan* seems to invite it.").

[40] *See, e.g.*, 1 HOWARD B. ABRAMS & TYLER T. OCHOA, THE LAW OF COPYRIGHT § 1:27.50 (2020) ("[I]t takes little imagination to project . . . that the Supreme Court would be hostile to any grant of rights that are functionally equivalent to copyright that could not be constitutionally validated within the sole confines of the Copyright-Patent clause."); Malla Pollack, *Unconstitutional Incontestability? The Intersection of the Intellectual Property and Commerce Clauses of the Constitution: Beyond A Critique of* Shakespeare Co. v. Silstar Corp., 18 SEATTLE U. L. REV. 259, 270 (1995) (arguing that Congress "may not bypass" the "limited Times" requirement by relying on the Commerce Clause); Wayne A. Kalkwarf, *The Commerce Clause Versus the Patent and Copyright Clause: A Battle of Constitutional Proportions*, 54 IDEA 351, 410–11 (2014) (arguing that the "limited Times" requirement restricts Congress's commerce powers in a manner similar to the Bankruptcy Clause as interpreted in *Railway Labor Executives' Association*, which is discussed *supra* note 7); Michael F. Finn, *"Just the Facts, Ma'am": The Effect of the Supreme Court's Decision in* Feist Publications, Inc. v. Rural Telephone Service Co. *on the Colorization of Black and White Films*, 33 SANTA CLARA L. REV. 859, 871 (1993) ("It seems likely that the same rationale present in [*Railway Labor Executives' Association*] would also bar any type of Commerce Clause legislation aimed at removing limitations of the Intellectual Property Clause."). Another question is whether Congress could rely on either its IP power or the commerce power to put in place a duration of protection for a patent or copyright that is itself so long as to violate the "limited Times" requirement. *See, e.g.*, Heald & Sherry, *supra* note 36, at 1172 ("To put the question pointedly, could Congress constitutionally enact a 100-billion-year copyright or patent term?"). For insights into how courts might use a functional approach to determine when a purportedly "limited Time" is not sufficiently "limited" for constitutional purposes, see *id.* at 1172–75; *see also* Jerome N. Epping, Jr., *Harmonizing the United States and European Community Copyright*

So just how far do the patent and copyright powers, and any resulting limits on other powers, reach?[41] As for copyrights, the Court has declared that Congress can afford monopoly-type protection only to "original" works and not to the mere gathering and presentation of

Terms: Needed Adjustment or Money for Nothing?, 65 U. CIN. L. REV. 183, 214–15 (1996); Abrams, *supra* note 39, at 521–23. For a further discussion of the extent to which the terms of the Intellectual Property Clause impede congressional use of the commerce power, see *infra* Section 10.B.2.

[41] One question about the scope of the power concerns whether the clause's opening phrase, "to promote the Progress of Science and useful Arts," has a legally significant, power-constraining effect. *See* Edward C. Walterscheid, *The Preambular Argument: The Dubious Premise of* Eldred v. Ashcroft, 44 IDEA 331, 331, 332 n.5 (2004) (stating that the Court "has never directly addressed this specific question" and "has indirectly addressed it in apparently conflicting ways"). For some relevant treatments of the matter, see *John Deere Co.*, 383 U.S. at 6 (suggesting that the clause embodies a "constitutional command" and adding that "[t]his is the standard expressed in the Constitution and it may not be ignored"); *Great Atlantic & Pacific Tea Co. v. Supermarket Equipment Corp.*, 340 U.S. 147, 154 (1950) (Douglas, J., concurring) ("The Congress does not have free rein, for example, to decide that patents should be easily or freely given. The Congress acts under the restraint imposed by the statement of purpose in Art. I, § 8. The purpose is 'To promote the Progress of Science and useful Arts.' "); Craig W. Dallon, *Original Intent and the Copyright Clause:* Eldred v. Ashcroft *Gets It Right*, 50 ST. LOUIS U. L.J. 307, 315–36 (2006) (contending that, contrary to the views of some, *see, e.g.*, Eldred v. Reno, 239 F.3d 372, 378 (D.C. Cir. 2001), *rev'd on other grounds*, 537 U.S. 186 (2003), the clause's introductory language is not merely "preambular"); Heald & Sherry, *supra* note 36, at 1153 (asking why the Framers would "not just give Congress the power 'to grant copyrights and patents' " if the opening language were not meant to establish some limitations). In *Eldred*, the Court sidestepped this debate by pointing out that "Congress, from the start, has routinely applied new definitions or adjustments of the copyright term." *Eldred*, 537 U.S. at 213. In essence, the challengers in that case had argued that extending copyright terms for already-protected works failed to "promote the Progress of . . . useful Arts" because such an extension "does not stimulate the creation of new works, but merely adds value to works already created." *Id.* at 211–12. The Court, however, rejected this argument by challenging its premise. It reasoned that Congress had a "rational basis," apart from simply enriching copyright holders, for extending the operative copyright terms because the newly extended terms served to bring American copyright protections more in line with international practice. *Id.* at 205–06, 213. Speaking to a closely related matter, the Court also found that term extensions for already-copyrighted materials did not violate any implied "quid pro quo" requirement—that is, the supposed requirement that "an author or inventor may not be given something for nothing." Heald & Sherry, *supra* note 36, at 1162. According to the Court, even assuming some such requirement exists, the prospect of later receiving a copyright extension can be viewed as part of the incentive for the creation of new works; in other words, what is traded to the authors who undertake to create works is a "a copyright not only for the time in place when protection is gained, but also for any renewal or extension legislated during that time." *Eldred*, 537 U.S. at 215; *see also* Dallon, *supra*, at 313 (noting the assumption of the Court in *Eldred* that "authors created their works in exchange for copyright protection with an expectation that they would also be entitled to future copyright extensions"). It remains to be seen whether the Court's dismissive treatment of the purpose-related preambular language of the Second Amendment in *District of Columbia v. Heller*, 554 U.S. 570, 577–79, 578 n.4, 595–601 (2008) (declaring that "a prologue can be used only to clarify an ambiguous operative provision" and "apart from that clarifying function, a prefatory clause does not limit or expand the scope of the operative clause"), will in any way inform the Court's approach to the opening language of the Intellectual Property Clause.

information already in existence.[42] Consider "data compilations," such as an alphabetized telephone book. Without question, the creation of such a work involves the investment of time, expense, and effort. Even so, the Court declared in *Feist Publications, Inc. v. Rural Telephone Service Co.*[43] that the "facts" gathered in data compilations cannot receive copyright protection because they "do not owe their origin to an act of authorship."[44] Thus, for example, Congress could not, under the Intellectual Property Clause, pass a law prohibiting a second telephone-book maker from copying all the factual information gathered by a first telephone-book maker, notwithstanding the "sweat of the brow" efforts that went into generating that expansive and useful initial publication.[45] In similar fashion, the Court has held that "ideas" are not copyrightable.[46] Thus, if *A* writes an essay that asserts, for the first time, that recent Montana wildfires resulted from Martian satellite attacks, federal copyright law neither can nor does preclude *B* from writing a second essay advancing the same theory. To be sure, Congress might validly

---

[42] *See* Feist Publ'ns, Inc. v. Rural Tel. Serv. Co., 499 U.S. 340, 345–47 (1991) (citing Goldstein v. California, 412 U.S. 546, 561–62 (1973), in describing originality as the "touchstone of copyright protection"). A work is sufficiently "original" if it was "independently created by the author" and it "possesses at least some minimal degree of creativity." *Id.* at 345. Notably, the Court has been clear in stating that "originality is a constitutional requirement," and not just a statutory one. *Id.* at 346; *see also* Paul J. Heald, *The Vices of Originality*, 1991 SUP. CT. REV. 143, 144 (noting the Court's repeated emphasis in *Feist* of the constitutional basis of the originality requirement).

[43] 499 U.S. 340 (1991).

[44] *Id.* at 347; *see also* Int'l News Serv. v. Associated Press, 248 U.S. 215, 234 (1918) (holding that federal copyright protection of a news article may not extend to the factual information it contains because that information "is not the creation of the writer, but is a report of matters that ordinarily are *publici juris*"). As explained by Justice O'Connor in *Feist*: "The distinction is one between creation and discovery: The first person to find and report a particular fact has not created the fact; he or she has merely discovered its existence." *Feist*, 499 U.S. at 347. Indeed, Justice O'Connor described this "fact/expression dichotomy" as "the essence of copyright," *id.* at 350, in that it reflects the underlying idea that copyright's primary objective is not to "reward the labor of authors" but instead "[t]o promote the Progress of Science and useful Arts." *Id.* at 349 (quoting U.S. CONST. art. I, § 8, cl. 8.). To be sure, factual compilations, such as the white pages of a phone book, may be copyrightable to the extent they reflect creative choices made by the compiler as to "which facts to include, in what order to place them, and how to arrange the collected data." *Id.* at 348. Even so, as the Court emphasized in *Feist,* copyright protection for factual compilations is "thin" because follow-on authors can take the facts that the first author laboriously collected and simply rearrange them in an "original" manner. *Id.* at 349. In *Feist* itself, the Court went one step further, concluding that the telephone company's alphabetization of names in the white pages did not enjoy copyright protection because it lacked even the "modicum of creativity" necessary to establish the base level of originality needed to qualify for federal copyright protection. *Id.* at 362.

[45] *Id.* at 349 (setting forth the "constitutional principle" that "much of the fruit of the compiler's labor may be used by others without compensation").

[46] *See* Baker v. Selden, 101 U.S. 99, 102 (1879). This constitutionally rooted mandate is now statutorily codified at 17 U.S.C. § 102(b). *See generally* Alfred C. Yen, *A First Amendment Perspective on the Idea/Expression Dichotomy and Copyright in a Work's "Total Concept and Feel,"* 38 EMORY L.J. 393, 395 (1989).

prohibit *B* from copying verbatim the words of *A*'s essay. But the idea that Martian satellites have caused the wildfires, even though wholly original to *A*, could not itself receive federal copyright protection.[47]

Along these same lines, patentability—which the Intellectual Property Clause makes available only for "Discoveries" by "Inventors"—reaches no further, at least as a general matter, than to safeguard creations that are "novel," "useful," and "nonobvious."[48] Building on this principle, the Court in 1853 barred Congress from making any "[l]aws of nature" patentable.[49] Later rulings have drawn on the same idea to hold that "the basic tools of scientific and

[47] *See* Nichols v. Universal Pictures Corp., 45 F.2d 119, 121 (2d Cir. 1930) ("Upon any work, and especially upon a play, a great number of patterns of increasing generality will fit equally well, as more and more of the incident is left out. The last may perhaps be no more than the most general statement of what the play is about, and at times might consist only of its title; but there is a point in this series of abstractions where they are no longer protected, since otherwise the playwright could prevent the use of his 'ideas,' to which, apart from their expression, his property is never extended.").

[48] These terms are embodied in the present-day statute, 35 U.S.C. § 101 *et seq.*, and (not surprisingly) the statutory formulation is designed to correspond with constitutional strictures. *See* David O. Taylor, *Confusing Patent Eligibility*, 84 TENN. L. REV. 157, 164 n.22 (2016); *see also* Diamond v. Chakrabarty, 447 U.S. 303, 308 (1980) (setting forth the text of the original statute, authored by Thomas Jefferson, attaching patentability to "any new and useful art, machine, manufacture, or composition of matter, or any new or useful improvement [thereof]" (quoting Act of Feb. 21, 1793, § 1, 1 Stat. 319)); *John Deere Co.*, 383 U.S. at 17 (addressing concerns that the first explicit congressional recognition of the non-obviousness standard did not come until 1952 by explaining that, nonetheless, the operative statute was "merely . . . a codification of judicial precedents"). One question regarding the "novelty" standard was raised by legislation, enacted in 2011, that shifted the award of patentable monopoly rights from the "first to invent" to the "first to file" regarding the invention. *See* Leahy-Smith America Invents Act, Pub. L. 112–29, 125 Stat. 284 (2011). On one theory, this shift in governing law was unconstitutional because a "first to file" claimant cannot be filing with regard to a "novel" invention if that person was not in fact the "first to invent." Andrew L. Sharp, Note, *Misguided Patent Reform: The Questionable Constitutionality of First-To-File*, 84 U. COLO. L. REV. 1227, 1244 (2013) (citing the Patent Act of 1790, ch. 7, 1 Stat. 110); *cf. also* Shantanu C. Pathak, Comment, *The AIA and the First-to-File Provision: Consequences and Constitutionality*, 28 TEMP. INT'L & COMP. L.J. 115, 139 (2014) (emphasizing the important role of the term "first and true inventor," which has its roots in the English Statutes of Monopolies of 1623, which in turn influenced the framing of the Intellectual Property Clause). For a contrary view, see *id.* at 138 (arguing that the Court has "left the details to Congress on how to 'promote the Progress of . . . useful Arts,' " thus establishing "a sufficiently broad approach to the definition of 'inventor' " as to leave "open the possibility of the first-to-file provision"); *see also* Jane C. Ginsburg, *No "Sweat"? Copyright and Other Protection of Works of Information After* Feist v. Rural Telephone, 92 COLUM. L. REV. 338, 378 (1992) (endorsing judicial deference in assessing the constitutionality of patent and copyright laws because "Congress is better situated than is the Court not only to make the policy determination of what constitutes the progress of knowledge, but to judge what means best achieve that goal").

[49] Le Roy v. Tatham, 55 U.S. 156, 174–75, 177 (1853); *see also* Mayo Collaborative Servs. v. Prometheus Labs., Inc., 566 U.S. 66, 70 (2012) (holding that "[l]aws of nature, natural phenomena, and abstract ideas" are not patentable" (quoting *Chakrabarty*, 447 U.S. at 309)).

technological work"—such as the physical properties of natural materials and mathematical formulas—are not patent-eligible.[50] For example, no patent could issue for the general operation of electricity, gravity, or magnetism.[51] This limitation, the Court has reasoned, ensures that the essential building blocks of invention are not monopolized in a way that would thwart, rather than promote, "the Progress of Science."[52]

Exemplifying these principles is the Court's ruling in *Ass'n for Molecular Pathology v. Myriad Genetics, Inc.*[53] There, the Court acknowledged that the discovery of the location and genetic sequence of two human genes, BRCA1 and BRCA2, may have been the product of a brilliant scientific effort that required the expenditure of millions of dollars. Even so, the Court held that the thus-unearthed information was not patentable because it was not an "invention"; instead, it was a "product of nature"—here, in the form of a "naturally occurring segment of . . . DNA"—that accordingly was not subject to patent-based protection "merely because it [was] isolated" from "the rest of the human genome."[54] At the same time, the discoverers of the gene sequence could secure patent protection for newly formed molecules created by a lab technician with information gained from the earlier genetic mapping effort.[55] Indeed, the Court emphasized

---

[50] Gottschalk v. Benson, 409 U.S. 63, 67 (1972); *see also* Funk Bros. Seed Co. v. Kalo Inoculant Co., 333 U.S. 127, 130 (1948); *Le Roy*, 55 U.S. at 175.

[51] *See* Christopher Beauchamp, *Patenting Nature: A Problem of History*, 16 STAN. TECH. L. REV. 257, 269 (2013) (citing OLIVER EVANS, EXPOSITION OF PART OF THE PATENT LAW BY A NATIVE BORN CITIZEN OF THE UNITED STATES 12–13 (1816)).

[52] *See* Alice Corp. v. CLS Bank Int'l, 573 U.S. 208, 216 (2014); Ass'n for Molecular Pathology v. Myriad Genetics, Inc., 569 U.S. 576, 589 (2013); Mayo Collaborative Servs. v. Prometheus Labs., Inc., 566 U.S. 66, 71 (2012)). Scholars have noted how these subject-matter limits on patentability parallel limits in copyright law based on differentiating expression from ideas and facts. Both sets of limits, so they assert, "operate to keep intellectual infrastructure in the public domain." Peter Lee, *The Evolution of Intellectual Infrastructure*, 83 WASH. L. REV. 39, 56 (2008); *see also* WILLIAM M. LANDES & RICHARD A. POSNER, THE ECONOMIC STRUCTURE OF INTELLECTUAL PROPERTY LAW 305–06 (2003) (stating that the legal inability to secure intellectual-property rights in the laws of nature, ideas, facts, and the like makes sense because it negates "both . . . the enormous potential for rent seeking that would be created if property rights could be obtained in them and . . . the enormous transaction costs that would be imposed on would-be users").

[53] 569 U.S. 576 (2013).

[54] *Id.* at 580, 591 ("[The patentee] did not create anything. To be sure, it found an important and useful gene, but separating that gene from its surrounding genetic material is not an act of invention.").

[55] *Id.* at 580 ("[W]e hold that a naturally occurring DNA segment is a product of nature and not patent eligible merely because it has been isolated, but that cDNA is patent eligible because it is not naturally occurring."). In other words, the patent applicant could not claim the exclusive right to find something in nature—that is, to isolate an individual's BRCA1 and BRCA2 genes—but the patent applicant could claim the exclusive right to manipulate something found in nature to make something else that was significantly different—that is, to create BRCA complementary DNA (cDNA) in a lab.

that the initial mappers were in an "excellent position" to claim patents on "new *applications* of knowledge" about the BRCA1 and BRCA2 genes,[56] including, as Professor Jorge Contreras has suggested, a built-out "method for assessing a person's risk of cancer based on the presence of certain mutations in [those] *BRCA* genes."[57]

2. Intellectual Property Clause Limits on Commerce-Power-Based Regulation of IP-Related Matters

As indicated above, an important constitutional question relating to the Intellectual Property Clause concerns the extent to which its existence and its terms restrict the ability of Congress to make use of the commerce power to deal with IP-related subjects.[58] One debate on this topic has involved a federal "anti-bootlegging" statute aimed at halting the copying of live performances, which are themselves not eligible for protection under the Intellectual Property Clause (so, at least, most analysts would agree) because they do not qualify as "Writings."[59] Critics of this legislation have argued that the inability of Congress to grant copyright protection to such works carries with it a companion inability to give copyright-like protection to live performers under the Commerce Clause. In *United States v. Moghadam*,[60] however, the Eleventh Circuit rejected this contention.[61] It reasoned that "[e]xtending quasi-copyright protection to unfixed live musical performances is in no way inconsistent with the Copyright Clause"; rather, protecting live performances from exploitive copying is "in harmony" with the clause in part because those performances "clearly satisf[y] the originality requirement."[62]

---

[56] *Id.* at 596 (emphasis added).

[57] Jorge L. Contreras, Association for Molecular Pathology v. Myriad Genetics: *A Critical Reassessment*, 27 MICH. TECH. L. REV. 1, 38 (2020).

[58] *See supra* note 40 and accompanying text.

[59] In particular, a work can qualify as a copyrightable "Writing" only if it is "reduced to a tangible form," which a live performance in and of itself cannot be. *See* United States v. Moghadam, 175 F.3d 1269, 1274 (11th Cir. 1999); *see also Feist*, 499 U.S. at 355 (quoting H.R. Rep. No. 94–1476, p. 51 (1976)).

[60] 175 F.3d 1269.

[61] *Id.* at 1281.

[62] *Id.* at 1280. For other decisions upholding the anti-bootlegging law, see *United States v. Martignon*, 492 F.3d 140, 149 (2d Cir. 2007) (reasoning that Congress impermissibly regulates copyright-related matters under the Commerce Clause only when "(1) the law it enacts is an exercise of the power granted Congress by the Copyright Clause and (2) the resulting law violates one or more specific limits of the Copyright Clause"), and Kiss Catalog, Ltd. v. Passport Int'l Prods., Inc., 405 F. Supp. 2d 1169, 1176 (C.D. Cal. 2005) (finding no "fundamental conflict" between the Intellectual Property Clause and the anti-bootlegging statute because "the question is not whether legislation empowered by the Copyright Clause—but invalid under it—can otherwise be empowered by the Commerce Clause"; instead "[t]he question is

Although the court in *Moghadam* upheld the anti-bootlegging statute, it recognized that not all federal statutes that exceed the power granted by the Intellectual Property Clause can pass constitutional muster simply because they comport with Commerce Clause rules.[63] But how far does this principle go? We have seen, for example, that Congress cannot use its power regarding copyrights to prelude Mr. B's replication of telephone "white pages" initially produced by Ms. A.[64] But could Congress turn to the commerce power to safeguard the "sweat of the brow" effort of the makers of such first-time-around works, thus encouraging their creation, by outlawing post-publication copying of them by the Mr. Bs of the world? Prominent scholars have contended that the answer is "no" in light of the balance struck by the Framers in the Intellectual Property Clause itself.[65]

---

whether matters not encompassed within the Copyright Clause can be addressed by the Commerce Clause free of the restrictions of the Copyright Clause").

63 One problem of this sort grows out of the Court's ruling in *Dastar Corp. v. Twentieth Century Fox Film Corp.*, 539 U.S. 23 (2003). There, relying in part on an earlier patent-law decision, *see* Sears, Roebuck & Co. v. Stiffel Co., 376 U.S. 225 (1964), the Court held that the right to copy a work, as to which the term of protection had expired, carried with it the right to copy without any attribution of the work's original creator, regardless of limits (imposed by the Lanham Act) in "passing off" others' work as one's own. The Court relied on principles of statutory interpretation in setting forth this principle in *Dastar*. There exists, however, a separate question whether the Constitution would command the same outcome even if federal legislation were to require attribution. The worry is that mandating attribution would in effect restrict use of materials as to which free access and re-use is constitutionally protected because, in keeping with their protection for only "limited Times," those materials now rest in the public domain. *See Dastar*, 539 U.S. at 34 (expressing concern about the creation of "a species of mutant copyright law that limits the public's 'federal right to copy and use' expired copyrights" (quoting Bonito Boats, Inc. v. Thunder Craft Boats, Inc., 489 U.S. 141, 165 (1989)) (other internal quotations omitted)). For one discussion of this question, see ABRAMS & OCHOA, *supra* note 40, at § 1:27.50 (expressing concern about maintaining the "balance . . . between the limited rights of copyright granted in the Copyright Act and essentially identical but broader rights . . . in a statute grounded on a different constitutional grant of power to Congress").

64 *See supra* note 45 and accompanying text.

65 For treatments noted earlier, see Heald & Sherry, *supra* note 36, at 1176–79; Heald, *supra* note 42, at 168–76; and Pollack, *supra* note 40. Additional treatments of the subject include Theodore H. Davis, Jr., *Copying in the Shadow of the Constitution: The Rational Limits of Trade Dress Protection*, 80 MINN. L. REV. 595 (1996); Rochelle C. Dreyfuss, *A Wiseguy's Approach to Information Products: Muscling Copyright and Patent into a Unitary Theory of Intellectual Property*, 1992 SUP. CT. REV. 195; Kevin J. Hickey, *The Copyright/Commerce Clause Collision: A Subject Matter Approach*, 82 U. CIN. L. REV. 1 (2013); John J. Flynn, *The Orphan Drug Act: An Unconstitutional Exercise of the Patent Power*, 1992 UTAH L. REV. 389; Thomas B. Nachbar, *Intellectual Property and Constitutional Norms*, 104 COLUM. L. REV. 272 (2004); Caroline T. Nguyen, Note, *Expansive Copyright Protection for All Time? Avoiding Article I Horizontal Limitations Through the Treaty Power*, 106 COLUM. L. REV. 1079 (2006); William Patry, *The Enumerated Powers Doctrine and Intellectual Property: An Imminent Constitutional Collision*, 67 GEO. WASH. L. REV. 359 (1999); Aaron K. Perzanowski, *The Penumbral Public Domain: Constitutional Limits on Quasi-Copyright Legislation*, 10 U. PA. J. CONST. L. 1081 (2008); Malla Pollack, *The Right to Know?: Delimiting Database Protection at the Juncture of the Commerce Clause, the*

3. A Dormant Intellectual Property Clause?

A related question (and one that might turn out to be of keen interest to both Ms. A and Mr. B) is whether works, such as data collections, that fall outside the coverage of the Intellectual Property Clause might nonetheless receive protection under *state* law. To be sure, in some cases, courts might conclude that Congress has preempted copyright-related restrictions embedded in state law by channeling some works, but not others, into the public domain.[66] *Feist,* however, suggests that data collections are not copyrightable as a matter of federal *constitutional* law, and that is the case regardless of how Congress deals with the subject by way of federal statute.[67] The question thus arises whether—wholly apart from the

---

Intellectual Property Clause, and the First Amendment, 17 CARDOZO ARTS & ENT. L.J. 47 (1999).

[66] For example, in *Bonito Boats,* the Court held invalid a Florida statute prohibiting the use of a production process called "direct molding" to copy the shape of unpatented boat hulls. *See* 489 U.S. at 144. The Court found that the law "substantially restrict[ed] the public's ability to exploit an unpatented design in general circulation" and thereby impermissibly disrupted a "scheme of federal regulation . . . so pervasive as to make reasonable the inference that Congress left no room for the States to supplement it." *Id.* at 167 (quoting Rice v. Santa Fe Elevator Corp., 331 U.S. 218, 230 (1947)); *see also* David E. Shipley & Jeffrey S. Hay, *Protecting Research: Copyright, Common-Law Alternatives, and Federal Preemption,* 63 N.C. L. REV. 125, 152–53 (1984) (discussing how "the court reversed a decision under state unfair competition law that prohibited the copying o[f] an unpatentable light fixture" in both *Sears,* 376 U.S. 225 (1964), and its companion case, *Campco Corp. v. Day-Brite Lighting, Inc.,* 376 U.S. 234 (1964), because "[a]llowing a state to forbid the copying of a work not subject to patent protection" would be preempted by federal patent law). *But cf.* Kewanee Oil Co. v. Bicron Corp., 416 U.S. 470, 479–95 (1974) (finding that federal patent law did not preempt the application of state trade-secret law, even as to patentable subject matter, because "the patent policy of encouraging invention is not disturbed by the existence of another form of incentive to invention"). *See generally* Paul J. Heald, *Federal Intellectual Property Law and the Economics of Preemption,* 76 IOWA L. REV. 959, 989 (1991) (suggesting that *Kewanee Oil, Bonito Boats, Sears, Campco,* and other cases together "firmly establish[ ] that any state law which upsets the balance struck between benefits to society and benefits to inventors by patent law is preempted"). Even so the interrelation of the power of the states and the Intellectual Property Clause standing alone remains murky. *See, e.g.,* Pollack, *supra* note 40, at 308 ("Even such luminaries as Story have found that the tie between the states and the Intellectual Property Clause is unclear." (citing JOSEPH STORY, COMMENTARIES ON THE CONSTITUTION OF THE UNITED STATES § 1154 (5th ed. 1891))). For one in-depth discussion of whether states can offer intellectual-property rights that Congress cannot offer, see Pollack, *supra* note 40, at 300–26 (arguing that the states may well be limited by the Intellectual Property Clause pursuant to several theories: "(1) statutory/constitutional preemption created by the Intellectual Property Clause in combination with any federal legislation under that Clause, or (2) narrow constitutional preemption by the Intellectual Property Clause acting alone, or (3) a dormant Intellectual Property Clause, or (4) the intersection of the Intellectual Property Clause and the Dormant Commerce Clause" (internal footnote omitted)).

[67] To be sure, Congress might choose to preempt by express legislation state protections of data collections. But absent such an express legislative take-down, it would be difficult to infer a congressional intent to preclude state legislation in this area. Indeed, even if Congress were to deny by statute copyright protection for such works, that denial might well signal nothing more than an appropriate adherence to

law of preemption—the Intellectual Property Clause of its own force operates to nullify state laws of certain kinds.[68] For example, may states enact laws that—even in the face of *Feist*—seek to protect federally unprotectible data collections on a fairness-based "sweat of the brow" property-law theory? The short answer to this question is that it remains largely unexplored.[69] Even so, the argument seems strong that some such constitutional limit on state lawmaking must exist. After all, if a core purpose of the Intellectual Property Clause is to ensure that otherwise-unprotectable materials move into and remain in the public domain, allowing state laws to prohibit the copying of materials otherwise located within the public domain

---

its own constitutional obligation not to give federal copyright protection to data collections, as opposed to legislating one way or the other with regard to state prerogatives on this matter. (Perhaps, in fact, a Congress constitutionally thwarted in its efforts to confer copyright protection on data collections would affirmatively approve of state-based attempts to do the same.)

[68] To be clear, the Court has long rejected the proposition that the Intellectual Property Clause *wholly* prohibits *all* state-based regulation of intellectual-property matters. In particular, a five-Justice majority in *Goldstein* upheld a state's ban on copying for resale musical recordings, which were not then protected under federal copyright law, even though the ban was unlimited in time. *See* 412 U.S. at 571. The majority relied in part on the idea that a single state's ban on copying was necessarily limited in its impact because it would not affect copying in any other states. Some passages in the Court's opinion, however, suggested that the Intellectual Property Clause standing alone might well bar state lawmaking with regard to copyright-related-matters under some circumstances. *See, e.g., id.* at 557 (indicating, after noting the distinction between "national" and "local" subjects for dormant Commerce Clause purposes, that the IP Clause does not "recognize[ ] . . . that state legislation is, *in all cases,* unnecessary or precluded" (emphasis added)); *id.* at 560 (adding that "[t]he subject matter to which the Copyright Clause is addressed may *at times* be of purely local concern," thus supporting the conclusion that "the States have not relinquished *all power* to grant to authors 'the exclusive right to their respective Writings' " (emphasis added)). In addition, the Court in *Kewanee Oil Co.,* 416 U.S. at 478—in the process of sustaining a state's application of traditional trade-secret-law principles to a patentable (but unpatented) invention—relied on *Goldstein* in broadly suggesting in a brief discussion that "[t]he only limitation on the States is that in regulating the area of patents and copyrights, they do not conflict with the operation of the laws in this area passed by Congress." *Id.* The Court, however, also framed the issue as involving only "whether the States are forbidden to act at all in the area of protection of the kinds of intellectual property which may make up the subject matter of trade secrets," *id.*, and it described *Goldstein* as holding that "in the case of writings, the States were not prohibited from encouraging and protecting the efforts of those within their borders *by appropriate legislation,*" *id.* at 478–79 (emphasis added). Viewed in their entirety, these authorities thus support the conclusion that the Court has not yet definitively weighed in on the extent to which, if at all, the Intellectual Property Clause of its own force precludes the adoption of state IP-related legislation.

[69] But not wholly unexplored. *See, e.g.,* Pollack, *supra* note 40, at 300–26; Nachbar, *supra* note 65, at 358–61; Julie E. Cohen, *Copyright and the Jurisprudence of Self-Help,* 13 BERKLEY TECH. L.J. 1089, 1129–33 (1998) (noting that "the Court has held that the Intellectual Property Clause does not bar states from enacting their own forms of intellectual property protection, even for works otherwise patentable or copyrightable," while also asserting that "where unpatentable know-how and uncopyrightable facts or principles are concerned, the same restrictions that bind Congress also bind the states").

would necessarily trench on the constitutional plan.[70] For this reason, the Court someday may endorse a constitutional principle not yet explicitly set forth in the pages of the U.S. Reports—namely, that there exists a "dormant Intellectual Property Clause," akin to the dormant Commerce Clause,[71] which requires invalidation of some state laws even in the absence of congressional preemption.[72]

4. The Intellectual Property Clause and the First Amendment

This discussion reveals that the constitutional law of copyrights and the constitutional law of patents closely track one another.[73]

---

[70] *See John Deere Co.*, 383 U.S. at 6 (suggesting the impermissibility of laws that "remove existent knowledge from the public domain, or . . . restrict free access to materials already available"); *Bonito Boats*, 489 U.S. at 146 ("The Patent Clause itself reflects a balance between the need to encourage innovation and the avoidance of monopolies which stifle competition without any concomitant advantage in the 'Progress of Science and useful Arts.' "); *see generally* Heald & Sherry, *supra* note 36, at 1165–66 (endorsing this view). Any doubt on the subject would seem to be dispelled by both common sense and constitutional history. As for common sense, could it possibly be that state law could grant copyright and patent protection of infinite duration even though the Intellectual Property Clause itself gives to Congress the power to provide such protections only for "limited Times"? If the answer is "no," then it follows necessarily that Intellectual Property Clause of its own force imposes some restrictions on state power, and the relevant question thus becomes how far that limit reaches. As for constitutional history, *The Federalist* provides telling guidance. It explains that the Framers gave the national Congress the power to pass laws on copyrights and patents because "[t]he States cannot separately make effectual provisions for either of the cases, and most of them have anticipated the decision of this point." THE FEDERALIST NO. 43 (Madison). Why does this passage matter? Because it is difficult to argue that Congress could, simply by declining to act, allow any state to pass any law it might like regarding copyrights and patents in light of the Framers' apparent belief that "the States *cannot* make effectual provisions" on these matters. *Id.* (emphasis added).

[71] *See infra* Chapters 16–22. Notably, if such a dormant Intellectual Property Clause exists, it would not be subject to the same (and important) congressional-consent exception that is a feature of dormant Commerce Clause law. *See infra* Section 20.B. This is the case because dormant Commerce Clause law proceeds from the view that Congress can permit states to impose rules regarding interstate commerce that Congress itself can impose. But from that proposition it does not follow that Congress can permit states to establish copyright and patent rules that—due to the irreducible protection given by the Constitution to the public domain—Congress itself *cannot* impose.

[72] Another possible takeaway may be that there now operates, in the field of patent and copyright law, such a distinctly vigorous approach to statutory preemption that questions about the state-law-displacing impact of the Intellectual Property Clause standing alone are of only academic interest. *See Bonito Boats*, 489 U.S. at 167 ("The patent statute's careful balance between public right and private monopoly to promote certain creative activity is a 'scheme of federal regulation . . . so pervasive as to make reasonable the inference that Congress left no room for the States to supplement it.' " (quoting *Rice*, 331 U.S. at 230)); *see also Sears, Roebuck & Co.*, 376 U.S. at 232–33; *Campco Corp.*, 376 U.S. at 237.

[73] This is not to say that these parallels are always exact. Judge Richard Posner, for example, has observed that: "Copyright law unlike patent law does not require substantial originality. In fact, it requires only enough originality to enable a work to be distinguished from similar works that are in the public domain." Assessment Techs.

There is, however, one deviation from this pattern of alignment. The difference arises because copyright rules, unlike patent rules, target communicative materials, thus bringing into play First Amendment protections against "abridging the freedom of speech, or of the press."[74] How the First Amendment and the Intellectual Property Clause fit together is a matter marked by significant uncertainty. There can be no doubt, however, that the First Amendment has exerted a gravitational pull on both congressional and judicial work in the copyright field.[75] Most notably, free-speech principles underlie the existing statutory defense for the "fair use" of copyrighted material, even by way of direct replication, insofar as that defense operates to foster self-expression and the search for truth.[76] Talk of the interaction between the Intellectual Property Clause and the First Amendment is part of a broader conversation about how multiple clauses of the Constitution can come together in defining the scope of both powers and rights.[77] Lawyers, accordingly, should be on the lookout for ways to argue that the joint operation of these two clauses works to limit how far Congress can go—especially in borderline cases, such as those involving highly transformative derivative works—in disallowing the "copying" of preexisting written creations.

---

of WI, LLC v. WIREdata, Inc., 350 F.3d 640, 643 (7th Cir. 2003) (citing *Feist*, 499 U.S. at 345–48; Bucklew v. Hawkins, Ash, Baptie & Co., 329 F.3d 923, 929 (7th Cir. 2003); and Alfred Bell & Co. v. Catalda Fine Arts, Inc., 191 F.2d 99, 102–03 (2d Cir. 1951)); *see also* Heald & Sherry, *supra* note 36, at 1164–65 (discussing the disparate treatment of "authors" under copyright law and "inventors" under patent law).

[74] *See* Neil Weinstock Netanel, *First Amendment Constraints on Copyright After* Golan v. Holder, 60 UCLA L. REV. 1082, 1084 (2013) (citing Melville B. Nimmer, *Does Copyright Abridge the First Amendment Guarantees of Free Speech and Press?*, 17 UCLA L. REV. 1180, 1181 (1970)).

[75] *See Eldred*, 537 U.S. at 219 ("[C]opyright's limited monopolies are compatible with free speech principles. Indeed, copyright's purpose is to *promote* the creation and publication of free expression."); Harper & Row, Publishers, Inc. v. Nation Enters., 471 U.S. 539, 558 (1985) ("[T]he Framers intended copyright itself to be the engine of free expression. By establishing a marketable right to the use of one's expression, copyright supplies the economic incentive to create and disseminate ideas.").

[76] The law of fair use is deeply complicated, and the subject ranges far beyond the scope of this book. Among other things, however, the doctrine can permit copying for purposes such as criticizing or clarifying the meaning of earlier works. *See* 17 U.S.C. § 107 (associating fair use with "criticism, comment, news reporting, teaching . . . scholarship, or research"). And this is even more the case when such copying is, for example, limited in its extent and not done for money-making purposes. *See id.* For one discussion of the impact of the First Amendment on fair-use doctrine, see Joseph P. Bauer, *Copyright and the First Amendment: Comrades, Combatants, or Uneasy Allies?*, 67 WASH. & LEE L. REV. 831, 848–62 (2010) (discussing the "First Amendment-copyright clash"). In Professor Bauer's view, existing fair-use doctrine "does not reach far enough to encompass all First Amendment concerns" and this "inadequacy is compounded by the often-cramped, and too-often-inconsistent, treatment it receives from the courts." *Id.* at 861.

[77] *See, e.g.*, Michael Coenen, *Combining Constitutional Clauses*, 164 U. PA. L. REV. 1067, 1082–83 (2016).

C. THE TREATY POWER

The Constitution's treatment of treaties, which is set forth in Article II, section 2, creates federal lawmaking power in two separate ways. First, it permits the federal government to create binding law in the form of self-executing treaties made by the President and approved by a two-thirds majority of then-gathered Senate members—that is, without any involvement by the House of Representatives at all.[78] Second, the Treaty Clause, in combination with the Necessary and Proper Clause, authorizes the enactment of bicameral legislation, not otherwise supported by the commerce power or any other enumerated congressional power, to carry into execution both self-executing and non-self-executing treaties.[79] The seminal case on this latter point is *Missouri v. Holland*,[80] which concerned a federal statute that prohibited individuals from hunting certain species of migratory birds. In that case, the Court assumed—not surprisingly, as the dispute arose in 1920—that this enactment did not embody a permissible exercise of the congressional commerce power. Nonetheless, in an opinion authored by Justice Holmes, the Court upheld the statute by relying on the Senate's prior approval of a treaty with Canada that called for protection of the bird species that the statute covered.[81] It did not matter, in other words, that an

---

[78] *See infra* Section 27.B (highlighting these requirements in further detail).

[79] *See generally supra* Chapter 6 (discussing the Necessary and Proper Clause). Although the Court has at times suggested that the treaty power may be exercised only in relation to subjects that are "properly the subject of negotiation with a foreign country," Geofroy v. Riggs, 133 U.S. 258, 267 (1890), *cited in* Asakura v. City of Seattle, 265 U.S. 332, 341 (1924), the Court has never invalidated a treaty on that basis, and some analysts doubt that it would ever do so. Indeed, the *Restatement (Third) of Foreign Relations Law* expressly stated that the "Constitution does not require that an international agreement deal only with 'matters of international concern,'" RESTATEMENT (THIRD) OF THE FOREIGN RELATIONS LAW OF THE UNITED STATES § 302 cmt. c (1987), although the *Restatement (Fourth)* stepped away from taking a position on the issue, treating it as "not . . . sufficiently addressed in judicial decisions and other relevant legal materials." *See* RESTATEMENT (FOURTH) OF FOREIGN RELATIONS LAW § 312 n.4 & n.8 (2018). Some commentators, however, have cast doubt on the idea that subject-matter limits "place any real constraints on the exercise of the treaty power." *See, e.g.*, Oona Hathaway, et al., *The Treaty Power: Its History, Scope, and Limits*, 98 CORNELL L. REV. 239, 288 (2013). *But cf. id.* at 290–92 (highlighting the to-date hypothetical possibility that courts might set aside a treaty on the related ground that it violates a constitutional "prohibition on the power of the federal government to enact a purely pretextual treaty"). On the other hand, some observers have expressed serious concerns about the possibility that the treaty power might be invoked to sustain federal laws that impinge too much on traditionally recognized state lawmaking powers. *See, e.g.*, Nicholas Quinn Rosenkranz, *Executing the Treaty Power*, 118 HARV. L. REV. 1867, 1871–73 (2005) (identifying, and also critiquing, scholarly arguments that the Religious Freedom Restoration Act, the Violence Against Women Act, and the Endangered Species Act are defensible treaty-implementing laws regardless of their sustainability under other grants of federal lawmaking power).

[80] 252 U.S. 416 (1920).

[81] *See* Migratory Bird Treaty Act, Pub. L. No. 65–186, 40 Stat. 755 (1918) (codified as amended at 16 U.S.C. §§ 703–712). As a technical matter, the treaty was made with

"earlier act of Congress that attempted by itself and not in pursuance of a treaty to regulate the killing of migratory birds within the States had been held bad."[82] Instead, the new act passed muster because it constituted "a necessary and proper means" to effectuate the duly ratified migratory-bird treaty.[83] The Court did not say that any treaty the nation might make would support any follow-on laws that Congress might enact based on the Necessary and Proper Clause. But here, that clause did support the challenged statute because that statute directly implemented a treaty that dealt with "a national interest of very nearly the first magnitude" concerning the cross-border movement of a major food supply.[84]

A near-century later, in a concurring opinion in *Bond v. United States*,[85] Justice Scalia urged the Court to abandon the Congress-empowering rule of *Holland*.[86] His argument centered on the assertion that the Court's ruling in that case rested on an "an ill-considered *ipse dixit* that enables the fundamental constitutional principle of limited federal powers to be set aside by the President and Senate's exercise of the treaty power."[87] Justice Scalia's view of things has supporters and detractors.[88] A majority of Justices in

---

Great Britain because Canada was then a part of the United Kingdom. *See* Convention for the Protection of Migratory Birds, U.S.-U.K., art. VIII, Aug. 16, 1916, 39 Stat. 1702. Congress passed the Migratory Bird Treaty Act implementing the treaty two years later. *See* Hathaway et al. *supra* note 79, at 255.

[82] *Holland*, 252 U.S. at 432 (discussing earlier lower court rulings).

[83] *Id.*

[84] *Id.* at 435. For a collection of lower-court rulings that have relied on this principle, see Rosenkranz, *supra* note 79, 1871 & n.11. Related to the question whether Congress can regulate certain *activities* pursuant to the treaty power that it cannot regulate pursuant to the commerce power is the separate question whether Congress can utilize regulatory *means* under the treaty power that it cannot deploy when it wields the commerce power. Might Congress, for example, be able to commandeer behavior by state officials pursuant to the treaty power even though it cannot commandeer such behavior pursuant to the commerce power? *See supra* Section 5.B. On the one hand, Court might hesitate to hand Congress a treaty-power tool with which to work around the anti-commandeering rule. On the other hand, while constitutional protections of individual rights appear to apply with full force to limit exercises of the treaty power, *see, e.g.*, Reid v. Covert, 354 U.S. 1, 17–18 (1957), external restraints rooted in concerns about state autonomy might not restrict exercises of that power in the same way. For a more detailed treatment of this subject, see *infra* Chapter 13.

[85] 572 U.S. 844 (2014).

[86] *Id.* at 866–82 (Scalia, J., concurring). Justice Scalia's opinion was joined by Justices Thomas and Alito.

[87] *Id.* at 881–82. *See generally* Rosenkranz, *supra* note 79, at 1881–92 (arguing that, while Congress may pass laws under the Necessary and Proper Clause to help federal authorities "make" treaties, it may not rely on that clause to enact laws unsupported by its other legislative powers to implement treaties that already have been "made").

[88] The literature on this subject is expansive. *See, e.g.*, Hathaway et al., *supra* note 79, 244–65; Rosenkranz, *supra* note 79; Thomas Healy, Note, *Is* Missouri v. Holland *Still Good Law? Federalism and the Treaty Power*, 98 COLUM. L. REV. 1726

Bond, however, found it unnecessary to address the question on which Justice Scalia wrote at length because they interpreted the operative statute as not covering the conduct at issue in the case. By taking this approach, the majority illustrated how already-existing doctrinal principles, grounded largely in federalism values, constrain congressional use of the treaty power to intrude on state prerogatives even in a world in which *Holland* remains good law. Indeed, three separate lines of doctrine operate in this way.

First, as the Court made clear in *Bond* itself, statutes enacted pursuant to the treaty power are subject to the same rule of statutory interpretation that requires a narrow reading of ambiguous commerce-power legislation when it trenches on traditional state regulatory authority.[89] That case arose out of the indictment of Carol Anne Bond, who allegedly spread two toxic chemicals on a mailbox, car, and door knob with the aim of causing her intended victim to develop a rash. A problem faced by federal prosecutors sprang from the Court's earlier suggestion in *United States v. Morrison*[90] that this sort of injury-causing conduct is not subject to federal regulation under the commerce power.[91] Federal prosecutors, however, argued that the operative statute—which criminalized the use of "chemical weapons"—was sustainable regardless of commerce-power limits because it implemented a federal treaty addressing the misuse of noxious substances of this kind. In the end, the Court ruled in Bond's favor by finding that the statute did not cover her conduct, and it did so by relying squarely on the clear-statement rule set forth in earlier commerce-power cases, such as *United States v. Bass*.[92] In particular, the Court observed that "we will not be quick to assume that Congress has meant to effect a significant change in the sensitive

---

(1998); Arthur E. Sutherland, Jr., *Restricting the Treaty Power*, 65 HARV. L. REV. 1305 (1952); Heather K. Gerken, *Slipping the Bonds of Federalism*, 128 HARV. L. REV. 85 (2014); Curtis A. Bradley, *The Treaty Power and American Federalism*, 97 MICH. L. REV. 390 (1998). For some defenses of the *Holland* rule (though not necessarily of the reasoning of *Holland* itself), see, e.g., LOUIS HENKIN, FOREIGN AFFAIRS AND THE UNITED STATES CONSTITUTION 191–94 (2d ed. 1996); Jean Galbraith, *Congress's Treaty-Implementing Power in Historical Practice*, 56 WM. & MARY L. REV. 59 (2014); David M. Golove, *Treaty-Making and the Nation: The Historical Foundations of the Nationalist Conception of the Treaty Power*, 98 MICH. L. REV. 1075 (2000); Martin S. Flaherty, *Are We to Be a Nation? Federal Power vs. "States' Rights" in Foreign Affairs*, 70 U. COLO. L. REV. 1277, 1305–1316 (1999); Michael J. Glennon & Robert D. Sloane, *The Sad Quiet Death of* Missouri v. Holland: *How* Bond *Hobbled the Treaty Power*, 41 YALE J. INT'L L. 51, 61–68 (2016); Gerald L. Neuman, *The Nationalization of Civil Liberties, Revisited*, 99 COLUM. L. REV. 1630, 2647–50 (1999); and David Sloss, Bond v. United States*: Choosing the Lesser of Two Evils*, 90 NOTRE DAME L. REV. 1583, 1589–1604 (2015).

89 *See Bond*, 572 U.S. at 857–58.

90 529 U.S. 598 (2000).

91 *See supra* Section 4.A.

92 404 U.S. 336 (1971). *See generally supra* Section 5.D (discussing this principle and its application in other cases).

relation between federal and state criminal jurisdiction,"[93] especially in a way that "dramatically intrude[s] upon traditional state criminal jurisdiction."[94] In short, the Court in *Bond* did not endorse Justice Scalia's state-authority-vindicating approach to defining the constitutional limits of the treaty power. But the majority's own state-authority-vindicating view of how to interpret treaty-based statutes led it to endorse exactly the same defendant-freeing result supported by the concurring Justices.[95]

Second, the same general principles that hold back Congress's ability to use the Necessary and Proper Clause in connection with other enumerated grants of authority operate no less forcefully with respect to the treaty power.[96] The point is illustrated by *United States v. Nagarwala,*[97] a lower-court decision involving provisions of the federally ratified International Covenant on Civil and Political Rights (ICCPR) that called for protecting both women and children from discrimination. Acting pursuant to this treaty, Congress passed legislation that outlawed female genital mutilation. In *Nagarwala*, however, a federal district court ruled that this enactment exceeded Congress's *Holland*-based authority under the Necessary and Proper Clause.[98] The key question, as the court framed it, was "whether the statute constitutes a means that is rationally related to the implementation of a constitutionally enumerated power" under the rule laid down in *United States v. Comstock*.[99] And here, the court concluded, there was "simply no rational relationship" between the challenged statute and the ICCPR.[100] One difficulty, according to the court, was that "protect[ing] girls aged seventeen and younger from a particular form of physical abuse" did not "effectuate the purposes" of the treaty's sweeping call for ensuring equality between men and

---

93 *Bond*, 572 U.S. at 349.

94 *Id.* at 350 (internal quotations and alterations omitted).

95 *Cf.* Glennon & Sloane, *supra* note 86, at 53 (contending that future adherence to the Court's approach to statutory interpretation in *Bond* would "effectively undermine" the rule of *Holland* in such a way as to ensure that "*Holland* survives in name only").

96 These general principles emanate, at least primarily, from restrictions that derive from the term "necessary" in the Necessary and Proper Clause. As noted earlier, *see supra* note 84, it is not clear whether Congress-constraining rules sometimes connected up with the term "proper"—in particular, the state-protective anti-commandeering doctrine and sovereign-immunity-based anti-liability principle—apply in the same way to the treaty power as they do, for example, to the commerce power. *See infra* Sections 13.A & 13.B.

97 350 F. Supp. 3d 613 (E.D. Mich. 2018).

98 The Court also rejected Congress's alternative claim of lawmaking authority under the Commerce Clause. *Id.* at 625–30. *See supra* Section 4.A.

99 *Nagarwala*, 350 F. Supp. 3d at 617 (quoting United States v. Comstock, 560 U.S. 126, 134 (2010)). For a detailed discussion of *Comstock*, see *supra* Section 6.A.2.

100 *Nagarwala*, 350 F. Supp. 3d. at 618.

women in the enjoyment of political and civil rights.[101] The court found an "arguably closer" relationship between the anti-mutilation statute and the ICCPR's separate prohibition on discrimination against minors. Again, however, the court determined that the challenged statute was not "necessary" to carry this aspect of the treaty into effect. The problem, it reasoned, was that the statutory prohibition on only one highly particularized form of physical mistreatment of only girls was too tenuously linked to a treaty that recognized generalized equality-based rights of all minors, regardless of gender.[102] The ruling in *Nagarwala*—which rests on a rare determination, by a single district-court judge, that Congress exceeded its power under the Necessary and Proper Clause—is debatable at the least. But what is not debatable is the fact that considerations of federalism shaped the result in the case. Indeed, on its way to detecting a constitutional violation, the court specifically emphasized—in keeping with the spirit of *Bond*—that "states possess primary authority for defining and enforcing criminal law."[103]

Finally, the long-recognized distinction between self-executing and non-self-executing treaties can work to safeguard state-autonomy values by rendering some Article II treaties—that is, those of the "non-self-executing" variety—judicially unenforceable within the United States unless and until Congress enacts separate legislation that implements their terms.[104] In *Medellín v. Texas*,[105] discussed further in Chapter 27, the Court pointedly declined to embrace an interpretive presumption in favor of self-execution,[106] thus leading some commentators to detect a federalism-focused course change in the direction of a more treaty-power-limiting juridical approach.[107] Moreover, and wholly apart from the principles set forth in *Medellín*, some constitutional provisions—most notably, the Article I, section 7 requirement that bills for raising revenue must "originate" in the House, and the Article I, section 9 requirement that "[n]o money shall be drawn from the Treasury, but in Consequence of Appropriations made by Law"[108]—may obligate Congress to enact implementing legislation on certain subjects

---

[101] *Id.*

[102] *See id.* ("As laudable as the prohibition of a particular type of abuse of girls may be, it does not logically further the goal of protecting children on a nondiscriminatory basis.").

[103] *Id.* at 618 (internal quotation omitted).

[104] *See infra* Section 27.B.2.a.

[105] 552 U.S. 491 (2008).

[106] *See* Curtis A. Bradley, *Intent, Presumptions, and Non-Self-Executing Treaties*, 102 AM. J. INT'L L. 540, 546 (2008) ("The Court in *Medellín* appears to have rejected any strong presumption in favor of self-execution.").

[107] *See infra* Section 27.B.2.a n.52 (collecting sources).

[108] *See* U.S. CONST. art. I, § 7, cl. 1; *id.* art. I, § 9, cl. 7.

regardless of whether a treaty purports to be self-executing.[109] These limiting principles operate to reduce federal interference with state authority by making it less likely that treaties will give rise to judicially enforceable federal-law rules that displace state-law requirements.[110] To be sure, non-self-executing treaties do have both practical and legal effects.[111] But courts can, and sometimes do, tip the balance of power in favor of the states by leaning on principles that favor the characterization of treaties as non-self-executing in nature.

D. THE WAR POWERS

The Constitution empowers Congress to "declare War," to "raise and support Armies," and to "provide and maintain a Navy."[112] There

---

[109] By way of example, Professor Tribe has observed that "[a] treaty which requires the appropriation of funds . . . cannot be self-executing; subsequent congressional appropriation of the funds is required" because of the special spending-related constitutional rules set forth in Article I, section 9. *See* TRIBE, *supra* note 25, § 4–4, at 644 & n.4 (citing Turner v. Am. Baptist Missionary Union, 24 F. Cas. 344 (C.C.D. Mich. 1853) (No. 14,251)); *accord* Edwards v. Carter, 580 F.2d 1055, 1058 (D.C. Cir. 1978) (per curiam) (noting that the goal of securing congressional spending "cannot be accomplished by self-executing treaty; implementing legislation appropriating such funds is indispensable"); Michael D. Ramsey, *A Textual Approach to Treaty Non-Self Execution*, 2015 BYU L. REV. 1639, 1643 (noting that, insofar as Congress has an exclusive power to appropriate funds, a treaty "purport[ing] to appropriate funds" would be "unconstitutional—but Congress can cure the violation by making the designated appropriation"); *see also* Retfalvi v. United States, 930 F.3d 600, 605–10 (4th Cir. 2019) (declining to read either the Article I Origination Clause or the Article I Taxing Clause as prohibiting the federal government from authorizing, by way of a self-executing treaty, the Internal Revenue Service to collect taxes owed to Canada by persons subject to U.S. jurisdiction). It has also been suggested that treaties cannot be self-executing in imposing criminal liability; instead, on this view, the establishment of criminal laws requires the enactment of follow-up legislation pursuant to the ordinary rules of bicameralism and presentment. *See* Hopson v. Kreps, 622 F.2d 1375, 1380 (9th Cir. 1980) (asserting that "[t]reaty regulations that penalize individuals . . . are generally considered to require domestic legislation before they are given any effect"). For further discussion of these matters, see RESTATEMENT (FOURTH), *supra* note 79, § 310 cmt. f & n.11 (2018).

[110] This is particularly so given that the follow-on legislation necessary to implement a non-self-executing treaty requires not only an effective reaffirmation of the treaty by the President and the Senate, but also a formalized buy-in by the House of Representatives—a buy-in that might sometimes never materialize.

[111] *See infra* Section 27.B.2.a.

[112] U.S. CONST. art. 1, § 8, cls. 11, 12 & 13. Other constitutional powers also have a close relation to the subject of military affairs. The treaty power, for example, provides the basis for creating military alliances. Article I, section 8, clause 14 vests in Congress (and not the President) the power to "make Rules for the Government and Regulation of the land and naval forces." *Id.* art. 1, § 8, cl. 14. The same clause that permits Congress to declare war also empowers it to "grant letters of Marque and Reprisal, and make rules concerning Captures on Land and Water." *Id.* Article I, section 8, clauses 15 and 16 give Congress wide-ranging authority over state militias (now the National Guard and Air National Guard), while clause 10 empowers Congress to "define and punish Piracies and Felonies committed on the high seas, and Offences against the law of Nations." *Id.* art. 1, § 8, cls. 10, 15–16. As with other grants of congressional power, these grants have an independent significance that

is a tendency to think of these powers as focused on preparing for and carrying out military campaigns outside the nation's boundaries, and a later chapter considers them from this perspective.[113] The Court, however, has also recognized that the enumerated war powers—especially when conjoined with the Necessary and Proper Clause—vest Congress with broad authority to regulate activity far removed from foreign shores.[114] Indeed, the war powers permit Congress to control many matters of daily life that do not involve military operations at all.[115] During World War I, for example, Congress enacted a pre-Eighteenth Amendment law that barred the sale of intoxicating beverages to each and every would-be drinker in the nation.[116] Although that ban may well not have been sustainable under the commerce power at that time, the Court nonetheless upheld it "as a means of increasing our war efficiency" on the ground that it fostered the sobriety, and hence the productivity, of the

---

undermines any suggestion that modern Commerce Clause jurisprudence has rendered the rest of Article I, section 8 an empty vessel. To take one example, the commerce power would not (or at least almost certainly would not) allow congressional regulation of noneconomic activity in the form of a prohibition on violent actions on U.S. soil by foreign military combatants, much less the displacement of Bill of Rights protections in trying those combatants (including U.S. citizens) for the thus-defined offenses. In *Ex parte Quirin*, 317 U.S. 1 (1942), however, the Court ruled that Congress had the power to take exactly these steps pursuant to its Article I power to enact "laws defining and punishing offenses against the law of nations, including those which pertain to conduct of war." *Id.* at 26; *see infra* Section 28.B.2.a.

[113] *See infra* Chapter 28. More broadly, that chapter considers the ways in which Congress's war-related powers under Article I intersect with the President's commander-in-chief powers under Article II and the ways in which both powers are restricted by other constitutional provisions, such as the Suspension Clause of Article I, section 9.

[114] A classic statement of the overarching proposition was offered by Chief Justice Chase, who insisted that the power to declare war "necessarily" carries with it a supplementary congressional authority to enact "all legislation essential to the prosecution of war with vigor and success, except such as interferes with the command of the forces and the conduct of campaigns." *Ex Parte* Milligan, 71 U.S. (4 Wall.) 2, 139 (1866) (Chase, C.J., concurring). One build-out of this idea would seem to be that the power to declare war gives rise to a measure of authority to make sure that any such war (even when none looms immediately on the horizon) can be prosecuted efficaciously. *See* Matthew C. Waxman, *The Power to Wage War Successfully*, 117 COLUM. L. REV. 613, 628–30 (2017) (discussing this idea in connection with a 1917 speech on the subject given by Chief Justice Hughes). Otherwise, declarations of war might be ill-advisedly discouraged, and declarations that do occur might well, contrary to all good sense, create engagements not destined for success. This principle in turn supports the enactment of some legislation, even with respect to commerce, that may not be supported by the commerce power itself. *See* Clallam Cty., v. United States, 263 U.S 341 (1923); Sloan Shipyards Corp. v. U.S. Shipping Bd. Emergency Fleet Corp., 258 U.S. 549 (1922).

[115] *Cf., e.g.*, Bowles v. Willingham, 321 U.S. 503, 521 (1944) (characterizing the establishment of World War II-era rent controls as a valid exercise of the "the war power"); Yakus v. United States, 321 U.S. 414, 422–23 (1944) (reaching a similar conclusion with respect to World War II-era price controls).

[116] War-Time Prohibition Act, ch. 212, 40 Stat. 1045, 1046 (1918).

American work force.[117] Indeed, securing these positive effects was deemed sufficiently justifiable during wartime to support the law's constitutionality despite what the Court later characterized as its "undoubtedly commercially crippling" effect on the nation's brewers, distillers, and liquor distributors.[118]

Even more indicative of the broad reach of the war powers are cases in which the Court has upheld domestic restrictions founded on those powers even after hostilities have ceased.[119] A leading case is *Woods v. Cloyd W. Miller Co.*,[120] in which the Court sustained congressionally imposed post-World War II rent controls still in operation three years after the surrender of the Axis powers. According to the Court in *Woods*, Congress's war-related powers allowed it to "remedy the evils which have arisen from [the war's] rise and progress,"[121] and the challenged statute permissibly addressed the post-war "deficit in housing which in considerable measure was caused by the heavy demobilization of veterans and by the . . . reduction in residential construction during the period of hostilities."[122] Under present-day law, it seems all-but-certain that the Commerce Clause would support such rent regulations on the basis that they target "economic activity."[123] But *Woods* illustrates how the defenders of other domestic measures, even if unable to

---

[117] Hamilton v. Kentucky Distilleries & Warehouse Co., 251 U.S. 146, 158–59 (1919).

[118] Andrus v. Allard, 444 U.S. 51, 67 n.24 (1979).

[119] Indeed, the Court upheld the World War I prohibition law itself not only with regard to the period of hostilities, but also following the conclusion of military operations. *See Hamilton*, 251 U.S. at 158–159. As the Court later explained, this result made sense because the challenged restrictions "conserved manpower and increased efficiency of production in the critical days during the period of demobilization, and helped to husband the supply of grains and cereals depleted by the war effort." Woods v. Cloyd W. Miller Co., 333 U.S. 138, 142 (1948) (discussing *Hamilton*, 251 U.S. 146 (1919); and *Jacob Ruppert, Inc. v. Caffey*, 251 U.S. 264 (1920)).

[120] 333 U.S. 138 (1948).

[121] *Id.* at 141 (quoting *Hamilton*, 251 U.S. at 161); *accord* Stewart v. Kahn, 78 U.S. (11 Wall.) 493, 507 (1870).

[122] *Woods*, 333 U.S. at 142. At the same time, there can be no doubt that the operation of Congress's war-related powers, as applied to domestic matters, does not endure forever. *Cf.* Chastleton Corp v. Sinclair, 264 U.S. 543, 548–49 (1924) (holding, albeit in the context of a due process-based challenge, that a 1919 federal rent-control law applicable to the District of Columbia, though upheld in its operation three years earlier, could no longer validly operate if the war-related emergency justifying its adoption had dissipated and thus remanding for a focused exploration of that question; reasoning that "[a] law depending upon the existence of an emergency or other certain state of facts to uphold it may cease to operate if the emergency ceases or the facts change even though valid when passed"). Justice Holmes, who wrote for the Court, "suggest[ed] strongly that the emergency had in fact expired, although he remanded to the trial court for factual findings on 'the condition of Washington at different dates in the past.' " *See* Adrian Vermeule, *Holmes on Emergencies*, 61 STAN. L. REV. 163, 167–68 (2008) (quoting *Chastleton Corp.*, 264 U.S. at 549).

[123] *See supra* Section 4.D.1.

persuade a court to sustain them under the Commerce Clause, might draw upon Congress's war-related powers for support.[124]

Supplementing Congress's capacious Article I authority to regulate civilian activities near in time to periods of war is its authority to regulate non-service members in times of peace if their actions threaten to impede the fighting-readiness of military forces.[125] More specifically, the Court has recognized Congress's ability to regulate entirely off-the-military-base civilian conduct—including in ways not subject to federal control under the Commerce Clause—when doing so is helpful, and thus permissible under the Necessary and Proper Clause, in enhancing troop morale, fitness, and discipline. Illustrative is *McKinley v. United States*,[126] in which Justice Day declared for a unanimous Court that "to guard and promote the health and efficiency of the men composing the army" Congress could criminalize the operation of a "house of ill fame" located within five miles of a military station.[127]

---

124 One other important difference between the war powers and Congress's other powers concerns the scope of Congress's ability to delegate authority without exposure to the ordinary reach of the nondelegation doctrine. *See* Hamilton v. Dillin, 88 U.S. (21 Wall.) 73, 97 (1875) (rejecting a claim that authority to impose a tax had been impermissibly delegated to the Secretary of the Treasury because: "[T]o impose such conditions upon commercial intercourse with an enemy in time of war . . . does not belong to the same category as the power to levy and collect taxes, duties, and excises. It belongs to the war powers of the government . . . ."); *see also* Lichter v. United States, 334 U.S. 742, 778–79, 782 (1948) ("This power [of delegation] is especially significant in connection with constitutional war powers under which the exercise of broad discretion as to methods to be employed may be essential to an effective use of its war powers by Congress."). In *Lichter*, given the pressing need for mobilization to "support armies" and to "maintain a navy," the highly discretionary "administrative authority . . . granted [in the challenged laws] was well within the constitutional war powers then being put to their predestined uses." *Id.* at 782–83. In addition, the specialized grant of the war powers supports forms of property confiscation hard to justify (to say the least) under the commerce power, especially in light of ordinarily operative rights-based limits on government interference with property interests. *See, e.g.*, Brown v. United States, 12 U.S. (8 Cranch) 110, 117 (1814) (opinion of Marshall, C.J.) (endorsing Congress's power to confiscate property within the reach of the enemy so long as the confiscation is undertaken pursuant to the war powers); Stoehr v. Wallace, 255 U.S. 239, 242 (1921) (relying on the congressional power to "make rules concerning captures on land and water" to support a broad view of federal authority to seize property without compensation in an effort to impede enemy efforts in the course of war); United States v. Pac. R.R., 120 U.S. 227 (1887) (invoking much the same principle to hold that there is no duty to provide compensation for property seized or destroyed to prevent its use by the enemy).

125 More fundamentally, Congress possesses far-reaching power to regulate service members themselves, including by establishing rules unsustainable under the commerce power because they directly map onto the sort of rules established by the states pursuant to their police powers. *See, e.g.*, 10 U.S.C. § 912 ("Any person subject to this chapter who is drunk on duty shall be punished as a court-martial may direct."); 10 U.S.C. § 933 ("Any commissioned officer, cadet, or midshipman who is convicted of conduct unbecoming an officer shall be punished as a court-martial may direct.").

126 249 U.S. 397 (1919).

127 *Id.* at 398–99 ("That Congress has the authority to raise and support armies and to make rules and regulations for the protection of the health and welfare of those

A similar line of war-powers reasoning supported, at least in part, the Court's validation of the federal law establishing the Bank of the United States in *McCulloch v. Maryland*.[128] It is noteworthy on this score that some advocates who challenged the "individual mandate" at issue in *NFIB* argued that Congress could not have relied on the commerce power, even when wedded to the Necessary and Proper Clause, to validate its chartering of the national bank.[129] These advocates did not suggest, however, that the Court in *McCulloch* erred in upholding that statute. Instead, they acknowledged that Congress could establish the bank pursuant to other powers, including its military powers, coupled with the Necessary and Proper Clause[130]—and understandably so, because the Court in *McCulloch* in fact relied on the distinct capacity of the geographically dispersed branches of the national bank to facilitate the movement of money needed to support the nation's troops. More specifically, as Chief Justice Marshall explained, "armies [will have] to be marched and supported" across "this vast republic," thus requiring that "treasure raised in the north should be transported to the south, that raised in the east, conveyed to the west, or that this order should be reversed."[131]

NFIB highlights another key point about the long reach of Congress's war-related authority. A central holding of that case was that there exist strict limits on Congress's ability to impose "individual mandates" pursuant to the commerce power.[132] Even as

---

composing them, is too well settled to require more than the statement of the proposition"). It is far from clear that Congress can enact *de facto* zoning rules pursuant to the Commerce Clause, at least with respect to a specific locale. *See supra* Section 4.D.1 (explaining that such localized rules might not be sustainable under the Commerce Clause because they do not address activity that, in the aggregate, has a substantial effect on interstate commerce). Under the principle of *McKinley*, however, it seems clear enough that that Congress could take even highly targeted action concerning a single facility—whether a brothel, a gambling hall, a marijuana parlor, or a late-night disco—if deemed helpful to supporting the fighting spirit of even a small number of service members.

128 17 U.S. (4 Wheat.) 316, 407–08 (1819).

129 *See* Transcript of Oral Argument at 64, *NFIB*, 567 U.S. 519 (No. 11–398 Mar. 27, 2012). These advocates found it necessary to make this argument because it aligned with their underlying theory that Congress could not leverage its power to "regulate" commerce to "create" commerce that did not already exist, *see supra* Section 4.E—which, so it seemed, is exactly what Congress had done by *creating* the Bank of the United States. Accordingly, because the result in *McCulloch* was not supportable under the commerce power on their theory of the case, these advocates had to point to some other power to support that result, so as to avoid having to concede that their theory required the overruling of that landmark case.

130 *See, e.g.*, Brief for Docs4PatientCare, et al., as Amici Curiae on the Minimum Coverage Provision Issue in Support of Respondents at 25–26, *NFIB*, 567 U.S. 519 (No. 11–398), 2012 WL 484068.

131 *McCulloch*, 17 U.S. at 408.

132 *See supra* Section 4.E.

it declared this principle, however, the Court made clear that Congress *could* impose individual mandates pursuant to its military powers.[133] Nor was that pronouncement surprising because the Court has long recognized that Congress may mandate service in the armed forces by enacting conscription laws—thus compelling millions of the nation's citizens to risk nothing less than death or severe injury—pursuant to its powers to "raise . . . an army" and to "provide . . . a navy."[134] Nor does Congress's ability to impose mandates under its war powers stop there. The Court also has upheld federal laws that subject civilians to government-imposed mandates as part of its effort to ensure success on the battlefield.[135]

The difference in the legal treatment of individual mandates under the commerce power and the war powers shines a light on two critical points about the law of constitutional federalism. First, it confirms the conclusion—also supported by earlier discussions of many other aspects of Article I—that Congress's non-commerce powers have an independent significance, including in present day.[136]

---

[133] *See id.*

[134] U.S. CONST. art. 1, § 8, cls. 12 & 13. *See* Arver v. United States (*Selective Draft Law Cases*), 245 U.S. 366 (1918).

[135] *See, e.g.*, United States v. Bethlehem Steel Corp., 315 U.S. 289, 305 (1942) (upholding Congress's authority not only "to draft men for battle service" but also to impose affirmative duties on "business organizations to support the fighting men" as well). Indeed, the Court has upheld laws such as those requisitioning food and fuel, as well as those requiring the takeover of factories, telephone systems, and rail lines as part of the war effort. *See Lichter*, 334 U.S. at 754–55 (upholding such laws as authorized by the "broad rather than restrictive" express power grant that places emphasis upon the supporting as well as upon the raising of armies" and explaining that "[w]ith the advent of . . . [global] warfare, mobilized property in the form of equipment and supplies became as essential as mobilized manpower"); *see also Bowles*, 321 U.S. at 519 ("A nation which can demand the lives of its men and women in the waging of . . . war is under no constitutional necessity of providing a system of price control on the domestic front which will assure each landlord a 'fair return' on his property"). Notably, the Third Amendment explicitly envisions one form of congressionally imposed individual mandate, of extreme invasiveness, by indicating that citizens can be compelled to quarter soldiers "in time of war . . . in a manner to be prescribed by law." U.S. CONST. amend. III.

[136] In fact, the treatment of the war powers offered here only begins to reveal why and how it has a freestanding impact regardless of the reach of the commerce power. It does so because one way in which some grants of power have a specialized impact is in clarifying *what arm of government* has authority to act on particular subjects, which is something that the Commerce Clause does not do. Under the law of England at the time of the framing, for example, the power to declare war and to raise military forces rested with the executive branch in the form of the king. In a move designed to counteract the abuse of these powers, however, the Framers assigned them to the more broadly accountable legislative branch, which can move forward only pursuant to cross-checking and deliberation-enhancing bicameral processes. In similar fashion, Article I, section 8, clauses 15 and 16 address the division of decision-making authority regarding the militia, which at the time of the framing operated almost entirely under the control of state authorities. In particular, clause 15 channeled power to Congress—and not the President—by specifying that the legislative branch was to "provide for calling forth the Militia to execute the Laws of the Union, suppress Insurrections and repel Invasions," *see* U.S. CONST. art. I, § 8, cl. 15, and clause 16 vested in Congress

Second, the importance of these other power grants has grown in recent decades as the Rehnquist and Roberts Courts have recognized and applied doctrines that increasingly have constrained the reach of the commerce power. And to the extent that this trend continues into the future, the separate work done by both the war powers and all other non-commerce powers will necessarily grow in importance.

E. INHERENT POWERS

It is often said that that the Constitution vests Congress with only "enumerated powers." Even so, the case law suggests that not all federal powers "depend upon the affirmative grants of the Constitution."[137] The underlying thought is that some areas of governance are "inherently inseparable from the conception of nationality" and therefore assigned to the federal government as a necessary concomitant of that government's very existence.[138] Some of these powers may flow to the executive branch.[139] But other such powers are held by Congress in light of its primacy as the law-giving agency of the nation. On one view, these powers rest with Congress because they must exist somewhere, and they cannot be (and/or have

(and again not in the President) other key militia-related powers, while leaving some such powers in the hands of the states, *id.* art. I, § 8, cl. 16. As the clause states, Congress has the power: "[t]o provide for organizing, arming, and disciplining, the Militia, and for governing such Part of them as may be employed in the Service of the United States, reserving to the States respectively, the Appointment of the Officers, and the Authority of training the Militia according to the discipline prescribed by Congress." *Id.* Building on this provision—and, in particular, its grant of power as to "organizing" the militia—Congress has created the Army National Guard and the Air National Guard, the units of which, while not on active federal duty, operate on a state-by-state basis and under the command of state-appointed officers. From time to time, challenges arise regarding federal efforts to control the activities of Guard units. In general, however, the courts have not given these challenges a warm welcome. *See, e.g.*, Perpich v. Dep't of Defense, 496 U.S. 334, 340 (1990) (concluding that, "read as a whole," Article I allows Congress to authorize the President to order National Guard members "to active duty for purposes of training outside the United States during peacetime without either the consent of a State Governor or the declaration of a national emergency"); *see also* Houston v. Moore, 18 U.S. (5 Wheat.) 1, 6 (1820) (noting that state power over militias, although extensive, is "subordinate nevertheless to the paramount law of the general government").

[137] United States v. Curtiss-Wright Exp. Corp., 299 U.S. 304, 318 (1936).

[138] *Id.*; *see also* Mackenzie v. Hare, 239 U.S, 299, 311 (1915) ("As a government, the United States is invested with all the attributes of sovereignty. As it has the character of nationality it has the powers of nationality, especially those which concern its relations and intercourse with other countries."); United States v. Lara, 541 U.S. 193, 201 (2004) (suggesting that Congress's broad power with respect to Native nations rests, at least in part, "not upon affirmative grants of the Constitution, but upon the Constitution's adoption of preconstitutional powers necessarily inherent in any Federal Government" (internal quotations omitted)); *see generally* Matthew L.M. Fletcher, *Preconstitutional Federal Power*, 82 TUL. L. REV. 509 (2007).

[139] *See infra* Section 27.A (discussing this subject, particularly in light of *Curtiss-Wright*).

never been in any serious way) wielded by the states.[140] On another view, Congress has these powers because simple logic suggests that the power to deal with any distinctly national subject must lie with national lawmaking authorities.[141] On yet another view, these powers spring from the Necessary and Proper Clause on the theory that their use helps to carry into execution "the aggregate of national powers" vested in the federal government.[142] Perhaps some unenumerated powers find support in one of these theories, while other unenumerated powers find support in another. In any event, there exists a cluster of congressional powers, often described as "inherent," that lack a readily discernible attachment to any specific textual grant.

1. Foreign Affairs

Most prominent among these powers is Congress's authority to legislate on the subject of foreign affairs.[143] It is far from clear, for

---

[140] *See Curtiss-Wright*, 299 U.S. at 317 ("The states were not 'sovereigns' in the sense contended for by some. They did not possess the peculiar features of sovereignty,—they could not make war, nor peace, nor alliances, nor treaties. Considering them as political beings, they were dumb, for they could not speak to any foreign sovereign whatever. They were deaf, for they could not hear any propositions from such sovereign. They had not even the organs or faculties of defence or offence, for they could not of themselves raise troops, or equip vessels, for war." (quoting 5 JONATHAN ELLIOT, DEBATES IN THE SEVERAL STATE CONVENTIONS ON THE ADOPTION OF THE FEDERAL CONSTITUTION 212 (1836) (statement of Rufus King))).

[141] On a related point, even Justices who tend to emphasize the key role of constitutional text have recognized nontextual limits on federal authority. *See supra* Chapter 4 (discussing, for example, non-textual limits on federal commandeering and abrogations of state sovereign immunity); *see also* U.S. Term Limits, Inc. v. Thornton, 514 U.S. 779, 848 (1995) (Thomas, J., dissenting) (acknowledging that some limits on state authority arise by "necessary implication"). These same authorities may support the notion that non-textual *powers*, within a narrow compass, likewise arise by way of structural reasoning or logical implication.

[142] TRIBE, *supra* note 25, § 5–3, at 806. *See generally* Coenen, *supra* note 77, at 1070 (suggesting the possibility that, in some instances, congressional authority under the Necessary and Proper Clause, even if not supportable by a single textual grant, might properly operate to carry into execution a combination of powers). Another possibility is that an implied power might, on close inspection, prove to be a necessary and proper extension of a single express power or limited subset of express powers. For a build-out of this line of thinking in evaluating the inherent congressional over foreign affairs, see *infra* note 143.

[143] With regard to the source of this authority, the Court in *Curtiss-Wright* relied in part on constitutional history in finding that the foreign-affairs power flowed naturally to the United States under the Constitution because it resided solely in the national government, and not the individual states, even under the Articles of Confederation. *Curtiss-Wright*, 299 U.S. at 317–18. According to another line of thinking, Congress's authority over foreign affairs properly emanates from one or more enumerated powers coupled with the Necessary and Proper Clause. Congress's generalized crafting of sound legislation regarding foreign relations, for example, might be seen as "beneficial," under the rule of *McCulloch*, 17 U.S. at 407–09, in setting the stage for salutary forms of regulating "Commerce with foreign Nations" or of "mak[ing] Treaties." Alternatively, it may be that Congress's foreign-affairs power is a sensible outgrowth of the constitutionally enumerated war powers. According to this

example, that Congress can rely on its power to "regulate Commerce with foreign Nations" to require state courts, in the face of contrary state legislation, to hear child-custody cases brought by non-citizens who reside abroad. Even so, it seems clear that Congress may pass such a statute because it deals with a matter of foreign relations. And precisely because Congress can pass such a law, it can—as this hypothesized case illustrates—preempt state-based decision-making that otherwise would operate in quintessentially police-power fields such as family law.[144]

Three features of Congress's specialized power over foreign affairs are particularly important to the law of constitutional federalism.[145] First, the broadly applicable "presumption against preemption" that generally guides courts in assessing the state-law-displacing impact of federal statutes[146] does not operate when those statutes concern foreign relations; indeed, in this legal domain, the Court often seems inclined, if not eager, to find that challenged state laws are incompatible with federal statutory schemes.[147] Second, and relatedly, some state laws impinge so much on federal authority over foreign affairs that they cannot stand even in the absence of preemptive federal legislation.[148] The leading case on this point is

---

line of thinking, strong relations with allies and roadblocks placed in the way of adversaries are likely to create the most propitious conditions for using the power to declare war and, more important, to engage in effective military action, including pursuant to the President's commander-in-chief power. Viewed from another angle, the power to declare war carries with it a power to keep the peace. And if that is so, it is hard to envision any means better suited for pursuing that objective than that of legislating in the field of foreign relations. Finally, the making of good legislation in this area might help Congress "raise *and support* Armies" and "provide *and maintain* a Navy," U.S. CONST. art. I, § 8, cl. 12, 13 (emphasis added), including by keeping fighting forces, to the greatest degree possible, out of harm's way.

[144] *See infra* Chapter 24 (discussing the law of federal preemption, including its especially broad application when Congress legislates in the area of foreign affairs).

[145] A fourth feature of this power—namely, that it gives Congress an especially wide berth in delegating policymaking authority to executive authorities—might sometimes affect the state-federal balance by facilitating federal executive action that that runs counter to state policy choices in a way not permitted when other powers are at play. Indeed, in the *Curtiss-Wright* case itself, the Court recognized that Congress had particularly broad authority to delegate policymaking authority to the executive branch in legislating with regard to foreign affairs. *See infra* Section 27.A (discussing this feature of *Curtiss-Wright*); *see also* United States *ex rel.* Knauff v. Shaughnessy, 338 U.S. 537, 542 (1950); *cf. supra* note 124 (citing other authorities supportive of a contracted view of the nondelegation doctrine when Congress acts pursuant to its war powers).

[146] *See infra* Section 24.C.

[147] *See* TRIBE, *supra* note 25, § 6–31, at 1210 (citing the field of foreign affairs, which "is traditionally deemed 'national,'" as one in which the Court is "extremely solicitous of the paramount federal interest in matters germane to foreign affairs" when applying preemption principles). *See generally infra* Section 24.C (further discussing this idea).

[148] For judicial rhetoric supportive of this notion, see *United States v. Pink*, 315 U.S. 203, 233 (1942) (stating that "[p]ower over external affairs is not shared by the

Zschernig v. Miller,[149] which involved an Oregon statute that disallowed the making of testamentary gifts to foreigners unless the beneficiary's home country met state-specified standards rooted in a hostility to communist regimes. In invalidating the law, the Court neither could nor did point to any preemptive federal statute. Instead, it struck down the challenged law because it constituted "an intrusion by the State into the field of foreign affairs which the Constitution entrusts to the President and the Congress."[150] Third, it is possible that federalism-based external limits applicable to the commerce power—specifically, state-protective rules regarding anti-commandeering and state sovereign immunity from suit—do not apply to laws enacted pursuant to the foreign-affairs power.[151] Might Congress, for example, mandate that state authorities turn over to foreign governments state-held prisoners if the President determines, pursuant to a delegation of authority made by way of federal statute, that doing so is necessary to achieve important foreign-policy objectives? Such a law, if passed solely under the commerce power, would have to face up to a serious challenge under the anti-commandeering principle. Perhaps, however, that principle should give way to choices made by federal decisionmakers tasked with pursuing critical national objectives in the "delicate field of international relations."[152]

2. Immigration

One aspect of Congress's foreign-affairs powers concerns the subject of noncitizens who are present, or seek to be present, in the

States; it is vested in the national government exclusively"). The resulting principle, according to *Trojan Techs., Inc. v. Pennsylvania*, 916 F.2d 903 (3d Cir. 1990), is that "any state law that involves the state in the actual conduct of foreign affairs is unconstitutional." *Id.* at 913.

[149] 389 U.S. 429 (1968).

[150] *Id.* at 432. Professor Tribe has suggested that the foreign-affairs power exerts such a powerful force that Congress cannot by statute affirmatively authorize enactment of the sort of state law struck down in *Zschernig*. TRIBE, *supra* note 25, § 6–35, at 1246 n.45. This position is defensible, especially if one views the power as centered on eradicating nonuniformity in the nation's dealing with foreign sovereigns. At the same time, Congress itself might choose to treat foreign nations in different ways in different circumstances, and it is not self-evident that it cannot approve state choices such as the one at issue in *Zschernig* in the process of doing so, just as it can consent to the enactment of state laws that otherwise would run afoul of the dormant Commerce Clause. *See infra* Section 20.B. Put differently, perhaps it should be open to the federal government to "speak with one voice" on the subject of foreign affairs, Michelin Tire Corp. v. Wages, 423 U.S. 276, 285 (1976), but to do so in a way that takes account of the values of local decision-making on subjects as to which, on the considered view of federal authorities, uniformity is not a matter of the highest urgency.

[151] *See supra* Section 5.B (discussing the application of these rules to commerce-power legislation).

[152] Benz v. Compania Naviera Hidalgo, S.A., 353 U.S. 138, 147 (1957). For further discussion this topic, see *infra* Section 13.B.

United States. Perhaps the Article I power over "Naturalization" naturally carries with it a companion power to regulate access to permanent resident status on the theory that the latter power qualifies as a "first cousin" of the former.[153] But many other features of the nation's treatment of actual or would-be foreign visitors—ranging over subjects as diverse as pre-border-crossing diversion, passport control, temporary student and worker visas, refugee status, asylum, and deportation—have no comparably close connection to the formal act of granting U.S. citizenship.[154] The Justices have filled the resulting textual lacuna by insisting that "every sovereign nation has the power, as inherent in sovereignty, and essential to self-preservation, to forbid the entrance of foreigners within its dominions, or to admit them only in such cases and upon such conditions as it may see fit to prescribe."[155] Indeed, the Court has embraced this notion with such enthusiasm that it once expressed the view that " 'over no conceivable subject is the legislative power of Congress more complete than it is over' the admission of aliens."[156] Drawing on this font of authority, Congress

---

[153] More specifically, the connection between obtaining naturalization and securing a green card may have an especially interlocking kinship because permanent resident status often is intended to be (in the view of both the individual and the legal system) a key step on the way to securing full citizenship.

[154] *See* Mary Ann McNulty, Comment, *A Doctrine Without Exception: Critiquing an Immigration Exception to the Anticommandeering Rule*, 169 U. PA. L. REV. 241, 251 (2020) (asserting that "the constitutional text . . . speaks only to the importance of *naturalization* to become a United States citizen, not immigration broadly"). To be sure, some regulations of travel into the United States might find support in Congress's power over "Commerce with foreign Nations." *See supra* Section 4.F.2. Even so, it seems difficult, according to the ordinary rules of linguistic usage, to shoehorn the full range of immigration-related matters into that doctrinal category.

[155] Ekiu v. United States, 142 U.S. 651, 659 (1892). *See generally* Toll v. Moreno, 458 U.S. 1, 10 (1982) (pointing out that the Court has "long recognized the preeminent role of the Federal Government with respect to the regulation of aliens within our borders").

[156] Fiallo v. Bell, 430 U.S. 787, 792 (1977). This principle is closely associated with the Court's notorious decisions in *Chae Chan Ping v. United States*, 130 U.S. 581 (1889), *Fong Yue Ting v. United States*, 149 U.S. 698 (1893), and others (sometimes collectively referred to as the *Chinese Exclusion Cases*), in which the Justices rejected several constitutional challenges to the Chinese Exclusion Act while recognizing for the federal government a broad and largely unreviewable power to disregard equal-protection and other rights-based constitutional guarantees when creating and enforcing federal immigration law. Although these decisions derived from openly expressed nativist and racist sentiments, they continue to exert precedential force to this day. *See* Avidan Y. Cover, *Quieting the Court: Lessons from* The Muslim Ban Case, 23 J. GENDER RACE & JUST. 1, 65–66 (2020) (emphasizing that the Court in *Trump v. Hawaii*, *see infra* note 158, employed a deferential standard of review derived from an earlier decision that drew upon the "xenophobic and judicially-enervating" rationale of *Chae Chan Ping* and *Fong Yue Ting*). For a broader overview of the Chinese Exclusion Act, the *Chinese Exclusion Cases*, and those cases' continuing doctrinal impact, see Gabriel J. Chin, Chae Chan Ping *and* Fong Tue Ying: *The Origins of Plenary Power*, *in* IMMIGRATION LAW STORIES 5–29 (David A. Martin & Peter H. Schuck, eds., 2005).

has put in place the vast network of laws that deal with the status of all categories of actual and prospective travelers to the United States. Moreover, the character of this power has informed the Court's development of individual rights. In particular—and in keeping with the sweeping reach of Congress's authority over immigration—when noncitizens assert rights-based claims, particularly claims founded on principles of equal-protection law, they are far less likely to succeed in challenging federal, as opposed to state, legislation.[157]

3. Self-Preservation: Presidential Elections and Anti-Insurrection Laws

Far removed from Congress's power over foreign affairs is the inherent power, recognized in *Burroughs v. United States*,[158] to safeguard the propriety of federal elections for President of the United States.[159] As the Court explained in upholding federal campaign-contribution disclosure rules in that case: "To say that Congress is without power to pass appropriate legislation to safeguard such an election from the improper use of money to influence the result is to deny to the nation in a vital particular the power of self-protection. Congress, undoubtedly, possesses that power, as it possesses every other power essential to preserve the departments and institutions of the general government from impairment or destruction, whether threatened by force or by corruption."[160] Along the same lines, the inherent power of national self-protection may provide the basis for federal legislation that outlaws dangerous forms of action or incitement aimed at overthrowing the federal government by violent means.[161]

---

157 *See, e.g.*, Mathews v. Diaz, 426 U.S. 67, 82 (1976) (recognizing the operation of a "a narrow standard of review of decisions made by the Congress or the President in the area of immigration and naturalization"); *see also* Reno v. Am.-Arab Anti-Discrimination Comm., 525 U.S. 471, 488 (1999) (ruling that "an alien unlawfully in this country has no constitutional right to assert selective enforcement as a defense against his deportation"); Kleindienst v. Mandel, 408 U.S. 753, 770 (1972) (holding that rights-based challenges to executive-branch actions undertaken pursuant to statutory delegations of immigration-related authority trigger a highly deferential standard of review, according to which the Court asks whether there exists a "facially legitimate and bona fide reason" for the government's action); Trump v. Hawaii, 138 S. Ct. 2392, 2418–20 (2018) (rejecting a religion-based-discrimination challenge to President Trump's "travel ban" targeting the citizens of several Muslim-majority countries).

158 290 U.S. 534 (1934).

159 The textual vacuum on this point exists because Article I, section 4, by its terms allocates power to Congress to oversee federal elections only for House and Senate seats, while no comparable power to oversee presidential elections is set forth in the Constitution. *See generally supra* Chapter 9.

160 *Burroughs*, 290 U.S. at 545.

161 *See* 18 U.S.C. § 2385. Some anti-insurrection laws might also be supported by Congress's power to enforce section 3 of the Fourteenth Amendment, which generally prohibits persons who participated in (or otherwise abetted) "rebellion" or

4. National Symbols

A related line of inherent-power reasoning may also provide support for federal legislation designed to safeguard national symbols.[162] At least in the absence of a preexisting treaty obligation, for example, it is not easy to find any constitutional text authorizing the enactment of a federal statute banning the "possession" of eagle feathers or the "disturb[ing]" of these majestic creatures.[163] Assuming (perhaps incorrectly) that the commerce power does not supply a proper basis for such laws, on what power might Congress rely?[164] Perhaps it is the inherent power of the nation to create a unifying set of national symbols, coupled with the logically companion authority to give those symbols protection. Such a view of federal power might even draw strength from certain federalism-based protections for the states. After all, if it makes sense to recognize an implied constitutional limit on the federal government's authority to meddle with key symbolic embodiments of a state's

---

"insurrection" against the United States from holding state or federal office. *See generally infra* Section 32.C (discussing this requirement).

[162] Another possibility is that such symbols might qualify as a specialized form of federal "property" that Congress can regulate pursuant to the Property Clause. *See supra* Section 10.A. *But cf.* TRIBE, *supra* note 25, § 6–10, at 1086 (noting, in light of *Hughes v. Oklahoma*, 441 U.S. 322 (1979), that the notion of "public ownership with respect to wildlife is a dead letter under contemporary Commerce Clause analysis").

[163] Bald and Golden Eagle Protection Act, 16 U.S.C. §§ 668, 668c. The essential difficulty is that both the possession of feathers and the disturbing of birds might be characterized as noneconomic activities, which are not ordinarily subject to regulation under the commerce power. *See supra* Section 4.D.1.

[164] The phrase "perhaps incorrectly" finds a place in this sentence because lines of argument are available for defending the law under the Commerce Clause. It might be, for example, that the migratory nature of eagles puts them in a special category, supporting something like a conclusive presumption of a previous border-crossing, thus allowing these sorts of regulations based on their embodiment of a specialized "jurisdictional element" or as "instruments" of interstate commerce (or users of the "channels" of interstate commerce) and distinctly subject to federal regulation on such a theory. *See Andrus*, 444 U.S. at 63 n.19 (describing as "clearly flawed" the suggestion that "the national commerce power does not reach migratory wildlife"). Perhaps most important, it may be that these prohibitions (and particularly the ban on possession) would be sustainable as part of an "integrated regulatory scheme" focused on blocking the purchase and sale of eagles and eagle parts and the harvesting of these animals for those purposes. See supra Section 4.D.2.a. In sum, specialized commerce-power considerations may, in the end, support the constitutionality of eagle-related laws of this kind. Even so, it is far from clear that all judges would endorse these theories and, regardless, any eagle-specific commerce-power rationale might well not apply to other national symbols, such as the American flag. *See* TRIBE, *supra* note 25, § 5–3, at 806 n.17 (noting that "[r]emarkably," in the case that resulted in invalidation of the federal flag desecration act under the First Amendment, neither the Court nor the parties "paused to address the seemingly anterior question of Congress' affirmative authority to enact the statute").

identity,[165] perhaps it makes no less sense to recognize an implied power in the federal government to safeguard symbols of its own.[166]

165 *See supra* Section 5.A (discussing the implied prohibition on congressional interference with the location of a state capitol).

166 A related point is that the power to safeguard distinctly national symbols cannot effectively reside in the states. More specifically, one might say that such a power was, in its nature, not "reserved to the States" by the Tenth Amendment because the power to deal with a matter intrinsically related to the national government—in this case, core national symbols—could not and did not come into being until the Constitution created the national government itself. Thus, such a power could not be "reserved to the States" under the Tenth Amendment because the term "reserved" envisions only the *retention* of powers held by the states before the new Constitution took effect. In sum, the power to protect national symbols must exist somewhere, and because it does not and cannot exist in the states, it must be lodged (even if by implication, rather than express grant) in the federal government. For a treatment of the word "reserved," as used in the Tenth Amendment, that lends support to this argument, see *U.S. Term Limits*, 514 U.S. at 802–03.

Chapter 11

THE FOURTEENTH AND FIFTEENTH AMENDMENT ENFORCEMENT POWERS

Analysis

Section 1 of the Fourteenth Amendment provides: "No State shall make or enforce any law which shall abridge the privileges or immunities of citizens of the United States; nor shall any State deprive any person of life, liberty, or property, without due process of law; nor deny to any person within its jurisdiction the equal protection of the laws."[1] At the heart of the development of U.S. constitutional law lies the Supreme Court's evolving interpretations of these fifty-two words. One part of that story is that the Court has defined very narrowly "the privileges or immunities of citizens of the United States," thus rendering that portion of the Fourteenth Amendment of limited significance in the constitutional scheme.[2] But the amendment's other safeguards of rights, embodied in the Due Process and Equal Protection Clauses, have provided the basis for many of the Court's most consequential rulings over the past 150 years.

The Court has read the Due Process Clause to provide two sweeping sets of protections against state action: (1) safeguards of "procedural due process," which entitle persons to fair proceedings whenever states seek to deprive them of life, liberty, or property; and (2) safeguards of "substantive due process," which block states from abridging rights deemed "fundamental," regardless of how much

---

1 U.S. CONST. amend. XIV, § 1.

2 *See* ERWIN CHEMERINSKY, CONSTITUTIONAL LAW: PRINCIPLES AND POLICIES 521–22 (5th ed. 2015) (stating that the Court's "extremely narrow interpretation of the privileges or immunities clause" in the *Slaughter-House Cases*, 83 U.S. 36 (1872), has "rob[bed the clause] of all meaning"). For further treatment of the clause, see *infra* Section 15.A.

procedural protection accompanies the challenged government action.[3] Of particular importance, the Court has invoked the "incorporation doctrine" to apply almost all of the protections of the Bill of Rights, which originally targeted only federal action,[4] in full measure to the states.[5] The result is that, by virtue of the Fourteenth Amendment, key procedural protections set forth in the first eight amendments (such as the Sixth Amendment rights of criminal defendants to the assistance of counsel, to an impartial jury, and to confront witnesses) and key substantive protections (such as the First Amendment rights of free speech and free exercise of religion and the Second Amendment right to bear arms) now constrain state authorities no less than their federal counterparts.[6]

The Equal Protection Clause supplements these protections by barring states from passing laws that embody impermissible forms of discrimination. The Commonwealth of Virginia, for example, had no duty to offer students the chance to attend a military college. But its choice to do so, coupled with the decision to afford that opportunity only to men, ran afoul of equal-protection limits on sex discrimination.[7] Key decisions of the Court under the Equal Protection Clause have struck down state laws that discriminated on the basis of race.[8] In other rulings, the Court has invalidated measures that discriminated on the basis of sexual orientation, citizenship status, and the marital status of one's parents, as well as laws that established discriminatory classifications lacking a "rational relationship to a legitimate state interest."[9] The Court also has held that having access both to the franchise and to judicial processes implicates interests of such distinct importance that especially robust equal-protection doctrines guard against discrimination in these contexts.[10] The bottom line is that the Fourteenth Amendment's Due Process and Equal Protection Clauses have shaped the course of constitutional law in profound ways. Those clauses underlie such high-profile rights-based rulings as *Brown v.*

---

[3] *See* CHEMERINSKY, *supra* note 2, at 569 (discussing how the Due Process Clause imposes both procedural and substantive limits).

[4] *See* Barron v. Baltimore, 32 U.S. (7 Pet.) 243, 250–51 (1833) (holding that the protections of these amendments apply only against federal actors).

[5] *See* CHEMERINSKY, *supra* note 2, at 529.

[6] *See id.* at 528–29.

[7] *See* United States v. Virginia, 518 U.S. 515, 534, 542 (1996).

[8] *See* CHEMERINSKY, *supra* note 2, at 719–82 (discussing many of these rulings).

[9] Ambach v. Norwick, 441 U.S. 68, 80 (1979). *See generally* CHEMERINSKY, *supra* note 2, at 800–03.

[10] *See id.* at 908–56 (discussing the Court's rulings on the right to vote and access to the courts).

Board of Education,[11] *New York Times Co. v. Sullivan*,[12] *Miranda v. Arizona*,[13] *Roe v. Wade*,[14] *Bush v. Gore*,[15] and *Obergefell v. Hodges*,[16] as well as countless other rulings of far-reaching significance.

Even more important for present purposes, section 5 of the Fourteenth Amendment vests Congress with the "power to enforce, by appropriate legislation, the provisions" of section 1.[17] This affirmative grant of authority to Congress—no less than other such grants, including those made by the Commerce, Taxing, and Spending Clauses—enables Congress to impose important regulatory controls. Indeed, section 5 lodges in Congress a form of lawmaking power that reaches beyond other key powers in a fundamental way. This is so because the powers granted by the original Constitution generally permit Congress to regulate individuals, corporations, and other private entities.[18] In contrast, section 5 enables Congress to impose duties on states themselves because of section 1's focus on limiting *state* action.[19]

Section 2 of the Fifteenth Amendment operates in much the same way as section 5 of the Fourteenth Amendment, albeit as to only one regulatory subject. Section 1 of that amendment provides: "The right of citizens of the United States to vote shall not be denied or abridged by the United States or by any State on account of race, color, or previous condition of servitude."[20] Echoing section 5 of the Fourteenth Amendment (which itself echoes section 2 of the Thirteenth Amendment),[21] section 2 goes on to provide that "Congress shall have power to enforce this article by appropriate legislation."[22] As a result, federal lawmakers can use the Fifteenth Amendment enforcement power, just as they can use the Fourteenth

---

11 347 U.S. 483 (1954).

12 376 U.S. 254 (1964).

13 384 U.S. 436 (1966).

14 410 U.S. 113 (1973).

15 531 U.S. 98 (2000).

16 576 U.S. 644 (2015).

17 U.S. CONST. amend. XIV, § 5.

18 *See supra* Section 5.B (noting the limits imposed by the anti-commandeering doctrine).

19 *See infra* notes 265–267 and accompanying text (discussing further the state-action doctrine).

20 U.S. CONST. amend. XV, § 1.

21 That amendment, which provides that "[n]either slavery nor involuntary servitude, except as a punishment for crime whereof the party shall have been duly convicted, shall exist within the United States, or any place subject to their jurisdiction," U.S. CONST. amend. XIII § 1, also confers on Congress the power to enforce its guarantee by "appropriate legislation," *id.* amend. XIII, § 2. *See infra* Chapter 12.

22 U.S. CONST. amend. XV, § 2.

Amendment enforcement power, to impose rights-vindicating restrictions on state governments.[23]

The Enforcement Clauses of the Fourteenth and Fifteenth Amendments have stirred controversy from their earliest days. Indeed, those controversies often have been particularly intense precisely because Congress can use and has used these grants of power to reshape core features of state self-governance, including state electoral processes. This feature of the enforcement powers has driven arguments, often made by or on behalf of state governments, that the Court should view these powers as having a narrow application.[24] But competing arguments for a broad interpretation have found support in three separate considerations: (1) the centrality to the Reconstruction project of establishing a system of expansive rights-based safeguards so as to facilitate active federal oversight of (and limits on) the powers of state governments; (2) the catastrophic injustices wrought by discrimination and subjugation, especially on the basis of race, throughout the nation's history; and (3) strong indications that the framers of the Fourteenth and Fifteenth Amendments meant for Congress to have a key role, independent of the courts, in shaping the protections those amendments afford.[25]

---

[23] *See* CHEMERINSKY, *supra* note 2, at 310–13 (discussing Congress's power under section 2 of the Fifteenth Amendment).

[24] This subject is a complex one, with different analysts taking different views of precisely how to balance the cross-cutting considerations in this field of law. For commentaries that nonetheless can be seen as leaning in the direction of safeguarding state-autonomy interests, see J. Randy Beck, *The Heart of Federalism: Pretext Review of Means-End Relationships*, 36 U.C. DAVIS L. REV. 407, 409 (2003) (generally defending the modern enforcement-power-limiting "congruence and proportionality" test on the ground that it "implements *McCulloch*'s promise to strike down pretextual exercises of congressional power"); Steven G. Calabresi & Nicholas P. Stabile, *On Section 5 of the Fourteenth Amendment*, 11 U. PA. J. CONST. L. 1431, 1434, 1437 (2009) (rejecting the deferential approach suggested by then-Judge Michael McConnell to the application of section 5 in part because of its drafters' use of the "the verb 'to enforce' "); Marci A. Hamilton & David Schoenbrod, *The Reaffirmation of Proportionality Analysis Under Section 5 of the Fourteenth Amendment*, 21 CARDOZO L. REV. 469, 479–87 (1999) (defending the congruence-and-proportionality test as properly connected up with judicial powers to shape equitable remedies for constitutional violations); Ronald D. Rotunda, *The Powers of Congress Under Section 5 of the Fourteenth Amendment After* City of Boerne v. Flores, 32 IND. L. REV. 163, 178–80 (1998) (arguing that the Court has properly narrowed Congress's Section 5 power, so as to permit the enforcement but not the redefinition of constitutional rights); Tracy A. Thomas, *Congress's Section 5 Power and Remedial Rights*, 34 U.C. DAVIS L. REV. 673, 704 (2001) (agreeing that, under a properly governing theory of rights, Congress's section 5 power should be limited in such a way as to deny Congress the authority to redefine the amendments' rights-based protections).

[25] *See, e.g.*, United States v. Guest, 383 U.S. 745, 783 n.7 (1966) (Brennan, J., concurring in part and dissenting in part) (citing JOSEPH B. JAMES, THE FRAMING OF THE FOURTEENTH AMENDMENT 184 (1956), ROBERT J. HARRIS, THE QUEST FOR EQUALITY 53–54 (1960), and Laurent B. Frantz, *Congressional Power to Enforce the Fourteenth Amendment Against Private Acts*, 73 YALE L.J. 1353, 1356 (1964), in

Against this backdrop, different sets of Justices—confronted with different political and social conditions—have sought to define the proper scope of the Fourteenth and Fifteenth Amendments' Enforcement Clauses. In traveling this road, the Court has dealt with three main topics: (1) Congress's power to directly remedy outright violations of Fourteenth and Fifteenth Amendment rights; (2) Congress's ability to enforce those rights prophylactically with laws that impose more far-reaching constraints on state regulatory prerogatives than are imposed by the amendments in and of themselves; and (3) Congress's authority to constrain private behavior (as opposed to state action) when federal lawmakers view that behavior as subversive of section 1 rights.

---

support of the proposition that "Congress, not the judiciary, was viewed as the more likely agency to implement fully the guarantees of equality, and thus it could be presumed the primary purpose of the Amendment was to augment the power of Congress, not the judiciary"); A. Christopher Bryant, *The Pursuit of Perfection: Congressional Power to Enforce the Reconstruction Amendments*, 47 HOUS. L. REV. 579, 612–15 (2010) (arguing that Congress has broad power to enact prophylactic legislation to ensure "perfect compliance" with the Reconstruction Amendments); Evan H. Caminker, *"Appropriate" Means-Ends Constraints on Section 5 Powers*, 53 STAN. L. REV. 1127, 1159–65 (2001) (critiquing the congruence-and-proportionality test embraced by the modern Court as contrary to the drafters' intentions regarding Congress's central role in implementing rights protections pursuant to the Reconstruction Amendments); Garrett Epps, *Interpreting the Fourteenth Amendment: Two Don'ts and Three Dos*, 16 WM. & MARY BILL OF RTS. J. 433, 455–56 (2007) (arguing that the framers of the Fourteenth Amendment had little reason to place trust in the federal courts that had issued decisions like *Dred Scott* and therefore sought to create a "legislative centrality" in safeguarding civil rights); Robert J. Kaczorowski, *Congress's Power to Enforce Fourteenth Amendment Rights: Lessons from Federal Remedies the Framers Enacted*, 42 HARV. J. ON LEGIS. 187, 189 (2005) (arguing that the Court's current conception of Section 5 power forgets "the Madisonian first principles of American constitutionalism . . . which recognized plenary congressional power to enforce constitutional rights and to remedy their violation"); Douglas Laycock, *Conceptual Gulfs in* City of Boerne v. Flores, 39 WM. & MARY L. REV. 743, 763–66 (1998) (emphasizing Congress's repudiation of past judicial work, especially the *Dred Scott* decision, as driving adoption of a broad empowerment of Congress in the Enforcement Clauses); Michael W. McConnell, *Institutions and Interpretation: A Critique of* City of Boerne v. Flores, 111 HARV. L. REV. 153, 171, 178 & n.153, 188 (1997) (arguing that section 5 allows Congress to legislate its own "good faith interpretations of the meaning of the Fourteenth Amendment" and that courts should review resulting laws by applying the "latitudinarian construction of congressional power" endorsed in *McCulloch v. Maryland*, 17 U.S. (4 Wheat.) 316, 421 (1819), while applying "particular deference" to rights-extending treatments of Bill of Right protections because "the federal government will bear no less cost and inconvenience than the states" as a result of such federal enactments); *see also* Steven A. Engel, Note, *The* McCulloch *Theory of the Fourteenth Amendment:* City of Boerne v. Flores *and the Original Understanding of Section 5*, 109 YALE L.J. 115, 117 (1999) (concluding that the drafters envisioned that "it would be Congress, and not the courts, that would be the . . . primary enforcer[ ] of the Fourteenth Amendment" and that courts would therefore employ the "deferential standard" of *McCulloch* in assessing exercises of the section 5 power). Noteworthy in this regard is a concern, famously reflected in *The Federalist*, that subversion of rights through tyrannical acts of majority "factions" presents a far greater danger at the state than at the national level. *See* THE FEDERALIST NO. 10 (Madison); *see also supra* Section 1.D.

A. DIRECT ENFORCEMENT OF SECTION 1 RIGHTS

One of the most important laws ever passed by Congress is now set forth at 42 U.S.C. § 1983. That statute's core prohibition, enacted in the immediate wake of the ratification of the Fourteenth Amendment, provides in relevant part that:

> Every person who, under color of any statute, ordinance, regulation, custom, or usage, of any State . . . subjects, or causes to be subjected, any citizen of the United States or other person within the jurisdiction thereof to the deprivation of any rights, privileges, or immunities secured by the Constitution and laws, shall be liable to the party injured in an action at law, suit in equity, or other proper proceeding for redress . . . .[26]

Every year, plaintiffs bring thousands of lawsuits under section 1983. These actions involve a sprawling range of claims of wrongful state action, including claims made by prisoners alleging cruel and unusual punishment, arrestees who assert the unconstitutional use of excessive force by police officers, and city, county, and state employees who attribute firings or demotions to their exercise of expressive or religious liberties. Section 1983 thus provides a key vehicle (and sometimes the only vehicle) for civil litigation based on claimed violations of the Fourteenth Amendment's far-reaching Due Process and Equal Protection Clauses. A companion provision, set forth at 18 U.S.C. § 242, also criminalizes such constitutional violations so long as prosecutors can offer proof that satisfies an especially demanding *mens rea* requirement.[27]

To the extent that these two statutes operate to vindicate the constitutional rights established by section 1 of the Fourteenth Amendment and section 1 of the Fifteenth Amendment, are they constitutional? Of course they are. This is the case because the congressional-power-granting clauses set forth in section 5 of the former amendment and section 2 of the latter amendment give Congress the power to "enforce" the rights they create, and nothing could more clearly "enforce" these rights than subjecting persons who directly violate those rights to civil and criminal redress.[28] Even so,

---

[26] 42 U.S.C. § 1983.

[27] *See* Screws v. United States, 325 U.S. 91, 104 (1945) (holding that "the specific intent required . . . is an intent to deprive a person of a right which has been made specific either by the express terms of the Constitution or laws of the United States").

[28] The Court also has allowed plaintiffs to seek civil redress under section 1983 for violations of rights established by provisions other than the Fourteenth and Fifteenth Amendments. *See, e.g.*, Dennis v. Higgins, 498 U.S. 439, 446 (1991) (holding

one important question regarding the relationship of the Enforcement Clauses and direct-enforcement statutes such as section 1983 went unanswered for many years—namely, whether Congress could subject states themselves, as opposed to individual state officials, to liability for the actions of their agents notwithstanding Eleventh Amendment-related principles of sovereign immunity.[29] The Court's decision in *Ex parte Young*[30] has long stood for the proposition that sovereign-immunity restrictions do not cover efforts to secure injunctive relief against state officials,[31] and the Court also has made it clear that this immunity does not apply to money-damages actions brought against municipalities[32] or individual state actors.[33] What if, however, a plaintiff seeks to recover damages directly from the state? Can Congress abrogate the state's sovereign immunity by relying on its Reconstruction Amendment enforcement powers—thus requiring states to pay money damage awards out of their own treasuries—even if it cannot do so under the Commerce Clause or some other provision of Article I?[34]

The Court took up these questions in *Fitzpatrick v. Bitzer*.[35] In that case, the state-employee plaintiffs sought money damages from the state pursuant to Title VII of the Civil Rights Act of 1964, based on allegations that the state's retirement plan discriminated on the basis of sex in violation of both the statute and the Equal Protection

that the dormant Commerce Clause "confers 'rights, privileges, or immunities' within the meaning of [section] 1983").

29 *See supra* Section 5.C.1. With respect to section 1983 itself, this question has been mooted by the Court's determination that the statute itself does not authorize suits in which the plaintiff seeks to recover damages directly from the state treasury. *See* Will v. Michigan Dept. of State Police, 491 U.S. 58 (1989).

30 209 U.S. 123, 167 (1908).

31 *See id.* at 159–60. In *Edelman v. Jordan*, 415 U.S. 651, 676–77 (1974), the Court clarified that principles of sovereign immunity did not bar a section 1983 action for prospective injunctive relief that effectively mandates action by the state—including very costly action by the state—so long as the pleading formally names a responsible state official, rather than the state itself, as the defendant. *See id.* at 668 (authorizing such suits even though "an ancillary effect on the state treasury is a permissible and often an inevitable consequence" of complying with resulting injunctions); *see also* Alabama v. Pugh, 438 U.S. 781, 782 (1978) (reaffirming that rule in a case improperly brought against the state and a state agency, as opposed to the proper individual-state-employee defendant).

32 *See* Owen v. City of Independence, 445 U.S. 622, 647–48 (1980) (holding that Congress permissibly had "abolished whatever vestige of the State's sovereign immunity that [municipalities had] possessed" in enacting section 1983).

33 *See* Alden v. Maine, 527 U.S. 706, 757 (1999) (noting that "a suit for money damages may be prosecuted against a state officer in his individual capacity for unconstitutional or wrongful conduct fairly attributable to the officer himself, so long as the relief is sought not from the state treasury but from the officer personally").

34 *See supra* Section 5.C.

35 427 U.S. 445 (1976).

Clause.[36] The state responded by invoking the sovereign-immunity defense, but the Court rejected the state's argument on the ground that Title VII's imposition of a money-damage remedy for sex discrimination by state employers was a permissible exercise of the Fourteenth Amendment enforcement power.[37]

The Court in *Fitzpatrick* glossed over the question whether the state's violation of Title VII also constituted a violation of the Fourteenth Amendment's Equal Protection Clause. But on one possible reading of the case, the Court assumed, for purposes of evaluating the section 5 issue, that such a violation of section 1 of the Amendment had occurred.[38] To the extent that this was the Court's view of the matter, it followed that Title VII, as applied, was not subject to challenge on the ground that it reached beyond "enforc[ing]" the Equal Protection Clause because *ipso facto* Congress can, at a minimum, deploy section 5 to outlaw direct abridgments of section 1.[39] As for the separate question regarding congressional abrogation of the states' Eleventh Amendment immunity from money-damages actions, the Court hinted that federal legislators might be unable to effectuate such an abrogation when acting pursuant to the Commerce Clause or other Article I grants of power.[40] Just as surely as the Eleventh Amendment post-dated Article I, however, the Fourteenth Amendment post-dated the Eleventh.[41] Even more important, the drafters and ratifiers of the Fourteenth Amendment meant for it to create broad new "limitations on state authority," thus effectuating a marked "shift in the federal-state balance."[42] As a result, the Court concluded, Congress could abrogate the states' otherwise-operative sovereign immunity pursuant to the enforcement powers embodied in the Reconstruction Amendments,

---

[36] *Id.* at 448. The plaintiffs in *Fitzpatrick* could not sue under section 1983 because of statutory-law limits on the reach of that provision later concretized in *Quern v. Jordan*, 440 U.S. 332, 338–42 (1979). *See infra* note 44; *see also Fitzpatrick*, 427 U.S. at 452 (suggesting, but not holding, that section 1983 did not, as a matter of statutory law, abrogate the sovereign immunity of states themselves).

[37] *See id.* at 456–57.

[38] *Cf. id.* at 452–53 (noting that section 1 of the Fourteenth Amendment prohibits state denials of "the equal protection of the laws"); *id.* at 456 n.11 (noting that the "state officials do not contend that the substantive provisions of Title VII as applied here are not a proper exercise of congressional authority under [section] 5 of the Fourteenth Amendment").

[39] *See supra* notes 28–34 and accompanying text.

[40] *See Fitzpatrick*, 427 U.S. at 452–53.

[41] *See id.* at 453.

[42] *Id.* at 455–56.

even if it could not abrogate that immunity by wielding the powers granted by Article I.[43]

In the wake of *Fitzpatrick*, the Court has continued to apply this principle. To be sure, the Justices have limited the practical impact of *Fitzpatrick* by interpreting section 1983 (in contrast to the Title VII prohibition at issue in *Fitzpatrick* itself) as not authorizing compensatory-damages actions against states as a matter of statutory law.[44] In keeping with the underlying principle of *Fitzpatrick*, however, the Court also held that Congress validly used its enforcement powers to abrogate state sovereign immunity when authorizing attorneys' fee awards against the state in federal civil rights actions.[45] This result made sense, the Justices concluded, because "Congress has plenary power," if it chooses to use that power, "to set aside the States' immunity from retroactive relief in order to enforce the Fourteenth Amendment."[46]

Some three decades later, a unanimous Court in *United States v. Georgia*[47] endorsed the same proposition. As Justice Scalia explained, "While the Members of this Court have disagreed regarding the scope of Congress's 'prophylactic' enforcement powers under § 5 of the Fourteenth Amendment, no one doubts that § 5 grants Congress the power to 'enforce . . . the provisions' of the Amendment by creating private remedies against the States for *actual* violations of those provisions."[48] Relying on that principle, the Court endorsed the recovery of money damages from states themselves, under Title II of the Americans with Disabilities Act, by

---

[43] *Id.* at 456 (concluding that "the Eleventh Amendment, and the principle of state sovereignty which it embodies, are necessarily limited by the enforcement provisions of § 5 of the Fourteenth Amendment" (internal citations omitted)).

[44] *See Quern*, 440 U.S. at 345 (holding that section 1983 "does not . . . indicate on its face an intent to sweep away the immunity of the States; nor does it have a history . . . which shows that Congress considered and firmly decided to abrogate the Eleventh Amendment immunity of the States"); *see also Will*, 491 U.S. at 71 (holding that "neither a State nor its officials acting in their official capacities are 'persons' " under section 1983). In contrast, the Court, in *Monell v. Department of Social Services*, 436 U.S. 658 (1978), both (1) reaffirmed that municipalities, even though they are subunits of the state, do not generally enjoy the Eleventh Amendment immunity afforded by that amendment to the states themselves; and (2) held that municipalities are "persons" within the meaning of section 1983, thus rendering them susceptible to money-damages liability under that statute in proper cases. *Id.* at 690 n.54, 694–701.

[45] *See* Hutto v. Finney, 437 U.S. 678, 691, 694, (1978) (holding that Congress had enforcement-power authority to abrogate state sovereign immunity when enacting the applicable fee-award statute, while also indicating that state sovereign immunity by its own terms does not bar fee awards issued as "ancillary to the federal court's power to impose injunctive relief").

[46] *Id.* at 693; *accord* Missouri v. Jenkins, 491 U.S. 274, 278–82 (1989) (reaffirming the *Hutto* rule, including in the face of arguments that it had been undermined by intervening decisions of the Court).

[47] 546 U.S. 151 (2006).

[48] *Id.* at 158 (emphasis in original) (internal citations omitted).

plaintiffs who could establish wrongdoing that violated both the statute and the Fourteenth Amendment itself. As Justice Scalia put the key point, "insofar as Title II creates a private cause of action for damages against the States for conduct that *actually* violates the Fourteenth Amendment, Title II validly abrogates state sovereign immunity."[49]

B. PROPHYLACTICALLY PROTECTING FOURTEENTH AND FIFTEENTH AMENDMENT RIGHTS

The most intensely debated questions raised by the Enforcement Clauses have concerned not Congress's efforts to legislate remedies for outright violations of section 1 rights, but rather its attempts to outlaw activities that range beyond judicially recognized section 1 violations. As with Congress's efforts to directly enforce section 1 rights, most laws of this kind have concerned the sweeping range of protections afforded by the Fourteenth Amendment, as opposed to the more targeted race-related-voting-rights protections established by the Fifteenth Amendment. Even so, section 2 of the latter amendment has played a key role in this set of cases for two reasons. First, some of the most important legislation passed by Congress pursuant to the Reconstruction Amendments has taken focused aim at race-based discrimination by the states in affording access to the ballot. Second, the Court has seemed to view Congress's remedial authority under section 5 of the Fourteenth Amendment as paralleling, at least roughly, its remedial authority under section 2 of the Fifteenth Amendment.[50] In light of these points, the ensuing discussion addresses cases involving both the Fourteenth and Fifteenth Amendment enforcement powers.

The basic question presented by these cases is easy to ask but hard to answer: To what extent can Congress prohibit state action that does not itself abridge, but nonetheless threatens or tends to undermine, the judicially enforceable section 1 rights established by the Fourteenth and Fifteenth Amendments? In other words, to what extent can Congress target state action that is not itself unconstitutional under those amendments in an effort to "enforce"

---

[49] *Id.* at 159 (emphasis in original).

[50] *See, e.g.*, Travis Crum, *The Superfluous Fifteenth Amendment*, 114 NW. U. L. REV. 1549, 1568 & n.99 (2020) (noting that "courts and commentators frequently treat Congress's enforcement authorities under the Reconstruction Amendments as coextensive," while also noting that some commentators have maintained that the power-limiting "congruence and proportionality" test that has frequently been applied in Fourteenth Amendment section 5 cases should not similarly apply in Fifteenth Amendment section 2 cases); *see also infra* note 135.

with "appropriate legislation" the protections that section 1 of each of those amendments puts in place?

1. *South Carolina v. Katzenbach* and the Remedial Theory

At the time of the adoption of the Reconstruction Amendments, many observers—including members of Congress who had crafted the operative texts—considered the enforcement powers to be of far-reaching importance. This view found support in the history of the amendments, which suggested that their drafters meant for their implementation to depend more on congressional enforcement than judicial application.[51] Against this backdrop, Congress moved swiftly to invoke its enforcement powers to vest individuals, especially those individuals recently freed from the bondage of slavery, with protections that reached beyond the amendments' already-judicially-enforceable section 1 safeguards. A hostile Supreme Court, however, proceeded to invalidate several resulting laws as beyond Congress's power to enact.[52] And with the passage of time, the priorities of Congress shifted away from the protections of liberty and equality enshrined in the Reconstruction Amendments, due in part to the growing influence in national politics of the Jim Crow South. The consequence was both legally significant and socially tragic: Congress's Fourteenth and Fifteenth Amendment enforcement powers fell into disuse for nearly a century.[53]

Political realities changed, however, as efforts to address the reality of entrenched and widespread state-sponsored race discrimination slowly gained traction with the rise of the Civil Rights Movement in the 1960s. One consequence of these transformational

---

[51] *See supra* note 25 and accompanying text.

[52] *See, e.g.*, United States v. Stanley (*The Civil Rights Cases*), 109 U.S. 3, 8 (1883) (holding that a recently enacted federal law that prohibited race discrimination in certain places of public accommodation fell outside the scope of Congress's powers to enforce the Reconstruction Amendments); United States v. Harris, 106 U.S. 629, 635–41 (1883) (holding that a provision of the Force Act of 1871, which authorized criminal penalties against persons who conspired to violate others' constitutional rights, fell outside the scope of Congress's power to enforce the Fourteenth Amendment). Indeed, in *Harris* the Court went so far as to indicate that "the amendment imposes no duty and confers no power upon Congress" except when "the state has been guilty of [violating section 1's] provisions." 106 U.S. at 639; *see also* Tennessee v. Lane, 541 U.S. 509, 564 n.4 (2004) (Scalia, J., dissenting) (reading *Harris* as suggesting that Congress could wield its Fourteenth Amendment enforcement powers only to address actual violations of substantive section 1 rights). Notably, even Justice Scalia, who took a far narrower view of the enforcement powers than most of his colleagues, rejected this approach as too narrow. *See id.* (observing that he did "not see the textual basis for this interpretation").

[53] *See* RICHARD KLUGER, SIMPLE JUSTICE: THE HISTORY OF *BROWN V. BOARD OF EDUCATION* AND BLACK AMERICA'S STRUGGLE FOR EQUALITY 166–67, 200 (1975) (detailing, for example, Black activists' push for, and Congress's failure to pass, anti-lynching laws throughout the early 1900s).

developments was a marked rise in support for responsive congressional action, though intense opposition from Southern Democrats dampened the prospects of legislative intervention, especially in the Senate. Then came the assassination of John F. Kennedy and Lyndon Johnson's succession to the presidency. Johnson, himself a Southern Democrat and former longtime Senate Majority Leader, took up the cause of pursuing civil-rights reform. These developments, and many others too, culminated in the enactment of two of the most important pieces of federal legislation in American history—the Civil Rights Act of 1964 and Voting Rights Act of 1965.[54] Key components of these statutes, however, soon encountered constitutional challenges.

In a pair of landmark rulings, the Supreme Court upheld Title II of the 1964 act, which bans racial discrimination by private businesses that operate places of public accommodation, as a permissible exercise of the commerce power.[55] The Voting Rights Act (VRA), however, was much more difficult to defend as a permissible exercise of Congress's authority to control interstate commerce.[56] Congress thus relied instead on its Fourteenth and Fifteenth Amendment enforcement powers in enacting that law, including its provisions that established rights enforceable against states that reached beyond the section 1 protections put in place by the amendments standing alone.

Key provisions of the VRA came before the Court in *South Carolina v. Katzenbach*.[57] One provision, set forth in section 4(b) of the act, established a "coverage formula" that in effect subjected only certain jurisdictions—namely, seven states in their entirety (Alabama, Alaska, Georgia, Louisiana, Mississippi, South Carolina,

---

[54] Among the other events were civil-rights demonstrations in the South, which prompted President Kennedy to encourage Congress to pursue legislative reforms. The March on Washington (on August 28, 1963) and the deadly bombing of the 16th Street Baptist Church in Birmingham (on September 15, 1963) also played important roles in spurring the Kennedy administration to increase pressure on congressional leaders to move forward on this front. The assassination of President Kennedy focused attention on his legislative goals, thus pushing forward the political movement that produced the 1964 and 1965 Acts. *See, e.g.*, Ted Gittinger & Allen Fisher, *LBJ Champions the Civil Rights Act of 1964*, 36 THE NATIONAL ARCHIVES: PROLOGUE MAGAZINE 2 (2004).

[55] *See supra* Section 3.C.3 (discussing the Court's rulings in *Heart of Atlanta Motel* and *Katzenbach v. McClung*).

[56] More specifically, under present-day law, it seems likely that the Voting Rights Act, or at least some portions of it, could not be sustained under the commerce power because (1) it requires action by state officials themselves, thus implicating the "anti-commandeering principle," *see supra* Section 5.B, and (2) voting, in any event, might not be characterized as an "economic activity" properly subject to aggregation under the limiting principle of *United States v. Lopez*, 514 U.S. 549 (1995), *see supra* Section 4.D.1.

[57] 383 U.S. 301 (1966).

and Virginia) and specific counties in four more states (twenty-six in North Carolina, three in Arizona and one each in Hawaii and Idaho)—to key restrictions imposed by the statute.[58] A second provision, set forth in section 4(a), required discontinuance in these covered jurisdictions of almost all voting-qualification restrictions, including any restrictions based on literacy-testing, which state officials long had used as a tool of race-based disenfranchisement.[59] A third provision, set forth in section 5 of the Act, mandated "preclearance" by the federal Department of Justice (subject to federal-court review) of any new "standard, practice, or procedure with respect to voting" proposed for adoption in any of these covered jurisdictions, so as to ensure continued adherence to federal-law requirements.[60] The VRA also included a "bail out" provision that allowed targeted states and localities to secure removal from the covered-jurisdiction list by proving that they had complied with federally imposed voting rules for a period of five years.[61]

In the face of a challenge brought by South Carolina, the Court upheld each of these restrictions in an opinion authored by Chief Justice Warren.[62] At the heart of the Court's analysis was a detailed treatment of the history of race-based voter suppression, particularly in the southern United States. The history recounted was one of voter-qualification sorting devices, including literacy tests, "which were specifically designed to prevent Negroes from voting."[63] Indeed, exclusionary practices of this sort were marked by such "variety and persistence" that they effectively wiped out voting by Black individuals in many jurisdictions going all the way back to the late 1800s.[64] To be sure, beginning in 1957, Congress had taken small steps in the direction of remediating actual violations of section 1 of

---

58 *Id.* at 318.

59 Voting Rights Act of 1965 § 4(a), codified at 52 U.S.C. § 10303(a).

60 *Id.* § 5, codified at 52 U.S.C. § 10304. In this regard, section 2 of the VRA blocked any jurisdiction, whether or not on the covered-jurisdiction list, from implementing a new standard, practice, or procedure that had the purpose or effect of diminishing the ability of citizens to vote on account of race. *Id.* § 2, codified at 52 U.S.C. § 10301.

61 *Id.* § 4(a), codified at 52 U.S.C. § 10303(a).

62 *South Carolina*, 383 U.S. at 307. The Chief Justice wrote for himself and seven other Justices. *Id.* In a separate opinion, Justice Black agreed with several key conclusions of the majority, including that the Congress had acted lawfully in singling out certain jurisdictions for the imposition of specialized voting-law-related duties. *Id.* at 355–56 (Black, J., concurring and dissenting). He dissented, however, from the majority's validation of the preclearance mechanism. *Id.* at 356. In his view, the Framers' conception of the federal-state relations left no room for a congressional command that state or local officials "beg" the attorney general to permit them to alter their jurisdiction's constitution or laws. *Id.*

63 *Id.* at 310 (majority opinion).

64 *Id.* at 311.

the Fifteenth Amendment.[65] But this legislation had "proved ineffective," both because states that had been successfully sued "merely switched to discriminatory devices not covered by the federal decrees" and because some local officials "defied and evaded court orders or . . . simply closed their registration offices to freeze the voting rolls."[66] The Court observed that by 1965 it had become clear that discrimination in determining voting qualifications was operating as "the principal method" of race-based voter suppression.[67] Among other indications of this problem, some jurisdictions required voters to establish their "good character," a standard "so vague and subjective that it has constituted an open invitation to abuse at the hands of voting officials."[68]

In addition to offering this legislation-supporting historical account, the Court made a significant doctrinal move by carrying over to the enforcement-power context the deferential approach to Congress's Article I authority rooted in *McCulloch v. Maryland*.[69] Building on this foundation, the Justices concluded that: (1) "Congress may use any rational means to effectuate the constitutional prohibition of racial discrimination in voting"; (2) this principle permits legislators to do "more than to forbid violations of the Fifteenth Amendment"; and (3) Congress can vindicate section 1 by "fashioning specific remedies" and "applying them to particular localities" free of "any need for prior adjudication."[70]

The Justices also fended off more focused attacks on each of the act's challenged strictures. As for Congress's singling out of only some jurisdictions for special forms of federal control, South Carolina urged both that "the coverage formula . . . violates the principle of the equality of States" and that it "is awkwardly designed in a number of respects and . . . disregards various local conditions which have nothing to do with racial discrimination."[71] The Court responded by

---

[65] *Id.* at 313. *See* The Civil Rights Act of 1957, codified at 42 U.S.C. § 1971 (barring race-based discrimination against otherwise-qualified voters and authorizing the Attorney General to sue to block such discrimination).

[66] *South Carolina*, 383 U.S. at 314. The Chief Justice recounted, for example, how (1) the Fifth Circuit had instructed Mississippi officials to furnish Black voters with the "same assistance" in registering to vote as white voters had received in the past, *id.* at 314 n.19; *see also* United States v. Lynd, 301 F.2d 818, 823 (5th Cir. 1962); and (2) the Mississippi legislature, in an attempt to thwart the efforts of would-be Black voters, responded by passing a law that required everyone to register to vote without assistance. *See South Carolina*, 383 U.S. at 314 n.19 (citing United States v. Mississippi, 220 F. Supp. 925, 996–97 (S.D. Miss. 1964) (Brown, J., dissenting)).

[67] *Id.* at 312.

[68] *Id.* at 311, 313.

[69] 17 U.S. (4 Wheat.) 316 (1819) (discussed *supra* Section 1.B); *see also South Carolina*, 383 U.S. at 326.

[70] *Id.* at 324, 327–28.

[71] *Id.* at 323, 329.

observing that this jurisdiction-specific feature of the VRA cut in favor of, rather than against, its constitutionality. More specifically, Congress's power to enact "appropriate" legislation under its enforcement powers fit hand-in-glove with the decision to "confine[ ] these remedies to a small number of States and political subdivisions" which were "familiar to Congress" as known violators of section 1 rights.[72] With regard to the preclearance requirement, South Carolina complained that subjecting each and every proposed state and local voting-law change to federal Justice Department review flouted basic principles of constitutional federalism.[73] The Court responded by emphasizing Congress's finding, based on "reliable evidence," that "case-by-case litigation was inadequate to combat widespread and persistent discrimination in voting."[74] In these circumstances, the Chief Justice declared, it was an "appropriate means of combatting the evil" for Congress to "shift the advantage of time and inertia from the perpetrators of the evil to its victims."[75]

Finally, with regard to the literacy test ban, South Carolina pointed to the Court's earlier and unanimous ruling in *Lassiter v. Northampton County Board of Elections*,[76] in which the Court had upheld a set of literacy tests against direct constitutional attack.[77] Chief Justice Warren, however, viewed *Lassiter* as cutting against South Carolina's position. In that very case, he explained, the Court had qualified its holding by declaring that "[o]f course a literacy test, fair on its face, may be employed to perpetuate that discrimination which the Fifteenth Amendment was designed to uproot."[78] Moreover, as it framed the 1965 act, Congress had specifically determined that within the covered jurisdictions, literacy tests had been widely "instituted with the purpose of disenfranchising" Black voters.[79]

In 1970, Congress amended the Voting Rights Act to prohibit literacy tests not only in covered jurisdictions but nationwide.[80] Responding to a challenge to this reform in *Oregon v. Mitchell*,[81] the Court unanimously upheld it as a proper exercise of Congress's

---

72 *Id.* at 328.

73 *See also id.* at 358–60 (Black, J., concurring and dissenting) (voicing similar concerns).

74 *Id.* at 328–29 (majority opinion).

75 *Id.* at 328.

76 360 U.S. 45 (1959).

77 *Id.* at 51–53.

78 *South Carolina*, 383 U.S. at 333 (quoting *Lassiter*, 360 U.S. at 53).

79 *Id.*

80 Voting Rights Act, Amendments of 1970 § 201(a), 52 U.S.C. § 10501(a).

81 400 U.S. 112 (1970).

enforcement powers.[82] Even Justice Harlan, who by then was the member of the Court who took the narrowest view of these powers, found that this "remedial" legislation did not reach too far. As he explained:

> Despite the lack of evidence of specific instances of discriminatory application or effect, Congress could have determined that racial prejudice is prevalent throughout the Nation, and that literacy tests unduly lend themselves to discriminatory application, either conscious or unconscious. This danger of violation of § 1 of the Fifteenth Amendment was sufficient to authorize the exercise of congressional power under § 2.[83]

2. *Katzenbach v. Morgan* and the One-Way-Ratchet Theory

Three months after handing down its decision in *South Carolina v. Katzenbach*, the Court again dealt with the Voting Rights Act in an opinion destined to stir intense debate about the nature of the enforcement powers. *Katzenbach v. Morgan*[84] concerned a portion of section 4(e) of the VRA, which generally prohibited states from enforcing language-based restrictions against otherwise eligible voters who had advanced through sixth grade in a U.S.-based school whose primary language of instruction was not English.[85] (The law was primarily aimed at addressing the disenfranchisement of Puerto Rican-born voters in New York City.) Again, the Court, in an opinion by Justice Brennan, rejected the argument that Congress could override state legislation "only . . . if the judicial branch determines that the state law is prohibited" by section 1—in this instance, section 1 of the Fourteenth Amendment (rather than the Fifteenth Amendment) because the statute did not specifically target race-based discrimination.[86] "Neither the language nor history of § 5" of the Fourteenth Amendment, the majority emphasized, supported giving Congress only such an "insignificant role."[87]

This reaffirmation of basic enforcement-power principles created an opening for the Justices to uphold section 4(e) of the VRA.

---

[82] *Id.* at 118, 131–34 (opinion of Black, J.). The case presented multiple issues, which in turn generated a checkerboard of opinions among the Justices. On the question of Congress's authority to outlaw literacy tests, however, the Justices were unanimous. *Id.* (noting, with respect to the conclusion that the literacy-test prohibition was valid, that "all of my Brethren join me in this judgment").

[83] *Id.* at 216 (Harlan, J., concurring in the judgment) (internal footnote omitted).

[84] 384 U.S. 641 (1966).

[85] *Id.* at 643.

[86] *Id.* at 648.

[87] *Id.* at 648–49.

And uphold it they did, in an opinion that endorsed two distinct theories of the section 5 enforcement power. First, building on the *South Carolina* case, Justice Brennan reasoned that section 4(e) furnished a remedy for past and ongoing unconstitutional discrimination suffered by the "Puerto Rican community residing in New York" in connection with the state's provision of schooling, housing, law-enforcement, and other public services.[88] In particular, as Justice Brennan explained,"[i]t was for Congress, as the branch that made this judgment, to assess and weigh the various conflicting considerations," including "the risk or pervasiveness of the discrimination in governmental services, the effectiveness of eliminating the state restriction on the right to vote as a means of dealing with the evil, the adequacy or availability of alternative remedies, and the nature and significance of [any countervailing] state interests."[89] Again citing *McCulloch*, Justice Brennan found it necessary only "to perceive a basis upon which the Congress might resolve the conflict as it did."[90] And applying this standard, he had no difficulty upholding the VRA's expansion of voting rights for non-English-speakers who had come to the mainland from Puerto Rico as a permissible means of remediating equal-protection violations against them. Indeed, he declared that doing otherwise "would require us to be blind to the realities familiar to the legislators."[91]

In a separate paragraph, however, Justice Brennan endorsed an alternative basis for validating Congress's challenged exercise of the enforcement power—a basis that reached beyond the violated-rights remediation theory launched in the *South Carolina* case.[92] According to this line of analysis, Congress could—regardless of what courts themselves might have said about the scope of section 1 protections—make its own independent "judgment that the application of New York's English literacy requirement to deny the right to vote [to persons covered by the statute] constituted an invidious discrimination in violation of the Equal Protection Clause."[93] In other words, Congress itself could deploy constitutional means-ends analysis in a court-like manner to identify state laws it found to be problematic under section 1. More specifically, it could do so even if the record revealed no pattern of past state violations of section 1 as

---

88 *See id.* at 652.

89 *Id.* at 653.

90 *Id.*; *see also id.* at 651 (reaffirming that "the *McCulloch v. Maryland* standard is the measure of what constitutes 'appropriate legislation' under § 5 of the Fourteenth Amendment").

91 *Id.* at 653.

92 *Id.* at 654–56.

93 *Id.* at 656.

interpreted by the courts.[94] That is, Congress could rely on its own independent assessment of constitutionally relevant considerations to enact legislation premised on the conclusion that the states' posited interests (here, in ensuring informed voting and incentivizing the study of English) did not "weigh" enough to override the "precious and fundamental" right to vote.[95]

In dissent, Justice Harlan, joined by Justice Stewart, assailed this aspect of the majority's reasoning. The Court, he explained, "reads § 5 of the Fourteenth Amendment as giving Congress the power to define the *substantive* scope of the Amendment."[96] This view of things, however, involved "the sacrifice of fundamentals in the American constitutional system," particularly "the separation between the legislative and judicial function."[97] Especially alarming to Justice Harlan was what he saw as a logical corollary to the majority's rationale. Given Congress's ability to define the scope of section 1 rights, he explained, "I do not see why Congress should not be able as well to exercise its § 5 'discretion' by enacting statutes so as in effect to dilute equal protection and due process decisions of this Court."[98]

In responding to this critique, Justice Brennan did not question Justice Harlan's understanding of the Court's alternative theory—namely, that section 5 supports judicial validation of "a legislative announcement that Congress believes a state law to entail an unconstitutional deprivation of equal protection" based on its own balancing of the protected right and countervailing state interests.[99] Justice Brennan, however, did directly repudiate the dissenters' claim that the majority's analysis opened the door to future congressional restrictions of Fourteenth Amendment rights. As he explained in footnote 10 of his opinion:

> Contrary to the suggestion of the dissent, § 5 does not grant Congress power to exercise discretion in the other direction and to enact "statutes so as in effect to dilute equal protection and due process decisions of this Court." We emphasize that Congress' power under § 5 is limited to

---

94 *Id.* at 654.

95 *Id.* at 653–54.

96 *Id.* at 668 (Harlan, J., dissenting).

97 *Id.* at 659.

98 *Id.* at 668. As to the Court's "alternative argument" that section 4(e) was properly tailored to remediate various forms of "unconstitutional discrimination," as defined by the courts under section 1, Justice Harlan reasoned that there was "no legislative record supporting § 4(e)." This fact rendered *South Carolina* readily distinguishable for him because, in connection with the VRA provisions challenged in that case, "such legislative findings were made." *Id.* at 668–69.

99 *Id.* at 669.

adopting measures to enforce the guarantees of the Amendment; § 5 grants Congress no power to restrict, abrogate, or dilute these guarantees.[100]

This exegesis touched off an avalanche of scholarly commentary.[101] The idea that footnote 10 laid out became known as the "one-way ratchet theory,"[102] and appropriately so because it authorized the elevating, but not the lowering, of judicially recognized protections embedded in the section 1 texts of the Fourteenth and Fifteenth Amendments. In post-*Morgan* cases, some later-appointed Justices echoed Justice Harlan's claim that the enforcement powers, if properly interpreted, supported only rights *remediation* and not rights *expansion*.[103] Meanwhile, both academics and politicians debated the theory's implications. Could Congress, for example, "ratchet up" the rights of the unborn by declaring them to be "persons" for purposes of the Fourteenth Amendment, thus affording them constitutional protections that would override judicially recognized abortion-related rights?[104] Or might Congress "ratchet up" the free-exercise rights of public school students by requiring states to allow them to pray in groups in classrooms, despite earlier rulings that such rituals run of afoul of the ban on

---

[100] *Id.* at 651 n.10 (majority opinion) (internal citations omitted).

[101] *See, e.g.*, Jeffery L. Yablon, *Congressional Power Under Section Five of the Fourteenth Amendment*, 25 STAN. L. REV. 885, 894 (1973) (describing Justice Brennan's' analysis as suggesting that "the section five powers of Congress operate like a ratchet," so that, "once the Court has found that an enactment or practice is violative of the fourteenth amendment, Congress is powerless to turn the wheel backwards"); William Cohen, *Congressional Power to Interpret Due Process and Equal Protection*, 27 STAN. L. REV. 603, 606–07 (1975) (noting that Justice Brennan's theory would not only broaden but also limit Congress's power to interpret the Fourteenth Amendment, while also offering criticisms of the theory).

[102] *See, e.g.*, J. Edmond Nathanson, *Congressional Power To Contradict the Supreme Court's Constitutional Decisions: Accommodation of Rights in Conflict*, 27 WM. & MARY L. REV. 331, 332 (1986) (internal quotations omitted).

[103] *See* City of Rome v. United States, 446 U.S. 156, 200 (1980) (Powell, J., dissenting) (citing *Morgan*, 384 U.S. at 667 (Harlan, J., dissenting), in support of the proposition that, "[u]nder § 2 of the Fifteenth Amendment, Congress may impose such constitutional deprivations only if it is acting to remedy violations of voting rights"); *cf. Mitchell*, 400 U.S. at 296 (Stewart, J., concurring in part and dissenting in part) (noting earlier agreement with Justice Harlan that the Equal Protection Clause does not grant Congress the power to "determine as a matter of substantive constitutional law what situations fall within the ambit of the clause" (citing *Morgan*, 384 U.S. at 667 (Harlan, J., dissenting))). *See generally* James Leonard, *A Damaged Remedy: Disability Discrimination Claims Against State Entities Under the Americans with Disabilities Act After* Seminole Tribe *and* Flores, 41 ARIZ. L. REV. 651, 677 n.232 (1999) (observing, among other things, that Justice Harlan "believed that an expansive view of congressional power under section 5 contradicted the normal process for amending the Constitution").

[104] *See Roe*, 410 U.S. at 153 (holding that the right to privacy is "broad enough to encompass a woman's decision whether or not to terminate her pregnancy").

state "establishment" of religion?[105] Almost all analysts agreed that the answer to these questions was "no," on the theory that Congress could not use its power to "ratchet up" constitutional protections in a manner that simultaneously operated to "ratchet down" section 1 rights already recognized by the Court.[106] But what would happen if Congress passed a law that expanded some Fourteenth Amendment rights without taking any others away? A much-changed Court would confront just such an enactment in *City of Boerne v. Flores*.[107]

3. *City of Boerne* and the "Congruence and Proportionality" Test

City of Boerne put before the Court the constitutionality of the Religious Freedom Restoration Act (RFRA), which Congress had enacted in the wake of the Court's landmark Free Exercise Clause ruling in *Employment Division v. Smith*.[108] Pre-*Smith* case law supported the view that a generally applicable statute (such as a general prohibition on all peyote use) could be challenged as applied to religious practitioners (such as members of a faith community that required sacramental use of peyote). Indeed, that earlier case law indicated that such a constitutional attack should succeed unless the state could show that the challenged application of the statute was supported by a "compelling state interest."[109] In *Smith*, however, the Court moved sharply away from this line of First Amendment

---

[105] *See* Engel v. Vitale, 370 U.S. 421, 424 (1962) (holding that school-sponsored prayer is "a practice wholly inconsistent with the Establishment Clause").

[106] *See* Christopher L. Eisgruber & Lawrence G. Sager, *Why the Religious Freedom Restoration Act Is Unconstitutional*, 69 N.Y.U. L. REV. 437, 441 (1994) ("Congress can no more overturn Supreme Court decisions defining the scope of religious freedom than it can those addressing the questions of flag-burning, school prayer, abortion, or school desegregation."); Samuel Estreicher & Margaret H. Lemos, *The Section 5 Mystique,* Morrison, *and the Future of Federal Antidiscrimination Law*, 2000 SUP. CT. REV. 109, 123 n.61 (explaining that "[t]he problem with the Human Life Bill was . . . that it explicitly authorized unconstitutional state action and shielded such action from judicial review" (citing Samuel Estreicher, *Congressional Power and Constitutional Rights: Reflections on Proposed "Human Life" Legislation*, 68 VA. L. REV. 333 (1982))); *see also Lane*, 541 U.S. at 564 (Scalia, J., dissenting) (noting, in discussing the enforcement power, that "I would not, of course, permit any congressional measures that violate other provisions of the Constitution"). Another separate reason for finding a want of congressional authority—at least in the persons-include-the-unborn hypothetical statute—focuses on the idea that such a statute does not involve an independent weighing of asserted state interests to expand a previously recognized right; instead, it involves giving an entirely new definition to a constitutional term of art (here the term "person"), as already defined by the Court, so as to displace a previously recognized right. *See Roe*, 410 U.S. at 158 ("[T]he word 'person,' as used in the Fourteenth Amendment, does not include the unborn.").

[107] 521 U.S. 507 (1997).

[108] 494 U.S. 872 (1990).

[109] Sherbert v. Verner, 374 U.S. 398, 403 (1963) (quoting NAACP v. Button, 371 U.S. 415, 438 (1963), in indicating that an "incidental burden on . . . free exercise" had to "be justified by a 'compelling state interest' "); *accord* Thomas v. Review Bd., 450 U.S. 707, 718 (1981).

authority. It held instead that, as a rule, the generally applicable character of a law would itself foreclose any free-exercise challenge to that law unless the challenger could show a hidden legislative design to target religious believers and their practices.[110] Thus, for example, the generally applicable character of an across-the-board prohibition on peyote use immunized it from a free-exercise challenge by even the most devout participant in a sacramental ingestion of that substance. And this was true no matter what a court might conclude about the lack of a need to apply the law across the board or the severity of the burden the law imposed on sincere religious practitioners.[111]

This ruling was unpopular, and pressure mounted on Congress to restore the as-applied protection of religious liberties that operated under pre-*Smith* free-exercise law. The result was that both Houses of Congress voted by overwhelming margins to enact RFRA, which restored by way of statutory command the pre-*Smith* constitutional regime.[112] In taking this step, Congress relied on the Fourteenth Amendment enforcement power insofar as it directed that act's strictures at state (as opposed to federal) action.[113] Congress's reliance on section 5 was premised on the well-settled proposition that section 1 made First Amendment free-exercise protections fully applicable to the states. But it also implicated Justice Brennan's not-so-well-settled assertion in *Morgan* that section 5 of the Fourteenth Amendment allowed federal lawmakers to ratchet up protections established by section 1 of that amendment.

The Court in *City of Boerne* was called on to assess the continuing efficacy of *Morgan*, and—in a watershed treatment of the

---

[110] *Smith*, 494 U.S. at 894. In an opinion penned by Justice Scalia, the Court offered an elaborate text-based and policy-based rationale in support of this result. *See id.* at 878, 885–86.

[111] Indeed, *Smith* itself involved just such a peyote law as challenged by just such a group of religious practitioners. *Id.* at 874. And in keeping with the principle articulated in the case, the Court upheld the law without engaging in any balancing of any kind. *See id.* at 890.

[112] A unanimous U.S. House of Representatives and a nearly unanimous (97–3) U.S. Senate passed the bill in 1993. *H.R. 1308—Religious Freedom Restoration Act of 1993*, CONGRESS.GOV, https://www.congress.gov/bill/103rd-congress/house-bill/1308/actions (last updated Nov. 16, 1993); *see also* Religious Freedom Restoration Act § 2, 42 U.S.C. § 2000bb (stating that the purpose of the Act was to "restore the compelling interest test" and "to guarantee its application in all cases where free exercise of religion is substantially burdened").

[113] To the extent the act applied to federal programs, the Fourteenth Amendment enforcement power—which concerns *state* behavior—was not relevant. Instead, Congress relied on the same powers that supported the enactment of any law as to which RFRA provided an exception as the proper source of power for enacting and thus applying RFRA itself. *See, e.g.*, Burwell v. Hobby Lobby Stores, 573 U.S. 682, 694 (2014) (holding that "[a]s applied to a federal agency, RFRA is based on the enumerated power that supports the particular agency's work").

enforcement powers—it definitively rejected Justice Brennan's one-way ratchet theory. Writing for himself and five other members of the Court, Justice Kennedy emphatically declared that "[t]he design of the Amendment and the text of § 5 are inconsistent with the suggestion that Congress has the power to decree the substance of the Fourteenth Amendment's restrictions on the States."[114] The core of the Court's reasoning on this point was simple: "Congress does not enforce a constitutional right by changing what the right is."[115] In addition, Justice Kennedy made the case that "[t]he Fourteenth Amendment's history confirms the remedial, rather than substantive, nature of the Enforcement Clause."[116] To be sure, *Morgan* "could be interpreted" as endorsing Congress's access to a non-remedial, rights-expanding authority under section 5.[117] But that was "not a necessary interpretation" according to Justice Kennedy,[118] and in any event it ran afoul of two principles established by no less of a landmark precedent than *Marbury v. Madison*.[119] First, it contravened the bedrock proposition that the Constitution is "superior paramount law, unchangeable by ordinary means."[120] Second, it clashed with the notion that, when it comes to interpreting the Constitution, it is "the province of the Judicial Branch . . . to say what the law is."[121]

Having dispatched the one-way ratchet theory of *Morgan*, Justice Kennedy turned to whether RFRA was sustainable as an "exercise of Congress' remedial or preventive power" under *South Carolina v. Katzenbach*.[122] In that case, he reasoned, the Court had rightly recognized that "[l]egislation which deters or remedies constitutional violations can fall within the sweep of Congress' enforcement power even if in the process it prohibits conduct which is not itself unconstitutional."[123] In addition, he reaffirmed that the Court in *South Carolina* had acted properly in upholding the VRA's literacy-test ban and other voting-rights safeguards because those laws—though they reached beyond addressing direct constitutional violations—responded to longstanding and still-rampant patterns of abridgments of constitutional voting rights.[124] Having thus set forth

---

114 *Boerne*, 521 U.S. at 519.

115 *Id.*

116 *Id.* at 520.

117 *Id.* at 527–28.

118 *Id.* at 528.

119 5 U.S. (1 Cranch) 137 (1803); *see infra* Section 34.A (discussing this decision).

120 *Boerne*, 521 U.S. at 529 (citing *Marbury*, 5 U.S. at 177).

121 *Id.* at 536 (citing *Marbury*, 5 U.S. at 177).

122 *Id.* at 529.

123 *Id.* at 518.

124 *Id.* at 525–26.

the key principles of enforcement-power doctrine, Justice Kennedy turned to the question whether RFRA was sustainable under now-governing, post-*Morgan* section 5 law.[125]

In a second watershed ruling, Justice Kennedy declared that RFRA did not pass muster because it "reflects a lack of proportionality or congruence between the means adopted and the legitimate end to be achieved"—that is, the "end" of responding to real-world violations of the Constitution as interpreted by the courts.[126] The problem was that Congress's imposition of RFRA's "stringent test" of legality reached "far" beyond providing a defensible response to "any pattern or practice of unconstitutional conduct under the Free Exercise Clause as interpreted in *Smith*."[127] Under *Smith*, after all, laws subject to invalidation under free-exercise principles included only those measures that "had the object of stifling or punishing free exercise."[128] In enacting RFRA, however, Congress had gathered no evidence indicating that generally applicable laws (such as across-the-board bans on peyote use) were commonly enacted pursuant to surreptitious plans to saddle religious practitioners with discriminatory burdens.

Adding to the case for a finding of remedial overkill was RFRA's "[s]weeping coverage," which rendered it applicable to "every level of government, displacing laws and prohibiting official actions of almost every description and regardless of subject matter."[129] Of particular significance, this every-state-or-local-action-you-can-think-of feature of the challenged law rendered it distinguishable from statutes validated in the Court's earlier enforcement-power cases. As Justice Kennedy explained, whereas the VRA requirements upheld in *South Carolina* had been "confined to those regions of the country where voting discrimination had been most flagrant, and affected a discrete class of state laws, i.e., state voting laws," and whereas the literacy-test-related prohibitions upheld in *Morgan* and *Mitchell* had "attacked a particular type of voting qualification," RFRA was a measure that "pervasively prohibits constitutional state action in an effort to remedy or to prevent unconstitutional state action."[130] Justice Kennedy disclaimed any suggestion that "§ 5 legislation requires termination dates, geographic restrictions or egregious

---

[125] *Id.* at 529.

[126] *Id.* at 533. Notably, the Court did not rely on the more deferential, *McCulloch*-derived standard that it had embraced in *South Carolina* and other earlier enforcement-power cases. *See supra* Sections 11.B.1 & 11.B.2.

[127] *Boerne*, 521 U.S. at 533–34.

[128] *Id.* at 534.

[129] *Id.* at 532.

[130] *Id.* at 532–33 (internal citations omitted).

predicates."[131] But he nonetheless insisted that a proper constitutional assessment of a law like RFRA required the Court "to ensure Congress' means are proportionate to ends legitimate under § 5."[132]

4. Post-*City of Boerne* Applications of the "Congruence and Proportionality" Test

In the wake of *City of Boerne*, the Court has applied the congruence-and-proportionality test across a broad range of cases that fall into three main categories. The first involves congressional abrogations of state sovereign immunity in connection with the operation of federal anti-discrimination statutes. The second also involve abrogations of sovereign immunity, albeit in connection with statutes purporting to enforce non-equality based Due Process Clause rights.[133] The final set of cases involves (as had *South Carolina*, *Morgan*, and *Mitchell*) the imposition on states of substantive duties—without regard to the abrogation of sovereign immunity—that reach beyond the judicially enforceable duties imposed directly by the Fourteenth and Fifteenth Amendments.[134] Following the lead of *City of Boerne*, the Court has applied the "congruence and proportionality" test across all three types of cases.[135]

---

[131] *Id.*

[132] *Id.*

[133] Beginning in 1996, the Court made clear that federal lawmakers lack the authority to abrogate state sovereign immunity while exercising the powers granted by the Commerce Clause. *See supra* Section 5.C (discussing the establishment and building out of this principle).

[134] Notably, Congress enacted a law of this ilk, the Religious Land Use and Institutionalized Persons Act (RLUIPA), 42 U.S.C. §§ 2000cc, in response to the Court's invalidation of RFRA in *Boerne*. *See* Cutter v. Wilkinson, 544 U.S. 709, 715 (2005). Moving sharply away from the earlier statute's targeting of all state and local laws, RLUIPA directed RFRA's compelling-state-interest approach at "only . . . regulations regarding land use and prison conditions." Guru Nanak Sikh Soc. of Yuba City v. Cty. of Sutter, 456 F.3d 978, 986 (9th Cir. 2006). In ensuing litigation, circuit courts distinguished *City of Boerne* in finding the statute to be a congruent and proportional exercise of the section 5 power. *See Guru Nanak Sikh Soc.*, 456 F.3d at 994–95 ("RLUIPA is a congruent and proportional response to free exercise violations because it targets only regulations that are susceptible, and have been shown, to violate individuals' religious exercise."); Midrash Sephardi, Inc. v. Town of Surfside, 366 F.3d 1214, 1239 (11th Cir. 2004) (holding RLUIPA to qualify as an appropriate use of section 5 authority because "Congress's findings regarding the widespread discrimination against religious institutions are plausible and provide a basis for concluding that RLUIPA remedies and prevents discriminatory land use regulations").

[135] The Court has not yet applied the "congruence and proportionality" test in a Fifteenth Amendment enforcement power case. *See* Shelby County v. Holder, 570 U.S. 529 (2013) (holding that the VRA's coverage formula—an exercise of the Fifteenth Amendment enforcement power—violated the "equal sovereignty" of the states, without mentioning the congruence-and-proportionality standard); *see also* Nw. Austin Mun. Util. Dist. No. One v. Mukasey, 557 U.S. 193, 204 (2009) [hereinafter *NAMUDNO*] (noting that "we need not resolve" questions concerning *City of Boerne*'s

a. Abrogating Sovereign Immunity to Support Anti-Discrimination Rights

As we have seen, in *Fitzpatrick v. Bitzer*, the Court had no difficulty upholding an award of monetary damages imposed on a state for violating Title VII of the Civil Rights Act of 1964, at least insofar as the protections provided by that act mirrored the protections afforded by the Equal Protection Clause.[136] In other words, the statute's establishment of a monetary remedy for state sex discrimination that violated section 1 of the Fourteenth Amendment was plainly "congruent and proportional" to the remediation of conduct that the Amendment made unlawful. *Fitzpatrick*, however, did not address how far Congress might go in using its Fourteenth Amendment section 5 authority to abrogate state sovereign immunity in other contexts, including under anti-discrimination laws that reached beyond "suspect" or "quasi-suspect" classifications such as race, ethnicity, and sex. Questions of this kind were temporarily rendered beside the point by a fractured Court's post-*Fitzpatrick* endorsement of the idea that Congress possessed broad authority to negate state sovereign immunity through the exercise of its commerce power.[137] This ruling was of great consequence because,

---

applicability to a Fifteenth Amendment enforcement power case because the challenged law "raise[d] serious constitutional questions" regardless of the test applied). In light of that fact, some commentators have suggested that the more deferential means-ends test of *South Carolina v. Katzenbach* continues to define the scope of Congress's power under section 2. *See, e.g.*, Crum, *supra* note 50, at 1568 (asserting that "[t]he Court has never applied [the congruence-and-proportionality standard] in a case involving the Fifteenth Amendment—or any case involving race or voting rights—and thus the deferential rationality standard for Congress's Fifteenth Amendment enforcement authority remains good law"); *see also* Caminker, *supra* note 25, at 1190–91 (noting that "Section 2 [of the Fifteenth Amendment] could not possibly give rise to a legitimate fear that, if construed to require only *McCulloch*-style means-ends tailoring, it would functionally award Congress a virtually plenary police power," while at the same time noting that "*Boerne* strongly suggests that Section 2 measures . . . are subject to stringent congruence and proportionality analysis"). Application of a more lenient standard, or at least a deferential version of the congruence-and-proportionality test, in Fifteenth Amendment cases could find justification in that Amendment's highly focused targeting of race discrimination in voting, as well as the textualist pull toward giving the Enforcement Clause of the Fifteenth Amendment a reading that is not duplicative of the Enforcement Clause of the Fourteenth Amendment. On the other hand, the Court in *City of Boerne* did not in any way indicate that such a doctrinal distinction exists and, indeed (as we have seen), wove into its discussion of the operation of the congruence-and-proportionality test in the Fourteenth Amendment context a detailed treatment of the Court's Fifteenth Amendment ruling in *South Carolina*. *See also* Bd. of Trustees of Univ. of Ala. v. Garrett, 531 U.S. 356, 373–74 & n.8 (2001) (invoking *South Carolina*, a Fifteenth Amendment enforcement power case, in the course of a discussing the Fourteenth Amendment enforcement power, while also noting that "Section 2 of the Fifteenth Amendment is virtually identical to § 5 of the Fourteenth Amendment").

[136] *See supra* Section 12.A.

[137] *See* Pennsylvania v. Union Gas Co., 491 U.S. 1 (1989); *see also supra* Section 5.C.2.

in reliance on the principle that it endorsed, Congress had over time made monetary-damage remedies recoverable from both private and public entities in connection with a variety of different statutory rights, including rights against employment discrimination based on age and disability status.[138] Just one year prior to its ruling in *City of Boerne*, however, the Court in *Seminole Tribe v. Florida*[139] abandoned this earlier view of the commerce power, squarely holding that Congress could not invoke that power to authorize the recovery of money damages from state defendants.[140] As a result, new issues under the Enforcement Clauses of the Fourteenth and Fifteenth Amendments leapt into view because, as a practical matter, those clauses now offered the only hope for defending monetary remedies imposed on states pursuant to federal anti-discrimination laws.

The Court's first encounter with this set of issues came in *Board of Trustees v. Garrett*.[141] That case raised the question whether Congress had unconstitutionally authorized damage awards against state defendants for violating the portion of the Americans with Disabilities Act (ADA)[142] that requires employers, including state employers, to provide reasonable accommodations to employees who have medical disabilities.[143] The Court in *Garrett* did not question Congress's ability to rely on the Commerce Clause to impose this duty of non-discrimination on both private and public employers. Nor was there any doubt that Congress could, as it did, saddle private-employer violators of the statute with money-damages liability. *Seminole Tribe*, however precluded the ADA's exposure of *state* defendants to monetary claims based on the commerce power. The result was that courts could entertain such money-damages claims only if their establishment was alternatively supported by section 5 of the Fourteenth Amendment.[144]

Applying the principles of *City of Boerne*, five Justices agreed that subjecting states to damages claims for employment-related ADA violations was not "congruent and proportional" to the goal of remediating abridgments of constitutionally imposed (as opposed to merely statutorily imposed) anti-discrimination duties regarding persons with disabilities.[145] The essential difficulty was that the

---

138 *See, e.g.*, Age Discrimination in Employment Act of 1967, 29 U.S.C. §§ 621–634; Americans with Disabilities Act of 1990, 42 U.S.C. §§ 12101–12213; Rehabilitation Act of 1973, 29 U.S.C. §§ 701–796.

139 517 U.S. 44, 47 (1996).

140 *See supra* Section 5.C.2.

141 531 U.S. 356 (2001).

142 *Id.* at 362–63.

143 *Id.* at 360–61.

144 *See supra* Section 5.C.2.

145 *Garrett*, 531 U.S. at 374.

Court had previously construed the Equal Protection Clause to permit discrimination against such persons only in exceptional circumstances, and in particular it had never suggested that the clause imposed on the states a generalized constitutional duty to afford "reasonable accommodations" of the sort mandated by the ADA.[146] To be sure, the Court had held that section 1 of the Fourteenth Amendment barred irrational discrimination against persons with disabilities (just as it bars irrational discrimination against anyone), and it was therefore possible, at least in theory, that the ADA remediated some forms of unconstitutional state discrimination.[147] According to the Court, however, the legislative record failed to support a finding that irrational discrimination of this sort was widespread.[148] Thus, the Court concluded, Congress lacked the constitutional authority to establish the ADA's employee-protecting abrogation of sovereign immunity based on the need to rectify genuinely *unconstitutional* activity.[149]

In later cases involving other anti-discrimination laws, the Court has taken the same approach. Most notably, in *Kimel v. Florida Board of Regents*,[150] the Court invalidated Congress's abrogation of state sovereign immunity for claims brought under the Age Discrimination in Employment Act (ADEA).[151] As in *Garrett*, the Court emphasized that age does not constitute a suspect or quasi-suspect classification for Fourteenth Amendment equal-protection purposes—a doctrinal proposition that greatly complicates efforts to establish the sort of recurring unconstitutional discrimination against members of this group that would support enforcement-power-based constitutional remediation.[152] Nor, according to the Court, had Congress come even close to filling the fact-finding gap by documenting a "pattern" of irrationally discriminatory treatment of elderly employees by the states.[153]

---

146 *Id.* at 367–68 (citing Cleburne v. Cleburne Living Center, Inc., 473 U.S. 432, 448 (1985)).

147 *Id.* at 367.

148 *Id.* at 368.

149 *Id.* at 373–74. Joined by three other Justices in the dissent, Justice Breyer argued that Congress had supplied a sufficient evidentiary record—centered on widespread, nationwide discrimination against individuals with disabilities—to support application of the ADA to the states, including in its abrogation of otherwise operative sovereign-immunity rules. *Id.* at 377–78 (Breyer, J., dissenting). Among other things, Justice Breyer emphasized the appropriateness of deferring to congressional judgments of this kind and expressed concern that the majority's approach to the case "saps § 5 of independent force." *Id.* at 388–89.

150 528 U.S. 62 (2000).

151 *Id.* at 66.

152 *Id.* at 83.

153 *See id.* at 89 (emphasizing that "Congress never identified any pattern of age discrimination by the States, much less any discrimination whatsoever that rose to

In contrast to its decisions in *Garrett* and *Kimel*, the Court in *Nevada Department of Human Resources v. Hibbs*[154] upheld the abrogation of state sovereign immunity implemented by the Family and Medical Leave Act of 1993 (FMLA). That law addresses the widespread difficulties confronted by family caregivers by requiring employers to excuse employees from otherwise-operative job duties for reasons related to the "serious health condition" of a spouse, child, or parent.[155] *Hibbs*, Chief Justice Rehnquist explained for a six-Justice majority, differed from *Garrett* and *Kimel* because it involved legislation aimed at discriminatory practices rooted in outmoded gender-role stereotypes, thus implicating a sex-based classification that triggers heightened protections under judicially established equal-protection doctrine.[156] To be sure, this law went beyond affording relief only for sure-enough violations of the Equal Protection Clause itself. But Congress's imposition of a remedial prophylaxis was permissible because the record showed that implementing this law, including insofar as it abrogated state sovereign immunity, was "congruent and proportional" to addressing workplace practices, including among public employers, rooted in impermissible stereotypes about the proper role of women as caregivers in the home.[157]

In *Coleman v. Court of Appeals*,[158] the Court found that the enforcement power did not support an abrogation of sovereign immunity effectuated by another provision of the FMLA, which authorizes up to twelve work weeks of unpaid leave for employees who themselves have encountered significant medical problems.[159] Four dissenters, in an opinion penned by Justice Ginsburg, argued that unconstitutional state-employer discrimination against women with medical challenges, especially as a result of pregnancy and maternity, "were hardly isolated incidents."[160] Justice Ginsburg also reasoned that a remedy that treated men and women equally, as opposed to singling out women for targeted relief, fit together best with the Congress's proper effort to lay "the foundation for a more egalitarian relationship at home and at work."[161] In the key opinion

---

the level of constitutional violation"). Writing for himself and three other members of the Court in dissent, Justice Stevens challenged the *Seminole Tribe* limit on the commerce power and thus did not address the proper operation of section 5 in this setting. *Id.* at 93 (Stevens, J., dissenting in part and concurring in part).

154 538 U.S. 721 (2003).

155 *Id.* at 724 (quoting 29 U.S.C. § 2612(a)(1)(C)).

156 *Id.* at 736–37.

157 *Id.*

158 566 U.S. 30 (2012).

159 *Id.* at 34.

160 *Id.* at 52 (Ginsburg, J., dissenting).

161 *Id.* at 65.

in the case, however, Justice Kennedy could discover neither a sex-based "pattern of state constitutional violations" to which the law responded nor "a remedy drawn in narrow terms to address" any problem of unconstitutional discrimination in affording sick-leave to state workers.[162]

b. Abrogating Sovereign Immunity to Support Due-Process Rights

As noted in the first sentence of this chapter, section 1 of the Fourteenth Amendment does not include only an Equal Protection Clause. It also declares that a state may not "deprive any person of life, liberty, or property, without due process of law."[163] While the Court's post-*City of Boerne* rulings in *Garrett, Kimel, Hibbs*, and *Coleman* explored the interaction of section 5 and the Equal Protection Clause, the Court also has considered the extent to which Congress can use section 5 to enforce section 1's due-process-based protections.[164] In particular, three post-*City of Boerne* cases—all involving due-process based protections of property rights—raised issues of this sort. In the first two cases, each brought by a plaintiff who claimed that Florida had unlawfully marketed a college-finance certificate scheme, the Court struck down federal statutes that abrogated state sovereign immunity for trademark and patent violations. In the third case, the Court struck down a statute that abrogated sovereign immunity for copyright infringements committed by the states.

In *College Savings Bank v. Florida Prepaid Postsecondary Education Expense Board* (*College Savings Bank*),[165] the plaintiff sought money damages from Florida based on the state's alleged violation of the Lanham Act's ban on "false representations in commerce."[166] The majority, however, rebuffed this attempt, making short work of the plaintiff's due-process-based defense of Congress's

---

[162] *Id.* at 37 (opinion of Kennedy, J.). Justice Kennedy wrote for four Justices. This group included Chief Justice Roberts, Justice Thomas, and Justice Alito, who had earlier replaced Justice O'Connor, a member of the five-Justice majority in *Hibbs*. Justice Scalia wrote separately to reemphasize his decision not to uphold duty-expanding enforcement-power legislation outside the race-discrimination context. *Id.* at 45 (Scalia, J., concurring in the judgment) ("As I have explained in greater detail elsewhere, outside of the context of racial discrimination (which is different for *stare decisis* reasons), I would limit Congress's § 5 power to the regulation of conduct that *itself* violates the Fourteenth Amendment." (citing *Lane*, 541 U.S. at 558–60) (emphasis in original)).

[163] U.S. CONST. amend. XIV, § 1.

[164] Indeed, *City of Boerne* itself involved a decision of this sort insofar as section 1's Due Process Clause makes applicable to the states the protections of religious freedom afforded by the First Amendment. *City of Boerne*, 521 U.S. at 519.

[165] 527 U.S. 666 (1999).

[166] *Id.* at 670.

abrogation of sovereign immunity for Lanham Act suits. The problem, Justice Scalia explained, was that any false representations made by the defendant, even if economically damaging to the plaintiff, had nothing to do with any "deprivation" of "property" for due-process purposes.[167] To be sure, a competitor's misstatements might hurt the overall value of a competitor's business. But for a constitutional deprivation of property to occur, there had to be a particular "business asset" that the state had "impinged upon."[168] As a result, the Lanham Act's false-representation provisions could not have been enacted pursuant to Congress's power to enforce the Fourteenth Amendment.[169] And because those provisions lacked any connection to property deprivations, there was no underlying set of constitutional violations to which to apply the congruence and proportionality test.[170]

The second case, *Florida Prepaid Postsecondary Education Expense Board v. College Savings Bank* (*Florida Prepaid*),[171] arose out of the same plaintiff's companion claim that state agents had infringed the patent it had secured for the financing methodology that undergirded its commercially-marketed college-savings prepayment plan.[172] In the Patent and Plant Variety Protection Remedy Clarification Act, Congress had authorized precisely this type of civil action against state defendants by expressly abrogating their immunity from money-damage claims based on patent infringement.[173] Again, however, the Court concluded that this abrogation was not sustainable under the Fourteenth Amendment enforcement power.[174] To be sure, patents did constitute "property" for Fourteenth Amendment purposes.[175] But, according to Chief Justice Rehnquist, who wrote for a five-Justice majority, to establish the requisite pattern of unconstitutional deprivations of such property, Congress had to show repeated acts of state patent infringement that were both willful and not subject to remediation

---

167 *Id.* at 674.

168 *See id.* at 675.

169 *Id.*

170 *Id.* Taking a broader view of what constitutes "property" for due-process purposes and emphasizing "the presumption of validity" of congressional enactments, Justice Stevens dissented from the Court's application of section 5. *Id.* at 692, 693 (Stevens, J., dissenting) (reasoning that "[a] State's deliberate destruction of a going business is surely a deprivation of property"). In a separate dissent, Justice Breyer (joined by Justices Stevens, Souter, and Ginsburg) defended the sovereign-immunity provision on commerce-power grounds. *See id.* at 693–705 (Breyer, J., dissenting).

171 527 U.S. 627 (1999).

172 *Id.* at 630–32.

173 Patent and Plant Variety Protection Remedy Clarification Act § 2(a), 35 U.S.C. § 296(a).

174 *Florida Prepaid*, 527 U.S. at 647–48.

175 *Id.* at 642.

under state tort and property law.[176] This was the case because already-existing case law established that (1) for a state to "deprive" someone of property for Fourteenth Amendment purposes, its action could not be merely negligent, much less entirely innocent,[177] and (2) even when willful infringements occur, states can afford "due process of law" by themselves providing an "adequate remedy" within their own legal systems for resulting deprivations of protected property interests.[178] Here, however, Congress had "identified no pattern of patent infringement by the States, let alone a pattern of constitutional violations."[179] Indeed, the relevant House Report had identified only two past lawsuits alleging patent infringement by a state, and the lower court could unearth only eight such suits brought in the past 110 years.[180] Adding to the difficulty was Congress's failure to fine-tune its response even to these supposed problems, such as by targeting only intentional state infringements, limiting abrogation to jurisdictions with a high incidence of violations, or targeting only those states shown not to have in place their own remedial processes for addressing wrongful patent-related property-taking.[181]

In the third case, *Allen v. Cooper*,[182] a company that mapped Blackbeard's sunken pirate ship off the coast of North Carolina claimed that the state had published that company's images of the

---

176 *Id.* at 642, 645.

177 *Id.* at 645.

178 *Id.* at 643.

179 *Id.* at 640.

180 *Id.* (citing H.R. REP. NO. 101–960, at 38 (1990) and Coll. Savings Bank. v. Fla. Prepaid Postsecondary Educ. Exp. Bd., 148 F.3d 1343, 1353–54 (Fed. Cir. 1998)).

181 *See, e.g.*, *id.* at 641. Justice Stevens dissented, joined by Justices Souter, Ginsburg, and Breyer. *Id.* at 648 (Stevens, J., dissenting). For him, the majority's handwringing about innocent or negligent infringement was beside the point because the plaintiff in this action had alleged willful wrongdoing. *Id.* at 653. Congress, he added, "did hear testimony about inadequate state remedies" and in any event could fairly conclude that state remedies would be inadequate for three reasons. *Id.* at 655. First, as to actions based on patent infringement itself, federal court jurisdiction had long been exclusive. *Id.* at 648–49. Second, and relatedly, state judges lacked experience in handling the sorts of questions that patent-related litigation routinely involves. *Id.* at 659. Third, and in any event, Congress could have concluded that state judges would not be free from all partiality in this set of actions, given that such actions would necessarily be brought against the state itself. *Id.* at 660. In addition, Justice Stevens rejected the assertion that *City of Boerne* somehow required a more nuanced and carefully calibrated abrogation than Congress had fashioned. *Id.* at 662–63. That case, he noted, involved an attempted exercise of section 5 authority that put a federal statutory overlay on every generally applicable rule directed at any form of conduct put in place by any state or local government anywhere in the nation. *Id.* at 661–62. In striking contrast, he reasoned, this challenged law—which reached no further than to abrogate state sovereign immunity for patent-infringement claims—took aim at only a "narrow category of cases." *Id.* at 662.

182 140 S. Ct. 994 (2020).

ship in violation of federal copyright law.[183] The case thus brought under the judicial microscope the Copyright Remedy Clarification Act of 1990 (CRCA), which specified that "a State 'shall not be immune, under the Eleventh Amendment [or] any other doctrine of sovereign immunity, from suit in Federal court' for copyright infringement."[184] Justice Kagan, writing for a seven-member majority, again insisted that "a congressional abrogation is valid under Section 5 only if it sufficiently connects to conduct courts have held Section 1 to proscribe."[185] And here, the challenged statute failed to fill the constitutional bill for the same reasons found dispositive in *Florida Prepaid*.[186] As with patents, Justice Kagan acknowledged, "[c]opyrights are a form of property."[187] But just like in *Florida Prepaid*, no meaningful record of genuinely remediable unconstitutional state conduct supported the CRCA. Indeed, Congress's pre-enactment investigation revealed that even state *statutory* violations of the copyright laws were "not widespread."[188] Even more important, the evidence of actual due-process violations—rooted in intentional infringements not remediated within the states' own legal systems—was, at best, "exceedingly slight."[189] Finally, just as in *Florida Prepaid*, Congress had not crafted a nuanced response directed at true constitutional problems; instead, once again, it had given the statute an "indiscriminate scope" by "extending [it] to every infringement case against a state."[190] In sum, there were no "material" differences between this case and *Florida Prepaid*, so that "the CRCA . . . must fail [the] 'congruence and proportionality' test."[191]

---

183 *Id.* at 999.

184 *Id.* (quoting 17 U.S.C. 511(a)).

185 *Id.* at 1004.

186 *Id.* at 1005 (noting that "*Florida Prepaid* . . . serves as the critical precedent").

187 *Id.* at 1004.

188 *Id.* at 1006 (noting the legislative record's documentation of only 12 instances of copyright infringement by states).

189 *Id.* at 1007.

190 *Id.*

191 *Id.* In a paragraph of the opinion joined by five other Justices, Justice Kagan added that the Court's ruling "need not prevent Congress from passing a valid copyright abrogation law" designed to "bring digital Blackbeards to justice" so long as such a law "link[ed] the scope of its abrogation to the redress or prevention of unconstitutional injuries—[while] creating a legislative record to back up that connection." *Id.* She also noted that Congress's failure to do so in enacting the statute struck down in the case was understandable because its enactment predated the Court's rulings in *Seminole Tribe* and *Boerne*. *Id.* Writing separately in an opinion joined by Justice Ginsburg, Justice Breyer criticized the majority's approach for failing to take proper account of the Intellectual Property Clause, which he viewed as authorizing congressional abrogation of sovereign immunity for state copyright infringements. *Id.* at 1008–09 (Breyer, J., concurring in the judgment). Nonetheless, he concurred in the judgment because he "recogniz[ed] that my longstanding view has

c. *Post-*City of Boerne *Primary-Conduct Rules:* Tennessee v. Lane

The key pre-*City of Boerne* enforcement-power cases—*South Carolina, Morgan,* and *Mitchell*—did not focus on the abrogation of state sovereign immunity. Instead, they dealt with congressional efforts to create new substantive rights (especially new voting rights) that Congress could not enact into law under the Commerce Clause or any other wellspring of Article I power.[192] Following *City of Boerne,* the Court encountered another substantive-rights-expanding use of the section 5 power in *Tennessee v. Lane.*[193] That case involved two plaintiffs who used wheelchairs for mobility and, as a result, were unable to access various Tennessee courthouses. (More specifically, one of the plaintiffs was sent to jail because he failed to appear in a second-floor courtroom after refusing to crawl or be carried up a stairway in a building without an elevator.[194]) All members of the Court seemed ready to assume that the case involved a violation of Title II of the ADA, which specifies that "no qualified individual with a disability shall, by reason of such disability, be excluded from participation in or be denied the benefits of the services, programs or activities of a public entity."[195] Notably, however, the Court in *Lane* did not assume that the Commerce Clause authorized Congress to impose this duty on the states themselves, perhaps because securing access to a state-operated courtroom might not be readily characterized as "economic activity" under the Court's commerce-power precedents.[196] The cornerstone question presented in the case

---

not carried the day, and that the Court's decision in *Florida Prepaid* controls this case." *Id.* at 1009.

192 *See supra* Sections 11.B.1–11.B.2.

193 541 U.S. 509.

194 *Id.* at 514. Another plaintiff in the case, who was "a certified court reporter, alleged that she has not been able to gain access to a number of county courthouses, and, as a result, has lost both work and an opportunity to participate in the judicial process." *Id.*

195 42 U.S.C. § 12132. In particular, this text and companion statutory provisions require implementation of "reasonable measures," including in certain circumstances the installation of elevators, to facilitate building access by individuals unable to walk. *Lane,* 541 U.S. at 531; *see also* 42 U.S.C. § 12132.

196 *Lane,* 541 U.S. at 516. *See supra* Section 4.D.1 (detailing the non-economic activity doctrine of *United States v. Lopez,* 514 U.S. at 559). Another Article I question looming over the case concerned whether, even on the assumption that the case involved an economic activity, external constraints on the commerce power would restrict Congress's ability to regulate the design of state courthouses. *See supra* Section 5.A (discussing the implications of the Court's ruling in *Coyle v. Smith,* 221 U.S. 559 (1911)). With regard to the matter of monetary remedies, it bears emphasis that the case in fact did arise out of a money-damage claim and that the majority spoke of the issue presented as involving Congress's abrogation of sovereign immunity. *Lane,* 541 U.S. at 514–15. The more fundamental question, however, was whether Congress could impose on states the substantive duty imposed by Title II. In a sense, as noted earlier, this distinction did not make a difference for constitutional purposes. To

thus was whether federal lawmakers could impose this substantive-law duty on the state pursuant to its section 5 power.

In *Garrett*, the Court had ruled that section 5 did not support applying to the states the employment-discrimination rules set forth in Title I of the ADA.[197] But the five-Justice majority in *Lane*, in an opinion written by Justice Stevens, held that Title II of the Act, regarding access to public places, was sustainable to the extent it applied to state courthouses.[198] Picking up on a theme regarding sex-based discrimination sounded earlier in *Hibbs*, the Court emphasized that Title I concerned an attempted congressional vindication of equal-protection rights subject only to a rational-basis test.[199] The relevant features of Title II, in contrast, implicated due-process-based access-to-court rights, the abridgements of which are "subject to more searching judicial review," thus creating a heightened likelihood that there existed constitutional problems that Congress could rightly remedy under the congruence-and-proportionality test.[200] Of particular importance, the Court's past access-to-court rulings had gone so far as to impose "affirmative obligations" on states—such as the need to provide free trial transcripts and appellate counsel to defendants in serious criminal cases—and these obligations paralleled in important respects the duties created by Title II to provide reasonable accommodations to persons with disabilities.[201] Also distinguishing *Garrett* was the fact that the legislative record in that earlier case had revealed at most a problem of discrimination in *private* employment,[202] whereas the record in *Lane* revealed a "pattern of unequal treatment in the administration of a wide range of *public* services," including in "the administration of justice."[203] Especially significant, according to Justice Stevens, was Congress's discovery "that many individuals, in many States across the country, were being excluded from courthouses and court proceedings by reason of their disabilities," in part because "76% of public services and programs housed in state-owned buildings were inaccessible" to persons unable to walk.[204] Finally, Justice Stevens emphasized that the remedy Congress had formulated to address

---

repeat: The Court has applied the same congruence-and-proportionality touchstone in evaluating cases that involve both the imposition of statutory duties that reach beyond what the Constitution requires and the authorization of monetary remedies for the violation of those duties.

[197] *See supra* notes 141–149 and accompanying text.

[198] *Lane*, 541 U.S. at 530–31.

[199] *Id.* at 521–22.

[200] *Id.* at 522–23.

[201] *Id.* at 532–33.

[202] *Garrett*, 531 U.S. at 371.

[203] *Lane*, 541 U.S. at 525 (emphasis added).

[204] *Id.* at 527.

these problems was "a limited one," in part because Title II and its implementing regulations imposed only a "reasonable modification requirement [that] can be satisfied in a number of ways."[205]

The principal dissent, written by Chief Justice Rehnquist and joined by Justices Kennedy and Thomas, challenged the Court's analysis on two main grounds.[206] First, these Justices declared themselves unmoved by what they saw as "a wide-ranging account of societal discrimination against the disabled."[207] The relevant point was that the legislative record did not reveal to them due-process violations at an adequate level of specificity because it failed to focus on state access denials that the Court had previously declared unconstitutional, such as abridgments of "the right to be present at criminal trials, . . . to be heard in civil cases, [to participate in] jury service, or . . . to attend criminal trials [as an observer]."[208] Second, the dissenters faulted the majority for failing to assess Title II as a

---

[205] *Id.* at 531–32. *See id.* at 532 (citing 28 C.F.R. §§ 35.151, 35.150(b)(1)). In particular, Justice Stevens emphasized that "in no event is the entity required to undertake measures that would impose an undue financial or administrative burden, threaten historic preservation interests, or effect a fundamental alteration in the nature of the service." *Id.* at 532 (citing 28 C.F.R. §§ 35.150(a)(2), (a)(3)).

[206] Justice Scalia dissented separately to advocate abandonment of the congruence-and-proportionality test. That "flabby" standard, he asserted, allowed the Justices to engage in "policy-driven decisionmaking" while also creating a deeply problematic clash with a coordinate branch by directing the Court to "regularly check Congress's homework to make sure that it has identified sufficient constitutional violations to make its remedy congruent and proportional." *Lane*, 541 U.S. at 557–58 (Scalia, J., dissenting). As a textual matter, he reasoned, a power to "enforce" a rights-creating constitutional provision did not properly permit Congress to pass "prophylactic legislation" that reached beyond vindicating the scope of constitutionally protected rights themselves. *Id.* at 559–60. To be sure, Congress could enforce these rights by, for example, requiring states to jump through the procedural hoop of reporting on rights-threatening activities in an effort to flush out actual rights violations. *Id.* at 560. But it could not, as he viewed things, "enforce" section 1 substantive rights by creating new and additional substantive rights. *Id.* At the least, he concluded, any congressional power to put in place such prophylactic protections should permit nothing more than congressional action that addressed the evil of race discrimination, which was the central concern of the Reconstruction Amendments. *Id.* at 560 n.2, 561.

[207] *Id.* at 541 (Rehnquist, C.J., dissenting).

[208] *Id.* at 543; *see also id.* at 541, 543–44 (finding that the majority could "identify only two reported cases finding that a disabled person's federal constitutional rights were violated" and that "nothing in the legislative record" established a meaningful denial of constitutional rights based on disability status). The Chief Justice added that a state's declining to make architectural adjustments to facilitate unaided movement was far removed, for example, from a state's refusal to provide appellate counsel to a criminal defendant following conviction for engaging in a serious crime. *See id.* at 546–47. In addition, the Chief Justice reasoned that, even in Mr. Lane's own case, court personnel had offered to provide him with access to the courtroom by carrying him up a stairway. *See id.* at 514; *see also id.* at 546–47 (asserting that that "[a] violation of due process occurs only when a person is actually denied the constitutional right to access a given judicial proceeding" and that "[w]e have never held that a person has a *constitutional* right to make his way into a courtroom without any external assistance").

whole. The majority, Chief Justice Rehnquist insisted, "posits a hypothetical statute, never enacted by Congress, that applies only to courthouses,"[209] thus "rig[ging] the congruence-and-proportionality test by artificially constricting the scope of the statute to closely mirror a recognized constitutional right."[210] Indeed, for the dissenters, the very fact that Title II "applies indiscriminately to all 'services,' 'programs,' or 'activities' of any 'public entity' " demonstrated its "massive overbreadth"—as opposed to its proportionality—with regard to remedying supposed instances of unconstitutional state behavior.[211]

As for the first line of criticism leveled by the dissenters, Justice Stevens appeared not to accept the premise of their position—namely, that the right of access reaches no further than to safeguard the ability of an individual with a disability to get into a courtroom in some way. Rather, Justice Stevens's opinion left open the possibility that section 1 of the Fourteenth Amendment provides a right that at least sometimes ensures workable and non-demeaning access to courthouse facilities for everyone, including those who cannot walk. But whatever right to courthouse access came within the reach of section 1, and thus was enforceable under section 5, "the sheer volume of evidence" presented to Congress supported, in the majority's view, the protections it had put in place.[212] As for the dissenters' second point, Justice Stevens saw no problem with subjecting Title II of the ADA to as-applied scrutiny in assessing its permissibility as an exercise of the Fourteenth Amendment enforcement power. In support of this conclusion, he pointed to *United States v. Raines*,[213] in which the Court had permitted enforcement of a race-related voting statute against state officials, even though the statute applied with equal force to private actors and in that respect may have exceeded the scope of Congress's power to enforce the Fifteenth Amendment.[214] In other words, the Court in *Raines* had upheld "an application of the statute," as alleged in "the complaint"—that is, specifically with regard to claimed acts of

---

209 *Id.* at 551.

210 *Id.*

211 *Id.* Such an omnibus statute, he reasoned, simply "is not susceptible of being carved up" to produce a lesser included "hypothetical statute narrowly tailored enough to constitute valid prophylactic legislation." *Id.*

212 *Id.* at 528 (majority opinion). In a separate concurrence, Justice Ginsburg added that she saw the dissenters' approach as requiring Congress "essentially to indict" each and every state for engaging in conduct of the most egregious sort whenever it chose to impose nationwide duties under section 5. *Id.* at 537 (Ginsburg, J., concurring). This approach, she asserted, was both unduly nitpicky and intrinsically unsound because "[m]embers of Congress are understandably reluctant to condemn their own States as constitutional violators." *Id.*

213 362 U.S. 17 (1960); *see Lane*, 541 U.S. at 531 (discussing *Raines*).

214 *Raines*, 362 U.S. at 27.

discrimination by public officials—without worrying about whether other potential applications of the statute may have fallen beyond Congress's enforcement authority.[215]

There is room to disagree about whether the majority in *Lane* could fairly rely on *Raines* to rebuff Chief Justice Rehnquist's disproportionality-based line of attack.[216] But whatever conclusion one reaches on that point, *Lane* creates opportunities for lawyers to defend at least some enactments against congruence-and-proportionality challenge, in part rather than as a whole, based on a still-protean as-applied theory of section 5.[217]

5. The VRA Revisited: From *City of Rome v. United States* to *Shelby County v. Holder*

The Voting Rights Act's preclearance provision, upheld by the Court in *South Carolina v. Katzenbach*, provoked widespread opposition in covered jurisdictions, and in 1980 a renewed attack on this feature of the law reached the Supreme Court. The case, *City of Rome v. United States*,[218] arose out of an effort to restructure the

---

[215] *Id.* at 24–25. Not surprisingly, Chief Justice Rehnquist rejected this argument, relying in part on the fact that *Raines* predated development of congruence-and-proportionality standard. *See Lane*, 541 U.S. at 551 (Rehnquist, C.J., dissenting). The Chief Justice also viewed *Raines* as presenting a distinguishable case because it "considered the constitutionality of [a law enacted under the Fifteenth Amendment] whose narrowly tailored substantive provisions could 'unquestionably' be applied to state actors." *Id.* at 552 n.11 (citing *Raines*, 362 U.S. at 25). Justice Stevens, however, viewed *Raines* as involving an analogous as-applied challenge. *See id.* at 531 n.19 (majority opinion) (citing *Raines*, 362 U.S. at 24–25). He also observed that "[i]n fact, the decision in *Garrett*, which severed Title I of the ADA from Title II for purposes of the § 5 inquiry, demonstrates that courts need not examine 'the full breadth of the statute' all at once." *Id.* at 530 n.18 (internal quotations omitted). Finally, he argued that, at least in this context, an as-applied inquiry made good sense because "[i]t is unclear what, if anything, examining Title II's application to hockey rinks or voting booths can tell us about whether Title II substantively redefines the right of access to the courts." *Id.*

[216] Apart from the points of disagreement canvassed in the preceding footnote, the Chief Justice argued that, if the Court could "arbitrarily constrict[ ] the scope of the statutes to match" the as-applied challenge, then *Garrett* would have "come out differently." *Id.* at 552 (Rehnquist, C.J., dissenting). An authority that might be even more supportive of the Chief Justice's position was the patent-related *Florida Prepaid* case. There, after all, Justice Stevens had argued in effect that the abrogation of sovereign immunity for patent violations should be upheld on a *pro tanto* basis with regard to willful wrongdoers. *See supra* note 181. The majority, however, did not embrace this approach and instead assessed the congruence and proportionality of the challenged patent-infringement-abrogation statute as a unitary whole. *See id.*

[217] *See* David L. Franklin, *Facial Challenges, Legislative Purpose, and the Commerce Clause*, 92 IOWA L. REV. 41, 51–52 (2006) (comparing the Court's tendency to review challenges to legislation under Congress's Commerce Clause powers as facial challenges while reviewing legislation under Congress's section 5 powers on an as-applied basis).

[218] 446 U.S. 156 (1980).

manner of electing local officeholders.[219] In addition, Rome had taken steps to annex several neighboring communities, even though doing so would dilute the voting strength of the city's Black residents.[220] Wielding his preclearance authority, the Attorney General rejected many of the election-related changes and some of the proposed annexations, relying on the statutory provision that barred approval of proposed laws that would "have the effect," even if not the purpose, of "abridging the right to vote on account of race or color."[221] In reviewing a challenge to that action, Justice Powell was prepared to invalidate the preclearance provision of the VRA as applied to Rome in part because, at that time, only Georgia as a whole—rather than individual cities and counties within the state—could pursue "bail out" relief under the act.[222] Two other dissenters, Justices Rehnquist and Stewart, would also have ruled for the city, finding it unjustifiable that the VRA's preclearance scheme required rejection of all voting laws found to discriminate "in effect" against Black voters when establishment of a constitutional violation required the far more difficult showing of discriminatory purpose.[223]

Six Justices in *City of Rome*, however, joined together to reaffirm the constitutionality of section 5, finding that the city was, as a practical matter, "asking us to do nothing less than overrule" *South Carolina v. Katzenbach*.[224] Writing for the Court, Justice Thurgood Marshall pointed to the danger of state action that "perpetuates the effects of past discrimination" in light of the "demonstrable history" of longstanding racial discrimination in Georgia and other covered jurisdictions.[225] Thus, he concluded, "the Act's ban on electoral changes that are discriminatory in effect is an appropriate method of promoting the purposes of the Fifteenth Amendment, even if it is assumed that § 1 of the Amendment prohibits only intentional discrimination in voting."[226]

In 1982, a sunset provision caused the VRA to expire, but Congress revived it for another 25-year period. Thereafter in 2006, Congress reinstalled the VRA once again, this time with a ten-year

---

219 *Id.* at 160–61.

220 *Id.* at 161–62.

221 *Id.* at 161–62, 167 (quoting the Voting Rights Act of 1965 § 5(a), 52 U.S.C. § 10304(a)).

222 *City of Rome*, 446 U.S. at 200 (Powell, J., dissenting).

223 *Id.* at 218 (Rehnquist, J., dissenting, joined by Stewart, J.).

224 *Id.* at 174 (majority opinion).

225 *Id.* at 176–77.

226 *Id.* at 177.

term of operation.[227] In *Shelby County v. Holder*,[228] however, a new set Justices held that section 4's coverage formula, as linked to section 5's preclearance provision, lay beyond the scope of Congress's power to enact, notwithstanding the Court's earlier rulings in *South Carolina* and *City of Rome*. The preclearance remedy, Chief Justice Roberts now declared for a five-Justice majority, was "a drastic departure from basic principles of federalism" and the covered-jurisdictions provision was "an equally dramatic departure from the principle that all States enjoy equal sovereignty."[229] Although "no one" could doubt that "voting discrimination still exists," he insisted that the "conditions that originally justified these measures no longer characterize voting in the covered jurisdictions."[230] In particular, some fifty years after the initial adoption of the 1965 Act, "the racial gap in voter registration and turnout [had become] lower in the States originally covered by § 5 than it was nationwide."[231] In addition, according to the Chief Justice, "[b]latantly discriminatory evasions of federal decrees are rare," and "minority candidates hold office at unprecedented levels."[232] Congress, in short, had failed to "identify those jurisdictions to be singled out on a basis that makes sense in light of current conditions."[233] Instead, the Chief Justice reasoned, the act's "extraordinary and unprecedented features were reauthorized" on a basis that was inattentive to present conditions—that is, "as if nothing had changed."[234]

Writing for herself and Justices Breyer, Sotomayor, and Kagan, Justice Ginsburg could only shake her head in disbelief. In her view, "the very success of § 5"[235] as applied to the covered jurisdictions supported its retention, especially in light of the need to address " 'second-generation barriers' to minority voting."[236] Those barriers included racial gerrymandering, adoption of "at-large voting in lieu of district-by-district voting" and "annexation [of] majority-white

---

[227] *See History of Federal Voting Rights Laws*, U.S. DEP'T OF JUSTICE (July 28, 2017), https://www.justice.gov/crt/history-federal-voting-rights-laws.

[228] 570 U.S. 529 (2013).

[229] *Id.* at 535.

[230] *Id.* (internal alteration omitted).

[231] *Id.* (citing *NAMUDNO*, 557 U.S. 193, 203–04 (2009)).

[232] *Id.* at 540 (citing *NAMUDNO*, 557 U.S. at 202).

[233] *Id.* at 553.

[234] *Id.* at 549. Notably, the majority left open the possibility that Congress could reinstall a preclearance rule by coupling it with a new coverage formula "based on current conditions." *Id.* at 557. In a separate concurrence, however, Justice Thomas expressed the view that the preclearance mechanism installed by section 5 was not justifiable in light of "current needs," so that for him no coverage formula that Congress might later put in place could support a finding of present-day constitutionality. *Id.* at 559 (Thomas, J., concurring) (internal quotations omitted).

[235] *Id.* at 559 (Ginsburg, J., dissenting).

[236] *Id.* at 592.

areas into city limits"[237]—all of which "prevent minority voters from fully participating in the electoral process."[238] Indeed, Justice Ginsburg declared, a "legislative record [that] filled more than 15,000 pages" established that very point.[239] The same legislative record also showed that case-by-case litigation continued to offer "an inadequate substitute for preclearance," particularly because it is costly and slow.[240] For the dissenters, the VRA's continued singling out of the covered jurisdictions made sense in light of their "unique history of problems with racial discrimination in voting . . . still in living memory."[241] Further support for a finding of remedial proportionality came from the 2006 act's inclusion of a much-reduced 10-year sunset period, as well as its retention of a covered-jurisdiction bail-out procedure, which had been successfully used in the past by nearly 200 government entities.[242]

Also of importance to the dissenters were three key legal propositions: (1) that "[w]hen confronting the most constitutionally invidious form of discrimination, and the most fundamental right in our democratic system, Congress' power to act is at its height";[243] (2) that, under the Court's landmark rulings in *McCulloch*, *South Carolina*, and *Morgan*,[244] the only question should have been whether Congress had acted "rationally" in seeking to address Fifteenth Amendment violations;[245] and (3) that, as the Court in *South Carolina* had emphatically declared, any supposed equal-sovereignty principle "applies only to the terms upon which States are admitted to the Union" and thus not to Enforcement Clause-

---

[237] *Id.* at 563–64.

[238] *Id.* at 566.

[239] *Id.* at 565.

[240] *Id.* at 572.

[241] *Id.* at 576.

[242] *Id.* at 579. That provision, after all, specifically provided each covered jurisdiction with a clear-cut pathway for escaping the supposed Sisyphean cycle of never-ending preclearance duties. No less important, it did so in a way that seemed directly aligned with the Court's previously endorsed focus-on-the-wrongdoers approach to the enforcement powers by permitting "innocent" jurisdictions to exempt themselves from the act's coverage by establishing their lack of remediation-justifying past wrongdoing in focused, jurisdiction-specific bail-out proceedings. *Id.* at 539. Indeed, the Court in another opinion penned by Chief Justice Roberts had only four years prior to *Shelby County* accorded to the bail-out provision a broadened reach, in part for the express purpose of alleviating constitutional concerns about the coverage formula's purportedly overinclusive scope. *See NAMUDNO*, 557 U.S. at 207–11 (holding that bail-out suits may be brought by "all political subdivisions" within a state as opposed to only states as a whole). The Court in *Shelby County*, however, never paused to explain why the now-expanded bail-out mechanism was insufficient to address its overinclusiveness-related constitutional concerns.

[243] *Shelby County*, 570 U.S. at 566 (Ginsburg, J., dissenting).

[244] *See supra* Sections 11.B.1–11.B.2.

[245] *Shelby County*, 570 U.S. at 568 (Ginsburg, J., dissenting).

based "remedies for local evils."[246] The dissenters complained that the majority had failed to give any serious attention to either of the first two principles.[247] And while the majority did focus on, and explicitly abandon, the third principle, that action, according to the dissenters, contravened even the legal doctrine set forth in *City of Boerne* itself.[248]

6. Enforcement-Power Legislation After *Shelby County*

The Court's decision in *Shelby County* produced a flood of commentary built in large part on challenges to the Court's reliance on its newly minted "equal sovereignty" principle,[249] critiques of its

---

[246] *Id.* at 587 (quoting *South Carolina*, 383 U.S. at 328–29).

[247] The majority did indicate that the coverage formula failed to satisfy *McCulloch*'s instruction that a "legislative means [must be] 'consistent with the letter and spirit of the constitution,'" *see id.* at 555–56 (majority opinion) (quoting *McCulloch*, 17 U.S. at 421 (internal alterations omitted)), but it neither expressly endorsed or nor expressly repudiated the dissenters' assertion that the rational-basis test supplies the proper touchstone for assessing congruence-and-proportionality questions. *See id.*

[248] *See id.* at 588–90 (Ginsburg, J., dissenting).

[249] For focused criticisms of the equal-sovereignty principle, see Leah M. Litman, *Inventing Equal Sovereignty*, 114 MICH. L. REV. 1207 (2016); Richard A. Posner, *The Supreme Court and the Voting Rights Act: Striking Down the Law is All About Conservatives' Imagination*, SLATE (June 26, 2013, 12:16 AM), https://slate.com/news-and-politics/2013/06/the-supreme-court-and-the-voting-rights-act-striking-down-the-law-is-all-about-conservatives-imagination.html (calling the Court's reliance on the equal-sovereignty principle an "indispensable prop" and reproving the Court for relying on that "imaginary" doctrine); and Zachary Price, *NAMUDNO's Non-Existent Principle of State Equality*, 88 N.Y.U. L. REV. ONLINE 24, 26 (2013) (raising similar concerns in criticizing the Court's pre-*Shelby County* ruling in *NAMUDNO*); *see also* Edward Cantu, *The Roberts Court and Penumbral Federalism*, 64 CATH. U. L. REV. 271, 311 (2015) (critiquing the Court's equal-sovereignty reasoning while suggesting that the result in *Shelby County* might alternatively be justified by reference to a theory of a "penumbral federalism"); Samuel Issacharoff, Comment, *Beyond the Discrimination Model on Voting*, 127 HARV. L. REV. 95, 100 (2013) (noting that "the equal dignity requirement may be of questionable original constitutional pedigree"); Samuel Spital, *A Doctrine of Sameness, not Federalism: How the Supreme Court's Application of the "Equal Sovereignty" Principle in* Shelby County v. Holder *Undermines Core Constitutional Values*, 34 N. ILL. U. L. REV. 561, 578–81 (2014) (challenging the Court's suggestion that "equal sovereignty" means that all states must be treated the same; urging in particular that this view "undermined the very federalism values the Court intended to protect"); Sandy Levinson, *Tendentious, Mendacious or Audacious? John Roberts Rewrites the 10th Amendment*, BALKINIZATION (June 30, 2013), http://balkin.blogspot.com/2013/06/tendentious-mendacious-or-audacious.html (rejecting the majority's federalism reasoning on the grounds that "the Constitution expressly does grant Congress the power to engage in all appropriate legislation to enforce the 15th Amendment's guarantee" and "the 10th Amendment has nothing whatsoever to do with the case"); *see generally* Cantu, *supra*, at 310 (noting that, "[a]ccording to a vast majority of commenters, equal sovereignty as a constitutional rule was implausible and the product of rhetorical trickery"); Neal Kumar Katyal & Thomas P. Schmidt, *Active Avoidance: The Modern Supreme Court and Legal Change*, 128 HARV. L. REV. 2109, 2133 n.103 (2015) ("The legal commentariat generally viewed the doctrine as an invention."). For a thoroughgoing defense of a constrained version of the equal-sovereignty principle, see Thomas B.

curious refusal to engage in that case with the congruence-and-proportionality test,[250] and claims that the majority failed to grapple in a serious way with persisting problems of race-related voter suppression in the United States.[251] In addition, the ruling raised profound concerns about the future of voting rights as a practical matter. Prior to *Shelby County*, for example, the Justice Department often declined to preclear voter-identification laws based on their disproportionate disadvantaging of minority voters. Following *Shelby County*, however, multiple previously-covered jurisdictions moved quickly to adopt new laws of this kind.[252] Along the same lines, states clamped down in other ways on ready access to the franchise, including by purging voter rolls based on a lack of voting activity in recent years.[253] To be sure, challenges to such measures can still be mounted in judicial proceedings in which plaintiffs allege direct

---

Colby, *In Defense of the Equal Sovereignty Principle*, 65 DUKE L.J. 1087, 1091–92, 1123, 1150–51, 1167, 1169 (2016) (arguing that "there is indeed a deep structural principle of equal sovereignty" that "is not just about new states [but] is about *all* states," while also insisting that this principle is "much less expansive . . . than . . . critics have feared" because it focuses only on laws that "grant more regulatory authority or capacity for self-government to some states than to others"; thus concluding, for example, that no problem under it arises when "the federal government spends money in ways that benefit some states more than others" and further concluding that "targeted departures" from the principle are justifiable, so that "[g]eographic tailoring" under the enforcement powers "is not only permissible [but] arguably *preferable*" (emphasis in original)).

[250] *See, e.g.*, Rick Hasen, *The Curious Disappearance of* Boerne *and the Future Jurisprudence of Voting Rights and Race*, SCOTUSBLOG (June 25, 2013), https://www.scotusblog.com/2013/06/the-curious-disappearance-of-boerne-and-the-future-jurisprudence-of-voting-rights-and-race (arguing that Chief Justice Roberts intentionally omitted any reference to the *Boerne* congruence-and-proportionality analysis in *Shelby County* in order to make it easier to strike down the preclearance formula).

[251] *See, e.g.*, Kareem Crayton & Jane Junn, *Five Justices, Section 4, and Three Ways Forward in Voting Rights*, 9 DUKE J. CONST. L. & PUB. POL'Y 113, 134–45 (2013) (detailing evidence of ongoing racial discrimination in voting in jurisdictions previously subject to preclearance under the VRA).

[252] *See, e.g.*, NOAH FELDMAN & KATHLEEN M. SULLIVAN, CONSTITUTIONAL LAW 913 (20th ed. 2019) (noting efforts of this kind in Texas, North Carolina, Alabama, and Mississippi).

[253] *See, e.g.*, Black Voters Matter Fund v. Raffensperger, 580 F. Supp. 3d 1283, 1288-89 (N.D. Ga. 2020) (detailing the plaintiffs' allegations that the Georgia Secretary of State unlawfully cancelled thousands of voter registrations from the state's rolls in the lead up to the 2020 election but finding no likelihood of success on the merits with respect to the plaintiffs' statutory and constitutional claims). For additional accounts of recent voting changes, see Ian Vandewalker & Keith G. Bentele, *Vulnerability in Numbers: Racial Composition of the Electorate, Voter Suppression, and the Voting Rights Act*, 18 HARV. LATINO L. REV. 99, 121–23 (2015) (making the case that recent state legislation that restricts access to voting is "correlated with minority population and turnout"); U.S. COMM'N ON CIV. RTS., AN ASSESSMENT OF MINORITY VOTING RIGHTS ACCESS IN THE UNITED STATES (2018), https://www.usccr.gov/pubs/2018/Minority_Voting_Access_2018. pdf (detailing data on voter registration pre- and post-*Shelby County* and documenting the use of restrictive voting laws in jurisdictions previously subject to preclearance).

violations of the VRA's terms.[254] Repudiation of the preclearance provision, however, has placed squarely on the shoulders of minority voters the burden of inertia that three separate Congresses had sought to lift from them.[255]

These events also raise questions about the extent to which Congress might act to reenergize minority voting rights in the much-changed post-*Shelby County* world.[256] In the wake of the 2020 elections, for example, Congress took up (but ultimately failed to pass) major legislative proposals designed to bolster the protections provided by the VRA, including by reinstalling the preclearance

---

[254] Notably, however, the Court has recently moved to rein in the protective reach of these terms as well. *See* Brnovich v. DNC, 141 S. Ct. 2321 (2021) (adopting a narrowed construction of section 2 of the Voting Rights Act and thereby making it more difficult for challengers to prevail on voting-discrimination claims under the statute).

[255] Since 2013, hundreds of suits have been filed around the country alleging violations of the VRA, including multiple cases related to formerly covered jurisdictions that have reached the Supreme Court. *See, e.g.*, Abbott v. Perez, 138 S. Ct. 2305 (2018); Cooper v. Harris, 137 S. Ct. 1455 (2017); Harris v. Ariz. Indep. Redistricting Comm'n, 578 U.S. 253 (2016); Ala. Legis. Black Caucus v. Alabama, 575 U.S. 254 (2015). These cases, in turn, raise questions about whether *City of Boerne* and follow-on rulings have placed in jeopardy the constitutionality of the results-centered restrictions imposed by section 2 of the VRA. Michael T. Morley, *Prophylactic Redistricting? Congress's Section 5 Power and the New Equal Protection Right to Vote*, 59 WM. & MARY L. REV. 2053, 2078 (2018) (assessing, among other things, the potential impact of *City of Boerne* on section 2 in light of the premise that that case "has jeopardized the VRA's constitutional underpinnings"). For academic work defending section 2 as a permissible exercise of the enforcement powers, see Joshua S. Sellers, *The Irony of Intent: Statutory Interpretation and the Constitutionality of Section 2 of the Voting Rights Act*, 76 LA. L. REV. 43, 46 (2015); Christopher S. Elmendorf, *Making Sense of Section 2: Of Biased Votes, Unconstitutional Elections, and Common Law Statutes*, 160 U. PA. L. REV. 377, 448–56 (2012); Janai S. Nelson, *The Causal Context of Disparate Vote Denial*, 54 B.C. L. REV. 579, 637 (2013); Pamela S. Karlan, *Section 5 Squared: Congressional Power to Extend and Amend the Voting Rights Act*, 44 HOUS. L. REV. 1 (2007); Pamela S. Karlan, *Two Section Twos and Two Section Fives: Voting Rights and Remedies After* Flores, 39 WM. & MARY L. REV. 725 (1998). For other discussions of this subject, see Luke P. McLoughlin, *Section 2 of the Voting Rights Act and* City of Boerne: *The Continuity, Proximity, and Trajectory of Vote-Dilution Standards*, 31 VT. L. REV. 39, 47–48 (2006), and Michael J. Pitts, *Congressional Enforcement of Affirmative Democracy Through Section 2 of the Voting Rights Act*, 25 N. ILL. U. L. REV. 185, 187–88 (2005). With regard to a kindred issue presented by application to the states of effects-related prohibition imposed by Title VII of the Civil Rights Act of 1964, see *In re Emp't Discrimination Litig.*, 198 F.3d 1305 (11th Cir. 1999) (concluding that, in allowing disparate-impact claims against states under Title VII of the Civil Rights of 1964 and in abrogating sovereign immunity for such claims, Congress crafted a permissibly congruent and proportional remedy for equal-protection violations even though the statutory proscription extends to non-purposeful discrimination).

[256] *See* Ryan P. Haygood, *Hurricane SCOTUS: The Hubris of Striking Our Democracy's Discrimination Checkpoint in* Shelby County *& the Resulting Thunderstorm Assault on Voting Rights*, 10 HARV. L. & POL'Y REV. S11, S49 (2016) (arguing for a threefold approach to combating voting discrimination: "(1) promotion of the Voting Rights Advancement Act ('VRAA'), (2) advocating for new procedures that uphold the right to vote, and (3) remaining vigilant and responsive to newly implemented discriminatory voting practices across the nation").

mechanism while altering the coverage formula to respond to the concerns about outdatedness expressed by the Court in *Shelby County*.[257] Another field of possible enforcement-power reform concerns partisan gerrymandering. Does Congress, for example, have the power under section 5 of the Fourteenth Amendment to establish nonpartisan standards for the drawing of state legislative maps or to force states to establish independent redistricting commissions to mitigate self-interested partisan influences?[258] In *Rucho v. Common Cause*,[259] the Court concluded that partisan gerrymandering claims present nonjusticiable political questions because no "judicially manageable standard" exists for addressing the legal issues they present.[260] As a result, the Court did not—because it decided it could not—lay down any due-process or equal-protection limits to rein in even the worst forms of partisan chicanery in drawing voting-district boundaries.[261] The question thus arises: Does Congress, because it need not worry about "*judicially* manageable standards," have authority under section 5 to step in to fill the constitutional gap?[262] Or are the hands of federal legislators tied because, in light of *Rucho*, there are no judicial guideposts to look to in seeking to forge a "congruent and proportional" enforcement-power remedy? The difficulty of enacting voting-law reforms (particularly in light of the Senate filibuster rules[263]) may render these questions of little more

---

[257] *See, e.g.*, Voting Rights Advancement Act, H.R. 4, 116th Cong. (2019) (proposing, among other things, a new coverage formula based on demonstrated voting rights violations during the past twenty-five years and the reinstatement of the preclearance requirements for thus-covered jurisdictions). Focusing on a pressing non-voting-related issue, Professors Jason Mazzone and Stephen Rushin have also urged Congress to wield its section 5 power to address the problem of "local police misconduct" by adopting legislation "modeled on the core provisions of the VRA." *See* Jason Mazzone & Stephen Rushin, *From Selma to Ferguson: The Voting Rights Act as a Blueprint for Police Reform*, 105 CAL. L. REV. 263, 268 (2017) (contending that, "given the magnitude of police misconduct and the failures of past responses to it, aggressive federal intervention is consistent with constitutional principles of federalism"). In their view, such a law "would set forth a coverage formula to identify police departments engaged in civil rights violations, and . . . impose targeted reforms upon those departments in order to prevent future violations." *Id.*

[258] There is little question that Congress possesses this power with respect to federal elections, given its separate Article I-based authority to regulate the "Times, Places and Manner of holding Elections for Senators and Representatives." U.S. CONST. art. I, § 4; *see also supra* Section 9.A.

[259] 139 S. Ct. 2484, 2491 (2019); *see also infra* Section 35.E (discussing *Rucho* in connection with the political-question doctrine).

[260] *Rucho*, 139 S. Ct. at 2506–07.

[261] *See id.* at 2502. In a dissent written by Justice Kagan, four Justices came together to challenge the Court's action, complaining that "[f]or the first time ever, this Court refuses to remedy a constitutional violation because it thinks the task beyond judicial capabilities." *Id.* at 2509 (Kagan, J., dissenting).

[262] *See, e.g.*, McConnell, *supra* note 25, at 186 (noting that "courts are particularly likely to defer to the judgments of representative bodies when there are no judicially manageable standards for decisionmaking").

[263] *See infra* Section 14.A.

than academic interest, at least in the present day. Even so, they illustrate how the judicial and legislative powers can interact in complex ways when Congress looks to invoke the Enforcement Clauses of the Fourteenth and Fifteenth Amendments.[264]

---

[264] Apart from the Fourteenth and Fifteenth Amendments, the Nineteenth Amendment (which bars voting discrimination "on account of sex") and the Twenty-sixth Amendment (which bars such discrimination "on account of age" for persons "eighteen years of age or older") include their own Enforcement Clauses. *See* U.S. CONST. amend. XIX, § 2; *id.* amend. XXVI, § 2. The practical effect of these separate enforcement powers remains uncertain because Congress has not sought to use either of them in any significant way. *But cf.* 52 U.S.C. §§ 10701–10702 (establishing specialized judicial procedures and remedial opportunities for cases involving claimed violations of Twenty-sixth Amendment rights). To the extent that state officials might meddle with voting laws for political purposes, however, possibilities arise that they could disadvantage persons protected by these amendments, such as young voters, male or female voters in general, or certain groups of male and or female voters, including on the basis of age. To be sure, such actions might support congressional remediation—including prophylactic remediation—pursuant to section 5 of the Fourteenth Amendment in light of the voting-rights protections that that amendment of its own force affords to *all* citizens. *See supra* note 10 and accompanying text; *cf.* Ball v. Brown, 450 F. Supp. 4, 8 (N.D. Ohio 1977) (suggesting that the "further guarantee of the right to vote" afforded by the Nineteenth Amendment "is encompassed within the fourteenth amendment guarantee of equal protection"). But there can be little doubt that, in some circumstances, the Nineteenth and Twenty-sixth Amendments give broader protections to the groups they cover than does the Fourteenth Amendment standing alone. *See, e.g.*, Reynolds v. Sims, 377 U.S. 538, 557 (1964) (noting that the Nineteenth Amendment restricts "a State from overweighting or diluting votes on the basis of . . . sex"); United States v. Texas, 445 F. Supp. 1245, 1248–49 (S.D. Tex. 1978) (finding a violation of the Twenty-sixth Amendment in the application to students of particularly onerous processes to establish local residence for voting purposes and collecting similar earlier rulings), *aff'd sub nom.* Symm v. United States, 439 U.S. 1105 (1979). Indeed, the Twenty-sixth Amendment was passed specifically because five Justices concluded that Congress could not provide state-election voting rights to young-adult voters pursuant to its section 5 power. *See Mitchell*, 400 U.S. at 119–31 (opinion of Black, J.); *see also id.* at 154–213 (Harlan, J., concurring in part and dissenting in part); *id.* at 293–96 (Stewart. J., concurring in part and dissenting in part). In the end, it is hard to envision what the practical effect of these specialized enforcement powers might be. But they could in time at least lead courts to afford federal lawmakers an amped-up measure of means-ends deference (as, perhaps, it has done in applying the Fifteenth Amendment) if federal lawmakers did enact voter-protection laws connected up specifically with age or sex. For reflections on these and related matters, see Richard L. Hasen & Leah M. Litman, *Thin and Thick Conceptions of the Nineteenth Amendment Right to Vote and Congress's Power to Enforce It*, 108 GEO. L.J. 27 (2020); Steve Kolbert, *The Nineteenth Amendment Enforcement Power (But First, Which One Is the Nineteenth Amendment, Again?)*, 43 FLA. ST. U. L. REV. 507, 534 (2016); Reva B. Siegel, *She the People: The Nineteenth Amendment, Sex Equality, Federalism, and the Family*, 115 HARV. L. REV. 947 (2002); and Eric S. Fish, Note, *The Twenty-Sixth Amendment Enforcement Power*, 121 YALE L.J. 1168, 1175 (2012). *Cf. Shelby County*, 570 U.S. at 567 n.2 (Ginsburg, J., dissenting) (reasoning that the "implication" of the Constitution's many protections of voting rights, including in the Nineteenth and Twenty-sixth Amendments, is that "Congress holds the lead rein in making the right to vote equally real for all U.S. citizens").

C. SECTION 5 AND PRIVATE ACTION

Section 1 of the Fourteenth Amendment declares that "[n]o *State* shall" deny to any person due-process and equal-protection rights.[265] In a long line of cases, the Court has drawn on this portion of the Amendment's text to hold that it restricts only "state action," as opposed to "merely private conduct, however discriminatory or wrongful."[266] In applying this principle, the courts sometimes view nominally private individuals or entities themselves to be state actors—for example, when persons not employed by the state conspire or collaborate with state employees to deprive targeted individuals of their constitutional rights.[267] In these cases, the action of the private person is in effect found not to be private action but instead to be state action within the meaning of section 1. In another set of cases, the Court has explored Congress's efforts to use section 5 to go one step further—that is, to limit private action, not itself unlawful under section 1, so as to ensure that the rights established by section 1 receive adequate protection.

Congressional efforts along these lines initially received a chilly judicial reception. In *United States v. Harris*,[268] for example, the

---

[265] U.S. CONST. amend. XIV, § 1 (emphasis added). In similar fashion, section 1 of the Fifteenth Amendment prohibits race-based abridgements of voting rights "by any *State*." *Id.* amend. XV, § 1 (emphasis added). Notably, in the *White Primary Cases*, the Court held that nominally private political parties qualified as state actors within the meaning of the Fifteenth Amendment and were thus constitutionally barred from discriminating on the basis of race in administering primary elections. *See, e.g.*, Smith v. Allwright, 321 U.S. 649, 662-66 (1944). Those decisions thus lend support to the idea that, as Professor Travis Crum has put it, the "Court . . . conceives of state action more broadly under the Fifteenth Amendment than under the Fourteenth Amendment." Travis Crum, *Reconstructing Racially Polarized Voting*, 70 DUKE L.J. 261, 327 (2020). Even so, the Court has not in any recent enforcement-power case considered the extent to which such a loosened state-action requirement might enhance Congress's power to target certain forms of private-party interference with Fifteenth Amendment-based rights, thus leaving unresolved the question whether Congress's section 2 authority to regulate private-party-conduct under the Fifteenth Amendment exceeds its parallel section 5 authority to regulate private-party conduct under the Fourteenth Amendment. *But cf. Ex parte* Yarbrough, 110 U.S. 651, 665–66 (1884) (upholding, in part by reference to the Fifteenth Amendment, a Reconstruction-era statutory prohibition that reached private-party conduct).

[266] Shelley v. Kraemer, 334 U.S. 1, 13 (1948).

[267] *See* United States v. Price, 383 U.S. 787, 795 (1966) (allowing the prosecution of private conspirators involved in the murder of civil rights workers because "state officers participated in every phase" of the criminal conduct and those "who took advantage of participation by state officers in accomplishment of the foul purpose alleged must suffer the consequences of that participation"). In addition, the Court has sometimes found state action to be present under circumstances in which nominally private parties carry out functions that are "traditionally exclusively reserved to the state." Jackson v. Metro. Edison Co., 419 U.S. 345, 352 (1974); *see also supra* note 265 (noting the Court's reliance on similar reasoning in the *White Primary Cases*). Overall, however, "very few" functions fall within the scope of this rule. Flagg Bros., Inc., v. Brooks, 436 U.S. 149, 158 (1978).

[268] 106 U.S. 629 (1883).

Court found unconstitutional section 2 of the Force Act of 1871, which outlawed conspiracies among private persons to deprive any individual of the equal protection of state laws.[269] As a result, the Justices required dismissal of an indictment of a group of white supremacists who had seized and beaten four Black men, killing one of them, because, according to the Court, the defendants were "private persons" not covered by the Fourteenth Amendment.[270] Likewise, in the *Civil Rights Cases*,[271] the Court struck down the Civil Rights Act of 1875, which prohibited race discrimination by private businesses engaged in the operation of inns, public conveyances, theatres, and amusement facilities.[272] It rooted this holding in the proposition that the "[i]ndividual [as opposed to state] invasion of individual rights is not the subject-matter of the amendment," so that section 5 did not authorize Congress to target the activities of private parties.[273]

---

[269] *Id.* at 639.

[270] *Id.* at 629–30. Quoting *Virginia v. Rives*, 100 U.S. 313, 318 (1880), the Court in *Harris* asserted along the way that "provisions of the Fourteenth Amendment have reference to State action exclusively, and not to any action of private individuals." *Harris*, 106 U.S. at 639–40. Thus, because "the section of the law under consideration is directed exclusively against the action of private persons, without reference to the laws of the states, or their administration by [state officers], we are clear in the opinion that it is not warranted by any clause in the fourteenth Amendment." *Id.* at 639; *see also* United States v. Cruikshank, 92 U.S. 542, 554 (1876) (observing that the Fourteenth Amendment "prohibits a State from depriving any person of life, liberty, or property, without due process of law; but this adds nothing to the rights of one citizen as against another").

[271] *The Civil Rights Cases*, 109 U.S. 3.

[272] *Id.* at 19.

[273] *Id.* at 11. In reaching this conclusion, as noted in Justice Harlan's powerful dissenting opinion in the case, the Court in the *Civil Rights Cases* gave short shrift to several plausible bases for upholding the law, including, for instance: (1) the suggestion that the law reflected a permissible exercise of the Thirteenth Amendment enforcement power insofar as it sought to eliminate the "badges and incidents" of slavery, *id.* at 39 (Harlan, J., dissenting); (2) the suggestion that the law functioned to enforce the Fourteenth Amendment's Citizenship Clause insofar as its anti-discrimination requirements helped to vindicate that Clause's guarantee of equal citizenship, *id.* at 46–47; and (3) the suggestion that, even insofar as application of a state-action requirement was warranted, that requirement was satisfied in light of the fact that "railroad corporations, keepers of inns, and managers of places of public amusement are agents of the State, because they are charged with duties to the public, and are amenable, in respect of their public duties and functions, to governmental regulation," *id.* at 58–59. Indeed, the weaknesses of the majority opinion in the *Civil Rights Cases*, combined with the disastrous effects of that ruling (and others like it, such as *Harris* and *Cruikshank*) in empowering white resistance to Reconstruction, have led some commentators to suggest that the *Civil Rights Cases* belong squarely within the constitutional "anti-canon," alongside such widely repudiated decisions as *Plessy v. Ferguson* and *Dred Scott v. Sanford*. *See, e.g.*, Matthew Norman & Christopher Bryant, *Why the* Civil Rights Cases *Belong in the Anti-Canon: Black Citizenship, the Fourteenth Amendment, and Judicial Interposition*, 12 CONLAWNOW 191 (2021). Nevertheless, and as the ensuing discussion demonstrates, the Court has never repudiated the *Civil Rights Cases* and, indeed, cited them with approval in

A measure of murkiness marked the scope of these rulings, particularly because the Court in the *Civil Rights Cases* noted that the challenged statute "does not profess to be corrective of any constitutional wrong committed by the States."[274] This passage had importance because it signaled that—at least maybe—Congress could target private actors if states, for example, facilitate private race discrimination by displacing otherwise operative common-law rules that broadly require inns, trains, and ferries to accommodate would-be customers in an equal fashion. In addition, the Court issued these rulings during the same post-Reconstruction era that gave rise to *Plessy v. Ferguson*[275] and other later-repudiated decisions that had upheld core elements of the Jim Crow apartheid regime.[276] Questions thus arose, particularly in the wake of *Brown v. Board of Education*,[277] as to whether the Justices might retreat from the limits on Congress's section 5 power suggested by these early precedents.[278]

The Court signaled a willingness to make just such a course change in *United States v. Guest*.[279] At issue in that case was a federal prosecution brought under 18 U.S.C. § 241, a key component of the Enforcement Act of 1870, which criminalizes conspiracies to "oppress, threaten, or intimidate any citizen in the free exercise or enjoyment of any right or privilege secured to him by the Constitution."[280] The indictment stemmed from the fatal 1964 shooting of Lemuel Penn, a Black reserve officer, as he was traveling to Washington, D.C.[281] According to the charges, the defendants conspired to oppress, threaten, and intimidate Penn and two other

---

United State v. Morrison, 529 U.S. 598, 621–22 (2000). *See infra* notes 289–300 and accompanying text.

[274] *The Civil Rights Cases*, 109 U.S. at 14.

[275] 163 U.S. 537 (1896) (upholding the provision of "separate but equal" public transportation).

[276] *See, e.g.*, Pace v. Alabama, 106 U.S. 583 (1883) (upholding Alabama laws that criminalized interracial marriage or cohabitation); Cumming v. Cty. Bd. of Educ. 175 U.S. 528 (1889) (refusing to find that a Georgia county board of education violated the Fourteenth Amendment by maintaining a high-school system that served only white students).

[277] 347 U.S. 483 (1954).

[278] *See* LAURENCE H. TRIBE, AMERICAN CONSTITUTIONAL LAW § 5–17, at 961 (3d ed. 1999) (noting that "when the Supreme Court began to reconsider the extent of congressional power under the Fourteenth Amendment in the 1960s a principal issue was thought to be whether, under a new theory of congressional power, Congress would be able to subject private conduct to Fourteenth Amendment limits"). These questions were driven forward in part by the fact that the first Justice Harlan had dissented in the *Civil Rights Cases*, just as he later would do in *Plessy*, *see* 163 U.S. at 552–64 (Harlan, J., dissenting). *See also supra* note 273.

[279] 383 U.S. 745 (1966).

[280] The Civil Rights Act (The Enforcement Act) of 1870 § 2, 18 U.S.C. § 241.

[281] *Lt. Col. Lemuel Penn*, THE GEORGIA CIVIL RIGHTS COLD CASES PROJECT AT EMORY UNIVERSITY, https://coldcases.emory.edu/lt-col-lemuel-penn/.

Black servicemembers with regard to their exercise of "[t]he right to the equal utilization, without discrimination upon the basis of race, of public facilities in the vicinity of Athens, Georgia."[282] This federal prosecution moved forward only after a jury had acquitted the defendants of state-law murder charges in a Georgia court.[283]

A unanimous Court overturned the lower court's dismissal of the federal indictment, but the case produced a mix of opinions. Writing for a six-Justice majority, Justice Stewart reasoned that the indictment's phrasing was "broad enough to cover a charge of active connivance by agents of the State," thus permitting prosecution based on the presence of state action directly prohibited by section 1 itself.[284] In a separate concurring and dissenting opinion, Justice Brennan, joined by Chief Justice Warren and Justice Douglas, deemed the prosecution permissible even in the absence of state action. In their view, it was "appropriate" for Congress, "in order adequately to protect the right to equal utilization of state facilities, . . . to punish other individuals—not state officers themselves and not acting in concert with state officers—who engage in . . . brutal conduct for the . . . misguided purpose" of depriving a victim of that protected right.[285] Finally, in another concurring opinion, which was joined by Justices Black and Fortas, Justice Clark criticized Justice Brennan's assessment of the precedential implications of the majority's state-action-centered analysis.[286] These same Justices, however, then proceeded to endorse Justice Brennan's key point, observing that "there now can be no doubt that the specific language of § 5 empowers the Congress to enact laws punishing all conspiracies—with or without state action—that interfere with Fourteenth Amendment rights."[287] Seven years later, in *District of*

---

282 *Guest*, 383 U.S. at 747 n.1, 753.

283 *Lt. Col. Lemuel Penn*, *supra* note 281.

284 *Guest*, 383 U.S. at 756.

285 *Id.* at 783–84 (Brennan, J., concurring and dissenting) (citing *Price*, 383 U.S. at 787, in support of the proposition that "§ 5 authorizes Congress to make laws that it concludes are reasonably necessary to protect a right created by and arising under that Amendment; and Congress is thus fully empowered to determine that punishment of private conspiracies interfering with the exercise of such a right is necessary to its full protection," as Congress did in enacting section 241).

286 *Guest*, 383 U.S. at 762 (Clark, J., concurring).

287 *Id.* Thus, as stated by Justice Brennan: "A majority of the members of the Court expresses the view today that § 5 empowers Congress to enact laws punishing all conspiracies to interfere with the exercise of Fourteenth Amendment rights, whether or not state officers or others acting under the color of state law are implicated in the conspiracy." *Id.* at 782 (Brennan, J., concurring in part, dissenting in part). He continued: "Although the Fourteenth Amendment itself, according to established doctrine, speaks to the State or to those acting under the color of its authority, legislation protecting rights created by that Amendment, such as the right to equal utilization of state facilities, need not be confined to punishing conspiracies in which state officers participate." *Id.* (internal quotations omitted).

Columbia v. Carter,[288] a much-altered set of Justices unanimously expressed their endorsement of this same principle.

The tables turned again, however, when the Rehnquist Court moved in *United States v. Morrison*[289] to rebalance federal and state authority not only under the Commerce Clause, but also under section 5 of the Fourteenth Amendment.[290] That case, as detailed earlier,[291] involved a provision of the Violence Against Women Act (VAWA) that created a federal damages action against private-citizen defendants who injure private-citizen plaintiffs by engaging in gender-motivated violence.[292] After first finding that the commerce power did not support this law, a five-Justice majority also concluded that it was unsustainable under section 5.[293] In essence, Chief Justice Rehnquist reasoned that *Harris* and the *Civil Rights Cases* had properly tied the reach of the section 5 power to the mast of state action, which was not an element of the cause of action created by the VAWA.[294] In addition, the Chief Justice reasoned that the rule of *Guest*—at least to the extent it retreated from the state-action limit laid down in the *Civil Rights Cases*—should not endure because it was built on "naked dicta" in the opinion of Justice Clark, which offered "no explanation whatever" as to why he and his colleagues agreed with Justice Brennan's view of Congress's authority to enact legislation under section 5.[295]

---

[288] 409 U.S. 418, 423–24 n.8 (1973).

[289] 529 U.S. 598 (2000).

[290] For a discussion of the Court's treatment of the commerce power in *Morrison*, see *supra* Section 4.A.

[291] *See id.*

[292] *Morrison*, 529 U.S. at 605–06 (describing the Violence Against Women Act § 40302, 42 U.S.C. § 13981).

[293] *Id.* at 627.

[294] *Id.* at 624.

[295] *Id.* (adding that "[t]his is simply not the way that reasoned constitutional adjudication proceeds," so that "Justice Clark's opinion, when added to Justice Brennan's opinion, [does not] cast any doubt upon the enduring vitality of the *Civil Rights Cases* and *Harris*"). *Id.* With regard to the Court's ensuing decision in *Carter*, he added: "A footnote in that opinion recites the same litany respecting *Guest* that petitioners rely on. This litany is of course entirely dicta [because the issue concerned whether the District of Columbia is a state for purposes of § 1983], and in any event cannot rise above its source." *Id.* The Chief Justice's back-of-the-hand treatment of these earlier authorities, however, was marked by serious problems. More specifically, in eschewing the Court's preexisting understanding of *Guest*—and particularly by brushing aside Justice Clark's concurrence in that case—Chief Justice Rehnquist failed to take account of all of the pre-*Guest* (but post-*Harris* and post-*Civil Rights Cases*) authorities on which Justice Brennan had relied. *See Guest*, 383 U.S. at 779–80 (Brennan, J., concurring in part, dissenting in part) (citing *Price*, 383 U.S. 787; United States v. Classic, 313 U.S. 299 (1941); *In re* Quarles and Butler, 158 U.S. 532 (1895); Logan v. United States, 144 U.S. 263 (1892); and *Yarbrough*, 110 U.S. 651). Moreover, there is every indication that Justice Clark was relying on exactly this same intervening body of law because he asserted that, notwithstanding the Court's earlier decisions in *Harris* and the *Civil Rights Cases*, "there *now* can be no doubt" that section

One complication confronted by the majority in *Morrison* was that the individual plaintiff in that case argued that she should win even if the *Civil Rights Cases*, rather than *Guest*, provided the proper touchstone for analysis.[296] This position made sense, so the argument went, because Congress had made elaborate findings before enacting the VAWA that supported viewing the challenged measure as an appropriate section 5 remedial response to unconstitutionally discriminatory state action in the form of under-investigating, under-prosecuting, and under-punishing sex-based violent crimes.[297] The majority, however, rejected this argument by declaring that, even if Congress had been trying to respond to state action in the form of sex discrimination by public officials, its chosen cure was not, as required by under *City of Boerne*, a "congruent and proportionate" remedy for the constitutional affliction.[298] The problem was that any proper legislative response to sex discrimination by public police officers, prosecutors, and judges had to take aim not at private malefactors, but instead at the wrongdoing state actors themselves.[299] In any event, the Chief Justice explained, Congress's across-the-board application of the VAWA to all acts of gender-based violence lacked the sort of fine-tuned targeting of particularly problematic states or localities that had led the Court to find in earlier decisions that enforcement-power prophylaxes satisfied the congruence-and-proportionality test.[300]

---

5 permits congressional regulation of rights-targeting private conspiracies. *Id.* at 762 (Clark, J., concurring) (emphasis added). The Chief Justice's indication that "reasoned constitutional adjudication" had not occurred in *Guest* (and that a unanimous Court had failed to pick up on this point in *Carter*) thus reflected a view of the work of his predecessors that was highly oversimplified at best.

296 *See Morrison*, 529 U.S. at 622.

297 *Id.* at 619–20. Thus, the Court in in *Morrison* confronted the argument that the case involved "gender-based disparate treatment by state authorities, whereas in [the *Civil Rights Cases*] there was no indication of such state action." *Id.* at 624; *see also The Civil Rights Cases*, 109 U.S. at 17 (distinguishing cases involving private conduct "sanctioned in some way by the State").

298 *Morrison*, 529 U.S. at 625–26.

299 *Id.* at 626 (reasoning in this respect that "Section 13981 is not aimed at proscribing discrimination by officials which the Fourteenth Amendment might not itself proscribe; it is directed not at any State or state actor, but at individuals who have committed criminal acts motivated by gender bias"). The Court also questioned the plaintiffs' efforts to distinguish the *Civil Rights Cases* based on congressional findings of widespread state wrongdoing offered in support of the VAWA. *Id.* at 625 (questioning this purported distinction because "abundant evidence [tends] to show that the Congresses that enacted the Civil Rights Acts of 1871 and 1875 had a purpose similar to that of Congress in enacting § 13981" in that "[t]here were state laws on the books bespeaking equality of treatment, but in the administration of these laws there was discrimination against newly freed slaves").

300 *Id.* at 626–27 (noting that the challenged VAWA provision "applies uniformly throughout the Nation" even though "the problem of discrimination against the victims of gender-motivated crimes does not exist in all States," whereas "the § 5 remedy upheld in *Katzenbach* v. *Morgan* was directed only to the State where the evil found

Is anything left of the idea, once vindicated by *Guest*, that section 5 sometimes permits Congress to go beyond targeting only those private persons who themselves qualify as section 1 state actors?[301] At least three possibilities remain in play.[302] First, as the

by Congress existed, and in *South Carolina v. Katzenbach* the remedy was directed only to those States in which Congress found that there had been discrimination" (internal citations omitted)). For some scholarly critiques of the Court's treatment of section 5 in the *Morrison* case, see Jack M. Balkin, *The Reconstruction Power*, 85 N.Y.U. L. REV. 1801, 1807 (2010) (arguing that Congress may "prevent private interference with federally guaranteed rights, including federal constitutional rights"); Evan H. Caminker, *Private Remedies for Public Wrongs Under Section 5*, 33 LOY. L.A. L. REV. 1351, 1353, 1357 (2000) (arguing that "[n]either text, precedent, nor federalism values guiding constitutional interpretation persuasively support limiting Congress's Section 5 powers" pursuant to the rationale applied in *Morrison*—whether or not the result in the case was defensible—because "the constitutionality of Section 5 enforcement does not hinge on a public/private distinction concerning the regulatory target"; reasoning, among other things, that the VAWA "does prevent the tangible consequences that flow from . . . unconstitutional state action" because, as a matter of but-for causation, "[w]omen are subject to gender-motivated violence by private actors in part because the state fails to deter such violence" due to unconstitutional enforcement-related discrimination); Estreicher & Lemos, *supra* note 106, at 115, 143–51 (arguing that the Court in *Morrison* both "misunderstood the state action limitation" and "misapplied the congruence and proportionality test").

[301] For a detailed treatment of the subject, see Robert C. Post & Reva B. Siegel, *Equal Protection by Law: Federal Antidiscrimination Legislation After* Morrison *and* Kimel, 110 YALE L.J. 441, 443 (2000) ("It is . . . unclear after *Morrison* whether and to what extent antidiscrimination legislation enacted under Section 5 can regulate the conduct of private actors."), and *id.* at 445 ("Although *Morrison* might be interpreted as announcing a per se rule forbidding the use of Section 5 power to regulate private parties, we argue that the decision is better read as requiring a case-by-case determination of whether Section 5 legislation is congruent and proportional to the constitutional violation it seeks to remedy."); *see also id.* at 444 (noting that future rulings could cause "the Court's Section 5 jurisprudence [to] develop in quite different directions").

[302] The term "at least" is included in this sentence in part because *Morrison* may not foreclose future application of even the very rule embraced by six Justices in *Guest* itself—that is, the rule that Congress can outlaw under section 5 "all conspiracies—with or without state action—that interfere with Fourteenth Amendment rights," *see supra* note 287 and accompanying text (quoting Justice Clark's concurring opinion), including "the right to equal utilization of state facilities," *see supra* note 285 and accompanying text (quoting Justice Brennan's concurring opinion), and perhaps non-conspiratorial private interferences with such rights as well. After all, *Morrison* itself involved no such claimed right, because it concerned only an alleged assault by one private person on another private person without any indication that the assault was connected up with any constitutional right against the state held, and then exercised or about to be exercised, by the victim. In addition, the majority in *Morrison* focused on rejecting "the view that the *Civil Rights Cases* were wrongly decided." *Morrison*, 529 U.S. at 622–23. But even if the *Civil Rights Cases* were rightly decided, that would not dictate a rejection of the Brennan-Clark position in *Guest* because that case—in contrast to both the *Civil Rights Cases* and *Morrison* itself—involved a claimed interference with a constitutional right (there, the right to equal access to state facilities) by the regulated wrongdoers themselves. To be sure, the Brennan-Clark position might lie in greater tension with the Court's ruling in *Harris*, on which the majority in *Morrison* also relied. *See supra* note 268–270 and accompanying text (discussing *Harris*). There was simply no need in *Morrison*, however, to resolve any disharmony between that ruling and the Court's later ruling in *Guest*, even assuming that some such disharmony existed.

Chief Justice himself implied in *Morrison*, more carefully crafted remedial statutes might pass muster if, for example, Congress takes aim at only those jurisdictions as to which the evidence reveals a longstanding history of unconstitutionally discriminatory non-enforcement practices by local law enforcement officials.[303] Second, Congress might be able to sanction private individuals who affirmatively disable public officials from affording rights-vindicating protections to victims of private individuals' wrongdoing.[304] Finally, it might be that the Court would distinguish *Morrison* in a case that concerns private-individual wrongdoing aimed at a victim already protected by a court order vindicating that victim's section 1 rights. Assume, for example, that a judge has enjoined the state from maintaining an all-male school and that a disgruntled private individual, for that reason, kidnaps a female student on her way to enroll in classes. Such an action—while not committed by a state actor—might strike a court as so directly disruptive of the victim's section 1 rights, because those rights have now been vindicated in a judicial order, that Congress can target that action pursuant to section 5.

Another question looms as well: Might the Court resuscitate the principle of *Guest* at some point in the future? Might it hold, for example, that the murder of a protestor by a mob of private citizens, because the protestor was on the way to a political rally, constitutes action that Congress can outlaw based on its "power to enforce, by appropriate legislation," the rights to speak and to assemble that are incorporated into section 1?[305] As the Court considers such questions,

---

[303] *See* 529 U.S. at 624. At the same time, the Court's subsequent embrace of the equal-sovereignty principle in *Shelby County* might complicate the fashioning of a narrowed statute along these lines. *See supra* Section 11.B.5.

[304] Consider, for example, a non-state-actor mob of private citizens who proceed to lock up a state officer who is trying to protect jailed prisoners before seizing and murdering the prisoners. Such a case might support punishment of the mob members pursuant to section 5 legislation because it involves facts not present in the group-acting-only-against-an-individual scenario posited by Justice Brennan in *Guest*. The theory would be that this mob interfered with the victim's constitutional rights in a particularly direct way by purposefully taking out the very state actor who was attempting to safeguard those very rights. One possible difficulty with this argument is that the indictment in *Harris* set forth similar facts and the Court in that case nonetheless found that the underlying prosecution was not constitutionally authorized by the enforcement power. But the Court in *Harris*—and certainly the Court in *Guest*—never focused on the potential significance of this piece of the constitutional puzzle, and it is possible, in particular, that the Court in *Harris* did not deem the interfering-with-a-state-official aspect of the case significant because it had nothing to do with the elements set forth in the governing statute. In this vein, it is noteworthy that the Court rejected a Thirteenth Amendment-based defense of the same statute on the ground that the measure, on its face, extended to many cases that reached beyond that amendment's properly understood concern about discrimination against persons recently liberated from bondage. *See Harris*, 106 U.S. at 640–41.

[305] The Court's willingness to rein in the section 5 power not only in *Morrison*, but also in *Shelby County*, *see supra* Section 11.5, suggests that the answer to this

it may find itself reflecting on another body of law that now does allow private-party-targeting legislation akin to the statutes long ago invalidated in *Harris* and the *Civil Rights Cases*—namely the body of law built around Congress's power to enforce the Thirteenth Amendment, to which the next chapter turns.

---

question, at least in the short term, may well be "no." In the longer term, however, a new set of Justices might have no more hesitance about abandoning *Morrison* than the Court that decided *Morrison* had about retreating from *Guest*, particularly in light of the intense criticism that decision has received at the hands of historians and legal scholars. *See, e.g.*, Post & Siegel, *supra* note 301, at 475–76, 478 (2000) (concluding that *Harris* and the *Civil Rights Cases* did not and do not support a sweeping ban on regulating private behavior under section 5 because in those cases "the court struck down legislation that prescribed 'rules for the conduct of individuals in society toward each other' without being 'corrective of any constitutional wrong committed by the States' " and thus were "largely irrelevant precedents" in *Morrison*; adding that, while the Court in the end did apply the congruence and proportionality test in a context-specific fashion to the VAWA, as opposed to viewing the law as *ipso facto* unconstitutional because it regulated private actors, the Court was "quite careless" in doing so, including because it failed to deal with the powerful case for applying a nationwide remedy in this context (quoting *The Civil Rights Cases*, 109 U.S. at 14)); Estreicher & Lemos, *supra* note 106, at 145–46 (explaining in detail why "it is far from clear that either [*Harris* or the *Civil Rights Cases*] supports the conclusion that congress may not target private conduct as a means to remedy or prevent unconstitutional state action"; emphasizing that the reasoning in each case provided "no basis for the conclusion that Congress lacks the power to legislate against private conduct as a means to remedy or prevent unconstitutional state action," such as the well-documented unconstitutional state action, in the form of discriminatory enforcement, on which Congress relied in enacting the VAWA); *id.* at 146 n.153 (also concluding that Professors Post and Siegel argue "persuasively" that "*Harris* and the *Civil Rights Cases* are best understood as relics of a bygone era").

Chapter 12

THE THIRTEENTH AMENDMENT ENFORCEMENT POWER

Analysis

Earlier chapters have detailed how the Court in *United States v. Morrison*[1] rebuffed attempts to defend the civil-remedy provision of the Violence Against Women Act (VAWA) as a permissible exercise of congressional power under both the Commerce Clause and section 5 of the Fourteenth Amendment.[2] But could there be another source of authority supportive of this enactment? In the wake of *Morrison*, some analysts suggested that the Thirteenth Amendment might fill the gap.[3] Section 1 of that Amendment abolished "slavery [and] involuntary servitude, except as a punishment for crime," throughout the United States.[4] Section 2 of the Amendment—in the mold of its companion post-Civil War provisions[5]—gives Congress the "power to enforce this article by appropriate legislation."[6] Section 1 of the

---

1 529 U.S. 598 (2000).

2 *See supra* Sections 4.A, 11.C.

3 *See* Lawrence G. Sager, Commentary, *A Letter to the Supreme Court Regarding the Missing Argument in* Brzonkala v. Morrison, 75 N.Y.U. L. REV. 150, 153 (2000) (stating that "the reasoning of *Jones*"—which is discussed *infra* Section 12.A—is "fully apt" as to *Morrison*); Alexander Tsesis, Symposium, *Gender Discrimination and the Thirteenth Amendment*, 112 COLUM. L REV. 1641, 1661–68 (2012) (addressing this subject in detail); Marcellene Elizabeth Hearn, Comment, *A Thirteenth Amendment Defense of the Violence Against Women Act*, 146 U. PA. L. REV. 1097, 1100 (1998) (arguing that the Thirteenth Amendment should be understood to "abolish any form of servitude found in the twentieth century" and that violence against women would qualify as an "incident" of such servitude); *see also* Lawrence G. Sager, *Congress's Authority to Enact the Violence Against Women Act: One More Pass at the Missing Argument*, 121 YALE L.J. ONLINE 629, 637 (2012). One of us floated this idea not long after the ruling in *Morrison* came down. *See* DAN T. COENEN, CONSTITUTIONAL LAW: THE COMMERCE CLAUSE 192–94 (2004) (raising the issue but also noting that "[t]he Court's sharp focus in *Jones* on the history of race discrimination provides a basis for arguing that its principle would not sustain the law concerning sex discrimination at issue in *Morrison* if that law were defended on Thirteenth Amendment grounds").

4 U.S. CONST. amend. XIII, § 1.

5 *See supra* Chapter 11.

6 U.S. CONST. amend. XIII, § 2. For a deep dive into the origins of the Thirteenth Amendment, including the possible implications for the application of section 2, see

Thirteenth Amendment is highly unusual in that the prohibition it establishes does not target only government actors; it also reaches purely *private* persons who subject others to slavery or involuntary servitude.[7] Building on this idea, the Court established as early as 1883 that the supplementary power given to Congress by section 2 permits federal lawmakers not only to impose punishment for holding others in bondage, but also to eradicate "all badges and incidents of slavery."[8] In that same ruling, however, the Court gave this phrase a circumscribed reach by declaring that explicit forms of race-based discrimination did not fall within its ambit.[9]

A. *JONES V. ALFRED H. MAYER CO.* AND ITS PRESENT-DAY IMPLICATIONS

A new vision of the Thirteenth Amendment took hold, however, with the Court's 1968 ruling in *Jones v. Alfred H. Mayer Co.*[10] In that case, the plaintiffs challenged private race discrimination in the sale of housing under a federal statute enacted close on the heels of emancipation.[11] In response, the Court again declared that Congress

---

James Gray Pope, *Section 1 of the Thirteenth Amendment and the Badges and Incidents of Slavery*, 65 UCLA L. REV. 426, 433–51 (2018).

[7] *See* United States v. Stanley (*The Civil Rights Cases*), 109 U.S. 3, 23 (1883) (stating that the Thirteenth Amendment "eradicate[d] all forms and incidents of slavery and involuntary servitude," and that this is true "whether sanctioned by State legislation or not"; Bray v. Alexandria Women's Health Clinic, 506 U.S. 263, 278 (1993) (noting that, among the "few such rights" that are "protected against private, as well as official, encroachment" are "the Thirteenth Amendment right to be free from involuntary servitude, and, in the same Thirteenth Amendment context, the right of interstate travel" (internal citations omitted)); LAURENCE H. TRIBE, AMERICAN CONSTITUTIONAL LAW § 5–15, at 924 (3d ed. 2000) (noting that "the Thirteenth Amendment differs from the Fourteenth . . . in that, even absent implementing legislation, it is not subject to a state action requirement"). Another constitutional right that the Court has sometimes described as protected against private, as well as public, action is the unenumerated "right to travel." *See* Saenz v. Roe, 526 U.S. 489, 498 (1999) (noting that this constitutional protection is "assertable against private interference as well as governmental action," thus giving rise to a "virtually unconditional personal right, guaranteed by the Constitution to us all" (quoting Shapiro v. Thompson, 394 U.S. 618, 643 (1969) (Stewart, J., concurring))). The ability of Congress to legislate in support of this right is shrouded in uncertainty, in part because both the source and the scope of the right are unclear and because federal lawmakers, in any event, have broad authority to safeguard interstate movement pursuant to the commerce power. *See supra* Section 4.B. For a suggestion that there may be a limited number of other constitutional rights enforceable against private actors, and thus potentially supportive of congressional authority to enact implementing federal legislation, see United States v. Guest, 383 U.S. 745, 772 (1966) (Harlan, J., concurring in part and dissenting in part).

[8] *The Civil Rights Cases*, 109 U.S. at 20–21.

[9] *See id.* at 24 (holding that the denial to Black citizens of equal access to public accommodations on the basis of their race did not qualify as a "badge of slavery").

[10] 392 U.S. 409 (1968).

[11] The plaintiff's civil action was brought under 42 U.S.C. § 1982, which specifies that "[a]ll citizens of the United States shall have the same right, in every State and Territory, as is enjoyed by white citizens thereof to inherit, purchase, lease, sell, hold,

could invoke section 2 to "pass all laws necessary and proper for abolishing all badges and incidents of slavery."[12] It then, however, departed from earlier case law by giving this proposition a much-broadened meaning. As Justice Stewart explained for himself and six other members of the Court, "exclusion of Negroes from white communities [had become] a substitute for the Black Codes," which themselves had served as a substitute for legalized enslavement.[13] Thus, Congress could "rationally . . . determine"[14] that the challenged practice of housing discrimination by private sellers was a "relic of slavery" permissibly banned by way of federal legislation enacted pursuant to the Thirteenth Amendment enforcement power.[15]

Later cases reaffirmed these principles.[16] Ensuing developments in Commerce Clause law, however, rendered the doctrine of *Jones* of

---

and convey real and personal property." *Id.* In *Jones*, the Court interpreted this text to ban private, as well as public, behavior. *Jones*, 392 U.S. at 413. In later cases, the Court likewise applied to private action an additional set of limits laid down by 42 U.S.C. § 1981, including its mandate that "[a]ll persons . . . shall have the same right . . . to make and enforce contracts . . . as is enjoyed by white citizens." *See* Runyon v. McCrary, 427 U.S. 160, 168, 193 (1976).

[12] *Jones*, 392 U.S. at 439 (quoting *The Civil Rights Cases*, 109 U.S. at 20) (emphasis omitted).

[13] *Id.* at 442.

[14] *Id.* at 440.

[15] *Id.* at 443.

[16] *See* Patterson v. McLean Credit Union, 491 U.S. 164, 189 (1989) (holding that 42 U.S.C. § 1981 validly applied to a private party's race-based refusal to promote a Black employee); *Runyon*, 427 U.S. at 172 (holding that 42 U.S.C. § 1981 validly applied to racial discrimination in private school admissions); Sullivan v. Little Hunting Park, Inc., 396 U.S. 229, 236–37 (1969) (holding that 42 U.S.C. § 1982 validly applied to a private corporation's race-based refusal to approve a member's transfer of shares to a Black assignee). It is important to note that the Court has not considered how its reformulation of Fourteenth Amendment law in *City of Boerne v. Flores*, 521 U.S. 507 (1997), *see supra* Section 11.B.3, might impact future application of the Thirteenth Amendment enforcement power. Not surprisingly, commentators have wondered whether the Court will adjust its approach to the Thirteenth Amendment enforcement power in light of this important post-*Jones* development. *See, e.g.*, Jennifer M. McAward, *The Scope of Congress's Thirteenth Amendment Enforcement Power after* City of Boerne v. Flores, 88 WASH. U. L. REV. 77, 81 (2010) ("In light of *City of Boerne*, *Jones* is arguably a remnant of the past. However, the Court itself has never explicitly questioned the *Jones* standard, and lower courts continue to invoke that standard to evaluate Thirteenth Amendment legislation."). *But see* Jack M. Balkin, *The Reconstruction Power*, 85 N.Y.U. L. REV. 1801, 1822 (2010) (indicating that, in keeping with the approach of *Jones*, "[t]he framers of the Thirteenth Amendment assumed that Congress would define the badges and incidents of slavery and decide what legislation was appropriate to eliminate them, and that the courts would defer to any reasonable construction"). Even if the Court were to apply Fourteenth-Amendment-like congruence-and-proportionality analysis to Thirteenth Amendment enforcement-power issues, however, there is reason to believe it would not retreat from the holding of *Jones*. To be sure, state-sanctioned chattel slavery no longer exists within the United States. But it seems incontestable that slavery itself was not the only form of oppression targeted by section 1. *See* Jack M. Balkin & Sanford Levinson, Symposium, *The Dangerous Thirteenth Amendment*, 112 COLUM. L. REV. 1459, 1499 (2012) (observing that existing doctrine fails to recognize the Thirteenth Amendment's proper application beyond the context of chattel slavery);

limited practical significance in economic-activity cases, such as *Jones* itself.[17] Even so, scholars have continued to ponder the present-day implications of that case.[18] Congress has taken note of the Thirteenth Amendment as well. Most notably, in 2009, it relied squarely on its section 2 power to enact a provision of the Matthew Shepard and James Byrd, Jr., Hate Crimes Prevention Act (the Shepard and Byrd Act) that outlaws acts of physical violence—

Pope, *supra* note 6, at 436–37 (detailing the historical case that the framers of the Thirteenth Amendment meant for Section 1 to ban not just chattel slavery, but also certain "badges and incidents" of slavery, including, according to many Republicans at the time, forms of private discrimination as set forth in the Civil Rights Act of 1866). In any event, during the centuries preceding adoption of the Thirteenth Amendment, chattel slavery itself had been institutionalized on a massive scale, the drafters of the Amendment envisioned congressional remediation of the practical consequences of such oppression, the "badges and incidents" test carried forward this idea, and forms of dehumanizing race-based discrimination remain widespread to this day. Against this backdrop, it would be entirely plausible for courts to conclude that the congressional prohibition of overt race-based discrimination in housing sales and other commercial activities continues to qualify as a "congruent and proportionate" remedial response to the chattel-slavery system and its persisting aftershocks. *See generally* Michael A. Lawrence, *Racial Justice Demands Truth and Reconciliation*, 80 U. PITT. L. REV. 69, 72 (2018) (discussing the "persistent, deeply-rooted systemic racism [that] has worked, without interruption, to oppress people of color on this continent," from "the earliest days of the slave markets of Virginia in 1619, to the economic disadvantages and disproportionately-skewed criminal justice system" of the present).

[17] *See, e.g.*, McAward, *supra* note 16, at 134 (suggesting that "much of the civil-rights-related legislation that Congress has passed under the Thirteenth Amendment . . . likely would be sustained as appropriate legislation under the Commerce Clause"). The overlap of the Commerce Clause and the Thirteenth Amendment has been noted by Professor George Rutherglen, who posits that Congress could have relied on its Section 2 power, apart from its Commerce Clause power, to support enactment of the Civil Rights Act of 1964. George Rutherglen, Symposium, *The Thirteenth Amendment, the Power of Congress, and the Shifting Sources of Civil Rights Law*, 112 COLUM. L. REV. 1551, 1563–68 (2012); *see also* George Rutherglen, Essay, *State Action, Private Action, and the Thirteenth Amendment*, 94 VA. L. REV. 1367, 1391 (2008) (claiming that "*Jones* . . . as a theoretical matter, . . . simply invoked the existing understanding of congressional power already established under the Commerce Clause"). In particular, because house selling and contract making would seem to entail "economic activity," modern-day commerce-power doctrine, *see supra* Section 4.D.1, lends powerful support to the validity of federal anti-discrimination laws, such as 42 U.S.C. §§ 1981 and 1982, *see supra* note 11, on a substantial-effects theory.

[18] *See, e.g.*, G. Sidney Buchanan, *The Quest for Freedom: A Legal History of the Thirteenth Amendment*, 12 HOUS. L. REV. 843, 852 (1975) (stating that *Jones* "leaves unanswered" whether the Thirteenth Amendment extends "into the inner circle of associational choice"); *see also* Balkin & Levinson, *supra* note 16, at 1499 (observing that the Thirteenth Amendment, even after *Jones*, has been largely neglected); Jamal Greene, *Thirteenth Amendment Optimism*, 112 COLUM. L. REV. 1733, 1760 (2012) ("The Thirteenth Amendment analysis in *Jones* . . . has done little important judicial work since."). For one recent treatment touching on the potential implications of section 2, see Ndjuoh MehChu, *Help Me to Find My Children: A Thirteenth Amendment Challenge to Family Separation*, 17 STAN. J. CIV. RTS. & CIV. LIBERTIES 133, 174–82 (2021) (contending that the Trump Administration's policy of involuntarily separating migrant families implicated Thirteenth Amendment-based guarantees and highlighting the possibility of section 2-based corrective legislation); *see also infra* note 25 (citing additional sources).

including violence that has no relation to any Commerce-Clause-related economic activity—based on the victim's race or ethnicity.[19]

As *Morrison* holds, Congress ordinarily cannot outlaw private acts of physical violence under either the Commerce Clause or the Fourteenth Amendment.[20] In *Griffin v. Breckenridge*,[21] however, the Court built on *Jones* to hold that Congress could, as it did in 42 U.S.C. § 1985(3), invoke the Thirteenth Amendment to create a statutory remedy for physical injuries inflicted on Black citizens who were "the victims of conspiratorial, racially discriminatory private action aimed at depriving them of the basic rights that the law secures to all free men."[22] Drawing on *Griffin*, lower courts have upheld the hate-crime prohibitions embodied in the Shepard and Byrd Act, at least insofar as they outlaw race-based conduct.[23] And there is powerful, if not incontrovertible, reason to conclude that they have been correct in doing so given the centrality of race-based physical violence to both

---

19 *See* 18 U.S.C. § 249. For further information on the operation of the act, see *The Matthew Shepard and James Byrd, Jr., Hate Crimes Prevention Act of 2009*, U.S. DEP'T OF JUSTICE (Aug. 6, 2015), https://www.justice.gov/crt/matthew-shepard-and-james-byrd-jr-hate-crimes-prevention-act-2009. Notably, that provision of the act also extends to violence based on the victim's religion. For a discussion of this feature of the act, see *infra* note 36 and accompanying text.

20 *See supra* Sections 4.A, 11.C.

21 403 U.S. 88 (1971).

22 *Id.* at 105.

23 The key provision is 18 U.S.C. § 249(a)(1), which imposes criminal penalties on "[w]hoever, whether or not acting under color of law, willfully causes bodily injury to any person . . . because of the actual or perceived race, color, religion, or national origin of any person." A related statute is 18 U.S.C. § 245(b)(2)(B), which criminalizes violence, motivated by "race, color, religion or national origin," engaged in with the goal of keeping the victim from "participating in or enjoying any benefit, service, privilege, program, facility or activity provided or administered by any State or subdivision thereof"); *see also* 18 U.S.C. § 247(c) (criminalizing vandalism or destruction of "religious real property because of the race, color, or ethnic characteristics of any individual associated with that religious property"). Among the cases upholding these provisions are *United States v. Nelson*, 277 F.3d 164, 181 (2d Cir. 2002) (deeming § 245(b)(2)(B), as applied to race-based interference with use of a public facility, to fall "comfortably within" the Thirteenth Amendment enforcement power), *United States v. Cannon*, 750 F.3d 492, 505 (5th Cir. 2014) (holding that § 249(a)(1) constitutes a valid exercise of Congress's section 2 power in the context of racially motivated violence), *United States v. Hatch*, 722 F.3d 1193, 1209 (10th Cir. 2013) (same), *United States v. Metcalf*, 881 F.3d 641, 645 (8th Cir. 2018) (same), and *United States v. Allen*, 341 F.3d 870, 884 (9th Cir. 2003) (holding that § 245(b)(2)(B) constitutes a valid exercise of Congress's section 2 power in the context of race-based interference with the use of a public park). *See also* United States v. Nicholson, 185 F. Supp. 2d 982, 992 (E.D. Wis. 2002) (holding, based in part on the Thirteenth Amendment, that Congress can outlaw race-based acts of arson). Notably, the constraints imposed by the Shepard and Byrd Act reach beyond those imposed by § 1985, which the Court upheld in *Griffin*, in part because that act does not require conspiratorial conduct. *See also Bray*, 506 U.S. at 269–77 (limiting the operation of section 1985 by ruling that the targeting of persons seeking an abortion does not entail invidious discrimination against women under the principle of *Griffin*).

the pre-emancipation slave system and the post-emancipation reign of terror that carried forward the legacy of human bondage.[24]

Congress in the future may look to wield its Thirteenth Amendment enforcement authority more aggressively than it has in the past. One interesting possibility is that federal legislators might seek to use the power to rein in forms of *state* action that it cannot now reach under the Fourteenth Amendment enforcement power.[25]

---

[24] *See, e.g.*, *Cannon*, 750 F.3d at 502–03 ("Just as master-on-slave violence was intended to enforce the social and racial superiority of the attacker and the relative powerlessness of the victim, Congress could conceive that modern racially motivated violence communicates to the victim that he or she must remain in a subservient position, unworthy of the decency afforded to other races." (quoting *Hatch*, 722 F.3d at 1206)); United States v. Roof, 225 F. Supp. 3d 438, 448 (D.S.C. 2016) (concluding that it "seems inarguable" that "racially motivated violence" is a "badge or incident of slavery"), *aff'd*, United States v. Roof, 10 F.4th 314, 391–93 (4th Cir. 2021). *But see* Gail Heriot & Alison Somin, *Sleeping Giant?: Section Two of the Thirteenth Amendment, Hate Crimes Legislation, and Academia's Favorite New Vehicle for the Expansion of Federal Power*, ENGAGE, Oct. 2012, at 31, 35 (arguing that courts should not uphold the Shepard and Byrd Act under the Thirteenth Amendment enforcement power because the act "does not attempt to remove a legal disability imposed on former slaves or slave descendants," but "simply adds federal penalties for conduct that was already illegal").

[25] *See supra* Section 11.B.4 (discussing the limits laid down by the Court in *City of Boerne*). For examples of how the Thirteenth Amendment might permit Congress to target state action related to race in a way that reaches beyond what may be possible under the remedial Fourteenth Amendment power as outlined in *City of Boerne*, see Alexander Tsesis, *The Problem of Confederate Symbols: A Thirteenth Amendment Approach*, 75 TEMP. L. REV. 539, 610–12 (2002) (arguing that, on a "badges and incidents" theory of section 2, Congress could pass legislation banning the use of Confederate symbols on state property); Douglas L. Colbert, *Challenging the Challenge: Thirteenth Amendment as a Prohibition Against the Racial Use of Peremptory Challenges*, 76 CORNELL L. REV. 1, 120–25 (1990) (suggesting, at least by implication, the possibility of section 2-based federal legislation outlawing peremptory challenges that have the effect of excluding Black citizens from juries, including for ostensibly race-neutral reasons); William M. Carter, Jr., *A Thirteenth Amendment Framework for Combating Racial Profiling*, 39 HARV. C.R.-C.L. L. REV. 17, 86–93 (2004) (advocating for the use of section 2 to impose federal limits on racial profiling by local law enforcement officers, perhaps including limits that reach beyond those Congress can impose pursuant to the Fourteenth Amendment enforcement power); *see also* Alexander Tsesis, *Congressional Authority to Interpret the Thirteenth Amendment*, 71 MD. L. REV. 40, 42–46, 58 (2011) (arguing, on originalist grounds, that section 2 supports a broad congressional power to pass legislation such as the Civil Rights Act of 1964 and the Shepard and Byrd Act and that, in any event, recent rulings that restrict the Fourteenth Amendment enforcement power pursuant to the remediation-based "congruency and proportionality" limit do not and should not carry over to Thirteenth Amendment cases). *But see* Jennifer M. McAward, *Congressional Authority to Interpret the Thirteenth Amendment: A Response to Professor Tsesis*, 71 MD. L. REV. 60, 64–79 (2011) (questioning Professor Tsesis's historical analysis and suggesting that the Court's rulings as to the Fourteenth Amendment enforcement power should help inform the scope of the Thirteenth Amendment enforcement power). For a proposed doctrinal approach that would fundamentally alter current law regarding public race-related affirmative-action programs by shifting attention from Fourteenth Amendment law to Thirteenth Amendment law, see Michael A. Lawrence, *The Thirteenth Amendment as Basis for Racial Truth and Reconciliation*, 62 ARIZ. L. REV. 637, 639 (2020) (advocating use of the Thirteenth Amendment enforcement power, especially in light of current obstacles to applying the Fourteenth Amendment, to remediate centuries-long and systemic racism, including through "the broad use of

No less important, Congress might seek to justify restraints on *private* behavior, not regulable under the commerce power, that reach beyond race-based physical violence. It might well, for example, be able to draw on section 2 to prohibit racially motivated threats or fighting words if it takes care to frame such legislation to avoid First Amendment problems.[26] Perhaps, as some scholars argue, Congress also can invoke the Thirteenth Amendment to pass some laws that outlaw forms of private action that, even though not explicitly race-based, involve the sort of dehumanizing treatment that lay at the core of antebellum slavery.[27] Some commentators have raised the possibility, for example, that Congress could deploy section 2 to outlaw purely private action that involves serious forms of child abuse.[28]

all manner of governmental remedies, including unapologetically race-conscious affirmative action measures"). For an exploration of how Section 2 might address state action concerning matters other than race discrimination, see, e.g., Andrew Koppelman, *Forced Labor: A Thirteenth Amendment Defense of Abortion*, 84 NW. U. L. REV. 480, 484 (1990) (suggesting that the Thirteenth Amendment imposes limits on state-based abortion restrictions because such restrictions make women "into a servant caste, a group which, by virtue of a status of birth, is held subject to a special duty to serve others and not themselves"; thus implying that federal legislation implementing this concept would be permissible).

[26] Along these lines, see Alexander Tsesis, Symposium, *Regulating Intimidating Speech*, 41 HARV. J. ON LEGIS. 389, 390 (2004) (advocating for the use of section 2 to pass a federal hate-speech ban); Akhil Reed Amar, Comment, *The Case of the Missing Amendment*: R.A.V. v. City of St. Paul, 106 HARV. L. REV. 124, 126 (1992) (positing that Congress might be able to prohibit certain forms of racist language and symbols under the Thirteenth Amendment enforcement power); *see also* William M. Carter, Jr., *The Thirteenth Amendment and Pro-Equality Speech*, 112 COLUM. L. REV. 1855, 1875 (2012) (urging that section 2 permits Congress to prohibit private retaliation undertaken in response to pro-equality speech). For an early case rejecting the idea that Congress could outlaw threats aimed at blocking Black citizens from seeking work, see *Hodges v. United States*, 203 U.S. 1, 18–19 (1906). *But see* Memphis v. Greene, 451 U.S. 100, 126 n.40 (1981) (indicating that the Court in *Jones* had overruled *Hodges* (citing *Jones*, 392 U.S. at 441 n.78)).

[27] *See* Taja-Nia Y. Henderson, *The Ironic Promise of the Thirteenth Amendment for Offender Anti-Discrimination Law*, 17 LEWIS & CLARK L. REV. 1141, 1147–48 (2013) (advocating for the use of section 2 to pass legislation barring many forms of private discrimination against persons with criminal records in light of the "civil death" convicted persons now face, which may include the loss of the right to vote, exclusion from jury service, and divestment from public pension programs). *But cf.* Richard Delgado, *Four Reservations on Civil Rights Reasoning by Analogy: The Case of Latinos and Other Nonblack Groups*, 112 COLUM L. REV. 1883, 1885–86 (2012) (sounding a "cautionary note" about efforts to "revitalize[ ]"the Thirteenth Amendment so as to "aid nonblack minorities, such as Latinos, Asian Americans, Native Americans, and Middle Eastern people, [in] gain[ing] relief from oppressive conditions," because such efforts might provoke a judicial narrowing of the Thirteenth Amendment, much as has happened with the Fourteenth Amendment).

[28] *See* Akhil Reed Amar & Daniel Widawsky, *Child Abuse as Slavery: A Thirteenth Amendment Response to* DeShaney, 105 HARV. L. REV. 1359, 1363–65 (1992) (contending that child abuse falls within section 1 of the Thirteenth Amendment and thus implying that Congress could impose sanctions on such behavior under section 2); Susan H. Bitensky, *An Analytical Ode to Personhood: The Unconstitutionality of Corporal Punishment of Children Under the Thirteenth*

B. QUESTIONS FOR THE FUTURE

These ruminations circle us back to the question, posed at the outset of this chapter, about whether the sex-based-violence provision of the VAWA might be sustainable as an exercise of the Thirteenth Amendment enforcement power.[29] The Court's clear-eyed focus on *race* discrimination in *Jones* and *Griffin* offers reason to conclude that the "badges and incidents" principle of those cases would not support a ban on *sex*-based abuse.[30] But a closer look reveals that things are not as simple as they might first seem. To begin, there is no doubt that section 1 of the Thirteenth Amendment outlaws all forms of "slavery" and "involuntary servitude," whether or not related to race.[31] In addition, as many analysts have noted, the history of the nation's treatment of women has a measure of connectedness to the history of American slavery.[32] Finally, *Griffin* declared that § 1985 requires a showing of "some racial, *or perhaps otherwise class-based,* invidiously discriminatory animus,"[33] and the Court later took care to reserve the question whether Congress could make forms of sex-based subjugation actionable under this

---

Amendment, 53 SANTA CLARA L. REV. 1, 14 (2013) (arguing that Congress holds the power under section 2 of the Thirteenth Amendment to legislate a ban on the corporal punishment of children). *But see* Greene, *supra* note 18, at 1742–44, 1748–49 (considering arguments that section 2 would support federal limits on child abuse and domestic violence but expressing skepticism that courts would accept such arguments in light of their potentially wide-ranging implications).

[29] For scholarly arguments to this effect, see the authorities collected *supra* note 3.

[30] This conclusion may gain added force from the Court's insistence in *Morrison* that "we can think of no better example of the police power, which the Founders denied the National Government and reposed in the States, than the suppression of violent crime and vindication of its victims." *Morrison*, 529 U.S. at 618.

[31] *See, e.g.*, *The Civil Rights Cases*, 109 U.S. at 24 (stating that "[t]he Thirteenth Amendment has respect, not to distinctions of race, or class, or color, but to slavery"); *see also* McDonald v. Santa Fe Trail Transp. Co., 427 U.S. 273, 288 n.18 (1976) (deeming § 1981 applicable to all discrimination based on race, regardless of the racial identity of the victim, in part because "Congress is authorized under the Enforcement Clause of the Thirteenth Amendment to legislate in regard to 'every race and individual' ").

[32] In the picture are both: (1) the linkage to the slave system of the pervasive sexual abuse of Black women, *see* Crystal N. Feimster, *"What If I Am a Woman": Black Women's Campaigns for Sexual Justice and Citizenship*, *in* THE WORLD THE CIVIL WAR MADE 249 (Gregory P. Downs & Kate Masur, eds. 2015) (offering a historical examination of "black women's resistance to sexual violence during the transition from slavery to freedom" and noting ways in which "their campaigns against rape shaped national debates about the emerging meanings of freedom and black citizenship"); and (2) the existence of some parallels between the law's historical imposition of disabilities on the basis of race and its historical imposition of disabilities on the basis of sex, *see* Frontiero v. Richardson, 411 U.S. 677, 685 (1973) (opinion of Brennan, J.) (suggesting that "in many respects" such parallels existed "throughout much of the 19th century"); *see also* Tsesis, *supra* note 3, at 1661–68 (discussing how the "rhetoric of the antislavery and women's rights movements often overlapped").

[33] *Griffin*, 403 U.S. at 102 (emphasis added).

principle.[34] Building on these ideas, lower courts have suggested that the principle of *Jones* could support federal hate-crime legislation targeting *religious* discrimination.[35] These authorities might furnish the basis for an argument for upholding the VAWA provision at issue in *Morrison* under the Thirteenth Amendment. After all, if religious discrimination is close enough to race discrimination when it comes to identifying the badges and incidents of slavery, then—perhaps even *a fortiori*—courts should view sex discrimination as close enough to race discrimination, too.[36]

The foregoing discussion shows why the Thirteenth Amendment continues to play an important role, independent of both the commerce power and the Fourteenth and Fifteenth Amendment powers, in defining congressional authority. So, too, does the post-*Jones* emergence of the anti-commandeering limit on the former font, but not the latter fonts, of federal lawmaking authority. Might Congress, for example, pass a law that requires states to adopt hate-crime laws that regulate private wrongdoers? Faced with such a statute, the Court could reason that restrictions on private conduct under the Thirteenth Amendment are akin to restrictions imposed under the commerce power and therefore subject to the anti-commandeering rule.[37] On the other hand, the Court might view the Thirteenth Amendment as more closely analogous to the Fourteenth and Fifteenth Amendments, as to which the anti-commandeering rule appears to be inapplicable.[38] These and other questions will be

---

34 *See Bray*, 506 U.S. at 269.

35 *See Nelson*, 277 F.3d at 190 (concluding "that § 245(b)(2)(B)'s prohibition against private violence motivated by the victim's race, religion, etc., and because of the victim's use of a public facility, etc., falls comfortably within Congress's power" (internal footnote omitted)); *Metcalf*, 2016 WL 827763, at *1 ("Congress could have rationally determined that violence motivated by 'actual or perceived race, color, religion, or national origin' was a badge or incident of slavery." (quoting 18 U.S.C. § 249(a)(1))). *But cf.* Baer v. Baer, 450 F. Supp. 481, 493 (N.D. Cal. 1978) (declining to "hold that § 2 of the Thirteenth Amendment empowered Congress to grant civil redress under § 1985(3) for private conspiracies denying freedom of religion"). *See generally Hatch*, 722 F.3d at 1205 (discussing this issue).

36 A counterargument rests on the idea that, in enacting the Shepard and Byrd Act, Congress found that "members of certain religious and national origin groups were . . . perceived to be distinct 'races' " at the time of the Thirteenth Amendment's adoption. Shepard and Byrd Act, Pub. L. No. 111–84 § 4702(8), 123 Stat. 2190, 2836 (2009). *See* St. Francis College v. Al-Khazraji, 481 U.S. 604, 612–13 (1987) (noting this point in discussing modern hate-crime legislation); *see also* Shaare Tefila Congregation v. Cobb, 481 U.S. 615, 617–18 (1987) (finding the relevant question to be whether a protected group was considered a "separate race" when § 1982 was created).

37 *See supra* Section 5.B.

38 *See Hatch*, 722 F.3d at 1202 (noting that the Thirteenth Amendment was "enacted after the Tenth Amendment" and that "[n]o party has cited, nor could we find, any authority stating that the Tenth Amendment nonetheless imposes limits on Congress's Thirteenth Amendment powers"). In a similar vein, it might be that the Thirteenth Amendment enforcement power provides a mechanism for side-stepping

decided in the future against the backdrop of a body of section 2 "badges and incidents" law that, while increasingly a subject of scholarly examination,[39] remains largely undeveloped in the work of the courts.[40]

limits on sovereign-immunity-based limits on Congress's ability to use the commerce power to impose damages liability on states for certain forms of behavior. *See infra* Section 13.A n.13 (citing authority for the inapplicability of sovereign-immunity principles to laws founded on the Thirteenth Amendment enforcement power). Might Congress, for example, draw on the Thirteenth Amendment to require all employers (including state employers) to pay all workers a "living wage," so as to extirpate oppressive working conditions? *See* Ruben J. Garcia, *The Thirteenth Amendment and Economic Justice: The Thirteenth Amendment and Minimum Wage Laws*, 19 NEV. L.J. 479, 479, 492 (2018) (arguing that the Thirteenth Amendment, at least when coupled with the Fourteenth Amendment, gives Congress authority to legislate the "equal application of minimum wage laws to all workers"; reasoning that the Thirteenth Amendment "explicitly addresses labor," has been interpreted "more broadly than the Fourteenth Amendment," and "applies to private action as well as government action"). If Congress can use the Thirteenth Amendment to pass a substantive prohibition of this kind, it would seem to follow that Congress could subject states to money-damage remedies for violating that same law, even though such remedies could not be imposed if the same law were enacted under only the Commerce Clause. *See supra* Section 11.B.4 (discussing the Court's indication that the Reconstruction Amendments, in part because they post-dated the Eleventh Amendment, allow congressional state-sovereign-immunity abrogations that are not permitted when Congress invokes only the commerce power).

[39] *See* Heriot & Somin, *supra* note 24, at 31 (noting the "growing movement in . . . academia . . . to use the Thirteenth Amendment's Section 2 to address a variety of social ills thought to be in some way traceable back to slavery").

[40] *But cf.* Greene, *supra* note 18, at 1734–35 (maintaining that while many proposed applications of the Thirteenth Amendment are "conceptually sound," it is "nearly self-evident that neither the current U.S. Supreme Court nor any presently imaginable U.S. Supreme Court is likely to accept any of [them]").

Chapter 13

EXTERNAL LIMITS ON NON-COMMERCE POWERS

Analysis

Sec.

As we have seen, multiple federalism-based "external" restraints cabin Congress's use of its power to regulate interstate commerce.[1] Two of these restraints have provided the basis for invalidating acts of Congress in high-profile Supreme Court cases: the sovereign immunity rule of *Seminole Tribe v. Florida*[2] and *Alden v. Maine*[3]; and the anti-commandeering principle of *New York v. United States*[4] and *Printz v. United States*.[5] In addition, the Court has signaled its willingness to impose political-process-based constraints on the commerce power,[6] and a new process-related constraint—the "equal sovereignty" principle of *Shelby County v. Holder*[7]—has recently been applied in a non-commerce-power case. One might assume that these external limits, like the external limits on federal authority imposed by the Bill of Rights, apply in equal measure to all congressional powers.[8] The governing doctrine turns out, however, to be considerably more complicated than that.

---

1 *See supra* Chapter 5.

2 517 U.S. 44 (1996).

3 527 U.S. 706 (1999).

4 505 U.S. 144 (1992).

5 521 U.S. 898 (1997).

6 *See supra* Section 5.A (discussing the Court's rulings in *National League of Cities v. Usery*, 426 U.S. 833 (1976), and *Garcia v. San Antonio Metropolitan Transit Authority*, 469 U.S. 528 (1985)).

7 570 U.S. 529 (2013).

8 U.S. CONST. art. I, § 8, cl. 3.

A. SOVEREIGN IMMUNITY AND THE ANTI-LIABILITY PRINCIPLE

Take sovereign immunity. Although Congress may not abrogate this Eleventh Amendment-tied immunity pursuant to its commerce power,[9] it is free to do so pursuant to its Fourteenth and Fifteenth Amendment enforcement powers.[10] Indeed, in recent years, litigation over the scope of the enforcement powers has centered on the operation of this very principle.[11] The later-enacted-amendment/state-action-constraining logic of these rulings carries over to other powers, too.[12] It would seem to indicate, in particular, that Congress can strip away state sovereign immunity when it legislates pursuant to the Thirteenth Amendment,[13] as well as when it wields its enforcement powers under the sex-related Nineteenth Amendment and the age-related Twenty-sixth Amendment.[14]

No less important, the Court has held that not all the powers given to Congress by the original Constitution are subject to state-sovereign-immunity-based limitations on their use. Most notably, in *Central Virginia Community College v. Katz*,[15] the Court held that the Bankruptcy Clause—despite its proximity to the Commerce Clause in Article I—permits, to the extent it is applicable, Congress to abrogate state sovereign immunity.[16] Aggrieved copyright holders quickly drew on this ruling to argue that its principle should carry over to the Intellectual Property Clause, thus authorizing Congress to expose states to money-damages actions for violations of federal

---

9 *See supra* Section 5.B.

10 *See Seminole Tribe*, 517 U.S. at 60, 65–66. With respect to the Fourteenth Amendment, the proposition rests on the idea that that amendment, which postdates the Eleventh Amendment, was intended to "expand[ ] federal power at the expense of state autonomy." *Id.* at 55. Although the Court has not yet explicitly weighed in on the matter, similar logic supports the idea that *Seminole Tribe* has no applicability to Congress's power to enforce the Fifteenth Amendment as well. *See* Alabama State Conf. of NAACP v. Alabama, 949 F.3d 647, 654 (11th Cir. 2020) (holding that "if § 5 of the Fourteenth Amendment permits Congress to abrogate state sovereign immunity, so too must § 2 of the Fifteenth Amendment"), *vacated on other grounds*, 141 S. Ct. 2618 (2021); Mixon v. Ohio, 193 F.3d 389, 398–99 (6th Cir. 1999) (similar); OCA-Greater Hous. v. Texas, 867 F.3d 604, 614 (5th Cir. 2017) (similar).

11 *See supra* Section 11.B.4.

12 *See id.* (discussing the reasoning of *Fitzpatrick v. Bitzer*, 427 U.S. 445 (1976)).

13 *See* United States v. Nelson, 277 F.3d 164, 181 n.17 (2d Cir. 2002) (noting that "the scope of Congress's power under Section Two of the Thirteenth Amendment to enforce the prohibition on slavery and its badges and incidents probably remains unaffected by *Seminole Tribe*'s holding").

14 *See supra* Section 11.B.6 n.264.

15 546 U.S. 356 (2006).

16 Susan E. Hauser, *Necessary Fictions: Bankruptcy Jurisdiction After* Hood *and* Katz, 82 TUL. L. REV. 1181, 1185 (2008) (discussing at length the Court's decision in this case).

copyright law. In *Allen v. Cooper*,[17] however, the Court rejected this contention, characterizing *Katz* as a "good-for-one-clause-only" holding and thus suggesting, at least for the moment, that the bankruptcy power is the only Article I authority not subject to the *Seminole Tribe* rule.[18] At the same time, the Court in *Allen* did not fully foreclose the possibility that the law of sovereign immunity might not apply in march-step fashion across all of Congress's Article I powers.

Consider in this respect the naturalization power, which is granted to Congress in a passage located not just next to, but in the very same clause as, the text that vests Congress with authority to regulate bankruptcy.[19] Does this constitutional architecture signal that the bankruptcy-based power to abrogate sovereign-immunity entails a naturalization-based power to do so as well? Another question is whether the rule of *Seminole Tribe* and *Alden* should govern when Congress acts in the field of foreign-relations.[20] At the least, this power might operate in this way in some contexts—for example, if Congress leverages the specialized "plenary power" doctrine that governs in the field of immigration control.[21] Of

---

17 140 S. Ct. 994 (2020).

18 *Id.* at 1003.

19 U.S. CONST. art. I, § 8, cl. 4.

20 *See, e.g.*, Peter S. Menell, *Economic Implications of State Sovereign Immunity from Infringement of Federal Intellectual Property Rights*, 33 LOY. L.A. L. REV. 1399, 1460–61 (2000) (arguing that, because "state sovereignty has never been understood to extend to international affairs," Congress may be able to abrogate that immunity in the international-law context under the Necessary and Proper Clause). One argument for Congress's sweeping authority in this area stems from the thought that the federal power over foreign affairs has an inherent-in-the-nature-of-things, pre-constitutional quality, thus rendering state-protective doctrines inapplicable in this context. *Cf.* United States v. Curtiss-Wright Export Corp., 299 U.S. 304, 316 (1936) ("[S]ince the states severally never possessed international powers, such powers could not have been carved from the mass of state powers but obviously were transmitted to the United States from some other source."). *See generally* Janet R. Carter, Note, *Commandeering Under the Treaty Power*, 76 N.Y.U. L. REV. 598, 623–24 (2001) (developing this point). *But see, e.g.*, Jack L. Goldsmith, *Federal Courts, Foreign Affairs, and Federalism*, 83 VA. L. REV. 1617, 1660 n.184 (1997) (highlighting academic criticisms of *Curtiss-Wright*'s theory of preconstitutional powers). More important—and regardless of abstract theories concerning the source of the federal foreign-affairs power—there is no question that this power has long operated with unusual potency to crowd out competing claims of state authority. *See, e.g.*, United States v. Pink, 315 U.S. 203, 233 (1942) ("No State can rewrite our foreign policy to conform to its own domestic policies. Power over external affairs is not shared by the States; it is vested in the national government exclusively."); United States v. Belmont, 301 U.S. 324, 331 (1937) ("[C]omplete power over international affairs is in the national government and is not and cannot be subject to any curtailment or interference on the part of the several states."); *see also* THE FEDERALIST NO. 42 (Madison) ("If we are to be one nation in any respect, it clearly ought to be in respect to other nations.").

21 Assume, for example, that Congress by statute prohibits states from discriminating against non-citizens. Might Congress rely on its power over immigration to abrogate state sovereign immunity for violations of this statute? It might be significant in this regard that the Court has long recognized an especially

particular significance, it remains to be seen whether Congress has authority to abrogate state sovereign immunity when it invokes the Article I Necessary and Proper Clause to implement federal treaties made under Article II.[22] A final set of issues concerns whether the rule of *Seminole Tribe* and *Alden* operates when Congress wields the limited number of powers vested in it by the original Constitution to regulate states themselves—specifically, the Article I power to regulate federal elections[23] and the Article IV power to ensure state compliance with the Full Faith and Credit Clause.[24] Rulings in other contexts leave open the possibility that, even in the wake of *Allen*, otherwise applicable state-sovereign-immunity rules might have to give way when these powers underlie immunity-abrogating congressional enactments.[25]

---

broad congressional power to legislate in the field. *See supra* Section 10.E.2. With regard to a related topic, see Henry Paul Monaghan, *The Sovereign Immunity "Exception,"* 110 HARV. L. REV. 102, 116–17 (1996) (arguing that Congress has the power to abrogate state sovereign immunity in cases brought by Native nations and criticizing the Court's ruling in *Seminole Tribe* for rejecting this view by failing to recognize "the special nature of Indian tribes and the unique nature of the congressional power under the Indian Commerce Clause" and by instead relying on "an intractable 'thereness' of an . . . unyielding principle of state sovereign immunity . . . incapable of and not needing justification").

[22] For a thoughtful exploration of the competing arguments on this point, compare Edward T. Swaine, *Does Federalism Constrain the Treaty Power?*, 103 COLUM. L. REV. 403, 434, 435 & n.131 (2003) (noting, among other things, that "[a]n historical argument against treaty power exceptionalism [in the sovereign-immunity context] was proffered in *Alden v. Maine*, which noted that Congress had refused to adopt an exception to the proposed Eleventh Amendment for cases arising under treaties"; also indicating that the Court in *Federal Republic of Germany v. United States*, 526 U.S. 111, 112 (1999) (per curiam), and *Breard v. Greene*, 523 U.S. 371, 377 (1998) (per curiam), "assumed that state sovereign immunity applies equally where treaties are concerned" and that some scholarly commentary supports this position), with *id.* at 436–37 (noting that *Missouri v. Holland*, 252 U.S. 416 (1920), offers some, though "not overwhelming," support for a power to abrogate sovereign immunity in the treaty-power setting), and *id.* at 437 (adding that finding a treaty-specific waiver of sovereign immunity by the states "in the plan of the convention" gains support from the idea that "in foreign affairs, unlike in domestic matters, the states were never sovereign"; that "[t]he Founders were greatly concerned, too, with the states' record of breaching treaties"; that "they took special steps to ensure that the treaty power would not be used to abuse state interests"; and that "treaty breaches may pose a graver risk to the national interest that requires more dramatic remedies to deter and make amends for state violations" (quoting Principality of Monaco v. Mississippi, 292 U.S. 313, 322–23 (1934))). For another thoroughgoing treatment of the issue, see Carlos Manuel Vázquez, *Treaties and the Eleventh Amendment*, 42 VA. J. INT'L L. 713 (2002) (concluding that, notwithstanding countervailing arguments under *Holland* and otherwise, no treaty-power exception to the *Seminole Tribe/Alden* rule exists).

[23] U.S. CONST. art. I, § 4, cl. 1.

[24] *Id.* art. IV, § 1.

[25] *See, e.g.*, Arizona v. Inter Tribal Council of Ariz., Inc., 570 U.S. 1, 14 (2013) (applying specialized preemption rules in connection with a law passed under the Elections Clause); *infra* note 31 and accompanying text (noting the Court's distinct treatment of the anti-commandeering doctrine when Congress wields the full-faith-and-credit power, as well as lower court rulings that hold that the prohibition on commandeering does not apply when Congress legislates pursuant to the Elections

B. THE ANTI-COMMANDEERING PRINCIPLE

The foregoing enumeration of already-recognized and potentially additional limits on the non-negatability of the state-sovereign-immunity defense underscores the key doctrinal point: The rule of *Seminole Tribe* and *Alden*, which was developed in cases involving the commerce power, does not necessarily carry over to all of Congress's other powers. This same proposition, as it turns out, applies with no less force to the operation of the state-protective anti-commandeering principle. Indeed, when Congress legislates pursuant to grants of authority apart from the Commerce Clause, it may be that the anti-commandeering principle is subject to even more limitations than is its sovereign-immunity-based counterpart.[26]

To begin with, notwithstanding the commerce-power-related rulings in *New York* and *Printz*, there is little doubt that Congress is free to commandeer state action when acting pursuant to its Fourteenth and Fifteenth Amendment enforcement powers[27] because

---

Clause). Another possibility along these lines is raised by the uniquely broad grant to Congress of the power to "exercise exclusive Legislation in all Cases whatsoever" as to the District of Columbia and federal properties acquired with the specialized consent of states. *See* U.S. CONST. art. I, § 8, cl. 17. Might Congress, for example, rely on the distinct phrasing and resulting comprehensiveness of this grant to subject states themselves to monetary liability on a *respondeat superior* theory when their agents wrongfully cause injuries within the District's boundaries? *See also infra* note 31 (raising the question whether Congress might have authority under the Law of Nations Clause to regulate states in much the same manner as it can under the Elections and Full Faith and Credit Clauses).

26 *See, e.g., infra* note 33 and accompanying text (noting that more limits on congressional authority may apply in sovereign-immunity cases than in anti-commandeering cases because the textual command of the state-protective Eleventh Amendment operates only in the former setting).

27 *See, e.g.*, Rebecca Aviel, *Remedial Commandeering*, 54 U.C. DAVIS L. REV. 1999, 2002 (2021) (concluding that anti-commandeering limits, "whatever their wisdom, coherence, or constitutional virtue [in other settings], do not restrain Congress in the exercise of its remedial powers under the Reconstruction Era Amendments"); *id.* at 2003–04, 2023–55 (supporting this position with arguments from the text, the sequence of amendment adoptions, and governing precedent, as well as on the theory that "the assumptions undergirding commandeering doctrine make little or no sense in the context of remedial legislation"); Evan H. Caminker, Printz, *State Sovereignty, and the Limits of Formalism*, 1997 SUP. CT. REV. 199, 238–42 (reasoning that the same logic that supports allowing the abrogation of state sovereign immunity under the enforcement powers likewise supports congressional commandeering pursuant to those powers); Robert A. Mikos, *Can the States Keep Secrets from the Federal Government?*, 161 U. PA. L. REV. 103, 171 (2012) ("Congress may commandeer the states pursuant to its powers under the Reconstruction Era Amendments."); *see also* Jason Mazzone & Stephen Rushin, *From Selma to Ferguson: The Voting Rights Act as a Blueprint for Police Reform*, 105 CAL. L. REV. 263, 332 (2017) (noting that the Voting Rights Act, which the Court upheld in 1966, worked "a significant commandeering of the states," including by requiring "the adoption of new state government administrative measures" and by requiring some states to "obtain federal approval before new voting policies could take effect"). *But cf.* Michael Paisner, Note, Boerne *Supremacy: Congressional Responses to* City of Boerne *v. Flores and the Scope of Congress's Article I Powers*, 105 COLUM. L. REV. 537, 579 (2005) (mentioning how

they specifically support congressional regulation of states themselves.[28] In similar fashion, whatever rules might apply in the sovereign-immunity context, it seems indisputable—as lower courts have recognized—that Congress can commandeer state authorities when it acts pursuant to the Elections Clause.[29] This is especially true because the Court itself offered powerful support for this conclusion in *Printz v. United States*[30] when it distinguished various early acts of congressional commandeering on the ground that those acts rested on Congress's closely analogous full-faith-and-credit power.[31] With regard to federal authority over foreign affairs, there

---

"RLUIPA and RLPA—in requiring that 'state and local laws and executive actions include religion-based exemptions in accordance with congressionally mandated criteria'—arguably regulate state and local governments in violation of Tenth Amendment federalism principles expounded in New York v. United States and Printz v. United States").

[28] *See* Vicki C. Jackson, *Federalism and the Uses and Limits of Law:* Printz *and Principle?*, 111 HARV. L. REV. 2180, 2210–11 (1998). Directly in line with this conclusion is the Court's ruling in *City of Rome v. United States*, 446 U.S. 156 (1980), decided during the era of the "integral activities" limit on the commerce power, *see supra* Section 5.A.1, that "principles of federalism that might otherwise be an obstacle to congressional authority are necessarily overridden by [Congress's] power to enforce the Civil War Amendments 'by appropriate legislation.' " *Id.* at 179. *Accord* EEOC v. Wyoming, 460 U.S. 226, 243 n.18 (1983).

[29] For case law on this point, see *supra* Section 9.A.1. *See also* Justin Weinstein-Tull, *Election Law Federalism*, 114 MICH. L. REV. 747, 782 (2016) (noting that courts have rejected state arguments that federal election laws violate the anti-commandeering principle "by distinguishing the source of congressional power in anticommandeering cases from that in voting cases"; observing more specifically that "[t]he anticommandeering cases are grounded in a Commerce Clause analysis, this reasoning goes, whereas the federal election statutes are enacted pursuant to Congress's Elections Clause authority").

[30] 521 U.S. 898 (1997).

[31] *Id.* at 908. The key consideration here is that the Elections Clause and the Full Faith and Credit Clause differ from the Commerce Clause (and other components of Article I, section 8) because they specifically envision congressional regulation of states qua states. Aviel, *supra* note 27, at 2045 (reasoning, from the Court's founding of the anti-commandeering limit on the idea that the Constitution "confers upon Congress the power to regulate individuals, not States," that "Congress may in fact have commandeering power whenever it regulates pursuant to a provision that gives it authority to directly regulate states, such as the Elections Clause, Article IV's Full Faith and Credit Clause, or Article I, Section 10, providing that state laws imposing import or [export] duties 'be subject to the revision and control of the Congress' " (first quoting *New York*, 505 U.S. at 160–61; then quoting U.S. CONST. art. 1, § 10, cl. 2)). Are there other textual grants of power of this kind? One possibility is the Guarantee Clause of Article IV. *See* Erwin Chemerinsky, *Cases Under the Guarantee Clause Should Be Justiciable*, 65 U. COLO. L. REV. 849, 877–88 (1994) (noting that "an exception [to the anti-commandeering principle] could be recognized for instances in which Congress acts to guarantee that states have a republican form of government" because the Guarantee Clause embodies a "specific grant of power to the federal government over state government structure and processes"); Carolyn Shapiro, *Democracy, Federalism, and the Guarantee Clause*, 62 ARIZ. L. REV. 183, 236 (2020) (agreeing that the anti-commandeering rule does not limit Congress's power under the Guarantee Clause). Another possibility is supplied by the Law of Nations Clause of Article I, section 8, clause 10 because (at least in general) the law of nations addresses itself to the actions of governments. To be sure, the text of that clause—which

is no apparent reason to conclude that Congress has less power to sidestep the *New York/Printz* anti-commandeering rule than it has to sidestep the *Seminole Tribe/Alden* rule regarding the abrogation of state sovereign immunity.[32] Indeed, Congress might well have more leeway when it comes to averting the anti-commandeering rule because the specialized text-based limits of the Eleventh Amendment come into play only in the state-sovereign-immunity context.[33]

This same consideration (among others) lends support to the conclusion that the anti-commandeering doctrine could be inapplicable when the federal government acts pursuant to its treaty-making power.[34] To be sure, some analysts have taken a different view.[35] At least some of those observers, however, seem simply to

---

authorizes Congress to "define and punish . . . Offences against the Law of Nations"—might be read to require Congress to target such offenses only by way of its own direct regulation of individual conduct. But the government-centric nature of the law of nations—especially when considered in tandem with Congress's broad power over foreign affairs as a general matter—might in some instances allow Congress to commandeer state behavior as it acts with "due diligence" to carry this particular power into execution. United States v. Arizona, 120 U.S. 479, 484 (1887).

[32] *See supra* note 20 and accompanying text (detailing the special considerations that apply in foreign-relations cases). One particular question concerns the extent to which the anti-commandeering doctrine limits Congress's ability to legislate with regard to immigration controls. For different views on this issue, compare *New York v. U.S. Dep't of Just.*, 951 F.3d 84, 112–14 (2d Cir. 2020) (suggesting that limits on the application of the anti-commandeering principle apply when Congress wields the immigration power because "[a] commandeering challenge to a federal statute depends on there being pertinent authority 'reserved to the states' " under the Tenth Amendment and because states can claim no reserved power to flout federal laws enacted to effectuate Congress's "preeminent" power in this area of law), with Mary Ann McNulty, Comment, *A Doctrine Without Exception: Critiquing an Immigration Exception to the Anticommandeering Rule*, 169 U. PA. L. REV. 241, 245 (2020) (critiquing the Second Circuit's decision and arguing that the "anticommandeering rule does not, and should not, have an exception for immigration related commands").

[33] *But cf. Alden*, 527 U.S. at 728 (asserting that "sovereign immunity derives not from the Eleventh Amendment but from the structure of the original Constitution itself").

[34] An extended discussion of this question appears in Carter, *supra* note 20, at 599–618. *See also* Swaine, *supra* note 22, at 423–28 (detailing arguments both for and against the position that the anticommandeering principle limits the treaty power). For additional treatments, see Gerald L. Neuman, *The Nationalization of Civil Liberties, Revisited*, 99 COLUM. L. REV. 1630, 1651–55 (1999); Carlos Manuel Vázquez, Breard, Printz, *and the Treaty Power*, 70 U. COLO. L. REV. 1317, 1350–59 (1999); and Thomas Healy, Note, *Is* Missouri v. Holland *Still Good Law? Federalism and the Treaty Power*, 98 COLUM. L. REV. 1726, 1755–56 (1998) (contending that while "a close reading of *Printz*, in particular, suggests that the treaty power . . . may be subject to some of the same [federalism-based] limits that have been applied to the Commerce Clause," the "importance of plenary federal power over foreign matters" should ultimately compel the conclusion that "in the exercise of the treaty power, the federal government should remain free from the concerns of federalism").

[35] *See, e.g.*, LOUIS HENKIN, FOREIGN AFFAIRS AND THE UNITED STATES CONSTITUTION 467 n.75 (2d ed. 1996) ("Presumably, the United States could not command state legislatures, or 'coopt' state officials by treaty, say a human rights convention that required state legislatures, as distinguished from Congress, to enact state procedures or provide state remedies, or an agreement that required state

have assumed that *New York* and *Printz* dictate this outcome, while other, more nuanced treatments offer arguments for deeming the anti-commandeering rule inapplicable, at least as a general matter, in the treaty-power context.[36] To be sure, one might note that the

officials to participate in international peace-keeping operations."). Note also Professor Swaine's observations about Professor Laurence Tribe's seemingly shifting position on this question: "To illustrate the uncertainty, compare 1 Tribe, Constitutional Law (3d ed.) . . . at 647–48 ('[A]lthough *Missouri v. Holland* establishes that a treaty may enlarge the substantive reach of congressional legislation, it appears that a treaty cannot give Congress authority to circumvent the structural limitations on such legislation—such as the ban on federal commandeering of state sovereignty recognized in *Printz v. United States* and *New York v. United States*.'), with Tribe, *Taking Text and Structure Seriously*, . . . at 1260 (asserting that the anticommandeering principle is 'not applicable, of course, to the treaty power')." Swaine, *supra* note 22, at 425 n.88.

[36] To begin with (as noted earlier), the specialized and capacious foreign-affairs power applies with full force in this setting. *See supra* note 20 and accompanying text. Even more important, however, additional and treaty-power-specific considerations also are at work. In particular: (1) with regard to the treaty power, *Missouri v. Holland* tellingly declares that "there may be matters of the sharpest exigency for the national well being that an act of Congress could not deal with but that a treaty followed by such an act could," 252 U.S. at 433; *see also* Swaine, *supra* note 22, at 478–79; (2) because the treaty power springs from Article II, rather than Article I, there is reason to question whether otherwise applicable limits imposed (including under the Article I Necessary and Proper Clause) properly apply to treaties (and perhaps treaty-based legislation), especially because federal action in this context involves effectuating not only the power of Congress but also the power of the President; (3) special political safeguards against federal overreaching vis-a-vis the states (and against unwise federal action in general) apply in the treaty context because of the requirement of supermajority Senate approval, *see, e.g., id.* at 437 n.138 (discussing this point); Carter, *supra* note 20, at 606–08 (same); and (4) critical elements of the reasoning that supported the Court's recognition of the anti-commandeering principle do not apply in this context, including because: (a) resort to the use of congressional conditional-spending and conditional-preemption programs will not work well in this setting because of the need to ensure compliance by state actors in the process of both establishing and thereafter enforcing treaty obligations with foreign partners; and (b) the option of having Congress (or individual states or groups of states) fill regulatory gaps with legislation that directly targets individuals is unavailable in this context to the extent that treaties place (or call for the placement of) obligations directly on states themselves. For a thoroughgoing elaboration of these points, see *id.* at 601, 605 (noting that the conditional-spending and conditional-preemption alternatives to commandeering "are largely unavailable when the federal plan involves a treaty" and "if a treaty beneficial to the United States cannot be made by the federal government because implementing it would violate states' rights, then that treaty cannot be made at all"); *id.* at 610–11 (noting that "while it is *possible* that domestic matters will be treated appropriately by the states acting individually" even in the absence of a commandeered response, "it is *impossible* that the United States will be able, through state action, to enter into formal treaty relations guaranteeing particular conduct from other countries"; adding that while "[c]oordinated state action" can provide "a noncommandeering means through which domestic programs . . . can be made," such coordinated action cannot take the place of treaties and that "[t]his discrepancy cuts in favor of enhancing the federal government's power to act directly on the states, when the national interest pursued involves a treaty"). *See generally id.* at 611–19 (further developing these ideas, including by arguing that applying the anti-commandeering principle in this context would restrict not only federally preferred "means" but also impose "what is functionally a limitation on [nationally desirable] ends"); Swaine, *supra* note 22, at 487 ("Doctrinal technicalities aside, the basic concern is that commandeering's alternatives may simply not work as well for treaties. For example, uncertainty as to whether states will accept conditioned moneys and the associated

modern-era expansion of the commerce power has reduced the independent significance of Congress's treaty-related lawmaking authority in many contexts.[37] On the other hand, the potential operation of the treaty power free of the anti-commandeering rule—and perhaps of the sovereign-immunity rule as well[38]—pointedly illustrates that power's persisting significance as a freestanding source of congressional lawmaking authority.[39]

One key doctrine limits the impact of both the anti-commandeering and the sovereign-immunity constraints on federal legislative authority: Congress may wield its Article I spending power to *induce* states to pass laws that Congress wants them to pass even though it cannot *force* them to enact those same measures under the Commerce Clause or other provisions of Article I.[40] Indeed, in *New York v. United States*,[41] the Court emphasized Congress's access to this conditional-spending-program option in the process of justifying its endorsement of the anti-commandeering rule.[42] To be sure, the Court made it clear in *NFIB v. Sebelius*[43] that the

---

obligations, or agree to preemption, may impair U.S. bargaining with other countries.").

[37] *Cf.* Nicholas Quinn Rosenkranz, *Executing the Treaty Power*, 118 HARV. L. REV. 1867, 1936 (2005) (noting that during the "decades when the Commerce Clause power was construed to be essentially limitless," questions concerning the scope of the treaty power were "almost entirely hypothetical" and that it was not until the Court's decision in *Lopez* that those questions began to "recover even potential practical significance"). For a general discussion of the treaty power, see *supra* Section 10.C.

[38] *See supra* note 22 and accompanying text.

[39] It merits emphasis that different forms of international agreements may carry with them different consequences with regard to how external constraints intersect with congressional power. In particular, the powers to make and to implement a treaty requires a supermajority Senate endorsement as to the content of the treaty itself, and they thus may well be distinguishable from, in particular, the power to implement congressional-executive agreements (which, as further discussed *infra* Section 27.C.1, can be accomplished entirely through the enactment of ordinary legislation). *See* Vázquez, *supra* note 34, at 725 (noting this distinction in assessing state sovereign-immunity abrogation). In addition, one might well argue that federal commandeering (and perhaps federal abrogation of state sovereign immunity as well) is permissible at least by way of self-executing treaties. These exertions of federal authority, after all, not only require supermajority Senate endorsement but also stem solely from the authority vested by Article II and thus do not bring into play any limits built into Article I, including any limits founded on the idea that Congress can enact only "proper" laws when it legislates pursuant to the Necessary and Proper Clause. *See* Swaine, *supra* note 22, at 421–22 (noting this point); *see also supra* Section 5.B (noting earlier suggestions that the anti-commandeering rule emanates from the term "proper" as used in the Necessary and Proper Clause).

[40] *See supra* Chapter 8.

[41] 505 U.S. 144 (1992).

[42] *Id.* at 167–68 (highlighting that the anti-commandeering rule does not unduly impinge on federal authority in part because Congress may place conditions on federal spending as a "permissible method of encouraging a State to conform with federal policy choices").

[43] 567 U.S. 519 (2012).

Constitution bars Congress from structuring conditional spending programs in ways that involve not mere encouragement but de facto commandeering.[44] In assessing such programs in the wake of *NFIB*, however, courts have been reluctant to find that this constitutional dividing line has been crossed.[45]

C. POLITICAL PROCESS CONSTRAINTS AND THE "EQUAL SOVEREIGNTY" PRINCIPLE

The now-most-prominent external constraint supported by political-process concerns lies in the notion that Congress, at least in deploying certain powers, faces serious obstacles in enacting legislation that favors some states in relation to others.[46] The Court gave impetus to this principle in *Coyle v. Smith*,[47] when it recognized that such a constraint hems in Congress's choices as it wields its power to admit new states to the Union.[48] And the Court gave effect to a more expansive version of this principle in *Shelby County v. Holder*,[49] when, in a stark departure from its prior decision in *South Carolina v. Katzenbach*,[50] it invalidated the coverage formula of the Voting Rights Act, relying in large part on the ground that that formula abridged the "fundamental principle of equal sovereignty" among the states.[51] As already noted, some lower courts have held that this principle—though now undoubtedly applicable to exercises of the Fifteenth Amendment enforcement power—does not restrict congressional use of the commerce power.[52] Moreover, the underlying reasoning of *Shelby County*—which emphasized the VRA's regulation of state choices about formulating their own voting-based self-governing systems—could ultimately drive forward the conclusion that the principle of that case, at least in its strongest form, is inapplicable to most exercises of Congress's Article I lawmaking powers.[53]

---

[44] *See supra* Section 8.C.

[45] *See supra* Section 8.D.

[46] *See id.*

[47] 221 U.S. 559 (1911).

[48] *Id.* at 566–68.

[49] 570 U.S. 529 (2013); *see supra* Section 11.B.5.

[50] 383 U.S. 301 (1966); *see supra* Section 11.B.1 (discussing the *South Carolina* decision in greater detail).

[51] *Shelby County*, 570 U.S. at 544 (internal quotations and citations omitted).

[52] *See supra* Section 5.A.2.b (collecting these cases and discussing in greater detail this line of doctrinal development).

[53] This sentence makes reference to "most," rather than "all," exercise of Article I powers because some form of the equal-sovereignty principle necessarily applies to exercises of those congressional powers (namely, the taxing, naturalization, and bankruptcy powers) that, per the express terms of Article I itself, support the enactment of only "uniform" laws. *See id.* (discussing the textual contrast in Article I

* * *

The foregoing discussion underscores a basic point—namely, that each of Congress's powers occupies its own doctrinal domain. More specifically, it shows that, despite temptations to assume otherwise, federalism-based limits on the authority of Congress do not apply in lockstep fashion to each of its granted powers.[54] Rather, when it comes to the operation of key external constraints—rooted in state sovereign immunity, the anti-commandeering doctrine, and the equal-sovereignty principle—the theme of governing law is one of difference rather than sameness in how those limits interact with the many and varying powers assigned to the legislative branch.

---

between those granted powers that explicitly call for geographic uniformity and those that do not).

[54] Of particular importance, different powers trigger the operation of different "quasi-constitutional" rules of statutory interpretation regarding the protection (or non-protection) of state-based autonomy interests. *See generally supra* Section 5.D. Of particular importance, when Congress acts to regulate interstate commerce a "presumption against preemption" of state law almost always dominates the scene. *See infra* Section 24.C. This presumption gives way, however, when Congress invokes other powers, such as its power to regulate federal elections. *See supra* note 25. In addition, when litigants advance preemption arguments based on statutes enacted pursuant to certain powers—most notably, the patent power, the Indian commerce power, and the broad structural power to regulate foreign affairs—the balance (at least in most cases) tilts the other way. Indeed, it may not be too much to say that, at least as a general matter, the presumption against preemption is replaced by a presumption in its favor within these federal regulatory fields. *See infra* Section 24.C.

Chapter 14

RULES OF PROCEEDINGS AND CONGRESSIONAL INVESTIGATORY POWERS

Analysis

A. THE RULES OF PROCEEDINGS CLAUSE

Article I, section 5 states that "[e]ach House may determine the Rules of its Proceedings." As a result, "all matters of method are open to the determination of [each] house."[1] Governing treatments of these "matters of method" find expression in formalized rules established independently by the House of Representatives, on the one hand, and by the Senate, on the other, and these rules bind each legislative body so long as they comport with "constitutional restraints," such as those embodied in the Bill of Rights.[2] One difference between House rules and Senate rules concerns their durability. Because House elections occur on a biennial basis, each set of just-elected members constitutes a newly formed body, which thus must adopt its own rules for its own two-year period of operation.[3] In contrast, because only one third of the Senate stands for election at any one time, it is viewed as a "continuing body," whose rules remain in effect without interruption absent affirmative displacement.[4] In some situations, this difference

---

1 United States v. Ballin, 144 U.S. 1, 5 (1892).

2 *Id.* (adding that there also must be "a reasonable relation between the mode or method of proceeding established by the rule and the result which is sought to be attained").

3 *See* McGrain v. Daugherty, 273 U.S. 135, 180–82 (1927) (describing the House of Representatives as a non-continuous body).

4 *Id.*; *accord* STANDING RULES OF THE SENATE, R. V.2, S. DOC. NO. 113–18, at 4 (2013) ("The rules of the Senate shall continue from one Congress to the next . . . ."); John C. Roberts, *Gridlock and Senate Rules*, 88 NOTRE DAME L. REV. 2189, 2205–07 (2013). *But see* Aaron-Andrew P. Bruhl, *Burying the "Continuing Body" Theory of the Senate*, 95 IOWA L. REV. 1401, 1431–44 (2010) (disputing the continuing-body theory).

has significance.[5] As a practical matter, however, the impact of the distinction is limited because recently elected House members—most of whom are incumbents—often reinstall the rules that prevailed from the previous term, with at most a few tweaks when each new session begins.[6]

The Rules of Proceedings of both the House and the Senate are highly consequential. By way of example, they establish the jurisdiction for each chamber's standing committees, which do the lion's share of work in sorting through legislative proposals.[7] These committees examine, evaluate, and sometimes revise proposed bills. They also almost always determine whether a bill subject to its review moves forward for full-chamber consideration.[8] Each legislative body's rules also deal with such matters as the selection of standing committee members and chairs, the establishment of special committees, the issuance of committee reports, the manner of discussing and amending bills in full-House or full-Senate proceedings, and the process for resolving differences in bills passed by the House and Senate on the same legislative subject.[9] The rules also address how to resolve interpretive disputes concerning the rules themselves and how to handle matters not explicitly addressed by those rules.[10] As a practical matter, the complexities that mark both

---

[5] *See, e.g.*, *id.* at 1458 (noting some commentators' suggestion that a subpoena issued by the House of Representatives expires at the end of the House's two-year term, whereas a subpoena issued by the Senate may not have a similar expiration date).

[6] *See, e.g.*, H.R. RES. 6, 116th Cong. (2019) (adopting nearly wholesale the rules of the 115th Congress with only limited amendments).

[7] The modern congressional structure for standing committees was created by the Legislative Reorganization Act of 1946, §§ 102–03, 121, 60 Stat. 812–30. Since 1946, each house has adjusted the number, tasks, and procedures of its committees by single-chamber resolution. *See, e.g.*, H.R. RES. 5, 94th Cong. (1975) (abolishing the standing House Committee on Internal Security—formerly the House Committee on Un-American Activities); S. RES. 445, 108th Cong. (2004) (altering the jurisdiction of the standing Senate Committee on the Budget); *see also* JANE A. HUDIBURG, CONG. RSCH. SERV., R45731, HOUSE RULES CHANGES AFFECTING COMMITTEE PROCEDURE IN THE 116TH CONGRESS (May 21, 2019) (noting the changes that H.R. Res. 6, 116th Cong. (2019), made to the names, jurisdiction, and procedures of certain House committees and the resolution's creation of two new select committees), *available at* https://crsreports.congress.gov/product/pdf/R/R45731.

[8] *See generally* MICHAEL WELSH, AN OVERVIEW OF THE DEVELOPMENT OF U.S. CONGRESSIONAL COMMITTEES (2008), https://www.llsdc.org/assets/sourcebook/cong-cmte-overview.pdf (providing a history of the U.S. congressional committee system and an overview of its modern operations).

[9] *See* STANDING RULES OF THE SENATE, S. DOC. NO. 113–18 (2013); RULES OF THE HOUSE OF REPRESENTATIVES, reprinted *in* H.R. DOC. NO. 115–177 (2019). For an analysis of the differences between Senate and House rules, see JUDY SCHNEIDER, CONG. RSCH. SERV., RL30945, HOUSE AND SENATE RULES OF PROCEDURE: A COMPARISON (2008), *available at* https://crsreports.congress.gov/product/details?prodcode=RL30945.

[10] For example, Jefferson's Manual of Parliamentary Practice "shall govern the House in all cases to which they are applicable and in which they are not inconsistent

House and Senate rules channel significant authority to each chamber's parliamentarian.[11]

In some instances, a violation of legislative rules threatens harm to individuals, as when an unlawful subpoena exposes a would-be witness to unwanted risks of public embarrassment or even follow-up charges of perjury. Persons who confront this situation can object to the subpoena's legality—for example, on the ground that the subject of inquiry falls outside the relevant committee's jurisdiction.[12] Under governing law, such aggrieved individuals can insist that legislators honor their own regulations (and other legal requirements), including by seeking to vindicate their rights in the context of judicial proceedings.[13]

---

with the Rules and orders of the House." RULES OF THE HOUSE OF REPRESENTATIVES, R. XXIX, *reprinted in* H.R. DOC. NO. 115–177, at 1035 (2019) (referencing JEFFERSON'S MANUAL OF PARLIAMENTARY PRACTICE, Sec. XV *reprinted in* H.R. DOC. NO. 115–177, at 174 (2019)).

[11] *See* VALERIE HEITSHUSEN, CONG. RSCH. SERV., RS20544, THE OFFICE OF THE PARLIAMENTARIAN IN THE HOUSE AND SENATE (2018), *available at* https://crsreports.congress.gov/product/pdf/RS/RS20544. Perhaps the most prominent example of the parliamentarian's authority concerns the budget reconciliation process, governed by Section 310 of the Congressional Budget and Impoundment Control Act of 1974, Pub. L. 93–344, 88 Stat. 297 (codified at 2 U.S.C. § 641), which exempts certain types of tax and spending-related measures from the ordinary operation of the Senate filibuster. Under the "Byrd Rule," a senator may make a point of order that a provision in a reconciliation bill is extraneous because it does not relate to taxation or spending. The Senate's presiding officer (either the Vice President or a member of the majority party presiding in the Vice President's absence) is then tasked with ruling on the point of order, but—under modern Senate practice—typically defers to the advice of the Senate parliamentarian. If the point of order is sustained, then the challenged provision is stricken from the bill, unless sixty Senators vote either to waive application of the Byrd Rule or to override the ruling. *See* Ellen P. Aprill & Daniel J. Hemel, *The Tax Legislative Process: A Byrd's Eye View*, 81 LAW & CONTEMP. PROBS. 99, 102–08 (2018). In practice, however, Senate leadership usually consults with the parliamentarian in advance and preemptively removes any measures deemed to be Byrd-Rule-noncompliant. *See id.* at 105.

[12] *See* Watkins v. United States, 354 U.S. 178, 198 (1957) (adding that it is "beyond the powers conferred upon the Congress" to conduct investigations into individual affairs that lack a relation to any valid legislative purpose).

[13] As Professor Tribe has put the point: "If government actors promulgate rules limiting their own conduct, they must comply with such rules." LAURENCE TRIBE, AMERICAN CONSTITUTIONAL LAW § 5–1, at 794 (3d. ed. 2000). On some occasions, courts have seen fit to stop the House, the Senate, and their committees from breaching internal rules in the course of conducting investigations. For example, in *Gojack v. United States*, 384 U.S. 702 (1966), the Court concluded that a subcommittee lacked investigatory power because the full committee never defined the scope of the subcommittee's investigatory authority. *Id.* at 706 (concluding that "[t]here is no resolution, minute or record of the Committee authorizing the inquiry with which we are concerned"). Similarly, a congressional committee's failure to follow its own rules on conducting an executive session was found to give rise to a valid defense to a charge of criminal contempt based on a failure to appear. *See* Yellin v. United States, 374 U.S. 109, 121 (1963). Related to the principle that congressional committees are bound by their own rules is the judicially established principle that congressional committees' demands for compliance with their investigative requests cannot be enforced if those demands lack adequate clarity. *See* Flaxer v. United States, 358 U.S. 147, 151 (1958).

Perhaps the best known and most consequential of all "Rules of Proceedings" is Senate Rule XXII, which concerns the so-called "filibuster." In essence, this provision allows 41 of the chamber's 100 senators to threaten to debate a proposed bill indefinitely, thus blocking a formal vote on its passage.[14] The operation of Rule XXII has changed greatly over the decades, and today the occurrence of true filibustering—that is, protracted speechmaking on the Senate floor itself—is extremely rare.[15] Instead, a "silent filibuster" system now exists, effectively allowing a group of Senators to stop the enactment of any pending bill, at least if they can demonstrate to the Senate Majority Leader that there are enough votes to defeat a "cloture" motion if an effort to vote on that matter were to arise.[16] There are, however, some important limits on the power of Senate coalitions to make use of Rule XXII. For example, that Rule no longer permits the filibustering of Senate votes on the confirmation of key executive officials or federal judges, including Justices of the Supreme Court.[17] In addition, Rule XXII has no effect with regard to "reconciliation" bills, which deal with debt-limit, revenue, and spending matters, unless those bills concern the Social Security Program.[18] Nor may Senators use the filibuster to preclude consideration of disapproval resolutions introduced pursuant to the Congressional Review Act, a statute that facilitates legislative repudiation of certain types of recently promulgated agency regulations.[19]

---

[14] *See generally* VALERIE HEITSHUSEN & RICHARD S. BETH, CONG. RSCH. SERV., RL30360, FILIBUSTERS AND CLOTURE IN THE SENATE (2017), *available at* https://crsreports.congress.gov/product/pdf/RL/RL30360.

[15] On the history of filibustering in the Senate, see generally Catherine Fisk & Erwin Chemerinsky, *The Filibuster*, 49 STAN. L. REV. 181, 187–214 (1997).

[16] *See id.* at 203–10.

[17] Dubbed the "nuclear option," this change to the Senate's rules came in two steps. First, in 2013, during the tenure of then-Senate Majority Leader Harry Reid, the Senate rendered the ordinary supermajority filibuster rule inapplicable to votes on the confirmation of all presidential appointments except appointments to the Supreme Court. Paul Kane, *Reid, Democrats Trigger 'Nuclear' Option; Eliminate Most Filibusters on Nominees*, WASH. POST, Nov. 21, 2013. Thereafter, in 2017, during the tenure of then-Senate Majority Leader Mitch McConnell, the threshold for ending debate on Supreme Court nominations was exempted from Rule XXII's supermajoritarian constraint, thus permitting the Senate to vote to confirm the appointment to the high Court of then-Judge Neil Gorsuch. *See* Matt Flegenheimer, *Senate Republicans Deploy 'Nuclear Option' to Clear Path for Gorsuch*, N.Y. TIMES, Apr. 6, 2017.

[18] Under 2 U.S.C. § 641(e)(2), debate on reconciliation bills is limited to 20 hours. For a thorough discussion of the Reconciliation Bill exception to the operation of Rule XXII, see Tonja Jacobi & Jeff VanDam, *The Filibuster and Reconciliation: The Future of Majoritarian Lawmaking in the U.S. Senate*, 47 U.C. DAVIS L. REV. 261, 291–99 (2013).

[19] *See* Jody Freeman & Matthew Stephenson, *The Untapped Potential of the Congressional Review Act*, 58 HARV. J. ON LEG. (forthcoming 2022) (offering an overview of the CRA and highlighting the statute's potential to operate as a filibuster-

The Senate's practice regarding filibusters raises two separate constitutional questions. The first concerns whether either chamber can impose upon itself a straightforward supermajority voting requirement, either in general or for particular categories of legislation.[20] Some analysts have urged that supermajority voting rules of this sort offend the constitutional plan put in place by the Framers.[21] Others, however, argue that supermajority voting rules pose no constitutional problem, at least so long as the legislative body can alter those rules by way of majority vote.[22] The second question concerns whether—assuming the Constitution does preclude each House from imposing supermajority voting requirements to pass bills themselves—Rule XXII runs afoul of that limitation. Defenders of the filibuster system's constitutionality argue that this rule addresses only when and how debate occurs and thus does not violate any requirement concerning the actual enactment of legislation.[23] Critics respond that this view elevates form over substance, at least in a world where silent filibusters can and do now operate to block legislative enactments without the occurrence of any debate at all.[24] Given the controversy that surrounds Rule XXII, one might suppose that courts would have weighed in on these foundational constitutional questions. But they have not. In a leading case, the D.C. Circuit rejected a challenge to Rule XXII on the ground that the plaintiffs' alleged injuries were not attributable to the defendants named in the complaint, such as the Senate's Sergeant at Arms, but instead to "an 'absent third party'—the Senate itself," whose

circumvention device when the same party controls the Senate and the Presidency), *available at* https://papers.ssrn.com/sol3/papers.cfm?abstract_id=3895427; *see also infra* Section 29.D.

20 By way of example, in 1995, the House of Representatives adopted House Rule XXI, which required the concurrence of three-fifths of voting House members to approve any income-tax increase. *See* Neals-Erik William Delker, *The House Three-Fifths Tax Rule: Majority Rule, the Framers' Intent, and the Judiciary's Role*, 100 DICK. L. REV. 341, 341 (1996).

21 *See, e.g.*, Dan T. Coenen, *The Originalist Case Against Congressional Supermajority Voting Rules*, 106 NW. L. REV. 1091, 1095–96 (2012) (arguing that the both the text and history of the Constitution indicate that the Framers rejected self-imposed supermajority voting requirements in the House and Senate); Bruce Ackerman et al., *An Open Letter to Congressman Gingrich*, 104 YALE L.J. 1539 (1995) (arguing that this three-fifth's majority requirement impermissibly undermines constitutional requirements of majority rule).

22 *See, e.g.*, John O. McGinnis & Michael B. Rappaport, *The Constitutionality of Legislative Supermajority Requirements: A Defense*, 105 YALE L.J. 483, 484 (1995) (arguing that the Rules of Proceedings Clause authorizes each House of Congress to adopt such rules, at least so long as the rules themselves are subject to majority-vote repeal).

23 *See, e.g.*, Michael J. Gerhardt, *The Constitutionality of the Filibuster*, 21 CONST. COMMENT. 445, 456–57 (2004) (positing that Rule XXII "does not require 60 votes to adopt a law; it requires at least 60 votes to end debate").

24 *See, e.g.*, Dan T. Coenen, *The Filibuster and the Framing, Why the Cloture Rule Is Unconstitutional and What to Do About It*, 55 B.C. L. REV. 39 (2014).

members could not be sued because of the Constitution's immunity-granting Speech or Debate Clause.[25]

B. EXCLUSIONS, EXPULSIONS, AND PUNISHMENTS FOR "DISORDERLY BEHAVIOR"

The Rules of Proceedings Clause does not stand alone in empowering each House to oversee its own operations. Key provisions of the Constitution, for example, deal with the initial seating and continued service of representatives elected (or said to be elected) by local voters. Article I, section 5, clause 1 decrees that "[e]ach House shall be the Judge of the Elections, Returns and Qualifications of its own Members."[26] In light of its reference to "Elections" and "Returns," this clause channels into each chamber of Congress (as opposed to state decision-making bodies) the power to resolve disputes about which candidate for federal legislative office received the most votes[27] and whether malfeasance rendered an election void, even if a result in favor of a particular candidate has been certified by state officials.[28] For example, the Senate was called upon to resolve a disputed senatorial contest in Iowa in 1924.[29] After a nail-bitingly close election, Iowa officials certified Smith W. Brookhart as the winner.[30] Daniel F. Steck, Brookhart's opponent, however, challenged that determination, alleging serious electoral

---

[25] Common Cause v. Biden, 748 F.3d 1280, 1285 (D.C. Cir. 2014). In particular, the court concluded that individual Senators who caused the plaintiff's alleged injury—by using the filibuster to prevent passage of the DREAM and DISCLOSE Acts—could not be sued because the Speech or Debate Clause bars suits against legislators for acts that fall "within the sphere of legitimate legislative activity." *Id.* at 1283 (quoting Eastland v. U.S. Servicemen's Fund, 421 U.S. 491, 503 (1975)). For a more detailed discussion of the Speech or Debate Clause, see *infra* Section 33.D.

[26] U.S. CONST. art. I, § 5, cl. 1.

[27] *See* Gammage v. Compton, 548 S.W.2d 1, 1–4 (Tex. 1977) (refusing to overturn the results in a congressional race due to the exclusive jurisdiction of the House of Representatives to settle such disputes).

[28] *See* Roudebush v. Hartke, 405 U.S. 15, 25–26 (1972) ("[Congress] is free to accept or reject the apparent winner in either [the state's initial count or recount], and, if it chooses, to conduct its own recount."); Joshua A. Douglas, *Procedural Fairness in Election Contests*, 88 IND. L.J. 1, 29 (2013) ("Ultimately, Congress has the final say in any dispute involving one of its own seats, making any 'conclusive' determination from a state entity actually advisory."). For insight into how early Congresses decided disputed elections, see Sean J. Wright, *The Origin of Disputed Elections: Case Studies of Early American Contested Congressional Elections*, 81 ALB. L. REV. 609, 630–46 (2018). For an analysis of more recent contested-election cases, see L. PAIGE WHITAKER, CONG. RSCH. SERV., 98–194, CONTESTED ELECTION CASES IN THE HOUSE OF REPRESENTATIVES: 1933 TO 2009 (2010), *available at* https://sgp.fas.org/crs/misc/98-194.pdf.

[29] *See Roudebush*, 405 U.S. at 27–28 (Douglas, J., dissenting) (discussing this case).

[30] *See* ANNE M. BUTLER & WENDY WOLFF, UNITED STATES SENATE ELECTION, EXPULSION, AND CENSURE CASES, 1793–1990, at 312 (1995).

irregularities.[31] In response, the Senate conducted its own independent recount after having all 900,000 ballots cast in the election transported to Washington to be examined by a Senate committee.[32] As a result of this process, the Senate declared Steck the winner and unseated Brookhart.[33]

Apart from exercising the power to resolve election contests, "[e]ach House may . . . punish its Members for disorderly Behaviour, and, with the Concurrence of two thirds, expel a Member."[34] The power of expulsion differs from the power not to seat an elected member in the first place based on a lack of "Qualifications."[35] Indeed, under the Constitution, it is both easier and harder to wield the former power than the latter. On the one hand, it is easier to expel than to exclude because the Court has held that exclusions for a lack of "Qualifications" can occur under only narrow circumstances—that is, if the elected member fails to meet a *constitutionally*-established standard for holding office, such as the age, citizenship, and residency standards laid down in Article I, sections 2 and 3.[36] On the other hand, it is harder to expel than to exclude because exclusion requires only a majority vote, whereas expulsion requires action by a two-thirds supermajority.[37] The chambers have successfully wielded the power of expulsion on twenty occasions over the course of American history.[38] The most recent instance involved the removal

---

31 *Id.* at 312–13.

32 *Id.* at 313.

33 *Id.*

34 U.S. CONST. art. I, § 5, cl. 2. This provision's express treatment of the manner of removing members of the two chambers of Congress has long been understood to render inapplicable to those officials the process of impeachment that governs legislative removal of executive and judicial officers. For a more detailed treatment of this matter, see *infra* Section 32.A.3.a.

35 U.S. CONST. art. I, § 2, cl. 2: *id.* § 3, cl. 3.

36 *See* Powell v. McCormack, 395 U.S. 486, 522 (1969) (holding that Congress lacks "authority to exclude any person, duly elected by his constituents, who meets all the requirements for membership expressly prescribed in the Constitution"). Though such occurrences have been rare, both the Senate and the House have excluded members-elect from their chambers; those exclusions, however, predated *Powell* and would not likely survive the standard set forth in that case. *See* Gerald T. McLaughlin, *Congressional Self-Discipline: The Power to Expel, to Exclude and to Punish*, 41 FORDHAM L. REV. 43, 58–59 (1972). For instance, Brigham Roberts was excluded by the House in 1899 for engaging in polygamy—an unconstitutional basis of exclusion under *Powell. See id.* at 59.

37 *See* McLaughlin, *supra* note 36, at 45. After Adam Clayton Powell, Jr., was excluded from the 90th Congress, he won reelection in the special election held to fill his vacant seat and then again was elected for another full term to the 91st Congress. The House denied Powell his seniority but did not take further steps to expel him following his reelection. U.S. HOUSE OF REPRESENTATIVES, *Powell, Adam Clayton, Jr.*, https://history.house.gov/People/Detail/19872 (last visited June 17, 2021).

38 *See* CYNTHIA BROWN & TODD GARVEY, CONG. RSCH. SERV., R45078, EXPULSION OF MEMBERS OF CONGRESS: LEGAL AUTHORITY AND HISTORICAL PRACTICE 10 (2018), *available at* https://sgp.fas.org/crs/misc/R45078.pdf. Moreover, most of these

from the House of James A. Traficant following his conviction on bribery charges in 2002.[39]

The House and the Senate also can respond to the misdeeds of their members with sanctions less serious than expulsion. To begin with, Article I, section 5, clause 2 authorizes each chamber to "punish its Members for disorderly Behavior."[40] In addition, the House and Senate sometimes take action against problematic conduct that does not involve "disorderly Behaviour," at least in the ordinary sense of the term. In 1954, for example, the upper chamber censured Senator Joseph R. McCarthy for refusing to cooperate with its investigation into the propriety of his actions in leading a Senate committee.[41] In 2010, the House censured Representative Charles B. Rangel after determining that he had engaged in financial improprieties and tax evasion.[42] And in 2021, the House censured Representative Paul Gosar for posting to social media an anime-style video depicting his engaging in violent behavior directed at Representative Alexandria Ocasio-Cortez and President Joseph Biden.[43] In unusual circumstances, sanctions more onerous than censure are imposed on members of the legislative body, and the chambers on rare occasions have censured (or attempted to censure) non-members as well.[44] In 1834, for example, the Senate censured President Andrew Jackson for abusing his powers in connection with his efforts to defund the Bank of the United States, though it would subsequently expunge the censure resolution after Jacksonian Democrats reclaimed the majority.[45]

---

expulsions occurred in the narrow time period immediately following the outset of the Civil War based on conduct indicative of disloyalty to the United States. *Id.*

39 *Id.* at 11. The most recent expulsion in the Senate was of Jesse D. Bright for disloyalty to the Union in 1862. *Id.* at 20.

40 U.S. CONST. art. I, § 5, cl. 2.

41 *See* BUTLER & WOLFF, *supra* note 30, at 404–06.

42 U.S. House of Representatives, *Rangel, Charles B.*, https://history.house.gov/People/Detail/20144 (last visited June 17, 2021).

43 Jonathan Weisman & Catie Edmondson, *House, Mostly Along Party Lines, Censures Gosar for Violent Video*, N.Y. TIMES (Nov. 16, 2021), https://www.nytimes.com/2021/11/17/us/politics/paul-gosar-video.html.

44 *See, e.g.*, JANE A. HUDIBURG & CHRISTOPHER M. DAVIS, CONG. RSCH. SERV. R45087, RESOLUTIONS TO CENSURE THE PRESIDENT: PROCEDURE AND HISTORY (2021), *available at* https://sgp.fas.org/crs/misc/R45087.pdf. As for other punitive actions taken against sitting representatives and senators, a member might also be punished through the taking away of seniority or the loss of other privileges, such as committee assignments.

45 *See id.* at 5–6.

C. INVESTIGATIONS, SUBPOENAS, AND CONTEMPT CITATIONS

The most common use of the congressional power to impose sanctions stems from each chamber's efforts to exercise due diligence as it discharges its law-shaping functions. As the Supreme Court has noted, "Congress has no enumerated constitutional power to conduct investigations or issue subpoenas."[46] Nonetheless, federal lawmakers, in keeping with pre-Constitution legislative practice,[47] have exercised the authority to gather information—including by subpoenaing witnesses and documents—from the earliest days of the republic.[48] One might suppose that this authority emanates from the Necessary and Proper Clause because no prerogative would seem to be more "helpful" in generating "beneficial" legislative measures[49] than that of securing relevant factual data and expert guidance in the process of shaping legislation.[50] Like other provisions of Article I, section 8, however, the Necessary and Proper Clause empowers

---

[46] Trump v. Mazars USA, LLP, 140 S. Ct. 2019, 2031 (2020).

[47] *See* James M. Landis, *Constitutional Limitations on the Congressional Power of Investigation*, 40 HARV. L. REV. 153, 166–68 (1926).

[48] *See Mazars*, 140 S. Ct. at 2031 (citing Congress's recognized power "to secure needed information" (quoting *McGrain*, 273 U.S. at 161)). This power was noted at the Constitutional Convention by George Mason, who observed that members of Congress "are not only Legislators but they possess inquisitorial powers" and thus "must meet frequently to inspect the Conduct of the public offices." 2 THE RECORDS OF THE FEDERAL CONVENTION OF 1787, at 206 (Max Farrand, ed. 1937). For more extensive treatments of the legislative branch's investigatory powers, see Louis Fisher, CONG. RSCH. SERV., RL31836, CONGRESSIONAL INVESTIGATIONS: SUBPOENAS AND CONTEMPT POWER (2003), *available at* https://sgp.fas.org/crs/misc/RL31836.pdf; JOSH CHAFETZ, CONGRESS'S CONSTITUTION: LEGISLATIVE AUTHORITY AND THE SEPARATION OF POWERS 152–200 (2017); JOEL D. ABERBACH, KEEPING A WATCHFUL EYE: THE POLITICS OF CONGRESSIONAL OVERSIGHT (1990); ROGER A. BRUNS, CONGRESS INVESTIGATES: A CRITICAL AND DOCUMENTARY HISTORY (David Hostetter & Raymond W. Smock eds., rev. ed., 2011); MORRIS S. OGUL, CONGRESS OVERSEES THE BUREAUCRACY: STUDIES IN LEGISLATIVE SUPERVISION (1976). With regard to the powers of House and Senate Committees to issue and enforce subpoenas in keeping with their delegated authority, see CHARLES DOYLE, CONG. RSCH. SERV., RL34304, OBSTRUCTION OF CONGRESS: AN ABRIDGED OVERVIEW OF FEDERAL CRIMINAL LAWS RELATING TO INTERFERENCE WITH CONGRESSIONAL ACTIVITIES 23 (2010), *available at* https://crsreports.congress.gov/product/pdf/RS/RS22784/6. For a treatment of the most infamous use of the investigatory power, which provides a pointed reminder of the risk of abuse this power raises, see ROBERT SHOGAN, NO SENSE OF DECENCY: THE ARMY–MCCARTHY HEARINGS (2009). For a treatment of one of the most celebrated examples of legislative investigation, see SAMUEL DASH, CHIEF COUNSEL: INSIDE THE ERVIN COMMITTEE—THE UNTOLD STORY OF WATERGATE (1976). For another illustration of the critical role played by the investigative power—in this case, following the onset of the Great Depression—see MICHAEL A. PERINO, THE HELLHOUND OF WALL STREET: HOW FERDINAND PECORA'S INVESTIGATION OF THE GREAT CRASH FOREVER CHANGED AMERICAN FINANCE (2010).

[49] United States v. Comstock, 560 U.S. 126, 134, 137 (2010).

[50] *See Mazars*, 140 S. Ct. at 2031 (noting that "[w]ithout information, Congress would be shooting in the dark, unable to legislate 'wisely or effectively' " (quoting *McGrain*, 273 U.S. at 175)).

Congress only to pass "laws" in a bicameral fashion, whereas "each House" independently possesses the "power of inquiry—with process to enforce it."[51] According to the prevailing theory, this unicameral authority exists by implication because it "is an essential and appropriate auxiliary to the legislative function."[52] On another view, the power emanates from the Rules of Proceedings Clause, on the theory that gathering information is a critical component of the "proceedings" engaged in by each chamber as it discharges its core law-shaping responsibilities.[53]

Either way, "[t]he congressional power to obtain information is 'broad,' " covering "inquiries into the administration of existing laws, studies of proposed laws, and 'surveys of defects in our social, economic or political system for the purpose of enabling the Congress to remedy them.' "[54] At the same time, the investigative power is "subject to several limitations."[55] First, as further explained in Chapter 33, specialized limitations come into play when the subpoena concerns presidential communications that might be subject to a claim of executive privilege or that otherwise implicate special separation-of-powers concerns.[56] Second, all targets of legislative investigation can assert their constitutional rights, such as the right against self-incrimination,[57] as well as testimonial privileges, including those based on attorney-client, doctor-patient, and priest-penitent relationships.[58] Third, questions posed by a

---

[51] *Id.* (quoting *McGrain*, 273 U.S. at 174).

[52] *McGrain*, 273 U.S. at 174. *See* TRIBE, *supra* note 13, § 5–1, at 790–91 (describing the investigatory power as "implicit or ancillary" in nature and, more particularly, "implicit in the general Article I, § 1, grant of 'legislative powers' to Congress").

[53] *Cf. Watkins*, 354 U.S. at 197 (describing the power as "justified solely as an adjunct to the legislative process.").

[54] *Mazars*, 140 S. Ct. at 2031 (quoting *Watkins*, 354 U.S. at 187, 215); *see also* Barenblatt v. United States, 360 U.S. 109, 111 (1959) (describing the "power of inquiry" as being "as penetrating and far-reaching as the potential power to enact [laws] and appropriate [money] under the Constitution").

[55] *Mazars*, 140 S. Ct. at 2031.

[56] *Id.* at 2034–35. *See generally infra* Section 33.A.

[57] *See, e.g.*, Quinn v. United States, 349 U.S. 155, 161 (1955). For cases concerning other constitutional rights, see, e.g., *United States v. Rumely*, 345 U.S. 41, 44–48 (1953) (indicating that the First Amendment could have precluded questioning about speech-related activities, but not reaching the question by narrowly construing the scope of the committee's permissible work partly in light of constitutional concerns); *McPhaul v. United States*, 364 U.S. 372, 382–83 (1960) (considering, but rejecting, a Fourth Amendment-based claim that a congressional subpoena was "unreasonable").

[58] *See, e.g.*, *Mazars*, 140 S. Ct. at 2032 (noting that recipients of subpoenas "have long been understood to retain common law and constitutional privileges with respect to certain materials, such as attorney-client communications"); United States v. Tobin, 195 F. Supp. 588, 610 (D.D.C. 1961) (asserting that privileges based on "certain relationships" extend to congressional proceedings), *rev'd on other grounds*, 306 F. 2d 270 (D.C. Cir. 1962). *See generally* Jonathan P. Rich, Note, *The Attorney-Client Privilege in Congressional Investigations*, 88 COLUM. L. REV. 145 (1988). An

congressional committee cannot reach beyond that body's delegated authority of inquiry, particularly when dangers arise regarding the provision of fair notice to a witness about the scope of an impending investigation.[59] Finally, "a congressional subpoena is valid only if it is 'related to, and in furtherance of, a legitimate task of the Congress,' "[60] which ordinarily means "it must concern[ ] a subject on which legislation could be had."[61] Corollaries to this principle establish that "[i]nvestigations conducted solely for the personal aggrandizement of the investigators" are off limits,[62] as are

---

interesting question is whether the chambers of Congress could choose to abrogate any subconstitutional privileges for purposes of their own proceedings. *See* TRIBE, *supra* note 13, § 5–1, at 793 n.27 (noting that "many committees have taken the position that recognition of such privileges is discretionary"); *see also* Michael D. Bopp & DeLisa Lay, *The Availability of Common Law Privileges for Witnesses in Congressional Investigations*, 35 HARV. J.L. & PUB. POL'Y 897, 907 (2012) (flagging as unlikely as a practical matter that the chambers of Congress would refuse to honor proper claims of attorney-client privilege).

59 *See Watkins*, 354 U.S. at 202–03 (holding that the Due Process Clause required dismissal of a criminal contempt-of-Congress prosecution because the defendant was not notified of the committee's subject of inquiry and thus could not prepare for pertinent questions); Deutch v. United States, 367 U.S. 456, 469–71 (1961) (finding, in connection with a contempt-of-Congress prosecution, that "the Government failed to prove the charge in the indictment that the questions which the petitioner refused to answer were pertinent to the question then under inquiry by the subcommittee before which he appeared" (internal quotations omitted)); Sacher v. United States, 356 U.S. 576, 577–78 (1958) (per curiam) (overturning a witness's contempt conviction because the portion of the hearing for which he was to be held in contempt was "not clearly pertinent" to the committee's subject of inquiry); *see also* TRIBE, *supra* note 13, § 5–1, at 794 n.30 (citing *Rumely*, *see supra* note 57, for the proposition that "[p]articularly exacting standards of clarity are applied whenever the congressional investigation appears to threaten First Amendment rights").

60 *Mazars*, 140 S. Ct. at 2031 (quoting *Watkins*, 354 U.S. at 187).

61 *Id.* (internal quotations omitted); *see also* Kilbourn v. Thompson, 103 U.S. 168, 192–93 (1880). Often attributed to then-Professor Woodrow Wilson is the idea that, apart from the role played by legislative investigations in informing the lawmaking process, such investigations are independently justifiable for the purpose of informing the citizenry about matters of recognized public importance. *See Rumely*, 345 U.S. at 43 (urging that "[t]he informing function of Congress should be preferred even to its legislative function" (citing WOODROW WILSON, CONGRESSIONAL GOVERNMENT 303 (1885))). Some observers might view the Court's focus in *Mazars* on inquiries spawned by matters "on which legislation could be had" as throwing cold water on this notion. *See Mazars*, 140 S. Ct. at 2033–35. As Professor Tribe has observed, however, "Congress undeniably has legitimate concerns in ensuring, on behalf of a watching nation, that appropriations are well spent and that creatures of legislative creation are adequately supervised through oversight hearings," even if such resulting proceedings "have only a tenuous link to future legislation." TRIBE, *supra* note 13, § 5–1, at 791. The broader point is that congressional watchdogging and congressional lawmaking are almost always (if not always) tied closely together, and especially so when it comes to the "pure and efficient administration" of government on which Wilson focused. WILSON, *supra*, at 303. This is so because Congress always can (and should) consider the prospect of addressing problematic conditions in the operation of government (or society as a whole) with remedial legislation. No less important, educating the public about potentially problematic conditions can create valuable feedback from the citizenry that in turn triggers ameliorative legislative action.

62 *Mazars*, 140 S. Ct. at 2032 (quoting *Watkins*, 354 U.S. at 187).

congressional efforts simply to pry into "the private affairs of the citizen"[63] or to do nothing more than "expose for the sake of exposure."[64] Federal legislators also cannot "use subpoenas to 'try' someone 'before [a] committee for any crime or wrongdoing.' "[65] To be sure, inquiries along these lines are permissible when matters of impeachment, legislative expulsion, or the sanctioning of members are on the table.[66] But subpoenas issued for the sole purpose of punishing wrongful conduct outside these specialized contexts are "indefensible" because the pursuit of justice through trial-type processes is a task constitutionally assigned to the executive and judicial branches.[67]

Not surprisingly, it is far easier to state these rules than to apply them. This is true in part because legislative-branch officials may bring varied motivations, both individually and collectively, to their investigatory work. In *Trump v. Mazars*,[68] for example, House Democrats asserted that subpoenas of the President's financial records were appropriately designed to develop information related to the possible need for legislation regarding tax-related and business-related disclosure requirements and conflict-of-interest restrictions for Presidents and/or presidential candidates. House Republicans, however, characterized the endeavor as an effort to

---

63 Interstate Commerce Comm. v. Brimson, 154 U.S. 447, 478 (1894).

64 *Mazars*, 140 S. Ct. at 2032 (quoting *Watkins*, 354 U.S. at 200); *see id.* (quoting *McGrain*, 273 U.S. at 173–74) (stating that Congress lacks a " 'general' power to inquire into private affairs and compel disclosures").

65 *Id.* (quoting *McGrain*, 273 U.S. at 179).

66 With regard to impeachment, see *Kilbourn*, 103 U.S. at 190 (recognizing that, when either House of Congress considers an impeachment-related matter, it has the "right to compel the attendance of witnesses, and their answer to proper questions, in the same manner and by the use of the same means that courts of justice can in like cases"). With regard to expulsion and related matters, see *In re* Chapman, 166 U.S. 661, 668–69 (1897) (affirming Congress's right to compel a witness's testimony in the course of an internal investigation into a member's misconduct). In similar fashion, each House of Congress may conduct investigations unrelated to lawmaking, including by issuing and enforcing subpoenas, when it exercises its constitutionally assigned power to serve as "the Judge of the Elections, Returns, and Qualifications of its own Members." U.S. CONST. art. I, § 5, cl. 1. *See* Barry v. United States *ex rel.* Cunningham, 279 U.S. 597, 616 (1929) ("In exercising the power to judge of the elections, returns, and qualifications of its members, the Senate acts as a judicial tribunal, and the authority to require the attendance of witnesses is a necessary incident of the power to adjudge."); Thomas v. Loney, 134 U.S. 372, 373–75 (1890) (vindicating the congressional power to pursue punishment for witnesses who commit perjury when providing evidence for the purposes of deciding a contested election).

67 *Mazars*, 140 S. Ct. at 2032 (quoting *Watkins*, 354 U.S. at 187); *accord Quinn*, 349 U.S. at 161 (rejecting congressional involvement in "law enforcement" because that power is reserved to the executive and judicial branches); *see also* Sinclair v. United States, 279 U.S. 263, 295 (1929) (noting, in particular, that "Congress is without authority to compel disclosures for the purpose of aiding the prosecution of pending suits").

68 *Mazars*, 140 S. Ct. at 2019.

embarrass the President and thereby gain a political advantage. A looming question—applicable not only to high-ranking government officials, but to every potential target of a congressional inquiry—is whether courts can dismiss a colorable assertion of valid legislative aims on the ground that it constitutes a pretext. On occasion, the Court has seen fit to attribute pretextual reasoning to government decisionmakers.[69] It seems improbable, however, that federal judges will frequently, if ever, question the good faith of members of a co-equal branch who can point to an objectively defensible reason for seeking information to help them discharge their lawmaking responsibilities.[70]

What remedies exist if would-be witnesses impede legislative efforts to secure information sought by the House or the Senate? Either chamber can find a witness in contempt, pursuant to a majority vote, if that person fails to respond properly to a summons to appear, a subpoena to produce documents, or a permissible question posed in a legislative hearing.[71] Questions of both legality and practicality have arisen as to each chamber's ability to use its own sergeant-at-arms to detain persons found to be in contempt.[72]

---

[69] *Cf.* Dept. of Commerce v. New York, 139 S. Ct. 2551, 2575 (2019) (finding, in the context of an APA-based challenge to the Commerce Department's preparation of the U.S. census questionnaire, that the Secretary of Commerce's decision to include an inquiry about citizenship was "incongruent with what the record reveals about the agency's priorities and decisionmaking process").

[70] *See McGrain*, 273 U.S. at 178 (finding "that the presumption should be indulged that [aiding the Senate's legislative duties] was the real object" for obtaining witness testimony); *see also Sinclair*, 279 U.S. at 295 (finding valid a subpoena in support of lawmaking even though it "may also be of use in [pending] suits"); Hutcheson v. United States, 369 U.S. 599, 613–616 (1962) (four-to-two decision) (rejecting the suggestion in the earlier *Kilbourn* case that "mere pendency of the state indictment ipso facto constitutionally closed [an otherwise relevant] avenue of interrogation" and thus permitting congressional inquiry of a defendant—who had already been criminally charged with using money to bribe a state official—to aid legislative efforts to curb the misuse of union funds).

[71] For treatments of each chamber's authority to wield the contempt sanction, see *Marshall v. Gordon*, 243 U.S. 521, 542 (1917) (finding that the power to punish for contempt comports with "the right to prevent acts which, in and of themselves, inherently obstruct or prevent the discharge of legislative duty or the refusal to do that which there is an inherent legislative power to compel in order that legislative functions may be performed"), and *Jurney v. MacCracken*, 294 U.S. 125, 147, 149–50 (1935) (rejecting the argument that a person who destroyed subpoenaed records could not be held in contempt on the theory that the sanction could not be used "solely qua punishment"; reasoning instead that contempt in such circumstances vindicates "the established and essential privilege of requiring the production of evidence"). In unusual cases, the houses of Congress may find ways, apart from the pursuit of contempt citations, to sanction refusals to cooperate with their work. *See, e.g.*, TRIBE, *supra* note 13, § 5–1, at 791 n.17 (noting the House Judiciary Committee's inclusion of an article of impeachment against President Nixon based on defiance of committee subpoenas).

[72] *See McGrain*, 273 U.S. at 173 (affirming Congress's authority, "through its own process, to compel a private individual to appear . . . and give testimony needed"); Anderson v. Dunn, 19 U.S. 204, 231 (1821) (indicating that legislative detention for

Problems along these lines, however, have to some extent been obviated because a statute enacted pursuant to the Necessary and Proper Clause now criminalizes most contumacious conduct, thus empowering the executive branch to bring charges against uncooperative congressional witnesses.[73] The legislative contempt power, however, is not subject to wholesale statutory relinquishment. As the Court declared in 1897, "[C]ongress could not d[i]vest itself, or either of its Houses, of the essential and inherent power to punish for contempt, in cases to which the power of either house properly extended."[74]

---

contempt is permissible but cannot continue beyond the date of the body's adjournment). One question that has arisen is whether Congress can itself act to detain executive-branch officials that it has held to be in contempt. *Compare* Josh Chafetz, *Executive Branch Contempt of Congress*, 76 U. CHI. L. REV. 1083, 1152 (2009) (arguing that the sergeant-at-arms can be used to detain executive-branch officers who are found in contempt), *with* Todd Peterson, *Contempt of Congress v. Executive Privilege*, 14 U. PA. J. CONST. L. 77, 120–21 (2011) (arguing, on both legal and practical grounds, that the sergeant-at-arms should not be used to detain executive-branch officials claiming executive privilege). The earliest case of deploying a sergeant-at-arms, in this case of the House, to detain the subject of a House investigation involved the arrest in 1795 of two non-members, Robert Randall and Charles Whitney, who had allegedly offered bribes to House members, but only one of whom (Randall) was ultimately found guilty of contempt. *See* Letter from James Madison to Thomas Jefferson (Jan. 10, 1796), https://founders.archives.gov/documents/Madison/01-16-02-0103 (last visited June 17, 2021) (discussing Randall's attempts at bribery). Randall and Whitney were detained during the pendency of the House investigation and were eventually released not long after its conclusion. *See* Chafetz, *supra*, at 1128–1129.

73 *See* 2 U.S.C. § 192. In particular, once a chamber charges an individual with contempt, it can request that the Department of Justice pursue a conviction under the criminal-contempt statute, as recently occurred in connection with the refusal of Steve Bannon to appear before the House Select Committee to Investigate the January 6 Attack on the United States Capitol. *See* Katie Brenner & Luke Broadwater, *Bannon Indicted on Contempt Charges Over House's Capitol Riot Inquiry*, N.Y. TIMES (Nov. 12, 2021), https://www.nytimes.com/2021/11/12/us/politics/bannon-indicted.html. The statute, however, does not afford as much promise when a contempt referral targets a member of a sitting President's administration (or another political ally of the President), given that the President's own Attorney General might simply decline to act on the referral. Another route open to the House or Senate is to seek a court order requiring compliance with the subpoena's instructions. *See* TODD GARVEY, CONG. RSCH. SERV., RL34097, CONGRESS'S CONTEMPT POWER AND THE ENFORCEMENT OF CONGRESSIONAL SUBPOENAS: LAW, HISTORY, PRACTICE AND PROCEDURE (2017), *available at* https://sgp.fas.org/crs/misc/RL34097.pdf. For a further discussion of these issues, *see infra* Section 33.A.1.c.

74 *In re* Chapman, 166 U.S. 661, 671–72 (1897).

Part II

STRUCTURAL CONSTITUTIONAL LIMITS ON THE POWERS OF STATES AND OTHER NONFEDERAL ENTITIES

Chapter 15

UNION-PROTECTING LIMITS ON STATE LAWMAKING POWER

Analysis

In cases such as *Seminole Tribe*, *Alden*, *New York*, and *Printz* the Court looked to the structure and history of the Constitution, much more so than its text, in identifying external limits on federal authority to protect state-autonomy values.[1] The theme of these rulings carries with it a "flip-side" implication. It suggests that the Court might likewise restrict state authority to the extent necessary to safeguard constitutional interests in national unification. The Constitution imposes some limits of this kind in express terms.[2] But other limits—in the fashion of kindred restrictions rooted in state-supporting federalism values—find expression in constitutional doctrines tied only loosely to the constitutional text.

A. EXPRESS LIMITS ON STATE AUTHORITY

By its express terms, the Constitution both mandates and restricts certain forms of interstate collaboration. As for express *requirements* that such collaboration occur, Article IV, section 2 specifies that state officials, upon receiving an appropriate demand, must send fugitives from justice back to the jurisdiction from which they fled.[3] Each state also must give "Full Faith and Credit . . . to the

---

[1] *See supra* Chapter 5.

[2] *See infra* Section 15.A.

[3] U.S. CONST. art. IV, § 2, cl. 2. A point of no small consequence, especially in the age of internet crimes, is that the constitutional duty to extradite applies only as to persons who "shall flee from Justice" out of the extradition-demanding state, as opposed to all persons properly subject to prosecution in such a state. *Id. See, e.g.*, Innes v. Tobin, 240 U.S. 127, 131 (1916) (applying this textual requisite to limit the clause's operation); Gee v. Kansas, 912 F.2d 414, 418 (10th Cir. 1990) (same). As originally ratified, this provision was attached to the infamous Fugitive Slave Clause of Article IV, section 2, which effectively obligated each state to honor the demands of other states' slaveholders for the return of any "Person[s] held to Service or Labour"

public Acts, Records, and judicial Proceedings of every other State."[4] And another textual command (which receives further treatment in a separate chapter)[5] provides that "[t]he Citizens of each State shall be entitled to all Privileges and Immunities of Citizens in the several States."[6]

As for express *restrictions* on interstate collaboration, Article 1, section 10 establishes that "No State shall enter into any Treaty, Alliance, or Confederation."[7] Not surprisingly, during the post-Civil War period, the Court observed that the southern states had violated this dictate when they purported to form their own confederacy.[8] More commonly litigated is the Compact Clause, which specifies that that "[n]o State shall, without the Consent of Congress, . . . enter into any Agreement or Compact with another State."[9] Disputes under the clause have arisen in part because the Court has refused to accord it as sweeping a prohibitory reach as a literal reading of its terms might support. This process of interpretive narrowing began with *Virginia v. Tennessee*,[10] in which the Court held that not every deal between states qualifies as an "Agreement" within the meaning of the

---

who had fled into its territory. U.S. CONST. art. IV, § 2, cl. 3. That provision was given broad effect by Congress with the Fugitive Slave Act of 1793, upheld by the Court in *Prigg v. Pennsylvania*, 41 U.S. (16 Pet.) 539 (1842), so as to render states powerless to prevent out-of-state "slave catchers" from kidnapping alleged "fugitives." *See* Jamal S. Greene, *The Anticanon*, 125 HARV. L. REV. 379, 428 (2011) (noting that the Court's decision in *Prigg* "abided the constant threat of enslavement experienced by free brown-skinned Americans in both the North and the South" and "worked a simultaneous assault on due process and on equal protection, the twin pillars of the modern Fourteenth Amendment"). For more on the tragedy of the Fugitive Slave Clause, the Fugitive Slave Act, and the *Prigg* decision, see Sanford Levinson, *Is* Dred Scott *Really the Worst Opinion of All Time? Why* Prigg *Is Worse Than* Dred Scott *(But Is Likely to Stay Out of the "Anticanon")*, 125 HARV. L. REV. F. 23 (2011), *responding to* Greene, *supra*.

[4] U.S. CONST. art. IV, § 1. The Full Faith and Credit Clause has generated a wide-ranging body of judicial decisions treated in detail in other places. *See, e.g.*, 18B CHARLES ALAN WRIGHT & ARTHUR R MILLER, FEDERAL PRACTICE AND PROCEDURE § 4467 (4th ed. Supp. 2021).

[5] *See infra* Chapter 23.

[6] U.S. CONST. art. IV, § 2.

[7] U.S. CONST. art. I, § 10.

[8] *See* Williams v. Bruffy, 96 U.S. 176, 182–83 (1878). Also not surprisingly, the clause has come into play in cases involving constitutional challenges to state arrangements that touch on relations with foreign nations. *Compare, e.g.*, Holmes v. Jennison, 39 U.S. 540, 579 (1840) (invoking the clause in finding that individual states lack authority to surrender to foreign nations fugitives from justice who have fled to the United States), *with* Skiriotes v. Florida, 313 U.S. 69, 79 (1941) (refusing to read the clause as disabling Florida from regulating its own residents' activities in sponge fishing even outside its own territorial waters). For another case in which the Court alluded to the clause, see *United States v. California*, 332 U.S. 19, 35 (1947) (discussed *infra* note 105).

[9] U.S. CONST. art. I, § 10, cl. 3.

[10] 148 U.S. 503, 518 (1893).

Compact Clause,[11] because "the object of the constitutional provision" was to target only those agreements that "tend to increase and build up the political influence of the contracting states, so as to encroach upon or impair the supremacy of the United States."[12] It logically followed, so the Court concluded, that congressional consent was required for only those interstate arrangements that would "lead . . . to the increase of the political power or influence of the states affected, and thus encroach . . . upon the full and free exercise of federal authority."[13] For example, the Compact Clause "may well" require congressional approval if, pursuant to an agreement between two states, the boundary between them were "so run as to cut off an important and valuable portion of a state," thus bolstering "the political power of the state enlarged."[14] On the other hand, boundary agreements do not require congressional consent when they serve only "to mark and define that which actually existed before, but was undefined and unmarked."[15] In later cases, the Court has grappled with how to apply this principle to both border-related and other forms of interstate deal-making.[16] In doing so, however, the Court

[11] *Id.* at 517–18 (recognizing that the terms of the clause, "taken by themselves, are sufficiently comprehensive to embrace all forms of stipulation, written or verbal, and relating to all kinds of subjects," but going on to reject this interpretation).

[12] *Id.* at 518.

[13] *Id.* at 520.

[14] *Id.*

[15] *Id.*; *see also id.* at 518–19 (identifying other interstate collaborations that would not require Congress's approval, such as the consensual transfer of a small parcel of land or a collaborative plan to drain a borderland swamp to stanch the spread of an insect-borne disease or otherwise address a shared public health emergency, which might arise even while Congress is not in session).

[16] *See* New Hampshire v. Maine, 426 U.S. 363 (1976) (holding that a consent decree affirming the boundary line between New Hampshire and Maine, though unapproved by Congress, did not violate the Compact Clause because it in no way increased any state's power or encroached on federal supremacy); U.S. Steel Corp. v. Multistate Tax Comm'n, 434 U.S. 452 (1978) (rejecting a challenge under the Compact Clause to the Multistate Tax Compact because it did not tend to increase the political power of the states in a way that threatened federal supremacy); Northeast Bancorp, Inc. v. Bd. of Governors of Fed. Reserve Sys., 472 U.S. 159, 160 (1985) (holding that a Massachusetts law that allowed out-of-state bank holding companies to do local business if reciprocal authorization were granted by their states did not meaningfully infringe on federal interests, even if the Compact Clause were deemed applicable to it); *see also* McComb v. Wambaugh, 934 F.2d 474, 478–82 (3d Cir. 1991) (holding that the Interstate Compact on Placement of Children did not require congressional consent because it focused on an area of the law historically within state control); S&M Brands, Inc. v. Caldwell, 614 F.3d 172, 175–76 (5th Cir. 2010) (holding that a settlement agreement involving multiple states, although not approved by Congress, passed muster under the Compact Clause because it did not encroach on federal supremacy); Bimber's Delwood, Inc. v. James, 496 F. Supp. 3d 760, 787–88 (W.D.N.Y. 2020) (finding that the plaintiffs had not shown a likelihood of success on the merits of their claim that an agreement between several states regarding COVID-19 mitigation efforts violated the Compact Clause); United States v. California, 444 F. Supp. 3d 1181, 1196 (E.D. Cal. 2020) (rejecting a Compact Clause-based challenge to California's cap-and-trade program, while noting that the program did not enhance California's power vis-à-vis the federal government); Koterba v. Dep't of Transp., 736

has never retreated from the policy-centered approach it launched in *Virginia v. Tennessee*, which continues to stand as a powerful example of the Court's now-and-again willingness to depart from the most natural (and bright-line) reading of the constitutional text to avoid "permanent inconvenience or public mischief."[17]

Interests in promoting national cohesion also underlie the Tonnage Clause and the Import-Export Clause of Article I, section 10, as well as the Privileges or Immunities Clause of the Fourteenth Amendment. The Tonnage Clause—which bars states from "lay[ing] any Duty of Tonnage" in the absence of congressional consent—promotes national cohesiveness by inhibiting states from imposing self-serving taxes on those who make use of harbors within their boundaries, thus safeguarding free-flowing maritime shipping.[18] In *Polar Tankers, Inc. v. City of Valdez*,[19] for example, the Court invalidated a municipality's "personal property tax" imposed, as a practical matter, only on oil tankers. To be sure, the city's levy was not based on "Tonnage" in the accepted linguistic sense of the weight or "the internal cubic capacity of a vessel."[20] The Court, however, deemed this disconnection inconsequential.[21] What mattered was that earlier rulings forbade "a State to do that indirectly which she is forbidden . . . to do directly."[22] Thus, the clause barred imposition of any ship-targeting tax, "regardless of [its] name or form, . . . which

A.2d 761, 764–66 (Comm. Ct. Pa. 1999) (finding that congressional consent was not required for a compact under which states shared driving records because the compact did not threaten the supremacy of the federal government).

17 *Virginia*, 148 U.S. at 519–20. Apart from questions about the need for congressional consent under the Compact Clause, issues regarding the proper form that such consent must take also have stirred debate. The Court addressed two important questions on this subject in *Virginia*, when it indicated that (1) congressional consent can either predate or postdate the making of the "Agreement or Compact"; and (2) while consent is often given in express terms, it also "may be implied." *Id.* at 521. For more recent rulings along these lines, see *Cuyler v. Adams*, 449 U.S. 433, 441 (1981) (holding that Congress may consent to an interstate compact "in advance or by giving expressed or implied approval" after the fact), and *Columbia River Gorge United-Protecting People and Property v. Yeutter*, 960 F.2d 110, 114 (9th Cir. 1992) (finding that Congress consented in advance to the Columbia River Gorge Compact). Another question concerns whether the Constitution requires presentment to the President—as it does for ordinary lawmaking—to effectuate a "Consent of Congress" for purposes of Article I, section 10, clause 3. For a detailed canvassing of this subject and an argument that such "Consent" does not require presentment, see James F. Blumstein & Thomas J. Cheeseman, *State Empowerment and the Compact Clause*, 27 WM. & MARY BILL OF RTS. J. 775, 792–826 (2019).

18 U.S. CONST. art. I, § 10, cl. 3.

19 557 U.S. 1, 9 (2009).

20 *Id.* at 6 (internal quotations omitted).

21 *Id.*

22 *Id.* (internal quotations omitted) (citing *The Passenger Cases*, 48 U.S. (7 How.) 283 (1849)); *see also* Smith v. Turner, 48 U.S. 283 (1849) (stating that "[t]he State may levy any tax which is not obviously a duty on imports, but it cannot, by indirection, do the precise thing forbidden").

operate[s] to impose a charge for the privilege of entering, trading in, or lying in a port."[23] Finally, the Court concluded that this principle controlled in *Polar Tankers* itself because the city had placed its levy on "ships and . . . no other property at all."[24]

The Import-Export Clause, meanwhile, specifies that "[n]o State shall, without the Consent of the Congress, lay any Imposts or Duties on Imports or Exports, except what may be absolutely necessary for executing its inspection Laws."[25] In *Woodruff v. Parham*,[26] the Court limited the reach of this provision by clarifying that it blocks state interference only with international, and not with interstate, trade.[27] In the same case, the Court also embraced the "original package" doctrine, which woodenly prohibited all state taxation—even pursuant to generally applicable laws—of imported goods not yet removed from the containers in which they had arrived.[28] This doctrine operated for many years, but the Court abandoned it in *Michelin Tire Corp. v. Wages*.[29] There, the Court pointed to the Framers' goals, in fashioning the Import-Export Clause, to help safeguard federal control over foreign affairs, to protect federal

---

[23] *Polar Tankers*, 557 U.S. at 8.

[24] *Id.* at 16. Notably, however, the Tonnage Clause does not prohibit state charges for the use of towing services, wharves, and other state-provided improvements, even when calculated according to the ship's true "tonnage"—that is, its total holding capacity or weight. *See* Dan T. Coenen, *State User Fees and the Dormant Commerce Clause*, 50 VAND. L. REV. 795, 816–17 (1997). The compatibility of state user fees, including fees of this kind, with the dormant Commerce Clause principle is addressed *infra* Section 21.E. For a comprehensive treatment of the Tonnage Clause, see JEROME R. HELLERSTEIN, WALTER HELLERSTEIN & JOHN A. SWAIN, STATE TAXATION ¶ 5.08 (3d ed. 1998 with 2021 cumulative supp.).

[25] U.S. CONST. art. I, § 10, cl. 2.

[26] 75 U.S. (8 Wall.) 123, 128 (1868).

[27] Justice Thomas has criticized this holding. *See* Camps Newfound/Owatonna, Inc. v. Town of Harrison, 520 U.S. 564, 609 (1997) (Thomas, J., dissenting). For an important academic treatment of the subject, see Brannon P. Denning, *Justice Thomas, the Import-Export Clause, and* Camps Newfound/Owatonna v. Harrison, 70 U. COLO. L. REV. 155, 164–66 (1999).

[28] *See Camps Newfound/Owatonna*, 520 U.S. at 633–34 (Thomas, J., dissenting) (discussing the Court's acceptance of the "original package" doctrine in *Woodruff* and in *Low v. Austin*, 80 U.S. (13 Wall.) 29 (1871), as well as its later demise). For illustrative cases applying the original-package doctrine, see *Brown v. Maryland*, 25 U.S. (12 Wheat.) 419, 442–46 (1827) (holding that requiring a license in order to import goods, in their original form or package, is prohibited by the Constitution as being a duty on imports), and *Cook v. Pennsylvania*, 97 U.S. 566, 573 (1878) (holding that a tax on an auctioneering sale is "a tax on the goods sold . . . and when applied to foreign goods sold in the original packages of the importer, before they have become incorporated into the general property of the country, the law imposing such tax is void as laying a duty on imports"). For a case illustrating the limitations of the doctrine, see *Youngstown Sheet & Tube Co. v. Bowers*, 358 U.S. 534, 536 (1959) (concluding that the Import-Export Clause did not cover goods—here, ore, lumber, and veneers—that had been so acted on in the manufacturing process "as to cause them to lose their distinctive character as imports").

[29] 423 U.S. 276 (1976).

revenue collections from undue state encroachment, and to impede states located on seaway trade routes from bilking citizens of other states "not situated as favorably geographically."[30] The Justices could detect no affront to these objectives in Georgia's placement of a nondiscriminatory ad valorem tax on imported tires even though they remained in their original packages. Indeed, the line drawn in *Woodruff* struck the Court in *Michelin Tire* as particularly unjustifiable because, once imported property was unloaded and warehoused in the state, it enjoyed the full benefit of public services such as state police and fire protection no less than functionally identical, but non-imported, goods subject to full-scale state taxation.[31]

The Privileges *or* Immunities Clause of the Fourteenth Amendment (which is not to be confused with the Privileges *and* Immunities Clause of Article IV) safeguards a corpus of long-implied rights that "owe their existence to the Federal government" and "its National character."[32] These rights include "free access to [the Nation's] seaports," the ability "to come to the seat of government to assert any claim" upon it, and the capacity "to use the navigable waters of the United States, however they may penetrate the territory of the several States."[33] A seminal application of these

---

[30] *Id.* at 285–86.

[31] *Id.* at 288. For an extensive discussion of the Import-Export Clause, see HELLERSTEIN, HELLERSTEIN & SWAIN, *supra* note 24, ¶¶ 5.01 to 5.07.

[32] *Slaughter-House Cases*, 83 U.S. (16 Wall.) 36, 79 (1873). The clause provides that "[n]o State shall make or enforce any law which shall abridge the privileges or immunities of citizens of the United States." U.S. CONST. amend. XIV, § 1. The *Slaughter-House Cases* have been roundly criticized based on the view that they embraced an understanding of the Privileges or Immunities Clause that was far more cramped than what the Framers of the Reconstruction Amendments had envisioned. *See* AKHIL REED AMAR, THE BILL OF RIGHTS: CREATION AND RECONSTRUCTION 210–13 (2008); *see also* Saenz v. Roe, 526 U.S. 489, 527–28 (1999) (Thomas, J., dissenting) (criticizing the *Slaughter-House Cases* on this basis and indicating that "I would be open to reevaluating [the Privilege or Immunities Clause's] meaning in an appropriate case").

[33] *Slaughter-House Cases*, 83 U.S. at 79. For a case illustrating the limits of the clause's operation—in particular, with regard to using the nation's navigable waters—see *Courtney v. Goltz*, 736 F.3d 1152, 1160–61 (9th Cir. 2013) (holding that the Privileges or Immunities Clause did not extend to the operation of a commercial ferry on a lake deemed navigable by the federal government, without a required state certificate, because conducting a profit-making ferry business involves "do[ing] more than simply navigat[ing] the waters" of a lake; noting that "[w]e have narrowly construed the rights incident to United States citizenship enunciated in the *Slaughter-House Cases*, particularly with respect to regulation of intrastate economic activities"). A significant limit on the clause's operation—and one that distinguishes it from the Fourteenth Amendment's companion protections of due-process and equal-protection rights—stems from the text-driven general understanding that the clause protects only "citizens," as opposed to all "persons," including noncitizens. *See, e.g.*, Richard A. Epstein, *Of Citizens and Persons: Reconstructing the Privileges or Immunities Clause of the Fourteenth Amendment*, 1 N.Y.U. J.L. & LIBERTY 334, 339–40 (2005); Derek Shaffer, Note, *Answering Justice Thomas in* Saenz: *Granting the Privileges or*

principles came in *Crandall v. Nevada*,[34] in which the Court held that states cannot tax citizens for traveling across their borders.[35] As then-Associate Justice Rehnquist would later explain, this ruling reflected "the theme that the power to obstruct totally the movements of people is incompatible with the concept of one Nation."[36] In *Saenz v. Roe*,[37] the Court shifted its attention from temporary interstate travel to indefinite interstate relocation, holding that states may not discriminate between recently-arriving and longer-term residents in administering a public benefits program.[38] Pointing to both the Privileges or Immunities Clause and its textual next-door neighbor, the Citizenship Clause, Justice Stevens declared for a seven-member majority that the Constitution "does not provide for, and does not allow for, degrees of [state] citizenship based on length of residence."[39] Otherwise, local authorities could inhibit relocation

---

Immunities Clause Full Citizenship Within the Fourteenth Amendment, 52 STAN. L. REV. 709, 741 (2000) (noting that the clause "by its terms applies only to U.S. citizens"); Michael Kent Curtis, *Historical Linguistics, Inkblots, and Life After Death: The Privileges or Immunities of Citizens of the United States*, 78 N.C. L. REV. 1071, 1149 (2000). *But see* JOHN HART ELY, DEMOCRACY AND DISTRUST 24–25 & n.51 (1981) (urging that, because "[i]t seems to be generally agreed that no conscious intention to limit the protection of the clause to citizens appears in the historical records," construing the Privileges or Immunities Clause to protect noncitizens "would better reflect what we know of the purpose"; also proposing an interpretation of the text that conforms with this view).

34 73 U.S. (6 Wall.) 35 (1868).

35 Notably, *Crandall* predated adoption of the Fourteenth Amendment. But the Court's ruling in the *Slaughter-House Cases* made it clear that the purpose of the Privilege or Immunities Clause was to enshrine in the constitutional text this set of nation-regarding rights, which previously had been set forth in in "no express provision of the Constitution." *Crandall*, 73 U.S. at 48.

36 Nevada v. Hall, 440 U.S. 410, 441 (1979) (Rehnquist, J., dissenting) (adding that "the constitutional framework demanded that the tax be proscribed"); *see also* United States v. Guest, 383 U.S. 745, 758 (1966) (suggesting that the right to free interstate movement was "conceived from the beginning to be a necessary concomitant of the stronger Union the Constitution created").

37 526 U.S. 489 (1999).

38 *Id.* at 511.

39 *Id.* at 506 (quoting Zobel v. Williams, 457 U.S. 55, 69 (1982) (Brennan, J. concurring)). The Citizenship Clause states: "All persons born or naturalized in the United States and subject to the jurisdiction thereof, are citizens of the United States and of the State wherein they reside." U.S. CONST. amend. XIV, § 1. Notably, in *Zobel* the Court reached a conclusion parallel to the one in *Saenz* when it invalidated an Alaska program that allocated government oil revenues to state citizens by means of a duration-of-residency-based system. Although the majority opinion (written by Chief Justice Burger) rested this result on the Equal Protection Clause, two other opinions (one written by Justice Brennan, joined by Justices Marshall, Blackmun, and Powell, and the other written by Justice O'Connor) explored additional possible sources of this "principle of free interstate migration," *Zobel*, 457 U.S. at 73–74 (Brennan, J., concurring), including the Citizenship Clause. *See id.* at 67; *see also* Kevin Maher, Comment, *Like a Phoenix from the Ashes:* Saenz v. Roe, *the Right to Travel, and the Resurrection of the Privileges or Immunities Clause of the Fourteenth Amendment*, 33 TEX. TECH L. REV. 105, 123 (2001); Tim A. Lemper, *The Promise and Perils of*

from one state to another in contravention of "the nature of our Federal Union," which is structured so as to let citizens vote with their feet.[40]

Several text-based limits on the authority of states serve to stifle their ability to interfere with the exercise of constitutionally granted federal powers. Thus, "[n]o State shall . . . grant Letters of Marque and Reprisal; coin Money; emit Bills of credit; [or] make any Thing but gold and silver Coin a Tender in Payment of Debts."[41] In addition,

---

"Privileges or Immunities": Saenz v. Roe, 119 S. Ct. 1518 (1999), 23 HARV. J.L. & PUB. POL'Y 295, 304 (1999).

[40] *Saenz*, 526 U.S. at 499 (quoting Shapiro v. Thompson, 394 U.S. 618, 629 (1969)). Prior to its ruling in *Saenz*, the Court (building on its 1969 ruling in *Shapiro*), handed down a line of rulings dealing with problems of this kind based on an application of the Equal Protection Clause. In some of those cases, the Court invalidated durational residency requirements imposed on persons who moved to the state with the stated intention to remain there indefinitely. *See* Dunn v. Blumstein, 405 U.S. 330 (1972) (invalidating a one-year residency requirement attached to voting eligibility); Memorial Hosp. v. Maricopa Cty., 415 U.S. 250 (1974) (invalidating a one-year residency requirement for persons to receive county-subsidized nonemergency hospitalization or medical care). In other cases, the Court upheld such laws. *See* Sosna v. Iowa, 419 U.S. 393, 407 (1975) (validating a one-year requirement for eligibility to file a divorce action by reference to a "reasonabl[e]" state interest in not becoming a "divorce mill"); Starns v. Malkerson, 326 F. Supp. 234 (D. Minn. 1970) (upholding a durational residency requirement for in-state higher-education tuition), *summarily aff'd*, 401 U.S. 985 (1971); *see also* Vlandis v. Kline, 412 U.S. 441, 452 n.9 (1973) (distinguishing *Starns*, as involving only a one-year residency requirement, in striking down an ongoing conclusive presumption of nonresidency for many, if not most, students coming from outside the state). In *Saenz*, while shifting attention away from equal-protection analysis, the Court distinguished earlier cases that involved "portable benefit[s], such as a divorce or a college education, that will be enjoyed after [persons receiving such benefits] return to their original domicile." *Saenz*, 526 U.S. at 505. For a sampling of post-*Saenz* commentary on the right of interstate migration and the broader implications of *Saenz*, see, e.g., Laurence H. Tribe, Saenz *Sans Prophesy: Does the Privileges or Immunities Revival Portend the Future—or Reveal the Structure of the Present?*, 113 HARV. L. REV. 110 (1999), Lawrence J. Conlan, Note, *Durational Residency Requirement for In-State Tuition: Searching for Access to Affordable Higher Learning*, 53 HASTINGS L.J. 1389 (2002), and John B. Schrader, Note, *Reawakening "Privileges or Immunities": An Originalist Blueprint for Invalidating State Felon Disenfranchisement Laws*, 62 VAND. L. REV. 1285 (2009).

[41] U.S. CONST. art. I, § 10, cl. 1. In treating one key portion of this clause, the Court has drawn on "the historical circumstances which are known to have led to [its] adoption" in holding that the term "Bills of credit" comprehends only "a paper medium intended to circulate between individuals, and between government and individuals"—that is, "to circulate as money." Poindexter v. Greenhow, 114 U.S. 270, 283–84 (1885) (internal quotations and citations omitted). Accordingly, the clause does not foreclose a state's issuance of bonds to fund its treasury, including by making available to bondholders transferrable coupons subject to use, in particular, to pay taxes. *Id.* at 283–85. The key point is that instruments of this kind are neither by design nor in practice "substitute[s] for money." *Id.* at 284. *Accord, e.g.*, Hous. & Tex. Central R.R. Co. v. Texas, 177 U.S. 66, 89 (1900). For an early and exceptional case in which the Court did find state-issued instruments to qualify as "Bills of credit," see *Craig v. Missouri*, 29 U.S. (4 Pet.) 410 (1830) (Marshall, C.J.). There, a four-to-three majority deemed it decisive that: "The denominations of the bills, from ten dollars to fifty cents, fitted them for the purpose of ordinary circulation; and their reception in payment of taxes, and debts to the government and to corporations, and of salaries and fees, would give them currency." *Id.* at 433. In addition, the relevant state law

no state may, without congressional approval, "keep Troops, or Ships of War in time of Peace, enter into any Agreement or Compact with . . . a foreign power, or engage in War, unless actually invaded, or in such imminent danger as will not admit of delay."[42]

Two other express provisions control state choices about their own institutional arrangements based on values of foundational, nationwide significance. One provision, set forth in Article I, section 10, bans state grants of "any Title of Nobility." This clause might seem quaint in the present day. In *The Federalist*, however, Alexander Hamilton described it as nothing less than "the corner-stone of republican government" due to its role in ensuring that "the government will be . . . that of the people."[43] Addressing the same theme in a more general way, Article IV, section 4 requires that "[t]he United States shall guarantee to every State in this Union a Republican Form of Government."[44] Although controversial principles of justiciability doctrine long have impeded judicial invocation of this clause, the provision's core directive remains both unmistakable and important: No state may properly—through the actions of its citizenry, its leaders, or an insurrectionist mob—abandon basic principles of popular self-rule.[45]

---

made specific reference to the "circulation" of these instruments. *Id.* On these facts, the majority deemed itself duty-bound to strike down the challenged law even though that law characterized the instruments as "certificates," rather than "bills of credit." Otherwise, Chief Justice Marshall observed, "the constitution, in one of its most important provisions, may be openly evaded by giving a new name to an old thing." *Id.*

[42] U.S. CONST. art. I, § 10, cl. 3.

[43] THE FEDERALIST No. 84 (Hamilton). Various other provisions of Article I, section 10 lay down limits on state authority that relate closely to individual rights and are thus not covered in any detail within this book. *See, e.g.*, U.S. CONST. art. I, § 10, cl. 1 (prohibiting states from "pass[ing] any Bill of Attainder, ex post facto Law, or Law impairing the Obligation of Contracts").

[44] U.S. CONST. art. IV, § 4.

[45] On the justiciability issues, see Luther v. Borden, 48 U.S. (7 How.) 1 (1849) (treating claims arising under the clause as presenting nonjusticiable political questions); *see also infra* Section 35.E (discussing the political-question doctrine). For further commentary on the Republican Form of Government Clause (or "Guarantee Clause"), see generally JACK M. BALKIN, LIVING ORIGINALISM 243 (2011) (arguing that "[t]he goal of the guarantee clause is to . . . to ensure that majorities rule and prevent aristocracy or oligarchy, [including as] the result of political machination"); LAURENCE H. TRIBE, AMERICAN CONSTITUTIONAL LAW § 5–12, at 909–10 (3rd ed. 2000) (noting Madison's view of the clause as rejecting "aristocratic or monarchical innovations" (quoting THE FEDERALIST NO. 43 (Madison)); citing treatments of the clause by Professors Merritt, Amar, Choper, and Linde; and concluding that "preserving federalism's capacity of institutional innovation probably requires a fairly narrow reading of the clause's restrictions"); Carolyn Shapiro, *Democracy, Federalism, and the Guarantee Clause*, 62 ARIZ. L. REV. 183, 184–85, 186, 194–96 (2020) (emphasizing that the clause derived from the Framers' fears that "departures from a republican form of government in one state would threaten the continued existence of republican government in other states," and contending that—although the clause is often viewed as unenforceable by the courts—it nonetheless constitutes a meaningful font of congressional power); Mark D. Rosen, *Can Congress Play a Role in Remedying*

B. IMPLIED LIMITS ON STATE AUTHORITY

The most important constitutional provision dealing with state-federal relations appears in Article VI, clause 2, which states that: "This Constitution, and the Laws of the United States which shall be made in Pursuance thereof; and all treaties . . . shall be the supreme Law of the Land, and the Judges in every State shall be bound thereby, any Thing in the Constitution or Laws of any State to the Contrary notwithstanding."[46] This provision has given rise to the Court's many decisions (addressed in detail in a later chapter) on the subject of "preemption"—that is, the interpretation of federal statutes, treaties, and agency regulations to displace, or not to displace, challenged state-law rules.[47] The Supremacy Clause, however, also has operated to restrict state power in a more subtle way because courts have drawn on it to rein in state prerogatives in cases that do not involve preemption in any ordinary sense of that word.

1. Federal Tax Immunity

Federal immunity from state taxation has its source in the Court's landmark ruling in *McCulloch v. Maryland*.[48] There, the Court held that Maryland's taxation of the Bank of the United States ran afoul of a principle that, although "not . . . stated in terms" in the Constitution, derived from a "fair construction" of the document as a whole, beginning with the Supremacy Clause.[49] The task of applying the tax-immunity rule first laid down in *McCulloch* has raised vexing questions for more than two centuries. Indeed, even while scuttling the Maryland tax at issue in that case, the Court injected nuance into the doctrine by indicating that this immunity would not "extend to a tax paid by the real property of the bank, in common with the other real property within the State, nor to a tax imposed on the interest

---

Dysfunctional Political Partisanship?, 50 IND. L. REV. 265, 271–72 (2016) (arguing that the clause authorizes Congress "to enact rules-of-the-road for state elections," so as "to preempt possible harm to republicanism"); Jacob M. Heller, Note, *Death by a Thousand Cuts: The Guarantee Clause Regulation of State Constitutions*, 62 STAN. L. REV. 1711, 1753–59 (2010) (arguing that the clause would support federal anti-corruption legislation and some laws that attack malapportionment and "legislative power grabs"); Jarrett A. Zafran, Note, *Referees of Republicanism: How the Guarantee Clause Can Address State Political Lockup*, 91 N.Y.U. L. REV. 1418 (2016) (arguing for the clause's use in combating power-maintaining "lockup" of state political authority). *But see* Ryan C. Williams, *The "Guarantee" Clause*, 132 HARV. L. REV. 602 (2018) (arguing, based on an international-law-based original-meaning analysis, that federal authorities can act under the Guarantee Clause only in response to a state's request for intervention).

[46] U.S. CONST. art. VI, cl. 2.

[47] *See infra* Chapter 24.

[48] 17 U.S. (4 Wheat.) 316 (1819) (discussed *supra* Section 1.B).

[49] *Id.* at 427.

which the citizens of Maryland may hold in this institution, in common with other property of the same description throughout the State."[50]

Building on this passage, later decisions have established that state taxes related to the work of the federal government abridge constitutional limits if (1) they target federal entities "directly," or (2) they "discriminate against the United States or those with whom it deals."[51] Applying the first of these limits—the so-called "legal incidence" requirement—the Court determined that a state property tax imposed on the Reconstruction Finance Corporation offended the Constitution because it fell on an "arm" of the federal government itself, notwithstanding the fact that a private lessee had agreed to reimburse the government for any state taxes it had to pay.[52] In keeping with this same principle, the Court also has held that states may impose a generally applicable tax on the income of private contractors derived from work on federal construction projects, even where the federal government has absorbed the cost of the tax by agreeing to indemnify the contractor for any levies to which it might be subject.[53] These cases confirm what the name of the "legal

50 *Id.* at 436. In *First Agricultural National Bank v. State Tax Commission*, 392 U.S, 339 (1968), the Court again considered the extent to which states can tax the operations of federally chartered banks—in this case by imposing on such institutions nondiscriminatory sales-and-use-tax-related obligations. The majority sidestepped a full-scale exploration of *McCulloch*'s operation in this context by finding that the challenged state tax was preempted by federal statutory law. In a dissent joined by Justices Harlan and Stewart, however, Justice Thurgood Marshall reasoned that federally chartered banks, given their "present functions," should not be "constitutionally immune from nondiscriminatory state taxation." *Id.* at 349 (Marshall, J., dissenting). In particular, he reasoned that "hoary cases," such as *Owensboro National Bank v. Owensboro*, 173 U.S. 668 (1899)—in which the Court, in an "alternative holding," had invoked *McCulloch* to invalidate the application to a national bank of "a nondiscriminatory franchise tax"—should not be deemed to preclude this result. *First Agricultural Nat'l Bank*, 392 U.S. at 350 (Marshall, J., dissenting). In support of this stance, Justice Marshall highlighted both Congress's ability to deal with state-taxation problems concerning national banks by way of legislative intervention and the Court's founding of the *McCulloch* principle "not . . . upon any specific provisions of the Constitution, but rather upon this Court's concepts of federalism." *Id.* at 351-52.

51 Cal. State Bd. of Equalization v. Sierra Summit, Inc., 490 U.S. 844, 848–50 (1989) (upholding a state sales tax as applied to a bankruptcy liquidation because it imposes an obligation on the bankruptcy estate, "not . . . the Federal Government," and it applies generally to in-state sales so that "[t]here is no claim . . . that the tax discriminates"). For a detailed treatment of these rules, see generally HELLERSTEIN, HELLERSTEIN & SWAIN, *supra* note 24, at ¶ 22.06.

52 Rohr Aircraft Corp. v. San Diego, 362 U.S. 628 (1960).

53 *See, e.g.*, United States v. California, 507 U.S. 746 (1993) (holding that an agreement by the federal government to indemnify a contractor does not create an immunity for the contractor from state taxation); *see also* United States v. New Mexico, 455 U.S. 720 (1982) (upholding a state tax as applied to federal contractors who managed the federal government's atomic laboratories); James v. Dravo Contracting Co., 302 U.S. 134 (1937) (allowing state taxation of the gross receipts of a contractor

incidence" principle implies: Judicial inquiries must focus on who bears *legal responsibility* for the tax and not on who, as a practical matter, bears the ultimate *economic burden* that the tax creates.

The second component of the tax-immunity doctrine—which focuses on nondiscrimination—centers, like the legal-incidence rule, on core notions that lack complexity. Thus, just as surely as a state may extend an across-the-board income tax to private contractors who work on federal government projects,[54] it likewise may apply such a tax to persons working directly for the federal government.[55] A state, however, may not impose its income tax or any other tax in a way that discriminates against federal contractors or federal employees.[56]

In applying these principles, courts sometimes encounter knotty problems of characterization. In *Davis v. Michigan Department of Treasury*,[57] for instance, former federal government workers launched a discrimination-based attack on a Michigan income tax exemption that covered the retirement income of only former state and local government employees. In assessing a challenge to the exemption mounted by these federal retirees, the Court confronted a conundrum: Was the proper point of reference for assessing the discrimination claim the state's treatment of the favored class of former state and municipal workers (in which case the existence of an uneven treatment of federal retirees was obvious), or was it the state's treatment of the much larger group of non-government retirees who, just like federal retirees, received no advantage from the challenged exemption (in which case no discrimination existed)? Writing in dissent, Justice Stevens opted for the latter view, urging that "[t]he fact that a State may elect to grant a preference . . . to a small percentage of its residents does not make the tax discriminatory in any sense that is relevant to the doctrine of intergovernmental tax immunity."[58] In addition, he argued that, even if constitutionally problematic discrimination somehow did inhere in the Michigan taxing scheme, that discrimination was

---

that built locks and dams for the federal government to the extent that the contractor's activities occurred in the taxing state).

[54] *See supra* note 53 and accompanying text.

[55] *See* Graves v. New York *ex rel.* O'Keefe, 306 U.S. 466 (1939). A statute enacted in the wake of *Graves*, 4 U.S.C. § 111, now specifically provides for this result. The Court in *Davis v. Michigan Dep't of Treasury*, 489 U.S. 803 (1989), noted that this statutory rule is "coextensive with the prohibition against discriminatory taxes embodied in the modern constitutional doctrine of intergovernmental tax immunity." *Id.* at 813.

[56] *See* Barker v. Kansas, 503 U.S. 594 (1992) (invalidating the state's uneven treatment of former federal military personnel in taxing retirement benefits).

[57] 489 U.S. 803 (1989).

[58] *Id.* at 821 (Stevens, J., dissenting).

justifiable because a state should have no less power to compensate its own former workers by lowering their state-imposed tax obligations than by raising their state-awarded retirement-benefit payments.[59] Eight members of the Court, however, found these arguments unpersuasive. Writing on behalf of this group, Justice Kennedy reasoned that increased benefits differed from decreased taxes because state grants of the former, but not of the latter, "would result in higher federal income tax payments."[60] Nor was the majority persuaded by Justice Stevens's there's-no-discrimination-in-the-first-place rationale. In its view, "it does not seem too much to require that the State treat those who deal with the [federal] Government as well as it treats those with whom it deals itself."[61]

2. Federal Regulatory Immunity

In keeping with the reasoning of *McCulloch*, the Court has immunized federal government operations not only from taxation but also from certain forms of state regulation. In *Johnson v. Maryland*,[62] for example, a unanimous Court relied on *McCulloch* in holding that a state could not apply a generally applicable drivers' license law to a federal postal employee. The Court acknowledged that the state could probably subject mail carriers to "for instance, a statute or ordinance regulating the mode of turning at the corners of streets."[63] The licensing law was unacceptable, however, because it "requires qualifications in addition to those that the [federal] Government has pronounced sufficient."[64] As it turns out, rulings that address federal immunity from state regulatory control are few in number. Even so, the Court's sporadic pronouncements on the subject suggest that its view of regulatory immunity parallels the doctrine of tax immunity as reflected in cases such as *Davis*.[65] And while the precise reach of

59 *Id.* at 823.

60 *Id.* at 814 n.4 (majority opinion).

61 *Id.*

62 254 U.S. 51 (1920).

63 *Id.* at 56.

64 *Id.* at 57. For an early case suggestive of limits on the principle of *Johnson*, see *United States v. Kirby*, 74 U.S. (7 Wall.) 482 (1868) (assuming the constitutional power of a state official to arrest a mail carrier, while on the job, for having committed the crime of murder despite a broadly phrased federal statute prohibiting interference with mail deliveries because "[t]he reason of the law in such cases should prevail over its letter" to avoid "an absurd consequence").

65 *See, e.g.*, North Dakota v. United States, 495 U.S. 423, 454 n.3 (1990) (opinion of Stevens, J., joined by three other Justices) (indicating, in keeping with modern tax-immunity precedents, that "[a] state regulation is invalid only if it regulates the United States directly or discriminates against the Federal Government or those with whom it deals"); *id.* at 454 n.3 (Brennan, J., concurring in the judgment in part and dissenting in part, joined by three other Justices) (agreeing that "state taxes and regulations are subject to the same restrictions under the federal immunity doctrine" but adding that "[r]egulations . . . present a wider range of possibilities for interference

both these tax-immunity and regulatory-immunity rules is uncertain, one governing principle is both sensible and well-established: Courts will find no undue interference with federal operations if federal law itself authorizes what the state has done.[66]

One specialized set of regulatory constraints imposed on state authorities concerns the so-called "Supremacy Clause immunity" afforded to federal officers subjected to state (as opposed to federal) judicial processes.[67] The Court launched this doctrine in *In re Neagle*,[68] when it affirmed a lower court's order discharging from state custody a federal officer charged in a state tribunal for murder.[69] The Court in *Neagle* did not go so far as to suggest that federal officers enjoyed a blanket immunity from state-level prosecution for state-law crimes. It did insist, however, that at least some level of immunity was necessary to prevent states from "paralyz[ing] the operations of the [federal] government."[70]

The Supremacy Clause immunity doctrine requires courts to sort between the actions of federal officials that merit protection from state interference due to their federal character and the actions of such officers that do not. Some lower courts have sought to lend structure to this process by developing a two-step doctrinal test. The first step requires the court to ask whether the officer who claims the immunity was engaging in a function authorized by federal law when that officer violated governing state-law rules. The second step requires the court to determine whether, even if the answer to the first question is "yes," the targeted conduct constituted a "necessary and proper" means for the officer to discharge the relevant federal-law function.[71]

As for the first inquiry, "the question is not whether federal law expressly authorizes violation of state law, but whether the federal official's conduct was reasonably necessary for the performance of his duties."[72] Courts have applied this standard liberally, evincing a

---

with federal activities than do taxes"). *See generally* TRIBE, *supra* note 45, § 6–34, at 1225–37.

66 *See* HELLERSTEIN, HELLERSTEIN & SWAIN, *supra* note 24, at ¶ 22.06.

67 Texas v. Kleinert, 143 F. Supp. 3d 551 (W.D. Tex. 2015), *aff'd*, 855 F.3d 305 (5th Cir. 2017).

68 135 U.S. 1 (1890).

69 *Id.* at 76.

70 *Id.* at 62.

71 *See, e.g.*, Kentucky v. Long, 837 F.2d 727, 744 (6th Cir. 1988); *see generally* Seth P. Waxman & Trevor W. Morrison, *What Kind of Immunity? Federal Officers, State Criminal Law, and the Supremacy Clause*, 112 YALE L.J. 2195, 2237 (2003).

72 Wyoming v. Livingston, 443 F.3d 1211, 1227–28 (10th Cir. 2006) (explaining that a federal agent and a federal contractor accused of wrongfully trespassing on private land had acted reasonably in pursuit of their work duties in monitoring the activities of wolves).

willingness to find it met even when officers violate federal law in the course of doing their jobs.[73] As a result, "most (if not all) Supremacy Clause immunity defenses" turn on the second prong of the operative test.[74] Moreover, according to most lower courts, the "necessary and proper" requirement is satisfied so long as the officer "had an honest and reasonable belief that what he did was necessary in the performance of his duty."[75] This approach, in turn, requires the court to carry out another two-part analysis: (1) a subjective analysis to determine if the officer honestly believed that the challenged conduct was justified and (2) an objective analysis to determine whether that honest belief was reasonable.[76] In *Texas v. Kleinert*,[77] for example, a U.S. district court took this approach in upholding a federal official's invocation of Supremacy Clause immunity in resisting a state-law prosecution for using excessive force in making an arrest. The court first emphasized that no evidence suggested that the officer was acting with any motive other than to carry out his law-enforcement duties. The court next found that the officer's actions fell within the range of reasonableness because the suspect had resisted apprehension and fled from the officer twice, resulting in an ensuing struggle during which the officer had to make a split-second decision.[78] In contrast, another district court found the Supremacy Clause immunity defense unavailable in *Arizona v. Files*.[79] There, the state charged a federal Wildlife Services employee with animal

---

[73] *See In re* Lewis, 83 F. 159, 161–62 (D. Wash. 1897) (granting immunity to federal marshals who wrongfully seized private papers while executing a search warrant); *see also* Clifton v. Cox, 549 F.2d 722, 728–30 (9th Cir. 1977) (holding that, even if the state's challenge to the legality of a search warrant was valid, the agent's actions during the warrant's execution fell within the general scope of that agent's federal authority).

[74] Arizona v. Files, 36 F. Supp. 3d 873, 878 (D. Ariz. 2014).

[75] *Clifton*, 549 F.2d at 729 (quoting *In re* McShane, 235 F. Supp. 262, 274 (N.D. Miss. 1964)). For similar formulations, see *Kleinert*, 855 F.3d at 314–15 (discussed *infra* notes 77–78 and accompanying text), and *Long*, 837 F.2d at 745 (noting that precedent does not require federal agents to show that a challenged action was necessary or justifiable but instead only requires a finding that they "*reasonably thought* it to be necessary and justifiable" (emphasis added)). In *Neagle* itself, the Court referenced the Necessary and Proper Clause in discussing this immunity, thus suggesting that—as with the Court's expansive reading of the clause in defining federal lawmaking authority, *see supra* Chapter 6—that the scope of federal-officer freedom from state control should be viewed broadly. *See Neagle*, 135 U.S. at 84.

[76] *See* New York v. Tanella, 374 F.3d 141, 147 (2d Cir. 2004). In assessing the officer's subjective belief, a court must determine that an officer "had no motive other than to discharge his duty." *In re McShane*, 235 F. Supp. at 274. In assessing the objective reasonableness of that belief, a court must determine that it was justifiable in light of the circumstances as they appeared to the officer at the time of the act. *See Livingston*, 443 F.3d at 1229.

[77] 143 F. Supp. 3d 551.

[78] *Id.* at 569. The court also found it "compelling" that the officer had violated only work guidelines, rather than formal policies. *Id.*

[79] 36 F. Supp. 3d 873 (referenced *supra* note 74).

cruelty based on his trapping of a neighbor's dog. More specifically, the court held both (1) that the officer, who claimed that the dog had become unduly aggressive, did not honestly believe his conduct was a justifiable part of his job responsibilities and (2) that there was no reasonable basis for officer to trap the dog in any event.[80] The essential difficulty was that the record indicated that the officer had misused his position as a federal officer to address a personal grievance.[81]

3. Federal Control of the Institutions of the Federal Government

The immunities founded on cases such as *McCulloch*, *Davis*, *Johnson*, and *Neagle* all have a connection to federal-government programs established by Congress. Sometimes, however, federal regulatory immunities attach to institutions established by the Constitution itself. In *U.S. Term Limits, Inc. v. Thornton*,[82] for example, the issue was whether states could establish term limits (or other qualifications apart from the age, citizenship, and duration-of-residence requirements specified in Article I, section 2, clause 2 and Article I, section 3, clause 3) for persons otherwise eligible to serve in the House of Representatives and the Senate. A four-Justice minority insisted that the power to impose such limits was "reserved" to the states by the Tenth Amendment in light of the absence of any express constitutional treatment of the subject.[83] Tracking Justice Story's view of the Tenth Amendment, however, the majority concluded that "no state can say, that it has reserved, what it never possessed."[84] It followed, according to the majority, that states could not fix qualifications for these federal legislative officials for a simple reason: The states "never possessed" pre-constitutional authority to regulate membership in the House and the Senate because those institutions did not even exist until the Constitution created them.[85] The majority added that strong historical evidence confirmed the exclusivity of the restrictions on eligibility set forth in Article I, thus precluding states from adding eligibility restrictions of their own.[86] This conclusion, it added, comported with the "fundamental

---

80 *Id.* at 880–81 (noting, among other things, that the defendant had been told by his supervisors to work with animal-control personnel).

81 *Id.* at 884.

82 514 U.S. 779 (1995).

83 *Id.* at 845 (Thomas, J., dissenting).

84 *Id.* at 802 (majority opinion) (quoting 1 JOSEPH STORY, COMMENTARIES ON THE CONSTITUTION OF THE UNITED STATES § 627 (2d ed. 1851)).

85 *Id.*

86 *Id.* at 806–19.

principle" that citizens of the United States should be free to "choose whom they please to govern them" in House and Senate elections.[87]

In *Cook v. Gralike*,[88] the Court encountered a Missouri constitutional provision that sought to promote the establishment of term limits for Senators and House members in a different way: The provision stipulated that ballots for federal elections had to include (1) the words "DISREGARDED VOTERS' INSTRUCTION ON TERM LIMITS" with the names of incumbent candidates who had not pushed for adoption of a state-endorsed constitutional term-limits amendment, and (2) the words "DECLINED TO PLEDGE TO SUPPORT TERM LIMITS" with the names of nonincumbent candidates who refused to take a state-formulated pledge to support that same proposed amendment if voters put them in office.[89] The Court in *Cook* invalidated this measure by invoking the same principle that it had applied in *U.S. Term Limits*, emphasizing in particular that Missouri had no "reserved" power to pass the law targeting federal offices that did not exist before the Constitution's ratification.[90] In addition, the Court rejected Missouri's alternative argument that its Article I, section 4 power to prescribe the "Times, Places and Manner of holding Elections for Senators and Representatives" authorized information-sharing on-the-ballot language of this sort. The problem with this latter theory, the Court explained, was that the challenged state law did not merely address the "Manner" of conducting elections by establishing a "procedural regulation,"[91] but instead sought, as a functional matter, to "dictate electoral outcomes"[92] by "favor[ing] candidates who are willing to support the particular form of a term limits amendment" that the state endorsed.[93]

Lower courts have applied these principles in other cases involving state ballot-access rules.[94] Moreover, the core rationale of

---

87 *Id.* at 793 (internal quotations omitted).

88 531 U.S. 510 (2001).

89 *Id.* at 525.

90 *Id.* at 522.

91 *Id.* at 523. *See id.* at 524 (citing past cases indicating that "Manner" rules have no role beyond "ensuring that elections are 'fair and honest,' and that 'some sort of order, rather than chaos, is to accompany the democratic process' ").

92 *Id.* at 526.

93 *Id.* at 524.

94 *See* Schaefer v. Townsend, 215 F.3d 1031, 1039 (9th Cir. 2000) (striking down a mandate of state residency prior to election day as reaching beyond Article I's exclusive qualifications; viewing *U.S. Term Limits* as foreclosing establishment of state rules that have "the likely effect of handicapping an otherwise qualified class of candidates"); Campbell v. Davidson, 233 F.3d 1229, 1235 (10th Cir. 2000) (invalidating a rule that required candidates for federal office to be registered voters, including because the state could not defend it as a regulation of only the "Manner of Elections"); Tex. Democratic Party v. Benkiser, 459 F.3d 582, 589 (5th Cir. 2006) (rejecting the

the *Term Limits* case—namely, that states have no "reserved" power to control any aspect of the national government created by the Constitution—holds the potential to inhibit state lawmaking on matters that reach well beyond the subject of excluding or disadvantaging would-be candidates for federal office.[95] But regardless of the broader implications of *U.S. Term Limits*, its essential holding is in and of itself one of foundational significance: States may not, either directly or indirectly, establish qualifications for holding office in either the House or the Senate that go beyond the limited set of restrictions established by the Constitution itself.

4. Limits on State Powers Derived from Grants of Federal Power

Cases such as *McCulloch*, *U.S. Terms Limits*, and *Cook* reflect doctrines built, at least in part, on texts located outside Article I, including the Supremacy Clause. Other cases have dealt with another question: To what extent do the many grants of power to Congress made by Article I impliedly limit certain forms of state lawmaking as to the matters covered by these grants regardless of whether Congress has passed preemptive legislation? In *Sturges v. Crowninshield*,[96] Chief Justice Marshall proclaimed a principle that has guided deliberations on this question ever since: "Whenever the terms in which a power is granted to Congress, or the nature of the power, require that it should be exercised exclusively by Congress, the subject is as completely taken from the State Legislatures, as if they had been expressly forbidden to act on it."[97]

The most well-known application of this doctrine concerns the "dormant Commerce Clause"—that is, the limit on state powers that emanates from the grant of Congress's power to regulate "Commerce with foreign Nations, and among the several States, and with the Indian Tribes."[98] Indeed, this dormancy doctrine plays such a dominant role in constitutional law that its treatment occupies seven

---

state's argument that its pre-election residency-requirement constituted only a "manner" regulation while reiterating the Court's assertion in *U.S. Term Limits* that the "Qualifications Clauses were intended to . . . fix as exclusive the qualifications in the Constitution" (quoting *U.S. Term Limits*, 514 U.S. at 806)).

[95] *See, e.g.*, Agre v. Wolf, 284 F. Supp. 3d 591 (E.D. Pa. 2018) (holding that a challenge to the Pennsylvania General Assembly's congressional redistricting plan presented a nonjusticiable political question; noting, however, that the state's reserved-power argument in defense of the plan was foreclosed by *U.S. Term Limits* because the "States' authority to redistrict [for congressional elections] is a power delegated by Art. I, § 4, and not a power reserved by the Tenth Amendment").

[96] 17 U.S. (4 Wheat.) 122 (1819).

[97] *Id.* at 193.

[98] U.S. CONST. art. I, § 8, cl. 3.

separate chapters of this book.[99] The dormant Commerce Clause, however, does not stand alone. For example, it has long been recognized that Congress's power over naturalization is exclusive, thus precluding state policymaking in this field of law.[100] There also exist strong reasons to conclude that the grant of power in the Intellectual Property Clause likewise places some limits on state authority over the same subject.[101]

To these limitations, the Court has added others. First, in the field of federal Indian law (including as to matters not involving commerce, at least as that term is generally understood), the Court has recognized important restrictions on state power even in the absence of preemptive congressional legislation.[102] Second, the Court has held that the Constitution's grant of federal authority over admiralty law broadly precludes the states from regulating matters regarding that same subject.[103] Finally, and in keeping with the

---

[99] *See infra* Chapters 16–22.

[100] *See* THE FEDERALIST NO. 32 (Hamilton).

[101] *See supra* Section 10.B.3 (discussing this topic). Another example of how "dormancy" principles might emanate from Article I grants of powers, apart from the Commerce Clause, is provided by *Fox v. Ohio*, 46 U.S. (5 How.) 410 (1847). There, state authorities prosecuted the defendant for passing a counterfeit federal coin to another person. In a dissenting opinion, Justice McLean expressed the view that this exercise of state authority was unconstitutional. His argument rested on the premise that Congress's power under Article I, section 8, clause 6 "[t]o provide for the Punishment of counterfeiting the Securities and current coin of the United States" was exclusive in nature. He reasoned in particular that "uniformity in the coin and its value" was "indispensable" and accordingly that "the regulation [of it] must be the result of the same discretion, and not of distinct and independent judgments . . . exercised by two governments." *Id.* at 436 (McClean, J., dissenting). Especially worrisome to Justice McLean was the prospect that states "may inflict, by virtue of [their] own sovereignty, punishment for the same act, as an offence against the State, which the federal government may constitutionally punish." *Id.* at 438–39. In a curious closing of his opinion, he added that "the lamented Justice Story," who had passed away shortly before the ruling came down, concurred in this view of the case "if I mistake not." *Id.* at 440. Notably, Justice Daniel, in writing for the majority, determined that it was unnecessary to address the question whether Congress's power to punish counterfeiters was exclusive, deeming it decisive that the state prosecution did not target *counterfeiting* itself, but instead took aim at only the *transferring* of counterfeit money. Distinguishing between these two types of activity made sense, he emphasized, because (1) Article I gives Congress the power prohibit counterfeiting, which is "an offence directly against the government," without addressing at all the subject of making use of counterfeit money, which is "a private wrong," and (2) "[t]he punishment of a cheat . . . within the State . . . is peculiarly and appropriately within [its] functions and duties." *Id.* at 433–34 (majority opinion).

[102] As stated in *New Mexico v. Mescolero Apache Tribe*, 462 U.S. 324 (1983), apart from the operation of the preemption doctrine, "[t]he exercise of state authority may also be barred by an independent barrier—inherent tribal sovereignty—if [that exercise of state authority] unlawfully infringes 'on the right of reservation Indians to make their own laws and be ruled by them.' " *Id.* at 334 n.16 (internal quotation omitted) (quoting Williams v. Lee, 358 U.S. 217, 220 (1959)). For a more extensive treatment of this principle, see *infra* Section 25.A.4.

[103] *See, e.g.*, S. Pac. Co. v. Jensen, 244 U.S. 205, 216 (1917) (declaring that "no [state] legislation is valid if it . . . works material prejudice to the characteristic

federal government's specialized role in overseeing international relations, there exist constitutional limits on the states' powers to legislate in the area of foreign affairs.[104] These principles have had

---

features of the general maritime law, or interferes with the proper harmony and uniformity of that law in its international and interstate relations"); Am. Dredging Co. v. Miller, 510 U.S. 443, 446–50 (1994) (recognizing and applying this doctrine); *see also* The Lottawanna, 88 U.S. (21 Wall.) 558, 574–75 (1874) (recognizing limits on state power over admiralty matters, thereby preserving the constitutional plan of "uniformity and consistency"); *see generally* David J. Bederman, *Uniformity, Delegation and the Dormant Admiralty Clause*, 28 J. MAR. L. & COM. 1, 7–14 (1997) (discussing further judicial development of the *Jensen* doctrine). With regard to Congress's ability to authorize state treatments of admiralty matters, see *Knickerbocker Ice Co. v. Stewart*, 253 U.S. 149, 164 (1920) (finding it "beyond the power of congress" to authorize state-by-state enforcement of workers' compensation statutes, which varied among themselves and that did not mirror traditional maritime compensation rules). *See generally* Garrick B. Pursley, *Dormancy*, 100 GEO. L.J. 497, 551–52 (2012) (defending the Court's rejection of a congressional-consent exception to the implied limit on state regulation of admiralty regulation in part by highlighting differences between this limitation and the dormant Commerce Clause, as to which such an exception applies; justifying the Court's different approach on the ground that "[i]n the interstate commerce context, instrumental considerations warrant allowing Congress, with its greater institutional competence and expertise on complex economic questions, to correct judicial errors," while no need for "a similar error-correcting role for Congress" exists in the admiralty context because "[c]ourts have the institutional advantage here" in light of historical practice and other factors).

[104] This limit on state power is distinct from the limit imposed by the dormant Foreign Commerce Clause. As to it, see *infra* Chapter 22. As to the dormant foreign-affairs power, a leading case is *Zschernig v. Miller*, 389 U.S. 429, 432 (1968) (invalidating a state law that limited inheritance by citizens of some foreign nations because the law reflected "an intrusion by the State into the field of foreign affairs which the Constitution entrusts to the President and the Congress"; also discussed *supra* Section 10.E.1). *See also* Henderson v. Mayor of N.Y., 92 U.S. 259, 273 (1875) (stating that a regulation "must of necessity be national in its character" when it affects "a subject which concerns our international relations, in regard to which foreign nations ought to be considered and their rights respected"). *See generally* TRIBE, *supra* note 45, § 4–5, at 656–57 (collecting additional cases). For an illustrative modern case in which an argument based on this principle was raised, see *Crosby v. Nat'l Foreign Trade Council*, 530 U.S. 363, 381 (2000) (invalidating a state's restriction on its own agencies' dealings with firms doing business with Myanmar; relying on a preemption rationale and thus noting the lack of any need to "get into any general consideration of limits of state action affecting foreign affairs," but also adverting to the "exclusively national power" in this area). *See also* Am. Ins. Ass'n v. Garamendi, 539 U.S. 396, 417–20 (2003) (citing the principle of *Zschernig* with approval in recognizing that state choices must sometimes yield to federal policy on foreign relations and invalidating, albeit on what was said to be preemption grounds, a state law concerning insurance-related matters for Holocaust survivors as incompatible with federal foreign policy in this field as reflected in executive agreements and statements by high-level members of the President's administration). In a number of cases, the lower courts have grappled with how to apply this implied restraint on state lawmaking power. *See* Nat'l Foreign Trade Council v. Natsios, 181 F.3d 38, 49 (1st Cir. 1999) (adverting to the grant of various powers in Article I as rightly providing the textual basis for the dormant foreign affairs doctrine), *aff'd on other grounds*, *Crosby*, 530 U.S. 363; Deutsch v. Turner Corp., 324 F.3d 692, 710–16 (9th Cir. 2003) (endorsing and applying *Zschernig*); Nat'l Foreign Trade Council, Inc. v. Giannoulias, 523 F. Supp. 2d 731, 744–45 (N.D. Ill. 2007) (reading *Zschernig* and *Garamendi* as "concerned with the practical effect a state law might have on the national government's ability to conduct foreign policy on behalf of the United States" and concluding that a state law directed at Sudan "unconstitutionally interfere[d] with the federal government's power to conduct

ripple effects in other constitutional domains, particularly by helping to shape governing principles of statutory preemption.[105] In addition, these limits have stirred controversy along the way because of both their nontextual moorings in the law and their constraining effect on state policymaking choices.[106] Against this backdrop, it is not surprising that the Court's willingness to apply these implied

foreign affairs"); *see also* Michael D. Ramsey, *The Power of States in Foreign Affairs: The Original Understanding of Foreign Policy Federalism*, 75 NOTRE DAME L. REV. 341, 358–65 (1999) (discussing lower-court decisions following *Zschernig*); Matthew Schaefer, *Constraints on State-Level Foreign Policy: (Re) Justifying, Refining and Distinguishing the Dormant Foreign Affairs Doctrine*, 41 SETON HALL L. REV. 201, 242–60 (2011) (similar); *see also id.* at 228 (discussing early Supreme Court authorities and noting that they "hinted at such a doctrine well before *Zschernig* and implicitly supported such a doctrine [based on the Court's recognition] that foreign affairs was an 'exclusive' federal domain in numerous opinions for well over a century before *Zschernig*").

[105] Thus, the Court has applied a super-charged form of preemption in relation to both foreign-affairs law and federal Indian law. As to the former, see, e.g., Carlos Manuel Vázquez, *W(h)ither* Zschernig?, 46 VILL. L. REV. 1259, 1304 (2001) (viewing the preemption analysis in *Crosby* as so aggressive that it "is virtually a dormant foreign affairs case in disguise"); *see generally infra* Chapter 22. As to the latter, see *Mescalero Apache Tribe*, 462 U.S. at 334 (noting that, in dealing with federal-law displacement of state controls regarding Native nations, the Court has "rejected a narrow focus on congressional intent to preempt state law as the sole touchstone" for analysis), and *infra* Section 25.A.4. *See generally infra* Chapter 24 (discussing both of these principles of modern-day preemption law). Concerns about the special role of the federal government in dealing with foreign affairs also occasionally have surfaced in cases that involve neither preemption nor the *Zschernig* rule. *See, e.g.*, United States v. California, 332 U.S. 19 (1947) (finding that states did not, as a matter of governing property law, despite strong history-based arguments to the contrary, have territorial control over a "three-mile belt" extending from their shorelines into the open ocean, thus denying them the ability to exploit oil reserves beneath sea floor; justifying this result by reference to a dominant federal interest, borne of relations with foreign nations, in controlling land and resources that lay below oceanic waters).

[106] In particular, there exists an extensive literature challenging the soundness of the Court's constitutional ban on state interference with foreign relations in the absence of preemptive legislation. *See, e.g.*, Ryan Baasch & Saikrishna Bangalore Prakash, *Congress and the Reconstruction of Foreign Affairs Federalism*, 115 MICH. L. REV. 47, 67–68 (2016) (deeming the judiciary "hardly equipped to judge whether a state law has disturbed a foreign nation" and looking back on *Zschernig* as "something of an embarrassment"); Curtis A. Bradley, *A New American Foreign Affairs Law?*, 70 U. COLO. L. REV. 1089, 1105 (1999) (anticipating a "shift away from foreign affairs exceptionalism, since there is now a reduced need for the national government to speak with one voice in international relations, and because many of the exceptionalism decisions, such as *Zschernig* . . . , clearly seem to be a product of the Cold War era"); Jack L. Goldsmith, *Federal Courts, Foreign Affairs, and Federalism*, 83 VA. L. REV. 1617, 1681–90 (1997) (challenging the legitimacy of and continued need for "judge-made foreign relations law"); Ramsey, *supra* note 104, at 379–88 (offering an originalist critique of judicial invalidations of state actions in the foreign-affairs field); Ernest A. Young, *Dual Federalism, Concurrent Jurisdiction, and the Foreign Affairs Exception*, 69 GEO. WASH. L. REV. 139, 188 (2001) ("'Foreign affairs' is no more sustainable a category than 'intrastate commerce' or 'state police power' was in 1937."); *see also* Schaefer, *supra* note 104 (offering a refined test for dormancy-based limits on state meddling with foreign-affairs matters in light of the confusion and uncertainty that marks the doctrine in its current form); Michael P. Van Alstine, *Federal Common Law in an Age of Treaties*, 89 CORNELL L. REV. 892, 943 nn.305–06 (2004) (discussing this controversy).

restrictions has ebbed and flowed over the long course of U.S. history. Through it all, however, there has been no retreat from the core idea that there do exist independent constitutional constraints, as opposed to principles of treaty-based and statute-based preemption, on state authority in the fields of Native American affairs, admiralty law, and foreign relations.

5. Constitutional Common Law

A final set of implied restrictions on state powers springs from the authority of the federal courts to craft common-law rules tethered only loosely, if at all, to the text of the Constitution and congressionally enacted statutes. To be sure, the Court's landmark ruling in *Erie R.R. Co. v. Tompkins*[107] repudiated the proposition that there exists a "federal general common law."[108] But this same declaration opened the door to judicial development of a body of "specialized federal common law"[109] that necessarily displaces state law in its area of operation.[110]

In *Clearfield Trust v. United States*,[111] for example, the federal government issued a check to an employee for services performed for the Works Progress Administration. A wrongdoing interloper stole the check, forged an endorsement, and then used it to purchase goods. The retailer, in turn, signed the check over to the retailer's bank which secured payment on it from the federal government, all of which set the stage for the federal government's follow-up effort to hold the bank liable for passing along the forgery-bearing instrument.[112] The bank's defense was that the federal government's claim for relief came too late under controlling state-law principles.[113] The Court, however, held that—notwithstanding *Erie* and even in the absence of any federal statute addressing the subject—"[t]he rights and duties of the United States on commercial paper which it issues are governed by federal rather than local law."[114] In the view of Justice Douglas, who wrote for a unanimous Court, the need for a one-size-fits-all approach to this set of problems dictated that "federal courts [must] fashion the governing rule."[115] As he explained:

---

107 304 U.S. 64 (1938).

108 *Id.* at 78.

109 United States v. Kin-Buc, Inc., 532 F. Supp. 699, 700 (D.N.J. 1982).

110 *Id.* at 700–01.

111 318 U.S. 363 (1943).

112 *Id.* at 364–66.

113 *Id.* at 366.

114 *Id.* at 366.

115 *Id.* at 367.

> The issuance of commercial paper by the United States is on a vast scale and transactions in that paper from issuance to payment will commonly occur in several states. The application of state law . . . would subject the rights and duties of the United States to exceptional uncertainty. It would lead to great diversity in results by making identical transactions subject to the vagaries of the laws of the several states. The desirability of a uniform rule is plain.[116]

Analysts have scratched their heads over cases like *Clearfield Trust.* One source of consternation stems from the view of some observers that "the Laws of the United States" accorded state-law-trumping effect by the Supremacy Clause rightly include only duly enacted federal statutes and duly adopted treaties, thus leaving no room for the displacement of state-imposed rules by federal common law.[117] Whatever one might think about these matters, however, two points are of critical significance. First, even if only in a narrow range of cases, the federal courts long have put to work a body of doctrine fairly described as "federal common law."[118] Second, that body of doctrine rests at bottom—in a way that circles all the way back to *McCulloch*—on implications drawn from the goal of safeguarding the value of nationhood within a federal system.

---

116 *Id.*

117 *See, e.g.*, Caleb Nelson, *The Legitimacy of (Some) Federal Common Law*, 101 VA. L. REV. 1, 3–4 (2015) (arguing that the Supremacy Clause's language regarding the "Laws of the United States" refers only "to federal statutes enacted through the process of bicameralism and presentment").

118 Boyle v. United Techs. Corp., 487 U.S. 500, 503–04 (1988) (collecting earlier cases in reaffirming that "a few areas, involving uniquely federal interests, are so committed by the Constitution and laws of the United States to federal control that state law is pre-empted and replaced" pursuant to "so-called federal common law"; applying this principle to suggest that a state wrongful death action based on allegations of a faulty helicopter escape-hatch design might require dismissal under the so-called "military-contractor defense" (internal quotations omitted)). One set of cases in which federal common law has played an important role has arisen out of the Court's sensible recognition that states may not supply their own rules of decision governing "disputes implicating the[ir] conflicting rights." Tex. Indus., Inc. v. Radcliff Materials, Inc., 451 U.S. 630, 641 (1981). Accordingly, for example, no state can apply its own law to interstate disputes over borders, Cissna v. Tennessee, 246 U.S. 289, 295 (1918), water rights, Hinderlider v. La Plata River & Cherry Creek Ditch Co., 304 U.S. 92, 110 (1938), or the contested interpretation of interstate compacts, Petty v. Tennessee-Missouri Bridge Comm'n, 359 U.S. 275, 278–279 (1959). While the states may have had the power to apply their own rules to such matters before they entered the Union, the Constitution implicitly forecloses such exercises of power because the "interstate . . . nature of the controversy makes it inappropriate for state law to control." *Texas Indus.*, 451 U.S. at 641. For an overview of federal common law, see 19 WRIGHT & MILLER, *supra* note 4, § 4514. For another significant scholarly treatment, see Bradford R. Clark, *Federal Common Law: A Structural Reinterpretation*, 144 U. PA. L. REV. 1245 (1996).

Chapter 16

THE DORMANT COMMERCE CLAUSE DOCTRINE: ITS ORIGINS, PURPOSES, AND STRUCTURE

Analysis

What is the "dormant Commerce Clause"? The term captures in a shorthand way an idea that some state laws are invalid simply because the Commerce Clause exists. In other words, some state legislation runs afoul of the Commerce Clause, or limiting principles implied from it, even though Congress has not affirmatively exercised its commerce power to preempt that legislation. The state law falls, without more, because the Commerce Clause is there, albeit in its dormant—that is, congressionally unactivated—state.

A. THE ORIGINS AND GOALS OF THE DORMANT COMMERCE CLAUSE PRINCIPLE

Not surprisingly, the core purpose of the dormant Commerce Clause principle lies in safeguarding the "Commerce . . . among the several States" that lay at the heart of the Framers' concerns about the Confederation-era system of governance.[1] In keeping with this aim, the Court has invalidated state laws that either "discriminate against"[2] or impose an "undue burden"[3] on interstate commerce. The difficulty is that the words "discriminate," "burden," and (most of all) "undue" are opaque. Their application thus requires courts to make contextual and sometimes controversial judgments about a wide range of state laws that bear on interstate trade.

---

[1] U.S. CONST. art. I, § 8, cl. 3. As for the Framers' concerns, the classic judicial treatment of the subject appears in Justice Jackson's opinion for the Court in *H.P. Hood & Sons v. Du Mond*, 336 U.S. 525 (1949).

[2] Tenn. Wine & Spirits Retailers Ass'n v. Thomas, 139 S. Ct. 2449, 2458 (2019).

[3] Dean Milk Co. v. City of Madison, 340 U.S. 349, 353 (1951).

1. The Tariff Paradigm

A good starting point for thinking about dormant Commerce Clause doctrine involves recognizing that some applications of it have long posed few difficulties. Take the case of a protective tariff, which operates to tax goods shipped into, but not comparable goods produced within, the tariff-imposing state. Such a law gives rise to paradigmatic violation of the dormant Commerce Clause rule because, as the Court explained in *West Lynn Creamery, Inc. v. Healy,*[4] it "violates the principle of the unitary national market by handicapping out-of-state competitors, thus artificially encouraging in-state production even when the same goods could be produced at lower cost in other States."[5]

A second step in understanding the dormant Commerce Clause involves recognizing that targeting tariffs alone would not adequately vindicate the principle that "our economic unit is the Nation."[6] To begin with, tariffs "are so patently unconstitutional that [the] cases reveal not a single attempt by any State to enact one."[7] No less important, laws other than tariffs may prove equally disruptive of "the unitary national market" that the dormant Commerce Clause principle protects. Common examples include export restrictions placed on goods much in demand in other states and discriminatory taxes other than tariffs that disadvantage interstate business operations.[8] Thus, to promote in a meaningful way the operation of a national common market, courts must be on the lookout for more than cross-border-trade-thwarting tariffs that one state imposes on other states' goods. And indeed, from the days of the Marshall Court onward, the Court has done just that, scrutinizing a wide range of state laws by reference to the principle that the nation constitutes a single "federal free trade unit" subject to judicial protection even in the absence of preemptive congressional action.[9]

2. The Legitimacy of the Dormant Commerce Clause Principle

Despite the Court's longstanding acceptance of the dormant Commerce Clause principle, challenges to its legitimacy surface from time to time. During his tenure on the Court, for instance, Justice Scalia was a prominent critic of the doctrine, and Justice Thomas

4 512 U.S. 186 (1994).

5 *Id.* at 193.

6 *Hood,* 336 U.S. at 537.

7 *West Lynn Creamery,* 512 U.S. at 194.

8 *Id.* at 193–94 (stating that cases addressing laws that seek to advantage local production through tax exemptions to local products "are legion").

9 *Hood,* 336 U.S. at 538.

long has voiced skepticism as well.[10] Their basic challenge to the doctrine centers on the observations that: (1) the Commerce Clause

---

[10] *See* Camps Newfound/Owatonna, Inc. v. Town of Harrison, 520 U.S. 564, 610–20 (1997) (Thomas, J., dissenting) (asserting that "[t]he negative Commerce Clause has no basis in the text of the Constitution" and has proven to be "virtually unworkable in application"); Oklahoma Tax Comm'n. v. Jefferson Lines, Inc., 514 U.S. 175, 200 (1995) (Scalia, J., concurring) (claiming that the "negative Commerce Clause" is " 'negative' not only because it negates state regulation of commerce, but also because it does *not* appear in the Constitution" (emphasis in original)); Tyler Pipe Indus., Inc. v. Washington State Dep't of Revenue, 483 U.S. 232, 261 (1987) (Scalia, J., concurring in part and dissenting in part) ("[T]he language of the Commerce Clause gives no indication of exclusivity. Nor can one assume generally that Congress' Article I powers are exclusive; many of them plainly coexist with concurrent authority in the States." (internal citation omitted)). Justice Gorsuch, who took Justice Scalia's place on the high Court bench, also has voiced some misgivings about the Court's dormant Commerce Clause jurisprudence. *See, e.g.*, *Tenn. Wine & Spirits Retailers Ass'n*, 139 S. Ct. at 2478 (Gorsuch, J., dissenting) (opining that, at least in the area of alcohol regulation, "we should not be in the business of imposing our own judge-made 'dormant Commerce Clause' limitations on state powers"); South Dakota v. Wayfair, Inc., 138 S. Ct. 2080, 2100–01 (2018) (Gorsuch, J., concurring) (noting that "[m]y agreement with the Court's discussion of the history of our dormant commerce clause jurisprudence . . . should not be mistaken for agreement with all aspects of the doctrine" while adding that a determination of the doctrine's legitimacy presents "questions for another day"). As of this writing, however, Justice Gorsuch has not rejected the doctrine, and it remains to be seen—particularly in light of the Court's recent and reasoned reaffirmation of it—whether he will do so. For scholarly critiques of the dormancy doctrine, see Julian N. Eule, *Laying the Dormant Commerce Clause to Rest*, 91 YALE L.J. 425 (1982); Richard D. Friedman, *Putting the Dormancy Doctrine Out of Its Misery*, 12 CARDOZO L. REV. 1745 (1991); Patrick C. McGinley, *Trashing the Constitution: Judicial Activism, the Dormant Commerce Clause, and the Federalism Mantra*, 71 OR. L. REV. 409 (1992); and Martin H. Redish & Shane V. Nugent, *The Dormant Commerce Clause and the Constitutional Balance of Federalism*, 1987 DUKE L.J. 569. *See also* DAVID P. CURRIE, THE CONSTITUTION IN THE SUPREME COURT: THE FIRST HUNDRED YEARS 1789–1888, at 234 (1985); Barry Friedman & Daniel T. Deacon, *A Course Unbroken: The Constitutional Legitimacy of the Dormant Commerce Clause*, 97 VA. L. REV. 1877, 1878–79 nn.6–7 (2011) (noting, in the context of defending the doctrine, that "[t]here is a long tradition of dormant Commerce Clause skepticism, much of it based in the argument that the doctrine has no foundation in text or Founding-era history"). For scholarly defenses of the doctrine, in addition to that of Friedman & Deacon, *supra*, see, e.g., LAURENCE H. TRIBE, AMERICAN CONSTITUTIONAL LAW § 6–2 (3d ed. 2000); Albert S. Abel, *The Commerce Clause in the Constitutional Convention and in Contemporary Comment*, 25 MINN. L. REV. 432 (1941); Ernest J. Brown, *The Open Economy: Justice Frankfurter and the Position of the Judiciary*, 67 YALE L.J. 219, 222 (1957); and Brannon P. Denning, *Reconstructing the Dormant Commerce Clause Doctrine*, 50 WM. & MARY L. REV. 417 (2008). *See also* Norman R. Williams, *Why Congress May Not "Overrule" the Dormant Commerce Clause*, 53 UCLA L. REV. 153 (2005). A partial response to Justice Scalia's criticisms appears in Mark V. Tushnet, *Scalia and the Dormant Commerce Clause: A Foolish Formalism?*, 12 CARDOZO L. REV. 1717 (1991). For some more recent scholarly reflections on these and related matters, see Edward A. Zelinsky, *Comparing* Wayfair *and* Wynne: *Lessons for the Future of the Dormant Commerce Clause*, 22 CHAP. L. REV. 55, 71–72 (2019) (noting that the recent cases of *South Dakota v. Wayfair* and *Comptroller of the Treasury v. Wynne* suggest "that the Court is unlikely to abandon the dormant Commerce Clause altogether"; but also observing that "the Justices who would forsake the dormant Commerce Clause can exercise critical influence in specific cases" addressing dormant Commerce Clause questions), and Daniel Francis, *The Decline of the Dormant Commerce Clause*, 94 DENV. L. REV. 255, 255 (2017) (arguing that "the dormant Commerce Clause is in remarkable decline," because, among other reasons, "the Court

by its own terms embodies only a grant of power to Congress and not a limit on the power of the states,[11] and (2) other provisions of Article I lay down explicit limits on state behavior that do not include any general restriction on interfering with interstate commerce.[12] It follows, according to this text-based critique, that no "dormant" limit on state legislative authority is properly grounded in the Constitution; instead, if federal interests justify stamping out state-based encroachments on cross-border trade, it is for Congress and Congress alone to protect those interests by exercising the legislative power that the Commerce Clause confers.[13]

---

has profoundly eroded the rule against discriminatory regulation" and "the Court has created and expanded exceptions to the reach of the doctrine with remarkable speed").

[11] *See Tyler Pipe*, 483 U.S. at 263 (Scalia, J., concurring in part and dissenting in part) (rejecting the idea of "reading the Commerce Clause to be other than what it says—an authorization for Congress to regulate commerce").

[12] *See id.* at 261 (noting that, with regard to the Commerce Clause, "there is no correlative denial of power over commerce to the States in Art. I, § 10, as there is, for example, with the power to coin money or make treaties"). For an early articulation of this idea, see *Thurlow v. Massachusetts* (*License Cases*), 46 U.S. (5 How.) 504, 579 (1847), (opinion of Taney, C.J.) ("[I]n many instances, after the grant [to Congress] is made, the constitution proceeds to prohibit the exercise of the same power by the States in express terms; in some cases absolutely, in others without the consent of Congress. And if it was intended to forbid the States from making any regulations of commerce, it is difficult to account for the omission to prohibit it, when that prohibition has been so carefully and distinctly inserted in relation to other powers, where the action of the State over the same subject was intended to be entirely excluded."), *overruled in part by Leisy v. Hardin*, 135 U.S. 100 (1890). *See also Camps Newfound/Owatonna*, 520 U.S. at 610 (Thomas, J., dissenting) (challenging the use of the dormancy doctrine to invalidate "discriminatory state taxation of interstate commerce" when "the Constitution would seem to provide an *express* check on the States' power to levy certain discriminatory taxes on the commerce of other States—not in the judicially created negative Commerce Clause, but in the Art. I, § 10, Import-Export Clause"); David P. Currie, *The Constitution in the Supreme Court: Contracts and Commerce, 1836–1864*, 1983 DUKE L.J. 471, 500–01 (1983).

[13] Also underlying challenges to the doctrine—particularly insofar as it targets facially nondiscriminatory laws—are worries about the capacity of judges to formulate workable rules in this field. *See, e.g., Camps Newfound/Owatonna*, 520 U.S. at 596 (Scalia, J., dissenting) (asserting that "[o]ur cases have struggled (to put it nicely) to develop a set of rules by which we may preserve a national market without needlessly intruding upon the States' police powers, each exercise of which no doubt has some effect on the commerce of the Nation"); *id.* at 618 (Thomas, J., dissenting) (commenting that "our negative Commerce Clause jurisprudence has taken us well beyond the invalidation of obviously discriminatory taxes" and that "[w]e have used the Clause to make policy-laden judgments that we are ill equipped . . . to make"); Am. Trucking Ass'ns v. Smith, 496 U.S. 167, 202 (1990) (Scalia, J., concurring in the judgment) (claiming that that dormant Commerce Clause law is a "quagmire," that has produced "arbitrary" and "conclusory" rulings and has "only worsened with age" (citations omitted)); Bendix Autolite Corp. v. Midwesco Enters., 486 U.S. 888, 897 (1988) (Scalia, J., concurring in the judgment) (noting that he would "leave essentially legislative judgments to the Congress" and rejecting in particular the "balancing" approach sometimes applied under the dormant Commerce Clause); CTS Corp. v. Dynamics Corp. of Am., 481 U.S. 69, 95 (1987) (Scalia, J., concurring in part and concurring in the judgment) (arguing that the current approach to analyzing state laws under the dormant Commerce Clause is a practice that "is ill suited to the judicial function and should be undertaken rarely if at all"). *But see* James M. McGoldrick, Jr., *The Dormant*

There are, however, serious difficulties with this position. To begin with, it has been widely accepted from the earliest days of the Republic that some grants of power to Congress in and of themselves preclude the states' exercise of that same power, or at least some components of it. Alexander Hamilton endorsed this position in *The Federalist No. 32*,[14] and Chief Justice Marshall (who himself had been a delegate to the Virginia ratification convention) likewise declared, in an early opinion for a unanimous Court, that the "nature of the power" to legislate without more sometimes dictates that "it should be exercised exclusively by Congress."[15] In addition, the establishment of an exclusive congressional power carries with it the logical corollary that state action fairly characterized as involving the exercise of that power is necessarily incompatible with the Constitution's commands, even where the state attempts to cast the action as involving the exercise of its police power or other related authority.[16] Giving decisive significance to the state's chosen label, after all, would glorify form over substance to such an extreme degree that it would render effectively meaningless the exclusivity of the relevant federal-power grant.[17] Put otherwise, and to borrow from a formulation offered by Justice Cardozo, "[f]ormulas and catchwords"

Commerce Clause: The Endgame—From Southern Pacific *to* Tennessee Wine & Spirits*—1945 to 2019*, 40 PACE L. REV. 44, 125 (2020) (rejecting Justice Scalia's critique by noting that, when it comes to the Court's balancing approach, "the Court is actually pretty good at it").

14 *See* THE FEDERALIST NO. 32 (Hamilton) (stating that, apart from text-based negations of state power, exclusivity exists when the Constitution "grant[s] an authority to the Union, to which a similar authority in the States would be absolutely and totally *contradictory* and *repugnant*," as opposed to instances "where the exercise of a concurrent jurisdiction might be productive of occasional interferences in the *policy* of any branch of administration, but would not imply any direct contradiction or repugnancy in point of constitutional authority" (emphasis in original)).

15 Sturges v. Crowninshield, 17 U.S. (4 Wheat.) 122, 193 (1819). *See* Garrick B. Pursley, *Dormancy*, 100 GEO. L.J. 497, 525–26 (2012) (noting that "the framing-era consensus seems to have been that *some* implied preclusions were, in fact, generated" by the creation of federal powers irrespective of whether any text denied the same power to the states (emphasis in original)). For one Supreme Court decision along these lines, see *DeCanas v. Bica*, 424 U.S. 351, 354 (1976) (declaring that the "[p]ower to regulate immigration is unquestionably exclusively a federal power"). For discussion of the related point that both the federal government and a state government may well be able to regulate the same activity, albeit pursuant to different powers, see *infra* note 48 and accompanying text.

16 *See. e.g.*, Pursley, *supra* note 15, at 514 (reasoning that, if a federal power is exclusive, it logically follows that there exists "an implied preclusion of state actions that undermine the national government's ability to exercise such a power exclusively, even if the state action does not purport to be a direct exercise of the exclusively national power" such as when the state purports to act "under [the] police power"); *see also* THE FEDERALIST NO. 32 (Hamilton) (explaining that the establishment of an exclusive federal power carries with it an "alienation[ ] of State sovereignty," so as to "extinguish" any "pre-existing" ability of the state to wield that power).

17 *See* Pursley, *supra* note 15, at 516 (noting that "no rational state government would openly claim" to be exercising the "exclusive portion of Congress's power to regulate interstate commerce").

must be "subordinate" to the "overmastering requirement" of such a power's exclusive nature.[18]

The question thus becomes whether the grant of the congressional *commerce* power is the type of grant that rightly qualifies as exclusive in the sense that its creation forecloses state efforts to exercise that same power.[19] And, contrary to the position

---

[18] Baldwin v. G.A.F. Seelig, Inc., 294 U.S. 511, 527 (1935). *See* Cooley v. Bd. of Wardens, 53 U.S. (12 How.) 299, 314 (1851) ("[I]t is the thing, and not the name, which is to be considered."); So. Pac. Co. v. Arizona, 325 U.S. 761, 780 (1945) (declaring that states cannot avoid the restraints of the dormant Commerce Clause by "simply invoking the convenient apologetics of the police power" (quoting Kansas City S. Ry. Co. v. Kaw Valley Drainage Dist., 233 U.S. 75, 79 (1914))). An example helps to make the key point. Assume a state passed a law that blocked the shipment across state lines of all grain produced in the state, thus prohibiting its sale to out-of-state buyers. Assume also that the state legislature included in the law the following statement of purpose: "We are a sovereign state which continues to have the power, just as we did under the Articles of Confederation, to regulate commerce among the several states. We emphasize that, in passing this law, we are exercising that power and only that power and not any police power, taxing power, or power to regulate intrastate trade. We expressly and proudly claim to retain the power to regulate interstate commerce and rely only on that power in passing this law." If there were no dormant Commerce Clause, this state law would be constitutional, even though such a result would be one that "those who framed and ratified the Constitution would surely find surprising." *Tennessee Wine & Spirits*, 139 S. Ct. at 2460. And if, conversely, one insists that such a state law must be unconstitutional, then one must accept at least some version of the principle underlying modern-day dormant Commerce Clause doctrine. No less important, once it is recognized that there must be a dormant Commerce Clause doctrine—tied to the notion that states cannot claim to exercise the same power over interstate commerce they possessed under the Articles of Confederation—then it becomes necessary to determine how to gauge the proper reach of its prohibitions. To be sure, one possible resolution of the matter would be to allow the courts to invalidate only state laws, such as this hypothesized law, that claim on their face to entail the regulation of interstate commerce. But the Court has eschewed that approach on the theory that it would render the exclusivity principle effectively meaningless, as states could evade its reach simply by relabeling their otherwise-invalid laws as exercises of the retained taxing or police powers. *Cf.* Weiss v. Stearn, 265 U.S. 242, 254 (1924) (noting in the context of a case about federal income taxation that "[q]uestions of taxation must be determined by viewing what was actually done, rather than the declared purpose of the participants" and that "we must regard matters of substance and not mere form.").

[19] Put a bit differently, one might think of the correct exclusivity inquiry as posing these questions: In laying its hands on the particular set of commercial activities dealt with in the challenged statute, has the state truly acted pursuant to its police (or other retained) powers? Or does the state's action, although defended on that ground, rightly fail to qualify as a mere exercise of the police (or other retained) powers, because it is so significantly injurious to interstate trade and so little justified by cognizable local interests that it can and must be recharacterized as a regulation of interstate commerce? Notably, this line of justification for the dormant Commerce Clause proceeds from the understanding—premised on more general principles put forward by Hamilton and Marshall, among others—that the Framers granted an exclusive power over interstate commerce to Congress, thus denying that same power in its entirety to the states. To be sure, other analysts have rooted the dormancy doctrine in somewhat different, though related, analytical approaches. One theory posits that the grant of the commerce power is rightly seen as partially, as opposed to wholly, exclusive—an approach that, in keeping with the Court's existing dormancy-doctrine jurisprudence, supports the displacement of state authority over "national" (as opposed to "local") matters connected up with interstate traffic and trade. *See infra*

espoused by Justice Scalia, Justice Thomas, and some academic commentators, the Constitution itself provides telling textual signals for concluding that it is. To begin with, Article I gives Congress authority "[t]o *regulate* Commerce . . . among the several States."[20] Although the Court in *Gibbons v. Ogden*,[21] found it unnecessary to rule definitively on the exclusivity question, Chief Justice Marshall on behalf of the Court went out of his way to note the significance of this terminology:

> It has been contended by the counsel for the appellant, that, as the word "to regulate" implies in its nature, full power over the thing to be regulated, it excludes, necessarily, the action of all others that would perform the same operation on the same thing. That regulation is designed for the entire result, applying to those parts which remain as they were, as well as to those which are altered. It produces a uniform whole, which is as much disturbed and deranged by changing what the regulating power designs to leave untouched, as that on which it has operated. *There is great force in this argument, and the Court is not satisfied that it has been refuted.*[22]

Two other features of the text lend support to the view that the grant of the commerce power is exclusive. First, the Framers' treatment of interstate commerce appears immediately after its treatment of commerce "with foreign nations,"[23] and it has long been accepted that the power to regulate foreign commerce belongs solely to the federal

---

notes 51–52 and accompanying text (discussing the ruling and reasoning in the *Cooley* case); *see also* Seminole Tribe v. Florida, 517 U.S. 44, 148 (1996) (Stevens, J., dissenting) (describing "the power over interstate commerce" as "concurrent" in the sense that states can "engage in *some* regulation of interstate commerce" (emphasis added)). Another theory posits that the dormant Commerce Clause finds its footing, much like the state-power-limiting principle of *McCulloch v. Maryland*, 17 U.S. (4 Wheat.) 316 (1819), in a proper understanding of the intrinsically national character of free cross-border commerce within the Framers' structural arrangement. *See* CHARLES BLACK, STRUCTURE AND RELATIONSHIP IN CONSTITUTIONAL LAW 21–22 (1969). On yet another theory, the Court has rightly recognized the dormant Commerce Clause as a central feature of "constitutional common law," so as to give practical (though congressionally displaceable) meaning to constitutional values of distinctive importance. *See* Henry Paul Monaghan, *Constitutional Common Law*, 89 HARV. L. REV. 1, 15–17 (1975). The critical and overarching point is that the case laid out in the ensuing pages for the dormant Commerce Clause principle—founded, as it is, on the Constitution's text, history, and purposes, coupled with deep-rooted precedent—offers strong support for recognition of that principle regardless of how, precisely, one conceives of its doctrinal origins.

20 U.S. CONST. art. I, § 8, cl. 3 (emphasis added).

21 22 U.S. (9 Wheat.) 1 (1824).

22 *Id.* at 209 (emphasis added); *see also Tennessee Wine & Spirits*, 139 S. Ct. at 2459–60 (noting this aspect of Chief Justice Marshall's opinion in *Gibbons*).

23 U.S. CONST. art. I, § 8, cl. 3.

government.[24] The principle that courts should construe clauses in light of the textual company they keep thus bolsters the conclusion that the power over interstate commerce should be viewed as exclusive lest it operate in a way that is oddly different from Congress's companion power over foreign commerce.[25] Second, Article I grants to Congress the power "[t]o regulate Commerce . . . *among* the several states."[26] This phrasing, it can be said, indicates that the Framers fundamentally reconceptualized the nature of the governmental power to regulate interstate trade as they moved to replace the Articles of Confederation with the far more nationally minded Constitution. More specifically, this language offers support for the conclusion—which also finds support in the historical materials[27]—that a system built on a hodgepodge of thirteen powers held by each state to regulate its own border-crossing transactions was being replaced by a new system premised on the idea that the proper subject of government control in this field was a unitary body of commerce "among" all the states. And to the extent that this conception of commerce drove the Framer's thinking, it corresponded with vesting the power over that unitary national subject in the single and unitary federal Congress.[28]

---

[24] *See supra* Section 10.E.1. To put the point another way, it would be odd to find a nonexclusive power over interstate commerce textually conjoined to an exclusive power over foreign commerce. And it would be especially odd to do so when one recalls that the Framers viewed these two powers as inextricably intertwined. *See* THE FEDERALIST NO. 42 (Madison) (explaining why, due to some states' abilities to exploit their control over key ports and trade routes, "without this supplemental provision [regarding interstate commerce], the great and essential power of regulating foreign commerce would have been incomplete and ineffectual"). The same point applies to the textual tying together of the power to regulate interstate commerce and the power to regulate "Commerce with the Indian Tribes," which the Framers again understood as being assigned exclusively to the federal Congress. *See, e.g.*, Friedman & Deacon, *supra* note 10, at 1910. *See generally infra* Section 25.A.4.

[25] *See, e.g.*, *Gibbons*, 22 U.S. at 193–94 (highlighting, in discussing the meaning of the term "commerce," that the Commerce Clause, "in its application to foreign nations, . . . must carry the same meaning throughout the sentence, and remain a unit, unless there be some plain intelligible cause which alters it").

[26] U.S. CONST. art. I, § 8, cl. 3 (emphasis added).

[27] See *infra* notes 33–37 and accompanying text.

[28] Put another way, this phrasing mattered because it would make no sense for any one state—far less each of them—to claim a power to regulate "Commerce . . . among the several states," thus permitting, for example, Georgia to regulate trade between Connecticut and New Hampshire. To the extent the Framers came to see the relevant subject of regulation in this field as a unitary and shared commerce "among" the states, it thus would seem to follow that control over that subject had to be placed exclusively in the hands of the federal government because the federal government alone was structurally suited for dealing with that subject in light of its intrinsically national character. This line of reasoning also may find support in the separate text of the Tenth Amendment that specifies that certain powers are "reserved" to the states, which the Court has read to mean that states retain under that amendment only those state powers that antedated the formation of the Constitution. *See* U.S. Term Limits v. Thornton, 514 U.S. 779, 802–05 (1995) (endorsing this reading of the provision). In other words, so the argument goes, the states could not "reserve," because they never

Whatever one might conclude about the significance of these specialized features of the constitutional text, the Court itself has concluded that the history of the framing mandates recognition of the dormant Commerce Clause principle. Thus, in *Tennessee Wine & Spirits Ass'n v. Thomas*,[29] Justice Alito emphasized for a seven-Justice majority that "without [the dormant Commerce Clause], we would be left with a constitutional scheme that those who framed and ratified the Constitution would surely find surprising."[30] More specifically:

> [R]emoving state trade barriers was a principal reason for the adoption of the Constitution. Under the Articles of Confederation, States notoriously obstructed the interstate shipment of goods. Interference with the arteries of commerce was cutting off the very life-blood of the nation. The Annapolis Convention of 1786 was convened to address this critical problem, and it culminated in a call for the Philadelphia Convention that framed the Constitution in the summer of 1787. At that Convention, discussion of the power to regulate interstate commerce was almost uniformly linked to the removal of state trade barriers, and when the Constitution was sent to the state conventions, fostering free trade among the States was prominently cited as a reason for ratification. In *The Federalist No. 7*, Hamilton argued that state protectionism could lead to conflict among the States, and in *No. 11*, he touted the benefits of a free national market. In *The Federalist No. 42*, Madison sounded a similar theme.[31]

---

had, the Framers' newly created power to "regulate Commerce . . . *among* the several States."

[29] 139 S. Ct. 2449 (2019).

[30] *Id.* at 2460.

[31] *Id.* (internal quotations, citations, and footnotes omitted). Professor Edmund Kitch has argued that the traditional depiction of widespread protectionism under the Articles of Confederation is overstated. *See, e.g.*, Edmund Kitch, *Regulation and the American Common Market, in* REGULATION, FEDERALISM, AND INTERSTATE COMMERCE (A. Tarlock ed. 1981). Professor Denning, on the other hand, has gathered evidence that challenges Professor Kitch's thesis. *See* Denning, *supra* note 10, at 479–81. But regardless of which of these analysts has the better side of the historical debate, the critical *legal* points are that: (1) the Framers themselves, as Justice Alito highlighted, viewed the problem of state-sponsored protectionism and escalating trade wars as acute; and (2) they responded to this perception by forging the Constitution and the Commerce Clause. *See, e.g.*, Friedman & Deacon, *supra* note 10, at 1890 ("[M]any people in the [founding] period, including but not limited to some of the most influential Framers, believed interstate discrimination to be an extremely serious problem meriting a profound response."); Donald H. Regan, *The Supreme Court and State Protectionism: Making Sense of the Dormant Commerce Clause*, 84 MICH. L. REV. 1091, 1114 n.55 (1986) (making the same point). Of particular importance in this regard, both Alexander Hamilton and James Madison voiced profound concern about already-escalating trade disputes among the states—disputes they viewed as

Accordingly, Justice Alito concluded, "our cases have long emphasized the connection between the trade barriers that prompted the call for a new Constitution and our dormant Commerce Clause jurisprudence."[32]

More specific features of the framing history bolster the conclusion, reached by Justice Alito and his six colleagues in *Tennessee Wine & Spirits*, that the Framers viewed the commerce power as foreclosing cross-border trade-restricting forms of state action.[33] For instance, as Professor Albert Abel documented nearly

---

portending such serious "outrages" that the nation stood on the brink of state-against-state "reprisals and wars." THE FEDERALIST NO. 7 (Hamilton); THE FEDERALIST NO. 42 (Madison) (discussing these problems as establishing the "[t]he necessity of a superintending authority over the reciprocal trade of confederated States").

[32] *Tennessee Wine & Spirits Ass'n*, 139 S. Ct. at 2461. In support of this assertion, Justice Alito pointed to, among other things, an 1880 ruling in which the Court reasoned that state protectionist measures, "if maintained by this court, would ultimately bring our commerce to that 'oppressed and degraded state,' existing at the adoption of the present Constitution, when the helpless, inadequate Confederation was abandoned and the national government instituted." *Id* (citing Guy v. Baltimore, 100 U.S. 434, 440 (1880)). He also pointed to *Granholm v. Heald*, 544 U.S. 460, 472 (2005), as "[m]ore recently" recognizing that "our dormant Commerce Clause cases reflect a 'central concern of the Framers that was an immediate reason for calling the Constitutional Convention: the conviction that in order to succeed, the new Union would have to avoid the tendencies toward economic Balkanization that had plagued relations among the Colonies and later among the States under the Articles of Confederation.'" *Tennessee Wine & Spirits Ass'n*, 139 S. Ct. at 2461 (internal quotations omitted in part). Notably, many other rulings of the Court have likewise emphasized the dormant Commerce Clause's sturdy historical roots. *See, e.g.*, *Baldwin*, 294 U.S. at 522 (noting that the chief concern of the "commerce clauses was the mutual jealousies and aggressions of the States, taking form in customs barriers and other economic retaliation" (internal quotations omitted)); Minnesota Rate Cases, 230 U.S. 352, 398 (1913) (focusing on the Framers' intention to respond to the "disastrous experience under the Confederation").

[33] With regard to history, critics of the dormant Commerce Clause principle rely primarily on the absence of specific endorsements of it in the records of the founding period. *E.g.*, FELIX FRANKFURTER, THE COMMERCE CLAUSE UNDER MARSHALL, TANEY, AND WAITE (1937); Currie, *supra* note 12, at 497–502; David P. Currie, *The Constitution in the Supreme Court: State and Congressional Powers, 1801–1835*, 49 U. CHI. L. REV. 887, 943–47 (1982); Redish & Nugent, *supra* note 10, at 585–88. One difficulty with this argument is that its underlying premise is shaky, as Professor Abel explained in his comprehensive treatment of the subject. *See* Abel, *supra* note 10, at 442–46. A second difficulty is that Federalist proponents of the Constitution (as in *The Federalist*) focused their attention on rebuffing Antifederalist arguments against ratification. Moreover, those arguments understandably focused on objections to specific terms of the document (particularly its express grants of federal power) together with the document's obvious omissions, particularly as to a Bill of Rights—as opposed to principles, such as the dormant Commerce Clause principle, derived by implication from the document's text, purposes, and history. (By way of comparison, writings from the framing period did not focus on, or perhaps even mention at all, the immunity of federally created banks from state taxation recognized in *McCulloch*. But that does not mean that the Court erred in recognizing such an immunity in that case.) Apart from pointing to a supposed lack of contemporaneous disquisition on the dormancy principle, a detractor might point to the contrast between the Articles of Confederation, which specified in express terms that powers given by the Articles to the federal government were exclusive, see ARTICLES OF CONFEDERATION OF 1781, art. II, and to the Constitution itself, which includes no similar textual passage. *Cf.*

seventy-five years ago, many leaders of the founding generation expressly endorsed the idea that "as to commercial regulation, Congress would or should be given 'full power,' 'absolute control,' and the like."[34] (Among the exponents of this view, moreover, were James Madison and James Wilson, two of the most important and actively engaged delegates at the Philadelphia Convention.[35]) In addition,

Douglas G. Smith, *An Analysis of Two Federal Structures: The Articles of Confederation and the Constitution*, 34 SAN DIEGO L. REV. 249, 281–83 (1997) (comparing these two provisions). This linguistic shift might be seen as supporting the suggestion, frequently asserted by critics of the dormant Commerce Clause principle, that the powers granted to Congress by the Constitution necessarily are nonexclusive unless the text specifies otherwise (for example, with regard to the taxation of imports). *See, e.g.*, Redish & Nugent, *supra* note 10, at 587–88. This line of reasoning, however, contravenes the suggestion of both *The Federalist* and the Marshall Court that the exclusivity of federal powers in some instances could and did arise in the absence of any text specifically disempowering state governments. *See supra* notes 14–15 and accompanying text. Another problem is that this line of reasoning effectively strips telling words of the Constitution itself—in this case, the words "regulate" and "among the several states"—of their otherwise operative significance. *See supra* note 20 and accompanying text. Finally, this argument from textual contrast turns the history of the founding on its head. It does so by insisting that the Constitution was more solicitous of preserving concurrent powers in the states than was the Articles of Confederation, despite the universally understood aim of the Framers to rearrange government powers in a way that diminished—indeed, diminished radically—the scope of state authority as federal authority was strengthened.

[34] Abel, *supra* note 10, at 491 (internal footnotes omitted); *see also id.* at 491 n.264 (citing, for example, the language of the Rhode Island merchants' address to the Convention); *id.* at 491 n.265 (collecting additional citations along these lines, including to the writings of Centinel and James Monroe's remarks at the Virginia Ratification Convention).

[35] According to Madison's notes of the Convention's proceedings, Wilson observed in particular that "[t]he natil. Govt. is one & [that] of the states another—Commerce, War, Peace, Treaties &c are peculiar to the former—certain inferior and local Qualities are the province of the Latter—there is a line of separation." 1 THE RECORDS OF THE FEDERAL CONVENTION OF 1787, at 416 (Max Farrand ed., 1911) [hereinafter FARRAND'S RECORDS]. As for Madison himself, he observed at the Convention that the commerce power "seem[s] to exclude this power of the States" in the context of addressing the question "[w]hether the States are . . . restrained from laying tonnage duties" in the absence of a specific restriction on such state action because, as he observed, the need for a clause imposing such a restriction "depends on the extent of the power 'to regulate commerce.' " *Id.* at 625, *quoted* in *Tyler Pipe*, 483 U.S. at 263 (Scalia, J., dissenting). As Professor Tushnet has noted, Justice Scalia viewed Madison's comments as offering a "mere shadow of historical support" for recognizing the dormant Commerce Clause principle. *See* Tushnet, *supra* note 10, at 1723 (quoting *Tyler Pipe*, 483 U.S. at 264 (Scalia, J., dissenting)). To be sure, Madison's statement was made only in the context of his questioning of the need for including the Tonnage Clause in the Constitution, and the Framers decided to include that clause in Article I anyway. *See Tyler Pipe*, 483 U.S. at 264 (Scalia, J., dissenting). For a variety of reasons, however, Justice Scalia's line of reasoning is subject to serious question. First, the delegates may well have worried that, regardless of constitutional limits on state powers to "regulate . . . Commerce," tonnage duties might be sustained by the courts under the states' separate *taxing* powers that would have unquestionably remained available in the absence of an express prohibition on their use. Second and relatedly, the felt need to specify express limits on state taxing authority (embodied in both the Tonnage Clause and the Import Export Clause) corresponded with the idea that the retained state power to tax was uniquely expansive—indeed, so much so that, in general, Congress could not displace state taxes even with affirmative legislation

that position dovetailed with the then-accepted understanding that certain powers—beginning, it seems clear, with the commerce power—needed to be granted to Congress because the states were "incompetent" to exercise them.[36] After all, it would make no sense to leave in the hands of the states a power that the Framers vested in Congress because the states were "incompetent" to exercise it. Finally, it bears emphasis that the dormant Commerce Clause can be seen as responding not only to the Framers' concerns about commerce standing alone, but also to their more general concerns about fostering national unification in the face of a worrisome post-

enacted pursuant to its own new taxing power (or any other power) in combination with the Necessary and Proper Clause. (Indeed, this view of the role of the Tonnage Clause was specifically endorsed by Alexander Hamilton in *The Federalist No. 32.*) Third, the Framers might well have felt that, even if the imposition of tonnage duties could qualify as a "regulation" of commerce, the evenhanded imposition of such charges on all ships (including locally owned or locally operated ships) by a state would not qualify as the sort of impermissible interference with interstate commerce clearly foreclosed by the Commerce Clause in its dormant state. Fourth, and of particular importance, the most likely explanation for the Framers' inclusion of the Tonnage Clause in the Constitution is that the Framers simply wanted to block the states from imposing tonnage charges—full stop. And obviously the best way to achieve that goal was to state in the constitutional document, in no uncertain terms, that such charges were impermissible. It was hardly unique for the Framers to include texts in the Constitution that nailed down the existence of principles that otherwise would have existed—albeit only by implication from other clauses—so as to leave no doubt about the operation of those constitutional rules. *See, e.g.*, *McCulloch*, 17 U.S. at 420–21 ("If no other motive for [the Necessary and Proper Clause's] insertion can be suggested, a sufficient one is found in the desire to remove all doubts respecting the right to legislate on that vast mass of incidental powers which must be involved in the constitution. . . ."). And this idea supported inclusion of the Tonnage Clause in Article I whether or not the delegates found merit in Madison's view of the state-limiting impact of the Commerce Clause.

36 *See* 1 FARRAND'S RECORDS, *supra* note 35, at 21 (highlighting James Madison's proposal, on which the enumeration of powers was later built, "[t]hat the National Legislature ought to be impowered . . . to legislate" both in all cases "in which the harmony of the United States may be interrupted by the exercise of individual Legislation" and "in all cases to which the separate States are incompetent"); *see also* Thomas B. Colby, *Revitalizing the Forgotten Uniformity Constraint on the Commerce Power*, 91 VA. L. REV. 249, 274–75 n.79 (2005) (noting that this vision of federal powers was set forth in "the Virginia Plan submitted by Edmund Randolph (though largely the work of Madison)"); Abel, *supra* note 10, at 492 (noting the "[f]airly widespread expression of the view that the states were incompetent to legislate in the field [of interstate commerce], whether because their action would be ineffectual or because it would not be disinterested"). A related point is that the intrinsically interstate nature of the Interstate Commerce Clause in and of itself supports the notion that the grant of power it embodies is exclusive to the federal government. *See* 2 THE DEBATES IN THE SEVERAL STATE CONVENTIONS ON THE ADOPTION OF THE FEDERAL CONSTITUTION AS RECOMMENDED BY THE GENERAL CONVENTION AT PHILADELPHIA 424 (Jonathan Elliot ed., 2d ed. 1836) (statement of James Wilson) ("Whatever object of government is confined, in its operation and effects, within the bounds of a particular state, should be considered as belonging to the government of that state; whatever object of government extends, in its operation or effects, beyond the bounds of a particular state, should be considered as belonging to the government of the United States.").

Revolution drift toward self-interested state policymaking and rising interstate hostility.[37]

Debate over the legitimacy of the dormant Commerce Clause principle is certain to persist notwithstanding the textual and historical arguments that support its longstanding recognition. (Some originalists, for instance, may continue to conclude that, on balance, the relevant sources cut more against rather than in favor of the view expressed by Justice Alito, while some nonoriginalists may view the discussion offered here to be wholly or largely beside the point.) At the very least, however, this account suggests that the text- and history-based case to be made on its behalf is significantly stronger than critics of the doctrine typically make it out to be. In addition, whatever any individual analyst might conclude about these arguments, it is a matter of no small consequence that Justices of widely varying ideologies have consistently recognized and applied the dormant Commerce Clause principle over many generations.[38] For this reason, the case for continuing to apply that principle pursuant to the doctrine of *stare decisis* is particularly strong.[39] And that case is bolstered by the fact that Congress, for well more than a century, has made decisions to legislate—or not to legislate—based on its background understanding that the courts, rather than it, would take the lead role in policing excessive state disruptions of a free-flowing interstate trade. Nor is this pattern of acceptance by Congress surprising, given that—as Justice Jackson observed in a classic treatment of the subject—judicial work with the dormant Commerce Clause has contributed to producing in the United States

---

[37] *See supra* note 31 (noting particular expressions of this concern from Alexander Hamilton and James Madison).

[38] *See, e.g.*, Freeman v. Hewitt, 329 U.S. 249, 252, 256 (1946) (invoking the dormancy doctrine to invalidate a state taxing system based on "that very freedom of commercial flow which for more than a hundred and fifty years has been the ward of the Commerce Clause" and citing "the course of adjudication unbroken through the Nation's history" through which the Court has applied "the Commerce Clause even without implementing legislation by Congress"); Gwin, White & Prince, Inc. v. Henneford, 305 U.S. 434, 441 (1939) (opining that the dormant Commerce Clause has operated to constrain state decisionmaking since the Court's 1827 decision in *Brown v. Maryland*, 25 U.S. (12 Wheat.) 419 (1827)). Indeed, even as of 1959 the Court was able to identify at least 300 cases in which it had applied the doctrine, and even that tabulation—made more than 60 years ago—included only cases involving challenges to state taxes. *See* Nw. States Portland Cement Co. v. Minnesota, 358 U.S. 450, 457–458 (1959).

[39] Indeed, even Justice Scalia concluded that the requirements of *stare decisis* bound him to apply already-established features of the dormancy doctrine. *See West Lynn Creamery*, 512 U.S. at 209–10 (Scalia, J., concurring) (commenting that the Court "formally adopted the doctrine of the negative Commerce Clause 121 years ago" and "[a]s a result, I will, on *stare decisis* grounds, enforce a self-executing 'negative' Commerce Clause in two situations: (1) against a state law that facially discriminates against interstate commerce, and (2) against a state law that is indistinguishable from a type of law previously held unconstitutional by this Court").

a level of "material success" fairly described as "the most impressive in the history of commerce."[40]

3. The Dormant Commerce Clause and Political Processes

The dormant Commerce Clause principle not only takes aim at the economic problems of protectionism, inefficiency, and trade wars; it also responds to the dangers of "faction" endemic in the processes of republican self-government.[41] Consider in this respect the principle's disallowance of state-imposed protective tariffs. According to constitutional thinking that focuses on the dangers of factional abuse, the dormant Commerce Clause's targeting of such actions makes sense because it responds to the tendencies of state legislatures to advance the well-being of "insider" interest groups (particularly in-state manufacturers) at the expense of "outsider" interest groups (particularly out-of-state manufacturers) that lack equivalent access to the levers of political influence. In other words, as the Court itself has explained, "to the extent that the burden falls on economic interests without the state, it is not likely to be alleviated by those political restraints which are normally exerted on legislation where it adversely affects interests within the state."[42]

Critics of the dormant Commerce Clause might respond to this expression of political-process-based concerns by pointing out that the national Congress is always in a position to remedy the malady of self-interested state overreaching by enacting preemptive legislation.[43] One difficulty with this line of reasoning, however, is that the many impediments to enacting any federal law reduce the chances that such curative legislation will materialize even when well-justified.[44] Another complication arises because federal

---

[40] *Hood*, 336 U.S. at 536–38.

[41] *See* THE FEDERALIST NO. 10 (Madison).

[42] McGoldrick v. Berwind-White Coal Mining Co., 309 U.S. 33, 45–46 n.2 (1940). For a critique of the use of representation-reinforcement theory in dormant Commerce Clause cases, at least as a dominant theme, see Regan, *supra* note 31, at 1160–63. For a defense of one form of representation-reinforcement-related analysis in this context, see Mark Tushnet, *Rethinking the Dormant Commerce Clause*, 1979 WIS. L. REV. 125.

[43] They might also make the related point that, relative to Congress, the Court is "ill equipped and arguably unauthorized to make" the sorts of "policy-laden judgments" that the dormant Commerce Clause doctrine requires. *Camps Newfound/Owatonna*, 520 U.S. at 618 (Thomas, J., dissenting).

[44] *See, e.g.*, Duckworth v. Arkansas, 314 U.S. 390, 400 (1941) (Jackson, J., concurring in the result) ("The sluggishness of government, the multitude of matters that clamor for attention, and the relative ease with which men are persuaded to postpone troublesome decisions, all make inertia one of the most decisive powers in determining the course of our affairs and frequently gives to the established order of things a longevity and vitality much beyond its merits."). *See generally infra* Section 29.D.2 (discussing, among other things, the challenges presented to enacting

legislators elected on a state-by-state basis may bring to the table an attitude of "I'll scratch your back if you scratch mine"—an attitude that might not only impede corrective congressional action, but also cause the numbers of isolationist state laws to multiply over time. No less important, there exists the related problem that, as Justice Jackson observed in *Duckworth v. Arkansas*,[45] "restraints [on interstate commerce] are individually too petty, too diversified, and too local to get the attention of a Congress hard pressed with more urgent matters," thus yielding "[t]he practical result . . . that in default of action by us [the states] will go on suffocating and retarding and Balkanizing American commerce, trade, and industry."[46]

Indeed, Congress's ability to wield the commerce power might well provide the basis for an argument *in favor of* the dormancy doctrine. According to this line of thinking, democracy-centered objections to the doctrine are undercut by the fact that dormant Commerce Clause decisions—unlike judicial decisions based on almost all other constitutional rules—are always subject to congressional override by way of the enactment of ordinary legislation. (That is, Congress can undo any unwanted dormant Commerce Clause ruling by exercising its commerce power so as to authorize whatever form of state-based commercial regulation that ruling disallowed.[47]) To be sure, judicial invocations of the dormancy doctrine still shift the burden of inertia in a consequential way, by making affirmative congressional intervention necessary to restore the thus-invalidated law. But it nonetheless remains true—and critical in assessing the supposed de-democratizing effect of the dormancy doctrine—that every judicial decision applying the doctrine to invalidate a state law invites Congress to respond to, including by overturning, that decision through the use of ordinary legislative processes.

A final concern about the dormancy doctrine rests on fears that it now provides a tool for massive displacement of state authority, even in the absence of preemptive legislation, given the post-New Deal jurisprudence that has greatly expanded Congress's affirmative lawmaking power under the Commerce Clause. Underlying this concern is the assumption that the scope of the dormant Commerce Clause principle must be tied in some way to the scope of the affirmative Commerce Clause power. But this assumption is wrong. The dormant Commerce Clause in fact has nothing to do with the

legislation by the constitutional presentment and bicameralism requirements); Section 14.A (also noting complications raised by self-imposed rules of procedure).

45 314 U.S. 390 (1941).

46 *Id.* at 400 (Jackson, J., concurring in the result).

47 *See generally infra* Section 20.B (discussing the congressional-consent exception to the dormant Commerce Clause rule).

breadth, or lack of breadth, of Congress's affirmative commerce power. Instead, it has to do with only one thing—whether a state law is so disruptive of interstate trade that it must be characterized as a *de facto* regulation of interstate commerce, as opposed to a permissible exercise of the state's retained police or taxing or other powers. Put another way, any concern that the effect that dormancy-doctrine restraints have become too sweeping because of the now-long reach of the affirmative commerce power reflects a fundamental category error.[48] The scope of the dormant Commerce Clause is wholly unrelated to the scope of Congress's legislative authority under the Commerce Clause. It has to do—and only has to do—with whether a court should recharacterize a particular law of a particular state, claimed to rest on its reserved powers, as instead resting on an unreserved power to regulate interstate commerce in light of the law's common-market-defeating character.[49]

---

[48] Indeed, Justice Rutledge observed, in the immediate post-New Deal period as the affirmative commerce power grew in robustness, that "[j]ust as in recent years the permissive scope for congressional commerce action has broadened . . . the prohibitive effect of the clause has been progressively narrowed." WILEY RUTLEDGE, A DECLARATION OF LEGAL FAITH 68 (1947).

[49] Put another way, the relevant inquiry has nothing to do with the scope of Congress's affirmative commerce power because that latter subject has to do with the making of federal statutory law. Instead, the relevant inquiry concerns only whether a state law interferes so greatly with cross-border trade that it must be characterized as a regulation of interstate commerce and not—as the state would have it—an ordinary exercise of its police (or other retained) powers. The Court's many dormant Commerce Clause decisions—addressing many laws over many years—have all in effect involved the application of this functional distinction, and two points about that line-drawing process merit emphasis here. First, the Court has (as the next five chapters highlight) developed a specialized set of constitutional decision rules to guide its work in drawing this line. Second, the location of the rightly drawn line does not hinge on whether the state has regulated an activity that Congress could regulate under its commerce power, including on the theory that the activity is itself "in interstate commerce." (Congress, for example, might well be able to regulate thefts from trucks hauling cargo on interstate trips on an in-commerce theory. But that would not mean that the state could not regulate that same wrongdoing pursuant to a generally applicable theft statute enacted pursuant to the state's police power.) As Justice Kennedy suggested in *Wayfair*, 138 S. Ct. at 2090–92, such a view of the Commerce Clause would go too far in restricting state authority and has never gained the support of the Court. Indeed, the Court's recognition of the irrelevance of Congress's affirmative commerce power to the contours of dormant Commerce Clause doctrine dates all the way back to the work of Chief Justice Marshall and his colleagues nearly two centuries ago. *See, e.g.* George L. Haskins, *John Marshall and the Commerce Clause of the Constitution*, 104 U. PA. L. REV. 23, 29 (1955) ("Although denying the power of a state to regulate interstate commerce, *Marshall* [in *Willson v. Blackbird Creek Marsh Co.*, 27 U.S. (2 Pet.) 245 (1829)] held that a state law enacted in the exercise of the state's police powers might validly operate on interstate commerce transactions, since this was not a regulation of the commerce itself and hence not an invasion of the field granted to Congress."); *see also* Norman R. Williams, *The Commerce Clause and the Myth of Dual Federalism*, 54 UCLA L. REV. 1847, 1853 (2007) (concluding that "[f]or close to two centuries, we have had two Commerce Clauses, one for the federal government and one for the states"; adding that "there never has been a unitary Commerce Clause, and, judged by its recent decisions, the Court is entirely uninterested in creating one").

For newcomers to constitutional law, the dormant Commerce Clause may seem arcane and peripheral, or at least lacking in the fascination routinely stirred by higher-profile areas of Supreme Court doctrine. Recalling both the core aspirations of the Framers and the practical effects of the dormancy doctrine, however, should remove any doubt about that doctrine's centrality to the law of constitutional structure. Indeed, the dormancy principle—perhaps more so than any other legal principle—has given life to the proposition that, as Justice Cardozo observed a near-century ago, the very "salvation" of the nation lies "in union and not division."[50]

B. BASIC DORMANT COMMERCE CLAUSE DOCTRINE

The Court has applied the dormancy doctrine throughout U.S. history, and the rhetoric that informs its application has evolved greatly from its first stirrings in the era of Chief Justice Marshall. In *Cooley v. Board of Wardens*,[51] for example, the Court drew a hard-to-pin-down constitutional dividing line between matters "in their nature national" and matters "local and not national."[52] Thereafter, the Court relied largely on an analytical touchstone that differentiated between laws that "directly" and "indirectly" affect interstate commerce.[53] For many years, the Court made use of the local/national standard and the direct/indirect distinction in applying the dormant Commerce Clause rule.[54] With ever-increasing insistence, however, legal-realist critics in the early twentieth century condemned these tests as unduly conclusionary and subject to judicial manipulation. As a consequence, building on opinions such as then-Associate Justice Stone's dissent in *Di Santo v.*

---

[50] *Baldwin*, 294 U.S. at 523.

[51] 53 U.S. (12 How.) 299 (1851).

[52] *Id.* at 319. *Accord, e.g.*, Wabash, St. Louis & Pac. Ry. Co. v. Illinois, 118 U.S. 557, 577 (1886) (striking down a state railroad rate rule as applied to the intrastate portion of interstate shipment based on the local-national distinction).

[53] Smith v. Alabama, 124 U.S. 465, 474 (1888) (pointing to this principle); *id.* at 482 (upholding the challenged law because it "affects transactions of commerce among the States . . . only indirectly, incidentally, and remotely").

[54] *E.g.*, Southern Ry. Co. v. King, 217 U.S. 524, 531 (1910); Di Santo v. Philadelphia, 273 U.S. 34, 37 (1927) (invalidating a state law that required "licenses to sell steamship tickets or orders for transportation to or from foreign countries" because "[t]he license fee and other things imposed by the act . . . constitute a direct burden on that commerce"); Silz v. Hesterberg, 211 U.S. 31, 40–41 (1908) ("That a state may not pass laws directly regulating foreign or interstate commerce has frequently been held in the decisions of this court. But . . . laws passed by the States in the exertion of their police power, not in conflict with laws of Congress upon the same subject, and indirectly or remotely affecting interstate commerce, are nevertheless valid laws."). Many cases decided during this period involved state laws related to railroads. For a detailed examination of these cases, see James W. Ely, Jr., *"The Railroad System Has Burst Through State Limits": Railroads and Interstate Commerce, 1830–1920*, 55 ARK. L. REV. 933, 937–60 (2003).

Pennsylvania,[55] the Court moved away from "doing little more than using labels."[56] The result of this process was the doctrinal approach, based on a more transparent evaluation of state and national interests, that dominates dormant Commerce Clause discourse today.

The Court's many modern decisions set out an overarching structure—complete with great chambers, meandering side halls, and nooks and crannies—for evaluating dormant Commerce Clause cases. At the center of the edifice stands the principle that broadly prohibits laws that *discriminate on their face* against interstate commerce. Facial discrimination takes many forms. States may check the inflow of commerce with taxes or regulatory laws that exclude incoming goods and services. Alternatively, they may block the outflow of commerce by imposing export bans or other hoarding measures that favor in-state over out-of-state buyers.[57] The Court has taken an intensely hostile view of all these acts of overt discrimination, subjecting them to a "virtually *per se* rule of invalidity."[58]

The dormant Commerce Clause prohibition, however, does not stop at outlawing the most patently protectionist measures. The Court also has declared that even a facially neutral state law will encounter a ramped-up form of judicial scrutiny if (1) the protectionist impact of the law is so apparent that it is functionally indistinguishable from a tariff or other facially discriminatory rule; (2) the law was adopted because of a protectionist purpose; or (3) the law generates distinctly worrisome "extraterritorial" effects.[59] In addition, the Court has held that ostensibly neutral, but commerce-disrupting, state laws will trigger application of the "*Pike* balancing test," even if those laws do not reflect facial, purposive, or in-effect discrimination or have a presumptively impermissible extraterritorial impact.[60] Applying this test, in turn, requires courts to weigh the burden the challenged state law places on interstate commerce against its "putative local benefits" for purposes of

55 273 U.S. 34 (1927).

56 *Id.* at 44 (Stone, J., dissenting) According to Justice Stone: "[I]nquiring whether the interference with commerce is direct or indirect seems to me too mechanical, too uncertain in its application, and too remote from actualities, to be of value. In thus making use of the expressions, 'direct' and 'indirect interference' with commerce, we are doing little more than using labels to describe a result rather than any trustworthy formula by which it is reached." *Id.*

57 For numerous other examples of facial discrimination, see *infra* Section 17.A.

58 City of Philadelphia v. New Jersey, 437 U.S. 617, 624 (1978).

59 *See infra* Chapter 19.

60 *Oregon Waste Sys.*, 511 U.S. at 100 (identifying the test set forth in *Pike v. Bruce Church, Inc.*, 397 U.S. 137 (1970)).

determining whether the former is "clearly excessive" in relation to the latter.[61]

Making matters even more complicated is the Court's recognition of a bevy of exceptions to these dormant Commerce Clause rules. Thus, states may at least sometimes adopt even blatantly discriminatory measures that involve (1) actions to which Congress has consented, (2) affirmative cash subsidization, (3) behavior by the state in its capacity as a "market participant," or (4) certain forms of "state self-promotion" that channel business activity to a state's own commercial operations.[62] As if this network of exceptions were not complex enough, the Court has developed important limitations on each of them—what we might well call "exceptions to the exceptions"—that guard against undermining particularly important dormant Commerce Clause values. Finally, and in addition to carving out full-scale exceptions to the dormancy doctrine, the Court has recognized that the doctrine applies in distinctive ways within particular contexts—including when foreign commerce is in the picture,[63] and when challengers target state and

---

[61] *Pike*, 397 U.S. at 142. *See generally infra* Chapter 18.

[62] All these exceptions are discussed *infra* Chapter 20.

[63] *See infra* Chapter 22. Another set of questions concerns the extent to which dormant Commerce Clause principles that restrain state action apply to territorial governments and the District of Columbia. Present-day case law supports the view that the dormancy doctrine does, or at least might, apply to the actions of local authorities in U.S. territories. *See* Trailer Marine Transp. Corp. v. Rivera Vazquez, 977 F.2d 1, 8 (1st Cir. 1992) (holding that dormant-Commerce-Clause limits apply to Puerto Rico because it "has sufficient actual autonomy to justify treating it as a public entity distinct from Congress," but also implying that the same conclusion might not apply to Guam if viewed as " 'an instrumentality' of the federal government"); JDS Realty Corp. v. Gov't of Virgin Islands, 824 F.2d 256 (3d Cir. 1987) (applying the dormancy doctrine to the Virgin Islands), *vacated on other grounds*, 484 U.S. 99 (1988); Anderson v. Mullaney, 191 F.2d 123, 127 (9th Cir. 1951) (applying that doctrine to the then-territory of Alaska), *aff'd on other grounds*, 342 U.S. 415 (1952). In similar fashion, the courts have held that the dormant Commerce Clause principle applies to actions taken by municipal authorities in the District of Columbia. *See, e.g.*, Milton S. Kronheim & Co., Inc. v. District of Columbia, 91 F.3d 193, 198–201 (D.C Cir. 1996); *see also* Electrolert Corp. v. Barry, 737 F.2d 110, 112–13 (D.C. Cir. 1984) (upholding a District ordinance that outlawed devices designed to detect police radar in the face of a dormant Commerce Clause attack); Am. Bus Ass'n, Inc. v. District of Columbia, 2 A.3d 203, 212–21 (D.C. 2010) (finding no dormant Commerce Clause violation in a permit law that afforded like treatment to District residents and others). On the other hand, laws passed by Congress itself, although concerning the District, are immune from dormant Commerce Clause challenge. *See, e.g.*, District of Columbia v. Helen Dwight Reid Educ. Found., 766 A.2d 28, 37 (D.C. 2001) ("While the dormant commerce clause may prohibit state legislatures and other non-federal legislative bodies from enacting burdens on interstate commerce, that clause imposes no limitations on Congress, even when Congress acts 'like a state legislature' in exercising its plenary power to legislate for the District of Columbia under art. I, § 8, cl. 17 of the Constitution.").

local taxing measures, as opposed to non-tax-based regulatory restrictions.[64]

This introduction to the dormant Commerce Clause principle reveals, if nothing else, its doctrinal complexity. What is more, this summary understates that complexity because the Court sometimes structures its analysis in ways that do not fit neatly within this framework. The Court may, for example, refer loosely to both discriminatory purpose and effect.[65] It may combine *Pike* balancing and extraterritoriality analysis.[66] It may even revert to *Cooley*'s local-versus-national rhetoric.[67] The Court's embrace of the modern-day *Pike* test also has given rise to some uncertainty about how the Court's past decisions concerning facially neutral laws fit together with present-day law in this field. But while the complexity of dormant Commerce Clause doctrine might sometimes seem to make it a muddle, that complexity also underlies a practical point of great importance: Lawyers who encounter a state law that imperils the free flow of interstate commerce almost always can find at least one way, and sometimes more than one way, to mount an argument against it.

---

64 *See infra* Chapter 21.

65 *See, e.g.*, *Baldwin*, 294 U.S. at 522.

66 *See, e.g.*, Edgar v. MITE Corp., 457 U.S. 624 (1982).

67 *See, e.g.*, Bob-Lo Excursion Co. v. Michigan, 333 U.S. 28, 37–40 (1948).

Chapter 17

DISCRIMINATION AGAINST INTERSTATE COMMERCE

Analysis

The core of the dormant Commerce Clause principle lies in its prohibition of state laws that discriminate against interstate commerce. But when is unlawful discrimination present? The answer, in short, is that state laws may qualify as discriminatory in three ways: (1) on their face;[1] (2) in effect;[2] or (3) in purpose.[3] Moreover, although the Court has indicated that a discriminatory law will survive constitutional attack if the state shows that the law provides a necessary means of achieving an important state goal, the Justices only once have found that this standard was satisfied.[4] For all practical purposes, then, the form of judicial scrutiny that applies to discriminatory state laws, while " 'strict' in theory," is "fatal in fact."[5]

A. FACIALLY DISCRIMINATORY LAWS

The most frequently applied component of the anti-discrimination rule is its ban on state and local laws that discriminate on their face against interstate commerce. In *City of*

---

[1] *See infra* Section 17.A.

[2] *See infra* Section 17.B.

[3] *See infra* Section 17.C. *See generally* James M. McGoldrick, Jr., *The Dormant Commerce Clause: The Endgame—From* Southern Pacific *to* Tennessee Wine & Spirits—*1945 to 2019*, 40 PACE L. REV. 44, 83 (2020) (asserting that the task of identifying discriminatory laws has proven to be so challenging that "the Court's decisions as to discrimination are a morass").

[4] *See* Maine v. Taylor, 477 U.S. 131 (1986) (discussed *infra* Section 17.D).

[5] Gerald Gunther, *The Supreme Court, 1971 Term—Foreword: In Search of Evolving Doctrine on a Changing Court: A Model for the Newer Equal Protection*, 86 HARV. L. REV. 1, 8 (1972) (employing this terminology in regard to equal-protection-based strict scrutiny).

Philadelphia v. New Jersey,[6] for example, the Court invoked the dormant Commerce Clause principle to invalidate a New Jersey statute that prohibited all deliveries of out-of-state solid waste for handling by in-state landfills. The Court saw the case as one involving a ban on the *importation* of out-of-state waste products, which the Court found to be "articles of commerce."[7] Others might have viewed the law as having prohibited the *exportation* of in-state waste-disposal services.[8] But what mattered in the end was the challenged measure facially (and unjustifiably) discriminated against out-of-state trash and thus ran afoul of the "virtually *per se* rule of invalidity" that applies when a state law "overtly blocks the flow of interstate commerce at a State's borders."[9]

Facially discriminatory statutes come in many shapes and sizes.[10] But most of them fall into one of three broad categories: export restrictions, import restrictions, and local processing requirements.

1. Facially Discriminatory Export Restrictions

Facially discriminatory restrictions on state exports take different forms, but the paradigmatic case involves the "export embargo."[11] In *Pennsylvania v. West Virginia*,[12] for example, the Court encountered a state law that permitted private firms to export natural gas only after local needs were satisfied. In dissent, Justice Holmes saw no reason "to prevent a State from giving a preference to

---

6 437 U.S. 617 (1978).

7 *Id.* at 627.

8 *Cf.* C & A Carbone, Inc. v. Town of Clarkstown, 511 U.S. 383, 392 (1994).

9 *City of Philadelphia*, 437 U.S. at 624; *see also* Baude v. Heath, 538 F.3d 608, 611 (7th Cir. 2008) ("A state law that discriminates explicitly ('on its face,' lawyers are fond of saying) is almost always invalid under the Supreme Court's commerce jurisprudence . . . ."). For scholarly commentary on the facial-discrimination concept, see, e.g., David S. Day, *The "Mature" Rehnquist Court and the Dormant Commerce Clause Doctrine: The Expanded Discrimination Tier*, 52 S.D. L. REV. 1, 47–50 (2007) (suggesting that, in determining whether to apply the facial-discrimination characterization, the Rehnquist Court sometimes looked beyond the text of the challenged law itself, including by considering the law's interaction with other regulatory measures).

10 For a discussion of one increasingly popular brand of state law that raises discrimination issues, see Andrew T. Hayashi & Richard M. Hynes, *Protectionist Property Taxes*, 106 IOWA L. REV. 1091, 1094–95 (2021) (addressing rising state and local efforts to target nonresidents with property taxation; concluding that "facially discriminatory property taxes are almost certainly unconstitutional," but that "facially neutral taxes on . . . second homes and vacant properties[ ] are likely to survive constitutional scrutiny" (internal footnote omitted)). For a more general discussion of discrimination in the context of state and local taxation, see *infra* Chapter 21.

11 Donald H. Regan, *The Supreme Court and State Protectionism: Making Sense of the Dormant Commerce Clause*, 84 MICH. L. REV. 1091, 1199, 1270 (1986) (noting that "[e]xplicit export embargoes . . . are virtually *per se* illegal").

12 262 U.S. 553 (1923).

its inhabitants in the enjoyment of its natural advantages."[13] The majority, however, offered powerful reasons to the contrary, emphasizing that, were such a measure to be upheld, "embargo may be retaliated by embargo, and commerce will be halted at state lines."[14] In more recent cases, the Court has drawn on this same principle to block state efforts to hoard local minnows,[15] electricity,[16] and water.[17] The Court also has held that a state may not overtly reserve for its own residents either services supplied by private firms within the state,[18] or valuable investment or other business opportunities.[19]

---

[13] *Id.* at 602 (Holmes, J., dissenting).

[14] *Id.* at 599 (majority opinion). For a doctrinal precursor, see *West v. Kansas Natural Gas Co.*, 221 U.S. 229 (1911) (invalidating an Oklahoma pipeline regulation that effectively barred exportation of locally produced natural gas).

[15] Hughes v. Oklahoma, 441 U.S. 322, 337–38 (1979) (stating that "[f]ar from choosing the least discriminatory alternative, Oklahoma has chosen to 'conserve' its minnows in the way that most overtly discriminates against interstate commerce").

[16] New Eng. Power Co. v. New Hampshire, 455 U.S. 331, 339 (1982) (holding that "the [New Hampshire] Commission's 'exportation ban' places direct and substantial burdens on transactions in interstate commerce" and that those "burdens cannot be squared with the Commerce Clause when they serve only to advance simple economic protectionism" (internal quotations omitted)).

[17] Sporhase v. Nebraska *ex rel.* Douglas, 458 U.S. 941, 943 (1982) (striking down a Nebraska law that restricted "the withdrawal of ground water from any well within Nebraska intended for use in an adjoining State").

[18] Camps Newfound/Owatonna, Inc. v. Town of Harrison, 520 U.S. 564 (1997) (invalidating a real-estate and personal property tax break made available to income-tax-exempt charitable entities, here privately operated summer camps, only so long as they directed most of their work toward state residents); *see also* Ky. Power v. Huelsmann, 352 F. Supp. 2d 777, 785 (E.D. Ky. 2005) (striking down as facially discriminatory a Kentucky law that required utility companies to take certain steps during emergency shortages because, "[a]lthough [the law] does not use the phrase 'Kentucky customers' to describe the class of customers favored by the statute, it is undisputed that only Kentucky customers can benefit from the curtailment priority set forth therein").

[19] *See* Lewis v. BT Inv. Managers, Inc., 447 U.S. 27 (1980) (invalidating a state law that facially discriminated against out-of-state firms with regard to opportunities to acquire or operate local investment-advisory and trust-related businesses). One important set of laws that can be seen as fitting this mold involves those that flatly discriminate between residents and nonresidents, or discriminate based on the duration of one's residency, with regard to conducting a business in the state. This form of discrimination has been repudiated by the Court, particularly in a leading decision on state alcohol regulation. *See infra* Section 20.F (discussing the *Tennessee Wine & Spirits* case). Even so, some states have tried—thus far in all but one case without success—to sidestep challenges to such discriminatory restrictions imposed with regard to engaging in now-burgeoning marijuana-related commercial activities. *See, e.g.*, NPG, LLC v. City of Portland, No. 2:20–CV–00208–NT, 2020 WL 4741913, at *9 (D. Me. Aug. 14, 2020) (preliminarily enjoining enforcement of Portland, Maine's cannabis-related residency requirements over the city's argument that anti-discrimination analysis should not apply to resident-preferred cannabis licensing because it "operates in a unique dimension" as a federally classified Schedule I drug); Lowe v. City of Detroit, 544 F. Supp. 3d 804, 816 (E.D. Mich. 2021) (finding a substantial likelihood of success of a plaintiff's challenge, on dormant Commerce Clause grounds, to an "Ordinance's facial favoritism toward Detroit residents of at

2. Facially Discriminatory Import Restrictions

The flip side of the facially discriminatory export restriction is the no-less-frowned-upon facially discriminatory state import restriction. In *Welton v. Missouri*,[20] for example, the Court invalidated a licensing tax levied only on peddlers of goods made in other states. Since then, the Court has consistently adhered to *Welton*'s instruction that a state may not "discriminat[e] in favor of goods, wares, and merchandise which are the growth, product, or manufacture of the State, and against those which are the growth, product, or manufacture of other states or countries."[21] In addition,

least 10–15 years" in the issuance of licenses for retailing, growing, processing and otherwise dealing with marijuana in commercial operations); Toigo v. Dep't of Health & Sr. Servs., 549 F. Supp. 3d 985, 990–94 (W.D. Mo. 2021) (granting a preliminary injunction that barred enforcement of one-year-residency rule regarding medical-marijuana-related businesses). The outlier case is *Original Investments, LLC v. Oklahoma*, 542 F. Supp. 3d 1230, 1234, 1237 (W.D. Okla. 2021) (describing the attack on a state law imposing residency requirements for issuance of cannabis licenses as "not frivolous," but declining to address the merits of the challenger's claim on the theory that it was foreclosed by the equitable "unclean hands" doctrine due to federal restrictions on cannabis production and sales). In *Northeast Patients Group v. Maine. Dep't of Admin. & Fin. Servs.*, 554 F. Supp. 3d 117 (D. Me. 2021), however, the court both noted and declined to follow the ruling in *Original Investments. See id.* at 184 n.10. For an appraisal of the intersection of cannabis regulation and the dormant Commerce Clause, see Robert A. Mikos, *Interstate Commerce in Cannabis*, 101 B.U. L. REV. 857 (2021). For other judicial repudiations of residency-related state laws, see *Cooper v. McBeath*, 11 F.3d 547, 554 (5th Cir. 1994) (preliminarily enjoining a requirement that corporate applicants for licenses to serve certain alcoholic beverages be majority-owned by state residents; reasoning that "[i]n this age of split-second communications by means of computer networks . . . and other technological marvels," if "Texas desires to scrutinize its applicants thoroughly, as is its right, it can devise nondiscriminatory means short of saddling applicants with the 'burden' of residing in Texas"); *Nationwide Biweekly Admin., Inc. v. Owen*, 873 F.3d 716, 736–37 (9th Cir. 2017) (invalidating a law that required an out-of-state company to incorporate in California in order to provide "prorating" services to California residents). For additional judicial work with the exportation-ban limit and associated principles, see *Jamgotchian v. Ind. Horse Racing Comm'n*, No. 1:16-cv-2344-WTL-TAB, 2017 WL 4168488 (S.D. Ind. 2017) (striking down as facially discriminatory an Indiana law that generally prohibited certain horses purchased in Indiana from racing outside Indiana for sixty days, while allowing the same horses to race in the state during that time period); *Mitchell v. Atkins*, 483 F. Supp. 3d 985, 998 (W.D. Wash. 2020) (applying *Pike* balancing analysis, *see infra* Chapter 18, in upholding a Washington law that prohibited in-person semiautomatic assault rifle sales to nonresidents; reasoning that the law did not discriminate against interstate commerce because it burdened the state's own economy—"the very opposite of economic protectionism"—and Washington's interest in safety outweighed any potential burden on interstate commerce).

[20] 91 U.S. 275 (1875).

[21] *Id.* at 277. *See, e.g.*, Wyoming v. Oklahoma, 502 U.S. 437, 440–41 (1992) (invalidating an Oklahoma law that "require[d] Oklahoma coal-fired electric generating plants producing power for sale in Oklahoma to burn a mixture of coal containing at least 10% Oklahoma-mined coal" for being facially discriminatory); New Energy Co. of Ind. v. Limbach, 486 U.S. 269, 271 (1988) (striking down an Ohio law "that award[ed] a tax credit against the Ohio motor vehicle fuel sales tax for each gallon of ethanol sold (as a component of gasohol) by fuel dealers, but only if the ethanol is produced in Ohio or in a State that grants similar tax advantages to ethanol

the Justices have recognized that this principle applies to restrictions on the importation of out-of-state services just as surely as it applies to restrictions on the importation of out-of-state goods.[22]

---

produced in Ohio"); Bacchus Imports, Ltd. v. Dias, 468 U.S. 263, 271 (1984) (deeming unconstitutional a Hawaii tax statute that discriminated against alcoholic beverages manufactured outside the state); Polar Ice Cream & Creamery Co. v. Andrews, 375 U.S. 361 (1964) (invalidating a set of Florida regulations that generally required milk distributors in the Pensacola area to purchase all Class I milk from local producers unless local production became inadequate); Hale v. Bimco Trading, Inc., 306 U.S. 375 (1939) (invalidating a Florida law that imposed significant inspection charges on foreign, but not local, cement). Many lower-court cases have applied this same rule. *See, e.g.*, Piazza's Seafood World, LLC v. Odom, 448 F.3d 744, 750 (5th Cir. 2006) (holding that "discrimination appears on the face of the statute: the Catfish Statute treats domestic catfish differently from foreign catfish to the benefit of the former and the detriment of the latter"); Prof'l Dog Breeders Advisory Council v. Wolff, No. 1:CV–09–0258, 2009 WL 2948527, at *6 (M.D. Pa. Sept. 11, 2009) (holding that "[b]ecause the Dog Law explicitly states that a $300 licensing fee will be imposed on out-of-state dog dealers with absolutely no indication that any sort of similar fee will be imposed on in-state dog dealers, the law is facially discriminatory"); Wal-Mart P.R., Inc. v. Zaragoza-Gomez, 834 F.3d 110, 126 (1st Cir. 2016) (striking down as facially discriminatory a Puerto Rico "expenses and tangible-property" tax designed to "prevent multistate corporations doing business in Puerto Rico from shifting profits off the island by purchasing goods and services from related mainland entities"). In recent years, courts have been especially active in invalidating facially discriminatory laws that disadvantage out-of-state liquor producers and distributors. *E.g.*, Tennessee Wine & Spirits Retailers Ass'n v. Thomas, 139 S. Ct. 2449, 2456 (2019) (striking down a Tennessee statutory durational-residency requirement for retail alcohol licenses as facially discriminatory); Granholm v. Heald, 544 U.S. 460 (2005) (striking down Michigan and New York regulatory schemes that allowed in-state wineries, but not out-of-state wineries, to ship alcohol directly to consumers); Freeman v. Corzine, 629 F.3d 146, 157–60 (3d Cir. 2010) (striking down a New Jersey law that, among other things, forbade out-of-state wineries to sell directly to consumers and imposed permit requirements on those seeking to import out-of-state wine as facially discriminatory); *see also* Anheuser-Busch v. Schnorf, 738 F. Supp. 2d 793 (N.D. Ill. 2010) (striking down a state licensure scheme for beer distribution as facially discriminatory). Notably, state reciprocity provisions do not save import-impeding state laws from invalidation under the anti-discrimination principle. The point is illustrated by *Great Atlantic & Pacific Tea Co. v. Cottrell*, 424 U.S. 366 (1976), in which the challenged measure stipulated that milk from other states could come into Mississippi, but only if those states authorized the importation of Mississippi milk. The Court invalidated this inhibition on importation from non-reciprocating states because "Mississippi may not use the threat of economic isolation as a weapon to force sister states to enter into even a desirable reciprocity agreement." *Id.* at 379. In effect, the Court declared that the proper response to import-impeding neighbors was to initiate legal actions under the dormant Commerce Clause—not to engage in just the sort of legislative retaliation that the Framers had found intolerable. *Accord Sporhase*, 458 U.S. at 958 n.18 (1982) (asserting that a "reciprocity requirement cannot, of course, be justified as a response to another State's unreasonable burden on commerce").

[22] *E.g.*, Boston Stock Exch. v. State Tax Comm'n, 429 U.S. 318 (1977) (invalidating an added increment of tax imposed on stock transfers unless effected through local brokers; noting that "[n]o State, consistent with the Commerce Clause, may 'impose a tax which discriminates against interstate commerce . . . by providing a direct commercial advantage to local business' " (quoting Nw. Cement Co. v. Minnesota, 358 U.S. 450, 458 (1959))). Lower courts, not surprisingly, have applied the same principle. *See, e.g.*, Tri-M Group, LLC v. Sharp, 638 F.3d 406, 413 (3d Cir. 2011) (striking down as facially discriminatory a Delaware regulation allowing in-state contractors to pay a lower "apprentice wage" than out-of-state contractors); Am. Trucking Ass'ns v. Whitman, 437 F.3d 313 (3d Cir. 2006) (striking down a New Jersey

3. Facial Discrimination and In-State Processing Requirements

A recurring form of regulation that runs afoul of the ban on facially discriminatory laws involves "in-state processing requirements."[23] In *Dean Milk Co. v. Madison*,[24] for example, the Court struck down a Madison, Wisconsin, ordinance that, in a purported effort to facilitate effective inspections to protect the health of local milk drinkers, required all milk sold in the city to be bottled within five miles of its central square. According to the Court, because the law erected "an economic barrier protecting a major local industry against competition from without the state," it could not stand as long as the Court could identify "reasonable nondiscriminatory alternatives, adequate to conserve legitimate local interests."[25] The Justices also found that such reasonable alternatives did exist because, for example, the city could send its inspectors to more distant bottling facilities and then charge their operators for any extra travel costs. Having concluded for this reason that Madison's rule was not "essential" to the protection of local milk drinkers' wellbeing, the Court declared it unconstitutional.[26]

Dean Milk is one of many cases in which courts have invalidated state laws because "they bar the import of the processing service" or (to put much the same point another way) "hoard a local resource . . . for the benefit of local businesses that treat it."[27] According to the

---

regulation requiring certain trucks to avoid local roads and congested areas as facially discriminatory because the regulation favored in-state businesses over out-of-state businesses); Daghlian v. DeVry Univ., Inc., 582 F. Supp. 2d 1231, 1242–43 (C.D. Cal. 2007) (striking down a California higher education law that "mandate[d] that postsecondary educational institutions that have not obtained [Western Association of Schools and Colleges] accreditation comply with several student protection provisions, but exempt[ed] WASC-accredited schools from such requirements entirely" because "DeVry would have had to operate its California campuses effectively as separate California-based subsidiaries"; reasoning, in light of Supreme Court precedent, that states cannot require out-of-state entities "to become residents in order to compete on equal terms" (quoting *Granholm*, 544 U.S. at 475) (alterations omitted)). At least some state laws that involve economic favoritism tied to the fact or duration of residency can be seen as limiting the importation of valuable services. For a listing of some such cases, see *supra* note 21.

23 South-Central Timber Dev., Inc. v. Wunnicke, 467 U.S. 82, 93 n.8 (1984).

24 340 U.S. 349 (1951).

25 *Id.* at 354.

26 *Id.* at 356. Notably, the Court in *Dean Milk* deemed the measure subject to exacting dormant Commerce Clause scrutiny even though it discriminated against *non-local*—as opposed to *out-of-state*—commerce. *See id.* at 354 n.4 (noting that it was "immaterial that Wisconsin milk from outside the Madison area is subjected to the same proscription as that moving in interstate commerce"). For a further discussion of this point, see *infra* notes 80–83 and accompanying text.

27 *Carbone*, 511 U.S. at 392. *See South-Central Timber Dev.*, 467 U.S. 82 (invalidating a regulation requiring Alaskan timber to be processed within the state prior to export); Pike v. Bruce Church, Inc., 397 U.S. 137 (1970) (invalidating a state

Court's most recent decisions, such overt discrimination renders in-state processing mandates subject to the "rule of virtual *per se* invalidity" laid down in *City of Philadelphia*.[28] Those decisions also establish that this strong presumption of unconstitutionality applies whether the challenged law favors a group of local processors, as in

law because it required local packaging of Arizona-grown cantaloupes prior to removing them from the state); Toomer v. Witsell, 334 U.S. 385, 403–06 (1948) (invalidating a South Carolina law requiring the unloading, packing, and stamping of shrimp caught within the state prior to export); Foster-Fountain Packing Co. v. Haydel, 278 U.S. 1 (1928) (highlighting constitutional defects in a Louisiana statute that prohibited the export of shrimp unless heads and hulls were removed within the state); Johnson v. Haydel, 278 U.S. 16 (1928) (reaching the same conclusion with respect to a similar Louisiana oyster processing law); Minnesota v. Barber, 136 U.S. 313 (1890) (invalidating a Minnesota law requiring that all animals to be sold as meat in-state, regardless of origin, be inspected in-state prior to being slaughtered). The reasoning used in *Dean Milk* also might have a bearing in cases involving state laws that prevent car manufacturers from selling their products to consumers without going through the intermediary of a local dealership. For example, in *Ford Motor Co. v. Texas Department of Transportation*, 264 F.3d 493 (5th Cir. 2001), Ford challenged a state law that prohibited car manufacturers from (1) owning an interest in a dealership, (2) operating a dealership, or (3) acting in the capacity of a dealer. When Ford attempted to sell cars in Texas through its online "Showroom," the Texas Department of Transportation prohibited the action, noting that it violated the state law that prohibited manufacturers from acting in the capacity of a dealer. *Id.* at 499. Ford responded by challenging the state law on the ground that it "discriminate[d] against out-of-state interests" and "unconstitutionally burden[ed] the flow of interstate commerce." *Id.* The Fifth Circuit, however, rejected Ford's challenge, holding that the state had a legitimate interest in "prevent[ing] vertically integrated companies from taking advantage of their incongruous market position" and that no discrimination inhered in the law because it took no account of the domicile of the manufacturer. *Id.* at 503. *See also* Int'l Truck & Engine Corp. v. Bray, 372 F.3d 717, 725 (5th Cir. 2004), *opinion corrected on denial of reh'g*, 380 F.3d 231 (5th Cir. 2004) (upholding a provision of the Texas Occupations Code that barred truck manufacturers from operating as dealers of used trucks). Despite the Fifth Circuit's rejection of Ford's dormant Commerce Clause challenge, Tesla has challenged similar laws under the dormant Commerce Clause, emphasizing that a key component of its business model involves selling cars directly to consumers. *See* Tesla Motors, Inc. v. Johnson, No. 1:16–CV–1158, 2017 WL 11500988, at *1 (W.D. Mich. Dec. 11, 2017); Cynthia Barmore, *Tesla Unplugged: Automobile Franchise Laws and the Threat to the Electric Vehicle Market*, 18 VA. J.L. & TECH. 185, 192 (2014) (noting that Tesla CEO Elon Musk has characterized the laws as a "perversion of democracy"); *see also* Daniel A. Crane, *Tesla, Dealer Franchise Laws, and the Politics of Crony Capitalism*, 101 IOWA L. REV. 573, 576 (2016). The impact of the Court's local-processing cases in this context is uncertain. Perhaps, as the Fifth Circuit has indicated, laws that target the vertical integration of manufacturing and retail-sales operations will survive constitutional challenge. But to the extent that a state requires (or favors) the sale of products at sites physically situated within its borders and/or operated by businesses with in-state ties, the analytical framework in *Dean Milk* may well come into play. *See* Rhode v. Becerra, 445 F. Supp. 3d 902, 950 (S.D. Cal. 2020) (finding a likely dormant Commerce Clause violation in a California law that required gun-ammunition sales by any seller to be funneled through a California resident vendor licensed to sell ammunition; reasoning that "[w]hat is important is that California's resident businesses are the only businesses that may sell directly to ammunition consumers" and that "[s]ales of any quantity, by all other sellers, anywhere else in the country, must be funneled through a California resident vendor licensed to sell ammunition"), *stay granted*, 2020 WL 9938296 (9th Cir. May 14, 2020).

[28] *South-Central Timber Dev. Inc.*, 467 U.S. at 100; *see also Carbone*, 511 U.S. at 392. *See generally infra* Section 17.D.

Dean Milk, or only a single local processor that is given a monopoly position. The latter situation arose in *C & A Carbone, Inc. v. Town of Clarkstown*,[29] which concerned a rule that required delivery of all solid waste within a town to a specific privately owned "transfer station." In the view of several Justices, because a single firm could exert less influence in favor of adopting protectionist legislation than a cabal of local operators, it made sense to reduce the intensity of judicial review when the state gives a single in-state processor monopoly power.[30] The majority disagreed, however, suggesting instead that the discrimination at issue in *Carbone* was even "more acute" than that involved in *Dean Milk*. In *Dean Milk*, after all, "[a]n out-of-state pasteurizer who wanted access to that market might have built a pasteurizing facility within the radius."[31] Here, by contrast, the ordinance "squelches competition in the waste-processing service altogether, leaving no room for investment from outside."[32]

The majority in *Carbone* was also unimpressed by the town's proffered justification for its forced-use rule. According to local officials, granting a monopoly to the transfer station served the purpose of ensuring its financial viability. As in *Dean Milk*, however, the majority determined that a less restrictive alternative was available to achieve this governmental goal. The town, the Court reasoned, could ensure the facility's financial stability by subsidizing its operations, as opposed to forcing all local residents to forgo all business dealings with all out-of-state waste handlers.[33]

B. FACIALLY NEUTRAL LAWS AND DISCRIMINATORY EFFECTS

Before developing its modern *Pike* balancing formula,[34] the Court dealt with problematic state laws unmarked by facial discrimination through use of analogistic reasoning. In effect, the Court declared that some facially neutral laws, although not overtly discriminatory, so closely parallel statutes that concededly violate the Constitution as to warrant an equally strong judicial rebuke. The leading decision in this line of cases is *Baldwin v. G.A.F. Seelig, Inc.*[35]

---

29 511 U.S. 383 (1994).

30 *Id.* at 411, 416–17 (Souter, J., joined by Rehnquist, C.J., and Blackmun, J., dissenting).

31 *Id.* at 392 (majority opinion).

32 *Id.*

33 *Id.* at 393–94.

34 *See infra* Chapter 18.

35 294 U.S. 511 (1935).

Baldwin arose after New York established minimum price levels for milk sold by in-state dairy farmers. To help ensure this program's success, the state also prohibited in-state retail sales of milk produced in other states unless the producer had been paid at least the same minimum price made applicable to sales by New York farmers. Even though this feature of the program gave the minimum price rule a uniform operation, a unanimous Court found it unconstitutional. The Court's reasoning was multifaceted. At its core, however, lay the thought that the law operated like a protective tariff in that it deprived efficient out-of-state sellers of the opportunity to undersell in-state competitors.[36] The analogy constructed by the Court was imperfect. After all, the law challenged in *Baldwin*—unlike a true tariff—was not a tax, did not generate funds for the state treasury, provided much-desired price increases for some nonresident dairy farmers, and (most important) did not discriminate on its face against anyone. It was precisely this set of factual differences, however, that revealed the potency of the Court's it's-enough-like-a-tariff analogistic-reasoning approach. According to the Court, because the state had "set up what is equivalent to a rampart of customs duties," the law was unconstitutional despite its seemingly neutral character.[37]

Just two years after *Baldwin*, the Court signaled that its *de facto* tariff rationale had important limits. In *Henneford v. Silas Mason Co.*,[38] the Court faced the argument that compensatory use taxes implicate the tariff-likeness principle first recognized in *Baldwin*. (A compensatory use tax applies to the in-state "use" of goods purchased from an out-of-state seller, thus eliminating any savings the user would have realized by avoiding, via the out-of-state purchase, the state's own sales-tax obligation.) In finding Washington's compensatory use tax constitutional in *Silas Mason*, Justice Cardozo reasoned for the majority that the incidence of the regulation in *Baldwin* fell on out-of-state sales, whereas the incidence of the use tax fell on the in-state use of goods.[39] This distinction seems questionable, however, because the law in each case targeted goods brought into the state after being purchased elsewhere. The Court also asserted that in *Silas Mason*, unlike in *Baldwin*, "[e]quality is the theme" of the statute.[40] Yet this attempted distinction also had something of a hollow ring because the "theme" of the same-

---

36 *Id.* at 521.

37 *Id.* at 527.

38 300 U.S. 577 (1937).

39 This aspect of the Court's reasoning in *Baldwin* and *Silas Mason* also raises questions about how far states may go in adopting regulations with "extraterritorial" effects. For a discussion of that topic, see *infra* Section 20.F.

40 *Silas Mason*, 300 U.S. at 583.

minimum-price law invalided in *Baldwin* seemed to be "equality" as well.[41] This is not to say that the outcome of *Silas Mason* was indefensible, however, because another, stronger distinction supported the underlying result: The compensatory use tax—unlike the minimum milk-price law—did not inhibit out-of-state sellers' ability to engage in efficiency-based price competition but rather functioned to remove an artificial state-created disadvantage that local sellers alone otherwise would have had to endure. For this reason—far more so than for the reasons most emphasized by Justice Cardozo—the compensatory use tax could be plausibly defended as not implicating *Baldwin*'s *de facto* tariff principle.

The Court in *Baldwin* never suggested that analogy-based discriminatory-effects reasoning properly extends only to tariff-like state measures, and it later applied much the same type of reasoning to a very different type of law in *H.P. Hood & Sons v. DuMond*.[42] At issue in *Hood* was an order by the New York Commissioner of Agriculture and Markets that blocked the opening of a milk-receiving station near the city of Troy, New York. The Commissioner denied the permit under a state law that prohibited the licensing of any station that would "tend to a destructive competition in a market already adequately served" or otherwise harm "the public interest."[43] In the view of the Supreme Court, however, the license denial amounted to an unconstitutional hoarding of the state's own resources because the Commissioners had acted in response to concerns that the proposed station would divert milk away from purchasers in the Troy area to purchasers in Boston, Massachusetts.

The dissenters found fault with the majority's readiness to condemn the state's action as inherently protectionist. Focusing on the facial neutrality of the statute (rather than on the particular agency action taken pursuant to it), Justice Black reasoned that state regulators would be equally bound to protect milk buyers in Boston or other areas outside New York if a future proposed receiving station threatened to divert milk away from out-of-state purchasers.[44] Without saying as much, the majority maintained that the New York law was highly unlikely to produce such an evenhanded result. And why was that? Because a New York law administered by a New York Commissioner would not reliably protect Massachusetts milk buyers against competing demands made by New York milk consumers who vote in New York elections.[45] In short, the Court concluded, the

---

41 *See infra* notes 36–37 and accompanying text.

42 336 U.S. 525 (1949).

43 *Id.* at 527 n.3.

44 *Id.* at 545–63 (Black, J., dissenting).

45 *See* Vincent Blasi, *Constitutional Limitations on the Power of States to Regulate the Movement of Goods in Interstate Commerce*, *in* 1 COURTS AND FREE MARKETS:

facially neutral licensing law, as applied in *Hood*, was so likely in effect to operate the same way as a facially discriminatory hoarding measure that it could not withstand dormant Commerce Clause attack.

Following the pattern of *Baldwin* and *Silas Mason*, however, the Court in *Hood* recognized limits on the *de facto* discrimination principle of that case. In particular, the Court there reaffirmed its earlier decision in *Milk Control Board v. Eisenberg Farm Products*,[46] which had upheld the application of a Pennsylvania minimum price rule to sales of milk made by Pennsylvania dairy farmers for shipment outside the state. Challengers of the law argued that it unconstitutionally disrupted local producers' abilities to compete successfully in out-of-state markets. The Court in *Eisenberg* however, found the argument unavailing, distinguishing *Baldwin* (which had also concerned a minimum price law) on the ground that the challenge in that earlier case had focused on a state law as applied to out-of-state, rather than in-state, behavior.[47]

There is reason to question the outcome in *Eisenberg* (and, by extension, the Court's reaffirmation of it in *Hood*). After all, one reason to promote a national common market is to protect local buyers (here, local buyers in states other than Pennsylvania) by facilitating price competition from out-of-state products; yet the rule challenged in *Eisenberg* plainly impeded out-of-state price competition between Pennsylvanian and non-Pennsylvanian milk producers by forcing Pennsylvania-based exporters to ratchet up their prices in response to the state's specified producer-price minimum.[48] No less important, from a policy perspective, a troubling asymmetry seems to mark *Baldwin* and *Eisenberg*, particularly in light of the Court's more recent declaration that state authorities "may not insist that producers *or consumers* in other States

PERSPECTIVE FROM THE UNITED STATES AND EUROPE 195 (T. Sandalow & E. Stein eds., 1982) (noting the possibility that "state laws are to be invalidated if they grant enforcement officials too much discretion to make judgments that might be influenced by hostility to out-of-state interests").

46 306 U.S. 346 (1939).

47 *Id.* at 353.

48 For similar reasons, one might question the correctness of *Parker v. Brown*, 317 U.S. 341 (1943), in which the Court upheld a similar effort by California to elevate the price of locally grown raisins and thus "prevent the demoralization of the industry." *Id.* at 367. Professor Tribe has suggested that the ruling in *Parker* is best explained as reflecting the Court's "substantial deference to *congressional* agricultural policy." LAURENCE H. TRIBE, AMERICAN CONSTITUTIONAL LAW § 6–30, at 1196 n.13 (3d ed. 2000) (emphasis added). There was no finding in *Parker*, however, that Congress had specifically consented to enactment of the California price-support program, and it is open to question whether the sort of "quasi-consent" logic extracted from the case by Professor Tribe would carry water today in light of now-operative clear-statement requirements. *See infra* Section 20.B (discussing the Court's rejection of a similar argument in *Maine v. Taylor*).

surrender whatever competitive advantages they may possess."[49] On the other hand, it is a stretch to view *Eisenberg* as a hoarding case in the mold of *Hood*. From all appearances, Pennsylvania was not trying to keep milk near at hand for the benefit of local consumers, who in fact were disadvantaged by the law insofar as it operated to elevate retail prices.[50] Rather, the law seemed genuinely to be aimed at fostering stability for a fragile industry, and—as the Court concluded—there was plausibility in the state's assertion that "uniform operation of the statute locally would be crippled and might be impracticable" if an exemption for out-of-state sales were put in place.[51] In addition, the law disadvantaged some Pennsylvania milk producers and distributors (namely, those in the out-of-state export business) but not others (namely, those not in that business), and both of these in-state groups enjoyed representation in the Pennsylvania state legislature where they were free to duke things out on an equal footing. In short, *Eisenberg* was a tricky case. It is therefore not surprising that it came on the heels of earlier decisions in which the Court found, albeit under the now-abandoned direct-

---

[49] Brown-Forman Distillers Corp. v. New York State Liquor Auth., 476 U.S. 573, 580 (1986) (emphasis added). In particular, the Pennsylvania law might (for example) have deprived prospective out-of-state buyers of the chance to capitalize on efficiencies they had achieved by purchasing large quantities of milk from Pennsylvania producers, who were barred from selling at volume-discount prices by the minimum-price law.

[50] The absence of a hoarding motive, standing alone, would have been determinative for Professor Regan. *See* Regan, *supra* note 11, at 1259 (arguing that the key to *Eisenberg* is that even though the minimum-price rule helped "Pennsylvania milk producers at the expense of out-of-state distributors and consumers," it did not protect Pennsylvania producers vis-à-vis non-Pennsylvania producers or Pennsylvania distributors and consumers vis-à-vis their counterparts in other states).

[51] *Eisenberg*, 306 U.S. at 353. In particular, state legislators had good reason to worry that the entire system of price supports would come to ruin as buyers for in-state resale pretended to purchase milk for out-of-state resale so that they could pay sub-minimum prices, especially given the fact that only "a small fraction of the milk produced . . . in Pennsylvania [was actually] shipped out of the Commonwealth." *Id.* Professor Tribe has suggested that the presence of a predominance of local buyers for the price-regulated product may have been the decisive factor in the case, perhaps because local consumers would logically oppose a law that increased prices for their milk unless powerful justifications for its enactment existed. TRIBE, *supra* note 48, § 6–8, at 1074–75. *But see* Regan, *supra* note 11, at 1258 (questioning the significance of this fact). In this same vein, Professors Nowak and Rotunda have suggested that the Court properly upheld the law challenged in *Eisenberg* because it "involved an inner political check." JOHN E. NOWAK & RONALD D. ROTUNDA, CONSTITUTIONAL LAW § 8.9 (6th ed. 2000). These commentators fail to note, however, that a similar consumer-based "check" on enactment of a minimum-price law did not save its application to out-of-state sellers in *Baldwin*. Moreover, Professors Nowak and Rotunda question the Court's seeming reliance on the large-local-consumer-base rationale in *Eisenberg* on the ground that the preponderance of local sales may well have resulted from the minimum-price law itself. *Id.* Finally, a rationale that focuses on the small amount of exported milk stands in tension with *Parker*, *see supra* note 48, because there the Court validated price-support rules for raisins imposed by the state even though the vast majority of consumers of this product were located outside its borders.

indirect test, that similar minimum-pricing rules did violate the dormancy doctrine.[52]

As the preceding discussion has shown, the Court has not restricted its application of strict scrutiny under the dormant Commerce Clause to cases that involve facially discriminatory laws. *Baldwin* and *Hood*, to be sure, are old cases, but more modern decisions continue to indicate that an ill-defined set of facially neutral state laws can sometimes have enough of a "discriminatory effect" to trigger scrutiny more exacting than deferential "*Pike* balancing" review.[53]

C. FACIALLY NEUTRAL LAWS AND DISCRIMINATORY PURPOSES

Another branch of dormant Commerce Clause doctrine suggests that state legislatures, at least as a rule, may not enact facially neutral laws if they do so because of a "discriminatory purpose."[54] This line of doctrine, like its "discriminatory effects" counterpart, is murky: In some cases, the Court has recognized but not applied the principle,[55] and in other cases (including *Baldwin*) the Court has

---

[52] *See* Lemke v. Farmers' Grain Co., 258 U.S. 50 (1922); Shafer v. Farmers' Grain Co., 268 U.S. 189, 201 (1925) (striking down a North Dakota law that regulated prices paid by out-of-state buyers of local grain because the regulations "directly interfere[d] with and burden[ed] interstate commerce").

[53] Minnesota v. Clover Leaf Creamery Co., 449 U.S. 456, 471 n.15 (1981). The leading case is *Hunt v. Washington State Apple Advertising Comm'n*, 432 U.S. 333 (1977), in which the Court found that the "practical effect" of a facially neutral law gave rise to the sort of "discrimination" that placed "the burden . . . on the State to justify [the law]." *Id.* at 353. A variety of lower-court cases seem to take much the same approach. *See* Island Silver & Spice, Inc. v. Islamorada, 542 F.3d 844 (11th Cir. 2008) (invalidating an ordinance that had the practical effect of preventing interstate chain retailers from establishing locations in the township); Family Winemakers of Cal. v. Jenkins, 592 F.3d 1, 11 (1st Cir. 2010) (striking down a Massachusetts law that conferred a "clear competitive advantage to 'small' wineries, which include all Massachusetts's wineries, and create[d] a comparative disadvantage for 'large' wineries, none of which are in Massachusetts"); Cherry Hill Vineyards, LLC v. Lilly, 553 F.3d 423, 423, 433 (6th Cir. 2008) (striking down a set of Kentucky restrictions that made it "financially infeasible for out-of-state wineries to sell directly to Kentucky residents"); Walgreen Co. v. Rullan, 405 F.3d 50, 56 (1st Cir. 2005) (invalidating a facially neutral Puerto Rican law requiring pharmacies seeking to open or relocate in Puerto Rico to apply for a certificate of necessity and convenience because the law created a competitive advantage for local pharmacies and had "discriminatory effects" because "[w]hile the Secretary has rejected virtually no unopposed applications, twenty-three percent of opposed applications have been denied" (internal footnote omitted)); *see also Anheuser-Busch, Inc.*, 738 F. Supp. at 805 (applying strict scrutiny in reviewing an Illinois alcoholic beverage distribution system because "[t]he bottom line is that in-state brewers are permitted to perform the distribution function in Illinois, while out-of-state brewers are precluded from doing the same").

[54] *Clover Leaf Creamery*, 449 U.S. at 471 n.15.

[55] *See, e.g.*, *Wash. State Apple Advert. Comm'n*, 432 U.S. at 352–53 (noting the challenger's assertion of a purpose-based argument but deciding the case on effect-based grounds instead); *see also* Caleb Nelson, *Judicial Review of Legislative Purpose*, 83 N.Y.U. L. REV. 1784, 1848–49 (2008) (stating that "[w]hile the Court occasionally

adverted to problematic state purposes only in combination with condemnatory references to a law's discriminatory effects.[56] Even so, it remains true that concerns about discriminatory purpose can sometimes be enough to render facially neutral laws subject to a heightened form of dormant Commerce Clause scrutiny.

1. Identifying Discriminatory Purposes

Sometimes it will be clear that the legislative motive underlying a state law qualifies as impermissibly discriminatory: Any court, for example, would look hard at a facially nondiscriminatory statute preceded by a preamble that proclaims a purpose of "promoting this truly awesome State's economy by shutting down commerce coming from other (far less awesome) states."[57] For much the same reason, tax breaks specifically designed to promote local industries, even if superficially neutral, may well trigger the same judicial response.[58] Other cases, however, pose trickier problems. For example, in *Cities Service Gas Co. v. Peerless Oil & Gas Co.*,[59] the state fixed a minimum price for the sale of natural gas extracted in the state to curtail demand, thus "preventing rapid and uneconomic dissipation of one of

---

held even nondiscriminatory statutes unconstitutional because of their effects on interstate commerce, most laws that the Court struck down under this prong of its test favored in-state interests at the expense of out-of-state interests and probably were designed to do so"; adding that Professor Regan "has persuasively described the Court's [effects-based] test as a means of rooting out state laws that were enacted for protectionist reasons" but also observing that "the Court did not justify its approach in these terms"). For a lower court case that scuttled a law based on perceived problems with its "intended effect," see *Alliance for Clean Coal v. Miller*, 44 F.3d 591, 595–96 (7th Cir. 1995) (striking down an Illinois law for having both the purpose and effect of discriminating against coal produced in other states, where the law required that "commissioners take account of the effect on the local coal industry when considering compliance plans" designed to meet environmental restrictions). *See also* Family of Winemakers of California v. Jenkins, 592 F.3d 1 (1st Cir. 2010) (determining that a Massachusetts law was discriminatory in both effect and purpose); Jones v. Gale, 470 F.3d 1261 (8th Cir. 2006) (invalidating a Nebraska law prohibiting farming or ranching by all but a few specific categories of corporations because the law was facially discriminatory and had a discriminatory purpose).

[56] *Baldwin*, 294 U.S. at 522 (noting the need for judicial intervention "when the avowed purpose of the obstruction, as well as its necessary tendency, is to suppress or mitigate the consequences of competition between the states").

[57] The statute in *Hood* did not include such a preamble, but the Court invalidated the state action in that case in part because it detected a purpose that might be set forth in closely analogous terms. *See Hood*, 336 U.S. at 532; *see also Bimco Trading*, 306 U.S. at 380 (noting that the state's asserted interest of neutralizing "the competitive effect of foreign cement in the Florida market" amounts to "a candid admission that the very purpose of the statute is to keep out foreign goods").

[58] *See Bacchus Imports*, 468 U.S. at 265, 271 (invalidating a wholesaling tax preference afforded to okolehao, "a brandy distilled from the root of . . . an indigenous shrub of Hawaii," primarily because "the purpose of the exemption was to aid Hawaiian industry"). Significant complexity, however, marks constitutional restrictions concerning state tax-based business development incentives. *See generally infra* Section 21.A.

[59] 340 U.S. 179 (1950).

[the state's] chief natural resources."[60] Was this law marked by a discriminatory purpose of hoarding? The Court said "no," reasoning in effect that the law constricted gas sales "whether destined for interstate or intrastate consumers" in a way reasonably designed to conserve a scarce resource for both classes of buyers in the future.[61]

Cities Service illustrates that not all "economic" purposes qualify as discriminatory, despite loose language in some opinions that might suggest otherwise.[62] Common sense confirms the soundness of this conclusion because innumerable state laws that guard against road wear, unfair trade practices, monopolization, and even theft have economic purposes that are entirely proper for states to pursue. It is a *protectionist* purpose—not an economic purpose—that brings the anti-discrimination rule into play.[63]

Another tricky question raised by the discriminatory-purpose line of cases has to do with the proper *characterization* of the purpose underlying a challenged law. In *Buck v. Kuykendall*,[64] for example, the Court found that an impermissible purpose drove the state's refusal to license the operation of a Portland-to-Seattle "auto stage line" on the ground that the route applied for was already adequately

---

60 *Id.* at 187.

61 *Id.* at 189. The Court went a step further in *Sporhase*, concluding that, in the unique context of groundwater regulation, a state could take steps "to conserve and preserve *for its own citizens* this vital resource in times of severe shortage." 458 U.S. at 956 (emphasis added). Even this specialized recognition of a seeming right to hoard, however, does not totally exempt state water-transfer restrictions from dormant Commerce Clause attack. In particular, the dormancy principle bars essentially gratuitous state water-transfer restrictions—for example, when they operate "[e]ven though the supply of water in a particular well may be abundant, or perhaps even excessive, and even though the most beneficial use of that water might be in another State." *Id.* at 958.

62 *See also Hood*, 336 U.S. at 526, 535 (endorsing a broad state authority to protect residents' "health and safety" but finding fault with a license denial that would "protect and advance local economic interests").

63 *See City of Philadelphia*, 437 U.S. at 624 (associating the "virtually *per se* rule of invalidity" with "simple economic protectionism"); *see also* Catherine Gage O'Grady, *Targeting State Protectionism Instead of Interstate Discrimination Under the Dormant Commerce Clause*, 34 SAN DIEGO L. REV. 571, 575 (1997) (contending that the primary concern in dormant Commerce Clause analysis should be "the long-recognized prohibition against resident economic protectionism" and that the question of protectionist purpose should precede the discrimination question, while also noting that courts, focusing largely on the latter question, tend to blur the two principles); *see also* Gillian E. Metzger, *Congress, Article IV, and Interstate Relations*, 120 HARV. L. REV. 1468, 1505 (2007) (arguing that "[m]easures can be facially discriminatory but not protectionist, and facially neutral measures may on closer inspection appear pernicious"); Jessica Berch, *If You Don't Have A Cow (or Chicken or Pig), You Can't Call It Meat: Weaponizing the Dormant Commerce Clause to Strike Down Anti-Animal-Welfare Legislation*, 2021 UTAH L. REV. 73, 98 (arguing for an approach, in the context of evaluating litigation brought by both meat producers and animal-welfare advocates, that would invalidate as protectionist labeling rules meant to advantage in-state meat producers while upholding animal-welfare laws enacted for non-protectionist reasons).

64 267 U.S. 307 (1925).

served. Justice McReynolds stood ready to uphold the state's action because, in his view, the state's purpose was to avert the risk that "chaotic conditions will quickly develop" on the highways.[65] For the rest of the Court, however, the permit denial violated the dormancy principle because the state's "primary purpose is not regulation with a view to safety or to conservation of the highways, but the prohibition of competition."[66] A similar problem lurked quietly in *Hood*, in which the Court spotted "an avowed purpose . . . of curtailing the volume of interstate commerce to aid local economic interests."[67] In a sense, this description was apt because in fact New York sought to avoid disruption of the City of Troy's milk supply due to the diversion of milk to Bostonians. But given the statutory scheme's ostensible aim of protecting all milk buyers (including buyers located outside the state), the Court might have characterized the law's purpose in a very different way—namely, as evenhandedly protecting the stability of access for *all* buyers of New York milk.

The Court in neither *Buck* nor *Hood* paused to justify the characterization choice it made, and the Court has not since offered much meaningful guidance—either for purposes of the dormant Commerce Clause or in other doctrinal contexts—as to what sorts of considerations ought to guide this determination.[68] These cases nonetheless serve to highlight the key point: The manner in which a state's purpose is described—narrowly or broadly, approvingly or pejoratively—inevitably shapes the application of legal rules that hinge on the presence or absence of an illicit motive.

2. The Doctrinal Relevance of a Discriminatory-Purpose Finding

For decades, judges and scholars have bemoaned the difficulties of discerning legislative purposes. The key problems are well-known. Different legislators vote for the same law for different reasons, including reasons that may have nothing to do with policy choices but everything to do with achieving compromise or simply getting reelected. In the usual case, identifying even a single legislator's purpose, much less the shared purpose of scores of legislators, involves a difficult exercise in mind reading. And a rule giving significance to a legislative body's purpose may further require some form of nose counting to see if enough members of that body acted with a no-go *mens rea*. Must a majority of legislators have a bad

---

65 George W. Bush & Sons Co. v. Maloy, 267 U.S. 325 (1925) (McReynolds, J., dissenting in both *Bush* and its companion case, *Buck*).

66 *Buck*, 267 U.S. at 315.

67 *Hood*, 336 U.S. at 530–31.

68 *See generally* Michael Coenen, *Characterizing Constitutional Inputs*, 67 DUKE L.J. 743 (2018).

motive? A substantial number? One legislator standing alone? These and other complexities have led many analysts to argue against purpose-driven analysis both inside and outside the dormant Commerce Clause field.[69]

On occasion, the Court has acceded to these pleas. But it more often has turned them away.[70] In particular, in dormant Commerce

---

[69] The following pieces are only a small fraction of the many scholarly treatments that deal with these matters and other complexities of motive-based analysis. *See, e.g.*, Michael Coenen, *Campaign Communications and the Problem of Government Motive*, 21 U. PA. J. CONST. L. 333, 341–56 (2018); Richard H. Fallon, Jr., *Constitutionally Forbidden Legislative Intent*, 130 HARV. L. REV. 525, 548 (2016); Kenneth Karst, *The Costs of Motive-Centered Inquiry*, 15 SAN DIEGO L. REV. 1163 (1978) (noting problems with motive review in the race-discrimination context); Richard L. Hasen, *Bad Legislative Intent*, 2006 WIS. L. REV. 843; Ashutosh Bhagwat, *Purpose Scrutiny in Constitutional Analysis*, 85 CAL. L. REV. 297 (1997); John F. Manning, *Inside Congress's Mind*, 115 COLUM. L. REV. 1911 (2015). *See generally* Dan T. Coenen, *A Constitution of Collaboration: Protecting Fundamental Values with Second-Look Rules of Interbranch Dialogue*, 42 WM. & MARY L. REV. 1575, 1757–59 (2001) (collecting many authorities, including Supreme Court opinions, that question the wisdom of purpose-centered doctrines for, among other things, the reasons set forth above). Addressing the dormant Commerce Clause cases, Professor Brannon Denning has observed that the Court "has never been transparent about how one ascertains discriminatory purpose," or "how one might go about proving discriminatory purpose, or even why purpose should be considered." Brannon P. Denning, *Reconstructing the Dormant Commerce Clause Doctrine*, 50 WM. & MARY L. REV. 417, 500, 502 (2008). *See also* Julian Cyril Zebot, Note, *Awakening a Sleeping Dog: An Examination of the Confusion in Ascertaining Purposeful Discrimination Against Interstate Commerce*, 86 MINN. L. REV. 1063, 1077–84 (2002) (cataloging and critiquing non-uniform discriminatory purpose analyses undertaken by federal courts of appeals).

[70] *See* Coenen, *supra* note 69, at 1759–64. Professor Denning has considered the possibility of restricting the anti-discrimination principle to laws that discriminate against interstate commerce on their face, but he has rejected that approach on the ground that it would leave the dormant Commerce Clause underenforced because states could easily craft facially neutral laws that produce desired discriminatory effects. *See* Denning, *supra* note 69, at 499–500. As a result, he has endorsed a "decision rules model," under which courts would plainly set forth standards for demonstrating discriminatory purpose, including by identifying types of evidence admissible to show such a purpose. *Id.* at 501–03. He also observes that some lower courts have fashioned sub-rules that move in this direction. *Id.* at 503; *see, e.g.*, S.D. Farm Bureau, Inc. v. Hazeltine, 340 F.3d 583, 593–95 (8th Cir. 2003) (focusing on direct evidence of discriminatory purpose and irregularities in the law-making process); Waste Mgmt. Holdings v. Gilmore, 252 F.3d 316, 336 (4th Cir. 2001) (looking at the historical background of the legislation, and the sequence of events leading up to its enactment, for signals of discriminatory purpose); *see also* Alexandra B. Klass & Jim Rossi, *Revitalizing Dormant Commerce Clause Review for Interstate Coordination*, 100 MINN. L. REV. 129, 172 (2015) (noting that "a statute may have both protectionist and non-protectionist motives" and proposing that courts should consider the state or local political processes leading to a law's adoption in determining whether an improper motive underlies it). Not surprisingly, some courts, in applying the dormant Commerce Clause, have drawn on the Supreme Court's identification of relevant considerations, set forth in *Village of Arlington Heights v. Metropolitan Housing Development Corp.*, 429 U.S. 252 (1977), for ferreting out wrongful purposes in the equal-protection context. *See, e.g.*, Smithfield Foods, Inc. v. Miller, 367 F.3d 1061, 1065 (8th Cir. 2004) (identifying such relevant evidence as including (1) "statements by lawmakers," (2) the "sequence of events leading up to a statute's adoption," (3) a state's "consistent pattern" of imposing a disparate impact on particular classes, (4) a statute's "historical background," including its connectedness with past

Clause cases, the Court has sometimes focused on legislative purpose—although it has done so with caution, looking almost exclusively to formal legislative materials or outright concessions in assessing whether an improper motivation tainted an otherwise permissible law.[71] In *Bacchus Imports v. Dias*,[72] for example, the Court relied on assertions made by the state's own supreme court—which in turn relied on published committee reports of the state legislature—in finding that the purpose that lay behind a challenged tax exemption for a product made from the roots of an indigenous Hawaiian plant was "to aid Hawaiian industry."[73] Usually, however, the Court has hesitated to focus solely on legislative purpose before invalidating state laws under the dormant Commerce Clause. Even in *Bacchus Imports*, for example, the Court also emphasized the highly discriminatory effect of the exemption, which "applie[d] only to locally produced beverages."[74] In addition, the Court sometimes

---

discrimination, and (5) a statute's "use of highly ineffective means to promote the legitimate interest asserted by the state").

[71] *Cf. Arlington Heights*, 429 U.S. at 268 n.18 (noting that in equal-protection purposive-discrimination cases, "[p]lacing a decisionmaker on the stand is . . . 'usually to be avoided' "). The classic defense of recognizing (and recognizing only) a purpose-centered approach to the dormant Commerce Clause principle (at least for cases other than those involving taxes or transportation) comes from Professor Regan, who has suggested that judicial use of the dormant Commerce Clause is "in fact better justified by a purpose-based theory than by any other." Regan, *supra* note 11, at 1098. Professor Regan further contends that an explicitly "purpose-based anti-protectionism principle" would not require courts to "sift the evidence looking for purpose case by case' " in the mode of a psychological examination aimed at discovering the inner workings of the minds of specific lawmakers. *Id.*; *see also* Fallon, *supra* note 69, at 548 n.115 (characterizing Professor Regan's thesis in a similar fashion). Rather, "the Court both should use and does use some per se rules or presumptions in its search for protectionist purpose" and "the per se rules or presumptions the Court uses can be justified by a purpose-based theory." Regan, *supra* note 11, at 1098. As a theoretical matter, the emphasis placed by Regan on wrongful purpose may make good sense and help both to justify and to explain the Court's dormant Commerce Clause jurisprudence, at least in its central dimensions. In particular, this line of thinking may validate current doctrine—particularly regarding discriminatory-effects and *Pike* balancing analysis—as reflecting the sort of "per se rules" and "presumptions" the Court "both should use and does use." *Id.* As a doctrinal matter, however, the Court has not meaningfully distinguished between laws that have problematic purposes and laws that have problematic effects, at least insofar as the Court has recognized that either one of these problems may result in a finding of unconstitutionality. As a practical matter, what this may ultimately mean is little more than this: Absent facial discrimination, courts will typically focus on problematic effects regarding interstate commerce and the state's justifications for creating them. However, in unusual cases, where evidence of a genuinely protectionist motivation for a law is exceptionally strong, the courts will stand ready to strike it down with nothing (or essentially nothing) more because, in such cases, any need to apply balancing tests and the like are not needed to establish the gravamen of the constitutional violation.

[72] 468 U.S. 263 (1984).

[73] *Id.* at 271; *cf. Maine*, 477 U.S. at 150 (finding "weak evidence of legislative intent" in "comments . . . made by a state administrative agency long after the statute's enactment").

[74] *Bacchus Imports*, 468 U.S. at 271.

has noted in passing indications of a problematic purpose while ultimately finding laws violative of the dormant Commerce Clause on other grounds.[75] In short, the ban on discriminatory purpose—even if wielded by the courts with neither frequency nor clarity—remains a part of the judicial "tool kit," available for use in cases in which distinctly suspicious facts suggest that facially evenhanded laws were in actuality the product of state efforts to squelch cross-border trade.

D. LIMITS (AND NON-LIMITS) ON THE ANTI-DISCRIMINATION RULE

In applying the anti-discrimination rule, the Court has fashioned a series of sub-rules that refine that principle and generally accord it a broad scope. To begin with, the Court has held that a law's ultimate aim, even if unobjectionable, will not save a statute otherwise marked by impermissible discrimination.[76] The Court also has made it clear that discrimination in favor of some, rather than all, in-state consumers or industry members is enough to trigger strict judicial scrutiny.[77] Applying much the same principle, the Court has held that both the anti-discrimination rule and the dormant Commerce Clause in general apply to local governments (which are sub-units of state governments) no less than they apply to state governments themselves. Thus, for instance, in *Fort Gratiot Sanitary Landfill, Inc. v. Michigan Department of Natural Resources*,[78] the Court held that the dormant Commerce Clause does not permit a local government to block interstate commerce by banning the local disposal of all out-of-county waste, even though the law disadvantaged all in-state-but-out-of-county waste producers no

[75] *See* Kassel v. Consol. Freightways Corp. of Delaware, 450 U.S. 662, 677 (1981) (plurality opinion) (deeming invalid an Iowa law that prohibited "the use of 65-foot double[-trailer trucks] within its borders" but provided exceptions for trucks coming in and out of bordering cities, thus leading the Court to comment that "Iowa's statute may not have been designed to ban dangerous trucks, but rather to discourage interstate truck traffic").

[76] The seminal case on this point is *City of Philadelphia*, in which the parties had debated at length whether the underlying goal of New Jersey's waste-exclusion law was, on the one hand, to safeguard the economic interests of in-state landfill users or, on the other hand, to effectuate beneficial environmental protection. For the Court, this debate was beside the point because "the evil of protectionism can reside in legislative means as well as legislative ends." *City of Philadelphia*, 437 U.S. at 626.

[77] In *Bacchus Imports*, for example, the fact that the statute favored only local fruit wine and okolehao producers, while treating local sake and fruit liqueur makers no better than their out-of-state competitors, did not stop the Court from invalidating the challenged liquor tax. *See Bacchus Imports*, 468 U.S. at 265.

[78] 504 U.S. 353 (1992).

less than it disadvantaged similarly situated out-of-state waste-service seekers.[79]

It is worth focusing on this last point because it sheds light on the Court's general approach to dormant Commerce Clause cases. One might well argue, for instance, that a *statewide* ban on out-of-state commerce at least typically will have more sweeping effects than a *local* prohibition on non-local commerce, thus justifying a doctrinal distinction between state-based and local measures. The critic might also contend that state-discrimination and local-discrimination cases present very different political-process considerations. A comparison of *City of Philadelphia* and *Fort Gratiot* reveals the critical point. In *City of Philadelphia* (which involved a statewide ban), the law ultimately adopted by New Jersey did not disadvantage any in-state generators of waste; thus, not a single in-state waste producer had any reason to lobby against the law and thereby operate as an indirect (or "virtual" or "surrogate") representative of the out-of-state waste producers that the law disadvantaged. In *Fort Gratiot,* however, all in-state waste generators, except the relatively few such generators located in the discrimination-practicing county, suffered the same fate as banned out-of-state waste producers.[80] The Court, however, has never made use of such surrogate-representation-based logic in this context, perhaps because in the world of local-government politics, non-local (but in-state) residents operate as poor substitutes for out-of-state residents.[81] The Justices' refusal to distinguish between these two types of cases also comports with the more general principle that there is no *de minimis* exception to the anti-discrimination rule.[82] In any event, the governing doctrinal proposition carries with it the

---

[79] *Dean Milk* and *Carbone*, which are discussed *supra* Section 17.A.3, also fall within this line of authority.

[80] *Fort Gratiot*, 504 U.S. 353.

[81] After all, so the argument goes, local officials have accountability only to the residents of the locality who actually elect them. To be sure, out-of-county/in-state victims of county-based discrimination may, in theory, seek relief from *state* officials and might thus be able to represent out-of-staters' interests in a meaningful way. But the prospect of a statewide legislative response to a local county or city's actions may often be unlikely enough as to render the benefits of surrogate representation more illusory than real. *See also supra* Section 16.A.3 (noting the possibility that subunits of government within a broader polity might adopt an I'll-scratch-your-back-if-you-scratch-mine mentality).

[82] *Camps Newfound/Owatonna*, 520 U.S. at 581 n.15; *accord, e.g.*, Oregon Waste Sys., Inc. v. Dep't of Envtl. Quality, 511 U.S. 93, 100 n.4 (1994) ("[O]ur precedents . . . clearly establish that the degree of a differential burden . . . on interstate commerce . . . 'is of no relevance to the determination whether a State has discriminated against interstate commerce.' " (quoting *Wyoming*, 502 U.S. at 455)); *see also Anheuser-Busch, Inc.*, 738 F. Supp. 2d at 807 (noting "[t]he absence of a *de minimis* exception" in striking down a discriminatory state law). *See generally* Christine A. Klein, *The Environmental Commerce Clause*, 27 HARV. ENVTL. L. REV. 1, 50 (2003) (noting the absence of a "de minimis exception").

benefit of straightforwardness and clarity: "[A] state (or one of its political subdivisions) may not avoid the strictures of the Commerce Clause by curtailing the movement of articles of commerce through subdivisions of the state, rather than through the state itself."[83]

What happens if a court concludes that a state law does, indeed, discriminate against interstate commerce? As we have seen, unless some exception to the dormancy doctrine applies, an initial determination of discrimination by the court triggers application of a "virtually *per se* rule of invalidity."[84] The accuracy of this description of the operative test finds strong support in the cases because only once, in the many decades that have passed since this standard's initial articulation, has the Court found that a discriminatory state law was supported by such a powerful state interest that it warranted validation. That case was *Maine v. Taylor*,[85] in which the issue was whether Maine's wholesale ban on the importation of baitfish violated the dormancy doctrine. Expounding on the doctrine's basic operation, the Court declared that the sort of facial discrimination presented by the Maine statute triggered "the strictest scrutiny," under which "the burden falls on the State to demonstrate both that the statute 'serves a legitimate local purpose,'

---

[83] *Fort Gratiot*, 504 U.S. at 361. With regard to concerns about straightforwardness and clarity, a failure to employ this bright-line rule would inevitably generate hard-to-answer questions—for example, when multiple (but not all) local governments adopt a local-residents-favoring rule or when a particularly large or politically powerful local government unit does so. It is not surprising, in light of these potential complications, that the Court has in effect concluded that the best course is to adhere to the now-governing rule that always equates interlocality discrimination with interstate discrimination.

[84] *City of Philadelphia*, 437 U.S. at 624. One question about whether the anti-discrimination rule does apply concerns what might be said to involve the "apples and oranges" problem. Put differently, the dormancy-doctrine ban on discrimination (like many such bans in other areas of law) focuses on ensuring that like things receive like treatment. But sometimes things that might seem "like" at first glance turn out, on close inspection, not to be "like" enough as to trigger anti-discrimination review. *See, e.g.*, Allco Fin. Ltd. v. Klee, 861 F.3d 82, 105 (2d Cir. 2017) (rejecting a challenge based on Connecticut's seemingly discriminatory treatment of power coming from a regional grid as opposed to other sources; relying largely on a state's ability to fashion its own property law, including in defining the nature of transferrable "renewable energy credits," in finding that the state had properly "treated as different" purportedly competing products). For a treatment of this subject in the context of dormant Commerce Clause tax-law cases, see *infra* Chapter 21, and for the role played by this idea in developing the state-self-promotion exception to the dormant Commerce Clause, see *infra* Section 20.E. For a treatment of two dormant Commerce Clause regulatory cases in which the circuit courts built on this idea, see Kevin Todd, Note, *The Dormant Commerce Clause and State Clean Energy Legislation*, 9 MICH. J. ENVTL. & ADMIN. L. 189, 210 (2019) (endorsing the courts' rulings in these cases, which involved state efforts to address problems of climate change; expressing concern that an "expansive reading" of the dormant Commerce Clause facial-discrimination principle to cover these and similar cases would unwisely threaten the constitutionality of innovative state environmental measures).

[85] 477 U.S. 131 (1986).

and that this purpose could not be served as well by available nondiscriminatory means."[86] In applying this test, the Court looked to the voluminous record developed at trial, which in its view indicated that no alternative means existed for achieving the state's goal of protecting Maine's native baitfish population from non-native parasites. In particular, because inspections and more targeted importation bans were unworkable—and because the "abstract possibility" of later "developing acceptable testing procedures" did not qualify as an "adequate[ ]" option—the Court concluded that the state had no practical choice but to retain the challenged program.[87] In dissent, Justice Stevens declared that there was "something fishy about this case" because "[a]mbiguity about dangers and alternatives should actually defeat, rather than sustain, the discriminatory measure."[88] For the eight-Justice majority, however, it sufficed to sustain the statute that the district court's findings with regard to these matters were not "clearly erroneous."[89]

Maine v. Taylor is an exceptional—indeed, extraordinary—case. In *City of Philadelphia*, for example, the Court readily found that New Jersey could adequately protect its interests in preserving undisrupted land and reducing groundwater-contaminating leachate by limiting, in a source-neutral fashion, the overall volume of materials buried in local landfills, rather than by excluding only out-of-state waste.[90] In other cases, as in *City of Philadelphia*, the Court has pointed to similarly nondiscriminatory alternatives in striking down facially discriminatory measures.[91] In short order, we will consider exceptions to the dormancy doctrine that can shield even explicitly discriminatory laws from the application of the "virtually per se rule."[92] There can be no doubt, however, that when that rule does apply, the challenged state law almost never survives constitutional attack.

---

86 *Id.* at 138.

87 *Id.* at 147.

88 *Id.* at 152 (Stevens, J., dissenting).

89 *Id.* at 146 (majority opinion).

90 *City of Philadelphia*, 437 U.S. at 626.

91 *See, e.g.*, *Hughes*, 441 U.S. at 337–38 (finding an outright ban on exportation not "the least discriminatory alternative," but in fact the most discriminatory approach, for conserving the local minnow population; citing the possible alternative of putting catch limits on licensed minnow dealers and emphasizing that the challenged law was "not a 'last ditch' attempt at conservation after nondiscriminatory alternatives have proved unfeasible"); *see also supra* Section 17.A.3 (discussing less-restrictive-means analysis in the *Dean Milk* and *Carbone* cases).

92 *See infra* Chapter 20.

Chapter 18

FACIALLY NEUTRAL LAWS AND THE *PIKE* BALANCING TEST

Analysis

Sec.

As we have seen, the Court has closely scrutinized state laws that discriminate against interstate commerce on their face, in their effect, or in their purpose. The Court, however, has not stopped there in its effort to protect the federal common market. Recognizing that interferences with that market may take "ingenious" forms,[1] the Court has provided that a state law may fall victim to a dormancy-doctrine challenge even if it "regulates evenhandedly."[2] In 1970, the modern iteration of this approach was set forth by Justice Stewart in an opinion for a unanimous Court in *Pike v. Bruce Church, Inc.*[3] As he wrote:

> Where the statute regulates even-handedly to effectuate a legitimate local public interest, and its effects on interstate commerce are only incidental, it will be upheld unless the burden imposed on such commerce is clearly excessive in relation to the putative local benefits. If a legitimate local purpose is found, then the question becomes one of degree. And the extent of the burden that will be tolerated will of course depend on the nature of the local interest involved, and on whether it could be promoted as well with a lesser impact on interstate activities.[4]

---

1 Best & Co. v. Maxwell, 311 U.S. 454, 455 (1940); *see also* Hunt v. Wash. Apple Advert. Comm'n, 432 U.S. 333, 350 (1977) (insisting that dormant Commerce Clause principle must go beyond "the rare instance where a state artlessly discloses an avowed purpose to discriminate against interstate goods" (quoting Dean Milk Co. v. City of Madison, 340 U.S. 349, 354 (1951))).

2 Hughes v. Oklahoma, 441 U.S. 322, 326, 331 (1979) (internal quotations omitted).

3 397 U.S. 137 (1970).

4 *Id.* at 142 (internal citations omitted).

The style of judicial balancing endorsed by the Court in *Pike* was long criticized by Justice Scalia largely on the ground that it improperly injects judges into a policymaking role that they are neither legally warranted nor institutionally well-equipped to handle.[5] *Pike* itself, however, was a unanimous decision, and the balancing methodology

---

[5] In *Bendix Autolite Corp. v. Midwesco Enterprises*, 486 U.S. 888 (1988), for example, Justice Scalia offered an influential critique of the *Pike* balancing test, deeming it "not really appropriate, since the interests on both sides are incommensurate," so that this analysis is no more satisfactory than "judging whether a particular line is longer than a particular rock is heavy." *Id.* at 895–98 (Scalia, J., concurring in the judgment); *see also* CTS Corp. v. Dynamics Corp. of Am., 481 U.S. 69, 95 (1987) (Scalia, J., concurring in part and dissenting in part) (noting that the current approach to analyzing state laws under the dormant Commerce Clause is a practice that "is ill suited to the judicial function and should be undertaken rarely if at all"). Justice Thomas has expressed similar concerns. *See* Camps Newfound/Owatonna, Inc. v. Town of Harrison, 520 U.S. 564, 618 (1997) (Thomas, J., dissenting) (commenting that "our negative Commerce Clause jurisprudence has taken us well beyond the invalidation of obviously discriminatory taxes" and that "[w]e have used the Clause to make policy-laden judgments that we are ill equipped and arguably unauthorized to make"). In an earlier time, Justice Black expressed the view that courts should invalidate only those laws that "discriminate" against interstate commerce, J. D. Adams Mfg. Co. v. Storen, 304 U.S. 307, 330 (1938) (Black, J., dissenting in part), lest the judiciary take on the role of a "super-legislature." S. Pac. Co. v. Arizona *ex rel.* Sullivan, 325 U.S. 761, 788 (1945) (Black, J., dissenting). Notably, Justice Gorsuch also voiced skepticism about the *Pike* test during his tenure on the Tenth Circuit. *See* Energy & Envtl. Legal Inst. v. Epel, 793 F.3d 1169, 1171 (10th Cir. 2015) (Gorsuch, J.) (calling *Pike* "a pretty grand, even 'ineffable,' all-things-considered sort of test, one requiring judges (to attempt) to compare wholly incommensurable goods for wholly different populations"). For illustrative academic critiques, see, e.g., Earl M. Maltz, *How Much Regulation Is Too Much—An Examination of Commerce Clause Jurisprudence*, 50 GEO. WASH. L. REV. 47, 58–64 (1981) (questioning *Pike* analysis on the ground that "if the balancing test is to be justified in terms of its flexibility, the flexibility must be related to the proper function of the judicial process"); Daniel A. Farber, *State Regulation and the Dormant Commerce Clause*, 3 CONST. COMMENT. 395, 407–10 (1986); Alan O. Sykes, *Regulatory Protectionism and the Law of International Trade*, 66 U. CHI. L. REV. 1, 43–45 (1999). Professor Regan and other observers have expressed concern about fixating on effects-centered analysis, advocating instead that judicial work with the dormant Commerce Clause should focus on the invalidation of state laws marked by a protectionist purpose (at least when the Court moves beyond the transportation and taxation contexts). *See* Donald H. Regan, *The Supreme Court and State Protectionism: Making Sense of the Dormant Commerce Clause*, 84 MICH. L. REV. 1091, 1102–07, 1131, 1141 (1986). As Professor Regan himself has recognized, however, judicial application of this principle can and should take account of the "evidence" of protectionist purpose based on a "protectionist effect," *id.*, including by investigating whether "the law seems to achieve nothing, or even very little, in the way of its articulated purpose." *Id.* at 1132–33; *see also id.* at 1137 (noting that "effect is often the best evidence of purpose"); *id.* at 1225 (recognizing that "issues of permissible benefits and less restrictive alternatives are relevant to direct motive review"). In sum, Professor Regan's methodology endorses the assessment of effect-centered evidence, and the lack of demonstrably neutral state justifications, to demonstrate unacceptable protectionism. His overall approach thus can be seen as consistent, at least to some degree, with the structured effect-based style of "balancing" analysis, particularly as limited by the clearly-excessive-burden requirement set forth in the *Pike* test. For a classic defense of judicial balancing in the dormant Commerce Clause setting, see Noel T. Dowling, *Interstate Commerce and State Power—Revised Version, in* SELECTED ESSAYS ON CONSTITUTIONAL LAW: 1938–1962 (1963). *See also* Noel T. Dowling, *Interstate Commerce and State Power*, 27 VA. L. REV. 1 (1940).

it reflects is a longstanding and recurring feature of constitutional law.[6] Thus, courts at all levels continue to apply the *Pike* formula on a routine basis in dormant Commerce Clause cases.[7]

---

[6] *See generally* Regan, *supra* note 5, at 1153 (noting that courts "balance frequently (or at least say they are balancing frequently)" outside the dormant Commerce Clause context).

[7] Recent decisions, however, may indicate a movement toward applying *Pike* balancing with a greater measure of deference than the Court has indulged in the past. *See* Dan T. Coenen, *Where* United Haulers *Might Take Us: The Future of the State-Self-Promotion Exception to the Dormant Commerce Clause Rule*, 95 IOWA L. REV. 541, 627 (2010) (commenting on the possible future contraction of the *Pike* test in light of *Kentucky Dep't of Revenue v. Davis*, 553 U.S. 338 (2008), in which a cross-section of Justices seemed to support limitations on the test's applicability); Brandon P. Denning, *Extraterritoriality and the Dormant Commerce Clause: A Doctrinal Post-Mortem*, 73 LA. L. REV. 979, 1005–06 (2013) (noting the "judicial hostility" or "indifference" of the Roberts Court to, among other things, *Pike* balancing); Garrick B. Pursley, *Dormancy*, 100 GEO. L.J. 497, 541 (2012) ("First, the relative infrequency of *Pike* cases suggests that courts are less willing to seriously entertain Dormant Commerce Clause challenges to nondiscriminatory state laws. Second, when *Pike* is applied, the judicial approach is deferential to state lawmakers on the nature and importance of the local interests served by the challenged measure." (internal footnote omitted)); *see also* Gen. Motors v. Tracy, 519 U.S. 278, 308–09 (1997) (suggesting, albeit outside the context of applying the *Pike* test, that "the Court is institutionally unsuited to gather the facts upon which economic predictions can be made, and professionally untrained to make them"; adding that "[w]e are consequently ill qualified to develop Commerce Clause doctrine dependent on any such predictive judgments"). Indeed, Professor Denning has gone so far as to claim that, for practical purposes, the Court has in recent years abandoned *Pike* balancing "sub silentio." Brannon P. Denning, *Reconstructing the Dormant Commerce Clause Doctrine*, 50 WM. & MARY L. REV. 417, 493 (2008); *see also* Norman R. Williams & Brannon P. Denning, *The "New Protectionism" and the American Common Market*, 85 NOTRE DAME L. REV. 247, 304 (2009) ("*Davis* further diluted . . . *Pike* to the point of abnegation, calling into question the future viability of balancing as a feature of the dormant Commerce Clause doctrine."). A different way of looking at things, however, is that the Court's repeated demonstration of caution in applying the *Pike* test helps to justify its continued operation. In other words, and in keeping with the terms of the *Pike* test itself, the Court's actions reveal a steady willingness to invalidate state laws only when federal interests in free-flowing commerce truly are "*clearly* excessive" in comparison to countervailing state interests, thus evidencing the Justices' capacity to avoid the use of the balancing methodology to become anything like "super-legislature." *See supra* note 5 (noting Justice Black's use of this term). *See generally* James M. McGoldrick, Jr., *The Dormant Commerce Clause: The Endgame—From* Southern Pacific *to* Tennessee Wine & Spirits—*1945 to 2019*, 40 PACE L. REV. 44, 125 (2020) (rejecting Justice Scalia's critique of the *Pike* methodology by asserting that, when it comes to the Court's balancing approach, "the Court is actually pretty good at it," including because "litigants are given good directions at what to emphasize" in *Pike*-type cases). In any event—and regardless of what the future might hold within the Supreme Court—the lower courts "continue to see the *Pike* balancing approach as 'deferential but not toothless.'" Alexandra B. Klass & Jim Rossi, *Revitalizing Dormant Commerce Clause Review for Interstate Coordination*, 100 MINN. L. REV. 129, 159 (2015) (quoting Colon Hlth. Ctrs. of Am. v. Hazel, 733 F.3d 535, 545 (4th Cir. 2013)).

A. BALANCING ANALYSIS AND THE TRANSPORTATION CASES

1. Early Decisions About Trains and Roadways

The Court moved with caution in its initial forays with *Pike*-type balancing analysis under the dormancy doctrine. In *Bradley v. Public Utilities Commission*,[8] for example, the Justices sustained Ohio's refusal to authorize a new motorized common-carrier service between Cleveland and western Michigan. Signaling a deferential approach, the Court accepted the state's argument that the affected highway was "so badly congested by established motor vehicle operations, that the addition of the applicant's proposed service would create and maintain an excessive and undue hazard to the safety and security of the travelling public."[9] This fact, the Court noted, distinguished its earlier ruling in *Buck v. Kuykendall*,[10] in which the Justices had struck down a similar licensing denial because the state there had relied primarily on economic, rather than safety-centered, concerns.[11]

The Court again sounded a theme of deference in *South Carolina State Highway Department v. Barnwell Bros*.[12] That case presented the question whether South Carolina could enforce motor vehicle width and weight limits that kept 85–90% of the nation's long-haul trucks off the state's roads. Although the district court found a constitutional violation, the Supreme Court reversed, finding a "rational basis" for the state's judgment that its regulations reduced highway accidents.[13] The Court bolstered its analysis by noting that "[u]nlike the railroads, local highways are built, owned, and maintained by the state."[14] It also reasoned that "the fact that [the regulations] affect alike shippers in interstate and intrastate commerce in large number within as well as without the state is a safeguard against their abuse."[15]

In *Southern Pacific Co. v. Arizona ex rel. Sullivan*,[16] however, the Court shifted gears, putting the balancing methodology to work in invalidating a facially neutral Arizona train-length law. The Court began by emphasizing that dormant Commerce Clause analysis must turn on "the relative weights of the state and national interests

---

[8] 289 U.S. 92 (1933).

[9] *Id.* at 93–94.

[10] 267 U.S. 307 (1925).

[11] *Bradley*, 289 U.S. at 92–93.

[12] 303 U.S. 177 (1938).

[13] *Id.* at 192.

[14] *Id.* at 187.

[15] *Id.*

[16] 325 U.S. 761 (1945).

involved."[17] As to the federal-interest side of the balance, there was "no doubt that the Arizona Train Limit Law impose[d] a serious burden on . . . interstate commerce" in that Arizona stood alone in barring passenger trains that included more than fourteen cars and was one of only two states that placed a 70-car length limit on freight trains.[18] Because of these distinctly restrictive features, the Arizona law in effect required either the costly breaking up of long trains before they entered the state or the costly rerouting of those trains to navigate around the state. In measuring the resulting burden on interstate commerce, the Court found it significant that around 95% of Arizona's rail traffic was interstate in nature; that the Arizona train-length rules cost railroad companies about $1 million per year; that the rules necessarily delayed many cross-border deliveries; and that the "practical effect" of the law was to "control train operations beyond the boundaries of the state" because railroad-company responses to the Arizona law required reconfiguring trains as far away as El Paso, Texas, and Los Angeles, California.[19] Meanwhile, on the state-interest side of the balance, the Court placed heavy weight on the trial court's findings "that the Arizona law had no reasonable relation to safety" and in fact "made train operation more dangerous."[20] Although the Arizona Supreme Court had rejected these determinations, the U.S. Supreme Court was persuaded that any safety advantage gained by shortening trains was effectively "offset by the increase in the number of accidents resulting from the larger number of trains when train lengths are reduced."[21] The Court also deemed it significant that the primary safety problems associated with long trains—so-called slack-action accidents—were "relatively the same" in Arizona as in Nevada, which handled "substantially the same amount of traffic" without regulating train lengths at all.[22]

The Court's opinion in *Southern Pacific* also revealed how judges could use fact-sensitive balancing analysis to sidestep precedent that might otherwise compel a contrary decision. In particular, the Court distinguished earlier cases upholding state laws that required locomotive headlights and full train crews both (1) because those laws genuinely "removed or reduced safety hazards" and (2) because they created no "substantial interference with the interstate movement of trains" in light of the ease with which railroad companies could adapt

---

17 *Id.* at 770.

18 *Id.* at 773–74.

19 *Id.* at 771, 772, 775.

20 *Id.* at 775.

21 *Id.*

22 *Id.* at 777.

to them.[23] In a similar vein, the Court found *Barnwell* distinguishable not only because it involved government-maintained highways but also because its stringent width and weight rules fell on intrastate and interstate truckers alike. In contrast, as Chief Justice Stone explained in *Southern Pacific*, "the burden of [Arizona's train-length] regulation [fell] on interests outside the state" so that it was "unlikely to be alleviated by the operation of those political restraints normally exerted when interests within the state are affected."[24]

In sum, the Court in *Southern Pacific* emphasized that a state could not avoid the restraints of the dormant Commerce Clause by "simply invoking the convenient apologetics of the police power."[25] Rather, "the decisive question is whether in the circumstances the total effect of the law as a safety measure in reducing accidents and casualties is so slight or problematical as not to outweigh the national interest in keeping interstate commerce free from interferences which seriously impede it."[26] The Arizona law flunked this test because it generated "at most" a "slight and dubious" safety advantage while "preventing the free flow of commerce by delaying it and by substantially increasing its cost and impairing its efficiency."[27]

2. *Kassel v. Consolidated Freightways Corp.* and the Modern Treatment of Roadways

The Court's decisions in *Barnwell* and *Southern Pacific* raised an intriguing question: Did the Court mean to erect a never-to-be-breached distinction between facially neutral state *road* laws and facially neutral state *train* laws for dormant Commerce Clause purposes? In *Bibb v. Navajo Freight Lines, Inc.*,[28] the Court answered "no," by invalidating an Illinois law that required trucks to use "contour" mudguards (as opposed to "straight" mudguards, which were either authorized or required by most other states).[29] In *Raymond Motor Transportation, Inc. v. Rice*,[30] the Court again found that a motor vehicle law—this one a Wisconsin restriction that

[23] *Id.* at 779.

[24] *Id.* at 767 n.2.

[25] *Id.* at 780 (quoting Kansas City S. Ry. Co. v. Kaw Valley Drainage Dist., 233 U.S. 75, 79 (1914)).

[26] *Id.* at 775–76.

[27] *Id.* at 779.

[28] 359 U.S. 520 (1959).

[29] *Id.* at 524–25. *See* John F. Preis, *The Dormant Commerce Clause as a Limit on Personal Jurisdiction*, 102 IOWA L. REV. 121, 144 (2016) (viewing *Bibb* as establishing that, in the face of a burden on interstate commerce, "where a state cannot show any local benefit, the state law violates the Dormant Commerce Clause").

[30] 434 U.S. 429 (1978).

generally limited truck lengths to 55 feet and thus prevented the challengers from using 65-foot double-trailer trucks—violated the dormant Commerce Clause. *Raymond*, however, was of limited precedential significance because the state had offered no evidence in opposition to the challengers' carefully presented case (1) that 65-foot double-trailer trucks were as safe as 55-foot single-trailer trucks and (2) that the exclusion of 65-foot "doubles" from Wisconsin roads imposed massive burdens on interstate commerce.[31]

The predictable sequel to *Raymond* was *Kassel v. Consolidated Freightways Corp.*[32] At issue was Iowa's generally applicable exclusion of trucks exceeding 60 feet in length, including 65-foot doubles, from most of its highways. Applying *Pike* balancing analysis to this facially neutral law, Justice Powell (writing for four Justices) conceded that Iowa in *Kassel* (unlike Wisconsin in *Raymond*) had offered some evidence of a safety justification.[33] He also found support in the record, however, for the district court's conclusion that 65-foot doubles were, all things considered, as safe as the 55-foot singles and 60-foot doubles that could legally traverse Iowa's highways.[34] Turning to the other side of the balance, Justice Powell concluded that the law placed a heavy burden on interstate commerce. In particular, because all other western and midwestern states authorized use of the same 65-foot doubles that Iowa excluded, the challenged law increased both costs and accidents as shippers added highway miles by circumventing Iowa or deployed an increased number of trucks to carry goods through the state.[35] Finally, the law raised suspicions because the burden it imposed on long-haul traffic—which primarily went through, rather than to or from, the state—fell "disproportionately on out-of-state residents and businesses."[36] This problem was magnified because the statute included exemptions (including for Iowa truck manufacturers and for cargo-carrying truck traffic with a starting or ending point in a limited number of Iowa cites, particularly cities located near the state's border) that "secure to Iowans many of the benefits of large trucks while shunting to neighboring states many of the costs associated with their use."[37] Considering all these matters, Justice Powell concluded that the Iowa law, as applied to 65-foot double-

---

31 *Id.* at 436–38.

32 450 U.S. 662 (1981).

33 *Id.* at 674 (opinion of Powell, J.).

34 *Id.* at 667–68.

35 *Id.* at 674–75.

36 *Id.* at 676.

37 *Id.*

trailer trucks, abridged the dormancy doctrine under the balancing principle of *Pike*.

Justice Brennan (who was joined by Justice Marshall) declined to sign on to Justice Powell's plurality opinion even though he agreed that the Iowa law offended constitutional requirements.[38] In Justice Brennan's view, the Powell opinion had "ask[ed] and answer[ed] the wrong question," in part because judicial second-guessing of legislative judgments "in the field of safety" was to be avoided at almost all costs.[39] Instead, Justice Brennan reasoned, the problem with the law lay in its impermissibly discriminatory purpose.[40] More specifically, he deemed the law's "actual purpose" to be "protectionist" because the Governor had vetoed an earlier (and more accommodating) truck-length requirement on the ground that it "would benefit only a few Iowa-based companies while providing a great advantage for out-of-state trucking firms . . . at the expense of our Iowa citizens."[41]

In dissent, then-Associate Justice Rehnquist (writing for himself and two other members of the Court) criticized the plurality's willingness to "compare safety benefits to commerce costs" and, in particular, to consider "incremental safety benefits from prohibiting 65-foot doubles as opposed to 60-foot doubles."[42] Justice Rehnquist argued that states must be free to enact some forms of truck-length rules; that these rules necessarily involve numerical cutoffs; and that "[l]ines drawn for safety purposes will rarely pass muster if the question is whether a slight increment can be permitted without sacrificing safety."[43] In staking out this position, Justice Rehnquist did not pause to consider that the particular increment involved in *Kassel* was fraught with practical consequences, given the widespread authorization in the West and Midwest of 65-foot trucks but the absence of any similar allowance of, say, 70- or 75-foot vehicle lengths. He did note, however, that, unlike Wisconsin in *Raymond*, Iowa in *Kassel* had offered evidence that 65-foot-long trucks pose distinct safety dangers, because, among other things, a "65-foot vehicle exposes a passing driver to visibility-impairing splash and

---

38 *Id.* at 679–87 (Brennan, J., concurring in the judgment).

39 *Id.* at 679, 686.

40 *See generally supra* Section 17.C.

41 *Kassel*, 450 U.S. at 685 (Brennan, J., concurring in the judgment). Justice Brennan emphasized that impermissible protectionism was not limited to disadvantaging out-of-state businesses; in his view, the nation-preserving purposes of the dormancy doctrine dictated that foisting the financial and safety costs of road use on other states constituted impermissible protectionism as well. *Id.* at 686.

42 *Id.* at 697 (Rehnquist, J., dissenting).

43 *Id.*

spray during bad weather for a longer period than do the shorter trucks permitted in Iowa."[44]

The fractured decision in *Kassel* reflected genuine differences of opinion. The three opinions in the case, however, also occupied some common ground. Each opinion started from the premise that safety-based highway laws warrant a "strong presumption of validity."[45] All nine Justices also agreed, however, that claimed safety justifications will not always support validation of commerce-burdening legislation. Most interestingly, all the opinion writers in the case, although proceeding from different points of reference, embraced much the same formula for assessing road-safety measures. The two concurring Justices proclaimed a willingness to jettison such laws if the safety benefit they created was "illusory, insubstantial, or nonexistent."[46] The three dissenters likewise stood ready to step in if the state's safety justification was "demonstrably trivial."[47] And even Justice Powell's opinion seemed hospitable to an approach under which state road laws would pass muster, at least as a general rule, so long as the state's safety justifications were "not illusory."[48]

Taken as a whole, these opinions thus lend support to a specialized version of the *Pike* balancing test as applied to highway safety (and perhaps all safety-related) cases. On this view, whenever a safety justification for a facially neutral road regulation is more than "insubstantial," "trivial," or "illusory"—presumably an easy standard for most such laws to meet—the case is at an end, at least in the absence of a showing of discriminatory purpose.[49] To be sure,

---

[44] *Id.* at 694.

[45] *Id.* at 670 (opinion of Powell, J.); *see id.* 685 (Brennan, J., concurring in the judgment); *id.* at 690 (Rehnquist, J., dissenting).

[46] *Id.* at 681 n.1 (Brennan, J., concurring in the judgment).

[47] *Id.* at 692, 697 n.8 (Rehnquist, J., dissenting).

[48] *Id.* at 670 (opinion of Powell, J.) (internal quotations omitted).

[49] *See* Preis, *supra* note 29, at 145 (pointing to cases that "demonstrate that, when a state can show some benefit, the Court will uphold the law without truly balancing the burden against the benefit because it is either unable or unwilling to perform such an analysis"). For an example of a case in which a lower court found a violation of the *Pike* rule in another context that at least touched on the subject of transportation, see *Florida Transportation Services, Inc. v. Miami-Dade County*, 703 F.3d 1230 (11th Cir. 2012). That case involved a county ordinance requiring the permitting of stevedores. While acknowledging that the local benefits of efficiency and safety motivating the ordinance were legitimate, the Eleventh Circuit nonetheless ruled that the permitting practices "d[id] not rationally contribute to the[ ] purported local benefits." *Id.* at 1260. Of particular importance, "[s]tevedore permits expired annually and a county ordinance required each stevedore company each year to reapply and be reassessed, along with any new applicants, as to competency, safety record, financial strength, and need." *Id.* at 1234. While this county ordinance seemed neutral on its face, the county in actual practice "rubber-stamp[ed] and automatically renew[ed] permits for all existing stevedore permit holders at the Port and automatically den[ied] permits to all new applicants." *Id.* In other words, the county's determination of whether or not a stevedore company would receive a permit turned on whether the company had

judges might sometimes fudge in applying this test by characterizing a state safety interest as "illusory" because a heavy burden on commerce hangs in the balance. Alternatively, judges might find some special reason to ratchet down the measure of deference applicable in a particular case—as the plurality in *Kassel* itself appeared to do because of the state's adoption of suspiciously self-serving exemptions from the supposedly general 60-foot rule.[50] In the end, however, the opinions in that case suggest that courts, as a rule, should apply a distinctly deferential version of *Pike* in highway-safety cases.[51]

Kassel raises interesting questions. Would the same truck-length law have survived constitutional challenge if it had been imposed by, say, Massachusetts or Maine? (Conceivably yes, given the law's lesser impact on interstate commerce because all New England states, and several nearby states as well, prohibited the use of 65-foot doubles.[52]) What about Hawaii? (Presumably yes, because the state's roads are not part of any interstate trucking route.) Would the Court have sustained an Iowa ban on 70-foot doubles? (Almost certainly yes, given the hypothesized rule's far lesser impact on interstate commerce and the greater safety problems it likely would address.) Does *Kassel*'s invalidation of a truck-safety regulation indicate that the result in *Barnwell* is no longer good law? (Probably no, because the weight-and-width statute at issue in *Barnwell*, though burdensome to interstate commerce, seemed to have

---

conducted in-state operations during the prior year, and not on the purported purposes of the ordinance such as safety and efficiency. *Id.* at 1257–58 (adding that a "protectionist motivation . . . underlying these practices" was reflected in the favoritism afforded to "incumbent stevedores" over new companies seeking to enter the market). After reviewing the county's application of the ordinance under a *Pike*-balancing analysis, the court concluded that "[t]he burden on interstate commerce—effectively removing the Port of Miami stevedore market from the local, state, and national markets and preserving it for a select few privileged permit holders—is significant, whereas the actual permitting practices did not further any local benefits." *Id.* at 1261–62.

50 *See* Waste Mgmt. Holdings, Inc. v. Gilmore, 252 F.3d 316, 344 (4th Cir. 2001) (declining to afford the "traditional deference that is due state legislation in the area of highway safety" where Virginia's General Assembly acted with a discriminatory purpose).

51 Notably, the Third Circuit has specifically declared that "non-discriminatory highway safety statutes must be given a more deferential treatment, and may not be overturned absent a showing that the safety benefits are slight, problematic, or illusory." Am. Trucking Ass'ns, Inc. v. Whitman, 437 F.3d 313, 319 (3d Cir. 2006) (citing Am. Trucking Ass'ns, Inc. v. Larson, 683 F.2d 787, 795 (3d Cir. 1982)). For judicial rhetoric that, although set forth in a road-related context, is suggestive of a deferential approach to safety laws in general, see *Electrolert Corp. v. Barry*, 737 F.2d 110, 112–113 (D.C. Cir. 1984) (holding that an ordinance banning devices to detect police radar did not violate the dormant Commerce Clause because, among other reasons, "state safety regulations are accorded particular deference in Commerce Clause analysis").

52 *See Kassel*, 450 U.S. at 688 (Rehnquist, J., dissenting).

something more than an "insubstantial," "trivial," or "illusory" safety justification.[53]) Whatever the answers to these questions, *Kassel* reveals that the dormant Commerce Clause is alive and well in the road-regulation context.[54]

B. FACIALLY NEUTRAL LAWS OUTSIDE THE TRANSPORTATION CONTEXT

Both *Raymond* and *Kassel* revealed the Court's openness to dormant Commerce Clause balancing under the *Pike* formula in transportation cases. Most judicial work with *Pike*-based analysis, however, has come in cases not involving transportation-related problems. Two significant points about the Court's handling of these cases merit mention at the outset. First, *Pike* itself presented an odd case in which to set forth a standard for assessing facially neutral laws because it involved the application of a state statute that, as applied, entailed overt discrimination in the form of a local processing requirement.[55] Second, although the *Pike* test has drawn much criticism on the ground that it serves as a vehicle for judicial activism, the Court has expressly relied on that test only once to invalidate a nondiscriminatory state law outside the road-safety

---

[53] *See Barnwell*, 303 U.S. at 192–96 (detailing the state's safety and road-maintenance evidence; noting, for example, with respect to the challenged width rule, that many South Carolina roads were too narrow to accommodate two 96-inch-wide trucks and that "as the width of trucks is increased it obstructs the view of the highway").

[54] *See, e.g.*, Martin Marietta Materials, Inc. v. City of Greenwood, No. 06–697–CV-W-W, 2008 WL 4832638, at *7 (W.D. Mo. Sept. 4, 2008) (finding that a city ordinance prohibiting through-truck traffic violated the dormant Commerce Clause under *Pike*). In particular, several lower courts have considered with care the application of the *Pike* balancing test to state toll-road laws. *See, e.g.*, Yerger v. Mass. Tpk. Auth., 395 F. App'x 878 (3d Cir. 2010) (holding that a toll discount program offered to subscribers of the Massachusetts Turnpike Authority's electronic toll payment system did not violate the dormant Commerce Clause); Selevan v. New York Thruway Auth., 711 F.3d 253, 256 (2d Cir. 2013) (holding that a toll-bridge discount available only to island residents did not violate the dormant Commerce Clause). Lower courts have applied *Pike* in non-road transportation contexts as well. *See, e.g.*, Francarl Realty Corp. v. Town of East Hampton, 400 F. App'x 605, 607 (2d Cir. 2010) (applying the *Pike* test to a town's ferry regulation and holding that it survived a dormant Commerce Clause challenge because the "incidental burden on interstate commerce" did not clearly outweigh the law's countervailing local benefits).

[55] In *Pike*, Arizona required a cantaloupe grower to package its product in crates within the state so that state authorities could ensure that those crates indicated the Arizona origins of the product. From a present-day vantage point, the operation of the Arizona law thus seemed to discriminate against interstate commerce by imposing an in-state processing requirement on the grower. *See supra* Section 17.A.3. Why, then, did the Court in that case not apply the virtually per se rule of unconstitutionality to wipe the Arizona law off the books? Perhaps because, at the time, the Court had not yet fully developed its modern analytical structure for assessing dormant Commerce Clause cases or (at least) had not yet seen fit to characterize all in-state-processing requirements as inherently discriminatory. For a careful analysis of *Pike*, including with regard to whether it was truly a discrimination case, see Regan, *supra* note 5, at 1209–20.

context.[56] Even so, the Court has never questioned the *Pike* formula, and one post-*Pike* case, *Hunt v. Washington State Apple Advertising Commission*,[57] invalidated a facially neutral state law using an analysis that—while tethered to a finding of discriminatory effect—so closely paralleled *Pike*-based review that it provides a worthy illustration of the Court's openness to dormant Commerce Clause balancing.[58]

In *Washington State Apple Advertising Commission*, the Court confronted a law passed by North Carolina, a leading apple-producing state, that prohibited the use of closed apple containers that bore any grading mark other than the U.S. Department of Agriculture (USDA) quality designation. Growers from Washington, another leading apple-producing state, challenged the law because they had developed their own grading system, which they routinely used in marking packages of produce shipped to every corner of the nation.[59] The challengers first argued that the North Carolina law

---

[56] That occasion came in *Edgar v. MITE Corp.*, 457 U.S. 624 (1982), in which five Justices came together (in Part V-B of the opinion) to invoke the *Pike* test in invalidating a state tender-offer statute; *see also infra* Section 19.C (discussing *Edgar* in further detail). Apart from *Edgar*, the Court on occasion has applied *Pike*'s balancing methodology in striking down *discriminatory* state laws. For example, in *Lewis v. BT Investment Managers, Inc.*, 447 U.S. 27 (1980), the Court drew on *Pike* in striking down a state law that overtly discriminated between in-state and out-of-state entities with regard to their ability to operate local investment-advisory businesses. Another post-*Pike* case is *Bendix Autolite Corp.*, in which the Court invalidated a rule that subjected a foreign corporation to indefinite tolling of all statutes of limitations unless it appointed an in-state agent to receive service of process, including with respect to actions over which the state could not otherwise exert personal jurisdiction. The Court—albeit without citing *Pike*—concluded that "the burden imposed on interstate commerce by the tolling statute exceeds any local interest that the state might advance." *Bendix Autolite Corp.*, 486 U.S. at 891. The Court, however, also observed along the way that "the Ohio statute imposes a greater burden on out-of-state companies than it does on Ohio companies," *id.* at 894, thus suggesting that the statutory scheme involved outright discrimination against interstate commerce. *See id.* at 898 (Scalia, J., concurring in the judgment) (concluding that the statute was "on its face discriminatory" against foreign corporations); *see also* Great Atl. & Pac. Tea Co. v. Cottrell, 424 U.S. 366, 375–77 (1976) (applying the *Pike* test to a Mississippi law under which, in seemingly discriminatory fashion due to its application to only imported goods, "milk and milk products from another State may be sold in Mississippi provided that . . . the other State . . . accepts Grade A milk and milk products produced and processed in Mississippi on a reciprocal basis" (internal quotations and alterations omitted)).

[57] 432 U.S. 333 (1977).

[58] To be clear, the Court in this case described the law, despite its facial neutrality, as so greatly burdensome for out-of-staters in comparison to in-staters that its "practical effect" entailed "discrimination." *Id.* at 350. Even so, the balancing process engaged in by the Court tracks *Pike*-based analysis in such a close way that it underscores both the relevance and the impact of this mode of judicial review—regardless of whether that analysis is put work in connection with a finding of discriminatory effect or judicial use of the intolerable-incidental-effects rhetoric of *Pike*. *See also id.* at 350 (adverting to *Pike* in referencing "the task of effecting an accommodation of the competing national and local interests").

[59] *Id.* at 336.

reflected nothing more than a thinly veiled purposeful effort to block competition from Washington apple producers. The Court, however, found it unnecessary to "ascribe an economic protection motive to the North Carolina legislature."[60] Instead, it ruled that a proper balancing of state and national interests showed that the law, although facially neutral, impinged unduly upon interstate trade.[61]

On the state-interest side of the ledger, the Court found little that counted. North Carolina argued that its law reduced confusion. The Court, however, found this proffered justification to be flimsy because: (1) closed containers were typically purchased by sophisticated resellers, rather than consumers in need of protection from getting too much information; (2) removal of the Washington grade in fact kept the very buyers the state supposedly was protecting from receiving potentially useful information; and (3) the risk of confusion created by inclusion of local grade marks, even for the most unsophisticated consumers, was small and speculative in any event.[62] The Court also emphasized that North Carolina could protect its claimed interests with less restrictive alternatives, including "by permitting out-of-state growers to utilize state grades only if they also marked their shipments with the applicable USDA label."[63]

On the other side of the ledger, the law put such a burden on Washington apple producers that it had the "practical effect" of "discriminating" against them.[64] This was so because (1) the law raised costs for Washington producers by forcing them to segregate crates destined for North Carolina from crates bound elsewhere; (2) the law stripped away from the Washington apple industry "advantages it has earned for itself through its expensive inspection and grading system"; and (3) the law effectively "downgrad[ed]" high-quality Washington apples to, at best, a lower designation supplied by the cruder USDA system.[65] The cumulative effect of these considerations led the Court to invalidate the facially neutral North Carolina labeling law. Even those Justices who would later dissent in *Kassel* (with the exception of Justice Rehnquist, who did not participate in the case) joined a unanimous opinion finding an affront to the dormant Commerce Clause principle.[66]

---

60 *Id.* at 352.

61 *Id.* at 353.

62 *Id.* at 353–54.

63 *Id.* at 354.

64 *Id.* at 350.

65 *Id.* at 351–52.

66 *Id.* at 354.

Lower courts, engaging in similar forms of analysis under the banner of *Pike*, have likewise found facially evenhanded state laws to violate the dormant Commerce Clause.[67] Consider, for example, *Yamaha Motor Corp., U.S.A. v. Jim's Motorcycle, Inc.*,[68] a Fourth Circuit decision concerning an amendment to Virginia's motorcycle franchise law. Under the earlier statute, motorcycle dealers had "the right to protest the establishment of a new dealership for the same line-make (brand) in its 'relevant market area,' defined as a seven to ten-, fifteen-, or twenty-mile radius around the existing dealer, depending on population density."[69] The challenged amendment, however, broadly expanded the statutory protest right by allowing any dealer located anywhere in Virginia to challenge the proposed establishment of any new dealership anywhere in the state.

In applying *Pike*-based review, the court first concluded that the "protection for motorcycle dealerships" from "excessive competition" was, as the state argued, a "legitimate purpose" for expanding the geographic scope of protest rights—albeit a purpose that gave rise to

---

[67] *See, e.g.*, Baude v. Heath, 538 F.3d 608, 608–12 (7th Cir. 2008) (striking down part of a facially neutral Indiana law that allowed wineries to sell directly to consumers only if they did not hold a wholesale-alcoholic-beverages license; reasoning that the law in effect advantaged in-state wineries, which were barred by Indiana from wholesaling, over out-of-state wineries whose states allowed them to engage in local wholesaling); PSINet, Inc. v. Chapman, 362 F.3d 227, 240 (4th Cir. 2004) (striking down under *Pike* a state law criminalizing the dissemination of harmful material to minors over the Internet; reasoning in part that, while "[t]here is no question that Virginia has a compelling interest in protecting the physical and psychological well-being of minors," the benefits of this statute "have not been proven" because minors still had a wide variety of avenues to access similar communications); Alliant Energy Corp. v. Bie, 330 F.3d 904, 912–14 (7th Cir. 2003) (finding an in-state incorporation requirement for public utility companies operating in the state unconstitutional under the *Pike* balancing formula because that requirement disadvantaged companies that were incorporated elsewhere with no discernible purpose for doing so); R & M Oil & Supply, Inc., v. Saunders, 307 F.3d 731, 736–37 (8th Cir. 2002) (identifying less commerce-burdening alternatives for state-imposed propane-storage regulations on the way to invalidating those regulations under *Pike* analysis); GoodCat, LLC v. Cook, 202 F. Supp. 3d 896, 916–17 (S.D. Ind. 2016) (finding that the burdens imposed by a challenged e-liquid law clearly exceeded any purported benefits where that law required manufacturers to comply with rigorous security standards to sell products in Indiana); Island Silver & Spice, Inc. v. Islamorada, Vill. of Islands, 475 F. Supp. 2d 1281, 1292–93 (S.D. Fla. 2007) (holding a zoning ordinance unconstitutional under *Pike* because it imposed strict, across-the-board size limitations that restricted national retail chains from entering the local market for no reason apart from fostering the "small town character" of a community that did not have "any small town character to preserve"), *aff'd on other grounds*, 532 F.3d 844 (11th Cir. 2008); Metro Produce Distribs. v. City of Minneapolis, 473 F. Supp. 2d 955, 963 (D. Minn. 2007) (concluding that the burden imposed by a Minneapolis noise ordinance that forced produce distributors to alter delivery schedules—thus prohibiting any distributor from "operat[ing] a refrigeration unit at night while parked outside an insulated building in a residential area"—outweighed any benefits produced for local residents by decreasing noise).

[68] 401 F.3d 560 (4th Cir. 2005).

[69] *Id.* at 563 (quoting VA. CODE ANN. § 46.2–1993).

only a "weak benefit."[70] In reaching this conclusion, the court took close account of the specialized features of motorcycle retailing business, including that (1) sales territories for such businesses exceed in size the territories of otherwise comparable automobile dealerships; and (2) motorcycle dealerships "typically sell within a forty-mile radius."[71] The court also found that the burdens placed by the statutory amendment on interstate commerce were "severe" because they created "a significant barrier to market entry."[72] Support for this conclusion came from key case-specific facts, including that (1) as a result of the new law, protests were almost certain to occur in response to every new-dealership proposal; (2) the law impeded the establishment of new dealerships by removing prior guidance as to where it would make the best sense to locate those dealerships; and (3) the evidence indicated that the costs of anticipating and defending against the much-expanded set of protests likely to be triggered by the new law would create a chilling effect on the creation of new dealerships.[73] The Court found it telling that Virginia's post-amendment law was "uniquely anti-competitive even as dealer protection laws go" because no comparably restrictive measure existed in any state.[74] It also emphasized that the law swept too broadly because a "less restrictive alternative" to it was near at hand: Instead of creating sweeping statewide protest rights, the Commonwealth's legislature "could have imposed some rational geographic limit on protest rights, but it did not."[75] In sum, because of the "weak benefit" and "substantial burden" created by this new law, the Fourth Circuit concluded that it could not stand in keeping with *Pike*-balancing principles.[76]

Jim's Motorcycle illustrates how *Pike*-based balancing, built on a thoroughgoing analysis of the specific features of the operation of the challenged statute, can lead to findings of constitutional invalidity. More subtly, the case shows how this methodology can generate judicial overrides of state laws in precisely those instances where there is strong reason to suspect that protectionist motivations (here on behalf of already-established local business operators) have been at work. It is critical to see, however, that the *Pike* test has built into it a self-restraining quality because it supports judicial

[70] *Id.* at 564, 568, 571.

[71] *Id.* at 571.

[72] *Id.*

[73] *Id.*

[74] *Id.*

[75] *Id.* at 571, 573.

[76] *Id.* at 573. For a later ruling that drew on this case, see *Colon Health*, 733 F.3d at 546 (noting that where the burdens of a state law "fall primarily on out-of-state economic interests," courts have held that "the state's political process cannot be relied upon to rectify legislative abuse" (citing *Jim's Motorcycle*, 401 F.3d at 573)).

intervention only when the burden a law places on interstate commerce is "clearly excessive" in relation to the state interests offered in support of the measure.[77] As a result, it is not surprising that *Pike*-based attacks very often—indeed, most often—meet with failure.[78] Indeed, the Court itself has rejected *Pike*-based challenges to state laws on multiple occasions.[79]

---

[77] *See Pike*, 397 U.S. at 142.

[78] Many lower court rulings illustrate the point. *See, e.g.*, Rosenblatt v. City of Santa Monica, 940 F.3d 439, 442, 451–53 (9th Cir. 2019) (upholding a city ordinance that prohibited certain types of "vacation rentals" while emphasizing that no evidence suggested that the law significantly burdened interstate commerce), *cert. denied*, 140 S. Ct. 2762 (2020); VIZIO, Inc. v. Klee, 886 F.3d 249, 258–60 (2d Cir. 2018) (holding that Connecticut's E-Waste law did not impose an undue burden on interstate commerce in part because the law's local benefits were "legion"); N.Y. Pet Welfare Ass'n v. City of New York, 850 F.3d 79, 91 (2d Cir. 2017) (holding that the plaintiff "fail[ed] sufficiently to allege that the burden of having to sell directly to City pet shops, rather than through distributors, will fall disproportionately on out-of-state breeders"); Safari Club Int'l v. Becerra, 702 F. App'x 607 (9th Cir. 2017) (holding that the plaintiffs failed to show that a law prohibiting importation, possession, or transportation of mountain lions into or in California imposed a substantial burden on interstate commerce); *Colon Health*, 813 F.3d 145 (holding that a Virginia law requiring medical service providers to obtain a certificate of need prior to establishing or expanding operations within the state satisfied the *Pike* balancing test because the benefits of improving healthcare quality, increasing access to healthcare for indigent individuals, and lowering general healthcare costs outweighed any burden on interstate commerce); Chinatown Neighborhood Ass'n v. Harris, 794 F.3d 1136 (9th Cir. 2015) (upholding California's Shark Fin Law because the local benefits—including "conserv[ing] state resources, prevent[ing] animal cruelty, and protect[ing] wildlife and public health"—outweighed the burden on interstate commerce, which was at most minimal); Fresenius Med. Care Holdings, Inc. v. Tucker, 704 F.3d 935, 942–44 (11th Cir. 2013) (upholding a Florida law that prohibited physicians from making referrals to services in which they had a financial interest because the burden imposed by the law on interstate commerce was not excessive in comparison to the benefits of protecting patients); Nat'l Ass'n of Optometrists v. Harris, 682 F.3d 1144, 1155 (9th Cir. 2012) (upholding a California law prohibiting opticians from establishing one-stop eyewear shops because the law did not impose a significant burden on interstate commerce under the *Pike* test); Pac. Merch. Shipping Ass'n v. Goldstene, 639 F.3d 1154, 1180–82 (9th Cir. 2011) (holding that California vessel-fuel-use regulations provided benefits in protecting residents' health from harmful emissions and that these benefits outweighed any incidental burden on interstate commerce); Brown v. Hovatter, 561 F.3d 357, 363–68 (4th Cir. 2009) (upholding Maryland's Morticians Act, which generally prohibited corporations from owning morticians' licenses and funeral establishments, because "mortuary science is inherently a local profession," the Act did not burden the flow of interstate commerce, and the law fostered "familiarity between an owner and his business"); Buss. for a Better N.Y. v. Angello, 341 F. App'x 701, 705 (2d Cir. 2009) (holding that New York scaffolding laws satisfied the *Pike* test because the benefits of protecting construction workers were not clearly outweighed by any burdens imposed on interstate commerce); Allstate Ins. Co. v. Abbott, 495 F.3d 151 (5th Cir. 2007) (concluding that, under the *Pike* test, a Texas statute that restricted car insurance companies' right to operate car body shops did not violate the dormant Commerce Clause because the benefits of protecting consumers were not clearly outweighed by the burden of preventing one interstate body-shop owner from expanding in Texas); Int'l Truck & Engine Corp. v. Bray, 372 F.3d 717 (5th Cir. 2004) (finding that a Texas law that forbade truck manufacturers from operating as dealers of vehicles did not impermissibly burden interstate commerce under *Pike*).

[79] *See* Nw. Cent. Pipeline Corp. v. State Corp. Comm'n, 489 U.S. 493 (1989) (rejecting a challenge to a generally applicable Kansas measure designed to encourage

C. RECURRING THEMES OF DORMANT COMMERCE CLAUSE DOCTRINE

What "big picture" lessons can one draw from the Court's non-discrimination and *Pike* balancing rulings? First, all these cases—including those involving outright discrimination against interstate commerce—require a weighing of state and federal interests. The Maine baitfish case, for example, reveals the Court's willingness to assess with care justifications offered by the state in support of even the most starkly discriminatory law.[80] This is not to say that the level of scrutiny lacks importance in dormant Commerce Clause litigation. Far from it. For example, in *Minnesota v. Clover Leaf Creamery Co.*,[81] a *Pike* balancing case, the Court was quick to accept the state's argument that a subsidy program would operate as an inadequate substitute for its ban on the use of nonreturnable plastic milk jugs in furthering the environmental and waste-disposal interests that the ban itself was said to promote.[82] When confronting the facially

---

efficient natural gas production); Arkansas Elec. Coop. Corp. v. Arkansas Pub. Serv. Comm'n, 461 U.S. 375, 395 (1983) (specifically citing *Pike*'s "clearly excessive" standard in upholding the state's rate regulation of a local power wholesaler, notwithstanding prior authority under the Court's direct-indirect jurisprudence barring such a regulation); Exxon Corp. v. Governor of Maryland, 437 U.S. 117 (1978) (discussed *infra* note 92); *cf. also* Huron Portland Cement Co. v. City of Detroit, 362 U.S. 440, 448–49 (1960) (upholding a nondiscriminatory pollution-control law as applied to ships operating in interstate commerce); Breard v. City of Alexandria, 341 U.S. 622 (1951) (discussed *infra* Section 21.A n.35). In *Minnesota v. Clover Leaf Creamery Co.*, 449 U.S. 456 (1981), for example, the Court upheld a state-imposed ban on the sale of milk in plastic nonreturnable containers. The challengers asked the Court to balance the law into oblivion, emphasizing that the resin used to make plastic jugs came entirely from outside the state, whereas the pulpwood used to make substituted paperboard containers came largely from in-state producers. The Court, however, declined to find the resulting burden on interstate commerce "clearly excessive" in relation to Minnesota's "substantial" state interest in reducing energy consumption, the generation of solid waste, and the depletion of the non-renewable resources used in making plastic. *Id.* at 473. The Court also characterized the law's burdens on interstate commerce as "relatively minor" because (1) it advantaged out-of-state pulpwood producers; (2) in-state plastic-container producers and users were adversely affected by the law; and (3) both the out-of-state and the in-state paperboard-carton industry benefited from the law in ways difficult to measure. *Id.* at 472–73. In addition, the Court pushed aside two purportedly preferable less-restrictive alternatives put forward by the law's challengers. First, "banning all nonreturnables" did not present a reasonable option because that restriction would place an even greater burden on interstate commerce than Minnesota's more limited ban on only some nonreturnable containers. *Id.* Second, a program of "providing incentives for recycling" did not offer a workable alternative because it was "less likely to be effective" than an outright prohibition. *Id.* at 473–74. Finally, and sounding the same representation-reinforcement theme that had surfaced in its earlier decisions, the Court emphasized that the law created problems for a number of local interest groups. *See id.* at 473 n.17 (noting that "the existence of major in-state interests adversely affected by the Act is a powerful safeguard against legislative abuse").

[80] *See* Maine v. Taylor, 477 U.S. 131 (1986) (discussed *supra* Section 17.D).

[81] 449 U.S. 456 (1981). *See supra* note 80 (discussing the case).

[82] *Clover Leaf Creamery*, 449 U.S. at 473–74.

discriminatory measure at issue in *Carbone*, however, the Court invalidated a challenged forced-use rule because local-government authorities could have relied on a subsidy program a "less restrictive means" for ensuring the effective operation of the waste transfer facility.[83] To be sure, these are only two cases, but they illustrate the key point—namely, that the analytical "mood" that courts bring to *Pike* balancing analysis differs dramatically from the one they display in applying the virtually per se rule triggered by discriminatory state measures.

Second, the Court has indicated that both the nature of the state's interest and its mode of advancing that interest have significant roles to play in determining a law's validity under modern-day dormant Commerce Clause doctrine. Thus, saving lives should count for more than ensuring that products work, which should count for more than merely averting some possibility of confusion among product purchasers. (Compare, for example, the Court's deference to the state's highway-safety interests in *Bradley* with the Court's pooh-poohing of the state's confused-fruit-buyer rationale in the *Washington State Apple Advertising* case.[84]) Likewise, the degree of fit between a challenged law and the interest it is said to promote is of analytical importance. A challenged rule may fail because it advances the state's interest too tenuously, because its effectiveness is too speculative or because it is affirmatively counterproductive. (Recall, for example, the Court's concern in *Washington State Apple Advertising* that the state's purchaser-protection law perversely deprived product purchasers of useful information.[85]) In addition, problems of overinclusiveness may place a state law in constitutional jeopardy.[86] The wholesale ban on

---

[83] *See* C & A Carbone, Inc. v. Town of Clarkstown, 511 U.S. 383 (1994) (discussed *supra* Section 17.A.3).

[84] *See supra* Section 18.B. The Court overtly suggested the sliding-scale importance of different state interests in *Washington State Apple Advertising* when it noted that such an interest, at least presumptively, "*is particularly strong* when the State acts to protect its citizenry in matters pertaining to the sale of foodstuffs." *Wash. State Apple Advert.*, 432 U.S. at 350 (emphasis added); *see also Pike*, 397 U.S. at 143 (noting that "[w]e are not . . . dealing here with state legislation in the field of safety or with an Act designed to protect consumers . . . from contaminated or unfit goods" but instead with a law enacted "simply to protect and enhance the reputation of growers within the state" (internal quotations and alterations omitted)); *id.* at 145–46 (describing this state interest as "tenuous," "minimal," and "certainly less substantial than a state's interest in securing employment for its people").

[85] *See supra* Section 18.B.

[86] A rule is overinclusive if it reaches more persons than those involved in the mischief it has the purpose of addressing. Assume, for example, that a state wishes to deal with the growing problem of used newspapers being left in public places. A law that prohibits the possession of newspapers outside one's own yard would obviously operate to cut down on this problem. But it would also be overinclusive because many persons who take newspapers outside their yards nonetheless properly dispose of them. A law that prohibits all purchases of newspapers would be even more

baitfish importation upheld in *Maine v. Taylor*,[87] for example, might well become unconstitutional if, in the future, scientists devise ways to identify and exclude only those particular fish that carry destructive parasites.[88] It is equally true that underinclusiveness may lead a court to invalidate a commerce-burdening statute. Excluding only non-locally-generated hazardous waste from state disposal facilities, for example, is unjustifiable if locally generated hazardous waste poses exactly the same environmental threat.[89] And it is likewise true that less-restrictive-alternatives analysis (and related doctrinal tools) often play a prominent role in dormant Commerce Clause cases.[90] In *Jim's Motorcycle*, for example, the court reasoned that a trimmed-down expansion of dealer-protest rights would have worked just as well to safeguard genuinely legitimate state interests in avoiding destructive oversaturation of localized motorcycle-distribution markets. Likewise, in *City of Philadelphia*,[91] New Jersey's ban on the importation of out-of-state waste was difficult to justify in light of a readily available less restrictive alternative that would have no less effectively addressed the state's asserted excess-waste-disposal problem—namely, a nondiscriminatory limit on the total volume of solid waste put in the state's ground.[92]

---

overinclusive, and a law that prohibits all littering would be overinclusive as well, so long as the law's purpose was to stop only newspaper littering. Given such a purpose, a law that simply outlawed newspaper littering would not be overinclusive (or at least not substantially so), but such a law might also not be very effective in rooting out the problem of visual blight caused by newspaper littering. *See generally* LOUIS MICHAEL SEIDMAN, CONSTITUTIONAL LAW, EQUAL PROTECTION OF THE LAWS 66–73 (2003).

[87] 477 U.S. 131 (1986) (discussed *supra* Section 17.D).

[88] *See id.* at 147 (noting that, "if and when such procedures are developed, Maine no longer may be able to justify its import ban").

[89] *See* Or. Waste Sys., Inc. v. Dep't of Envtl. Quality, 511 U.S. 93, 105–07 (1994).

[90] *See generally* Jud Mathews & Alec Stone Sweet, *All Things in Proportion? American Rights Review and the Problem of Balancing*, 60 EMORY L.J. 797, 814–20 (2011) (suggesting that less-restrictive-means analysis first surfaced in the Court's nineteenth-century dormant Commerce Clause jurisprudence before spreading to other areas of the law and that the Court adopted this form of "testing as a means of 'smoking out' protectionist motives" masked by a claimed "important or compelling public interest").

[91] *See infra* Section 17.A.

[92] A related point is that, in some cases, less restrictive alternatives may be functionally unavailable even when burdens on interstate commerce are severe, thus effectively foreclosing successful dormancy-doctrine challenges, at least in balancing cases. Illustrative of the point is *Exxon Corp. v. Governor of Maryland*, 437 U.S. 117 (1978). There, the Court upheld a Maryland law that barred all petroleum producers and refiners from operating local gas stations. At least at first glance, the burden imposed by the law on interstate commerce seemed great because the law's practical effect fell solely on out-of-state businesses in that no gas was produced or refined in Maryland. The majority, however, found no impermissible burden on interstate commerce, making much of the fact that the law did not preclude service-station ownership by *all* out-of-state businesses because out-of-state non-producer/non-refiner firms could continue to operate gas stations in Maryland. *Id.* at 126 & n.15. As Justice

Third, just as surely as courts will carefully consider the precise state interests cited in support of challenged legislation, they also will look closely at the precise burden the challenged law places on interstate commerce. In *Southern Pacific*, for example, the Court emphasized the variety of ways in which Arizona's train-length law raised costs (for both carriers and neighboring states) and delayed cross-border deliveries.[93] Likewise, in *Clover Leaf Creamery*, the Court refused to oversimplify the case by focusing myopically on only the harms suffered by out-of-state plastic resin producers that generated material used in making the disposable plastic jugs that were targeted by the challenged restriction. Instead, the Court was careful to consider the law's positive impact on out-of-state milk bottlers, pulp producers, and dairy farmers, some of whom gained new business opportunities as a result of the enactment of that same law.[94] The key point is that these cases have less to do with the incantation of legal platitudes than with close, and highly contextual, factual analysis.[95] Lawyers called on to handle dormant Commerce Clause cases must roll up their sleeves, closely probe the particular law's underlying purposes and practical effects, seek to identify less

---

Blackmun observed in dissent, however, the state legislature's failure to engage in "universal discrimination" against out-of-state entities was not controlling. *Id.* at 146–47 (Blackmun, J., dissenting). In *Washington State Apple Advertising*, for example, the Court had found a dormant Commerce Clause violation because Washington apple producers were disadvantaged by a North Carolina packaging law even though that law had no ill effects on the many other out-of-state apple producers who had not put in place a distinctive grading and package-marking system. *See id.* at 146 n.14. Indeed, in one sense, the Maryland law at issue in *Exxon* seemed more onerous for would-be out-of-state market entrants than the apple-packaging restrictions imposed by North Carolina because the Maryland law *flatly excluded* many out-of-state businesses from the local market, as opposed to (as in the *Washington Apple* case) simply complicating out-of-staters' efforts to compete with local producers. Perhaps the key to understanding *Exxon* lies in Maryland's claimed state interest in countering vertical integration in the gasoline-distribution industry to solve such problems as unfair discrimination against non-vertically-integrated gas stations in allocating products in times of shortage. But if that is so, then the key point is this: By recognizing the prevention of vertical integration as a significant state interest, the Court ensured that any further balancing in a case such as *Exxon* would be all but unnecessary. Even though the Maryland law disproportionately burdened non-local gas station owners, there was simply no way to avoid that result (given the pre-existing location of refiners and producers) if the practice of vertical integration was to be discontinued. For this reason, although the Court's analysis in *Exxon* is open to criticism, the majority may not have overreached in concluding that Maryland's statute did not "impermissibly" burden interstate commerce. *Id.* at 127; *see also* Regan, *supra* note 5, at 1239 (asserting that "[c]ertainly there is a much more plausible legitimate purpose to credit . . . in *Exxon* than . . . in" the Washington apple case).

93 *See supra* Section 18.A.

94 *See supra* notes 81–82 and accompanying text.

95 *See, e.g.*, *Colon Health*, 813 F.3d at 151, 157–59 (noting the "fact-intensive quality" of dormant Commerce Clause analysis and then probing in detail the alleged burdens on interstate commerce imposed by West Virginia's certificate-of-need requirement for establishing and expanding medical facilities before finding the requirement valid).

restrictive alternatives, build a supportive evidentiary record with respect to the law's burdens and benefits, and do all this while attending to scores of legal precedents that provide rich opportunities for argument by analogy and by distinction.[96] In short, "Commerce Clause adjudication must depend in large part 'upon the thoroughness with which the lawyers perform their task in the conduct of constitutional litigation.' "[97]

Fourth, as courts assess the constitutionality of any particular state law, the surrounding *legal* environment may play a key role. In *Southern Pacific* and *Kassel*, for example, the Court relied heavily on the commerce-burdening effects that flowed from the challenged measure's interaction with the laws of nearby states.[98] The interaction of state and federal law will sometimes matter too. For

---

[96] Complicating this process is the fact that the Court sometimes uses slippery rhetoric in deciding discrete dormant Commerce Clause questions that litigants must grapple with in handling later cases. In *Exxon*, for instance, the Court proclaimed that nothing in "the Commerce Clause protects the particular structure or methods of operation in a retail market." 437 U.S. at 127. But what does this statement mean? Surely it does not signify that a state may freely control all "methods of operation" in any market without worrying about the dormancy doctrine. The Court invalidated the law in *Washington State Apple Advertising*, for example, even though it involved "methods of operation" with respect to product packaging. *See supra* Section 18.B. This statement also cannot mean that the Court will never invalidate state laws that control business ownership structures. Just two years after *Exxon*, for example, the Court invalidated a Florida law that outlawed ownership of local investment advisory firms by out-of-state bank holding companies. *See Lewis*, 447 U.S. at 44. Perhaps the best reading of *Exxon*'s "particular structures or methods" language is that existing businesses, including out-of-state businesses, have no vested right to keep in place any pre-existing laws, including pre-existing laws about the permissibility of vertical integration. Just as surely as "variations in the experiences or habits of different communities may well call for different legislative regulations as to methods and manners of doing business," *Breard*, 341 U.S. at 641, so too may shifts in conditions and values that take place in the same state with the passage of time.

[97] *Raymond Motor Transp., Inc.*, 434 U.S. at 448 n.25 (quoting Dowling, *supra* note 5, at 27–28); *see also* Stephanie Tai, *When Natural Science Meets the Dismal Science*, 42 ARIZ. ST. L.J. 949, 997–98 (2010) (emphasizing that courts addressing state and local waste regulations have looked for "economic evidence regarding the impact of challenged state regulations on out-of-state businesses, as well as evaluating economic theories regarding market impact").

[98] *See also Bibb*, 359 U.S. at 529–30 (emphasizing that "a design out of line with requirements of almost all the other States may sometimes place a great burden of delay and inconvenience on those interstate motor carriers entering or crossing its territory"). This consideration played a significant role in pre-*Brown v. Board of Education* efforts to attack generally applicable racial-segregation requirements to the extent they applied to interstate transportation. *See* Morgan v. Virginia, 328 U.S. 373, 377, 381 (1946) (striking down a segregation requirement as applied to interstate bus passengers in light of "related statutes of other states"; finding that the law "unduly burdens [interstate] commerce in matters where uniformity is necessary" in part because, especially for sleeping or resting passengers, "reseating would be disturbing"). *Cf.* Colo. Anti-Discrimination Comm'n v. Cont'l Air Lines, Inc., 372 U.S. 714, 718–22 (1963) (rejecting an airline's challenge to the application of a general state ban on race discrimination in hiring; noting that hiring is more "localized" than transporting passengers and that, unlike in *Morgan*, the "threat of diverse and conflicting regulation" was "virtually nonexistent").

example, in *Edgar v. MITE, Corp.*,[99] the Court downplayed the state's interest in according shareholders of take-over-target corporations "withdrawal, proration, and equal consideration rights" because the federal Williams Act already protected those same interests to a significant degree.[100] Although the Illinois statute went beyond the Williams Act in requiring corporate disclosures, the Court reasoned that—in light of the federal law's significant, freestanding disclosure requirements—any marginal benefits supplied by the Illinois statute were too "speculative" to justify the substantial burdens the statute placed on interstate transactions.[101]

Finally, it is important to see that dormant Commerce Clause cases do not always fit into a single, tidy pattern. Facially neutral laws, for example, may be evaluated under the *Pike* balancing test, under the specialized *Pike* rule apparently applicable in road-safety cases, under a category-based approach that asks whether the law has a "discriminatory effect" or "discriminatory purpose," or (as we soon will see) under an inquiry that focuses on its "extraterritorial" impact.[102] What remains true across the board is that at least one of these analytical pathways will likely lead to a finding of constitutional invalidity if there is a solid basis for concluding that the challenged state law significantly impedes the free flow of interstate commerce for no good reason. In other words, if a law threatens the national-common-market values that have driven the application of the dormancy principle over the years, without providing any meaningful countervailing benefit, there exist multiple doctrinal hooks upon which to hang the finding of a constitutional violation.

---

99 457 U.S. 624 (1982).

100 *Id.* at 644.

101 *Id.* at 644–45.

102 *See infra* Chapter 19.

Chapter 19

THE DORMANCY-DOCTRINE EXTRATERRITORIALITY RULE

Analysis

The dormancy doctrine's anti-discrimination and *Pike*-balancing restrictions are supplemented by a third, freestanding prohibition that precludes states from engaging in "extraterritorial regulation."[1] This limitation stems from a cluster of constitutional policies. To begin with, the extraterritoriality doctrine focuses largely on promoting "horizontal" federalism.[2] The core idea is simple: Fully safeguarding any particular state's autonomy in controlling activities within its own borders requires not only shielding that state from federal overreaching, but also—and no less importantly—from comparable overreaching by other states.[3] In addition, the

---

1 Healy v. Beer Inst., Inc., 491 U.S. 324, 332 (1989). Notably, a separate set of extraterritoriality-based limits on state regulatory authority emanates from the Due Process Clause of the Fourteenth Amendment. The relation between due-process and dormant Commerce Clause extraterritoriality requirements is not well-developed. In some state-tax cases, however, the Court has given the so-called "nexus" limitation developed under the dormant Commerce Clause a longer reach than the extraterritoriality restriction imposed by the Due Process Clause, *see infra* Section 21.A, and it seems clear that the dormancy doctrine's extraterritoriality limit on state regulatory measures likewise limits state authority to a greater degree than due-process-based rules.

2 *See, e.g.*, Am. Libraries Ass'n v. Pataki, 969 F. Supp. 160, 175–76 (S.D.N.Y. 1997) (noting that the extraterritoriality limit not only "subordinates each state's authority over interstate commerce to the federal power of regulation (a vertical limitation)," but also "mandates that one state not expand its regulatory powers in a manner that encroaches upon the sovereignty of its fellow states (a horizontal limitation)"). For one of many treatments of the subject of horizontal federalism, see JOSEPH F. ZIMMERMAN, HORIZONTAL FEDERALISM: INTERSTATE RELATIONS (2011).

3 *See* IMS Health Inc. v. Mills, 616 F.3d 7, 30 n.29 (1st Cir. 2010) (noting the appropriateness of limitations on state regulation of extraterritorial commerce because "one State's power to impose burdens on the interstate market . . . is also constrained by the need to respect the interests of other States" (quoting BMW of North America, Inc. v. Gore, 517 U.S. 559, 571 (1996)), *judgment vacated sub nom.* IMS Health, Inc. v. Schneider, 564 U.S. 1051 (2011); Midwest Title Loans, Inc. v. Mills, 593 F.3d 660, 667–68 (7th Cir. 2010) ("Suppose Illinois thinks title loans . . . shouldn't be restricted in the way that Indiana thinks they should be. To allow Indiana to apply

extraterritoriality doctrine addresses concerns that one state's undue meddling with activities in other states creates special threats to a well-functioning federal system. More specifically, the doctrine addresses risks that state-based extraterritorial regulation, if allowed to operate unchecked, will: (1) effectively impede or undermine choices made by firms and individuals to "vote with their feet" by locating business operations in one state rather than another in response to the mix of differentiated regulatory regimes that a vibrant federal system envisions;[4] (2) inhibit cross-border trade by subjecting commercial actors to a crazy quilt of differing state regulatory regimes;[5] and (3) permit outlier jurisdictions—both perversely and inefficiently—to establish *de facto* national commerce-constricting rules as firms make practical choices to conform operations to the most restrictive set of state regulatory controls.[6]

A. THE SUPREME COURT'S EXTRATERRITORIALITY JURISPRUDENCE

Complexities in evaluating extraterritoriality problems arise because countless state laws have cross-border impacts without implicating the anti-extraterritoriality principle.[7] At the same time, the Court has made clear that the principle does indeed exist and that, if applicable, it triggers a level of judicial scrutiny far more demanding than that of the *Pike* balancing test.[8] The Court, however,

---

its law against title loans when its residents transact in [Illinois] would be arbitrarily to exalt the public policy of one state over that of another.").

4 *See generally* Ilya Somin, *Foot Voting, Federalism, and Political Freedom*, 55 NOMOS: AM. SOC'Y POL. LEGAL PHIL. 83, 83 (2014) ("[F]oot voting is . . . a tool for enhancing political freedom: the ability of the people to choose the political regime under which they wish to live.").

5 *See Healy*, 491 U.S. at 336–37 ("[T]he Commerce Clause protects against inconsistent legislation arising from the projection of one state regulatory regime into the jurisdiction of another State."); Jack L. Goldsmith & Alan O. Sykes, *The Internet and the Dormant Commerce Clause*, 110 YALE L.J. 785, 807 (2001) (explaining that overlapping state regulations sometimes cause "regulatory compliance costs [to] increase significantly for no good reason").

6 *See infra* Section 19.C (discussing cases presenting problems of this sort).

7 Goldsmith & Sykes, *supra* note 5, at 795 (explaining that, while "many state regulations of transjurisdictional activities," such as the laws that allow "products liability actions against out-of-state manufacturers," create "out-of-state costs," the "dormant Commerce Clause plainly does not strike down all such local regulations simply because of their extraterritorial effect"); Gillian E. Metzger, *Congress, Article IV, and Interstate Relations*, 120 HARV. L. REV. 1468, 1521 (2007) (observing that "in practice, states exert regulatory control over each other all the time"); Mark D. Rosen, *Extraterritoriality and Political Heterogeneity in American Federalism*, 150 U. PA. L. REV. 855, 862 (2002) (claiming that "[m]eaningful empowerment" of states requires permitting them to pass laws with extraterritorial effects).

8 Indeed, for some courts, placing a state law in the extraterritorial-regulation category supports subjecting it to a "per se" rule of unconstitutionality, thus removing the need for any balancing or means-ends analysis at all. *See, e.g.*, Am. Beverage Ass'n

has offered little guidance regarding the precise scope of the extraterritoriality doctrine, having discussed it in only a small number of fact-bound decisions.[9] In particular:

1. In *Baldwin v. G.A.F. Seelig, Inc.*,[10] the Court invalidated a New York statute that barred the local retailing of milk purchased from out-of-state farmers for less than a minimum price established by New York authorities. The Court offered a variety of reasons for this result, but one was that "New York has no power to project its legislation into Vermont by regulating the price to be paid in that state for milk acquired there."[11]

2. In *Brown-Forman Distillers Corp. v. New York State Liquor Authority*,[12] the Court drew on *Baldwin* to undo a New York law requiring every liquor distiller to ensure that the price it charged for any sale in the state did not exceed the lowest price charged for that same

---

v. Snyder, 735 F.3d 362, 376 (6th Cir. 2013); *see also* Int'l Dairy Foods Ass'n v. Boggs, 622 F.3d 628, 645–46 (6th Cir. 2010) (discussing different views of different circuit courts on this question, while emphasizing that characterizing a challenged law as "extraterritorial" at least brings into play the same "virtually per se" rule of illegality, discussed *supra* Section 17.D, applicable to laws that discriminate against interstate commerce).

[9] *See also* Katherine J. Florey, *State Courts, State Territory, State Power: Reflections on the Extraterritoriality Principle in Choice of Law and Legislation*, 84 NOTRE DAME L. REV. 1057, 1060, 1068 (2009) (observing that "the Supreme Court has not developed a uniform standard for assessing the proper scope of state legislative jurisdiction"); Goldsmith & Sykes, *supra* note 5, at 789 (remarking that the extraterritoriality-related "aspects of the dormant Commerce Clause [doctrine] are unsettled and poorly understood"). Analysts often bemoan the difficulty of distinguishing between laws that do and do not have impermissibly extraterritorial effects. *See, e.g.*, *Snyder*, 735 F.3d at 379–80 (Sutton, J., concurring) (explaining that it is "exceedingly difficult to understand which extraterritorial effects exceed [constitutional] bounds and which do not").

[10] 294 U.S. 511 (1935).

[11] *Id.* at 521. For a more detailed discussion of *Baldwin*, see *supra* Section 17.B. The Court in later cases has specifically relied on extraterritoriality logic. Most notably, in *C & A Carbone, Inc. v. Town of Clarkstown*, 511 U.S. 383 (1994), the Court struck down a law that required the delivery of all waste generated in a defined area to a local, privately operated, high-quality recycling-and-disposal center. On its way to invalidating the law, the Court observed: "Nor may Clarkstown justify the flow control ordinance as a way to steer solid waste away from out-of-town disposal sites that it might deem harmful to the environment. To do so would extend the town's police power beyond its jurisdictional bounds. States and localities may not attach restrictions to exports or imports in order to control commerce in other States." *Id.* at 393 (citing *Baldwin* in support of this proposition); *see also* Henneford v. Silas Mason Co., 300 U.S. 577, 585 (1937) (distinguishing *Baldwin* on extraterritoriality grounds in upholding a compensatory use tax). In addition, in *Edgar v. MITE Corp.*, 457 U.S. 624 (1982), although the full Court did not reach the issue, four Justices agreed that a state anti-takeover law violated the Commerce Clause extraterritoriality rule. *Id.* at 641–43 (opinion of White, J.). For a further discussion of the case, see *infra* notes 59–64 and accompanying text.

[12] 476 U.S. 573 (1986).

product anywhere in the nation, with the lowest price being fixed on the first day of each month. In the Court's view, this liquor-sale analogue of most-favored-nation status improperly projected New York's regulatory power into other jurisdictions because "[o]nce a distiller has posted prices in New York, it is not free to change its prices elsewhere in the United States during the relevant month."[13] Following the lead of *Brown-Forman*, the Court in *Healy v. Beer Institute, Inc.*[14] struck down a Connecticut measure that barred any beer distributor from charging a price within the state that exceeded, at the moment of sale, the lowest price that it was then charging in any adjacent state.[15] According to the Court, "because volume discounts are permitted in Massachusetts, New York, and Rhode Island, but not in Connecticut," the challenged law had the impermissible consequence of "deter[ring] volume discounts in each of these other States."[16]

3. In *Pharmaceutical Research & Manufacturers of America v. Walsh* (*PhRMA-Maine*),[17] the Court considered a Maine program put in place to reduce prescription drug costs for many state residents. In general, states hold down the prices paid for prescription drugs supplied through their own Medicaid programs by wielding their market power as large-volume buyers, while private insurers likewise leverage their repeat-player purchasing status to secure volume discounts for drug-buying policyholders. The program at issue in *PhRMA-Maine* was set up to generate similar pricing relief for persons who had neither private insurance nor Medicaid coverage. It operated in this way by pressuring drug manufacturers to pay local pharmacies "rebates" with regard to drugs sold to uninsured/non-Medicaid buyers by those pharmacies, which in turn had to reduce prices for these buyers in an amount equivalent to the rebates they received. Pressure on drug manufacturers to agree to pay rebates existed because, if they failed to do so, they became subject to a "prior authorization"

---

13 *Id.* at 582.

14 491 U.S. 324 (1989).

15 *Id.* at 326–27.

16 *Id.* at 339.

17 538 U.S. 644 (2003).

requirement for the dispensing of their products within the state Medicaid program.[18] In other words, any doctor's prescription of a drug for any Maine Medicaid recipient would have to run the gauntlet of a review process conducted by a state-appointed medical board, which could substitute another drug for the patient's use.[19] The district court found that this feature of the Maine law violated the principle of *Baldwin* because paying rebates to in-state pharmacies "limit[ed] the revenue" that manufacturers otherwise were able to realize on out-of-state sales made to drug wholesalers.[20] The Supreme Court, however, rejected this analysis because—unlike in *Baldwin*—the challenged law "does not insist that manufacturers sell their drugs to a wholesaler for a certain price" so that it "does not regulate the price of any out-of-state transaction."[21]

B. THE LOWER COURTS' WORK WITH THE EXTRATERRITORIALITY RULE

In the wake of *PhRMA-Maine*, some commentators expressed the view that the end of meaningful extraterritoriality review was imminent.[22] These predictions, however, have proven incorrect because lower courts continue to find extraterritoriality violations in post-*PhRMA-Maine* cases. To begin with, those courts have not retreated from applying the core rules set forth in *Baldwin*, *Brown-Forman*, and *Healy*.[23] Even more important, at least for now, the

---

18 *Id.*

19 *Id.* at 655.

20 Pharm. Rsch. & Mfrs. of Am. v. Comm'r, Me. Dep't of Human Servs., No. Civ. 00–157–B-H, 2000 WL 34290605, at *1, *4 (D. Me. Oct. 26, 2000), *rev'd*, 249 F.3d 66 (1st Cir. 2001), *aff'd*, 538 U.S. 644.

21 *Id.* (internal citations omitted).

22 *See* Brannon P. Denning, *Extraterritoriality and the Dormant Commerce Clause: A Doctrinal Post-Mortem*, 73 LA. L. REV. 979, 980 (2013) (describing the extraterritoriality principle as "dead"); *see also* Ass'n for Accessible Meds. v. Frosh, 887 F.3d 664, 681 (4th Cir. 2018) (Winn, J., dissenting) (noting that "several circuits have questioned the continuing vitality of the extraterritoriality doctrine following the Supreme Court's decision in [*PhRMA-Maine*]"). In addition, some commentators have seized on *PhRMA-Maine*, among other decisions, in advocating for an abandonment of the doctrine. *See* David M. Driesen, *Must the States Discriminate Against Their Own Producers Under the Dormant Commerce Clause?*, 54 HOUS. L. REV. 1, 46 (2016) (suggesting that "lower courts should follow the Supreme Court's lead and let the extraterritoriality doctrine die"); *see also* Alexandra B. Klass & Elizabeth Henley, *Energy Policy, Extraterritoriality, and the Dormant Commerce Clause*, 5 SAN DIEGO J. CLIMATE & ENERGY L. 127, 184 (2014) (viewing *PhRMA-Maine* as indicating that courts are "declining to extend the extraterritoriality doctrine").

23 *See, e.g.*, *Ass'n for Accessible Meds.*, 887 F.3d at 672 (invalidating, albeit over a dissent, a state's ban on "unconscionable" manufacturer pricing of drugs on the ground

extraterritoriality doctrine remains alive and well in three additional categories of cases.

1. Leveraging In-State Activity to Regulate Related Out-of-State Transactions

First, in some rulings, lower courts have built on the principle of *Baldwin* to limit a state's ability to leverage in-state activity (in *Baldwin* itself, in-state retail purchases of milk) to regulate related out-of-state contractual activity (in *Baldwin*, the out-of-state purchase by wholesalers from producers of the milk later sold in those retail transactions). In *Dean Foods Co. v. Brancel*,[24] for example, the Seventh Circuit invalidated a Wisconsin law that barred all in-state milk producers from making volume-discount sales to the extent that their sales occurred outside the state. It was not enough, according to the court, that the milk production itself and "preliminary negotiations" for the relevant sale occurred in Wisconsin, or that the occurrence of volume-discount transactions, wherever they took place, tended to drive small Wisconsin farmers out of business.[25] Instead, the extraterritoriality principle operated to exempt the relevant transactions from Wisconsin's volume-discount prohibition because, as to each of them, the offer, acceptance, and performance of the milk-sale contract all "indisputably" occurred in Illinois.[26] Some courts have refused to take the principle that underlies *Dean Foods* as far as it might go, particularly in the now-common setting of computer-based consumer transactions.[27] In another line of cases, courts have rejected the view

that the ban was "effectively a price control statute [as to] transactions that do not take place in Maryland"); Pharm. Rsch. & Mfrs. of Am. v. District of Columbia, 406 F Supp. 2d 56, 71 n.15 (D.D.C. 2005) (striking down a similar law in part because "the inevitable effect of the D.C. Act *is* to regulate the price of out-of-state transactions" (emphasis in original)), *aff'd on other grounds sub nom.* Biotech Indus. Org. v. District of Columbia, 496 F.3d 1362 (D.C. Cir. 2007). *But see* Energy & Env't Legal Inst. v. Epel, 793 F.3d 1169, 1173 (10th Cir. 2015) (questioning whether "the *Baldwin* line of cases is really a distinct line of dormant commerce clause jurisprudence at all" in light of the focus in those cases on undermining competitive advantages in the interstate market, thus fitting them within the "*Philadelphia* anti-discrimination rule"); IMS Health Inc. v. Mills, 616 F.3d 7, 30–31 (1st Cir. 2010) (highlighting the presence of protectionism, not just regulation of out-of-state behavior, in *Baldwin*), *judgment vacated sub nom.* IMS Health, Inc. v. Schneider, 131 S. Ct. 3091 (2011). One question regarding the scope of the *Baldwin* price-related extraterritoriality principle has to do with whether it constrains the application of state antitrust law to out-of-state price-fixing agreements that have in-state price-elevating effects. *Compare In re* Brand Name Prescription Drugs Antitrust Litig., 123 F.3d 599, 613 (7th Cir. 1997) (Posner, J.) (concluding that it does not), *with Ass'n for Accessible Meds.*, 887 F.3d at 688 (Winn, J., dissenting) (concluding that, under the majority's ruling, it does).

24 187 F.3d 609 (7th Cir. 1996).

25 *Id.* at 619–20.

26 *Id.* at 611–12, 619.

27 *See* Quik Payday, Inc. v. Stork, 549 F.3d 1302, 1308 (10th Cir. 2008) (rejecting an extraterritoriality challenge to an application of Kansas payday-lending

that *Baldwin* mandates the invalidation of laws that effectively require producers of items sold into the state to use certain production methods (such as low-carbon-impact fuel use) in their out-of-state operations even though those methods have nothing to do with intrinsic safety or quality of the imported items themselves.[28] Other courts, however, have followed the lead of *Dean Foods*, including by finding violations of the extraterritoriality principle in cases that do not, like that case, involve producer-targeting pricing controls.[29]

---

restrictions to a Utah-based internet lender based on its dealings with state residents); State *ex rel.* Swanson v. Integrity Advance, LLC, 870 N.W.2d 90, 95 (Minn. 2015) (finding, in a case involving a Minnesota payday lending law, that an approach that would give decisive weight to "where [parties] sign[ ] the contract . . . is unjustifiably narrow"). These rulings may find support in the Court's tax-nexus-expanding decision *South Dakota v. Wayfair*, 138 S. Ct. 2080 (2018) (discussed *infra* Section 21.B), particularly because the Court in that case emphasized that, by way of "targeted advertising and instant access" via the internet, "a business may be present in a State in a meaningful way" whether or not that presence is "physical in the traditional sense of the term." *Id.* at 2095 (quoting Direct Mktg. Ass'n v. Brohl, 575 U.S. 1, 17–18 (2015) (Kennedy, J., concurring)).

[28] *See Epel*, 793 F.3d at 1174 (finding no dormant Commerce Clause problems in a law that restricted sales of electric power in Colorado, even if generated outside the state, that was not produced in conformance with state-imposed carbon-footprint-reducing environmental standards); Rocky Mountain Farmers Union v. Corey, 730 F.3d 1070, 1104 (9th Cir. 2013) (upholding a California law limiting in-state sales of ethanol regardless of "the physical structure of a product" and even though, unlike in product-liability tort cases, its "harmful properties" existed only as a consequence of its production—here, by means of greenhouse-gas-generating coal-based electricity); Am. Fuel & Petrochemical Mfrs. v. O'Keefe, 903 F.3d 903, 916–17 (9th Cir. 2018) (reaffirming and applying the principle of *Rocky Mountain* in upholding a set of Oregon greenhouse-gas-targeting fuel rules); *see also* Ass'n des Eleveurs de Canards et d'Oies du Quebec v. Harris, 729 F.3d 937, 941–43, 952–53 (9th Cir. 2013) (upholding a ban on in-state sales of certain foods derived from force-fed birds); Nat'l Pork Prods. Council v. Ross, 6 F. 4th 1021, 1025, 1028 (9th Cir. 2021) (affirming the dismissal of an extraterritoriality-based challenge to a California prohibition on the sale of "whole pork meat" not produced in compliance with specified "sow-confinement restrictions," while reasoning that *Baldwin*, *Brown-Forman*, and *Healy* were not controlling because the challenged law "is neither a price-control nor price-affirmation statute, as it neither dictates the price of pork products nor ties the price of pork products sold in California to out-of-state prices"), *cert. granted*, No. 21-468, 2022 WL 892100 (Mar. 28, 2022). Some judges have taken a different view by finding case-dispositive extraterritoriality problems in statutes of this kind. *See* North Dakota v. Heydinger, 825 F.3d 912, 922 (8th Cir. 2016) (invalidating Minnesota rules designed to reduce the carbon footprint of electricity produced outside the state because they "seek to reduce emissions that occur outside Minnesota" and "their practical effect is to control activities taking place *wholly* outside Minnesota" (emphasis in original)); *Rocky Mountain Farmers Union*, 740 F.3d at 518 (Smith, J., dissenting).

[29] *See, e.g.*, North Dakota v. Heydinger, 15 F. Supp. 3d 891, 912 n.12, 919 (D. Minn. 2014) (rejecting any reading of *PhRMA-Maine* that makes extraterritoriality limits inapplicable "beyond price control laws"), *aff'd*, 825 F.3d 912 (agreeing with this conclusion based on "well-established Supreme Court jurisprudence"); Publius v. Boyer-Vine, 237 F. Supp. 3d 997, 1024 (E.D. Ca. 2017) (same). *But see Energy & Env't Legal Inst.*, 793 F.3d at 1173 (declining to entertain an extraterritoriality-based challenge to a state law that "isn't a price control statute [and] doesn't link prices paid in Colorado with those paid out of state"). A leading case that tracks the approach of *Dean Foods* is *Midwest Title Loans, Inc. v. Mills*, 593 F.3d 660 (7th Cir. 2010). There,

2. Leveraging In-State Activity to Regulate Unrelated Out-of-State Transactions

Cases like *Dean Foods* constrain a state's capacity to regulate a transaction even though it is connected to an in-state activity, such as the local making or sale of a particular product. In a second set of extraterritoriality cases, the state goes a long step further by seeking to leverage an in-state activity to regulate out-of-state transactions that have no connection to the particular good or service that the in-state transaction involves. Consider, for example, *American Beverage Association v. Snyder*.[30] That case grew out of Michigan's effort to discourage the landfilling of bottles and cans by making a state-issued payment for each such container turned in for recycling. To ensure that payments were made only for containers from Michigan,

an Illinois-based firm made loans, secured by motor vehicles, to consumers who lived in Indiana. *Id.* at 662. The lender had no physical presence in the Hoosier state, and all loan contracts were finalized, and all lent funds were remitted, during face-to-face meetings at the lender's office in Illinois. *Id.* at 662–63. Even so, the lender dealt directly with the Indiana Bureau of Motor Vehicles to perfect its security interests, and (not surprisingly) it enforced those security interests when defaults occurred, although it did so by engaging a third-party Indiana-based company to repossess the collateralized cars. *Id.* at 663. While acknowledging that loans of this kind could "trap borrowers in a cycle of debt," the court ruled that Indiana could not apply to this Illinois lender the same statutory interest-rate limits that applied to Indiana-based lenders. *Id.* at 661 (internal quotations and citation omitted). As the court explained, the fact that "[t]he contract was . . . made and executed in Illinois," sufficed "to show that [application of the Indiana statute] violates the commerce clause." *Id.*; *see also* Carolina Trucks & Equipment, Inc. v. Volvo Trucks of N. Am., Inc., 492 F.3d 484, 494 (4th Cir. 2007) (narrowly construing, in light of extraterritoriality concerns, a South Carolina law so as to prevent it from prohibiting a manufacturer's direct sale of a vehicle to a South Carolinian who physically left the state to buy the vehicle off a Georgia lot); Legato Vapors, LLC v. Cook, 847 F.3d 825 (7th Cir. 2017) (finding an extraterritoriality violation in a state law, concerning the production of vapor liquids, that directed at producers "unprecedented" and "detailed" rules "for sinks, cleaning products, and even the details of contracts with outside security firms and the qualifications of those firms' personnel"); Healthcare Distrib. All. v. Zucker, 353 F. Supp. 3d 235, 261 (S.D.N.Y. 2018) (finding that the extraterritoriality principle would prohibit a rule that precluded manufacturers compelled to make payments into a state opioid fund from passing along those charges to out-of-state buyers because, among other things, "[a]n opioid manufacturer based in Maine that wished to pass on the surcharge it paid on New York transactions by selling opioids at a markup to a pharmacy in New Mexico could face a million-dollar penalty from New York State"), *rev'd in part on other grounds sub nom.* Ass'n for Accessible Medicines v. James, 974 F.3d 216 (2d Cir. 2020), *cert denied sub nom.* Healthcare Distrib. All. v. James, 142 S. Ct. 87 (2021); *cf.* Sam Francis Found. v. Christies, Inc., 784 F.3d 1320, 1323 (9th Cir. 2015) (concluding "easily" that the dormant Commerce Clause renders invalid a California mandatory-payment-sharing-with-the-artist law "as applied to out-of-state sales by California residents" based solely on their residency—for example, when "a California resident has a part-time apartment in New York, buys a sculpture in New York from a North Dakota artist to furnish her apartment, and later sells the sculpture to a friend in New York"). A canvassing of earlier cases, including *Midwest Title*, appears in *Eric M. Berman, P.C. v. City of New York*, 895 F. Supp. 2d 453, 483 (E.D.N.Y. 2012), *vacated and remanded on other grounds*, 796 F.3d 171 (2d Cir. 2015).

[30] 735 F.3d at 375–76.

the governing law (1) required all bottlers, wherever located, to place a distinguishing mark on each container meant for delivery into the state; and (2) restricted the delivery of thus-marked bottles and cans into other states. Reviewing this law, the Sixth Circuit had no problem with its first requirement. That restriction, after all, fell comfortably in line with routinely validated measures that saddle manufacturers, wherever they might be located, with safety, quality, and labeling requirements for goods sent into the state.[31] In the court's view, however, the second requirement was a bridge too far because it stipulated what out-of-state manufacturers had to do in making products destined for sale and use in states other than Michigan. Nor was the court moved by the state's insistence that, if Michigan-marked bottles and cans could freely circulate in other states, opportunistic money-seekers would track them down and haul them into Michigan to cash in on the state's recycling subsidies, thus causing Michigan effectively to remediate non-Michigan waste-disposal problems. Whatever the force of that logic might be, the court explained, no fair reading of the relevant precedents allowed

---

[31] *See, e.g.*, *Epel*, 793 F.3d at 1173, 1175 (deeming the extraterritoriality limit inapplicable to state rules that "regulate[ ] the quality of a good sold to in-state residents," such as "health and safety regulations that require out-of-state manufacturers to alter their designs or labels"). In a related set of cases—which bear a measure of resemblance to *PhRMA-Maine*—courts have allowed states to impose specialized duties on manufacturers, reaching beyond the control of product-qualities themselves, in light of the harms that products might generate within the state. *See, e.g.*, VIZIO, Inc. v. Klee, 886 F.3d 249, 255–56 (2d Cir. 2018) (upholding a Connecticut law that required television producers to contribute to a recycling fund for problematic component parts, even though assessments were based on national—rather than state—market share and even though most recycling efforts focused on parts not included in the plaintiff's products; finding that the law did not violate extraterritoriality limits because it "merely influence[d] national pricing decisions" by driving up the cost of local activities as "one of 'innumerable valid state laws affect[ing] pricing decisions in other States' " (quoting *Healy*, 491 U.S. at 345 (Scalia, J., concurring in part and concurring in the judgment))); Star Scientific, Inc. v. Beales, 278 F.3d 339, 354–55 (4th Cir. 2018) (upholding Virginia's imposition of a per-cigarette-sold-in-the-state escrow-payment obligation despite the manufacturer's objection that the law required it "to make payments on cigarettes sold by it to independent distributors in other states if the cigarettes are later sold into Virginia"; finding unpersuasive the manufacturer's claims that the law "attempts to regulate aspects of the stream of commerce that occur upstream, outside the State's borders"); Freedom Holdings Inc. v. Spitzer, 357 F.3d 205, 220–21 (2d Cir. 2004) (upholding a state law requiring that "cigarettes sold at retail must have been produced only by manufacturers in certified compliance with New York's Escrow Statute," even though that meant that "importers such as appellants must buy more expensive, 'certified' cigarettes (in their out-of-state transactions) if they wish to sell to New York retailers"; reasoning that "[t]he extraterritorial effect described by appellants amounts to no more than the upstream pricing impact of a state regulation" and "a similar pricing impact might result from any state regulation of a product"); *see also* Pharm. Rsch. & Mfrs. of Am. v. Cty. of Alameda, 768 F.3d 1037, 1039–40, 1045 (9th Cir 2014) (rejecting an extraterritoriality challenge to an ordinance requiring manufacturers of drugs sold in the county to maintain facilities for the disposal of unused drugs).

State A to restrict the sending of products labeled a certain way from State B into State C.[32]

3. Regulating In-State Activity in a Manner That Creates Problematic Spillover Effects

A problem fundamentally different from the ones presented in *Dean Foods* and *Snyder* marks a final set of extraterritoriality cases, which involve a state's targeting of an activity that unquestionably occurs within its own borders. In these cases, the constitutional difficulty stems from the fact that the state law, as a practical matter, creates spillover effects that threaten to induce out-of-state businesses to reshape their operations, often on a nationwide scale. Courts sometimes have struck down laws of this kind, particularly in cases concerning (a) sports leagues, (b) the internet, and (c) the would-be unitary marketing of products across multiple states.

a. The Sports-League Cases

The sports-league cases have their origin in *Flood v. Kuhn*,[33] in which the Court held that a single state could not apply its own antitrust law to invalidate Major League Baseball's reserve-clause requirement, which strictly limited the ability of players to move

[32] *See Snyder*, 735 F.3d at 375–76. For another application of the same principle, see *National Solid Waste Management Ass'n* v. *Meyer*, 63 F.3d 652 (7th Cir 1995), which involved a Wisconsin law barring the in-state handling of out-of-state waste unless the state from which that waste came adopted the same recycling rules made applicable by Wisconsin to in-state waste handlers. Indeed, this law created an even more serious extraterritoriality problem than the law at issue in *Snyder* because Wisconsin in effect insisted on controlling *all* waste-related activity by *anyone* in that other state, as opposed to targeting only those persons engaged in sending goods into Wisconsin. *See id.* at 655, 658, 661–62. In *Daniels Sharpsmart, Inc. v. Smith*, 889 F.3d 608 (9th Cir. 2018), the court invalidated a California law requiring incineration of medical waste generated in California, regardless of the site of its disposal, by invoking a similar theory—reasoning that, absent this result, a state could control "the use or disposal of any item . . . everywhere in the country if it had its origin in [that state]." *Id.* at 616. The use of this rationale in that case was questionable, however, at least if one characterizes the challenged state law as targeting the importation of waste services into the state. *See C & A. Carbone*, 511 U.S. at 390–91. A constitutional principle that allows state regulation only of such importation, after all, is a far cry from one that supports state regulation of "the use or disposal of any item . . . everywhere in the country" of any item originating in the state. For another case akin to *National Solid Waste Management Ass'n*, see *Air Transportation Ass'n of America v. City & County of San Francisco*, 992 F. Supp. 1149, 1661–64 (N.D. Cal. 1998) (holding invalid on extraterritoriality grounds a San Francisco ordinance that barred public contracting with companies that discriminated anywhere in the United States, and not just in California, between married couples and domestic partners in operating employee-benefit programs); *see also* Levon Klugman, *The Beginning of an Economic Civil War: The Unconstitutionality of State-Implemented Travel Bans*, 22 U. PA. J. CONST. L. 409, 427–30, 444–47 (2020) (arguing that bans on state-employee travel to other states that refuse to embrace certain policies—including such bans recently put in place by New York and California—violate the extraterritoriality rule and are not saved by the market-participant exception to the dormancy doctrine).

[33] 407 U.S. 258, 284 (1972).

from one team to another. As stated by the Court, "because national 'uniformity (is required) in any regulation of baseball and its reserve[ ] system,' . . . 'the burden on interstate commerce outweighs the states' interests in regulating [that] system.' "[34] Put otherwise, if any given major-leaguer could become a free agent under one state's antitrust law, then other teams in other states would have to award their players free agency, too. And this result was intolerable because the "national uniformity" that "is required" in operating a far-flung sports league should not be attributable, as a matter of fairness or logic, to the dictates of a single state.[35] The Second Circuit in *Flood* had captured the critical point when it observed that the enforcement of such local laws "requires the enterprise to comply with the *strictest standard* of several states in order to continue an interstate business extending over many states," and this "extra-territorial effect . . . constitutes, absent a strong state interest, an impermissible burden on interstate commerce."[36] Not surprisingly, the lower courts have applied this same "strictest standard" extraterritoriality principle in other sports-league cases, including in the context of professional football[37] and intercollegiate athletics.[38]

---

[34] *Id.* at 284–85 (internal citations omitted) (quoting Flood v. Kuhn, 316 F. Supp. 271, 280 (S.D.N.Y. 1970), and then quoting Flood v. Kuhn, 443 F.2d 264, 268 (2d Cir. 1971)).

[35] *Id.* at 284 (internal quotations marks omitted).

[36] *Flood*, 443 F.2d at 267 (emphasis added).

[37] *See* Partee v. San Diego Chargers Football Co., 668 P.2d 674 (Cal. 1983) (citing other post-*Flood* cases in which "state antitrust regulation has been held inapplicable to professional basketball . . . and professional football" because "differing state antitrust decisions if applied to the enterprise would likely compel all member teams to comply with the laws of the strictest state").

[38] *See* NCAA v. Miller, 10 F.3d 633 (9th Cir. 1993) (overturning a Nevada statute mandating elaborate hearing procedures whenever the NCAA moved to sanction local institutions, coaches, athletes, and boosters for alleged rule violations because the NCAA's need for "uniform enforcement procedures" would force it "to apply Nevada's procedures to enforcement proceedings throughout the country . . . regardless of whether the statute's extraterritorial reach was intended by the [state] legislature"); NCAA v. Roberts, No. TCA 94–40413–WS, 1994 WL 750585, at *1 (N.D. Fla. Nov. 8, 1994) (following *Miller* in invalidating a Florida statute that required a similarly heightened set of process-based safeguards). Notably, courts have applied this same principle in dealing with issues outside both the labor-relations and the hearing-process contexts. *See, e.g.*, City of San José v. Office of the Comm'r of Baseball, No. 13–CV–02787 RMW, 2013 WL 5609346, at *10 (N.D. Cal. Oct. 11, 2013) (relying on *Flood* to reject a challenge under state antitrust law to Major League Baseball's refusal to permit relocation of a professional team); New Orleans Pelicans Baseball, Inc. v. Nat'l Ass'n of Prof'l Baseball Leagues, Inc., No. 93–253, 1994 WL 631144, at *9 (E.D. La. Mar. 1, 1994) (same); *see also* Bowers v. NCAA, 151 F. Supp. 2d 526, 539 (D.N.J. 2001) (not reaching the question whether *Miller* and similar cases precluded application of New Jersey's anti-discrimination law in the NCAA-sports context because Congress consented to that regulation).

b. *Internet Regulation*

Some courts have taken a similar approach in policing state internet regulations. The pathbreaking treatment of this subject came in *American Libraries Ass'n v. Pataki*,[39] which concerned a New York law that criminalized any use of the internet to disseminate material with sexual content "harmful to minors."[40] A federal district court overturned this law under the extraterritoriality principle, reasoning that "geography . . . is a virtually meaningless construct on the Internet" because posted content "is available to all other Internet users worldwide."[41] The court worried, for example, that the challenged New York law would catch in its web a California artist with an online studio who primarily targeted buyers in Oregon.[42] The difficulty, in other words, was that no one who posted material in any state "could avoid liability . . . given that there is no feasible way to preclude New Yorkers from accessing a Web site, receiving a mail exploder message or a newsgroup posting, or participating in a chat room."[43] Courts have followed the lead of *American Libraries Ass'n* by vindicating challenges targeting similar state laws designed to shield minors from communications with sexual content[44] and additional state-imposed internet restrictions as well.[45] Some courts,

[39] 969 F. Supp. 160.

[40] *Id.* at 163 (internal quotations omitted).

[41] *Id.* at 167, 169.

[42] *Id* at 176.

[43] *Id.* at 171. For commentary that seems generally supportive of this line of thinking, see, e.g., Dan L. Burk, *Federalism in Cyberspace*, 28 CONN. L REV. 1095, 1123–34 (1996); Bruce P. Keller, *The Game's the Same: Why Gambling in Cyberspace Violates Federal Law*, 108 YALE L.J. 1569, 1593–96 (1999); and Glenn Harlan Reynolds, *Virtual Reality and "Virtual Welters": A Note on the Commerce Clause Implications of Regulating Cyberporn*, 82 VA. L. REV. 535, 537–42 (1996). For a critical assessment, see Goldsmith & Sykes, *supra* note 5, at 823 (concluding, among other things, that "the court's logic [in *American Libraries Ass'n*] would condemn an extraordinary array of state laws as applied to cross-border activity that no one heretofore viewed as problematic").

[44] *See, e.g.*, ACLU v. Johnson, 194 F.3d 1149, 1161 (10th Cir. 1999) (following *American Libraries Ass'n* in finding a "per se" violation); PSINet Inc. v. Chapman, 108 F. Supp. 2d 611, 615, 627 (W.D. Va. 2000) (entering a preliminary injunction against enforcement of a Virginia "harmful to juveniles" law because a "California website owner would have to alter his commercial materials in all states in order to comply with the rigors of the Virginia statute"): Cyberspace, Commc'ns, Inc. v. Engler, 55 F. Supp. 2d 737, 751 (E.D. Mich. 1999) (noting that "virtually all Internet speech is . . . available everywhere including Michigan"), *aff'd*, 238 F.3d 420 (6th Cir. 2000).

[45] *See* Backpage.com, LLC v. McKenna, 881 F. Supp. 2d 1262, 1285–86 (W.D. Wash. 2012) (preliminarily enjoining enforcement of a Washington statute that barred transmission of a message reasonably understood to be an advertisement of paid-for sex in the state with a minor because in effect it would require internet-using firms to engage in a "screening process [that] would" require a "costly change to the business operations of these corporations that have little to no connection with the State of Washington"); Backpage.com, LLC v. Cooper, 939 F. Supp. 2d 805, 841–42 (M.D. Tenn. 2013) (preliminarily enjoining enforcement of a similar Tennessee law); Publius v. Boyer-Vine, 237 F. Supp. 3d 997, 1012–13, 1029 (E.D. Cal. 2017) (preliminarily

however, have upheld state laws targeting internet communications on the ground that those laws serve important purposes.[46] While reconciling these many rulings is not an easy task, one point is clear: To the extent that these laws face a special brand of extraterritoriality challenge, it is because courts see them as posing—like in the sports-league cases—a special set of spillover-effect problems.[47]

---

enjoining enforcement of a California law that blocked e-transmission of personal addresses or phone numbers of California public officials; reasoning that California in effect foisted its restriction "onto the rest of the nation" because, for example, it required "a Massachusetts resident, to remove a post from his online forum . . . even if the only people accessing the forum are New Hampshire residents (or citizens of states other than California)"); McLemore v. Gumucio, No. 3:19–cv–00530, 2019 WL 3305131, at *8–9 (M.D. Tenn. July 23, 2019) (preliminarily enjoining enforcement of a Tennessee law requiring registration by online e-auctioneers based on the court's understanding that "the mere existence of an online auction website" triggered its operation "even if the auctioneer and the products being auctioned are 'wholly outside of the State's borders' " because an internet auctioneering company "cannot simply turn off its website at the Tennessee border" (quoting *Healy*, 491 U.S. at 336)). Notably, the rhetoric of some internet-related extraterritoriality rulings is extremely broad. *See, e.g.*, Nat'l Fed'n of the Blind v. Target Corp., 452 F. Supp. 2d 946, 958 (N.D. Cal. 2006) (noting that "[c]ourts in several circuits have invalidated state laws regulating the internet on the grounds that *any* regulation of the internet regulates conduct occurring outside the borders of the state" (emphasis in original)); *see generally* Goldsmith & Sykes, *supra* note 5, at 787 ("[U]nder the logic of *American Libraries Ass'n*, nearly every state regulation of Internet communications will have the extraterritorial consequences the court bemoaned. This explains why the dormant Commerce Clause has been called 'a nuclear bomb of a legal theory' against state Internet regulations." (quoting Declan McCullagh, *Brick by Brick*, TIME DIGITAL DAILY, Jan. 31, 1997)).

46 *See* Greater L.A. Agency on Deafness v. CNN, Inc., 742 F.3d 414, 433 (9th Cir. 2014) (rejecting a challenge to the state's mandate that websites provide captioning of audio content to assist in-state hearing-impaired persons because, "[e]ven though CNN.com is a single website, the record before us shows that CNN could enable a captioning option for California visitors to its site"); *Target Corp.*, 452 F. Supp. 2d at 961 (rejecting an e-retailer's extraterritoriality challenge to state sales-related regulations because it "could choose to make a California-specific website" and even if it changed "its entire website in order to comply with California law, this does not mean that California is regulating out-of-state conduct"); *see also Quik Payday*, 549 F.3d at 1302 (upholding a state requirement that internet lenders register with state authorities, thus potentially subjecting them to additional forms of state regulation because "[r]egulation of one-to-one commercial exchanges via the Internet . . . is quite a different matter" than the regulation of sexually explicit Internet communications involving minors); State v. Heckel, 24 P.3d 404, 412–13 (Wash. 2001) (finding "no 'sweeping extraterritorial effect' " in the application of a spam-distribution-prohibiting statute against an out-of-state resident (quoting *Edgar*, 457 U.S. at 642)). The courts have looked with particular disfavor on extraterritoriality challenges directed at state laws that target e-communications made with the aim of luring minors to engage in sex. *See, e.g.*, Hatch v. Superior Court, 94 Cal. Rptr. 2d 453, 472, 485–86 (Cal. Ct. App. 2000) (reasoning that such laws do not regulate "legitimate commerce" or demonstrably trench on other states' policies when the elements of the crime occur in the prosecuting state); People v. Foley, 731 N.E.2d 123, 132–33 (N.Y. 2000) (noting that the court in *American Library Ass'n* observed that the case did not involve such a "luring" law).

47 For one treatment of how courts should approach cases of this sort, see Goldsmith & Sykes, *supra* note 5, at 787 n.12 (asserting that "one cannot assess the validity under the dormant Commerce Clause of state Internet regulations taken as a

c. *Other Strictest-Standard Problems*

In theory, courts could strike down many state laws because, in effect, they pressure multistate actors to comply with their commands on a nationwide basis. In general, however, courts have eschewed this approach.[48] From time to time, however, courts detect a strictest-standard-based extraterritoriality problem in assessing state laws outside the sports-league and internet contexts.[49] *Knoll*

---

whole; rather, the analysis depends very much on the type of Internet service, the costs of geographical identification and filtering associated with that service, the type of regulation, the nature of the penalties, and more").

[48] *See, e.g.*, Nat'l Elec. Mfrs. Ass'n v. Sorrell, 272 F.3d 104, 110 (2d Cir. 2001) (allowing enforcement of a light-bulb labeling law challenged by a trade association that asserted that, "[g]iven the . . . systems used by its members . . . if its members continue selling in Vermont, they would also be forced as a practical matter to label lamps sold in every other state"; rejecting that complaint on the ground that industry members "could arrange their . . . processes to produce labeled lamps solely for the Vermont market"); Int'l Dairy Foods Ass'n v. Boggs, 622 F.3d 628, 647 (6th Cir. 2010) (upholding an Ohio milk-labeling law challenged by bottlers on the ground that it "force[d] them to create a nationwide label in accordance with Ohio's requirements"); *Epel*, 793 F.3d at 1173–74 (indicating that "*Baldwin*'s near *per se* rule doesn't apply" when "one or more states impose quality mandates [and] manufacturers . . . find the cheapest way to comply isn't to produce a special product for them but to redesign their product as it's sold nationwide, with an increased cost felt by consumers everywhere"); *Snyder*, 735 F.3d at 379 (Sutton, J., concurring) (suggesting that no extraterritoriality problems would be posed by an exacting California fuel-emission law even though it might cause car-makers to "sell only California-compliant cars and pass the higher costs of production on to consumers nationwide"). For other cases involving unsuccessful extraterritoriality-based challenges mounted by national distributers of manufactured products, see *Rocky Mountain Farmers Union*, 730 F.3d at 1102–03 (ethanol); *SPGGC, LLC v. Blumenthal*, 505 F.3d 183, 195–96 (2d Cir. 2007) (prepaid gift cards); *Hampton Feedlot, Inc. v. Nixon*, 249 F.3d 814, 819 (8th Cir. 2001) (livestock); and *Cotto Waxo Co. v. Williams*, 46 F.3d 790, 793 (8th Cir. 1995) (petroleum-based sweeping compounds).

[49] *See, e.g.*, *Heydinger*, 825 F.3d at 922 (invalidating a set of Minnesota rules that blocked the sale into the state of high-fossil-fuel-produced electricity in part because, "[l]ike persons who post information on an out-of-state internet website, out-of-state utilities entering into purchases and sales of electricity in the [regional] transmission grid 'cannot prevent [electricity users in Minnesota] from accessing the [electrons]' "; thus producers must either "unplug" from the "regional grid" or seek special approval from Minnesota to engage in activity on that grid in violation of *Brown-Forman*'s dictate that "[f]orcing a merchant to seek regulatory approval in one State before undertaking a transaction in another directly regulates interstate commerce" (quoting *Brown-Forman*, 476 U.S. at 582)); Spoofcard v. Burgum, 499 F. Supp. 3d 647, 656–57 (D.N.D. 2020) (invalidating North Dakota's ban on telephone number "spoofing" on the ground that it had "the practical effect of regulating interstate commerce because it is impossible for Plaintiffs to determine whether a call recipient is physically within North Dakota"); City of Boston v. Smith & Wesson Corp., No. 199902590, 2000 WL 1473568, at *13 n.57 (Mass. Super. Ct. July 13, 2000) (postponing to "a later stage of litigation" the evaluation of a firearms manufacturers' argument that the issuance of injunctive relief, under state law, regarding corporate practices said to facilitate diversion of weapons to unlawful owners, would "have the effect of forcing [them] to change [their] practices nationwide"); *see also Ass'n des Eleveurs*, 729 F.3d at 950 (signaling the possible applicability of the sports-league cases in the product-generation context but finding no indication that the regulated producers had to alter broadly their production techniques in light of the challenged state regulation); *cf. BMW*, 517 U.S. at 572 n.18 (noting, in the due-process context, that "[t]he record

Pharmaceutical Co. v. Sherman[50] illustrates the point. That case arose after the manufacturer of a weight-loss drug, recently approved for distribution by the FDA, put together a "massive" national advertising campaign promoting the drug's use.[51] Unfortunately for the seller, Illinois law banned any advertising of any controlled substance, and that state moved to block the manufacturer's promotional efforts to the extent they occurred inside the state's borders.[52] A federal district court, however, rebuffed Illinois's effort. The difficulty, according to the court, was that there was no way for the drug-maker to engage in its ad campaign—which reached across "all major television network and cable programming," as well as print advertising in at least three nationally circulated newspapers—except on a national basis.[53] And because controlling precedents dictated that "Illinois may not impose its policy choices on other states," the law could not stand because it "would preclude the general public in most states from receiving accurate, non-misleading information about an FDA-approved prescription drug."[54] To be sure, cases like *Knoll Pharmaceutical* are unusual.[55] But that ruling highlights a critical point—namely, that exactly the same underlying concerns that have driven judicial application of the strictest-standard principle in the sports-league and internet contexts sometimes crop up in other contexts as well.

C. EXTRATERRITORIALITY AND THE *PIKE* BALANCING TEST

Even when courts find no extraterritoriality-based violation, they routinely consider a challenged law's out-of-state effects as they engage in dormant Commerce Clause balancing.[56] In *Southern Pacific Railway* v. *Arizona ex rel. Sullivan*,[57] for example, the Court emphasized that the challenged Arizona train-length law both (1) diverted train traffic into neighboring states and (2) caused railroad companies to operate shorter trains than they otherwise would have

---

discloses no basis for [the plaintiff's] contention that BMW could not comply with Alabama's law without changing its nationwide policy").

50 57 F. Supp. 2d 615, 622–24 (N.D. Ill. 1999).

51 *Id.* at 618.

52 *Id.* at 619–20.

53 *Id.* at 618, 623–24.

54 *Id.* at 623–24 (footnote omitted).

55 *See supra* note 48 and accompanying text.

56 *See, e.g.*, Freedom Holdings, Inc. v. Cuomo, 624 F.3d 38, 64 n.18 (2d Cir. 2010) (noting that "a court may analyze a claim that a state statute is invalid because it regulates commerce extraterritorially either as a disproportionate burden on commerce under the [*Pike*] balancing test . . . or . . . 'independently' ").

57 325 U.S. 761 (1945).

in states other than Arizona.[58] More nuanced is the manner in which the Court sometimes draws on extraterritorial consequences in assessing the strength of proffered justifications for challenged state laws. Consider *Edgar v. MITE Corp.*,[59] in which the Court assessed the constitutionality of an Illinois corporate-takeover statute. That law placed limits on such takeovers, including those involving foreign corporations, so long as (1) Illinois residents owned at least 10% of the target company's stock or (2) the corporate target had its principal office in Illinois and specified amounts of its assets were located there.[60] The Court invalidated this law under the *Pike* balancing test, emphasizing that the state had "no legitimate interest" in regulating transactions between non-Illinois corporations and non-Illinois shareholders—which was exactly what the statute did in many of its applications.[61] In contrast, the Court upheld Indiana's takeover statute in *CTS Corp. v. Dynamics Corp. of America*,[62] distinguishing *Edgar* on the ground that Indiana's statute (unlike Illinois's) applied only when a corporation chartered by the state became the target of a takeover bid. In this context, the Court held, no dormant Commerce Clause problem existed because of (1) the entity's voluntarily assumed relationship with the charter-issuing state and (2) long-accepted understandings about what state should oversee the governance of a chartered corporation, including as to the rights of its shareholders.[63] Together, *Edgar* and *CTS* may stand for something like the flipside of the principle that drove the Court's decisions in *Brown-Forman* and *Healy*: Just as surely as a state may not impose rules that effectively structure the terms of private trade in other jurisdictions, it may not justify its burdening of interstate commerce by relying on supposed regulatory benefits that accrue primarily to persons with whom the state lacks a meaningful connection.[64]

---

58 *See supra* Section 18.A.1.

59 457 U.S. 624 (1982).

60 *Id.* at 626–27.

61 *Id.* at 644.

62 481 U.S. 69 (1987).

63 *Id.* at 93.

64 *See Edgar*, 457 U.S. at 644 (noting that "[w]hile protecting local investors is plainly a legitimate state objective, the State has no legitimate interest in protecting nonresident shareholders," so that that interest cannot be "weighed in the balance").

Chapter 20

EXCEPTIONS TO THE DORMANT COMMERCE CLAUSE PRINCIPLE

Analysis

From the earliest days of the dormancy doctrine, the Court has recognized important limitations on its operation. Three such limitations have long occupied prominent places in the structure of dormant Commerce Clause doctrine: the congressional-consent exception, the subsidy exception, and the market-participant exception. Two other doctrines—one that involves what might be called the state-self-promotion exception and another that deals with the distinct subject of alcohol regulation—have more recently received the Court's attention. No less important, as these limitations on the dormancy principle have taken hold, other previously recognized limitations have fallen away either in whole or in part. We begin this chapter with an overview of those now-marginalized exceptions. And we then turn to the five carve-outs that are of greatest prominence today.

A. THE MODERN MOVEMENT AWAY FROM CATEGORICAL DORMANT COMMERCE CLAUSE EXCEPTIONS

Notwithstanding the dormancy doctrine's far-reaching anti-discrimination principle, the Court indicated in a string of early decisions that states could adopt "quarantine" laws that flatly ban the importation of "noxious" items, such as "rags . . . infected with the germs of yellow fever" or "animals having contagious or infectious diseases."[1] The Court retained, but narrowed, this quarantine exception when it struck down the prohibition on solid waste importation at issue in *City of Philadelphia v. New Jersey*.[2] The dissenters in that case argued that the "fact of life that New Jersey must somehow dispose of its own noxious items does not mean that it must serve as a depository for those of every other State."[3] Writing for the majority, however, Justice Stewart indicated that import-restricting quarantine laws are permissible only when the "very movement" of the excluded goods "risked contagion and other evils."[4]

---

1 Bowman v. Chicago & Nw. Ry. Co., 125 U.S. 465, 488, 491–92 (1888) (reasoning in part that, because "[s]uch articles are not merchantable," it follows that "[t]hey are not legitimate subjects of trade and commerce"); *see, e.g.*, Mintz v. Baldwin, 289 U.S. 346, 350 (1933) (upholding a prohibition on the importation of cattle unless certified as coming from herds free of the highly infectious Bang's Disease; concluding without difficulty that this limitation did not "so unnecessarily burden[ ] interstate transportation as to contravene the commerce clause"). It is important to distinguish true "quarantine" cases from cases that take account of the dangerous qualities of a regulated product in, for example, applying *Pike* balancing analysis. In other words, there is a fundamental difference between the sort of inherently "noxious" items subject to the quarantine exception (germ infested rags, for example) and the many kinds of ordinary products (gas, oil, cars, etc.) that can and do present health and safety problems. Occasionally, however, lower courts have upheld non-quarantine laws by invoking reasoning that bears a resemblance to the reasoning that underlies the quarantine exception. *See, e.g.*, Portland Pipe Line Corp. v. City of South Portland, 332 F. Supp. 3d 264, 306 (D. Me. 2018) (upholding a city ordinance that prohibited loading tar-sands-based crude oil onto tankers where "there [was] evidence that the City considered tar sands to be a dangerous article with greater health and environmental risks than other types of crude oils and intended to alleviate the risks from transporting and loading tar sands crude oil 'whatever its origin' " (internal alterations omitted)). In *Rocky Mountain Farmers Union v. Corey*, 730 F.3d 1070 (9th Cir. 2013), the Ninth Circuit rejected a dormancy-doctrine challenge to a law that limited local use of fuels because their manner of production exacerbated the dangers of climate change. In doing so, the court made reference to *Oregon-Washington Railroad & Navigation Co. v. Washington*, 270 U.S. 87 (1926), "an older case rejecting a dormant Commerce Clause challenge to a Washington State regulation that blocked shipments of alfalfa, except in sealed containers, from neighboring states whose fields had been infested with alfalfa weevils." *Rocky Mountain*, 730 F.3d at 1095. As the court recognized, however, *Oregon-Washington* presented a very different type of case because the "existence of th[e] pest and its geographical location ma[de] the law a real quarantine law and not a mere inhibition against importation of alfalfa." *Id.* at 1095 (quoting *Oregon-Washington*, 270 U.S. at 96). Notably, the earliest articulations of the "quarantine" principle also supported state authority to "exclude from its limits convicts, paupers, idiots, and lunatics," all of whom the Court inhumanely likened to "persons afflicted by contagious or infectious diseases." *Bowman*, 125 U.S. at 492. The Court, however, abandoned this stance in *Edwards v. California*, 314 U.S. 160 (1941). In invalidating a California law that criminalized bringing any "indigent" nonresident into the state, the Court reasoned that "the transportation of persons is 'commerce,' " *id.* at 172; that providing assistance to the needy and "the social phenomenon of large-scale interstate migration" were matters "of national concern," *id.* at 175; and that, whatever one may have thought a century earlier, "we do not think that it will now be seriously contended that because a person is without employment and without funds he constitutes a 'moral pestilence,' " *id.* at 177.

2 437 U.S. 617 (1978). For additional discussion of this case, see *supra* Section 17.A.

3 *Id.* at 632 (Rehnquist, J., joined by Burger, C.J., dissenting).

4 *Id.* at 629 (majority opinion).

Because the key problems targeted by New Jersey's solid-waste restriction—including the polluting effects of groundwater-disturbing leachate, the proliferation of vermin, and green-space loss—arose as a result of placing that waste in the ground, the Court deemed the quarantine exception inapplicable.

In *Chemical Waste Management, Inc. v. Hunt*,[5] the Court further cabined the quarantine exception when it struck down an Alabama law that imposed a special charge on the importation of hazardous waste produced in other states. Without considering the dangers posed by such waste while in transit, the Court concluded that the challenged rule was far removed from a genuine quarantine measure because "Alabama permits both the generation and landfilling of hazardous waste . . . and the importation of still more hazardous waste subject to payment of the additional fee."[6]

After *City of Philadelphia* and *Chemical Waste Management*, the quarantine exception may be moving toward something like the following principle: A state may foreclose the importation of items only if (1) they are marked by a noxious condition that threatens infection or similar dangers in the process of movement, and (2) the state has, within its own borders, sought to stamp out the noxious condition, including by aggressively minimizing exposure to it by people or property that might be put at risk by the threat it poses. According to this view, the Court in *Chemical Waste Management* properly invalidated the challenged statute not only because the state tolerated the generation and movement of hazardous waste as a foreseeable by-product of local business operations, but also because the grant of authority to transport out-of-state waste for an added fee was inconsistent with an intention to extirpate any and all exposure to it.[7]

Other once-vibrant exceptions to the dormancy doctrine have met an even harsher fate. In a nineteenth-century case, *Geer v.*

---

[5] 504 U.S. 334 (1992).

[6] *Id.* at 346–47.

[7] Loosely related to the quarantine exception have been recent attempts to exempt from dormant Commerce Clause scrutiny state laws regarding trade in marijuana. States have (even if with some measure of internally inconsistent behavior) allowed trade in marijuana products while simultaneously seeking to fend off dormant Commerce Clause challenges to starkly resident-favoring regulations of the thus state-authorized trade by relying on (now largely unenforced) federal laws that prohibit even marijuana possession. In one such case, a federal district court dismissed a challenge to a starkly discriminatory state marijuana-licensing law on the theory that general equitable principles barred a would-be federal-law violator from seeking the aid of a federal tribunal. In other cases, however, courts have not hesitated to uphold discrimination-based dormant Commerce Clause challenges in cases of this kind. *See generally supra* Section 17.A.1 n.19 (collecting relevant cases).

Connecticut,[8] the Court shielded from Commerce Clause attack laws regulating the hunting of wild game—including a flatly discriminatory prohibition on killing ducks and geese for shipment outside the state—on the theory that those laws targeted a form of "common property" subject to heightened state authority.[9] In *Hughes v. Oklahoma*,[10] however, the Court overruled *Geer*, describing its "state ownership" rationale as a "legal fiction" that ignored "practical realities."[11] Drawing on *Hughes*, the Court also abandoned its earlier endorsement of a wholesale exemption from Commerce Clause scrutiny for state water-export restrictions in *Sporhase v. Nebraska*.[12] The Court concluded that "[a]lthough [the state's] greater ownership interest may not be irrelevant to Commerce Clause analysis, it does not absolutely remove [regulation of local] ground water from such scrutiny."[13]

Other modern cases carry forward the tendency reflected in both *Hughes* and *Sporhase*. In *Bacchus Imports, Ltd. v. Dias*,[14] for example, the Court torpedoed the state's effort to rely on an exception for discriminatory state laws (here, in the form of a discriminatory tax law) that the legislature had crafted in an effort to bolster start-up or struggling local industries. Although arguments occasionally surface for state favoritism in this context,[15] the Court declared that "the propriety of economic protectionism may not be allowed to hinge upon the State's—or this Court's—characterization of the industry as either 'thriving' or 'struggling.' "[16]

More than a decade later, in a case that closely divided the Court, a majority of Justices declined to apply a dormant Commerce Clause exception to a tax break given by Maine to only those

---

8 161 U.S. 519 (1896).

9 *Id.* at 523.

10 441 U.S. 322 (1979).

11 *Id.* at 335–36.

12 458 U.S. 941 (1982) (refusing to follow *Hudson Cty. Water Co. v. McCarter*, 209 U.S. 349, 357 (1908), which in turn had relied on *Geer*).

13 *Id.* at 951. At the same time, the Court in *Sporhase* endorsed a distinctly deferential approach to water regulations, including ostensibly discriminatory efforts by a state "to conserve and preserve *for its own citizens* this vital resource in times of severe shortage." *Id.* at 956 (emphasis added). In adopting this specialized approach, the Court relied in substantial part on the idea that water "has some indicia of a good publicly produced and owned" by the state as a result of conservation efforts. *Id.* at 957. This logic bears a kinship to the reasoning that underlies the market-participant exception to the dormancy doctrine, which is discussed later in this chapter. *See infra* Section 20.D.

14 468 U.S. 263 (1984).

15 *See* Donald H. Regan, *The Supreme Court and State Protectionism: Making Sense of the Dormant Commerce Clause*, 84 MICH. L. REV. 1091, 1138 (1986) (noting the argument for infant-industry protectionism).

16 *Bacchus Imports*, 468 U.S. at 273.

"benevolent and charitable institutions" that primarily served residents of the state.[17] Challenged by a religious summer camp that dealt with many nonresidents, the law fell victim to the anti-discrimination principle. In the view of the dissenters, the Court should have used the case to endorse a "domestic charity exception" for resident-serving nonprofit institutions on the theory that they deliver "social services" that the state could limit to its own residents if the state provided those services itself.[18] The majority, however, rejected that position. The opinion of the Court, written by Justice Stevens and joined by four other Justices, was built on the idea that there is no justification for distinguishing for-profit from not-for-profit enterprises in applying the dormant Commerce Clause principle because "[e]ntities in both categories are major participants in interstate markets."[19] In addition, Justice Stevens reasoned, "[i]f there is need for a special exception for nonprofits, Congress . . . has the power to create it."[20]

B. THE CONGRESSIONAL-CONSENT EXCEPTION

The congressional-consent exception is simple in its basic operation: If Congress so provides, state laws that otherwise would offend the dormant Commerce Clause principle are immune from challenge under it. Because this doctrine permits Congress to overturn ostensibly constitutional rulings without resort to the constitutional amendment process, it has sparked controversy.[21] Indeed, in the seminal *Cooley* decision, the Court asserted that "[i]f the Constitution excluded the States from making any law regulating commerce, certainly Congress cannot re-grant, or in any manner re-convey to the States that power."[22] This dictum, however, has not kept the Court from allowing Congress to authorize the operation of state laws that otherwise would violate the dormancy doctrine. Most notably, in *Prudential Insurance Co. v. Benjamin*,[23] the Court declared in no uncertain terms that Congress could exercise its power to regulate interstate commerce, including by subjecting it to

---

[17] Camps Newfound/Owatonna, Inc. v. Town of Harrison, 520 U.S. 564, 568 (1997).

[18] *Id.* at 605, 608 (Scalia, J., dissenting) (internal quotation marks omitted); *see id.* at 602–08.

[19] *Id.* at 586 (majority opinion).

[20] *Id.* at 588.

[21] *See, e.g.*, Norman R. Williams, *Why Congress May Not 'Overrule' the Dormant Commerce Clause*, 53 UCLA L. REV. 153 (2005) (questioning Congress's power to authorize state enactment of laws otherwise violative of the dormant Commerce Clause principle).

[22] Cooley v. Bd. of Wardens, 53 U.S. (12 How.) 299, 318 (1851).

[23] 328 U.S. 408 (1946).

limitations and disadvantages, "in conjunction with coordinated action by the states."[24] Applying this principle, the Court went on to conclude that the federal McCarran-Ferguson Act exempted from dormant-Commerce-Clause scrutiny even plain-as-day state discrimination in the taxation of nondomiciliary insurance companies.[25]

Although the modern Court has unwaveringly endorsed the congressional-consent exception, it has also applied that exception with restraint. As explained in *Maine v. Taylor*,[26] "because of the

---

[24] *Id.* at 434. One might say, to put the same point another way, that the Commerce Clause is no longer "dormant" once Congress has spoken, including by declaring that particular state laws do not impede interstate trade in either an undue or unjustifiable way. For a leading scholarly defense of the congressional-consent rule, see William Cohen, *Congressional Power to Validate Unconstitutional State Laws: A Forgotten Solution to an Old Enigma*, 35 STAN. L. REV. 387 (1983). For a critique of Professor Cohen's view, see Williams, *supra* note 21, at 204–05 (asserting that "there are several flaws in Cohen's approach," including the problem that it "is at odds with the Supreme Court's understanding of the Constitution" and, in particular, that "[o]utside of the Dormant Commerce Clause context, the Court has never recognized the power of Congress to waive federalism-based limitations on state authority").

[25] *Prudential*, 328 U.S. at 431. In keeping with this principle, the lower courts have applied the congressional-consent exception to uphold state laws in a wide variety of settings. *See, e.g.*, Mabey Bridge & Shore, Inc. v. Schoch, 666 F.3d 862, 873–74 (3d Cir. 2012) (rejecting a Commerce Clause challenge to a Pennsylvania steel production law that imposed more stringent requirements on foreign materials in part because Congress had explicitly consented to such requirements in the Buy America Act); Tarrant Reg'l Water Dist. v. Herrmann, 656 F.3d 1222 (10th Cir. 2011) (rejecting a challenge to a set of Oklahoma water statutes because the Red River Compact insulated the statutes against dormant Commerce Clause attack), *aff'd*, 569 U.S. 614 (2013); Life Partners, Inc. v. Morrison, 484 F.3d 284 (4th Cir. 2007) (rejecting a Commerce Clause challenge to a Virginia law that regulated certain aspects of insurance settlements because Congress had consented to state regulation in the McCarran-Ferguson Act); Maryeli's Lovely Pets, Inc. v. City of Sunrise, No. 14–61391–Civ–Scola, 2015 WL 11197773, at *2 (S.D. Fla. June 25, 2015) (rejecting a dormant Commerce Clause attack on a city ordinance regulating pet sales because Congress had consented to such regulation via the Animal Welfare Act); Dairy v. Bonham, No. C–13–1518 EMC, 2013 WL 3829268, at *3–*4 (N.D. Cal. July 23, 2013) (rejecting a challenge to a crab trap limit in California because Congress had expressly precluded dormant Commerce Clause challenges to the limit in the Reaffirmation Act of 2005); G.B. v. Rogers, 703 F. Supp. 2d 724, 732–33 (S.D. Ohio 2010) (holding that an Ohio sex-offender-registration scheme could not violate the dormant Commerce Clause because Ohio had put in place the scheme pursuant to the federal Adam Walsh Act); Cent. Valley Chrysler-Jeep v. Witherspoon, 456 F. Supp. 2d 1160, 1185 (E.D. Cal. 2006) (upholding California regulations that burdened interstate commerce by regulating greenhouse-gas emissions because Congress had given California "permission" to do so in the Clean Air Act). In other cases, however, the courts have found the exception inapplicable. *See, e.g.*, Tri-M Group, LLC v. Sharp, 638 F.3d 406, 431 (3d Cir. 2011) (invalidating a set of Delaware regulations that did not extend certain labor protections to out-of-state registered apprentices in part because the Fitzgerald Act did not "expressly authorize[ ] the states to enact apprenticeship regulations that discriminate against out-of-state interests"); Mary Hitchcock Mem'l Hosp. v. Cohen, No. 15–cv–453–LM, 2016 WL 1735818, at *5 (D.N.H. May 2, 2016) ("[N]either the Medicaid Act nor the Borne Amendment . . . allows states to impose Medicaid rates that favor in-state hospitals over out-of-state hospitals.").

[26] 477 U.S. 131 (1986).

important role the Commerce Clause plays in protecting the free flow of interstate trade, this Court has exempted state statutes from the implied limitations of the Clause only when the congressional direction to do so has been unmistakably clear."[27] Citing this principle, the Court in *Taylor* itself declined to rely on the congressional-consent principle to uphold a challenged ban on baitfish imports at issue in that case, rejecting in particular the state's half-a-loaf argument that the federal government's extensive regulation of commerce in wildlife—while not amounting to outright consent—warranted a watered-down form of dormant Commerce Clause review. Instead, citing the "risk that unrepresented interests will be adversely affected by restraints on commerce," the Court found the "clear expression" rule fully applicable "regardless of whether the purported authorization takes the form of a flat exemption from Commerce Clause scrutiny or the less direct form of a reduction in the level of scrutiny."[28]

The Court limited the impact of the congressional-consent exception, at least to a small degree, with its application of the Fourteenth Amendment's Equal Protection Clause in *Metropolitan Life Insurance Co. v. Ward*.[29] There, a foreign corporation challenged a state tax law that discriminated on its face in favor of domestic insurers. Writing for a five-Justice majority, Justice Powell conceded that the law was immune from dormant Commerce Clause challenge under the congressional-consent exception and the McCarran-Ferguson Act. He went on, however, to find the law unconstitutional under the Fourteenth Amendment's Equal Protection Clause (which is not subject to any congressional-consent exception) because, he reasoned, "penalizing foreign insurers" to effectuate "parochial discrimination" was not the sort of "legitimate state purpose" that even the most deferential form of equal-protection review requires.[30]

As other analysts have noted, "[t]he implications of *Metropolitan Life* remain uncertain."[31] The decision drew a rebuke from an unusual coalition of four dissenting Justices (namely, Justices Brennan, Marshall, Rehnquist, and O'Connor), who described as "astonishing" the majority's unwillingness to view as legitimate the

---

27 *Id.* at 139 (internal quotations omitted); *accord, e.g.*, Hillside Dairy, Inc. v. Lyons, 539 U.S. 59, 66 (2003).

28 477 U.S. at 139.

29 470 U.S. 869 (1985).

30 *Id.* at 877–78.

31 KATHLEEN M. SULLIVAN & GERALD GUNTHER, CONSTITUTIONAL LAW 327 (14th ed. 2001); *see also* William Cohen, *Federalism in Equality Clothing: A Comment on* Metropolitan Life Insurance Company v. Ward, 38 STAN. L. REV. 1, 27 (1985) (noting that "[l]ower courts that rely on *Ward* outside the field of insurance regulation or taxation risk reversal, at least so long as this Court, or some future Court, remembers the context of the decision").

state's purpose of "encourag[ing] capital investment within its borders."[32] In addition, later in the same term, the Court cabined the principle of *Metropolitan Life* when it upheld a congressionally authorized program established by Massachusetts and Connecticut that entirely barred the local operation of banks headquartered in any of the other 48 states.[33] Perhaps most significantly, the Court's reasoning in *Metropolitan Life* itself may signal that states can sidestep equal-protection difficulties by simply coming up with some explanation for tax discrimination other than outright protectionism. States, for example, might seek to justify heightened taxation of non-resident firms on a theory that it roughly equalizes tax burdens placed on resident corporations by way of local property and other taxes. Such a justification—which almost always fails for dormant Commerce Clause purposes[34]—may nonetheless work for equal-protection-clause purposes to avert a fatal characterization of the law as "purely and completely discriminatory."[35]

C. THE SUBSIDY EXCEPTION

Prior discussion has shown that discriminatory tax laws, unless authorized by Congress, routinely violate the dormant Commerce Clause because they provide favored in-state firms with a competitive edge.[36] Basic "tax expenditure theory" teaches, however, that tax exemptions, credits, and deductions are, as an economic matter, functionally indistinguishable from outright monetary grants.[37] Does it follow that cash subsidies for in-state businesses are unconstitutional because—just like discriminatory tax laws—they provide local firms with advantages *vis-à-vis* out-of-state competitors?

---

[32] *Metro. Life Ins. Co.*, 470 U.S. at 883 (O'Connor, J., dissenting).

[33] *See* Ne. Bancorp, Inc. v. Bd. of Govs. of Fed. Reserve Sys., 472 U.S. 159 (1985). Seeming to grasp at analytical straws, the Court reasoned that, unlike in *Metropolitan Life*, neither Massachusetts nor Connecticut had excluded all interstate commerce (because each state permitted competition coming from the other) and that banking was (for some reason) a matter of distinctly "profound local concern." *Id.* at 177 (internal quotations omitted).

[34] *See infra* Section 21.B.

[35] *Metro. Life Ins. Co.*, 470 U.S. at 878. Supportive of the idea that equal-protection law puts fewer restraints than the dormancy doctrine on the states' ability to adopt these sorts of "compensatory" taxes is *Associated Indus. v. Lohman*, 511 U.S. 641, 651–52 (1994).

[36] *See supra* Chapter 17; *see also infra* Chapter 21 (discussing dormant Commerce Clause rules for tax laws in greater detail).

[37] *See, e.g.*, Stanley S. Surrey, *Tax Incentives as a Device for Implementing Government Policy: A Comparison with Direct Government Expenditures*, 83 HARV. L. REV. 705, 717 (1970) ("A dollar is a dollar—both for the person who receives it and the government that pays it, whether the dollar comes with a tax credit label or a direct expenditure label.").

Although the Supreme Court has left itself wiggle room to reconsider the matter,[38] its precedents suggest that the answer to this question is "no."[39] Given the recurring theme that "practical realities" should guide dormant Commerce Clause decisionmaking,[40] how can it be that the Court has failed to equate discriminatory tax breaks with outright monetary subsidies that produce functionally equivalent financial effects? One explanation lies in the constitutional text. On this view, the Commerce Clause by its terms deals with the power to "regulate" interstate commerce, which forecloses taxation that "burdens" such commerce but not affirmative subsidization that operates only to "benefit" intrastate actors.[41] Another explanation lies in constitutional history. According to this account, it was not fear of unfair subsidization, but concern about "taxation without representation," that dominated worries at the time of both the Revolution and the Philadelphia Convention.[42]

The best explanation, however, seems to lie in the very same considerations of "practical consequences"[43] that the most forceful critiques of the subsidy exception invoke. This account posits that that tax breaks and subsidies, although not *economically* different, are *politically* different in critical ways. In particular, monetary subsidies are likely to encounter distinctive political obstacles to enactment because they involve straightforward and visible government spending; they are typically subject to reconsideration in each year's budgeting process; and they lack the built-in appeal, for many, of government tax reduction.[44] As a result, the tax-break/subsidy distinction dovetails with the notion that courts should reduce the level of intensity with which they apply the dormancy doctrine when a "State's own political processes will act as a check on local regulations that unduly burden interstate commerce."[45]

When does a government program or rule fall within the subsidy exception? One governing principle is that the exception does not reach any form of discriminatory *tax* relief afforded by state law, regardless of whether that relief takes the form of a favorable

---

[38] *See Camps Newfound/Owatonna*, 520 U.S. at 589 (noting that "[w]e have 'never squarely confronted the constitutionality of subsidies' . . . and we need not address these questions today" (quoting West Lynn Creamery, Inc. v. Healy, 512 U.S. 186, 199 n.15 (1994)).

[39] *See, e.g.*, Dan T. Coenen, *Business Subsidies and the Dormant Commerce Clause*, 107 YALE L.J. 965, 977–78 (1998) (discussing the relevant case law).

[40] Hughes v. Oklahoma, 441 U.S. 322, 335 (1979).

[41] For a criticism of this view, see Coenen, *supra* note 39, at 1013–14.

[42] *See id.* at 980–81.

[43] Nippert v. City of Richmond, 327 U.S. 416, 431 (1946).

[44] *See* Coenen, *supra* note 39, at 984–97.

[45] Raymond Motor Transp., Inc. v. Rice, 434 U.S. 429, 447 (1978).

exemption, deduction, credit, rebate, or refund.[46] A more difficult question, which was squarely presented in *West Lynn Creamery, Inc. v. Healy*,[47] is whether there are instances in which a benefit characterized by the state as a "subsidy" or "payment" should be recharacterized by the courts as an unconstitutionally discriminatory tax break.[48]

West Lynn Creamery involved a two-part Massachusetts program designed to aid the state's struggling dairy-farming industry. Under the first part of the program, the state imposed a tax on milk dealers (that is, primarily non-producer milk wholesalers) for all sales they made to local retailers, whether or not the milk they sold had been produced within the state. Under the second part of the program, the state then turned over the revenue raised by this tax to in-state dairy farmers. According to the dissenting opinion of Chief Justice Rehnquist, who was joined by Justice Blackmun, the state's program was constitutional because it embodied (1) a permissible nondiscriminatory tax and (2) state pay-outs that were unobjectionable under the subsidy exception to the dormant Commerce Clause.[49] The Court as a whole, however, rejected this analysis. Reasoning that the two features of the challenged program could not be viewed in isolation, five Justices, in an opinion by written by Justice Stevens, recharacterized the state's payments to its dairy farmers as discriminatory tax refunds or rebates.[50] It was inconsequential, Justice Stevens explained, that the supposed tax relief went to beneficiaries (that is, dairy farmers) who were not the target of the tax (that is, milk dealers). The overarching problem was that the Massachusetts program "in its practical operation" violated "the cardinal principle that a State may not 'benefit in-state economic interests by burdening out-of-state competitors.' "[51]

The *de facto* refund principle of *West Lynn Creamery* raises troublesome problems of legal labeling. To begin with, the Court in that case focused on the subsidy program's unusually close linkage with a specialized state tax. But how should courts decide whether any particular tax-subsidy linkage is close enough to raise a constitutional red flag? Must the payment program and tax program

---

46 *See* Dan T. Coenen & Walter Hellerstein, *Suspect Linkage: The Interplay of State Taxing and Spending Measures in the Application of Constitutional Antidiscrimination Rules*, 95 MICH. L. REV. 2167, 2203–14 (1997) (developing this principle and noting possible qualifications to it).

47 512 U.S. 186 (1994).

48 *Id.* at 194.

49 *Id.* at 212 (Rehnquist, C.J., dissenting).

50 *Id.* at 197 (majority opinion). Justices Scalia and Thomas separately concurred only in the judgment. *See id.* at 207 (Scalia, J., concurring in the judgment).

51 *Id.* at 199 (majority opinion (quoting New Energy Co. v. Limbach, 486 U.S. 269, 273–74 (1988)).

appear in the same law? Must they be enacted simultaneously or at least close in time? Can an adequate linkage exist only when, as Justice Scalia claimed in a concurring opinion, the tax proceeds never find their way into the general treasury but instead go directly into a segregated fund from which all local-business-favoring payments are then made?[52] These and other questions about the requisite connection between subsidies and taxes loom on the horizon of dormant Commerce Clause law.[53]

D. THE MARKET-PARTICIPANT EXCEPTION

1. A Basic Overview

Closely related to the Court's treatment of subsidies is its recognition of the "market participant" exception to the dormancy doctrine. Indeed, the Court first applied the market-participant exception in *Hughes v. Alexandria Scrap Corp.*[54] to validate a novel cash-subsidy program. The case involved a challenge to a Maryland law under which the state made payments to scrap processors as part of an effort to rid local roadsides of unsightly junk cars. The fly in the ointment was that Maryland subjected out-of-state scrap-processing firms to a more extensive and costly set of documentation requirements for obtaining the available subsidies. The Court, however, rejected an out-of-state processor's challenge to this patently discriminatory feature of the Maryland scheme. According to Justice Powell, who wrote for six Justices, the non-discrimination rule had no role to play in the case because the state had not sought to regulate private market behavior. Instead, because Maryland had itself entered "the market as a purchaser, in effect," it was free to choose its own trading partners.[55] The dissenters worried that the

---

[52] *Id.* at 211 (Scalia, J., concurring in the judgment).

[53] For detailed treatments of these questions, as well as related questions raised in the tax-immunity context, see Coenen & Hellerstein, *supra* note 46, at 2215–27; and Coenen, *supra* note 39, at 1037–53. For a recent and narrowing gloss on *West Lynn Creamery*, see *Pharmaceutical Research & Manufacturers of America v. Walsh*, 538 U.S. 644, 670 (2003) (refusing to apply the *West Lynn Creamery* rule where payments effectively required by Maine from out-of-state drug manufacturers resulted in a financial benefit to local pharmacies and consumers; finding the *de facto* tariff principle inapplicable because "payments to the local pharmacists provide no special benefit to competitors of [out-of-state] manufacturers," which would receive no benefit from the program even "by opening production facilities in Maine"), and *DirecTV, Inc. v. Treesh*, 487 F.3d 471, 480 (6th Cir. 2007) (holding that a Kentucky tax/benefit scheme for cable television operators was not an impermissible tariff-like tax-and-subsidy program; reasoning that "[t]he instant case differs from *West Lynn Creamery* in several important respects," one of them being that "the claimed subsidy is not a direct monetary subsidy, but is instead only the right to conduct business and use local rights-of-way without local taxation or fees" in a manner analogous to unimpeded use of state roads).

[54] 426 U.S. 794 (1976).

[55] *Id.* at 808.

Court had taken a wrong turn by "treating what is essentially a problem of striking a balance between competing interests as an exercise in absolutes."[56] For the majority, however, the governing principle was straightforward: "Nothing in the purposes animating the Commerce Clause prohibits a State, in the absence of congressional action, from participating in the market and exercising the right to favor its own citizens over others."[57]

The Court consolidated the market-participant exception in *Reeves, Inc. v. Stake*[58] by holding that South Dakota could restrict sales from a state-owned cement plant to South Dakota residents. Then, in *White v. Massachusetts Council of Construction Employers, Inc.*,[59] the Court invoked the exception to uphold a Boston law that required building contractors engaged by the city to give a specified minimum percentage of resulting jobs to in-city, and thus in-state, residents. In effect, the Court's decision in *White* embodied two separate holdings. First, the Court effectively shielded from dormant Commerce Clause scrutiny the common practice of favoring state or municipal residents in hiring state or municipal employees. Second, the Court extended this principle to permit a city to force a *private* contractor that was working on a city construction project to favor local residents in its own hiring for that project. The Court justified this second holding by reasoning that persons employed to work on a city construction project, although paid and supervised by a private firm, were "in a substantial, if informal, sense, 'working for the city.' "[60]

The market-participant exception, like the congressional-consent and subsidy exceptions, has proven controversial. Each of the Court's rulings—in *Alexandria Scrap*, *Reeves*, and *White*—came from a divided Court, leading Justice Brennan to suggest that the Court's recurring disagreements "point up the inherent weakness of the doctrine."[61] Commentators have also challenged the exception on

---

[56] *Id.* at 819 (Brennan, J., dissenting) (quoting H. P. Hood & Sons, Inc. v. Du Mond, 336 U.S. 525, 564 (1949) (Frankfurter, J., dissenting)).

[57] *Id.* at 810 (majority opinion) (internal footnote omitted).

[58] 447 U.S. 429 (1980).

[59] 460 U.S. 204 (1983).

[60] *Id.* at 211 n.7.

[61] South-Central Timber Dev., Inc. v. Wunnicke, 467 U.S. 82, 101 (1984) (Brennan, J., concurring). The Court's ruling in *Reeves* came in a five-to-four decision, and Justice Powell, who had written for the majority in *Alexandria Scrap*, wrote the dissenting opinion. The Court's ruling in *White* came in a seven-to-two decision, and Justice Blackmun, who had written for the majority in *Reeves*, wrote the dissenting opinion. The Court's later ruling in *South-Central Timber*, to which Justice Brennan specifically alluded, in effect resulted from a four-to-two vote on the dormant Commerce Clause issue, due both to the filing of a separate concurrence by Justice Powell, joined by Chief Justice Burger, that did not address the market-participant question, and to Justice Marshall's non-participation in the case. Then-Associate

various grounds, including by pointing out that it threatens efficiency and creates incentives for states to engage in business operations best handled by private firms.[62] Even so, the market-participant rule seems well-entrenched.[63] Nine different Justices contributed to the majorities that handed down the decisions in *Alexandria Scrap*,

---

Justice Rehnquist, who had written for the Court's majority in *White*, penned the dissent in *South-Central Timber*.

[62] *See, e.g.*, Christine H. Kellett, *The Market Participant Doctrine: No Longer "Good Sense" or "Sound Law,"* 9 TEMP. ENVTL. L. & TECH. J. 169, 172–79 (1990) (emphasizing the uncertain legal basis for the exception and the difficulties of determining what state actions are subject to it); Richard H. Seamon, Note, *The Market Participant Test in Dormant Commerce Clause Analysis-Protecting Protectionism?*, 1985 DUKE L.J. 697, 697–99 (arguing that the exception shelters protectionist state actions that otherwise would be disallowed); Edward W. Greason, Note, *Garbage and the Constitution: Solid Waste Disposal, the Dormant Commerce Clause, and the Market Participant Exception*, 3 FORDHAM ENVTL. L. REP. 1, 13 (1991) (noting that the market-participation exception "makes it easy for a state to avoid Commerce Clause scrutiny . . . through the use of government enterprises" and expressing concern that this exception is in actuality "becoming the rule"). Professor Tribe has written that "[t]he Court's reasoning in these cases is in some respects problematic," LAURENCE H. TRIBE, AMERICAN CONSTITUTIONAL LAW § 6–11, at 1090 (3d ed. 2000), and also has collected additional authorities critical of the exception, *id.* at 1090 n.20. For a defense of the exception, see Dan T. Coenen, *Untangling the Market-Participant Exemption to the Dormant Commerce Clause*, 88 MICH. L. REV. 395, 398, 431–33 (1989) (arguing that attacks on the exception are "misplaced" because it stems from the Court's "sound, if complex, accommodation of competing constitutional values").

[63] Lower courts have applied the market-participant rule in a variety of factual contexts, although not all market participation arguments have fared well. *See, e.g.*, Asante v. Cal. Dep't of Health Care Servs., 886 F.3d 795 (9th Cir. 2018) (holding that California was a market participant when it set reimbursement rates to hospitals for those insured under California's Medicaid participation program because the state was acting like a private insurer and not a market regulator); Associated Builders & Contractors, Inc. v. City of Jersey City, 836 F.3d 412 (3d Cir. 2016) (finding that the exception did not apply to a city ordinance that imposed requirements for private-developer tax exemptions because the ordinance involved market regulation rather than market participation); Mason & Dixon Lines Inc. v. Steudle, 683 F.3d 289, 293–94 (6th Cir. 2012) (holding that Michigan was acting as a participant in the road construction market when it closed off public access to a bridge and thus impeded interstate movement); Antilles Cement Corp. v. Fortuño, 670 F.3d 310, 326–31 (1st Cir. 2012) (holding, for purposes of the dormant Foreign Commerce Clause, *see infra* Chapter 22, that Puerto Rico acted as a market participant when it prohibited Commonwealth-funded construction projects from using non-Puerto Rican cement, but that it was acting as a regulator and not a market participant, when it imposed cement labeling requirements); United Healthcare Ins. Co. v. Davis, 602 F.3d 618, 624–27 (5th Cir. 2010) (rejecting a dormant Commerce Clause challenge to a Louisiana statute that set out guidelines for state healthcare administrators and insurance contracts because the state was acting as a market participant by listing preferred business partners in the process of contracting for administrative services); Brooks v. Vassar, 462 F.3d 341, 355–60 (4th Cir. 2006) (upholding a Virginia law that required state-owned-and-operated liquor stores to sell only Virginia-produced wine because the state was itself acting as a free-market actor in making choices for only its own stores, as opposed to regulating private operators).

Reeves, and *White*.[64] And no Justice who later joined the Court has expressed a negative view of the doctrine.

So just what considerations justify recognition of the market-participant exception? In *Reeves* the Court pointed to history, conventional understanding, fairness, and federalism in claiming that the exception reflects "good sense and sound law."[65] As to history, the Court reasoned that the Commerce Clause grew out of concerns about the imposition of obstructive taxes and regulations directed at private parties engaged in private transactions, as opposed to acts of government favoritism toward state residents when the state itself engages in buying and selling.[66] As to conventional understandings, the Court cited the "long recognized right of trader or manufacturer, engaged in an entirely private business, freely to exercise his own independent discretion as to parties with whom he will deal."[67] As to fairness, the Court reasoned that state citizens should be able to reap where they have sown, including by insisting that the state should "limit[ ] benefits generated by a state program to those who fund the State treasury."[68] Finally, as to federalism, the Court reasoned that the market-participant rule comports with the value of fostering state experimentation.[69] The Court's actual experience in applying the market-participant exception may also lend aid to the case for retaining it: In particular, and as the next section shows, the Court has wielded the exception with restraint by surrounding it with an array of significant limits, thus undercutting parade-of-horribles-type arguments about the exception's susceptibility to abuse.

2. Limits on the Market-Participant Exception

Just as surely as the Court has invoked the market-participant exception in deciding several cases, it has declined to apply it in

---

64 The Justices joining various majorities in *Alexandria Scrap*, *Reeves*, and *White* were Chief Justice Burger and Justices Blackmun, Brennan, Marshall, O'Connor, Powell, Rehnquist, Stevens, and Stewart.

65 *Reeves*, 447 U.S. at 436. *See generally* Coenen, *supra* note 62.

66 *Reeves*, 447 U.S. at 437.

67 *Id.* at 438–39 (quoting United States v. Colgate & Co., 250 U.S. 300, 307 (1919)).

68 *Id.* at 442. The Court also noted that state proprietary activities commonly are subject to the same restrictions applicable to private business; thus "[e]venhandedness suggests that, when acting as proprietors, States should similarly share existing freedoms from federal constraints, including the inherent limits of the Commerce Clause." *Id.* at 439.

69 In *Reeves*, for instance, Justice Blackmun noted that the South Dakota cement plant had benefited both the state and the region since the early 1900s, while gesturing towards the question whether South Dakota would have built the plant in the first place if it had known that it would have to hold back supplies from its own residents to fill orders from out-of-state buyers in times of greatest need. *See id.* at 441.

others. In *New England Power Co. v. New Hampshire*,[70] for example, the state sought to rely on its "ownership" of the Connecticut River in passing a law that restricted the ability of privately-owned plants located on the river to export hydroelectric power to would-be buyers in other states. The Court responded by invalidating the law, reasoning that the federal government—not the state—had primary control over navigable waterways and that the challenged law, in any event, targeted electricity and not the waters of the river itself.[71] In *Camps Newfound/Owatonna*,[72] a state again tried to shoehorn an overtly discriminatory measure—here in the form of tax relief provided only to a set of non-profit corporations that favored the state's own residents—into the market-participant category. A five-Justice majority, however, failed to see how affording tax breaks to a private party based on its contracting choices with other private parties somehow allowed the tax-imposing state to deem itself a market participant.[73] The majority also observed that the challenged tax exemption differed from the "discrete" program at issue in *Alexandria Scrap* and the "narrow" program in *Reeves* because "it sweeps to cover broad swathes of the nonprofit sector."[74]

Most important, a plurality opinion in *South-Central Timber Co. v. Wunnicke*[75] pointed to three possible constraints on applying the market-participant principle. At issue in that case was an Alaska statute that required purchasers of the state's standing timber to process that timber within the state prior to exportation. In striking down this law, a plurality of Justices emphasized that it (1) involved

---

[70] 455 U.S. 331 (1982).

[71] *Id.* at 338 n.6.

[72] 520 U.S. 564, 568 (1997); *see also supra* note 17 and accompanying text.

[73] *Camps Newfound/Owatonna*, 520 U.S. at 589.

[74] *Id.* at 594. The Court's "broad swathes" rationale may well surface again as the Court grapples with market-participant issues in other contexts. It could, for example, influence the Court's evaluation of an issue that has divided the circuit courts—namely, whether states may require all local governments to put in place buy-local and similar proprietary programs. *Compare* W.C.M. Window Co. v. Bernardi, 730 F.2d 486, 494–96 (7th Cir. 1984) (holding that such state laws are not sustainable on a market-participant theory), *with* Nat'l Solid Waste Mgmt. Ass'n v. Williams, 146 F.3d 595, 599 (8th Cir. 1998) (declining to follow *W.C.M. Window*); Trojan Tech., Inc. v. Pennsylvania, 916 F.2d 903, 911 (3d Cir. 1990) (similar); Smith Setzer & Sons, Inc. v. S.C. Procurement Rev. Panel, 20 F.3d 1311, 1319–20 (4th Cir. 1994) (similar); Big Country Foods, Inc. v. Bd. of Educ., 952 F.2d 1173, 1179 (9th Cir. 1992) (agreeing "with the Third Circuit in *Trojan Technologies*" in explicitly rejecting the holding of *W.C.M. Window*). For a more recent case discussing this matter, see *Lakeside Roofing Co. v. Nixon*, No. 4:10CV1761 JCH, 2012 WL 709276, at *9 (E.D. Mo. Mar. 5, 2012) (holding that because "local government action constitutes state action for purposes of Commerce Clause analysis," the state's application of an "Excessive Unemployment Law" to local governments fell within the exception). *See generally* Coenen, *supra* note 62, at 481–84 (addressing this issue and endorsing the *W.C.M. Window* approach in light of the policies that underlie the market-participant exception).

[75] 467 U.S. 82 (1984).

a natural resource; (2) impeded international, as well as interstate, commerce; and (3) not only imposed restrictions on the state's choice of trading partners as it sold state-owned timber but also "impose[d] conditions downstream in the timber-processing market."[76] In addition, and wholly apart from *South Central Timber*, a long line of Supreme Court rulings suggests that, at least sometimes, a fourth limitation on the market-participant exception is operative when the state seeks to restrict access to channels of commerce that the state itself owns. We now turn to each of these four possible "exceptions to the exception" that find support in the Court's market-participant rulings.

a. Natural Resources

In *Reeves*, the Court distinguished cement—the product of an elaborate manufacturing process that works on raw materials—from natural resources located "by happenstance" within the state.[77] The Court thus implied that two mutually reinforcing justifications might support recognition of a natural-resources exception to the market-participant doctrine. First, the lucky break that landed valuable natural resources in a state gives that state a greatly diminished earned-right claim to hoard those resources pursuant to the doctrine's fairness-based reap-what-you-sow rationale. Second, restricting out-of-staters' access to natural resources threatens interstate commerce in a heightened way because those resources constitute the essential building blocks of production. As usual, these justifications have spawned critiques. The extraction of natural resources, for example, often itself requires complex work and substantial financial outlays, and buyers denied access to state-owned resources can always look elsewhere for market substitutes. In *South-Central Timber*, however, the Court's plurality reiterated and relied on the proposition that special considerations arise if "a natural resource 'like coal, timber, wild game, or minerals' [is] involved" in the case.[78]

Assuming a natural-resource exception exists, borderline questions will crop up about whether particular state transactions fall within it. Take the case of state-owned landfills. Does land constitute a natural resource so that a state may deny nonresidents access to any landfill that the state itself owns and operates? The

---

76 *Id.* at 95. Arguably, the Court in that case looked at these factors in the aggregate. But *South-Central Timber* and other cases as well lend support to the view that each of these "factors" may independently limit the operation of the market-participant exception.

77 *Reeves*, 447 U.S. at 444.

78 *South-Central Timber*, 467 U.S. at 96 (opinion of White, J.) (quoting *Reeves*, 447 U.S. at 444).

better answer is "no." Whatever else one might say about land, after all, all states have it. It thus follows that the key justifications for recognition of a natural-resources exception—based on happenstance and scarcity—do not apply with much force in this context, as multiple lower courts in effect have concluded.[79]

b. Foreign Commerce

In *South-Central Timber*, Justice White's plurality opinion emphasized that a great deal of Alaskan timber was exported to Japan and that, for this reason, the state's processing restriction significantly impeded international, as well as interstate, commerce. The plurality reasoned that this fact helped support invalidation of the law because it brought into play the specialized consideration that "the Federal Government [should] speak with one voice when regulating commercial relations with foreign governments."[80] These few words leave it unclear whether a full-fledged foreign-commerce "exception" to the market-participant doctrine might someday gain recognition. The Court, however, has paid attention to this factor in other contexts,[81] and it is likely to follow the lead of the *South-Central Timber* plurality by giving it at least some weight in applying the market-participant doctrine.[82]

---

[79] *E.g.*, Swin Resource Sys., Inc. v. Lycoming Cty., 883 F.2d 245, 251–55 (3d Cir. 1989) (applying the dormant Commerce Clause to assess whether impermissible discrimination marked the operation of a publicly owned waste facility, but ultimately holding that the county's attempt to preserve landfill capacity by charging a higher price for disposing of non-local waste fell within the market-participant exception); Cty. Comm'rs v. Stevens, 473 A.2d 12, 20 (Md. 1984) (holding that a county was a market participant and that the "natural resource" exception did not apply to the county owned and operated landfill facility); Evergreen Waste Sys., Inc. v. Metro. Serv. Dist., 643 F. Supp. 127, 132 (D. Or. 1986) ("[A] complex metropolitan landfill operation is not a natural resource to which commerce clause scrutiny should apply. Like the cement plant in *Reeves, Inc.*, the District has developed a complex plant. The District is not hoarding raw land, it is providing a public service to its residents."), *aff'd*, 820 F.2d 1482 (9th Cir. 1987); Whitehouse v. New Eng. Ecological Dev., Inc., No. 98–4525, 1999 WL 1001188, at *3 (R.I. Super. Oct. 28, 1999) ("Although the Central Landfill is referred to as a 'public resource,' this Court finds that it is a state-created resource rather than a natural resource since landfills are not found in this State by pure fortuity and require a degree of expenditure to produce them.").

[80] *South-Central Timber*, 467 U.S. at 100 (quoting Michelin Tire Corp. v. Wages, 423 U.S. 276, 285 (1976)).

[81] *See generally infra* Chapter 22 (discussing the special features of the dormant Foreign Commerce Clause).

[82] *See* Nat'l Foreign Trade Council v. Natsios, 181 F.3d 38, 66 (1st Cir. 1999) ("Contrary to the Third Circuit's view in *Trojan Technologies*, we believe that the risks inherent in state regulation of foreign commerce—including the risk of retaliation against the nation as a whole and the weakening of the federal government's ability to speak with one voice in foreign affairs—weigh against extending the market participation exception to the Foreign Commerce Clause." (internal citation omitted)), *aff'd on other grounds sub nom.* Crosby v. Nat'l Foreign Trade Council, 530 U.S. 363 (2000); Brannon P. Denning & Jack H. McCall, Jr., *The Constitutionality of State and Local "Sanctions" Against Foreign Countries: Affairs of State, States' Affairs, or a Sorry*

c. *Downstream Restraints*

Writing for the Court's four-Justice plurality in *South-Central Timber*, Justice White emphasized the special threats to a free-flowing commerce posed by the "State's attachment of restrictions on dispositions subsequent to the goods coming to rest in private hands."[83] According to Justice White, the imposition of such "downstream restrictions" properly negates application of the "market *participant*" label because they have the "*regulatory* effect" of controlling the behavior of purely private trading partners—in *South-Central Timber*, private log owners and private timber processors.[84] Building on this point, Justice White observed: "The limit of the market-participant doctrine must be that it allows a State to impose burdens on commerce within the market in which it is a participant, but allows it to go no further."[85] He added that the market that the state has entered must be "relatively narrowly defined" lest the market-participant exception "swallow[ ] up" the dormant Commerce Clause rule.[86] Justice White then applied these principles by contrasting the facts that drove its earlier ruling in *White* with those of *South-Central Timber*. In *White*, he explained, Boston had entered the market for employment because construction workers employed by private contractors "substantial[ly] . . . work[ed] for the City" in "the course of an ongoing commercial relationship in which the city retained a continuing proprietary interest."[87] In *South-Central Timber*, by contrast, Alaska was not "participating in the processed timber market"; instead, it merely "restrict[ed] the post-purchase activity of the purchaser" while "participat[ing] in no way in the actual processing."[88]

As the Court's effort to distinguish these two cases reveals, application of the "downstream restraint" principle is complicated by the wide variety of forms that restraints of this nature can take.[89] If a state gives high school graduates scholarships for strong performance, but only if they attend in-state colleges, has it imposed

---

State of Affairs, 26 HASTINGS CONST. L.Q. 307, 351–68 (1999) (suggesting that the market-participant exception should not apply in foreign-commerce cases).

83 *South-Central Timber*, 467 U.S. at 98.

84 *Id.* at 97 (emphasis added).

85 *Id.*

86 *Id.* at 97–99.

87 *Id.* at 94–97, 97 n.10.

88 *Id.* at 98–99.

89 *See, e.g.*, New England Power Co. v. New Hampshire, 455 U.S. 331, 338 n.6 (1982) (invalidating a state ban on a private company's exportation of hydroelectric power generated by a river the state claimed to own by pointing out that, among other things, the law restricted "the sale of electric energy, a product entirely distinct from the river waters used to produce it").

a discriminatory restriction on a "market in which it is not a participant"? Does the answer to the question depend on whether the program benefits private-college, as well as public-college, students? (The argument seems strong, after all, that states are participants in the market for public education, but far less strong that they are participants in the private-education market as well.) Are downstream restraint problems negated if the state issues checks directly to in-state private schools, rather than to students, because this form of payment makes the state a participant in the private-education market in its capacity as a payor-buyer? (Note, in this regard, Justice White's unwillingness in *South-Central Timber* "to say that the State could evade the reasoning of this opinion by merely including a provision . . . that title [to the timber] does not pass until the processing is complete" because "the substance of the transaction . . . governs."[90]) Does the state remain a participant in both the public-education and private-education markets, so that there is no downstream-restraint problem, if it monitors student performance following the award grant with a view to assessing continuing eligibility for scholarship grants? Is talk about "markets" entirely irrelevant in the cash-grant scholarship context because it involves a subsidy, rather than a market-participant, problem?[91] And for that matter, is talk about state participation in particular markets ever appropriate, given that the ruling in *South-Central Timber* came from a mere plurality of four Justices?[92]

d. Channels of Commerce

A final exception to the market-participant doctrine appears to apply when the state grants access to the channels of commerce in which it maintains a proprietary interest. Consider the road-related cases covered in the previous chapter—cases such as *Bibb*, *Raymond*, and *Kassel*.[93] Basic doctrine condemns state laws that discriminate against or unduly burden interstate users of roadways. Yet states pay for, build, and own state roads, so that—at least as a matter of theory—courts might choose to apply the market-participant exception in this context. One senses that a refusal to apply the market-participant exception in these cases reflects the special importance of the infrastructure of commerce to interstate movement

---

[90] 467 U.S. at 99 n.11.

[91] *See supra* Section 20.C (discussing the subsidy limit on the dormant commerce clause).

[92] *But see* David Q. Cross, Note, *Dormant Danger?: A Potential Constitutional Challenge to Georgia's Hope Scholarship*, 34 GA. L. REV. 1381, 1393 (2000) (noting that "although Justice White's discussion of downstream restraints occurs in a plurality opinion, both federal appellate courts and commentators have favored adopting a downstream restraint exception" (internal footnote omitted)).

[93] *See supra* Section 18.A.

and trade.[94] But how far does this "exception to the exception" extend? Without saying as much, one federal court of appeals appeared to apply the channels-of-commerce exception in holding invalid a state's discriminatory treatment of nonresident vendors who sought to rent space in a state-owned farmers' market.[95] Another application of this exception has come in decisions addressing the constitutionality of highway and airport "user fees."[96] The bottom line seems clear enough: In some cases involving access to the corridors of trade and travel, courts have declined to let the state, despite its ownership of those corridors, claim that it is a "participant" in a relevant "market" so as to escape the operation of the dormancy doctrine in a field of state action in which that doctrine long has done much of its most important work.

E. THE STATE-SELF-PROMOTION EXCEPTION

In *United Haulers Ass'n v. Oneida-Herkimer Solid Waste Management Authority*,[97] the Court endorsed a previously unrecognized limit on the dormant Commerce Clause principle. That case arose out of a trash-handling program put in place by two counties in New York State. Seeking to address a "solid waste

---

[94] *See generally* Louis Cholden-Brown, *Planes, Trains and Trucks: Applying the Market Participant Exception to the Government as Proprietary Owner of Hubs of Commerce*, 14 CHARLESTON L. REV. 1 (2020). This is not to say that every state law that has anything to do with roads is properly subject to application of the market-participant-limiting channels-of-commerce principle. *See Mason & Dixon Lines Inc.*, 683 F.3d at 294 (holding that Michigan was acting as a participant in the "road construction market" when it declined, at the behest of a participating contractor (and, at a later stage, at the behest of others), to open certain lanes of a highway subject to a massive road-improvement project as quickly as the participating contractor wanted in an overall effort properly to "ensur[e] the completion of a contract").

[95] *See* Smith v. Dep't of Agric., 630 F.2d 1081 (5th Cir. 1980); *see also* Fla. Transp. Serv., Inc. v. Miami-Dade Cty., 757 F. Supp. 2d 1260, 1282 (S.D. Fla. 2010) ("Like Georgia in . . . *Smith*, the County simply provides a suitable market place that it owns—the Port—for stevedores to offer their services"; thus concluding that "[o]wnership of the Port does not make the County a participant in the stevedore market any more than ownership of the farmers' market made Georgia a participant in the produce market"), *aff'd sub nom.* Fla. Transp. Servs., Inc. v. Miami-Dade Cty., 703 F.3d 1230 (11th Cir. 2012); Coenen, *supra* note 62, at 451–53 (analyzing the *Smith* case along these same lines). *But see* Four T's, Inc. v. Little Rock Mun. Airport Comm'n, 108 F.3d 909, 912–13 (8th Cir. 1997) (adopting the dissenter's approach in *Smith* in concluding that a municipal airport commission's practice of charging concession fees to car rental companies fell within the market-participant exception).

[96] *See infra* Section 21.E. *But see* Owner-Operator Indep. Drivers Assn., Inc. v. Holcomb, 990 F.3d 565, 567–68 (7th Cir. 2021) (applying the market-participant exception to rebuff a challenge to the state's increase to a user-fee charge for accessing a state highway based on the history of private operation of tollways and the court's earlier ruling in *Endsley v. Chicago*, 230 F.3d 276, 284–86 (7th Cir. 2000); suggesting that this result makes sense "even if [the charge is] treated as discriminating against interstate commerce" but also suggesting that the law would not in fact qualify as discriminatory because it "treats everyone alike"), *cert. denied*, 142 S. Ct. 351 (2021).

[97] 550 U.S. 330 (2007).

'crisis,'" these localities established a public authority "to purchase and develop facilities" to process local refuse.[98] These facilities, in turn, were to engage in such activities as "composting," "recycling . . . 33 kinds of materials," and providing "household hazardous waste disposal."[99] To pay for these expanded services, the authority set fees for delivery of waste to this processor at levels that "significantly exceeded [amounts] charged for waste removal on the open market."[100] In addition, to ensure that customers would not flee the program due to these elevated charges, local officials mandated "that all solid waste generated within the Counties be delivered to the Authority's processing sites."[101] Not surprisingly, out-of-state waste-service firms (as well as haulers to their facilities) challenged this local-processing requirement under the dormant Commerce Clause.[102]

There was good reason to believe that this challenge would succeed. After all, the counties' program seemed to have exactly the same "essential vice" as the waste-handling program struck down in *C & A Carbone, Inc. v. Town of Clarkstown*[103] because it "bar[red] the import of the processing service" and thereby "deprive[d] out-of-state businesses of access to a local market."[104] Nonetheless, a six-Justice majority upheld the local-processing mandate, with Chief Justice Roberts authoring the decisive opinion in the case.[105] According to his

---

98 *Id.* at 334–35.

99 *Id.* at 336.

100 *Id.*

101 *Id.*

102 *Id.* at 337.

103 511 U.S. 383, 392 (1993). *Carbone* is discussed *supra* Section 17.A.3.

104 *Carbone,* 511 U.S. at 390, 392. Indeed, *Carbone* supplied an *a fortiori* argument for the challengers in *United Haulers*: If (as in *Carbone*) a local ordinance excluding all but one private operator animated protectionist concerns, then an ordinance that excludes *all* private operators would seem to move the needle even further in the direction of pointing toward protectionist behavior. *See* Dan T. Coenen, *Where* United Haulers *Might Take Us: The Future of the State-Self-Promotion Exception to the Dormant Commerce Clause Rule,* 95 IOWA L. REV. 541, 550–51 (2010) (developing this point). Additionally, if governments can implement competition-excluding programs only through the use of government-owned facilities (as *Carbone* and *United Haulers,* viewed together, would indicate) then state and local governments have a powerful incentive to replace private-market operators with publicly owned facilities. *See United Haulers,* 550 U.S. at 364 n.3 (Alito, J., dissenting) ("[T]he Court sends a bold and enticing message to local governments throughout the United States: Protectionist legislation is now permissible, so long as the enacting government excludes all private-sector participants from the affected local market."); *see also* Coenen, *supra,* at 551–52 (discussing the implications of the public-facility/private-facility distinction, especially in connection with a Court supportive in other contexts of the operation of private markets).

105 *See United Haulers,* 550 U.S. at 334. Concurring in the judgment, Justice Thomas declared that he would no longer invalidate any state or local law under the dormant Commerce Clause. *Id.* at 349 (Thomas, J., concurring in the judgment). Concurring in part, Justice Scalia found the challenged program permissible under his

analysis, the anti-discrimination rule focuses on rooting out "protectionism."[106] And for him that label did not readily apply to a program that favored a local *government* operation, as opposed to a local *private* business. Put another way, it made sense here—as it did in *Carbone* and does in all dormant Commerce Clause cases—to compare with care the supposedly benefited and burdened parties in deciding whether discrimination was present. Having done so, the Chief Justice concluded that treating government entities and private business operators as comparable actors, at least in this context, involved an impermissible lumping together of constitutional apples and oranges.[107]

The Chief Justice also suggested, albeit obliquely, that ordinary political processes might well operate more effectively to mitigate abuses when a public program, as opposed to a private business, stands to gain from an in-state processing requirement.[108] The difference exists, he suggested, because *all* private industry members could be expected to line up against the sort of government-favoring program at issue in *United Haulers*. In *Carbone*, in contrast, *at least one* private entity—perhaps one with significant political clout—would be laser-focused on supporting government action that would result in the grant of a monopoly position.[109] All these distinctions led the Court to deem *Carbone* beside the point when a local processing requirement applies to facilities "owned and operated" by an arm of the state,[110] at least when the challenged operation involves a "typically and traditionally . . . local government function," such as "waste disposal."[111]

United Haulers has generated a truckload of questions, one of which came before the Court in *Department of Revenue v. Davis*.[112] There, the Court held that a state can exempt from its own income

approach to applying the dormant Commerce Clause, which in effect called for the invalidation of a state regulation of commerce only when required by an on-all-fours past authority. Pursuant to that principle, he reasoned, the government program at issue in *United Haulers* had to be upheld because it failed to qualify as "indistinguishable from [the] type of law previously held unconstitutional by [the] Court." *Id.* at 348 (Scalia, J., concurring in part) (quoting *West Lynn Creamery*, 512 U.S. at 210 (Scalia, J., concurring in the judgment)).

[106] *Id.* at 338 (majority opinion).

[107] *See id.* at 339 ("[F]avoring local government is by its nature different from favoring a particular private company.").

[108] *United Haulers*, 550 U.S. at 345.

[109] *See* Coenen, *supra* note 104, at 557–59 (stating that this consideration made it "easier—perhaps far easier—in *United Haulers* than in *Carbone* to justify judicial nonintervention").

[110] *United Haulers*, 550 U.S. at 334.

[111] *Id.* at 344 (quoting United Haulers Ass'n v. Oneida-Herkimer Solid Waste Mgmt. Auth., 261 F.3d 245, 264 (2d Cir. 2001) (Calabresi, J., concurring)).

[112] 553 U.S. 328 (2008).

taxing program interest paid on bonds issued by it and its subunits, even while taxing comparable bond interest paid out by other state and local jurisdictions. In accounting for this result on behalf of a seven-Justice majority, Justice Souter contended that the "logic" of *United Haulers* "applies with even greater force to laws favoring a State's municipal bonds, given that the issuance of debt securities to pay for public projects is a quintessentially public function, with [a] venerable history" and that "[b]ond proceeds are . . . the way to shoulder the cardinal civic responsibilities listed in *United Haulers*: protecting the health, safety, and welfare of citizens."[113] In light of these facts—and the additional fact that *Davis* involved a "century-old taxing practice . . . presently employed by 41 states"[114]—the Court was unmoved by the taxpayer's efforts to distinguish *United Haulers*. In particular, Justice Souter rejected the argument that *Davis* involved a state's straightforward discrimination because its tax exemption favored its own bonds vis-à-vis "substantially similar" *public* bonds issued by other states, in contrast to favoring the government's monopolistic waste-handling operation in *United Haulers* over not-substantially-similar *private*-market would-be waste-handling competitors.[115]

Even so, "the Court in *Davis* followed the lead of *United Haulers* by emphasizing the existence of limits on the state-self-promotion doctrine,"[116] thus bringing into view a range of follow-up conundrums. What if, for example, the favored local entity is run not solely by the government itself or by a private business standing alone, but instead by a public-private joint venture? This question presents complications in part because the organizational structure of programs like those involved in *Carbone* and *United Haulers* can take many forms. Indeed, as it turns out, the programs at issue in those very cases each involved a measure of public-private

---

[113] *Id.* at 341–42 (internal citations and footnotes omitted).

[114] *Id.* at 342 (internal citations and footnotes omitted).

[115] *See* Coenen, *supra* note 104, at 560–62 (noting four additional distinctions between the two cases, including the tariff-like nature of the program in *Davis* and the presence of a potentially stronger political-process justification for judicial intervention in *Davis* than in *United Haulers*).

[116] *Id.* at 562. For a wide-ranging challenge to both *United Haulers* and *Davis*, which directs a particularly harsh line of criticism at the no-discrimination component of the Court's reasoning, see Norman R. Williams & Brannon Denning, *The New Protectionism and the American Common Market*, 85 NOTRE DAME L. REV. 247, 251 (2013) (arguing that the "new exception to the dormant commerce clause" recognized in *United Haulers* and *Davis* is "profoundly misguided," largely because the Court's characterization of state self-promotion as not involving discrimination "blinks reality"; also expressing concern that these rulings invite "truly breathtaking" incursions on the dormant Commerce Clause principle by "open[ing] the door to governmental efforts to protect private enterprises from out-of-state competition through cleverly constructed public-private partnerships").

collaboration.[117] In general, however, the reasoning of *United Haulers* suggests that joint-venture programs that involve a substantial element of private-firm involvement should fall on the *Carbone*, rather than the *United Haulers*, side of the constitutional divide.[118]

Another line-drawing problem created by *United Haulers* and *Davis* stems from the Court's suggestion in both cases that the state-self-promotion exception operates only with regard to programs that involve "traditional," as opposed to "nontraditional," government activities. What if, for example, a city requires local businesses to deal with a city-owned waterworks, thus precluding a resident manufacturing business from importing water through pipes that cross a state line? In such a case, the "traditional government function" label would seem to apply because cities commonly provide water services, and that is so even though (just as in *United Haulers*) the forced-use rule itself might not comport with traditional practice.[119] Would the Court take a different view of things, however, if a local government built its own cement plant (hardly a "traditional" government undertaking) and then ordered local builders to use only that plant's products, thus excluding out-of-state suppliers from the in-state market?[120] Perhaps the Court would use such a case to abandon altogether the project of distinguishing

---

[117] *See* Coenen, *supra* note 104, at 570–72.

[118] This approach makes sense because the Court in *United Haulers* never questioned the core Commerce Clause policy of safeguarding out-of-state private businesses from protectionism-based favoritism for local private competitors. Moreover, in the joint-venture context, political-process worries remain acute because of the likely ability of well-positioned local private firms to wield self-serving influence among local political leaders. *See id.* (exploring the joint-venture issue in greater detail).

[119] *See id.* at 558–59 (noting the Court's characterization of the relevant government activity in *United Haulers* as "waste disposal"); *see also* Bradford Mank, *The Supreme Court's New Public-Private Distinction Under the Dormant Commerce Clause: Avoiding the Traditional Versus Nontraditional Classification Trap*, 37 HASTINGS CONST. L.Q. 1, 5 (2009) (emphasizing the difficulty in distinguishing between traditional and nontraditional government activities and suggesting that the validity of a law under the dormant Commerce Clause should turn on "whether it appropriately favors the government's provision of public services, or inappropriately prefers local private interests"); Norman R. Williams, *The Foundations of the American Common Market*, 84 NOTRE DAME L. REV. 409, 462 (2008) (criticizing the Court's focus on traditional government activities on the ground that it invites a "wide-ranging, roving, *Lochner*-esque process" and needlessly so because judicial review under the dormant Commerce Clause historically has been "of highly limited scope, which affords ample room to and respect for state autonomy"); Wentong Zheng, *Untangling the Market and the State*, 67 EMORY L.J. 243, 261, 268 (2017) (criticizing sharply the Court's tradition-based approach to state-self-promotion cases on the ground that any form of tradition-centered analysis tends to become "overly formalistic and easily circumventable" and fails to recognize that government functions change over time, thus "rendering the determination of what constitutes traditional governmental functions not subject to objective criteria").

[120] *See* Coenen, *supra* note 104, at 589–90 (analyzing this question).

between traditional nontraditional government activities, following the reasoning—famously put to work in *Garcia v. San Antonio Metropolitan Transit Authority*[121]—that engaging in this form of constitutional line-drawing is neither wise nor judicially manageable.[122] For two reasons, however, that outcome seems unlikely. First, notwithstanding *Garcia*, the Court has continued to apply the traditional/nontraditional distinction in a variety of settings involving constitutional federalism.[123] Second, and more important, the Court highlighted—indeed, highlighted repeatedly—the "traditional" character of the activity at issue in both *United Haulers* and *Davis*, thus signaling its endorsement of the significance of this analytical touchstone in state-self-promotion cases.[124]

A final question concerns the relationship between *Pike* balancing and the state-self-promotion limit on the dormant Commerce Clause rule.[125] Notably, after finding that this limit foreclosed a discrimination-based challenge to the compelled-use rule in *United Haulers*, a plurality of Justices proceeded to subject that rule to *Pike*-based scrutiny.[126] Thereafter, in *Davis*, a majority of the Court again took this same approach.[127] In so doing, the Court underscored the important point that the state-self-promotion exception is not so much an exception to the dormant Commerce Clause rule as it is to the dormant Commerce Clause-based prohibition on *discrimination*. Does this aspect of the rulings in these cases make sense? The argument that it does stems from the idea that a state, "as a public entity, does not have to treat itself as being 'substantially similar' to the other [participants] in the market."[128] Put another way, the Court's specialized safeguarding of the state

---

[121] 469 U.S. 528, 545 (1985).

[122] *See id.* at 531 ("Our examination of this 'function' standard applied . . . over the last eight years now persuades us that the attempt to draw the boundaries of state regulatory immunity in terms of 'traditional governmental function' is not only unworkable but is also inconsistent with established principles of federalism . . . ."). *See generally supra* Section 5.A.1.

[123] *See, e.g.*, Bates v. Dow Agrosciences LLC, 544 U.S. 431, 449 (2005) (reiterating that, when preemption is at issue, "[i]n areas of traditional state regulation, we assume that a federal statute has not supplanted state law unless Congress has made such an intention 'clear and manifest' "); United States v. Lopez, 514 U.S. 549, 580–83 (1995) (Kennedy, J., concurring) (deeming the Gun Free School Zones Act unconstitutional in part because it impeded state regulation of education, an area of "traditional" state concern); *see also* Edmonson v. Leesville Concrete Co., 500 U.S. 614, 624 (1991) (observing that, in assessing whether the use of peremptory challenges involves state action, the Court considers "whether the action in question involves the performance of a traditional function of the government").

[124] See *supra* notes 103–115 and accompanying text.

[125] *See supra* Chapter 18 (discussing *Pike*).

[126] *United Haulers*, 550 U.S. at 346 (opinion of Roberts, C.J.).

[127] *Davis*, 553 U.S. at 338–40.

[128] *Id.* at 343.

actors involved in both *United Haulers* and *Davis* sprang from the Court's determination that there was no discrimination against out-of-state competitors in either case. Under basic dormant Commerce Clause principles, however, a judicial finding that a law does not *discriminate* against interstate commerce does not preclude a separate finding that that the law subjects interstate commerce to an *undue burden*.[129]

Notwithstanding the Court's endorsement of this two-step methodology, it is hard to hypothesize cases in which the Court first would apply the state-self-promotion rule to establish the absence of discrimination but then declare the challenged program unconstitutional under the *Pike* balancing test. Indeed, the Court in *Davis* rendered this possibility especially remote by pointing to special problems it saw as applicable when judges put the already-deferential *Pike* standard test to work in the state-self-promotion context.[130] At least for now, however, it remains true as a doctrinal matter that the state-self-promotion exception is, in an important point of contrast to the subsidy and market-participant exceptions, only an exception to the anti-discrimination principle's "virtually *per se* rule of illegality."[131] That is, even when it is obviously applicable,

---

[129] *See supra* Chapter 18.

[130] *See Davis*, 553 U.S. at 353, 355–56 (reasoning that "the Judicial Branch is not institutionally suited to draw reliable conclusions of the kind that would be necessary for the Davises to satisfy a *Pike* burden in this particular case" in part because of the inherent difficulty of answering "cost-benefit questions" in this setting and "the unsuitability of the judicial process and judicial forums for making whatever predictions and reaching whatever answers are possible at all"; adding that "Congress has some hope of acquiring more complete information than adversary trials may produce, and an elected legislature is the preferable institution for incurring the economic risks of any alteration in the way things have traditionally been done").

[131] *Id.* at 338. The "for now" qualifier warrants two additional points. First, the *Pike* test itself might now be in jeopardy of abandonment by the Court or at least in jeopardy of a generalized effort to harness further its already limited operation. *See supra* Chapter 18. Second, one way of viewing the *Pike* rule is that it sets forth a test designed to flush out a hidden discriminatory purpose. *See supra* Section 17.C.2 n.71 (detailing this view of the dormant Commerce Clause advanced by Professor Regan). *Cf.* Elena Kagan, *Private Speech, Public Purpose: The Role of Governmental Motive in First Amendment Doctrine*, 63 U. CHI. L. REV. 413, 416 (1996) (positing that, in similar fashion, "a wide range of [Free Speech Clause] rules—indeed the essential structure of the doctrine—are best and most easily understood as devices to detect the presence of illicit motive"); *id.* at 414 (describing First Amendment law as built around "a series of tools to flush out illicit motives and to invalidate actions infected with them"). If the Court comes to view the *Pike* standard in this way, the no-discrimination basis of the state-self-promotion exception may logically dictate that that test has no role to play at all once the court determines that the exception applies. After all, if the challenged law *necessarily* involves no discrimination based on an apples-and-oranges rationale, then there would seem to be no sense in applying a prophylaxis designed only to "flush out" such discrimination because it is otherwise difficult to detect.

the state self-promotion exception does not automatically defeat the operation of *Pike*'s undue-burden principle.[132]

F. THE CURIOUS CASE OF STATE ALCOHOL REGULATION

1. The Twenty-First Amendment and the Continued Applicability of the Dormant Commerce Clause

The Twenty-first Amendment includes two substantive sections. The first overturns the Eighteenth Amendment's ill-fated experiment with nationwide prohibition.[133] The second declares that the "transportation or importation into any State, Territory, or possession of the United States for delivery or use therein of intoxicating liquors, in violation of the laws thereof, is hereby prohibited."[134] The Court's earliest treatments of section 2 held that it rendered otherwise operative dormant Commerce Clause restraints wholly inapplicable to state alcohol regulations.[135] In later rulings, however, the Court abandoned this position. A key step came in *Bacchus Imports, Ltd. v. Dias*.[136] There, a five-Justice majority concluded that a tax benefit afforded to sellers of in-state, but not out-of-state, fruit wine had no purpose except "to promote a local industry."[137] Thus, the state's action, even though it dealt specifically with alcohol, offended the dormancy doctrine because it did not "promote temperance" or otherwise address any "clear concern of the Twenty-first Amendment."[138]

Twenty-one years later, in *Granholm v. Heald*,[139] the Court reaffirmed *Bacchus Imports* on its way to invalidating two laws, one

---

[132] *See supra* Chapter 18.

[133] U.S. CONST. amend. XXI, § 1.

[134] *Id.* XXI, § 2.

[135] *See, e.g.*, State Bd. of Equalization v. Young's Market Co., 299 U.S. 59, 62 (1936) (holding that Section 2 negates the operation of dormant Commerce Clause restraints because it "confer[s] upon the State the power to forbid all importations which do not comply with the conditions which it prescribes").

[136] 468 U.S. 263 (1984).

[137] *Id.* at 273. The opinion, written by Justice White, was joined by Chief Justice Burger and Justices Marshall, Blackmun, and Powell. Justices Stevens, Rehnquist and O'Connor dissented, and Justice Brennan did not participate in the case.

[138] *Id.* at 276. For a critical assessment of *Bacchus Imports*, see Brannon P. Denning, *Smokey and the Bandit in Cyberspace: The Dormant Commerce Clause, the Twenty-First Amendment, and State Regulation of Internet Alcohol Sales*, 19 CONST. COMMENT. 297, 319, 339–40 (2002) (exploring in detail the course of Supreme Court decision-making in this field and arguing that the Twenty-first Amendment was intended to disable the application of the dormant Commerce Clause principle to state liquor-import restrictions).

[139] 544 U.S. 460 (2005).

from Michigan and one from New York, that let local, but not non-local, wineries ship products directly to resident buyers. Justice Kennedy, again writing for a five-Justice majority, set forth four key doctrinal pronouncements.[140] First, although the "in violation of the laws thereof" text of section 2 might seem to have a categorical quality, it did not create a liquor-law exception to *all* constitutional restrictions on state power.[141] Second, with regard to dormant Commerce Clause restraints, the underlying goal of section 2 was to return the states to the position they occupied before enactment of the Eighteenth Amendment.[142] Third, section 2 thus constitutionalized the pre-1919 authority of states to enact their own prohibition laws and other similarly "evenhanded" alcohol-related measures.[143] Fourth, at the same time, that section did not displace limits imposed by the dormant Commerce Clause on state liquor laws that impeded interstate commerce because those limits had applied prior to 1919 with no less robustness to alcohol-related state laws than to non-alcohol-related state laws.[144]

Against this backdrop, the Court in *Granholm* determined that Michigan's and New York's facially discriminatory direct-shipment statutes abridged the "virtually *per se* rule of invalidity,"[145] because those measures advanced no "legitimate local purpose that cannot be adequately served by reasonable nondiscriminatory alternatives."[146]

---

140 Justice Kennedy's opinion was joined by Justices Scalia, Souter, Ginsburg, and Breyer. Justice Thomas's dissent was joined by Chief Justice Rehnquist and Justices Stevens and O'Connor. Justice Stevens's dissent was joined by Justice O'Connor.

141 *Granholm*, 544 U.S. at 486–87.

142 *Id.* at 487.

143 *Id.* at 487–88, 493. Notably, the pre-Eighteenth Amendment landscape included two federal statutes, the Wilson Act and the Webb-Kenyon Act, of critical significance to the majority in mapping out the contours of Section 2. The key impact of these statutes was to displace the so-called "original package doctrine" insofar as it applied to alcoholic beverages. That doctrine—an important component of the Court's then-operative (but no-longer operative) dormant Commerce Clause jurisprudence, precluded the imposition of state restrictions on the transportation of goods coming from outside the state, so long as those goods remained in their original packages. Prior to Congress's intervention, this doctrine had safeguarded the activities of nonresident liquor sellers, thus affording them an advantage over would-be resident sellers and greatly complicating efforts to effectuate statewide prohibition policies by excluding all alcoholic beverages from the state. The idea behind the federal statutes was to remedy these problems by permitting states to treat out-of-state and in-state liquor purveyors in an "evenhanded" way by outlawing all local sales and all transit of alcoholic beverages, whether they came from inside or outside the state and whether or not those beverages were in their original packages. *Granholm*, 544 U.S. at 478–81. In keeping with this focus on evenhandedness, however, nothing in the pre-Eighteenth Amendment legal regime permitted states to enact laws, including liquor laws, meant to favor in-state businesses over out-of-state competitors. *Id.* at 486.

144 *See id.* at 476–77.

145 *Id.* at 476 (quoting Philadelphia v. New Jersey, 437 U.S. 617, 624 (1978)).

146 *Id.* at 489 (quoting New Energy Co. of Ind. v. Limbach, 486 U.S. 269, 278 (1988)).

The Court was particularly unimpressed by the states' effort to defend these restrictions as prophylaxes fashioned to forestall illicit alcohol buying by tech-savvy minors. As Justice Kennedy explained, requiring an adult signature for any direct home delivery of wine provided a less restrictive way to address this problem, assuming it was a problem at all.[147] Nor was the majority moved by the dissenters' claim that these laws made sense because, in their absence, out-of-state wineries could effectively sidestep state health-and-safety-based regulatory controls.[148] The right way to address this concern, the Court reasoned, was for states to deploy the "alternative of an evenhanded licensing requirement."[149]

---

[147] *Id.* at 490–91.

[148] More specifically, Justice Thomas argued in his dissenting opinion that "State officials can better enforce their regulations by inspecting the premises and attaching the property of in-state entities; '[p]resence ensures accountability.'" *Id.* at 523 (Thomas, J., dissenting) (alteration in original) (quoting Swedenburg v. Kelly, 358 F.3d 223, 237 (2d Cir. 2004)). He also read preexisting law—and, indeed, the majority opinion in *Granholm* itself—as establishing that states can favor local wholesalers and retailers (as opposed to producers) over their out-of-state counterparts because doing so "make[s] regulating liquor easier." *Id.* at 524. Justice Thomas continued: "If allowing a State to require all wholesalers and retailers to be in-state companies is a core concern of the Twenty-first Amendment, so is allowing a State to select only in-state manufacturers to ship directly to consumers, and therefore act, in effect, as their own wholesalers and retailers." *Id.* For a further discussion of Justice Thomas's underlying assumption about states' ability to limit wholesaling and retailing to resident businesses, see *infra* note 179 and accompanying text.

[149] *Id.* at 492 (majority opinion). Building on this analysis, post-*Granholm* lower-court decisions have emphasized the key role of nondiscrimination in the states' imposition of liquor regulations. *See, e.g.*, Black Star Farms LLC v. Oliver, 600 F.3d 1225, 1234 (9th Cir. 2010) (reading "*Granholm* to permit States to limit direct shipment from wineries *so long as the limitations treat in-state and out-of-state wineries in the same manner*, and do not impose new burdens on out-of-state wineries" (emphasis in original) (internal citation omitted)); Arnold's Wines, Inv. v. Boyle, 571 F.3d 185, 190 (2d Cir. 2009) ("It is only where states create discriminatory exceptions to the three-tier system, allowing in-state, but not out-of-state, liquor to bypass the three regulatory tiers, that their laws are subject to invalidation based on the Commerce Clause."); Jelovsek v. Bredesen, 545 F.3d 431, 436 (6th Cir. 2008) ("[T]he logical corollary to evenhanded permissiveness is evenhanded restrictiveness—a State may choose to ban direct shipment of wine." (quoting Jelovsek v. Bredesen, 482 F. Supp. 2d 1013, 1019 (E.D. Tenn. 2007))). In a similar vein, Professor William Green views *Granholm* as implicitly endorsing the Model Direct Shipping Bill, promulgated by the National Conference of State Legislatures (NCSL) to establish a governing framework for state liquor regulation. *See* William C. Green, *Creating a Common Market for Wine: Boutique Wines, Direct Shipment, and State Alcohol Regulation*, 39 OHIO N.U. L. REV. 13, 38 (2012). This model bill, among other things, requires wineries "to obtain a direct shipping permit, to submit sales reports, and remit taxes." *Id.* at 29. When the Court decided *Granholm*, thirteen states had already moved to establish nondiscriminatory regulatory structures regarding direct shipments of wine—three by enacting laws permitting direct shipment by all producers of wine on equal terms, and ten by prohibiting all direct shipments of wine. *Id.* at 38–39. Other states, however, had in place rules that disadvantaged out-of-state producers. *Id.* at 39. As Professor Green has observed, states that had implemented such discriminatory policies had two options after *Granholm*: They could either "level up" their regulations (perhaps by adopting the NCSL model bill) to allow both in-state and out-of-state wineries to ship

Then came *Tennessee Wine & Spirits Retailers Ass'n v. Thomas*,[150] which concerned a law that limited eligibility for retail liquor licenses to applicants who already had resided in the state for at least two years. Few doubted that this facial disadvantaging of interstate-business ownership conflicted with general dormancy-doctrine principles.[151] The state argued, however, that the Twenty-first Amendment rendered those principles inapplicable to the challenged statute.[152] Justice Alito responded by rejecting this position in an opinion for himself and six other members of the Court.[153] Relying on an elaborate historical exegesis, Justice Alito began by reaffirming *Granholm*'s core conclusion that section 2 did not undo all dormant Commerce Clause restraints on state liquor regulations.[154] He next nixed the state's effort to limit *Granholm*'s holding to commerce-impeding laws aimed at "*products and producers*," as opposed to in-state retailing.[155] This proffered distinction fell flat because it had no grounding in "the States' power to regulate alcohol that prevailed before Prohibition," which "§ 2 was meant to 'constitutionaliz[e].' "[156]

This back-to-the-future view of section 2 might suggest that dormant Commerce Clause restraints will henceforth apply to discriminatory state liquor laws in precisely the same way they apply to all other state laws because that was how things worked before the Eighteenth Amendment took hold. Notably, Justice Kennedy seemed to endorse this position without qualification in *Granholm*,[157] and (as the preceding paragraph shows) Justice Alito sounded similar notes in his own opinion in *Tennessee Wine & Spirits*.[158] At other points, however, Justice Alito seemed to back away from endorsing a full-

on equal terms or " 'level down' their regulations and prohibit all direct shipping." *Id.* at 39–40.

150 139 S. Ct. 2449 (2019).

151 *See id.* at 2458 (noting the Tennessee Attorney General's repeated determinations to this effect).

152 *Id.* at 2472.

153 For a more recent doctrinal build-out of this holding, see *Fine Wine & Spirits v. Cook*, 459 F. Supp. 3d 1157 (S.D. Ind. 2020) (enjoining enforcement of an Indiana law requiring alcohol retailers to be Indiana residents).

154 *Id.* at 2467–69.

155 *Id.* at 2471–72 (emphasis in original).

156 *Id.* at 2467–68 (alteration in original) (quoting Craig v. Boren, 429 U.S. 190, 206 (1976)); *see also id.* at 2468 (noting the amendment's design to reaffirm the judicial power to strike down "protectionist measures" that was "recognized during that period").

157 *See supra* note 143; *see also Granholm*, 544 U.S.at 524 (Thomas, J., dissenting) (describing the majority opinion as "employing otherwise-applicable negative Commerce Clause scrutiny and giving no weight to the Twenty-first Amendment").

158 *See also Tennessee Wine & Spirits*, 139 S. Ct. at 2470 (describing *Granholm* as "declin[ing] to read § 2 as allowing the States to violate the 'nondiscrimination principle' ").

bore application of otherwise-applicable dormant Commerce Clause constraints in the alcohol-regulation context. Thus, in one key passage, he wrote: "Since the 2-year residency requirement discriminates on its face against nonresidents, it could not be sustained if it applied across the board to all those seeking to operate any retail business in the State. *But because of § 2, we engage in a different inquiry*."[159] Seeming to drive this same point home, he added that "Section 2 gives the States regulatory authority . . . they would not otherwise enjoy."[160]

2. Dormant Commerce Clause Scrutiny in the Shadow of the Twenty-First Amendment

Just what is this additional Twenty-first Amendment-based "regulatory authority" that, according to these passages, states "would not otherwise enjoy"? Justice Alito left behind few clues about the proper answer this question. But he did make several rhetorical moves that are sure to engage the attention of judges and lawyers in future alcohol-related litigation. First, he asserted that section 2 "allows each State leeway to enact the measures that its citizens believe are appropriate to address the public health and safety effects of alcohol use and to serve other legitimate interests."[161] Building out this thought, he suggested that the decisive question is "whether the challenged requirement can be justified as a public health or safety measure or on some other legitimate nonprotectionist ground."[162] Next, he indicated that the answer to this inquiry will hinge on whether "the *predominant effect* of a law is protectionism."[163] Finally,

---

[159] *Id.* at 2474 (emphasis added) (citations omitted). Justice Alito also observed that "§ 2 grants States latitude with respect to the regulation of alcohol." *Id.* at 2470.

[160] *Id.* at 2474.

[161] *Id.*

[162] *Id.*; *see also id.* (noting that the dormant Commerce Clause "does not license the States to adopt protectionist measures with no demonstrable connection to those interests"). The Court's core idea seemed to be that the goal of "§ 2 was not to give States a free hand to restrict the importation of alcohol for purely protectionist purposes," so that the key inquiry thus became whether the challenged law's "overall purpose and effect is protectionist" as opposed to "serv[ing] a State's legitimate § 2 interests." *Id.* at 2469, 2475; *see id.* at 2472 (noting agreement "with the dissent that, under § 2, States 'remai[n] free to pursue' their legitimate interests in regulating the health and safety risks posed by the alcohol trade" (alteration in original)). One way to view this aspect of the Court's reasoning is that it flipped the script with regard to the traditional method of dormant Commerce Clause inquiry. The traditional rule, after all, calls on courts initially to determine whether the challenged state law is discriminatory in its terms, its purpose, or its effect, and then to apply strict means-ends scrutiny if one of these earmarks of protectionism is present. In contrast, the Court in *Tennessee Wine & Spirits* seemed to see its role in applying means-ends analysis as focused on determining whether a challenged law qualifies as protectionist. *See supra* note 132.

[163] *Tennessee Wine & Spirits*, 139 S. Ct. at 2474, 2476 (emphasis added) (concluding, after applying means-ends analysis, that "the predominant effect of the 2-year residency requirement is simply to protect the Association's members from out-

he noted that assessing a law's "predominant effect" requires courts to evaluate the means-ends fit of the state's action, with the operative inquiry apparently focusing on whether the challenged enactment is "*reasonably necessary* to protect the States' asserted interests."[164] Applying these principles, the Court in *Tennessee Wine & Spirits* struck down the two-year-residency rule for alcohol retailers because it had "no demonstrable connection" to health and safety interests.[165] Indeed, in the majority's view, the state had offered nothing on this score apart from "unsupported assertions" and "mere speculation."[166]

---

of-state competition [and that] therefore . . . this provision violates the Commerce Clause and is not saved by the Twenty-first Amendment"); *accord id.* at 2474 ("Where the predominant effect of a law is protectionism, not the protection of public health or safety, it is not shielded by § 2.").

[164] *Id.* at 2470 (emphasis added). Notably, the Court cited *Granholm* in support of this formulation even though the formulation appeared nowhere in the *Granholm* opinion itself. Indeed, Justice Alito's phrasing of the operative means-ends inquiry could easily be seen as diluting, rather than tracking, the "exacting" means-ends test put to work by Justice Kennedy in that case. *See, e.g.*, *Granholm*, 544 U.S. at 492–93 ("The Court has upheld state regulations that discriminate against interstate commerce only after finding, based on concrete record evidence, that a State's nondiscriminatory alternatives will prove unworkable. Michigan and New York have not satisfied this exacting standard." (citation omitted)).

[165] *Tennessee Wine & Spirits*, 139 S. Ct. at 2474 (emphasis added). For example, Tennessee sought to defend the law on the ground that local operators of liquor stores would be in the best position to monitor other local residents' alcohol misuse. The two-year residency requirement, they argued, "makes it more likely that retailers will be familiar with the communities served by their stores, and this . . . will lead to responsible sales practices." *Id.* at 2475–76; *see also* Byrd v. Tenn. Wine & Spirits Retailers Ass'n, 883 F.3d 608, 633 (6th Cir. 2018) (Sutton, J., concurring in part and dissenting in part) ("Requiring individual retailers to reside in one place for a sustained, two-year period ensures that they will be knowledgeable about the community's needs and committed to its welfare. . . . The same is true with respect to a residency requirement for officers and directors of the retailer. It ensures that they are familiar with the community and in a position to alter or influence the retailer's behavior based on that understanding."); S. Wine & Spirits of Am., Inc. v. Div. of Alcohol & Tobacco Control, 731 F.3d 799, 811 (8th Cir. 2013) (upholding a residency requirement for wholesalers because "a wholesaler governed predominantly by Missouri residents is more apt to be socially responsible and to promote temperance, because the officers, directors, and owners are residents of the community and thus subject to negative externalities . . . that liquor distribution may produce"). This justification failed, however, in part because the law "applie[d] to those who hold a license, not to those who actually make sales," and because "it require[d] residence in the State, not in the community that a store serve[d]." *Tennessee Wine & Spirits*, 139 S. Ct. at 2476. Thus, the state could not "explain why a proprietor who lives in Bristol, Virginia, will be less knowledgeable about the needs of his neighbors right across the border in Bristol, Tennessee, than someone who lives 500 miles away in Memphis." *Id.* In any event, it was strained to believe that a neighborhood-watch approach to retail liquor sales would, especially in the modern day, somehow effectively curb alcohol misuse. *Id.* at 2475.

[166] *Tennessee Wine & Spirits*, 139 S. Ct. at 2474 (quoting *Granholm*, 544 U.S. at 490, 492); *see also id.* (observing that "the record is devoid of any 'concrete evidence' showing that the 2-year residency requirement actually promotes public health or safety; nor is there evidence that nondiscriminatory alternatives would be insufficient to further those interests" (quoting *Granholm*, 544 U.S. at 490, 492)); *id.* (concluding that the challenged rule "has at best a highly attenuated relationship to public health or safety").

In sum, Tennessee's effort to justify its statute on non-protectionist grounds was "implausible on its face."[167]

Where, then, has dormant-Commerce-Clause law come to rest in the wake of *Tennessee Wine & Spirits*? One observer has suggested that Justice Alito's opinion shifts the level of scrutiny applicable to laws that discriminate against interstate commerce from "strict" to "intermediate" when those laws deal with alcoholic beverages.[168] A problem with this assessment, however, is that the Court in *Tennessee Wine & Spirits* never deployed the verbiage of "intermediate scrutiny." Another observer has read the decision to suggest that lower courts now must assess state alcohol laws under a review standard of "rational basis with bite."[169] Again, however, there was no talk of such a standard—far less an endorsement of it—in Justice Alito's opinion, and such a test would travel a long distance away from the version of strict scrutiny usually applied to state laws that discriminate against interstate commerce.[170] In the end, one

[167] *Id.* at 2475. To be clear, nothing in *Tennessee Wine & Spirits* signaled that the Court meant to establish such a deferential standard for evaluating state liquor laws that judges now can strike them down *only* when there is "no demonstrable connection" between means and ends or the claimed means-end connection is "implausible on its face." *Id.* at 2474–75. Rather, these characterizations fully fit the particular facts of *Tennessee Wine & Spirits*, and the Court—both accurately and appropriately—thus made use of them in emphasizing the weakness of the means-end nexus between the challenged law and its purported objectives. Stated otherwise, there is no reason to conclude that the Court meant for these pejorative descriptive phrases to define the outer limits of the predominant-effect/reasonably-necessary inquiry. Rather, these characterizations simply captured the idea that the challenged law easily failed to meet whatever standard might govern such cases as a general matter.

[168] McDermott Will & Emery, *Implications of the Supreme Court's Tennessee Retailers Decision*, ALCOHOL L. ADV. (July 8, 2019), https://www.alcohollawadvisor.com/2019/07/implications-of-the-supreme-courts-tennessee-retailers-decision/.

[169] Braden H. Boucek, *That's Why I Hang My Hat in Tennessee: Alcohol and the Commerce Clause*, 2019 CATO SUP. CT. REV. 119, 151–52 ("Under *Tennessee Wine*, a law must have a 'real and substantial' relation to an actual public health or safety goal. That looks a lot like the rational basis with bite used by the Supreme Court in [an earlier equal-protection ruling].").

[170] Another possible reading of *Tennessee Wine & Spirits* (and *Granholm* as well) would require the Court to negate the operation of otherwise applicable features of modern dormant Commerce Clause doctrine by displacing them, albeit only in the alcohol-regulation context, with those (now-antiquated) dormancy-doctrine rules that operated in the immediate pre-1919 period. This result would make sense, so the argument goes, because of the emphasis laid in those cases on section 2's goal of reinstating "the basic structure of federal-state alcohol authority that prevailed prior to the Eighteenth Amendment's adoption." *Tennessee Wine & Spirits*, 139 S. Ct. at 2463. On this view, for example, it might be that the Court could not reinstate the operation, with regard to state alcohol regulation, of the now-long-forgotten original-package doctrine, which had hamstrung state temperance efforts and, for that reason, was repudiated by federal statute as to state alcohol rules in the pre-1919 timeframe. *See supra* note 143. A more significant build-out of this "old-law lock-in" theory might lead the Court to conclude that state alcohol laws—unlike all other laws—should be exempt from *Pike* balancing analysis because the principle of that case was not laid down until 1970. On the better view, however, this approach should be rejected because (1) as the Court in *Tennessee Wine & Spirits* itself acknowledged, pre-

thing seems clear enough: The majority in *Tennessee Wine & Spirits*, even if unwittingly, opened the door to recognizing some form of a liquor-law limitation on otherwise-applicable dormant Commerce Clause rules. More specifically its rhetoric invites a possible ratcheting down, at least in some measure, of the "virtually *per se* rule" of invalidity ordinarily directed at discriminatory state laws.[171]

3. The Future of Three-Tiered Liquor Distribution Regimes

Particularly in light of questions raised by *Tennessee Wine & Spirits*, dormancy-doctrine litigation concerning alcohol laws is sure to persist. Future cases are especially likely to implicate longstanding state regulatory regimes built around "three-tiered

---

Eighteenth Amendment dormant Commerce Clause jurisprudence plainly supported invalidation of many laws that burdened interstate commerce even while not discriminating on their face, 139 S. Ct. at 2464 (emphasizing that, prior to 1919, "the Commerce Clause prevented States from passing facially neutral laws that placed an impermissible burden on interstate commerce" (quoting *Granholm*, 544 U.S. at 477)), and (2) the *Pike* test simply carries forward this same limitation in a form marked by a theme of judicial restraint. *See supra* Chapter 18; *see also Tennessee Wine & Spirits*, 139 S. Ct. at 2649 ("We have examined whether state alcohol laws that burden interstate commerce serve a State's legitimate § 2 interests."). It might be that some courts will extract from Justice Alito's opinion some support for tamping down, even if not abandoning altogether, *Pike*-based review of facially neutral state alcohol laws. *Cf.* Lebamoff Enters., Inc. v. Huskey, 666 F.3d 455, 462 (7th Cir. 2012) (noting that, in the case at hand, the "absence of even an incidental effect on interstate commerce" removed any need to apply *Pike* analysis to a law described by the court as lying "within the Twenty-First Amendment's gravitational field"). The Fifth Circuit, however, recently did not hesitate to apply garden-variety *Pike* analysis on its way to upholding a Texas law that placed a blanket ban on the issuance of liquor-sale permits to corporate entities. Wal-Mart Stores, Inc. v. Tex. Alcoholic Beverage Comm'n, 945 F.3d 206, 222 n.26, 224 (5th Cir. 2019), *cert. denied*, 141 S. Ct. 874 (2020).

171 The Sixth Circuit, in *Lebamoff Enters. Inc. v. Whitmer*, 956 F.3d 863, 870 (6th Cir. 2020), *cert. denied* 141 S. Ct. 1049 (2021), for example, found compatible with the dictates of *Tennessee Wine & Spirits* a law that discriminated between in-state and out-of-state retailers by allowing only the former to make direct deliveries to in-state customers. *Id.* at 868. In reaching this result, the court rejected the challenger's claim "that ordinary dormant Commerce Clause analysis applies," asserting instead that "the States' authority to regulate 'importation,'" recognized in the Twenty-first Amendment, must "slight[ ] the dormant Commerce Clause's efforts to halt barriers to free commerce" because otherwise section 2 of the Amendment "would be a dead letter." *Id.* at 873 (quoting Bridenbaugh v. Freeman-Wilson, 227 F.3d 848, 853 (7th Cir. 2000)). Quoting from *Tennessee Wine & Spirits*, the court continued: "That's why a 'different' dormant Commerce Clause test applies to alcohol regulations. The Twenty-first Amendment 'gives states regulatory authority that they otherwise would not otherwise enjoy.'" *Id.*; *see also id.* (quoting *Bridenbaugh*, 227 F.3d at 854, in asserting that "[a]llowing States to 'channel' alcohol sales through in-state wholesalers is 'precisely what § 2 is for'"; also quoting *Tennessee Wine & Spirits*, 139 S. Ct. at 2474). Building on these principles, the court in *Lebamoff* went on to find that the law "promote[d] plenty of legitimate state interests, [including] promoting temperance and controlling the distribution of alcohol" and that "limits on [the] free market of alcohol distribution flow from the kinds of traditional regulations that characterize this market, not state protectionism." *Id.* at 871 (quotations omitted). Notably, *Lebamoff* was authored by Judge Jeffrey Sutton—the lone dissenter in the Sixth Circuit decision upheld by the Court in *Tennessee Wine & Spirits*.

systems" of liquor distribution.[172] These systems center on prohibiting vertical integration in the liquor industry. In other words, liquor producers must sell their products to separately owned liquor wholesalers, which in turn must sell them to separately owned liquor retailers, which then sell them to local buyers.[173] In *Granholm*, the Court emphasized that "the three-tier system itself is 'unquestionably legitimate.' "[174] But in *Tennessee Wine & Spirits* the Court noted that *Granholm* "did not suggest that § 2 sanctions every discriminatory feature that a State may incorporate into its three-tiered scheme" so that "each variation must be judged based on its own features."[175] What if, for example, a state law mandates that liquor wholesalers distribute their products from facilities located within the state or that retail sales can occur only at local stores, thus barring resident buyers (for example) from purchasing alcohol in a neighboring state and spiriting it back home? Such laws, on their

---

[172] *Tennessee Wine & Spirits*, 139 S. Ct. at 2457. *See, e.g.*, Missouri Broads. Ass'n v. Schmitt, 946 F.3d 453, 459 (8th Cir. 2020) (upholding a First Amendment challenge to a law that prohibited alcohol producers and distributors from engaging in retail-level advertising, imposed as part of that state's three-tier system, while at the same time reasoning that *Tennessee Wine & Spirits* and *Granholm* make clear that "[t]he Twenty-first Amendment allows states to regulate alcohol only if the regulations 'do not . . . violate rights secured by the Constitution of the United States,' " including through their use of the three-tiered system).

[173] *See Tennessee Wine & Spirits*, 139 S. Ct. at 2457 (explaining that "[p]roducers may sell only to licensed wholesalers; wholesalers may sell only to licensed retailers or other wholesalers; and only licensed retailers may sell to consumers").

[174] *Granholm*, 544 U.S. at 489 (quoting North Dakota v. United States, 495 U.S. 423, 432 (1990)); *accord, e.g., Lebamoff Enters.*, 956 F.3d at 869 (reading *Granholm* as leaving in its wake "no drama about the issue" of the Twenty-first Amendment's authorization of three-tier systems and echoing earlier Sixth Circuit rulings on this point).

[175] 139 S. Ct. at 2471–72. The Court went on to state: "At issue in the present case is not the basic three-tiered model of separating producers, wholesalers, and retailers, but the durational-residency requirement that Tennessee has chosen to impose on new applicants for liquor store licenses. Such a requirement is not an essential feature of a three-tiered scheme." *Id.* at 2471. Not surprisingly, later court cases have raised a variety of questions about what does and does not qualify as such an "essential feature." *See Lebamoff Enters.*, 956 F.3d at 872–74 (rejecting a challenge to a state restriction on in-state activities of out-of-state retailers on the ground that it "would create a sizeable hole in the three-tier system" and "a discriminatory *exception* to a three-tier system" (emphasis in original)). One case involving such a contextual inquiry is *Wal-Mart Stores*, in which the Fifth Circuit upheld a Texas law that, as part of the state's three-tier alcohol scheme, prohibited all publicly held corporations, regardless of domicile, from holding a certain class of liquor sales permits. 945 F.3d at 211–12. The court began its analysis by declaring that, in *Tennessee Wine & Spirits*, the Supreme Court "reaffirmed what this court had previously concluded: Section 2 does not grant states the power to violate the 'nondiscrimination principle' of the dormant Commerce Clause." *Id.* at 213 (internal footnotes omitted) (quoting *Tennessee Wine & Spirits*, 139 S. Ct. at 2470). The court also recognized that "[v]arious nondiscriminatory laws passed under three-tier systems place at least some burden on interstate commerce," and "*Pike* balancing might be decisive in many cases." *Id.* at 222 n.26. After applying *Pike* analysis to the challenged restriction, however, the Fifth Circuit found no impermissible burden on interstate commerce. *Id.* at 224.

face, starkly constrain interstate commercial activity, thus raising major problems under traditional dormant Commerce Clause analysis. But would such state laws, because they take aim at liquor, pass muster under a now-operative alcoholic-beverages limitation on the dormancy doctrine?[176]

The most sensible approach to questions of this kind might be to allow states to keep in place their vertical-integration-thwarting, three-tiered systems, while disallowing licensing schemes that permit the wholesaling and retailing of liquor to occur only from facilities physically situated within the state.[177] *Granholm* provides some support for this synthesis. There, after all, the majority was unimpressed by the claim that states should be able to allow direct local wine sales only by in-state wine producers because of the supposedly added obstacles regulators would face in policing the operations of nonresident vineyards.[178] In other words, if a state can adequately police out-of-state producers—as the Court in *Granholm* suggested it could—why can it not adequately police out-of-state wholesalers (at least) and out-of-state retailers (as well)?[179] Academic

---

[176] One form of the three-tiered system involves retail distribution exclusively through state-owned-and-operated stores. As we have seen, the Court has relied on the "state self-promotion exception" to uphold laws that compel local citizens to use state-owned facilities, at least when those programs involve a traditional government function. *See supra* Section 20.E. In the state-alcohol-retailing context, states that grant themselves a store-ownership monopoly position thus might go so far as to prohibit local citizens from traveling across state lines to purchase alcoholic beverages as part of a state-self-promoting scheme that forces all liquor buyers to deal only with state-owned retailers. Challengers of such a restriction would have a high hill to climb in light of the Court's validation of the forced-use rule concerning the operation of a self-awarded publicly operated monopoly in *United Haulers*. *See supra* Section 20.E.

[177] *See* Exxon Corp. v. Governor of Maryland, 437 U.S. 117, 133 (1978) (upholding a state prohibition aimed at preventing vertical integration in the oil and gas industry despite the prohibition's significant impact on interstate commerce); *see also* Ford Motor Co. v. Tex. Dep't of Transp., 264 F.3d 493, 502 (5th Cir. 2001) (upholding a Texas statute prohibiting vertical integration in auto manufacturing and retailing because it did "not discriminate *among* in-state and out-state" businesses, as the statute merely "prevent[ed] manufacturers, regardless of their domicile, from entering the retail market" (emphasis in original)). In *Ford Motor Company*, Judge Jones concurred in the dormant Commerce Clause analysis only because she viewed *Exxon* as requiring the court to uphold the Texas statute. In her opinion, however, "*Exxon* seems woefully out of step with the Court's more recent cases," and the Texas statute, which created an "outright prohibition on retail competition from out-of-state auto manufacturers," was "about as negative toward interstate commerce as legislative action can get." *See id.* at 512 (Jones, J., specially concurring).

[178] *Granholm*, 544 U.S. at 490–92 ("In summary, the States provide little concrete evidence for the sweeping assertion that they cannot police direct shipments by out-of-state wineries.").

[179] On the other hand, *Granholm* might cut against this conclusion because the majority opinion in that case included a citation to Justice Scalia's separate opinion in *North Dakota*, 495 U.S. 423, with the following parenthetical appended to it: "The Twenty-first Amendment . . . empowers North Dakota to require that all liquor sold for use in the State be purchased from a licensed *in-state* wholesaler." 544 U.S. at 489 (emphasis added) (quoting 495 U.S. at 447 (Scalia, J., concurring in the judgment)).

commentators have expressed mixed views on questions of this kind.[180] So too have lower courts.[181] One thing, however, is certain: Given the prevalence, economic importance, and unsettled constitutional status of state-based liquor-regulation regimes, additional cases involving the intersection of the dormant Commerce

---

Moreover, as previously noted, Justice Thomas read the majority opinion in *Granholm* as validating state laws that require wholesalers to use local facilities. *Id.* at 518 (Thomas, J., dissenting) (stating that the majority "concedes" this point). *But see* Brief of 23 Wine Consumers as *Amici Curiae* in Support of Petitioners at 6, Lebamoff Enters., Inc. v. Whitmer, 141 S. Ct. 1049 (2020) (No. 20–47) ("*Granholm* requires that states grant privileges to in-state and out-of-state stakeholders on an equal basis and prohibits states from requiring that out-of-state stakeholders establish a physical presence as a condition of exercising such privileges. States thus cannot act in a way which benefits local interests but prevents out-of-state competition. New technologies now enable alcoholic beverage retailers the opportunity to offer novel purchasing and delivery options to consumers. States have shown an increasing willingness to embrace these novel options, but only for in-state retailers. *Amici* assert this violates *Granholm* and *Thomas*.").

[180] *See, e.g.*, Jerry Ellig & Alan E. Wiseman, *Price Effects and the Commerce Clause: The Case of State Wine Shipping Laws*, 10 J. EMPIRICAL LEGAL STUD. 196, 197–98 (2013) (finding that laws restricting out-of-state retailers, but permitting out-of-state wineries to ship alcohol directly to consumers, "have noticeable effects on price competition in local markets," principally by depriving consumers of price savings); Susan Lorde Martin, *Wine Wars—Consumers and Mom-and-Pop Wineries vs. Big Business Wholesalers: A* Citizens United *Example*, 21 KAN. J.L. & PUB. POL'Y 1, 24 (2011) (noting that, after *Granholm*, "states are still trying to regulate in ways that favor their own wine producers and wholesalers"); Jonathan M. Rotter & Joshua S. Stambaugh, *What's Left of the Twenty-First Amendment?*, 6 CARDOZO PUB. L. POL'Y & ETHICS J. 601, 628–29 (2008) ("While practically necessary for control, perhaps from a doctrinal perspective, disadvantaging out-of-state retailers is . . . unacceptable. A state may have every right to insist that liquor purchased within its borders passes through the three-tier system, but it may not have power to regulate liquor that is purchased in other states and subsequently brought into the state by the consumer.").

[181] For example, in *Brooks v. Vassar*, 462 F.3d 341 (4th Cir. 2006), the plaintiffs challenged a portion of Virginia's liquor regulation that prohibited Virginia residents from importing more than one gallon of alcohol for personal use. *Id.* at 344. The plaintiffs argued that "[b]ecause only *retailers* in Virginia may now sell directly to consumers . . . in-state *retailers* are favored over out-of-state *retailers*." *Id.* at 352 (emphasis in original). Nevertheless, the Fourth Circuit reasoned that "an argument that compares the status of an in-state retailer with an out-of-state retailer—or that compares the status of any other in-state entity under the three-tier system with its out-of-state counterpart—is nothing different than an argument challenging the three-tier system itself." *Id.* Thus, because the three-tier system was "unquestionably legitimate" under *Granholm*, the court rejected the plaintiffs' challenge. *Id.*; *see also* Wine Country Gift Baskets.com v. Steen, 612 F.3d 809 (5th Cir. 2010) (holding that a Texas law permitting in-state alcohol retailers, but prohibiting out-of-state retailers, to ship to Texas consumers did not violate dormant Commerce Clause); Arnold's Wines, Inc. v. Boyle, 571 F.3d 185, 187, 191 (2d Cir. 2009) (holding that a New York law permitting in-state alcohol retailers to sell directly to customers, but prohibiting out-of-state retailers from doing so without "ship[ping] to state-licensed wholesalers within the three-tier system" did not violate dormant Commerce Clause restrictions because *Granholm*'s "exceptions to the states' three-tier systems" applied to producers, not retailers); Siesta Vill. Mkt., LLC v. Granholm, 596 F. Supp. 2d 1035 (E.D. Mich. 2008) (holding that a Michigan law prohibiting only out-of-state wineries from shipping to in-state consumers was discriminatory and unconstitutional).

Clause and the Twenty-first amendment will continue to furnish new opportunities for doctrinal clarification.

Chapter 21

THE DORMANCY DOCTRINE AND STATE TAX LAWS

Analysis

The Supreme Court has wrestled with state and local taxes under the Commerce Clause in much the same way that it has wrestled with state and local regulatory measures.[1] Applying a variety of verbal formulae, the Court has struck down scores of such tax-related measures while upholding scores of others, sometimes drawing debatable distinctions between one law and another.[2] In *Complete Auto Transit, Inc. v. Brady*,[3] the Court sought to bring some order to this field by fashioning an overarching synthesis, based on "economic realities," of its dormancy-doctrine taxation jurisprudence.[4] Pulling together different strands of pre-existing doctrine, the Court declared that a state tax law can survive a dormant Commerce Clause challenge only so long as each of four requirements is satisfied—namely, that the challenged tax (1) "does not discriminate against interstate commerce"; (2) "is applied to an activity with a substantial nexus with the taxing State"; (3) "is fairly apportioned"; and (4) "is fairly related to the services provided by the State."[5] This set of requirements remains in effect today, and the modern cases reflect an attentiveness to tax-law policies that comport

---

[1] From the earliest years of the dormancy doctrine, the Court has recognized that state taxation may qualify as "in effect, a regulation" subject to displacement by the grant to Congress of authority to "regulate" interstate and international commerce. *See* Walling v. Michigan, 116 U.S. 446, 455 (1886).

[2] *Compare* Ry. Express Agency, Inc. v. Virginia, 347 U.S. 359, 364 (1954) (holding that a tax for "the privilege of doing business in this state" is unconstitutional), *with* Ry. Express Agency, Inc. v. Virginia, 358 U.S. 434, 440 (1959) (allowing for a similar tax when renamed a "franchise tax").

[3] 430 U.S. 274 (1977).

[4] *Id.* at 279.

[5] *Id.* at 278.

with the same unitary-market values that the Court has sought to vindicate in the regulatory context.[6] In particular, the Court's guiding principle has been to ensure that interstate commerce bears no more than its "fair share" of state and local tax levies.[7]

The *Complete Auto Transit* test applies to all forms of state and local taxation—income taxes, sales taxes, license taxes, real estate taxes, and any other type of tax that comes down the pike.[8] It also takes into account all features of the state's taxing scheme, focusing attention not only on the definition of tax bases and apportionment formulas but also on deductions, exemptions, credits, and other forms of tax relief.[9] In short, the Court's *Complete Auto Transit* jurisprudence—particularly as refined in recent decisions applying the so-called "internal consistency" and "external consistency" tests—provides a roadmap for exploring the compatibility of any state taxing law with the dormant Commerce Clause principle.[10] We turn now to a more detailed examination of each of the *Complete Auto Transit* test's components, beginning with the "nondiscrimination" requirement, and then turning to the substantial-nexus, fair-apportionment, and fair-relation requirements.[11] This chapter

---

6 *See generally supra* Chapter 16.

7 Goldberg v. Sweet, 488 U.S. 252, 261 (1989).

8 *See, e.g.*, Camps Newfound/Owatonna, Inc. v. Town of Harrison, 520 U.S. 564, 574–75 (1997) (concluding that a "tax on real estate, like any other tax, may impermissibly burden interstate commerce"). For an illustrative case applying the *Complete Auto Transit* test—here, in evaluating a timeshare-occupancy tax implemented by the Virgin Islands—see *American Resort Development Association v. Government of Virgin Islands*, 848 F. App'x 79, 83 (3d Cir. 2021) (holding that no dormant Commerce Clause violation was shown because, among other things, "the Territory taxes resident and non-resident taxpayers at equal rates" and "apportions its tax based on consumption" in a way that does not create discriminatory effects).

9 *See, e.g.*, Maryland v. Louisiana, 451 U.S. 725, 756 (1981) (invalidating a state's "first use" tax on natural gas because it "unquestionably discriminates against interstate commerce in favor of local interests as the necessary result of various tax credits and exclusions").

10 It is not surprising that the core requirement of nondiscrimination that this test directs at taxes parallels the nondiscrimination rule applicable to state regulatory constraints. *See supra* Chapter 17. On the other hand, *Pike* balancing analysis is *not* a part of the *Complete Auto Transit* framework. *See supra* Chapter 18. This difference in approach makes sense because, among other things, (1) states always have a legitimate interest in raising revenue, and imposing taxes in any form necessarily advances that goal; (2) it is accordingly not possible to engage in anything like *Pike*-based contextualized means-ends inquiries in the tax-law context; and (3) as a practical matter, the *Complete Auto Transit* requirements that do not deal with discrimination—most notably, the fair-apportionment requirement as supplemented by the internal-consistency and external-consistency tests—provide a workable "stand in" for *Pike* analysis in tax-related cases not involving discrimination.

11 This treatment offers nothing more than an introduction to a highly complex subject. The leading scholarly treatment appears in Volume I, Part III of JEROME R. HELLERSTEIN, WALTER HELLERSTEIN & JOHN A. SWAIN, STATE TAXATION ¶¶ 4.01 to 4.24 (3d ed. 1998 with 2021 cumulative supp.). The leading casebook in this field is

concludes with a brief discussion of the Court's specialized application of the *Complete Auto Transit* test to state-based user fees.

A. THE NONDISCRIMINATION REQUIREMENT

The "nondiscrimination" prong of the *Complete Auto Transit* test extends to tax cases the same core feature of the dormancy doctrine that operates with regard to state regulatory measures.[12] The Court, for example, has not hesitated to invalidate facially discriminatory taxing measures, including when it is claimed that they have caused no injury to interstate business operators because these operators "pass on" added tax increments to third parties. In particular, the Court has eschewed such an "economic incidence analysis" as likely to create an unwanted doctrinal "morass" marked by "a certain potential for error."[13] In similar fashion, the Court has rejected efforts to skirt the rule of strict equality based on assertions that: (1) the challenged tax involves only "*de minimis*" discrimination;[14] (2) the discriminatory feature of the law affects only a small number of taxpayers;[15] and (3) the challenged tax relief involves subsidy-like business development incentives for start-up or struggling local enterprises.[16]

Indeed, the Court's many applications of the nondiscrimination rule have given rise to only one specialized limitation. Under the so-called compensatory-tax doctrine, the state may lay a specialized tax

---

WALTER HELLERSTEIN, KIRK J. STARK, JOHN A. SWAIN & JOAN M. YOUNGMAN, STATE AND LOCAL TAXATION, CASES AND MATERIALS (11th ed. 2020).

[12] As noted earlier, *see supra* text accompanying note 6, the Court's tax-related anti-discrimination jurisprudence bears a close resemblance to its regulation-related anti-discrimination jurisprudence. Lawyers, accordingly, should be on the lookout for opportunities to draw on precedents from either field as they handle cases that involve the other. The point is well-illustrated by the fact that a leading tax case, *Bacchus Imports, Ltd. v. Dias*, 468 U.S. 263 (1984), also provides a key precedent for assessing discriminatory purpose and effect in applying the dormant Commerce Clause to state regulations. *See supra* Chapter 17.

[13] Fulton Corp. v. Faulkner, 516 U.S. 325, 342 (1996); *accord, e.g.*, *Bacchus Imports*, 468 U.S. at 272.

[14] *Fulton Corp.*, 516 U.S. at 333 n.3.

[15] New Energy Co. v. Limbach, 486 U.S. 269, 276–77 (1988) (stating, in a case in which the challenged law affected only one local firm and one non-local firm, that "the size or number of the in-state businesses favored or the out-of-state businesses disfavored [is not] relevant to our determination"; reasoning that "[v]arying the strength of the bar against economic protectionism according to the size and number of in-state and out-of-state firms" would produce undesirable complexity).

[16] *See Bacchus Imports*, 468 U.S. at 272–73. For discussions of this subject, see Peter D. Enrich, *Saving the States from Themselves: Commerce Clause Constraints on State Tax Incentives for Business*, 110 HARV. L. REV. 377 (1996); Walter Hellerstein & Dan T. Coenen, *Commerce Clause Restraints on State Business Development Incentives*, 81 CORNELL L. REV. 789 (1996); and Philip M. Tatarowicz & Rebecca F. Mims-Velarde, *An Analytical Approach to State Tax Discrimination Under the Dormant Commerce Clause*, 39 VAND. L. REV. 879 (1986). As this set of treatments reveals, this subject is marked by both disagreement and complexity.

on interstate transactions to equalize tax burdens placed on comparable intrastate activity.[17] Thus, in *Henneford v. Silas Mason Co.*,[18] the Court upheld a "use tax" directed at persons who bought goods outside the state for in-state consumption. This tax was proper, in the Court's view, because it was part of a broader taxing scheme under which all goods—whether purchased inside or outside the state—were subject to nondiscriminatory taxation notwithstanding the fact that the tax on in-state purchases was structured as a "sales," rather than a "use," tax.[19] Later cases, however, have put the compensatory-tax limitation on such a short leash that it almost never operates outside the sales-and-use-tax setting.[20] In this way, the Court has advanced its more general agenda of avoiding "the creation of new uncertainties in an already complex field."[21]

Unlawful tax discrimination is often stark.[22] In *New Energy Co. v. Limbach*,[23] for example, Ohio sought to defend a sales-tax credit

---

17 Perhaps it is technically inaccurate to characterize the compensatory tax doctrine as a "limitation" on the nondiscrimination rule. Another way to look at the use-tax cases is to view them as reflecting the proposition that in substance, regardless of formal appearances, no discrimination is present at all.

18 300 U.S. 577 (1937).

19 *See supra* Section 17.B (discussing *Silas Mason* case in greater detail).

20 In particular, the Court in *Fulton Corp.*, *see supra* note 13, drew on its prior decision in *Oregon Waste Systems, Inc. v. Department of Environmental Quality*, 511 U.S. 93 (1994), to declare that the exception applies only if three conditions are met: "First, a State must, as a threshold matter, identify the intrastate tax burden for which the State is attempting to compensate. Second, the tax on interstate commerce must be shown roughly to approximate—but not to exceed—the amount of the tax on intrastate commerce. Finally, the events on which the interstate and intrastate taxes are imposed must be substantially equivalent; that is, they must be sufficiently similar in substance to serve as mutually exclusive proxies for each other." 516 U.S. at 332–33 (internal quotation marks and citations omitted) (quoting *Oregon Waste Systems*, 511 U.S. at 103, and then quoting Armco Inc. v. Hardesty, 467 U.S. 638, 643 (1984)). For a pre-*Silas Mason* case in which the Court upheld a compensatory use tax, see *Hinson v. Lott*, 75 U.S. (8 Wall.) 148 (1869) (upholding a tax on imported liquor because it compensated for a tax imposed on all liquor distilled in the state). In *Fulton Corp.*, the Court identified *Hinson* as providing the "only exception" to its pattern of applying the compensatory tax doctrine exclusively to "traditional sales/use taxes." 516 U.S. at 342 n.8. *See generally* Walter Hellerstein, *Complementary Taxes as a Defense to Unconstitutional State Tax Discrimination*, 39 TAX LAW. 405 (1986).

21 New Energy Co. v. Limbach, 486 U.S. 269, 277 (1988).

22 *See, e.g.*, *Oregon Waste Systems*, 511 U.S. 93 (invalidating a law that imposed a surcharge on out-of-state waste that was more than 2.5 times greater than the charge imposed for identical in-state waste); Chemical Waste Mgmt., Inc. v. Hunt, 504 U.S. 334 (1992) (invalidating waste disposal fees that applied only to out-of-state waste); Tyler Pipe Indus., Inc. v. Wash. State Dep't of Revenue, 483 U.S. 232 (1987) (invalidating a manufacturing tax imposed, in practical effect, on goods sold outside the state but not on goods sold inside the state); Westinghouse Elec. Corp. v. Tully, 466 U.S. 388, 407 (1984) (holding unconstitutional tax credits for in-state businesses because they "discriminate[d] against export shipping from other States"); Boston Stock Exch. v. State Tax Comm'n, 429 U.S. 318 (1977) (invalidating a stock transfer tax that was higher for out-of-state sales than for in-state sales).

23 486 U.S. 269.

for ethanol-based gasoline. The Court, however, struck down the exemption because the state granted it only for ethanol produced in Ohio or in a state that afforded Ohio ethanol similarly favorable tax treatment. The reciprocity provision, the Court explained, did not save the exemption because Ohio could not pass a law, even with the aim of generally stimulating interstate ethanol sales, that in effect punished other states for not treating an Ohio product as favorably as Ohio would have liked.[24] Nor did it matter that Ohio had acted with the salutary goals of reducing pollution and promoting a more environmentally friendly energy source as compared to traditional gasoline. States are free to pursue such aims, the Court proclaimed, but they may not do so with programs that overtly discriminate against interstate commerce.[25]

In other cases, the Court has detected unlawful discrimination even though it is not immediately apparent on the face of the challenged tax law. In *South Central Bell Telephone Co. v. Alabama*,[26] for example, the Court struck down a franchise tax calculated for Alabama corporations that was based on the par value of their stock and calculated for non-Alabama corporations based on the actual value of their capital within the state. A unanimous Court found that this scheme violated the nondiscrimination rule because in-state firms could set par value at any level they wished under Alabama corporation law, thus reducing their tax liability to minimal amounts by way of a unilateral choice.[27] A trickier tax-discrimination issue came before the Court in *Associated Industries v. Lohman*.[28] At issue in that case was the constitutionality of a Missouri taxing scheme marked by two key components. First, the state imposed a sales tax, triggered by the in-state purchase of goods, that varied from 4.225% to 7.725% of the purchase price depending on whether the local government exercised an option under state law to raise the operative base rate. Second, the state imposed a uniform 5.725% use tax, triggered by the local use of goods purchased outside the state, which was designed to make up for forgone sales-tax revenue pursuant to the principle of *Silas Mason*.[29] Focusing on the fact that "over 93% of the dollar volume of sales in the State occurred in

---

[24] *Id.* at 274–76; *see also supra* Section 17.A.2 n.21 (discussing the judicial treatment of reciprocity statutes in the non-tax context, including the statute invalidated in *Great Atlantic & Pacific Tea Co. v. Cottrell*, 424 U.S. 366 (1976)).

[25] *New Energy*, 486 U.S. at 278–79.

[26] 526 U.S. 160 (1999).

[27] The Court thus in effect took account of how the state's tax law and its corporation law operated together in finding that "[t]he tax . . . facially discriminates." *Id.* at 169.

[28] 511 U.S. 641 (1994).

[29] *See supra* notes 17–21 and accompanying text.

jurisdictions where the local sales tax exceeded the use tax,"[30] the Missouri courts had upheld the taxing scheme. The Supreme Court, however, rejected this overall-impact approach. Instead, citing *Dean Milk* and its progeny,[31] the Court required a comparison of tax burdens on a locality-by-locality basis and invalidated the taxing scheme as applied to each place where the local government had not imposed a sales tax equal to or greater than the 5.725% use-tax rate. Again sounding a theme of simplicity and straightforwardness, the Court reasoned that "patent discrimination in part of the operation of a tax scheme can[not] be rendered inconsequential for Commerce Clause purposes by advantages given to interstate commerce in other facets of a tax plan or in other regions of a State."[32]

The Court probably has pushed the anti-discrimination rule to its furthest point in striking down facially non-discriminatory charges placed on door-to-door sellers, sometimes called "drummers," who solicit orders for delivery at a later time. In *Robbins v. Taxing District of Shelby County*,[33] the Court reasoned that, as a practical matter, "the tax on drummers operates greatly to [out-of-state firms'] disadvantage in comparison with the merchants and manufacturers of Memphis" because those local operators typically sell their wares from "regular licensed houses of business."[34] Placing an important limit on this principle, the Court in later cases distinguished taxes that target "drummers" from taxes placed on "peddlers" who carry goods with them in an effort to finalize sales on the spot. The Court appears to have justified its differing approach to these cases by relying on the somewhat shaky theory that drummers almost always work for out-of-state suppliers while peddlers more often represent local businesses.[35]

---

[30] *Associated Industries*, 511 U.S. at 645.

[31] *See supra* Section 17.A.3.

[32] *Associated Industries*, 511 U.S. at 649.

[33] 120 U.S. 489 (1887).

[34] *Id.* at 498; *accord, e.g.*, Nippert v. City of Richmond, 327 U.S. 416 (1946); Best & Co. v. Maxwell, 311 U.S. 454 (1940).

[35] *See, e.g.*, Caskey Baking Co. v. Virginia, 313 U.S. 117, 119–20 (1941) (allowing Virginia to collect a peddler tax imposed on an out-of-state baker); Wagner v. City of Covington, 251 U.S. 95, 102–04 (1919) (collecting authorities and noting that goods sold by a peddler "might just as well have been manufactured within the State"); *see also* Dunbar-Stanley Studios, Inc. v. Alabama, 393 U.S. 537, 542 (1969) (holding that a state tax imposed at a higher rate on transient photographers than on fixed-location photographers did not unlawfully discriminate against interstate commerce). A related case is *Breard v. City of Alexandria*, 341 U.S. 622 (1951), in which the Court upheld a general prohibition on door-to-door solicitation, as applied to a drummer, against a dormant Commerce Clause challenge. How can one reconcile this ruling with *Robbins*? At least three possibilities come to mind. First, the ordinance in *Breard* did not involve a tax at all and was said to be supported by a weighty state interest in safeguarding residential privacy. Second, the *Breard* ordinance (unlike the law at issue in *Robbins*) did not place cumulative unapportioned tax obligations on

Even while recognizing few limits on the nondiscrimination rule, the Court has been careful to restrict its application to cases that involve "a comparison of substantially similar entities."[36] In *Alaska v. Arctic Maid*,[37] for example, the Court considered a state statutory scheme as applied to the taxation of salmon fishing, according to which (1) fishing operators had to pay a 4% tax on the value of salmon frozen on ships for transport and later canning outside the state and (2) fishing operators had to pay a 1% tax for salmon brought on shore for later local sale as freshly frozen fish. Despite allegations of discrimination offered up by freezer-ship operators, the Court found that their constitutional challenge involved a faulty attempt to equate economically dissimilar business operations. After all, the Court explained, freezer ship operators sold fish to canners and thus did not compete at all in the retail fresh-frozen fish market to which the 1% tax applied. The dormant Commerce Clause, the Court continued, simply does not impose an " 'iron rule of equality' between taxes laid by a State on different types of business."[38]

As *Lohman*, *Robbins*, and *Arctic Maid* reveal, the Court's conscientious efforts to simplify the nondiscrimination rule have not removed from this legal field all difficulties of characterization and line drawing. Taxing schemes come in so many shapes and sizes that hard questions about the presence or absence of discrimination inevitably arise. The existence of some subtleties, however, should not obscure the overarching message of the Court's decisions: "[I]n the process of competition no state may discriminatorily tax the products manufactured or the business operations performed in any other state."[39]

---

commercial operators (including small operators) who happened to operate in a variety of jurisdictions; rather, its constraint "affected interstate drummers and local drummers in exactly the same way—both were put out of business." Donald H. Regan, *The Supreme Court and State Protectionism: Making Sense of the Dormant Commerce Clause*, 84 MICH. L. REV. 1091, 1199 (1986). Finally, the law at issue in *Breard* appeared to reach both drummers and peddlers. Thus, although *Breard* itself involved a challenge by drummers, the Court might have found the constitutional challenge to the ordinance controlled by its peddling-fee cases, rather than its drumming-fee cases, in part because the law's application to peddlers tended to ensure a greater measure of local opposition to its enactment.

36 General Motors Corp. v. Tracy, 519 U.S. 278, 298 (1997).

37 366 U.S. 199 (1961).

38 *Id.* at 205. Another application of this principle came in *General Motors Corp. v. Tracy*, 519 U.S. 278 (1997). There the Court upheld a state's imposition of different tax rates on sales of natural gas by local utilities and sales by independent operators, most of whose operations took place outside the state. Relying on *Arctic Maid*, the Court reasoned that the differential tax rates did not offend dormant-Commerce Clause principles because regulated utilities and nonregulated independent sellers operate in separate markets. *See id.* at 300–02.

39 Boston Stock Exch. v. State Tax Comm'n, 429 U.S. 318, 337 (1977).

B. THE SUBSTANTIAL-NEXUS RULE

In much the same way that due-process principles require "minimum contacts" for a state to assert personal jurisdiction over a nonresident,[40] the dormant Commerce Clause principle prohibits states from asserting tax-based jurisdiction over any person or firm with whom they lack a sufficiently close connection. Indeed, the Court in *Quill Corp. v. North Dakota*[41] declared that the dormant Commerce Clause imposes an even stricter nexus rule than does the Due Process Clause standing alone. The issue in that case was whether a state could require a mail-order business to collect and remit a use tax on items sold for delivery into that state. Reaffirming *National Bellas Hess, Inc. v. Department of Revenue*,[42] the Court rejected this assertion of state authority on the ground that the seller lacked a local "physical presence" in the form of facilities or company personnel.[43] In so ruling, however, the Court took care to rely only on the dormant Commerce Clause and not on due-process principles—a move that carried with it significant consequences in light of the "congressional consent" exception to the dormancy doctrine.[44] In other words, *Quill* left Congress "free to decide whether, when, and to what extent the States may burden interstate mail-order concerns with a duty to collect use taxes."[45] Congress, however, never passed

---

40 Int'l Shoe Co. v. Washington, 326 U.S. 310, 316 (1945).

41 504 U.S. 298 (1992).

42 386 U.S. 753 (1967).

43 *Quill*, 504 U.S. at 317–18. In a number of earlier cases, the Court had found a sufficient physical presence to support the exercise of state tax-related authority over out-of-state firms. *See, e.g.*, Nat'l Geographic Soc'y v. Cal. Bd. of Equalization, 430 U.S. 551 (1977) (upholding the imposition of an obligation on an out-of-state company to collect use taxes because the company had advertising offices in the taxing state, even though those offices were unrelated to the company's mail-order sales); Scripto, Inc. v. Carson, 362 U.S. 207 (1960) (allowing the state to impose use-tax-collection duties on an out-of-state business because it employed in-state independent contractors to solicit sales); Gen. Trading Co. v. State Tax Comm'n, 322 U.S. 335 (1944) (upholding the imposition of a duty to collect a use tax for items ordered as the result of solicitations made by traveling salespeople sent into the state by the out-of-state company); Nelson v. Sears, Roebuck & Co., 312 U.S. 359 (1941) (allowing the state to impose obligations to collect use taxes based on an out-of-state corporation's mail order sales because it had retail stores in the state, even though those stores did not account for the mail-order catalogue sales that triggered the use tax).

44 *See supra* Section 20.B.

45 *Quill*, 504 U.S. at 318. Related to these decisions are cases that involve dormancy-based restraints on state power to force out-of-state corporations to register to do business, thus subjecting themselves to the general personal jurisdiction and taxing authority of the state. These cases require application of the "manipulable and at times anachronistically metaphysical" principle, LAURENCE H. TRIBE, AMERICAN CONSTITUTIONAL LAW § 6–14, at 1104 (3d ed. 2000), that a state may not demand registration of a firm that engages solely in "interstate commerce" but may demand registration if the firm "is engaged in intrastate as well as interstate aspects of the . . . business." Eli Lilly & Co. v. Sav-On-Drugs, 366 U.S. 276, 279 (1961) (upholding a qualification requirement for a foreign corporation that, in addition to selling drugs to

a law authorizing the imposition of such a duty, and the Court eventually chose to revisit the issue in *South Dakota v. Wayfair*.[46]

In *Wayfair*, the Court overruled *Quill*, choosing to abandon the physical-presence requirement as "artificial" and "arbitrary," especially in light of the "far-reaching systemic and structural changes" created by modern computer-based retailing.[47] One problem, according to Justice Kennedy, who wrote for a five-Justice majority, was that the *Quill* rule had deterred sellers from engaging in the most efficient business choices, including by avoiding the employment of local workers in local facilities, simply to avoid incurring tax-collection obligations.[48] No less problematic was *Quill's* creation of strange forms of differential treatment—for example, by placing tax-collection duties on an out-of-state mom-and-pop business that kept a tiny amount of inventory in an in-state warehouse while placing no duty on an e-commerce mega-firm that stored massive volumes of inventory just across the state line.[49] Finally, the goal of heightened simplicity that underlay *Quill* had faded with time, as new questions emerged about whether physical presence could arise by way of such actions as an e-retailer's installation of "cookies" in local buyers' computers, the downloading onto cellphones by in-state buyers of a retailer's app, or even the retailer's simple transmission via the internet of its website into the state.[50]

New Jersey wholesalers, also maintained an office and had 18 employees promoting its product to hospitals and pharmacies in the state). A key decision in this line of rulings, *Allenberg Cotton Co. v. Pittman*, 419 U.S. 20 (1974), concerned a corporate cotton merchant, headquartered in Tennessee, that (1) contracted, through a Mississippi broker, to buy Mississippi farmers' cotton; (2) took title under those contracts in Mississippi, where the cotton was stored in warehouses; and (3) shipped the cotton to buyers located outside Mississippi. The Court ruled that—whether or not Mississippi could tax the firm for local storage of the cotton or for other in-state components of these transactions, *see id.* at 33–34—it could not require registration. In reaching this conclusion, the Court emphasized that the corporate cotton merchant had no local office; did not own or operate the local warehouses; had no employees working in Mississippi "on a regular basis"; and essentially operated through an independent broker who lacked authority to contract on the corporation's behalf. *See id.* at 33.

46 138 S. Ct. 2080 (2018).

47 *Id.* at 2095, 2097 (quoting Direct Mktg. Ass'n v. Brohl, 575 U.S. 1, 18 (2015) (Kennedy, J., concurring)).

48 *Wayfair*, 138 S. Ct. at 2094. Justice Kennedy emphasized the resulting costs in terms of states' financial and autonomy interests, especially in light of the centrality of sales and use taxes to supporting critical state programs and the magnified revenue losses caused by the explosion in recent years of internet-based retail sales. *Id.* at 2092, 2095. In dissent, the Chief Justice challenged these points, pointing to data suggesting that any harm to state treasuries caused by the intersection of *Quill* and e-commerce "is apparently receding with time." *Id.* at 2103 (Roberts, C.J., dissenting).

49 *Id.* at 2098–99 (majority opinion).

50 *Id.* at 2095.

In a dissent joined by Justices Breyer, Sotomayor, and Kagan, Chief Justice Roberts faulted the majority for failing to adhere to principles of stare decisis. He argued that it was especially wrong-minded for the Court to overrule a decision that had itself reaffirmed a preexisting and longstanding precedent, especially because the rule of those cases was (and had always been) subject to congressional retooling by way of ordinary legislation.[51] Expanding on this point, the Chief Justice emphasized Congress's specialized competence—and the Court's lack of competence—to evaluate the subject of state taxation of a "critical segment of the economy" that remained in the midst of radical change.[52] For the majority, however, present-day conditions left no doubt that the "formalistic" distinction between physical presence and functionally meaningful, even if non-physical, presence "simply makes no sense."[53]

One question left behind by *Wayfair* is whether anything remains of the dormant Commerce Clause "nexus" requirement—that is, to the proposition that dormancy-based nexus requirement imposes limits not already established by its due process-based counterpart.[54] On this score, the majority noted that the two separate limits "may not be identical or coterminous,"[55] but it did not elaborate on the point. At the same time, Justice Kennedy did emphasize that the challenged statute included an exemption for non-physically-present businesses that did not generate either $100,000 in total sales or 200 separate purchase transactions on an annual basis.[56] This feature of the law, he explained, tended to undermine reliance-based arguments against the overruling of *Quill* in *Wayfair*: After all, as Justice Kennedy explained, the smallest sellers faced with the greatest risk of suffering reliance-based harms remained protected by an exemption built into the challenged state law itself.[57] This aspect of the Court's reasoning could portend a future doctrinal development—namely, that the Court will continue to apply the dormant Commerce Clause nexus rule, even if it cannot draw on the less protective due-process limit, to safeguard out-of-state retailers (perhaps even if they somehow meet the pre-*Wayfair* physical-presence test) whose sales activity creates a connection with a would-

---

51 *Id.* at 2102 (Roberts, C.J., dissenting).

52 *Id.* at 2101.

53 *Id.* at 2092 (majority opinion). *See* Adam B. Thimmesch, *A Unifying Approach to Nexus Under the Dormant Commerce Clause*, 116 MICH. L. REV. ONLINE 101, 102 (2018) (endorsing the elimination of "any special nexus requirement under the dormant Commerce Clause").

54 *See Wayfair*, 138 S. Ct. at 2092–93.

55 *Id.* at 2093.

56 *Id.* at 2089, 2099.

57 *Id.* at 2099.

be collection-duty-imposing state that turns out to be minimal, unintended, or spasmodic.[58]

C. THE REQUIREMENT OF FAIR APPORTIONMENT

Closely connected to the requirement of "substantial nexus" is the separate *Complete Auto Transit* principle that mandates "fair apportionment" of state taxes. To take a simple example, assume that a multistate firm, Mega-Metal Fabricating Corporation, does 10% of its business in the state of Taxomania. Common sense (if not common decency) suggests that Taxomania should not be able to tax 100% of the net profits generated by Mega-Metal's nationwide activities even though the state clearly has taxing "jurisdiction" over the firm under *Wayfair* and other nexus-based rulings. The essential problem is this: If Taxomania can tax 100% of Mega-Metal's income, many other states can do so as well. The consequence would be that Mega-Metal would pay a heavy price for engaging in interstate commerce because it would have to bear a far heavier tax burden than a firm that generated exactly the same revenues and profits but operated in only one jurisdiction.

To counter this "risk of multiple taxation,"[59] the Court has insisted that states may tax only "that aspect of the interstate commerce to which the State bears a special relation."[60] As a result, states long have limited their imposition of property taxes on instrumentalities of interstate commerce that move through multiple jurisdictions (*i.e.*, railroads, delivery trucks, and the like) and have used apportionment formulas for calculating income-based tax obligations for firms with unitary multistate operations. Historically, the most common of these income-tax apportionment formulas has given equal weight to three separate factors: sales, property, and payroll. For example, if Taxomania used this three-factor formula, it could tax 10% of Mega Metal's total income if 15% of the firm's total

---

[58] One problem with recognizing such a limitation is that it would introduce a layer of uncertainty into this field of law—although challenging issues of line-drawing are hardly unusual in the tax context. In any event, it seems clear that any specialized dormant Commerce Clause "small operator" nexus rule would, if recognized, not reach very far. *See* HELLERSTEIN, HELLERSTEIN & SWAIN, *supra* note 11, ¶ 6.03 ("Although future litigation may well reveal distinctions between *Wayfair*'s Commerce Clause nexus test of 'availing' oneself of the 'substantial privilege of carrying on business in a state' and the Court's pre-existing Due Process Clause nexus test of 'purposefully availing' oneself of 'the benefits of an economic market in the state,' we cannot identify such distinctions for the moment and, in light of the Court's reasoning in *Wayfair*, doubt that significant distinctions between Due Process Clause nexus and Commerce Clause nexus will emerge in the future." (internal footnote omitted)).

[59] *Quill*, 504 U.S. at 309.

[60] Central Greyhound Lines v. Mealey, 334 U.S. 653, 661 (1948).

sales, 10% of its total property and 5% of its total payroll were attributable to that state.[61]

Not all states, however, use this three-factor-apportionment approach, and some deviations from it have given rise to fair-apportionment-based challenges.[62] In *Moorman Manufacturing Co. v. Bair*,[63] for example, an interstate firm challenged Iowa's single-factor formula, which calculated the state's share of taxable income by reference to *only* the percentage of nationwide *sales* that were attributable to that state. The firm argued that this sales-only approach offended the dormant Commerce Clause goal of fostering "tax-neutral decisions"[64] by rewarding firms that located their physical facilities and work force within, rather than outside, the taxing state. (After all, unlike in three-factor states, Iowa did not in any way disadvantage a firm, by way of an elevated income-tax obligation, for locating employees and property within the state.) The Court, however, rejected this argument, emphasizing the difficulties presented by judicial micro-management of facially non-discriminatory apportionment methodologies.[65]

1. The Internal Consistency Test

Moorman Manufacturing comports with the historic inclination of the Court to uphold apportionment techniques unless they raise very obvious problems of fairness.[66] In more recent years, however, the Court has devised a new approach for assessing both apportionment problems and related difficulties: the so-called internal-consistency test.[67] A state law satisfies this test if, but only if, "the imposition of a tax identical to the one in question by every other State would add no burden to interstate commerce that intrastate commerce would not also bear."[68] For example, the tax challenged on fair-apportionment grounds in *Oklahoma Tax Commission v. Jefferson Lines, Inc.*[69] passed the internal-consistency

---

[61] *See* Butler Bros. v. McColgan, 315 U.S. 501 (1942) (upholding the standard three-factor apportionment formula).

[62] Indeed, most states today give greater weight to the sales factor than to other factors, and several states have adopted the single-factor sales formula described below.

[63] 437 U.S. 267 (1978).

[64] *Boston Stock Exch.*, 429 U.S. at 331.

[65] *Moorman Mfg.*, 437 U.S. at 278.

[66] *See, e.g.*, Norfolk & W. Ry. Co. v. Mo. State Tax Comm'n, 390 U.S. 317, 326 (1968) (invalidating a tax where the state's methodology led to a "grossly distorted" tax levy).

[67] *See generally* Walter Hellerstein, *Is "Internal Consistency" Foolish?: Reflections on an Emerging Commerce Clause Restraint on State Taxation*, 87 MICH. L. REV. 138 (1988).

[68] Okla. Tax Comm'n v. Jefferson Lines, Inc., 514 U.S. 175, 185 (1995).

[69] *Id.*

test with flying colors. There, Oklahoma had imposed a 4% sales tax on ticket purchases for every bus trip that originated in the state regardless of the trip's destination. The tax raised a knotty fair-apportionment problem because it applied in full to ticket purchases for all Oklahoma-originating bus trips, regardless of whether 1% or 100% of the trip occurred within the state. The tax, however, posed no problem under the internal-consistency test because any particular bus trip, whether interstate or intrastate, can originate in only one jurisdiction. Thus, even assuming that all states imposed this same taxing scheme, each bus trip would be subject to one, and only one, tax payment so that interstate bus operators would fare no worse than similarly situated intrastate competitors.[70]

In contrast, the Court in *American Trucking Associations, Inc. v. Scheiner*,[71] found that a flat, unapportioned "axle tax," which applied to any large truck that operated in Pennsylvania without regard to mileage traveled, ran afoul of the internal-consistency mandate. The problem was apparent: If all states exacted the same fixed fee, a truck that traveled through all of the contiguous United States during the tax year would pay 48 times the tax paid by a truck that traveled exactly the same distance solely within Pennsylvania. The Court in *Scheiner* noted that "the Commerce Clause does not require the States to avoid flat taxes when . . . the use of a more finely gradated user-fee schedule would pose genuine administrative burdens."[72] In *Scheiner* itself, however, the state could easily have tied its charge for highway use to miles actually traveled, in keeping with the practice of many other states (and of Pennsylvania itself for other truck-tax purposes).[73]

State laws sometimes raise internal-consistency problems because they are phrased in the disjunctive. In *Goldberg v. Sweet*,[74] for example, the Court confronted an Illinois tax that applied to phone calls *either* sent to *or* sent from the state. Had the law stopped there, it would have violated the internal consistency test because, if adopted by all states, it would have imposed twice the tax burden on interstate calls as on otherwise indistinguishable intrastate calls. In fact, however, the law did not stop there because it specified that the tax applied only to those calls that were billed to an Illinois service

---

70 The taxing scheme challenged in *Moorman Manufacturing* also posed no internal-consistency problem. If every state applied a single-factor sales-based apportionment formula, every multistate firm would be taxed on 100%, but no more than 100%, of its total income, just as surely as a firm that made all its sales intrastate would pay tax on 100% of its income.

71 483 U.S. 266 (1987).

72 *Id.* at 296.

73 *Id.* at 291.

74 488 U.S. 252 (1989).

address. This feature of the law removed internal-consistency problems because, as the Court explained, "if every State taxed only those interstate phone calls which are charged to an in-state service address, only one State would tax each interstate telephone call."[75] Another technique that states may use to avoid internal-consistency problems is to provide a credit for taxes paid in other jurisdictions.[76] Indeed in *Goldberg* itself, although the Court did not focus on the point, the challenged law included a credit provision that reduced the Illinois telecommunications tax to the extent that the taxpayer made tax payments to other states. This credit provision, no less than the law's billing address limitation, negated internal-consistency problems because if every state taxed every phone call, but gave a full credit for taxes on the same call paid anywhere else, the taxpayer involved in either an interstate or intrastate call would end up paying only one tax.[77]

In its most recent internal-consistency ruling, *Comptroller of the Treasury v. Wynne*,[78] the Court lauded "the economic bona fides" of the test.[79] At issue in the case was a feature of Maryland law that denied state residents a full credit for income taxes paid to other states,[80] thus effectively subjecting out-of-state income to double taxation.[81] Writing for the majority, Justice Alito emphasized that

---

75 *Id.* at 261.

76 *See* D.H. Holmes Co. v. McNamara, 486 U.S. 24, 31 (1988) (concluding that the "Louisiana taxing scheme is fairly apportioned, for it provides a credit against its use tax for sales taxes that have been paid in other States").

77 *Cf. Goldberg*, 488 U.S. at 264 (noting, although in a portion of the opinion not focusing specifically on internal-consistency concerns, that "the credit provision contained in the Tax Act operates to avoid actual multiple taxation").

78 575 U.S. 542 (2015).

79 *Id.* at 563 (emphasizing that the internal-consistency test enables courts to distinguish between: "(1) tax schemes that inherently discriminate against interstate commerce without regard to the tax policies of other States, and (2) tax schemes that create disparate incentives to engage in interstate commerce (and sometimes result in double taxation) only as a result of the interaction of two different but nondiscriminatory and internally consistent schemes"); *see also* Michael S. Knoll & Ruth Mason, *The Dormant Foreign Commerce Clause After* Wynne, 39 VA. TAX REV. 357, 359 (2020) ("Although the Supreme Court has applied the internal consistency test by name for more than three decades, *Wynne* was the first case to acknowledge its 'economic bona fides' as a test for protectionism." (footnote omitted)); Ruth Mason, *Identifying Illegal Subsidies*, 69 AM. U. L. REV. 479 (2019) (arguing that the "internal consistency test" can and should be utilized as a means to identify illegal tax subsidies).

80 *Wynne*, 575 U.S. at 545–48. Like many states, Maryland taxed the income its residents earned both inside and outside the state, along with the income that nonresidents earned from Maryland-based sources. *Id.* With respect to residents, Maryland imposed its income tax in two parts: a "state" income tax and a "county" income tax. *Id.* The critical feature of this scheme—and its critical defect in the Court's view—was that Maryland gave residents paying income taxes to another jurisdiction a credit against the *state* tax but not against the *county* tax. *Id.*

81 *Id.* at 556.

the statute "created a powerful incentive to engage in intrastate rather than interstate economic activity."[82] He also observed that if every state adopted a similar scheme, residents would be less likely to seek income from out-of-state activities to avoid overlapping taxes, thus directly constraining socially valuable interstate work.[83] Indeed, the Court viewed this feature of Maryland's tax rule as so "inherently discriminatory" as to make it, in practical effect, "operate[ ] as a tariff."[84]

2. The External Consistency Test

The Court's modern cases carry forward the traditional requirement of fair apportionment by requiring not only internal consistency but "external consistency" as well.[85] Under this aspect of the Court's jurisprudence, even the most internally consistent tax will run afoul of the Commerce Clause if it lacks "all appropriate proportions to the business transacted . . . in that State, or has led to a grossly distorted result."[86] In practice the Court has seldom condemned state taxes on this ground. In an important line of cases,

[82] *Id.* at 561–62.

[83] *Id.* at 564–65.

[84] *Id.* at 565. For reflections on the Court's rationale in *Wynne*, see Knoll & Mason, *supra* note 79, at 367 (arguing that the Court in *Wynne* showed itself to be "[c]ommitted to the internal consistency test as a means of verifying whether state taxes function economically equivalently to tariffs"), and Michael S. Knoll & Ruth Mason, *The Economic Foundation of the Dormant Commerce Clause*, 103 VA. L. REV. 309, 333 (2017) (stating that the *Wynne* Court "affirm[ed] the usefulness of the internal consistency test in identifying the tariff-like impact of the Maryland tax"). *See also* Edward A. Zelinsky, *The Enigma of* Wynne, 7 WM. & MARY BUS. L. REV. 797, 805–08 (2016) (discussing Justice Alito's tariff analogy and adding that it is "powerful" in that "state-imposed tariffs are the quintessential evil against which the dormant Commerce Clause is aimed," but also "limitless" in that that most state action has a "tariff-like effect" and the analogy lacks a logical confining principle). Notably, the quoted language from Justice Alito's opinion seems to suggest a relocation of the internal-consistency inquiry from the fair-apportionment component of the *Complete Auto Transit* test to that test's anti-discrimination component. *See* Adam B. Thimmesch, *The Unified Dormant Commerce Clause*, 92 TEMP. L. REV. 331, 365 (2020) (arguing that the Court in *Wynne* folded the "internal consistency test into its nondiscrimination analysis rather than analyze internal consistency as part of the fair-apportionment prong"). The important point, however, does not concern the words on the banner under which the internal-consistency requirement now marches. Rather, it is simply that the Court remains committed to the internal-consistency test itself. *See generally* Bradley W. Joondeph, *The States' Multiple Taxation of Personal Income*, 71 CASE W. RES. L. REV. 121 (2020) (offering a post-*Wynne* treatment of multiple-taxation problems); *see also* Wal-Mart P.R., Inc. v. Zaragoza-Gomez, 834 F.3d 110, 113, 126 (1st Cir. 2016) (striking down a Puerto Rico tax whose underlying purpose was "to prevent multistate corporations doing business in Puerto Rico from shifting profits off the island"; reasoning that "its identical application by every State in the Union would place interstate commerce at a disadvantage as compared with commerce intrastate" (quoting *Wynne*, 575 U.S. at 562)).

[85] *Jefferson Lines*, 514 U.S. at 185.

[86] *Id.* at 195 (quoting Container Corp. v. Franchise Tax Bd., 463 U.S. 159, 170 (1983)).

for example, the Justices have upheld the implementation of the "conventional sales tax," imposed at a flat rate on a local transfer of goods, even when the transferred product has close connections with other states.[87] Nonetheless, internally consistent taxes occasionally run afoul of the external-consistency requirement.[88]

Consider a flat $500 tax placed on any train trip, but only if the trip's longest intrastate segment occurs within the taxing state. Such a tax would be internally consistent because every train trip—whether interstate or intrastate in nature—can have only one longest intrastate segment. The practical effect of such a tax, however, would be to give an artificial taxing advantage to geographically large states by permitting them to tax *in toto* many train trips that occur largely, or even primarily, in other states. In times gone by, the Court might have dealt with this problem by blocking state taxation of cross-border train trips altogether, perhaps on the theory that states lack the ability to tax interstate commerce "directly."[89] In the modern era, however, the Court would likely hold that such a tax violates the principle of "external consistency" by unfairly permitting large states to cash in on out-of-state attributes of only quasi-intrastate train traffic.

A leading "external consistency" case is *Norfolk & Western Railway Co. v. Missouri State Tax Commission*.[90] There the Court confronted a property tax made applicable to the rolling stock of railroad companies. Because train engines and cars constantly moved in and out of Missouri, the state adopted a convenient

---

[87] *Id.* at 188. *See, e.g.*, State Tax Comm'n v. Pac. State Cast Iron Pipe Co., 372 U.S. 605, 606 (1963) (upholding full application of a generally applicable sales tax even though the particular sold items were to be immediately shipped outside the state); *see also* Browning v. Waycross, 233 U.S. 16, 23 (1914) (holding that the state may fully tax a local installer of lightning rods even though they were manufactured outside the state). *See generally* Walter Hellerstein, Michael J. McIntyre & Richard D. Pomp, *Commerce Clause Restraints on State Taxation After* Jefferson Lines, 51 TAX L. REV. 47, 86 (1995) (noting both this aspect of dormant Commerce Clause law and the inherent differences between sales-based and income-based taxes).

[88] Notably, it has been suggested that the Court's failure to mention the external-consistency concept in *Wynne* may indicate that that test, at least in essence, is now a relic of the past. *See* Knoll & Mason, *supra* note 79, at 406–09 (flagging this question and noting that "[w]e agree with the Utah Supreme Court that the current status of the external consistency test is unclear, especially after cases like *Quill* and *Wayfair* that suggest that nexus issues will be resolved under the due process clause rather than the dormant commerce clause"); Zelinsky, *supra* note 84, at 808–10 (pondering whether *Wynne* signals "the [d]eath of [e]xternal [c]onsistency"). Notably, the Utah Supreme Court seems to have concluded that, with *Wynne*, the external-consistency test has given up the ghost. *See* Steiner v. Utah State Tax Comm'n, 449 P.3d 189, 196–97 (Utah 2019) (noting that "[w]hatever life external consistency might have left, it is highly unlikely that it continues to apply in the context of an individual taxpayer's challenge to a state's taxation system"), *cert. denied*, 140 S. Ct. 1114 (2020).

[89] Freeman v. Hewit, 329 U.S. 249, 258 (1946).

[90] 390 U.S. 317 (1968).

apportionment formula based on track length. In particular, the state multiplied the total value of all the company's rolling stock by a ratio determined by comparing all track "owned, leased, or controlled by the N & W . . . in Missouri" to all track owned, leased or controlled by the company anywhere in the United States.[91] The problem was that, due to substantial real-world traffic-density variations, this formula subjected 8.2824% of the firm's rolling stock to state taxation even though in actuality only about 3.16% of its total fleet (in terms of its taxable value) was located in Missouri on an average day. While acknowledging that states are entitled to "broad tolerance" in fashioning apportionment formulas, the Court found the Missouri statute unconstitutional as applied because it generated "a grossly distorted result."[92] The governing principle, in the Court's view, was that the Constitution would not "tolerate any result, however distorted, just because it is the product of a convenient mathematical formula which, in most situations, may produce a tolerable product."[93]

Did the Illinois telephone-call tax involved in *Goldberg* offend the "external consistency" standard because it assigned to the party billed for a call a levy based on 100% of its cost even though the telephonic signals sent back and forth by the parties moved in large measure outside Illinois? Distinguishing physical-movement cases such as *Scheiner*, the Court said "no" because an "apportionment formula based on mileage or some other geographic division of individual telephone calls would produce insurmountable administrative and technological barriers."[94] What about the law involved in *Jefferson Lines*, which imposed a flat 4% sales tax on the price of all bus trips that originated in the state, whatever the distance traveled inside or outside Oklahoma? In its earlier decision in *Central Greyhound Lines, Inc. v. Mealey*,[95] the Court had mandated mileage-based apportionment of a New York "gross receipts tax" laid on all revenues obtained "by reason of any sale . . . made" in the state by a bus line operator.[96] Because aggregate in-state ticket "sales" under the Oklahoma statute equaled aggregate "gross receipts" under the New York formula, the dissenters in *Jefferson Lines* could see no reason not to extend the external-consistency-based ruling in *Central Greyhound* to the *Jefferson Lines*

---

[91] *Id.* at 321.

[92] *Id.* at 326–27.

[93] *Id.* at 327.

[94] *Goldberg*, 488 U.S. at 264–65.

[95] 334 U.S. 653 (1948).

[96] *Id.* at 664 (Murphy, J., dissenting).

case.[97] Even while acknowledging the "striking" similarities of the cases, however, the majority found no external-consistency problem. According to Justice Souter, because a "sale of goods is most readily viewed as a discrete event facilitated by the laws and amenities of the place of sale"[98] and because a "sale of services can ordinarily be treated as a local state event just as readily as a sale of tangible goods,"[99] a state that places a sales tax on the transfer of a bus ticket is permitted to ignore the interstate elements of the service that the ticket represents. To the dissenters, the difference between the sales tax and the gross receipts tax was purely "formal" because both exactions "as a practical matter" required sellers to remit unapportioned tax payments calculated by focusing on exactly the same tax base.[100] The majority, however, was prepared to declare that "economic equivalence alone has . . . not been (and should not be) the touchstone of Commerce Clause jurisprudence."[101] This division within the Court reflected competing visions of what is required by a dormant Commerce Clause jurisprudence that the Court often has declared to be properly focused on "practical effects."[102] The result in the case, however, left no doubt about the Court's continuing hesitation to carry over to the sales-tax context a jurisprudence of fair apportionment developed to deal, at least primarily, with taxes based on income and property values.

D. THE FAIR-RELATION REQUIREMENT

In theory, the *Complete Auto Transit* test requires states to ensure that taxes are "fairly related to the services provided by the state" in support of the activity being taxed.[103] In practice, however, the Court has never insisted that levies paid by a taxpayer and services received by that taxpayer match one another in any meaningful sense. In *Commonwealth Edison Co. v. Montana*,[104] for example, the Court considered Montana's imposition of a severance tax for coal, 90% of which was shipped outside the state. The challengers asserted that the tax violated the fair-relation requirement because it brought into the state's coffers about 100 times the amount that the state had to spend for roads, police protection, and other services attributable to intrastate coal

---

[97] *Jefferson Lines*, 514 U.S. at 201, 203–07 (Breyer, J., joined by O'Connor, J., dissenting).

[98] *Id.* at 186 (majority opinion).

[99] *Id.* at 188.

[100] *Id.* at 204 (Breyer, J., dissenting).

[101] *Id.* at 196 n.7 (majority opinion).

[102] *Id.*

[103] *Complete Auto Transit*, 430 U.S. at 279.

[104] 453 U.S. 609 (1981).

mining.[105] The Court, however, found that the challengers, in making this argument, "completely misunderstood the nature of the inquiry under the fourth prong," which Montana had satisfied simply by tying its tax to the amount of coal extracted from the earth.[106] It is not surprising, in light of this holding, that a leading authority has written that "[t]he 'fairly related test' appears to have little independent significance."[107]

In *Commonwealth Edison*, however, the Court signaled that the fair-relation requirement might well continue to play a meaningful role in judicial assessments of state user fees. Distinguishing earlier decisions involving such exactions, the Court emphasized that *Commonwealth Edison* itself did not involve "user charges," but instead concerned a "true" tax in the "technical sense."[108] The Court also suggested that the dormant Commerce Clause might require a tighter linkage between the value of services provided and the level of user fees exacted in connection with those services because such fees partake "of a rent charged by the State, based upon its proprietary interest in its public property."[109] This seemingly simple pronouncement, however, has given rise to a significant analytical conundrum, to which we now turn.

E. THE DORMANCY DOCTRINE AND STATE USER FEES

As *Commonwealth Edison* illustrates, the Court's rulings indicate that the *Complete Auto Transit* test extends to state-imposed user fees—that is, fees of the sort that the state might impose on individuals who make use of its landfill services, college education programs, parks, and so forth. Indeed, the Court in *Commonwealth Edison* went one step further, by suggesting that these fees are subject to an even more probing scrutiny under the *Complete Auto Transit* test than applies to ordinary taxes, at least with regard to the fair-relation requirement. There is reason to conclude, however, that this suggestion makes no sense. After all, the imposition of state user fees would seem to fit squarely within the rubric of "market participation," which (as we have seen) is *wholly exempt* from *any* dormant Commerce Clause review.[110] Put another way, the Court's distinctly activist Commerce Clause user-fee jurisprudence seems to

---

105 *Id.* at 620 n.10.

106 *Id.* at 621.

107 Walter Hellerstein, *State Taxation and the Supreme Court,* 1989 SUP. CT. REV. 223, 244–45.

108 *Commonwealth Edison,* 453 U.S. at 622 n.12 (internal quotations omitted).

109 *Id.* (internal quotations omitted).

110 *See supra* Section 20.D.

be set on a "collision course" with its distinctly hands-off approach to state market participation.[111] What is going on here?

According to one account, the underlying problem stems from the fact that the Court has not shown care in its use of the user-fee label. It has broadly proclaimed, for example, that the term embraces any "charges imposed by the State for the use of state-owned or state-provided transportation *or other facilities and services*."[112] In actuality, however, the Court has never invoked, and could not logically invoke, the dormant Commerce Clause to invalidate resident-favoring price discrimination in the sale of items such as educational services or state-made products.[113] In *Reeves, Inc. v. Stake*,[114] for example, the Court held that South Dakota could totally prohibit non-residents from purchasing the state's cement. Because the greater power of total exclusion must include the lesser power of partial exclusion, it seems obvious that the state could let out-of-state buyers enter this market even while charging them a higher price than it might impose on its own residents.

What, then, is one to make of cases like *Commonwealth Edison*, which suggest that the *Complete Auto Transit* test applies—and, indeed, applies with an elevated potency—in the user-fee context? Close inspection reveals that the Court has taken this approach *only* in assessing the constitutionality of user fees charged in making available to interstate operators the *channels of interstate commerce*.[115] The underlying idea thus seems to be that a state, just as surely as it may not invoke the market-participant label to dodge the dormant Commerce Clause in roadway-regulation cases such as *Kassel v. Consolidated Freightways Corp.*,[116] likewise may not invoke the market-participant exception as it seeks to charge discriminatory user fees for access to state-owned highways, wharves, or airports. Indeed, the national interest in keeping these channels of commerce wide open is so strong that, as *Commonwealth Edison* indicates, the Court has intensified the "fair relationship" inquiry in this context.[117]

---

111 Dan T. Coenen, *State User Fees and the Dormant Commerce Clause*, 50 VAND. L. REV. 795, 802 (1997).

112 *Or. Waste Sys.*, 511 U.S. at 103 n.6 (internal quotation and alteration omitted).

113 *See* Coenen, *supra* note 111, at 807 n.60.

114 447 U.S. 429 (1980).

115 *See* Coenen, *supra* note 111, at 816–23 (emphasis added).

116 450 U.S. 662 (1981).

117 *See generally supra* Section 20.D.2.d (discussing in greater detail the channels-of commerce limit on the market-participant exception to the dormant Commerce Clause doctrine, including by noting user-fee rulings from the Seventh Circuit that, while failing to discuss this posited channels-of-commerce limit, seem to cut back on it, if not reject it altogether).

The bottom line is that the market-participant rule will shelter from dormant Commerce Clause attack many, perhaps most, state decisions about setting prices for goods and services that a state chooses to sell. When, however, the state charges "user fees" for access to roads and other components of the national transportation infrastructure, not only does the market-participant exception fall away but an amped-up version of the fair-relationship test seems to mandate that the "rent charged by the state" must align with the actual value of the property or service that the state provides.[118]

118 *Commonwealth Edison*, 453 U.S. at 622 n.12 (internal quotations omitted).

Chapter 22

THE DORMANT FOREIGN COMMERCE CLAUSE

As the previous several chapters have documented, the courts have applied the dormant Commerce Clause in many cases to invalidate state laws that discriminate against or unduly burden interstate commerce. But Article I, section 8, clause 3 addresses not just "Commerce . . . among the several states"; it also targets "Commerce with foreign Nations . . . and with the Indian Tribes."[1] A question thus arises: To what extent do the dormancy-doctrine rules forged by the Court to handle interstate-commerce cases carry over to state regulations of foreign and Indian commerce? A later chapter deals with state-based encroachments on Native nations' commercial (and noncommercial) affairs.[2] The remainder of this chapter considers the constitutional rules that govern state laws that impede commerce in the international arena.

The Court's treatment of state laws that impinge on foreign commerce reflects two core ideas. First, the grant of the power over foreign commerce renders invalid, of its own force, state laws that clash with Congress's properly exclusive role in this field.[3] Second, state interferences with foreign commerce receive a stricter examination than would apply to similar interferences with interstate trade.[4] The cornerstone case on both points is *Japan Line, Ltd. v. County of Los Angeles*,[5] in which the Court encountered a challenge to the application of a county-imposed tax on shipping containers used exclusively to move goods across international borders.[6] The levy targeted the value of the containers present in the county on a specified day, which was fairly illustrative of the value of

---

1 U.S. CONST. art. I, § 8, cl. 3.

2 *See infra* Section 25.A.4.

3 *See* Buttfield v. Stranahan, 192 U.S. 470, 492–93 (1904) (describing congressional power over foreign commerce as "exclusive"); Bd. of Trustees of Univ. of Ill. v. United States, 289 U.S. 48, 56–57 (1933) (describing Congress's foreign commerce power as "exclusive and plenary"). *See generally* Barry Friedman & Daniel T. Deacon, *A Course Unbroken: The Constitutional Legitimacy of the Dormant Commerce Clause*, 97 VA. L. REV. 1877, 1910 (2011) (noting general recognition of the Framers' intention to assign the foreign commerce power exclusively to Congress).

4 *See, e.g.*, Bowman v. Chi. & Nw. Ry., 125 U.S. 465, 482 (1888) (noting that "[i]t may be argued that . . . the inference to be drawn from the absence of legislation by [C]ongress on the subject excludes state legislation affecting commerce with foreign nations more strongly than that affecting commerce among the states").

5 441 U.S. 434 (1979).

6 *Id.* at 436.

the containers present in the county on each day of the year.[7] In an opinion written by Justice Blackmun, the Court first concluded that this taxing methodology fully satisfied each of the four requirements applicable to interstate commerce under the *Complete Auto Transit* framework.[8] But Justice Blackmun's majority opinion then went on to hold that, because this tax targeted foreign commerce, it had to surmount two additional constitutional hurdles. Specifically, the county had to show that the tax would neither (1) expose the taxpayer to overlapping international tax obligations nor (2) "impair federal uniformity in an area where federal uniformity is essential."[9] These additional requirements, the Court explained, sprang from the particular concern that a state law that failed to meet these supplementary demands would result in extreme unfairness for businesses engaged in multinational activity and prevent the "Nation from 'speaking with one voice' in regulating foreign commerce."[10]

As to the first of these two additional requirements, Justice Blackmun began by observing that judicial enforcement of *Complete Auto Transit*'s fair-apportionment standard tended to ensure that "multiple burdens . . . cannot occur" even when different states impose a levy on the same tax base.[11] When it came to international taxation, however, "the same conclusion . . . logically cannot be drawn."[12] This complication arose from the inability of federal courts to subject foreign nations to made-in-America fair-apportionment rules. As Justice Blackmun explained: "Due to the absence of an authoritative tribunal capable of ensuring that the aggregation of taxes is computed on no more than one full value, a state tax, even though 'fairly apportioned' to reflect an instrumentality's presence within the State, may subject foreign commerce 'to the risk of a double tax burden to which [domestic] commerce is not exposed and which the commerce clause forbids.' "[13] Indeed, the facts of *Japan Line* itself vividly illustrated this difficulty because the Los Angeles County tax, though fairly apportioned, turned out to be unquestionably duplicative in its real-world impact. This doubling-up problem arose because Japan taxed the full value of the same shipping containers, with no apportionment at all, and the federal courts could not lift a finger to alter that sovereign nation's taxing choice. Thus, *Japan Line* in effect added a fifth, overlapping-tax-

---

7 *Id.* at 437.

8 *Id.* at 445.

9 *Id.* at 447–48.

10 *Id.* at 451 (quoting Michelin Tire Corp. v. Wages, 423 U.S. 276, 285 (1976)).

11 *Id.* at 447 (quoting Dep't of Revenue v. Ass'n of Wash. Stevedoring Cos., 435 U.S. 734, 746–747 (1978)).

12 *Id.*

13 *Id.* at 447–48 (quoting *Evco v. Jones*, 409 U.S. 91, 94 (1972)).

minded requirement to the ordinary *Complete Auto Transit* framework, and the challenged Los Angeles County levy turned out, particularly in light of Japan's taxing policy, to run afoul of this specialized foreign-commerce-related rule.

The Court also concluded that the county's levy abridged the dormant Foreign Commerce Clause's newly installed sixth requirement for state taxes—namely, that the tax not "impair federal uniformity in an area where federal uniformity is essential."[14] In this case, special difficulties arose because both the United States and Japan had entered into a customs convention that exempted shipping containers temporarily within the borders of a signatory nation from "all duties and taxes whatsoever chargeable by reason of importation."[15] No less important, the purpose of the convention was to free up signatory states to impose just the sort of unapportioned container tax that Japan had put in place. Against this backdrop, the Court found that the challenged exaction impermissibly compromised the "attainment of federal uniformity" because it "create[d] an asymmetry in international maritime taxation operating to Japan's disadvantage."[16] The Justices were especially concerned that "[t]he risk of retaliation by Japan, under these circumstances, is acute, and such retaliation of necessity would be felt by the Nation as a whole."[17]

In some later cases, courts have traveled the same route as *Japan Line* in finding that state or local tax laws offend the

---

[14] *Id.* at 448.

[15] *Id.* at 453.

[16] *Id.*

[17] *Id.* Notably, and importantly, the Court did not purport to rest this conclusion on a determination—at least in the orthodox sense—that the convention itself preempted state law. *See generally infra* Chapter 24. Nonetheless, the convention, in setting forth national "policy" regarding international shipping containers, obviously played a key role in establishing the unlawfulness of the challenged local tax under the essential-uniformity test. *Japan Line*, 441 U.S. at 453. The broader point may be that preemption analysis and dormant Commerce Clause analysis can act in synergistic ways. And to the extent that these two modes of analysis differ in this context, it is more than fair to describe the distinction—in the apt words of the leading authorities on the subject—as "a mystifying one at best." JEROME R. HELLERSTEIN, WALTER HELLERSTEIN & JOHN A. SWAIN, STATE TAXATION ¶ 4.21[2] (3d ed. 1998 with 2021 cumulative supp.); *see also* Walter Hellerstein, *States' Power to Tax Foreign Commerce Dominates Supreme Court's 1978 Agenda*, 51 J. TAX'N 106 (1979). For suggestions that the Court has retreated from its endorsement in *Japan Line* of the essential-uniformity test, see Jack L. Goldsmith, *Federal Courts, Foreign Affairs, and Federalism*, 83 VA. L. REV. 1617, 1705 (1997) (indicating that, "[a]s for the one-voice test in dormant Foreign Commerce Clause cases," the Court's later decision in *Barclays Bank PLC v. Franchise Tax Board*, 512 U.S. 298 (1994), "effectively eliminated it"); and Matthew Schaefer, *Constraints on State-Level Foreign Policy: (Re)Justifying, Refining and Distinguishing the Dormant Foreign Affairs Doctrine*, 41 SETON HALL L. REV. 201, 279–82 (2011) (stating that "it appears that the Court is gradually moving towards giving up the entire exercise of engaging in analysis under prong two of *Japan Line*").

specialized foreign-commerce-tax rules laid down in that seminal decision.[18] In other cases, the courts have distinguished *Japan Line* by finding that the challenged taxing measure satisfies all six constitutional requisites that now apply in this context.[19] Courts also

---

[18] *See, e.g.*, Harris Cty. Appraisal Dist. v. Transamerica Container Leasing, Inc. 920 S.W.2d 678 (Tex. App.1995), discussed *infra* note 19. One question that has arisen in the wake of *Japan Line* concerns the interaction between its teachings and the nondiscrimination prong of the *Complete Auto Transit* test. Extensive litigation has resulted, for example, from California's decision to exempt imported goods from its ad valorem tax, thus placing interstate shippers of such goods at a competitive disadvantage in relation to foreign competitors. Challenges to this taxing structure pinged-ponged through the courts, including the Supreme Court of the United States, culminating in a ruling by the California Supreme Court that this brand of uneven treatment does indeed violate the non-discrimination principle. *See* Star-Kist Foods, Inc. v. Cty. of Los Angeles, 719 P.2d 987, 995 (Cal. 1986). For further treatment of this litigation, see HELLERSTEIN, HELLERSTEIN & SWAIN, *supra* note 17, ¶ 4.24. For another application of the anti-discrimination rule in the foreign-commerce context, see *Kraft General Foods v. Iowa Department of Revenue & Finance*, 505 U.S. 71, 79–81 (1992) (invalidating an Iowa law that treated as taxable income dividends received from foreign but not domestic subsidiaries). *But see* Michael T. Fatale, *Foreign Commerce Clause Discrimination*, 72 BAYLOR L. REV. 47 (2020) (urging reconsideration of *Kraft General Foods* in light of intervening legal developments).

[19] For an important case of this genre, see *Itel Containers Int'l Corp. v. Huddleston*, 507 U.S. 60 (1993). There the state applied its sales tax to the in-state transfer of international shipping containers. In upholding the tax, the court found *Japan Line* distinguishable on two grounds. First, it turned out that—unlike in *Japan Lines* itself—no actually duplicative foreign tax existed, thus greatly reducing multiple-taxation worries. Second, the state granted a credit against the tax for any other proper tax payments made (including to foreign nations) as a result of the same sale transaction, thus addressing even the limited possibility that multiple international taxation might occur. In these circumstances, the Court concluded that "*Japan Line* does not require forbearance" by the state in a way that is "so extreme or so one-sided." *Id.* at 74 (internal quotations omitted); *see also* Air China Ltd. v. San Mateo Cty., 93 Cal. Rptr. 3d 893, 899 (Cal. Ct. App. 1st Dist. 2009) (finding no constitutional violation in a county property tax applied to Air China's interests, including landing rights, tied to the San Francisco International Airport "because the property being taxed is fixed permanently within the County and not subject to taxation in any other location, including the [People's Republic of China]"). In *Harris County, see supra* note 18, the Court found *Japan Line* controlling and *Itel* distinguishable because the challenged property tax imposed on international shipping containers neither (1) targeted only discrete transactions occurring within the state because it instead applied to items that in their nature routinely move through international commerce, nor (2) afforded any credit for the payment of overlapping taxes. *Harris Cty.*, 920 S.W.2d at 684–85; *see also* Container Corp. of America v. Franchise Tax Board, 463 U.S. 159, 193 (1983) (upholding a scheme for apportioning corporate income despite some evidence of multiple taxation; distinguishing *Japan Line* on the ground that it involved clear multiple taxation tied to the use of instrumentalities of foreign commerce and refusing in the end "to require California to give up one allocation method that sometimes results in double taxation in favor of another allocation method that also sometimes results in double taxation"); *Barclays Bank*, 512 U.S. 298 (carrying over the state-tax-supporting principles of *Container Corp* from domestically based multinational conglomerates to foreign-based conglomerates); Mobil Oil Corp. v. Commissioner of Taxes, 445 U.S. 425, 448 (1980) (rejecting challenges to Vermont's taxation of the foreign-source dividend income of an international petroleum firm, pursuant to apportionment on a unitary-business theory, in the face of an argument that only allocation of this income to a single state could adequately reduce the danger of duplicative taxation by state and foreign-nation taxing authorities; distinguishing *Japan Line* based on (1) the capacity of U.S. courts

have drawn on *Japan Line* in cases involving state regulatory measures.[20] Of particular importance, the Court has signaled the need for hesitation in applying the market-participant exception to the dormant Commerce Clause when foreign, rather than interstate, commerce is disrupted by a challenged state law.[21] Building on this line of authority, the First Circuit has gone so far as to suggest that the exception is wholly inapplicable to cases involving foreign commerce.[22]

---

to guard against any risk of such duplicative taxation by requiring fair apportionment of the unitary-business tax base among Vermont and other income-tax-imposing states; (2) the inappropriateness of carrying over to the income-tax context *Japan Line's* treatment of a property tax applied to "instrumentalities of foreign commerce"; and (3) the absence of any real-world duplicative taxation attributable to Vermont's taxation of its fairly apportioned share of the firm's foreign-dividend income). For a case in which the Court found no abridgment of the essential-uniformity test, see *Wardair Can., Inc. v. Fla. Dep't of Revenue*, 477 U.S. 1, 7–13 (1986) (declining to invalidate a Florida tax on sales of aviation fuel used by international carriers on this basis because "the United States has at least acquiesced in state taxation" of such transactions over a long stretch of time); *see also Air China Ltd.*, 93 Cal Rptr. 3d at 900 (rejecting the "one voice" challenge because the operative tax concerned property and the relevant treaty addressed only "income and profits"). For a post-*Japan Line* case in which a one-voice problem took center stage, see *Springfield Rare Coin Galleries, Inc. v. Johnson*, 503 N.E.2d 300, 307 (Ill. 1986) (emphasizing the one-voice principle in invalidating a state's removal of South African coins and medallions from an otherwise applicable sales-tax exemption because "disapproval of the political and social policies of a foreign nation does not provide a valid basis for a tax classification by this State"; relying in the end, however, on the requirement of "reasonable classification" imposed by the state constitution, rather than the dormant Commerce Clause to strike down the challenged measure). For a more general treatment of the subject, see HELLERSTEIN, HELLERSTEIN & SWAIN, *supra* note 17, ¶¶ 8.17[3][a] & [b] (questioning, among other things, why state taxes that interact with foreign nations' taxes should be treated similarly to state taxes that interact with other state taxes and suggesting that courts might instead analogize taxes imposed by foreign nations to taxes imposed by the United States itself, thus removing constitutional concerns about multiple international taxation since overlapping state and federal taxation plainly do not raise constitutional concerns of this kind).

20 *See* Antilles Cement Corp. v. Calderon, 288 F. Supp. 2d 187, 195–96 (D.P.R. 2003) (applying the *Japan Line* methodology in invalidating a ban on the use of non-Puerto Rican cement in government-funded construction projects), *rev'd sub nom.* Antilles Cement Corp. v. Fortuno, 670 F.3d 310 (1st Cir. 2012) (finding *Japan Line* inapplicable in light of the antecedent conclusion that Puerto Rico had acted as a market participant); Portland Pipe Line Corp. v. City of S. Portland, 332 F. Supp. 3d 264, 316 (D. Maine 2018) (upholding local oil tanker regulations as they did not "interfere with the federal government's ability to 'speak with one voice' when regulating commercial relations with foreign governments" (quoting *Japan Line*, 441 U.S. at 449)); Cavel Int'l, Inc. v. Madigan, 500 F.3d 551, 558–59 (7th Cir. 2007) (upholding an Illinois ban on slaughtering horses for human consumption in part because there was little threat of the kind of international retaliation the Court feared in *Japan Line*).

21 *See supra* Section 20.D.

22 *See* Nat'l Foreign Trade Council v. Natsios, 181 F.3d 38, 66 (1st Cir. 1999) (expressing disagreement with the Third Circuit on this point), *aff'd on other grounds sub nom.* Crosby v. Nat'l Foreign Trade Council, 530 U.S. 363 (2000); *see generally* Brannon P. Denning & Jack H. McCall, Jr., *The Constitutionality of State and Local "Sanctions" Against Foreign Countries: Affairs of State, States' Affairs, or a Sorry State*

The broader lesson of these cases is apparent: Whenever a state law impinges on foreign affairs, lawyers challenging that law can advance at least one of three separate lines of attack. First, the facts might support a claim that the law offends implied constitutional limits that apply in an across-the-board fashion to all state measures that interfere unduly with federal authority in this field.[23] Second, a preemption-based argument might find support in specialized state-disfavoring rules that apply when the case involves international relations.[24] Third, *Japan Line* may provide a basis for attacking the law not only under doctrines that limit state interference with foreign affairs as a general matter, or based on a theory of statutory preemption, but also under the constitutional restraint that targets in a focused way those state laws that threaten the free flow of international trade.[25]

---

of Affairs, 26 HASTINGS CONST. L.Q. 307, 351–68 (1999) (arguing that the market-participant exception should not apply in foreign-commerce cases).

[23] *See supra* Section 15.B.4.

[24] *See infra* Chapter 24.

[25] For some reflections on how these three separate doctrines intersect, see Goldsmith, *supra* note 17, at 1637 (suggesting that the "so-called one-voice test" applicable in general to state interferences with foreign affairs "is functionally identical to dormant foreign relations preemption"); Schaefer, *supra* note 17, at 209, 269 (commenting on this similarity and noting that "the relationship between the dormant foreign affairs doctrine and the dormant Foreign Commerce Clause is not well-understood").

Chapter 23

THE PRIVILEGES AND IMMUNITIES CLAUSE

Analysis

Sec.

The dormant Commerce Clause does not stand alone as a constitutional bulwark against state interferences with the goal of fostering union. Several express prohibitions set forth in the Constitution—including the Full Faith and Credit, Import-Export, and Tonnage Clauses—operate in more targeted ways to promote the same end.[1] One clause of the Constitution, however, has done particularly heavy lifting in transforming the residents of diverse states into citizens of a single, unitary nation: the Privileges and Immunities Clause of Article IV, section 2. That Clause declares that "Citizens of each State shall be entitled to all Privileges and Immunities of Citizens in the several states,"[2] thus ensuring that, as the Court has put it, "a citizen of State A who ventures into State B [has] the same privileges which the citizens of State B enjoy."[3] Thus, for instance, the clause bars states from denying basic police protection, or access to local doctors' offices or stores, to nonresidents simply because they are nonresidents.[4] There are, however,

---

1 *See supra* Section 15.A.

2 U.S. CONST. art. IV, § 2.

3 Toomer v. Witsell, 334 U.S. 385, 395 (1948). It merits emphasis that the Privileges *and* Immunities Clause of Article IV, which focuses on ensuring the *equal treatment* of nonresidents present within a state vis-à-vis state residents, is to be distinguished from the Privileges *or* Immunities Clause of the Fourteenth Amendment, which affords to all citizens at all times an entirely separate (though limited) set of *substantive rights* against state infringement. For a brief discussion of the Privileges or Immunities Clause, see *supra* Section 15.A.

4 *See* LAURENCE H. TRIBE, AMERICAN CONSTITUTIONAL LAW § 6–37, at 1264 (3d ed., 2000); *see also* Jonathan D. Varat, *State "Citizenship" and Interstate Equality*, 48 U. CHI. L. REV. 487, 539 (1981) (discussing the Privileges and Immunities Clause and related constitutional limits in detail). For detailed historical treatments of the clause, see Stewart Jay, *Origins of the Privileges and Immunities of State Citizenship under*

Article IV, 45 LOY. U. CHI. L.J. 1, 15–19 (2013), and Kurt T. Lash, *The Origins of the Privileges or Immunities Clause, Part I: "Privileges and Immunities" as an Antebellum Term of Art*, 98 GEO. L.J. 1241, 1258–1263 (2010) (highlighting the background of the Privileges *and* Immunities Clause of Article IV in the context of a broader discussion of the Privileges *or* Immunities Clause of the Fourteenth Amendment). In keeping with the clause's focus on barring discrimination against outsiders by self-interested states, the courts have held that it does not apply to actions taken by the federal government, *see* Pollack v. Duff, 793 F.3d 34, 40–45 (D.C. Cir. 2015) (collecting supportive rulings from other circuits and providing an extended discussion of the historical evidence on this point, including some evidence that cuts against the court's position); Robinson v. Huerta, 123 F. Supp. 3d 30, 44 (D.D.C. 2015) (noting that the Clause is "inapplicable to a suit against the federal government"); Maynard v. U.S. Dist. Court, 701 F. Supp. 738, 740 (C.D. Cal. 1988) ("[T]he Privileges and Immunities Clause has been construed as a limitation on powers of the states and not on powers of the Federal Government."), *aff'd*, 915 F.2d 1581 (9th Cir. 1990), even when it legislates with regard to local matters concerning the District of Columbia. *See* Duehay v. Acacia Mut. Life Ins. Co., 105 F.2d 768, 775 (D.C. Cir. 1939) (holding that the Privileges and Immunities Clause "is a limitation upon the powers of the states and in no way affects the powers of Congress over the territories and the District of Columbia"); Neild v. District of Columbia, 110 F.2d 246, 249 n.3 (D.C. Cir. 1940) (following *Duehay*). Several additional questions have long been raised by the clause. One is whether the clause applies to laws made applicable in the District not by the nationally representative Congress but instead by local D.C. officials exercising powers delegated to them by prior congressional action. *See* Metro. Washington Chapter v. District of Columbia, 57 F. Supp. 3d 1, 20–21 (D.D.C. 2014) (assuming that the clause is applicable, without resolving the question, in light of the litigation position taken by the District). A related question concerns the extent to which the Privileges and Immunities Clause is applicable to laws adopted by territorial legislatures, which likewise are empowered to act by Congress. In *Haavik v. Alaska Packers' Ass'n*, 263 U.S. 510 (1924), the Court appeared to declare that the Privileges and Immunities Clause did not, of its own force, preclude actions by territorial governments under which "[o]nly residents of the territory are preferred," so that "citizens of every state are treated alike." *Id.* at 515. *See* Anderson v. Mullaney, 191 F.2d 123, 134 (9th Cir. 1951) (viewing *Haavik* as holding that "Article IV, Sec. 2, had no application" to the then-territory of Alaska), *aff'd*, 342 U.S. 415 (1952). In its ruling in the just-cited *Mullaney* case, however, the Supreme Court raised significant questions about this view of *Haavik* by describing the "real issue," and the resulting "constitutional holding," in that case as involving only whether there is a "power of Congress *to relieve* the Territory of some of the restrictions applicable to a state." *Mullaney*, 342 U.S. at 419 (emphasis added). As it turns out, however, this is largely a moot issue because Congress has generally subjected territorial governments by way of statute to the same duties that the Privileges and Immunities Clause places on the states. *See, e.g.*, Barnard v. Thorstenn, 489 U.S. 546, 552 (1989) (noting that Congress by statute extended Privileges and Immunities Clause protections to nonresidents of the Virgin Islands); Chase Manhattan Bank v. South Acres Dev. Co., 434 U.S. 236, 238 (1978) (reaching the same conclusion as to Guam): Mailloux v. Mailloux, 554 F.2d 976, 978 (9th Cir. 1977) ("Congress intended that Guam should be treated as if it were a state for the purpose of applying the privileges and immunities clause.") *rev'd on other grounds sub nom.* Chase Manhattan Bank v. South Acres Dev. Co., 434 U.S. 236 (1978); Romeu v. Cohen, 265 F.3d 118, 127 & n.3 (2d Cir. 2001) (finding no need to decide whether Article IV protections apply when nonresidents travel to territories because, in any event, "Congress has extended the Privileges and Immunities Clause to Puerto Rico"). A further question concerns whether residents of the District of Columbia or of U.S. territories are protected by the Privileges and Immunities Clause when they travel into states, and the answer to that question—in tit-for-tat fashion—might well hinge on whether courts determine that the clause does put limits on the District and on territorial governments. A final question concerns whether the Privileges and Immunities Clause—as opposed, for example, to the Equal Protection Clause—protects non-U.S. citizens who reside in one state when they visit another. The clause's repeated reference to "Citizens," in contrast to its use of the words important limits on the protective scope of the Privileges and Immunities Clause, and these limits—together with other features of its operation—cause it to differ from the dormant Commerce Clause rule in significant ways.

A. THE PRIVILEGES AND IMMUNITIES CLAUSE AND THE DORMANT COMMERCE CLAUSE: AN INTRODUCTORY COMPARISON

How do the restrictions placed on states by the Privileges and Immunities Clause differ from those imposed by the dormancy doctrine?[5] First, the Privileges and Immunities Clause, in contrast to the dormant Commerce Clause principle, affords no protection to corporations or other non-individual plaintiffs.[6] Thus, for example, Reeves, Inc. (a Wyoming corporation) could not have challenged under the Privileges and Immunities Clause South Dakota's overtly discriminatory ban on cement sales to nonresidents, even though its corporate status did not foreclose a dormant Commerce Clause challenge.[7] Second, the Privileges and Immunities Clause targets only a state's *discriminatory treatment* of nonresidents, while dormant Commerce Clause doctrine reaches further by rendering facially neutral laws subject to invalidation pursuant to the *Pike*-balancing formula.[8] For this reason, even individual truck operators,

---

"person" or "persons" in other settings, suggests that the answer is "no." But the Court's repeated declarations that "the terms 'citizen' and 'resident' are essentially interchangeable" for purposes of the clause, *see* Austin v. New Hampshire, 420 U.S. 656, 662 n.8 (1975)—together, perhaps, with considerations of basic decency—might provide a basis for reaching the opposite conclusion.

5 *See generally* Brannon P. Denning, *Why the Privileges and Immunities Clause of Article IV Cannot Replace the Dormant Commerce Clause Doctrine*, 88 MINN. L. REV. 384 (2003) (detailing differences between the clauses).

6 *See* Tenn. Wine & Spirits Retailers Ass'n v. Thomas, 139 S. Ct. 2449, 2460–61 (2019) (striking down a two-year durational-residency requirement for retail alcohol licenses on dormant Commerce Clause grounds while expressly noting that "the Privileges and Immunities Clause has been interpreted not to protect corporations"). The seminal ruling on this point is *Paul v. Virginia*, 75 U.S. (8 Wall.) 168 (1868).

7 *See* Reeves, Inc. v. Stake, 447 U.S. 429 (1980) (discussed *supra* Section 20.D). Of course, this principle forecloses use of the Privileges and Immunities Clause by the large numbers of other corporate plaintiffs that typically (and often successfully) bring dormant Commerce Clause challenges. *See, e.g.*, Dean Milk Co. v. City of Madison, 340 U.S. 349 (1951).

8 *See supra* Chapter 18. With regard to the separate question whether, if ever, the Privileges and Immunities Clause outlaws measures that discriminate only in effect against nonresidents, the Court has offered very little guidance, although it has indicated that some laws will run afoul of the clause even if they do not distinguish in express terms between residents and nonresidents. Thus, in *Chalker v. Birmingham & Northwest Railway Co.*, 249 U.S. 522 (1919), the Court invoked the clause to invalidate a state tax imposed at a higher level on individuals whose principal office was located outside the state, whether or not they resided in the state, because "the chief office of an individual is commonly in the State of which he is a citizen." *Id.* at 527. In *Hillside Dairy, Inc. v. Lyons*, 539 U.S. 59 (2003), the Court reaffirmed that successful pursuit of a Privileges and Immunities Clause claim does not require "an

who could have prevailed on a dormant Commerce Clause theory in a truck-length case like *Kassel v. Consolidated Freightways Corp.*,[9] would not be able to successfully invoke the Privileges and Immunities Clause in such a case, at least unless the challenged rule somehow generated discrimination in "practical effect" between in-state and out-of-state residents.[10] Third, while only the nonresidents of a state enjoy protections against it under the Privileges and Immunities Clause,[11] both residents and nonresidents can also

---

express statement in [state] laws and regulations identifying out-of-state citizenship as a basis for disparate treatment." *Id.* at 67. The Court added that: "Whether *Chalker* should be interpreted as merely applying the Clause to classifications that are but proxies for differential treatment against out-of-state residents, or as prohibiting any classification with the practical effect of discriminating against such residents, is a matter we need not decide." *Id.*

9 450 U.S. 662 (1981); *see also supra* Section 18.A.1 (discussing the decision).

10 *See supra* note 8. For a lower-court ruling that touches on this subject, see *Schoenefeld v. Schneiderman*, 821 F.3d 273, 280, 284 (2d Cir. 2016) (reading the Supreme Court's *McBurney* decision, *see infra* note 35, to bar state laws "only [when] enacted for the protectionist purpose of burdening out-of-state-citizens"; also finding that the state law at issue, which required nonresident lawyers to maintain an office in New York, although residents could work from their homes, was not marked by a protectionist purpose because it was initially enacted to expand, rather than contract, nonresidents' practice opportunities; also reasoning that, even today, the law "place[s] admitted resident and nonresident attorneys on an equal footing" by requiring that "*every* attorney . . . must have a presence in the state in the form of a physical premises" (emphasis in original) (internal quotations omitted)). For an earlier case that upheld a similar restriction without focusing on concerns about a protectionist purpose, see *Kleinsmith v. Shurtleff*, 571 F.3d 1033, 1044 (10th Cir. 2009) (upholding a statute that required all Utah-based attorneys acting as trust-deed trustees to "maintain a place" within the state despite the challenger's claim that the law favored residents who could work from home; reasoning that "[r]esident and nonresident attorney trustees alike are subject to the same requirement: they must maintain a place in Utah where the trustor can meet with the trustee to request information and deliver money and documents"). Another possible problem with applying the Privileges and Immunities Clause to practically burdensome but facially nondiscriminatory laws emanates from its textual protection only of nonresidents "*in* the several states." For example, the nonresident road users primarily disadvantaged by the Iowa truck-length law at issue in *Kassel*, *see supra* Section 18.A.2, were not discriminated against, if at all, during the times in which they were physically present in Iowa. Rather, they were disadvantaged precisely because they did not drive through Iowa at all as result of facially neutral Iowa and non-Iowa laws that caused truck travel to move through neighboring jurisdictions. *See* Donald H. Regan, *The Supreme Court and State Protectionism: Making Sense of the Dormant Commerce Clause*, 84 MICH. L. REV. 1091, 1203–05 & n.236 (1986). It might well be that the Court would authorize the bringing of actions based on claimed mistreatment of this sort if the plaintiff could establish that the thus-induced circumvention of the state's roadway network constituted (as it seemingly would) a remediable injury in fact for jurisdictional purposes. *See infra* Section 35.D. It remains to be seen, however, whether the Court might draw upon the "in the . . . states" text of Article IV, in this sort of suit or in other cases to limit the protections that the Privileges and Immunities Clause affords.

11 *See, e.g.*, Bradwell v. Illinois, 83 U.S. 130, 138 (1873) ("The protection designed by that clause, as has been repeatedly held, has no application to a citizen of the state whose laws are complained of. If the plaintiff was a citizen of the State of Illinois, that provision of the Constitution gave her no protection against its courts or its legislation."); *accord, e.g.*, Chadwick v. Kelley, 187 U.S. 540, 546–47 (1903).

secure relief against a state under the dormant Commerce Clause.[12] Indeed, it is not uncommon for residents a state who engage in interstate commerce to succeed on dormancy-doctrine claims because they are treated less favorably than other residents of that state who do not engage in such commerce.[13] Fourth, the Privileges and Immunities Clause differs from the dormancy doctrine in that the latter, but not the former, is clearly subject to a congressional-consent exception. That is, while Congress may legislatively authorize states to enact laws that would otherwise violate the dormant Commerce Clause, it cannot similarly authorize state actions that would run afoul of Article IV.[14] Fifth, the Court has

---

[12] A corollary of this point would seem to be that courts cannot apply the Privileges and Immunities Clause to strike down laws on the theory that they improperly *favor* nonresidents. In *Paradise Point, LLC v. Prince George's County*, 540 F. Supp. 3d 524 (D. Md. 2021), the court may have lost sight of this idea. That case involved a Maryland law that required Prince George's County, Maryland, to hold a specialized "limited" auction when selling tax-delinquent properties, with access to that auction granted only to county residents, in-county workers, veterans, and federal employees, thus excluding most nonresidents. The court first held that the challenged law implicated "the fundamental right of acquiring property within the state." *Id.* at 530; *see infra* Section 23.B (discussing the "fundamental interest" requirement). It then upheld the law insofar as it favored county residents and in-county workers on the theory that they "are more likely to make improvements on the distressed properties" than typical nonresidents. *Paradise Point,* 540 F. Supp. 3d at 532. The Court, however, did not stop there. It reasoned that, because this better-caretaker rationale did not support applying the statute in general to veterans and federal employees—including to the extent they lived outside the state—the law "failed to satisfy the Privileges and Immunities Clause" as applied to them. *Id.* at 533. The ruling is subject to criticism because, in effect, it drew upon the Privileges and Immunities Clause, which is designed to protect nonresidents from unfavorable treatment, to block the state from treating certain nonresidents—namely, veterans and federal employees—in a favorable way. Stated otherwise, while the nonresident-disfavoring result reached by the court might conceivably have been justified under the Equal Protection Clause, its nonresident-burdening effects make the outcome difficult to justify under the Privileges and Immunities Clause.

[13] *See, e.g.*, Comptroller of the Treasury v. Wynne, 575 U.S. 542 (2015) (upholding individual residents' challenge to a Maryland tax measure that disadvantaged them in relation to other residents). Another distinction would arise were courts to agree that noncitizens are *ipso facto* not "*Citizens* of [a] State" within the meaning of Article IV regardless of their state of residence. *See supra* note 4. There is no reason why, however, noncitizens injured by an impermissible burdening of interstate or foreign commerce cannot seek a remedy for such state overreaching under generally available dormancy rules. *See, e.g.*, Japan Line, Ltd. v. Cty. of Los Angeles, 441 U.S. 434 (1979); *see also supra* Chapter 22 (discussing this decision).

[14] Of particular importance, the core justification for recognizing the exception in the dormant Commerce Clause context—namely, that it is a sensible build-out of Congress's granted power to determine how interstate commerce should operate, *see supra* Section 16.A—has no application to the rights-establishing (and thus presumably irrevocable) protection afforded by the Privileges and Immunities Clause. *See* Piper v. Sup. Ct. of N.H., 723 F.2d 110, 113 (1st Cir. 1983) (en banc) (stating that Congress cannot override the protections afforded by the Privileges and Immunities Clause), *aff'd*, 470 U.S. 274 (1985); *see also* United States v. Wheeler, 254 U.S. 281, 294 (1920) (noting that the Privileges and Immunities Clause, like Article 4 of the Articles of Confederation, was meant to preserve national uniformity "not by lodging

declined to extend the "market participant" exception, recognized in dormant Commerce Clause cases, to its application of the Privileges and Immunities Clause—though, as we will see at the end of this chapter, there may be less to this distinction than first meets the eye.[15] A final distinction between these two protections has to do with the range of conduct at which they take aim. In particular, the dormant Commerce Clause, in contrast to the Privileges and Immunities Clause, deals only with commercial activity.[16] At the same time (and as detailed in the next section), the operation of the Privilege and Immunity Clause is restricted by a subject-matter coverage limit of its own: That Clause outlaws not all forms of state discrimination against nonresidents, but only such discrimination that touches on interests "which are, in their nature, fundamental"[17] or (to put the same point another way) are "basic to the maintenance or well-being of the Union."[18]

---

power in Congress" but instead by "inhibiting the power [of states] from being used to discriminate").

[15] *See infra* Section 23.D.

[16] It would seem to follow from *United States v. Lopez,* 514 U.S. 549 (1995), *see supra* Section 4.A (discussing the decision), that the Court lacks authority to disrupt nonresident-disfavoring state legislation concerning gun possession near schools by invoking the Commerce Clause in its dormant state, *but cf.* TRIBE, *supra* note 4, § 6–5, at 1050 n.1 (suggesting that a ban on possessing nonlocally, but not locally, produced guns might violate the dormant Commerce Clause), even though such a law would raise obvious Privileges and Immunities Clause problems. *See infra* notes 19–25 and accompanying text (noting the clause's safeguarding of nonresident's interests in "tak[ing], hold[ing] and dispos[ing] of property"). This is not to say that such a claim would present a slam-dunk case, and courts might well conclude that such a law concerns a non-fundamental, as opposed to a clause-protected fundamental interest. *See supra* note 33 (discussing past judicial treatment of nonresident-disfavoring concealed-weapon laws). In particular, one might characterize the relevant interest in this instance either broadly (that is, as the interest in using one's property in a gun) or narrowly (that is, as an interest in bringing a gun into a specifically defined and highly regulated area such as a school zone), and the result might well turn on which characterization the court endorses. In any event, the key point is simply that the Privileges and Immunities Clause may permit the Court to overturn some forms of noneconomic regulation that lay beyond the grasp of the dormant Commerce Clause principle. *See also* Lunding v. N.Y. Tax Appeals Tribunal, 522 U.S. 287 (1998) (invalidating under the Privileges and Immunities Clause a state law that provided a tax deduction for alimony payments only to residents and thus implicating a family-law related matter that may today fall outside the scope of the Commerce Clause's coverage).

[17] Corfield v. Coryell, 6 F. Cas. 546, 551 (C.C.E.D. Pa. 1823) (No. 3230) (Washington, J., Circuit Justice). *See., e.g.*, Austin v. New Hampshire, 420 U.S. 656, 661 (1975) (describing *Corfield* as "the first, and long the leading, explication of the Clause").

[18] Baldwin v. Fish and Game Comm'n, 436 U.S. 371, 388 (1978).

B. THE FUNDAMENTAL-INTEREST REQUIREMENT

What sorts of interests qualify as sufficiently basic to the Union to warrant Article IV protection? From the outset, courts have held that these interests include the right to ply a private trade, "to institute and maintain actions of any kind in the courts of the state," "to take, hold and dispose of property," and to be free of "higher taxes or impositions than are paid by the . . . citizens of the state."[19] In *Toomer v. Witsell*,[20] for example, the Court deemed the interest in engaging in commercial shrimping sufficiently fundamental to support invalidation of a state licensing fee imposed on nonresident shrimpers that was 100 times greater than the fee laid upon similarly situated resident competitors.[21] In *Supreme Court of New Hampshire v. Piper*,[22] the Court likewise struck down a law limiting bar membership to state residents after finding that the "opportunity to

---

19 *Corfield*, 6 F. Cas. at 552. With regard to the fundamental nature of having access to local courts, see *Miles v. Ill. Cent. R.R. Co.*, 315 U.S. 698, 704 (1942) ("To deny citizens from other states . . . access to its courts would, if it permitted access to its own citizens, violate the Privileges and Immunities Clause."), and *McKnett v. St. Louis & S.F. Ry. Co.*, 292 U.S. 230, 233 (1934) ("The privileges and immunities clause requires a state to accord to citizens of other states substantially the same right of access to its courts as it accords to its own citizens." (internal citations omitted)).

20 334 U.S. 385 (1948).

21 *Id.* at 389. A case in which a court distinguished *Toomer* was *Marilley v. Bonham*, 844 F.3d 841, 855 (9th Cir. 2016). There, the Ninth Circuit held that the Privileges and Immunities Clause did not bar California from charging higher fees to nonresidents than to residents for registrations, licenses, and permits for commercial fishing vessels. In Fiscal Year 2010–11, California had subsidized its commercial fishing industry, and the extra fees paid by nonresidents—varying between 2.6 and 3.3 times the fees paid by residents—offset by approximately $435,000 the resulting subsidy outlays they had received. The court found that the nonresident fees were "relatively modest" and that the revenue from the differentials was less than the amount that California had channeled to nonresidents as part of its subsidy program. *Id.* at 852. The court also noted the very different character of the unconstitutional commercial fishing fees in *Toomer* (involving a fee differential that was 100 times greater), and *Mullaney* (involving a differential that was 10 times greater). More specifically, it read *Toomer* as supporting state choices to charge varying fees so long as the added amounts paid by nonresidents served to provide fair compensation for state-provided benefits, as was the case in *Marilley*. Steering a somewhat different course, the Supreme Court of Alaska in *State v. Carlson*, 191 P.3d 137, 142–48 (Alaska 2008), struck down a 3:1 nonresident-resident fee-differential for state commercial-fishing licenses. The court determined that, in order to pass constitutional muster, the state—even though it could take some account of the differing overall tax-based contributions made to the state by residents and nonresidents—was duty-bound to produce a fee-charging scheme that bore a sufficiently close relationship to the goal of "equalizing the economic burden." *Id.* at 140. Applying this standard, the court found that the Alaska fee program was unsustainable because, even in those instances where the differential fee did tend to equalize overall benefits and burdens, that was solely "a matter of fortuity and nothing else." *Id.* at 145.

22 470 U.S. 274 (1985).

practice law" qualified as "fundamental."[23] And in *Doe v. Bolton*,[24] the Court overturned a Georgia residency requirement for obtaining abortions from privately operated hospitals and clinics on the ground that, if the clause "protects persons who enter other states to ply their trade, so must it protect persons who enter Georgia seeking the medical services that are available there."[25]

Cases such as *Toomer*, *Piper*, and *Doe* reveal that the Court's definition of "fundamental interests" is broad and multifaceted.[26] In *Baldwin v. Fish and Game Commission*,[27] however, the Court made clear that this legal category also has its limits. *Baldwin* concerned the common state practice of subjecting nonresidents to elevated fees

---

[23] *Id.* at 281. *Accord* Supreme Court of Va. v. Friedman, 487 U.S. 59 (1988) (relying largely on *Piper* to invalidate a Virginia rule that permitted residents but not nonresidents to secure admission to the bar based on past practice experience and without having to take the bar examination); *see also* Fraizer v. Heebe, 482 U.S. 641 (1987) (drawing in part on the Court's privilege-and-immunities rulings in overturning, based on its supervisory powers, a federal district court's membership rules that disadvantaged nonresidents).

[24] 410 U.S. 179 (1973).

[25] *Id.* at 200 (internal citations omitted).

[26] An additional illustration of the point, founded squarely on the nation-unifying purposes of the Privileges and Immunities Clause is provided by *Nelson v. Geringer*, 295 F.3d 1082 (10th Cir. 2002). There, the court held that service in the National Guard qualifies as a fundamental interest for purposes of the Privileges and Immunities Clause primarily because there are "few activities comparable to participating in national military service that tend to constitute United States citizens as 'one people' and to promote a sense and a mission of national unity." *Id.* at 1090. Building on this proposition, the court went on to hold that exclusion of nonresidents from serving in the second highest ranking National Guard positions in Wyoming bore upon a fundamental interest on its way to striking down a state law that excluded nonresidents from service in these roles. *Id.* at 1090–95. The Court rejected the argument that these positions implicated in a special way "the state's ability to function as a sovereign body," thus justifying resident-favoring discrimination in this context. *Id.* at 1090. The problem with this argument, according to the court, was that the National Guard in fact is "a dual state-federal organization" within which "the [second-in-command] position is, overall, primarily federal in nature." *Id.* at 1093. The court also rejected the state's effort to invoke the Article I, section 8, clause 16 text "reserving to the States respectively, the Appointment of the Officers" of the militia. The court concluded, albeit with little explanation, that this specialized state-protective provision did not create a "stand-alone exception for state national guard officers" when it came to applying the Privileges and Immunities Clause. *Id.* at 1092. On this score, the court might have pointed out that the Framers' deployment of the term "reserving" in the Militia Clause creates a parallel with the Tenth Amendment's use of the term "reserved." And because the reservation of powers to the states under the Tenth Amendment plainly does not create any exception to the operation of the state-power-trumping, rights-vesting Privileges and Immunities Clause, neither should the reservation to the states of the power to appoint National Guard officers under the Militia Clause. Put another way, just as the enumeration of certain powers in the federal government cannot and does not override those rights set forth in the Constitution for the very purpose of hemming in the exercise of those enumerated federal powers, neither can nor should the reservation of certain powers in the states operate to override those rights set forth in the Constitution for the very purpose of hemming in the exercise of those reserved state powers.

[27] 436 U.S. 371 (1978).

for hunting licenses. In deeming this stark form of discrimination immune from Privileges and Immunities Clause attack, the Court reasoned that bagging game is "not a means to the nonresident's livelihood"[28] and that "[w]hatever rights or activities may be 'fundamental' under the Privileges and Immunities Clause, . . . elk-hunting by nonresidents in Montana is not one of them."[29]

The proper result in *Baldwin* was hardly self-evident in light of the nation-building purposes of the Privileges and Immunities Clause.[30] Some citizens, after all, might miss the chance to experience in full measure the nation's natural diversity if blocked by individual states from the pleasures of roaming hunting grounds, bird habitats, and fishing streams.[31] Nonetheless, the result in *Baldwin* was understandable. Given the Court's longstanding insistence that the "fundamental interest" principle puts some restraints on Article IV protections, the Justices found themselves unable to apply that rubric to an activity that was only "a recreation and a sport."[32] In other cases, too, courts have declined to invalidate nonresident-disfavoring laws because the interests at stake failed to qualify as fundamental. Among these interests have been the claimed rights to carry a concealed handgun,[33] to invoke the same

---

28 *Id.* at 388.

29 *Id.* The Eighth Circuit drew directly on *Baldwin* in later upholding North Dakota waterfowl and pheasant hunting regulations that favored residents over non-residents. *See* Minnesota *ex rel.* Hatch v. Hoeyen, 456 F.3d 826, 834 (8th Cir. 2006). The *Hoeven* court also entertained, but rejected, the separate argument that hunting rights fall within the Privileges and Immunities Clause's protection of property rights—that is, the property rights of nonresident owners or lessees of local land—on the theory that the ability to hunt on one's own land is not "a part of the bundle of property rights accompanying the ownership or lease of land." *Id.* at 836.

30 *See, e.g.*, *Baldwin*, 436 U.S. at 394 (Brennan, J., dissenting) (worrying about Montana's "invidiously discriminating against nonresidents seeking to enjoy natural treasures it alone among the 50 States possesses").

31 *Cf.* Varat, *supra* note 4, at 511 ("It is easy to imagine a nonresident feeling greater hostility towards a state that excludes him totally from, or charges him vastly more for, a recreational activity available to residents than towards a state that charges a little more for a commercial fishing license than can be justified by the fact of nonresidence.").

32 *Baldwin*, 436 U.S. at 388.

33 *See* Peterson v. Martinez, 707 F.3d 1197, 1215–16 (10th Cir. 2013) (upholding Colorado's resident-only concealed handgun licensing regime because "carrying a concealed weapon is not a privilege or immunity protected under Article IV," as the activity is not "sufficiently basic to the livelihood of the Nation" (quoting *Friedman*, 487 U.S. at 64)). *But cf.* Culp v. Raoul, 921 F.3d 646, 657 (7th Cir. 2019) (upholding Illinois's concealed carry law, under which only nonresidents living in states with licensing standards "substantially similar" to Illinois's can be issued Illinois licenses, but limiting its analysis to avoid "taking a position" on whether nonresidents have a fundamental right "to carry a concealed firearm in another state"), *cert. denied*, 141 S. Ct. 109 (2020); Bach v. Pataki, 408 F.3d 75, 87, 91 (2d Cir. 2005) (holding that "New York's interest in monitoring gun licensees" is sufficiently weighty that the state could restrict the issuance of licenses "to residents and persons working primarily within

protections afforded residents by state statutes of limitations,[34] and to demand documents under a state Freedom of Information Act.[35] In addition, courts have rejected on fundamental-interest grounds challenges to court-access requirements found to disadvantage nonresidents to only a modest extent.[36]

C. THE SUBSTANTIAL-JUSTIFICATION REQUIREMENT

The fundamental-interest requirement sets forth a necessary, but not sufficient, condition for establishing a violation of the Privileges and Immunities Clause. This is so because, "[l]ike many other constitutional provisions, the [Clause] is not an absolute."[37] Rather, even in cases that involve fundamental interests, the clause bans discrimination against nonresidents only if "there is no substantial reason for the discrimination beyond the mere fact that they are citizens of other states."[38] In other words, to rule against the

---

the State" while "assum[ing], without deciding, that entitlement to a New York carry license is a privilege under Article IV").

34 *See, e.g.*, State v. McGuire, 786 N.W.2d 227, 236 (Wis. 2010).

35 *See* McBurney v. Young, 569 U.S. 221 (2013). In *Lee v. Minner*, 458 F.3d 194, 195 (3d Cir. 2006), the Third Circuit had concluded that there was, for Article IV purposes, a fundamental right to access public information, reasoning in particular that "political advocacy is an 'essential activity' which 'bear[s] upon the vitality of the Nation as a single entity' " and that "access to public records is necessary to the ability to engage in that activity." *Id.* at 200 (quoting *Baldwin*, 436 U.S. at 387). In *McBurney*, however, the Supreme Court rejected that proposition, finding fault with the "sweeping claim" made by challengers of Virginia's residents-only freedom-of-information law that the Privileges and Immunities Clause grants noncitizens "the right to access public information on equal terms with citizens of the Commonwealth." 569 U.S. at 232. The Court noted that no such right existed in either English or American common law on its way to holding that access to public records was not "basic to the maintenance or well-being of the Union." *Id.* at 233–34 (quoting *Baldwin*, 436 U.S. at 388). The Court also determined that Virginia's law did not, in a constitutionally direct enough way, abridge the challengers' fundamental interests in pursuing a common calling, in owning and transferring property, or in securing access to the Virginia courts. *Id.* at 226–27. It added that the challenged law did "not impermissibly burden noncitizens' ability to access [those] courts" in part because nonresidents had access to "most of the information that they sought" through other means. *Id.* at 232.

36 *See, e.g.*, Clement v. Durban, 115 N.E.3d 614, 346 & n.5 (N.Y. 2018) (holding that a New York statute requiring nonresident, but not resident, plaintiffs to post $500 as security for later possible assessments of court costs did not implicate a fundamental interest because it did not impair "reasonable and adequate access to New York courts"; emphasizing that the law provided an exemption for plaintiffs who "qualify for poor persons' status"; relying on early Supreme Court rulings such as *Canadian Northern Railway Co. v. Eggen*, 252 U.S. 553 (1920); and noting that this result "aligns with a national understanding," as established by a "nearly uniform body of decisions," with the only outlier case having involved the "significantly more burdensome" imposition of a "$6,000 security requirement").

37 *Toomer*, 334 U.S. at 396.

38 *Id.* at 396, 398. In building out these principles, the Court in *Piper* stated that "[i]n deciding whether the discrimination bears a close or substantial relationship to the State's objective, [we consider] the availability of less restrictive means." 470 U.S.

state on a privileges-and-immunities claim, a court must find *both* the existence of residency-based discrimination with respect to a fundamental interest *and* the absence of a "substantial" justification for the discriminatory treatment itself.

Consider in this respect *Hicklin v. Orbeck*,[39] which concerned an Alaska program that forced private firms to prefer residents in any employment that was "a result of" oil-and-gas and pipeline projects involving the state.[40] The Court had no difficulty concluding that nonresidents' losses of private jobs, pursuant to the statute, implicated a fundamental interest.[41] But that point alone did not dispose of the case because the Court also had to consider whether a "substantial reason" supported the discriminatory rule that Alaska had put in place.[42] On this point too, the Court decided against the state, reasoning that nonresident workers were not a "peculiar source" of the widespread unemployment Alaska supposedly sought to rectify because local joblessness was instead primarily attributable to a lack of training and a dearth of specialized work skills among Alaska's local labor force.[43] The Court also refused to approve the

---

at 284. The Court then determined that New Hampshire's refusal to afford nonresidents bar-admission privileges failed to satisfy this "close or substantial relationship" test. *Id.* Among other things, the Court concluded that the state-residency rule bore only the most tenuous relationship to ensuring that bar members were well-versed in local law. In addition, far more sensible and less-restrictive ways existed to advance this interest—for example, through the use of bar examinations and CLE requirements. The Court also pointed out that lawyers who take the time, make the effort, and incur the expense needed to join the New Hampshire bar can reasonably be presumed to live in locations "reasonably convenient to New Hampshire." *Id.* at 287. The lower courts have picked up this theme. For example, in invalidating a Nevada statute that required nonresident insurance brokers to jump through costly regulatory hoops not applicable to resident brokers, the Ninth Circuit observed that Nevada could reasonably obtain pertinent information from nonresident brokers without bogging them down with unnecessarily burdensome requirements. Council of Ins. Agents & Brokers v. Molasky-Arman, 522 F.3d 925, 936 (9th Cir. 2008). Likewise, in *Connecticut v. Crotty*, 346 F.3d 84 (2d Cir. 2008), the Second Circuit struck down a New York law that blocked nonresidents from lobstering in a "Restricted Area" in Long Island Sound. In reaching this result, the court relied in part on the state's failure to utilize less discriminatory alternatives, such as overall harvesting limits, to achieve its professed conservation goals. *Id.* at 100. Notably in this regard, the case law indicates that the burden shifts to the state to show that the substantial-relationship test is satisfied once the measure's challenger establishes that it discriminates regarding a fundamental interest. *See, e.g., Friedman*, 487 U.S. at 67–68 (referencing Virginia's "burden of showing that the discrimination is warranted by a substantial state objective" after concluding that the residency requirement in question unduly interfered with "a privilege protected by the Privileges and Immunities Clause"); W.C.M. Window Co., Inc. v. Bernardi, 730 F.2d 486, 498 (7th Cir. 1984) (citing the Supreme Court's ruling in *Hicklin v. Orbeck*, discussed *infra* notes 39–47 and accompanying text, in support of this proposition).

39 437 U.S. 518 (1978).

40 *Id.* at 529.

41 *See id.* at 524.

42 *Id.* 525 (quoting *Toomer*, 334 U.S. at 396).

43 *Id.* at 526 (quoting Toomer, 334 U.S. at 3968).

"Alaska-hire" program on the ground that it properly operated to steer the value of the state's own oil-and-gas-related assets into the hands of its own residents. While acknowledging the "often . . . crucial" importance of "a State's ownership of the property with which the statute is concerned," the Court found that Alaska had chosen a means to advance its supposed sow-and-reap purpose that swept too broadly.[44] The problem was that the law covered "employers who have no connection whatsoever with the State's oil and gas, perform no work on state land, have no contractual relationship with the State, and receive no payment from the State," reaching even "suppliers who provide goods or services to subcontractors who, in turn, perform work for contractors despite the fact that none of these employers may themselves have direct dealings with the State's oil and gas or ever set foot on state land."[45] Put simply, the law amounted to "an attempt to force virtually all businesses that benefit in some way from the economic ripple effect of Alaska's decision to develop its oil and gas resources to bias their employment practices in favor of the State's residents."[46] And under these circumstances, "Alaska's ownership of the oil and gas" supplied an "insufficient justification for the pervasive discrimination against nonresidents that the Act mandates."[47]

---

44 *Id.* at 529.

45 *Id.* at 530.

46 *Id.* at 531.

47 *Id. See also Barnard*, 489 U.S. 546 (invalidating a residency requirement for membership in the Virgin Islands bar; rejecting state justifications based on the geographical isolation of the territory and the resulting complications regarding scheduling, appearance on short notice, and the need to meet with and represent indigent defendants pursuant to local bar rules on the ground that these problems were largely subject to remediation through association by nonresident lawyers with local counsel; also dismissing concerns about the workability of such a system as involving too much "speculation" to "justify a blanket exclusion of nonresidents"); *Molasky-Arman*, 522 F.3d at 935 (finding that no substantial interest supported Nevada's requirement that insurance policies be signed by a resident agent and that the law failed the "closely related" requirement in any event because, as stated in *Council of Insurance Agents & Brokers v. Gallagher*, 287 F. Supp. 2d 1302, 1312 (N.D. Fla. 2003), "the notion that an agent cannot provide [follow-up] assistance outside his home state is nonsense; whatever may have been said when people traveled by horseback and communicated by regular mail, today people communicate by telephone and facsimile and e-mail and overnight courier [so that] state boundaries pose no obstacle"; adding that this justification also failed because it illogically disadvantaged nearby, but across-the-border, agents to the benefit of agents who lived in the state but at great distance from insurance purchasers). For a case in which the court found that the state's discrimination was justifiable even if it implicated a fundamental interest, see *Bach*, 408 F.3d at 92–93 (deeming the state's interest in having the ability to continuously monitor handgun licensees for purposes of discretionary license revocations to be sufficiently weighty to warrant limiting the issuance of licenses to state residents; reflecting more broadly on how residency requirements sometimes correlate with state interests in effective policing while at other times they do not, such as when nonresidents are little, if any, less subject to state watchdogging than residents because they continuously work in or have a place of business in the state).

The Court's recurring resort to means-ends analysis in applying the Privileges and Immunities Clause likens its operation to that of the dormant Commerce Clause principle.[48] In each setting, the Court seeks to determine whether the state has a good enough reason for laying a special burden on outsiders who lack representation equivalent to favored insiders in local government institutions. Absent such a reason—in *Toomer* and *Hicklin* no less than in *City of Philadelphia*[49] and *Dean Milk*[50]—the Court has stood ready to require the sort of evenhanded treatment of nonresidents that the state's political decisionmakers have failed to provide.

D. THE RELEVANCE OF MARKET PARTICIPATION

As noted earlier, the Privilege and Immunities Clause differs from the dormant Commerce Clause in that it lacks an explicitly recognized market-participant exception. As it turns out, however, something of a *de facto* version of this exception may well operate with regard to privileges-and-immunities law, because the Court has indicated that the Article IV clause applies with lesser force to discriminatory measures implemented by states as market participants.

The Court's cornerstone treatment of these matters came in *United Building & Construction Trades Council v. Mayor & Council of Camden*.[51] That case concerned a Camden, New Jersey ordinance that required contractors dealing with the city both to hire a minimum percentage of local residents to work on city building projects and to ensure that their subcontractors did the same.[52] As we saw in an earlier chapter,[53] the Court in *White v. Massachusetts Council of Construction Employers, Inc.*[54] had previously rejected a dormant Commerce Clause-based attack directed at a functionally identical requirement on the theory that the claim targeted only

---

48 *See supra* Section 18.C (discussing the significance of judicial assessments of less restrictive alternatives and means-ends fit in applying the dormant Commerce Clause). For an analysis based on the proposition that sometimes even stark discrimination between residents and nonresidents can survive means-ends analysis under both the Privilege and Immunities Clause and the dormant Commerce Clause, see Brannon P. Denning, *One Toke Over the (State) Line: Constitutional Limits on 'Pot Tourism' Restrictions*, 66 FLA. L. REV. 2279, 2289 (2013) (arguing that Colorado would have a strong likelihood of success in justifying its rule allowing residents to purchase more marijuana than nonresidents in retail sales transactions, especially in light of "the lack of any explicit (or covert) protectionist motive" for the law).

49 City of Philadelphia v. New Jersey, 437 U.S. 617 (1978).

50 Dean Milk Co. v. City of Madison, 340 U.S. 349 (1951).

51 465 U.S. 208 (1984).

52 *Id.* at 211–12.

53 *See supra* Section 20.D.

54 460 U.S. 204 (1983).

market participation by the state. *Camden*, however, involved a claim under the Privileges and Immunities Clause, and the Court in that case pointedly declined to invoke the same exception as a basis for upholding the challenged law in the face of this alternative line of constitutional challenge. In particular, the Court in *Camden* reasoned that, while the Commerce Clause by its terms gives rise to limits on the state's power to "regulate" (as opposed to participate in) the interstate market, the Privileges and Immunities Clause focuses on ensuring equal treatment of nonresidents as a general matter.[55] The Court further held that, because working for a private construction firm involved the "fundamental" interest of pursuing a "common calling," the plaintiffs faced no out-of-the-gate obstacle to invoking the Article IV clause.[56]

What the Court in *Camden* gave with one hand, however, it seemed ready, at least largely, to take away with the other. This was so for several reasons. First, in defining what interests qualify as fundamental under the Privileges and Immunities Clause, the Court sharply distinguished Camden's restriction on private firms' hiring of private workers to carry out public works contracts from a preference given to residents in hiring by the city itself. By thus indicating that genuinely public employment does not qualify as a "fundamental right,"[57] the Court invited recognition of a broad exception to the Privileges and Immunities Clause that mirrored the market-participant exception in its application to the most direct, and probably the most common, form of resident-hiring preference.[58] Second, the *Camden* decision left no doubt that the universe of non-fundamental government-bestowed interests, unprotected by the Privileges and Immunities Clause, stretches beyond state employment.[59] In particular, the Court suggested that the clause would not bar price differentials for (or even total exclusions of non-residents from) public educational services and other benefits provided directly by the state itself.[60] In doing so, the Court signaled

---

55 *Camden*, 465 U.S. at 220.

56 *Id.* at 219–20.

57 *Id.* at 219.

58 *See* Salem Blue Collar Workers Ass'n v. City of Salem, 33 F.3d 265, 270 (3d Cir. 1994) ("[W]e hold that direct public employment is not a privilege or fundamental right protected by the Privileges and Immunities Clause of Article Four."); Morgan v. City of Wheeling, 516 S.E.2d 48, 57 (W. Va. 1999) (holding that an out-of-state applicant had no fundamental right, for Privileges and Immunities Clause purposes, to work as a city police officer in the face of an ordinance limiting hiring to local residents).

59 *See* TRIBE, *supra* note 4, § 6–37, at 1263 (suggesting that this principle, which flows from a state's constitutional nature as a "separate political community," extends to state discrimination in affording access to "public libraries, public schools, state universities, state-supported hospitals, and other public welfare programs" (internal quotations and footnotes omitted)).

60 *Camden*, 465 U.S. at 221.

that its application of the fundamental-interest touchstone of Privileges and Immunities Clause analysis would take broad account of the same resident-favoring sow-and-reap logic that underpins the market-participant exception to the dormancy doctrine.[61]

Finally, the Court—while declining to dismiss the case on market-participant grounds—did not invalidate the challenged private-resident-employee hiring preference. Instead, the Court remanded the case for further proceedings, noting that the lower courts had not yet considered whether the law was "necessary to counteract [the] grave economic and social ills" that had led Camden to enact it—that is, whether the challenged discrimination against nonresidents bore a "close relation" to a "substantial" state interest.[62] In addition, the Court emphasized that "caution is particularly appropriate" in applying this form of means-ends analysis when the challenged program, as in this case, involves dispensing the state's own resources.[63] Thus, as the Court emphasized in describing the analysis to be applied by the lower court on remand, "[t]he fact that Camden is expending its own funds . . . is certainly a factor—perhaps the crucial factor—to be considered in evaluating whether the statute's discrimination violates the Privileges and Immunities Clause."[64] As it turns out, the *Camden* case was settled before the

---

[61] *See supra* Section 20.D (discussing the sow-and-reap concept). In particular, the Court noted that the case did not involve a state's direct use of its own resources, but instead involved "efforts to bias private employment decisions." *Camden*, 465 U.S. at 221; *see also Marilley*, 844 F.3d at 850 (observing that "Commerce Clause decisions are relevant to the Privileges and Immunities Clause because the two clauses share the same underlying concerns").

[62] *Camden*, 465 U.S. at 222.

[63] *Id.* at 221–23.

[64] *Id.* at 221. *See generally Marilley*, 844 F.3d at 849–50 (noting that "the Supreme Court has stated that a state's expenditures may justify discrimination against nonresidents that would otherwise be impermissible"). In *State v. Antonich*, 694 P.2d 60 (Wyo. 1985), the court relied heavily on this aspect of the reasoning in *Camden* in upholding a challenged law that "requires merely that governmental funds, allocated to public-works projects, be used to hire qualified, available residents in preference to nonresidents." *Id.* at 64. More specifically, the court reasoned that nonresident workers did "constitute the peculiar source of the evil identified by the State"—that is, the evil of "a qualified Wyoming worker's remaining unemployed while a nonresident goes to work on a government-funded construction project." *Id.* at 63. In addition, the court found that the law targeted this "evil" in a reasonable way because it did not wholly foreclose the hiring of nonresidents; rather, it authorized their employment so long as the public-works contractor first made sure, in consultation with the local employment office, that no qualified resident workers were available to fill job openings. *Id.* at 64. Indeed, in a concurring opinion, Chief Justice Thomas was prepared to give the Court's specialized treatment of state resource-distribution programs in *Camden* such a broad reading that he deemed it "inappropriate to invoke the Privileges and Immunities Clause" whenever the state is "a market participant pursuing essentially a proprietary function." *Id.* at 65 (Thomas, C.J., concurring) (adding that this result comported with the "mutually reinforcing relationship" between the dormant Commerce Clause principle and the Privileges and Immunities Clause, as well as federalism concerns reflected in the Tenth Amendment). *But see*

lower courts could turn to these matters. Nonetheless, some other tribunals (though by no means all of them) have since drawn on the "certainly a factor" rhetoric of *Camden* in upholding challenged rules that require private firms that enter into public contracts to favor residents as they hire project workers.[65] In sum, although the Court

Robison v. Francis, 713 P.2d. 259, 269 (Alaska 1986) (declaring that the exclusion of "non-residents from public construction jobs so that more jobs will be available to Alaskans . . . is not a permissible justification for discrimination under the privileges and immunities clause").

65 *Antonich*, discussed *supra* note 64, illustrates how a court can read certain passages of *Camden* broadly to authorize laws of this kind. *See also Metro. Washington Chapter*, 57 F. Supp. 3d at 23, 25–26 (observing that, while "virtually every other residence preference law that has been challenged on Privileges and Immunities grounds has been found to be unconstitutional," further proceedings were necessary to explore whether the distinctive character of the District of Columbia, particularly in light of its congressionally imposed inability to tax nonresidents who work in the District, justifies its imposition of such a residents-preference rule on public-works contractors, including because *Camden* cut in favor of affording the District "some deference" in controlling the use of its own funds). For a sharply contrasting approach, see *A.L. Blades & Sons, Inc. v. Yerusalim*, 121 F.3d 865 (3d Cir. 1997). There, the Third Circuit cited six earlier (but mostly pre-*Camden*) state appellate-court rulings in invalidating a Pennsylvania statute that required public-works contractors to employ only Pennsylvania residents. *Id.* at 873 n.12. The court first rejected the state's effort to justify the law based on "alleviating high unemployment" because "unemployment among Pennsylvania construction workers" was not marked by any "distinguishing characteristic," *id.* at 871–72, and because removing the law would "increase[ ] unemployment in the construction industry by only .093%," *id.* at 872. The court also rejected the state's alternative theory that the statute properly guarded against the "loss of economic benefits resulting from the expenditure of Commonwealth funds on nonresident workers." *Id.* at 871. Again, the court reasoned that any benefit-retaining impact of the residence-based hiring requirement was "minimal at best," and it added that, in any event, the program was fatally underinclusive with regard to this goal in that the disadvantaged nonresident construction workers' actions did not differ from those of "the legions of [other] nonresident employees who remove their income from the Commonwealth daily." *Id.* at 875. More generally, the court worried that (1) the state's theory overlooked offsetting benefits it might well receive in the form of lowered costs on construction projects if the law did not exist, *id.* at 875 n.16; (2) "discrimination against nonresidents because they choose to spend their incomes in their states of residence would appear to be the type of discrimination the Privileges and Immunities Clause was drafted to eliminate," *id.* at 875 n.14; and (3) there existed a danger that at least in the absence of more focused evidence of an unusual problem, "the migration of economic benefits theory would validate virtually every employment residency requirement," *id.* at 875. (The court also might have noted that the principle it vindicated served to facilitate the migration of benefits *into* Pennsylvania by ensuring that its own residents could earn wages in other states and then bring them back home.) Of particular importance, the court found that *Camden* presented no obstacle to its ruling. In that case, the court observed, the Supreme Court did nothing more than remand the case for a determination whether "nonresident employees were the peculiar source of Camden's urban decay and high unemployment," while in this case, the overarching point of the court's analysis was to show that nonresident construction workers were not, as the Privileges and Immunities Clause requires, a "peculiar source" of any unemployment-related or benefit-retention-related problems that the state purportedly sought to address. *Id.* at 876; *see also Robison*, 713 P.2d. at 267, 269 (flagging "differences between the local hire act here and the ordinance in *Camden*" based on Alaska's "dynamic and growing economy," as opposed to Camden's "condition of decay," the fact that "[p]ublic works account for the majority of commercial construction activity in Alaska," and the difference between the "90% to 100%" hiring preference operative in Alaska versus the 40% "goal, not a requirement"

in *Camden* refused to import the dormant Commerce Clause's market-participant exception into Privileges and Immunities Clause doctrine in full-force fashion, the policy concerns that underlie that exception have influenced judicial application of the clause in significant ways.

at issue in *Camden;* also explaining, with respect to the "peculiar source of the evil" requirement that Alaskan unemployment was largely attributable to factors such as "climatic extremes" and "lack of training prevalent among rural Alaskans"); 1st Westco Corp. v. Sch. Dist. of Phila., 811 F. Supp. 204, 208 (E.D. Pa. 1993) (invalidating a similar resident-preference requirement imposed on public contractors because it at best reduced local unemployment by only .037%, thus indicating that nonresident workers were not a "peculiar source" of a properly targeted local problem), *rev'd on other grounds,* 6 F.3d 108 (3d Cir. 1993); Laborers Local Union No. 374 v. Felton Constr. Co., 654 P.2d 67, 70–71 (Wash. 1982) (en banc) (likewise rejecting a public-contractor resident-preference requirement because of the "paucity of evidence [that] nonresidents might otherwise drain the economy"; also reasoning that the government's defense of the law on the theory that "local economies will be strengthened . . . is an example of the highly protectionist economic policies the privileges and immunities clause was designed to protect against" (internal quotations omitted)).

Chapter 24

THE SUPREMACY CLAUSE AND FEDERAL PREEMPTION DOCTRINE

Analysis

Article VI provides that "[t]his Constitution, and the Laws of the United States which shall be made in Pursuance thereof; and all Treaties made . . . under the Authority of the United States, shall be the supreme Law of the Land . . . , any Thing in the Constitution or Laws of any State to the Contrary notwithstanding."[1] The Supreme Court has given life to this pronouncement by ruling in many cases that actions of the federal government preempt the operation of conflicting state laws. Each of these decisions—and there are hundreds of them—hinges on the distinctive features of the particular federal and state provisions at issue in the case.[2] The situation-specific character of these rulings frustrates efforts to encapsulate preemption doctrine in a few short pages,[3] but key themes merit close attention.[4]

---

[1] U.S. CONST. art. VI, cl. 3.

[2] *See* LAURENCE H. TRIBE, AMERICAN CONSTITUTIONAL LAW § 6–31, at 1210 n.27 (3d ed. 2000) (noting that "[i]n the end, . . . preemption analysis is (or ought to be) so thoroughly a function of the federal statute's specific text and history that rigid and elaborate doctrinal decision trees are more likely to hinder than to advance the necessary task of sound statutory interpretation").

[3] A more detailed and comprehensive, though also somewhat more dated, discussion appears in the Tribe treatise. *See id.* §§ 6–28 to 6–32.

[4] Preemption doctrine also plays a distinctive role in the law of civil procedure. Specifically, under the well-pleaded-complaint rule, federal-question jurisdiction must derive from the federal-law nature of a *plaintiff*'s claims—that is, it cannot be grounded in federal-law defenses asserted by the opposing party in response to the plaintiff's complaint. *See* Louisville & Nashville R.R. Co. v. Mottley, 211 U.S. 149, 152 (1908). Under the "complete preemption" doctrine, however, federal-question jurisdiction is proper when the state-law cause of action is so thoroughly preempted by federal law as to render the plaintiff's claim one that is "in reality based on federal law." Beneficial Nat. Bank v. Anderson, 539 U.S. 1, 8 (2003). For an in-depth analysis

To begin with, preemption rulings—unlike, for example, dormant Commerce Clause or Privilege and Immunities Clause rulings—hinge on the prescriptions of sub-constitutional law, usually as set forth in federal statutes.[5] In addition, the overarching task of the courts in applying these materials is simple to state: In each case, the judge must determine whether an "act of Congress, fairly interpreted, is in actual conflict with the law of the State."[6] In practice, however, deciding whether such a conflict exists often gives rise to difficult legal questions, thanks largely to the fact that Congress, as it enacts legislation, seldom anticipates the sort of highly particularized preemption questions that later give rise to litigated disputes. Consequently, courts must employ a mixed bag of

---

of the complete-preemption doctrine, see 14C CHARLES ALAN WRIGHT, ARTHUR R. MILLER & EDWARD H. COOPER, FEDERAL PRACTICE AND PROCEDURE § 3722.2 (rev. 4th ed. 2021).

[5] For at least three reasons, this point does not mean that the Constitution is beside the point in such cases. First, as Professor Tribe has noted, "[m]ost problems pertaining to federal preemption have arisen in close connection with the Commerce Clause" because they arise in cases "involving federal legislation enacted pursuant to that clause." TRIBE, *supra* note 2, § 6–28, at 1173. Second, courts may well look to rules of statutory interpretation grounded in constitutional policy in determining whether federal laws have state-law-displacing effects. *See, e.g.*, *supra* Section 5.D (discussing the avoidance canon). Third, litigants in preemption cases may assert companion arguments under the dormant Commerce Clause, and it may be that, in some such cases, federal laws—even if not preemptive in and of themselves—help inform dormancy-doctrine analysis. *See, e.g.*, *supra* Section 19.B.3 (suggesting the role of federal antitrust policy in the Court's application of the dormant Commerce Clause in *Flood v. Kuhn*, 407 U.S. 258 (1972)).

[6] Savage v. Jones, 225 U.S. 501, 533 (1912). In addition to statutes passed pursuant to Article I of the Constitution, other types of federal enactments can also preempt state legislation. *See* Missouri v. Holland, 252 U.S. 416, 432 (1920) (discussing preemption of state law by a federal treaty); Hughes v. Talen Energy Mktg., LLC, 136 S. Ct. 1288 (2016) (considering preemption of state law by federal agency regulation); Tarrant Reg'l Water Dist. v. Herrmann, 569 U.S. 614 (2013) (considering whether a congressionally approved interstate compact preempted state law). The Court has also given preemptive effect to binding executive agreements, *see* United States v. Pink, 315 U.S. 203, 229–30 (1942), despite the protestation of some observers that the Supremacy Clause itself speaks only of the "Constitution," "Laws," and "Treaties." *See, e.g.*, Brannon P. Denning & Michael D. Ramsey, American Insurance Association v. Garamendi *and Executive Preemption in Foreign Affairs*, 46 WM. & MARY L. REV. 825, 906–15 (2004) (arguing against the preemptive effect of executive agreements because "the Constitution contains a strong negative implication that it does not contain additional allocations of preemptive power" beyond the Constitution itself, "Laws of the United States," and treaties, thus signaling that "preemptive power is, fundamentally, a legislative power"); *see also* David Sloss, *International Agreements and the Political Safeguards of Federalism*, 55 STAN. L. REV. 1963, 1967, 1970 (2002) (asserting that "textual analysis [of Articles I, II and VI of the Constitution] supports the inference that nontreaty agreements should not have the same domestic legal force as treaties," although "both Presidential practice and judicial precedent support" the alternative view); *Pink*, 315 U.S. at 230 ("All constitutional acts of power, whether in the executive or in the judicial department, have as much legal validity and obligation as if they proceeded from the legislature." (citing THE FEDERALIST NO. 64 (Jay) (internal quotations omitted))); LOUIS HENKIN, FOREIGN AFFAIRS AND THE UNITED STATES CONSTITUTION 226–28 (2d ed. 1996) (concluding that "executive agreements, too, are supreme law of the land").

tools in determining whether the relevant federal law, when given a proper interpretation, has preemptive effect. In an effort to guide this judicial work, the Court has organized preemption doctrine into decision-tree-type categories, drawing a line between express- and implied-preemption cases, while further distinguishing in implied-preemption cases between "conflict" and "field" preemption.

A. EXPRESS PREEMPTION

In express-preemption cases, the parties battle over the scope of a federal statutory provision—often known as a "preemption clause"—that explicitly provides for the displacement of some types of state laws. Consider in this respect the Federal Cigarette Labeling and Advertising Act (FCLAA), which both: (a) mandates that manufacturers print the now-familiar "Surgeon General's Warning" on every pack of cigarettes sold in the United States,[7] and (b) expressly preempts any "requirement or prohibition based on smoking and health . . . imposed under State law with respect to the advertising or promotion of any cigarettes the packages of which are labeled in conformity with [the statute's rules]."[8] In *Cipollone v. Liggett Group, Inc.*,[9] the Court held that the FCLAA's preemption clause displaces state tort-law regimes (whether founded on statutory law, common law, or both) to the extent that they authorize recoveries based on the marketer's failure to warn of product dangers in communications designed to promote cigarette sales. The Court also held, however, that the federal statute did not negate state-law causes of action for breach of express warranty because the "requirement" that gives rise to such a claim is not " 'imposed under State law', but rather imposed *by the warrantor*."[10] Placing a further gloss on the FCLAA's express preemption provision, the Court in *Cipollone* concluded that its text did not affect state-law claims based on fraudulent statements made in cigarette advertising, on the theory that such claims arise not out of "a duty 'based on smoking and health' " but instead out of "a more general obligation—the duty not to deceive."[11] Finally, the Court found that the statutory preemption provision did not bar actions based on failures to warn of product dangers in communications made to governing bodies such as an "administrative agency."[12] Again focusing on the preemption provision's precise terms, the Court concluded that, even if these

---

7 15 U.S.C. §§ 1331–1340.

8 15 U.S.C. § 1334(b).

9 505 U.S. 504 (1992).

10 *Id.* at 525 (emphasis in original).

11 *Id.* at 528–29.

12 *Id.*

suits involve a "requirement . . . based on smoking and health"[13] within the meaning of the statutory text, they remained available because of their focus on failures "to disclose . . . facts through channels of communication other than advertising or promotion."[14] As these differing conclusions reached in *Cipollone* help to illustrate, express-preemption issues often require a highly contextual analysis to determine whether particular state rules fall within or without the federal statutory mandate of displacement.[15]

B. IMPLIED PREEMPTION

More controversial than cases like *Cipollone* are those presenting claims that federal legislation displaces state law even in the absence of a preemption clause.[16] In addressing these "implied preemption" disputes, the Court has identified two main types of federal statutory preeminence. The first involves "field preemption," which applies when federal regulation of a given subject is "so pervasive" or federal interests with respect to it are "so dominant" that "state laws on the same subject" should not operate.[17] The

---

[13] *Id.* at 526.

[14] *Id.* at 528.

[15] *See* TRIBE, *supra* note 2, § 6–31, at 1210 n.27. For a few of the Court's many recent express-preemption rulings, see, e.g., *National Meat Ass'n v. Harris*, 565 U.S. 452, 455 (2012) (finding that the Federal Meat Inspection Act's express preemption clause rendered inoperative the California Penal Code's regulation of "nonambulatory" animals); *Dan's City Used Cars, Inc. v. Pelkey*, 569 U.S. 251 (2013) (finding that the Federal Aviation Authorization Act's express preemption clause did not preempt state law claims concerning the storage of a tow truck); and *Rutledge v. Pharmaceutical Care Management Ass'n*, 141 S. Ct. 474 (2020) (ruling that the Employee Retirement Income Security Act's express preemption clause did not displace an Arkansas pharmaceutical statute).

[16] Notably, sometimes the Court will consider whether a federal statute impliedly preempts a state law even if the federal statute includes an express preemption provision that does not cover that state measure. *See* Hillman v. Marrieta, 569 U.S. 483, 490 (2013) (noting that "[a]lthough [the Federal Employees' Group Life Insurance Act of 1954] contains an express pre-emption provision" but considering, in light of the ruling below, "only whether Section D is pre-empted under conflict pre-emption principles"; going on to find that the Virginia law at issue was impliedly preempted by the act). Put another way, the mere existence of an express preemption clause in a federal statute does not automatically create a negative implication that precludes a finding that the same statute impliedly preempts some state laws. *See also* Geier v. American Honda Motor Co., 529 U.S. 861, 870 (2000) (declining to conclude that the relevant "pre-emption provision, the saving provision, or both together, create some kind of 'special burden' beyond that inherent in ordinary pre-emption principles—which 'special burden' would specially disfavor [implied] pre-emption here").

[17] English v. Gen. Elec. Co., 496 U.S. 72, 79 & n.5 (1990) (internal quotations omitted). For illustrative cases addressing field preemption, see, e.g., *Chamber of Com. of U.S. v. Brown*, 554 U.S. 60, 66 (2008) (finding the National Labor Relations Act created "a zone protected and reserved for market freedom," which preempted a California law that placed restrictions on spending related to union organizing (internal quotations omitted)), and *Kurns v. R.R. Friction Prods. Corp.*, 565 U.S. 625, 637 (2012) (finding that the petitioner's state-law design-defect and failure-to-warn claims were preempted because they fell "within the field of locomotive equipment

second involves "conflict preemption," which operates when a state law clashes with the purpose, as opposed to the express command, of a federal enactment.[18] The Court has noted that these two categories are not "rigidly distinct," and one might indeed fairly characterize both inquiries as concerned with the same, bottom-line question whether state law "stands as an obstacle to the accomplishment and execution of the full purposes and objectives of Congress."[19]

An illustrative implied-preemption case is *Burbank v. Lockheed Air Terminal, Inc.*[20] There, the Court struck down a city ordinance that prohibited jet takeoffs from a local airport between 11:00 p.m. and 7:00 a.m. Enforcement of this ordinance, the Court concluded, would conflict with the Federal Aviation Act, even though that act included no express preemption provision, because the city's "timing of takeoffs and landings would severely limit the flexibility of FAA in

---

regulation" covered by the Locomotive Inspection Act). For cases rejecting claims of field preemption, see, e.g., *Altria Grp., Inc. v. Good*, 555 U.S. 70 (2008) (concluding that the Federal Cigarette Labeling and Advertising Act, as implemented by the Federal Trade Commission, did not support a field-preemption theory with respect to certain types of state-law fraud claims), *Oneok, Inc. v. Learjet, Inc.*, 575 U.S. 373 (2015) (declining to find that a set of "state antitrust claims fall within the field pre-empted by the Natural Gas Act"), and *Kansas v. Garcia*, 140 S. Ct. 791, 804–07 (2020) (determining that state-law fraud convictions of noncitizens for using false social security numbers on employment forms were not displaced on a field preemption theory by the Immigration Reform and Control Act).

18 *English*, 496 U.S. at 79 n.5. For a sampling of cases addressing conflict preemption, see, e.g., *Pharmaceutical Research & Manufacturers of America v. Walsh*, 538 U.S. 644, 666–69 (2003) (addressing whether a Maine drug law conflicted with federal Medicaid regulations), *Entergy Louisiana, Inc. v. Louisiana Public Service Comm'n*, 539 U.S. 39 (2003) (ruling that an order issued by a Louisiana electric utility contravened Federal Energy Regulatory Commission interstate pricing regulations), *PLIVA, Inc. v. Mensing*, 564 U.S. 604, 618–19 (2011) (deeming state tort claims for drug labeling defects preempted by Food and Drug Administration labeling rules), *Chamber of Commerce v. Whiting*, 563 U.S. 582, 600–07 (2011) (finding that an Arizona law requiring employers to verify the immigration status of their employees did not conflict with the Immigration Reform and Control Act), and *Williamson v. Mazda Motor of America, Inc.*, 562 U.S. 323 (2011) (ruling that California law claims were not preempted by a set of seatbelt-related safety standards promulgated by the U.S. Department of Transportation).

19 *English*, 496 U.S. at 79 (quoting Hines v. Davidowitz, 312 U.S. 52, 67 (1941)). Put another way, "field pre-emption may be understood as a species of conflict pre-emption" in that a "state law that falls within a pre-empted field conflicts with Congress' intent . . . to exclude state regulation" from that field. *Id.* at 79 n.5. One highly specialized—and rare—subspecies of conflict preemption is "impossibility preemption," which occurs when a regulated party literally cannot adhere to state law without violating federal law. *See* Wyeth v. Levine, 555 U.S. 555 (2009) (noting that "[i]mpossibility pre-emption is a demanding defense"); *see also* JAY B. SYKES & NICOLE VANATKO, CONG. RSCH. SERV., R45825, FEDERAL PREEMPTION: A LEGAL PRIMER 24 (2019) ("To illustrate this principle, the Court has explained that a hypothetical federal law forbidding the sale of avocados with *more* than 7% oil content would preempt a state law forbidding the sale of avocados with *less* than 8% oil content, because avocado sellers could not sell their products and comply with both laws." (citing Fla. Lime & Avocado Growers v. Paul, 373 U.S. 132, 142–43 (1963))), *available at* https://sgp.fas.org/crs/misc/R45825.pdf.

20 411 U.S. 624 (1973).

controlling air traffic flow."[21] In addition, the "pervasive nature of the scheme of federal regulation of aircraft noise" supported a finding that the local rule would not fly because it obstructed the effective operation of the overarching federal scheme.[22]

On the other hand, the Court in *Pacific Gas & Electric Co. v. State Energy Resources Conservation & Development Commission* (*PG&E*)[23] declined to find that the federal Atomic Energy Act preempted a moratorium on building new nuclear power plants put in place by California to address the lack of a workable disposal mechanism for radioactive waste. The Court first rejected the would-be plant operator's contention that the moratorium conflicted with federal occupation of "the entire field of nuclear safety concerns."[24] To be sure, the Court acknowledged, Congress through the statute had assumed exclusive control of nuclear safety matters, and the spent fuel rods generated by nuclear plants did indeed pose safety risks as they built up in cooling ponds on plant sites.[25] Nonetheless, the Court concluded that congressional occupation of the nuclear *safety* field did not have the effect of undoing the state moratorium because California had adopted it for the permissible *economic* purpose of avoiding the power disruptions that would occur if ever-mounting waste-storage problems required future plant shutdowns.[26] The Court also found unpersuasive PG&E's separate argument that the moratorium was unlawful because "a primary purpose of the Atomic Energy Act was, and continues to be, the promotion of nuclear power."[27] The problem with this argument was that it missed the point that Congress never meant to promote nuclear power "at all costs."[28] Rather, by specifically permitting states to regulate the economic elements of nuclear-power production and distribution, Congress had signaled its willingness to tolerate just the sort of non-safety-based restriction adopted by California.[29]

---

[21] *Id.* at 639; *see also id.* at 633 (noting that "[t]here is, to be sure, no express provision of pre-emption in the 1972 Act").

[22] *Id.* at 633.

[23] 461 U.S. 190 (1983).

[24] *Id.* at 212.

[25] *Id.* at 212–13.

[26] *Id.* at 213–16 (emphasis added).

[27] *Id.* at 221.

[28] *Id.* at 222 (internal quotations omitted).

[29] In finding a congressional intent not to preempt state economic regulation related to nuclear plants, the Court relied in part on a federal statutory mandate that "[n]othing in this section shall be construed to affect the authority of any state or local agency to regulate activities for purposes other than protection against radiation hazards." *Id.* at 210 (quoting 42 U.S.C. § 2021(k)). These sorts of non-preemption or "savings" clauses appear with frequency in federal enactments and can play a key role in decisions concerning whether state law must give way in the face of Congress's exercise of its powers. *See, e.g.*, New Eng. Power Co. v. New Hampshire, 455 U.S. 331,

In the preemption context, as elsewhere, the level of generality at which courts characterize legislative purposes often proves all-important. In *PG&E*, for example, the Court had declared in seemingly broad terms that the Atomic Energy Act occupied the field of nuclear-power safety. In *Silkwood v. Kerr-McGee Corp.*,[30] however, the Court found that a state-law punitive damages award against a nuclear-plant operator for recklessly exposing an employee to radiation injuries was not subject to preemption. The majority reasoned that Congress's plan to occupy the nuclear-safety field did not extend so far as to interfere with traditional "state tort remedies."[31] That characterization of the preempted field, however, differed greatly from the one adopted by the dissenters, who instead insisted that Congress had at least meant to preempt state punitive-damages awards (as opposed to compensatory-damages awards) because of their essentially "regulatory" purpose of penalizing and deterring safety-related lapses.[32] Indeed, one might well have advanced an even more state-limiting position—namely, that the "comprehensive" safety-related federal authority recognized in *PG&E* mandated preemption of even compensatory remedies for a nuclear-plant safety breach.[33] Each of these three positions, in keeping with *PG&E*, acknowledges that Congress has roped off an "impliedly preempted field" with regard to nuclear power safety.[34] Each position, however, also reflects a different view about how far Congress meant for that roped-off area to extend. Fortunately for the plaintiff in *Silkwood*, five Justices embraced the view most hospitable to the retention of state authority—namely, that the federal-law purpose of ensuring federal safety control was hemmed in by the countervailing goal of honoring state tort-law remedies.

---

343 (1982) (discussing the effect of a statutory " 'nonpre-emption' clause" and distinguishing its effect from that of a statute that affirmatively consents to the operation of state laws that otherwise violate the dormant Commerce Clause principle—a subject discussed *supra* Section 20.B).

30 464 U.S. 238 (1984).

31 *Id.* at 253.

32 *Id.* at 274–75 (Powell, J., dissenting).

33 *Cf. id.* at 281 (noting the Act's "comprehensive" treatment of safety-related matters). The nuclear-power operator in fact did make this argument before the Tenth Circuit. Silkwood v. Kerr-McGee Corp., 667 F.2d 908, 920–21 (10th Cir. 1981) (rejecting this claim), *rev'd*, 464 U.S. 238. It opted, however, not to appeal from the Tenth Circuit's refusal to set aside the compensatory damages award, perhaps because that award was small in comparison to the amount of punitive damages recovered in the case. *See* Brief for Appellees at 18, *Silkwood*, 464 U.S. 238 (No. 81–2159) ("The only compensatory verdict remaining in this case is the property damage award of $5,000—the stipulated value of Silkwood's furnishings—from which Kerr-McGee has not appealed.").

34 *Pac. Gas & Elec. Co.*, 461 U.S. at 205.

C. THE PRESUMPTION AGAINST PREEMPTION

On its way to rejecting the claim of preemption in *Silkwood*, the Court relied on a rule of restraint that surfaces often in its preemption decisions. Beginning with its decision in *Rice v. Santa Fe Elevator Corp.*,[35] the Court has hewed to the view that when "Congress legislate[s] . . . in [a] field which the States have traditionally occupied, . . . we start with the assumption that the historic police powers of the States were not to be superseded by the Federal Act unless that was the clear and manifest purpose of Congress."[36] This presumption, to be sure, is sometimes overcome.[37] In general, however, its operation bodes ill for litigants seeking to escape the grip of state law.[38]

Sometimes the Court sidesteps application of this presumption by finding that the challenged measure lies outside a field

---

[35] 331 U.S. 218 (1947) (holding that the federal Warehouse Act displaced state warehousing laws because a preemptive purpose was shown).

[36] *Id.* at 230. *Accord, e.g.*, United States v. Locke, 529 U.S. 89, 108 (2000) (citing the " 'assumption' of nonpre-emption" endorsed in *Rice*). *See generally* NORMAN J. SINGER & J.D. SHAMBIE SINGER, STATUTES AND STATUTORY CONSTRUCTION § 36:9 (7th ed. 2007) (discussing the presumption against preemption); ANTONIN SCALIA & BRYAN GARNER, READING LAW: THE INTERPRETATION OF LEGAL TEXTS 290 (2012) ("It is a reliable canon of interpretation—though sometimes dishonored in the breach—to presume that a federal statute does not preempt state law."). Moreover, in some cases, the presumption may apply with elevated intensity. *See, e.g.*, *Walsh*, 538 U.S. at 666 ("The presumption against federal pre-emption of a state statute designed to foster public health has special force when it appears . . . that the two governments are pursuing common purposes." (internal citations and quotations omitted)).

[37] *See, e.g.*, Crosby v. Nat'l Foreign Trade Council, 530 U.S. 363, 374 n.8 (2000) (invalidating a state law that restricted trade with firms that dealt with Myanmar in light of a federal statutory treatment of the same subject matter even while "[a]ssuming, *arguendo*, that some presumption against preemption is appropriate" in this context (emphasis in original)); Egelhoff v. Egelhoff *ex rel.* Briener, 532 U.S. 141, 151–52 (2001) (invalidating a Washington life-insurance law because, even though "[t]here is indeed a presumption against pre-emption in areas of traditional state regulation such as family law," the "presumption can be overcome where, as here, Congress has made clear its desire for pre-emption"); Hillman v. Maretta, 569 U.S. 483, 490 (2013) (invaliding a Virginia life-insurance-beneficiaries statute that conflicted with the Federal Employees' Group Life Insurance Act, even though "[t]he regulation of domestic relations is traditionally the domain of state law" and "[t]here is therefore a 'presumption against pre-emption' of state laws governing domestic relations" (internal citations omitted)).

[38] *See, e.g.*, De Buono v. NYSA-ILA Med. & Clinical Serv. Fund, 520 U.S. 806, 814 (1997) (stating that "[r]espondents . . . bear the considerable burden of overcoming 'the starting presumption that Congress does not intend to supplant state law' "; relying on the presumption in finding that the Employee Retirement Income Security Act did not preempt a New York state tax law); *Wyeth*, 555 U.S. at 565–66 (noting that the Court "start[s] with the assumption that the historic police powers of the States were not to be superseded by the Federal Act unless that was the clear and manifest purpose of Congress" and finding the relevant federal law not to preempt state tort-law rules that gave rise to the plaintiff's failure-to-warn claims).

"traditionally occupied" by the states.[39] In other words, when putatively preemptive federal laws address "national subjects," the Court is "more vigilant in striking down what would amount to state incursions into subjects that Congress may have validly reserved to itself."[40] For example and not surprisingly, the Court has deemed the field of foreign affairs to be "national" in nature,[41] and it has thus within this area taken a high-octane approach to recognizing the preemption of state laws that in any way "conflict or interfere with, curtail or complement, the federal law, or enforce additional or auxiliary regulations."[42] The Court likewise has taken a broad view of the preemptive effect of federal laws and treaties that concern

---

[39] *Locke*, 529 U.S. at 108 (declining to apply the *Rice* anti-preemption presumption to a state oil-tanker regulation because "Congress has legislated in the field [of maritime transport] from the earliest days of the Republic").

[40] TRIBE, *supra* note 2, § 6–31, at 1210 & n.29 (listing "national subjects" that the Supreme Court has identified, including as in *Toll v. Moreno*, 458 U.S. 1, 10 (1959) (the treatment of noncitizens), *North Dakota v. United States*, 460 U.S. 300, 309 (1983) (migratory bird protection), and *San Diego Building Trades Council v. Garmon*, 359 U.S. 236 (1959) (labor-management relations)); *see also Arizona v. Inter Tribal Council of Arizona, Inc.*, 570 U.S. 1, 13–14 (2013) (finding the presumption inapplicable when Congress wields its power to regulate the "Times, Places and Manner" of elections for federal office pursuant to Article I, section 4).

[41] *See, e.g.*, United States v. Curtiss-Wright Export Corp., 299 U.S. 304, 316–320 (1936) (comparing the federal government's "plenary" power over foreign affairs with its limited, enumerated powers over internal affairs). This dominance stems in part from the Court's recognition that states are entirely foreclosed, in some respects, from regulating foreign affairs even in the absence of preemptive laws or treaties. *See supra* Section 15.B.4 (discussing, among other cases, *Zschernig v. Miller*, 389 U.S. 429, 430–38 (1968)). The important point here, however, is that—even when state action in the foreign-affairs field is not foreclosed by the Constitution standing alone—the Court may view the preemptive effects of federal actions more capaciously than it would when the presumption against preemption applies.

[42] *Hines*, 312 U.S. at 66–67. For example, in *American Insurance Ass'n v. Garamendi*, 539 U.S. 396 (2003), the Court denied enforcement, on preemption-based grounds, of a California statute that required insurance companies to disclose information about Holocaust-era insurance policies. In part, this result was supported by a recent executive agreement between President Bill Clinton and German Chancellor Gerhard Schröder, which finalized a set of German reparation payments for victims of Nazi persecution in exchange for President Clinton's expressed willingness to work toward limiting German exposure to lawsuits in U.S. courts. *Id.* at 405. Notably, the agreement did not include an express preemption clause. *Id.* at 417. Nor did it require state courts to dismiss such claims. *Id.* at 406 (noting that the agreement in itself did not "provide an independent legal basis for dismissal" but rather compelled the Government to tell courts "that U.S. policy interests favor dismissal on any valid legal ground" (internal quotation marks omitted)). Instead, the Court found that the California statute was impliedly preempted based on the "clear conflict between the policies." *Id.* at 421; *see also id.* at 423–24 (adding that " 'a different, state system of economic pressure,' . . . undercuts the President's diplomatic discretion and the choice he has made exercising it"). For a lower-court ruling along the same lines, see *Odebrecht Construction, Inc. v. Secretary of Florida Department of Transportation*, 715 F.3d 1268 (11th Cir. 2013) (deeming preempted, in part by reference to the President's "discretionary authority" with respect to Cuba, a Florida statute that prevented the state government from awarding contracts to companies that conducted business operations in that country).

indigenous peoples,[43] emphasizing that "[t]he unique historical origins of tribal sovereignty make it generally unhelpful to apply to federal enactments regulating Indian tribes those standards of pre-emption that have emerged in other areas of the law."[44]

Although the Court has historically applied the presumption against preemption with equal force across both express- and implied-preemption cases,[45] recent decisions may signal a change in this position.[46] Most notably, in *Puerto Rico v. Franklin Cal. Tax-Free Trust*,[47] the Court declared that, "because the statute contains an express pre-emption clause, we do not invoke any presumption against pre-emption but instead focus on the plain wording of the clause, which necessarily contains the best evidence of Congress' pre-emptive intent."[48] The difficulty presented by this passage is that it is subject to different interpretations. On one reading, it indicates that the presumption against preemption no longer operates at all in express-preemption cases. But on another reading, the passage means that express-preemption cases are different from implied-preemption cases only in the sense that express-preemption cases in their nature require the interpretation of preemption clauses whose wording, if "plain," necessarily will overcome the anti-preemption presumption.

Lower courts (not surprisingly) have disagreed about which view is correct,[49] and for now the Court's position on the matter remains

---

[43] As noted elsewhere in this book, the Court's application of preemption doctrine in this context often overlaps with its recognition of a freestanding (though congressionally defeasible) immunity from state-based regulation that exists as a basic component of tribal sovereignty. *See generally infra* Section 35.A.4.

[44] White Mountain Apache Tribe v. Bracker, 448 U.S. 136, 143 (1980) (adding that "[t]he tradition of Indian sovereignty over the reservation and tribal members must inform the determination whether the exercise of state authority has been pre-empted by operation of federal law").

[45] In *Cipolline*, for example, Justice Stevens insisted on behalf of the majority that "we must fairly but—in light of the strong presumption against pre-emption—narrowly construe the precise language" set forth in the express-preemption provision of the federal cigarette-labeling law. 505 U.S. at 523. *Accord, e.g., Altria Grp., Inc.*, 555 U.S. at 77 ("[W]hen the text of a pre-emption clause is susceptible of more than one plausible reading, courts ordinarily 'accept the reading that disfavors pre-emption.' " (quoting Bates v. Dow Agrosciences, LLC, 544 U.S. 431, 449 (2005)) (internal quotations marks omitted)).

[46] *See Altria Grp., Inc.*, 555 U.S. at 99 (2008) (Thomas, J., dissenting) (asserting that, "[s]ince *Cipollone*, the Court's reliance on the presumption against pre-emption has waned in the express pre-emption context").

[47] 579 U.S. 115 (2016).

[48] *Id.* at 116 (internal quotations omitted).

[49] Thus, in *Dialysis Newco, Inc. v. Community Health Systems Group Health Plan*, 938 F.3d 246, 257–59 (5th Cir. 2019), the Fifth Circuit rejected a narrow reading of *Franklin* and found that the presumption against preemption no longer applies in express-preemption cases. *Accord* Air Evac EMS v. Cheatham, 910 F.3d 751, 762 (4th Cir. 2018) (cabining the presumption against preemption to implied-preemption cases; stating that for express-preemption cases "our task is simply to interpret the words as

unclear.[50] Given the muscularity of the presumption against preemption, the issue is consequential. Indeed, its eventual resolution could have significant ripple effects across other areas of federal statutory-interpretation law.[51]

D. THE FRONTIERS OF PREEMPTION DOCTRINE

Modern-day commentators have raised new questions about the proper nature and scope of federal preemption doctrine. For example, some critics of now-operative doctrine have suggested that courts should dramatically limit, and perhaps eliminate altogether, findings

---

they are written"); Atay v. County of Maui, 842 F.3d 688, 699 (9th Cir. 2016) (tracking the language of *Franklin*); Watson v. Air Methods Corp., 870 F.3d 812, 817 (8th Cir. 2017) (similar); *see also* Joseph Alberts et al., *Survey of Recent Developments in Indiana Product Liability Law*, 50 IND. L. REV. 1305, 1323 (2017) (stating that *Franklin* undid the presumption against preemption for express preemption cases); Alice Kaswan, *Statutory Purpose in* the *Rollback Wars*, 71 HASTINGS L.J. 1179, 1195 n.115 (2020) (highlighting this possibility but also noting ambiguity in the Court's statement). On the other hand, in *Shuker v. Smith & Nephew, PLC*, 885 F.3d 760 (3d Cir. 2017), the Third Circuit held that that the presumption against preemption did apply to its reading of a statutory preemption clause because *Franklin* did not address "preemption of claims invoking 'historic . . . state regulation of matters of health and safety,' " and so did not eliminate the presumption for "the products liability claims at issue here." *Id.* at 770, 771 n.9; *see also* EagleMed LLC., v. Cox, 868 F.3d 893, 903 (10th Cir. 2017) (deeming the presumption against preemption inapplicable only if the express clause is unambiguous); *see also* FMS Nephrology Partners N. Cent. Ind. Dialysis Ctr., LLC. v. Meritain Health, Inc., 144 N.E.3d 692, 702 (Ind. 2020) ("Despite the statement in *Franklin* that the Court's preemption analysis 'begins and ends' with the clause's text, there is reason to think the Court continues to apply a different, atextual preemption standard in ERISA cases."). *See generally* Matthew N. Metz & Janelle London, *State Vehicle Electrification Mandates and Federal Preemption*, 9 MICH. J. ENVTL. & ADMIN. L. 433, 473 (2020) (suggesting that the presumption against preemption still exists when there is "ambiguity as to coverage of the express preemption clause").

[50] The Court has addressed express-preemption clauses in several decisions handed down since *Franklin* but has not yet addressed the question flagged here. *See, e.g.*, Gobeille v. Liberty Mut. Ins. Co., 577 U.S. 312, 325–26 (2016) (ignoring the presumption-based argument because "[a]ny presumption against pre-emption, whatever its force in other instances, cannot validate [the challenged state law]"); Coventry Health Care of Mo., Inc. v. Nevils, 137 S. Ct. 1190, 1198 (2017) (referencing but not directly engaging with a presumption-based argument, while ultimately relying on the "text, context, and purpose" of a federal statute to conclude that it preempted the relevant state law); *Rutledge*, 141 S. Ct. 474 (making no reference to the presumption in concluding that ERISA did not preempt an Arkansas law).

[51] The problem arises because the presumption against preemption—including relation to express-preemption statutes—is closely tied to a more general principle of statutory interpretation, *see supra* Section 5.D, that favors narrow readings of federal laws that touch upon areas of traditional state control. *See* Raygor v. Regents of the Univ. of Minn., 534 U.S. 533, 543–44 (2002) (highlighting the Court's state-favoring interpretive approach that equally "applies when Congress 'intends to pre-empt the historic powers of the States' or when it legislates in 'traditionally sensitive areas' that 'affec[t] the federal balance' " (quoting Will v. Mich. Dept. of State Police, 491 U.S. 58, 65 (1989))). A question thus exists as to whether this more general principle, despite its longstanding acceptance, can and will continue to operate if the Court abandons application of the presumption against preemption in the express-preemption context.

of implied preemption because such findings rest only on inferential judgments and thus (so it is argued) intrinsically clash with the presumption against preemption.[52] Even the sometimes-federalism-minded Rehnquist and Roberts Courts, however, have stuck with the longstanding view that judges can find state laws impliedly preempted by federal statutes, at least so long as Congress's "purpose" to preempt is clearly discernible.[53] Other analysts have

---

[52] *See* Stephen Gardbaum, *Rethinking Constitutional Federalism*, 74 TEX. L. REV. 795, 828–29 (1996) (suggesting that this result would follow from the recognition of a congressional duty to engage in focused deliberation for any would-be preemptive action in order for that action to qualify as "proper" under the Necessary and Proper Clause); Betsy J. Grey, *Make Congress Speak Clearly: Federal Preemption of State Tort Remedies*, 77 B.U. L. REV. 559, 607 (1997) (arguing that, "when state tort law is at stake," the Court should "find preemption only when Congress has explicitly referred to state tort actions in 'clear and unmistakable' language or when compliance with both state tort law and federal law would be impossible"); Caleb Nelson, *Preemption*, 86 VA. L. REV. 225, 265–90 (2000) (arguing against "obstacle" preemption as an unconstitutional expansion of the Supremacy Clause). Justice Thomas has expressed support for doctrinal reform along these lines. *See Wyeth*, 555 U.S. at 582–604 (Thomas, J., concurring in the judgment) (arguing for a preemption doctrine rooted in a law's text and thus critiquing the Court's current implied-preemption doctrine). *But see* Daniel J. Meltzer, *Preemption and Textualism*, 112 MICH. L. REV. 1, 56–57 (2013) (arguing that implied preemption is necessary because "Congress can rarely craft statutory language that will adequately resolve the full range of preemption issues").

[53] *See, e.g.*, *Geier*, 529 U.S. at 881–82 (2000) (concluding that a Federal Motor Vehicle Safety Standard impliedly preempted state tort rules authorizing a no-airbag negligence action, even though no express statutory preemption provision covered such common-law claims); Arizona v. United States, 567 U.S. 387, 401–07 (2012) (both endorsing and applying principles of implied field-based and conflict-based preemption in invalidating multiple features of an Arizona law); Gade v. Nat'l Solid Wastes Mgmt. Ass'n, 505 U.S. 88 (1992) (finding that state licensing requirements for hazardous waste workers were impliedly preempted by the federal Occupational Safety and Health Act); *see also Williamson*, 562 U.S. at 326–37 (reaffirming and applying the preemption principles of *Geier*, but arriving at a different conclusion with regard to a Federal Motor Vehicle Safety Standard concerning the installation of seat belts). Indeed, commentators on occasion have observed that some of the Justices most closely identified with a pro-federalism perspective have seemed, perhaps ironically, most inclined to find that federal statutes preempt state laws. *See* Richard H. Fallon, Jr., *The "Conservative" Paths of the Rehnquist Court's Federalism Decisions*, 69 U. CHI. L. REV. 429, 432, 462–63 (2002) (describing the "unwillingness of the Rehnquist Court consistently to enforce a robust presumption against preemption"); Ernest A. Young, *"The Ordinary Diet of the Law": The Presumption Against Preemption in the Roberts Court*, 2011 SUP. CT. REV. 253, 341 (asserting that this trend has continued in the Roberts Court, and that, "[w]hile some of the conservative Justices . . . have been willing to restrict preemption, most have tended to favor broad preemption of state law"); *see also* TRIBE, *supra* note 2, § 6–30, at 1204 n.66 (noting that "a Justice's states' rights orientation is surprisingly unpredictive of that Justice's readiness to find federal preemption absent a clear statement of congressional intent"). One possible explanation for this result is that these Justices (or at least some of them) may tend to value private freedom from regulatory controls more than they value local regulatory autonomy. On this view, these Justices are drawn to a robust set of preemption rules because their typical effect is to exempt business and other interests from state-imposed constraints that reach beyond, if not far beyond, parallel controls imposed by federal law. *See* Fallon, *supra*, at 471 ("Because federal preemption eliminates state regulatory burdens, preemption rulings have a tendency—welcome to substantive conservatives—to minimize the regulatory requirements to which businesses are subject."); Young, *supra*, at 342 (noting that "[f]ederal preemption is

sought to draw on a political-process-based rationale, along the lines of the approach put to work in *Garcia v. San Antonio Metropolitan Transit Authority*,[54] in an effort to cabin federal preemption based on agency rules, as opposed to congressional enactments.[55] In particular, these commentators assert that administrative rulemaking lacks the same built-in state-protective structural features that operate when Congress considers adopting potentially preemptive laws. Thus, so the argument goes, the Court should seldom, if ever, give preemptive effect to the pronouncements of federal agencies.[56] Once again, however, the Court has not embraced this state-protective mode of analysis, at least in its strongest forms,[57] and it has in fact gone so far as to give implied preemptive effect to agency action not embodied in formally and finally promulgated regulations.[58] At the same time, the Justices have

---

generally deregulatory—that is, preemption cases typically arise only where a state government has regulated more strictly than has the national government" and that "[p]reemption cases . . . thus pit the deregulatory impulses of conservative Justices against their sympathy for the states").

[54] 469 U.S. 528 (1985).

[55] *See generally supra* Section 5.A (discussing the Court's political-process-based limits on federal power).

[56] *See, e.g.*, Calvin R. Massey, *Etiquette Tips: Some Implications of "Process Federalism,"* 18 HARV. J. L. & PUB. POL'Y 175, 193, 213 (1994); Nina A. Mendelson, *A Presumption Against Agency Preemption*, 102 NW. U. L. REV. 695, 698 (2008) ("Despite agencies' expertise in implementing their own programs, no presumptive deference should be due because agencies lack both institutional expertise on important issues of state autonomy and federalism and adequate statutory guidance regarding preemption questions."); Thomas W. Merrill, *Preemption and Institutional Choice*, 102 NW. U. L. REV. 727, 755 (2008) (reasoning that agencies "are unlikely to have much knowledge—or even care—about larger questions concerning the division of authority between the federal government and the states").

[57] Indeed, the Court has allowed agencies to preempt state law even when Congress has not directly authorized a federal agency to do so. *See Wyeth*, 555 U.S. at 556 (going on to observe that "[w]here, as here, Congress has not authorized a federal agency to pre-empt state law directly, the weight this Court accords the agency's explanation of state law's impact on the federal scheme depends on its thoroughness, consistency, and persuasiveness").

[58] *See Geier*, 529 U.S. at 861; *id.* at 887, 907–10 (Stevens, J., dissenting) (complaining that the majority's decision to recognize the preemption of state airbag suits was "the product of the Court's interpretation of the final commentary accompanying an interim administrative regulation and the history of airbag regulation generally"). At the same, in cases decided prior to *Geier*, the Court signaled hesitancy in finding state laws to be impliedly preempted by agency regulations, while justifying that approach by reference to the need to protect the "federal-state balance" and a recognition that "agencies normally address problems in a detailed manner [so that] we can expect that they will make their intentions clear if they intend for their regulations to be exclusive." Hillsborough Cty. v. Automated Med. Labs., Inc., 471 U.S. 707, 717–18 (1985) (refusing to find county ordinances preempted by FDA regulations); *see also* Cal. Coastal Comm'n v. Granite Rock Co., 480 U.S. 572, 583 (1987) (citing *Hillsborough County* in observing that "it is appropriate to expect an administrative regulation to declare any intention to pre-empt state law with some specificity"). The majority in *Geier*, however, distinguished those cases on the ground that they did not involve a circumscribed claim of purpose-based conflict preemption but instead involved an assertion of field preemption of "*all* state law in a particular

balked at recognizing the preemption of state laws by agency rules primarily attributable to the actions of private industry groups.[59]

area" due to "the mere 'volume and complexity' of agency regulations." *Geier*, 529 U.S. at 884 (emphasis in original) (quoting *Hillsborough Cty.*, 471 U.S. at 717).

[59] *See Fla. Lime & Avocado Growers*, 373 U.S. at 150–51 (refusing to give a federal regulation preemptive effect in part because it had been drafted not "by impartial experts in Washington or even in Florida, but rather by the South Florida Avocado Administrative Committee"). For a far-reaching criticism of the ways in which private actors empowered by the federal government can secure "preemptive effects" over state law, see Craig Konnoth, *Privatization's Preemptive Effects*, 134 HARV. L. REV. 1937, 1940 (2021) (exploring in detail mechanisms through which the federal government channels power to private entities to override or undermine the effects of state regulation, including through direct delegation of the power to preempt state law; challenging this growing practice on the ground that private entities "are generally more well insulated from transparency mechanisms and meaningful legal review than are federal entities, [thus reducing] democratic accountability" when such transfers of authority occur).

Chapter 25

OTHER GOVERNMENTAL ENTITIES: NATIVE NATIONS, U.S. TERRITORIES, AND THE DISTRICT OF COLUMBIA

Analysis

To proclaim that "the Framers split the atom of sovereignty"[1] as between the states and the federal government is to offer an incomplete account of the U.S. constitutional order.[2] In actuality, the "dual federalism" that governs federal-state relations exists alongside structural arrangements concerning other governmental entities—in particular, Native nations, federal territories, and the District of Columbia. In varied ways, moreover, these entities' incorporation into the governing structures of the Constitution are reflective of colonialist and imperialist practices that stand in stark tension with traditional constitutional narratives about a "more Perfect union" established by "We the People."[3] Native nations were excluded from the Constitution's ratification process,[4] and have

---

1 *See* U.S. Term Limits, Inc. v. Thornton, 514 U.S. 779, 838 (1995) (Kennedy, J., concurring).

2 *See* Gregory Ablavsky, *Empire States: The Coming of Dual Federalism*, 128 YALE L.J. 1792, 1795 (2019) (noting that the "origin story" underlying the dual-federalism account "is a partial and incomplete account of federalism and the constitutional moment known as the Founding").

3 U.S. CONST. preamb; *cf.* Aziz Z. Rana, *How We Study the Constitution: Rethinking the* Insular Cases *and Modern American Empire*, 130 YALE L.J. FORUM 312, 318 (2020) (highlighting key ways in which the United States was established as a "settler empire . . . systematically organized around efforts to claim Indigenous territory exclusively for insider communities" and emphasizing that "[t]here are populations that continue to this day to experience direct colonial subjugation, from Native peoples throughout the country to local communities specifically in the territories").

4 *See* Seth Davis, *American Colonialism and Constitutional Redemption*, 105 CAL. L. REV. 1751, 1756 (2017) (noting that the "story of popular consent that our Constitution is based upon cannot be told about American Indians and Alaska Natives, who did not consent as peoples to the Constitution"). This is not to say that Native

experienced colonial subjugation for much of U.S. history.[5] The Commonwealth of Puerto Rico and other federal territories entered the Union as conquered lands,[6] and their residents to this day lack the full degree of participatory and substantive rights that extend to the residents of U.S. states.[7] And while Article I, section 8 explicitly designates the District of Columbia as the "Seat of Government of the United States,"[8] the District continues to lack voting representation in Congress and other basic privileges of U.S. statehood.[9] In these and other ways, the rules governing these entities' relationship to the federal and state governments continue to raise pressing questions about the promise and reach of popular sovereignty, democratic representation, equality before the law, and other constitutional ideals.

A. NATIVE NATIONS

The field of federal Indian law emanates from a complex body of constitutional-law, international-law, common-law, statutory, regulatory, and treaty-based rules that, as described by a leading treatise on the subject, "mediat[e] the . . . intergovernmental relationships among the Indian nations, the United States, and the states of the Union."[10] The subject is often taught as a stand-alone law-school class, but many of its overarching principles directly implicate bigger-picture aspects of U.S. constitutional law (and especially U.S. constitutional structure).[11] An overview of this field thus is important not only for its own sake, but also because it sheds light on key organizational features of the U.S. constitutional system.

---

nations took no interest in the framing of the Constitution. To the contrary, representatives of the Cherokee, Chickasaw, and Choctaw Nations held official meetings with George Washington and other delegates of the Convention in June of 1787. *See* Mary Sarah Bilder, *Without Doors: Native Nations and the Convention*, 89 FORDHAM L. REV. 1707 (2021) (detailing the circumstance of this visit).

[5] *See* Michalyn Steele, *Indigenous Resilience*, 62 ARIZ. L. REV. 305, 313 (2020) ("Perhaps until the 1970s, the common presumption of American policymakers was that tribes and separate indigenous identity would (and should) inevitably yield to the superior civilization and might of the United States.").

[6] *See* Andrew Hammond, *Territorial Exceptionalism and the American Welfare State*, 119 MICH. L. REV. 1639, 1656–59 (2021) (briefly recounting the circumstances leading to the acquisition of the five permanently inhabited territories that are today a part of the United States).

[7] *See infra* Section 25.B.

[8] *See* U.S. CONST. art. I, § 8.

[9] *See infra* Section 25.C.

[10] 1 COHEN'S HANDBOOK OF FEDERAL INDIAN LAW 1 (Nell Jessup Newton et al., eds 2019) [hereinafter COHEN'S HANDBOOK].

[11] *See, e.g.*, Maggie Blackhawk, *Federal Indian Law as Paradigm Within Public Law*, 132 HARV. L. REV. 1787, 1797 (2019) (noting, among other things, that "the paradigm of Indian law unsettles many of public law's current presuppositions about how best to distribute and limit power in order to protect minorities").

1. The Historical Foundations of Federal Indian Law

At the time of the founding, "powerful Native nations owned and governed much of the territory mapmakers labeled 'United States.' "[12] White settlers, meanwhile, clamored for territorial expansion, with the result being that many states acted on their own initiative to expropriate indigenous lands, often in disregard of federal treaties already in effect. Indian affairs thus weighed heavily on the minds of the Framers, who, broadly speaking, entertained two competing visions of how the newly created federal government should engage with Native nations. On one view, which Professor Gregory Ablavsky has termed the "Madisonian" position, a strengthened federal government would work to suppress state-based interference with federal Indian policy and thereby facilitate westward expansion through contractual purchases of Native lands and other treaty-based arrangements.[13] On the competing, "Hamiltonian" view, by contrast, a strengthened federal government would use both the threat and the exercise of military force to "dominate the borderlands at the Indians' expense."[14]

The Madisonian and Hamiltonian approaches to westward expansion would both find expression in the document that emerged from the Philadelphia Convention,[15] but proponents of ratification

---

[12] Greg Ablavsky, *The Savage Constitution*, 63 DUKE L.J. 999, 1003–04 (2014).

[13] *See id.* at 1006–07.

[14] *Id.* at 1007.

[15] The paternalistic ambitions of the Madisonian view were reflected in: (1) the Indian Commerce Clause, *see* U.S. CONST. art. I, § 8, cl. 3 (authorizing Congress to "regulate commerce . . . with the Indian tribes"); *see also supra* Section 4.F.2; (2) the Treaty Clause, *see* U.S. CONST. art. II, § 2 (authorizing the President, with the consent of two-thirds of the Senate, to "make Treaties"); (3) the Supremacy Clause, *see* U.S. CONST. art. VI; *see* Ablavsky, *supra* note 12, at 1042 (noting that the Supremacy Clause, by assigning "supreme law" status to both "treaties made" and treaties "which shall be made," established that pre-1789 federal treaties with Native Nations would continue to have binding effect); (4) the Compact Clause, *see* U.S. CONST. art. I, § 10 (providing that "[n]o state shall enter into any Treaty, Alliance, or Confederation"); (5) the Territory Clause, *see id.* § 3 (providing that the federal government shall "make all needful Rules and Regulations respecting the Territory . . . belonging to the United States"); *see also* Ablavsky, *supra* note 12, at 1044 (noting that this provision helped to ensure that Congress had the power to "criminalize illegal settlement on Indian lands and, under Article III, to prosecute violators in new federal courts far from sympathetic local juries"); and (6) various other provisions aimed at strengthening the federal government's ability to negotiate, implement, and enforce treaty-based arrangements with Native nations free from state-based obstruction and interference. *See generally id.* at 1039–45. The militaristic ambitions of the Hamiltonian view, meanwhile, were reflected not only in the various war- and military-related powers vested in Congress and the President, *see, e.g.*, U.S. CONST. art. I, § 8, cls. 13–14 (authorizing Congress to "raise and support Armies" and to "provide and maintain a Navy"); *id.* art. II, § 2 (making the President the "Commander in Chief of the Army and Navy of the United States, and of the Militia of the several States, when called into the actual Service of the United States"), but also in the Guarantee Clause, which

quickly recognized the political expedience of emphasizing the latter at the expense of the former. Thus, as Professor Ablavsky has observed: "Although few Federalists were rabid Indian-haters of the sort common on the frontier, they . . . sold the Constitution by promising to use federal power against Indians rather than, as Madison had anticipated, to restrain states."[16] And "[t]he history of national violence against Indians that followed ratification fulfilled the Hamiltonian vision, as the dispossession and settlement of western lands became one of the central projects of the new federal state."[17]

Even as the newly created federal government began to pursue the Hamiltonian program, some states continued to pursue their own aggressive policies of displacement. Georgia in particular had voted to ratify the Constitution with the expectation that it would receive uncompromising federal assistance in its ongoing efforts to expel Native peoples from their lands.[18] In the wake of ratification, however, state officials remained unplacated by federal "removal" initiatives and therefore embarked on a violent removal program of their own. Of particular significance were several Georgia laws adopted in the late 1820s that sought, as Chief Justice Marshall would later put it, to "annihilate the Cherokees as a political society, and to seize, for the use of Georgia, the lands of the nation which have been assured to them by the United States in solemn treaties repeatedly made and still in force."[19] These state laws precipitated a series of legal challenges, and these challenges gave the Chief Justice an early opportunity to set forth his views regarding the status of Native nations within the new constitutional order.

---

committed the federal military to "protect each [state] against invasion," *see id.* art. IV, § 4; *see also* Ablavsky, *supra* note 12, at 1047 (noting that an earlier draft of the clause referenced a federal power to protect states against "foreign" invasions but that the word "foreign" was subsequently stricken from its language), and in provisions that sought to bolster states' claims to and demands for western lands, *see, e.g.*, U.S. CONST. art. IV, § 3 (stipulating that "[n]othing in this Constitution shall be so construed as to Prejudice any Claims of the United States, or of any particular State," and prohibiting the federal government from carving new states out of territories of existing states without those existing states' legislative consent); *see also* Ablavsky, *supra* note 12, at 1046–48.

16 *Id.* at 1008.

17 *Id.*

18 *See* Robert N. Clinton, *The Dormant Indian Commerce Clause*, 27 CONN. L. REV. 1055, 1160–61 (1995); *see also* Ablavsky, *supra* note 12, at 1067–71.

19 *See* Cherokee Nation v. Georgia, 30 U.S. (5 Pet.) 1, 15 (1831). Those laws had already resulted in the summary execution of a Cherokee citizen that was done in defiance of an earlier Supreme Court order. *See* JILL NORGREN, THE CHEROKEE CASES: TWO LANDMARK FEDERAL DECISIONS IN THE FIGHT FOR SOVEREIGNTY 60–62, 95–98 (2004) (describing Georgia's refusal to abide by the Court's issuance of a writ of error following its arrest of George "Corn" Tassel).

In *Cherokee Nation v. Georgia*,[20] the Court disposed of the first of these challenges on jurisdictional grounds, with several Justices concluding that the underlying dispute did not involve a conflict between a state (i.e., Georgia) and a "foreign state" (i.e., the Cherokee Nation) within the meaning of Article III, section 2.[21] Writing for a plurality of Justices,[22] the Chief Justice declared that the Cherokee Nation was a "a distinct political society, separated from others, capable of managing its own affairs and governing itself."[23] But he did not recognize the Cherokee Nation as a "foreign" state for purposes of Article III. Rather, the Chief Justice maintained, "[t]he relation of the Indians to the United States is marked by peculiar and cardinal distinctions which exist no where else."[24] Using paternalist language, he went on to characterize Native nations as being "in a state of pupilage" and in a "relation to the United States resembl[ing] that of a ward to his guardian."[25] He continued: "They look to our government for protection; rely upon its kindness and its power; appeal to it for relief to their wants; and address the president as their great father."[26] Harkening back to an earlier decision from the Court (*Johnson v. M'Intosh*),[27] he also emphasized that Native

---

[20] 30 U.S. (5 Pet.) 1, 15 (1831).

[21] *See* U.S. CONST. art. III, § 2 (noting that "the Court shall have original jurisdiction" in "all cases . . . in which a state shall be a party," including "controversies . . . between a state . . . and foreign states").

[22] The Court in *Cherokee Nation* was badly fragmented. For a breakdown of the votes, see Matthew L.M. Fletcher, *The Iron Cold of the Marshall Trilogy*, 82 N.D. L. REV. 627, 639 (2006).

[23] *Cherokee Nation*, 30 U.S. at 16.

[24] *Id.*

[25] *Id.* at 17.

[26] *Id.*

[27] 21 U.S. (8 Wheat.) 543 (1823). In *Johnson*, the Court "first attempted to address the basic question of colonization and constitutionalism" by considering a series of questions related to property rights over indigenous lands. Philip P. Frickey, *Marshalling Past and Present: Colonialism, Constitutionalism, and Interpretation in Federal Indian Law*, 107 HARV. L. REV. 381, 385 (1993). In so doing, the Court incorporated into U.S. law a common-law property doctrine, the "doctrine of discovery," that, it claimed, had furnished an organizing principle for European colonial powers' earlier dealings with Native nations. *See Johnson*, 21 U.S. at 572–73. *But see* STUART BANNER, HOW THE INDIANS LOST THEIR LAND: LAW AND POWER ON THE FRONTIER 12 (2005) (contending that early English colonists did not embrace the discovery doctrine and instead had "normally acknowledged that Indian land had to be obtained by contract, not by force"). According to the discovery doctrine, as Chief Justice Marshall described it, the "discovery" of aboriginal land "gave title to the government by whose subjects, or by whose authority, it was made, against all other European governments, which title might be consummated by possession." *Johnson*, 21 U.S. at 573. This in turn meant that "the rights of the original inhabitants were . . . to a considerable extent, impaired." *Id.* at 574. More specifically, although Native nations remained "rightful occupants of the soil," their "rights to complete sovereignty, as independent nations, were necessarily diminished, and their power to dispose of the soil at their own will, to whomsoever they pleased, was denied." *Id.* The injustice of this rule was manifest, and even Marshall himself voiced misgivings about the "extravagant . . . pretension of converting the discovery of an inhabited country into conquest." *See id.*

nations "occupy a territory to which we assert a title independent of their will."[28] All told, he concluded that Native nations—though states in some sense of the word—were neither states of the Union nor states outside the Union. Instead, in language frequently quoted by courts to this day, Marshall asserted that they were "perhaps" best characterized as "domestic dependent nations."[29]

As it turned out, the Court's dismissal of *Cherokee Nation* only briefly forestalled a merits-based ruling on the validity of Georgia's anti-Cherokee laws. That ruling came one year later in *Worcester v. Georgia*,[30] in which the Chief Justice unambiguously declared for the Court that Georgia had acted unlawfully by "interfer[ing] forcibly with the relations established between the United States and the Cherokee nation, the regulation of which . . . are committed *exclusively* to the government of the union."[31] In addition, he continued, the Georgia laws were "in direct hostility with treaties" between the Cherokee Nation and the United States—treaties that "guaranty to [the Cherokees] all the land within their boundary; solemnly pledge the faith of the United States to restrain their citizens from trespassing on it; and recognize the pre-existing power of the nation to govern itself"—and "in equal hostility with the acts of congress for regulating this intercourse, and giving effect to the treaties."[32] In short, the challenged Georgia measures were "repugnant to the constitution, laws, and treaties of the United States."[33]

The majority opinion in *Worcester* also offered an account of tribal sovereignty that departed sharply from the "ward/guardian" model that Chief Justice Marshall had earlier set forth in *Cherokee Nation*.[34] Appealing to the "settled doctrine of the law of nations," the

---

at 591. Nonetheless, the Court has never disavowed the discovery doctrine, *see* Joseph William Singer, *Indian Title: Unraveling the Racial Context of Property Rights, or How to Stop Engaging in Conquest*, 10 ALB. GOV'T L. REV. 1, 3 (2017) (noting that *Johnson* "has been interpreted and altered by both case law and statutes, but it remains a foundational case in the field of federal Indian law"), and federal courts continue to invoke *Johnson* in resolving cases today. *See* BANNER, *supra*, at 12 (noting that "*Johnson* . . . might be the only member of th[e] anti-canon that remains the law, and that is still cited as authority by lower courts several times a year").

[28] *Cherokee Nation*, 30 U.S. at 13.

[29] *Id.*

[30] 31 U.S. (6 Pet.) 515 (1832).

[31] *Id.* at 561 (emphasis added).

[32] *Id.* at 562.

[33] *Id.*

[34] *See* Hope M. Babcock, *A Civil-Republican Vision of "Domestic Dependent Nations" in the Twenty-First Century: Tribal Sovereignty Re-Envisioned, Reinvigorated, and Re-Empowered*, 2005 UTAH L. REV. 443, 480 (noting that Chief Justice Marshall in *Worcester* "made it clear that the tribes' relationship to the federal government was governed by consent and the concept of dependency as it was then

Chief Justice now denied that Native nations' had ever "surrender[ed]" their "independence" by "associating with a stronger [nation], and taking its protection."[35] He continued: "The Cherokee nation, then, is a distinct community occupying its own territory, with boundaries accurately described, in which the laws of Georgia can have no force, and which the citizens of Georgia have no right to enter, but with the assent of the Cherokees themselves."[36] The challenged Georgia law, in other words, clashed not only with the supremacy of federal law, but also with the sovereignty of the Cherokee Nation itself. This was stronger language than anything Marshall had previously offered on the subject of Native nations' sovereign status; indeed, as Professor Matthew Fletcher has noted, "[t]here had not been a stronger statement of respect for the legal authority of Indian tribes—and there have been few statements of the kind since."[37]

---

understood in international law, not by any wardship or subordination arising out of Indians' nature or primitive condition").

[35] *Worcester*, 31 U.S. at 560–61.

[36] *Id.* at 561.

[37] *See* MATTHEW L.M. FLETCHER, PRINCIPLES OF FEDERAL INDIAN LAW 31 (2017). Apart from its importance in thus propounding important state-power-confining principles of law, the majority opinion in *Worcester* was also noteworthy for what it said about the doctrine of discovery. *See supra* note 27. Though not purporting to overrule *Johnson* directly, the Chief Justice in *Worcester* offered an account of the doctrine that appeared to be narrower than the account offered in *Johnson* itself. In particular, Marshall no longer maintained that "discovery gave title," *see Johnson*, 21 U.S. at 573; rather, as he now put it in *Worcester*, discovery afforded to a colonizing government only "the exclusive right to *purchase*" (exclusive, that is, vis-à-vis other colonial powers) discovered land while "not affect[ing] the rights of those already in possession." *Worcester*, 31 U.S. at 544 (emphasis added). Thus, as Professor Blake Watson has put it, whereas *Johnson* had indicated that "Indian tribes retained possession of their lands after discovery, but no longer owned the land," *Worcester* instead indicated that "Indian tribes retained ownership *and* possession of their lands after discovery, but no longer held unlimited disposition rights." *See generally* Blake A. Watson, *Discovery and the Definition of Indian Title*, 15 LEWIS & CLARK L. REV. 995, 999 (2011). *But cf.* Singer, *supra* note 27, at 24–36 (suggesting that *Johnson* itself is compatible with the full-ownership view and that *Worcester* merely helped to "clarify" some of *Johnson*'s "ambiguous" language). Notwithstanding the Chief Justice's apparent change of course on this issue, however, the Court would over a century later endorse a version of the discovery doctrine marked by a harshness that exceeded even that of *Johnson* itself. *See* Tee-Hit-Ton Indians v. United States, 348 U.S. 272, 279 (1955) (holding that the discovery doctrine permitted the United States government to divest the Tee-Hit-Ton Indians of their lands "without any legally enforceable obligation to compensate the Indians," notwithstanding the dictates of the Fifth Amendment's Takings Clause); *see also* Singer, *supra* note 27, at 39 ("*Tee-Hit-Ton* contradicts the Marshall Court rulings that hold that Indian nations possess 'Indian title' and that their property rights 'are as sacred as the fee simple of the whites' " (quoting Mitchel v. United States, 34 U.S. 711, 745 (1835))); Davis, *supra* note 4, at 1766 (characterizing the *Tee-Hit-Ton* holding as one that "*Johnson* neither portended nor supported"); Milner S. Ball, *John Marshall and Indian Nations in the Beginning and Now*, 33 JOHN MARSHALL L. REV. 1183, 1190 (2000) (contending that the *Tee-Hit-Ton* rule "can be derived from *Johnson* only by first importing interpretive devices from Wonderland and then employing them to do real harm to real tribes").

On its face, *Worcester* seemed to reflect a victory for the Madisonian vision of federal-tribal relations. But the case's legacy is more complex. In the short term, the decision did little to halt the expulsion of the Cherokee Nation from its lands. Instead of acting in accordance with the Court's ruling,[38] President Andrew Jackson pressed on with the federal government's own "Indian removal" program, leading eventually to the forced relocation of the Cherokee people along the Trail of Tears. As for the longer-term impact of the ruling, although the Court continues to cite to *Worcester* with approval, it has watered down key aspects of the case's holding. Perhaps most important, while the Court in *Worcester* insisted that state law could "have no force" within Indian country,[39] the Court today applies a more qualified version of this rule.[40] Indeed, by 1992 the doctrinal ground had shifted so much that the Court would remark without any apparent misgivings that "[t]he 'platonic notions of Indian sovereignty' that guided Chief Justice Marshall have, over time, lost their independent sway."[41]

2. Modern Tribal Sovereignty and the Means of Its Defeasance

Even so, the concept of tribal sovereignty remains a key element of federal law, and the Court continues to recognize that Native nations retain the "inherent powers of a limited sovereignty which has never been extinguished."[42] These powers include the power to establish and structure a system of government,[43] to determine membership within the political community,[44] to exercise civil and criminal jurisdiction over members and territory,[45] and to exclude

---

[38] *Worcester* is the subject of a phrase often attributed to Jackson: "John Marshall has made his decision; now let him enforce it." *See* COHEN'S HANDBOOK, *supra* note 10, § 1.03. While it is doubtful that Jackson spoke these precise words, the spirit of the quote rings true insofar as the President "did nothing . . . to protect the Cherokees from increasing abuse from white settlers." *Id.*

[39] *Worcester*, 31 U.S. at 561.

[40] *See infra* Section 25.A.4.

[41] County of Yakima v. Confederated Tribes & Bands of Yakima Indian Nation, 502 U.S. 251, 258 (1992) (quoting McClanahan v. Arizona State Tax Comm'n, 411 U.S. 164, 172 (1973)).

[42] United States v. Wheeler, 435 U.S. 313, 322 (1978) (quoting FELIX COHEN, HANDBOOK OF FEDERAL INDIAN LAW 122 (1945) (emphasis omitted)).

[43] *See, e.g.*, Williams v. Lee, 358 U.S. 217, 223 (1978) (recognizing the "right of the Indians to govern themselves" and the "authority of Indian governments over their reservations").

[44] *See, e.g.*, Williams v. Gover, 490 F.3d 785, 789 (9th Cir. 2007) (noting that "[a]n Indian tribe has the power to define membership as it chooses").

[45] *See, e.g.*, United States v. Mazurie, 419 U.S. 544, 556–57 (1975) (recognizing that "Indian tribes are unique aggregations possessing attributes of sovereignty over both their members and their territory"); *see also id.* at 558 (noting that "[t]he cases in this court have consistently guarded the authority of Indian governments over their reservations"); Merrion v. Jicarilla Apache Tribe, 455 U.S. 130, 160 (1982) (Stevens,

nonmembers from tribal land.[46] Tribal sovereignty also carries with it a general immunity from suit in state and federal court,[47] and, as Chief Justice Marshall first recognized in *Worcester*, a presumptive immunity, at least as a general matter, from the operation of state law within tribal boundaries.[48] These powers and immunities, moreover, are "pre-constitutional," in the sense that they derive from a sovereign status that predates the Constitution itself.[49] At the same time, the sovereignty of Native nations is subject to a rule of "complete defeasance" under federal law and may be diminished in one of three ways.[50] First, Congress may abrogate that sovereignty by statute; second, Native nations may relinquish their sovereignty via treaty (or some other type of binding agreement); and third (and most controversially), federal courts may recognize "implicit divestitures" of tribal sovereignty as a matter of judge-made federal common law.

a. Statutory Abrogation

The Court has recognized in Congress a "plenary and exclusive" authority to "legislate in respect to Indian tribes."[51] As a consequence, the sovereignty of Native nations "exists only at the sufferance of Congress," meaning that Congress may at any time enact laws that deprive those Nations of the sovereignty they

---

J., dissenting) ("Over its own members, an Indian tribe's sovereign powers are virtually unlimited").

[46] *See Merrion*, 455 U.S. at 159. *But see infra* Section A.2.c (discussing limits on tribal powers to regulate nonmember conduct on "fee lands"). For a more detailed overview of the powers that flow from tribal sovereignty, *see* COHEN'S HANDBOOK, *supra* note 10, § 4.01[2].

[47] *See* Michigan v. Bay Mills Indian Cmty., 572 U.S. 782, 788 (2014) (characterizing tribal sovereign immunity as "[a]mong the core aspects of sovereignty that tribes possess"). The rules and exceptions governing the scope of this immunity mirror in some respects the rules and exceptions governing the scope of state sovereign immunity, but there are some important differences as well. *See, e.g.*, Regents of the Univ. of Minn. v. LSI Corp., 926 F.3d 1327, 1340 (Fed. Cir. 2019) (noting that "tribal sovereign immunity is subject to the superior and plenary control of Congress, whereas state sovereign immunity can only be abrogated under a valid grant of constitutional authority" (quoting Santa Clara Pueblo v. Martinez, 436 U.S. 48, 58 (1978), and then quoting Kimel v. Fla. Bd. of Regents, 528 U.S. 62, 73 (2000))). For a more detailed overview of these rules, see generally COHEN'S HANDBOOK, *supra* note 10, § 7.

[48] *See Worcester*, 31 U.S. at 561. *But see infra* Section 25.A.4 (discussing exceptions to this rule).

[49] Most important, as the Court has long recognized, the restrictions imposed by the Bill of Rights do not directly limit the powers of tribal governments, *see* Talton v. Mayes, 136 U.S. 376 (1896), although Congress has imposed many analogous restrictions by way of federal statute, *see* Indian Civil Rights Act of 1968, 25 U.S.C. § 1302 (2018).

[50] *See Wheeler*, 435 U.S. at 323.

[51] United States v. Lara, 541 U.S. 193, 200 (2004) (internal quotations omitted); *see also infra* Section 25.A.3.a.

inherently possess.[52] Most controversially, Congress's power to abrogate tribal sovereignty extends even to those tribal interests and authorities that the U.S. government had previously pledged by treaty to preserve.[53]

Although Congress thus has wide-ranging authority to abrogate tribal sovereignty by statute, the federal courts have developed and often deploy canons of construction that discourage statute-based determinations that such abrogations have occurred. Known collectively as the "Indian canons,"[54] these legal principles provide that courts should construe statutes, treaties, and other legal materials "generously in order to comport with . . . traditional notions of [tribal] sovereignty and with the federal policy of encouraging tribal independence."[55] The Indian canons, moreover, often take precedence over competing canons that would otherwise favor constructions adverse to tribal interests.[56] Those canons thus enable

---

52 *See Wheeler*, 435 U.S. at 323. Congress has exercised this authority throughout U.S. history, often to devastating effect. For example, during the late 1800s and early 1900s, Congress enacted a series of statutes that overrode many communal land ownership systems, requiring instead that reservation land be divided into small parcels eventually to be held by individual (and, as it would often turn out, non-Native) landowners. (This "allotment program" reduced the tribal land base from some 135 million acres in 1887 to less than 50 million acres by 1934.) *See* COHEN'S HANDBOOK, *supra* note 10, § 1.04. In addition, during the 1950s, Congress enacted a series of measures that purported to "terminate" many Native nations, while also authorizing (via Public Law 280) many U.S. states to assert criminal and civil jurisdiction in Indian country without tribal consent. *See* FLETCHER, *supra* note 37, at 77–78. Many, though not all, of these termination decrees have subsequently been restored, and Congress has since amended Public Law 280 to include a tribal-consent requirement. *Id.* at 77.

53 *See, e.g.*, Lone Wolf v. Hitchcock, 187 U.S. 553 (1903). For scholarly criticisms of this opinion, see, for example, Joseph William Singer, Lone Wolf, *Or How to Take Property by Calling It a "Mere Change in the Form of Investment,"* 38 TULSA L. REV. 37 (2002); WALTER R. ECHO-HAWK, IN THE COURTS OF THE CONQUEROR: THE 10 WORST INDIAN LAW CASES EVER DECIDED 161–88 (2010).

54 For scholarly overviews, see, for example, Alex Tallchief Skibine, *Textualism and the Indian Canons of Statutory Construction*, 55 MICH. J. L. REF (forthcoming 2022); Philip P. Frickey, *Marshalling Past and Present: Colonialism, Constitutionalism, and Interpretation in Federal Indian Law*, 107 HARV. L. REV. 381, 412–28 (1993).

55 White Mountain Apache Tribe v. Bracker, 448 U.S. 136, 143–44 (1980); *see also* Minnesota v. Mille Lacs Band of Chippewa Indians, 526 U.S. 172, 202 (1999) ("Congress may abrogate Indian treaty rights [by statute], but it must clearly express its intent to do so."); United States v. Dion, 476 U.S. 734, 739 (1986) (refusing to construe a federal statute as abrogating Indian treaty rights absent "clear and plain" evidence of a congressional intent to do so); *Bay Mills Indian Cmty.*, 572 U.S. at 790 (applying a similar rule in connection with the claimed congressional abrogation of tribal sovereign immunity).

56 For instance, the Indian canons can override application of the presumption against repeals by implication, *see, e.g.*, Montana v. Blackfeet Tribe, 471 U.S. 759, 766 (1985) (holding that Congress impliedly revoked a taxing authority it had previously granted to U.S. states over certain royalty interests owned by Native nations under federal oil and gas leases, while finding that normally applicable interpretive presumptions "against repeals by implication" and "especially an implied repeal of a specific statute by a general one" did not apply because "the standard principles of

courts to play a "continuing role in safeguarding the inherent sovereign powers of Indian tribes" by precluding the recognition of statutory abrogations of tribal sovereignty in "cases where Congress has not acted clearly."[57]

b. Treaty-Based Relinquishment

Federal law also permits the divestiture of tribal sovereignty by way of agreement between Native nations and the United States. From the Revolutionary Era until 1871, these agreements most often took the form of treaties, many of which involved cessions of indigenous lands in exchange for federally provided goods, services, and/or property rights over other lands.[58] (These agreements, it should be noted, often were not—even remotely—the product of free, fair, arms-length negotiation, as federal agents often resorted to fraud, bribery, and military coercion to secure their counterparties' signatures.[59]) Congress declared an end to federal-Indian treatymaking with the Appropriations Act of 1871, and no more treaties with Native nations have been ratified since that time.[60] But the 1871 statute left untouched treaties that already were in effect, and scores of these treaties remain on the books today.[61] As a result, many eighteenth- and nineteenth-century treaties continue to bear

---

statutory construction do not have their usual force in cases involving Indian law"), the rule that statutory exemptions from taxation must be clearly expressed, *see, e.g.*, Choate v. Trapp, 224 U.S. 665, 675 (1912) (noting that, although "tax exemptions are strictly construed" as a general matter, the "rule is exactly the contrary" as applied to "the government's dealings with the Indians"), and (according to some lower courts) the principle of *Chevron* deference in administrative law, *see, e.g.*, Cobell v. Norton, 240 F.3d 1081, 1102 (D.C. Cir. 2001) (justifying a "departure from the *Chevron* norm" in federal Indian law cases). *But see* COHEN'S HANDBOOK, *supra* note 10, § 2.02 (noting that courts have sometimes "simply ignored the Indian law canons").

[57] *Id.* § 4.02. It also bears noting that, just as Congress may use its "plenary powers" to abrogate tribal sovereignty, so too may it use those powers to "affirm" aspects of tribal sovereignty that it (or the courts) had previously taken away. Congress did this, for instance, when it acted to afford official federal recognition to several Native nations that it had previously "terminated," *see, e.g.*, United States v. Long, 324 F.3d 475, 482 (7th Cir. 2003) (characterizing the Menominee Restoration Act in these terms), and it also acted in this way when it superseded by statute a series of Supreme Court rulings that had utilized the "implicit divestiture" doctrine to curtail tribal sovereignty, *see, e.g.*, *Lara*, 541 U.S. at 204 (recognizing Congress's power to "relax restrictions on tribal sovereignty").

[58] *See* FLETCHER, *supra* note 37, at 7.

[59] *See, e.g.*, RESTATEMENT (THIRD) OF THE LAW OF AMERICAN INDIANS § 6 cmt. a (2022) ("Indian treaty negotiations often involved duress, coercion, fraud, and other illegitimate efforts by the federal government and others to influence tribal treaty negotiators.").

[60] *See* 16 Stat. 566 (1871), codified at 25 U.S.C. § 71.

[61] In addition, and notwithstanding the 1871 statute, the federal government continues to negotiate agreements with Native nations, which it now implements through a combination of executive-branch actions and Article I statutes. *See* Antoine v. Washington, 420 U.S. 194, 203–04 (1975); *see also infra* Section 27.C (discussing congressional-executive agreements and sole executive agreements).

upon modern-day federal Indian law disputes. And in resolving these disputes, courts have often insisted, much as in the statutory context, that any treaty-based relinquishment of tribal sovereignty be expressed in unambiguous terms.[62]

c. *Implicit Divestiture*

The third means of diminishing tribal sovereignty stands in stark tension with the Indian canons. Whereas those canons discourage courts from finding that a statute or treaty has impliedly diminished a Native nation's sovereignty, the theory of implied divestiture renders some aspects of tribal sovereignty subject to curtailment by way of judge-made rulings rooted in principles of federal common law.[63] The resulting doctrinal inconsistency is clear: While ostensibly allowing Congress to abrogate tribal authority only by way of clear statutory or treaty-based language, the Court has asserted for itself a standalone power to recognize such "implicit divestitures" in instances where the relevant statutes or treaties do not speak, even arguably, to the matter at hand.[64]

The implied-divestiture doctrine traces its origins to the Court's 1978 ruling in *Oliphant v. Suquamish Indian Tribe*.[65] That case arose out of the effort of the Suquamish Tribe to bring tribal-court prosecutions against two non-Indian defendants who had violated tribal law while on tribal land. Although no federal statute or treaty prohibited the tribal court's exercise of jurisdiction, the Court nonetheless ruled that the Suquamish Tribe—and Native nations more generally—lacked the authority to prosecute and punish non-Indians for violations of tribal law. In particular, as then-Associate Justice Rehnquist explained for a six-Justice majority, "by submitting to the overriding sovereignty of the United States," Native nations had "necessarily give[n] up their power to try non-Indian citizens of the United States except in a manner acceptable to

---

[62] *See, e.g.*, County of Oneida v. Oneida Indian Nation, 470 U.S. 226, 247 (1985) ("[T]reaties should be construed liberally in favor of the Indians, with ambiguous provisions interpreted to their benefit." (internal citations omitted)); *see also* Winters v. United States, 207 U.S. 564, 576–77 (1908) (noting that "ambiguities occurring [within treaties] will be resolved from the standpoint of the Indians"); McGirt v. Oklahoma, 140 S. Ct. 2462, 2470 (2020) (noting the rule that "treaty rights are to be construed in favor, not against, tribal rights"); *see also* Herrera v. Wyoming, 139 S. Ct. 1686, 1699 (2019) (asserting that "the words of a treaty must be construed 'in the sense in which they would naturally be understood by the Indians' " (quoting Washington v. Wash. State Comm. Passenger Fishing Vessel Ass'n, 443 U.S. 658, 676 (1979))).

[63] *See Wheeler*, 435 U.S. at 326 (referencing "that part of sovereignty which the Indians implicitly lost by virtue of their dependent status").

[64] *See, e.g.*, Richard B. Collins, *Never Construed to Their Prejudice: In Honor of David Getches*, 84 U. COLO. L. REV. 1, 55 (2013) (noting that the "canons have been shunted aside" in the Court's implied divestiture jurisprudence).

[65] 435 U.S. 191 (1978).

Congress."[66] And this remained true even where, as here, the underlying crime had been committed within the tribal territory, against tribal officers, and in clear violation of properly enacted tribal law.

Notwithstanding powerful scholarly critiques of the Court's reasoning in *Oliphant*,[67] the decision remains in effect today. In fact, the Court in 1990 expanded the reach of its holding by concluding in *Duro v. Reina*[68]—again pursuant to a theory of "implied divestiture"—that tribal courts lack criminal jurisdiction over not just non-Indians but also "nonmember Indians" as well.[69] Congress,

---

[66] *Id.* at 210.

[67] To a nearly universal degree, the Court's ruling in *Oliphant* has been condemned by scholars of federal Indian law. *See, e.g.*, ROBERT A. WILLIAMS, LIKE A LOADED WEAPON: THE REHNQUIST COURT, INDIAN RIGHTS, AND THE LEGAL HISTORY OF RACISM IN AMERICA 115 (2005) (opining that "*Oliphant* has to be regarded as one of the most racist Indian law opinions written by a justice of the Supreme Court in the post-*Brown* era"). Among other things, these commentators have noted inaccuracies in *Oliphant's* historical analysis, *see, e.g.*, Robert N. Clinton, *There Is No Federal Supremacy Clause for Indian Tribes*, 34 ARIZ. ST. L.J. 113, 214–15 (2002) (highlighting the "revisionist nature of the history in the *Oliphant* opinion"), while also raising serious doubts about the Court's treatment of precedents and statutes relevant to the case, *see, e.g.*, John P. LaVelle, *Implicit Divestiture Considered: Outtakes from the* Cohen's Handbook *Cutting-Room Floor*, 38 CONN. L. REV. 731, 737, 739 (2006) (noting that "*Oliphant's* 'incorporation' theory is contradicted by the text and reasoning of the Marshall cases" and that the "*Oliphant* Court did not identify any provisions of positive law clearly inconsistent with the exercise of tribal power"). They have also highlighted ways in which the decision appeared to be "motivated in part by claims about the lawlessness of Indian tribes," Elizabeth A. Reese, *The Other American Law*, 73 STAN. L. REV. 555, 634 (2021); *see also* COHEN'S HANDBOOK, *supra* note 10, § 4.02[b] (noting that the Court's decision "may have been influenced by [its] assumption that the non-Indian majority on the Port Madison reservation would not be treated fairly by the tribal minority"), with the Court's reasoning thus reflecting and reinforcing "the European colonial-era principle of white racial supremacy," WILLIAMS, *supra*, at 112. Still others have emphasized the Court's failure to take account of the serious practical difficulties that the decision poses for criminal law enforcement in Indian Country. COHEN'S HANDBOOK, *supra* note 10, § 4.02 (noting that the Court's holding in *Oliphant* has left tribes "unable to respond when non-Indians commit crimes such as sale of illegal drugs and domestic violence that endanger the tribal community"); *see also* Hallie Bongar White, Kelly Gaines Stoner & James G. White, *Creative Civil Remedies Against Non-Indian Offenders in Indian Country*, 44 TULSA L. REV. 427 (2008) (offering an account of Native nations' post-*Oliphant* efforts to confront these difficulties). And they have more fundamentally questioned the Court's willingness to engage in any sort of "implicit divestiture" analysis at all, given Congress's already-existent (and plenary) power to regulate and limit tribal courts' criminal jurisdiction on its own. *Cf.* Lavelle, *supra*, at 739 (noting that "[j]udicial initiative in creating policy-driven limitations on inherent tribal powers is in tension . . . with the federal courts' traditional deference to Congress with respect to policymaking in Indian affairs")

[68] 495 U.S. 676 (1990).

[69] *Id.* at 690. Again, the Court reasoned—this time in an opinion by Justice Kennedy—that its ruling found support in the "Tribe's dependent status," which (so he said) precluded its power of "criminal enforcement" from "extend[ing] beyond internal relations among members." *Id.* at 688. In addition, and as in *Oliphant*, the Court noted its "hesita[nce] to adopt a view of tribal sovereignty that would single out another group of citizens . . . for trial by political bodies that do not include them." *See*

however, responded to this ruling with legislation that superseded *Duro*'s expansion of *Oliphant* (but not *Oliphant* itself),[70] and the Court upheld this legislation in *United States v. Lara*[71] as a valid exercise of Congress's power to affirm aspects of tribal sovereignty that the Court had previously refused to recognize. The result of this series of judicial and congressional actions is that federal law today prohibits all tribal courts from exercising criminal jurisdiction over non-Indians,[72] while permitting the courts of one Native nation to exercise jurisdiction over both that nation's members and the members of other such nations as well.

The Court has put the "implicit divestiture" theory to work not only in the criminal-law context, but also in several civil cases. The foundational decision in this area is *Montana v. United States*,[73] which arose from a challenge to the Crow Nation's regulation of hunting and fishing on non-Indian "fee lands" (i.e., lands owned in fee simple by non-Indians) located on reservation territory. In an opinion authored by Justice Stewart, a six-member majority ruled that the distinct character of these lands precluded the Crow Nation from regulating nonmember' activities on them.[74] As in *Oliphant*, the Court imposed this restriction on tribal authority even though no federal statute or treaty spoke directly to the question presented by the case.[75] In marked contrast to *Oliphant*, however, the Court in *Montana* did not purport to set forth a categorically prohibitive rule. Acknowledging that "Indian tribes retain inherent sovereign power to exercise some forms of civil jurisdiction over non-Indians on their

---

id. at 693. Also, as in *Oliphant*, the Court failed to reconcile its position with its longstanding willingness to permit state courts to exercise criminal jurisdiction over non-state citizens. *See* Matthew L.M. Fletcher, *Race and American Indian Tribal Nationhood*, 11 WYO. L. REV. 295, 319 & n.144 (2011) (noting this inconsistency, while also noting the broader irony of justifying divestitures of tribal sovereignty by reference to concerns about a lack of political representation or consent).

70 25 U.S.C. § 1301(2) (2018).

71 541 U.S. 193 (2004).

72 More recently, the 2013 reauthorization of the Violence Against Women Act effectuated a partial abrogation of *Oliphant*, by authorizing tribal courts to exercise "special domestic violence criminal jurisdiction" over non-Indian offenders. *See* Violence Against Women Reauthorization Act of 2013, Pub. L. No. 113–4, §§ 901–910, 127 Stat. 54, 118–26.

73 450 U.S. 544 (1981).

74 *See id.* at 565 ("[T]he principles on which [*Oliphant*] relied support the general proposition that the inherent sovereign powers of an Indian tribe do not extend to the activities of nonmembers of the tribe.").

75 The Court did reject the Crow Tribe's specific argument that various treaties and statutes had conferred on it an affirmative authority to regulate nonmember conduct on fee lands, but it did not further hold that those materials explicitly divested the Tribe of its authority to do so. *See id.* at 550–57. Instead, it concluded that the Tribe lacked the "inherent sovereignty" to regulate nonmember conduct on the lands because that authority was "inconsistent with the dependent status of the tribes." *Id.* at 564.

reservation," Justice Stewart identified two types of circumstances in which Native nations could continue to regulate nonmember conduct, "even on non-Indian fee lands."[76] First, "[a] tribe may regulate, through taxation, licensing, or other means, the activities of nonmembers who enter consensual relationships with the tribe or its members, through commercial dealing, contracts, lease, or other arrangements."[77] Second, tribal authorities "retain inherent power to exercise civil authority over the conduct of non-Indians on fee lands within its reservation when that conduct threatens or has some direct effect on the political integrity, the economic security, or the health or welfare of the tribe."[78]

The *Montana* rule and its two "*Montana* exceptions" have generated many follow-on decisions.[79] While a full recounting of these decisions lies beyond the scope of this book, two of them warrant a brief mention here. First, in *Strate v. A-1 Contractors Inc.*,[80] the Court extended the *Montana* rule to cover not only the regulatory powers of tribal lawmakers and agencies, but also the adjudicative powers of tribal courts in civil cases. More specifically, in a unanimous opinion authored by Justice Ginsburg, the Court barred the Tribal Court for the Three Affiliated Tribes of the Fort Berthold Reservation from adjudicating a tort claim involving two nonmember defendants that arose from a car accident on a public right-of-way located within tribal land.[81] In reaching this result, Justice Ginsburg downplayed the significance of two earlier decisions in which the Court had seemed to recognize broad tribal authority to adjudicate civil cases of this kind,[82] finding those precedents not to "expand or stand apart from *Montana*'s instruction on 'the inherent sovereign powers of an Indian tribe.' "[83] In addition, she reasoned that, when it came to applying the thus-controlling *Montana* rule, there was no reason to conclude that "a tribe's adjudicative jurisdiction [should] exceed its legislative jurisdiction."[84]

---

[76] *Id.* at 565.

[77] *Id.* at 566. In support of this exception, the Court cited to its earlier decision in *Williams v. Lee*, 358 U.S. 217 (1959), in which it had made clear that the Navajo Courts of Indian Offenses could exercise civil jurisdiction over a suit arising from a commercial transaction that had taken place between a nonmember merchant and a member buyer on tribal land. *See infra* Section 25.A.4.

[78] *Montana*, 450 U.S. at 566.

[79] *See generally* COHEN'S HANDBOOK, *supra* note 10, § 4.02[c].

[80] 520 U.S. 438 (1997).

[81] *Id.* at 442.

[82] *See* Nat'l Farmers Union Ins. Cos. v. Crow Tribe, 471 U.S. 845 (1985); Iowa Mut. Ins Co. v. LaPlante, 480 U.S. 9 (1987).

[83] *Strate*, 520 U.S. at 453 (quoting *Montana*, 450 U.S. at 565).

[84] *Id. Strate* also broadened the divestiture accomplished by *Montana* in two ways: First, the Court found it immaterial that the allegedly tortious conduct had

The second decision is *United States v. Cooley*,[85] in which the Justices unanimously upheld a tribal police officer's exercise of authority "to detain temporarily and to search a non-Indian on a public right-of-way that runs through an Indian reservation."[86] Given the criminal-law nexus of the challenged detention, the Court might have applied *Oliphant*. Ultimately, however, it did not, instead holding that *Montana* supplied the applicable rule and that the second *Montana* exception—*i.e.*, the exception that covers nonmember conduct threatening the "political integrity, the economic security, or the health or welfare of the tribe"[87]—"fits the present case, almost like a glove."[88] That was so, the Court explained, because it would be "difficult for tribes to protect themselves against ongoing threats," such as those posed by "non-Indian drunk drivers, transporters of contraband, or other criminal offenders operating on roads within the boundaries of a tribal reservation" unless their officers had some power to detain non-Indians, at least until state or federal officers arrive on the scene.[89]

In one sense, the Court's decision in *Cooley* was a narrow one, as Justice Alito's separate concurrence in the case took pains to point out.[90] But the decision is potentially significant for two reasons. First,

---

occurred not on fee lands (as in *Montana* itself), but rather on a reservation land encumbered by a public right of way. That fact the Court maintained, did not matter because it was willing to treat the roadway as a form of "alienated, non-Indian land" fully subject to the *Montana* rule. *Id.* at 454. Second, the Court refused to apply either one of *Montana*'s two exceptions and instead chose to describe the exceptions in narrow terms. In particular, while the Court in *Montana* had recognized a retained tribal authority to regulate nonmembers who were in "consensual relationships with the tribe . . . through commercial dealing," the Court in *Strate* found no significance in the fact that the sued company had been an active commercial subcontractor of the Tribes, reasoning instead that the accident itself involved individuals who were not parties to the relevant commercial contracts. *See id.* at 457; *see also* Atkinson Trading Co. v. Shirley, 532 U.S. 645, 656 (2001) ("A non-member's consensual relationship in one area . . . does not trigger tribal civil authority in another—it is not in for a penny, in for a pound." (internal quotations omitted)). Similarly, while the Court in *Montana* had recognized a retained tribal jurisdiction to deal with conduct that "threatens . . . the health and welfare of the tribe," *Montana*, 450 U.S. at 566, the Court in *Strate* refused to apply that exception on the ground that the challenged exercise of civil jurisdiction was not in its view "*crucial* to the 'political integrity, the economic security, or the health or welfare of the Three Affiliated Tribes.' " *Strate*, 520 U.S. at 459 (quoting *Montana*, 450 U.S. at 459) (emphasis added); *see also* COHEN'S HANDBOOK, *supra* note 10, § 4.02[3][c][i] n.75 (suggesting that under the "elevated threshold" set forth by the Court in *Strate*, "tribal power must be necessary to avert catastrophic consequences" in order to fall within *Montana*'s second exception).

85 141 S. Ct. 1638 (2021).

86 *Id.* at 1642.

87 *Montana*, 450 U.S. at 566.

88 *Cooley*, 141 S. Ct. at 1643.

89 *Id.*

90 *Cooley*, 141 S. Ct. 1646 (Alito, J., concurring) (suggesting that the Court had decided nothing more than "the following: On a public right-of-way that traverses an Indian reservation and is primarily patrolled by tribal police, a tribal police officer has

as Professor Elizabeth Reese has noted, the Court—by applying *Montana* rather than *Oliphant* in *Cooley*—"blur[red] the lines between the court's civil and criminal jurisdiction jurisprudence," thus suggesting that *Montana* may now operate as its "favored Indian sovereignty test."[91] Second, as Professor Reese also has observed, *Cooley* marks the first-ever case in which the Court found *Montana*'s second exception applicable, and it thus runs counter to the thrust of a long line of post-*Montana* decisions that had operated to undermine rather than vindicate values of tribal sovereignty.[92] It remains to be seen whether the decision reflects a blip on the radar or the start of a meaningful new trend, but it is possible that *Cooley* marks the beginning of a retreat from *Oliphant* and its theory of implied divestiture.

3. Federal Power and Responsibility with Respect to Indian Affairs

a. *The "Plenary Power" Doctrine*

"The Constitution," the Court has declared, "grants Congress broad general powers to legislate in respect to Indian tribes, powers that we have consistently described as 'plenary and exclusive.' "[93] This idea reaches back to a spate of late nineteenth-century cases in which the Court, invoking racist and colonialist notions about the "weakness and helplessness" of Native nations,[94] claimed for Congress an absolute and effectively unreviewable authority to pass laws concerning tribal matters.[95] By way of these early "plenary power" rulings, the Court permitted Congress to violate preexisting treaty obligations, abrogate core aspects of tribal sovereignty, dispossess Native people of their lands (without paying just compensation), and otherwise intrude on and interfere with native Nations' internal operations. The plenary power doctrine thus bears

---

the authority to (a) stop a non-Indian motorist if the officer has reasonable suspicion that the motorist may violate or has violated federal or state law, (b) conduct a search to the extent necessary to protect himself or others, and (c) if the tribal officer has probable cause, detain the motorist for the period of time reasonably necessary for a non-tribal officer to arrive on the scene").

91 Elizabeth Reese, *Affirmation of Inherent Tribal Power to Police Blurs Civil and Criminal Indian Law Tests*, SCOTUSBLOG (Jun. 7, 2021), https://www.scotusblog.com/2021/06/affirmation-of-inherent-tribal-power-to-police-blurs-civil-and-criminal-indian-law-tests/.

92 *Id.*

93 *Lara*, 541 U.S. at 200 (quoting Washington v. Confederated Bands & Tribes of Yakima Indian Nation, 439 U.S. 463, 470–71 (1979)).

94 *See, e.g.*, United States v. Kagama, 118 U.S. 375, 384 (1886).

95 *See Lone Wolf*, 187 U.S. at 565 (noting that "[p]lenary authority over the tribal relations of the Indians has been exercised by Congress from the beginning, and the power has always been deemed a political one, not subject to be controlled by the judicial department of the government").

a close linkage to some the worst tragedies in the history of federal Indian policy.[96]

It is noteworthy that the Court has never repudiated—and indeed continues to cite approvingly to—these early "plenary power" cases.[97] But the use of that power has evolved in line with Congress's shift, beginning in the late 1960s, toward a federal policy grounded in the values of tribal autonomy and self-determination.[98] During this "self-determination era," Congress has invoked its plenary power over Indian affairs to adopt laws that "affirm" features of tribal sovereignty (including features previously denied by Congress or the courts),[99] that delegate to Native nations policy-making powers under federal law,[100] that restore recognition of previously

---

[96] *See, e.g.*, Blackhawk, *supra* note 11, at 1797 (noting that the plenary power doctrine was the "constitutional law underlying" the federal government's "violent dispossession of Native peoples," "internment of Natives into reservation camps," and "efforts to 'kill the Indian and save the man' by forcing Indian children into boarding schools run by the federal government" (citing ROBERT ANDERSON ET AL., AMERICAN INDIAN LAW: CASES AND COMMENTARY 124–26 (3d ed. 2015))).

[97] *See, e.g.*, *Lara*, 541 U.S. at 200. The term "plenary power" can carry different connotations. In its broadest sense it describes a power whose exercise is not subject to any otherwise applicable constitutional limits (such as the rights-based protections of the Bill of Rights) or is at least not judicially reviewable in relation to those limits. Alternatively, it might mean, as Professor Nell Jessup Newton has described it, a power that remains subject to other negative limits but is at least "unlimited as to the objectives Congress might pursue." *See* Nell Jessup Newton, *Federal Power Over Indians: Its Sources, Scope, and Limitations*, 132 U. PA. L. REV. 195, 196 n.3 (1984) (citing David Engdahl, *State and Federal Power Over Federal Property*, 18 ARIZ. L. REV. 283, 363–66 (1976)). The Court's earliest plenary power decisions were more in line with the former conception, *see, e.g.*, *Lone Wolf*, 187 U.S. at 568 (suggesting that Congress's power over Indian affairs "has always been deemed a political one, not subject to be controlled by the judicial department of the government" and that "[w]e must presume that Congress acted in perfect good faith in the dealings with the Indians of which complaint is made"), but its more recent decisions are more in line with the latter. *See, e.g.*, Del. Tribal Bus. Comm. v. Weeks, 430 U.S. 73, 83 (1977) (noting that "the statement in *Lone Wolf* . . . has not deterred this Court, particularly in this day, from scrutinizing Indian legislation to determine whether it violates the equal protection component of the Fifth Amendment"); United States v. Sioux Nation, 448 U.S. 371, 413 (1980) (noting that the *Lone Wolf* suggestion "has long since been discredited in takings cases"); Hodel v. Irving, 481 U.S. 704 (1987) (striking down portions of the Indian Land Consolidation Act of 1983 as violative of the Takings Clause). That is, the Court today understands Congress's power to be "plenary" in the sense that, while subject to other constitutional limits, it encompasses the "authority to legislate for the Indian tribes in all matters." *Wheeler*, 435 U.S. at 319.

[98] *See* FLETCHER, *supra* note 37, at 81–87.

[99] *See supra* Section 25.2.A (discussing the *Duro* fix).

[100] For example, a variety of federal environmental statutes, including the Clean Air Act, the Clean Water Act, and the Comprehensive Environmental Response, Compensation, and Liability Act, confer on tribal governments the same general regulatory authorities that they confer on state governments. *See* Judith V. Royster & Rory SnowArrow Faussett, *Control of the Reservation Environment: Tribal Primacy, Federal Delegation, and the Limits of State Intrusion*, 64 WASH. L. REV. 581, 619–21 (1989) (describing these regulatory regimes). *See generally Mazurie*, 419 U.S. at 546 (holding that Congress may validly delegate federal powers to tribal governments).

"terminated" Tribes,[101] that protect indigenous peoples against both public and private forms of discrimination and abuse,[102] and that promote economic development and the provision of government services on tribal lands.[103] For this reason, the Court's recognition of a broad congressional authority over Indian affairs is today viewed by some commentators as serving salutary purposes in the present, notwithstanding the "plenary power" doctrine's profoundly problematic past.[104]

The source of Congress's "plenary power" over Indian affairs has always been uncertain. Although the Court has offered different theories at different times, it most recently suggested that the doctrine derives from three interlocking sources. The first is the Indian Commerce Clause of Article I, section 8, which, though referencing only a power to "regulate *commerce* . . . with the Indian tribes,"[105] has been viewed as supporting congressional authority to "regulate tribal affairs" more generally.[106] The second is the Treaty Clause of Article II, which, though "not literally authoriz[ing] Congress to act legislatively," supports Congress's wide-ranging authority to implement via statutory enactments founded on the Necessary and Proper Clause the many treaties with Native nations that remain on the books.[107] The third source is the "inherent" authority of the national government to engage in dealings with

---

101 *See, e.g.*, *Lara*, 541 U.S. at 203 (noting Congress's "re-recognition" of the Menominee Tribe—a Tribe that "it previously had terminated").

102 *See, e.g.*, Indian Child Welfare Act. 25 U.S.C. §§ 1901 *et seq.*; Indian Civil Rights Act, 25 U.S.C. §§ 1901 et seq. (2018); American Indian Religious Freedom Act, 42 U.S.C. § 1996 (2018).

103 *See, e.g.*, Indian Gaming Regulatory Act of 1988, 25 U.S.C. §§ 2701 et seq. (2018); Indian Health Care Improvement Act, 25 U.S.C. §§ 1601.

104 *See, e.g.*, Leah Litman & Matthew L.M. Fletcher, *The Necessity of the Indian Child Welfare Act*, THE ATLANTIC (Jan. 22, 2020), https://www.theatlantic.com/ideas/archive/2020/01/fifth-circuit-icwa/605167 (noting that the Court's foundational plenary-power decisions have "over time, . . . come to produce different results" and that it has "empowered Congress, in recent years, to protect Native families from various new and old forms of discrimination, imperialism, and white supremacy"). At the same time, the idea of a plenary congressional power to regulate Native nations stands in tension with the basic notion of tribal sovereignty, and some scholars and advocates have continued to voice skepticism of the idea. *See generally* Michalyn Steele, *Plenary Power, Political Questions, and Sovereignty in Indian Affairs*, 63 UCLA L. REV. 666, 670 & n.11 (2016) (collecting citations for the proposition that "many Indian law scholars view the plenary power doctrine . . . as a tool that fosters and formalizes the legal oppression of Indian people by an unchecked federal government").

105 U.S. CONST. art. I, § 8, cl. 3.

106 Ramah Navajo Sch. Bd., Inc. v. Bureau of Revenue of N.M., 458 U.S. 832, 837 (1982); *see also* Cotton Petroleum Corp. v. New Mexico, 490 U.S. 163, 192 (1989) (noting that the "central function of the Indian Commerce Clause is to provide Congress with plenary power to legislate in the field of Indian affairs").

107 *Lara*, 541 U.S. at 201; *see also id.* (citing Missouri v. Holland, 252 U.S. 416, 433 (1920)).

other sovereigns,[108] an authority that, according to the Court, "rest[s] in part . . . on powers that this Court has described as 'necessary concomitants of nationality.' "[109]

In recent years, however, the constitutional underpinnings of the plenary-power doctrine have been subject to question, with critics maintaining that the Indian Commerce Clause in particular points the way to a very different (and significantly) narrower scope of congressional authority with respect to tribal affairs.[110] Of particular note, this line of scholarship has caught the eye of Justice Thomas, who, in series of solo opinions filed over the past two decades, has questioned the textual bona fides of the plenary-power doctrine[111] and criticized it as fundamentally at odds with the idea of tribal sovereignty.[112] It remains to be seen whether this position will win over additional adherents—particularly from among Justices Gorsuch, Kavanaugh, and Barrett, none of whom as of this writing have participated in a case directly involving the plenary-power doctrine. But recent changes in the Court's composition, coupled with Justice Thomas's unflinching opposition to the doctrine, raise the

---

[108] *See generally supra* Section 10.E.

[109] *Lara*, 541 U.S. at 201 (quoting United States v. Curtiss-Wright Export Corp., 299 U.S. 304, 315–322 (1936)). On the origins of this idea—as applied not just to Congress's Indian affairs powers, but also to its powers with respect to foreign affairs, federal territories, and immigration, see Sarah H. Cleveland, *Powers Inherent in Sovereignty: Indians, Aliens, Territories, and the Nineteenth Century Origins of Plenary Power Over Foreign Affairs*, 81 TEX. L. REV. 1 (2002).

[110] *See, e.g.*, Robert G. Natelson, *The Original Understanding of the Indian Commerce Clause*, 85 DENV. U. L. REV. 201, 241–44, 250 (2007); Saikrishna Prakash, *Against Tribal Fungibility*, 89 CORNELL L. REV. 1069, 1089 (2004). *But see* Matthew L.M. Fletcher, *ICWA and the Commerce Clause* (contending that the relevant historical evidence "points to an inescapable conclusion—the original intent and meaning of the Indian Commerce Clause was to make Congressional authority plenary and exclusive as to the states" (emphasis added)), *in* FACING THE FUTURE: THE INDIAN CHILD WELFARE ACT AT 30, at 28, 31 (Matthew L.M. Fletcher et al. eds, 2009); Gregory Ablavsky, *Beyond the Indian Commerce Clause*, 124 YALE L.J. 1012, 1021 (2015) (contending that "many early actors located supreme federal authority in Indian affairs in a holistic interpretation of the Constitution"); Jack M. Balkin, *Commerce*, 109 MICH. L. REV. 1, 24–26 (2010) (noting that Congress's adoption of the Trade and Intercourse Acts beginning in 1790 evidenced a reading of the Indian Commerce Clause that authorized federal regulation of a wide range of noneconomic activities). For further discussion of the Indian Commerce Clause, see *supra* Section 4.F.1.

[111] *See, e.g.*, Adoptive Couple v. Baby Girl, 133 S. Ct. 2552, 2565–71 (2013) (Thomas, J., concurring); *Lara*, 541 U.S. at 224–25 (Thomas, J., concurring in the judgment).

[112] *See id.* at 226 (Thomas, J., concurring in the judgment) (questioning the idea that the federal government can "regulate the tribes through ordinary domestic legislation and simultaneously maintain that the tribes are sovereigns in any meaningful sense"); United States v. Bryant, 136 S. Ct. 1954, 1969 (2016) (Thomas, J., concurring) (describing the plenary power doctrine as based on "a paternalistic theory that Congress must assume all-encompassing control over the 'remnants of a race' for its own good" (quoting *Kagama*, 118 U.S. at 384)).

possibility that a judicial rethinking of this core feature of Native nation law might be on the horizon.[113]

b. The Indian Trust Doctrine

While the plenary-power doctrine gives Congress broad discretion in regulating Indian affairs, the "Indian trust doctrine," reins in the authority of both Congress and other federal decisionmakers. This doctrine, to be sure, does not directly override the plenary-power principle because it imposes only "prudential"—and thus nonbinding—constraints on Congress's legislative authority.[114] The principles that underlie the Indian trust doctrine, however, find expression in a wide range of treaties,[115] and "[n]early every piece of modern legislation dealing with Indian tribes contains a statement reaffirming the trust relationship between tribes and the federal government."[116] Against this backdrop, the Indian trust doctrine operates primarily as a principle that supports challenges to *executive-branch* decision-making, by empowering courts to set aside agency action on the ground that it violates legislatively recognized fiduciary duties of care, loyalty, and protection owed to Native nations by the federal government.[117] In addition, even though the doctrine is not legally enforceable against Congress, its focused endorsement of federal authorities' trustee-like obligations furnishes

---

113 Such a shift would potentially result in "a wholesale reshaping of the law that has governed Indian affairs for the past century and a half." Ablavsky, *supra* note 111, at 1016; *see also* FLETCHER, *supra* note 37, at 39 ("Undermining the theoretical foundations of federal plenary power might serve to limit federal authority over Indian affairs, but it might also destroy much of what Indian people and tribes relied upon as their best hopes for a remedy.").

114 *See* COHEN'S HANDBOOK, *supra* note 10, at § 5.04[3][b].

115 Mary Christina Wood, *Indian Land and the Promise of Native Sovereignty: The Trust Doctrine Revisited*, 1994 UTAH L. REV. 1471, 1497, 1503 (noting that many of the earliest treaty arrangements between the federal government and Native nations embodied a "sovereign trust" relationship).

116 *See* COHEN'S HANDBOOK, *supra* note 10, § 5.04. For much of U.S. history, this doctrine served the perverted purpose of helping to justify the Court's deference to the federal government's catastrophically harmful (and affirmatively non-fiduciary) treatment of indigenous peoples. *See* Raymond Cross, *The Federal Trust Duty in an Age of Indian Self-Determination: An Epitaph for a Dying Doctrine*, 39 TULSA L. REV. 369, 376 (2003) (noting that during much of the nation's past the federal courts, "far from inhibiting or channeling the overweening growth of this federal power over the Indian peoples, actively abetted and aided its growth by crafting judicial principles that rendered it impervious to the Indian peoples' legal or political challenge"); Seth Davis, *The False Promise of Fiduciary Government*, 89 NOTRE DAME L. REV. 1145, 1186 (2014) (noting that "courts have often treated the trust relationship as a shield for government action, not a sword to challenge it"). Perhaps the most notorious decision in this vein was *Lone Wolf*, 187 U.S. 553, in which the Court managed to invoke the trust relationship as providing a justification for, rather than fixing a limit on, the federal government's authority to unilaterally disregard its treaty responsibilities to Native nations. *See* Davis, *supra*, at 1186.

117 *See* COHEN'S HANDBOOK, *supra* note 10, § 5.04[3][b].

a "source of persuasive arguments by tribes urging passage of legislation or seeking oversight of executive agencies."[118]

4. Tribal-State Relations

We conclude our overview of federal Indian law by considering the extent to which states may exercise their own regulatory powers over Native nations and peoples located within state territorial boundaries. Notwithstanding Chief Justice Marshall's early declaration in *Worcester* that Georgia laws could "have no force" within Cherokee territory,[119] the Court today recognizes only a qualified prohibition on state-based regulations of this sort.[120] Modern case law on this subject is often said to begin with the Court's 1959 decision in *Williams v. Lee*.[121] The dispute in *Williams* arose from a state-court action brought by a non-Indian plaintiff against two members of the Navajo Nation—members who, the plaintiff alleged, owed him money for items purchased from his store on the Navajo Reservation.[122] The defendants resisted the suit on jurisdictional grounds, claiming that the case belonged in tribal court,[123] and all nine Justices agreed.[124] In his majority opinion for the Court,[125] however, Justice Black characterized the "basic policy"

---

118 *Id.* In addition, the trust doctrine has long been cited as providing a justification for the Indian canons of construction, which in turn provide their own safeguards against implicit legislative encroachments on tribal sovereignty. *See, e.g.*, County of Oneida v. Oneida Indian Nation of N.Y. State, 470 U.S. 226, 247 (1985) ("The canons of construction applicable in Indian law are rooted in the unique trust relationship between the United States and the Indians.").

119 *Worcester*, 31 U.S. at 561; *see also In re* Kansas Indians, 72 U.S. 737, 756 (1866) (relying on *Worcester* in holding that, absent a federal statute or treaty to the contrary, Native nations "enjoy the privilege of total immunity from [s]tate taxation").

120 *See, e.g.*, *Bracker*, 448 U.S. at 141–42 (noting that "[l]ong ago the Court departed from Mr. Chief Justice Marshall's view that 'the laws of [a State] can have no force' within reservation boundaries" (quoting *Worcester*, 31 U.S. at 562)).

121 358 U.S. 217 (1959); *see, e.g.*, Richard D. Pomp, *The Unfulfilled Promise of the Indian Commerce Clause and State Taxation*, 63 TAX LAW. 897, 994 (2011) ("In the 20th century, the Supreme Court was fairly quiescent on matters of Indian sovereignty until *Williams v. Lee*. . . .").

122 *Williams*, 358 U.S. at 217–18.

123 *Id.* at 218.

124 *Id.*

125 *Williams*'s historical legacy is complicated. On the one hand, as Professor Pomp has pointed out, Justice Black wrote *Williams* "during the termination era" and "Indian law scholars and Indian sympathizers [had] feared for the worst." Pomp, *supra* note 121, at 1004. From that perspective, *Williams* has been celebrated as a victory for the cause of tribal sovereignty and a decision that "helped create a legal foundation for tribal self-determination." Bethany R. Berger, Williams v. Lee *and the Debate Over Indian Equality*, 109 MICH. L. REV. 1463, 1468 (2011) (noting that "Justice Black . . . perceived a link between *Williams* and *Brown v. Board of Education*, and wrote an opinion that strongly affirmed not only tribal rights but also the prerogative of the federal government to protect those rights against state intrusion" (internal footnotes omitted)). From another perspective, however, as Professor Milner Ball described it, Justice Black's reworking of *Worcester* helped to "set in motion a fundamental shift in

of *Worcester* as standing only for the more limited principle that "absent governing Acts of Congress, the question has always been whether the state action *infringed on the right of reservation Indians to make their own laws and be ruled by them*."[126] And while the answer to that question was "yes" as applied to the facts of *Williams* itself,[127] the Court's reframing of *Worcester*'s central dictate in terms of an open-ended "infringement test" would end up laying the groundwork for a series of subsequent rulings in the other direction.[128]

The outcome of *Williams* derived from background (though congressionally defeasible) principles of tribal sovereignty not directly linked to federal statutory law. Today, however, those principles more often operate to inform courts' evaluation of questions concerning federal *statutes'* preemptive effects on states' powers to regulate with respect to Indian affairs.[129] That is, rather than ask whether a state law directly violates *Williams*'s "infringement test," courts more often treat the concerns underlying that test as a "backdrop" against which to construe federal statutes and treaties in determining their state-law displacing effects.[130] The two inquiries have thus come to share an overlapping doctrinal space.[131] And what occupies this space can be thought of as a form of

---

language and approach" that would eventually "encourage and sanction state forays into Indian country," forays that subsequent Justices would uphold under the *Williams* "infringement" standard. *See* Ball, *supra* note 37, at 1186–87.

126 *Williams*, 358 U.S. at 219–20 (emphasis added).

127 *Id.* at 223 (holding that there could be "no doubt" that allowing the state court to exercise jurisdiction would impermissibly interfere with "the right of the Indians to govern themselves."); *see also id.* (noting that it was "immaterial that the [plaintiff] is not an Indian" because "[h]e was on the Reservation and the transaction with an Indian took place there").

128 *See* Pomp, *supra* note 121, at 1007 (noting that "[i]n the hands of an ally like Justice Black, the threat to Indian sovereignty was minimal, but other justices would soon prove to be less protective").

129 *See McClanahan*, 411 U.S. at 172 (noting that the "trend" of the case law "has been away from the idea of inherent Indian sovereignty as a bar to state jurisdiction and toward reliance on federal pre-emption" instead).

130 *Id.* This trend, to be sure, is not entirely uniform, and the Court still sometimes purports to treat tribal sovereignty as a standalone source of legal protection against state-based regulation. *See, e.g.*, *Blackfeet Tribe*, 471 U.S. at 764 ("The Constitution vests the Federal Government with exclusive authority over relations with Indian tribes. As a corollary of this authority, *and in recognition of the sovereignty retained by Indian tribes even after formation of the United States*, Indian tribes and individuals generally are exempt from state taxation within their own territory." (internal citations omitted) (emphasis added)).

131 To be sure, there is a big conceptual difference in theory between: (a) treating the *Williams* test as a component of federal preemption doctrine; and (b) treating the *Williams* test as establishing a limit that exists separate and apart from preemption doctrine, as only the latter treatment of *Williams* would afford protections to tribal sovereignty where statutes and treaties fail to speak to the challenged state action. The Court, however, has suggested that the "extent of . . . residual Indian sovereignty in the total absence of federal treaty obligations or legislation" is "generally of little

constitutional common law—attributable in part to the penumbral implications of federal enactments and in part to stand-alone principles of tribal sovereignty and federal exclusivity, but subject at all times to congressional revision and repeal.

As might be predicted, the Court's decision-making in this area is marked by unpredictability, if not incoherence.[132] Different majorities of Justices, operating with different statutes and treaties in view, have reached different conclusions regarding the scope of tribal immunity from state-based regulations, yielding a complex patchwork of holdings that resist easy synthesis. Even so, a few general principles seem to have emerged from the Court's varied rulings. First, with a few notable exceptions,[133] the Court has concluded that states may not exercise jurisdiction over *tribal institutions and members within Indian country*,[134] unless explicitly authorized to do so by a federal statute or treaty.[135] At least as a default rule, that is, tribal governments hold the exclusive power to prohibit, penalize, tax, and otherwise regulate member conduct within their respective territories, and states cannot generally interfere with that power by enforcing their own prohibitions,

more than theoretical importance," as "in almost all cases federal treaties and statutes define the boundaries of federal and state jurisdiction." *McClanahan*, 411 U.S. at 172 n.8.

[132] For an especially thoughtful and comprehensive treatment of these issues—and one whose 326-page length pointedly attests to their complexity—see Pomp, *supra* note 121.

[133] *See, e.g.*, Moe v. Confederated Salish & Kootenai Tribes, 425 U.S. 463, 479 (1976) (permitting states to require tribal sellers operating on tribal land to collect sales-tax-related payments from non-Indian buyers of cigarettes); *see also* Washington v. Confederated Tribes of the Colville Indian Reservation, 447 U.S. 134, 159–60 (1980) (extending *Moe* to authorize additional sales-tax related reporting and certification requirements); Dep't of Taxation & Fin. v. Milhelm Attea & Bros Inc., 512 U.S. 61 (1994) (further extending *Moe* and *Colville* to cover a suite of regulations concerning the collection and reporting of cigarette taxes); *cf. County of Yakima*, 502 U.S. 251 (permitting states to tax tribal land that was rendered fully alienable by the General Allotment Act of 1887 and the 1906 Burke Act, even if owned by tribal members); Cass Cty. v. Leech Lake Band of Chippewa Indians, 524 U.S. 103 (1998) (permitting a similar form of taxation on similarly alienable lands, even where not expressly authorized by the 1906 Burke Act); City of Sherrill v. Oneida Indian Nation of N.Y., 544 U.S. 197 (2005) (applying a similar rule to land re-acquired by the Onieda Nation after having previously been sold in fee to a non-member buyer); Erik M. Jensen, *Taxation and Doing Business in Indian Country*, 60 ME L. REV. 1, 84 (2008) (citing *County of Yakima*, *Cass County*, and *Oneida Nation* for the proposition that "[t]axability follows alienability, unless a contrary intent is clearly manifested" (internal quotations omitted)).

[134] The term "Indian country" has been statutorily defined to encompass "all land within the limits of any Indian reservation under the jurisdiction of the United States Government," "all dependent Indian communities within the borders of the United States," and "all Indian allotments, the Indian titles to which have not been extinguished." *See* 18 U.S.C. § 1151.

[135] *See* COHEN'S HANDBOOK, *supra* note 10, § 6.01.

penalties, taxes, and regulations.[136] Second, and at the opposite end of the spectrum, the Court has taken a highly permissive approach to state regulation of *tribal members outside of Indian country*, with the end result being that "[a]bsent express federal law to the contrary, Indians going beyond reservation boundaries have generally been held subject to non-discriminatory state law otherwise applicable to all citizens of the State."[137] Here, in other words, the presumption that prevails within Indian country is effectively flipped on its head: whereas states must find affirmative authorization in federal statutes or treaties to justify the regulation of tribal members in tribal territory, the absence of a federal statutory or treaty-based prohibition will generally suffice to permit state regulation of Native Americans operating outside Indian country.[138] Finally, with respect to *Williams*-like cases involving state-based exercises of authority of nonmember conduct within Indian country, the Court now applies a framework derived from its 1980 decision in *White Mountain Apache Tribe v. Bracker*.[139] That framework calls for "a particularized inquiry into the nature of the state, federal, and tribal interests at stake,"[140] and it has over time "morph[ed] into a balancing test" that has proven not especially favorable to tribal interests and claims.[141]

---

[136] *See, e.g.*, *McClanahan*, 411 U.S. at 165 (holding that Arizona lacked the authority to tax income earned "wholly from reservation sources" by a tribal member who lived on tribal land).

[137] Mescalero Apache Tribe v. Jones, 411 U.S. 145, 148–49 (1973).

[138] Federal prohibitory measures of this kind do exist, and courts accordingly have set aside on preemption-related grounds some state regulations of out-of-Indian-country activities by tribal members. *See, e.g.*, *Herrera*, 139 S. Ct. 1686 (holding that the Crow Tribe's 1868 treaty with the United States prohibited Wyoming from criminally prosecuting the Tribe's members for hunting on unoccupied lands within the state and refusing to construe the subsequent statute granting statehood to Wyoming as abrogating this treaty-based protection).

[139] 448 U.S. 136 (1980).

[140] *Id.* at 145.

[141] *See* Pomp, *supra* note 121, at 1130. Thus, for instance, the interest-balancing exercise has enabled the Court to conclude that a state's revenue-raising interests can justify its taxation of nonmember activities within Indian country, even where state taxation is likely to depress commercial activity within tribal boundaries and therefore impair countervailing tribal interests in economic development and revenue raising. *See, e.g.*, *Colville*, 447 U.S. at 156. It also has enabled the Court to suggest that a state's provision of services in Indian country might operate to enhance the state's taxation authority within Indian country, even where the economic value of those services is admittedly "disproportionate to" the burden imposed by the tax. *See, e.g.*, *Cotton Petroleum Corp.*, 490 U.S. at 185–86 (declining to impose "a proportionality requirement"); *see id.* at 204 (Blackmun, J., dissenting) (noting that, "[u]nder the majority's approach, there is no pre-emption unless the States are *entirely* excluded from a sphere of activity and provide *no* services to the Indians or to the lessees they seek to tax"); *cf. also Ramah Navajo Sch. Bd., Inc.*, 458 U.S. at 843 (holding that the state's inability to tax nonmember-owned construction firms hired to build a school on tribal land derived in part from the state's own failure "to take any responsibility for the education" of Navajo children). At the same time, the Court has sometimes applied the *Bracker* framework in reaching pro-tribal results. *See, e.g.*, *Mescalero*, 462 U.S. 324

In other words—and putting statutory and treaty-based specifics to one side—the extent of a state's authority to regulate in relation to Native nations and their members now depends largely on two variables: (1) the place in which the regulated conduct occurs, and (2) the status of the regulated party as a tribal member or nonmember.[142] States generally *may not* exercise jurisdiction over tribal members in Indian country; they generally *may* exercise jurisdiction over tribal members outside of Indian country;[143] and their power to exercise jurisdiction over nonmembers in Indian country depends on the open-ended "interest-balancing" framework that *Bracker* and its progeny have established. Needless to say, this complicated patchwork of rules marks a substantial departure from the Court's simpler-seeming insistence in *Williams* that states could not "infringe[ ] on the right of reservation Indians to make their own laws and be ruled by them."[144] And it is an even farther cry from the Court's original proclamation in *Worcester* that state laws "have no force" in Indian country.[145]

(prohibiting New Mexico from enforcing state-law restrictions on hunting and fishing against both members and nonmembers engaging in such conduct on tribal land); California v. Cabazon Band of Mission Indians, 480 U.S. 202, 216 (1987) (prohibiting California from regulating bingo and poker games operated on Indian reservations and "played predominantly by non-Indians").

[142] With regard to state tax laws, the question of "where" and "against whom" a tax applies is not always easy to answer. In working through questions of this sort, the Court's general approach has been to emphasize the "legal" rather "economic" incidence of the tax in question. *See* Jensen, *supra* note 133, at 60 (noting that what matters in this context is not a tax's "economic reality" but rather the law's own formal characterizations of "*what* [is] being taxed and *where* the *what* [is]"). Thus, for instance, in *Oklahoma Tax Commission v. Chickasaw Nation*, 515 U.S. 450 (1995), the Court treated an Oklahoma motor-vehicle fuel excise tax as a tax on Chickasaw Nation-owned gas retailers, because the tax's "legal incidence" fell on retailers and not on the consumers to whom those retailers passed on the tax's underlying cost. *Id.* at 457–60. Similarly, in *Wagnon v. Prairie Band Potawatomi Nation*, 546 U.S. 95 (2005), the Court treated as presumptively permissible a Kansas tax levied on a distributor's off-reservation receipt of fuel, even though the fuel itself was destined for delivery to an on-reservation retail gas station owned by the Potawatomi Nation. *Id.* at 106, 102–10 (deeming it irrelevant that the tax, in its real-world operation, increased the on-reservation price of the fuel, including to tribe members and to the tribe's own obvious detriment, because the tax targeted "the distributor's off-reservation receipt of the motor fuel, and not any subsequent event" in terms of its legal incidence). In similar fashion, it did not matter in *Moe*, *see supra* note 133, that a Montana tax on cigarette sales was to be collected and remitted by tribal sellers doing business on tribal lands; instead, the Court drew attention to the Montana law's stipulation that the tax fell "on the retail consumer," which in turn meant that, insofar as it covered "sales by Indians to non-Indians," the tax did not unlawfully interfere with tribal affairs. 425 U.S. at 482–83.

[143] An unresolved question is whether a similarly categorical bar applies to a state's interference with tribal governments' regulation of nonmember Indians within Indian country. For a discussion of this question, see COHEN'S HANDBOOK, *supra* note 10, § 6.01.

[144] *Williams*, 358 U.S. at 220.

[145] *Worcester*, 31 U.S. at 561. A further potential limit on the ability of states to interfere with tribal affairs stems from the Indian Commerce Clause of Article I. *See*

U.S. CONST. art. I, § 8, cl. 3 (setting forth Congress's power "[t]o regulate Commerce with foreign Nations, and among the several States, and with the Indian Tribes"); *see generally supra* Chapters 16–22 (discussing the dormancy doctrines developed pursuant to the Commerce Clauses' treatment of interstate and foreign commerce). Some confusion has arisen as to whether that clause gives rise to a dormancy-based restriction on state action akin to the limits imposed by the interstate- and foreign-commerce-related features of Article I, section 8, clause 3. *See, e.g.*, Ward v. New York, 291 F. Supp. 2d 188, 199–200 (W.D.N.Y. 2003) (indicating, albeit in some tension with other aspects of the overall analysis in the case, that while "the Interstate Commerce Clause . . . has a dormant or negative aspect, the Indian Commerce Clause does not"). *See generally* Clinton, *supra* note 18, at 1220–21 (suggesting, as a doctrinal matter, that there are "no judicially enforceable limitations" under the Indian Commerce Clause but also forcefully challenging the legal basis for that result). The main source of this confusion is *Cotton Petroleum Corp.*, 490 U.S. 163, in which the Court considered a challenge to a New Mexico severance tax as applied to minerals extracted from land subject to the jurisdiction of the Jicarilla Apache Nation ("the Nation"). The tax presented a problem for would-be private-company drillers because the Nation also collected its own severance tax based on the same activity, thus creating an allegedly "unlawful multiple tax burden on interstate commerce." *Id.* at 187–88 (citing the Brief for Appellants). The Court, however, found no constitutional difficulty based on this interstate-commerce-based argument, emphasizing that Native nations do not constitute "States" within the meaning of the Commerce Clause, while adding along the way that "the Interstate Commerce and Indian Commerce Clauses have very different applications." *See id.* at 191–93 (noting in this regard that the clause itself "draws a clear distinction between 'States' and 'Indian Tribes' " and that different considerations apply, including as a matter of the framing history, to competition among geographically separate states as opposed to conflicts between "States and tribes [that] have concurrent jurisdiction over the same territory"). The only issue before the Court in *Cotton Petroleum Corp.*, however, concerned a claimed burdening of *interstate* commerce, and the Justices therefore neither had to nor did repudiate the earlier-established principle that Article I's treatment of Indian commerce, like its parallel treatment of interstate and foreign commerce, imposes some limits of its own force on state action. *See, e.g.*, *Colville*, 447 U.S. at 156–58 (observing that the dormancy doctrine "may have a more limited role to play in preventing undue discrimination against, or burdens, on Indian Commerce" while still applying that doctrine to find no impermissible state action in that case); *see also* Thunderhawk v. Cty. of Morton, 483 F. Supp. 3d 684, 747–48 (D.N.D. 2020) (stating that "[i]t remains unclear if the Supreme Court has recognized a dormant aspect to the Indian Commerce Clause" but assessing, in keeping with *Colville*, whether the challenged law produced "undue discrimination against, or burdens on, Indian commerce"); HCl Distribution, Inc. v. Peterson, 360 F. Supp. 3d 910, 919–922 (D. Neb. 2018) (concluding that "the plaintiffs' Indian Commerce Clause claims may not be resolved on a summary basis," albeit while not clearly distinguishing those claims from claims resting on generalized principles of tribal sovereignty). Indeed, seven years after handing down *Cotton Petroleum Corp.*, at least eight, and probably all nine, Justices effectively endorsed the proposition that "the regulation of Indian commerce . . . is under the exclusive control of the Federal Government," thus "vest[ing] in Congress complete lawmaking authority over [this] particular area." Seminole Tribe v. Florida, 517 U.S. 44, 72 (1996); *accord id.* at 148 (Souter, J., dissenting, joined by Ginsburg and Breyer, JJ.) (building on this exclusivity principle to conclude that "States have no sovereignty in the regulation of commerce with the tribes"); *see also id.* at 100 (Steven, J., dissenting) (detailing his own common-law-centered view of state sovereign immunity, but also stating that he dissented for "these reasons, as well as those set forth in [Justice Souter's opinion]"). To be sure, the dormant Indian Commerce Clause has had little practical impact in recent decades because of the Court's movement toward evaluating tribal-state conflicts by reference to federal-law preemption principles and the standalone protections of tribal sovereignty. Even so, and regardless of *Cotton Petroleum Corp.*, it remains open to courts to find that some state laws abridge the dormancy doctrine because of their specialized connection to *commerce* in particular. For this reason, when state laws do impinge Native nations' commercial activities—

B. U.S. TERRITORIES

1. A General Overview

Article IV, section 3 empowers Congress "to dispose of and make all needful Rules and Regulations respecting the Territory or other Property belonging to the United States."[146] At the time of the founding, this clause reflected a widespread expectation that the newly created nation would acquire additional land areas to be administered by the federal government as something other than full-fledged states.[147] This expectation was soon borne out, as the federal government laid claim to a growing number of "territories," first across the North American mainland and later overseas. Many of these territories would in time become states. Others would win their independence. Still others retain their territorial status to this day.

As of now, five permanently inhabited territories remain a part of the United States—American Samoa, Guam, the Northern Mariana Islands, Puerto Rico, and the U.S. Virgin Islands. Some 3.5 million people live in these territories, with the vast majority (some 3.3 million) living in the Commonwealth of Puerto Rico.[148] All of these territories have their own governments that, pursuant to congressional delegations of authority, make and administer their own local law.[149] At the same time, and as the Article IV Territory Clause suggests, the territories remain subject to the "plenary power" of Congress, which may act to supersede the dictates of territorial law (including as embodied in territorial constitutions) by way of federal statutes.[150]

---

and especially if such laws discriminate against those commercial activities—lawyers should look for chances to mount challenges based on not only generalized principles of preemption law and tribal sovereignty, but also the dormant Indian Commerce Clause as well.

146 U.S. CONST. art. IV, § . 3.

147 In addition, at the time, the federal government already exerted control over some areas—including the Northwest Territory—that lay outside the boundaries of any then-existing state. *See* Ordinance of 1787: The Northwest Territorial Government, *reprinted in* 1 U.S.C. at XLV (2012).

148 *See* U.S. DEPARTMENT OF THE INTERIOR, OFFICE OF INSULAR AFFAIRS, 2020 ISLAND AREAS CENSUSES (2020), *available at* https://www.doi.gov/sites/doi.gov/files/uploads/oia-02202020-census-in-the-territories.pdf; U.S. Census Bureau, Quick Facts: Puerto Rico, https://www.census.gov/quickfacts/PR (last visited Oct. 13, 2021).

149 *See* United States v. Lebrón-Caceres, 157 F. Supp. 3d. 80, 96-97 (D.P.R. 2016) (noting that "territorial governments are entirely a creation of Congress," which "owe all their powers to the statutes of the United States conferring on them the powers which they exercise").

150 *See, e.g.*, United States v. Vaello-Madero, 956 F.3d 12, 17 (1st Cir. 2020) (noting the "plenary powers granted to Congress under the Territory Clause"), *cert. granted*, 141 S. Ct. 1462 (2021). Although it might seem to follow from this point that Congress may reclaim for itself some (or even all) of those conferred powers at any time, Justice

Pointing to Congress's plenary control over the creation and operation of federal territories, the Court has held that such territories, in contrast to both states and Native nations, do not qualify as "separate sovereigns" within the U.S. constitutional system.[151] This distinction, to be sure, is not totally clear-cut: Most notably, all U.S. territories and most U.S. states (37 of 50, to be precise) share the important feature of having been brought into the nation by legislative act rather than the vote of an Article VII ratifying convention.[152] Similarly, U.S. territories resemble Native nations in that they too operate against the backdrop of a "plenary" federal legislative authority.[153] Even so, territorial governments remain institutionally distinctive in that they alone: (a) were brought into the Union by way of congressional legislation (like most states but unlike Native nations); (b) are subject to Congress's "plenary" legislative authority (unlike states but like Native nations); and (c) possess, as a matter of governing default rules, only those powers that Congress has affirmatively granted to them (unlike states and unlike Native nations).

In four of the five territories—namely, Guam, the Northern Mariana Islands, Puerto Rico, and the U.S. Virgin Islands—

Sotomayor recently suggested otherwise, at least with respect to Puerto Rico, reasoning that international-law obligations, among other things, may limit the federal government's authority to unilaterally alter the terms of a 1950 statute guaranteeing to Puerto Rico a republican form of government and the prerogatives of self-rule. *See* Fin. Oversight & Mgmt. Bd. for P.R. v. Aurelius Inv., LLC, 140 S. Ct. 1649, 1676–77 (2020) (Sotomayor, J., concurring in the judgment).

[151] In addition to being of some conceptual significance, this point carries immediate *doctrinal* importance in guiding the operation of the Fifth Amendment's Double Jeopardy Clause, which the Court has long interpreted as barring successive prosecutions by the *same* sovereign, while permitting such prosecutions by "separate sovereigns." *See* Heath v. Alabama, 474 U.S. 82, 88 (1985). Thus, for instance, it would not violate the Double Jeopardy Clause for the federal government to prosecute a defendant on charges for which the defendant was already prosecuted in state or tribal court. *See, e.g.*, United States v. Lanza, 260 U.S. 377, 382 (1922) (state law); *Wheeler*, 435 U.S. 313 (tribal law). But it would violate the Double Jeopardy Clause for the federal government to prosecute someone already prosecuted under territorial law, because, as the Court has held, a prosecution under that law is, in effect, also a prosecution under federal law as well. *See* Puerto Rico v. Sanchez Valle, 136 S. Ct. 1863 (2016). *But see id.* at 1880 (Breyer, J., dissenting) (contesting this conclusion on the ground that the Commonwealth of Puerto Rico has "gained sufficient sovereign authority to become the 'source' of power behind its own criminal laws"). In addition, the sovereign status of territorial governments has figured into disputes about their power to invoke sovereign immunity. *See generally* Adam D. Chandler, Comment, *Puerto Rico's Eleventh Amendment Status Anxiety*, 120 YALE L.J. 2183 (2011) (canvassing the case law concerning Puerto Rico's sovereign immunity, while also describing related decisions concerning other federal territories and the District of Columbia); 13 CHARLES ALAN WRIGHT & ARTHUR R. MILLER, FEDERAL PRACTICE AND PROCEDURE § 3524.2 (3d ed. Supp. 2021) (similar).

[152] *See Sanchez Valle*, 136 S. Ct. at 1871 (acknowledging this point).

[153] *See id.* at 1872 (noting this similarity).

territorial citizens possess U.S. citizenship.[154] (By contrast, the residents of American Samoa qualify as noncitizen U.S. nationals.[155]) This citizenship, however, carries with it a dramatically diminished set of rights of political participation. Pursuant to statute, the territories may elect "delegates" to the U.S. House of Representatives, but those delegates lack the core power possessed by actual House members in that they cannot vote on federal legislation or any other matters (such as impeachments or internal rulemaking) that come before the body.[156] Territories also lack any representation in the U.S. Senate. And while citizens who live in territories may be allowed by political parties to participate in presidential primaries, they play no role at all in the actual selection of presidential electors.[157] Thus, although the inhabitants of territories are fully subject to the powers of the federal government—indeed, because of the plenary authority vested in Congress by Article IV, even more so than inhabitants of the states—they have no electoral say in how these powers are exercised.

2. The *Insular Cases* and the Doctrine of Territorial Incorporation

Exacerbating (and to some extent underscoring) territorial citizens' lack of political representation is the Court's long-stated position—first set forth in a group of decisions known collectively as the *Insular Cases*—that the Constitution affords only incomplete protection to the residents of "unincorporated" territories. Although the Court has recently signaled doubts about the soundness of these decisions, it has not overruled them.[158] Moreover, because all present-day inhabited territories qualify as "unincorporated,"[159]

---

154 *See* 8 U.S.C. § 1402 (2018) (Puerto Rico); *id.* § 1406(b) (U.S. Virgin Islands); *id.* § 1407(b) (Guam); Act of Mar. 24, 1976, 90 Stat. 265 (Northern Mariana Islands).

155 *See* Tuaua v. United States, 788 F.3d 300, 302 (D.C. Cir. 2015) (noting the absence of statutorily-conferred citizenship for American Samoans and holding that citizenship was not independently conferred by the Citizenship Clause of the Fourteenth Amendment), *cert. denied*, 136 S. Ct. 2461 (2016); *see also American Samoa and the Citizenship Clause: A Study in* Insular Cases *Revisionism*, *in Developments in the Law—The U.S. Territories*, 130 HARV. L. REV. 1680 (2017).

156 *See* CHRISTOPHER M. DAVIS, CONG. RSCH. SERV., R40555, DELEGATES TO THE U.S. CONGRESS: HISTORY AND CURRENT STATUS (2015), *available at* https://sgp.fas.org/crs/misc/R40555.pdf.

157 In addition, the inhabitants of U.S. territories often receive less in the way of federal benefits than do the inhabitants of U.S. states, and indeed are sometimes altogether excluded from the ambit of federal benefits programs. *See* Tom C.W. Lin, *Americans, Almost and Forgotten*, 107 CAL. L. REV. 1249, 1266–67 (2019).

158 *See Aurelius*, 140 S. Ct. at 1665 (declining to reconsider the *Insular Cases*, while characterizing the cases as "much-criticized").

159 Indeed, the uninhabited atoll of Palmyra has since 1959 been the only territory of the United States formally designated as "incorporated." *See* Joseph Blocher & Mitu Gulati, *Puerto Rico and the Right of Accession*, 43 YALE J. INT'L L. 229, 241 n.84 (2018). *But see infra* note 184 and accompanying text (noting a recent U.S. district court

their millions of residents (the vast majority of whom are U.S. citizens) must continue to endure the "second-class treatment" that the Court in the *Insular Cases* endorsed.[160]

The *Insular Cases* arose in the aftermath of the Spanish-American War and the 1898 Treaty of Paris. In that treaty, Spain ceded to the United States its former territories of Puerto Rico, Guam, and the Philippines.[161] But in contrast to prior territorial-annexation treaties, which had extended the full guarantees of U.S. citizenship to territorial residents together with assurances of future U.S. statehood,[162] the 1898 treaty left it up to Congress to determine the "civil rights and political status" of the "native inhabitants" of Puerto Rico, Guam, and the Philippines.[163] Congress, however, chose not to act on this authority,[164] thus leaving the legal status of the residents of those territories in a "nebulous and undefined" state.[165]

It was against this backdrop that the *Insular Cases* were decided. In them, the Court established that the Constitution had

---

decision advocating for the conclusion that Puerto Rico has become an incorporated territory).

160 *See* Stacey Plaskett, *The Second-Class Treatment of U.S. Territories Is Un-American*, THE ATLANTIC (Mar. 11, 2021), https://www.theatlantic.com/ideas/archive/2021/03/give-voting-rights-us-territories/618246.

161 *See* Treaty of Paris, U.S.-Spain, Dec. 10, 1898, 30 Stat. 1754.

162 *See, e.g.*, Christina D. Ponsa-Kraus, *A Perfectly Empty Gift*, 119 MICH. L. REV. 1223, 1233 (2021) (noting that "prior treaties of annexation had included promising citizenship to the inhabitants of annexed territories"), *reviewing* SAM ERMAN, ALMOST CITIZENS: PUERTO RICO, THE U.S. CONSTITUTION, AND EMPIRE (2019).

163 *See* Treaty of Paris, *supra* note 161, art. 9 ("The civil rights and political status of the native inhabitants of the territories hereby ceded to the United States shall be determined by the Congress.").

164 For example, in the Foraker Act of 1900, Congress punted on the issue of territorial citizenship by referring to the inhabitants of Puerto Rico as the "citizens of Porto Rico." Organic (Foraker) Act of 1900, §§ 1–3, 6–9, 31 Stat. 77, 79 (1900) (codified as amended in scattered sections of 48 U.S.C.).

165 Christina Duffy Ponsa-Kraus, *When Statehood Was Autonomy*, *in* RECONSIDERING THE INSULAR CASES: THE PAST AND FUTURE OF AMERICAN IMPERIALISM, 1, 27 (Gerald L. Neuman & Tomiko-Brown Nagin eds., 2015). Congress's inaction on this front was driven largely by political resistance to full-scale annexation of the newly acquired territories. As Judge Juan Torruella once observed, these territorial acquisitions were different from most prior acquisitions not just in the sense that they involved far-off places with "almost no United States citizens residing therein when the change in sovereignty took place," but also in that "much if not most of the large native populations inhabiting these islands were non-white." Juan R. Torruella, *The* Insular Cases: *The Establishment of a Regime of Political Apartheid*, 29 U. PA. J. INT'L L. 283, 289 (2007). That fact, coupled with the widespread understanding that the territories would provide a locus for "economic exploitation" and "the establishment of strategic coaling and naval bases," *id.* at 289–90, led many ruling elites to view the territories in terms of "a typical European colonial relationship of the late nineteenth century." *Id.* at 290. At the same time, because "the term 'colonialism' was anathema" to the American ruling class, there arose the need to cloak the territories' colonial status "in an American constitutional mantle of facial respectability." *Id.* This is largely what the Court in the *Insular Cases* would seek to do.

limited applicability in the newly acquired territories, meaning that their residents did not enjoy the full benefit of its rights-based protections. That result ran directly counter to earlier rulings in which the Court had embraced the proposition that, as anti-imperialists of the time liked to put it, "the Constitution follows the flag."[166] In other words, the Court distinguished away what seemed to be controlling precedent, and it did so by conjuring up a newfangled distinction between "incorporated" territories, on the one hand, and "unincorporated" territories, on the other.[167]

Concurring in *Downes v. Bidwell*,[168] in an opinion later endorsed by a majority of the Court,[169] then-Associate Justice E.D. White explained the theory as follows: For territories that Congress had "deemed" to have "reached that state where it is proper that [they] should enter into and form a part of the American family"—i.e., *incorporated territories*—it was indeed true that the Constitution followed the flag.[170] But as for territories that existed only as "foreign to the United States in a domestic sense" (whatever that meant) and were therefore "merely appurtenant [to the United States] as a possession"—i.e., *unincorporated territories*—the follow-the-flag rule

---

166 *See, e.g.*, William Jennings Bryan, Imperialism: Flag of an Empire (Aug. 8, 1900). Ironically, one of the highest-profile precedents offering support for this proposition was Chief Justice Roger Taney's majority opinion in *Dred Scott v. Sandford*, 60 U.S. (19 How.) 393 (1857). There, in holding that the Fifth Amendment's Due Process Clause barred Congress from banning slavery in U.S. territories, Taney seemed to reject the idea that the Constitution's protections applied with lesser force in U.S. territories. *Id.* at 446–48. More generally, he suggested that Congress could take possession of territories only for the purpose of admitting them into the Union as states and that "no power is given to acquire a Territory to be held and governed permanently in that character." *Id.* at 46; *see also* Rana, *supra* note 3, at 319 (noting that "Taney's opinion defended racial subordination in part through claims that Congress did not enjoy discretionary power in the territories and was instead bound by constitutional constraints"). The Taney opinion thus took on outsize significance in the *Insular Cases*, particularly in *Downes v. Bidwell*, 182 U.S. 244 (1901), where, as Jack Balkin and Sanford Levinson have noted, "*Dred Scott* [was] extensively cited—without shame—by both sides." *See* Jack M. Balkin & Sanford Levinson, *Thirteen Ways of Looking at* Dred Scott, 82 CHICAGO-KENT L. REV. 49, 85 (2007). The "Constitution follows the flag" position also received support in an earlier, Marshall-era case, *Loughborough v. Blake*, 18 U.S. (5 Wheat.) 317 (1820), in which the Court treated the Constitution's Uniformity Clause as applicable to a tax that operated in the District of Columbia. In his opinion for the Court, Chief Justice Marshall reasoned that the term "United States," as used in the Constitution, "is the name given to our great republic, which is composed of States and territories." *Id.* at 319.

167 In so doing, the Court relied on a legal-academic theory that had recently been introduced in the pages of the *Harvard Law Review*. *See* Abbott Lawrence Lowell, *The Status of Our New Territories*, 12 HARV. L. REV. 365 (1899). For a modern-era reflection on the *Law Review*'s role in shaping the outcome of the *Insular Cases*, see *Developments in the Law—The U.S. Territories*, *supra* note 155, at 1680.

168 182 U.S. at 287 (White, J., concurring).

169 *See* Balzac v. Porto Rico, 258 U.S. 298, 309 (1922).

170 *Downes*, 182 U.S. at 339 (White, J., concurring).

did not apply.[171] Instead, the residents of these territories enjoyed only those protections that stemmed from "inherent, although unexpressed, principles which are the basis of all free government."[172]

As noted earlier, the *Insular Cases* remain in effect today, and the theory of "territorial incorporation" continues to breed uncertainty and confusion in the law. For example, the Court has still not made pellucid precisely what distinguishes an "incorporated" from "unincorporated" territory.[173] In addition, there remains the challenge of determining the precise extent to which the Constitution applies in unincorporated territories. Citing language from *Downes*, for instance, courts have generally understood the operative principle to distinguish between "certain natural rights enforced in the Constitution," which do apply in unincorporated territories, and "artificial or remedial rights . . . peculiar to our own system of

---

[171] *Id.* at 341–42.

[172] *Id.* at 290–91. As is perhaps already apparent, the doctrine of "territorial incorporation" derived far less from a dispassionate parsing of constitutional text, history, and precedent than it did from racist assumptions about the "alien races" inhabiting these newly acquired lands. *See, e.g.*, José A. Cabranes, *Citizenship and the American Empire*, 127 U. PA. L. REV. 391, 440 (1978) ("The doctrine of territorial incorporation . . . was based on precisely the same considerations that determined the nature of the 1900 legislation for Puerto Rico: an apprehension that the peoples of the new insular territories were aliens and a belief that the United States ought not to try to deal with them as though they were Americans."). Indeed, it was in this respect no coincidence that many of the Justices who supported the outcome of the *Insular Cases* had, just a few years earlier, endorsed the similarly tendentious and destructive caste-based logic of "separate but equal" in *Plessy v. Ferguson*, 163 U.S. 537 (1896). *See* Adriel I. Cepada Derieux & Neal C. Weare, *After* Aurelius: *What Future for the* Insular Cases?, 130 YALE L.J. FORUM 284, 286 (2020) (noting that "the *Insular Cases* . . . continue to implicitly serve as a basis for Congress to maintain discriminatory laws that treat residents of the territories as second-class citizens, much as *Plessy* did for laws that discriminated against African Americans").

[173] Justice White in *Downes* initially suggested that U.S. citizenship was a key factor—*i.e.*, that by conferring U.S. citizenship on a territory's residents, Congress would necessarily render that territory "incorporated" rather than "unincorporated." *See, e.g.*, *Downes*, 182 U.S. at 333 (White, J., concurring) (suggesting that Congress had acted to incorporate both the Louisiana and Northwest Territories "by bestowing the privileges of citizenship"). The Court, however, soon abandoned this idea, insisting rather cryptically in *Balzac v. Porto Rico*, 258 U.S. 298 (1922), that "[i]t is locality that is determinative of the application of the Constitution . . . and not the status of the people who live in it." *Id.* at 308–09; *see also* Ballentine v. United States, No. CIV.1999-130, 2001 WL 1242571, at *6 (D.V.I. Oct. 15, 2001) (reasoning that, according to the Court's holding in *Balzac*, "the bundle of rights of citizenship grows and diminishes as the citizen travels from one location to another within the physical geographic boundaries of the United States of America"). Other more recent decisions from the Court, meanwhile, have suggested that "incorporated" status depends primarily on whether a territory is "clearly destined for statehood," United States v. Verdugo-Urquidez, 494 U.S. 259, 268 (1990) (citing Dorr v. United States, 195 U.S. 138, 148 (1904)), and that "[i]t may well be that over time the ties between the United States and any of its unincorporated Territories strengthen in ways that are of constitutional significance," Boumediene v. Bush, 553 U.S. 723, 758 (2008).

jurisprudence," which do not.[174] Judicial application of that test, however, has yielded unsteady results.[175] And making matters even more confusing is the Court's recent suggestion that judicial applications of this "fundamentality test" should take into account the question "whether judicial enforcement of the [constitutional] provision would be 'impracticable and anomalous,' "[176] leading one lower court to suggest that the "impracticable and anomalous" standard has now become "the lodestar of the *Insular* framework."[177]

Hovering over all of these matters are first-order questions about the "continued validity" of the *Insular Cases* themselves.[178] More than a few Justices have signaled their willingness to jettison those decisions,[179] and a rising chorus of scholars, advocates, and

[174] *See Downes*, 182 U.S. at 268, 291; *see also Balzac*, 258 U.S. at 312 (holding that inhabitants of unincorporated territories are entitled to "guaranties of certain fundamental personal rights declared in the Constitution"). Recent scholarship has suggested that this binary "fundamental"/"non-fundamental" framing of the test reflects a misunderstanding of the *Insular Cases*, which never in fact suggested that " 'only' certain 'fundamental' rights apply to residents of the territories." *See* Derieux & Weare, *supra* note 172, at 288 (contending that this reading of the *Insular Cases* "turns the actual language from these cases on its head"); *see also* Christina Duffy Burnett, Untied *States: American Expansion and Territorial Deannexation*, 72 U. CHI. L. REV. 797, 804 (2005) (suggesting that the *Insular Cases* have been widely misunderstood in this respect and that "far from carving out a largely 'extraconstitutional zone' for the unincorporated territories, the *Insular Cases* simply perpetuated, with slight modification, an already ambiguous jurisprudence on the applicability of constitutional provisions in the territories of the United States").

[175] The Court itself has held, for instance, that the right to a jury trial is not "fundamental" within the meaning of the *Insular Cases*, *see Balzac*, 258 U.S. at 304–05, even though it has long treated that same right as sufficiently "fundamental" to warrant its incorporation against the states, *see, e.g.*, Ramos v. Louisiana, 140 S. Ct. 1390, 1397 (2020) ("This Court has long explained that the Sixth Amendment right to a jury trial is 'fundamental to the American scheme of justice' and incorporated against the States under the Fourteenth Amendment." (quoting Duncan v. Louisiana, 391 U.S. 145, 148–50 (1968))). Along the same lines, two circuit courts have held that even the Fourteenth Amendment's express guarantee of birthright citizenship is nonfundamental under the *Insular Cases*, *see Tuaua*, 788 F.3d at 308–09; Fitisemanu v. United States, 1 F.4th 862, 878–79 (10th Cir. 2021), even though the plain text of the Fourteenth Amendment guarantees citizenship to "*[a]ll persons* born or naturalized in the United States, and subject to the jurisdiction thereof." *See* U.S. CONST. amend. XIV, § 1 (emphasis added). *But see Tuaua*, 788 F.3d at 305 (concluding that "birthright citizenship does not simply follow the flag").

[176] *See Boumediene*, 553 U.S. at 759 (quoting Reid v. Covert, 354 U.S. 1, 74–75 (1957) (Harlan, J., concurring in the result)).

[177] *See Fitsemanu*, 1 F.4th at 879.

[178] *Aurelius*, 140 S. Ct. at 1666.

[179] *See, e.g.*, *Reid*, 354 U.S. at 14 (opinion of Black, J.) (cautioning that "neither the cases nor their reasoning should be given any further expansion"); Torres v. Puerto Rico, 442 U.S. at 475–76 (Brennan, J., concurring in the judgment) (contending that the cases should no longer serve as "authority for questioning the application of the Fourth Amendment—or any other provision of the Bill of Rights—to the Commonwealth of Puerto Rico"); *cf. Boumediene*, 553 U.S. at 765 ("The Constitution grants Congress and the President the power to acquire, dispose of, and govern territory, not the power to decide when and where its terms apply."); *Aurelius*, 140 S. Ct. at 1666 (characterizing the cases as "much-criticized," while noting but not

lower-court judges have advocated for precisely that result.[180] Meanwhile, some members of Congress have sought to trigger a judicial abandonment of the doctrine by declaring that body's official opposition to the theory of territorial incorporation.[181] (Another approach has been to try to pretermit the doctrine's operation as to Puerto Rico by conferring on it full-scale statehood.[182]) Waiting in the wings might also be a stealth overruling of the *Insular Cases* on the theory that the ties between the United States and all (or at least some) of its territories have so greatly "strengthened" with the passage of time that the transformative shift from unincorporated to incorporated status has now occurred.[183] That one district court recently reached this conclusion with respect to Puerto Rico[184] points to the possibility that other courts might likewise choose to do so in the future.

C. THE DISTRICT OF COLUMBIA

In many ways, the constitutional status of the District of Columbia mirrors that of the territories. Most important, just as surely as Congress has plenary power over the territories,[185] it has a similarly wide-ranging authority over the District of Columbia.[186]

---

deciding the question of whether to overrule them). *But see* Blocher & Gulati, *supra* note 159, at 247 (noting that "[p]erhaps not since the *Insular Cases* have the constitutional implications of colonialism been so central to the Supreme Court's docket—and the Justices have essentially re-affirmed the status quo, one in which the people of territories like Puerto Rico and Guam have second class status").

180 *See* Dereiux & Weare, *supra* note 172, at 291–92 (noting that a "scholarly consensus and the ever-growing number of lower courts wrestling with the *Insular Cases'* uglier implications increasingly show that the cases cannot be separated from their racialized justifications. Sanford Levinson is correct: the cases should rightly be viewed as 'central documents in the history of racism' " (footnotes omitted) (citing Sanford Levinson, *Why the Canon Should Be Expanded to Include the* Insular Cases *and the Saga of American Expansionism*, 17 CONST. COMMENT. 241, 245 (2020))).

181 *See* H.R. Res. 279, 117th Cong. (introduced on Mar. 26, 2021).

182 *See* H.R. 1522, 117th Cong. (introduced on Mar. 2, 2021).

183 *See Boumediene*, 553 U.S. at 757–58 (highlighting this possibility).

184 *See* Consejo de Salud Playa de Ponce, v. Rullan, 586 F. Supp.2d 22, 40–43 (D.P.R. 2008), *as corrected* (Nov. 10, 2008). *But see* Aurelius Inv., LLC v. Puerto Rico, 915 F.3d 838, 848 (1st Cir. 2019) (referring to Puerto Rico as "an unincorporated territory," notwithstanding the earlier district court decision in *Consejo*), *rev'd on other grounds*, 140 S. Ct. 1649 (2020).

185 *See* District of Columbia v. Thompson, 346 U.S. 100, 105–07 (1953) (equating congressional power to vest home-rule authority in locally elected District officers with its power to do the same with respect to territorial officers). For a broader comparison of the territories and the District of Columbia, particularly in terms of their treatment by Congress over time due to their very different physical locations, see *District of Columbia v. Carter*, 409 U.S. 418, 429–32 (1973).

186 *See* U.S. CONST. art. I, § 8, cl. 17 (authorizing Congress "[t]o exercise *exclusive* Legislation *in all Cases whatsoever*, over such District (not exceeding ten Miles square) as may, by Cession of particular States and the Acceptance of Congress, become the Seat of Government of the United States" (emphasis added)); *see also* Berman v. Parker, 348 U.S. 26, 31 (1954) (observing that "[t]he power of Congress over the

Also, in parallel fashion to its handling of the territories, Congress has assigned many of these powers to locally elected government officials.[187] And again as with the territories, Congress has created—with the Court's blessing—specialized courts to handle local disputes, even though those courts' members lack the life-tenure and salary-continuance protections afforded to Article III judges.[188]

Residents of the District, like residents of federal territories, do not have voting representation in the U.S. House or Senate,[189] and they are not eligible to participate (through the actions of their elected representatives) in the constitutional amendment process.[190] Even so, District residents do enjoy a more complete set of constitutional protections than do the residents of federal territories. For one thing, nothing like the principle of *Insular Cases* compromises the constitutional rights of the District's residents, who instead enjoy the full range of guarantees set forth in the Bill of Rights and elsewhere in the Constitution.[191] Meanwhile, with regard to political participation, the Twenty-third Amendment, which was ratified in 1961, directly empowers District residents to participate in presidential elections by giving it the same number of electoral votes "to which [it] would be entitled if it were a State, but in no event more than the least populous state"—a number that today comes out to three.[192]

District of Columbia includes all the legislative powers which a state may exercise over its affairs").

[187] See *Carter*, 409 U.S. at 429 n.25. The establishment of the local government was foreseen by members of the founding generation, including James Madison, who observed that "a municipal legislature for all local purposes, derived from [local residents'] own suffrages will of course be allowed to them." THE FEDERALIST No. 43 (Madison).

[188] *See* Palmore v. United States, 411 U.S. 389 (1973) (affirming Congress's power to establish non-Article III courts for the District of Columbia); *see also infra* Section 29.C (discussing non-Article III courts more generally). To be sure, Congress is free to wield its plenary powers as to territories and the District in different ways, including by treating one but not the other in the same way as states for certain statutory purposes. *See, e.g., Carter*, 409 U.S. at 423 (holding that the District of Columbia is not a "State or Territory" within the statutory meaning of 42 U.S.C. § 1983, even though it is a "State or Territory" within the meaning of 42 U.S.C. § 1982).

[189] As with federal territories, the District does elect a non-voting delegate to the House. *See* District of Columbia Delegate Act, Pub. L. No. 91–405, 84 Stat. 845 (1970).

[190] *See* U.S. CONST. art. V (limiting participation in the ratification of amendments to the legislatures or specially appointed conventions "of the several states").

[191] Indeed, the Court in the *Insular Cases* themselves made it clear that the District of Columbia fell outside the scope of the principle that those cases established. *See, e.g., Downes*, 182 U.S. at 261 (noting that "the Constitution had attached to [the District] irrevocably"); *see also Loughborough*, 18 U.S. at 319.

[192] U.S. CONST. amend. XXIII.

While Congress could at any time confer statehood on Article IV territories by statute,[193] its power to do the same with respect to the District raises a more complicated set of issues. To begin with, any effort by Congress to confer statehood directly on the District as a whole would likely violate the terms of Article I, section 8, which, by vesting in Congress the "exclusive" power over the "seat of Government,"[194] seems to require that the nation's capital—and thus some geographic area not included in a state—remain at all times subject to exclusive federal control.[195] Cognizant of that limit, proponents of D.C. statehood have advocated for reducing the size of the District down to little more than the Capitol complex and then transforming the remainder of the old District into a new state of its own.[196] This plan, however, has stirred its own set of questions, with critics contending (among other things) that the Twenty-third Amendment implicitly precludes such a maneuver by guaranteeing to the "[t]he district constituting the seat of Government" a minimum of three electoral votes.[197] More specifically, so the argument goes,

---

193 *Id.* art. IV, § 3 ("New states may be admitted by the Congress into this union. . .").

194 *Id.* art. I, § 8, cl. 17 (emphasis added).

195 *See* Allen Erbsen, *Constitutional Spaces,* 95 MINN. L. REV. 1168, 1212 n.59 (2011) ("[I]f Congress 'admitted' the District as a state under Article IV, could Congress retain 'exclusive jurisdiction' over the District under Article I? The answer seems to be no because the existence of federal plenary power is inconsistent with states having 'reserved' powers." (quoting U.S. CONST. amend. X)). *But see* Johnny Barnes, *Towards Equal Footing: Responding to the Perceived Constitutional, Legal and Practical Impediments to Statehood for the District of Columbia,* 13 U. D.C. L. REV. 1, 25 (2010) (contending that "[b]y delegating exclusive control of the District, the Constitution enables Congress to address all issues whatsoever that concern the District" and that "Congress may do with the District what it thinks best, including designating it as a state" (internal footnotes omitted)).

196 *See* Washington, D.C. Admission Act, H.R. 51, 117th Congress (2021) (designating the proposed new state as "the State of Washington, Douglass Commonwealth"); *see also* Peter Raven-Hansen, *The Constitutionality of D.C. Statehood,* 60 GEO. WASH. L. REV. 160, 163 (1991) (describing a similar plan to "shrink [the District] to an enclave of federal buildings and installations called the National Capital Service Area, and then to admit the balance of what is now D.C. as the new state of New Columbia").

197 U.S. CONST. amend. XXIII. (More specifically, the amendment guarantees to the District "[a] number of electors of President and Vice President equal to the whole number of Senators and Representatives in Congress to which the District would be entitled if it were a State," U.S. CONST. amend. XXIII, a number that must at least be three—*i.e.,* one Representative plus two Senators.) Other objections to the plan include the suggestion that Article I, section 8 prohibits Congress from "abandon[ing] its exclusive authority over *any part* of the District." OFFICE OF LEGAL POLICY, U.S. DEP'T OF JUSTICE, REPORT TO THE ATTORNEY GENERAL ON THE QUESTION OF STATEHOOD FOR THE DISTRICT OF COLUMBIA iii (1987) (emphasis added). *But see* Raven-Hansen, *supra* note 196, at 167, 167–77 (offering a rejoinder to this argument). Another critique maintains that Article IV, section 3 would require Maryland to consent to any such effort, *see* U.S. CONST. art. IV, § 3 (providing that "no new State shall be formed or erected within the Jurisdiction of any other State . . . without the Consent of the Legislatures of the States concerned"), on the theory that the newly created state would encompass land that once belonged to Maryland. *See* Raven-Hansen, *supra* note

any effort by Congress to relocate virtually all of the District's current residents into a new state would yield the absurd result of affording the handful of remaining residents of the much-diminished federal district (the First Family, perhaps, and maybe a few others[198]) a degree of representation in the electoral college wildly out of proportion to their (infinitesimal) share of the U.S. population.[199] In response, statehood proponents have contested this reading of the Twenty-third Amendment,[200] while also proposing statutory refinements that would eliminate absurd results.[201] In any event, transforming the District of Columbia into a state appears for now to be politically unachievable. Although the U.S. House of Representatives voted in favor of a D.C. statehood in 2021,[202] the bill was filibustered in the Senate and thus never reached the President's desk.

196, at 177–83 (scrutinizing and expressing skepticism about the argument, while also noting that, as a practical matter, official opposition to D.C. statehood from Maryland "could well defeat it").

[198] *See* Charlie Savage & Emily Cochrane, *White House Is Said to Quietly Push Change to D.C. Statehood Bill*, N.Y. TIMES (May 13, 2021), https://www.nytimes.com/2021/05/13/us/politics/biden-dc-statehood.html (noting that under the proposed D.C. statehood bill "[t]he only residence in the rump federal enclave would be the White House").

[199] *See* Derek T. Muller, *Twenty-Third Amendment Problems Confronting District of Columbia Statehood*, HARV. J. L. & PUB. POL'Y PER CURIAM 3–8 (Sept. 3, 2021), https://www.harvard-jlpp.com/twenty-third-amendment-problems-confronting-district-of-columbia-statehood-derek-t-muller/.

[200] *See, e.g.*, Philip G. Schrag, *The Future of District of Columbia Home Rule*, 39 CATH. U. L. REV. 311, 348–49 (1990) (contending that "the twenty-third amendment was not self-executing" and that Congress could therefore deprive the federal enclave of any electoral-college representation by repealing the federal statute that implements its terms); *see also* Raven-Hansen, *supra* note 196, at 188–89 (noting that no one would likely have standing to challenge the validity of a statute denying electoral-college representation to the federal enclave). *But see* Muller, *supra* note 199, at 5–6 (contesting this claim).

[201] One possible workaround would be to require by statute that all residents of the federal enclave establish a domicile in another state and that the enclave's electors cast their vote for whichever candidate won the greatest number of the remaining electoral votes. *See, e.g.*, Letter from Law Professors to Congressional Leaders 5 (May 22, 2021), https://www.scribd.com/document/509015647/Letter-to-Congressional-Leaders-on-Constitutionality-of-Statehood-for-Washington-D-C-May-2021 (outlining this idea).

[202] *See* Washington, D.C. Admission Act, H.R. 51, 117th Congress (2021).

Part III

THE ALLOCATION OF POWER WITHIN THE FEDERAL GOVERNMENT

Chapter 26

THE SEPARATION OF POWERS AND THE POWERS OF THE PRESIDENT

Analysis

Sec.

A. AN INTRODUCTION TO THE SEPARATION OF POWERS

Most of the preceding chapters have focused on the Constitution's *vertical* allocation of power between the federal government and the states. Of no less importance is Constitution's *horizontal* "separation of powers" across different institutions of the federal government. The core features of this plan are simple to state: The enumerated *legislative powers* belong to a Congress (which is itself further divided into a House and a Senate),[1] the *executive power* belongs to the President (who oversees a now-sprawling executive branch),[2] and the *judicial power* belongs to the federal courts (headed up by the Supreme Court of the United States).[3] The basic objective of this scheme is similarly straightforward: By dispersing federal power across separate, independent, and distinctive branches of government,[4] the Framers sought to avoid the "tyranny" that, they feared, would inevitably result from an "accumulation of all powers, legislative, executive, and judiciary" in a single governing entity.[5]

---

1 *See* U.S. CONST. art. I, § 1 ("All legislative Powers herein granted shall be vested in a Congress of the United States, which shall consist of a Senate and House of Representatives.").

2 *Id.* art. II, § 1 ("The executive power shall be vested in a President of the United States of America.").

3 *Id.* art. III, § 1 ("The judicial Power of the United States, shall be vested in one supreme Court, and in such inferior Courts as the Congress may from time to time ordain and establish.").

4 *See* Jon D. Michaels, *An Enduring, Evolving Separation of Powers*, 115 COLUM. L. REV. 515, 525 (2015) (noting that the different branches were "answerable to different sets of constituencies and subject to different temporal demands").

5 *See* THE FEDERALIST NO. 47 (Madison) ("The accumulation of all powers, legislative, executive, and judiciary, in the same hands, whether of one, a few, or many,

That, however, was not the entirety of the idea. A scheme of purely separated powers, after all, could remain vulnerable to tyrannical overreaching, in that any one of the three branches might abuse the particular subset of powers placed in its possession: The legislative branch might enact oppressive laws; the executive might pursue abusive prosecutions; and the judiciary might overreach when resolving cases or controversies. Aware of these possibilities, the delegates to the Philadelphia Convention thus added a second key feature to the federal government's design, known as the system of "checks and balances." The idea here was to pierce the walls of separation between the branches by creating mechanisms through which each of the branches could act to constrain the actions of its institutional counterparts.[6] For example, the veto power would enable the executive branch to block efforts by the legislative branch to pass power-aggrandizing laws,[7] the legislative branch's impeachment powers would enable it to remove from office executive and judicial officials who abused their authority,[8] the federal courts' review-related powers would enable them to thwart overreaching actions of the legislative and executive branches by denying them effect in judicial proceedings,[9] and so forth.[10] The hope, in short, was that each branch, in an effort to safeguard (or even expand) its own powers, would utilize the checking tools at its disposal to rein in the

---

and whether hereditary, self-appointed, or elective, may justly be pronounced the very definition of tyranny.").

6 *See* Peter L. Strauss, *The Place of Agencies in Government: Separation of Powers and the Fourth Branch*, 84 COLUM. L. REV. 573, 578 (1984) (noting that the system of checks and balances "seeks to protect the citizens from the emergence of tyrannical government by establishing multiple heads of authority in government, which are then pitted one against another in a continuous struggle").

7 *See* U.S. CONST. art. I, § 7 (providing that "[e]very bill which shall have passed the House of Representatives and the Senate, shall, before it becomes a law, be presented to the President of the United States; if he approve he shall sign it, but if not he shall return it, with his objections to that House in which it shall have originated").

8 *See id.* art. I, § 2 (vesting in the House "the sole Power of impeachment"); *id.* art. I, § 4 (vesting in the Senate the "sole Power to try all Impeachments"). *See generally infra* Section 32.A.

9 *See* U.S. CONST. art. III, § 2 (providing that the "judicial power shall extend to all cases, in law and equity, arising under this Constitution, the laws of the United States, and treaties made, or which shall be made, under their authority"). To be clear, Article III does not explicitly vest in federal courts the power to refuse enforcement of unconstitutional laws and executive actions, but that authority has long been understood to be implied by the basic structural arrangement. For more on the origins, scope, and desirability of the judicial-review power, see *infra* Chapter 34.

10 For example, the President could use the appointment power to influence the composition of the federal courts, *see* U.S. CONST. art. II, § 2, the Senate could use its "advice and consent" authority to prevent the President from making unwise or irresponsible appointments (and treaties), *id.*, and the legislature could reduce the extent of the President's executive power (and the courts' judicial power) by cutting annual appropriations, *see* U.S. CONST. art. I, § 8, cl. 1 (vesting in Congress the power of the purse).

excesses of its institutional counterparts. By thus seeking to make "[a]mbition . . . counteract ambition," as James Madison famously put it, the Framers sought to achieve an equilibrium of balanced governance notwithstanding—and, indeed, by way of—the power-maximizing desires of the people operating within it.[11]

This mixed structure of separated powers and checks and balances has long been celebrated as a major accomplishment of the Constitution's creators.[12] The overall soundness and continued viability of the plan, however, remains open to question. For one thing, the structural architecture put in place by the Framers may turn out to be *overly* responsive to the risk of governmental tyranny, yielding levels of gridlock, paralysis, and governmental inaction that threaten individual and societal wellbeing.[13] Put another way, if we take seriously the idea that the federal government can do harm *both* by over-regulating (and hence tyrannizing the people) *and* by under-regulating (and hence leaving the people exposed to threats, harms, and deprivations that only coordinated and aggressive federal action can mitigate),[14] then we might well worry that the U.S. constitutional system, by striving so hard to prevent government tyranny, has gone too far in the direction of promoting stasis and neglect.[15]

---

11 *See* THE FEDERALIST NO. 51 (Madison).

12 *See, e.g.*, Wellness Int'l Network Ltd. v. Sharif, 135 S. Ct. 1932, 1954 (2015) (Roberts, C.J., dissenting) ("By diffusing federal powers among three different branches, and by protecting each branch against incursions from the others, the Framers devised a structure of government that promotes both liberty and accountability.").

13 *See, e.g.*, Sanford Levinson, *How I Lost My Constitutional Faith*, 71 MD. L. REV. 956, 966 (2012) (noting that the "structural provisions of the Constitution, for better and, I believe, very much for worse, make it nearly impossible to pass legislation that truly addresses the major problems of our time").

14 There is another point too: One upshot of the system of checks and balances is that it makes it harder for present-day political majorities to undo the legislative actions of their predecessors (including those actions that managed to increase the scope of federal power writ large). Thus, it is not clear whether even hard-core libertarians ought to favor a system of government that places so many veto points in the way of the making (and hence un-making) of federal law. Over the short run, to be sure, such a system might succeed at preventing the federal government from creating new taxes, regulatory schemes, benefits programs, and so forth. But over the long run, the system might more reliably operate to entrench initiatives of this kind, whenever enacted, against subsequent repeal, with the end result being a gradual (but generally unidirectional) accretion of federal regulatory power. In other words, as then-Professor and now-Judge Richard Myers has put the point, "the Framers' obstructionist system of checks and balances is libertarian if laws are being written on a blank slate, but not once the laws are on the books." *See* Richard E. Myers, *Responding to the Time Based Failures of the Criminal Law Through a Criminal Sunset Provision*, 49 B.C. L. REV. 1327, 1333 (2008).

15 Indeed, as Eric Posner and Adrian Vermeule have suggested, this defect might eventually operate to undermine even the primary constitutional goal of preventing government tyranny. After all, if "checks and balances create gridlock and make it difficult to pass necessary reforms," then a frustrated public might come to "demand[ ] or at least accept[ ] a dictator who can sweep away the institutional obstacles to

Another criticism has to do with political parties.[16] A well-organized and highly polarized party structure, this argument posits, does not map well onto a constitutional system that seeks to leverage *interbranch* (rather than interparty) competitions for power as the primary safeguard against tyranny and abuse. The problem, more specifically, is that when parties become dominant, partisan interests trump institutional interests, meaning that legislators and governmental officials will tend to focus on maximizing the political fortunes of their respective parties, rather than maximizing the strength and autonomy of the institutions in which they serve.[17] Thus, in contrast to the framers' expectation that the power-hungry members of each arm of the federal government would be inclined to guard their own branch's turf against encroachments by institutional rivals, the on-the-ground reality is closer to one in which the branches collude and compete in the service of party-empowering goals. Co-partisans located in different branches might for this reason decline to check one another in light of their shared political goal of increasing party power.[18] And where different parties control different branches, federal officials might overuse the checking and balancing tools at their disposal for the sole purpose of inflicting maximum political pain on their partisan adversaries.[19] Ambition, in short, may still operate to counteract ambition, but not necessarily in a manner that generates a healthy equilibrium of interbranch authority.

---

reform." *See* Eric A. Posner & Adrian Vermeule, *Tyrannophobia*, *in* COMPARATIVE CONSTITUTIONAL DESIGN 338 (Tom Ginsburg, ed., 2012).

[16] *See generally* Daryl J. Levinson & Richard H. Pildes, *Separation of Parties, Not Powers*, 119 HARV. L. REV. 2311 (2006) (outlining this critique in detail).

[17] *See id.* at 2313 (noting that "[a]s competition between the legislative and executive branches was displaced by competition between two major parties, the machine that was supposed to go of itself stopped running").

[18] *See* James A. Gardner, *Democracy Without a Net? Separation of Powers and the Idea of Self-Sustaining Constitutional Constraints on Undemocratic Behavior*, 79 ST. JOHN'S L. REV. 293, 313–14 (2005) (noting that, with the emergence of parties, "the power necessary to act tyrannically is assembled not by centralizing it in the hands of a single branch, but by achieving partisan control of all three branches of government, separate though they may be").

[19] *See, e.g.*, Michael Coenen & Seth Davis, *Minor Courts, Major Questions*, 70 VAND. L. REV. 777, 837–38 (2017) (noting that polarized conditions create heightened risks of "legislative paralysis, brinkmanship, and interbranch warfare" when different parties control different branches, while correspondingly diminishing the risk of "meaningful oversight and/or resistance" to abusive executive-branch actions during times of unified government).

B. THE PRESIDENT'S POWERS AND DUTIES UNDER ARTICLE II

The first sentence of Article II provides that "[t]he executive Power shall be vested in a President of the United States."[20] Other clauses of that article further define the nature of this office, providing for a four-year term,[21] establishing baseline eligibility requirements,[22] and outlining a convoluted (and sometimes countermajoritarian) selection process involving the state-based appointment of delegates to cast votes as members of what is now called the "Electoral College."[23] In addition, the Constitution guarantees to the President a "[c]ompensation" that shall "neither be [i]ncreased nor diminished" during that President's term,[24] and it prohibits the President from "receiv[ing] within that Period any other Emolument from the United States, or any of them" or (like other federal officers) "accept[ing] any present, Emolument, Office, or Title from any King, Prince or foreign State."[25]

---

[20] U.S. CONST. art. II, § 1, cl. 1.

[21] *Id.* art. II, § 1, cl. 1.

[22] In particular, the President must be at least 35 years old, be a "natural born Citizen" of the United States, and have had at least 14 years of residence within the United States. *Id.* art. II, § 1, cl. 5.

[23] *Id.* art. II, § 1, cl. 3, *superseded in part by id.* amend. XII. As initially envisioned, the electoral college system was liable to yield undemocratic results insofar as the electors themselves might cast votes for presidential candidates disfavored by the nation as a whole. *See* Ray v. Blair, 343 U.S. 214, 232 (1952) (Jackson, J., dissenting) (emphasizing that "the plan originally contemplated" was that "electors would be free agents, to exercise an independent and nonpartisan judgment as to the men best qualified for the Nation's highest offices"). *But see* Keith E. Whittington, *Originalism, Constitutional Construction, and the Problem of Faithless Electors*, 59 ARIZ. L. REV. 903, 905 (2017) (suggesting that the electors were "expected to exercise a discretionary choice in casting their ballots only when the people at large were unable to decide on a president"). That specific problem does not exist today, as electors pledge themselves to particular presidential candidates ahead of time (and thus almost invariably cast their votes in accordance with the popular vote in their respective states). *See* Chiafalo v. Washington, 140 S. Ct. 2316, 2319–20 (2020) (upholding as consistent with Article II and the Twelfth Amendment the practice of many states to "compel electors to pledge in advance to support the nominee of that party"). Instead, the more immediate problem is that the states' near-universal practice of awarding their electoral votes on a winner-take-all basis can result (and often has resulted) in the election of a President who has lost, even by a substantial measure, the nationwide popular vote. *See, e.g.*, Ganesh Sitaraman, Morgan Ricks & Christopher Serkin, *Regulation and the Geography of Inequality*, 70 DUKE L.J. 1763, 1781–82 (2021) (noting that "Democrats have won the popular vote in seven of the last eight elections, yet have only held the presidency for five of eight terms").

[24] U.S. CONST. art. II, § 1, cl. 7.

[25] *Id.*; *id.* at art. I, § 9, cl. 8. These prohibitions became a source of litigation during Donald Trump's presidency. Several challengers alleged in particular that President Trump had violated at least one of these clauses by continuing to hold an ownership interest in various businesses that served clients representing foreign governments and the U.S. government. *See, e.g.*, Citizens for Responsibility & Ethics in Wash. v. Trump, 953 F.3d 178, 186–88 (2d Cir. 2019) (describing the plaintiff's

Our primary focus in the next few chapters, however, will be on the powers and duties of the President. In contrast to the Vesting Clause of Article I, which confers on Congress "all legislative powers *herein granted*,"[26] the Vesting Clause of Article II confers on the President "the executive Power," full stop.[27] At the same time, Article II does not leave the President's executive power unspecified, as various provisions of the article outline particular responsibilities with which the President has been entrusted. Among other things, Article II designates the President as "Commander in Chief" of the armed forces,[28] empowers the President to issue "reprieves and pardons for Offences against the United States,[29] and generally authorizes the President to "appoint," with the Senate's "advice and consent,"[30] executive-branch officials and federal judges.[31] In addition, that article sets forth (in a provision known as the "Take Care Clause") the further, catch-all instruction that the President "shall take care that the Laws be faithfully executed," thus alluding to a set of *duties* that the executive power seems to entail.[32]

The remainder of this chapter will consider these matters in the following way: First, we will discuss in general terms the relationship between the scope of the President's "executive power" and the substance of the laws that Congress has enacted—a relationship that courts have long analyzed through the lens of Justice Jackson's famous concurring opinion in *Youngstown Sheet & Tube Co. v. Sawyer* (also known as the *Steel Seizure Case*).[33] Second, we will offer an introductory overview of the more particularized aspects of presidential power that Article II explicitly enumerates—several of

---

claims under the domestic and foreign emoluments clauses based on the operation of the Trump International Hotel in Washington, D.C.), *vacated as moot by* 141 S. Ct. 1262 (2021); Blumenthal v. Trump, 949 F.3d 14, 16–17 (D.C. Cir. 2020) (describing the challengers' Foreign Emoluments Clause allegations involving the President's "vast business holdings around the world"), *cert. denied*, 141 S. Ct. 553 (2020). Although one federal district court denied the President's motions to dismiss such a challenge, *see* Blumenthal v. Trump, 335 F. Supp. 3d 45 (D.D.C. 2018) (denying the motion to dismiss on grounds of Article III standing), *rev'd and remanded by* 949 F.3d 14 (D.C. Cir. 2020); Blumenthal v. Trump, 373 F. Supp. 3d 191 (D.D.C. 2019) (denying the motion to dismiss for failure to state a claim), *rev'd and remanded*, 949 F.3d 14 (D.C. Cir. 2020), none of the cases ultimately resulted in a final merits judgment either for or against the President, and the Court itself held that the issues had become moot at the conclusion of President Trump's term. *See Citizens for Responsibility & Ethics in Wash.*, 141 S. Ct. 1262.

[26] U.S. CONST. art. I, § 1 (emphasis added).

[27] *Id.* art. II, § 1.

[28] *Id.* art. II, § 2; *see also infra* Section 28.A.

[29] U.S. CONST. art. II, § 2; *see also infra* Section 26.B.2.c.

[30] U.S. CONST. art. II, § 2.

[31] *See infra* Chapter 30.

[32] U.S. CONST. art. II, § 3.

[33] 343 U.S. 579 (1952).

which will receive further attention in later chapters of this book. Finally, we will turn our focus to the Take Care Clause, considering in particular the extent to which the constitutionally prescribed duty to "take care that the laws be faithfully executed" operates to limit the President's discretion in: (a) prioritizing enforcement of some federal laws over others; (b) declining to enforce laws the President believes to be unconstitutional; and (c) refusing to spend money that Congress has appropriated.

1. Toward a General Doctrinal Framework: Justice Jackson's Three Categories

a. *The* Youngstown *Decision*

The *Youngstown* case arose from a labor dispute involving the United Steelworkers of America and the owners of steel mills located throughout the country. On April 4, 1952, the union announced a nationwide strike, scheduled to begin just a few days later.[34] Hours before the scheduled start of the strike, President Truman issued an executive order directing his Secretary of Commerce, Charles Sawyer, to seize the steel mills and operate them on the nation's behalf.[35] President Truman defended this order as necessary to ensure that a steady supply of weapons and other equipment would remain available to U.S. troops then fighting in Korea.[36] But the steel-mill owners were unmoved. They sued, seeking an injunction prohibiting enforcement of the order on the theory that, in calling for its issuance, the President had exceeded the scope of his powers.

The case moved quickly through the courts, resulting in a final decision from the Supreme Court on June 2, 1952. By a 6–3 vote, the Court held that President Truman had in fact reached beyond his Article II powers. More specifically, as Justice Black explained, "[t]he President's power, if any, to issue the order must stem either from an act of Congress or from the Constitution itself."[37] And here, he continued, neither a federal statute nor the provisions of Article II supported the President's action. With respect to any supposed legislative imprimatur, Congress in fact had *refused* to authorize "the seizure technique to solve labor disputes in order to prevent work stoppages."[38] Likewise, with respect to the Constitution itself, the

---

[34] *Id.* at 583.

[35] *Id.*

[36] *See* Exec. Order No. 10,340, 17 Fed. Reg. 3139, 3141 (Apr. 8, 1952).

[37] *Youngstown*, 343 U.S. at 585.

[38] *Id.* at 586. More specifically, Justice Black noted that Congress had explicitly rejected an amendment to the Taft-Hartley Act that would have permitted a presidential short-circuiting of labor-disputes through "seizures in cases of emergency." *Id.* (noting that Congress instead "sought to bring about settlements by use of the customary devices of mediation, conciliation, investigation by boards of

President could rely on neither the Commander-in-Chief authority (because his actions had occurred outside the "theater of war")[39] nor the "executive power" more generally (because he was not "direct[ing] that a congressional policy be executed in a manner prescribed by Congress").[40] In sum, Justice Black concluded, what the President had attempted to do amounted "to lawmaking, a legislative function which the Constitution has expressly confided to the Congress and not to the President."[41]

Several other Justices wrote separately.[42] But of all the opinions issued in *Youngstown* (including the majority opinion of Justice Black), it was ultimately Justice Jackson's concurrence that would achieve the most widespread and lasting influence. That opinion framed its analysis in terms of a "somewhat over-simplified" grouping of "practical situations in which a President may doubt, or

---

inquiry, and public reports," in addition to "temporary injunctions . . . to provide cooling-off periods").

39 *Id.* at 587.

40 *Id.* at 588.

41 *Id.* at 582.

42 Justice Frankfurter, for instance, urged that the underlying dispute required an analysis that was "more complicated and flexible than may appear from" the majority opinion, *id.* at 589 (statement of Frankfurter, J.), while emphasizing that President Truman's actions were not reflective of (and were thus unsupported by) "a systematic, unbroken, executive practice, long pursued to the knowledge of the Congress and never before questioned." *Id.* at 610–11 (Frankfurter, J., concurring) (suggesting that such a practice could operate as a doctrinally significant "gloss on 'executive Power' "). *See generally* Curtis A. Bradley & Neil S. Siegel, *Historical Gloss, Constitutional Conventions, and the Judicial Separation of Powers*, 105 GEO. L.J. 255, 261–65 (2017) (offering a broader overview of Justice Frankfurter's theory of "historical gloss" and its continued relevance to modern-day separation-of-powers disputes). Justice Douglas also concurred, suggesting that the Fifth Amendment's Takings Clause had a role to play in guiding the separation-of-powers analysis because Congress, and not the President, was responsible for securing funds to pay "just compensation" for the taking of private property. *See Youngstown*, 343 U.S. at 631–32 (Douglas, J., concurring). Justice Clark concurred only in the judgment, characterizing the President's actions as inconsistent with three separate congressional statutes that "furnish the guideposts for decision in this case," *id.* at 665–66 (Clark, J., concurring in the judgment). Justice Burton, while joining the majority opinion, also authored a separate concurrence highlighting the "controlling fact" that Congress had "prescribed for the President specific procedures, exclusive of seizure, for his use in meeting the present type of emergency." *Id.* at 659–60 (Burton, J., concurring). Meanwhile, Chief Justice Vinson (joined by Justices Reed and Minton) dissented, contending that the President had permissibly "acted to preserve" various "defense programs" that Congress had put in place, and that Congress's failure to act in response to the seizure evidenced its acceptance of what the President had done. *See id.* at 709–10 (Vinson, C.J., dissenting); *see also* Jack Goldsmith & John F. Manning, *The President's Completion Power*, 115 YALE L.J. 2280, 2284 (2006) (noting that "Vinson described the legislative program at a high level of generality and implicitly conceded that it contained no mandate, express or implied, to seize the steel mills in the circumstances before the Court," while also noting that "in Vinson's judgment, the successful execution of a vast body of legislative commitments depended upon the President's ability to keep the mills functioning").

others may challenge, his powers,"[43] with each type of situation carrying a different set of implications for the overall constitutional analysis. In the first category (Category One) were those instances in which the "President acts pursuant to an express or implied authorization of Congress" and in which the President's power was therefore "supported by the strongest of presumptions and the widest latitude of judicial interpretation."[44] Conversely, in the third category (Category Three) were those instances in which "the President takes measures incompatible with the expressed or implied will of Congress."[45] In these situations, the President's power was at "its lowest ebb," meaning that he could "rely only upon his own constitutional powers minus any constitutional powers of Congress over the matter."[46] Finally, the middle category (Category Two) encompassed circumstances in which the "President acts in absence of either a congressional grant or denial of authority."[47] More specifically, Justice Jackson explained that presidential conduct neither authorized nor prohibited by statute fell within a "zone of twilight, in which [the President] and Congress may have concurrent authority, or in which its distribution is uncertain" and in which "congressional inertia, indifference or quiescence may sometimes, at least as a practical matter, enable, if not invite, measures on independent presidential responsibility."[48]

The case at hand, Justice Jackson continued, fit into Category Three. Echoing the observations of both Justice Black and other members of the *Youngstown* majority, he noted that Congress had not "left seizure of private property an open field" but instead had "covered it by three statutory policies inconsistent with" what the President had done here.[49] Thus, the seizure could be justified "only by the severe tests under the third grouping," meaning that it could not pass muster unless it fell "within [the President's] domain and beyond control by Congress."[50] And this, Jackson continued, was clearly not the case. Like Justice Black, Justice Jackson found the Commander-in-Chief power beside the point because President Truman's action concerned "internal affairs" far afield from the

---

[43] *Youngstown*, 343 U.S. at 635 (Jackson, J., concurring).

[44] *Id.* at 635–37.

[45] *Id.* at 637–38.

[46] *Id.*

[47] *Id.*

[48] *Id.* For a broader examination of Justice Jackson's middle category, with a particular focus on how lower-courts have evaluated "twilight-zone" forms of presidential action, see Michael Coenen & Scott M. Sullivan, *The Elusive Zone of Twilight*, 62 B.C. L. REV. 741 (2021).

[49] *Youngstown*, 343 U.S. at 639 (Jackson, J., concurring).

[50] *Id.* at 640.

theater of combat.[51] Also significant was the Constitution's express grant to Congress (and not to the President) of the powers to "raise *and support* Armies" and to "*provide* and *maintain* a Navy,"[52] an allocation of authority that cut strongly against the President's claim of unilateral authority to seek to ensure an uninterrupted flow of armaments to the nation's military forces.[53] In light of all this, Justice Jackson concluded that the President's "lowest ebb" claim of executive power could not overcome the strong constitutional presumption against its validity.

b. The Court's Adoption of the Jackson Framework: Dames & Moore v. Regan

Justice Jackson spoke only for himself in the *Youngstown* case, but all nine members of the Court in the 1981 case of *Dames & Moore v. Regan*[54] endorsed his tripartite framework as offering an "analytically useful" tool for evaluating presidential-power disputes.[55] In negotiating an end to the Iran hostage crisis, President Jimmy Carter had reached an agreement with the Iranian government that put in place a complex process for the settlement of unresolved legal claims asserted by U.S. nationals against Iran in U.S. courts. Those negotiations resulted in a series of executive orders purporting: (a) to nullify existing attachment orders in then-pending judicial proceedings involving these claims (the "attachment nullification" order); and (b) to suspend the adjudication of these claims in judicial tribunals so that they could instead be resolved by a specially constituted arbitral panel created by the agreement (the "claims suspension" order).[56] *Dames & Moore* presented a constitutional challenge to both of these actions, with the challengers contending that the President lacked the authority to undertake them without an explicit congressional sign-off.

Writing for the majority, then-Associate Justice Rehnquist (who, as it turned out, had served as a law clerk for Justice Jackson while *Youngstown* was before the Court) applied the Jackson framework to both the attachment-nullification and claims-suspension terms of the agreement.[57] His treatment of the attachment-nullification order was

---

[51] *Id.* at 641, 645–46.

[52] *See* U.S. CONST. art. I, § 8 (emphasis added).

[53] *Youngstown*, 343 U.S. at 643 (Jackson, J., concurring).

[54] 453 U.S. 654 (1981).

[55] *Id.* at 669.

[56] *Id.* at 665–68. More specifically, President Reagan ratified several orders previously issued by President Carter, while issuing a new order concerning the suspension of claims. *See id.*

[57] While applying the framework, Rehnquist also cautioned against an overly formalistic approach to it, noting that "executive action in any particular instance falls, not neatly in one of three pigeonholes, but rather at some point along a spectrum

straightforward: That pronouncement, Justice Rehnquist explained, fell comfortably within the statutory authority granted to the President under the International Emergency Economic Powers Act (IEEPA) and was accordingly valid as a an uncontroversial exercise of "Category One" authority.[58] The claims-suspension order, however, required a more extended analysis. The IEEPA, the Court conceded, could not "be read to authorize the suspension of claims."[59] Nor could such an authority be derived from a provision of another statute, the Hostage Act, on which the government had relied.[60] But having found that neither statute "constitutes specific authorization of the President's action suspending claims," the Court nonetheless regarded both to be "highly relevant" to the order's validity "in the looser sense of indicating congressional acceptance of a broad scope for executive action in circumstances such as those presented in this case."[61] More specifically, the "general tenor of Congress's legislation in this area," combined with a "history of congressional acquiescence" in international claims settlement by past Presidents,[62] could be considered to " 'invite' [such] 'measures on independent presidential responsibility' " within the meaning of Justice Jackson's middle category.[63] Put differently, Congress had not statutorily authorized the suspension order, but it had not prohibited it either. And a host of contextual factors, including the general thrust of the statutes themselves, was enough to tip the scale in the President's favor,

---

running from explicit congressional authorization to explicit congressional prohibition." *Id.* at 669. That point of caution, however, has had little practical effect. Rather, even after *Dames & Moore*, judges have tended to treat the framework's three categories as formally distinct and mutually exclusive. *See* Coenen & Sullivan, *supra* note 47, at 752 n.56.

58 *Id.* at 670–74 (noting that this order was taken pursuant to "specific congressional authorization" and that "[u]nder the circumstances of this case, we cannot say that petitioner has sustained th[e] heavy burden" of overcoming " 'the strongest of presumptions and the widest latitude of judicial interpretation' " in favor of the statute (quoting *Youngstown*, 343 U.S. at 637 (Jackson, J., concurring)).

59 *Id.* at 677.

60 *Id.*

61 *Id.*

62 *Id.* at 678–79. Although the Court did not cite to *Youngstown* on this point, this aspect of the Court's reasoning tracked the logic of Justice Frankfurter's *Youngstown* concurrence, which had pointed to longstanding congressional acceptance of a form of executive-branch conduct as a factor that militated in favor of that conduct's validity. *See Youngstown*, 343 U.S. at 613 (Frankfurter, J., concurring) (emphasizing that President Truman's actions were constitutionally suspect in large part because they did not "come to us sanctioned by long-continued acquiescence of Congress giving decisive weight to a construction by the Executive of its powers").

63 *Dames & Moore*, 453 U.S. at 678–79 (quoting *Youngstown*, 343 U.S. at 637 (Jackson, J., concurring)).

justifying the conclusion that Congress could "be considered to have consented to the President's action in suspending claims."[64]

Dames & Moore thus solidified the status of the Jackson framework as a go-to test for evaluating exercises of presidential power. But the decision itself deviated from that of *Youngstown* in ways that highlight the limits of the framework's analytical utility. This is particularly true with respect to the Court's upholding of the suspension order, whose relationship to background statutory law was in many respects quite similar to that of the seizure order invalidated in *Youngstown*. Both of these actions had arisen against a statutory backdrop that, as Professor Kristen Eichensehr has put it, qualified as "close but not quite"—that is, both President Truman's seizure of the steel mills and President Reagan's suspension of claims managed to implicate, but not find explicit support in, various legislative provisions that dealt with the subjects at hand.[65] In the two cases, however, the Court drew polar opposite inferences from the close-but-not-quite statutes that Congress had put on the books. In *Youngstown*, the Court saw the statutes as indicating Congress's *disapproval* of the steel mill seizure, on the theory that Congress could have added, but tellingly chose not to add, the unilateral seizure of manufacturing facilities to the strike-confronting toolkit it had placed in the executive's hands. In *Dames & Moore*, by contrast, the Court saw the background statutes as indicating *de facto* congressional "acceptance" of the claims suspension order, on the theory that the IEEPA and Hostage Act evinced a "general tenor" in favor of claims-settlement agreements.[66] Both decisions thus illustrate the substantial amount of discretion that the Jackson framework gives to the courts—both with respect to the task of assigning presidential action to one of the three categories and with

[64] *Id.* at 674. Some commentators have characterized this portion of the *Dames & Moore* opinion as involving a Category-One analysis reflecting the Court's conclusion that the order had been *impliedly authorized* by Congress. *See, e.g.*, Andrew Coan & Nicholas Bullard, *Judicial Capacity and Executive Power*, 102 VA. L. REV. 765, 810 (2016) (noting that "the Court placed the suspension of claims in Justice Jackson's first category"); Kristen E. Eichensehr, *The* Youngstown *Canon: Vetoed Bills and the Separation of Powers*, 70 DUKE L.J. 1245, 1278 (2021) (characterizing *Dames & Moore* as "the most significant case in which the Court has found implied authorization" under Category One). The better reading, however, is that the opinion involved a Category-Two analysis of a type of presidential action about which Congress's longstanding silence could be construed as a form of unofficial acquiescence. *See* Coenen & Sullivan, *supra* note 47, at 756 n.76 (defending this reading); *accord* E. Garrett West, *A* Youngstown *for the Administrative State*, 70 ADMIN. L. REV. 629, 643 (2018).

[65] *See* Eichensehr, *supra* note 64, at 1278.

[66] *See, e.g.*, Stephen I. Vladeck, *Congress, the Commander-in-Chief, and the Separation of Powers After* Hamdan, 16 TRANSNAT'L & CONTEMP. PROBS. 933, 948–49 (2007) ("In finding clear statutory acquiescence in President Carter's actions in a statute that was, at best, ambiguous, Justice Rehnquist effectively vitiated Jackson's taxonomy—or, at least, turned it on its head.").

respect to evaluating that action within the applicable category. In this respect, the Jackson framework, though a much-celebrated aspect of the Court's separation-of-powers jurisprudence,[67] may offer less in the way of guidance for the resolution of difficult constitutional cases than it does a vocabulary for describing outcomes that derive ultimately from independent and unstated considerations.

2. Explicitly Conferred Components of Presidential Power

The Court in both *Youngstown* and *Dames & Moore* focused on the President's generally conferred power to execute the law. As already noted, however, Article II does more than simply vest an undefined "executive power" in the President; it also elaborates on the nature of that power by authorizing the President to take specified actions and, in some cases, by setting forth subrules about the way in which these powers must be wielded. The ensuing discussion offers a brief overview of these enumerated presidential authorities—several of which receive more detailed treatment in other chapters of this book.[68]

a. The Commander-in-Chief Power

Article II, section 2 provides that "[t]he President shall be Commander in Chief of the Army and Navy of the United States, and of the Militia of the several States, when called into the actual Service of the United States."[69] The Court has long made it clear that this "Commander-in-Chief" Clause confers on the President substantial operational control over the military, and most (though not all)

---

[67] *See* Edward T. Swaine, *The Political Economy of* Youngstown, 83 S. CAL. L. REV. 263, 265 (2010) (noting that "*Youngstown* is one of the most celebrated cases dealing with the separation of powers" and that "Justice Jackson's concurrence is even more beloved").

[68] As we will see, the powers described below can give rise to disagreements of two types. The first set of disagreements goes to a given power's *scope*—that is, they concern the question of what sorts of actions a particular power authorizes (and does not authorize) the President to take. For example, President Truman's invocation in *Youngstown* of the Commander-in-Chief power raised an important question of scope: To what extent did that power authorize the President to regulate domestic industry for purposes of supporting a war effort on foreign soil? The second set of disagreements, meanwhile, goes to the designated power's *exclusivity*—that is, they concern the question whether the power at issue belongs to the President alone or is a power that Congress may concurrently exercise, including in ways that restrict the President's own authority. The Reception Clause of Article II, for instance, clearly empowers the President to "receive Ambassadors and other public Ministers," *see* U.S. CONST. art. II, § 3, but there remains the question whether Congress could specify by statute that, for example, meetings between the President and certain ambassadors should never occur or that such meetings should take place only in particular locations and/or at particular times. *See infra* Section 27.D.

[69] U.S. CONST. art. II, § 2.

commentators believe that at least the core exercises of this power are beyond Congress's authority to regulate or restrict.[70] As a later chapter will make clear, however, many questions exist about the scope and exclusivity of this power, particularly in relation to Congress's own authority pertaining to military affairs.[71]

b. *The Opinions Power*

Article II, section 2 empowers the President to "require the Opinion, in writing, of the principal Officer in each of the executive Departments, upon any Subject relating to the Duties of their respective Offices."[72] Though the Clause does not set forth a significant power in itself, its existence has proven relevant to broader debates about the President's relationship to the rest of the executive branch. At the very least, the Opinions Clause provides one textual indicator (among others) of the Framers' expectation that the President would oversee a broader administrative apparatus consisting of "Departments" headed up by "principal" officers.[73] In addition, and at least for some analysts, the clause's express grant of a limited-seeming "opinion-requiring" power in relation to other executive officers undercuts the suggestion that the President must at all times enjoy an illimitable and unitary control over all persons and departments within the executive branch.[74] We further consider these matters in a later chapter.[75]

c. *The Pardon Power*

Article II, section 2 vests in Presidents the power "to grant Reprieves and Pardons for Offences against the United States, except

---

70 *See infra* Section 28.A n.8.

71 *See infra* Section 28.A.

72 U.S. CONST. art. II, § 2.

73 *See, e.g.*, Ronald J. Krtoszynski, Jr., *Transcending Formalism and Functionalism in Separation-of-Powers Analysis: Reframing the Appointments Power After* Noel Canning, 64 DUKE L.J. 1513, 1526 (2015) (pointing to the Opinions Clause in noting that "Article II plainly presupposes that the President will enjoy the assistance of subordinates").

74 *See* Lawrence Lessig & Cass R. Sunstein, *The President and the Administration*, 94 COLUM. L. REV. 1, 38 (1994). More specifically, the suggestion here is that *if* the President enjoyed an illimitable inherent power to direct executive officers to act however the President might like, there would have been no need to separately vest in the President a considerably weaker power to require those officers to issue their opinions on various subjects. *Id.* Others, however, reject this suggestion, treating the Opinions Clause as supportive of the idea that the President possesses full and exclusive control over all the operations of the executive branch. *See, e.g.*, Steven G. Calabresi & Saikrishna B. Prakash, *The President's Power to Execute the Laws*, 104 YALE L.J. 541, 584 (1994) (contending that "[n]otions of hierarchy and of the unitary Executive are . . . implicit in the Opinions Clause" because the clause "empowers the President to obtain information in writing on government matters precisely so he will be able to issue binding orders to his subordinates").

75 *See infra* Section 31.A.

in Cases of Impeachment."[76] Several points about this power are clear. First, the clause's specific reference to the "Offences against the United States" establishes that the power extends only to criminal, not civil, matters and only to federal, not state, crimes.[77] Second, the carve-out for "Cases of Impeachment" indicates at a minimum that the President may not use the pardon power to undo the outcome of a congressionally conducted impeachment proceeding.[78] Third, it is well-established that the President may issue *preemptive pardons* for charges not yet brought or convictions not yet secured, although the power does not extend to crimes not yet committed.[79] Fourth, the President may condition the issuance of a pardon on recipients' willingness to fulfill certain requirements upon their release.[80] Finally, the Supreme Court has indicated that the pardon power belongs exclusively to the President and is therefore not subject to "modification or regulation by Congress."[81]

Other aspects of the power remain uncertain. Scholars disagree, for instance, as to whether the Pardon Clause requires a baseline level of specificity in a pardon's description of the persons and offenses to which it applies.[82] Another question goes to the use of

---

76 U.S. CONST. art. II, § 2.

77 *See, e.g.*, Peter L. Markowitz & Lindsay Nash, *Pardoning Immigrants*, 93 N.Y.U. L. REV. 58, 64–65 (2018) (noting this point).

78 *See* Brian C. Kalt, *The Constitutional Case for the Impeachability of Former Officials: An Analysis of the Law, History, and Practice of Late Impeachment*, 6 TEX. REV. L. & POL. 13, 78–80 (2001) (discussing the scope of the "cases of impeachment" exception to the pardon power).

79 In other words, the President may preemptively pardon *X* in connection with future potential charges stemming from *X*'s conduct yesterday, but the President may not pardon *X* in connection with future potential charges stemming from *X*'s (contemplated) conduct tomorrow. *See Ex parte* Grossman, 267 U.S. 87, 120 (1925) (noting that "[t]he executive can reprieve or pardon all offenses after their commission, either before trial, during trial or after trial"); *Ex parte* Garland, 71 U.S. (4 Wall.) 333, 380 (1867) (similar).

80 *See generally* Note, *The President's Conditional Pardon Power*, 134 HARV. L. REV. 2833 (2021).

81 *See Grossman*, 267 U.S. at 120; *see also* United States v. Klein, 80 U.S. (13 Wall.) 128, 147–48 (1871) (holding that Congress could not "impair[ ] the effect of a pardon" by stipulating that ex-Confederate recipients of a presidential pardon were not, because of the pardon, entitled to recover compensation for lands that had been seized from them). *But see supra* Section 6.C (exploring whether wholly excluding Congress from involvement in the pardon process comports with Article I's Necessary and Proper Clause).

82 *See* Aaron Rappaport, *An Underappreciated Constraint on the President's Pardon Power*, 52 CONN. L. REV. 271 (2020). On this view, for instance, a serious constitutional problem was raised by President Gerald Ford's preemptive pardon of his predecessor, Richard Nixon, for "all offenses against the United States which he . . . has committed or may have committed or taken part in." Proclamation No. 4311, 39 Fed. Reg. 32,601, 32,601–02 (Sept. 10, 1974). *But see* Frank O. Bowman, III, *Purpose, Not Specificity, Limits the Pardon Power: A Rejoinder to Rappaport*, JUST SECURITY (Dec. 28, 2020), https://www.justsecurity.org/74010/purpose-not-specificity-limits-the-pardon-power-a-rejoinder-to-rappaport/ (suggesting that Professor

conditional pardons that might implicate other constitutional guarantees: May a President, for instance, pardon an individual on the condition that the individual never publicly criticize the government, or would such a pardon be subject to attack on First Amendment grounds?[83] Another question concerns the extent to whether certain exercises of the pardon power, though operative in freeing up the pardoned individual, might expose the President to criminal liability. Could the President be prosecuted, for example, for issuing a pardon in exchange for the pardon recipient's giving of perjurious testimony, or would the existence of the pardon power itself somehow serve to insulate the President from a finding of criminal wrongdoing?[84] Finally, there remains the long-disputed (but, to date, unresolved) question of whether the President could validly execute a "self-pardon,"[85] or whether such a maneuver would

---

Rappaport's claim is undermined by the historical practice of U.S. presidents of issuing "non-specific pardons for over two hundred years with the express approval of the federal courts"). The Court, for its own part, has never recognized such a specificity requirement, but it has not explicitly repudiated the idea either.

[83] *See* Hoffa v. Saxbe, 378 F. Supp. 1221, 1234 (D.D.C. 1974) (noting that pardons must be "directly related to the public interest" and "not unreasonably infringe on the individual commutee's constitutional freedoms"); *see also* Shick v. Reed, 419 U.S. 256, 263 (1974) ("[T]he pardoning power is an enumerated power of the Constitution and . . . its limitations, if any, must be found in the Constitution itself."); *see also The President's Conditional Pardon Power*, *supra* note 80 (exploring the extent to which the conditional pardon power might be subject to certain constitutional limits).

[84] *See* 2 ROBERT S. MUELLER, U.S. DEP'T OF JUSTICE, OFFICE OF SPECIAL COUNSEL, REPORT ON THE INVESTIGATION INTO RUSSIAN INTERFERENCE IN THE 2016 PRESIDENTIAL ELECTION 173 (2019) (noting that "the promise of a pardon to corruptly influence testimony would not be a constitutionally immunized act"). Of course, the President could attempt to avoid such an outcome by issuing a supplemental self-pardon covering the earlier, potentially criminal act. The validity of this maneuver would depend on the validity of self-pardons in general.

[85] *See, e.g.*, RICHARD A. POSNER, AN AFFAIR OF STATE: THE INVESTIGATION, IMPEACHMENT, AND TRIAL OF PRESIDENT CLINTON 108 (1999) (noting that "it has generally been inferred from the breadth of the constitutional language that the President can indeed pardon himself"); Robert Nida & Rebecaa L. Spiro, *The President as His Own Judge and Jury: A Legal Analysis of the Presidential Self-Pardon Power*, 52 OKLA. L. REV. 197, 217 (1999) ("[If] the Framers had intended the text to restrict the pardon power even more, they most likely would have made this intention apparent from the plain meaning of the Constitution."); John Yoo & Saikrishna Prakash, *For Trump, Self-Pardon Would Equal Self-Immolation*, PHILA. INQUIRER (July 27, 2017), http://www2.philly.com/philly/opinion/commentary/for-trump-self-pardon-would-equal-self-immolation-20170727.html (contending that the "text [of the Pardon Clause] shows that the Framers knew how to make exceptions to the pardon power" and that "[i]f the Framers had wanted to prevent presidents from pardoning themselves, they had only to add another exception"); *cf. also* Paul F. Eckstein & Mikaela Colby, *Presidential Pardon Power: Are There Limits and, If Not, Should There Be?*, 51 ARIZ. ST. L.J. 71, 100 (2019) (noting that the "textual argument is strong, especially given the Supreme Court's view that the constitutional text gives the President plenary pardon power"); *cf. also* Donald J. Trump (@realDonaldTrump), TWITTER (June 4, 2018, 8:35 AM), https://www.thetrumparchive.com (search for "pardon myself") ("As has been stated by numerous legal scholars, I have the absolute right to PARDON myself, but why would I do that when I have done nothing wrong?").

instead be null and void,[86] either because it falls beyond the scope of the power granted by the Pardon Clause[87] or because it runs afoul of some other, superseding constitutional rule.[88]

d. The Treaty Power

Article II authorizes the President "by and with the Advice and Consent of the Senate, to make Treaties, provided two thirds of the Senators present concur."[89] As qualified by the important condition of a supermajoritarian senatorial sign-off, this power channels to the President the power to make a form of law that is fully binding under the Supremacy Clause,[90] and (as we have seen in an earlier chapter) even to do so on some subjects that Congress itself cannot regulate by enacting bicameral legislation.[91] A separate chapter of this book considers the treaty power in further detail, addressing in particular such matters as how validly enacted treaties interact with conflicting statutes, how validly enacted treaties may be terminated, and the extent to which federal actors can make and implement international agreements by way of statute, executive order, and other legal mechanisms not involving the treaty power itself.[92]

---

[86] The Justice Department's Office of Legal Counsel has articulated but not extensively defended the position that the Constitution would prohibit a self-pardon. *See* Memorandum from Mary C. Lawton, Acting Assistant Attorney General, Office of Legal Counsel, *Presidential or Legislative Pardon of the President*, 1 Op. O.L.C. Supp. 370, 370 (1974) ("Under the fundamental rule that no one may be a judge in his own case, it would seem that the question [of whether self-pardons are valid] should be answered in the negative.").

[87] *See, e.g.*, BRIAN C. KALT, CONSTITUTIONAL CLIFFHANGERS: A LEGAL GUIDE FOR PRESIDENTS AND THEIR ENEMIES 42–46 (2012) (highlighting, without necessarily endorsing, various text-based arguments that a prosecutor might offer on behalf of the claim that the Pardon Clause does not authorize self-pardons). For a broader examination of the self-pardon issue from the same author, see Brian C. Kalt, Note, *Pardon Me?: The Constitutional Case Against Self-Pardons*, 106 YALE L.J. 779 (1996).

[88] *See* Ethan J. Leib & Jed Handelsman Shugerman, *Fiduciary Constitutionalism: Implications for Self-Pardons and Non-Delegation*, 17 GEO. J.L. & PUB. POL'Y 463, 469–77 (2019) (suggesting that the President's duty of faithful execution under the Take Care Clause would preclude self-pardons done "chiefly for the narrow self-interest of the President and clearly against the public interest"); Kalt, *supra* note 87, at 806–07 (noting the tension between the idea of a self-pardon and the longstanding principle that "no man is allowed to be a judge in his own cause" (internal quotation omitted)). Another question of relevance to this issue is whether the President could circumvent a ban on self-pardons by simply resigning from office (or declaring temporary incapacity under Section 3 of the Twenty-fifth Amendment, *see infra* Section 32.B) and then *receiving* a pardon from a colluding Vice President (who, by virtue of the resignation or incapacity declaration, would at that point possess the full powers of the Presidency).

[89] U.S. CONST. art. II, § 2.

[90] *See* U.S. CONST. art. VI (listing "treaties" as among the various types of enactments that constitute "the Supreme Law of the Land").

[91] *See supra* Section 10.C (discussing the Court's holding in *Missouri v. Holland*, 252 U.S. 416 (1920)).

[92] *See infra* Chapter 27.

e. *The Appointment Power (and a Note on Removal)*

Another power that the President shares with the Senate is the power to "appoint" certain officials to federal-government positions. In particular, the Article II Appointments Clause provides that the President "shall nominate, and by and with the Advice and Consent of the Senate, shall appoint Ambassadors, other public Ministers and Consuls, Judges of the supreme Court, and all other Officers of the United States, whose Appointments are not herein otherwise provided for, and which shall be established by Law."[93] That basic rule, however, is qualified in important ways, as Article II provides that "Congress may by Law vest the Appointment of such inferior Officers, as they think proper, in the President alone, in the Courts of Law, or in the Heads of Departments"[94] and further provides that "[t]he President shall have Power to fill up all Vacancies that may happen during the Recess of the Senate, by granting Commissions which shall expire at the End of their next Session."[95] This cluster of provisions, which has yielded a complex set of doctrinal rules, is the subject of a later chapter.[96]

Related to the President's power to appoint executive officers is the complementary power to *remove* executive-branch officials. This authority, unlike its appointment-based counterpart, receives no express mention in Article II, and in part for this reason has long engendered judicial and scholarly debate. Most analysts acknowledge that the President enjoys some power to remove executive-branch officials as an incident of the Article II "executive power." But the *exclusivity* of that power remains disputed: In particular, judges and scholars have long disagreed on the question whether Congress may impose statutory restrictions on the President's power to remove certain types of executive-branch officials (and thus, in effect, afford those officials a level of independence from direct presidential control).[97] A later chapter considers these debates in connection with the Supreme Court's unsteady efforts to hash out a doctrinal resolution.[98]

---

[93] U.S. CONST. art. II, § 2, cl. 2.

[94] *Id.*

[95] *Id.* art. II, § 2, cl.3.

[96] *See infra* Chapter 30.

[97] *Compare, e.g.*, Seila Law v. CPFB, 140 S. Ct. 2183, 2226–38 (2020) (Kagan, J., concurring in the judgment with respect to severability and dissenting in part), *with id.* at 2204–08 (majority opinion).

[98] *See infra* Chapter 31.

f. The Reception Power (and a Note on Recognition)

The Article II Reception Clause provides that the President "shall receive Ambassadors and other public Ministers."[99] Though that grant of authority might appear to be a trivial one, the Court has relied on it—in conjunction with other features of Article II—as supporting the existence of a broader authority in the President to "recognize" foreign nations on behalf of the United States.[100] That power, in turn, has given rise to a variety of important questions, particularly as to how this recognition power interacts with congressional powers that, if exercised, might undermine the effect of a particular recognition decision. A later chapter considers these questions.[101]

g. The Veto Power

In contrast to the above-mentioned executive authorities, the President's "veto" power finds its source not in Article II, but in the provisions of Article I that detail how legislative bills become—or do not become—binding law. The mechanics of the veto process are straightforward: After both Houses of Congress vote to pass a bill, that bill goes to the President, who then has ten days (excluding Sundays) within which either to sign the bill (and thus cause it to become law) or "return it" to Congress "with his Objections" (at which point Congress can attempt to override the veto by supermajority vote).[102] If the President does not act within ten days, the bill becomes law *unless* Congress has adjourned during that time period, in which case presidential inaction operates as a *de facto* veto. In other words, the President can exercise what is known as a "pocket veto" by simply waiting for Congress to adjourn and, if such an adjournment occurs within the ten-day period, doing nothing at all.[103]

---

99 U.S. CONST. art. II, § 3.

100 *See, e.g.*, Zivotofsky v. Kerry, 576 U.S. 1, 13 (2015) (noting that "the Reception Clause provides support, although not the sole authority, for the President's power to recognize other nations").

101 *See infra* Section 27.D.

102 *See* U.S. CONST. art. I, § 7.

103 More specifically, Article I, section 7 provides that a bill "shall not be a Law" if "the Congress by their Adjournment prevent its Return" by the President. *Id.* Given that language, one might maintain that the pocket veto is available to the President only under the limited circumstances in which a congressional adjournment literally precludes a President from "returning" the bill to Congress (as might be the case, for instance, if there is no one physically present at the Capitol to receive the bill on Congress's behalf). In *The Pocket Veto Case*, 279 U.S. 655 (1929), however, the Court rejected this position, instead construing the clause to mean that any adjournment of Congress necessarily precludes a "return" of the bill and thus enables the President to exercise the pocket-veto power. *See id.* at 682–88; *see also id.* at 683–84 (finding "no substantial basis for the suggestion that although the House in which the bill originated is not in session the bill may nevertheless be returned, consistently with the constitutional mandate, by delivering it, with the President's objections, to an

The President's veto power is sweeping in the sense that Article I imposes no constraints on the reasons the President might invoke for making any veto decision.[104] But the Court has recognized one important limit on the power—namely, that the veto must apply to the *entirety* of a presented bill, rather than to only some provisions within it. This feature of the power provided the basis for the Court's 1998 decision in *Clinton v. New York*.[105] Seeking to rein in what it viewed as excessive federal spending, Congress passed the Line Item Veto Act of 1996, which authorized the President, upon determining that certain statutorily specified conditions were met, to "cancel in whole" particular budgetary grants and/or tax benefits included in duly enacted legislation.[106] Literally speaking, and notwithstanding the name of the law, the Line Item Veto Act did not permit the President to veto portions of laws that Congress presented; rather, under the terms of the statute, the President would sign the entirety of a presented bill into law and then invoke the act to block specified tax-benefit or budget-related provisions in it from having legal effect.[107] Nevertheless, the Court held that the statute involved the President in the lawmaking process in an impermissible way. As Justice Stevens explained in an opinion signed onto by five other members of the Court, the law could be seen as permitting the President to "amend" the measure that had just become law by excising from it one or more of its provisions.[108] That result, Justice Stevens explained, did not comport with the lawmaking requirements of Article I, because those requirements did not "authorize[ ] the President to enact, to amend, or to repeal statutes."[109] Nor could the law be sustained as compatible with the veto power because a veto requires "the constitutional return . . . of the entire bill," as opposed to "the statutory cancellation . . . of only a part."[110] The Court's decision in *Clinton* thus makes clear that the President's veto power must always be applied in a non-piecemeal fashion.[111]

---

officer or agent of the House, for subsequent delivery to the House when it resumes its sittings at the next session").

[104] J. Richard Broughton, *Rethinking the Presidential Veto*, 42 HARV. J. ON LEGIS. 91, 92 n.10 (2005) (noting the longstanding view that the President's veto power is in this respect "wholly discretionary").

[105] 524 U.S. 417 (1998).

[106] *Id.* at 436 (citing 2 U.S.C. § 691(a) (1994 ed., Supp. II)).

[107] *See id.* at 474 (Breyer, J., dissenting) (noting this distinction).

[108] *Id.* at 438 (majority opinion).

[109] *Id.* at 439.

[110] *Id.*; *see also id.* at 451 (Kennedy, J., concurring) ("The law is the functional equivalent of a line item veto and enhances the President's powers beyond what the Framers would have endorsed.").

[111] On its face, *Clinton* seems to establish a bright-line rule. In actuality, however, Congress and the President might pursue various workarounds to the holding—at

3. Faithful Execution and the Take Care Clause

Article II, section 3 specifies that the President "shall take Care that the Laws be faithfully executed."[112] This provision, known as the "Take Care Clause," might in one sense be seen as confirming what the Article II, section 1 Vesting Clause previously declared—namely, that the President has the power to execute the law. Its more specialized text, however, adds something more: It indicates that the President has not only a *power* to execute the law, but also a *duty* to

least in statute-specific drafting—that allow for the functional equivalent of a line-item veto. For example, a statute might validly authorize the President to spend "up to $1 billion" on a particular budgetary item, and the President might then exercise that authority by deciding to spend $0.00. *See* Elizabeth Garrett, *Accountability and Restraint: The Federal Budget Process and the Line Item Veto Act*, 20 CARDOZO L. REV. 871, 885 (1999) ("As all the justices acknowledged, Congress can appropriate money for particular projects but allow the Executive discretion as to whether all such funds should be obligated and spent."). Similarly, Congress might make a set of tax obligations set forth in a broader bill conditional on the President's determination that certain vaguely defined conditions have been met, thus effectively empowering the President to prevent those obligations from taking effect. *Cf Clinton*, 524 U.S. at 474–75 (Breyer, J., dissenting) (noting the potential for other similar workarounds). *But see infra* Section 29.B (highlighting the non-delegation doctrine, which might in some instances operate to limit Congress's power to vest such wide-ranging discretion in the President). In addition, and more controversially, Presidents have sometimes sought to achieve the functional equivalent of a line-item veto through the use of "signing statements" that declare the President's intention not to enforce certain provisions of a signed bill (usually based on the President's assertion that those provisions are unconstitutional). Some commentators have questioned this practice, contending that, while it is true that the President has the power (if not the responsibility) to scrutinize the constitutionality of proposed legislation before signing it, *see infra* Section 26.B.3.b, it is also true that Article I requires, particularly in the wake of *Clinton*, that the proper response to any constitutional objection is a formal exercise of the veto power, rather than the signing of a law with the stated intention to enforce only a part of it. *See, e.g.*, Christopher N. May, *Presidential Defiance of 'Unconstitutional' Laws: Reviving the Royal Prerogative*, 21 HASTINGS CONST. L.Q. 865, 984 (1994) (noting that, "[i]n disregarding the allegedly invalid sections of a law, the President, through self-help, exercises a negative considerably more powerful than the proposed item veto," particularly in that "the item veto is subject to congressional override" whereas the nonenforcement decision is not); *see also* AMERICAN BAR ASS'N, REPORT OF THE TASK FORCE ON PRESIDENTIAL SIGNING STATEMENTS AND THE SEPARATION OF POWERS DOCTRINE 22 (2006) ("To sign a bill and refuse to enforce some of its provisions because of constitutional qualms is tantamount to exercising the line-item veto power held unconstitutional . . . in [*Clinton*]."). Others, by contrast, have rejected this position, noting that the Presidents have long used signing statements in this way, *see* Steven G. Calabresi, Mark E. Berghausen & Skyler Albertson, *The Rise and Fall of the Separation of Powers*, 106 NW. U. L. REV. 527, 538 n.54 (2012) (suggesting that "two centuries of practice have established that the President may decline to enforce unconstitutional provisions of statutes that he or a former President has signed"), and that it would in any event be "unrealistic" to impose such a requirement "in an age of omnibus legislation," Curtis A. Bradley & Eric A. Posner, *Presidential Signing Statements and Executive Power*, 23 CONST. COMMENT. 307, 339–41 (2006) (noting that "presidents are often presented with dozens and even hundreds of provisions in a bill, often on multiple subjects, and as a political matter they will not be able to veto such bills simply because of constitutional concerns about a particular provision").

112 *See* U.S. CONST. art. II, § 3.

do so "faithfully."[113] Thus, for instance, on any plausible theory of the Take Care Clause, the President would act unconstitutionally by letting all federal statutes go unexecuted,[114] by pursuing only personal enrichment in carrying out official duties,[115] or by directing the Attorney General to bring criminal prosecutions against political enemies but not political allies.[116] In cases involving less extreme circumstances, by contrast, there arise difficult structural questions about the scope, content, and nature of the President's "take care" duties.

a. Enforcement Discretion vs. Law Dispensation

An initial difficulty posed by the clause is that, read literally, it appears to demand the impossible. As Professor Zachary Price has noted, the Take Care Clause "seems to require the President to fully enforce all congressional enactments,"[117] even though the executive branch has nowhere near enough resources to achieve that result (and would in any event encounter a range of intractable problems in investigating and prosecuting every potential violation of every federal enactment).[118] In light of this reality, courts have long understood the Take Care Clause to countenance (if not require) a substantial degree of presidential discretion in developing enforcement priorities with respect to the dictates of federal law.[119]

---

[113] For an in-depth, historical examination of the meaning of the phrase "faithful execution," see Andrew Kent, Ethan J. Leib & Jed Handelsman Shugerman, *Faithful Execution and Article II*, 132 HARV. L. REV. 2111, 2178 (2019) (suggesting that the phrase has three major components, which respectively contemplate, a duty not to act in violation of the law, a duty not to misappropriate governmental property, and a duty to execute the law in a manner that is "diligent, careful, [in] good faith, and impartial").

[114] *See, e.g.*, Evan D. Bernick, *Faithful Execution: Where Administrative Law Meets the Constitution*, 108 GEO. L.J. 1, 32–33 (2019) (noting that "the Laws" encompassed by the Take Care Clause "uncontroversially include[ ] federal statutes," while further contending that Presidents are not "obliged to enforce statutes that they believe to be unconstitutional").

[115] *See, e.g.*, Kent, Leib & Shugerman, *supra* note 113, at 2188–90.

[116] *See generally* Andrew McCanse Wright, *The Take Care Clause, Justice Department Independence, and White House Control*, 121 W. VA. L. REV. 353, 358 (2018) (contending that "the Take Care Clause obligates the President to protect the integrity of that criminal investigation from political interference, including interference by the President himself").

[117] Zachary S. Price, *Enforcement Discretion and Executive Duty*, 67 VAND. L. REV. 671, 673 (2014).

[118] Among other things, such an injunction would require the President to focus just as much attention on technical slip-ups as obvious and major offenses, thus generating not only grave misallocations of scarce resources but obvious injustices and departures from the real-world views of the public at large. *See generally* Kate Stith, *The Arc of the Pendulum: Judges, Prosecutors, and the Exercise of Discretion*, 117 YALE L.J. 1420, 1423 (2008) (emphasizing that "[r]esource constraints as well as prudence dictate the conclusion that the federal criminal law cannot be applied in its full rigor").

[119] *See, e.g.*, Heckler v. Chaney, 470 U.S. 821, 832 (1985) (noting that "an agency's refusal to institute proceedings shares to some extent the characteristics of the

But while the Take Care Clause undoubtedly accommodates executive-branch enforcement discretion, it also, as Professors Jack Goldsmith and John Manning have put it, stands as a "negation of any presidential power to dispense with or suspend federal law."[120] In other words, while some amount of enforcement discretion is baked into the concept of executive power,[121] too much enforcement discretion—particularly when exercised in a categorical and sweeping manner—might well encroach upon Congress's authority to delineate the *substance* of federal law. The difficult question thus becomes how much is too much? Or, to ask the question another way, how does one distinguish, for Take Care Clause purposes, between the permissible presidential prioritization of some law-enforcement responsibilities over others and the impermissible casting aside of duly enacted statutory commands?

Consider in this respect President Obama's "Deferred Action for Childhood Arrivals" (DACA) and "Deferred Action for Parents of Americans and Lawful Permanent Residents" (DAPA) programs, both of which outlined general administrative policies that discouraged the bringing of removal proceedings against designated categories of undocumented immigrants.[122] Defenders of these programs viewed them as unobjectionable and much-warranted exercises of enforcement discretion.[123] Opponents, however,

---

decision of a prosecutor in the Executive Branch not to indict—a decision which has long been regarded as the special province of the Executive Branch, inasmuch as it is the Executive who is charged by the Constitution to 'take Care that the Laws be faithfully executed' "); United States v. Armstrong, 517 U.S. 456, 464 (1996) (noting that federal prosecutors have a "latitude" not to bring criminal charges because "they are designated by statute as the President's delegates to help him discharge his constitutional responsibility to 'take Care that the Laws be faithfully executed' "); *see also* Kate Andrias, *The President's Enforcement Power*, 88 N.Y.U. L. REV. 1031, 1070 (2013) (noting that "presidents have long used enforcement as a tool to advance their policy goals").

[120] Jack L. Goldsmith & John F. Manning, *The Protean Take Care Clause*, 164 U. PA. L. REV. 1835, 1837 (2016); *see also* Kendall v. United States, 37 U.S. (12 Pet.) 524, 613 (1838) (rejecting the idea that "the obligation imposed on the President to see the laws faithfully executed implies a power to forbid their execution").

[121] *See* Price, *supra* note 117, at 683 (noting that "courts and executive-branch lawyers have come to see prosecutorial discretion as a central constitutional function of the executive branch").

[122] *See* Memorandum from Janet Napolitano, U.S. Dep't of Homeland Sec., to David Aguilar, Acting Comm'r, U.S. Customs & Border Protection, et al., Exercising Prosecutorial Discretion with Respect to Individuals Who Came to the United States as Children (June 15, 2012) (outlining the DACA program); Memorandum from Jeh Charles Johnson, U.S. Dep't Homeland Sec., to León Rodriguez, Director, U.S. Citizenship & Immigration Services, et al., Exercising Prosecutorial Discretion with Respect to Individuals Who Came to the United States as Children and with Respect to Certain Individuals Whose Parents are U.S. Citizens or Permanent Residents (Nov. 20, 2014) (DAPA).

[123] *See, e.g.*, Lauren Gilbert, *Obama's Ruby Slippers: Enforcement Discretion in the Absence of Immigration Reform*, 116 W. VA. L. REV. 255, 284–89 (2013); David

characterized them as *de facto* executive revisions of federal immigration law.[124] Both camps had a point: Proponents were correct that DACA and DAPA communicated new enforcement priorities, and opponents were correct that DACA and DAPA reflected, at least to some degree, a substantive revision of federal immigration policy—indeed, a revision that President Obama himself described (in an admittedly off-the-cuff remark about DAPA in particular) as "action to change the law."[125] But as far as the constitutionality of the President's actions was concerned, only one of these two answers could qualify as correct: Either DACA and DAPA counted as exercises of enforcement discretion, in which case the Take Care Clause permitted them, or they qualified as instances of law dispensation, in which case they could not be implemented.

Although the Supreme Court would at one point order briefing on the question whether DAPA violated the Take Care Clause,[126] it never rendered a definitive ruling on the issue, and the program was ultimately rescinded.[127] (DACA, meanwhile, remains on the books, and constitutional challenges to the program continue to work their way through the courts.[128]) More generally, the Court has not yet put in place a doctrinal framework for hashing out the distinction between permissible non-enforcement decisions and impermissible law-negation decisions. And while others have worked to fill the void,[129] it is unlikely that a straightforward and satisfactory

---

Martin, *A Defense of Immigration-Enforcement Discretion: The Legal and Policy Flaws in Kris Kobach's Latest Crusade*, 122 YALE L.J. ONLINE 167, 182–84 (2012).

[124] *See, e.g.*, Robert J. Delahunty & John C. Yoo, *Dream On: The Obama Administration's Nonenforcement of Immigration Laws, the DREAM Act, and the Take Care Clause*, 91 TEX. L. REV. 781, 783–84 (2013); Josh Blackman, *The Constitutionality of DAPA Part II: Faithfully Executing the Law*, 19 TEX. REV. L. POL. 213 (2015).

[125] Press Release, Office of the Press Sec'y, Remarks by the President on Immigration—Chicago IL (Nov. 25, 2014), https://obamawhitehouse.archives.gov/the-press-office/2014/11/25/remarks-president-immigration-chicago-il.

[126] *See* 577 U.S. 1101 (2016).

[127] The DAPA program was held unlawful by the Fifth Circuit on both procedural and substantive (statutory) grounds, *see* Texas v. United States, 809 F.3d 134 (5th Cir. 2015), and that decision was subsequently affirmed by an equally divided court, *see* United States v. Texas, 136 S. Ct. 2271 (2016).

[128] The Trump Administration attempted to rescind the DACA program, but the Court ultimately held that the rescission order had been implemented in an "arbitrary and capricious" manner and thus violated the federal Administrative Procedure Act. *See* Dep't of Homeland Sec. v. Regents of Univ. of Cal., 140 S. Ct. 1891 (2020). Of particular note, while the Trump Administration had pointed to DACA's likely unconstitutionality under the Take Care Clause as a basis for the rescission order, the Court found its deliberations on this score to be inadequate. *Id.* at 1910–15. At the same time, the Court did not express a final view as to the question of DACA's substantive legality. *See id.* at 1910 (declining to "evaluate the claims challenging the . . . correctness of the illegality conclusion").

[129] Professor Price, for instance, has suggested the need for a categorical bar (in the absence of statutory authorization) on the President's ability to pursue "[p]rospective nonenforcement"—that is, "an announced promise of declining

resolution of this conundrum will emerge. In addition, the practical difficulties of challenging a non-enforcement decision—for example, finding a plaintiff with Article III standing, dodging problems of ripeness, and steering clear of statutory limits on judicial review—may afford the executive branch a greater degree of *de facto* discretion to suspend the operation of federal law than any concrete doctrinal formulation would suggest.[130] This is not to say that Presidents can, far less should, freely disregard the Take Care Clause when deciding how aggressively to enforce a particular statutory command. But it is to say that the clause's applicability to such decisions is more likely to be guided by the largely unarticulated judgments of executive-branch actors than by any set of detailed doctrinal dictates laid down by the courts.[131]

---

enforcement of a law in the future." Price, *supra* note 117, at 706. *But see* Goldsmith & Manning, *supra* note 120, at 1864 (questioning "why the executive's articulation of such limits makes the exercise invalid"). Robert Delahunty and John Yoo, meanwhile, have more broadly suggested that any "deliberate decision to leave a substantial area of statutory law unenforced or underenforced is a serious breach of presidential duty." Delahunty & Yoo, *supra* note 124, at 784–85. *But see* Price, *supra* note 117, at 678 (contending that Delahunty and Yoo "give insufficient weight to countervailing considerations that support a presumption of case-by-case enforcement discretion"). And in its own evaluation of the DACA and DAPA programs, the Obama-era Justice Department proposed a four-pronged test, according to which a presidential non-enforcement decision would avoid Take Care Clause difficulties only if it: (1) reflected factors within the expertise of the enforcing agency; (2) did not involve an "effective[ ] rewrit[ing of] the laws to match [the President's] policy preferences"; (3) did not involve a policy that is "so extreme as to amount to an abdication of" statutory responsibilities; and (4) did not "foreclose[ ] the exercise of case-by-case discretion." *See* Memorandum from Karl R. Thompson, *The Department of Homeland Security's Authority to Prioritize Removal of Certain Aliens Unlawfully Present in the United States and to Defer Removal of Others*, 38 Op. O.L.C. 39, 45–47 (Nov. 19, 2004).

130 To take a notable example, the Justice Department has for nearly a decade adhered to a policy of declining to bring prosecutions under the federal Controlled Substances Act against various categories of producers, distributors, and users of marijuana who act in accordance with their respective states' laws. *See* Memorandum from James M. Cole, Deputy Att'y Gen., to U.S. Att'ys, Guidance Regarding Marijuana Enforcement 3 (Aug. 29, 2013). Some commentators have suggested that this nonenforcement policy amounts to a violation of the Take Care Clause insofar as it amounts to a *de facto* repeal of certain provisions of a federal statute. *See, e.g.*, Zachary C. Bolitho, *The Constitution, the U.S. Department of Justice, and State Efforts to Legalize Marijuana*, 4 LINCOLN MEM. U. L. REV. 2 (2017). *But see* Price, *supra* note 117, at 758–59 (noting that the current policy is "defensible insofar as it promises only to focus resources on particular types of cases, not to avoid prosecution altogether in other circumstances"). Procedural obstacles to challenging the policy have thus far operated to forestall judicial review of the policy's underlying legality. *See, e.g.*, West v. Holder, 60 F. Supp. 3d 197 (D.D.C. 2015) (declining to assess a challenge on the ground that the plaintiff lacked Article III standing and that the policy in any event reflected an "unreviewable exercise of prosecutorial discretion."), *aff'd sub nom.* West v. Lynch, 845 F.3d 1228 (D.C. Cir. 2017).

131 *See* Goldsmith & Manning, *supra* note 120, at 1864 ("[I]dentifying the line between a permissible exercise of prosecutorial discretion and an impermissible dispensation of the law seems very much like a matter of degree, the limits of which are subjective and difficult to define in a principled way.").

b. *A Duty to Enforce (and Defend?) Unconstitutional Laws*

The foregoing discussion focused on presidential nonenforcement decisions based on policy-based priorities. Suppose, however, that the President harbors *constitutional* objections to a statute. Under those circumstances, one might argue, the Take Care Clause not only permits, but requires, the President to refuse to enforce it. The "laws" to be faithfully executed, after all, include the Constitution itself, and the Supremacy Clause makes clear that constitutional commands take precedence over conflicting statutory rules.[132] At the same time, recognition of a wide-ranging authority not to enforce unconstitutional laws might facilitate easy evasion of the law-execution duties imposed by the Take Care Clause, as Presidents would be tempted to conjure up pretextual constitutional objections to laws that they actually wished to dispense with on unrelated grounds. Put another way, if one takes seriously the idea that the President lacks the power to suspend the operation of congressional statutes for policy-based reasons, one must also worry about the potential that an "I think it's unconstitutional" exception will swallow the overarching rule.[133]

Although different administrations have taken different positions on these issues,[134] a common recent approach has been to treat the Take Care Clause as requiring executive actors to enforce laws they regard as constitutionally suspect but not to defend those laws when they are challenged in court. For example, and as is further discussed elsewhere,[135] the Obama Administration chose to enforce but not to defend section 3 of the Defense of Marriage Act (DOMA), concluding that such an approach was "consistent with the Executive's obligation to take care that the laws be faithfully executed."[136] President Trump took a similar "enforce-but-don't-defend" approach to the Affordable Care Act. In particular, while the IRS and Department of Health and Human Services generally doled out benefits and imposed penalties as required by the statute,[137] the

---

[132] *See* Bernick, *supra* note 114, at 32–33 (laying out this argument).

[133] *See* Aziz Z. Huq, *Enforcing (But Not Defending) 'Unconstitutional' Laws*, 98 VA. L. REV. 1001, 1078–85 (2012) (noting that a presidential power not to enforce unconstitutional laws "carries a risk of executive branch self-dealing," particularly where "the legal basis of nonenforcement relates to the President's Article II powers").

[134] *See* Neal Devins & Saikrishna Prakash, *The Indefensible Duty to Defend*, 112 COLUM. L. REV. 507, 513–21 (2012) (offering a historical overview).

[135] *See supra* Section 35.D.4.

[136] Letter from Eric H. Holder, Jr., U.S. Attorney Gen., to the Hon. John A. Boehner, Speaker of the House (Feb. 23, 2011).

[137] To be sure, the Administration's enforcement of these requirements was sufficiently halting, uneven, and half-hearted as to lead at least one commentator to characterize it as a form of "administrative sabotage," in potential violation of the

Justice Department expressly sided with its challengers as they sought invalidation of the law in court, thus leaving it to other parties to defend the statute's constitutionality.[138]

Does this position make sense? Commentators have expressed a range of views,[139] and the debate is not likely soon to reach a

President's take-care duties. *See* David L. Noll, *Administrative Sabotage*, 120 MICH. L. REV 753, 761–62 (2022). The important point for present purposes, however, is that the Administration never espoused the position that the President's take-care duties empowered it to cease enforcing the statute altogether.

[138] *See* California v. Texas, 141 S. Ct. 2104, 2113 (2021) (noting that the United States "took the side of the plaintiffs" while the case was being argued in the lower courts and that several States, along with the District of Columbia, "intervened in order to defend the Act's constitutionality").

[139] Some scholars, for instance, criticized the Obama administration's non-defense of DOMA, with one observer suggesting that the action was "a power grab disguised as academic constitutional interpretation" and maintaining that the proper course of action would have been for the DOJ to adhere to its past policy of "defend[ing] the constitutionality of all federal statutes if it has a reasonable basis to do so." Orin Kerr, *The Executive Power Grab in the Decision Not to Defend DOMA*, THE VOLOKH CONSPIRACY (Feb. 23, 2011), http://volokh.com/2011/02/23/the-executive-power-grab-in-the-decision-not-to-defend-doma. For a more general suggestion that the President has a duty not just to enforce but also to defend constitutionally suspect laws, see EDWARD S. CORWIN, THE PRESIDENT: OFFICE AND POWERS 1787–1984, at 72 (Randall W. Bland et al. eds., 5th rev. ed. 1984) ("[O]nce a statute has been duly enacted, whether over his protest or with his approval, [the President] must promote its enforcement by all the powers constitutionally at his disposal unless and until enforcement is prevented by regular judicial process." (emphasis added)). Other scholars have attacked the enforce-but-don't-defend approach from the opposite direction, advocating for a robust executive power, *see, e.g.*, Frank H. Easterbrook, *Presidential Review*, 40 CASE W. RES. L. REV. 905, 922–23 (1990), or even a *duty* not to enforce (as well as not to defend) statutes that the President regards as unconstitutional. *See, e.g.*, Saikrishna Bangalore Prakash, *The Executive's Duty To Disregard Unconstitutional Laws*, 96 GEO. L.J. 1613, 1617–18 (2008); *see also* Gary Lawson & Christopher D. Moore, *The Executive Power of Constitutional Interpretation*, 81 IOWA L. REV. 1267, 1303 (1996) (suggesting that "[m]odern departmentalists" are "right" to contend that a President "[m]ust . . . refuse to enforce" a statute that the President determines is unconstitutional); Devins & Prakash, *supra* note 124, at 510 ("[E]ven if one shrinks from our broad claim about the duty to enforce, meaning that one believes the President should enforce statutes that he believes are unconstitutional, there are absolutely no good constitutional reasons to preserve the duty to defend."). Still others have proposed a range of middle-ground positions. *See, e.g.*, Dawn E. Johnsen, *Presidential Non-Enforcement of Constitutionally Objectionable Statutes*, 63 L. & CONTEMP. PROBS. 7, 11 (2000) (contending that the Constitution "neither preclude[s] nor authorize[s] all presidential refusals to enforce constitutionally objectionable laws" and that Presidents must sometimes make "difficult evaluations that depend on the specific statutory provision and the circumstances surrounding its enactment"); Daniel J. Meltzer, *Executive Defense of Congressional Acts*, 61 DUKE L.J. 1183, 1209, 1228 (2012) (characterizing the relevant question as "one of judgment" that requires executive branch decisionmakers to take account of "an extant and reasonably stable set of institutional practices and expectations," while cautioning about the dangers of a system in which "each administration views itself as having significant latitude to refuse to enforce and defend acts of Congress"); Huq, *supra* note 133, at 1007 (suggesting that "enforcement-litigation gaps" should qualify as "presumptively permissive when the executive defends an Article II value" and "presumptively disfavored when any other kind of value, including an individual rights question, is at stake").

definitive resolution. But as the debate continues, two points bear emphasis. First, the Executive's refusal to defend a law in court does not mean that the law will receive no defense at all. Already-in-effect statutes enable either house of Congress to defend a federal law on its own initiative,[140] and even where a law lacks a congressional defender, other state-based or private beneficiaries might participate as intervening parties (or, even if they lack standing, submit *amicus briefs* on behalf of the challenged law). Second, even assuming the absence of a presidential authority to decline enforcement and/or defense of a law on constitutional grounds, the President might still express concerns about a law's constitutionality in various other ways. The President might, for instance, veto legislation that the President regards as unconstitutional, offer pardons to individuals convicted under a constitutionally disputed criminal statute, utilize prosecutorial discretion to deprioritize enforcement of a suspect law, and so forth. The availability of these alternative avenues of redress does not in itself refute the idea that there exists a broader, wholesale presidential discretion not to enforce and/or defend allegedly unconstitutional laws. But it serves as part of the backdrop against which any exercise, or attempted exercise, of such discretion is to be assessed.

c. *Impoundment*

A special sort of presidential "nonenforcement" decision involves the refusal to spend congressionally appropriated funds. Suppose, for example, that the President believes that a particular line item in an appropriations bill reflects an especially obnoxious form of pork-barrel politics. May the President, by drawing an analogy to more orthodox instances of "enforcement discretion," properly claim the authority to "impound" the appropriated funds and thus prevent them from going to their congressionally intended destination? Might, in other words, the Take Care Clause permit the President to decline to adhere to a budgetary line-item mandate on the ground that doing so is in the best interest of the United States? Or does the exercise of a claimed power to impound such funds show that the President has failed to "faithfully" execute the law?

Conflicts over presidential impoundment came to a head in the 1970s, when President Nixon announced a policy of "not spend[ing] money if the Congress overspends."[141] The President's advisors

---

140 *See id.* at 1028 n.85 (describing the relevant statutory rules).

141 *See* PUBLIC PAPERS OF THE PRESIDENTS OF THE UNITED STATES: RICHARD NIXON 62 (1973). This policy gave rise to a handful of lower-court decisions concerning the validity of Nixon's impoundment policy. For instance, in *State Highway Commission v. Volpe*, 479 F.2d 1099 (8th Cir. 1973), the Eighth Circuit held that the certain statutory provisions of the Federal-Aid Highway Act of 1956 did not permit the withholding of various federal highway funds and that the Secretary of

insisted that the policy did not run afoul of the Take Care Clause, of Article I's vesting of the spending power to Congress, or of any other provision of the Constitution.[142] An unconvinced Congress, however, responded by enacting the Impoundment Control Act of 1974 (ICA),[143] which President Nixon, whose resignation was then imminent, reluctantly signed into law.[144] That statute limited the President's power to withhold appropriated funds, by generally requiring: (1) that all *permanent* impoundments (referred to by the Act as "rescissions") receive an explicit congressional sign-off; and (2) that certain categories of *temporary* impoundments (referred to by the Act as "deferrals") may be made by the President alone, provided that they are reported to Congress.[145]

That statute, which remains in effect today, has largely mooted constitutional questions related to the extent of the President's

---

Transportation's authority was "limited to carrying out the law according to its terms." *Id.* at 1111. Likewise, in *National Council of Community Mental Health Centers, Inc. v. Weinberger*, 361 F. Supp. 897 (D.D.C. 1973), a federal district court held that the executive branch had "no residual constitutional authority to refuse to spend" funds appropriated by Congress to support the construction and staffing of community health centers, while rejecting in particular the President's "assertion of inherent constitutional power . . . to decline to spend in the face of a clear statutory intent." *Id.* at 901, 903. The Supreme Court for its own part confronted an impoundment-related case in 1975, holding in *Train v. New York*, 420 U.S. 35 (1975), that the EPA Administrator had unlawfully refused to spend funds appropriated under the Water Pollution Control Act because the Act itself conferred no impoundment discretion. *See id.* at 45–46. To be sure, the Court in *Train* did not explicitly address any *constitutional* issues related to the scope of the President's impoundment authority. Nonetheless, as Professors Nowak and Rotunda have noted, "[b]y rejecting the [statutory] authority of the administration to impound, . . . the Court [in *Train*] impliedly rejected a constitutional authority to impound in the face of a congressional mandate to the contrary and in the context of a program where the President could not reasonably claim special powers as the Commander-in-Chief or an inherent power limited to foreign affairs." *See* RONALD D. ROTUNDA & JOHN E. NOWAK, 1 TREATISE ON CONSTITUTIONAL LAW: SUBSTANCE & PROCEDURE § 7.4(e) (5th ed. 2021 Update).

[142] *Impoundment of Appropriated Funds by the President: Joint Hearings on S. 373 Before the Ad Hoc Subcomm. on Impoundment of Funds of the S. Comm. on Gov't Operations & the Subcomm. on Separation of Powers of the S. Comm. on the Judiciary*, 93d Cong., 1st Sess. 365, 369 (1973) (statement of Joseph T. Sneed, Deputy Att'y Gen. of the United States) (characterizing the program as an effort "to promote fiscal stability" and "in the great tradition of checks and balances upon which our Constitution is based").

[143] Pub. L. 93–344, 88 Stat. 297, codified at 31 U.S.C. §§ 1001 *et seq.*

[144] *See* Presidential Statement on Signing the Congressional Budget and Impoundment Control Act of 1974, 10 WEEKLY COMP. PRES. DOC. 800 (July 12, 1974) (noting that various provisions of the statute "may well limit the ability of the Federal Government to respond promptly and effectively to rapid changes in economic conditions").

[145] *See* Gillian E. Metzger, *Taking Appropriations Seriously*, 121 COLUM. L. REV. 1075, 1088–89 (2021) (describing the mechanics of the statute); Christian I. Bale, Note, *Checking the Purse: The President's Limited Impoundment Power*, 70 DUKE L.J. 607, 610–11 (2020) (similar).

authority to impound.[146] But it is not difficult to imagine how questions of this sort might surface in the future. Suppose, for instance, that an appropriations statute requires the President to spend money on a military computer system that the President, as Commander in Chief, views as likely to create security vulnerabilities. Can the President under those circumstances invoke in inherent (and exclusive) constitutional authority under the Commander-in-Chief Clause to impound the funds and not install the system?[147] Or suppose that Congress requires the President to spend funds on the construction of a U.S. embassy within a foreign country whose sovereignty the President has not yet recognized? If (as the Court now has held) the President enjoys an exclusive power to "recognize" foreign sovereigns,[148] might that power carry with it a companion authority to disregard in this setting the commands of the ICA?[149] To put the point more generally, the ICA, by evincing a clear congressional disapproval of impoundment decisions, has the effect of placing presidential impoundment decisions within Category 3 of Justice Jackson's *Youngstown* framework. But presidential actions within this category are only presumptively invalid. Thus, to the extent that an executive impoundment decision connects up with the exercise of a clear and exclusive Article II authority of the President,

---

[146] The ICA proved relevant to President Trump's withholding of some $400 million in statutorily appropriated funds for military assistance to Ukraine—an action best known for triggering the first of his two impeachments. Much of Congress's impeachment inquiry centered on the question whether the President attempted to secure a "quid pro quo" for the release of the funds, *see* Articles of Impeachment Against Donald John Trump, H.R. Res. 755, 116th Cong. (2019) (enacted) (charging that the President conditioned the release of these funds on Ukraine's willingness to launch a criminal investigation of Joseph Biden, Trump's eventual successor in office), but the withholding of the money also gave rise to impoundment-related problems. Indeed, the U.S. Government Accountability Office (GAO) would eventually conclude that the hold-back of these monies violated the ICA. *See In re* Off. of Mgmt. & Budget-Withholding of Ukr. Sec. Assistance, B-331564, 2020 WL 241373, at *6 (Comp. Gen. Jan. 16, 2020). Put differently, because Congress had appropriated this monetary aid without affording the President discretion to withhold it, the President could have moved to impound the money in keeping with the ICA only by seeking a rescission or by utilizing a notice-based deferral. The President, however, took neither action, claiming instead an inherent authority to block any expenditure that "could conflict with the President's foreign policy." *Id.* at *5 (quoting Letter from General Counsel, OMB, to General Counsel, GAO (Dec. 11, 2019)). In the GAO's view, however, that was an invalid rationale because "[f]aithful execution of the law does not permit the President to substitute his own policy priorities for those that Congress has enacted into law." *Id.* at *6.

[147] *Cf. generally* Roy E. Brownell II, *The Constitutional Status of the President's Impoundment of National Security Funds*, 12 SETON HALL CONST. L.J. 1, 8 (2001) (laying out the case for an exclusive Presidential authority to impound "national security-related funds").

[148] *See Zivotofsky*, 576 U.S. at 32.

[149] *See* Bale, *supra* note 145, at 621 (2020) (suggesting, largely on the basis of the *Zivotofsky* decision, that the President "may impound appropriations that invade his recognition power").

the ICA's dictates may have to take a backseat to overriding constitutional commands.

Chapter 27

INTERNATIONAL RELATIONS AND THE SEPARATION OF POWERS

Analysis

Sec.

This chapter addresses questions about the Constitution's allocation of legislative and executive authority over international relations. It begins by examining the Court's curious ruling in *United States v. Curtiss-Wright Export Corp.*,[1] which has underlaid developments in this area for nearly a century.[2] The rest of the chapter considers the respective roles of the President and Congress in navigating international relations, highlighting in particular the rules governing the making of Article II treaties,[3] congressional-executive agreements,[4] and sole-executive agreements,[5] while also considering the Court's recent decision in *Zivotofsky v. Kerry (Zivotofsky II)*[6] regarding the President's authority to "recognize" foreign nations.[7]

A. *CURTISS-WRIGHT* AND THE IDEA OF FOREIGN AFFAIRS EXCEPTIONALISM

The Court's 1936 decision in *Curtiss-Wright* concerned a federal statute that authorized the President to prohibit (via criminally enforceable orders) the sale of weapons to governments involved in a

---

1 299 U.S. 304 (1936).

2 *See infra* Section 27.A.

3 *See infra* Section 27.B.

4 *See infra* Section 27.C.1.

5 *See infra* Section 27.C.2.

6 576 U.S. 1 (2015); *see also* Zivotofsky v. Clinton (*Zivotofsky I*), 566 U.S. 189 (2012) (holding that the underlying dispute did not raise a nonjusticiable political question).

7 *See infra* Section 27.D.

South American armed conflict.[8] The challengers asserted that the statute improperly assigned Article I lawmaking power to the President in violation of the nondelegation doctrine.[9] The Court, however, rejected this claim in an seven-to-one ruling,[10] finding "sufficient warrant for the broad discretion vested in the President . . . [by] the statute."[11] In itself, this holding was of limited significance.[12] But along with it came a wide-ranging and still-influential set of musings about the federal government's power to deal with foreign nations.[13]

Justice Sutherland began his analysis by drawing a stark distinction between the federal government's authority "in respect of foreign or external affairs" and "in respect of domestic or internal affairs."[14] These "two classes of power," he explained, were "different, both in respect of their origin and their nature."[15] More specifically, whereas the federal government's domestic powers were limited to those "specifically enumerated in the Constitution, and such implied powers as are necessary and proper to carry into effect the enumerated powers," its foreign-affairs authority embraced all "the powers of external sovereignty," which "did not depend upon the affirmative grants of the Constitution."[16] No less important, Justice Sutherland continued, the President, as "sole organ of the nation in its external relations,"[17] had a "very delicate, plenary and exclusive power" in foreign affairs that did not depend on legislative authorization as "a basis for its exercise."[18]

---

[8] 299 U.S. at 312.

[9] *See id.* at 315. For more on the nondelegation doctrine, see *infra* Section 29.B.

[10] Justice Stone did not participate in the case because he was ill at the time it arose. *See* Edward A. Purcell, Jr., *Understanding* Curtiss-Wright, 31 L. & HIST. REV. 653, 657 (2013). But he later voiced misgivings about the Court's opinion. *See id.* at 704–09.

[11] *Curtiss-Wright*, 299 U.S. at 329.

[12] *See* David M. Driesen & William C. Banks, *Implied Presidential and Congressional Powers*, 41 CARDOZO L. REV. 1301, 1316 (2020) (characterizing *Curtiss-Wright* as an "otherwise unremarkable case").

[13] *See* Ganesh Sitaraman & Ingrid Wuerth, *The Normalization of Foreign Relations Law*, 128 HARV. L. REV. 1897, 1914 (2015).

[14] *Curtiss-Wright*, 299 U.S. at 315.

[15] *Id.*

[16] *Id.* at 315–16, 316, 318.

[17] *Id.* at 319 (quoting 10 ANNALS OF CONG. 613 (1800) (statement of Rep. John Marshall on Mar. 7, 1800)).

[18] *Id.* at 320. The Court did go on to note that such powers must nonetheless "be exercised in subordination to the applicable provisions of the Constitution," *id.*, thus suggesting, for instance, that the President's "sole organ" authority did not encompass a power to abridge individual rights, suspend habeas corpus at will, or contravene other external constitutional limits on federal authority. *See* Am. Ins. Ass'n v. Garamendi, 539 U.S. 396, 416 n.9 (2003) (noting *Curtiss-Wright*'s acknowledgment of this point).

These were bold claims,[19] and the Court has retreated from some of the opinion's more extravagant flourishes.[20] In important respects, however, the spirit of the decision lives on. For one thing, *Curtiss-Wright* still receives approving citations from the Court and lower courts in support of the principle that the nondelegation doctrine operates in a watered-down way in the field of foreign affairs.[21] Of greater significance, the judicially abstemious mood of the opinion remains reflected in the work of the courts in foreign-affairs cases. *Curtiss-Wright*, as Professors Ganesh Sitaraman and Ingrid Wuerth have noted, was "the most important" in a "series of cases" that together lay the foundation" of "foreign affairs exceptionalism"[22]—that is, the practice of treating the political branches' (and especially the President's) exercise of foreign-affairs as entitled to special accommodation by the courts. This practice, to be sure, has not foreclosed judicial intervention in cases involving the foreign-affairs powers, and it may (at least in some respects) now be on the wane.[23]

---

[19] These claims were also, in the view of many scholars, significantly ahistorical. *See, e.g.*, LOUIS HENKIN, FOREIGN AFFAIRS AND THE UNITED STATES CONSTITUTION 19–20 (2d ed. 1996) (contending that the idea that "the new United States government was to have major powers outside the Constitution is not intimated in the Constitution itself, in the records of the Convention, in the Federalist Papers, or in contemporary debate").

[20] *See, e.g.*, *Ex parte* Quirin, 317 U.S. 1, 25 (1942) (noting that "Congress and the President, like the courts, possess no power not derived from the Constitution"); Youngstown Sheet & Tube Co. v. Sawyer, 343 U.S. 579, 632 n.2 (1952) (Jackson, J., concurring) (noting that much of the *Curtiss-Wright* opinion was "dictum" and that the case was properly understood as going no further than rejecting a "strict limitation upon congressional delegations of power . . . in external affairs"); *Zivotofsky II*, 576 U.S. at 21 (noting that *Curtiss-Wright*'s "description of the President's exclusive power was not necessary to the holding" of the case, while emphasizing (albeit also in dicta) that "[t]he Executive is not free from the ordinary controls and checks of Congress merely because foreign affairs are at issue").

[21] Most notably, Justice Gorsuch cited approvingly to *Curtiss-Wright* in his dissenting opinion in *Gundy v. United States*, 139 S. Ct. 2116 (2019), which, for reasons we consider elsewhere, *see infra* Section 29.B.2, may soon form the basis for a major reworking of the nondelegation doctrine. *Curtiss-Wright*, Justice Gorsuch explained, supported the idea of an expanded congressional ability to assign to the executive branch authority that is related to the "many foreign affairs powers [that] are constitutionally vested in the president under Article II." 139 S. Ct. at 2137 (Gorsuch, J., dissenting).

[22] *See* Sitaraman & Wuerth, *supra* note 13, at 1915. As Professors Sitaraman and Wuerth note, *see id.* at 1906, the term "foreign affairs exceptionalism" originates from the scholarship of Professor Curtis Bradley, who coined the phrase in a 1998 article. *See* Curtis A. Bradley, *The Treaty Power and American Federalism*, 97 MICH. L. REV. 390, 461 (1998).

[23] *See generally* Sitaraman & Wuerth, *supra* note 13, at 1901 (noting several recent decisions in which "the Supreme Court has rejected the idea that foreign affairs are different from domestic affairs," thus indicating that "foreign relations law is being normalized"). *But see* Carlos M. Vázquez, *The Abiding Exceptionalism of Foreign Relations Doctrine*, 128 HARV. L. REV. F. 305, 305 (2015) (contending that, while "[t]here have indeed been some recent Supreme Court decisions that seem to lack the exceptional deference to the Executive that had characterized judicial decisionmaking

Even so, this sort of exceptionalism remains an important feature of foreign-affairs cases,[24] manifesting itself in, among other things, a special judicial willingness to treat such cases as nonjusticiable,[25] a reluctance in such cases to second-guess the government's (and especially the President's) purported justifications for encroachments on individual rights,[26] a diminished commitment to vindicating state-autonomy interests,[27] and a heightened tolerance for flexibility and innovation in federal (and especially presidential) policymaking.[28] In other words, while *Curtiss-Wright*'s most expansive rhetoric regarding federal (and especially federal executive) power no longer holds sway, the "fundamental" distinction that Justice Sutherland posited between "internal" and "external" affairs certainly remains relevant to modern-day constitutional law.

B. TREATIES

1. Treaty Formation

The Article II Treaty Clause provides that the President "shall have Power, by and with the Advice and Consent of the Senate, to make Treaties, provided two thirds of the Senators present concur."[29] Several features of this arrangement differ from the Article I mechanism for creating federal statutory law: First, the President's formal involvement occurs at the *beginning* rather than *end* of the process. Second, whereas any piece of Article I legislation must receive the assent of the House of Representatives, that body plays no formal role in making treaties. Finally, while Article I imposes no supermajority voting rules for enacting ordinary legislation (except with respect to veto overrides), the Treaty Clause requires supermajority action in the Senate for any treaty to take effect.

---

in the foreign affairs area in previous years," many areas of "foreign affairs doctrine remain[ ] resolutely exceptionalist").

[24] *See* Sitamaran & Wuerth, *supra* note 13, at 1904 (noting that the "normalization of foreign relations law is ongoing, not complete").

[25] *See, e.g.*, Goldwater v. Carter, 444 U.S. 996 (1979) (declining to adjudicate on the merits a question related to the President's unilateral termination of an Article II treaty); *see infra* Section 27.B.3 (discussing the decision in greater detail).

[26] *See, e.g.*, Trump v. Hawaii, 138 S. Ct. 2392 (2018) (rejecting a set of religious-discrimination challenges to an executive order barring the citizens of several Muslim-majority countries from entering the United States).

[27] *See, e.g.*, Crosby v. Nat'l Foreign Trade Council, 530 U.S. 363, 376 (1994) (holding that a set of state-law sanctions on Burma were preempted by federal statute, while noting that the President's "plenitude of Executive authority" within this area "controls the issue of preemption here").

[28] *See infra* Section 27.C.2 (discussing the courts' willingness to uphold sole executive agreements as a valid exercise of the President's inherent Article II authority).

[29] U.S. CONST. art. II, § 2.

Other aspects of the treaty-making process have long stirred debate. One issue concerns the scope of the Senate's "advice and consent" function. This feature of the Treaty Clause's text makes clear that the Senate enjoys a *de facto* veto power over any treaty that the President has negotiated. But does the "advice and consent" function entail something more? Some commentators have argued that it does, emphasizing Article II's reference not just to the Senate's "consent" but also to its "advice."[30] Whatever the merits of that view might be, the Senate has long chosen not to involve itself in the treaty-making process until after negotiations have concluded, and the Court in turn has recently suggested (albeit in passing) that "[t]he President has the *sole power* to negotiate treaties."[31]

Another question concerns the Senate's power to condition its "consent" to a treaty on the making of modifications to its terms. The Court has endorsed the idea that the Senate enjoys such a conditional-consent authority,[32] and the Senate has exercised this authority in the past.[33] In addition, the Senate has sometimes voted

---

[30] *See* HENKIN, *supra* note 19, at 177 ("As originally conceived, no doubt, the Senate was to be a kind of Presidential council, affording him advice throughout the treaty-making process and on all aspects of it—whether to enter negotiations, who shall represent the United States, what should be the scope of negotiations, the positions to be taken, the responses to be made, the terms to be accepted."); *see also* THE FEDERALIST NO. 84 (Hamilton) (explaining that, under the Article II treaty-making process, the President would engage in "foreign negotiations . . . according to general principles concerted with the Senate"); THE FEDERALIST NO. 64 (Jay) (suggesting that the President could "at any time convene" the Senate for "advice and consent" as treaty negotiations were unfolding). *See generally* Jean Galbraith, *Prospective Advice and Consent*, 37 YALE J. INT'L L. 247, 251–63 (2012) (canvassing the founding-era evidence).

[31] *Zivotofsky II*, 576 U.S. at 13 (emphasis added); *see also Curtiss-Wright*, 299 U.S. at 319 (contending that "[i]nto the field of [treaty] negotiation the Senate cannot intrude"). *But see* Louis Fisher, *The Staying Power of Erroneous Dicta: From* Curtiss-Wright *to* Zivotofsky, 31 CONST. COMMENT. 149, 207 (2016) (characterizing the language from *Zivotofsky II* as "erroneous dicta" that the Court should not have "left in place"). In keeping with this executive-centric view of the treaty-making power, lower courts have occasionally declined to enforce congressional enactments purporting to require the President to initiate treaty negotiations on various subjects. *See, e.g.*, Earth Island Inst. v. Christopher, 6 F.3d 648, 652–54 (9th Cir. 1993) (declining to enforce a statutory provision that would have required the Secretary of State to negotiate a treaty to protect sea turtles because the requirement "impinges upon power exclusively granted to the Executive Branch under the Constitution" and therefore "violates the separation of powers").

[32] *See* Haver v. Yaker, 76 U.S. (9 Wall.) 32, 35 (1869) (noting that the Senate may condition its consent by demanding that the negotiating parties "modify or amend" the treaty in question); *see also* Fourteen Diamond Rings, 183 U.S. 176, 183 (1901) (Brown, J., concurring) (noting that the Senate "may refuse its ratification, or make such ratification conditional upon the adoption of amendments to the treaty").

[33] For example, the Senate in 1795 consented to a highly controversial treaty that Chief Justice John Jay had negotiated with Great Britain on President Washington's behalf, but only subject to the condition "that there be added to the said treaty an article whereby it shall be agreed to suspend the operation of so much of the 12th article, as respects the trade which his said Majesty thereby consents may be carried on, between the United States and his islands in West Indies." S. Exec. Journal, 4th

to approve treaties while setting forth "reservations, understandings, and declarations" reflecting its (often limited) expectations as to how the treaty will operate on the ground.[34] Some scholars have raised concerned about the use of such "RUDs,"[35] but the courts have determined that these instruments have legal significance and can be relevant to the interpretation of the treaties to which they attach.[36]

2. Treaty Implementation

The Supremacy Clause of Article VI designates as part of the "supreme Law of the Land" "all Treaties made, or which shall be made, under the Authority of the United States."[37] As a result, a duly ratified treaty constitutes a part of federal law that, to the extent it applies to any particular matter, is capable of both preempting state law[38] and imposing judicially enforceable domestic-law obligations.

Cong., Special Sess., June 24, 1795, at 186. Great Britain accepted the modification, and the treaty was accordingly ratified. *See* Curtis A. Bradley & Jack L. Goldsmith, *Treaties, Human Rights, and Conditional Consent*, 149 U. PA. L. REV. 399, 406 (2000) (citing RALSTON HAYDEN, THE SENATE AND TREATIES, 1789–1817, at 87 (1920)). In contrast, when the Senate conditioned its consent to an 1803 boundary treaty on the making of an additional modification, the British government would not accept the proposed change, and the treaty thus never took effect. *See id.* at 407 (citing HAYDEN, *supra*, at 145–56).

[34] *See* Bradley & Goldsmith, *supra* note 33, at 401, 416–24.

[35] *See, e.g.*, John Quigley, *The Rule of Non-Inquiry and Human Rights Treaties*, 45 CATH. U. L. REV. 1213, 1234 (1996) (contending that the Treaty Clause gives to the Senate only a "veto power, not a power of revision"); Louis Henkin, *U.S. Ratification of Human Rights Conventions: The Ghost of Senator Bricker*, 89 AM. J. INT'L L. 341, 349 (1995) (contending, with respect to the use of RUDs in connection with various human rights treaties, that they "threaten[ ] to undermine a half-century of effort to establish international human rights standards as international law"); *see also* Bradley & Goldsmith, *supra* note 33, at 442–46 (noting that "some commentators" contend that certain RUDs "infringe on the constitutional role of the judiciary" but responding that "there is no merit to the claim").

[36] *See* Kristen E. Eichensehr, *Treaty Termination and the Separation of Powers*, 53 VA. J. INT'L L. 247, 250 (2013) ("As part of its 'advice and consent' function, the Senate's power to attach reservations, understandings, and declarations (RUDs) to treaties is long-standing and undisputed."); *see also* Eric Chung, Note, *The Judicial Enforceability and Legal Effects of Treaty Reservations, Understandings, and Declarations*, 126 YALE L.J. 170, 176 (2016) (finding, on the basis of a comprehensive survey of recent case law, that "U.S. courts and international courts consistently enforce RUDs, except for international courts reviewing treaties that expressly prohibit their use").

[37] U.S. CONST. art. VI.

[38] Though acknowledging that treaties can preempt conflicting state law, the Court has also suggested that treaties and their implementing statutes should be construed narrowly when necessary to avoid encroaching on traditional areas of state regulation. *See, e.g.*, Bond v. United States, 572 U.S. 844, 859 (2014) (finding that a statute implementing the Chemical Weapons Convention Implementation Act did not authorize the federal government to prosecute a defendant for committing a "purely local crime," in light of the Court's general unwillingness to construe federal law as encroaching on "areas of traditional state responsibility"); *see also supra* Section 5.D. A related problem concerns whether the principles of state sovereign immunity and

In some respects, however, treaties can present special enforcement-related complications. First, some U.S. treaties (or provisions within treaties) turn out to be "non-self-executing," meaning that Congress must pass implementing legislation in order to render them judicially enforceable within U.S. courts. Second, Congress sometimes enacts statutes that conflict with the terms of previously ratified treaties (and vice versa), thus raising the question whether the statute or the treaty should take priority.

a. *Self-Executing vs. Non-Self-Executing Treaties*

Although all U.S. treaties qualify as part of the "supreme Law of the Land," only some of those treaties—known as "self-executing" treaties—on their own give rise to judicially enforceable domestic-law obligations.[39] Other treaties, by contrast, are non-self-executing. Pursuant to the Supremacy Clause, a duly concluded non-self-executing treaty constitutes a full and formal part of federal law.[40] But unless and until it is implemented by Congress, any such treaty will "depend[ ] for the enforcement of its provisions on the interest and the honor of the governments which are [p]arty to it."[41] In other words, as Chief Justice Marshall once explained, whereas a self-executing treaty, like an ordinary statute, creates rights and obligations that private parties and government officials may rely upon when litigating cases in U.S. courts, a non-self-executing treaty "addresses itself to the political, not the judicial department; and the legislature must execute the contract before it can become a rule for the Court."[42]

The question of treaty self-execution is one of treaty interpretation. In other words, deciding whether a treaty counts as

---

the prohibition on congressional commandeering of state authorities apply in the treaty-law context. For a discussion of that subject, see *supra* Section 13.A.

[39] *See, e.g.*, Asakura v. City of Seattle, 265 U.S. 332 (1924) (holding that that a treaty between Japan and the United States of its own force entitled a Japanese national to work as a pawnbroker in Seattle, notwithstanding a city ordinance that prohibited non-U.S. citizens from engaging in such work); *see also* Kolovrat v. Oregon, 366 U.S. 187 (1961) (holding that a treaty between the United States and Yugoslavia entitled Yugoslavian nationals to inherit money from two deceased residents of Oregon, notwithstanding the contrary dictates of Oregon state law).

[40] *See* Michael D. Ramsey, *A Textual Approach to Treaty Non-Self-Execution*, 2015 BYU L. REV. 1639, 1647 (noting that even if "U.S. treatymakers may prefer that a treaty provision not have [supreme-law] status . . . the Constitution commands (rightly or wrongly) that all treaties must have this status (unless displaced by a superior form of law)"); Ernest A. Young, *Treaties as "Part of Our Law,"* 88 TEX. L. REV. 91, 113 (2009) (noting that "[t]he idea that some treaties are not self-executing . . . is wholly consistent with the notions that treaties are 'part of our law,' " while analogizing non-self-executing treaties to "statutes [that] are simply contracts between the states and the federal government, the performance of which are governed largely by politics and the good faith of the parties").

[41] *The Head Money Cases*, 112 U.S. 580, 598 (1884).

[42] Foster v. Neilson, 27 U.S. (2 Pet.) 253, 314 (1829) (Marshall, C.J.).

self-executing or non-self-executing requires courts to consult the text of the treaty, related materials, and surrounding circumstances to determine whether the makers of that treaty understood themselves to be bringing into immediate effect judicially enforceable domestic-law obligations.[43] In the real-world, treaties often fail to address this matter in clear terms,[44] and courts thus must exercise substantial interpretive discretion in determining whether to give effect to treaty-based rules.

Exercising this discretion, the Roberts Court recently signaled a reluctance to infer self-execution in the face of textual silence. More specifically, in *Medellín v. Texas*,[45] the Court held that Article 94(1) of the United Nations Charter, which set forth the signatory nations' commitment to "undertake[ ] to comply" with decisions rendered by the International Court of Justice (ICJ), did not of its own force obligate U.S. courts (including state courts) to abide by the judgments of the ICJ on certain international-law matters.[46] Most notably, and contrary to the position then outlined by the *Restatement (Third) of Foreign Relations Law*,[47] the Court in

---

[43] *See* Carlos Manual Vázquez, *Treaties as Law of the Land: The Supremacy Clause and the Judicial Enforcement of Treaties*, 122 HARV. L. REV. 599, 631 (2008) (noting that, in the United States, the "need for implementing legislation has its source in the treaty itself"). *But see* David L. Sloss, *Executing* Foster v. Neilson: *The Two-Step Approach To Analyzing Self-Executing Treaties*, 53 HARV. INT'L L.J. 135, 137–38 (2012) (noting that "[i]n the vast majority of cases, there is nothing in the treaty text, negotiating history, or ratification record that specifies which domestic legal actors have the power or duty to implement the treaty" and that courts should avoid the search for a "a fictitious intent" and instead consider the self-execution question by reference to "domestic laws delineating the powers and duties of various government officials and institutions" implicated by the treaty's substantive terms).

[44] *See id.* at 137 n.6 (noting, with respect to multilateral treaties, that express textual guidance regarding treaty enforcement is almost always absent because "it would be virtually impossible for the drafters of [such a] treaty to agree on treaty language specifying which domestic government institutions have the power and/or duty to implement the treaty").

[45] 552 U.S. 491 (2008).

[46] *Id.* at 508; *see also* Sanchez-Llamas v. Oregon, 548 U.S. 331, 354 (2006) (holding that Article 36 of the Vienna Convention on Consular Relations does not require U.S. courts to waive otherwise applicable domestic-law procedural-default rules as necessary to vindicate the treaty's protections, notwithstanding the ICJ's embrace of a contrary position, while emphasizing that "[n]othing in the structure or purpose of the ICJ suggests that its interpretations were intended to be conclusive on our courts").

[47] *See* RESTATEMENT (THIRD) OF FOREIGN RELATIONS LAW OF THE UNITED STATES § 111 reporters' n.5 (1987). One might defend such a presumption as justified by the text of the Supremacy Clause itself, which, by according "supreme Law" status to treaties *and* statutes, can be read as evincing an expectation that the binding domestic-law force of a treaty should not, at least ordinarily, hinge on the later enactment of a statute. *See, e.g.*, Vázquez, *supra* note 43, at 602, 606. *But see* David H. Moore, *Law(makers) of the Land: The Doctrine of Treaty Non-Self Execution*, 122 HARV. L. REV. F. 32, 35–36 (2008) (suggesting that "attempting to answer the self-execution question by placing primary emphasis on the Supremacy Clause is misguided" and that other constitutional provisions militate in favor of a more flexible approach).

Medellín pointedly declined to embrace an interpretive presumption in favor of self-execution[48] and instead employed what it described as a "textual approach" to the self-execution question.[49] As applied to *Medellín* itself, that approach dictated the conclusion that the treaty on its own terms did not render the ICJ's judgments binding on domestic courts, and that in turn meant that the Court could not, on the basis of that treaty, set aside a Texas state-court conviction and capital sentence that (the ICJ had found) violated the Vienna Convention on Consular Relations.[50] To be sure, the majority in so holding did not go so far as to endorse an explicit interpretive presumption in favor of non-self-execution.[51] Even so, the "textual

---

48 *See* Curtis A. Bradley, *Intent, Presumptions, and Non-Self-Executing Treaties*, 102 AM. J. INT'L L. 540, 546 (2008) ("The Court in *Medellín* appears to have rejected any strong presumption in favor of self-execution.").

49 *Medellín*, 552 U.S. at 514.

50 *See Avena and Other Mexican Nationals (Mexico v. United States)*, 2004 ICJ Rep. 12 (Mar. 31), *reprinted in* 43 ILM 581 (2004). The Court in *Medellín* also denied effect to President George W. Bush's unilateral attempts to require state-court compliance with the ICJ judgment at issue through the issuance of a memorandum announcing the nation's commitment to "hav[e] State courts give effect to the decision." *See Medellín*, 552 U.S. at 503. Applying the tripartite framework from Justice Jackson's *Youngstown* concurrence, *see supra* Section 26.B.1, the Court reasoned, in light of the non-self-executing nature of the relevant treaty provisions, that the President's attempted "assertion of authority" was contrary to the treatymakers' intent and thus fell "within Justice Jackson's third category." *See Medellín*, 552 U.S. at 527. *But see* Ingrid Wuerth, Medellín: *The New, New Formalism*, 13 LEWIS & CLARK L. REV. 1, 6 (2009) (noting that "it is very difficult to see how the Senate could have had any particular understanding of what the fact of non-self-execution (itself implied, not stated) would mean for the President's executive power"). The Court also rejected the related argument that the President's actions reflected a valid exercise of his established authority "to settle foreign claims pursuant to an executive agreement." *See Medellín*, 552 U.S. at 531 (citing Dames & Moore v. Regan, 453 U.S. 654, 679–80 (1981)). That argument failed, the Court concluded, because *Dames & Moore* and the other "claims-settlement cases" involved a "narrow set of circumstances" not present in *Medellín*, and the Government had not "identified a single instance in which the President has attempted (or Congress has acquiesced in) a Presidential directive issued to state courts, much less one that reaches deep into the heart of the State's police powers and compels state courts to reopen final criminal judgments and set aside neutrally applicable state laws." *Id.* at 531–32; *see infra* notes 92–96 and accompanying text (discussing this aspect of the Court's holding in greater detail). None of this meant, the Court hastened to add, that the President altogether lacked the authority to promote compliance with the terms of a non-self-executing treaty. *Medellín*, 552 U.S. at 531. But it was clear to the Court that the President "may not rely upon a non-self-executing treaty to establish binding rules of decision that preempt contrary state law." *Id.* (internal quotations omitted); *cf.* Wuerth, *supra*, at 8 (noting that the opinion "leaves open the question of whether the President could enforce a non-self-executing treaty in domestic courts if the Senate and President attached a declaration to a treaty stating that the treaty was not self-executing but could nevertheless be enforced by the President in domestic courts").

51 *See* Bradley, *supra* note 48, at 540–41 (contending that, while "some commentators may claim that the decision supports a strong presumption against self-execution," a "careful reading of the decision suggests that this is not a fair construction"); John Quigley, *A Tragi-Comedy of Errors Erodes Self-Execution of Treaties:* Medellín v. Texas *and Beyond*, 45 CASE W. RES. J. INT'L. L. 403, 430–33 (2012) (finding that *Medellín*'s impact has been muted, particularly in connection with

approach" the Court employed was enough to strike the dissenters (and several commentators in the case's aftermath) as one that stacked the deck against domestic judicial enforcement of treaty-based norms.[52]

b. Treaties, Statutes, and the Last-in-Time Rule

A second distinctive challenge posed by treaty enforcement relates to conflicts that arise between Article II treaties and Article I statutes. Suppose, for instance, that the President and the Senate have put in place an explicitly self-executing treaty whose domestic-law requirements conflict with those set forth by an earlier Article I statute. Or suppose conversely that Congress seeks to nullify an existing (and also self-executing) Article II treaty by enacting a statute that abrogates its terms. Under these circumstances, which of the two enactments ought to prevail? Should treaty-based requirements always supersede statutory requirements?[53] Should statutory requirements always supersede treaty-based requirements?[54] Or should the two types of enactments generally

---

private-law treaties, because some lower courts have continued to "disregard[ ]" the decision's instructions regarding self execution).

[52] *Medellín*, 552 U.S. at 546 (Breyer, J., dissenting) (maintaining that the relevant case law "make[s] clear that, insofar as today's majority looks for language about 'self-execution' in the treaty itself and insofar as it erects 'clear statement' presumptions designed to help find an answer, it is misguided"); *see also* Gráinne de Búrca, *International Law Before the Courts: The EU and the US Compared*, 55 VA. J. INT'L L. 685, 713–14 (2015) ("The Court in *Medellín* rendered a particularly forceful ruling with respect to whether international treaties could be treated as self-executing, introducing something akin to a strong presumption against self-execution."); Daniel Abebe & Aziz Z. Huq, *Foreign Affairs Federalism: A Revisionist Approach*, 66 VAND. L. REV. 723, 741 (2013) (understanding *Medellín* to endorse "the idea that treaties are not 'self-executing,' in the sense of creating domestic legal obligations, absent a clear statement to that effect"); Moore, *supra* note 46, at 46 ("While the Court did not expressly adopt a presumption against self-execution, the separation of powers presumptions employed in *Medellín* make it more likely that courts will find treaties to be non-self-executing when the treatymakers do not expressly indicate otherwise."); *cf.* Sloss, *supra* note 43, at 137 (suggesting, with respect to debates between "nationalists" and "transnationalists" on treaty-related matters, that the Court in *Medellín* "threw its substantial weight behind the nationalist camp").

[53] *See* Carlos Manuel Vázquez, *Treaty-Based Rights and Remedies of Individuals*, 92 COLUM. L. REV. 1082, 1114 n.126 (1992) (suggesting that "there is strong (though not conclusive) evidence that the Framers intended that treaties be lexically superior to statutes").

[54] *Cf.* AKHIL REED AMAR, AMERICA'S CONSTITUTION: A BIOGRAPHY 302–07 (2005) (raising this possibility by reference to, among other things, the fact that the Supremacy Clause lists "the laws of the United States" prior to "treaties" in defining the "supreme Law of the Land" and the suggestion that statutes, which (unlike treaties) receive the assent of *both* the House and the Senate, have a "superior democratic pedigree"); *cf.* Vasan Kesavan, *The Three Tiers of Federal Law*, 100 NW. U. L. REV. 1479, 1633 (2006) (suggesting, among other things, that "the Founding generation would have been absolutely shocked to learn that the President and Senate, feared to be monarchical and aristocratic, respectively, would, by treaty, have the power to repeal the existing Laws of the United States, which necessarily include the judgments of the People's branch of the legislature, without the consent of Congress").

qualify as hierarchically equivalent, with treaty-statute conflicts to be resolved on the basis of some other rule of decision?[55]

Different commentators have proposed different approaches to this problem, but the Court has settled on the last of these options, holding that treaties and statutes are "placed on the same footing" by the Supremacy Clause[56] and that treaty-statute conflicts should be resolved by reference to a "last-in-time" rule.[57] That is, a statute adopted today will take precedence over a conflicting treaty adopted yesterday, and a treaty adopted tomorrow will take precedence over the conflicting statute adopted today. Treaty-statute conflicts are thus resolved no differently from statute-statute (and treaty-treaty) conflicts: Recency dictates priority.

To this point, however, we should add two qualifications. First, to the extent that a (more recent) *non-self-executing* treaty conflicts with a (less recent) federal statute, the statute's operation will remain undisturbed.[58] That conclusion follows from the concept of non-self-execution: Because courts cannot enforce a non-self-executing treaty, they also cannot rely on such a treaty as providing a legally sufficient basis for declining enforcement of any statutes with which it is said to conflict.[59] Second, several important canons of construction can play a pro-treaty role in guiding threshold

---

[55] *See, e.g.*, Julian G. Ku, *Treaties as Laws: A Defense of the Last-In-Time Rule for Treaties and Federal Statutes*, 80 IND. L.J. 319, 353 (2005) (construing the text of the Supremacy Clause to indicate that "the drafters of the Constitution understood that the last-in-time rule would apply to different forms of enacted law, even with respect to law enacted by different lawmaking institutions," and marshalling additional historical support for that reading).

[56] *See* Whitney v. Robertson, 124 U.S. 190, 194 (1888). Prior to its decision in *Whitney*, the Court had squarely rejected the proposition that treaties trump statutes, holding in the *Head Money Cases*, that there was not "anything in [a treaty's] essential character, or in the branches of the government by which the treaty is made" that "gives it [a] superior sanctity" over statutes. 112 U.S. at 599. That holding appeared to leave the door open to a rule of categorical priority for statutes over treaties. *Cf. id.* (noting that "if there be any difference" between treaties and statutes, "it would seem to be in favor of an act in which all three of the bodies participate"). But *Whitney* slammed that door shut, instead making clear that no categorical priority rule privileged either type of instrument.

[57] *See Whitney*, 124 U.S. at 194 (noting that if a statute and a treaty are "inconsistent, the one last in date will control the other").

[58] *See id.* (noting that the last-in-time rule applies subject to the key qualification that "the stipulation of the treaty on the subject is self-executing").

[59] *See* Emily S. Bremer, *The Dynamic Last-in-Time Rule*, 22 IND. INT'L & COMP. L. REV. 27, 44 (2012) (noting that "[i]f the treaty is non-self-executing, there is no conflict" because the treaty has not produced any binding, domestic-law norms at odds with those of the statute itself). To be sure, Congress can change that state of affairs by enacting legislation that executes the previously non-self-executing treaty. Once it has done so, the resulting conflict in the legal materials would, strictly speaking, be a conflict that arises between two statutes—the older, superseded statute, and the newer, implementing statute. And that conflict, like most inter-statute conflicts, would itself be resolved in accordance with the last-in-time rule.

determinations about whether treaties and statutes do in fact dictate irreconcilable results. For example, the so-called *Charming Betsy* rule provides that "an act of Congress ought never to be construed to violate the law of nations if any other possible construction remains,"[60] and that instruction often leads courts eschew a "finding [of] implicit repeal of a treaty in ambiguous congressional action."[61] Likewise, the "Indian canons" of statutory construction often discourage courts from finding that a statute impliedly abrogates a federal-tribal treaty.[62] Overall, then, canons of this sort can afford to treaties a sort of soft lexical priority over statutes: Although the last-in-time rule dictates that a newer statute takes precedence over an older conflicting treaty, courts may well seek to construe the newer statute so as to avoid any interference with the older treaty's effects.

3. Treaty Termination

While Article II, section 2 establishes that treaties can come into being only through the joint action of the President and two-thirds of the Senate, that provision says nothing about who can terminate treaties currently in effect. A few points on the subject, however, are clear.[63] First, as we have just seen, the last-in-time rule gives

---

[60] *See* Murray v. Schooner Charming Betsy, 6 U.S. (2 Cranch) 64, 118 (1804).

[61] *See, e.g.*, Trans World Airlines, Inc. v. Franklin Mint Corp., 466 U.S. 243, 252 (1984); *see also* Curtis Bradley, *The* Charming Betsy *Canon and Separation of Powers: Rethinking the Interpretive Role of International Law*, 86 GEO. L.J. 479, 488 (1998) (linking this rule to the *Charming Betsy* canon).

[62] *See, e.g.*, Minnesota v. Mille Lacs Band of Chippewa Indians, 526 U.S. 172, 202 (1999) ("Congress may abrogate Indian treaty rights [by statute], but it must clearly express its intent to do so."). *See generally supra* Section 25.A.2.a.

[63] It bears emphasizing throughout this discussion that we are here considering only the question of what procedures suffice, as a domestic-law matter, to effectuate a U.S. withdrawal from an international agreement. That question, however, is distinct from the question of what *international law* requires as a precondition to a valid treaty withdrawal. *See* Curtis A. Bradley, *Treaty Termination and Historical Gloss*, 92 TEX. L. REV. 773, 776 (2014) (noting that the question "whether a nation's treaty commitments are terminated is determined by international law, not U.S. law"); Jean Galbraith, *Rejoining Treaties*, 106 VA. L. REV. 73, 87 (2020) (contrasting the "well-developed standards for determining when withdrawal is consistent with *international law*" with the Constitution's silence on the question of "what domestic legal process is necessary for treaty withdrawal"). *See generally* Vienna Convention on the Law of Treaties (VCLT), *opened for signature* May 23, 1969, 1155 U.N.T.S. 331 (laying out various conditions under which a party's termination of a treaty is justified as a matter of international law); STEPHEN P. MULLIGAN, CONG. RSCH. SERV., RL32528, TREATIES AND OTHER INTERNATIONAL AGREEMENTS: THE ROLE OF THE UNITED STATES SENATE, S. REP. NO. 106–71, at 45 (2001) (noting that, although the United States has not ratified the VCLT, its "rules governing treaty relationships . . . are recognized as general principles of international law by the executive and judicial branches of the United States"), *available at* https://www.govinfo.gov/content/pkg/CPRT-106SPRT66922/html/CPRT-106SPRT66922.htm. To put the point another way, the domestic-law issues we consider here involve only the issue of who can declare, on behalf of the United States, that it no longer intends to honor an otherwise-operative set of treaty obligations. But that is different from asking whether such a declaration comports with the terms of the treaty being terminated and/or some other source of

Congress a *de facto* power to terminate U.S. treaties by passing statutes that abrogate or supersede any domestic-law rights and obligations that those treaties set-forth.[64] Second, there is no serious question that Article II permits the President and two-thirds of the Senate (again, only as a domestic-law matter) to decide collectively to withdraw the United States from a treaty into which it previously entered.[65] One other issue, however, remains formally unresolved: May the President, as the "sole organ" of U.S. foreign policy, act unilaterally to withdraw the United States from a treaty that, in the President's view, no longer serves the nation's interests?[66] Or does Article II, by requiring both presidential and senatorial consent as a prerequisite to treaty formation, impliedly require a similar (if not identical) degree of consensus as a precondition to any act of treaty termination?[67]

---

international law. Just because an act of treaty termination meets the procedural requirements of U.S. constitutional law does not mean that the termination itself meets the requirements of international law. And if it does not, the act of termination might result in an adverse international-law consequences for the United States itself.

[64] *See supra* Section 27.B.2.b; *see also* Galbraith, *supra* note 63, at 103 (noting that, pursuant to the last-in-time rule, Congress can use its Article I authority in a manner that "effectively invalidates a Senate resolution of advice and consent"). One possible exception to this principle applies in connection with self-executing treaties that, along the lines of *Missouri v. Holland*, 215 U.S. 416 (1920), *see supra* Section 10.C, touch on domestic-law subjects that Congress lacks the power to regulate under Article I. Under these circumstances, there is some question as to whether Congress would have the Article I power to abrogate the treaty by statute. *See, e.g.*, Curtis A. Bradley, *The Treaty Power and American Federalism*, 97 MICH. L. REV. 390, 457 (1998) (highlighting this question and pointing to its existence as a reason to doubt the correctness of *Missouri v. Holland*).

[65] Galbraith, *supra* note 63, at 103 (noting that "the Senate has reconsidered a resolution of advice and consent or itself approved the President's decision to withdraw from a treaty," albeit only on "rare occasions").

[66] *See, e.g.*, Alexander Hamilton, *Pacificus No. 1* (June 29, 1793), *reprinted in* 15 THE PAPERS OF ALEXANDER HAMILTON 33, 42 (Harold C. Syrett et al. eds., 1969) (noting, with respect to certain U.S. treaties with France, that "though treaties can only be made by the President and Senate, their activity may be continued or suspended by the President alone"); Louis Henkin, *Litigating the President's Power to Terminate Treaties*, 73 AM. J. INT'L L. 647, 652 (1979) ("The constitutional basis of [the treaty termination] authority may be the 'Executive Power' clause of Article II, as suggested by Alexander Hamilton, or the President's role as 'sole organ,' as suggested by John Marshall; or his authority may result from the sum of other powers." (citing *Curtiss-Wright*, 299 U.S. at 320)).

[67] *See, e.g.*, THE FEDERALIST No. 64 (Jay) (noting, with respect to the President and Senate, "that as the consent of both was essential to [treaty] formation at first, so must it ever afterwards be to alter or cancel [treaties]"); *see also* James J. Moriarty, *Congressional Claims for Treaty Termination Powers in the Age of the Diminished Presidency*, 14 CONN. J. INT'L L. 123, 136–37 (1999) (developing this argument). Militating against this view, albeit indirectly, are precedents concerning the President's removal power. In particular, the Court has never indicated that the Appointments Clause's "advice and consent" requirement imposes on the President a parallel obligation to secure the Senate's approval before removing an officer whom the Senate previously confirmed. *See infra* Chapter 30. Thus, one might argue, a similar rule ought to obtain with respect to the relationship between treaty formation and treaty termination: Just because the Treaty Clause requires the Senate's advice

The Court had an opportunity to answer this question in the 1979 case of *Goldwater v. Carter*,[68] in which Senator Barry Goldwater and others sought judicial nullification of President Jimmy Carter's unilateral termination of a defense agreement with Taiwan. Ultimately, the Justices ordered a dismissal of the case without reaching the merits,[69] and it has not since then weighed in on any similar treaty-termination dispute.[70] In the face of this silence,

---

and consent as a precondition to the making of treaties, it does not follow that such advice and consent is also necessary for the termination of treaties previously made. *But see* Moriarty, *supra*, at 59 (characterizing the analogy as "potentially problematic because the treaty provision is obviously quite different from the appointment provision"). *See generally* Eichensehr, *supra* note 36, at 269–75 (exploring in depth the removal-power analogy). A related argument draws on the Supremacy Clause: If, per that provision, a treaty has law-like status akin to that of a federal statute, then (so the argument goes) a federal statute should be required to rescind that treaty (in much the same way that a federal statute is required to supersede another statute). *See, e.g.*, Raoul Berger, *The President's Unilateral Termination of the Taiwan Treaty*, 75 NW. U. L. REV. 577, 620–22 (1980) (developing this argument).

68 444 U.S. 996 (1979).

69 Then-Associate Justice Rehnquist and three other Justices would have held that the case presented a nonjusticiable political question involving "the authority of the President in the conduct of our country's foreign relations." *See Goldwater*, 444 U.S. at 1003 (Rehnquist, J., concurring in the judgment); *see also id.* at 1004 (contending that this outcome was supported by the Court's holding in *Curtiss-Wright*, which plainly discouraged federal-court second-guessing of executive-branch decisions in matters "entirely external to the United States" (quoting *Curtiss-Wright*, 299 U.S. at 315 (internal quotation omitted))). But Justice Powell, who provided a fifth vote for dismissal, explicitly disclaimed reliance on the political-question doctrine—which, he argued, was inapplicable in light of the "Court's willingness on previous occasions to decide whether one branch of our Government has impinged upon the power of another." *Id.* at 1001 (Powell, J., concurring) (citing, among other cases, Buckley v. Valeo, 424 U.S. 1 (1976), United States v. Nixon, 418 U.S. 683 (1974), and Myers v. United States, 272 U.S. 52 (1926)). Instead, Justice Powell argued that "prudential considerations" favored dismissal on *ripeness*-based grounds, given the critical fact that neither the Senate alone nor both houses together had purported to block the President from terminating the treaty unilaterally. *Id.* at 996. With that point in mind, he concluded that the preferable course of action was for the judicial branch to stand back, at least for a time, and give "the normal political process . . . the opportunity to resolve the conflict." *Id.*

70 A handful of lower court opinions have continued to grapple with the issue. Thus, for instance, in *Beacon Products Corp. v. Reagan*, 633 F. Supp. 1191 (D. Mass. 1986), *aff'd on mootness grounds*, 814 F.2d 1 (1st Cir. 1987), a U.S. district court invoked the *Goldwater* plurality opinion in holding that a challenge to President Reagan's unilateral termination of a commercial treaty with Nicaragua presented a nonjusticiable political question. *See id.* at 1198–99. Similarly, in *Kucinich v. Bush*, 236 F. Supp. 2d 1 (D.D.C. 2002), another district court noted that, while *Goldwater* had yielded "no obviously binding holding," Justice Rehnquist's plurality opinion nonetheless furnished a persuasive rationale for dismissing on political-question grounds a challenge to President Bush's unilateral termination of the 1972 Anti-Ballistic Missile Treaty with Russia. *See id.* at 13–18. In addition, as some commentators have noted, the Court more recently has hinted at a willingness to consider treaty-termination questions on the merits. *See* Michael D. Ramsey, *War Powers Litigation After* Zivotofsky v. Clinton, 21 CHAP. L. REV. 177, 179 (2018) (noting that "the *Zivotofsky* majority opinion did not discuss Rehnquist's concurring opinion in *Goldwater*—and Rehnquist's analysis in *Goldwater* seems inconsistent with it"); Kristen E. Eichensehr, *The* Youngstown *Canon: Vetoed Bills and the Separation of Powers*, 70 DUKE L.J. 1245, 1308 (2020) (citing *Zivotofsky* for the proposition that

Presidents have consistently asserted (at least post-*Goldwater*) that they do have the authority to terminate treaties on their own, and neither Congress as a whole nor the Senate in particular has offered meaningful resistance to this assertion of executive power.[71] As a result, it is now, in the words of Professor Curtis Bradley, "widely (although not uniformly) accepted that presidents have a unilateral power of treaty termination."[72] That understanding, however, has never received the explicit sign-off of the courts.[73]

C. ALTERNATIVES TO TREATIES

Treaties do not provide the only mechanism for dealing by agreement with other nations. Two other devices also exist, and they often prove attractive to federal decisionmakers because their use is not constrained by a need to secure supermajority Senate approval. The first is the "congressional-executive agreement," through which Congress agrees to effectuate the terms of a treaty-like arrangement by enacting a statute under Article I. The second is the "sole executive agreement," through which the President alone concludes such an arrangement based on a claim of Article II authority.

1. Congressional-Executive Agreements

Congressional-executive agreements have long played an important role in implementing American foreign policy.[74] They can generally be effectuated in one of two ways: First, Congress might, via statutory enactment, *prospectively* authorize the President to

"[r]ecent doctrinal shifts suggest that courts might be prepared to adjudicate the merits of future treaty termination cases").

71 *See* Bradley, *supra* note 63, at 814–16.

72 *Id.* at 773. *But see* Harold Hongju Koh, *Presidential Power to Terminate International Agreements*, 128 YALE L.J. FORUM 432, 434–35 (2018) (maintaining that "the conventional wisdom is wrong" and rests "not on constitutional text, structure, or Supreme Court precedent, but on the thin reed of historical practice that followed the Court's summary disposition [in *Goldwater*]").

73 Another largely unaddressed aspect of the question relates to the extent of Congress's (or the Senate's) power to prescribe by statute (or by the terms of a particular treaty) a rule against unilateral presidential termination. In particular, one might contend that the Constitution permits the President to terminate treaties as a default matter while also permitting Congress as a whole (or the Senate in particular) to override the default rule by prospectively reserving for itself a role to play in any withdrawal decision. In other words, the applicable rule might provide that, where treaties say nothing about the processes of termination, then the President, acting within Category Two of Justice Jackson's *Youngstown* framework, can unilaterally terminate. But that rule would further provide that where codified withdrawal instructions place the President within Category Three, unilateral treaty termination would no longer be permitted. *See* Bradley, *supra* note 63, at 824 (highlighting this possibility).

74 For a historical overview, see Oona A. Hathaway, *Treaties' End: The Past, Present, and Future of International Lawmaking in the United States*, 117 YALE L.J. 1236, 1274–1307 (2008).

negotiate and consummate an agreement that, once completed, automatically carries binding domestic-law effect.[75] Alternatively, Congress might give its approval *ex post*, effectively codifying as U.S. statutory law the terms of a deal struck between the President and representatives of other nations.[76] In either event, the key feature of the agreement is that it acquires domestic-law force by way of the Article I lawmaking process. Congressional-executive agreements, in other words, become a part of the "supreme Law of the Land" not as treaties that were "made" pursuant to the procedures of Article II, section 2, but rather by way of "laws of the United States" that were enacted pursuant to the procedures set forth by Article I, section 7.

The elephant-in-the-room question about congressional-executive agreements is whether the Constitution permits their use at all. The basic argument against them is that the document explicitly deals with international agreements by way of a single provision—the Treaty Clause—that requires supermajority Senate consent. In other words, so the argument goes, the standalone existence of the Treaty Clause implicitly prohibits Congress and the President from pursuing treaty-like arrangements by means of procedures that do not satisfy that clause's procedural requirements. If the making of formal treaties requires the advice and consent of at least two-thirds of the Senate, then would-be "laws" that are the functional equivalent of treaties ought to be subject to the same requirement as well. Otherwise, the argument goes, Congress and the President could achieve a too-easy end-run around the Article II requirement of supermajoritarian senatorial approval.[77]

---

[75] *See* Oona A. Hathaway, *Presidential Power Over International Law: Restoring the Balance*, 119 YALE L.J. 140, 145 (2009).

[76] This was the case, for instance, with the recent United States-Mexico-Canada Agreement ("USMCA"), *see* United States-Mexico-Canada Agreement Implementation Act, Pub. L. No. 116–113, 134 Stat. 11 (2020), and the North American Free Trade Agreement ("NAFTA"), *see* North American Free Trade Agreement Implementation Act., Pub. L. No. 103–182, 107 Stat. 2057 (1993).

[77] For a lengthy articulation of this view, see Laurence H. Tribe, *Taking Text and Structure Seriously: Reflections on Free-Form Method in Constitutional Interpretation*, 108 HARV. L. REV. 1221, 1249–78 (1995), *responding to* Bruce Ackerman & David Golove, *Is NAFTA Constitutional*, 108 HARV. L. REV. 799 (1995). Other scholars, by contrast, have suggested that congressional agreements might (or even must) be used in connection with some subjects but not in connection with others. *See, e.g.*, John C. Yoo, *Laws as Treaties?: The Constitutionality of Congressional-Executive Agreements*, 99 MICH. L. REV. 757, 763–64 (2001) (contending that "the normal statutory mode must be used to approve international agreements that regulate matters within Congress's Article I powers," whereas treaties "are required for the national government to act in areas that are the subject of the concurrent powers of the executive and legislative branches"); Peter J. Spiro, *Treaties, Executive Agreements, and Constitutional Method*, 79 TEX. L. REV. 961, 996 (2001) (suggesting, based largely on historical practice, a baseline (but potentially changeable) presumption according to which congressional-executive agreements operate as the primary instrument for trade agreements, whereas Article II treaties operate as the primary instrument for

Whatever the abstract merits of this argument might be,[78] it does not find much support in either historical or present-day practice.[79] Congressional-executive agreements date all the way back to the founding era, and the Court has never expressed any qualms about their validity.[80] In addition (and as we soon will see), the Court has explicitly validated the President's making of *sole executive agreements*,[81] thus rebuffing (at least indirectly) the suggestion that the Treaty Clause operates as the exclusive mechanism for international deal-making.[82] Given this reality, and given the fact that it is often easier for a President to secure majoritarian support

---

"defense-related and human rights agreements"). *But see* Hathaway, *supra* note 74, at 1253 (suggesting that Professor Spiro's synthesis fails to capture, at least as descriptive matter, the full range of purposes to which congressional-executive agreements have been put).

[78] A textual basis for resisting the conclusion comes from Article I, section 10's stipulations that "[n]o state shall enter into any Treaty, Alliance, or Confederation" and that "[n]o state shall, without the Consent of Congress, . . . enter into any Agreement or Compact with another State." *See* U.S. CONST. art. I, § 10. That these provisions refer to both treaties and other types of inter-sovereign agreements might furnish grounds for concluding that treaties *qua* treaties do not exhaust the full range of agreement-making options at a government's disposal. *See, e.g.*, Hathaway, *supra* note 74, at 1287 ("This [provision] has long been taken as tacit acknowledgment that international agreements other than treaties can and do exist."). *But see* Yoo, *supra* note 77, at 769–70 (casting doubt on the practice of "reading prohibitions on the states as empowering the federal government to do the opposite").

[79] *See* Curtis A. Bradley, *Exiting Congressional-Executive Agreements*, 67 DUKE L.J. 1615, 1627 (2018) ("Presidential use of congressional-executive agreements in lieu of Article II treaties is generally assumed to be constitutionally permissible.").

[80] For example, in *Weinberger v. Rossi*, 456 U.S. 25 (1982), the Court interpreted a federal statute's use of the term "treaty" to encompass certain "executive agreements concluded by the President"—including agreements that the President negotiated pursuant to a congressional statute—without evincing any doubts as to the constitutionality of such agreements. *Id.* at 26; *see also* B. Altman & Co. v. United States, 224 U.S. 583, 601 (1912) (holding that a congressional-executive agreement qualified as a "treaty" under the terms of a jurisdictional statute, while noting that the agreement, though "not technically a treaty requiring ratification [by 2/3rds of the Senate]," was "nevertheless . . . a compact authorized by the Congress of the United States, negotiated and proclaimed under the authority of its President"). In addition, in *Field v. Clark*, 143 U.S. 649 (1892), the Court signaled its acceptance of congressional-executive agreements by finding that a grant to the President of reciprocal tariff-making authority did not invalidly delegate legislative power to the President, *see infra* Section 29.B.1, and also that it did not invalidly "invest[ ] the president with treaty-making power," *id.* at 694. To the extent that courts have confronted direct constitutional challenges to congressional-executive agreements, they have sometimes relied on the political-question doctrine to avoid reaching the merits of the issue. *See, e.g.*, Made in the USA Found. v. United States, 242 F.3d 1300, 1311–20 (11th Cir. 2001) (concluding, "in the context of international commercial agreements such as NAFTA," that "the issue of what kinds of agreements require Senate ratification pursuant to the Art. II, § 2 procedures presents a nonjusticiable political question").

[81] *See infra* Section 27.C.2.

[82] Indeed, one might argue that the validity of congressional-executive agreements follows *a fortiori* from the validity of their "sole executive" counterparts. That is, if even the President alone can circumvent the strictures of the Treaty Clause, then surely the President and Congress together can do the same.

in both houses than supermajoritarian support in the Senate, congressional-executive agreements have become, by far, the most common method of international agreement-making in the United States today.[83]

2. Sole-Executive Agreements

A different type of non-treaty-based international agreement—commonly referred to as the sole-executive agreement—involves the President's exercise of Article II powers other than the section 2 power to "make . . . Treaties" with the Senate's advice and consent.[84] Suppose, for instance, that the President negotiates an armistice that ends a war. Must that armistice receive the Senate's "advice and consent"? On one view, the answer is "yes" because the armistice on its face embodies an international agreement that (so the argument goes) must conform to Article II's requirements for treaty-making. On a different view, however, the answer is "no" because the armistice is independently justified by the President's "Commander in Chief" power, which the President can wield without input from the legislative branch.[85] Put differently, this argument concedes that any presidential exercise of the power to "make . . . Treaties" requires senatorial advice and consent. But it also posits that the President may rely on *other* Article II powers to enter into international agreements—that is, "sole executive agreements"—unencumbered by any restrictions that the Treaty Clause might otherwise impose.

In a long line of rulings, the Court has agreed. The foundational case is *United States v. Belmont*,[86] in which the Court upheld a sole-executive agreement between the United States and the Soviet Union as a valid exercise of President Franklin Roosevelt's Article II powers

---

83 *See, e.g.*, Curtis A. Bradley & Neil S. Siegel, *Historical Gloss, Madisonian Liquidation, and the Originalism Debate*, 106 VA. L. REV. 1, 29 (2020) (noting that such agreements "represent the vast majority of the international agreements concluded by the United States since World War II"). It is worth noting, however, that whereas the federal government's authority to effectuate congressional-executive agreements remains limited by the scope of Congress's enumerated powers, its authority to make Article II treaties is not so limited. *See supra* Section 10.C (discussing the Court's decision in *Missouri v. Holland*, 252 U.S. 416 (1920)).

84 *See* U.S. CONST. art. II, § 2. Sole executive agreements are not always easily distinguishable from congressional-executive agreements, particularly those of the *ex ante* variety. But the key distinction involves the source of the power to conclude the agreement in question. In particular, to the extent the President relies on a statutorily conferred authority to conclude an agreement with another country, then the agreement itself is better characterized as the completion of an *ex ante* congressional-executive agreement that Congress set into motion when it delegated the agreement-making authority to the President. In contrast, when the President relies on inherent Article II authorities to conclude the agreement, the agreement is better characterized as a sole-executive agreement instead.

85 *See* U.S. CONST. art. II, § 2 ("The President shall be Commander in Chief of the Army and Navy. . . .").

86 301 U.S. 324 (1937).

to "establish[ ] . . . diplomatic relations" with foreign nations.[87] Five years later, in *United States v. Pink*,[88] the Court again rejected a challenge to the same U.S.-Soviet agreement, with Justice Douglas reiterating that the Article II power to "determine the policy . . . to govern the question of recognition" of the Soviet government carried with it the authority, "without consent of the Senate, to determine the public policy of the United States" with respect to the various Russian actions addressed by the agreement.[89] Then again in 1981, the Court in *Dames & Moore v. Regan*[90] had no trouble upholding a sole-executive agreement made between the United States and Iran—in this case pursuant to Justice Jackson's *Youngstown* methodology—while specifically noting that "the President does have some measure of power to enter into executive agreements without obtaining the advice and consent of the Senate."[91]

More recently, the Court has signaled an inclination to police more aggressively the boundaries of the President's sole-executive-

---

[87] *See id.* at 330–31. In particular, Justice Sutherland reasoned that, while a treaty "signifies a compact," it was not conversely true that a "compact . . . is . . . always a treaty." *Id.* at 331 (internal quotation marks omitted). And because here "the Executive had authority to speak as the sole organ of [the U.S.] government," the "assignment and the agreements in connection therewith did not, as in the case of treaties . . . require the advice and consent of the Senate." *Id. But see* Michael D. Ramsey, *Executive Agreements and the (Non)Treaty Power*, 77 N.C. L. REV. 133, 145–54 (1998) (criticizing several aspects of this reasoning). In addition, Justice Sutherland concluded for the Court that the agreement itself was binding and preempted state law. *Id.* at 331. In so holding, he found it of no significance that the Supremacy Clause omits reference to sole-executive agreements in defining the "supreme Law of the Land" whose application overrides "the Constitution or Laws of any State to the Contrary." U.S. CONST. art. VI; *see Belmont*, 301 U.S. at 331 (noting that while the preemptive effect of Article II treaties was established by "the express language" of Article VI, "the same rule would result in the case of all international compacts and agreements from the very fact that complete power over international affairs is in the national government" (citing *Curtiss-Wright*, 299 U.S. at 316)). *But see* Ingrid Brunk Wuerth, *The Dangers of Deference: International Claim Settlement by the President*, 44 HARV. INT'L L.J. 4, 13 (2003) (suggesting that "the text of the Constitution seems clear that only treaties have the force of domestic law" and noting that "[b]ecause the Supremacy Clause applies to treaties and *not* to non-treaty agreements (like 'Compacts,' 'Agreements,' and 'Alliances') mentioned elsewhere in the Constitution, such other agreements do not come within [its] plain language"); *see also* Bradford R. Clark, *Domesticating Sole Executive Agreements*, 93 VA. L. REV. 1573, 1637 (2013) (suggesting that, while *Belmont* and *United States v. Pink*, 315 U.S. 203 (1942), "contain language suggesting that [sole executive agreements] . . . are capable of preempting state law," the cases are better read as indicating that "it was the President's exercise of his independent constitutional power to recognize the Soviet Union—rather than his agreement to do so—that operated to displace state law in those cases").

[88] 315 U.S. 203 (1942).

[89] *Id.* at 228–29.

[90] 453 U.S. 654 (1981).

[91] *Id.* at 682; *see also* Am. Ins. Ass'n v. Garamendi, 539 U.S. 396, 415–17 (2003) (endorsing the President's "authority to make executive agreements with other countries" and emphasizing that "valid executive agreements are fit to preempt state law, just as treaties are" (internal quotations omitted)).

agreement-making authority. Of particular importance, the Court in *Medellín* refused to give effect to a presidential memorandum that would have required state courts to abide by the ICJ's judgments, while specifically rejecting the President's effort to justify that order as a "valid exercise of the President's foreign affairs authority to resolve claims disputes with foreign nations."[92] In so doing, the Court characterized *Pink*, *Belmont*, and others of its prior sole-executive-agreement cases as involving a "narrow set of circumstances: the making of executive agreements to settle civil claims between American citizens and foreign governments or foreign nationals."[93] In other words, according to the Court in *Medellín*, these cases did not recognize a broad Article II power vested in Presidents to put in place sole executive agreements on any subject pertaining to foreign affairs; instead, they gave effect only to "[t]he Executive's narrow and strictly limited authority to settle international claims disputes pursuant to an executive agreement" in certain circumstances[94]—an authority that did not itself encompass orders "that reach[ ] deep into the heart of the State's police powers and compel[ ] state courts to reopen final criminal judgments and set aside neutrally applicable state laws."[95] To be sure, the Court in *Medellín* did not go so far as to question altogether the President's Article II authority to conclude sole executive agreements. But it did suggest, as several commentators have noted, that the scope of that authority is more circumscribed than several of the Court's earlier cases had suggested, particularly insofar as the President's actions encroach upon the "police powers" of the states.[96]

D. THE RECOGNITION POWER

The Court's executive-agreement rulings in *Belmont* and *Pink* relied on the President's Article II power to "recognize" foreign nations and governments. The Constitution itself nowhere grants this power in explicit terms, but the Court has endorsed the "inference that the President exercises the recognition power" by pointing to both historical practice[97] and various provisions of the

---

92 *Medellín*, 552 U.S. at 530.

93 *Id.* at 531.

94 *Id.* at 532.

95 *Id.*

96 *See, e.g.*, Daniel Bodansky & Peter Spiro, *Executive Agreements+*, 49 VAND. J. TRANSNAT'L L. 885, 925 (2016) (noting that "[i]n *Medellín*, the Roberts Court hinted at narrowing the conventional conception of sole executive agreements"); David H. Moore, *The President's Unconstitutional Treatymaking*, 59 UCLA L. REV. 598, 634 (2012) (noting "*Medellín*'s cabining of sole executive authority").

97 Most notable in this respect was a decision by President Washington during the course of the French Revolution to receive a minister from the republic of France—an act that was widely understood to signify official U.S. recognition of the newly

constitutional text—most notably, Article II's vesting in the President of the power to "receive Ambassadors and other public Ministers."[98]

Questions relating to both the scope and the exclusivity of the President's recognition power recently came to the fore in litigation concerning U.S. passports and the diplomatic status of Jerusalem. That city has long been made subject to conflicting claims of sovereignty from Israel and Palestine, and most recent U.S. Presidents have adhered to a general policy of not taking an official position with respect to the dispute.[99] Consistent with this approach, the State department adopted a practice of designating, on U.S. passports "Jerusalem"—as opposed to "Israel" or "Palestine"—as the place of birth for U.S. citizens born in the city.[100] In 2002, however, Congress passed a bill that, in addition to "urg[ing] the President to immediately begin the process of relocating the United States Embassy in Israel to Jerusalem," also required the Secretary of State "upon the request of [a Jerusalem-born citizen] or the citizen's legal guardian, [to] record the place of birth as Israel" on passports and related consular documents.[101] President Bush signed this bill into law, but indicated in a separate signing statement that he construed the passport measure as merely "advisory" rather than "mandatory."[102] Thus, when Menachem Binyamin Zivotofsky's parents applied on behalf of their son for a U.S. passport that designated "Israel" as his country of birth, the State Department denied the request and listed "Jerusalem" instead.[103] That decision triggered the bringing of a lawsuit by the child's parents, who argued that the State Department could not rely on the recognition power as

---

installed French government. *See* Saikrishna B. Prakash & Michael D. Ramsey, *The Executive Power over Foreign Affairs*, 111 YALE L.J. 231, 312–14 (2001).

[98] *See Zivotofsky II*, 576 U.S. at 13 (quoting U.S. CONST. art. II, § 3). The case for recognizing the recognition power also draws support from the President's explicit Article II authority to make treaties with other nations and to appoint public ministers and ambassadors to engage in diplomatic business with such nations, *see* U.S. CONST. art. II, § 2—each of which might be used (or not used) for recognition-granting (or recognition-denying) purposes. *Zivotofsky II*, 576 U.S. at 13–14; *see also* Jack L. Goldsmith, Zivotofsky II *as Precedent in the Executive Branch*, 129 HARV. L. REV. 112, 115 (2015) (noting that, prior to the Court's express validation of the recognition power in *Zivotofsky II*, "[n]o one seriously questioned that the President possessed this power").

[99] *See* Mark Landler, *Trump Recognizes Jerusalem as Israel's Capital and Orders U.S. Embassy to Move*, N.Y. TIMES (Dec. 6, 2017) (noting the Trump Administration's abandonment of this policy in favor of official U.S. recognition of Jerusalem as Israel's capital).

[100] *See Zivotofsky II*, 576 U.S. at 6–7.

[101] *See* Foreign Relations Authorization Act Fiscal Year 2003, Pub. L. No. 107–228, § 214(d), 116 Stat. 1350 (2002).

[102] *See* Statement on Signing the Foreign Relations Authorization Act, Fiscal Year 2003, 2002 Pub. Papers 1697, 1698 (Sept. 30, 2002).

[103] *Zivotofsky II*, 576 U.S. at 8.

the basis for its refusal to comply with the statutory requirement that "Israel" be listed as Zivotofsky's place of birth.

In *Zivotofsky II*,[104] the Court rejected Zivotofsky's claim of right (and Congress's claim of power) on the merits.[105] Writing for himself and four colleagues, Justice Kennedy began his analysis by characterizing the challenged exercise of presidential authority—*i.e.*, the listing of "Jerusalem" as Zivotofsky's birthplace—as implicating Category Three of Justice Jackson's *Youngstown* framework.[106] This conclusion was hard to dispute, given that the birthplace designation ran directly contrary to Congress's statutory instructions. And it followed from this conclusion that the President's refusal to implement the statute had to be "scrutinized with caution"; stated otherwise, the President's "asserted power [had to] be both 'exclusive' and 'conclusive' on the issue" in order for him to prevail.[107] Under the circumstances of this case, the Court declared, such a showing had indeed been made. More specifically, Justice Kennedy explained, the birthplace designation decision qualified as a *bona fide* exercise of the President's recognition power, because that designation could be construed as a "formal statement[ ] by the Executive Branch acknowledging the legitimacy of a state or government and its territorial bounds."[108] Indeed, as Justice Kennedy further explained, "[t]he weight of historical evidence indicates Congress has accepted that the power to recognize foreign states and governments and their territorial bounds is exclusive to the Presidency."[109] Taken together, these two propositions meant that the 2002 statute was unconstitutional because (1) the statute targeted an exercise of the recognition power, and (2) the recognition power belonged exclusively to the President. Thus, the statute impermissibly encroached on a power that only the President could wield.[110]

Each of the premises underlying this determination drew objection from the dissenters. With respect to the majority's conclusion that the recognition power was exclusive, Chief Justice Roberts (joined by Justice Alito) contended that the position was

---

[104] 576 U.S. 1 (2015).

[105] Prior to so holding, the Court had in an earlier decision determined that the case did not raise a nonjusticiable political question because, even though the underlying issue "might have 'political implications,' " the case at its core concerned a claim of "statutory right." *Zivotofsky I*, 544 U.S. at 195–96 (quoting INS v. Chadha, 462 U.S. 919, 943 (1983)). On the political question doctrine more generally, *see infra* Section 35.E.

[106] *Zivotofsky II*, 576 U.S. at 10.

[107] *Id.* (quoting *Youngstown*, 343 U.S. at 637–38 (Jackson, J. concurring)).

[108] *Id.* at 32; *see also id.* at 30 (noting "the longstanding treatment of a passport's place-of-birth section as an official executive statement implicating recognition").

[109] *Id.* at 28.

[110] *Id.*

textually undermined by the Appointments Clause (which extends to diplomatic officials) and the Treaty Clause of Article II, in that both provisions conditioned recognition-related presidential authority on the advice and consent of the Senate.[111] In addition, the Chief Justice argued, the historical evidence in favor of exclusivity had been overhyped by Justice Kennedy. It was true, as the majority opinion noted, that past Presidents often acted unilaterally in recognizing foreign nations.[112] But it was also true that past Congresses often tried to restrain or even dictate presidential recognition determinations by way of Article I enactments.[113] All told, these materials revealed to the dissenters that the President's "authority over recognition," though real, did not rise to the level of "the 'conclusive and preclusive' power required to justify defiance of an express legislative mandate."[114]

Chief Justice Roberts's dissent (along with a separate dissent by Justice Scalia) also trained its focus on the other key premise of the majority's reasoning—namely, the idea that the challenged-passport designation statute infringed on the recognition power.[115] The problem with that conclusion, as Justice Scalia put it, was that the underlying statute, far from "mak[ing] (or requir[ing] the President to make) a commitment accepting Israel's sovereignty over Jerusalem," simply called on the State Department to extend "deference to private requests" regarding passport designations.[116] In addition, both the Chief Justice and Justice Scalia asserted that the majority's reasoning proved "far too much."[117] Congress, after all,

---

111 *Id.* at 62 (Roberts, C.J., dissenting) (noting that the President's powers "to make treaties and appoint ambassadors . . . are *shared* with Congress, so they hardly support an inference that the recognition power is *exclusive*" (emphasis added) (internal citation omitted)).

112 *Id.* at 23–28 (majority opinion) (highlighting examples).

113 *Id.* at 63–64 (Roberts, C.J., dissenting). To take one example, acknowledged by the *Zivotofsky II* majority itself, President Andrew Jackson largely acceded to Congress's demand that he recognize Texas's secession from Mexico, and Congress responded by appropriating funding for a "diplomatic agent to be sent to the Republic of Texas, whenever the President of the United States shall deem it expedient to appoint such [a] minister." *Id.* at 25–26 (internal quotations and alterations omitted). *See generally* Robert J. Reinstein, *Recognition: Is the President's Recognition Power Exclusive?*, 86 TEMP. L. REV. 1, 50–52 (2013) (suggesting that the Constitution's "post-ratification history weighs against the President's recognition authority being exclusive").

114 *Zivotofsky II*, 576 U.S. at 64 (Roberts, C.J., dissenting) (quoting *Youngstown*, 343 U.S. at 638 (Jackson, J., concurring)).

115 *Id.* at 67 (Scalia, J., dissenting); *see also id.* at 64–67 (Roberts, C.J., dissenting) (emphasizing that "even if the President does have exclusive recognition power, he still cannot prevail in this case, because the statute at issue *does not implicate recognition*" (emphasis in original)).

116 *Id.* at 72–76 (Scalia, J., dissenting).

117 *Id.* at 65 (Roberts, C.J., dissenting); *see also id.* at 72 (Scalia, J., dissenting).

possessed sweeping Article I authority to "declare War,"[118] to "establish an uniform Rule of Naturalization,"[119] and to take numerous other types of actions that, as the majority itself conceded, might cause a "[f]ormal recognition [to] seem a hollow act."[120] That being so, it was difficult to see the logic of striking down a narrow and relatively obscure set of passport-preparation rules while, at the same time, recognizing Congress's far-reaching ability to "create more severe perceived contradictions with Presidential recognition decisions" through the exercise of explicitly enumerated powers.[121]

The overall import of *Zivotofsky II* is hard to assess. From one angle, the case looks like a major victory for proponents of a robust presidential role in foreign affairs: The majority not only declared that the President's recognition power is exclusive but also gave that power a scope that reaches well beyond the confines of issuing recognition declarations.[122] But from another angle, the majority's ruling can be seen as one that was, in Justice Scalia's words, "blatantly gerrymandered to the facts of this case."[123] Particularly ambiguous was the Court's treatment of *Curtiss-Wright*: On the one hand, Justice Kennedy unflinchingly repudiated Justice Sutherland's broadest dicta about presidential power as "not necessary to the holding" of that case and also emphasized that "[t]he Executive is not free from the ordinary controls and checks of Congress merely because foreign affairs are at issue."[124] On the other hand, the majority seemed to breathe new life into *Curtiss-Wright*'s endorsement of specialized executive authority in the realm of foreign relations—particularly by emphasizing the President's "unique role in communicating with foreign governments" and by

---

118 *See* U.S. CONST. art. I, § 8, cl. 10.

119 *Id.* art. I, § 8, cl. 4.

120 *Zivotofsky II*, 576 U.S. at 16.

121 *Id.* at 65 (Roberts, C.J., dissenting).

122 What is more, as the Chief Justice noted, *Zivotofsky II* was the first-ever decision in which the Court "allow[ed] the President to defy an Act of Congress in the field of foreign affairs." *Id.* at 67.

123 *Id.* at 76 (Scalia, J., dissenting). Of particular significance in this respect was the majority's acknowledgement of a continued congressional authority to adopt measures that—although not direct regulations of the President's recognition authority—could severely undermine, if not altogether negate, the effect of presidential recognition decisions. *See* Marty Lederman, *Thoughts on* Zivotofsky, *Part Three: The Broad Consensus on Presidential* and *Congressional Foreign Affairs Authorities*, JUST SECURITY (June 11, 2015), https://www.justsecurity.org/23702/thoughts-zivotofsky-part-three-broad-consensus/ (noting that "all of the Justices except Justice Thomas agreed that . . . Congress has substantial constitutional powers to control U.S. foreign affairs—including authorities that can, as a practical matter, undermine a President's recognition decision").

124 *Zivotofsky II*, 576 U.S. at 21; *see also* Michael Dorf, Zivotofsky *May Be Remembered as Limiting Exclusive Presidential Power*, DORF ON LAW (June 8, 2015), https://perma.cc/C772-2X8F (pointing to this feature of *Zivotofsky II* as an indicator that it was ultimately a pro-Congress ruling).

defending the need for the nation, through its President, to speak "with one voice" on at least some matters of international affairs.[125] For these reasons, the longer term influence of *Zivotofsky II* remains up in the air.

---

[125] *Zivotofsky II*, 576 U.S. at 21, 30; *see* Goldsmith, *supra* note 98, at 130 (contending that "*Zivotofsky II* affirms *Curtiss-Wright's* functional approach to exclusive presidential power").

Chapter 28

WAR AND MILITARY AFFAIRS

Analysis

When it comes to war-related powers, the overall constitutional design is one of shared authority between Congress and the President. Article II designates the President as "Commander in Chief" of the armed forces, thus vesting in that office day-to-day managerial control over the military's activities.[1] At the same time, Article I vests in Congress the powers to "declare war,"[2] to "raise and support Armies,"[3] to "provide and maintain a Navy,"[4] and "to make Rules for the Government and Regulation of the land and naval forces,"[5] among other things.[6] Further complicating matters is the existence of several important limits on the war-related powers of the federal government, including, most notably, Article I's guarantee that "the Privilege of the Writ of Habeas Corpus shall not be suspended, unless when in Cases of Rebellion or Invasion the public Safety may require it."[7]

---

1 *See* U.S. CONST. art. II, § 2, cl. 1.

2 *Id.* art. I, § 8, cl. 11.

3 *Id.* art. I, § 8, cl. 12.

4 *Id.* art. I, § 8, cl. 13.

5 *Id.* art. I, § 8, cl. 14.

6 Article I also vests in Congress the powers to "define and punish . . . Offences against the Law of Nations," *id.* art. I, § 8, cl. 10, to "grant Letters of Marque and Reprisal," *id.* art. I, § 8, cl. 14, to "make Rules concerning Captures on Land and Water," *id.*, to "provide for calling forth the Militia to execute the Laws of the Union, suppress Insurrections and repel Invasions," *id.* art. I, § 8, cl. 15, and to "provide for organizing, arming, and disciplining, the Militia, and for governing such Part of them as may be employed in the Service of the United States," *id.* art. I, § 8, cl. 16.

7 *Id.* art. I, § 9. The war-related powers of Congress and the President are also qualified by various protections provided by the Bill of Rights, and the Court has occasionally invalidated war and national security-related measures on rights-based grounds. *See, e.g.*, New York Times v. United States, 403 U.S. 713, 719 (1971) (disallowing an injunction against the publication of the "Pentagon Papers" in light of the principle that any government effort to impose a prior restraint on speech, even for claimed national-security purposes, is subject to "a heavy burden of showing justification for the imposition of such a restraint" (internal quotations omitted)); Hamdi v. Rumsfeld, 542 U.S. 507, 510 (2004) (opinion of O'Connor, J.) (concluding that

Some implications of this arrangement are clear. Article I establishes that Congress controls the structure, organization, and broad-brush policies of the military departments, meaning (for example) that the President cannot singlehandedly amend the Uniform Code of Military Justice, eliminate the Air Force, or double the Army's annual budget. The President, meanwhile, presides in the Situation Room and has broad authority to order troop deployments, to develop battle plans, and to manage operational matters.[8] In many

---

the military detention of an individual alleged to be an "enemy combatant" violated that person's Fifth Amendment due-process rights because he had not been afforded "a meaningful opportunity to contest the factual basis for that detention before a neutral decisionmaker"); Reid v. Covert, 354 U.S. 1, 3 (1957) (holding that rights-based principles prohibited the federal government from relying on a court martial to try and convict the wife of a U.S. servicemember for crimes committed on a U.S. military base in the United Kingdom). At the same time, however, the Court's commitment to civil liberties during wartime has been less than ironclad, as the Justices have sometimes pointed to the existence of a military conflict as justification for permitting severe encroachments on civil liberties. *See, e.g.*, Korematsu v. United States, 323 U.S. 214 (1944) (upholding against equal-protection attack a racially discriminatory exclusion order issued in connection with President Roosevelt's internment of Americans of Japanese ancestry during World War II).

[8] While most scholars agree that the Commander-in-Chief Clause authorizes such actions when undertaken in the face of congressional silence, there is less agreement on the question whether it precludes Congress from involving itself in decisions of this kind. *Compare, e.g.*, LOUIS HENKIN, FOREIGN AFFAIRS AND THE CONSTITUTION 103–104 (1987) ("It would be unthinkable for Congress to attempt detailed, tactical decision, or supervision, and as to these the President's authority is effectively supreme."), *with* David J. Barron & Martin S. Lederman, *The Commander in Chief at the Lowest Ebb—Framing the Problem, Doctrine, and Original Understanding*, 121 HARV. L. REV. 689, 696 (2008) [hereinafter Barron & Lederman, *Lowest Ebb I*] (contending that "there is surprisingly little Founding-era evidence supporting the notion that the conduct of military campaigns is beyond legislative control and a fair amount of evidence that affirmatively undermines it"), *and* David J. Barron & Martin S. Lederman, *The Commander in Chief at the Lowest Ebb—A Constitutional History*, 121 HARV. L. REV. 941, 947 (2008) [hereinafter Barron & Lederman, *Lowest Ebb II*] (marshalling evidence in support of the view that, over the course of American history, "Congress has been an active participant in setting the terms of battle (and the conduct and organization of the armed forces and militia more generally), to an extent that war powers scholarship has not fully acknowledged"); *see also* Little v. Barreme, 6 U.S. (2 Cranch) 170 (1804) (holding that the President lacked the authority to disregard an act of Congress that impliedly prohibited the capture of naval vessels sailing out of French ports). Another ongoing matter of debate involves the extent to which the President's Commander-in-Chief authority might—at least during times of war—authorize the President unilaterally to implement other domestic measures not directly involving the military. *Cf. supra* Section 26.B.1 (highlighting this issue in connection with the *Youngstown* decision). Consider in this respect the Emancipation Proclamation. In particular, as President Lincoln argued, even though he might have lacked the authority to abolish slavery during times of peace, the emergence of the war and the quite plausible connection between emancipation and a hastened Union victory provided a strong basis for treating the matter as within the scope of his Commander-in-Chief authority. *See* ABRAHAM LINCOLN, SPEECHES AND WRITINGS 1859–1865, at 368–70, 424–25 (1989); *see also* Michael Stokes Paulsen, *The Emancipation Proclamation and the Commander in Chief Power*, 40 GA. L. REV. 807, 814–23 (2006) (expanding on this argument). *But see* Sanford Levinson, *The David C. Baum Memorial Lecture: Was the Emancipation Proclamation Constitutional? Do We/Should We Care?*, 2001 U. ILL. L. REV. 1135, 1148–49 (suggesting that prominent constitutional defenses of the Proclamation

settings, however, the balance of congressional and executive power (as qualified by the Suspension Clause and other negative constitutional limits) has engendered uncertainty and debate.

This chapter considers two such areas of ongoing controversy: (1) the extent to which the President may use military force in the absence of congressional authorization; and (2) the extent to which either the President alone or the President and Congress together may prescribe the use of summary military procedures to detain, try, and convict persons captured in the course of military operations.

A. INITIATING MILITARY ACTION

1. Background Constitutional Principles and Practices

On its face, Article I's vesting in Congress of the power to "declare war" suggests that the legislative branch alone enjoys the power to initiate military action by issuing formal declarations of war.[9] As it turns out, however, that position misdescribes modern-day constitutional practice in at least five different ways. First, as the Court has long recognized, the Commander-in-Chief Clause gives the President unilateral authority to use defensive force without congressional authorization when responding to a sudden attack.[10] Second, to the extent that Congress does take action for the purpose of permitting the President to use military force, it need not always do so (and very often has not done so) by way of formal declarations of war; instead (and particularly in the post-World War II era),

---

"present a reading of the presidential prerogative wholly at odds with the far more restricted reading adopted by the Court in *Youngstown*," while still acknowledging that the Proclamation remains "one of the truly great acts in our history").

9 *See* Aziz Z. Huq, *The Constitutional Law of Agenda Control*, 104 CAL. L. REV. 1401, 1429 (2016) (noting that the Declare War Clause "appears to repose in Congress the power to initiate armed hostilities and then to regulate comprehensively their execution," while also noting the "general belie[f] that the Framers intended the presidency to have power to 'repel sudden attacks' on its own initiative" (quoting JAMES MADISON, NOTES OF DEBATES IN THE FEDERAL CONVENTION OF 1787, at 475–77 (W.W. Norton & Co. 1966) (1840))).

10 *See The Prize Cases*, 67 U.S. 635, 668 (1862) (noting that while "Congress alone has the power to declare a national or foreign war," the President is "not only authorized but bound to resist force by force" if "a war be made by invasion of a foreign nation"). Of equal significance, the Court in the *Prize Cases* also observed, in language that would foreshadow a future judicial reluctance to intervene in similar disputes, that it was for the President and the President alone to "determine what degree of force the crisis demands" and that "this Court must be governed by the decisions and acts of the political department . . . to which this power was entrusted." *Id.* at 670; *see also* Campbell v. Clinton, 203 F.3d 19, 27 (D.C. Cir. 2000) (Silberman, J., concurring) ("I read the *Prize Cases* to stand for the proposition that the President has independent authority to repel aggressive acts by third parties even without specific congressional authorization, and courts may not review the level of force selected.").

Congress has adopted "force authorization" statutes[11] that authorize the President to engage in specified military activities without explicitly declaring the existence of a "war" with another nation.[12] Third, modern Presidents have assigned a sweeping meaning to these force-authorization statutes (some of which are quite broadly worded),[13] to other legal instruments, and to the Article II Commander-in-Chief Clause in claiming wide-ranging power to commence and conduct military actions without an *explicit* congressional sign-off.[14] Fourth, when confronted with presidential uses of military force that are not specifically authorized by statute or undertaken in response to a sudden attacks, Congress often has done little to push back, thus enabling Presidents, as a practical

[11] Courts have long upheld these statutes as a permissible exercise of Congress's Article I powers. *See, e.g.*, Bas v. Tingy, 4 U.S. (4 Dall.) 37, 40–41 (1800) (opinion of Washington, J.) (recognizing that Congress had validly given effect to an "imperfect" war with France (known as the Quasi-War) by enacting laws that "authori[zed] . . . hostilities" while failing to formally declare war on France); *see also* Mitchell v. Laird, 488 F. 2d 611, 615 (D.C. Cir. 1973) ("We are unanimously agreed that it is constitutionally permissible for Congress to use another means than a formal declaration of war to give its approval to a war such as is involved in the protracted and substantial hostilities in Indo-China.").

[12] Part of the reason for this development, as Professors Curtis Bradley and Jack Goldsmith have explained, is that "the international law role for declarations of war has largely disappeared," as multilateral treaties such as the United Nations Charter and the Geneva Conventions of 1949 have largely obviated the need for sovereign entities to declare war as a precondition to triggering application of *jus in bello* rules. *See* Jack M. Goldsmith & Curtis A. Bradley, *Congressional Authorization and the War on Terrorism*, 118 HARV. L. REV. 2047, 2061–62 (2005); *see also id.* at 2062 (noting that "in light of the longstanding political branch practice of initiating war without a formal declaration of war, consistent judicial approval of this practice, changes in international law that render war declarations less relevant, and general scholarly consensus, it seems clear that Congress need not issue a formal declaration of war in order to provide its full authorization for the President to prosecute a war").

[13] For example, the force-authorization statute enacted by Congress in the wake of the 9/11 attacks empowers the President to "[u]se all necessary and appropriate force against those nations, organizations, or persons he determines planned, authorized, committed, or aided the terrorist attacks that occurred on September 11, 2001, or harbored such organizations or persons, in order to prevent any future acts of international terrorism against the United States by such nations, organizations or persons." Authorization for Use of Military Force, Pub. L. No. 107–40, 115 Stat. 224 (2001). That statute remains in effect today and, over the course of its two-decade existence, has been frequently relied on by Presidents in claiming authorization to conduct a wide range of military actions. *See, e.g.*, Curtis A. Bradley & Jack L. Goldsmith, *Obama's AUMF Legacy*, 110 AM. J. INT'L L. 628, 629 (2016) (noting the 2001 AUMF's "transformation . . . from an authorization to use force against the 9/11 perpetrators who planned an attack from Afghanistan into a protean foundation for indefinite war against an assortment of terrorist organizations in numerous countries"). *See generally* Scott M. Sullivan, *Interpreting Force Authorization*, 43 FLA. ST. U. L. REV. 241, 271–73 (2015).

[14] For example, in sending U.S. troops to the Korean peninsula, President Truman pointed to various resolutions issued by the United Nations Security Council, combined with existing U.S. treaty obligations under the U.N. charter, as providing a sufficient legal basis for his actions. *See generally* Louis Fisher, *The Korean War: On What Legal Basis Did Truman Act?*, 89 AM. J. INT'L L. 21, 32–35 (1995) (describing and criticizing this rationale).

matter, to pursue military actions that rest on tenuous claims of statutory and/or constitutional authority.[15] Finally, courts have likewise hesitated to second-guess presidential decisions to use military force,[16] dismissing the vast majority of constitutional challenges to such actions as nonjusticiable under principles of standing,[17] ripeness,[18] and/or the political-question doctrine.[19] In these and other ways—and arguably in tension with the text of Article I—the force-initiation powers of the President are, as a real-world matter, very broad indeed.

2. The War Powers Resolution

On one notable occasion, Congress attempted to effectuate a large-scale rebalancing of this power relationship. In 1973, shortly after the withdrawal of troops from Vietnam, and at the "high-water mark of congressional reassertion in national security affairs,"[20] Congress adopted over the veto of President Nixon a statute commonly referred to as the War Power Act (WPA).[21] This law, which remains in force, sets forth an overarching framework meant to

---

[15] For example, while members of Congress voiced strong opposition to the expansion of U.S. military involvement in Vietnam and Cambodia during the late 1960s and early 1970s (with many of them contending that Presidents Johnson and Nixon had acted beyond the scope of the powers conferred by the Gulf of Tonkin Resolution), Congress throughout that period continued to fund these operations and for much of that period permitted extensions of the military draft. *See* JOHN HART ELY, WAR AND RESPONSIBILITY: CONSTITUTIONAL LESSONS OF VIETNAM AND ITS AFTERMATH 20–27 (1993).

[16] *See, e.g.*, Michael J. Glennon, *The Executive's Misplaced Reliance on War Powers "Custom"* 109 AM. J. INT'L L. 551, 556 (2015) (noting that "war powers disputes arising in recent years have been regularly dismissed as nonjusticiable").

[17] *See, e.g.*, *Campbell*, 203 F.3d at 27.

[18] *See, e.g.*, Doe v. Bush, 323 F.3d 133 (1st Cir. 2003); *see also* Dellums v. Bush, 752 F. Supp. 1141, 1149-52 (D.D.C. 1990) (denying on prudentially-based ripeness grounds a motion for a preliminary injunction against President Bush's prosecution of the war in Iraq).

[19] *See, e.g.*, Al-Aulaqi v. Obama, 727 F. Supp.2d 1 (D.D.C. 2010) (dismissing on standing and political-question grounds (among others) a challenge to the executive's authority to carry out "targeted killings" of U.S. citizens outside of the country); Orlando v. Laird, 443 F.2d 1039, 1043–44 (2d Cir. 1971) (holding that, while "the constitutional delegation of the war-declaring power to the Congress contains a discoverable and manageable standard imposing on the Congress a duty of mutual participation in the prosecution of war," the "constitutional propriety of the means by which Congress has chosen to ratify and approve the protracted military operations in Southeast Asia is a political question"); Crockett v. Reagan, 720 F.2d 1355, 1356–57 (D.C. Cir. 1983) (holding that the district court properly dismissed as nonjusticiable a war-powers dispute concerning U.S. military intervention in El Salvador and noting the lower court's observation that it "did not have the resources or expertise to resolve the particular factual disputes involved in this case"). For a general overview of these justiciability-related doctrines, see *infra* Chapter 35.

[20] Louis Fisher & David Gray Adler, *The War Powers Resolution: Time to Say Goodbye*, 113 POL. SCI. Q. 1, 1 (1998).

[21] Pub. L. No. 93–148, 87 Stat. 555 (1983) (codified at 50 U.S.C. §§ 1541–1548 (2018)). The law is sometimes also referred to as the War Powers Resolution.

govern the President's introduction of the armed forces into military "hostilities."[22] Specifically, it provides that: (1) that the President must *report* to Congress any action involving the introduction of troops into such hostilities, typically within 48 hours of taking that action;[23] (2) the President then generally has 60 days within which to secure from Congress a declaration of war, statutory authorization of the actions, or an extension of the 60-day period;[24] and (3) Congress may at any time order the removal of military forces by "concurrent resolution" (*i.e.*, a resolution not subject to a Presidential veto).[25] The statute thus in effect countenances a *temporary* period of unilateral military engagement by the President, subject to the key statutory restraints (1) that Congress alone can issue a stand-down order by concurrent resolution at any time and (2) that any continuation of the action beyond the statutorily prescribed window period must receive affirmative legislative approval.

President Nixon's veto message attacked the WPA as "unconstitutional and dangerous,"[26] and proponents of a robust presidential war power have echoed these concerns.[27] As a practical matter, however, the statute has proven more controversial than consequential: Presidents have routinely managed to circumvent its

---

22 *Id.* § 2(c).

23 *Id.* § 4.

24 *Id.* § 5(b). Section 5(b) further provides that the 60-day period "shall be extended for not more than an additional thirty days if the President determines and certifies to the Congress in writing that unavoidable military necessity respecting the safety of United States Armed Forces requires the continued use of such armed forces in the course of bringing about a prompt removal of such forces." *Id.*

25 *Id.* § 5(c). The constitutionality of this provision was thrown into doubt by the Court's 1983 decision in *INS v. Chadha*, 462 U.S. 919 (1983); *see also infra* Section 29.B.2, which generally forecloses Congress from blocking executive action with "legislative vetoes" that do not satisfy the bicameralism and presentment requirements of Article I. *See Chadha*, 462 U.S. at 944–51; *see also id.* at 967 (White, J., dissenting) (implying that the majority's decision in *Chadha* likely spelled doom for the concurrent-resolution provision of the War Powers Resolution). *But see* Stephen L. Carter, *The Constitutionality of the War Powers Resolution*, 70 VA. L. REV. 101 (1984) (suggesting that *Chadha* might not apply to the War Powers Resolution on the theory that a concurrent resolution "commanding the President to bring troops home is not a part of the general article I legislative power, but an exercise instead of an extraordinary legislative power—the specific article I power to vote on whether to go to war," while conceding that the "argument is admittedly a shaky one"); *see also* Cyrus R. Vance, *Striking the Balance: Congress and the President Under the War Powers Resolution*, 133 U. PA. L. REV. 79, 86–87 (1984) (suggesting that the War Powers Act is distinguishable from the legislative veto provision invalidated in *Chadha* because it reflects "an attempt to reassert the authority of Congress in an area where legislative and executive functions are not susceptible of sharp delineation").

26 *See* Richard Nixon, Veto of the War Powers Resolution, Pub. Papers 893, 893 (Oct. 24, 1973).

27 *See* Carter, *supra* note 25, at 108 (canvassing without endorsing the traditional constitutional critiques of the statute).

limits,[28] Congress has never successfully utilized its concurrent resolution procedure to block military action within the initial 60-day period,[29] and the courts have shown little interest in mandating executive-branch compliance with the statutory timetable.[30] Indeed, some commentators have suggested that the WPA has had the counterintuitive effect of *enhancing* presidential authority by effectively—even if unintentionally—authorizing in a *carte blanche* fashion unilateral military intervention for at least 60 days.[31] Thus, although the WPA in theory seems to indicate that major military operations must involve interbranch deliberation and decisionmaking, the real-world arrangement continues be one in which the executive branch dominates the scene.[32]

B. MILITARY DETENTION AND TRIAL BY MILITARY COMMISSION

Although courts have generally declined to resolve disputes concerning the scope of the President's power to use military force, they have played a more active role in policing other aspects of the President's and Congress's war-related authorities. A key set of cases centers on efforts by Presidents, sometimes with the support of Congress, to provide for the summary detention, military trial, and

---

[28] For example, Presidents have contended that some overseas deployments do not involve the introduction of troops into "hostilities," thus rendering the War Powers Resolution and its 60-day time-limit inapplicable. *See, e.g.*, Charlie Savage & Mark Landler, *White House Defends Continuing U.S. Role in Libya Operation*, N.Y. TIMES (June 15, 2011), https://www.nytimes.com/2011/06/16/us/politics/16powers.html (noting the Obama administration's reliance on this argument in connection with U.S. military operations in Libya); *see also* John Hart Ely, *Suppose Congress Wanted a War Powers Act That Worked*, 88 COLUM. L. REV. 1379, 1381 (1988) (highlighting other Presidents' reliance on this strategy).

[29] *See* Scott S. Barker, *Reforming the War Powers Relationship Between Congress and the President*, 89 DENV. L. REV. FORUM 1, 17 (2021) (noting that "Congress has never successfully invoked the War Powers Resolution to stop military action initiated by the President without congressional authorization").

[30] *See, e.g.*, *Campbell*, 203 F.3d at 23 (D.C. Cir. 2000) (declining, on Article III standing grounds, to adjudicate a WPR-based challenge to U.S. military involvement in Kosovo); *see also* Elad. D. Gil, *Totemic Functionalism in Foreign Affairs Law*, 10 HARV. NAT'L SEC. J. 316, 353–54 (2019) (highlighting other examples of the courts' "reluctance to adjudicate disputes relating to the War Powers Resolution").

[31] Indeed, as Elad Gil has recently noted, Presidents have sometimes used the War Powers Act as "an instrument for enhancing presidential war powers" by arguing that the statute effectively "recognizes an independent presidential authority to introduce the military into hostilities for up to sixty days without congressional authorization." *See* Gil, *supra* note 30, at 353 & n. 185; *see also* Lori Fisler Damrosch, *The Clinton Administration and War Powers*, 63 L. & CONTEMP. PROBS. 125, 133–34 (2000) (discussing the Clinton administration's arguments to this effect in connection with a planned military operation in Haiti).

[32] *Cf.* HAROLD H. KOH, THE NATIONAL SECURITY CONSTITUTION: SHARING POWER AFTER THE IRAN-CONTRA AFFAIR 117 (1990) (characterizing the real-world state of affairs as one of "executive initiative, congressional acquiescence, and judicial tolerance").

ensuing punishment of persons captured during military operations. Some of the courts' work in this area lies beyond the scope of this book, as it involves the direct enforcement of rights-based protections laid out in the Bill of Rights. Other judicial rulings, however, squarely concern structural limitations on government authority, including with regard to the "Privilege of the Writ of Habeas Corpus" referenced by the Suspension Clause of Article I, section 9.[33] These rulings are considered here.

1. The Suspension Clause

Tracing its origins to the English common law, the writ of habeas corpus provides a vehicle for the judicial oversight of executive acts of arrest and imprisonment.[34] In particular, when individuals are held by the government against their will, they may file with a court petitions for habeas corpus and thereby obtain judicial review of their detentions' legality.[35] In the modern era, much federal-court habeas litigation occurs in the wake of state-court and federal-court criminal convictions and direct appeals, with the habeas action creating an additional layer of judicial review (often called "collateral review") of prior court proceedings.[36] In other contexts, however—and particularly in the context of military detentions—habeas petitions operate as a critical means (if not the only means) of *initiating* judicial review of summary arrests, convictions, and punishments that might otherwise bypass the courts altogether. For this reason, habeas corpus has long been described as a "vital instrument for the protection of individual liberty."[37]

The Constitution's sole reference to habeas corpus appears in the text of the Suspension Clause, which provides that the "Privilege

---

[33] *See* U.S. CONST. art. I, § 9 (providing that "[t]he Privilege of the Writ of Habeas Corpus shall not be suspended, unless when in Cases of Rebellion or Invasion the public Safety may require it").

[34] *See* Amanda L. Tyler, *The Forgotten Core Meaning of the Suspension Clause*, 125 HARV. L. REV. 901, 924 (2012) (noting that "in England, the writ of habeas corpus enjoyed special status as, to borrow from Blackstone, a 'bulwark of our liberties' and the embodiment of the 'natural inherent right' of the 'personal liberty of the subject' " (quoting 1 WILLIAM BLACKSTONE, COMMENTARIES *133, *126, *131)).

[35] *See* Preiser v. Rodriguez, 411 U.S. 475, 485 (1973) (noting that "the traditional function of the writ is to secure release from illegal custody").

[36] *See, e.g.*, 28 U.S.C. § 2254 (providing for federal-court habeas review in connection with petitions brought by persons being held pursuant to a state-court judgment); 28 U.S.C. § 2255 (providing for federal-court habeas review in connection with petitions brought by persons being held pursuant to a federal-court judgment). These and other statutory avenues for postconviction relief are subject to a tremendously complex array of statutory (and judge-made) restrictions, which collectively make it extremely difficult for petitioners to prevail in such proceedings. For a helpful overview of this area of the law, see, for example, JAMES E. PFANDER, PRINCIPLES OF FEDERAL JURISDICTION 317–48 (4th ed. 2021).

[37] Boumediene v. Bush, 553 U.S. 723, 742 (2008).

of the Writ of Habeas Corpus shall not be suspended, unless when in Cases of Rebellion or Invasion the public Safety may require it."[38] That language makes clear that no "suspension" of habeas corpus may occur unless justified by a "Rebellion or Invasion." But other questions linger. For example, courts and commentators have long debated whether only Congress may suspend the privilege or whether the President might also enjoy a residual authority, at least under certain circumstances, to authorize suspensions without explicit congressional approval.[39] Another set of questions goes to the limits (if any) that the clause imposes on the executive's power to detain persons without charges or judicial review when the privilege itself remains in effect.[40] Furthermore, although the Court had previously indicated that the clause operates as an affirmative guarantee of the habeas privilege's availability,[41] it very recently raised doubts about the continued vitality of that proposition, suggesting instead that the clause might serve only the more limited purpose of restricting the circumstances in which Congress (or the President) can exercise its suspension authority when access to the privilege is otherwise available.[42] These and other issues are considered further in the discussion below.

a. Who Can Suspend?

The "who can suspend" question became a flashpoint of debate during the Civil War, when President Lincoln acted to suspend

---

[38] U.S. CONST. art. I, § 9, cl. 2.

[39] *See infra* Section 28.B.1.a.

[40] *See infra* Section 28.B.1.b. A related question goes to the legal consequences that follow from a decision to suspend the habeas privilege. In particular, there is some debate as to whether an act of suspension *formally expands executive power*, by authorizing the President to ignore the various other legal rights and protections (such as, for instance, the Fifth Amendment's Due Process Clause) that would otherwise limit executive detentions, or whether the act of suspension merely disempowers courts from issuing a particular type of judicial remedy, without in any way altering the substantive-law backdrop against which the President proceeds. For differing views on the question, compare, e.g., Amanda L. Tyler, *Suspension as an Emergency Power*, 118 YALE L.J. 600, 608–09 (2009) (defending the view that "the suspension authority represents an emergency power of considerable consequence, as it 'frees the Executive from the legal restraints on detention that would otherwise apply' " (quoting David L. Shapiro, *Habeas Corpus, Suspension, and Detention*, 82 NOTRE DAME L. REV. 59, 89 (2006), and *Hamdi*, 542 U.S. 507 at 556–58, 578 n.6 (Scalia, J., dissenting) (suggesting that an act of suspension would "justify indefinite imprisonment without trial")), with Trevor W. Morrison, *Suspension and the Extrajudicial Constitution*, 107 COLUM. L. REV. 1533, 1536 (2007) (arguing that an act of suspension does not "convert an otherwise unlawful detention into a lawful one"), and *Ex parte* Milligan, 71 U.S. (4 Wall.) 2, 115 (1866) ("The suspension of the writ does not authorize the arrest of any one, but simply denies to one arrested the privilege of this writ in order to obtain his liberty.").

[41] *Boumediene*, 553 U.S. at 798.

[42] *See* Lee Kovarsky, *Habeas Privilege Origination and* DHS v. Thuraissigiam, 121 COLUM. L. REV. FORUM 23, 32 (2021).

habeas corpus without first seeking congressional authorization to do so.[43] Most prominent among the objectors to Lincoln's actions was Chief Justice Roger Taney, who, only four years after issuing his infamous *Dred Scott* opinion,[44] held in *Ex Parte Merryman*[45] (albeit only for himself and not on behalf of the Court) that President Lincoln had acted unconstitutionally because the suspension power belongs solely to Congress.[46] That conclusion, the Chief Justice reasoned, made sense in light of the Suspension Clause's placement in Article I, which is "devoted to the legislative department of the United States, and has not the slightest reference to the executive department."[47] He further maintained that various features of Article II, including the "short term" for which the President is elected and the "narrow limits to which his power is confined," revealed a "jealousy and apprehension of future danger which the framers of the constitution felt in relation" to the executive branch.[48] This "jealousy and apprehension" signified to the Chief Justice that the Framers did not mean to place a power of such consequence in the hands of the President alone,[49] thus leading him to proclaim that there is "no ground whatever for supposing that the president, in any emergency, or in any state of things, can authorize the suspension of the privileges of the writ of habeas corpus."[50]

In effect, however, Taney's decision in *Merryman* was ignored by federal officials, who continued to hold Merryman in custody,

---

[43] More specifically, the President authorized Commanding General Winfield Scott to suspend habeas "[i]f at any point on or in the vicinity of any military line which is now or which shall be used between the city of Philadelphia and the city of Washington you find resistance which renders it necessary to [do so] for the public safety." Order from Abraham Lincoln to General Winfield Scott (Apr. 27, 1861), *available at* https://www.presidency.ucsb.edu/documents/executive-order-465.

[44] 60 U.S. (19 How.) 393 (1857).

[45] 17 F. Cas. 144 (C.C.D. Md. 1861) (No. 9487).

[46] *Id.* at 144–45, 152–53. Although conventional wisdom holds that the Chief Justice heard *Merryman* while riding circuit, it is more likely that Taney entertained the petition in his capacity as an individual Justice authorized to dispose of habeas petitions submitted directly to the Court itself. *See* Edward A. Hartnett, *The Constitutional Puzzle of Habeas Corpus*, 46 B.C. L. REV. 251, 279–80 (2005). What is unmistakably clear, however, is that *Merryman* was not in and of itself a Supreme Court decision and therefore lacks the full force of binding Supreme Court precedent. At the same time, however, the Court has at least suggested (in a pre-*Merryman* decision) that the President may not suspend the habeas privilege without congressional authorization. *See Ex parte* Bollman, 8 U.S. 75, 101 (1807) ("If at any time the public safety should require the suspension of the powers vested by this act in the courts of the United States, it is for the legislature to say so.").

[47] *Merryman*, 17 F. Cas. at 148. The latter part of this statement is puzzling, given that Article I does in fact contain several references to the executive branch. *See, e.g.*, U.S. CONST. art. 1, § 7, cl. 3 (establishing the President's veto power).

[48] *Merryman*, 17 F. Cas. at 148.

[49] *Id.*

[50] *Id.* at 149.

notwithstanding the Chief Justice's protestations.[51] Moreover, President Lincoln would later offer a constitutional defense of his actions,[52] emphasizing, *contra* Taney, that the Suspension Clause was in fact "silent as to which or who is to exercise the power" (the clause, recall, merely uses the passive-voice formulation "*be . . . suspended*") and contending that, "as the provision was plainly made for a dangerous emergency, it can not be believed the framers . . . intended that in every case the danger should run its course until Congress could be called together."[53] In other words, while acknowledging that Congress possessed a superseding power to override any presidential suspension decision with which it disagreed, Lincoln insisted that there exists a residual authority to act unilaterally in emergency circumstances, particularly when Members of Congress are away from the Capitol and the body is thus unable to authorize suspension on its own.[54]

The issue posed by *Merryman* became moot when Congress later voted to ratify Lincoln's earlier suspension order, thus depriving the full Court of any chance to weigh in on the validity of the President's earlier action.[55] Moreover, no later President has attempted to

---

[51] *But see* Seth Barrett Tillman, Ex Parte Merryman: *Myth, History, and Scholarship*, 224 MIL. L. REV. 481, 495 (2016) (emphasizing that President Lincoln never "ignored or defied a judicial *order* from Chief Justice Taney to *release* John Merryman" because no such order had ever been issued). For a broader examination of Lincoln's response to *Merryman* through the lens of the judiciary's law-declaration authority, *see infra* Section 34.C.1.

[52] *See* Abraham Lincoln, Message to Congress in Special Session (July 4, 1861), https://millercenter.org/the-presidency/presidential-speeches/july-4-1861-july-4th-message-congress.

[53] *Id.* And even if, he continued, the clause had "to a very limited extent [been] violated," the violation was obviously justified by the grave threat that the nation then confronted. In an oft-quoted passage, Lincoln would rhetorically ask: "Are all the laws but one to go unexecuted, and the Government itself go to pieces lest that one be violated?" *Id.*

[54] *See* Barron & Lederman, *Lowest Ebb II*, *supra* note 8, at 999–1000 (noting that "Lincoln was careful to insist that Congress retained ultimate control, and he readily conceded that his bold initiatives, including those regarding the suspension of habeas, were subject to statutory qualification or override"). Put in the parlance of Justice Jackson's *Youngstown* framework, *see supra* Section 26.B.1, that is, Lincoln's suggestion here was that unilateral suspension of habeas by the President might sometimes constitute an appropriate form of Category-Two action (that is, action undertaken in the face of congressional silence) but could never constitute an appropriate form of Category-Three action (that is, action undertaken in the face of a statutory prohibition).

[55] *But see* Stephen I. Vladeck, *The Field Theory: Martial Law, the Suspension Power, and the Insurrection Act*, 80 TEMP. L. REV. 391, 408 (2007) (noting that other courts "confronted some form of the legal question raised in *Ex parte Merryman*, and virtually all of them reached a similar conclusion—i.e., that President Lincoln's extralegislative suspension of habeas corpus was unconstitutional" (internal footnote omitted)). For a general overview of Lincoln's wartime actions involving habeas corpus and related matters, see MARK NEELY, JR., THE FATE OF LIBERTY: ABRAHAM LINCOLN AND CIVIL LIBERTIES (1991).

suspend the habeas privilege without congressional authorization, thus leaving the "who can suspend" question formally unresolved.[56] As a practical matter, however, three points seem clear: First, given the weighty and consequential nature of any suspension decision, Presidents contemplating such an action will often have a strong political incentive to seek congressional authorization, even if they do not regard such an authorization as legally required. Second, the justification offered by President Lincoln to act unilaterally under the emergency circumstances presented by *Merryman* may well not have the same weightiness today, as changes in communications and transportation technology have made it significantly easier for Congress to reconvene on short notice in order to consider an urgent presidential request to suspend the privilege.[57] Finally (and nonetheless), any future President sufficiently determined to pursue a unilateral suspension order may well be able to get away with it, given the practical and political difficulties that any court would face in attempting to enforce a judgment against a defiant executive under the fraught circumstances of a national emergency. For this reason, the most significant feature of the *Merryman* decision may lie not in the Chief Justice's insistence that Presidents lack legal authority to suspend without *ex ante* congressional permission, but rather in his concession that his ruling had been "resisted by a force too strong for me to overcome."[58]

b. *Indefinite Detention During Times of Nonsuspension: The* Hamdi *Decision*

To what extent does the Suspension Clause operate to limit executive-branch conduct during times of non-suspension? Consider in this respect the Court's 2004 decision in *Hamdi v. Rumsfeld*.[59] In the wake of the 9/11 attacks, President George W. Bush claimed that, even in the absence of a congressional suspension of habeas corpus, he possessed the power to hold without charges individuals who had been captured in connection with ongoing U.S. military actions in Iraq and Afghanistan.[60] Yaser Esam Hamdi, a U.S. citizen who had

---

56 *See generally* Amy Coney Barrett, *Suspension and Delegation*, 99 CORNELL L. REV. 251, 258 n.13 (2014) (noting that while "lower court opinions are the only ones that address the question directly, dicta and separate opinions from the Supreme Court are consistent with th[e] view" that only Congress has the power to suspend the writ (citing *Hamdi*, 542 U.S. at 562 (Scalia, J., dissenting), and *Bollman*, 8 U.S. at 101)).

57 To be sure, other circumstances—including, for instance, a direct attack on the Capitol—might render Congress unable to convene, in which case a President's exercise of an emergency suspension authority might remain defensible.

58 *Merryman*, 17 F. Cas. at 152.

59 542 U.S. 507 (2004).

60 In particular, the President argued that this power flowed both from his Article II Commander-in-Chief responsibilities and from the 2001 Authorization for the Use

come into U.S. custody in the course of military operations in Afghanistan, was one such detainee.[61] Hamdi, having been designated an "enemy combatant" by the Bush Administration, was being held without trial in a naval brig in U.S. territory.[62] Faced with these circumstances, Hamdi's father filed a federal-court habeas action on his son's behalf.[63]

In an opinion by Justice O'Connor, a plurality of Justices concluded that the government had violated the Fifth Amendment's Due Process Clause by affording Hamdi insufficient notice of and an insufficient opportunity to contest the basis of the enemy-combatant designation that gave rise to his confinement.[64] At the same time, the plurality rejected the broader suggestion that, as long as the habeas privilege remained unsuspended, the "only options" at the government's disposal were "congressional suspension of the writ of habeas corpus or prosecution for treason or some other crime" in an Article III court.[65] Instead, the plurality concluded that Congress had here authorized the President to detain enemy combatants "for the duration of the relevant conflict," and that this authorization—though not itself a suspension of habeas—was enough to justify the President's detention without trial of U.S. citizens captured fighting alongside enemy forces on a battlefield abroad.[66] In other words, the plurality appeared to indicate that, if the President afforded such a citizen-detainee a constitutionally sufficient process for contesting the factual basis of an "enemy combatant" designation (with the sufficiency of that process to be adjudged by means of a multi-factor balancing test) and if such a designation was subject to a constitutionally sufficient form of judicial review, then neither the

---

of Military Force, which, he argued, furnished him with independent statutory authority to detain enemy combatants captured in connection with the "war on terror." *See id.* at 516–17 (opinion of O'Connor, J.).

[61] *Id.* at 510.

[62] *Id.*

[63] *Id.*

[64] *See id.* at 524–39. The plurality opinion was joined by Chief Justice Rehnquist and by Justices Kennedy and Breyer. Justices Souter and Ginsburg took the position in a separate opinion that the President lacked the requisite statutory authorization to detain Hamdi. *See id.* at 545–53 (Souter, J., concurring in part, dissenting in part, and concurring in the judgment). Nevertheless, those two Justices chose to "join with the plurality in ordering remand," so as to give "practical effect to the conclusions of eight members of the Court rejecting the Government's position." *Id.* at 553.

[65] *Id.* at 523 (opinion of O'Connor, J.). The plurality did, however, note the parties' agreement that "absent suspension, the writ of habeas corpus remains available to every individual detained within the United States." *Id.* at 525. Thus, because Congress had not suspended the writ, Hamdi was at least entitled to federal habeas review of his underlying claims. *Id.*; *see also infra* Section 28.B.1.c (exploring in greater detail the extent to which the Suspension Clause operates as an affirmative guarantee of habeas review during times in which the writ has not been suspended).

[66] *Hamdi*, 542 U.S. at 525 (opinion of O'Connor, J.).

Suspension Clause nor any other constitutional provision categorically obligated the President to bring formal criminal charges while the underlying military conflict persisted.[67]

This analysis provoked a dissent from Justice Scalia (joined by Justice Stevens), who instead saw the case as governed by a more straightforward rule: "Where the Government accuses a citizen of waging war against it, our constitutional tradition has been to prosecute him in federal court for treason or some other crime."[68] In addition, "[w]here the exigencies of war prevent that, the Constitution's Suspension Clause allows Congress to relax the usual protections temporarily."[69] Here, however, the federal government had taken neither of these steps; instead, the President, with no suspension order in effect, held a U.S. citizen in indefinite military custody without prosecuting him for a federal crime. Put differently, Justice Scalia understood the Suspension Clause to furnish the *exclusive* mechanism through which Congress could authorize the military's detention without trial of U.S. citizens "within the territorial jurisdiction of a federal court,"[70] meaning that, as long as the habeas privilege remained unsuspended, Hamdi should have been "entitled either to criminal trial or to a judicial decree requiring his release."[71]

The fractured nature of the *Hamdi* decision (along with the fact-specific nature of the plurality's analysis) has generated uncertainty regarding its bottom-line doctrinal takeaway.[72] What is clear from

---

67 *Id.* at 519 (finding "no bar to this Nation's holding one of its own citizens as an enemy combatant").

68 *Id.* at 554 (Scalia, J., dissenting).

69 *Id.* at 554 (internal citation omitted). For a historically oriented defense of this position, see Amanda L. Tyler, *The Forgotten Core Meaning of the Suspension Clause*, 125 HARV. L. REV. 901 (2012).

70 *Hamdi*, 542 U.S. at 577 (Scalia, J., dissenting).

71 *Id.* at 572. Pointing to this "territorial jurisdiction" qualification, Justice O'Connor noted that Justice Scalia's proposed rule would "create[ ] a perverse incentive" by causing "[m]ilitary authorities faced with the stark choice of submitting to the full-blown criminal process or releasing a suspected enemy combatant captured on the battlefield" to "simply keep citizen-detainees abroad." *Id.* at 524 (opinion of O'Connor, J.).

72 *See id.* at 576–77 (Scalia, J., dissenting). Among the many questions left open by *Hamdi* was whether a similar result should obtain in connection with the detention on U.S. soil of a citizen-detainee who had been captured in U.S. territory rather than "in a foreign combat zone." *See id.* at 523–24 (opinion of O'Connor, J.). This was no hypothetical question, as another U.S. citizen, Jose Padilla, was then being held under such circumstances. Prior to the Court's decision in *Hamdi*, the Second Circuit, relying in part on the Suspension Clause, had held that the President lacked statutory authorization to detain Padilla as an enemy combatant. *See* Padilla v. Rumsfeld, 352 F.3d 695, 715 (2d Cir. 2003). But the Court reversed that decision, holding that Padilla had filed his habeas petition in the wrong federal district court. *See* Rumsfeld v. Padilla, 542 U.S. 426 (2004). Padilla then successfully re-filed for habeas corpus in the right district court, *see* Padilla v. Hanft, 389 F. Supp. 2d 678 (D.S.C. 2005), but then

the decision, however, is that the plurality opinion and the Scalia dissent reflected "starkly opposed visions of habeas corpus and the Suspension Clause."[73] More specifically, as Professor Trevor Morrison has noted, whereas the *Hamdi* plurality viewed the clause as doing nothing more than "preserv[ing] for the courts a vital role in ensuring that individual exercises of the detention authority comport both with the scope of the statutory grant [of that detention authority] and with the constitutional demands of due process," Justices Scalia and Stevens instead understood it to achieve the more categorical result of prohibiting Congress, absent a suspension of the writ, from "authoriz[ing] the executive detention of U.S. citizens outside the criminal justice system," at least when held in U.S. territory.[74] This is not to say that one opinion was necessarily more liberty-protective than the other.[75] But whereas one opinion saw the Suspension Clause as of limited significance in defining the extent to which the President could hold "enemy combatants" without trial, the other saw the clause as rendering the President's power to detain U.S. citizens on U.S. soil decisively dependent on whether Congress had acted in pursuance of the clause's terms.

---

saw that decision reversed by the Fourth Circuit, which concluded that "the AUMF as interpreted by the Supreme Court in *Hamdi*" authorized his detention regardless of the "locus of capture." *See* Padilla v. Hanft, 423 F.3d 386, 391, 392 (4th Cir. 2005). Padilla then sought review in the Supreme Court, but while his petition was pending, the government at long last charged him with a crime, and the Court voted to deny certiorari largely on that basis. *See* Padilla v. Hanft, 547 U.S. 1062, 1063 (2006) (Kennedy, J., concurring) (noting that the Court's action was warranted in light of the fact that "[e]ven if the Court were to rule in Padilla's favor, his present custody status would be unaffected"). *But see id.* at 1064 (Ginsburg, J., dissenting) (noting that the Court should have answered a "question of profound importance to the Nation"—namely, "[d]oes the President have authority to imprison indefinitely a United States citizen arrested on United States soil distant from a zone of combat, based on an executive declaration that the citizen was, at the time of his arrest, an "enemy combatant" (internal quotations and citations omitted)).

[73] *See* Trevor W. Morrison, Hamdi*'s Habeas Puzzle*, 91 CORNELL L. REV. 411, 412 (2006).

[74] *Id.* at 415.

[75] *See, e.g., id.* at 415–16 (contending that "although Justice Scalia's *Hamdi* opinion has been widely hailed as the most liberty-protective of all the opinions in the case, [it] in fact . . . could, if adopted more broadly, pose a serious threat to the safeguards of liberty built into the law of habeas corpus" by making a suspension of the writ "both a necessary and a sufficient condition for authorizing this form of extraordinary detention"). In addition, the Scalia dissent was careful to clarify that only U.S. citizens received the benefit of its proposed rule, whereas the plurality opinion left the door open to extending its contemplated due-process-based safeguards to noncitizens as well.

c. *The Scope and Reach of the Suspension Clause's Protections: The* Boumediene *Decision*

The Suspension Clause figured prominently in another war-on-terror decision, *Boumediene v. Bush*,[76] which (in contrast to *Hamdi*) concerned the President's ongoing detention at the U.S. naval base in Guantanamo Bay, Cuba, of noncitizens alleged to be enemy combatants. Prior to *Boumediene*, the Court had held in *Rasul v. Bush*[77] that a federal statute enabled Guantanamo detainees to file habeas petitions in federal court. The subsequently enacted Military Commissions Act of 2006 (MCA),[78] however, amended this law so as to deprive federal courts of jurisdiction over all habeas petitions filed by any noncitizen "enemy combatant," regardless of the place of detention.[79] Pointing to this enactment, the government sought dismissal of several then-pending habeas actions filed by Guantanamo detainees. The Court in *Boumediene*, however, rebuffed that effort, holding that Congress, through the MCA, had effectuated an "unconstitutional suspension of the writ."[80]

The Court's decision in *Boumediene* is complex and confusing, and a full discussion of it lies beyond the scope of this book.[81] Three points, however, are worth mentioning here. First, the Court held in no uncertain terms that the Suspension Clause had "full effect" as applied to noncitizens being held at Guantanamo Bay. In arguing otherwise, the government had relied on a 1950 decision, *Johnson v. Eisentrager*,[82] in which the Court, while denying habeas review to

---

[76] 553 U.S. 728 (2008).

[77] 542 U.S. 466 (2004).

[78] Pub. L. 109–366, 120 Stat. 2600.

[79] *See id.* § 7. Prior to enacting the MCA, Congress had sought to curb the federal courts' habeas jurisdiction with the Detainee Treatment Act of 2005 (DTA), Pub. L. 109–148, 119 Stat. 2739. In *Hamdan v. Rumsfeld*, 548 U.S. 557 (2006), however, the Court chose to construe that provision narrowly, holding in particular that it did not apply to habeas proceedings that had been filed in federal court prior to the DTA's enactment. *Id.* at 576–77. By contrast, the MCA's jurisdiction-stripping provision, which was adopted in *Hamdan*'s wake, left no doubt that it applied with full force to (and thus required the dismissal of) any then-pending cases. *See Boumediene*, 553 U.S. at 736–37.

[80] *Boumediene*, 553 U.S. at 733. Importantly, the government nowhere attempted to defend the statute as a formal suspension of the habeas privilege that had been authorized by the existence of a "rebellion" or "invasion" and thus appeared to acknowledge that the statute's jurisdiction-stripping provisions amounted to something other than a formal suspension of the writ. *See* Br. for the Boumediene Pet'rs at 9, *Boumediene*, 553 U.S. 723 (No. 06-1195), 2007 WL 2441590 (noting that "[t]he government has never contended in this case that the MCA meets the requirements for a valid suspension of the writ").

[81] *See* Kovarsky, *supra* note 42, at 32 (noting that "*Boumediene* is an intricate opinion with many moving parts," including an "internally inconsistent discussion of the constitutional habeas guarantee").

[82] 339 U.S. 763 (1950).

noncitizens held at a military prison in ally-occupied Germany, had emphasized that petitioners were not "within any territory over which the United States is sovereign."[83] But Justice Kennedy (writing for himself and four colleagues) rejected the idea that *Eisentrager* had established a categorical bar on extraterritorial habeas petitions filed by or on behalf of noncitizens.[84] Instead, as he explained, "at least three factors are relevant in determining the reach of the Suspension Clause: (1) the citizenship and status of the detainee and the adequacy of the process through which that status determination was made; (2) the nature of the sites where apprehension and then detention took place; and (3) the practical obstacles inherent in resolving the prisoner's entitlement to the writ."[85] Applying those factors to the facts presented by *Boumediene*, Justice Kennedy concluded that the Suspension Clause was fully applicable to the Guantanamo detainees at issue in the case.[86]

---

[83] *See id.* at 778.

[84] *See Boumediene*, 553 U.S. at 726 (declining to read *Eisentrager* as establishing a "formalistic, sovereignty-based test").

[85] *Id.* at 766. In another case decided the same day, the Court unanimously held, among other things, that the general federal habeas statute broadly authorized federal jurisdiction over petitions brought by U.S. citizens "held overseas by American forces operating subject to an American chain of command," even where being held by a multinational coalition force. *See* Munaf v. Geren, 553 U.S. 674, 680 (2008). That statutory holding has, for the time being, obviated any need to consider whether U.S. citizens enjoy a similarly broad *constitutional* entitlement to habeas review. For a scholarly argument in favor of the position that they do, see Richard H. Fallon, Jr. & Daniel J. Meltzer, *Habeas Corpus Jurisdiction, Substantive Rights, and the War on Terror*, 120 HARV. L. REV. 2029, 2054–55 (2007); *see also* Richard H. Fallon, Jr., *The Supreme Court, Habeas Corpus, and the War on Terror*, 110 COLUM. L. REV. 352, 381 (2010) (noting that "[p]re-War on Terror authority had also made clear that federal habeas is available to citizens detained by federal officials outside the United States, as the Constitution probably mandates that it must be" (internal footnote omitted)).

[86] In particular, Justice Kennedy explained, the first factor, concerning "citizenship and status," militated in the petitioners' favor because, although they were not U.S. citizens, they did vigorously contest their designation as "enemy combatants" and, unlike the petitioners in *Eisentrager*, had not been afforded any "rigorous adversarial process to test the legality of their detention." *Boumediene*, 553 U.S. at 767. As for the second factor, concerning the "nature of the sites," the Court emphasized that, although the petitioners were "similarly situated to the *Eisentrager* petitioners in that the sites of their apprehension and detention are technically outside the sovereign territory of the United States," there were "critical differences" between the prison facilities at issue in each case, particularly in light of the key fact that "Guantanamo Bay . . . is no transient possession" and "is within the constant jurisdiction of the United States." *See id.* at 768–69. Finally, with respect to the third factor, concerning "practical obstacles," the Court emphasized that, while "there are costs to holding the Suspension Clause applicable in a case of military detention abroad," the Government had presented "no credible arguments that the military mission at Guantanamo would be compromised if habeas corpus courts had jurisdiction to hear the detainees' claims." *Id.* at 769. Notably, while the Court's application of these factors came out in the petitioners' favor, other courts' post-*Boumediene* applications of these factors have not always yielded pro-petitioner results. *See, e.g.*, Al Maqaleh v. Gates, 605 F.3d 84, 94–99 (D.C. Cir. 2010) (concluding, based on an application of the *Boumediene* factors, that the Suspension Clause's

Second, the Court held that the MCA's jurisdiction-stripping provisions violated the Suspension Clause because Congress had neither suspended habeas corpus nor furnished "adequate substitute procedures" for habeas-like review.[87] Although the Court did "not endeavor to offer a comprehensive summary of the requisites for an adequate substitute," it did emphasize that "the necessary scope of habeas review in part depends upon the rigor of any earlier proceedings."[88] In addition, the Court stressed that "[w]here a person is detained by executive order, rather than, say, after being tried and convicted in a court, the need for collateral review is most pressing."[89] In keeping with this principle, the Court went on to hold that the administrative processes afforded to "enemy combatant" detainees presented a "considerable risk of error" and thus required a form of after-the-fact judicial process that "[i]ncludes some authority to assess the sufficiency of the Government's evidence against the detainee."[90] The existing mechanism for judicial oversight that Congress had elsewhere put in place, however, did not allow for the exercise of a sufficiently rigorous form of sufficiency-of-the-evidence review,[91] and the statutorily-prescribed review process thus was "inadequate" to qualify as a constitutionally sufficient substitute for the habeas privilege itself.[92]

Finally, and perhaps most significantly, the Court in *Boumediene* made a pronouncement that it had never before explicitly embraced—namely, that the Suspension Clause "*ensures* that, except during periods of formal suspension, the Judiciary will have a time-tested device . . . to maintain the 'delicate balance of governance' that is itself the surest safeguard of liberty."[93] The Court, to be sure, had come close to endorsing this idea in earlier cases. Most notably, in *INS v. St. Cyr*,[94] it had narrowly construed a federal immigration statute to permit habeas review of certain deportation-related claims so as to avoid what it characterized as the "serious

---

protections did not extend to noncitizens held at the U.S.-occupied Bagram Air Base in Afghanistan).

87 *Boumediene*, 553 U.S. at 772.

88 *Id.*

89 *Id.* at 783.

90 *Id.* at 786.

91 In particular, while the DTA authorized the D.C. Circuit to determine whether the government had utilized valid "standards and procedures" in designating a detainee as an enemy combatant, the Court held that that law did not afford "an opportunity for the detainee to present relevant exculpatory evidence that was not made part of the record in the earlier proceedings." *Id.* at 789.

92 *Id.* at 792.

93 *Id.* at 745 (quoting *Hamdi*, 542 U.S. at 536 (opinion of O'Connor, J.)) (emphasis added).

94 533 U.S. 289 (2001).

Suspension Clause issue" that would arise from a contrary reading of the law.[95] But while the Court in *St. Cyr* merely hinted at a Suspension Clause-based limit on Congress's power to circumscribe habeas review, the Court in *Boumediene* left no doubt that it viewed the clause as *guaranteeing* the availability of the privilege (or at least an adequate substitute for habeas) for as long as Congress has not validly authorized suspension.[96] For post-*Boumediene* commentators, this was a big deal. As Professor Gerald L. Neuman put the point, proponents of a robust right to habeas could "breathe easier" after *Boumediene* because the Court had made it clear that "[t]he Suspension Clause not only regulates temporary suspension of the privilege of the writ, but permanently requires a right to habeas corpus, with a certain minimum content, when the writ has not been suspended."[97]

Just over a decade after *Boumediene*, however, the Court provided renewed reason for holding one's breath: In *Department of Homeland Security v. Thuraissigiam*,[98] a 2020 case concerning habeas review in the immigration context, the Court raised fresh doubts about its willingness to embrace a privilege-protecting reading of the Suspension Clause. Writing for a five-Justice majority, Justice Alito dropped a puzzling footnote, indicating that the Court was not in that case "revisit[ing]" the question "whether the Clause independently guarantees the availability of the writ or simply restricts the temporary withholding of its operation."[99] That was a

---

95 *Id.* at 305. Justice O'Connor's plurality opinion in *Hamdi* had also hinted at this idea, at least insofar as it suggested that, "[a]bsent suspension of the writ by Congress, a citizen detained as an enemy combatant" was "entitled" to "make his way to court with a challenge to the factual basis for his detention by his government." *Hamdi*, 542 U.S. at 536–37 (opinion of O'Connor, J.).

96 *See* Kovarsky, *supra* note 42, at 24, 29; *see also* Fallon, *supra* note 85, at 378 (noting that the Court in *Boumediene* "clearly held, for the first time, that the Suspension Clause protects a right to habeas at least as broad as that which existed in 1789, and that it does not merely prohibit complete withdrawals of whatever habeas rights Congress might have chosen to provide at any particular time"); Gerald Neuman, *The Supreme Court's Attack on Habeas Corpus in* DHS v. Thuraissigiam, JUST SECURITY (July 2, 2020), https://www.justsecurity.org/72104/the-supreme-courts-attack-on-habeas-corpus-in-dhs-v-thuraissigiam (noting that the Court in *Boumediene* held that the clause "guarantee[d] habeas corpus or an equivalent means of judicial inquiry into the legality of executive detention").

97 Gerald L. Neuman, *The Habeas Corpus Suspension Clause After* Boumediene v. Bush, 110 COLUM. L. REV. 537, 541 (2010); *see also* Jonathan Hafetz, *Calling the Government to Account: Habeas Corpus in the Aftermath of* Boumediene v. Bush, 57 WAYNE L. REV. 99, 144–45 (2011) (explaining how *Boumediene*'s ruling on the Suspension Clause ensured a constitutionally mandated judicial inquiry into the legality of military detentions at Guantanamo).

98 140 S. Ct. 1959 (2020).

99 *Id.* at 1969 n.12 ("The original meaning of the Suspension Clause is the subject of controversy. In [*St. Cyr*], the majority and dissent debated whether the Clause independently guarantees the availability of the writ or simply restricts the temporary withholding of its operation. We do not revisit that question." (internal citations

telling suggestion, and it was made all the more so by the absence of any discussion of or even citation to *Boumediene* within the footnote itself. To be sure, the Court in *Thuraissigiam* did not reject outright the idea that the Suspension Clause "guarantees the availability of the writ," and one might read other language in the opinion as endorsing at least a narrow version of that position.[100] But the important signal seemingly being sent was that at least five Justices now view as open for reconsideration an issue that *Boumediene* had earlier appeared to put to rest.[101]

2. Trial by Military Commission

Several of the Court's Suspension Clause cases involved the indefinite detention, without trial, of alleged enemy combatants by military personnel. Sometimes, however, executive authorities do more than simply detain persons said to be captured in connection with military operations; they also take the further step of using military tribunals to convict these persons of federal-law offenses. This practice raises obvious separation-of-powers problems in that it involves the use of Article II-based institutions to discharge quintessentially Article III-related tasks—namely, the trial, conviction, and sentencing of persons for federal crimes.[102] In addition, the summary procedures utilized by military tribunals do not conform with the rights-based safeguards provided by the Fifth Amendment, the Sixth Amendment, and other provisions of the Bill of Rights. Nevertheless, the Court has not categorically barred the President from using military commissions to secure war-related convictions and sentences. Instead, it has held that the President, at least with Congress's support, may sometimes—but not always—use

---

omitted)); *see also id.* at 1997 n.1 (Sotomayor, J., dissenting) (noting that "[t]he Court wisely declines to explore whether the Suspension Clause independently guarantees the availability of the writ or simply restricts the temporary withholding of its operation").

[100] *See id.* at 1969 (noting, though not necessarily endorsing, the Court's previous recognition that "the Clause, at a minimum, 'protects the writ as it existed in 1789,' when the Constitution was adopted" (quoting *St. Cyr*, 533 U.S. at 301)).

[101] *See* Kovarsky, *supra* note 42, at 24 (noting that the Court in *Thuraissigiam* "unceremoniously declared American law's existential habeas question—whether detainees are constitutionally entitled to habeas process—unsettled"); *see also* Amanda L. Tyler, Thuraissigiam *and the Future of the Suspension Clause*, LAWFARE (July 2, 2020), https://www.lawfareblog.com/thuraissigiam-and-future-suspension-clause (noting that the "*Thuraissigiam* majority apparently reopens" the question "whether the Suspension Clause creates an affirmative right to review," thus "beg[ging] the question of just what, if any, of the *Boumediene* majority opinion remains good law").

[102] To some extent, the case law addressed here intersects with a broader set of cases, discussed *infra* Section 29.C, concerning Congress's power to establish non-Article III tribunals. The cases covered here, however, raise distinctive issues insofar as they involve criminal proceedings and the President's Commander-in-Chief powers.

military commissions to try military detainees, including U.S. citizens.

a. Foundational Cases: **Ex Parte Milligan** *and* **Ex Parte Quirin**

In 1864, a U.S. military tribunal in Indiana convicted Lambdin Milligan on charges related to his aiding and abetting of the Confederate rebellion.[103] Milligan petitioned for habeas corpus, contending that the commission lacked the constitutional authority to try him. In *Ex parte Milligan*,[104] a decision handed down not long after the Civil War's conclusion, the Supreme Court agreed. While it left open the possibility that "the laws and usage of war" might under extreme circumstances permit the use of military tribunals to try and convict U.S. citizens on U.S. soil,[105] it emphatically rejected the government's attempt to use such a commission here.[106] In particular, the Court reasoned, "the laws and usages of war . . . can *never* be applied to citizens in states which have upheld the authority of the government, and where the courts are open and their process unobstructed."[107] Because Milligan was such a citizen and because Indiana was such a state, it followed that the only way for the government to secure a conviction against him was to prosecute him in an Article III court, subject to all the procedural safeguards that the Bill of Rights guaranteed.[108]

---

[103] *Ex parte Milligan*, 71 U.S. at 6–7 (1866) (reporter's syllabus) (noting that Milligan's charges stemmed from his joining of a "secret society . . . for the purpose of overthrowing the Government," "holding communication with the enemy," "conspiring to seize munitions of war" to "liberate prisoners of war," and "resisting the draft").

[104] 71 U.S. (4 Wall.) 2 (1866).

[105] *Id.* at 121. Of note, the Court in *Milligan* recognized that there might be "occasions when martial rule can be properly applied." *Id.* at 127. In particular, it cited the example of Virginia during the Civil War, where, for a time, "the national authority was overturned and the courts driven out." *Id.* But just because martial law "could have been enforced in Virginia," it did not follow "that it should obtain in Indiana, where [federal] authority was never disputed, and justice was always administered." *Id.*

[106] *Id.*

[107] *Id.* at 121.

[108] The Court in *Milligan* also addressed the applicability of an 1863 statute through which Congress had conferred on President Lincoln a qualified authority to suspend habeas corpus in connection with certain categories of military detainees. *See* Act of Mar. 3, 1863, ch. 81, §§ 1–3, 12 Stat. 755, 755–56. That statute, the Court concluded, was inapplicable to Milligan and thus did not bar him from pursuing habeas relief. *See Milligan*, 71 U.S. at 115–17. That conclusion, however, did not stop the Court in *Milligan* from further suggesting, contrary to the position subsequently set forth in Justice Scalia's *Hamdi* dissent, *see supra* Section 28.B.1.b, that a suspension of habeas would not in itself have *authorized* the President to detain Milligan without trial. *See Milligan*, 71 U.S. at 115 ("The suspension of the writ does not authorize the arrest of any one, but simply denies to one arrested the privilege of this writ in order to obtain his liberty."); *see also* Morrison, *supra* note 40, at 433 (noting that "the Court [in *Milligan*] divided five to four on the precise question

Milligan offered support for the view that the President lacks the power to convene military commissions to try U.S. citizens during times when and in places where the civilian courts are open. Nearly 80 years later, however, the Court significantly qualified this proposition in its next major military-commission ruling, *Ex parte Quirin*.[109] There, the Court unanimously upheld the conviction by a military commission of eight alleged Nazi saboteurs (one of whom was a U.S. citizen) who had traveled to the United States with plans to carry out attacks on domestic munitions facilities.[110] As in *Milligan*, the arrest and trial of these individuals had taken place on U.S. soil, outside "the theatre or zone of active military operations" and in a place where the civilian courts were open.[111] Even so, the Court held, the saboteurs differed from Milligan in that they were actively-serving "enemy belligerents" who had been charged with "an offense against the law of war."[112] In other words, while the Court in *Milligan* had declared that military commissions could never be used against "citizens in states . . . where the courts are open,"[113] the Court in *Quirin* chose to "construe" that statement "as having particular reference to the facts" of that case.[114] And whereas Milligan himself had been a mere civilian not actively carrying out military operations on behalf of the Confederacy, the petitioners here had "without uniform come[ ] secretly through the lines for the purpose of waging war by destruction of life or property," pursuant to a plan put in place by German military officials.[115] That distinction, the Court now held, was enough to make a constitutional difference.

In addition, although its reasoning was more oblique on this point, the Court in *Quirin* gestured towards a further ground for distinguishing the two cases: Unlike the commission at issue in *Milligan*, the use of which had not been authorized by Congress, the commission in *Quirin* had, in the Court's view, been properly

---

whether Congress could, by suspending the writ as to Milligan, authorize his detention" and that the majority's answer "was a clear no").

109 317 U.S. 1 (1942).

110 *Id.* at 22–23.

111 *Id.* at 38.

112 *Id.* at 46.

113 *Id.* at 45 (quoting *Milligan*, 71 U.S. at 121).

114 *Id.* at 31. Although *Quirin* itself was not a Suspension Clause case, the *Hamdi* plurality would later rely on the decision in concluding that the Suspension Clause did not bar the President from holding citizen-detainees as enemy combatants without trial. *See Hamdi*, 542 U.S. at 519 (opinion of O'Connor, J.) (noting, with respect to *Quirin*, that "[w]hile [a U.S. citizen] was tried for violations of the law of war, nothing in [that case] suggests that his citizenship would have precluded his mere detention for the duration of the relevant hostilities"). *But see id.* at 569–72 (Scalia, J., dissenting) (noting that *Quirin* "was not this Court's finest hour" and that the decision was in any event distinguishable).

115 *Quirin*, 317 U.S. at 31.

convened pursuant to Article 15 of the Articles of War, the precursor statute to the Uniform Code of Military Justice.[116] Consequently, the use of a military commission in *Quirin* (but not *Milligan*) reflected not just an exercise of the President's Article II powers,[117] but also an exercise of Congress's Article I "authority to define and punish offenses against the law of nations by sanctioning, within constitutional limitations, the jurisdiction of military commissions."[118] To be sure, the Court in *Quirin* did not spell out how important this fact was in supporting its bottom-line ruling in the case.[119] But its discussion of the point pointed to the potential doctrinal relevance of the statutory backdrop against which a military commission proceeds. That variable, it turned out, would prove critical to the Court's first (and only) military-commission decision of the "war on terror" era.[120]

---

[116] *See id.* at 26–28; *see also* Stephen I. Vladeck, *The Laws of War as a Constitutional Limit on Military Jurisdiction*, 4 J. NAT'L SECURITY L. & POL'Y 295, 315 (2010) (noting that the *Quirin* Court found congressional authorization for military commissions (which had been lacking in *Milligan*) in a statute that was "charitably, ambiguous" on this score); *see also* Jonathan Hafetz, *Policing the Line: International Law, Article III, and the Constitutional Limits of Military Jurisdiction*, 2014 WISC. L. REV. 681, 695–96 (highlighting the ways in which international-law norms supported Congress's authorization of the President to try the *Quirin* defendants for law-of-war violations).

[117] *Cf. Milligan*, 71 U.S. at 121 (noting that the military commission could not be "justif[ied] on the mandate of the President, because he is controlled by law, and has his appropriate sphere of duty, which is to execute, not to make, the laws"). Notably, the majority in *Milligan* did go on to suggest that the particular commission at issue in *Milligan* would have remained unlawful even if Congress had authorized its use, *see id.* at 125 (describing the constitutional safeguards associated with a full-scale criminal trial and emphasizing that "[n]ot one of these safeguards can the President or Congress or the Judiciary disturb, except the one concerning the writ of habeas corpus"), although four Justices noted their disagreement with this conclusion, *see id.* at 137 (opinion of Chase, C.J.) ("We think that Congress had power, though not exercised, to authorize the military commission which was held in Indiana.").

[118] *Quirin*, 317 U.S. at 28.

[119] *See* David P. Currie, *The Constitution in the Supreme Court: The Second World War, 1941–1946*, 37 CATH. U. L. REV. 1, 5 n.29 (1987) (noting that it was "unnecessary [in *Quirin*] to decide whether, contrary to the suggestion of Chief Justice Chase [in *Milligan*], the President had inherent authority to establish such tribunals by virtue of his position as Commander-in-Chief in the absence of 'controlling necessity' " (quoting *Milligan*, 71 U.S. at 139–40 (opinion of Chase, C.J.))).

[120] Some four years after *Quirin*, and with the war recently concluded, the Court in *In re Yamashita*, 327 U.S. 1 (1946), took up a question that presented a variation on the theme. Tomoyuki Yamashita was a Japanese general who had been captured by the U.S. army in the Philippines and had there been tried by a military commission for war crimes. *Id.* at 5. Yamashita challenged his conviction on the ground that (among other things) his trial occurred *after* the cessation of wartime hostilities, thus necessitating (so he said) adjudication by a duly constituted federal court. In an opinion by Chief Justice Stone, the Court ruled that the timing of the trial did not matter. "The war power," it explained, "is not limited to victories in the field, but carries with it the inherent power to guard against the immediate renewal of the conflict, and to remedy, at least in ways Congress has recognized, the evils which the military operations have produced." *Id.* at 12. At the least, the Court added, the executive branch could try war crimes by military commission "until peace has been

b. *Military Commissions and the "War on Terror":* Hamdan v. Rumsfeld *and Its Aftermath*

Hamdan v. Rumsfeld[121] concerned President George W. Bush's use of military commissions to try several alleged "enemy combatants" held at Guantanamo Bay.[122] One of these individuals was Salim Ahmed Hamdan, a Yemeni national who faced "conspiracy" charges based on his alleged work as the "bodyguard and personal driver" of Osama bin Laden.[123] Like the detainees in *Milligan* and *Quirin*, Hamdan sought and obtained Supreme Court review of the question whether a military commission had the authority to convict him.[124] But unlike the litigants in those earlier cases, Hamdan relied heavily on claimed *statutory* deficiencies in the commission's operation. In particular, and in several different respects, Hamdan argued that the Guantanamo commission made use of procedures that contravened congressionally established law—law that the President, despite his status as Commander-in-Chief, was constitutionally required to follow.

In a five-three decision, the Court ruled for *Hamdan* on some, but not all, of his statutory claims.[125] The Court's analysis thus had

officially recognized by treaty or proclamation." *Id.* at 12. For other post-World War II cases, see *Duncan v. Kahanamoku*, 327 U.S. 304, 26 (1946) (holding as statutorily invalid the use of "provost courts" in the then-territory of Hawaii to try civilians); *Madsen v. Kinsella*, 343 U.S. 341 (1952) (upholding the use of a military commission to adjudicate a homicide charge under the German Criminal Code against the wife of a U.S. soldier who had been stationed in ally-occupied Germany); and *Reid*, 354 U.S. at 3 (invalidating the use of a military commission to try a U.S. citizen for crimes committed on a U.S. military base abroad). *See also id.* at 82 (Burton, J., dissenting) (maintaining that *Madsen* and *Reid* were "practically indistinguishable" and that the distinction "that in one case the trial was by court-martial and in the other by a military commission is insubstantial").

121 548 U.S. 557 (2006).

122 *Id.* at 566.

123 *Id.* at 570.

124 *Id.* at 566. Hamdan had not yet been tried or convicted on these charges; rather, his petition sought prospectively to "challenge the Executive Branch's intended means" of prosecuting him. *Id.*

125 In particular, the Court held that the commission violated Article 36 of the Uniform Code of Military Justice (UCMJ), which mandated that the rules for military commissions and courts martial should be "uniform insofar as practicable," because the President had not justified the commission's "variances from the procedures governing courts-martial." *Id.* at 622. In addition, the Court held that the commission was not a "regularly constituted court" as required by Common Article 3 of the Geneva Convention, which had been fully incorporated into U.S. law by way of the UCMJ. *See id.* at 627–28 (noting that the rights conferred by the Geneva Convention were "part of the law of war" and that "compliance with the law of war is the condition upon which the authority set forth in Article 21 [of the UCMJ] is granted"). And the Court further rejected the President's contention that Congress had effectively superseded these restrictions by enacting the 2001 Authorization for the Use of Force and the 2005 DTA, finding that neither statute could be construed to furnish "specific, overriding authorization for the very commission that has been convened to try Hamdan." *Id.* at 593.

the effect, as Justice Kennedy put it in a separate concurrence, of placing the case "within Justice Jackson's third category, not the second or first," where the President's power, at its "lowest ebb," was insufficient to overcome the relevant statutory constraints.[126] That aspect of the Court's ruling, however, also left the door open for a congressional response. In particular, and as Justice Breyer noted (also in a separate concurrence), the majority's ruling "ultimately rests upon a single ground: Congress has not issued the Executive a 'blank check.' "[127] Thus, he continued, nothing in the ruling would "prevent[ ] the President from returning to Congress to seek the authority he believes necessary."[128]

And that is just what the President did. Only months after *Hamdan* came down, and at the President's urging, Congress passed the MCA, which (wholly apart from its later-invalidated treatment of habeas jurisdiction[129]) expressly authorized the President to use military-commission procedures similar to the ones that the Court had held unlawful in *Hamdan* itself.[130] What the Court had previously found to be an exercise of presidential authority at its "lowest ebb" had thus been elevated to the "maximum" level of the President's Article II authority instead.[131] As a result, it is not surprising that no court since the MCA's passage has held that

---

126 *See id.* at 638 (Kennedy, J., concurring in part); *see also id.* at 593 n.23 (majority opinion) ("Whether or not the President has independent power, absent congressional authorization, to convene military commissions, he may not disregard limitations that Congress has, in proper exercise of its own war powers, placed on his powers." (citing Youngstown Sheet & Tube Co. v. Sawyer, 343 U.S. 579, 637 (1952) (Jackson, J., concurring))).

127 *See id.* at 636 (Breyer, J., concurring).

128 *Id.*

129 *See supra* Section 28.B.1.c (discussing the Court's holding in *Boumediene*).

130 *See* Jana Singer, Hamdan *as an Assertion of Judicial Power*, 66 MD. L. REV. 759, 760 (2007) (characterizing the MCA as "something very close to the 'blank check' to which Justice Breyer refers").

131 *Youngstown*, 343 U.S. at 635 (Jackson, J., concurring); *see* Michael Stokes Paulsen, *The War Power*, 33 HARV. J.L. & PUB. POL'Y 113 (2010) (noting that "Presidential actions consistent with the MCA fall within the safest harbor of *Youngstown*'s 'Category One' of most-indisputably-authorized presidential actions").

Guantanamo commissions are wholly unlawful.[132] And those commissions remain in operation to this day.[133]

[132] To be sure, courts have continued to litigate a variety of issues concerning particular charges brought before the commissions, *see, e.g.*, Al Bahlul v. United States, 840 F.3d 757 (D.C. Cir. 2016) (en banc) (per curiam) (considering whether Congress was authorized to make "conspiracy to commit war crimes an offense triable by military commission"), and specific procedural issues related to individual cases, *see, e.g.*, *In re* Al-Nashiri, 921 F.3d 224, 262 (D.C. Cir. 2019) (finding that a military judge who was a member of the commissions had "created a disqualifying appearance of partiality" by applying for a position with the U.S. Department of Justice; thus vacating "all orders issued" by that judge after he applied for the job). But the President's general authority to use the commissions for purposes of prosecuting enemy-combatant cases, based on claimed violation of the laws of war, has not been subject to question.

[133] Though salvaged by the MCA, the Guantanamo commissions have suffered a number of serious setbacks in the years since the statute's enactment, resulting in the extraordinarily slow processing of the cases and leaving many of the Guantanamo detainees in legal limbo for years if not decades. For a recent overview of the commissions' many failures, see Steve Vladeck, *It's Time to Admit That the Military Commissions Have Failed*, LAWFARE (Apr. 16, 2019), https://www.lawfareblog.com/its-time-admit-military-commissions-have-failed (noting, as of 2019, that "in 13 years under the Military Commissions Act regime, and 17 years total, the commissions have produced a grand total of eight convictions").

Chapter 29

CONGRESS AND THE ADMINISTRATIVE STATE

Analysis

Although Article II directly establishes only the offices of the President and Vice President, the Constitution as a whole makes clear the Framers' expectation that these officials would exercise their executive powers in collaboration with a complex administrative apparatus.[1] That expectation has proven well-founded. The modern-day executive-branch comprises 15 Cabinet-level departments (State, Defense, Treasury, Commerce, Homeland Security, etc.),[2] scores of standalone agencies (such as the National Labor Relations Board, the Federal Communications Commission, the Environmental Protection Agency, and the Securities and Exchange Commission),[3] and many other offices and working groups

---

[1] In particular, various provisions of the document make reference to "Officers" and "Offices" within the executive branch, *see, e.g.*, U.S. CONST. art. II, § 2 (setting forth rules for the appointment of "Officers of the United States"), "executive Departments," *see id.* (providing that the President "may require the Opinion, in writing, of the principal Officer in each of the executive Departments"), "Heads" of departments, *see id.* (providing that "Congress may by Law vest the Appointment of such inferior Officers, as they think proper, in the President alone, in the Courts of Law, or in the Heads of Departments"), and "Ambassadors" and "other public Ministers and Consuls," *see id.* (referencing the President's power to appoint such individuals).

[2] These Departments are further subdivided into numerous "organizationally distinct bureaus." *See* JENNIFER L. SELIN & DAVID E. LEWIS, ADMINISTRATIVE CONFERENCE OF THE UNITED STATES, SOURCEBOOK OF UNITED STATES EXECUTIVE AGENCIES 36 (2018) (noting that "[t]he modern executive departments are comprised of anywhere from three to 40 organizationally distinct bureaus, with most housing 10–15"). For example, the Department of Transportation has within it the Federal Aviation Administration, the Federal Highway Administration, and the National Highway Traffic Safety Administration, among others. *See id.* at 130 app. A-1.

[3] *See id.* at 42 tab. 3. Some of these non-Cabinet agencies enjoy a measure of independence from presidential influence, guaranteed to them by statutory restrictions on the President's ability to remove their leaders from office. *See id.* (listing 24 such "independent commissions"). As detailed further in a later chapter, the

(including the Office of Management and Budget, the Council of Economic Advisors, and the Office of Science and Technology Policy) that together participate on a day-to-day basis in the execution of federal law.[4] Altogether, these entities employ some 4.1 million individuals (with several thousand serving in leadership positions),[5] while receiving well over $1 trillion in annual appropriations.[6] These government workers perform tasks that range from conducting investigations to prosecuting enforcement actions to adjudicating claims to making contracts to negotiating international agreements to issuing licenses to promulgating regulations to engaging in countless other actions on behalf of the executive branch. Their work touches on nearly every conceivable societal concern, from education to environmental protection to taxation to immigration to national security to financial regulation to disease prevention to space exploration and beyond. Indeed, one would be hard pressed to identify any modern-day domestic enterprise that is not in some way affected by the actions of the federal administrative state.

This chapter focuses on the relationship between Congress and the many administrative agencies within the executive branch. As the first section details, federal agencies are "creatures of statute" because they owe their existence to Article I enactments (frequently referred to as "organic" or "enabling" acts) and possess only those

---

constitutionality of such "independent agencies" has long been a subject of disagreement and debate. *See infra* Section 31.A. In addition, some Cabinet Department subunits (such as the Federal Energy Regulatory Commission within the Department of Energy) have long been understood to enjoy independent-agency status. *See id.* at 14 n.52.

[4] *See id.* at 23. These agencies are formally a part of the Executive Office of the President (EOP). Employees of these agencies, as a recent report describes it, "see it as their job to work for the President" rather than for a departmental Secretary or other agency head. *Id.* at 18.

[5] Roughly 2.7 million of these individuals serve in the civilian workforce, while the remaining 1.4 million serve as uniformed military personnel. *See* OFFICE OF MGMT. & BUDGET, EXEC. OFFICE OF THE PRESIDENT, ANALYTICAL PERSPECTIVES, BUDGET OF THE UNITED STATES GOVERNMENT, FISCAL YEAR 2022, at 44 tab. 5-2 (2021). It should also be noted, however, that while the size of the federal workforce may seem large in absolute terms, it is, as a percentage of population, smaller than it used to be, and considerably smaller than the workforces of other developed democracies. *See* Fiona Hill, *Public Service and the Federal Government*, BROOKINGS INSTITUTE (May 27, 2020), https://www.brookings.edu/policy2020/votervital/public-service-and-the-federal-government/.

[6] *See* CONG. BUDGET OFFICE, THE FEDERAL BUDGET IN FISCAL YEAR 2020: A CLOSER LOOK AT DISCRETIONARY SPENDING (2021) (estimating $1.6 trillion in discretionary outlays for fiscal year 2020, with $914 billion going to nondefense programs and $714 billion going to defense-related programs), *available at* https://www.cbo.gov/system/files/2021-04/57172-discretionary-spending.pdf. These totals do not include some $4.6 trillion in federal dollars that went to such "nondiscretionary" entitlement programs as Social Security, Medicare, Medicaid, and so forth. *See* CONG. BUDGET OFFICE, THE FEDERAL BUDGET IN FISCAL YEAR 2020: A CLOSER LOOK AT MANDATORY SPENDING (2021), *available at* https://www.cbo.gov/system/files/2021-04/57171-mandatory-spending.pdf.

powers that Congress has conferred on them.[7] No one seriously contests Congress's general authority to establish (and to disestablish) federal agencies by statute, but other aspects of the Congress-agency relationship present complexities that the remainder of this chapter addresses. One set of questions, which we canvass in the second section, concerns the "nondelegation" doctrine, which sets forth limits on Congress's authority to confer *rulemaking* and other policymaking powers on the agencies it creates. A further set of questions, canvassed in the third section, concerns the extent to which Article III limits Congress's authority to confer *adjudicative* powers on administrative agencies and other non-Article III institutions. A final set of questions, which we canvass in the final section, concerns the extent to which Congress can monitor and override agency actions by way of mechanisms outside the Article I lawmaking process.

A. CONGRESS'S POWER TO CREATE ADMINISTRATIVE AGENCIES

Although Article I does not in terms give Congress the power to create executive agencies,[8] it has long been recognized that the Necessary and Proper Clause supports a wide-ranging authority to create and empower agencies to help carry out the laws that it enacts.[9] This authority flows from the core principle recognized in *McCulloch v. Maryland*[10]: If the existence of a particular agency would be "useful" or "conducive" to carrying into execution one of Congress's enumerated powers, then Congress can establish that

---

[7] *See* Judge Rotenberg Educ. Ctr. Inc. v. FDA, 3 F.4th 390, 399–400 (D.C. Cir. 2021) ("Federal agencies are creatures of statute. They possess only those powers that Congress confers upon them. If no statute confers authority to a federal agency, it has none. If Congress has forbidden an agency from taking an action, the agency cannot so act." (internal citations omitted)).

[8] To be sure, Article I does explicitly authorize the creation of a few specific entities within the executive branch. *See, e.g.*, U.S. CONST. art. 1, § 8, cl. 7 (authorizing Congress to "establish Post Offices"); *id.* art. 1, § 8, cl. 12 (authorizing Congress to "raise and support Armies"); *id.* art. 1, § 8, cl. 13 (authorizing Congress to "provide and maintain a Navy"). But it does not contain a generalized enumerated power to establish administrative agencies.

[9] *See, e.g.*, Anne Joseph O'Connell, *Bureaucracy at the Boundary*, 162 U. PA. L. REV. 841, 897–98 (2014) (noting that "[u]nder the Necessary and Proper Clause, Congress can enact laws needed to carry out its legislative powers, which include the delegation of intelligible tasks to the administrative state" (internal footnote omitted)). Indeed, one need look no further than *McCulloch v. Maryland*, 17 U.S. (4 Wheat.) 316 (1819), for affirmation of the point: There, recall, Chief Justice Marshall characterized the national bank (an agency of sorts) as an entity that might assist Congress in the exercise of its various powers to lay and collect taxes, borrow money, regulate commerce, raise and support armies, and declare war. *See id.* at 408–09. That finding in turn supported his conclusion that the statute creating the bank fell comfortably within the scope of Congress's legislative authority. *See supra* Section 1.B.

[10] 17 U.S. (4 Wheat.) 316 (1819).

agency and put it to work.[11] Thus, for instance, Congress's authority to create an Internal Revenue Service emanates from its enumerated power to lay and collect taxes.[12] Congress's authority to create a U.S. Postal Service is implied by its enumerated power to establish post offices and roads.[13] And Congress's authority to create a Food and Drug Administration, Securities and Exchange Commission, Consumer Financial Protection Bureau, Environmental Protection Agency, and countless other entities involved in regulating aspects of the nation's economy arises from its enumerated power to regulate interstate commerce.[14] Broadly speaking, if Article I authorizes Congress to enshrine a particular set of substantive requirements into federal law, then the Necessary and Proper Clause authorizes it to create an agency for the purpose of helping to implement those requirements.

The Necessary and Proper Clause does another job as well. It permits Congress—again, for purposes of facilitating the "useful" and "conducive" implementation of the governing laws—to put in place rules about the structure, organization, and procedures of the agencies that it creates.[15] If Congress may create Agency *X* on the theory that the agency will help to carry into execution of Congress's enumerated powers, then Congress may also enact additional laws designed to ensure that Agency *X* does that job effectively. For some agencies, this might mean being headed by a multi-member board of individuals rather than a single individual. For other agencies, it might mean having one unit within the agency exercise oversight in connection with the activities that other units undertake. For still other agencies, it might mean creating mechanisms through which interested parties and the public at large can participate in decisionmaking processes.[16] Rules of this sort may not themselves involve the direct execution of any enumerated power. But they fall

---

11 *Id.* at 418–19.

12 U.S. CONST. art. I, § 8, cl. 1.

13 *Id.* art. I, § 8, cl. 7.

14 *Id.* art. I, § 8, cl. 3.

15 *See* John F. Manning, *The Supreme Court, 2013 Term—Foreword: The Means of Constitutional Power*, 128 HARV. L. REV. 1, 6 (2014) (emphasizing that the Necessary and Proper Clause "delegates to Congress broad and explicit (though not limitless) discretion to compose the government and prescribe the means of constitutional power").

16 Some of these requirements are *agency-specific* in that they derive from a particular agency's enabling statute and apply only to the exercise of that agency's statutory powers. Other such requirements, by contrast, stem from generally applicable statutes that cover a wide range of agencies. The most important of these statutes is the federal Administrative Procedure Act of 1946 (APA), 5 U.S.C. §§ 551 *et seq.*, which generally regulates agency rulemaking and adjudication (among other things), while also creating avenues for and restrictions on judicial review of agency action.

comfortably within Congress's purview as measures that are necessary and proper to facilitate the sound operation of the agencies that Congress has the power to create.[17]

B. THE NONDELEGATION DOCTRINE

What sorts of policymaking powers can Congress bestow on the agencies it has established? More specifically, can Congress authorize agencies to do anything and everything related to their substantive areas of focus, or are there limits on the breadth of policymaking discretion that Congress can confer? According to modern-day case law, such limits do in theory exist: In particular, the "nondelegation doctrine" holds that Congress may not delegate any of its *legislative* powers to administrative agencies, which instead may only be tasked with executing laws that Congress alone can create.[18] For most of its existence, the nondelegation rule has had more bark than bite: Even as Congress has passed thousands of laws concerning the powers of agencies—including some conferring on agencies wide-ranging authority to promulgate statute-like administrative regulations—the Court has not identified a single violation of the nondelegation doctrine since 1935.[19] Recent rumblings among the now-sitting Justices, however, indicate that a rethinking of nondelegation doctrine may be in the offing, carrying with it major implications for the future of the federal administrative state.

1. A Brief History of the Nondelegation Doctrine

During the decades leading up to the New Deal,[20] the Court rejected numerous nondelegation-based challenges to congressional

---

[17] Notably, Congress's ability to structure agencies may also find support in that feature of the Necessary and Proper Clause that permits Congress to pass laws that carry into execution the powers of the federal government as a whole, including the powers of the President. For a discussion of this topic, see *supra* Section 6.C.

[18] *See* Whitman v. Am. Trucking Ass'ns, 531 U.S. 457, 472–73 (2001) (explaining that the Article I Vesting Clause "permits no delegation of [Congress's legislative] powers" and that "when Congress confers decisionmaking authority upon agencies *Congress* must 'lay down by legislative act an intelligible principle to which the person or body authorized to [act] is directed to conform' " (quoting J.W. Hampton, Jr., & Co. v. United States, 276 U.S. 394, 409 (1928))).

[19] *See* Gundy v. United States, 139 S. Ct. 2116, 2130–31 (2019) (Alito, J., concurring in the judgment) (noting, though not necessarily with approval, that "since 1935, the Court has uniformly rejected nondelegation arguments and has upheld provisions that authorized agencies to adopt important rules pursuant to extraordinarily capacious standards").

[20] For an overview of the Court's first encounters with delegation-related ideas, see Keith E. Whittington & Jason Iuliano, *The Myth of the Nondelegation Doctrine*, 165 U. PA. L. REV. 379, 392–96 (2017) (discussing the Marshall Court's decisions in *Cargo of the Brig Aurora v. United States*, 11 U.S. (7 Cranch) 382, 382–85 (1813), *Wayman v. Southard*, 23 U.S. (10 Wheat.) 1 (1825), and *Bank of the United States v. Halstead*, 23 U.S. (10 Wheat.) 51, 61–62 (1825), while also noting that "[t]he Court had

enactments that conferred rulemaking powers on administrative agencies.[21] In deciding these cases, however, the Court did not explicitly endorse the idea that Congress could cede its lawmaking authority to the executive branch. Instead, as the Court put the point in *Field v. Clark*,[22] there existed a critical constitutional difference between "the delegation of power to make the law, which necessarily involves a discretion as to what it shall be," and the conferral of "authority or discretion as to its execution, to be exercised under and in pursuance of the law."[23] In other words, the Vesting Clause of Article I, as the Court understood it, prohibited Congress from handing off its "legislative Powers" to anyone else, including agencies within the executive branch. From that proposition, however, it did not follow that Congress lacked the ability to task other governing bodies with the *executive* responsibility of "fill[ing] up the details" of the laws that it created.[24]

The $64,000 question raised by these pronouncements was easy to spot but hard to answer: How does one distinguish between laws that (impermissibly) delegate legislative power to agencies and laws that (permissibly) authorize agencies to execute Congress's legislative commands? In its 1928 decision in *J.W. Hampton, Jr. & Co. v. United States*,[25] the Court set forth the still-applicable doctrinal sorting device, known as the "intelligible principle" requirement. According to Chief Justice Taft's majority opinion in that case, the question to ask in nondelegation cases is whether Congress has "la[id] down by legislative act an *intelligible principle* to which the person or body authorized [to act] is directed to

---

remarkably little to say regarding the delegation of legislative power from the late Marshall Court through the remainder of the nineteenth century").

[21] *See, e.g.*, Field v. Clark, 143 U.S. 649, 692–93 (1892) (upholding a provision of the Tariff Act of 1890 that authorized the President to impose reciprocal tariffs on certain types of goods); Buttfield v. Stranahan, 192 U.S. 470 (1904) (upholding provisions of the Tea Inspection Act that conferred on the Secretary of the Treasury various regulatory powers with respect to setting standards for imported tea); Union Bridge Co. v. United States, 204 U.S. 364, 366 (1907) (upholding a federal statute that authorized the Secretary of War to order modifications to bridges posing "an unreasonable obstruction" to navigable waters). For further discussion of these and other early twentieth-century cases, see generally Whittington & Iuliano, *supra* note 20, at 396–405.

[22] 143 U.S. 649.

[23] *Id.* at 693–94 (internal quotation omitted).

[24] United States v. Grimaud, 220 U.S. 506, 517 (1911) (emphasizing that the nondelegation doctrine did not bar Congress from empowering agencies "to fill up the details" of its statutory schemes (quoting *Wayman*, 23 U.S. at 31, 43)).

[25] 276 U.S. 394 (1928). *J.W. Hampton* involved the Tariff Act of 1922, which authorized the President to impose tariffs aimed at "equaliz[ing]" the differences in costs of production between U.S. products and competing products from foreign countries. *Id.* at 401–02. The Court upheld the provision, concluding that it communicated a congressional "plan" that was "perfectly clear and perfectly intelligible." *Id.* at 404–05.

conform."[26] If so, then the agency's discretion qualifies as sufficiently cabined to ensure that its actions involve only the execution, rather than the making, of federal law. If not, then the agency's discretion—because it is so unbounded—gives rise to an authority to make the law and thus to wield the legislative power that, so the nondelegation doctrine holds, only Congress can exercise. The Court's decision in *J.W. Hampton* thus established that the validity of a congressional grant of agency authority hinges on the open-endedness of the enabling act's terms. But little else about the operative test was made apparent (dare we say intelligible?) by the Court's ruling, particularly with respect to the question of how "intelligible" the underlying statutory directive must be.

Post-*J.W. Hampton*, the Court has not steered an altogether steady course in applying the intelligible-principle requirement. Of particular significance, in a pair of New Deal-era decisions from 1935, the Justices concluded that two key provisions of the National Industrial Recovery Act (NIRA) lacked sufficient specificity to survive nondelegation attack. First, in *Panama Refining Co. v. Ryan*,[27] the Court invalidated section 9 of the statute, which authorized the President to prohibit the interstate distribution of petroleum (and petroleum-related products) produced in excess of state-law quotas.[28] That provision, as Chief Justice Hughes explained for an 8–1 majority, involved an improper delegation of legislative power because it set forth "no requirement, no definition of circumstances and conditions in which the transportation is to be allowed or prohibited."[29] Second, in *Schechter Poultry Corp. v. United States*,[30] the Court invalidated section 3 of the NIRA, which authorized the President to promulgate "codes of fair competition"—including on such matters as minimum-wage, maximum-hour, workplace safety, and collective bargaining requirements—based on

26 *Id.* at 409 (emphasis added).

27 293 U.S. 388 (1935).

28 *Id.* at 407–08.

29 *Id.* at 430. Justice Cardozo noted in dissent that the statute did impose at least one such limit on the President's discretion—namely, the requirement that products targeted by the President must have been made "in excess of state permission." *See id.* at 434–35 (Cardozo, J., dissenting) (noting that, under the statute, the President "is not left to roam at will among all the possible subjects of interstate transportation, picking and choosing as he pleases," but was rather limited to "a particular commodity, and to that commodity when produced or withdrawn from storage in contravention of the policy and statutes of the states"). On the majority's view, however, the specificity of the triggering criterion was not enough: The difficulty was that the President remained free to decide whether or not to prohibit distribution of products that met the applicable standard, and the President's discretion was in that sense unbounded. *See id.* at 430 (majority opinion).

30 295 U.S. 495 (1935). As we have discussed elsewhere, the Court in *Schechter Poultry* also (and alternatively) found that Congress had acted beyond the scope of its authority to regulate interstate commerce. *See supra* Sections 2.B & 2.C.

recommendations received from industry groups and trade associations.[31] Once again and this time for a unanimous Court, the Chief Justice explained that the statute conferred on the President "an unfettered discretion to make whatever laws he thinks may be needed or advisable for the rehabilitation and expansion of trade or industry."[32] Instead of "prescribing rules of conduct," section 9 thus unconstitutionally "authorize[d] the making of codes to prescribe" such rules by the President himself.[33]

The Court's decisions in *Panama Refining* and *Schechter Poultry* signaled a judicial willingness to strike down federal statutes on nondelegation grounds. But as in other fields of constitutional law, the mood (and composition) of the Court shifted following the reelection of Franklin Roosevelt in 1936. In the ensuing decades, the Court repeatedly distinguished away its 1935 decisions in rejecting

---

[31] *See id.* at 521 n.4. The Court's decision in *Schechter Poultry* helped to spawn a separate but related line of decisions involving congressional delegations of power to *private* entities. *See generally* Calvin R. Massey, *The Non-Delegation Doctrine and Private Parties*, 17 GREEN BAG 2D 157, 160 n.15 (2014). *Schechter Poultry* itself involved an arrangement of this sort insofar as Section 3 of the NIRA empowered industry groups and trade associations to recommend fair-competition standards for the President to prescribe. *See* 295 U.S. at 521. And while much of the Court's decision in that case involved the application of general nondelegation principles, Chief Justice Hughes's majority opinion did go out of its way to note the special problems raised by the statute's empowerment of private delegees. *See id.* at 537. The next year, moreover, the Court would again endorse this idea by holding in *Carter v. Carter Coal Co.*, 298 U.S. 238 (1936), that a provision of the Bituminous Coal Conservation Act involved "legislative delegation in its most obnoxious form" by empowering designated groups of coal producers to establish minimum-wage and maximum-hour requirements for their industry. *Id.* at 311. And although the private delegation doctrine would lie mostly dormant for the next several decades, *see, e.g.*, Gillian E. Metzger, *Privatization as Delegation*, 103 COLUM. L. REV. 1367, 1439 (2003) (indicating that, as of 2003, "while *Carter*'s constitutional prohibition on private delegations . . . remains alive in theory, it is all but dead in practice"), it was recently given new life when the D.C. Circuit held that Congress had violated the private nondelegation doctrine by authorizing Amtrak, along with the Federal Railway Administration (FRA), to set "metrics and standards" for passenger rail services. *See* Ass'n of Am. Railroads v. U.S. Dep't of Transp., 721 F.3d 666, 673–88 (D.C. Cir. 2013). The Supreme Court granted certiorari and vacated that decision, but on the narrower ground that Amtrak was in fact a governmental entity and thus not the sort of "autonomous private enterprise" that implicated the rule against delegation to private parties. *See* U.S. Dep't of Transp. v. Ass'n of Am. Railroads, 575 U.S. 43, 53 (2015). In a concurring opinion, however, Justice Alito raised concerns about another rule requiring Amtrak and the FRA to submit to binding arbitration any disputes regarding the metrics and standards being set. *See id.* at 58–64 (Alito, J., concurring). That provision, Justice Alito argued, would be unconstitutional "[i]f the arbitrator can be a private person" because "handing off regulatory power to a private entity is 'legislative delegation in its most obnoxious form.'" *Id.* at 60–62 (Alito, J., concurring) (quoting *Carter Coal*, 298 U.S. at 311); *see also id.* at 87–88 (Thomas, J., concurring in the judgment) (emphasizing that "the Vesting Clauses would categorically preclude [a private entity] from exercising the legislative, executive, or judicial powers of the Federal Government").

[32] *Schechter Poultry*, 295 U.S. at 537–38.

[33] *Id.* at 541; *see also id.* at 533 (Cardozo, J., concurring) ("This is delegation running riot.").

subsequent nondelegation claims.[34] Indeed, this line of rulings was so consistent that by 1989 the Court could observe that "our jurisprudence has been driven by a practical understanding that in our increasingly complex society, replete with ever changing and more technical problems, Congress simply cannot do its job absent an ability to delegate power under broad general directives."[35] And the trend would continue into the new millennium, with Justice Scalia acknowledging for the Court in 2001 that "we have 'almost never felt qualified to second-guess Congress regarding the permissible degree of policy judgment that can be left to those executing or applying the law.' "[36] In sum, while the Court has never repudiated the proposition that Congress cannot delegate legislative power to administrative agencies, it has for nearly a century understood the requirement to impose only minimal limits on Congress's ability to vest administrative agencies with regulatory authority.[37] As the next

[34] *See, e.g.*, Currin v. Wallace, 306 U.S. 1, 6 (1939) (upholding provisions of the Tobacco Inspection Act conferring on the Secretary of Agriculture the power to establish standards regarding the quality and inspection of tobacco sold in interstate commerce); United States v. Rock Royal Co-op., 307 U.S. 533, 574–76 (1939) (upholding a provision of the Agricultural Marketing Agreement Act of 1937 that authorized the Secretary of Agriculture to issue orders concerning designated agricultural commodities aimed at effectuating the statute's goal of maintaining adequate purchasing power for farmers); Opp Cotton Mills Inc v. Administrator, 312 U.S. 126, 144 (1941) (upholding provisions of the Fair Labor Standards Act of 1938 that authorized the Administrator of the Wage and Hour Division of the Department of Labor to establish, within a statutorily prescribed range, minimum wage levels for industries engaged in interstate commerce); Nat'l Broadcasting Co. v. United States, 319 U.S. 190, 225–26 (1943) (rejecting a nondelegation challenge to the broadcast licensing powers granted to the Federal Communications Commission); Yakus v. United States, 321 U.S. 414, 426 (1944) (holding that Congress did not violate the nondelegation doctrine when it delegated to an agency official called the Price Administrator the power to fix maximum prices for commodities and rents as necessary to confront the emergency economic conditions posed by the second World War); Am. Power & Light Co. v. SEC, 329 U.S. 90, 104–06 (1946) (holding that Section 11(b)(2) of the Public Utility Holding Company Act, which gave to the Securities and Exchange Commission certain powers related to the regulation of corporate structures for utility holding companies, did not violate the nondelegation doctrine because "a veritable code of rules reveals itself for the Commission to follow in giving effect to the standards of [the statute]").

[35] Mistretta v. United States, 488 U.S. 361, 372 (1989).

[36] *Whitman*, 531 U.S. at 474–75 (citation omitted).

[37] To be sure, the Court and its Justices have sometimes sought to enforce the dictates of the nondelegation doctrine *indirectly*, by treating delegation-based concerns (alongside the canon of constitutional avoidance) as a reason to construe enabling statutes narrowly rather than broadly. *See, e.g.*, Indus. Union Dep't v. Am. Petroleum Inst., 448 U.S. 607, 646 (1980) (opinion of Stevens, J.) (construing an enabling statute narrowly so as to reject an alternative reading that would produce "such a 'sweeping delegation of legislative power' " as to render the law potentially unconstitutional under [*Schechter Poultry* and *Panama Refining*]"); *see also* Nat'l Cable Television Ass'n v. United States, 415 U.S. 336, 342 (1974) ("Whether the present Act meets the requirement of *Schechter* and *Hampton* is a question we do not reach. But the hurdles revealed in those decisions lead us to read the Act narrowly to avoid constitutional problems.").

section shows, however, recent developments at the Court indicate that a revival of the nondelegation doctrine may be in the works.

2. The *Gundy* Decision

The Court's 2019 decision in *Gundy v. United States*[38] concerned a provision of the federal Sex Offender Registration and Notification Act (SORNA) that authorizes the Attorney General to "specify the applicability of" the statute's "initial registration" requirements for "sex offenders" whose qualifying convictions had occurred prior to SORNA's enactment.[39] The Second Circuit had upheld that provision against nondelegation attack, reasoning that it supplied a sufficiently intelligible principle.[40] That judgment was ultimately affirmed, but with no majority opinion and with only eight Justices participating in the case.[41] Justice Kagan (joined by Justices Ginsburg, Breyer, and Sotomayor) authored a plurality opinion that endorsed the thrust of the Second Circuit's reasoning,[42] while Justice Gorsuch (joined by Chief Justice Roberts and Justice Thomas) filed a lengthy dissent urging a wholesale reconsideration of the Court's nondelegation jurisprudence.[43] The decisive vote thus came from Justice Alito, who explained that, while he would generally "support [an] effort" to "reconsider the approach [to the nondelegation doctrine] we have taken for the past 84 years," he was unwilling to do so in *Gundy* because no majority of the Court, as constituted for purposes of that case, supported the taking of that step.[44]

Gundy itself thus revealed the existence of four likely votes in favor of a revamped and far less Congress-friendly nondelegation doctrine. Shortly after the decision, moreover, Justice Kavanaugh, who had recently joined the Court, expressed openness to embracing the position espoused by the *Gundy* dissenters.[45] Not long after that, Justice Barrett replaced Justice Ginsburg, one of the four members

---

38 139 S. Ct. 2116 (2019).

39 *See* 34 U.S.C. § 20913(d).

40 *See* United States v. Gundy, 695 Fed. App'x 639, 641 n.2 (2d Cir. 2017) (citing United States v. Guzman, 591 F.3d 83, 91–94 (2d Cir. 2010)).

41 Justice Kavanaugh, whose elevation to the Court had occurred after oral argument in *Gundy*, did not participate in the case.

42 *Gundy*, 139 S. Ct. at 2121 (opinion of Kagan, J.).

43 *See id.* at 2131–48 (Gorsuch, J., dissenting).

44 *See id.* at 2130–31 (Alito, J., concurring in the judgment) ("If a majority of this Court were willing to reconsider the approach we have taken for the past 84 years, I would support that effort. But because a majority is not willing to do that, it would be freakish to single out the provision at issue here for special treatment.").

45 *See* Paul v. United States, 140 S. Ct. 342, 342 (2019) (Kavanaugh, J., statement respecting the denial of certiorari) (noting that "Justice Gorsuch's scholarly analysis of the Constitution's nondelegation doctrine in his *Gundy* dissent may warrant further consideration in future cases").

of the *Gundy* plurality.[46] Thus, while *Gundy* itself produced a 5–3 vote in favor of a no-nondelegation-problem affirmance, there now appear to be at least five (and perhaps six) votes in favor of reinvigorating the doctrine, most likely along the lines suggested by Justice Gorsuch's *Gundy* dissent.

Three features of that dissenting opinion bear emphasis here. The first is its heavily originalist orientation: Justice Gorsuch decried the modern-day nondelegation doctrine (and, by extension, the modern-day administrative state) as "at war with [the Constitution's] text and history,"[47] because, he contended, the Framers never intended to allow Congress to "announce vague aspirations and then assign others the responsibility of adopting legislation to realize its goals."[48] As many commentators have noted, however, Justice Gorsuch's originalist case for abandoning the present-day nondelegation doctrine is by no means airtight.[49] To be sure, the opinion offers much in the way of generalized, founding-era statements about "liberty" and the separation of powers.[50] But it is thin on specific evidence that the Framers would have disapproved

---

[46] Unlike Justice Kavanaugh, Justice Barrett has not, as of this writing, penned an opinion addressing the nondelegation doctrine. In her prior life as a legal academic, however, she once did endorse an approach to the nondelegation doctrine that was "more demanding" in relation to suspensions of habeas corpus than it was in connection with "the vast field of social and economic legislation in which the Necessary and Proper Clause gives Congress the authority to implement its Article I powers as it sees fit." *See* Amy Coney Barrett, *Suspension and Delegation*, 99 CORNELL L. REV. 251, 319 (2014). Thus, as Professor Lisa Heinzerling has noted, then-Professor Barrett seemed to "allude to the possibility that [the nondelegation principle] might permit a sliding-scale approach in which the Court's scrutiny becomes more intense in areas where 'the Constitution's allocating of authority reflects particular wariness of executive power.' " *See* Lisa Heinzerling, *Nondelegation on Stilts*, 29 N.Y.U. ENVTL. L.J. 379, 381 n.9 (2021) (quoting Barrett, *supra*, at 319).

[47] *Gundy*, 139 S. Ct. at 2131 (Gorsuch, J., dissenting).

[48] *Id.* at 2133. That sort of arrangement, Justice Gorsuch maintained, would have been anathema to the founding generation, which had exercised the "sovereign choice to vest the legislative power in Congress alone" and which had deliberately made the lawmaking process difficult so as to "protect their liberties, minority rights, fair notice, and the rule of law." *Id.* at 2135.

[49] *See, e.g.*, Kevin Arlyck, *Delegation, Administration, and Improvisation*, 97 NOTRE DAME L. REV. 243, 253 (2021) (noting that "the historical evidence [Justice Gorsuch] cited in *Gundy* does little to support his proposed version of nondelegation").

[50] *Gundy*, 139 S. Ct. at 2133 (citing to Chief Justice Marshall's opinion in *Wayman*, 23 U.S. at 42–43, for the proposition that the founding generation believed that "Congress may not 'delegate . . . powers which are strictly and exclusively legislative' " and citing to Madison's *Federalist No.* 47, for the proposition that "[t]here can be no liberty where the legislative and executive powers are united in the same person, or body of magistrates"). To be sure, Justice Gorsuch did note that "[j]udges and scholars representing a wide and diverse range of views have condemned [the requirement] as resting on 'misunderstood historical foundations,' " *id.* at 2139–40 (quoting *Ass'n of American Railroads*, 575 U.S. at 82 (Thomas, J., concurring in the judgment) (internal alterations omitted)), but he did not identify any primary sources that explicitly supported his suggestion that the intelligible-principle requirement itself reflects a departure from the Framers' views.

of the "intelligible principle" test itself, much less that they ever intended for the federal courts to aggressively police the size and powers of the administrative state.[51] Even assuming, moreover, that the relevant historical sources do in fact support Justice Gorsuch's position, the *Gundy* dissent does little to defend its operating methodological premise—namely, that eighteenth-century expectations about the role of agencies in federal governance under profoundly different circumstances ought to supplant the longstanding (and democratically-established) practices, understandings, and conventions that underlie the modern-day operation of the federal government.[52]

The second noteworthy feature of the *Gundy* dissent relates to its proposed alternative framework for evaluating nondelegation issues. Rather than having courts continue to apply the "intelligible principle" requirement in its "abused" modern-day form, Justice Gorsuch would have them rely on three "important guiding

---

[51] *Id.* at 2139. A lengthy historical argument against the position of the *Gundy* dissent (and indeed, against the basic tenets of the nondelegation doctrine more broadly) was recently set forth in Julian Davis Mortenson & Nicholas Bagley, *Delegation at the Founding*, 121 COLUM. L. REV. 277 (2021). *See also* Jerry L. Mashaw, *Recovering American Administrative Law: Federalist Foundations, 1787–1801*, 115 YALE L.J. 1256, 1295 (2006) (highlighting several examples of "broad delegations of authority" made by the early Congresses, "often to the President, but with full knowledge that his discretion would of necessity be sub-delegated to others"); Nicholas R. Parrillo, *A Critical Assessment of the Originalist Case Against Administrative Regulatory Power: New Evidence from the Federal Tax on Private Real Estate in the 1790s*, 130 YALE L.J. 1288, 1304 (2021) (drawing on the 1798 "direct tax" statute, which authorized regional boards of tax-commissioners to evaluate and adjust assessors' valuations of taxable property "as shall appear to be just and equitable," to rebut claims that the early Congresses' actions carry no broad implications for the nondelegation doctrine because its delegations of power all involved either foreign affairs or the administration of federal benefits and privileges). For contrary historical positions, see, e.g., Ilan Wurman, *Nondelegation at the Founding*, 130 YALE L.J. 1490, 1494, 1554 (2021) (contending that "[a]lthough the history is messy, there is significant evidence that the Founding generation adhered to a nondelegation doctrine, and little evidence that clearly supports the proposition that the Founding generation believed that Congress could freely delegate its legislative power," while also noting that the statutes of the First Congress "were not nearly as broad as recent scholars have claimed"); Aaron Gordon, *Nondelegation*, 12 N.Y.U. J.L. & LIBERTY 718, 729, 738 (2019) (gathering historical evidence from the Philadelphia Convention, the ratification debates, and the early Congresses in support of the contention that "grants of rulemaking power to agencies very often constitute delegations of legislative authority, and such delegations violate the Constitution"); and Gary Lawson, *Delegation and Original Meaning*, 88 VA. L. REV. 327, 398–403 (2002) (suggesting that the statutes of early Congresses "are at best weak evidence of original meaning" but that those statutes in any event did not "clearly vest legislative power in executive or judicial actors").

[52] In addition, one might criticize the dissent as proceeding from an impoverished conception of "individual liberty," which perceives the only potential threat to such liberty as stemming from government-based regulation of private conduct. Another view might be that liberty is also threatened by forms of private conduct that, if not adequately checked by a functioning administrative apparatus, would impair health, safety, financial security, and other key components of individual wellbeing.

principles" that, in his view, the Framers "offered."[53] First, although Congress may "authorize another branch to 'fill up the details' " of a statutory scheme, Justice Gorsuch would require that Congress alone can "make[ ] the policy decisions" underlying that scheme.[54] Second, while acknowledging that Congress may make the "application" of a rule regulating private conduct "depend on executive fact-finding," Justice Gorsuch would require that Congress "prescribe[ ] the rule" itself.[55] Finally, and in some tension with the first two principles, Justice Gorsuch *would* allow Congress to "confer[ ] wide discretion to the executive" in connection with Article II authorities "separately vest[ed]" in the executive branch, such as powers related to the military or foreign affairs.[56] These proposed guideposts, to be clear, have not (yet) received a formal sign-off from a majority of Justices. But they provide at least a rough approximation of what a revised nondelegation doctrine might well soon provide.

Finally, the *Gundy* dissent is noteworthy for the potentially transformative changes it presages for the federal administrative state.[57] Many areas of modern-day federal governance—on matters ranging from the environment to education to disease prevention to immigration and beyond—have arisen and evolved alongside the Court's traditionally deferential approach to reviewing congressional grants of authority to executive-branch agencies. A reinvigorated nondelegation doctrine would render those agencies' powers vulnerable to constitutional attacks—attacks that, if successful, would substantially compromise the ability of agencies to regulate the activities they oversee. Further raising the stakes of the issue is the reality that growing levels of paralysis and polarization in Congress might well render that institution unable to occupy the regulatory voids left behind by delegation-based nullifications of agency-empowering laws.[58] In other words, whatever the originalist

---

53 *Gundy*, 139 S. Ct. at 2135–36 (Gorsuch, J., dissenting).

54 *Id.* at 2136 (quoting *Wayman*, 23 U.S. at 31, 43).

55 *Id.* at 2136–37.

56 *Id.* at 2137 (citing, among other decisions, Youngstown Sheet & Tube Co. v. Sawyer, 343 U.S. 579, 635 (1952) (Jackson, J., concurring), and United States v. Curtiss-Wright Export Corp., 299 U.S. 304, 320 (1936)).

57 *See, e.g.*, Mortenson & Bagley, *supra* note 51, at 287 (noting that the Court's adoption of the *Gundy* dissent "could prove immensely destabilizing").

58 To take one example: If Congress is no longer able to task the EPA with specifying which particular types of chemical toxins (and at what particular concentrations) industrial actors are prohibited from emitting into the atmosphere, the upshot may be a regulatory landscape in which individuals are severely underprotected against the health hazards of air-pollution. In theory, of course, Congress could specify the types and levels on its own; in practice, however, the difficulty of reaching agreement on such particularities may mean that no such prohibitions are ever established in the first place. And even if a compromise is reached at Time 1, the emergence of a new, threatening toxin at Time 2 would require a whole new round of legislative action.

credentials of the position espoused by Justice Gorsuch's dissent, that position could—if applied with sufficient vigor—severely constrain the federal government's ability to deal with and respond to the complexities of the modern world. To be sure, the devil is in the details,[59] and much will depend on the extent to which the Court chooses to follow through on Justice Gorsuch's suggestions. But it is certainly possible that the *Gundy* dissent will eventually be seen as marking the beginning of a major—and potentially destabilizing—judicial reworking of the structure and operation of the federal executive branch.

C. AGENCY ADJUDICATION AND NON-ARTICLE III COURTS

A related set of constitutional questions surrounds Congress's authority to confer *adjudicative* powers on administrative agencies and other non-Article III actors. Although Article III requires that the "judicial Power of the United States" be exercised by judges with constitutional guarantees of (essentially) life tenure and salaries that cannot be "diminished" during their time in office,[60] Congress has nonetheless authorized a range of *agency* officials lacking in these protections to render judge-like, individualized determinations in connection with the statutes they administer.[61] In addition, Congress has created a range of specialized "courts"—such as the Tax Court, federal Bankruptcy Courts, and military courts martial—that act in

[59] For a skeptical assessment of the suggestion that the *Gundy* dissent presages the demise of the administrative state, see, e.g., Jonathan H. Adler & Christopher J. Walker, *Nondelegation for the Delegators*, REGULATION 14–15 (Spring 2020) (noting that "a nondelegation revival may target newly enacted outliers without doing much at all to curb those delegations that are already on the books").

[60] *See* U.S. CONST. art. III, § 1 (noting that "[t]he judges, both of the supreme and inferior courts, shall hold their Offices during good behaviour, and shall, at stated Times, receive for their Services, a Compensation, which shall not be diminished during their Continuance in Office").

[61] For example, administrative law judges (ALJs) within the U.S. Social Security Administration render thousands of decisions each year about individuals' eligibility for disability benefits under the federal Social Security Act, *see* JERRY L. MASHAW, BUREAUCRATIC JUSTICE: MANAGING SOCIAL SECURITY DISABILITY CLAIMS 18 (1983), ALJs within the National Labor Relations Board (in addition to the Board itself) render scores of annual decisions about employees' collective-bargaining rights (and related matters) under federal labor law, *see Administrative Law Judge Decisions*, NAT'L LABOR RELATIONS BOARD, https://www.nlrb.gov/cases-decisions/decisions/administrative-law-judge-decisions (last visited Oct. 31, 2021), and immigration judges within the U.S. Department of Justice render thousands of decisions each year about individuals' eligibility for asylum and related forms of relief under federal immigration law, *see* U.S. DEP'T OF JUSTICE EXEC. OFFICE FOR IMMIGRATION REVIEW, STATISTICS YEARBOOK: FISCAL YEAR 2018 (2019) (noting that immigration judges within the Justice Department's Office for Executive Office for Immigration Review adjudicated some 200,000 removal-related cases in 2018). *See generally* Christopher J. Walker & Melissa F. Wasserman, *The New World of Agency Adjudication*, 107 CAL. L. REV. 141, 153–57 (2019) (offering an overview of modern-day agency adjudication).

a judicial role while lacking Article III status.[62] The upshot of these arrangements is that a large volume of federal adjudicative work is today performed by institutions outside the Article III apparatus.[63] And that fact stands in some tension with the Constitution's vesting of the federal judicial power in the "judicial" rather than "executive" branch.

Nevertheless, the Court has recognized that Congress possesses substantial, though not absolute, authority to authorize adjudication outside of Article III. Several of the relevant decisions—particularly with respect to non-Article III-based territorial courts,[64] non-Article III based local courts for the District of Columbia,[65] and non-Article III courts martial (and other military tribunals)[66]—can be

---

[62] *See* ANDREW NOLAN & RICHARD M. THOMPSON II, CONG. RSCH. SERV., R43746, CONGRESSIONAL POWER TO CREATE FEDERAL COURTS: A LEGAL OVERVIEW 12 (2015) (highlighting several examples of non-Article III courts), *available at* https://crsreports.congress.gov/product/pdf/R/R43746.

[63] Indeed, the upshot of current constitutional doctrine is that "most federal adjudication occurs outside the Article III courts." F. Andrew Hessick, *Consenting to Adjudication Outside the Article III Courts*, 71 VAND. L. REV. 715, 716 (2018); *see also* William Baude, *Adjudication Outside Article III*, 133 HARV. L. REV. 1511, 1516 (2020) (noting that if recognized forms of non-Article III adjudication "are unlawful, then much of what we accept today as the law of federal jurisdiction is unlawful").

[64] *See* American Ins. Co. v. 356 Bales of Cotton, 26 U.S. 511, 545 (1828) (Marshall, C.J.) (reasoning that territorial courts are "legislative Courts" whose jurisdiction is "not a part of that judicial power . . . defined in the 3d article of the Constitution"). For criticisms of the Chief Justice's opinion in this case (which is more commonly referred to as *American Insurance Co. v. Canter*), see, e.g., Gary Lawson, *Territorial Governments and the Limits of Formalism*, 78 CAL. L. REV. 853, 892 (1990) (emphasizing that "Marshall offered no substantial support for his assertion that article III does not apply to the territories"). *But see* Baude, *supra* note 62, at 1527–33, 1533 (suggesting that territorial courts are not governed by Article III because they merely "exercise the judicial power of their respective territories" rather than the "judicial power of the United States" and that territorial courts "therefore fall outside of Article III for the same textual reason that state courts do").

[65] *See, e.g.*, Palmore v. United States, 411 U.S. 389, 410 (1973); *see also* Stephen I. Vladeck, *Military Courts and Article III*, 103 GEO. L.J. 933, 972 (2015) (noting that "*Canter* was at the heart of" the Court's reasoning in *Palmore*). *But see* James Durling, *The District of Columbia and Article III*, 107 GEO. L.J. 1205, 1241–44 (2019) (suggesting that the early Congresses' divergent treatment of court systems in the District of Columbia and the federal territories lends support to the proposition that D.C. courts should be governed by Article III).

[66] *See also* Northern Pipeline Constr. Co. v. Marathon Pipe Line, 458 U.S. 50, 66 (1982) (opinion of Brennan, J.) (suggesting that the legitimacy of courts martial (and other military tribunals) "strongly resembles the situation with respect to territorial courts" in that it is supported by an Article I power that "has been historically understood as giving the political Branches of Government extraordinary control over the precise subject matter at issue"); Ortiz v. United States, 138 S. Ct. 2165, 2175–76 (2021) (noting that "the constitutional foundation of courts-martial . . . is not in the least insecure"); *see also* Stern v. Marshall, 564 U.S. 462, 504–05 (2011) (Scalia, J., concurring) (articulating the view that "an Article III judge is required in all federal adjudications, unless there is a firmly established historical practice to the contrary" and acquiescing to the legitimacy of military courts on this basis). For a recounting of the relevant history, see generally David A. Schlueter, *The Court-Martial: An Historical Survey*, 87 MIL. L. REV. 129, 145–55 (1980).

straightforwardly summarized as involving specialized applications of legislative powers that the court has long described as unusually plenary in character. Other aspects of the case law, however, are considerably more difficult to explain and/or describe.[67]

Especially noteworthy in this respect is the Court's long-running suggestion, dating back to its 1856 decision in *Murray's Lessee v. Hoboken Land & Improvement Co.*,[68] that Congress may authorize non-Article III adjudication of claims that involve "public" as opposed to "private" rights. The central difficulty here has been the Court's ever-shifting understanding of what constitutes a "public right" and why Congress may assign claims regarding such rights to non-Article III adjudicators. For example, the Court has sometimes characterized "public rights" as rights that an individual holds *against the federal government directly*—rights, that is, that Congress may validly assign to non-Article III courts by way of a conditional or partial waiver of the federal government's otherwise-applicable sovereign immunity to suit.[69] In recent decades, however,

---

[67] For a useful attempt to work through the difficulties, see generally Baude, *supra* note 62. For more on military tribunals, see *supra* Section 28.B.2.

[68] 59 U.S. (18 How.) 272, 284 (1856) (noting that "there are matters, involving *public rights*, . . . which congress may or may not bring within the cognizance of the courts of the United States, as it may deem proper"). For a detailed overview of *Murray's Lessee*, see generally James E. Pfander & Andrew Borrasso, *Public Rights and Article III: Judicial Oversight of Agency Action*, 82 OHIO ST. L.J. 493, 532–39 (2021) (contending that the Court in *Murray's Lessee* decided less than has traditionally been supposed and that, far from recognizing a broad new category of "public rights" claims amenable to non-Article III resolution, it merely weighed in on the appropriateness of pursuing certain types of executive actions prior to an exercise of Article III review). *See also* JAMES E. PFANDER, ONE SUPREME COURT: SUPREMACY, INFERIORITY, AND THE JUDICIAL POWER OF THE UNITED STATES 115 (2009) (suggesting that *Murray's Lessee* is best read not as a wide-reaching invitation to Congress to place large categories of "public rights" matters beyond the reach of Article III courts, but instead as "affirming the Court's power to deploy Article III and established common-law remedies to preserve the individual's right to a judicial contest of government exactions").

[69] In particular, the argument goes, the federal government's greater power to resist altogether suits brought against it in federal court implies a lesser power to consent to such suits on the condition that they be adjudicated outside of the Article III apparatus. *See Ex parte* Bakelite Corp., 279 U.S. 438, 452 (1929) (holding that "Congress may attach to its consent such conditions as it deems proper, even to requiring that the suits be brought in a legislative court specially created to consider them"); *see also Northern Pipeline*, 458 U.S. at 67–68 (opinion of Brennan, J.) (noting that the public-rights exception "may be explained in part by reference to the traditional principle of sovereign immunity, which recognizes that the Government may attach conditions to its consent to be sued"); Granfinanciera v. Nordberg, 492 U.S. 33, 68 (1989) (Scalia, J., concurring in part and concurring in the judgment) ("[W]hat we meant by public rights [in *Murray's Lessee*] were not rights important to the public, or rights created by the public, but rights *of the public*—that is, rights pertaining to claims brought by or against the United States."); *cf.* Oil States Energy Servs., Inc. v. Greene's Energy Grp., LLC, 138 S. Ct. 1365, 1373 (2018) (affirming Congress's power under the public-rights exception to provide for the non-Article III-based *inter partes* review of patents previously issued by the U.S. Patent and Trademark Office, on the theory that such disputes concern a matter "aris[ing] between the government and

the Court has extended the exception to cover some purely private-party cases, with the Justices more broadly suggesting that a public-rights case is one in which "the claim at issue derives from a federal regulatory scheme, or in which resolution of the claim by an expert Government agency is deemed essential to a limited regulatory objective within the agency's authority."[70] On this account of the "public rights" exception, Congress may authorize non-Article III adjudication of claims as an incident of its statutory power to establish complex regulatory schemes and "essential" agency processes.[71] (Consider, for instance, Congress's heavy reliance on non-Article III "Bankruptcy Courts" to administer the complex array of federal statutory rules concerning the liquidation and distribution of assets in a bankruptcy proceedings.)[72] But it may not do the same

---

persons subject to its authority in connection with the performance of the constitutional functions of the executive or legislative departments" (internal quotations and citations omitted)). *But see id.* at 1378 n.5 (conceding that such disputes do not implicate any waiver of the government's sovereign immunity).

[70] *Stern*, 564 U.S. at 490.

[71] This theory too involves a greater-includes-the-lesser type of logic: More specifically, so the argument goes, Congress's greater power to create rights by statute encompasses a lesser power to involve non-Article III actors in the adjudicative aspects of those rights' implementation. *Cf.* Thomas v. Union Carbide Agric. Prods. Inc., 473 U.S. 568, 589 (1985) (noting that "Congress has the power, under Article I, to authorize an agency administering a complex regulatory scheme to allocate costs and benefits among voluntary participants in the program without providing an Article III adjudication"). This position, however, raises difficulties. For one thing, the "public rights are federal rights" position fails to account for the Court's occasional willingness in the public-rights context to treat the federal-law status of a claim as one of "a number of factors, none of which has been deemed determinative," that must be considered by reference to "the practical effect that the congressional action will have on the constitutionally assigned role of the federal judiciary." Commodities Futures Trading Corp. v. Schor, 478 U.S. 833, 851 (1986); *see also Thomas*, 473 U.S. at 589 (suggesting that the exception captures the "pragmatic" idea that "when Congress selects a quasi-judicial method of resolving matters that 'could be conclusively determined by the Executive and Legislative Branches,' the danger of encroaching on the judicial powers is reduced" (quoting *Northern Pipeline*, 458 U.S. at 68 (opinion of Brennan, J.))). In addition, that position likely overstates the scope of the exception in that the Court has never suggested that the federal-law status of a claim automatically suffices to justify adjudication by a non-Article III-forum, perhaps for fear that a general equating of federal rights with public rights would render the exception so broad as to swallow the Article III rule, *see, e.g.*, Kent Barnett, *Due Process for Article III—Rethinking* Murray's Lessee, 26 GEO. MASON L. REV. 677, 684 (2019) (noting that "if Congress can evade Article III whenever it has the substantive authority to regulate, Article III becomes a dead letter"), and it is in any event difficult to reconcile with Article III's stipulation that the "judicial Power of the United States" extends to "*all Cases* . . . arising under . . . the Laws of the United States," U.S. CONST. art. III, § 2 (emphasis added).

[72] *But see Stern*, 564 U.S. at 488 (finding that the public-rights exception did not authorize a non-Article III bankruptcy court to adjudicate a state-law counterclaim involving tortious interference); *Granfinanciera*, 492 U.S. at 56 (concluding that the exception did not authorize non-Article III adjudication of a fraudulent-conveyance claim arising out of a federal bankruptcy proceeding because "fraudulent conveyance actions by bankruptcy trustees . . . are quintessentially suits at common law that more nearly resemble state-law contract claims").

with respect to "the stuff of . . . traditional actions at common law tried by the courts at Westminster in 1789."[73] (Consider, for instance, a Bankruptcy Court's adjudication of a state-law breach-of-contract claim that arises in connection with the underlying bankruptcy proceeding.)[74]

The slippery contours of the public-rights exception exist alongside two other long-recognized (but equally muddled) propositions about non-Article III adjudication. First, in the New Deal-era case of *Crowell v. Benson*,[75] the Court allowed agency adjudication of a *private-rights* claim by pointing to the availability of after-the-fact Article III review.[76] According to this line of reasoning, Congress may permissibly empower non-Article III tribunals to operate as adjuncts to the Article III courts, provided that the review mechanism itself preserves for the Article III court the "essential attributes of the judicial power."[77] Second, initially in *Commodities Futures Trading Comm'n. v. Schor*,[78] and then more

---

[73] *Stern*, 564 U.S. at 484 (quoting *Northern Pipeline*, 458 U.S. at 90 (Rehnquist, J., concurring in the judgment)).

[74] *See, e.g.*, *Northern Pipeline*, 458 U.S. at 69–72 (opinion of Brennan, J.) (deeming the public-rights exception inapplicable to a state-law breach-of-contract claim arising in connection with a bankruptcy proceeding).

[75] 285 U.S. 22 (1932).

[76] *Id.* at 60.

[77] *Id.* at 51, 60–62 (noting that the agency's decisions were final only with respect to factual determinations that were not "fundamental" or "jurisdictional" in nature and that "[i]n cases brought to enforce constitutional rights, the judicial power of the United States necessarily extends to the independent determination of all questions, both of fact and law, necessary to the performance of that supreme function"). The adjunct theory (and its underlying "essential attributes" test) rests in uneasy relation to the long-established principle that courts should defer to agencies' reasonable constructions of ambiguous terms in their respective enabling statutes. *See* Chevron v. Nat. Res. Def. Council, Inc., 467 U.S. 837 (1984). Critics of "*Chevron* deference" have argued that the rule infringes on the federal courts' judicial power by according to executive-branch agencies interpretive primacy on questions concerning the meaning of the statutes they administer. *See, e.g.*, Gutierrez-Brizuela v. Lynch, 834 F.3d 1142, 1153 (10th Cir. 2016) (Gorsuch, J., concurring) (contending that, under *Chevron*, "*courts* are not fulfilling their duty to interpret the law and declare invalid agency actions inconsistent with those interpretations in the cases and controversies that come before them" (emphasis in original)). But a more targeted critique of the practice—focused specifically on courts' use of *Chevron* deference when reviewing agency adjudications—might stem from *Crowell* instead. If, as the Court would later put it, *Crowell* merely permits non-Article III actors "to make specialized, narrowly confined *factual* determinations regarding a particularized area of law" that are not subject to independent judicial review, *see Stern*, 564 U.S. at 489 n.6 (emphasis added), then any deference afforded to an agency adjudicator on a question of law would have the effect of rendering that adjudicator something more than an adjunct. *See* Christopher J. Walker, *Constitutional Tensions in Agency Adjudication*, 104 IOWA L. REV. 2679, 2692 (2019) (noting that, under *Stern*'s description of the "essential attributes" test, "it appears that *Chevron* deference would no longer be available for legal interpretations adopted" in an agency adjudication).

[78] 478 U.S. 833, 848 (1986).

recently in *Wellness International Network Inc. v. Sharif*,[79] the Court has held that "[t]he entitlement to an Article III adjudicator is a 'personal right' and thus ordinarily 'subject to waiver.' "[80] In other words, the Court in these cases indicated that individual litigants can often (though not necessarily always) *consent* to forms of adjudication that the Constitution would otherwise disallow.[81] Both of these theories raise vexing questions of their own—the Court has long struggled to articulate, for instance, what qualifies as an "essential attribute of the judicial power" under *Crowell*,[82] and both *Schor* and *Wellness International* are murky with respect to defining the non-"ordinary" circumstances in which the presumption of waivability is overridden.[83] The bigger picture point, however, is that both lines of decision, particularly when understood in connection with the "public rights" cases, afford Congress substantial discretion to place adjudicative responsibilities in the hands of administrative agencies and other non-Article III actors.[84]

---

79 575 U.S. 665 (2015).

80 *Id.* at 678 (quoting *Schor*, 478 U.S. at 848).

81 *See generally* Hessick, *supra* note 62 (highlighting and critiquing this line of cases).

82 Thus, for instance, a plurality of justices in *Northern Pipeline* found the adjunct theory inadequate to justify the federal bankruptcy courts' resolution of certain private-rights claims, reasoning that while Congress had "substantial discretion" to "assign[] to an adjunct [] some functions historically performed by judges," the substantial powers exercised by the bankruptcy courts were enough to deprive their Article III counterparts of the "essential attributes" to which they were entitled. 458 U.S. at 80 (opinion of Brennan, J.) (distinguishing *Crowell* on the grounds that (1) the subject-matter jurisdiction of the bankruptcy courts encompassed far more than "specialized, narrowly confined factual determinations regarding a particularized area of law"; (2) the bankruptcy courts engaged in more than just "factfinding functions" because in they actually "exercis[ed] *all* of the jurisdiction conferred by the Act on the district courts"; (3) the bankruptcy courts enjoyed "all ordinary powers of district courts" rather than a more "limited power to issue compensation orders pursuant to specialized procedures"; (4) judgments of the bankruptcy courts were "apparently subject to review only under the . . . clearly erroneous standard"; and (5) the bankruptcy courts' orders were "binding and enforceable even in the absence of an appeal" (internal quotations omitted)); *see also Stern*, 564 U.S. at 500–01 (noting that a bankruptcy court "can no more be deemed a mere 'adjunct' of the district court than a district court can be deemed such an 'adjunct' of the court of appeals").

83 Particularly confusing in this respect was the Court's suggestion in *Wellness International* that "allowing Article I adjudicators to decide claims submitted to them by consent does not offend the separation of powers *so long as Article III courts retain supervisory authority over the process*," *Wellness International*, 575 U.S. at 678 (emphasis added)—a suggestion that seemed to elide the waivability question at issue in that case with the *Crowell*-based question whether the presence of Article III supervision suffices to create a permissible "adjunct" arrangement. *Cf.* Aziz Z. Huq & Jon D. Michaels, *Cycles of Separation of Powers Jurisprudence*, 126 YALE L.J. 346, 371 (2016) (noting that the Court in *Wellness International* "reached across domains, citing and centrally relying on precedent from the agency adjudication context that . . . employed a much more flexible standard" than the Court's prior cases).

84 Conversely, the Court also has suggested that Congress may sometimes place *nonjudicial* responsibilities in the hands of Article III actors. *See* Mistretta v. United States, 488 U.S. 361, 404 (1989) (finding no separation-of-powers problem in the

D. CONGRESS'S POWERS OF AGENCY SUPERVISION AND OVERSIGHT

Suppose that Congress, having previously created and bestowed power on an agency, has become dissatisfied with the agency's work. How might federal lawmakers respond?

1. Superseding Legislation

As a "creature of statute," an administrative agency possesses "only those authorities conferred upon it by Congress."[85] Thus, any power Congress has given to an agency is also a power that Congress can take away. For instance, if the EPA promulgates a new air-quality standard that Congress opposes, Congress can revise the Clean Air Act to specify that the new air quality standard is no longer operative. If Congress more broadly disapproves of the EPA's performance in promulgating air-quality standards, it can go further and reassign the task to a different agency or simply reclaim for itself the power to set those standards directly. Indeed, were Congress to become particularly disquieted by the EPA's actions, it could simply abolish the agency altogether. Other possibilities also exist: Congress might, for instance, require the agency to follow a more rigorous set of procedures when promulgating air-quality standards; it might impose new substantive limits on what sorts of air-quality standards are permissible; or it might empower another agency to veto the EPA's air-quality standards by reference to congressionally established criteria. These and other forms of redress all lie within Congress's reach.[86]

Congress, however, often confronts a practical problem when attempting to check agency action by enacting Article I statutes. The difficulty is that agencies operate within the executive branch, which is overseen by the President, and therefore tend to act in ways that align with the President's agenda. That in turn means that the President, who holds the veto power, will typically have no interest

---

structure of the U.S. Sentencing Commission, which promulgates the U.S. Sentencing Guidelines and which includes among its members Article III judges; reasoning more broadly that "the principle of separation of powers does not absolutely prohibit Article III judges from serving on commissions" of this sort while cautioning that not "every kind of extrajudicial service under every circumstance necessarily accords with the Constitution").

85 Atlantic City Elec. Co. v. FERC, 295 F.3d 1, 8 (D.C. Cir. 2002) (internal quotations and citations omitted).

86 *See* Eric A. Posner & Adrian Vermeule, *Interring the Nondelegation Doctrine*, 69 U. CHI. L. REV. 1721, 1752–53 (2002) (noting, with illustrative examples, Congress's ability to enact laws that "reverse the decisions of agencies," "weaken their powers," "abolish whole agencies," "confine [agency] discretion," and "give interest groups the ability to alert Congress when the agency goes astray").

in undoing those agencies' policy choices.[87] Put simply, if Congress seeks to enact legislation that would nullify agency action the President endorses, then it will need to muster a veto-overriding supermajoritarian consensus that, on any matter of consequence, is highly unlikely to materialize.[88]

Another practical impediment to statute-based oversight of agency action is the Senate filibuster, which today operates to impose a *de facto* 60-vote threshold for the enactment of most federal legislation and which can thus stymie forms of legislative action that have the support of the President, the House, and a majority (but not supermajority) of the Senate.[89] Under a limited set of circumstances, however, Congress may sidestep the filibuster by invoking a 1996 statute, the Congressional Review Act (CRA),[90] which establishes a filibuster-proof procedure for Senate passage of any "resolution of disapproval" that targets a recent "major rule" of a federal administrative agency.[91] In addition, for legislators seeking to undo

---

[87] This point applies most forcefully where the relevant agency is subject to direct presidential control. Independent agencies, by contrast, might sometimes pursue policies that *both* the President and Congress oppose, thus eliminating the Article I presentment requirement as an obstacle to superseding legislation.

[88] *See* William N. Eskridge, Jr. & John Ferejohn, *The Article I, Section 7 Game*, 80 GEO. L.J. 523, 534–40 (1992) (highlighting this point). Even so, congressional majorities are sometimes able to exert their will, even in the face of presidential resistance. For example, most agencies receive funding from Congress through the enactment of annual appropriations statutes, *see* U.S. CONST. art. I, § 7 (providing that "[n]o Money shall be drawn from the Treasury, but in Consequence of Appropriations made by Law"), and while appropriations bills remain subject to the Article I presentment requirement, they often reach the President's desk with a "must-pass" character that can effectively force the President to stomach some unwanted restrictions on agency action. *See* Zachary S. Price, *Funding Restrictions and Separation of Powers*, 71 VAND. L. REV. 357, 367 (2018) ("Through the ingenious practice, begun with the very first Congress, of appropriating funds only one year at a time, Congress has ensured that presidents must always come back every year seeking money just to keep the government's lights on."); *see also id.* at 368 (noting that "the president's ability to advance his own agenda is constantly beholden to Congress's willingness to fund it, and Congress accordingly holds ongoing leverage over executive policy"). *But see id.* (noting that some past Presidents have "succeeded in laying blame for appropriations lapses . . . on their congressional adversaries," thus changing the overall bargaining dynamic in the President's favor). In addition, as Professor Jack Beerman has noted, the omnibus nature of appropriations bills, coupled with special congressional processes for the insertion of "riders" into such bills, might sometimes enable members of Congress to impose restrictions on agency action that "fly below the political radar." *See* Jack M. Beerman, *Congressional Administration*, 43 SAN DIEGO L. REV. 61, 88–89 (2006).

[89] *See supra* Section 14.A.

[90] *See* 5 U.S.C. §§ 801 et seq.

[91] *See id.* § 801; *see also* Note, *The Mysteries of the Congressional Review Act*, 122 HARV. L. REV. 2162, 2168 (2009) (noting that the statute "prohibits filibusters of disapproval resolutions in the Senate, setting time limits for debate and eliminating many procedural hurdles"). Why, one might ask, would a CRA resolution prove necessary when the President already opposes an agency's regulatory initiative? If, after all, the President opposes the regulatory initiative, the President could simply order the agency not to pursue it and thus obviate the need for any CRA resolution at

a recently-promulgated agency regulation, a CRA resolution carries with it the added benefit of not just canceling the targeted regulation but also barring the promulgation of any *future rules* that are "substantially the same" as the one that Congress has undone.[92] Congress can thus deploy the statute, so long as it has presidential support, to channel power back to itself to deal with the specific subjects that the disapproved rule purported to address.[93]

2. The Legislative Veto and *INS v. Chadha*

Given the practical constraints imposed by the complexities of the Article I lawmaking process, it is not surprising that Congress has experimented with agency-checking devices that do not require

---

all. This indeed will often be the case, and it helps to explain why Congress's invocations of the CRA are relatively infrequent. Under some circumstances, however, Presidents will have reason to rely on the CRA. Most importantly, a newly inaugurated President may call on Congress to use the CRA to undo last-minute regulatory actions undertaken by the predecessor administration. *See* Bethany A. Davis Noll & Richard L. Revesz, *Regulation in Transition*, 104 MINN. L. REV. 1, 19–21 (2019) (noting the Trump Administration's heavy reliance on the CRA to secure legislative override of many Obama-era regulatory initiatives). In addition, use of the CRA might be appealing to Presidents seeking to undo rules issued by "independent agencies"—that is, agencies whose actions the President is unable directly to control. *See id.* at 20 n.89 (noting this possibility). Finally, as noted below, a statutory invocation of the CRA differs from an executive rescission of a rule in that only the former has the effect of preventing the agency from subsequently enacting the rule or any other rule that is "substantially the same." *See infra* note 92 and accompanying text.

92 *See* 5 U.S.C. § 801(b)(2). For an examination of the courts' role in enforcing this "substantially the same" requirement, see, e.g., Michael J. Cole, *Interpreting the Congressional Review Act: Why the Courts Should Assert Judicial Review, Narrowly Construe "Substantially the Same," and Decline to Defer to Agencies Under* Chevron, 70 ADMIN L. REV. 53, 77–104 (2018).

93 Republicans in Congress have recently pushed for the enactment of another statute that would dramatically enhance Congress's ability to deny effect to unwanted agency regulations. The proposed "REINS Act" would essentially flip the CRA on its head, by providing that no "major rule" of an administrative action would take effect unless "approve[d]" by joint resolution. *See* Regulations from the Executive In Need of Scrutiny, S.68, 117th Cong. (2021). In effect, that is, the statute would require affirmative consent from Congress and the President (or supermajorities of each House) as a precondition to any "major rule" taking effect. For a debate over the constitutionality of the REINS Act, compare Bill Funk, *Why the REINS Act Is Unconstitutional*, CPRBLOG (Feb. 14, 2017), https://progressivereform.org/cpr-blog/why-the-reins-act-is-unconstitutional (contending that the REINS Act violates the separation of powers by empowering Congress to "approve" a rule rather than enact new law of its own), with Jonathan R. Siegel, *The REINS Act and the Struggle to Control Agency Rulemaking*, 16 LEG. & PUB. POL'Y 131, 171 (2014) (noting that, while "[t]he REINS Act would be a very substantial departure from current arrangements . . . it would not represent an assertion of too much power by Congress"). Whatever uncertainty there might be about the REINS Act's constitutionality, there is little doubt that the statute, if enacted, would have a seismic impact on administrative governance. Requiring explicit congressional approval of any "major" agency action will in many instances be effectively the same thing as disempowering the agency from pursuing such action in the first place, and the adoption of the REINS Act would thus amount to an across-the-board revocation of large swaths of agency rulemaking authority.

bicameral agreement and presidential approval. The most well-known mechanism of this sort, known as the "legislative veto," works this way: Congress, while conferring power on an administrative agency, also reserves to each of its Houses (or to both Houses together, or to one or more legislative committees) the power to overturn any particular exercise of that power, thus eliminating the need to enact a full-blown statute under Article I. The idea, in other words, is for Congress by statute to delegate to itself (or a part of itself) the power to override the relevant agency decision.

In a landmark case from 1983, however, the Court held that legislative-veto arrangements of this sort violate the separation of powers. *INS v. Chadha*[94] concerned the Immigration and Nationality Act, which, subject to certain exceptions, authorized the Attorney General to "suspend deportation" of certain persons otherwise deportable under federal law, while reserving to either House of Congress the authority to override the Attorney General's decision.[95] In effect, the statute put in place a three-step process: First, a lower-level immigration official would identify an individual as subject to deportation under the substantive terms of the INA. Second, the individual would apply to the Attorney General for a suspension of deportation, which the Attorney General could then "in his discretion" choose to grant.[96] Finally, if the Attorney General granted the application, either House of Congress could veto the Attorney General's decision and require that the deportation move forward.[97]

Why did Congress design this scheme in this way? In a nutshell, it was attempting to qualify the generally applicable rules governing deportation determinations with a process that facilitated the waiver of those rules on a case-by-case basis. In earlier times, Congress had achieved this result by way of a "private bill" procedure, through which it would enact full-fledged, Article I-compliant statutes that exempted named individuals from deportation. This practice, however, proved unwieldly, leading Congress to transfer this authority to the Attorney General.[98] As it did so, however, Congress also sought to retain a continued role in the process, and it achieved this result by empowering each of its two chambers to block any suspension order that the Attorney General issued. The overall arrangement thus reflected a compromise: Congress would give to an

94 462 U.S. 919 (1983).

95 *Id.* at 924–26.

96 *See id.* at 923 (quoting 8 U.S.C. § 1254(a)(1)).

97 *Id.* at 925 (quoting 8 U.S.C. § 1254(c)(2)).

98 *See* David J. Barron & Todd D. Rakoff, *In Defense of Big Waiver*, 113 COLUM. L. REV. 265, 289 (2013) (noting that the statutory provisions at issue in *Chadha* had been passed by Congress in an effort "to spare itself the burden of passing private bills to suspend deportations").

executive-branch actor (namely, the Attorney General) a broad set of powers previously exercised by Congress alone but only on the condition that those powers became subject to a workably nimble method of legislative review.[99]

In *Chadha*, however, the Court ruled that that this was not a compromise that Article I allowed. According to Chief Justice Burger, who wrote for himself and five colleagues, the INA's veto procedures called for an exercise of "legislative power" because it involved "action that ha[s] the purpose and effect of altering the legal rights, duties and relations of persons."[100] The problem, he continued, was that any exercise of the "legislative power" had to satisfy the twin constitutional requirements of joint action by the House and the Senate (i.e., "bicameralism") and submission to the President for a signature or veto (i.e., "presentment"),[101] and the INA's legislative veto satisfied neither. Instead, it permitted a *unicameral* override of suspension orders by *either* the House *or* the Senate, and it allowed that override to take effect without any presidential involvement at

---

99 *Cf. Chadha*, 462 U.S. at 968 (White, J., dissenting).

100 *Id.* at 952 (majority opinion). By singling out actions of this sort, the Court in *Chadha* signaled that Congress could continue to rely on non-Article I procedures to pursue various forms of non-binding action. *See also id.* at 952 ("Not every action taken by either House is subject to the bicameralism and presentment requirements of Art. I."). Thus, for instance, the Court's holding in *Chadha* does not preclude either House of Congress from forgoing bicameralism and presentment when passing nonbinding resolutions that simply express its approval or disapproval of a given executive action, so long as those resolutions do not actually compel anyone to do anything. *Cf.* Thomas M. Franck & Clifford A. Bob, *The Return of Humpty-Dumpty: Foreign Relations Law After the* Chadha *Case*, 79 AM. J. INT'L L. 912, 935 (1985) (noting that *Chadha* "could be interpreted as having converted the numerous legislative veto provisions into nonbinding sense of Congress resolutions"). Nor for that matter did the Court purport to question the power of either House to make rules for its own proceeding, *see* U.S. CONST. art. I, § 5, without satisfying the bicameralism and presentment requirements of Article I, section 7. *See Chadha*, 462 U.S. at 955 n.21 ("Each House has the power to act alone in determining specified internal matters."). A lingering conceptual difficulty concerns the relationship between *Chadha*'s "rights, duties and relations" formulation and the investigative powers of congressional committees. The Court in *Chadha* maintained that its "internal matters" exception "only empowers Congress to bind itself." *Id.* But congressional committees routinely issue subpoenas that "command the presence of witnesses" and "attach consequences to their failure to cooperate." Peter L. Strauss, *Was There a Baby in the Bathwater? A Comment on the Supreme Court's Legislative Veto Decision*, 1983 DUKE L.J. 789, 795. In this one sense, at least, the individual Houses of Congress have continued to alter the "private rights, duties, and obligations" of individuals outside the Article I lawmaking process, and no court has held that *Chadha* requires otherwise. *See generally supra* Section 14.C. *But see infra* Section 33.A (highlighting various separation-of-powers based restrictions on Congress's ability to demand information from (and/or pertaining to) the President and other executive-branch actors). But why precisely this is the case remains unclear—that is, on the logic of *Chadha* itself, the issuance of an investigative subpoena would seem to be just as much an exercise of "legislative power" than any other legislative act. *See* Strauss, *supra*, at 796 (noting that subpoenas and other investigative actions are "not readily distinguished from the legislative veto on the formal grounds the Court chose").

101 *See* U.S. CONST. art. I, § 7.

all. As a result, Congress had failed to abide by the "single, finely wrought and exhaustively considered, procedure" that Article I required it to use.[102]

The majority's reasoning in *Chadha* thus rested on a simple syllogism: Article I requires Congress to legislate in only one way; Congress tried to legislate in a different way; therefore, Congress violated Article I. Who could argue with that? One person who did was Justice White, who attacked the majority's reasoning as frustratingly formalistic. To begin with, Justice White questioned the Chief Justice's major premise—namely, that the issuance of the legislative veto involves an exercise of the legislative power.[103] For Justice White, that assertion did not hold water because there existed a world of difference between *creating new legislation where none existed before* (a genuine exercise of the "legislative power") and *exercising a power granted by already-enacted legislation* (which simply implements an exercise of the legislative power that previously and properly occurred).[104] In addition, Justice White

---

[102] *Chadha*, 462 U.S. at 951. Concurring in the judgment, Justice Powell expressed "hesitan[ce] to conclude that every veto is unconstitutional on the basis of the unusual example presented by this litigation." *Id.* at 960 n.1 (Powell, J., concurring in the judgment). In particular, Powell reasoned, the law at issue in *Chadha* was "unusual" because, by permitting one House of Congress to override the Attorney General's decision to suspend a deportation—an action that in and of itself had very little to do with the traditionally legislative business of "prescrib[ing] rules of general applicability"—the INA had invalidly empowered the legislative branch to perform a "judicial function" exclusively reserved to the courts under Article III. *Id.* at 963, 966. But Justice Powell stood alone in this view. Indeed, Chief Justice Burger explicitly rejected this line of reasoning, contending that any "attempted analogy between judicial action and the one-House veto is less than perfect" because "[f]ederal courts do not enjoy a roving mandate to correct alleged excesses of administrative agencies." *Id.* at 957 n.22 (majority opinion); *see also id.* at 1001 (White, J., dissenting) (maintaining that the statute did not "infringe on the judicial power" because "[c]ongressional action does not substitute for judicial review of the Attorney General's decisions").

[103] *See id.* at 980 ("The power to exercise a legislative veto is not the power to write new law without bicameral approval or presidential consideration.").

[104] A related complication raised by the legislative-power characterization was this: According to Chief Justice Burger, Congress exercised "legislative power" when vetoing suspension orders under the INA. *Id.* at 952. But if that was true, then it would seem to follow that the Attorney General had similarly (and impermissibly) exercised legislative power when issuing such orders in the first place. The Court, however, rejected that conclusion, contending instead that the Attorney General's suspension of deportations constituted an "executive action under legislatively delegated authority" that merely "resemble[d] 'legislative' action in some respects." *Id.* at 953 n.16. But this conclusion raised a major problem of its own. It was as if, as Professor Laurence Tribe has put the point, "the mere fact of statutory delegation obviates the need for formal classification of the power delegated when the recipient of such power is *outside* the legislative branch, while the fact of delegation somehow becomes irrelevant in assessing an exercise of delegated power by part of the legislative branch itself." Laurence H. Tribe, *The Legislative Veto Decision: A Law by Any Other Name*, 21 HARV. J. ON LEGIS. 1, 10 (1984). An alternative possibility would have been to characterize the legislative veto as an invalid exercise of *executive* power by the legislative branch. *See* Bowsher v. Synar, 478 U.S. 714, 736 (1986) (noting "the command of the Constitution that the Congress play no direct role in the execution of the laws"); *see*

challenged the majority's claim that its holding was necessary "to preserve freedom . . . by making the exercise of power subject to the carefully crafted restraints spelled out in the Constitution."[105] Indeed, he argued, far from "preserv[ing] freedom," the majority's ruling threatened to exacerbate the risk of liberty-abridging executive overreach. Why? Because if, as the majority itself had put it, Congress could only exercise agency oversight through procedures that were "clumsy, inefficient, even unworkable,"[106] then Congress would in effect lack the ability to check "the unavoidably expanding power of the agencies."[107]

---

also Metropolitan Wash. Airports Auth. v. Citizens for the Abatement of Aircraft Noise, 501 U.S. 252, 254 (1991) (holding that Congress's creation of an airport review board consisting of nine members of Congress, whose members were appointed with direct congressional input, violated the separation of powers because, insofar as the board's powers were "executive," the arrangement offended the principle that the Constitution "does not permit an agent of Congress to exercise [executive power]"; also noting that, insofar as the Board's powers were "legislative" in nature, the arrangement violated *Chadha*'s requirement that all exercises of "legislative power" must be "in conformity with the bicameralism and presentment requirements of Art. I, § 7"). This argument too, however, might have proven too much. It would have suggested, for instance, that the "private bill" procedure on which Congress had previously relied was also unconstitutional because the decision whether to suspend a deportation proceeding is a decision that is inherently "executive" in nature. At the same time, however, a proponent of the "executive power" rationale might have avoided the "proves too much" difficulty by reframing the constitutional conclusion as follows: What makes a legislative veto an impermissible exercise of executive power by Congress has nothing to do with *what* the veto accomplishes. Rather it has to do with the fact that the veto derives from an effort by Congress to *confer statutory powers on itself*. Put differently, one might freely concede that "a particular function, like a chameleon, will often take on the aspect of the office to which it is assigned," *Bowsher*, 478 U.S. at 749 (Stevens, J., concurring in the judgment), while at the same time insisting that the Constitution should always prohibit Congress from enacting statutes that devolve law-execution responsibilities on Congress or any of its component parts. *See* Tribe, *supra*, at 10–11 ("The only imaginable justification for what Justice White called 'this odd result' lies in a principle never expressly articulated by the majority: 'that the legislature can delegate authority to others *but not to itself*.' " (quoting *Chadha*, 462 U.S. at 987 (White, J., dissenting))).

105 *Id.* at 959. He also wondered whether the legislative veto provision at issue in *Chadha* required, as a functional matter, exactly the sort of tripartite agreement among the House, the Senate, and the President that the Framers had endorsed. Under the previously operative "private bill" procedure, after all, the House, Senate, and President all needed to agree (via the Article I lawmaking process) to suspend the deportation of a person otherwise qualifying as deportable. But that was also true under the legislative veto scheme at issue in *Chadha*. The President's consent was necessary in that only an agent of the President (i.e., the Attorney General) could suspend a deportation proceeding. *Id.* at 994. And the consent of both Houses was necessary in that both Houses of Congress needed to "indicate their approval of the Executive's action by not passing a resolution of disapproval." *Id.* Thus, "[t]he effect on the rights and obligations of the affected individuals and upon the legislative system [was] precisely the same as if a private bill were introduced but failed to receive the necessary approval." *Id.* at 995.

106 *Id.* at 959 (majority opinion).

107 *Id.* at 1002 (White J., dissenting). To put the point differently, what the Court in *Chadha* did was to raise the stakes of any decision by Congress to delegate powers to the executive branch. Pre-*Chadha*, Congress could pursue a middle-ground solution,

Ironically, this last criticism of the *Chadha* decision might point the way to a functionalist argument in its favor: On this view, the ruling may enhance efficient and responsive governmental decisionmaking by disabling Congress from meddling too much in executive-branch operations, particularly under conditions of extreme political polarization. More specifically, if the Presidency is controlled by one party and at least one chamber of Congress is controlled by the other party, the rule of *Chadha* will serve the salutary goal of preventing an opposition-controlled House or Senate from engaging in bad-faith obstruction of a President's agenda. That justification, to be sure, will not sit well with observers who worry, along the lines of Justice White's dissent, about the accumulation of executive power at Congress's expense. But for those who regard policymaking by specialist agencies as a second-best solution to the problems posed by congressional dysfunction and paralysis,[108] the *Chadha* decision might in fact serve to advance the very set of efficiency-related values that Justice White and others perceived it to be undermining. Far from saddling the federal government with policymaking procedures that were "clumsy, inefficient, even unworkable,"[109] the Court in *Chadha* might in fact have helped to liberate administrative policymaking from a procedural albatross around the neck—one that threatened to keep government from responding to problems in an adequately responsive way.[110] The Court in *Chadha* saw itself as elevating considerations of negative

---

giving expanded authority to agencies and agency officials while at the same time retaining for itself an active supervisory role. Post-*Chadha*, Congress would face "a Hobson's choice: either to refrain from delegating the necessary authority, leaving itself with a hopeless task of writing laws with the requisite specificity to cover endless special circumstances across the entire policy landscape, or in the alternative, to abdicate its law-making function to the executive branch and independent agencies." *Id.* at 968. Perhaps, when faced with such a choice, Congress would be more disinclined to delegate any such power to agencies in the first place, in which case *Chadha* could be credited with cabining the expansion of executive authority. But if Congress (perhaps driven by internal gridlock or a desire to evade responsibility for hard policy choices) continued to empower agencies with wide-ranging regulatory authority, the only lasting effect of the *Chadha* decision would be to eliminate a potentially powerful (and useful) legislative constraint on executive-branch action. *See* Jonathan R. Macey, *Separated Powers and Positive Political Theory: The Tug of War Over Administrative Agencies*, 80 GEO. L.J. 671, 697 (1992) (discussing the strategic dimensions of this choice).

[108] *Cf., e.g.*, Jody Freeman & David B. Spence, *Old Statutes, New Problems*, 163 U. PA. L. REV. 1, 6 (2014) (noting that "typical statutory obsolescence made worse by atypical congressional dysfunction puts tremendous pressure on agencies to do *something* to address new problems").

[109] *Chadha*, 462 U.S. at 959.

[110] *But cf.* Curtis A. Bradley, *Reassessing the Legislative Veto: The Statutory President, Foreign Affairs, and Congressional Workarounds*, 13 J. LEGAL ANALYSIS 439, 441, 458–66 (2021) (maintaining that "the availability of the veto was less important before *Chadha* to congressional-executive relations than is commonly assumed" and that the existence of functional workarounds to the veto has largely managed to replicate the pre-*Chadha* status-quo).

liberty over those of governmental efficiency. But the more lasting consequence of the decision might in fact have been to promote precisely the opposite result.

3. Legislative Oversight in *Chadha*'s Wake

Congress predictably responded to the *Chadha* decision by modifying several of the legislative veto provisions that were then on the books.[111] But it also, perhaps less predictably, refused to abandon legislative vetoes altogether. Many of its pre-*Chadha* legislative-veto provisions never were repealed.[112] Even more curiously, Congress enacted additional legislative-veto laws even after the ruling in *Chadha* came down. Indeed, according to a 1993 study by Professor Louis Fisher, over a period of some ten years following that decision, Congress "enacted more than two hundred new legislative vetoes," most of which "require[d] the executive branch to obtain the approval of specified committees" before undertaking the designated action.[113] These provisions were of dubious (if not obvious) unconstitutionality at the time of their enactment,[114] thus rendering it unlikely that they ever would be judicially enforced. Nevertheless, these enactments, as well as their still-on-the-books pre-*Chadha* predecessors, have met with substantial compliance from the agency decisionmakers they target.

---

[111] One strategy was to provide for legislative vetoes effectuated by joint resolution of Congress (i.e., a resolution satisfying bicameralism and presentment), *See, e.g.*, L. ELAINE HALCHIN, CONG. RSCH. SERV., R98–805, NATIONAL EMERGENCY POWERS 20 (2021) (describing such a change with respect to the National Emergencies Act of 1974). With another statute, by contrast, Congress flipped the default rule on its head: Rather than permitting executive action to take effect unless vetoed by one House of Congress, the revised statute prohibited such action from taking effect *unless* authorized by a joint resolution of approval enacted in keeping with the requirements of bicameralism and presentment. *See, e.g.*, Edward H. Stiglitz, *Unitary Innovations and Political Accountability*, 99 CORNELL L. REV. 1133, 1152–53 (2014) (describing such a change in connection with the Reorganization Act of 1977).

[112] Most notable in this regard was a provision of the War Powers Act, which empowered Congress to pass a *concurrent resolution* (i.e., a resolution without Presidential signature) that would require the President to withdraw troops from military hostilities. *See supra* Section 28.A.2; *see also Chadha*, 462 U.S. at 970–71 (White, J., dissenting) (highlighting this provision of the War Powers Act as jeopardized by the Court's decision in *Chadha*). *But see* Louis Fisher, *The Legislative Veto: Invalidated, It Survives*, 56 LAW & CONTEMP. PROBS. 273, 287 (1993) (noting the possibility that the War Powers Act is "technically not a legislative veto covered by *Chadha*" because it does not involve a "condition placed on delegated authority"); *see also supra* Section 28.A.2 n.25 (citing additional arguments on behalf of the WPA's post-*Chadha* constitutionality).

[113] Fisher, *supra* note 112, at 288.

[114] Several accompanying presidential signing statements would highlight this point. *See id.* at 288 (noting President Bush's declaration that a bill's legislative veto provisions were "similar to those declared unconstitutional" in *Chadha* and that "I will treat them as having no legal force or effect in this or any other legislation in which they appear); *id.* at 288–89 (noting President Reagan's statement that he would treat a bill's legislative-veto provisions "in a manner consistent with the *Chadha* decision").

The key dynamic at play here is, as Fisher explains, that "[a]gencies cannot risk . . . collisions with the committees that authorize their programs and provide funds."[115] In particular, while *Chadha* affords agencies a strong constitutional basis for defying a committee-level veto of their actions, countervailing pragmatic concerns about the dangers of ruffling congressional feathers militate in favor of agency quiescence. This is especially true because, even if a House or Senate committee cannot force an agency to honor a legislative veto, it can retaliate against noncooperative agencies in other ways. For example, the committee might insert into the next year's appropriations statute a draconian set of restrictions on the agency's powers—restrictions that the President might be forced to swallow as part of a much larger-scale budgetary compromise. Or the committee might decline to authorize a new program that the agency wishes to pursue. Especially on matters of low-level political salience, agencies have good reason to remain in the good graces of the committees that oversee their operations. And that fact gives those committees leverage to demand continued adherence to existing (though judicially unenforceable) legislative-veto arrangements. In this respect, the Court's decision in *Chadha* may not so much have eliminated the legislative veto as it simply ended up "driv[ing] underground a set of legislative and committee vetoes that formerly operated in plain sight."[116]

Congress also has other implements in its agency-oversight toolbox. Its committees, for example, have wide-ranging subpoena powers,[117] and they can use these powers to publicly pressure agency officials to alter their decisions and programs.[118] Members of Congress also can try to influence agency officials through private

---

[115] *Id.* at 288.

[116] *Id.* at 292. In addition, as Professor Bradley notes, Congress has relied on other substitute mechanisms for constraining executive conduct, including narrower delegations of statutory authority, sunset provisions attached to enabling statutes, consultation and reporting requirements, or veto-like powers over agency action vested in other administrative agencies. *See* Bradley, *supra* note 110, at 463–66.

[117] *See supra* Section 14.C. *But see infra* Sections 33.A.1.c & 33.A.2.b (discussing executive privilege and other separation-of-powers-based limits on Congress's oversight powers).

[118] To take one example, during the run-up to the 2020 presidential election, the U.S. Postal Service began to implement changes to its mail delivery services that threatened to delay the delivery of absentee ballots, thus raising concerns about the widespread disenfranchisement of persons who planned to vote by mail. When Democrats in Congress caught wind of these developments, they went public with their concerns by holding committee hearings on the issue, and those hearings in turn prompted Postmaster General Louis DeJoy to commit publicly to prioritizing the delivery of mail-in ballots. *See* Catie Edmondson, et al., *Key Highlights of Louis De Joy's Testimony to a House Panel*, N.Y. TIMES (Aug. 24, 2020), https://www.nytimes.com/2020/08/24/us/politics/postal-service-dejoy-testimony.html.

communications and informal political horse trading.[119] Some such legislator-administrator communications might target narrow matters—as, for example, when a congressional staffer contacts an agency employee in an effort to help a constituent pursue a claim for Social Security benefits. Other exchanges, however, might well involve higher-profile issues.[120] And while different members of Congress undoubtedly enjoy different levels of influence in terms of bending agency decisionmakers to their will, the deft utilization of these sorts of informal oversight mechanisms can, under the right conditions, trigger significant administrative changes of course.

---

[119] *See* Beerman, *supra* note 88, at 130 ("The public face of oversight and hearings exists against the background of a network of informal, often private contacts through which members of Congress attempt to influence the execution of the law by communicating directly with agency personnel.").

[120] *See, e.g.*, Jeffrey A. Love & Arpit K. Garg, *Presidential Inaction and the Separation of Powers*, 112 MICH. L. REV. 1195, 1232–33 (2014) ("[M]embers of Congress can monitor executive action by communicating directly with agency staff to express their preferences, a practice known as 'jawboning.' " (internal footnote omitted)).

Chapter 30

THE APPOINTMENT POWER

Analysis

Among the most consequential decisions that a President makes are those that concern the staffing of the executive branch. Because no one person can directly monitor all of the federal bureaucracy's vast and varied activities, the President must rely on a large team of individuals—known as the President's *administration*—to oversee and carry out those activities on the President's behalf. Decisions about who should hold high-ranking executive-branch positions thus carry major implications for what the federal government does and how effectively it operates. Government offices led by competent and experienced allies of the President will be well positioned to pursue the President's agenda; offices led by incompetent or inexperienced personnel are likely to bungle their responsibilities; and those led by outright or closet adversaries might well undermine the President's regulatory goals.

Article II sets forth the rules governing the President's appointment of executive-branch—as well as judicial-branch—officials. First and foremost, the Appointments Clause of Article II, section 2 establishes as a baseline matter that presidential appointments must be made "by and with the Advice and Consent of the Senate"[1]—language long understood to require Senate confirmation as a precondition to an appointee's assumption of office.[2] But the clause also empowers Congress "by Law" to override

[1] *See* U.S. CONST. art. II, § 2, cl. 2 ("[The President] shall nominate, and by and with the Advice and Consent of the Senate, shall appoint Ambassadors, other public Ministers and Consuls, Judges of the supreme Court, and all other Officers of the United States, whose Appointments are not herein otherwise provided for, and which shall be established by Law: but the Congress may by Law vest the Appointment of such inferior Officers, as they think proper, in the President alone, in the Courts of Law, or in the Heads of Departments.").

[2] *Id.* This confirmation requirement, as Hamilton noted, was intended to serve as a "check upon a spirit of favoritism in the President," with the hope that the Senate's advice-and-consent function would "tend greatly to prevent the appointment of unfit characters from State prejudice, from family connection, from personal attachment, or from a view to popularity." THE FEDERALIST NO. 76 (Hamilton).

this confirmation requirement with respect to "inferior Officers," so long as the power to appoint them is thereby vested "in the President alone, in the Courts of Law, or in the Heads of Departments."[3] In addition, the Recess Appointments Clause permits the President to forgo Senate confirmation when "fill[ing] up all Vacancies that may happen during the Recess of the Senate."[4] That clause also stipulates, however, that any such recess appointment must expire at the end of Congress's "next Session."[5]

This cluster of provisions has given rise to a range of issues. The first set of issues goes to the scope and substance of the Appointments Clause itself—in particular, with regard to: (a) which types of officials qualify as the "Officers of the United States" whose appointments are governed by the clause; (b) who among these "Officers" qualify as "inferior" (as opposed to "principal") officers whose manner of appointment may be prescribed by Congress; and (c) with respect to these inferior officers, what types of appointment arrangements Congress may prescribe by law. A second set of issues concerns the extent to which a President may circumvent the Senate's advice-and-consent function by pursuing alternative appointment mechanisms. In particular, we consider below several questions that arose in connection with President Barack Obama's (ultimately unsuccessful) attempt to rely on recess appointments as a means of bypassing Senate Republicans' refusal to confirm many of his nominees. We also consider kindred questions raised by President Donald Trump's frequent (and somewhat more successful) attempts to use a federal statute called the Vacancies Reform Act to install political loyalists as "acting" officials and thus to effectuate the *de facto* appointment of temporary officeholders while sidestepping the process of senatorial review.

A. THE APPOINTMENTS CLAUSE

1. "Officers of the United States"

The Appointments Clause governs the appointment of "Ambassadors, other public Ministers and Consuls, Judges of the supreme Court, and all other Officers of the United States."[6] The key term here is "Officers of the United States." We know from the text of the clause that this term encompasses "Ambassadors," "other

---

[3] U.S. CONST. art. II, § 2, cl. 2.

[4] *Id.* art. II, § 2, cl. 3.

[5] *Id.* ("The President shall have Power to fill up all Vacancies that may happen during the Recess of the Senate, by granting Commissions which shall expire at the End of their next Session.").

[6] U.S. CONST. art. II, § 2, cl. 2.

public Ministers and Consuls," and "Judges of the supreme Court." But how much farther does it reach?[7]

a. Officers of the United States vs. Officers of Congress

An initial question raised by the term "Officers of the United States" is whether it encompasses only persons who serve in the executive and judicial branches. More specifically, to what extent may Congress create subunits of government accountable to the *legislative branch* that are headed by individuals whose appointments are not governed by the Appointments Clause at all? That was a central question addressed by the Court's 1976 decision in *Buckley v. Valeo*.[8] At issue in that case was the constitutionality of a federal statute that, among other things, created a new agency, the Federal Election Commission (FEC), which was tasked with implementing a variety of statutory rules governing federal election campaigns.[9] The FEC was to consist of six voting members—two nominated by the President, another two nominated by the Speaker of the House, and the remaining two nominated by the President *pro tempore* of the Senate—all six of whom were subject to confirmation through votes of both Houses of Congress.[10] At issue in *Buckley* was whether these appointment-related provisions comported with the Constitution's scheme of separated powers.

As far as the Appointments Clause was concerned, the answer to this question clearly seemed to be "no." The Clause, after all, makes no reference to either the Speaker of the House or the President *pro tempore* of the Senate as appointing authorities,[11] thus

---

[7] A separate question is whether the Appointments Clause requires the renomination and reconfirmation of officials whose powers and duties have been legislatively altered by Congress. The answer, in short, is: "It's complicated." In particular, the Court has indicated that a new appointments process is warranted when Congress has vested preexisting officials with "additional duties" that are not "germane to the offices already held by them." *See* Shoemaker v. United States, 147 U.S. 282, 300–01 (1893); *see also* Weiss v. United States, 510 U.S. 163, 174 (1994) (noting the "principle of germaneness" set forth in *Shoemaker* (internal quotation omitted)); *see also* Lo Duca v. United States, 93 F.3d 1100, 1110 (2d Cir. 1996) ("Where Congress provides additional duties that are 'germane' to an already existing position, the Appointments Clause does not require a second appointment."). Thus, while not every statutory modification to an officer's powers and duties will require the President to make a new Article II appointment, the Appointments Clause does require reappointment to any office whose newly added duties qualify as "dissimilar to, or outside of the sphere of" the duties affixed to the office at the time the original appointment was made. *Shoemaker*, 147 U.S. at 301.

[8] 424 U.S. 1 (1976).

[9] *See* Federal Election Campaign Act of 1971, Pub. L. No. 92–225, 86 Stat. 3, as amended by the Federal Election Campaign Act Amendments of 1974, Pub. L. No. 93–443, 88 Stat. 1263.

[10] *Buckley*, 424 U.S. at 5.

[11] In particular, as the Court noted, neither of these officials could qualify as "Heads of Departments," because the "Departments referred to [by the Appointments

indicating that four of the Commission's six members had assumed their positions in an unconstitutional manner.[12] Nevertheless, the law's defenders argued that that the Necessary and Proper Clause authorized Congress to prescribe, at least for these officers, appointment procedures not set forth in Article II.[13] The Court, however, emphatically rejected that argument, and, in a *per curiam* opinion, left no doubt that that "[u]nless their selection is elsewhere provided for [by the Constitution], all Officers of the United States are to be appointed in accordance with the [Appointments] Clause."[14] Put differently, as long as the FEC's Commissioners qualified as "Officers of the United States," and no other constitutional provision authorized their appointment in a different manner, Congress had no constitutional authority to depart from the appointment-related rules that the clause itself set forth.

But were the FEC Commissioners "Officers of the United States"? In a nutshell, the majority's answer to this question was both "yes" and "no." On the one hand, the Court noted that the Commission performed certain functions that were "essentially of an investigative and informative nature," so that its members—to the extent they engaged in only these activities—did not qualify as "Officers of the United States," but instead exercised the sorts of "powers which Congress might delegate to one of its own committees."[15] (Indeed, insofar as the Commission carried out these functions on Congress's behalf, its members were perhaps better regarded as "Officers of the Congress," appointed pursuant to each legislative chamber's own separate Article I authority to "chuse" its own officers.)[16] On the other hand, the Court emphasized that the bulk of the Commission's work involved the exercise of "more substantial powers,"[17] including powers to promulgate regulations,

Clause] are themselves in the Executive Branch or at least have some connection with that branch." *Id.* at 127.

[12] The Court also hinted that the other two Commissioners nominated by the President posed potential Appointment Clause problems insofar as their nominations were subject to "confirmation not merely by the Senate, but by the House of Representatives as well." *Id.*

[13] *Id.* at 132 (noting the Commission's argument that "because Congress has been given explicit and plenary authority to regulate a field of activity, it must therefore have the power to appoint those who are to administer the regulatory statute").

[14] *Id.*; *see also id.* at 274 (White, J. concurring in part and dissenting in part) (agreeing with the majority's rejection of "the proposition that because the FEC is implementing statutory policies with respect to the conduct of elections, which policies Congress has the power to propound, its members may be appointed by Congress").

[15] *Id.* at 137–38 (majority opinion).

[16] *Id.* at 127–28 (citing U.S. CONST. art. I, § 2, cl. 5 ("The House of Representatives shall chuse their Speaker and other Officers . . . ."), and U.S. CONST. art. I, § 3, cls. 4–5 ("[T]he Vice President of the United States shall be President of the Senate, but . . . [t]he Senate shall chuse their other Officers.")).

[17] *Id.* at 138.

issue advisory opinions, and bring enforcement actions against alleged violators of federal campaign finance law.[18] And insofar as the Commission performed these "administrative functions," it was not "operat[ing] merely in aid of congressional authority to legislate" and was therefore not "sufficiently removed from the administration and enforcement of the public law" to escape the operation of the Appointments Clause.[19] In short, the Court held that "most of the powers conferred" on the Commission were powers that could "be exercised only by 'Officers of the United States.' "[20] Accordingly, those powers could not be exercised "by the Commission as presently constituted."[21]

This aspect of the Court's ruling in *Buckley* both vindicated and constrained congressional authority. The vindication came with the Court's recognition that Congress could disregard the Appointments Clause when exercising what Justice White in a separate opinion described as the "power to appoint its own inferior officers to carry out appropriate legislative functions."[22] But the constraint came with the Court's insistence that this power did not extend to officers who "perform[ ] a significant governmental duty exercised pursuant to a public law."[23]

b. *Officers of the United States vs. Local/Territorial Officers*

The Court recently recognized a second important carve-out to the Appointments Clause, predicated on the distinction between "Officers of the United States" and "local" officers of federally established territories. In *Financial Oversight & Management Board for Puerto Rico v. Aurelius Investment, LLC*,[24] the Justices confronted the question whether Congress had validly granted to the President

---

18 *Id.* at 110–13.

19 *Id.* at 141; *see also id.* at 269–70 (White, J., concurring in part and dissenting in part) ("By no stretch of the imagination can [the FEC's] various functions in this respect be considered mere adjuncts to the legislative process. . . .").

20 *Id.* at 143 (majority opinion).

21 *Id.*

22 *Id.* at 280 (White, J., concurring in part and dissenting in part). Consider, for instance, the Director of the Congressional Budget Office, who is currently appointed jointly by the Speaker of the House and the President pro tempore of the Senate. *See* 2 U.S.C. § 601(a). This arrangement is generally understood not to raise Appointments Clause issues, because the CBO itself plays no role in *enforcing* or *administering* the statutes that Congress enacts. The same is true of other legislatively appointed officers, including the House and Senate Sergeants at Arms, the Chief of the Capitol Police, the Director of the Office of Congressional Workplace Rights, and the Director of the Congressional Research Service. *See generally* IDA A. BRUDNICK, CONG. RSCH. SERV., RL42072, LEGISLATIVE BRANCH AGENCY APPOINTMENTS: HISTORY, PROCESSES, AND RECENT ACTIONS (2019), *available at* https://sgp.fas.org/crs/misc/R42072.pdf.

23 *Buckley*, 424 U.S. at 141.

24 140 S. Ct. 1649 (2020).

the power to appoint, without Senate confirmation, seven individuals to serve on an oversight board tasked with "representing Puerto Rico in bankruptcy proceedings and supervising aspects of Puerto Rico's fiscal and budgetary policies."[25] The First Circuit had invalidated the arrangement, concluding that the Board's members qualified as "principal" rather than "inferior" officers whose appointments required Senate confirmation.[26] But the Supreme Court reversed, reasoning that the Board's members were not "Officers of the United States" at all and that the Appointments Clause therefore "says nothing about them."[27]

Key to the outcome of *Aurelius* was the Court's determination that the phrase "Officers *of the United States*" was one that "suggests a distinction between federal officers—officers exercising power of the National Government—and nonfederal officers—officers exercising power of some other government."[28] This distinction, the Court explained, made structural sense in light of Congress's specialized and expansive regulatory powers over federal territories and the District of Columbia.[29] In exercising these powers, Congress had "both made local law directly and also created structures of local government, staffed by local officials, who themselves have made and enforced local law."[30] The Court's prior validation of these congressional actions further supported the notion that "when Congress creates local offices using these two unique powers, the officers exercise power of the local government, not the Federal Government," thus rendering them something other than "Officers of the United States."[31]

---

[25] *Id.* at 1655.

[26] *See* Aurelius Inv., LLC v. Fin. Oversight & Mgmt. Bd., 915 F.3d 838 (1st Cir. 2019), *rev'd* 140 S. Ct. 1649 (2020).

[27] *Aurelius*, 140 S. Ct. at 1658.

[28] *Id.* at 1659. The Court did take pains to emphasize, however, that its posited distinction between local and federal officials did not render the Appointments Clause inapplicable to the appointment of *all* officials "with duties in or related to the District of Columbia or an Article IV entity." *Id.* at 1661. Rather, the clause was inapplicable only to those officials, like the PROMESA members, in whom Congress had vested "primarily local duties." *Id.*; *see also id.* at 1670 (Thomas, J., concurring in the judgment) (expressing disagreement with the majority's "amorphous test" and instead advocating for an approach that would deem the Appointments Clause inapplicable to officers who "perform ongoing statutory duties under *only* Article IV" (emphasis added)).

[29] *See* U.S. CONST. art. IV, § 3, cl. 2 (empowering Congress to "make all needful Rules and Regulations respecting the Territory or other Property belonging to the United States"); *id.* art. I, § 8, cl. 17 (authorizing Congress to "exercise exclusive Legislation in all Cases whatsoever" regarding the District of Columbia). For a broader discussion of these authorities, see *supra* Sections 25.B & 25.C.

[30] *Aurelius*, 140 S. Ct. at 1658–59.

[31] *Id.* at 1659. The Court's application of this "federal"/"local" distinction in *Aurelius* also drew support from Puerto Rico's "longstanding practice of selecting

It bears emphasis that, although *Aurelius* itself concerned a financial oversight board, the scope and reach of the Court's posited distinction between national and local/territorial officers carries broader implications for democratic self-governance in Puerto Rico, other overseas territories, and the District of Columbia. Had the Court held that all local/territorial officers were subject to the dictates of the Appointments Clause, its decision might well have meant that even the now-elected officials of these governments—for example, the Governor of Puerto Rico, the Mayor of D.C., and the like—would qualify as "Officers of the United States" (and likely principal ones at that) whose assumption of office accordingly could occur only by way of the exceedingly non-democratic means of appointment by the President (for whom territorial citizens are unable to vote) and confirmation by the Senate (in which neither territorial citizens nor the citizens of D.C. have any representation).[32] To be sure, the Court's holding in *Aurelius* does not guarantee democratic accountability insofar as it still empowers Congress to prescribe appointment arrangements for local/territorial officials—such as the arrangement at issue in *Aurelius* itself—that do not involve direct or indirect input from local/territorial citizens. Nonetheless, the decision at least affords Congress the opportunity to put in place a democratic, voting-based selection process for offices that logically call for their use.[33]

---

public officials with important local responsibilities in ways that the Appointments Clause does not describe." *Id.* at 1659–61.

[32] *See id.* at 1661 ("[T]o read Appointments Clause constraints as binding Puerto Rican officials with primarily local duties would work havoc with Puerto Rico's (federally ratified) democratic methods for selecting many of its officials."). *But cf. Aurelius*, 915 F.3d at 859 (contending that, even if PROMESA members qualified as "Officers of the United States" the "elected officials" of territorial governments would fall outside the scope of that term because they would "exercise significant authority" pursuant to their own territorial law and not, as required, "*pursuant to the laws of the United States*" (quoting *Buckley*, 424 U.S. at 126) (emphasis added)).

[33] At the same time, however, the Court in *Aurelius* did not pursue other lines of reasoning that might have yielded a considerably more protective holding for territories and their citizens. For example, though the Court had been urged by the challengers to overturn the *Insular Cases*, in which it had earlier held that territorial citizens are not fully protected by the U.S. Constitution, *see supra* Section 25.B.2 (discussing these cases in greater detail), the Court ultimately dodged the issue, deeming it unnecessary to consider whether it ought to "overrule the much-criticized" decisions. *Aurelius*, 140 S. Ct. at 1665; *see also* Adriel I. Cepeda Derieux & Neil C. Weare, *After* Aurelius: *What Future for the* Insular Cases?, 130 YALE L.J. FORUM 284, 286 (2020) (faulting the Court for its refusal to reconsider the *Insular Cases* in *Aurelius*, while noting that "the Court's discussion of the *Insular Cases* . . . raises significant questions about those decisions' future"). In addition, and as Justice Sotomayor noted in her separate concurrence, the Court in *Aurelius* did not consider the separate question whether the powers granted to the Board conflicted with the terms of Public Law 600, a 1950 statute "in the nature of a compact," through which the Federal Government had extended to the Commonwealth of Puerto Rico a "grant of self-rule." *Aurelius*, 140 S. Ct. at 1672 (Sotomayor, J., concurring) (quoting Act of July 3, 1950, § 1, 65 Stat. 319); *see also* Christina D. Ponsa-Kraus, *Political Wine in a*

c. *Officers of the United States vs. Governmental Employees*

The federal government employs more than 4 million people[34]—soldiers, staff attorneys, meat inspectors, postal workers, park rangers, tax auditors, and on and on. Even though almost all of those individuals fall within the purview of the federal executive branch, most secure their positions through hiring processes that do not comport with the requirements of the Appointments Clause.[35] How can this be? The answer, according to the Court, is that such "lesser functionaries," much like legislative-branch and local/territorial officials, fail to qualify as "Officers of the United States" for purposes of that constitutional provision.[36] Instead, they are merely "employees," whose methods of appointment are accordingly not subject to Appointment-Clause constraints.[37]

With this basic principle in mind, the Court has worked to elaborate on the distinction between federal "officers," on the one hand, and federal "employees," on the other. In so doing, the Justices have focused attention on two variables of central importance. First, as the Court explained in *Lucia v. SEC*,[38] in order to qualify as an officer rather than an employee, one must generally occupy a position that is "continuing and permanent" rather than "occasional or temporary."[39] Thus, for instance, the Court in *United States v. Germaine*[40] held that a surgeon who provided periodic medical examinations for the U.S. Commissioner of Pensions was not an "Officer" for purposes of the Appointment Clause because he would "only . . . act when called on by the Commissioner . . . in some special case" and was "required to keep no place of business for the public

Judicial Bottle: Justice Sotomayor's Surprising Concurrence in Aurelius, 130 YALE L.J. FORUM 101, 102 (2020) (criticizing Justice Sotomayor's concurrence as taking sides "with respect to the debate over Puerto Rican decolonization" and suggesting that her "decision to shore up the 'compact theory' . . . severely exacerbates the considerable legal ambiguity that has defined and prolonged Puerto Rico's colonial condition for well over a century").

34 *See* U.S. Exec. Office of the President, Office of Mgmt. & Budget, Analytical Perspectives: Budget of the U.S. Government Fiscal Year 2022, at 44 (2021), https://www.govinfo.gov/content/pkg/BUDGET-2022-PER/pdf/BUDGET-2022-PER.pdf.

35 The hiring of non-military federal employees is governed by a complex array of statutory and regulatory requirements, known generally as "civil service" laws. For a brief overview, see U.S. Office of Personnel Management, Hiring Authorities, https://www.opm.gov/policy-data-oversight/hiring-information/hiring-authorities (last visited Nov. 3, 2021).

36 *See Buckley*, 424 U.S. 1, 127 n.162 (1976).

37 *See id.*

38 138 S. Ct. 2044 (2018).

39 *Id.* at 2051 (quoting United States v. Germaine, 99 U.S. 508, 512 (1879)).

40 99 U.S. 508 (1879).

use."[41] Along the same lines, as the U.S. Department of Justice has more recently argued, the logic of *Germaine* suggests that the clause does not govern the appointment of "special diplomatic agents, short-term contractors, *qui tam* relators, and many others in positions that have authority on an ad hoc or temporary basis."[42]

In addition to serving in a full-time rather than part-time capacity, Appointment Clause-covered "Officers" differ from Appointment Clause-uncovered "employees" in that such individuals exercise "*significant* authority" on behalf of the United States.[43] As to what counts as "significant authority," the Court's opinions provide a few analytical guideposts.[44] For example, the FEC Commissioners at issue in *Buckley* fell outside the category of mere "employees" because, in exercising their rulemaking, adjudicative, and law-enforcement functions, they were not "subject to the control or direction of any other executive, judicial, or legislative authority."[45] Similarly, in *Freytag v. Commissioner*,[46] the Court held that special trial judges of the Tax Court (a non-Article III tribunal) qualified as officers rather than employees because, in handling trials, ruling on evidentiary issues, and compelling compliance with discovery requests, they exercised "significant discretion" and were entrusted

---

41 *Id.* at 512.

42 *See Officers of the U.S. Within the Meaning of the Appointments Clause*, 31 Op. O.L.C. 73, 77 (2007). *But see* U.S. Dep't of Transp. v. Ass'n of Am. Railroads, 575 U.S. 43, 63–64 (2015) (Alito, J., concurring) (contending that an arbitrator appointed to resolve a dispute on behalf of the Surface Transportation Board qualified as an "Officer" under the Appointments Clause and thus suggesting that long-term tenure is not a *sine qua non* of Officer status); Ass'n of Am. Railroads v. U.S. Dep't of Transp., 821 F.3d 19, 37–38 (D.C. Cir. 2016) (agreeing with Justice Alito's position on remand); *see also* James A. Heilpern, *Temporary Officers*, 26 GEO. MASON L. REV. 753, 755–56 (2019) (noting the tension between *Lucia*'s treatment of the temporary-tenure factor and the D.C. Circuit's conclusion that the arbitrator was an "Officer," while also contending more generally that *Lucia*'s treatment of the factor creates a "significant loophole in this Constitutional scheme").

43 *See Buckley*, 424 U.S. at 126 (emphasis added). For a recent originalist critique of the "significant authority" test, see Jennifer L. Mascott, *Who Are "Officers of the United States"?*, 70 STAN. L. REV. 443, 451 (2018) (adducing historical evidence to suggest that "the most likely eighteenth century meaning of 'officer' was significantly broader than the modern 'significant authority' test implies" and that the term was in fact "commonly understood to encompass any individual who had ongoing responsibility for a governmental duty").

44 *See generally* Stacy M. Lindstedt, *Developing the Duffy Defect: Identifying Which Government Workers Are Constitutionally Required To Be Appointed*, 76 MO. L. REV. 1143, 1157 (2011) (noting that the question of what counts as "significant authority" "remains relegated to definition by example," while suggesting that "[a] few common factors can be discerned: an actor that executes or administers public laws in a nonministerial manner exercises significant authority, with finality and discretion playing at least some role").

45 *Buckley*, 424 U.S. at 127 n.162.

46 501 U.S. 868 (1991).

with "more than ministerial tasks."[47] Drawing on this holding, the Court in *Lucia* ruled that administrative law judges who work on behalf of the Securities and Exchange Commission also qualify as "Officers" because they enjoy a degree of "discretion" similar to that of the trial judges in *Freytag* while in some respects playing an even "more autonomous role."[48] To date, then, the Court's approach to applying the "significant authority" test has depended primarily on fact-intensive and position-specific assessments of "the extent of power an individual wields in carrying out his assigned functions."[49]

2. Principal vs. Inferior Officers

Under the Appointments Clause, not all "Officers of the United States" receive the same legal treatment. Rather, the clause distinguishes between "inferior Officers" and what have come to be known as their "principal officer" counterparts.[50] Specifically, while the clause mandates presidential nomination followed by Senate confirmation for all principal officers, it permits Congress "by law" to vest the appointment of inferior officers "in the President alone, in the Courts of Law, or in the Heads of Departments."[51] The underlying idea is straightforward: Some officials—namely, principal officers—enjoy a degree of power and responsibility so great as to require at all times both presidential selection and the second-look review inherent in the process of Senate confirmation. When it comes to inferior officers, however, the more restricted nature of their powers and responsibilities is said to justify the choice to use less

47 *Id.* at 881–82; *see also Weiss*, 510 U.S. at 169 ("The parties do not dispute that military judges, because of the authority and responsibilities they possess, act as 'Officers' of the United States.' ").

48 138 S. Ct. at 2053. As Justice Kagan noted for the majority, whereas the Tax Court judges in *Freytag* rendered decisions that were subject to *mandatory* review by supervising authorities, the ALJs at issue in *Lucia* had their decisions subject to only the discretionary review of the SEC itself. *Id.* at 2054. Thus, unlike the "Officers" in *Freytag*, the SEC's ALJs could sometimes issue decisions of behalf of the agency without securing any other official's sign-off on the merits. This "last-word capacity," Justice Kagan noted, thus presented the Court with an "*a fortiori* case," meaning that if the judges at issue in *Freytag* were officers, "then the Commission's ALJs must be too." *Id.*

49 *Id.* at 2051. For additional lower-court applications of this test, see, e.g., *Burgess v. Fed. Deposit Ins. Corp.*, 871 F.3d 297, 302–03 (5th Cir. 2017) (finding that FDIC ALJs, whose job duties entailed taking testimony, conducting trials, and ruling on the admissibility of evidence, are "Officers," rather than mere "employees," because "their broad authority . . . closely resembles the authority wielded by United States Commissioners—the forerunners of Magistrate Judges—who the Supreme Court held were officers" (citing Rice v. Ames, 180 U.S. 371, 378 (1901)) (internal footnote omitted)), and *Tucker v. Comm'r*, 676 F.3d 1129, 1134 (D.C. Cir. 2012) (holding that IRS "Appeals employees," who are responsible for reviewing tax liability and collection procedures, are mere employees, and not "Officers" because their "discretion is highly constrained").

50 U.S. CONST. art. II, § 2, cls. 1–2.

51 *Id.*

"cumbersome" appointment procedures in the interest of "administrative convenience."[52]

What distinguishes principal from inferior officers? The Court's first extended discussion of this question came in *Morrison v. Olson*,[53] a case concerning the independent-counsel provisions of the Ethics in Government Act.[54] That statute required the Attorney General, upon a preliminary finding of criminal misconduct by a high-ranking federal official, to "apply" to a panel of Article III judges (known as the Special Division), "for the appointment of an independent counsel" to investigate the alleged wrongdoing.[55] The Special Division could then appoint an "appropriate" individual to serve in that role.[56] Thus, as the statute made clear, neither the President nor the Senate played any role in the independent-counsel's appointment, meaning that the statute's appointment-related provisions could pass muster only if the independent-counsel qualified as an inferior officer rather than a principal officer.

"Several factors" led the Court in *Morrison* to conclude that the independent counsel "falls on the 'inferior officer' side of that line."[57] First, the holder of that office was "subject to removal by a higher Executive Branch official"—namely, the Attorney General—for "good cause,"[58] thus rendering her "to some degree 'inferior' in rank and authority."[59] In addition, the independent counsel was assigned "only certain, limited duties" in that her authority was confined to handling the alleged acts of wrongdoing flagged by the Special

---

52 Edmond v. United States, 520 U.S. 651, 660 (1997).

53 487 U.S. 654 (1988).

54 For pre-*Morrison* attempts to work through the principal-inferior distinction, see, e.g., *Go-Bart Importing Co. v. United States*, 282 U.S. 344, 352–54 (1931) (finding that a "United States commissioner" in district-court proceedings was an inferior officer), *Ex parte Siebold*, 100 U.S. 371, 397–98 (1880) (treating an election supervisor as an inferior officer), and *Ex parte Hennen*, 38 U.S. (13 Pet.) 225, 229 (1839) (treating a district court clerk as an inferior officer).

55 *Morrison*, 487 U.S. at 661.

56 *Id.*

57 *Id.* at 671.

58 *See* 28 U.S.C. § 596(a)(1) (1982 ed., Supp. V) (permitting the Attorney General to remove the independent counsel "only for good cause, physical disability, mental incapacity, or any other condition that substantially impairs the performance of such independent counsel's duties").

59 *Morrison*, 487 U.S. at 671. The for-cause limit on the Attorney General's removal power, as Justice Scalia argued, might have been seen as supporting a finding of principal-officer status. *See id.* at 671 (Scalia, J., dissenting) ("I fail to see how the fact that appellant is more difficult to remove than most principal officers helps to establish that she is an inferior officer."). *See also infra* Section 31.B.4 (discussing in greater detail the constitutional issues raised by these removal restrictions). The majority, however, viewed the Independent Counsel's susceptibility to removal, even if only for cause, as one factor supporting a finding of inferior-officer status.

Division.[60] Finally, the independent counsel's appointment, though not subject to a designated "time limit," was in its nature restricted in duration insofar as it concerned only the "single task" of investigating and (if appropriate), prosecuting specifically designated conduct.[61] In sum, the "tenure, duration and duties" associated with the independent counsel position operated together to establish the inferior status of the office.[62]

Less than a decade after *Morrison*, however, the Court moved away from this multi-factor approach to determining "inferior officer" status. Writing for the majority in *Edmond v. United States*,[63] Justice Scalia, who had been the lone dissenter in *Morrison*, downplayed the significance of that precedent by suggesting that it "did not purport to set forth a definitive test for whether an office is 'inferior.' "[64] On the proper view, he reasoned, the relevant inquiry is in fact much simpler than the Court in *Morrison* had suggested. In particular, although the Court's prior decisions had not "set forth an exclusive criterion for distinguishing principal and inferior officers,"[65] it was, "[g]enerally speaking," the case that "[w]hether one is an 'inferior' officer depends on whether he has a 'superior.' "[66] More specifically, the decisive question was whether the officer's "work is *directed and supervised* at some level by others who were appointed by Presidential nomination with the advice and consent of the Senate."[67]

---

60 *Morrison*, 487 U.S. at 671.

61 *Id.* at 672 (internal quotation omitted). This last component of the *Morrison* analysis stands in some tension with the Court's subsequent suggestion in *Lucia, see supra* Section 30.A.1.c, that persons serving in a temporary capacity generally qualify as "employees" and thus could not qualify as inferior *officers*. *See* Heilpern, *supra* note 42, at 770–76 (noting this tension and exploring ways in which to "harmonize *Lucia* and *Morrison*).

62 *Id.* (quoting *Germaine*, 99 U.S. at 509) (internal alterations omitted).

63 520 U.S. 651 (1997).

64 *Id.* at 661.

65 *Id.*

66 *Id.* at 662. *Edmond*'s repudiation of *Morrison* was made even clearer by the Court's explicit recognition that, unlike the independent counsel at issue in *Morrison*, the Coast Guard judges occupied a position that was not "limited in tenure" or "limited in jurisdiction," at least in the sense that the Court in *Morrison* had used those terms. *Id.* at 661. Under *Morrison*'s "tenure, duration, and duties" test, after all, those two distinctions would have militated in favor of treating the judges as principal rather than inferior officers. *See Morrison*, 487 U.S. at 672. But the Court in *Edmond* paid no attention to these features of the office, instead homing in on the single, all-controlling fact that other, higher-ranking officers exercised "supervision over their work." *Edmond*, 520 U.S. at 666; *see also* Tuan Samahon, *Are Bankruptcy Judges Unconstitutional? An Appointments Clause Challenge*, 60 HASTINGS L.J. 233, 266 (2008) (noting that if the *Edmond* rule "were applied in *Morrison*" it "would reverse its outcome").

67 *Edmond*, 520 U.S. at 663 (emphasis added). *Edmond* did not purport to overrule *Morrison* directly, thus leading to some uncertainty in the lower courts as to whether the *Edmond* "supervision" test had fully eclipsed the *Morrison* "tenure, duration, and duties" test. *See, e.g.*, Samahon, *supra* note 66, at 258–66 (highlighting

If so, the officer is "inferior." If not—if, that is, no one other than the President directly supervises the officer's work—then (and only then) does the "principal officer" label apply. Making use of this new test in evaluating the status of the officers at issue in *Edmond* itself—military judges on the Coast Guard Court of Criminal Appeals—the Court had no difficulty deciding the case: Because these officers were subject to the joint supervision of the Judge Advocate General and the Court of Appeals for the Armed Forces, they were "inferior" rather than principal officers.[68] Accordingly, the Appointments Clause did not require the joint participation of the President and the Senate in the process of those judges' selection.

3. Rules for Inferior Officers

Inferior-officer status does not in itself cut the Senate out of the advice-and-consent loop: Rather, when it comes to inferior officers, Congress may choose to—though it need not—override the generally applicable requirements of presidential nomination and Senate confirmation. Even when it exercises this option, however, Congress remains constrained in that inferior-officer appointments may be

---

competing views regarding the test's continued vitality); *see also* Nick Bravin, Note, *Is* Morrison v. Olson *Still Good Law? The Court's New Appointments Clause Jurisprudence*, 98 COLUM. L. REV. 1103 (1998) (analyzing this question not long after *Edmond* was decided). More recent decisions from the Court, however, leave little doubt that it now regards *Edmond* as setting forth the operative approach. *See* United States v. Arthrex, Inc., 141 S. Ct. 1970, 1981 (2021) (holding that Administrative Patent Judges of the U.S. Patent Trials and Appeal Board did not qualify as inferior officers because these judges had the power " 'to render a final decision on behalf of the United States' without any . . . review by their nominal superior or any other principal officer in the Executive Branch" (quoting *Edmond*, 529 U.S. at 665)); Free Enterprise Fund v. Public Co. Accounting Oversight Bd., 561 U.S. 477, 510–11 (2010) (relying on *Edmond*—and not *Morrison*—in concluding that members of the Public Company Accounting Oversight Board were inferior officers because they were subject to the "oversight authority" of the SEC).

68 *Edmond*, 520 U.S. at 664. Does the *Edmond* approach make sense? Simplicity in application and predictability of results are points in its favor, because application of the test often requires little more than a quick look at the relevant agency's organization chart. On the other hand, a supervision-focused sorting device might occasionally produce troubling outcomes. For instance, the rule of *Edmond* would seem to allow Congress to empower either the President or the Secretary of Defense, as one of the "Heads of Departments," to appoint the Secretary of the Army, the Secretary of the Navy, and other top-ranking Pentagon officials without any involvement by the Senate, on the theory that these officials are "directed and supervised" by the Secretary of Defense. Indeed, *Edmond*, if read for all it is worth, would seem to permit Congress to vest the appointment of all federal lower-court judges in the President alone (or in the Supreme Court), on the theory that those judges perform work that is "directed and supervised" by the nation's highest tribunal. *See* Tuan Samahon, *The Judicial Vesting Option: Opting Out of Nomination and Advice and Consent*, 67 OHIO ST. L.J. 783, 826–32 (2006) (contending that, under *Edmond*, lower court judges should qualify as "inferior officers"). *But cf.* Andrew Croner, Morrison, Edmond, *and the Power of Appointments*, 77 GEO. WASH. L. REV. 1002, 1011–14 (2009) (noting that the *Edmond* test "has been criticized for being overinclusive," but defending the test on the ground that it "place[s] the decision as to who require[s] the more cumbersome appointments process used for principal officers back in Congress's hands").

vested only in: (a) the "President alone"; (b) the "Courts of Law"; or (c) "the Heads of Departments." This limitation, in turn, has raised two sets of interpretive issues—one concerning the specific meaning of these terms (particularly "Courts of Law" and "Heads of Departments"), and the other concerning the permissibility of "interbranch appointments."

a. Defining Appointing Authorities: "Heads of Departments" and "Courts of Law"

Everyone knows what it means to vest an inferior officer's appointment in the "President alone." But the terms "Courts of Law" and "Heads of Departments" are not so clear. Consider *Freytag*, which involved a constitutional challenge to a law authorizing the Chief Judge of the United States Tax Court to appoint "special trial judges" to preside over and render preliminary decisions in tax-related disputes.[69] The Court had little difficulty classifying the special trial judges as "inferior officers" under the Appointments Clause.[70] That conclusion, however, gave rise to the separate and more difficult question whether "the Chief Judge of the Tax Court [could] constitutionally be vested by Congress with the power to appoint."[71]

The difficulty arose from the Tax Court's non-Article III status. Indeed, that tribunal had taken over the duties of a now-defunct executive-branch agency, and its judges did not enjoy the life-tenure or salary protections that Article III guarantees.[72] Thus, to uphold the statutory appointments arrangement, the Court needed to reach one of two conclusions: Either the Tax Court qualified as a "Court[ ] of Law" (despite its non-Article III status), or the Tax Court was a "Department[ ]" whose "Head[ ]" was the Chief Judge.

In an opinion for a five-member majority, Justice Blackmun opted for the first of these two conclusions, holding that the Tax Court qualified as a "Court[ ] of Law" and that the Chief Judge could therefore appoint inferior officers on that "Court's" behalf. The "Head of Department" theory did not work, he reasoned, because that term referred to persons who lead "divisions like the Cabinet-level departments" and not to " 'inferior commissioners and bureau officers' " like the Tax Court's Chief Judge.[73] By contrast, the "Court[ ] of Law" designation made sense. True, the Tax Court was

69 501 U.S. at 870–71.

70 *Id.* at 880–81.

71 *Id.* at 884.

72 *Id.* at 885. For more on non-Article III courts, see *supra* Section 29.C.

73 *Id.* at 886 (quoting *Germaine*, 99 U.S. at 511).

not formally part of the Article III judiciary.[74] But that fact was not dispositive of the issue, Justice Blackmun explained, because it remained true that the Tax Court's "function and role in the federal judicial scheme closely resemble those of the federal district courts."[75] In other words, even though the Tax Court did not formally qualify as an Article III tribunal, it still operated enough like such a tribunal to render it a "Court[ ] of Law" for Appointments Clause purposes.[76] And because it was a "Court[ ] of Law," it could validly make inferior-officer appointments through the actions of its Chief Judge.[77]

Writing for himself and three colleagues, Justice Scalia found that the majority had reached the right result but for the wrong reason.[78] In his view, the challenged provision was valid not because it channeled appointment authority to a "Court of Law," but instead because the Chief Judge of the Tax Court was a "Head of Department." As for the "Courts of Law" question, Justice Scalia could not understand the majority's willingness to look beyond the Tax Court's non-Article III status. For him, the Appointments Clause's reference to "*the* Courts of Law" signaled that the term did not embrace all " 'Bodies exercising judicial Functions' or even 'Courts of Law' generally"; rather, this terminology was, in his view, most naturally read to reference only "those courts of law envisioned by the Constitution"—that is, Article III tribunals.[79] Nonetheless, Justice Scalia concluded—again, in direct disagreement with the majority—that the Tax Court could and did qualify as a "Department," with the Chief Judge as its "Head." The term "Department," as he understood it, encompassed more than just "Cabinet-level" arms of the government; instead, it covered any "agenc[y] immediately below the President in the organizational structure of the Executive Branch."[80] The Tax Court, he added, fit this description because: (1) as a formal matter, it exercised "executive," rather than "judicial," power; and (2) as a functional matter, it was not subject to the supervision by any executive authority apart from the President.[81] Thus, Justice Scalia concluded,

---

[74] *Id.* at 888.

[75] *Id.* at 891.

[76] *Id.*

[77] *Id.*; *see also* James E. Pfander, *The Chief Justice, the Appointment of Inferior Officers, and the "Court of Law Requirement,"* 107 NW. U. L. REV. 1125, 1136–37 (2013) (noting that the Justices in *Freytag* "did not contest the power of the chief judge to act for the court" under the Appointments Clause, while questioning the soundness of this position on historical and structural grounds).

[78] *Freytag*, 501 U.S. at 892 (Scalia, J., concurring in part and concurring in the judgment).

[79] *Id.* at 901–02.

[80] *Id.* at 919.

[81] *Id.* at 915 (noting that the Tax Court "is a free-standing, self-contained entity in the Executive Branch, whose Chief Judge is removable by the President (and, save

the Chief Judge of the Tax Court was the "Head" of a "Department" to whom Congress could assign the authority to appoint inferior officers.

Notwithstanding Justices Scalia's protestations, Justice Blackmun's capacious conception of the term "Courts of Law" won the day in *Freytag* and remains still-governing law. With respect to the proper definition of "Heads of Departments," however, the view of the majority in *Freytag* has since lost out. The change came in *Free Enterprise Fund v. Public Company Accounting Oversight Board*,[82] in which the Court directly invoked Justice Scalia's *Freytag* concurrence in holding that the Securities Exchange Commission qualifies as a "Department" under the Appointments Clause, even though the SEC is not one of the " 'Executive departments' (*e.g.*, State, Treasury, Defense)" represented in the President's cabinet.[83] Thus, it now appears that, under current law, courts must embrace *both* the broader view of "Courts of Law" propounded by the *Freytag* majority (and rejected by the *Freytag* concurrence) *and* the broader view of "Heads of Departments" propounded by the *Freytag* concurrence (and rejected by the *Freytag* majority).[84] The curious consequence of this doctrinal synthesis is that these two terms now carry a collective doctrinal meaning that is likely more capacious than any one of the nine Justices in *Freytag* would have preferred.[85]

---

impeachment, no one else)"). The Tax Court's rulings, to be sure, were reviewable and reversible by Article III courts, *see id.* at 891–92 (majority opinion) (noting that the Tax Court's rulings are reviewable by the federal courts of appeals), but this fact did not undermine Justice Scalia's key point that the Tax Court itself was not subject to the direct authority of any other *executive-branch* entity.

82 561 U.S. 477 (2009).

83 561 U.S. at 510. The Court in *Free Enterprise Fund* also rejected the claim that Congress had violated the Appointments Clause by authorizing the Commissioners of the SEC to collectively appoint members of the Board, rather than by vesting that appointment authority specifically in a single individual designated as the "Head" of the agency. *Id.* at 512–13. That position was not sustainable, according to the Court, because there was "no reason why a multimember body may not be the 'Hea[d]' of a 'Departmen[t]' that it governs." *Id.*

84 It is not quite so simple as this because, as Professor Kent Barnett has noted, the Court in *Free Enterprise Fund* "failed to clarify exactly which reasoning in the *Freytag* concurring opinion it adopted and which portion, if any, of the majority opinion in *Freytag* remains good law." *See* Kent H. Barnett, *The Consumer Financial Protection Bureau's Appointment With Trouble*, 60 AM. U. L. REV. 1459, 1472 (2011). Broadly speaking, however, the Court's express reliance on Justice Scalia's *Freytag* concurrence to conclude that the SEC qualified as a "Department" signaled a general acceptance of that concurrence's broader understanding of the term "Heads of Departments" (and, correspondingly, a general rejection of the *Freytag* majority's narrower understanding of the same term).

85 Technically, the Court in *Free Enterprise Fund* did not overrule the *Freytag* majority opinion on the "Heads of Department" point insofar as that opinion contained dicta suggesting that the SEC, as "one of the principal agencies," might be functionally similar enough to a Cabinet-level Department as to qualify as a "Department" within the meaning of the Appointments Clause. *See Freytag*, 501 U.S. at 868; *see also id.* at

b. The Permissibility of Interbranch Appointments

To what extent can Congress utilize its authority under the Appointments Clause to authorize the appointment of inferior officers located in one branch of the government by individuals who work in another? Recall *Morrison*. The law at issue in that case authorized a panel of Article III judges to appoint an Independent Counsel to engage in investigatory and prosecutorial work in the executive branch under the auspices of the Department of Justice.[86] The Independent Counsel, as we have seen, was deemed to be an "inferior officer," and the judicial panel granted appointment authority was deemed to be a "Court[ ] of Law."[87] Even so, the challenger in *Morrison* argued that this statutory arrangement was unconstitutional because it authorized an *interbranch appointment* by enabling officers of one branch (here, the judicial branch) to appoint an inferior officer of another branch (here, the executive branch) and thus to impermissibly meddle in that other branch's business.[88]

In the view of the Court, however, this argument clashed with the text of the Appointments Clause, which on its face indicates that congressional decisionmakers can pick and choose "as they think proper" among the listed options of appointing authorities.[89] At the same time, the Court left open the possibility that some interbranch appointments might create a constitutionally intolerable "incongruity" between the functions of the appointing authority and the functions of the officer being appointed.[90] (To take a few hypothetical examples, Congress might not be permitted to vest the appointment of the Assistant Secretary of State for Consular Affairs in the Supreme Court of the United States or to vest the appointment of federal magistrate judges in the Secretary of Veterans Affairs.) In *Morrison*, however, there was no "inherent incongruity about a court having the power to appoint prosecutorial officers."[91] To the contrary, longstanding and routine "judicial experience with prosecutors in criminal cases" rendered the statutory appointment process for the

---

916 (Scalia, J., concurring in part and concurring in the judgment) (noting that the majority opinion in *Freytag* "reserves the right to consider as 'Cabinet-like' and hence as 'Departments' " certain non-Cabinet entities, including the SEC). Still, insofar as the Court in *Free Enterprise Fund* relied on Justice Scalia's *Freytag* concurrence rather than Justice Blackmun's *Freytag* majority opinion to defend this conclusion, it offered a more general rebuke of the *Freytag* majority's effort to confine the "Department" designation to only Cabinet-level (as well as, perhaps, Cabinet-like) entities.

86 *See supra* Section 30.A.2.

87 *Morrison*, 487 U.S. at 678–79.

88 *Id.* at 673.

89 *Id.* (quoting U.S. CONST. art. II, § 2, cl. 2).

90 *Id.* at 676 (quoting *Siebold*, 100 U.S. at 398).

91 *Id.*

independent counsel nonproblematic.[92] Thus, while the Constitution might block Congress from vesting the appointment power in officials with "no special knowledge or expertise" regarding the relevant inferior office, no such difficulty was presented by the Independent Counsel Act.[93]

B. CIRCUMVENTING SENATE CONFIRMATION

Notwithstanding the requirements of the Appointments Clause, individuals sometimes assume high-ranking executive-branch positions without going through the Senate confirmation process. This can occur in either of two ways: (1) through the President's making of temporary "recess appointments" under the Article II Recess Appointments Clause; or (2) through the designation of individuals to serve as "acting officials" while an executive-branch office remains unoccupied.

1. Recess Appointments

After setting forth the baseline rules for the appointment of both principal and inferior officers, Article II, section 2 goes on to provide that "[t]he President shall have Power to fill up all Vacancies that may happen during the Recess of the Senate, by granting Commissions which shall expire at the End of their next Session."[94] As noted by Alexander Hamilton in *The Federalist No. 67*, this Clause established "an auxiliary method of appointment" for use "in cases to which the general method was inadequate."[95] More specifically, circumstances could arise in which an adjournment of the Senate, perhaps for a lengthy period, would render that body unable to confirm nominations that required prompt action. It thus made sense to enable the President to deal with vacancies "which it might be necessary for the public service to fill without delay."[96]

---

92 *Id.* (noting the courts' past appointments of (1) "private attorneys to act as prosecutor for judicial contempt judgments," (2) "United States commissioners, who exercise[ ] certain limited prosecutorial powers," (3) federal marshals, and (4) interim U.S. Attorneys).

93 For a thoughtful proposal regarding how courts might implement this "incongruity" limit on the ground, see Kent Barnett, *Resolving the ALJ Quandary*, 66 VAND. L. REV. 797, 840–44 (2013) (proposing that courts first "determin[e] whether a significant reason for the interbranch appointment exists," then "consider[ ] whether the interbranch appointment impedes the central functioning of the appointing branch," and finally "consider[ ] whether the appointment impedes the central function of the competing branch").

94 U.S. CONST. art. 2, § 3, cl. 3. A "Session" of the Senate corresponds roughly to a calendar year, meaning that a recess appointee's term can last anywhere between one to two years, depending on when, relative to the "next Session," the appointment is made.

95 *See* THE FEDERALIST NO. 67 (Hamilton).

96 *Id.* The Court has not directly addressed the question whether the President's power to make recess appointments only applies to executive-branch officials or also

Today, because advances in communications and transportation technology have made it much easier to call the Senate back into session at even a moment's notice (and because the Senate is in any event much more frequently in session), this justification for the Recess Appointments Clause has lost much of its force. Even so, Presidents have continued to invoke the clause—often for purposes very different from those that Hamilton described. In particular, the recess-appointments power today functions primarily as a means of securing the appointment of nominees that the Senate refuses to confirm.[97] In other words, when confirmation-related problems arise, the President can simply wait for the Senate to adjourn and then make a recess appointment while the body is out of session. To be sure, a temporary recess appointment is not the same thing as the appointment of a fully confirmed member of the President's closest group of advisors. But from the President's perspective, the recess appointment of an unconfirmable ally will often prove preferable to no appointment at all.

---

extends to federal judges. *See* Louis Fisher, CONG. RSCH. SERV., RL31112, RECESS APPOINTMENTS OF FEDERAL JUDGES 24 (2001) (noting the "unsettled" status of the issue). By its own terms, however, the Recess Appointments Clause makes no distinction between executive and judicial branch officials, and several lower courts have upheld judicial recess appointments for this reason. *See, e.g.*, Evans v. Stephens, 387 F.3d 1220, 1223–24 (11th Cir. 2004) (en banc) (noting as of 2004 that over 300 such appointments had been made, including fifteen recess appointments of Supreme Court Justices); United States v. Woodley, 751 F.2d 1008 (9th Cir.1985) (en banc); United States v. Allocco, 305 F.2d 704 (2d Cir. 1962). Some analysts nonetheless have raised the question whether judicial recess appointments violate Article III's life-tenure guarantee insofar as they authorize individuals to serve as judges for only a temporary period of time. *See Woodley*, 751 F.2d at 1024 (Norris, J., dissenting) (contending that "the principles that animate the salary and tenure provisions of Article III—judicial independence and separation of powers—clearly outweigh the concerns of expediency and efficiency that underlie the Recess Appointments Clause"). *But see* Edward A. Hartnett, *Recess Appointments of Article III Judges: Three Constitutional Questions*, 26 CARDOZO L. REV 377, 428–29 (2005) (noting as of 2005 that "[a]ll but six of our presidents have made recess appointments to Article III courts" and that "the judges who accepted such recess appointments include Bushrod Washington, Benjamin Curtis, Earl Warren, William Brennan, Potter Stewart, Augustus Hand, Irving Kaufman, William Hastie, David Bazelon, Thurgood Marshall, Wilfred Feinberg, Griffin Bell, A. Leon Higginbotham, Spottswood Robinson, and Roger Gregory"; also urging that "[w]e should hesitate long before reaching th[e] conclusion" that "every one of those presidents violated the Constitution" and that "every one of those judges did so as well").

[97] In fact, this sort of strategic use of the recess appointments power dates back to the earliest days of the republic. *See* Nicole Schwartzberg, *What is a "Recess"?: Recess Appointments and the Framers' Understandings of Advice and Consent*, 28 J.L. & POL. 231, 264 (2013) (noting that many of the earliest recess appointments, including George Washington's recess appointment of John Rutledge as Chief Justice of the United States, and James Madison's recess appointments of Albert Gallatin, John Quincy Adams, and James A. Bayard to serve as special envoys to negotiate a peace treaty with Great Britain, were made in the face of "vigorous Senate opposition").

That at least was where things stood leading up to the presidency of Barack Obama, who, like many of his predecessors, turned to the recess appointments power in an attempt to bypass a hostile Senate's refusal to confirm his nominees. Senate Republicans, however, responded by attempting to block these appointments by punctuating otherwise long-term adjournments of the body with brief, *pro forma* sessions held every few days.[98] These sessions typically involved little more than a single Senator banging the gavel before a mostly (if not entirely) empty Senate chamber. But the ritual sufficed, Republicans argued, to prevent there from being any "recess" long enough in duration to trigger application of the President's recess-appointments power. The President saw things differently, however, and, in January of 2012, while the Senate was conducting only *pro forma* sessions, made three recess appointments to the National Labor Relations Board.[99]

These appointments prompted a constitutional challenge, and that challenge resulted in the Court's first (and to date its only) in-depth treatment of the Recess Appointments Clause. The case was *NLRB v. Noel Canning*,[100] in which a Pepsi distributor sought to nullify an NLRB order by arguing that, due to the alleged invalidity of the President's recess appointments, a majority of the Board's membership had not been properly installed.[101] The employer's central argument tracked the Senate Republicans' logic: The President's appointments were unlawful because the continuous holding of *pro forma* sessions meant that there had never been a period of adjournment long enough to support an exercise of the recess appointment power.[102] The employer also advanced two alternative arguments that, it claimed, showed why the recess appointments were invalid in any event. First, it urged that the clause authorized appointments only during the once-per-year recess

---

98 In so doing, they were taking a page from the playbook of Senate Democrats, who had earlier utilized the "pro forma sessions" maneuver in an effort to block various attempted recess appointments by President George W. Bush. *See* Alexander M. Wolf, Note, *Taking Back What's Theirs: The Recess Appointments Clause, Pro Forma Sessions, and a Political Tug of War*, 81 FORDHAM L. REV. 2055, 2067–68 (2013).

99 See Press Release, White House, President Obama Announces Recess Appointments to Key Administration Posts (Jan. 4, 2012), http://www.whitehouse.gov/the-press-office/2012/01/04/President-obama-announces-recess-appointments-key-administration-posts. The President on the same day announced the recess appointment of Richard Cordray to serve as Director of the Consumer Financial Protection Bureau. *Id.* Unlike the NLRB appointees, however, Cordray was eventually confirmed by the Senate to serve in the post. *See* Binyamin Appelbaum, *Vote Ushers in New Era in Oversight of Lending Practices*, N.Y. TIMES (July 16, 2013), https://www.nytimes.com/2013/07/17/business/cordray-confirmed-as-head-of-financial-watchdog-after-long-wait.html.

100 573 U.S. 513 (2014).

101 *Id.* at 520.

102 *Id.* at 520–21.

that separates one "Session" of Congress from the next. (The argument, if accepted by the Court, would have meant a victory for the employer because President Obama's NLRB appointments had occurred during an intra-session rather than inter-session adjournment of Congress.)[103] Second, the employer argued that the clause's reference to "Vacancies that may *happen* during the Recess" permitted recess appointments only to offices that had *become vacant* during the pendency of the recess itself. (This proposition too would have doomed the NLRB appointments because they involved vacancies that had arisen prior to, rather than in the midst of, the operative Senate recess.) The Court thus had before it three separate questions regarding the scope of the Recess Appointments Clause: First, did the clause permit appointments during only intersession recesses or during both inter- and intra-session recesses? Second, did the clause permit the President to fill vacancies that had arisen before a recess? And third, did the Senate's holding of regular *pro forma* sessions work to defeat the President's invocation of the recess appointment power?

In an opinion written by Justice Breyer, the Court ruled in favor of the President on the first two questions but against him on the last. As to intra-session recesses, Justice Breyer acknowledged that the text of the clause (and in particular its use of the term "*the* Recess of the Senate") was "ambiguous," but he ultimately concluded that confining the recess-appointments power to only inter-session recesses would undermine the clause's "purpose" of "ensur[ing] the continued functioning of the Federal Government when the Senate is away."[104] As for the claim that the power does not extend to pre-recess vacancies, the Court instead endorsed a broader reading of the clause, construing its reference to vacancies that "may happen during the recess" as encompassing all vacancies in existence during a

---

[103] *Id.* at 521–22; *see also* NLRB v. Noel Canning, 705 F.3d 490, 499–507 (D.C. Cir. 2013) (embracing this theory to hold that the President's recess appointments were invalid), *aff'd on other grounds*, 573 U.S. 513.

[104] *Noel Canning*, 573 U.S. at 528. In other words, it made little sense to treat inter-session absences differently than intra-session absences, given the Framers' underlying goal of giving the President ample staffing flexibility when the Senate is unable to quickly reconvene. At the time of the Founding, after all, either type of absence would have presented difficulties with regard to prompt return. Moreover, past presidents had frequently made use of intra-session appointments, and the Senate had "done nothing to deny the validity of this practice for at least three-quarters of a century." *Id.* at 529–34. Thus, the Court concluded, the intra-session nature of President Obama's NLRB appointments did not undercut their legitimacy. *But see Noel Canning*, 573 U.S. at 576 (Scalia, J., concurring in the judgment) (contending that, during the founding era, " 'the phrase 'the Recess' always referred to the gap between sessions' " (quoting Robert G. Natelson, *The Origins and Meaning of "Vacancies that May Happen During the Recess" in the Constitution's Recess Appointments Clause*, 37 HARV. J.L. & PUB. POL'Y 199, 213 (2014))).

period of adjournment, regardless of when they had initially arisen.[105]

That left the issue of the *pro forma* sessions. And now, having sided with the President on the two first two issues, the Court sided with the challengers instead. The *pro forma* sessions, Justice Breyer declared, were not meaningless; instead, because they counted as live sessions of the Senate under its own rules and—critically, in the Court's view—preserved the upper chamber's "capacity to transact Senate business," they were enough to defeat the President's attempted exercise of the recess-appointments power.[106] In addition, the Court stressed the appropriateness of deferring to the Senate's view of its own operations in light of the Constitution's "broad delegation of authority" to the Senate of the power to establish its own "Rules of . . . Proceedings."[107] In short, the *pro forma* sessions qualified, for constitutional purposes, as actual and legitimate convenings of the Senate itself, and they thus had the effect of denying to the President a period of Senate adjournment that was long enough to trigger application of the recess appointments power.[108]

Although the Court in *Noel Canning* handed down a mixed verdict on the meaning of the Recess Appointments Clause, its ruling was in a more practical sense a defeat for the office of the President. True, the Court interpreted the clause to authorize recess appointments under a broader set of circumstances than the challengers would have liked. But none of that much mattered because the Court's rejection of the President's substance-over-form

---

[105] *Noel Canning*, 573 U.S. at 538. To be sure, as Justice Breyer acknowledged, the "most natural meaning" of the phrase was the one that favored the challengers' position. *Id.* But the text still permitted the "broader interpretation," and considerations of purpose and historical precedent cut strongly in its favor. In particular, the Court worried that an endorsement of the challenger's position would "prevent the President from making any recess appointment that arose before a recess, no matter who the official, no matter how dire the need, no matter how uncontroversial the appointment, and no matter how late in the session the office fell vacant," whereas the broader interpretation was "more consistent with the Constitution's 'reason and spirit.' " *Id.* at 543 (quoting *Executive Authority to Fill Vacancies*, 1. OP. ATTY. GEN. 631, 632, 632 (1821)). As for historical practice, the broader reading found support in several past recess appointments (coupled with the Senate's apparent acquiescence to those appointments). *See id.* at 543–49; *see also* Hartnett, *supra* note 96, at 381–407 (citing numerous historical examples of past recess appointments involving pre-recess vacancies). *But see* Michael B. Rappaport, *The Original Meaning of the Recess Appointments Clause*, 52 UCLA L. REV. 1487, 1502–40 (2005) (offering a lengthy defense of the narrower, "arise interpretation" of the clause).

[106] *Noel Canning*, 573 U.S. at 550.

[107] *Id.* at 551 (quoting U.S. CONST. art. I, § 5).

[108] The Court more generally appeared to indicate, while leaving itself some wiggle room, that a recess would need to last at least 10 days before triggering application of the power. *See id.* at 536–38 (suggesting that "a recess of more than 3 days but less than 10 days is presumptively too short to fall within the Clause").

argument gave the Senate just the sort of self-serving authority it had sought to exercise. In effect, the Court endorsed the view that the Senate has a near-total power to prevent recess appointments from ever being made. In one sense, this has always been true: The Senate controls its own calendar, after all, and it undoubtedly has the prerogative to remain in session for the explicit purpose of denying to the President any recess-appointment opportunities. But there is a difference between actually remaining in session (and bearing the costs of being indefinitely stuck in D.C.) and effectively pretending to stay in session (and, except for the handful of nearby Senators who "preside" over *pro forma* sessions, suffering no inconvenience at all). By validating the Senate's use of *pro forma* sessions in January 2012, the Court in *Noel Canning* gave to that body an essentially costless means of preventing unwanted recess appointments from ever being made. And with the Senate now able to remain in session with no real impact on its members, the recess-appointments power is unlikely to be of much use to future Presidents who confront political resistance to their nominees.

2. Acting Officials and the Federal Vacancies Reform Act

Although the recess-appointments power has now been marginalized, a different sort of "confirmation-avoidance" technique remains at the President's disposal. This strategy involves the Federal Vacancies Reform Act of 1998 (Vacancies Act) and various related statutes that set forth rules regarding the selection of "acting" officials to discharge on a temporary basis the functions of agency positions that formally remain vacant.[109] Ostensibly designed to ensure the smooth and continued functioning of agencies in the wake of sudden leadership departures,[110] the Vacancies Act has proven to be a useful tool for Presidents determined to place unconfirmable political allies in high-ranking positions of power.[111] The strategy is simple: Rather than acting to fill a vacancy, the President simply leaves that vacancy in place and then uses the Vacancies Act (or, in some instances, an agency-specific statute with similar vacancy-related rules) to ensure that powers of the vacant office devolve on a person of the President's non-Senate-approved choosing.

Of particular significance in this respect is section 3345 of the Vacancies Act, which specifies that, when an office becomes vacant,

---

[109] 5 U.S.C. §§ 3345 *et seq.*

[110] *See* Anne Joseph O'Connell, *Actings*, 120 COLUM. L. REV. 613, 625–27 (2020) (describing the predecessors to the 1998 Vacancies Act and the circumstances of its adoption).

[111] *See id.* at 619–23 (canvassing President Trump's many uses of the Vacancies Act and related statutes to circumvent the Senate's advice-and-consent function).

the "first assistant" to the holder of that office shall immediately assume the office's "functions and duties."[112] That default rule, however, is subject to override by the President, who may "direct" that the acting position be occupied by either: (a) someone who has already been confirmed by the Senate to serve in any other executive-branch position; or (b) a sufficiently high-ranking "officer or employee" already working within the relevant agency.[113] These rules are subject to several qualifications, including a limit on the duration of an acting official's tenure[114] and a prohibition on acting service by a person formally nominated to fill the position.[115] Even so, the Vacancies Act in overall operation confers significant discretion on the President to control the management of agencies whose leadership positions are unoccupied.

Earlier-serving presidents sometimes used this strategy to make *de facto* appointments outside the Senate confirmation process. But President Trump took the practice to a new level, relying frequently and openly on the Vacancies Act as a confirmation-avoidance device.[116] In turn, several of his "acting" appointments gave rise to litigation,[117] leading some lower courts to hold that certain appointments violated the Vacancies Act or related statutory or

---

[112] 5 U.S.C. § 3345(a). Notably, the rules set forth by the Vacancies Act do not apply to all vacancies; for example, they do not cover vacancies on multimember boards or commissions, or on non-Article III courts. *See id.* §§ 3345(a), 3349c. In addition, the Vacancies Act does not apply to offices covered by agency-specific line-of-succession statutes that "expressly" supersede the Act's terms. *See id.* § 3347(a).

[113] *Id.* §§ 3345(a)(2), 3345(a)(3). More specifically, the "officer or employee" of the agency must have served for at least 90 days in a position whose "rate of pay" is "equal to or greater than the minimum rate of pay payable for a position at GS-15 at the General Schedule," the highest grade of the federal general pay schedule. *Id.*

[114] *See* O'Connell, *supra* note 110, at 628–31.

[115] 5 U.S.C. § 3346(a)(1). In general, the law permits an acting official to serve for up to 210 days after the vacancy's creation, while also allowing for various extensions in the event that a nomination to fill the vacancy has been submitted to the Senate. *Id.* These extensions can work to lengthen an acting official's tenure well beyond the baseline period of 210 days; indeed, if the President and Senate leadership play their cards right, a single acting official can serve under the Vacancies Act for over two-and-a-half years. *See* O'Connell, *supra* note 110, at 631.

[116] As President Trump himself said of his acting officials: "I sort of like 'acting.' It gives me more flexibility; do you understand that? I like 'acting.' " Felicia Sonmez, *Trump Says He's "In No Hurry" To Replace Acting Cabinet Members*, WASH. POST (Jan. 6, 2019), https://www.washingtonpost.com/politics/trump-says-hes-in-no-hurry-to-replace-acting-cabinet-members/2019/01/06/afac5fea-11e4-11e9-b6ad-9cfd62dbb0a8_story.html.

[117] *See, e.g.*, Guedes v. Bureau of Alcohol, Tobacco, Firearms & Explosives, 356 F. Supp. 3d 121, 137–55 (D.D.C 2019) (rejecting a legal challenge to Matthew Whitaker's authority to serve as acting Attorney General under the Vacancies Act), *aff'd*, 920 F.3d 1 (D.C. Cir. 2019), *cert. denied*, 140 S. Ct. 789 (2020); English v. Trump, 279 F. Supp.3d 307 (D.D.C. 2018) (finding that the President's designation of Mick Mulvaney to serve as acting Director of the Consumer Financial Protection Bureau was likely valid under the Vacancies Act, notwithstanding the prior Director's effort to designate another individual, Leandra English, to serve as acting Director instead).

agency-promulgated rules.[118] For the most part, however, these judicial decisions did not address—and have thus left unresolved—key *constitutional* questions concerning the Vacancies Act and other statutes like it.[119]

The most important of these question concerns the relationship between the Vacancies Act and the Appointment Clause's advice-and-consent requirement. Some judges, including Justice Thomas, have expressed the view that the Vacancies Act violates the Appointments Clause insofar as it permits the President to designate persons not previously confirmed by the Senate (and who sometimes do not even qualify as "officers") to assume the acting duties of principal officers.[120] The standard response to this contention, which draws some support from the Court's 1898 opinion in *United States v. Eaton*,[121] is that the temporary nature of an acting appointment renders the acting official an "inferior officer," who accordingly can be appointed by the "President alone."[122] That argument, however, rests uneasily alongside the Court's more recent ruling in *Edmond*, which indicates that the principal/inferior officer distinction depends mainly (if not exclusively) on the officer's *place* in the agency hierarchy and not—as the Court had earlier suggested in both *Eaton* and *Morrison*—on the *length of time* for which that officer serves.[123]

---

[118] *See* L.M.-M v. Cuccinelli, 442 F. Supp. 3d 1, 24–29 (D.D.C. 2020) (holding that Ken Cuccinelli's ascension to the position of acting Director of USCIS was likely invalid under the Vacancies Act because Cuccinelli, who had been appointed to a "first assistant" position *after* the Director position had become vacant, never in fact "serve[d] in a subordinate role" to anyone else within the agency and was thus ineligible to become acting Director of the agency); Casa de Maryland, Inc. v. Wolf, 486 F. Supp. 3d 928, 957–60 (D. Md. 2020) (finding that Chad Wolf's designation as acting Secretary of Homeland Security pursuant to an DHS succession order was invalid, because the succession order itself had been issued by an earlier acting Secretary of Homeland Security, Kevin McAleenan, whose designation had also been *ultra vires*); Bullock v. U.S. Bureau of Land Mgmt., 489 F. Supp.3d 1112, 1126–30 (D. Mt. 2020) (holding that the U.S. Secretary of Interior had delegated to William Perry Pendley a set of powers that made him the *de facto* acting Director of the U.S. Bureau of Land Management and that the delegation was improper because Pendley lacked the authority to serve as acting Director under both the Vacancies Act and the Appointments Clause).

[119] *See, e.g.*, O'Connell, *supra* note 110, at 661 (noting that "the Supreme Court has not ruled on the constitutional status of acting officials in principal offices since 1898").

[120] *See* NLRB v. S.W. General, Inc., 137 S. Ct. 929, 946 (2017) (Thomas, J., concurring).

[121] 169 U.S. 331, 338 (1898) (noting that a subordinate officer "charged with the performance of the duty of the superior for a limited time" was not "thereby transformed into the superior and permanent official").

[122] U.S. CONST. art. II, § 2; *see also Guedes*, 356 F. Supp. 3d at 153–54 (holding that Matthew Whitaker's service as acting Attorney General did not violate the Appointments Clause because Whitaker, who served "for a mere 100 days," did not ever "become a principal officer under the Appointments Clause").

[123] *See* Thomas A. Berry, S.W. General: *The Court Reins in Unilateral Appointments*, 2017 CATO SUP. CT. REV. 151 (noting the tension between *Edmond* and

After *Edmond*, for example, it would seem that an acting Attorney General (including one who had not previously received Senate confirmation) would qualify as a principal officer no less than a permanent Attorney General would so qualify, given that both acting and permanent Attorneys General operate subject to the direct supervision of the President and no one else.[124] And if the acting-Attorney General cannot be characterized as an inferior officer, then the Appointments Clause would seem to forbid any non-Senate confirmed individual from exercising power in that capacity.[125]

Constitutional issues also arise when already-Senate-confirmed officials assume new "acting" duties. Consider the case of Mick Mulvaney, who, having been confirmed by the Senate as Director of the Office of Management and Budget (OMB), was later designated under the Vacancies Act to serve as acting Director of the Consumer Financial Protection Bureau (CFPB).[126] At first glance, Mulvaney's taking on of these new duties might not seem to have posed an Appointments Clause problem; even assuming, after all, that the acting Director of the CFPB counts as a principal officer, Mulvaney himself had already been confirmed by the Senate and thus seemed to satisfy the relevant constitutional prerequisite.[127] But a potential difficulty arises when one notes that the Senate confirmed Mulvaney to serve in a position (Director of the OMB) quite different from the one into which he later was placed (Director of the CFPB). Did many (if any) of the Senators who voted to confirm Mulvaney's OMB

---

the "limited tenure" rationale for concluding that acting officials have inferior-officer status); *Edmond*, 520 U.S. at 662–63. On the other hand, the Court in *Edmond* did note its previous holding in *Eaton* that "a vice consul charged temporarily with the duties of the consul" counted as an "inferior officer." *See Edmond*, 520 U.S. at 661 (citing *Eaton*, 169 U.S. at 343). It is not clear, however, whether that citation was intended to signal the Court's continued approval of the underlying logic of the *Eaton* decision or whether it instead merely served the descriptive purpose of recounting a prior Appointments Clause holding.

[124] *Cf. S.W. General, Inc.*, 137 S. Ct. at 947–48 (Thomas, J., concurring) (implicitly rejecting the suggestion that an acting official's temporary service sufficed to render that official an inferior rather than principal officer).

[125] In addition, even if one concedes that all acting officials are "inferior" rather than "principal" officers, there remains the question whether the Appointments Clause permits a "first assistant" to *automatically* assume the duties of a vacant office without any explicit Presidential appointment of any kind. The problem arises because, under the Appointments Clause, even inferior officers must be "appoint[ed]" by someone. U.S. CONST. art. II, sec. 2. One potential way around this objection would be to treat a first-assistant's ascension to the role of an acting official as a contingent feature of the office to which that person was originally appointed. That is, we might understand that any individual who has been validly appointed to serve as Deputy Secretary of State has also been validly (if contingently) to serve as acting Secretary of State to the extent warranted by the Vacancies Act.

[126] *See, e.g.*, *English*, 279 F. Supp. 3d at 313–15 (recounting the circumstances of the Mulvaney appointments).

[127] *See id.* at 330 (noting Mulvaney's prior confirmation to the post of OMB Director).

appointment understand themselves to be contingently signing off on Mulvaney's later taking charge of the CFPB? And if not, could Mulvaney's assignment to the CFPB really be said to have been done with the Senate's "advice and consent"? The Court, to be sure, has not spoken directly on these questions. But it has elsewhere indicated that amending a statute to significantly alter, and thus expand, a principal officer's responsibilities is impermissible in the absence of a fresh nomination and confirmation.[128] And, under that principle, it is hard to see why a new nomination and confirmation would not similarly be required when a principal officer is assigned to a position that bears little relation to the one for which that officer was originally confirmed.[129]

Hovering other these constitutional questions is the obvious practical need to ensure that federal administrative agencies, many of which serve critical public functions, continue to operate smoothly when their leadership positions become vacant. The Vacancies Act, in many cases, serves this purpose well. It also helps to ensure democratic responsiveness during presidential transitions by giving newly elected Presidents some flexibility to install interim agency leaders as their formal nominations make their way through the Senate. The statute may also have value as a safeguard against Senate obstruction; under some circumstances, the President might manage to wield the threat of a senatorially unwanted Vacancies Act designation for the purpose of bringing opposition Senators to the negotiating table. On the other hand, countervailing dangers also exist. Put to work in all-out fashion, the Vacancies Act holds the potential to support an Appointments Clause "exception" of such breadth as to effectively swallow that clause's advice-and-consent rule.[130]

---

[128] *See supra* note 7 (noting the Court's decisions in *Shoemaker*, 147 U.S. 282, and *Weiss*, 510 U.S. 163).

[129] *See* Berry, *supra* note 123, at 178–79 (noting the potential doctrinal relevance of the question whether the duties of an acting office are "germane" to those of the office to which the acting official was originally appointed).

[130] For a recently scholarly proposal to limit Vacancies Act-based circumvention of the Article II advice-and-consent requirement, see Ronald J. Krotoszynski, Jr. & Atticus DeProspo, *Squaring a Circle: Advice and Consent, Faithful Execution, and the Vacancies Reform Act*, 55 GA. L. REV. 731, 742–43 (2021) (advocating for a reading of the Vacancies Act that would permit acting principal officers to serve only in a "caretaker" capacity, meaning that such officers could perform "essential or necessary tasks," but not "any discretionary actions").

Chapter 31

THE REMOVAL POWER

Analysis

Sec.

The Constitution speaks with only ambiguity-laden brevity to the subject of removing federal officeholders. As for legislative officials, Article I, section 5, permits each chamber, "with the Concurrence of two thirds, [to] expel a Member."[1] And as for executive and judicial officials, the document's only explicit removal-related provisions concern the subject of impeachment.[2] But while most observers view impeachment as the sole vehicle for removing federal judges from office in light of their enjoyment of lifetime appointments,[3] a very different set of questions arises when it comes to the removal of officeholders in the executive branch. What if, for example, the President has lost faith in the Secretary of State's ability to implement the President's foreign-policy agenda? May the President fire the Secretary of State on that basis alone? What if the firing is based on jealously or a personal grudge? Do presidential removal orders require the approval of Congress, or at least of the Senate? Does it matter whether the Senate previously confirmed the appointment of the officer the President wants to fire? Even if no such constitutional limits exist, can Congress impose prospective restrictions on the President's power to remove some or all executive branch officials—providing by statute, for instance, that specified officers may be fired only "for good cause"? If it may impose such restrictions for only some executive officers, which ones may it choose to protect? On these and other related questions, the constitutional text offers no explicit guidance.

---

1 U.S. CONST. art. I, § 5; *see also supra* Section 14.B.

2 *See infra* Section 32.A.

3 *But see infra* Section 32.A.3.a n.41 (highlighting scholarship that defends the possibility of removing federal judges through other means).

The Constitution's taciturnity on these issues hardly means they are unimportant. To the contrary, questions about removal are of great significance to the operation of the federal government. The power to remove, after all, carries with it the power to control; if *A* can remove *B* from office at any time for any reason, then that fact gives *B* strong reason to act in strict accordance with *A*'s wishes. By the same token, if *A* can remove *B* under only limited (if any) circumstances, then *B* will enjoy some level of independence from *A*'s control. Thus, when we ask who gets to remove whom and for what, we are in effect asking how to allocate decisionmaking power among Congress, the President, and the federal administrative state.

A. THE THEORETICAL DEBATE

Questions about removal implicate two competing theories regarding the nature of the presidency. The first theory, often called the "unitary executive" theory, posits that the Vesting and Take Care Clauses of Article II give the President complete control over the departments and agencies that wield executive power. This does not mean that the President must personally render every law-execution decision on behalf of every unit of the executive branch; that would be a logistical impossibility. It means instead that, when individuals other than the President exercise executive power, they always must do so from a position that is subject to unfettered presidential oversight and control.[4] Put differently, while Article II might not forbid Congress from dispersing law-execution responsibilities among different executive-branch officials, proponents of the unitary executive theory insist that those officials must always discharge their responsibilities as subordinate assistants to the President, rather than as autonomous or even semi-autonomous actors. Unitarians thus reject both the view that the Constitution by its own terms imposes any limits on the President's power to remove and even the more flexible view that Congress may, but need not, impose some such limits by statute. Restrictions of any kind, proponents of the unitary-executive theory insist, operate to deprive the President of complete supervisory control over the officials to whom they apply. And without complete supervisory control over all executive officials, the President lacks the full and unfettered "executive power" that, they claim, Article II vests exclusively in "a President of the United States" and no one else.

---

4 *See, e.g.*, Morrison v. Olson, 487 U.S. 654, 705 (1988) (Scalia, J., dissenting) (contending that the Article II reference to the "executive power" of the President "does not mean *some of* the executive power, but *all of* the executive power"); Steven G. Calabresi & Saikrishna B. Prakash, *The President's Power to Execute the Laws*, 104 YALE L.J. 541, 544 (1994) (noting that "[t]he claim made by unitary executivists" is "that the Constitution creates only three branches of government and that the President must be able to control the execution of all federal laws").

The alternative view reflects what might be called the "congressionalist" or "non-unitarian" position. Proponents of this approach ascribe a less absolutist significance to Article II, and they instead place emphasis on *Article I*'s vesting in Congress of the power to make all laws that are "necessary and proper for carrying into execution" the powers of the federal government, including the executive powers. Put differently, if, as the Necessary and Proper Clause suggests, the Constitution empowers Congress to establish departments and agencies for the purpose of administering the laws that Congress chooses to enact, then it naturally follows that Congress has a companion power to structure those departments and agencies in sensible ways, including by insulating them, in appropriate cases, from full-bore presidential control. Congress, in particular, might sometimes have very good reasons to make such a choice—most notably, when an official's law-enforcement functions would benefit from the application of apolitical expertise.[5] Statutory removal restrictions, on this view, are no more remarkable than the variety of other detailed legislative provisions that Congress might regard as "helpful" and "conducive" to carrying into execution the powers that the Constitution creates.[6]

As we will see, Supreme Court doctrine reflects some ambivalence in choosing between these two views.[7] On the one hand,

---

[5] Consider, for instance, the oft-cited suggestion that members of the Federal Reserve Board need to have a measure of independence from the President in order to "stop[ ] a President trying to win a second term from manipulating interest rates." Seila Law, LLC v. CPFB, 140 S. Ct. 2183, 2237 (2020) (Kagan, J., concurring in the judgment with respect to severability and dissenting in part).

[6] *See, e.g.*, Lawrence Lessig & Cass R. Sunstein, *The President and the Administration*, 94 COLUM. L. REV. 1, 68 (1994) (maintaining that the Necessary and Proper Clause gives Congress "the power to define the means to carry into effect any power of the federal government" and that "it is Congress that is vested with the power to determine how to structure the administration and how it is to function"); John Manning, *Separation of Powers as Ordinary Interpretation*, 124 HARV. L. REV. 1939, 1967 (2011) ("Because [the Necessary and Proper Clause] expressly grants Congress at least some authority to structure the way the executive and judicial powers are 'carried into Execution,' one cannot establish a constitutional violation simply by showing that Congress has constrained the way 'the executive Power' is implemented." (internal footnotes omitted)); *see also Seila Law*, 140 S. Ct. at 2227 (Kagan, J., concurring in the judgment with respect to severability and dissenting in part) (noting that "Article II presumes the existence of 'Officer[s]' in 'executive Departments' but "does not . . . give the President authority to decide what kinds of officers—in what departments, with what responsibilities—the Executive Branch requires" and maintaining that "[i]nstead, Article I's Necessary and Proper Clause puts those decisions in the legislature's hands"). For more on the Necessary and Proper Clause as a source of congressional power, see *supra* Chapter 6.

[7] We here note two other potential approaches to the removal power that have never gained much doctrinal traction. First, one might maintain that the Constitution by negative implication dictates that the only way to remove an executive official is by means of impeachment for high crimes and misdemeanors. A few members of the First Congress endorsed this position, *see* Saikrishna Prakash, *New Light on the Decision of 1789*, 91 CORNELL L. REV. 1021, 1035–36 (2006), but it has since then generally been

and consistent with the unitary executive theory, the Court has held that the President enjoys some measure of a constitutional entitlement to at-will removal, and it has invalidated some statutory removal restrictions on the ground that they impermissibly encroach upon the President's Article II authority to oversee the executive branch. On the other hand, and consistent with the congressionalist position, the Court has never gone so far as to suggest that Congress has no power to restrict the President's ability to fire executive-branch officials, and it has upheld some congressionally created removal restrictions against constitutional attack. In short, modern-day removal-power doctrine holds that the Constitution *sometimes but not always* prohibits Congress from interfering with the President's power of removal. The central doctrinal challenge thus involves distinguishing between those circumstances in which Congress's imposition of such restrictions is permissible, and those in which it is not.

We begin our examination of the Court's work in this area by considering a quartet of cases—*Myers v. United States*, *Humphrey's Executor v. United States*, *Bowsher v. Synar*, and *Morrison v. Olson*—that together establish the foundations of removal-power doctrine. Then, we turn to a pair of more recent decisions—*Free Enterprise Fund v. Public Company Accounting Oversight Board* and *Seila Law v. CFPB*—in which the Roberts Court has substantially reworked governing doctrine in this field, pushing it in a decidedly, but not yet categorically, unitarian direction.

---

rejected on the ground that an impeachment-only approach would confer on executive officials an effective guarantee of life tenure—an outcome that seems both (1) practically unworkable (imagine the number of holdover officials represented in each new President's cabinet/administration) and (2) difficult to reconcile with the constitutional text (which explicitly confers life tenure on federal judges while saying nothing about life tenure for executive-branch officials). *See id.* at 1035–36. Second, one might attempt to infer from the Appointments Clause a rule requiring the Senate's consent to any attempted removal of a principal officer (and perhaps also of other officers appointed with Senate confirmation). *See* FEDERALIST NO. 77 (Alexander Hamilton) (gesturing towards this view). *But see* Letter of William Loughton Smith to Edward Rutledge (June 21, 1789) (reporting word that Hamilton "had *changed his opinion* & was now convinced that the President alone should have the power of removal at pleasure" (emphasis in original)), *reprinted in* 69 S.C. HIST. MAG. 1, 8 (1968); Seth Barrett Tillman, *The Puzzle of Hamilton's* Federalist *No. 77*, 33 HARV. J.L. & PUB. POL'Y 149, 165 (2009) (suggesting that Hamilton had intended only to suggest that Senate consent was necessary to *replace* one officer with another and that Hamilton "never conceded any role for the Senate in *removals*, qua *removal*" (emphasis in original)). Textually speaking, however, this senatorial-signoff approach to removal may well read too much into the Appointments Clause, the operative language of which, after all, addresses only *appointments*, *see* Prakash, *supra*, at 1037–38, and one might also criticize this position on the structural ground that it accords to the Senate too powerful of a role in monitoring executive-branch activities. *Id.*

B. THE FOUNDATIONAL CASES

1. *Myers v. United States*

The Court's first major treatment of the removal power came in 1926, with its decision in *Myers v. United States*.[8] That case involved a challenge to the removal of a postmaster first-class (Myers) effectuated by the Postmaster General at the behest of President Woodrow Wilson.[9] Myers (and later his estate) sought backpay, contending that his ouster violated the terms of the federal statute that both established his office and required a senatorial sign-off on any removal of postal officials of Myers's rank. The Wilson administration did not seek or receive the Senate's consent before ordering Myers's removal and thus contravened the dictates of the governing statute.[10] Nonetheless, government attorneys defended the President's actions, contending in effect that Myers's removal was valid because the statute that prohibited it abridged controlling constitutional separation-of-powers principles.[11]

In a 6–3 decision, the Court struck down the statute.[12] Writing for the majority, Chief Justice (and former President) William

---

8 272 U.S. 52 (1926).

9 *See* Jonathan L. Entin, *The Curious Case of the Pompous Postmaster:* Myers v. United States, 65 CASE WES. RES. L. REV. 1059 (2015). *Myers*, to be sure, was not the very first Supreme Court case that dealt with removal-power issues. For example, in *United States v. Perkins*, 116 U.S. 483 (1886), the Court upheld a statutory removal restriction attached to certain inferior officers whose appointment had been vested in the Secretary of the Navy (who was then understood to be a Department Head within the meaning of the Appointments Clause), holding that "when congress, by law, vests the appointment of inferior officers in the heads of departments it may limit and restrict the power of removal as it deems best for the public interest." *Id.* at 485. Thereafter, in *Shurtleff v. United States*, 189 U.S. 311 (1903), the Court refused to construe a statute that authorized the removal of General Appraisers "for inefficiency, neglect of duty, or malfeasance in office" as impliedly prohibiting at-will removal by the President, noting that "[t]he right of removal would exist if the statute had not contained a word upon the subject," while also suggesting that such a right might be "limited by Constitution or statute." *Id.* at 313, 316. For another early case involving the interpretation of a removal-related statute, see *Parsons v. United States*, 167 U.S. 324 (1897), in which the Court rejected the claim of a former U.S. "district attorney" that his removal by the President violated a congressional enactment that granted to him a four-year term of appointment. The Court reached this result by reading the statute "as providing absolutely for the expiration of the term of office at the end of four years, and not as giving a term that shall last at all events for that time." *Id.* at 339.

10 Entin, *supra* note 9, at 1065.

11 *See id.* at 1073 (noting that the government challenged the statute by arguing that "Congress could not reserve a formal place for itself in the removal process but might set standards governing removals by the President").

12 For more on the historical context of the *Myers* decision, see Nikolas Bowie & Daphna Renan, *The Separation-of-Powers Counterrevolution*, 131 YALE L.J. (forthcoming 2022), manuscript at 5–6, 44–49 (characterizing the Court's decision in *Myers* as a centerpiece of the backlash to Reconstruction and emphasizing that Chief Justice Taft was "[s]teeped in Lost Cause historiography").

Howard Taft issued an aggressive endorsement of the unitarian position, contending that, with one narrow qualification, Congress lacked the authority to limit the President's power to remove executive-branch officials.[13] The majority opinion drew heavily on historical considerations, with the Chief Justice according "the greatest weight" to early statutory arrangements created by the First Congress and to the practices of subsequent Congresses and Presidents—all of which, he argued, cut in favor of the unitarian view.[14] In addition, Chief Justice Taft laid weight on the constitutional text,[15] invoking in particular Article II's vesting of

---

[13] Highlighting an earlier Supreme Court decision concerning the removal of inferior officers, Taft acknowledged that Congress could restrict the removal of such officers whose appointment it had chosen to "vest . . . in some one other than the President with the consent of the Senate." *See Myers*, 272 US. at 162 (citing *Perkins*, 116 U.S. at 483). In so doing, however, Taft also seemed to suggest that Congress might lack the power to limit removal of any inferior officer whose appointment it had vested in the President alone. *See id.* at 161–62 ("Whether the action of Congress in removing the necessity for the advice and consent of the Senate, and putting the power of appointment in the President alone, would make his power of removal in such case any more subject to Congressional legislation than before is a question this Court did not decide in the *Perkins* case. Under the reasoning upon which the legislative decision of 1789 was put, it might be difficult to avoid a negative answer, but it is not before us and we do not decide it.").

[14] *Myers*, 272 U.S. at 174–75. The First Congress's debates had centered on legislation establishing a Department of Foreign Affairs, to be headed by a Secretary who, according to some initial language in the bill, would be removable by the President. *See* Prakash, *supra* note 7, at 1030. A motion was made to strike the "removable by the President" language from the statute, at which point members of the House of Representatives engaged in a lengthy back-and-forth about what they understood the Constitution to permit and prohibit in terms of presidential removal. *See id.* at 1031. Ultimately, the House (and later the Senate) would vote to replace the "removable by the President" language with something more cryptic—namely, a provision instructing the Chief Clerk of the Department to take possession of departmental records "whenever the [Secretary] *shall be removed by the president, or a vacancy in any other way shall happen.*" *See id.* (emphasis added). Taft's view was that this language signaled Congress's understanding that the President enjoyed an inherent power of removal. But the language was at the least ambiguous on this point. Most important, the amendment's text left it unclear whether Congress was simply recognizing a constitutional power that the President already possessed or was instead bestowing on the President a power that Congress might alternatively have chosen to withhold. *Cf. Myers*, 272 U.S. at 284 (Brandeis, J. dissenting) (contending that the Decision of 1789 established, at most, that "the Senate does not, in the absence of legislative grant thereof, have the right to share in the removal of an officer appointed with its consent, and that the President has, in the absence of restrictive legislation, the constitutional power of removal without such consent"); *compare also* Prakash, *supra* note 7, at 1063 (suggesting that the relevant historical evidence "supports Chief Justice Taft"), *with* Jed Handelsman Shugerman, *The Decisions of 1789 Were Anti-Unitary: An Originalism Cautionary Tale* (Aug. 27, 2021), Fordham L. Legal Studies Rsch. Paper No. 3597496, unpublished manuscript at 12, papers.ssrn.com/sol3/papers.cfm?abstract_id=3597496 (contending that Madison drafted the relevant language of the 1789 statute in order to create a "strategic ambiguity" regarding the constitutional status of the President's removal power—an ambiguity that was necessary to win the votes of different congressional factions with different constitutional views).

[15] *Myers*, 272 U.S. at 163–64. One textual provision that Taft did not seriously consider was the Opinions Clause of Article II, section 2, which empowers the President to "require the Opinion, in writing, of the principal Officer in each of the

"[t]he executive power" in the President and maintaining that a congressional power to restrict removal would "would make it impossible for the President, in case of political or other difference with the Senate or Congress, to take care that the laws be faithfully executed."[16] The Court's ruling in *Myers* thus seemed to be a sweeping one, leaving Congress with, at best, a strictly limited role to play in regulating presidential removal decisions.[17] That at least

---

executive Departments, upon any Subject relating to the Duties of their respective Offices." *See* U.S. CONST. art. II, § 2. By expressly conferring on the President a relatively insubstantial power over other executive-branch officials, the clause might be read to imply that the President *lacks* a highly generalized and nontextual "directory" power with respect to other aspects of those officials' conduct—a conclusion flatly inconsistent with the unitarian conception of the President's role. *See Myers*, 272 U.S. at 207 (McReynolds, J., dissenting) ("[I]t is beyond the ordinary imagination to picture [the framers] vainly discussing, in the heat of a Philadelphia summer, whether express authority to require opinions in writing should be delegated to a President in whom they had already vested the illimitable executive power here claimed [by the majority]."); *see also* Peter L. Strauss, *Overseer, or 'The Decider'? The President in Administrative Law*, 75 GEO. WASH. L. REV. 696, 703 (2007) (noting that "Article II in terms gives the President only the right to seek from those officers a written opinion about their exercise of those duties (i.e., it does not say he may command their exercise of the duties assigned to them)"). *But see* Akhil Reed Amar, *Some Opinions on the Opinion Clause*, 82 VA. L. REV. 647, 652 (1996) (maintaining that the Opinions Clause merely "*exemplif[ies]* and *clarif[ies]* the President's role and powers" and thus does not carry any obvious negative implications regarding other presidential powers not expressly conferred (emphasis in original)); THE FEDERALIST No. 74 (Hamilton) ("This I consider as a mere redundancy in the plan, as the right for which it provides would result of itself from the office.").

16 *Myers*, 272 U.S. at 164. Not all aspects of that executive power, Taft conceded, were subject to the President's exclusive, unilateral control—that much was clear, from Article II's stipulation, for instance, that the Senate must play a role in the appointment of some executive-branch officials and in the making of treaties. *See id.* at 164. But these carve outs, according to the Court, were merely exceptions that helped to prove the rule: Constitutional "checks" on the executive power, the Chief Justice explained, were "limitations to be strictly construed, and not to be extended by implication," and the absence of any express check on presidential removal served only to bolster the conclusion that removal decisions remained within the President's exclusive domain. *Id.* at 164–65.

17 Chief Justice Taft also briefly dealt with one source from the early Republic that seemed to cut against his position—namely, the Court's opinion in *Marbury v. Madison*, 5 U.S. (1 Cranch) 137 (1803). That case, which is discussed in greater detail in Section 34.A, arose from the appointment by President John Adams of certain individuals to serve a five-year term as "justices of the peace"—a position that, notwithstanding its judicial-sounding name, involved the exercise of some executive powers. *See* David F. Forte, Marbury*'s Travail: Federalist Politics and William Marbury's Appointment as Justice of the Peace*, 45 CATH. U. L. REV. 349, 354 (1996) (noting that "Congress modeled the office of justice of the peace for the District of Columbia after Maryland's version of the position," one that involved an amalgam of "judicial, executive, and legislative powers"). Prior to dismissing the case for lack of jurisdiction, the Court declared that the appointees had a "right" to their commissions—a right that Adams's successor, President Thomas Jefferson, and Jefferson's Secretary of State, James Madison, were bound to honor. *Marbury*, 5 U.S. at 154. At the same time, the Court's opinion suggested that a different conclusion would have obtained if Congress had not given "the officer a right to hold [the office] for five years, independent of the executive." *Id.* at 162. Put differently, the "vested" nature of the appointees' right to their commissions depended on Congress's willingness to guarantee to justices of the peace a fixed term of office, and the Court's

was the prevailing understanding of *Myers* at the time the decision came down.[18] It was, however, an understanding that the Court itself would soon unsettle.

2. *Humphrey's Executor v. United States*

Less than a decade after *Myers*, the Court considered a case brought on behalf of William Humphrey,[19] a former member of the Federal Trade Commission (FTC) who had been fired by President Franklin Roosevelt in a manner that, the challenger claimed, violated a governing set of statutory limits on removal.[20] In defending the President's action, the Justice Department maintained that these removal restrictions were unconstitutional under *Myers*, which it saw, with much justification, as having recognized a broad presidential power to terminate the service of executive officials at will.[21] Charting a new course,[22] however, the Court rejected the

recognition of this right thus impliedly validated a congressional power to insulate executive officials against at-will presidential removal. *See Myers*, 227 U.S. at 217 (McReynolds, J., dissenting) (emphasizing this point); *see id.* at 242–43 (Brandeis, J., dissenting); *see also* Jed Handelsman Shugerman, *Presidential Removal: The* Marbury *Problem and the Madison Solutions*, 89 FORDHAM L. REV. 2085 (2021) (developing a detailed historical account of the (non-unitarian) understanding of the President's removal power that likely undergirded the Court's decision in *Marbury*). *But see Myers*, 227 U.S. at 142 (majority opinion) (suggesting that any implications to drawn from *Marbury* stemmed from the "mere statement of" a conclusion "without any examination of the discussion which went on in the First Congress" and thus concluding that *Marbury* "cannot be regarded as authority in considering the weight to be attached" to the actions of the First Congress).

18 *See* Entin, *supra* note 9, at 1075–76 ("Initially *Myers* was thought to have made clear that the President has unfettered power to remove all nonjudicial civilian appointed officials.").

19 Humphrey's Executor v. United States, 295 U.S. 602 (1935). Humphrey himself died shortly after the removal decision, but the executors of his estate proceeded with the action in an effort to collect backpay. *See id.* at 617.

20 The statute establishing the FTC guaranteed to each Commissioner a seven-year term, during which time the President could pursue removal only for "inefficiency, neglect of duty, or malfeasance in office." *Id.* at 620. President Roosevelt, however, did not invoke any of these grounds as the basis for his removal decision. Instead, he made it clear to Humphrey that the decision was based on his sense that "I do not feel that your mind and my mind go along together on either the policies or the administering of the Federal Trade Commission." *Id.* at 619.

21 *Id.* at 626.

22 How, in such a short time period, did the Court move away from a resoundingly pro-President stance on the removal power to the more Congress-friendly, officer-specific framework endorsed in *Humphrey's Executor*? Changes in judicial personnel provide part of the explanation—Chief Justice Taft, for instance, was no longer on the Court—but those changes do not tell the whole story, as four members of the *Humphrey's Executor* majority (including Justice Sutherland himself) had voted with Taft in *Myers*. So why did these Justices change their minds? One possibility is that, by 1933, members of the Court had developed new concerns about the scope of presidential power in light of New Deal-era expansions of the administrative state. *See Morrison*, 487 U.S. at 723 (Scalia, J., dissenting) (noting that *Humphrey's Executor* "was considered by many at the time the product of an activist, anti-New Deal Court bent on reducing the power of President Franklin Roosevelt"); *see also* Peter L.

government's position.[23] The opinion in *Myers*, Justice Sutherland explained for the majority, may have "examine[d] at length the historical, legislative, and judicial data bearing upon the question" of removal, but the "narrow point actually decided" in that case "was only that the President had power to remove a postmaster of the first class, without the advice and consent of the Senate."[24] In addition, although Chief Justice Taft's opinion in *Myers* had contained "expressions . . . which tend to sustain the government's contention," those expressions ultimately were "beyond the point involved" in that case and thus not entitled to *stare decisis* effect.[25] In short, Justice Sutherland, now writing for a unanimous Court, dismissed almost all of Chief Justice Taft's exhaustive, unitary-executive-celebrating analysis as beside-the-point dicta.[26]

But what about the actual holding of *Myers*? If Congress could not restrict the President's power to remove postmasters first-class, on what basis could Congress restrict the President's seemingly analogous power to dismiss members of the Federal Trade Commission? The answer, the Court explained, had to do with the different types of duties that each set of officers performed. Postmasters, on the one hand, were "restricted to the performance of executive functions" wholly unrelated to either "the legislative or

---

Strauss, *Formal and Functional Approaches to Separation-of-Powers Questions—A Foolish Inconsistency?*, 72 CORNELL L. REV. 488, 514 (1987) (noting that *Humphrey's Executor* came down on the same day as the Court's Congress-limiting decision in *Schechter Poultry Corp. v. United States*, 295 U.S. 495 (1935), and characterizing the date of both decisions—May 27, 1935—as "perhaps the New Deal's blackest day"). Another hypothesis connects the decision to growing concerns about totalitarianism abroad. In particular, by the time of the *Humphrey's Executor* decision, both Hitler and Mussolini had assumed dictatorial control, thus raising the salience of "the potential dangers of strong centralized executive government." PETER L. STRAUSS, TODD D. RAKOFF, GILLIAN E, METZGER, DAVID J. BARRON & ANNE JOSEPH O'CONNELL, GELLHORN AND BYSE'S ADMINISTRATIVE LAW: CASES AND COMMENTS 921 n.39 (12th ed. 2018).

23 The opinion also departed from prior rulings insofar as it interpreted the relevant statutory language as setting forth an exhaustive, rather than illustrative, list of grounds for removal. The Court had in an earlier decision construed similar language as *not precluding* at-will removal, *see Shurtleff*, 189 U.S. at 318, and it had gone out of its way to reaffirm that point in *Myers*, *see Myers*, 272 U.S. at 171–72. Nevertheless, the Court in *Humphrey's Executor* took a different view of things, characterizing the statute at issue in *Shurtleff* as "exceptional" and concluding that the identically worded FTC statute now before it was "definite and unambiguous" with regard to the President's lack of at-will removal authority. *Humphrey's Executor*, 296 U.S. at 624.

24 *Id.* at 626.

25 *Id.*

26 *See* Michael C. Dorf, *Dicta and Article III*, 142 U. PA. L. REV. 1997, 2020 (1994) ("Significantly, the *Humphrey's Executor* Court did not claim that the considerations justifying a departure from stare decisis were present; instead, the Court treated the rationale of *Myers* as outside the rule of stare decisis.").

judicial power."[27] Federal Trade Commissioners, on the other hand, could not "in any proper sense be characterized as an arm or an eye of the executive."[28] The FTC was tasked, for instance, with "making investigations and reports thereon for the information of Congress," which rendered it a "*quasi* legislative" agency acting "in aid of the legislative power."[29] The FTC also was tasked with acting as a "master in chancery under rules prescribed by the court," thus rendering it a "*quasi* judicial" agency as well.[30] Thus, whereas the postmaster in *Myers* had been a "purely executive" official "inherently subject to the exclusive and illimitable power of removal by the Chief Executive," the FTC held powers that could be exercised, pursuant to the choice of Congress, "independently of executive control."[31]

Both as an analytical matter and as a form of *ex ante* guidance, this *ratio decidendi* left much to be desired.[32] One thing, however, was clear: With *Humphrey's Executor* on the books, *Myers*'s rigidly

---

27 *Humphrey's Executor*, 295 U.S. at 627.

28 *Id.* at 628.

29 *Id.* at 628–29 (emphasis added).

30 *Id.* (emphasis added).

31 *Id.* at 630.

32 For scholarly criticism of the distinction (and of subsequent scholarly efforts to hash it out), see Bowie & Renan, *supra* note 12, at 57–60 (suggesting generally that any effort to distinguish between "core" and "peripheral" exercises of executive power will fail to "supply a judicially-manageable standard"). A deeper analytical difficulty lies in the Court's suggestion in *Humphrey's Executor* that Congress could vest "quasi-legislative" and "quasi-judicial" powers in agencies that were, as Justice Sutherland put it, "wholly disconnected from the executive department." *Id.* at 630; *see also id.* at 629 (characterizing the FTC as "an agency of the legislative or judicial departments of the government"). At a minimum, this description of the agency's "quasi-legislative" authority rested uneasily alongside the Court's earlier suggestions that Congress could not delegate its own legislative power to other decisionmakers. *See supra* Section 29.B (discussing the nondelegation doctrine); *see also* Stephen L. Carter, *The Independent Counsel Mess*, 102 HARV. L. REV. 105, 128 (1988) (noting that, in *Humphrey's Executor*, "[t]he constitutional basis for the delegation (or indeed, the existence) of these 'quasi' powers was not specified"). What is more, by characterizing the FTC as "an agency of the legislative *and* judicial departments," the Court seemed to signal its approval of the blending of constitutionally distinct powers within a single governmental institution, thus embracing a position in tension with its insistence elsewhere (indeed, even elsewhere in *Humphrey's Executor* itself) on "[t]he fundamental necessity of maintaining each of the three general departments of government entirely free from the control or coercive influence, direct or indirect, of either of the others." *Humphrey's Executor*, 295 U.S. at 629; *see also* Peter L. Strauss, *The Place of Agencies in Government: Separation of Powers and the Fourth Branch*, 84 COLUM. L. REV. 573, 611 (1984) (noting that the *Humphrey's Executor* opinion "tells us that the agency is in both the legislative and the judicial branches, because of the functions it performs, but not how an agency can at the same moment reside in both the legislative and the judicial branches, consistent with the 'fundamental necessity' " of separated powers endorsed in that case (quoting *Humphrey's Executor*, 295 U.S. at 629)). The Court in *Humphrey's Executor* thus managed to sidestep the dictates of *Myers* only because it chose to recharacterize the nature of executive-branch agencies in a confusing and structurally dubious way.

unitarian philosophy no longer held sway,[33] and a new and more flexible framework—focused on the "character of the office" subject to the removal restriction—had taken its place.[34] In a nutshell, "purely executive" offices would remain subject to the Congress-inhibiting holding of *Myers*, while "quasi-legislative" and "quasi-judicial" offices would fall within Congress's power to protect. The context-specific nature of this test, as the Court candidly acknowledged, would inevitably create a "field of doubt" as to its application.[35] But the hope was that "future consideration and determination" of other removal-power cases would generate additional clarity.[36]

3. *Bowsher v. Synar*

Although the Court's decision in *Humphrey's Executor* deviated in important ways from its earlier decision in *Myers*, it did not purport to disturb a narrower proposition of law that the *Myers* opinion, if only in passing, had appeared to endorse. Recall that the statute at issue in *Myers* required direct senatorial approval of any contemplated removal order, thus empowering the Senate to

---

33 *See* Dorf, *supra* note 26, at 2020 (noting that "the *Humphrey's Executor* Court adopted the functional approach [to removal] that the *Myers* Court had expressly rejected").

34 *Humphrey's Executor*, 295 U.S. at 631.

35 *Id.* at 632. Even so, the opinion did perhaps offer a few hints as to what the Court had in mind. For example, the Court dismissed the significance of the Decision of 1789 by pointing out that "the office under consideration by Congress" at the time—i.e., the Secretary of Foreign Affairs—"was not only purely executive, but . . . responsible to the President, and to him alone, in a very definite sense." *Id.* at 631. The Court also noted with approval James Madison's apparent endorsement of "a different rule in respect of executive removal" for the Comptroller of the Treasury, "since the duties of that office were not purely of an executive nature but partook of the judiciary quality as well." *Id.* at 631 (internal citations omitted)). Elsewhere, the Court analogized the FTC to the "Interstate Commerce Commission and the Court of Claims" (then a non-Article III tribunal) and added that the "illimitable power of removal is not possessed by the President in respect of officers of the character of those just named." *Id.* at 629. Finally, in a brief discussion of *Marbury*, the Court made clear its understanding that William Marbury, as "a justice of the peace for the District of Columbia was not removable at the will of the President," because "there was a distinction between such an officer and officers appointed to aid the President in the performance of his constitutional duties." *Id.*

36 *Id.* at 632. One such future case was *Wiener v. United States*, 357 U.S. 349 (1958), in which the Court reaffirmed *Humphrey's Executor*'s distinction between officers who are "part of the Executive establishment" and those "whose tasks require absolute freedom from Executive interference." *Id.* at 353. Applying that distinction to a federal statute establishing the federal War Claims Commission—a federal agency tasked with distributing compensatory benefits to individuals who had suffered injuries and property damage in connection with World War II—the Court held not only that Congress *could have* restricted the President's power to remove the Commission's members but also that it *had in fact done so* even though the statute lacked any express language to that effect. *Id.* at 354. That is, the Court relied on "the philosophy of *Humphrey's Executor*" to support a statutory presumption in favor of removal restrictions with respect to the particular type of officer whose removability was at issue in the case. *See id.* at 356.

participate directly in decisions about whether to remove individual postmasters. And while Chief Justice Taft in his sprawling opinion for the Court had spoken in very general terms about the impropriety of congressional meddling of any sort with the President's removal prerogatives, he also separately noted that Congress had acted unconstitutionally in that case by "*draw[ing] to itself* . . . the power to remove or the right to participate in the exercise of that power."[37] This isolated passage, to be sure, did not play a front-and-center role in *Myers*, given the Court's extensive defense of and reliance on the unitary-executive theory. But the Court's subsequent retreat from that theory in *Humphrey's Executor* put back on the table the question whether *Myers* remained good law to the extent it suggested that Congress could never give "itself" the ability to "participate in the exercise of [the removal] power."[38]

In *Bowsher v. Synar*,[39] the Court answered this question. That case concerned a statute (the Gramm-Rudman-Hollings Act) that empowered the Comptroller General of the United States to order (under certain circumstances) program-by-program spending reductions across the federal budget.[40] The statute itself did not directly address removal, but an older law that was still in effect separately prescribed that the Comptroller General's removal could occur only by way of a joint resolution of Congress.[41] Taken together, the Court concluded in *Bowsher*, these statutes produced a fatal separation-of-powers problem. The difficulty was that Congress (by way of the Gramm-Rudman-Hollings Act) had conferred executive power on an official who (due to the removal rules set forth in the earlier legislation that created the Comptroller General's office) performed his duties subject to "control[ ] by Congress."[42] As a result,

---

37 *Myers*, 272 U.S. at 161.

38 *Id.*

39 478 U.S. 714 (1986).

40 *Id.* at 717–19.

41 *Id. at* 728. In addition, the statute provided that any removal decision must be predicated on a finding of "permanent disability," "inefficiency," "neglect of duty," "malfeasance," or "a felony or conduct involving moral turpitude." *Id.*

42 *Id.* at 726. Not all the Justices agreed that the statute delegated "executive" power to the Comptroller General. Justices Stevens and Marshall concurred only in the judgment, reasoning that the sequestration-order provisions in fact delegated to the Comptroller General qualified as "legislative" in nature. *See id.* at 751–52 (Stevens, J., concurring in the judgment) (contending that the power to issue sequestration orders "may appropriately be labeled 'legislative' even if performed by the Comptroller General or by an executive agency"). That conclusion, however, simply functioned to replace one constitutional problem with another. While no longer delegating "executive power" to a "legislative official," Congress could now be understood as providing for the exercise of legislative power in a manner that circumvented the bicameralism and presentment requirements of Article I. *Id.* at 758–59. Justices Stevens and Marshall thus saw no need to get into the question of the Comptroller General's removal, as they regarded the statute as more fundamentally

Congress had attempted to "reserve for itself the power of removal of an officer charged with the execution of the laws."[43] But this it could not do because "[t]o permit the execution of the laws to be vested in an officer answerable only to Congress would, in practical terms, reserve in Congress control over the execution of the laws"[44] in violation of Article II's assignment of the executive power to the President.[45]

Of particular significance, the Court in *Bowsher* cast in categorical and unqualified terms the earlier suggestion in *Myers* that Congress could not "draw to itself" the power to remove.[46] Thus, what emerged from the decision was a sharp and still-operative distinction between: (a) statutes that lay down judicially enforceable substantive limits on presidential removal decisions (which are *sometimes* permissible); and (b) statutes that grant power to Congress, or an arm of Congress, to make or block particular removal decisions (which are *always* impermissible). Put simply, while Congress may in certain circumstances restrict the President's power to remove another executive-branch officer, that same body remains absolutely prohibited from "reserv[ing] for itself" the power to participate directly in such removal decisions.[47]

---

in conflict with the Court's earlier holding in *INS v. Chadha*, 462 U.S. 91 (1983). *See supra* Section 29.D.2 (discussing the *Chadha* decision).

[43] *Bowsher*, 478 U.S. at 726.

[44] *Id.*

[45] *Id.* ("The structure of the Constitution does not permit Congress to execute the laws; it follows that Congress cannot grant to an officer under its control what it does not possess.").

[46] *Id.* at 724 (citing *Myers*, 272 U.S. at 161). It also (if adventurously) found support in *Humphrey's Executor*, which, it claimed, had implicitly "reaffirm[ed] [*Myers*'s] holding that congressional participation in the removal of executive officers is unconstitutional" by not questioning that point while "distinguish[ing] *Myers*" on other grounds. *Id.* at 725. This line of analysis involved no small measure of inventiveness because the Court in *Humphrey's Executor* nowhere explicitly mentioned *Myers*'s alternative holding that Congress lacked the power to involve itself in removal decisions. Indeed, that omission was arguably quite telling, given that the Court in *Humphrey's Executor* could have distinguished (but evidently chose not to distinguish) *Myers* on the straightforward ground that that case, unlike *Humphrey's Executor*, involved an effort by Congress to "draw to itself" the power to remove. That the Court in *Humphrey's Executor* chose not to draw this distinction—and chose instead to steer clear of *Myers* by reference to a convoluted distinction between purely-executive and quasi-legislative/quasi-judicial officials—suggests that the Court in *Humphrey's Executor* was not eager to legitimate (much less reaffirm) the suggestion in *Myers* that Congress could not ever participate in a discrete removal decision.

[47] *Id.* at 726. Dissenting in *Bowsher*, Justice White questioned the extent to which the removal rules at issue there in fact rendered the Comptroller General subservient to Congress. *See Bowsher*, 478 U.S. at 765 (White, J., dissenting). The rules at issue provided for removal by *joint resolution*, which required compliance with the standard bicameralism and presentment requirements of Article I. Thus, a Comptroller General who retained the President's support could remain in office for as long as Congress lacked the requisite two-thirds support in both Houses necessary to override a Presidential veto. Mustering that level of support, moreover, would require "a feat of

4. *Morrison v. Olson*

Bowsher lent some clarity to the Court's removal-power jurisprudence by establishing a bright-line prohibition on congressional participation in the removal of executive-branch officials. The next major removal-power decision, however, threw new uncertainty into the mix, by casting doubt on the continued vitality of the distinction between "purely executive" and non-"purely executive" officers. That decision was *Morrison v. Olson*,[48] which involved a separation-of-powers-based attack on the independent-counsel provisions of the 1978 Ethics in Government Act. As noted in the previous chapter,[49] the Court in *Morrison* rejected a constitutional challenge to the manner of the independent counsel's appointment on the ground that the independent counsel qualified as an "inferior" rather than a principal officer, who thus could be validly selected by a Special Division of Article III judges.[50] That holding, however, left unresolved the constitutionality of the statute's *removal* provisions, according to which the Attorney General could terminate a thus-appointed independent counsel "only for good cause, physical disability, mental incapacity, or any other condition that substantially impairs the performance of [that individual's] duties."[51]

Under then-operative doctrine, this removal restriction seemed wide-open to constitutional attack. After all, as Justice Scalia emphasized in dissent, the independent counsel performed the "quintessentially executive function" of "[g]overnmental investigation and prosecution of crimes."[52] Thus, while no one could articulate the precise contours of the distinction between a "purely executive" officer (whose removal was reserved to the President alone) and a "quasi-legislative/quasi-judicial" officer (whose removal was subject to congressional regulation), everyone seemed to agree that the independent counsel fell comfortably on the "purely executive" side of the line.[53] Taken at face value, then, even the

bipartisanship more difficult than that required to impeach and convict." *Id.* at 771. (Impeachment requires a mere majority vote in the House, and conviction requires a two-thirds supermajority in the Senate. *See infra* Section 32.A.) Justice White thus concluded that, at least as far as the Comptroller General was concerned, "[t]he incremental *in terrorem* effect of the possibility of congressional removal in the face of a Presidential veto" was "exceedingly unlikely to have any discernible impact on the extent of congressional influence." *Id.* at 771–72.

48 487 U.S. 654 (1988).

49 *See supra* Section 30.A.2 (discussing the Appointments Clause portion of the *Morrison* opinion).

50 *Morrison*, 487 U.S. at 670–77.

51 *Id.* at 664.

52 *Id.* at 706 (Scalia, J., dissenting).

53 More specifically, in writing for the majority, Chief Justice Rehnquist acknowledged that "[t]here is no real dispute that the functions performed by the

Court's Congress-friendly ruling in *Humphrey's Executor* seemed to suggest that the independent counsel, as a "purely executive" officer, had to remain at all times subject to removal by the President at will.

Once again, however, the Court took removal-power doctrine in a new direction. Writing for an eight-member majority, Chief Justice Rehnquist conceded that the Court in *Humphrey's Executor* "undoubtedly" had relied "on the terms 'quasi-legislative' and 'quasi-judicial'" in defining the scope of Congress's authority to limit presidential removal.[54] Nonetheless, he reported, the Court's "present considered view is that the determination of whether the Constitution allows Congress to impose a 'good cause'-type restriction . . . cannot be made to turn on whether or not that official is classified as 'purely executive.'"[55] Instead, the "real question" was "whether the removal restrictions are of such a nature that they impede the President's ability to perform his constitutional duty."[56] And here the answer to that question was "no," meaning that the removal provision set forth in the independent counsel statute posed no constitutional problem.[57]

In his dissent, Justice Scalia asserted that the case should have been "over" as soon as the majority acknowledged the independent counsel's purely-executive status.[58] That acknowledgment left no doubt that the statute's removal restrictions infringed on the President's executive authority, and, in Justice Scalia's (strongly

---

independent counsel are 'executive' in the sense that they are law enforcement functions that typically have been undertaken by officials within the Executive Branch." *Id.* at 691 (majority opinion).

[54] *Id.* at 690.

[55] *Id.* at 689; *see also* Michael Abramowicz & Maxwell Stearns, *Defining Dicta*, 57 STAN. L. REV. 953, 1046 (2005) ("Using the euphemism of 'present considered view' to describe the Court's new position, Rehnquist rewrote longstanding doctrine by effectively ignoring broad positions in the prior cases to arrive at an otherwise unattainable result.").

[56] *Morrison*, 487 U.S. at 689.

[57] In support of this conclusion, the Court pointed to features of the measure that, in its view, substantially mitigated the risk of undue interference with executive-branch prerogatives. To begin with, the independent counsel was "an inferior officer under the Appointments Clause, with limited jurisdiction and tenure and lacking policymaking or significant administrative authority." *Id.* at 696. In addition, the statute did not prohibit removal altogether. Instead, it permitted removal for "good cause," thus ensuring that the President, "through the Attorney General, retain[ed] ample authority to assure that the counsel is competently performing his or her statutory responsibilities in a manner that comports with the provisions of the Act." *Id.* at 692. On top of that, "the congressional determination to limit the removal power . . . was essential, in the view of Congress, to establish the necessary independence of the office." *Id.* at 693. All things considered, the Chief Justice concluded, these specialized "features" of the statute sufficed to ensure that the removal limit did not so greatly "deprive[ ] the President of control over the independent counsel" as "to interfere impermissibly with his constitutional obligation to ensure the faithful execution of the law." *Id.*

[58] *Id.* at 708 (Scalia, J., dissenting) (quoting *id.* at 695).

unitarian) view, no infringement on that authority—however diminutive—was permissible under Article II.[59] Justice Scalia also faulted the majority for misapplying its own newly-fashioned test, which focused on whether Congress had "interfere[d] impermissibly" with presidential power. In words that would soon prove prophetic,[60] he warned that the statute placed a potent weapon in the hands of the Chief Executive's political adversaries, enabling them to gin up "massive and lengthy investigations" of the President (and/or the President's political allies) and thus to disrupt the focused work of the Chief Executive on matters of the gravest national importance.[61] Indeed, he argued, the arrangement posed acute constitutional dangers precisely because it eliminated the "primary check against prosecutorial abuse"—namely, political accountability.[62] Whereas federal prosecutors removable at will by the President had every reason to avoid taking actions whose "unfairness will come home to roost in the Oval Office," a renegade independent counsel would have no reason to worry about political backlash.[63] The statute, Justice Scalia predicted, would thus exert a "harmful effect upon our system of government, and even upon the nature of justice received by those men and women who agree to serve in the Executive Branch."[64]

The Court's ruling in *Morrison* created new questions about the contours of Congress's power to limit the President's power of removal. One set of questions concerned the relationship between the "impermissibly interfere" test that *Morrison* introduced and the "character of the office" test that *Humphrey's Executor* had earlier set

---

[59] *Id.* (Scalia, J., dissenting) (maintaining that it was not the Court's business "to determine . . . how much of the purely executive powers of government must be within the full control of the President" because "[t]he Constitution prescribes that they *all* are" (internal alterations omitted)).

[60] Justice Scalia issued his dissent some six years before Kenneth Starr would begin his controversial and consequential tenure as independent counsel. *See, e.g.*, Kent H. Barnett, *Avoiding Independent Agency Armageddon*, 87 NOTRE DAME L. REV. 1349, 1355–56 (2012) (noting that the "backlash against independent counsel Kenneth Starr's investigation into the Whitewater matter had vindicated much of Justice Scalia's dissenting position in *Morrison*," as "Starr's investigation had evidenced the dangers of having such a powerful figure with only one objective (and limited oversight) investigating executive officers, including the President").

[61] To be clear, the statute authorized the Attorney General (presumably an ally of the President) to initiate investigations while giving Congress no formal authority to apply for or appoint an independent counsel on its own initiative. But, as Justice Scalia saw things, Congress could easily use its oversight powers to *pressure* the Justice Department to act on tenuous charges. Indeed, he argued that Congress had, in the case of Olson himself, "effectively compelled a criminal investigation of a high-level appointee of the President in connection with his actions arising out of a bitter power dispute between the President and the Legislative Branch." *See Morrison*, 487 U.S. at 702–03 (Scalia, J., dissenting).

[62] *Id.* at 728.

[63] *Id.* at 729.

[64] *Id.*

forth in the process of distinguishing *Myers*. What role, if any, did the *Morrison* Court's "present considered view" of removal power doctrine envision for the *Myers/Humphrey's Executor* quasi-legislative/quasi-judicial framework going forward?[65] Another set of questions concerned the substance of the "impermissibly interfere" test. In particular, as lower courts applied that test, how were they to go about determining how much interference was too much interference for purposes of gauging a removal restriction's constitutionality?[66] And to the extent the *Myers/Humphrey's*

---

[65] For example, did *Morrison* in effect override *Humphrey's Executor* (and *Myers*) by establishing that Congress now had broad authority to afford protections against removal even with respect to "purely executive" officers? *See, e.g.*, Thomas W. Merrill, *Capture Theory and the Courts: 1967–1983*, 72 CHI.-KENT L. REV. 1039, 1110 (1997) (suggesting that the Court in *Morrison* "discarded *Myers'* categorical rule that all executive officers must be subject to dismissal at the will of the President"); *see also Morrison*, 487 U.S. at 725 (Scalia, J., dissenting) (suggesting that the Court's preexisting removal-power case law had been "swept into the dustbin of repudiated constitutional principles"). Did the Court also depart from *Humphrey's Executor* by signaling that one's status as a "quasi-legislative" or "quasi-judicial" official no longer of itself supported the constitutionality of congressionally crafted for-cause removal restrictions? *See, e.g.*, John O. McGinnis, *Models of the Opinion Function of the Attorney General: A Normative, Descriptive, and Historical Prolegomenon*, 15 CARDOZO L. REV. 375, 433 n.217 (1993) (contending that "*Morrison* eliminates the safe-harbor that [*Humphrey's Executor* and *Wiener*] gave to quasi-legislative and quasi-judicial agencies"). Or was *Morrison* best viewed as a ticket-good-for-one-day-only decision, which in effect said nothing of consequence about any subject other than the independent-counsel statute itself? *Cf.* Earl C. Dudley, Morrison v. Olson: *A Modest Assessment*, 38 AM. U. L. REV. 255, 271–72 (1989) (contending that "Justice Scalia was wrong when he called the *Morrison v. Olson* majority opinion 'revolutionary' " and that "the Justices correctly perceived that the constitutional issue was of less significance than the immediate political symbolism of the result"); *see also* Myriam E. Gilles, *Reinventing Structural Reform Litigation: Deputizing Private Citizens in the Enforcement of Civil Rights*, 100 COLUM. L. REV. 1384, 144 (2004) (noting in the context of a discussion about *Morrison*'s Appointments Clause ruling that "one could argue that the highly politicized *Morrison* case is fairly regarded as *sui generis*").

[66] *See* Richard W. Murphy, *The DIY Unitary Executive*, 63 ARIZ. L. REV. 439, 461–62 (2021) (characterizing *Morrison* as establishing a "don't-interfere-too-much" test). More specifically, did the Court envision a holistic evaluation of removal restrictions on a case-by-case basis, or did it expect lower courts to develop defined categories of removal statutes that Congress could or could not enact? *See, e.g.*, Lee S. Liberman, Morrison v. Olson: *A Formalistic Perspective of Why the Court Was Wrong*, 38 AM. U. L. REV. 313, 341 (1989) (suggesting that the Court in *Morrison* "depart[ed] from *Myers'* broad prohibition on removal restrictions in favor of a case-by-case assessment"). Did the Court's new test require (or at least permit) courts to scrutinize the *justifiability* of Congress's choice to establish decisionmaking independence for the particular office under review? *See, e.g.*, Leu v. Int'l Boundary Comm'n, 523 F. Supp. 2d 1199, 1207 (W.D. Wash. 2007) ("The removal cases instruct that Congress may limit the President's removal power where independence from the executive is warranted."), *vacated on other grounds*, 605 F.3d 693 (9th Cir. 2010). And if so, did that test allow (or even require) courts to weigh the benefits of an officer's decisionmaking independence against the costs of the thus-curtailed presidential removal authority? *See, e.g.*, Ronald J. Krotoszynski, Jr., Johnjerica Hodge & Wesley W. Wintermyer, *Partisan Balance Requirements in the Age of New Formalism*, 90 NOTRE DAME L. REV. 941, 945 n.14 (2014) ("So long as *Morrison* remains good law, when Congress limits the President's removal power over an executive officer (whether the officer holds a principal or an inferior office), the operative analysis involves balancing the remaining

Executor framework lived on, its still-vexing distinction between "purely executive" and "quasi-legislative"/"quasi-executive" officers remained largely undeveloped. In the decades following *Morrison*, the Court was mostly silent on these and other removal-power issues. But further guidance would eventually come from the Roberts Court.

C. THE REMOVAL POWER AND THE ROBERTS COURT

1. The Rule Against Multiple "For-Cause" Layers

The Roberts Court took its first look at removal power law in the 2010 case of *Free Enterprise Fund v. Public Company Accounting Oversight Board*.[67] This case involved a mix of statutes that governed the removal of members of the Public Company Accounting Oversight Board (PCAOB), a regulatory agency tasked with overseeing the work of accounting firms involved in auditing publicly traded companies.[68] Members of the Board were removable only "for good cause shown" and only by the members of another administrative agency, the Securities and Exchange Commission.[69]

Overhanging the dispute, and largely driving the lower courts' analysis the case,[70] were the differing doctrinal frameworks that had undergirded the Court's decisions in *Myers*, *Humphrey's Executor*, and *Morrison*. Writing for himself and four colleagues, however, Chief Justice Roberts found none of cases to be of much relevance, because each of them dealt with a removal regime "quite different" from the one that applied to the PCAOB.[71] Specifically, in the earlier cases, "only one level of protected tenure separated the President from an officer exercising executive power."[72] Here, by contrast, *two* such layers insulated the Board's members from the President's control. This was the case because the PCAOB's members could be removed only for cause by the SEC and because (so the Court assumed for purposes of deciding this case) the SEC's Commissioners

degree and scope of presidential control, the nature of the office (whether it resides at the core or the periphery of executive branch functions), and the policy objectives that animated Congress's decision to attenuate presidential control.").

67 561 U.S. 477 (2010).

68 *Id.* at 484–89. The Board was created by the Sarbanes-Oxley Act of 2002, in the aftermath of high-profile accounting scandals at Enron and WorldCom. *See* 116. Stat. 745.

69 *Free Enter. Fund*, 561 U.S. at 486. Another provision of the statute identified the particular grounds that would constitute "good cause" for removal, such as a Board Member's "willful[ ] violat[ion]" of applicable laws, "willful[ ] abuse[ ]" of "authority," or "fail[ure] to enforce compliance" of applicable rules and regulations. *Id.*

70 *See, e.g.*, Free Enter. Fund v. Pub. Co. Accounting Oversight Bd., 537 F.3d 667, 679–84 (D.C. Cir. 2008), *aff'd in part and rev'd in part*, 561 U.S. 477 (2010).

71 *Free Enter. Fund*, 561 U.S. at 496.

72 *Id.* at 495.

also could be removed only for cause by the President.[73] According to the Chief Justice, this multi-tiered limit on presidential removal authority "does not merely add to the Board's independence, but transforms it."[74]

The Court's decision in *Free Enterprise Fund* hinged on the premise that multi-layer limits on the removal of executive officials create a categorically different level of agency independence from presidential control in comparison to "single-layer" arrangements. But is that premise sound? All else equal, it might make sense to suppose that "two-layer" officials enjoy more independence than do their "one-layer" counterparts.[75] All else, however, is often not equal,

---

[73] *Id.* at 488. In fact, the relevant statutes were far from clear on the question whether the President could remove members of the SEC only for good cause. But the Court chose to "decide the case with th[e] understanding" that this statutory restriction existed because none of the parties had argued otherwise. *See id.* at 487–88. This maneuver provoked a befuddled response from Justice Breyer, whose dissenting opinion accused the majority of "creat[ing] a constitutional defect in a statute and then rely[ing] on that defect to strike a statute down as unconstitutional." *Id.* at 545–46 (Breyer, J., dissenting). For scholarly reflections about this debate and the more general problem posed by party-based stipulations of subsidiary legal conclusions, see, e.g., Amanda Frost, *The Limits of Advocacy*, 59 DUKE L.J. 447, 470–71, 477–82 (2009) (maintaining that "courts must retain control of the interpretive process and thus cannot cede to the parties the sources and arguments that will be used to interpret statutory or constitutional texts"); Gary Lawson, *Stipulating the Law*, 109 MICH. L. REV. 1191, 1196 (2011) (asserting that "Justice Breyer is correct that standard American practice does not generally allow parties to stipulate to legal conclusions," but also maintaining that "it should, and *Free Enterprise Fund* was therefore jurisprudentially right to take the state of the law as the parties jointly offered it"); Henry Paul Monaghan, *On Avoiding Avoidance, Agenda Control, and Related Matters*, 112 COLUM. L. REV. 665, 719–20 (2012) (contending that "Professor Lawson's . . . inflexible insistence upon an unyielding dispute resolution model is far too idiosyncratic to serve as a vehicle for thinking sensibly about our constitutional order").

[74] *Free Enter. Fund*, 561 U.S. at 497.

[75] But maybe not. As Justice Breyer pointed out in dissent, it is by no means obvious that a two-layer for-cause arrangement affords the President a lesser measure of control over the work of a subordinate official than does an alternative arrangement in which that official is subject to at-will removal by other officials subject to for-cause removal by the President. Consider, for instance, a scenario in which the President demands that the members of SEC act to remove an individual from the PCAOB. If the members of SEC enjoy for-cause removal protection vis-à-vis the President, they can simply ignore the President's demands, and accordingly it will not matter whether PCAOB members are subject to at-will or for-cause removal by the SEC itself. *Id.* at 526 (Breyer, J., dissenting). Conversely, suppose that the President demands that the SEC *not act* to remove a PCAOB member that the SEC's members would instead prefer to get rid of. Under this scenario, a second layer of for-cause protection would actually "*help[ ] the President*" by "hinder[ing] the Commission's ability to dismiss" the PCAOB member against the President's wishes. *Id.* at 526 (Breyer, J., dissenting) (emphasis in original). *But see id.* at 497 n.4 (majority opinion) (noting that "[w]ithout a second layer of protection, the Commission has no excuse for retaining an officer who is not faithfully executing the law," whereas "[w]ith the second layer in place, the Commission can shield its decision [with a] finding that good cause is absent—a finding that, given the Commission's own protected tenure, the President cannot easily overturn.").

as other independence-affecting variables may also enter the analytical picture.[76] Nevertheless, the Court in *Free Enterprise Fund* pushed all other factors aside, opting instead to focus fixedly on the multi-layer nature of the removal arrangement it confronted.

One might defend the Court's decision to act in this way on the ground that, in doing so, it at least brought into the law of removal a clear and straightforward doctrinal sorting device. But it is important not to overhype the brightness of this supposedly bright-line rule. To be sure, several passages in Chief Justice Roberts's opinion implied that the Court was imposing a categorical bar on

---

[76] Suppose, for instance, that a "two-layer" official directs an agency that heavily depends on the White House in shepherding its annual budgeting requests through Congress, whereas a "one-layer" official directs an agency that relies on its own sources of funding (for example, from program revenues) and thus does not need White House assistance in the appropriations process. *See* Lisa Schultz Bressman & Robert B. Thompson, *The Future of Agency Independence*, 63 VAND. L. REV. 599, 611 (2010) (noting that "[s]everal of the financial independent agencies have funding sources, usually from users and industry, which frees them from dependence on congressional appropriations and annual budgets developed by the executive branch"); *cf.* Eloise Pasachoff, *The President's Budget as a Source of Agency Policy Control*, 125 YALE L.J. 2182, 2205 (2016) (highlighting ways in which the White House's control over agency budgeting requests can furnish a "powerful tool for presidential control," even in connection with agencies whose heads enjoy statutory removal protections). Under these conditions, would the two-layer official—whose funding situation depends critically on securing the President's support—really be freer to deviate from the President's political agenda than the one-layer overseer of the financially freestanding agency? Or what if Congress attaches a ten-year statutory term to a one-layer office (thus forcing Presidents to work with holdover appointees from prior administrations), while attaching a two-year statutory term to a two-layer office (thus guaranteeing to Presidents the power to switch out such appointed officeholders, regardless of removal restrictions, on a regular basis)? *Cf., e.g.*, Neomi Rao, *Removal: Necessary and Sufficient for Presidential Control*, 65 ALA. L. REV. 1205, 1253 (2014) (noting that "a statutory term may reinforce a culture of independence and imply a sort of presumption against removal during the term, raising the political costs of removal for the President"). What if the actions of a two-layer official require the express consent of the supervising agency, thus diluting that official's authority vis-à-vis the President and everyone else, whereas the actions of a one-layer official take effect automatically? *Cf. Free Enter. Fund*, 561 U.S. at 528–30 (Breyer, J., dissenting) (noting this feature of the PCAOB's rulemaking and adjudicative authority and arguing that it helped to give the SEC "virtually absolute" "control over the Board's investigatory and legal functions"). Or what if a single-layer arrangement authorizes removal under only an exceptionally narrow range of circumstances, whereas a two-layer arrangement permits removal far more easily at each of the two layers? If nothing else, these examples illustrate that many factors can and do shape the degree of independence from the President that any given agency and its members enjoy. *See also* Adrian Vermeule, *Conventions of Agency Independence*, 113 COLUM. L. REV. 1163, 1166 (2013) (noting that "legally enforceable for-cause tenure protection is neither necessary nor sufficient for operational [agency] independence" and that "unwritten conventions" can play an important role in "constrain[ing] political actors from attempting to bully or influence" agency officials). By lending one such factor dispositive doctrinal significance (or at least near-dispositive such significance, *see infra* notes 77–82 and accompanying text), the Court in *Free Enterprise Fund* arguably ran the risk of generating distorted doctrinal results.

multi-layer for-cause removal arrangements.[77] Other portions of his opinion, however, left the door open for potentially significant carve-outs,[78] with the Chief Justice suggesting, among other things, that the rule did not necessarily apply to existing multi-layer arrangements involving millions of governmental *employees* (as opposed to "officers") within the federal civil service,[79] tens of thousands of commissioned officers within the U.S. military,[80] and some 1,500 administrative law judges (ALJs) serving across a range of different federal agencies.[81] These and other portions of the Chief

---

77 *Free Enter. Fund*, 561 U.S. at 483–84 ("May the President be restricted in his ability to remove a principal officer, who is in turn restricted in his ability to remove an inferior officer, even though that inferior officer determines the policy and enforces the laws of the United States? We hold that such multilevel protection from removal is contrary to Article II's vesting of the executive power in the President."); *id.* at 514 ("While we have sustained in certain cases limits on the President's removal power, the Act before us imposes a new type of restriction—two levels of protection from removal for those who nonetheless exercise significant executive power. Congress cannot limit the President's authority in this way.").

78 Scholars have divided on the question of just how much *Free Enterprise Fund* decided. *Compare, e.g.*, Kevin M. Stack, *Agency Independence After* PCAOB, 32 CARDOZO L. REV. 2391, 2393 (2011) (maintaining that the Court in that case did not adopt a bright-line rule against multi-layer for-cause removal arrangements because doing so would have meant "swe[eping] aside the constitutional foundation for good-cause protections for the many adjudicators operating in independent agencies who also have two layers of good-cause protection" and that the decision instead turned on the Board's relatively unique "combination" of "rulemaking, enforcement, and adjudicative functions"), *with* Neomi Rao, *A Modest Proposal: Abolishing Agency Independence in* Free Enterprise Fund v. PCAOB, 79 FORDHAM L. REV. 2541, 2544 (2011) (contending that "[t]he Court's reasoning [in *Free Enterprise Fund*] fails to explain how two layers of removal protection differ from one," thus setting the stage even for the possible overruling of *Humphrey's Executor* and adoption of an across-the-board prohibition on all removal restrictions).

79 *See Free Enter. Fund*, 561 U.S. at 506 (noting that the Court was not deciding "whether 'lesser functionaries subordinate to officers of the United States' must be subject to the same sort of control as those who exercise 'significant authority pursuant to the laws' " (quoting Buckley v. Valeo, 424 U.S. 1, 126 n.162 (1976))).

80 *See id.* at 507 (suggesting that military officers might implicate a different rule because they are already "broadly subject to Presidential control through the chain of command and through the President's powers as Commander in Chief").

81 *Id.* at 507 n.10 (suggesting that ALJs might be viewed differently than PCAOB members (1) because they are not "necessarily 'Officers of the United States' " and might simply be mere "employees" instead; (2) because they "perform adjudicative rather than enforcement or policymaking functions"; and (3) because they possess "purely recommendatory powers"). A few years after its decision in *Free Enterprise Fund*, the Court appeared to extinguish the first of these three potential distinctions by holding in *Lucia v. SEC*, 138 S. Ct. 2044 (2018), that the agency's own ALJs were "Officers" rather than employees for Appointments Clause purposes. *See supra* Section 30.A.1.c. The Court's holding in *Lucia* thus raised anew the question whether its bar on multi-layer removal arrangements spelled doom for the constitutional removal protections that ALJs currently enjoy. *See Lucia*, 138 S. Ct. at 2059–62 (Breyer, J., concurring in the judgment in part and dissenting in part) (noting that "[t]he majority here removes the first distinction" that the Court in *Free Enterprise Fund* offered in defense of its conclusion that ALJs were outside the scope of that opinion).

Justice's opinion thus raised nettlesome follow-on questions about the decision's precise import and scope.[82]

From a bigger picture perspective, however, it is certainly true that the Court's holding in *Free Enterprise Fund* inserted into removal-power doctrine a new and broadly applicable prohibition on Congress's ability to limit presidential removal: Generally speaking, any statutory arrangement that places an executive official at more than one layer of for-cause removal away from the President is highly suspect, if not automatically prohibited.[83] Perhaps some of the qualifications hinted at by the Chief Justice will take hold in future cases. But the overarching reasoning of his opinion suggests that down-the-road endorsements of such qualifications will be few and far between, at least so long as the Court's current tilt toward unitarianism remains unchanged.[84]

2. The Rule for Single-Director Agencies

Ten years after *Free Enterprise Fund*, the Court forged another significant limit on Congress's ability to restrict presidential removal. *Seila Law v. Consumer Financial Protection Bureau*[85] involved a challenge to the structure of a recently-created federal agency, the Consumer Financial Protection Bureau (CFPB), whose Director was terminable only for "inefficiency, neglect of duty, or malfeasance in office."[86] As he had done in *Free Enterprise Fund*, Chief Justice Roberts (again writing for a five-Justice majority) disclaimed any intent to "revisit our prior decisions allowing certain limitations on the President's removal power."[87] Rather, the Chief Justice once again trained his focus on a "novel" aspect of the challenged removal arrangement in finding a separation-of-powers violation.[88] In particular, Congress had fashioned the CFPB in a way

---

[82] *See, e.g.*, Kent Barnett, *Regulating Impartiality in Agency Adjudication*, 69 DUKE L.J. 1695, 1719 (2020) (noting the still-unresolved status in the wake of both *Free Enterprise Fund* and *Lucia* of ALJs' and other agency adjudicators' relationship to the *Free Enterprise Fund* rule).

[83] *See, e.g.*, Aziz Z. Huq & Jon D. Michaels, *The Cycles of Separation-of-Powers Jurisprudence*, 126 YALE L.J. 346, 364 (2016) (suggesting that the Court in *Free Enterprise Fund* adopted "what seems for the moment to be a rule-like carve-out from the *Morrison* standard, at least in special cases of double insulation," and characterizing the Court as holding "that two layers were per se unconstitutional").

[84] Indeed, the Court itself has already begun to describe its *Free Enterprise Fund* holding in categorical-seeming terms. *See Seila Law*, 140 S. Ct. at 2198 ("Although we had previously sustained congressional limits on [the removal] power in certain circumstances, we declined [in *Free Enterprise Fund*] to extend those limits to 'a new situation not yet encountered by the Court'—an official insulated by *two* layers of for-cause removal protection.' " (quoting *Free Enterprise Fund*, 561 U.S. at 483)).

[85] 140 S. Ct. 2183 (2020).

[86] *Id.* at 2193.

[87] *Id.* at 2192.

[88] *Id.*

that "deviated from the structure of nearly every other independent administrative agency in our history," by attaching the for-cause removal restriction to a "single Director" of the agency, rather than to leaders sharing power on a "board with multiple members."[89] Thus, the CFPB's director, had "no boss, peers, or voters to report to," even though he "wield[ed] vast rulemaking, enforcement, and adjudicatory authority over a significant portion of the U.S. economy."[90] Faced with this "new configuration"—that is, "an independent agency that wields significant executive power and is run by a single individual"—the Court was unwilling "to take th[e] step" of "extend[ing its] precedents" to validate the a for-cause removal restriction.[91]

Why did removal protections for a flying-solo officeholder—as opposed to each member of a squadron of agency overseers—make a decisive constitutional difference? For one thing, according to the Chief Justice, the arrangement smacked of unorthodoxy.[92] Indeed, lower-court judges, litigants, and amici had turned up "only a handful of isolated incidents in which Congress had provided good-cause tenure to principal officers who wield power alone rather than as members of a board or commission."[93] In addition, removal protections for single-Director agencies struck the Court as raising an especially worrisome problem of democratic accountability. As the lone leader of a powerful governmental body, the CFPB Director could act "*unilaterally*" with "no colleagues to persuade, and no boss or electorate looking over her shoulder."[94] This set-up, the Chief

---

89 *Id.*

90 *Id.*

91 *Id.*

92 For a general criticism of the Roberts Court's frequent embrace the idea that "a federal statute's novelty[ ] speaks to whether that statute is constitutional," see Leah M. Litman, *Debunking Antinovelty*, 66 DUKE L.J. 1407, 1410 (2017).

93 *Seila Law*, 140 S. Ct. at 2201 (internal quotation omitted). *But see id.* at 2241 (Kagan, J., concurring in the judgment with respect to severability and dissenting in part) (noting that the "CFPB's single-director structure has a fair bit of precedent behind it"). In addition, the Chief Justice reasoned, the Court itself had never before confronted, much less approved of, any regime of this nature. *Humphrey's Executor*, for example, had "recogniz[ed] an exception" only "for *multimember bodies* with 'quasi-judicial' or quasi-legislative' functions." *Id.* at 2199 (majority opinion). And although *Morrison* did involve a "single Director" structure of sorts (in that only a single person served as the independent counsel and thus alone oversaw the office's staff), that arrangement was distinguishable because it involved "an inferior officer" who "lacked policymaking or administrative authority." *Id.* at 2200. *See infra* Section 31.C.3 (discussing this aspect of the *Seila Law* opinion in greater detail).

94 *Id.* at 2203 (emphasis in original). Then-Judge Brett Kavanaugh also endorsed the idea during his tenure on the D.C. Circuit. *See* PHH Corp. v. CFPB, 881 F.3d 75, 165 (D.C. Cir. 2018) (en banc) (Kavanaugh, J., dissenting) ("Multi-member independent agencies do not concentrate all power in one unaccountable individual, but instead divide and disperse power across multiple commissioners or board

Justice reasoned, contravened a basic principle of the system of checks and balances, which—with the significant exception of a President who is persistently watchdogged by and directly accountable to the citizenry as a whole—"scrupulously avoids concentrating power in the hands of any single individual."[95]

Much as in *Free Enterprise Fund*, the Court never fully explained why the single-director structure of an independent agency should operate as a standalone and categorical constitutional deal-breaker. As we have already noted, the extent of an agency's independence is a complex phenomenon that depends on a host of institutional variables.[96] And Congress's manipulation of some of those variables—such as the grounds for removal, the procedural steps (and judicial reviewability) of a removal decision, the length (and renewability) of an official's presumptive term of office, and so forth—might well mean that some agencies run by a managerial team are in fact more independent as a practical matter than other agencies supervised by a single director. Indeed, single-leader structures might even in their nature be *more* rather than *less* conducive to direct Presidential control. If, as Justice Kagan observed in her partial dissent, it is "easier to get one person to do what you want than a gaggle," then it should similarly be "harder for [a President] to oversee, to influence—or to remove, if necessary—a group of five or more commissioners than a single director."[97] Viewed in this light, the Court's past willingness to uphold removal restrictions for multimember agencies, far from undercutting the validity of single-director removal restrictions, might have served as a source of *a fortiori* support.

That, however, was not how the majority saw things, and its decision in *Seila Law*, like its decision in *Free Enterprise Fund*, reined in Congress's removal-restricting authority by laying down a new and sharply delineated rule. Under that rule, Congress may not—apparently under any circumstances—limit the President's ability to remove "principal officers who, acting alone, wield significant executive power."[98] Rather, to the extent that *Humphrey's*

---

members. The multi-member structure thereby reduces the risk of arbitrary decisionmaking and abuse of power, and helps protect individual liberty.").

95 *Seila Law*, 140 S. Ct. at 2202.

96 *See id.* at 2242 (Kagan, J., concurring in the judgment with respect to severability and dissenting in part) (noting that "Presidential control . . . can operate through many means—removal to be sure, but also appointments, oversight devices (*e.g.*, centralized review of rulemaking or litigating positions), budgetary processes, personal outreach, and more").

97 *Id.*

98 *Id.* The Court reaffirmed this rule in *Collins v. Yellen*, 141 S. Ct. 1761 (2021), when it treated *Seila Law* as "all but dispositive" in a challenge to the structure of the Federal Housing Finance Agency (as established by the Housing and Economic

Executor continues to permit removal restrictions for "quasi-legislative" and quasi-judicial" officials, these permissions apply only in connection with "*multimember* expert agencies."[99]

3. The Marginalization of *Morrison*

In addition to fashioning new rules regarding multi-layer removal protections and single-Director agencies, *Free Enterprise Fund* and *Seila Law* together effectuated an additional doctrinal shift. Recall that the Court in *Morrison v. Olson* had linked the constitutionality of a challenged removal restriction to the question whether it "impermissibly interfere[d] with" the President's constitutional responsibilities.[100] On its face, that holding seemed to signal a substantial if not wholesale repudiation of the nature-of-the-office-based categorization scheme that *Humphrey's Executor* had previously set forth, suggesting instead that courts should adjudicate *all* future removal-power cases by reference to *Morrison*'s open-ended "impermissibly interfere" test. But *Free Enterprise Fund* and *Seila Law* put an end to that possibility. Instead, the Court in those cases made clear that the *Morrison* test now applies *only* to laws governing

Recovery Act of 2008). *Seila Law* controlled, the Court explained, because "[t]he FHFA (like the CFPB) is an agency led by a single Director, and the Recovery Act (like the Dodd-Frank Act) restricts the President's removal power." *Id.* at 1784. In addition, the Court rejected several posited distinctions between the FHFA and CFPB as irrelevant to *Seila Law*'s applicability. It did not matter, for instance, that the FHFA's authority might have been "more limited than that of the CFPB," because "the nature and breadth of an agency's authority is not dispositive in determining whether Congress may limit the President's power to remove its head." *Id.* (This was potentially the most significant aspect of the Court's holding in *Collins*, given an earlier suggestion from the Court in *Seila Law* that the rule against single-director removal restrictions would apply only in connection with agencies that exercise "significant executive power." *Seila Law*, 140 S. Ct. at 2192; *see Collins*, 141 S. Ct. at 1801 (Kagan, J., dissenting) (noting that "today's majority careens right past [the significant executive power] boundary line" by instead holding that "[a]ny agency led by a single Director, no matter how much executive power it wields, now becomes subject to the requirement of at-will removal" (internal quotations omitted)).) Nor was it of any relevance, the majority reasoned, that the FHFA exercised regulatory authority over other "Government-sponsored enterprises" (most notably, Fannie Mae and Freddie Mac, both federally chartered mortgage companies), because "the President's removal power serves important purposes regardless of whether the agency in question affects ordinary Americans by directly regulat[ing] them or by taking actions that have a profound but indirect effect on their lives." *Id.* at 1786 (majority opinion). It was similarly immaterial that the FHFA's director enjoyed a more "modest" set of tenure protections than the CFPB's director, because the *Seila Law* rule applied with full force to *all* single-Director removal restrictions, no matter how "modest" they might be. *Id.* In these and other ways, the Court's decision in *Collins* left little doubt that it today understands the *Seila Law* prohibition as a bright-line rule that outlaws all single-director removal restrictions for all principal officers.

99 *Seila Law*, 140 S. Ct. at 2199 (emphasis added); *see also* Murphy, *supra* note 66, at 466–67 (noting that *Seila Law* "contains language and themes that store up trouble for the future of [multimember] agencies even if the Court continues to leave *Humphrey's Executor* and *Morrison* damaged but in place").

100 *Morrison*, 487 U.S. at 660.

the removal of officers that are *inferior* (and not principal) in nature.[101]

This reading of *Morrison* may have had the virtue of fostering doctrinal simplicity and, for unitarians, minimizing the influence of one of the Court's most Congress-friendly removal-power precedents. But it also had the vice of playing fast and loose with the actual reasoning of *Morrison* itself. The majority in that case, to be sure, did conclude that the independent counsel was an inferior, rather than a principal, officer.[102] But it did so for purposes of explaining why the *appointment-related* provisions of the Independent Counsel Act passed muster—not for purposes of cabining the scope of the removal-related test it subsequently set forth.[103] Indeed, with respect to that matter, the Court in *Morrison* paid scant attention to the independent counsel's inferior-officer status, identifying it as only one of several factors militating in favor of its conclusion that the Ethics in Government Act's removal restrictions did not "impermissibly interfere[ ] with the functions of the Executive Branch."[104] Thus, far from treating inferior-officer status as an on-off trigger determinative of the operation of the "impermissibly interfere" test, the Court in *Morrison* regarded that status as merely one among many factors for courts to consider when applying the test itself.[105]

---

101 *See Free Enter. Fund*, 561 U.S. at 483 (characterizing *Morrison* as a case in which the Court considered "restrictions on the power of principal executive officers—themselves responsible to the President—to remove their own inferiors"); *Seila Law*, 140 S. Ct. at 2192 (noting that in *Morrison*, "we held that Congress could provide tenure protections to certain *inferior* officers with narrowly defined duties").

102 *Morrison*, 487 U.S. at 671 (holding that the independent counsel "clearly falls on the 'inferior side' of th[e] line").

103 *See id.* at 669–77.

104 *Id.* at 654, 691 (noting that the challenged removal restrictions did not impermissibly interfere with the President's executive authority because, among other things, the independent counsel was an "inferior officer under the Appointments Clause, with limited jurisdiction and tenure and lacking policymaking or significant administrative authority"); *see also Seila Law*, 140 S. Ct. at 2235–36 (Kagan, J., concurring in the judgment with respect to severability and dissenting in part) ("In the eight pages addressing the removal issue, the Court constantly spoke of 'officers' and 'officials' in general. By contrast, the Court there used the word 'inferior' in just one sentence (which of course the majority quotes), when applying its general standard to the case's facts." (internal citations omitted)).

105 Indeed, Justice Scalia made this same point clear in his *Morrison* dissent, when he lamented that the Court's new framework had declared "open season upon the President's removal power for *all executive officers*." *Morrison*, 487 U.S. at 727 (Scalia, J., dissenting) (emphasis added). There is another point too: If the Court in *Morrison* had wanted to issue an opinion that applied only to inferior officers, it very easily could have done so. For one thing, rather than confusingly declare that the *Humphrey's Executor* test no longer accorded with its "present considered view" of removal power doctrine, the Court in *Morrison* could have distinguished *Humphrey's Executor* by reference to the simple fact that that case had involved principal officers, whereas *Morrison* involved an inferior officer. In addition, and as Justice Scalia himself noted

This aspect of *Morrison*, however, was swept away by the *Free Enterprise Fund* and *Seila Law* opinions, which instead declared that the Court in *Morrison* had both "considered the status of inferior officers"[106] and recognized an "exception[ ]" for "inferior officers with limited duties and no policymaking or administrative authority."[107] These characterizations of *Morrison*, as Justice Kagan put it in her partial dissent in *Seila Law*, were simply "not true to the decision" itself.[108] But they are ones that the Court has now embraced. And in this sense, the Court's recent marginalization of *Morrison* reflects what has by now become a common maneuver within the Court's removal-power jurisprudence—namely, that of attributing to a predecessor opinion a far narrower scope of operation than the opinion itself seems to suggest. Much as *Humphrey's Executor* circumscribed *Myers*, and much as *Morrison* circumscribed *Humphrey's Executor*, so too did *Free Enterprise Fund* and *Seila Law* circumscribe *Morrison* in turn. They recast the decision as one that accomplished far less than it actually meant to do.

D. WHERE THINGS NOW STAND: AN ATTEMPTED RESTATEMENT

As the many jurisprudential twists and turns recounted in this chapter reveal, it is not much easier to capture the content of the Court's removal-power doctrine than it is to "keep a wave upon the

---

in his dissent, the Court in *Morrison* could have upheld the independent-counsel arrangement by relying on its (much earlier) decision in *Perkins*, 116 U.S. at 484, in which it had already conceded to Congress a wide-ranging power to restrict the removal of inferior officers appointed by Department Heads. *See Morrison*, 487 U.S. at 724 (Scalia, J., dissenting) (noting that the Court "could have resolved the removal power issue in [*Morrison*] by simply relying upon its erroneous conclusion that the independent counsel was an inferior officer, and then extending our holding that the removal of inferior officers appointed by the Executive can be restricted, to a new holding that even the removal of inferior officers appointed by the courts can be restricted"); *see also Seila Law*, 140 S. Ct. at 2236 (Kagan, J., concurring in the judgment with respect to severability and dissenting in part) (noting that, if the independent-counsel's inferior-officer status had been "*Morrison*'s basis," then "a simple citation [to *Perkins*] would have sufficed"). In fact, to the extent the Court's opinion in *Morrison* had carried any implications about inferior officers, those implications most plausibly cut in favor of a *restricted* congressional power to limit presidential removal. That is, in suggesting that removal restrictions for both principal and inferior officers were subject to a "impermissibly interfere" test, the Court in *Morrison* seemed to signal that it no longer regarded *Perkins* as conferring on Congress a *carte blanche* authority to restrict presidential removal of inferior officers whose appointment had been vested in Department Heads. *Perkins*, in other words, had seemed to indicate that at least some inferior-officer removal restrictions were subject to a rule of *per se* constitutional validity. But the Court in *Morrison*, by not relying on *Perkins*, instead seemed to imply that, as with removal restrictions for principal officers, no such safe harbor would henceforth be available.

106 *Free Enter. Fund*, 561 U.S. at 494.

107 *Seila Law*, 140 S. Ct. at 2299–2200.

108 *Id.* at 2235–36 (Kagan, J., concurring in the judgment with respect to severability and dissenting in part).

sand."[109] Even so, thanks largely to the Court's recent pronouncements in *Free Enterprise Fund* and *Seila Law*, that doctrine—for now—seems to have crystallized into something along the following lines:

1. *For all executive officers:*

   a. If a removal-power restriction attached to any executive officer gives Congress a role to play in the removal decision itself, then that restriction is unconstitutional under *Bowsher*.

   b. If an officer is subject to for-cause removal by another officer who is in turn subject to for-cause removal by the President, then the arrangement is likely unconstitutional under the no-multi-layer rule of *Free Enterprise Fund*. Such an arrangement, however, might be permissible if the Court determines that there are exceptions to the *Free Enterprise Fund* rule (particularly for military officials and/or administrative law judges)—a possibility that the Court in *Free Enterprise* did not foreclose.

2. *For principal officers:*

   a. If a principal officer is the sole director of an agency, then a removal restriction attached to that officer is unconstitutional under *Seila Law*.

   b. If a principal officer belongs to a multimember board that oversees an agency, then a removal restriction attached to that officer may or may not be constitutionally permissible. More specifically: (i) if the agency performs "purely executive" functions, then the removal restriction will likely be impermissible under *Myers* (and notwithstanding *Morrison*); whereas (ii) if the agency performs "quasi-legislative" or "quasi-judicial" functions, then the restriction will likely be permissible under *Humphrey's Executor* (and notwithstanding both *Myers* and *Morrison*).

3. *For inferior officers:* If an inferior officer is subject to only a single layer of for-cause removal protection, then the removal restriction *might be constitutionally permissible*, depending on whether the arrangement

---

[109] "How Do You Solve a Problem Like Maria?", *in* RODGERS AND HAMMERSTEIN'S THE SOUND OF MUSIC (Twentieth Century-Fox Film Corp. 1965).

"impermissibly interferes" with the President's executive power under *Morrison*.[110]

Although this restatement of removal-power doctrine is no doubt oversimplified, it reflects at least a rough approximation of the current state of the law. This broad-brush summary also reveals that the doctrine today turns out to operate much as it did in the immediate aftermath of *Myers*, with the applicable rules prohibiting congressional restrictions on presidential removal except in narrow circumstances. The Court's removal-power jurisprudence has traveled a long and winding road, but in recent years the Roberts Court has steered it back to a point not far removed from where the Taft Court left it nearly a century ago.

110 A lingering question has to do with whether the *Humphrey's Executor* character-of-the-office test, as opposed to the *Morrison* "impermissibly interfere" test, would apply in connection with (one-layer) removal restrictions made applicable to inferior officers who sit on multimember boards. *Seila Law* seems to indicate that the answer is "no" insofar as it characterizes *Humphrey's Executor* as having held that "Congress could create expert agencies led by a group of *principal officers* removable by the President only for good cause," *Seila Law*, 140 S. Ct. at 2192 (emphasis added), thus implying that the test has no applicability to a multimember, inferior-officer scenario. But the opinion is not definitive on the issue.

Chapter 32

CONSTITUTIONAL MECHANISMS FOR CONFRONTING OFFICIAL MISCONDUCT, PRESIDENTIAL INABILITY, AND PAST PARTICIPATION IN INSURRECTION

Analysis

A cluster of constitutional clauses addresses the possibility that Presidents, cabinet Secretaries, judges, and other governmental officials might engage in behavior or suffer an affliction that warrants a power-stripping intervention. At the head of this list of provisions are those that deal with the impeachment and conviction of high-ranking officeholders who commit "high Crimes and Misdemeanors."[1] Also in the picture, though less prominently, are two clauses that create alternative pathways for disempowering persons who reveal themselves to be unfit for office: (1) section 4 of the Twenty-fifth Amendment, which deals with the problem of a President who is "unable" to discharge the powers of office;[2] and (2) section 3 of the Fourteenth Amendment, which provides for the disqualification of officials who "have engaged in insurrection or rebellion" against the United States or who have "given aid or comfort to the enemies thereof."[3]

A. IMPEACHMENT AND REMOVAL

Anticipating that Presidents and other high-ranking officials might act in ways fundamentally incompatible with their constitutional responsibilities, the Framers created a mechanism

---

1 U.S. CONST. art. II, § 4.

2 *Id.* amend. XXV, § 4.

3 *Id.* amend. XIV, § 3.

through which Congress could remove these officials from office. The substantive standard for intervention is set forth in Article II, section 4, which provides that "the President, Vice President and all civil Officers of the United States, shall be removed from Office on Impeachment for, and Conviction of, Treason, Bribery, or other high Crimes and Misdemeanors."[4] The procedural rules for securing removal on these grounds are set forth in a pair of Article I provisions, which confer on the House the "sole power of Impeachment,"[5] and the Senate the "sole power to try all Impeachments," while also making conviction in the Senate dependent on "the Concurrence of two thirds of the members present."[6] Finally, as to remedies, Article I, section 3 specifies that "[j]udgment in Cases of impeachment shall not extend further than to removal from Office, and disqualification to hold and enjoy any office of honor, Trust or Profit under the United States."[7] In short, when the House has reason to believe that an official has committed "Treason, Bribery, or other high Crimes and Misdemeanors," it may proceed by majority vote to *impeach* that official. Any such vote to impeach places the case before the Senate, which then holds a trial on the question whether to *convict* on the charges, set forth under longstanding practice in formal "articles of impeachment," issued by the House.[8] If at least two-thirds of the Senators present for the trial

---

4 *Id.* art. II, § 4.

5 *Id.* art. I, § 2.

6 *Id.* art. I, § 3. That section also provides that the "Chief Justice shall preside" over any Senate impeachment trials involving the President. *Id.* The thinking that gave rise to this provision was that the Vice President, who normally presides over the Senate, would have an obvious conflict of interest in any proceeding whose outcome "could vault him into the Presidency." Akhil Reed Amar, *On Impeaching Presidents*, 28 HOFSTRA L. REV. 291, 297 (1999).

7 U.S. CONST. art. I, § 3. The provision goes on to make clear that "the Party convicted shall nevertheless be liable and subject to Indictment, Trial, Judgment and Punishment, according to Law." *Id.* Notably, Article II also prohibits the President from using the pardon power in "Cases of Impeachment," *id.* art. II, § 2, meaning that the President may not use the pardon power to halt an ongoing impeachment proceeding or to undo the effects of a past impeachment proceeding. *See, e.g.*, Frank O. Bowman, *Presidential Pardons and the Problem of Impunity*, 23 N.Y.U. J. LEGIS. & PUB. POL'Y 425, 480–85 (2021) (emphasizing that "the exclusion for impeachments merely prohibits a president from nullifying with a pardon the Senate's conviction in an impeachment case" and does not further prohibit the President from issuing pardons in connection with criminal proceedings for offenses that either have qualified or would qualify as impeachable misconduct).

8 *See* 3 LEWIS DESCHLER, DESCHLER'S PRECEDENTS OF THE U.S. HOUSE OF REPRESENTATIVES ch. 14, § 3 (1994) (noting that "[w]hen the House determines that grounds for impeachment exist, and they are adopted by the House, they are presented to the Senate in 'articles' of impeachment"). An open question is whether an impeachment vote by the House obligates or merely authorizes the Senate to hold a trial on the Articles of Impeachment. For a recent take on the question, see Bob Bauer, *Can the Senate Decline to Try an Impeachment Case*?, LAWFARE (Jan. 21, 2019), https://www.lawfareblog.com/can-senate-decline-try-impeachment-case (suggesting that the

vote to convict, the impeached official "shall be removed from office" and may, depending on the judgment of the Senate, also be disqualified from ever holding office again.[9]

1. Impeachment as a Political Question

According to conventional wisdom, decisions about both whether and how to carry out impeachment proceedings are exclusively for Congress to make. To date, the Court's treatment of impeachment-related issues is consistent with this view, as evidenced by its decision in *Nixon v. United States*.[10] That case involved not the almost-impeached former President Richard M. Nixon, but rather a federal judge named Walter Nixon. Judge Nixon, who recently had been impeached by the House and convicted by the Senate on perjury-related charges, sought judicial nullification of this action on the ground that the Senate did not "try" his case in a procedurally valid manner.[11] The Court, however, ruled that the case was subject to dismissal because it presented a nonjusticiable "political question."[12] For Chief Justice Rehnquist, who wrote for himself and five colleagues, the constitutional text was dispositive. In particular, by vesting in the Senate the "*sole* power to try all impeachments,"[13] Article I reflected a "textual commitment" to the upper chamber (and not the courts) of the power to decide upon the "procedures used . . . in trying impeachments."[14] This conclusion found additional support in the "history and contemporary understandings of the impeachment provisions"—especially because Judge Nixon could point to no "evidence . . . that even alludes to the possibility of judicial review in the context of the impeachment powers."[15] Nor was this lack of evidence surprising in light of the practical problems that judicial review of impeachment convictions would create. Of greatest concern was the danger that delays by judicial review in finally resolving impeachment controversies—which might well involve the

---

Senate is constitutionally obligated to try impeachment charges but that it likely could, as a practical matter, get away with choosing not to do so).

9 The Senate has long treated the removal sanction as automatically triggered by a vote to convict a sitting officer, while treating disqualification as contingent on a separate vote (subject only to a majority threshold) following the vote to convict. *See* 3 DESCHLER, *supra* note 8, ch. 14, § 18.17 (tracing the precedent back to the 1936 impeachment trial of Judge Halsted Ritter).

10 506 U.S. 224 (1993).

11 *Id.* at 228–29. Nixon's specific contention was that the Senate had not complied with its constitutional obligation to "try" all impeachments because it delegated to a committee of Senators the tasks of receiving evidence and taking testimony in the case. *Id.*

12 On the political-question doctrine more generally, *see infra* Section 35.E.

13 U.S. CONST. art. I, § 3 (emphasis added).

14 *Nixon*, 506 U.S. at 236.

15 *Id.* at 233.

President—could "expose the political life of the country to months, or perhaps years, of chaos."[16]

Some language in *Nixon* supports the conclusion that courts altogether lack the power to adjudicate impeachment-related disputes.[17] But this reading of the decision may go too far. Concurring only in the judgment in *Nixon*, Justice Souter suggested that the political-question bar was *not* absolute and that under "different and unusual circumstances"—circumstances involving, say, a decision to convict "upon a coin toss, or upon a summary determination that an officer of the United States was simply 'a bad guy' "—"a more searching review of impeachment proceedings" by the judicial branch might be proper.[18] Even more important, Justice Souter's view of things found some support in the majority opinion itself, which went out of its way to flag "several difficulties" with Nixon's specific claim that the Senate's reliance on committee proceedings to gather evidence in the case was inconsistent with the textual dictate that the Senate "try all impeachments."[19] A plausible takeaway from these portions of the opinion was that the Court's invocation of the political question doctrine had something to do with the Justices' collective sense that no *obvious* constitutional misstep had occurred in the Senate's processing of the case.[20] On this reading of *Nixon*, then, it remains possible that a future case involving egregiously out-of-bounds action by the House or Senate, especially as to matters not related to those bodies' chosen procedures, might surmount *Nixon*'s political-question bar.

Even so, the broader point remains: Throughout U.S. history the federal courts have said almost nothing about the constitutional law of impeachment. As a result, to the extent that any "precedents" on these issues exist, they are precedents that derive from past determinations reached by the House and the Senate in performing their respective roles. And while these precedents are not binding on

---

16 *Id.* at 236 (quoting Nixon v. United States, 938 F.2d 239, 246 (D.C. Cir. 1991)).

17 *See, e.g., id.* at 234 (noting particular "reasons why the Judiciary, and the Supreme Court in particular, were not chosen to have any role in impeachments").

18 *Id.* at 253–54 (Souter, J., concurring).

19 *See id.* at 229 (majority opinion).

20 *See* Vikram David Amar & Jason Mazzone, *The Power to "Try" "Cases of Impeachment": Some Reflections on the Finality, Transparency and Integrity of Senate Adjudications of Presidential Impeachments (Including that of Donald J. Trump)*, 95 CHI.-KENT L. REV. 455, 458–59 (2020) ("[E]ven though Chief Justice Rehnquist's majority opinion in *Nixon* does not explicitly embrace Justice Souter's approach—and instead purports to adopt a bright-line rule of no judicial review—the fact that the majority does opine on the meaning of the word 'try,' and how the Senate's definition of that word is a permissible one, suggests more agreement with Justice Souter than the majority itself acknowledges.").

future Congresses, they might at least sometimes come to carry significant persuasive force.[21]

2. What Offenses Are Impeachable?

Article II, section 4 identifies three categories of impeachable offenses: (1) "Treason"; (2) "Bribery"; and (3) "other high Crimes and Misdemeanors."[22] "Treason" itself is further defined by Article III, which stipulates that the offense "consist[s] only in levying War against [the United States], or in adhering to their Enemies, giving them Aid and Comfort."[23] And while "Bribery" lacks a comparable definition in the text of the Constitution, the term today is generally understood to track the statutory definition that an early Congress laid down in the federal criminal code.[24] These first two categories of impeachable offenses thus represent forms of misconduct that—while not free from ambiguity—have established definitional elements.

The third category is different. A late addition to the constitutional text, the phrase "high Crimes and Misdemeanors" was inserted at the urging of delegates who worried that limiting impeachment to only treason and bribery would render unduly narrow the congressional power of removal. In light of this concern, George Mason proposed adding "maladministration" to the list,[25] but James Madison objected on the ground that the term was "[s]o vague" as to "be equivalent to a tenure during pleasure of the Senate."[26] As a result, the delegates went with the more restrictive (but still open-

---

[21] *See* Michael J. Gerhardt, *Non-Judicial Precedent*, 61 VAND. L. REV. 713, 751 (2008) (noting that "the federal impeachment process is rife with final congressional judgments on constitutional questions, such as the appropriate burden of proof, rules of evidence, and procedures for impeachment trials").

[22] U.S. CONST. art. II, § 4.

[23] *See id* art. III, § 3; *see also* 18 U.S.C. § 2381 (adopting a similar definition for purposes of federal criminal law). It is not altogether clear whether impeachment trials are subject to Article III's further requirement that "[n]o Person shall be convicted of Treason unless on the Testimony of two Witnesses to the same overt Act, or on Confession in open Court," U.S. CONST. art. III, § 3, but a textual case can be made for this position. Article II, after all, speaks of the Senate's vote to "convict[ ]" in an impeachment trial, *id.* art. II, § 4, and the Treason Clause applies to any person who might be "*convicted* of Treason," *id.* art. III, § 3; *cf.* Brief of Petitioner, *Nixon*, 506 U.S. 224 (No. 91–740), 1992 WL 511933, at *27 ("[B]ecause treason is an impeachable offense, the treason clause would permit the Senate to 'convict' in treason cases only after hearing the testimony of at least two accusing witnesses.").

[24] *See* 18 U.S.C. § 201; *see also* MICHAEL J. GERHARDT, THE FEDERAL IMPEACHMENT PROCESS: A CONSTITUTIONAL AND HISTORICAL ANALYSIS 108 (3d ed. 2019) (noting that this statute "codifies an impeachable offense because bribery is expressly designated as such in the Constitution").

[25] 2 MAX FARRAND, RECORDS OF THE FEDERAL CONVENTION OF 1787, at 550 (rev. ed. 1911) (statement of George Mason).

[26] *Id.* (statement of James Madison).

ended) formulation of "other high crimes and misdemeanors."[27] The choice of this phrase reflected an attempt to travel a middle course between two undesirable extremes. It afforded Congress the desired capacity to remove officers who engaged in misconduct that, though serious, did not qualify as treason or bribery, while avoiding such a broadening of the grounds for impeachment as to authorize the equivalent of a parliamentary "no confidence" vote.[28] The phrase, in other words, captured not any and all acts of governmental mismanagement, but rather, as Charles Black once put it, the more limited class of "offenses having about them some flavor of criminality."[29]

The open-endedness of the "high Crimes and Misdemeanors" standard affords Congress much discretion in deciding for itself whether an official's actions rise to the level of impeachable misconduct. But that discretion is cabined in at least three ways. First, the constitutional standard presupposes a baseline threshold of severity that a wide range of official actions obviously would not meet.[30] (No one would seriously argue, for instance, that the President commits a high crime or misdemeanor by showing up late for a meeting.[31]) Second, abuses of the impeachment process might provoke political backlash, and fears of that backlash might deter Representatives and Senators from overreaching in invoking their powers to impeach and remove.[32] Finally, and of perhaps greatest importance, the two-thirds supermajority requirement for conviction in the Senate all but guarantees that any successful impeachment effort must have wide bipartisan support—support unlikely to manifest itself in obviously unsupportable or even borderline cases.

---

27 *Id.*

28 *See* CHARLES L. BLACK, JR., IMPEACHMENT: A HANDBOOK 30 (2d ed. 1998).

29 *Id.* at 29; *see also* GERHARDT, *supra* note 24, at 106 (noting that "the framers and ratifiers apparently shared a common understanding of impeachment as a political proceeding and impeachable offenses as political crimes").

30 A common formulation finds expression in Alexander Hamilton's *Federalist No. 65*, which characterized impeachable misconduct as an "abuse or violation of some public trust." *See* THE FEDERALIST NO. 65 (Hamilton). Put another way, in contrast to standard-fare criminal misconduct, which typically involves the infliction of injury on other individuals, impeachable misconduct causes an injury "immediately to the society itself," resulting from an abuse of the powers or duties with which a constitutional official has been entrusted. *Id.* One consequence of this understanding is that "the offences . . . to which the power of impeachment has been, and is ordinarily applied, as a remedy, are of a political character" and thus encompass more than "crimes of a strictly legal character." 2 JOSEPH STORY, COMMENTARIES ON THE CONSTITUTION § 762 (Thomas M. Cooley, ed., 4th ed. 1873).

31 *See* LAURENCE TRIBE, AMERICAN CONSTITUTIONAL LAW § 2–7, at 155 (3d ed. 2000) (noting that "[n]early everyone would concur, for example, that the misdemeanor of driving above the speed limit . . . could not constitute grounds for impeachment").

32 Motivating at least some members' reluctance to pursue frivolous impeachment proceedings might also be their oath of office, which obliges all House and Senate "to support this Constitution." *See* U.S. CONST. art. VI.

Indeed, as several commentators have recently argued, current conditions of political polarization may make this final safeguard against abuse of the impeachment-related powers significantly more exacting than it ought (and was intended) to be.[33]

3. Who Can Be Impeached and Convicted?

As the foregoing discussion shows, the "high Crimes and Misdemeanors" standard gives rise to complex questions about *what sort of conduct* qualifies as impeachable. But another feature of the constitutional text raises a separate question about *who* is subject to removal by way of impeachment. Article II, section 4 stipulates that the persons eligible for impeachment are "the President, Vice President and all civil Officers of the United States."[34] That language, however, leaves two major issues unaddressed. First, who qualifies as a "civil Officer[ ] of the United States"? And second, does Congress's power to impeach and to convict extend to *former* officials (including former Presidents) who have resigned or completed their terms of office?

a. *"Civil Officers of the United States"*

Generally accepted governing principles dictate that many types of government officials do *not* qualify as "civil Officers of the United States" within the meaning of the Article II Impeachment Clause. For example, the term obviously does not extend to state and local government officials, who, though perhaps "civil Officers" in a general sense, are not "civil Officers *of the United States*."[35] In addition, the term "*civil* Officers" is widely understood not to include federal *military* officers, who instead are subject to disciplinary procedures laid out in the Uniform Code of Military Justice and related statutes and rules.[36] Finally, and in keeping with the Court's

---

[33] *See, e.g.*, Jelani Cobb, *Why Impeachment Doesn't Work*, THE NEW YORKER (Feb. 22, 2021), https://www.newyorker.com/news/daily-comment/why-impeachment-doesnt-work (noting that, under current conditions, "[i]mpeachment is, at best, a tool that can deliver justice when a President's party is a congressional minority, and, at its worst, a mechanism whose bar for success is so high as to nullify its own utility"). *But see* Brian C. Kalt, *Presidential Impeachment and Removal: From the Two-Party System to the Two-Reality System*, 27 GEO. MASON L. REV. 1, 24–27 (2020) (contending that even under conditions of extreme polarization, it remains possible to "imagine offenses . . . that break through the reality barrier separating the two sides" and that the impeachment power therefore still serves the critical purpose of deterring egregiously severe (but otherwise uncheckable) acts of official misconduct).

[34] U.S. CONST. art. II, § 4.

[35] *See* Jennifer L. Mascott, *Who Are "Officers of the United States"?*, 70 STAN. L. REV. 443, 473–74 (2018) (noting that the Appointments Clause's use of the identical term "Officers of the United States" was intended to serve as "a reference to the general category of federal officers, as opposed to state officers").

[36] *See* 2 STORY, *supra* note 30, § 790 ("The reason for excepting military and naval officers is, that they are subject to trial and punishment according to a peculiar military code, the laws, rules, and usages of war."); *see also* Zachary S. Price,

interpretation of the Appointments Clause,[37] the term "Officers" does not appear to encompass the many "lesser functionaries" who work for the federal government as mere "employees."[38]

What about federal judges? The Impeachment Clause does not refer in express terms to judicial officials, and one might infer from the clause's placement in Article II that only executive-branch officials fall within its scope. But Congress has long rejected that position, treating members of the judicial-branch as no less subject to impeachment than their executive-branch counterparts.[39] Congress's position on the matter draws textual support from Article III's stipulation that judges "shall hold their Offices during good Behaviour"[40]—language that might well prove meaningless in the absence of some sort of mechanism for the removal of misbehaving holders of judicial office.[41] And because the Constitution fails to

---

Congress's Power Over Military Offices, 99 TEX. L. REV. 491, 500 (2021) (noting that "Congress lacks the power to impeach and remove military officers" because the relevant constitutional language makes reference "only to '[t]he President, Vice-President, and all civil [i.e., nonmilitary] officials of the United States' " (quoting U.S. CONST. art. II, § 4) (alterations in original)).

[37] *See supra* Section 30.A.1 (discussing the meaning of the term "Officers of the United States" in the context of the Appointments Clause).

[38] *Cf.* Lucia v. SEC, 138 S. Ct. 2044, 2051 (2018) (distinguishing, for Appointments Clause purposes, between "Officers of the United States" and "employees of the Federal Government"); *see also* Cong. Rsch. Serv., *Offices Eligible for Impeachment*, CONSTITUTION ANNOTATED, https://constitution.congress.gov/browse/essay/artII-S4-1-2-1/ALDE_00000689 (last visited Nov. 15, 2021) ("Assuming [the Appointments Clause] line of cases serves as a guide in deciding who is a civil officer subject to impeachment, it appears that 'employees,' as non-officers, are not subject to impeachment, while principal officers, such as the head of a cabinet-level executive department, are. In between these two categories, historical practice does not indicate whether an inferior officer is subject to impeachment, as the House has never impeached such an individual.").

[39] Indeed, the first person removed from office via impeachment was a federal judge, *see* Lynn W. Turner, *The Impeachment of John Pickering*, 54 AM. HIST. REV. 485 (1949), and 15 of the 20 officials ever to have been impeached by the House of Representatives have been Article III judges. *See Impeachment*, U.S. HOUSE OF REPRESENTATIVES, HISTORY, ART & ARCHIVES (last visited Nov. 15, 2021), https://history.house.gov/Institution/Origins-Development/Impeachment/; *see also id.* (noting that all eight of the Senate's past judgments of conviction have concerned judges).

[40] *See* U.S. CONST. art. III, § 1. This position finds additional support in the Appointments Clause, which, in referencing "Judges of the supreme Court" along with "*other* Officers of the United States," indicates that federal judges also qualify as "Officers of the United States." *See id.* art. II, § 2 (emphasis added); *see also id.* art. II, § 4 (subjecting all "civil Officers of the United States" to Congress's powers of impeachment).

[41] Some scholars have argued that, while impeachment constitutes a permissible mechanism for removing federal judges, the "good behavior" standard allows for other, statutorily prescribed removal processes as well. *See, e.g.*, Saikrishna Prakash & Steven D. Smith, *How to Remove a Federal Judge*, 116 YALE L.J. 72, 74, 78 (2006) (challenging the conventional wisdom that "impeachment is the only means of removing a federal judge" and contending that "Congress, using its authority under the Necessary and Proper Clause, may establish any number of mechanisms for determining whether a judge has forfeited her office through misbehavior" (internal

specify any other means of terminating a judge's tenure, it makes sense—so the argument goes—to read the Good Behavior Clause as premised on the legislature's ability to impeach and remove judges.[42]

Another "who can be impeached" question concerns members of the House and Senate. Congress confronted this question shortly after ratification, when Senator William Blount of Tennessee was implicated in a wild-eyed conspiracy to help the British gain control of the then-Spanish territories of Florida and Louisiana.[43] The conspiracy itself went nowhere, but both Houses of Congress were quick to act when its details came to light. The House moved first, with an immediate vote in favor of impeachment.[44] The Senate soon thereafter exercised its Article I authority to *expel* Blount from the body,[45] with the upshot being that Blount no longer held his seat when the House's articles of impeachment arrived in the Senate.[46] The Senate then attempted, but failed, to secure Blount's appearance for the impeachment trial (by then, he had made tracks back to Tennessee), thus setting the stage for the upper chamber's final action in the case: By way of a fourteen-to-eleven vote, the Senate dismissed the case, having concluded that "this Court ought not to hold jurisdiction of the said impeachment."[47] In issuing this pronouncement, the Senate did not elaborate on its reasons for refusing to proceed.[48] The general view, however, is that the vote

---

footnote omitted)). Others, however, have contested this view. *See, e.g.*, James E. Pfander, *Removing Federal Judges*, 74 U. CHI. L. REV. 1227, 1230–34 (2007).

[42] A harder question is whether the "good behavior" standard sets forth a substantive criterion of impeachability that differs from (or puts a distinctly judiciary-specific gloss on) the high-crimes-and-misdemeanors standard. More specifically, does the clause—or the distinctive role played by Article III judges—permit Congress to impeach and convict for any and all instances of bad behavior, or must those instances of bad behavior clear the seemingly higher "high Crimes and Misdemeanors" bar that unquestionably applies to executive-branch officials? *See* Brian C. Kalt, *The Constitutional Case for the Impeachability of Former Federal Officials*, 6 TEX. REV. L. & POL. 13, 63 n.198 (2001) (collecting commentary on the issue and noting that, while there is debate among commentators as to whether judges should be formally subject to a different test, Congress has in practice held judges to a "lower standard").

[43] *See generally* BUCKNER F. MELTON, THE FIRST IMPEACHMENT: THE CONSTITUTION'S FRAMERS AND THE CASE OF SENATOR WILLIAM BLOUNT (1998).

[44] 3 JOURNAL OF THE HOUSE OF REPRESENTATIVES OF THE UNITED STATES OF AMERICA 72–73 (Washington: Gales & Seaton 1826).

[45] *See* U.S. CONST. art. I, § 5 (providing that each House of Congress "may . . ., with the concurrence of two-thirds, expel a member"); *see also supra* Section 14.B (discussing the expulsion mechanism in greater detail).

[46] 2 JOURNAL OF THE SENATE OF THE UNITED STATES OF AMERICA 392 (Washington: Gales & Seaton 1820).

[47] 8 ANNALS OF CONG. 2319 (Washington: Gales & Seaton 1851).

[48] Even so, the Senate had to some extent shown its cards, in that it had already rejected (also by a 14–11 margin) a resolution that would have stipulated that "William Blount was a civil officer of the United States, within the meaning of the Constitution of the United States, and therefore, liable to be impeached by the House of Representatives." *Id.* at 2318. *But see* Buckner F. Melton, Jr., *Let Me Be Blunt: In*

reflected the body's determination that Senators and Representatives are not subject to impeachment at all.[49] And whatever the precise justification of the dismissal ruling might have been, the House and Senate have never since then wavered from the view that their own members, while subject to expulsion, are not subject to impeachment.

In sum, under present-day law, the term "Civil Officers of the United States" encompasses (1) nonmilitary federal executive-branch officials and (2) life-tenured federal judges. Other officials (including members of Congress) might still be held accountable for their misdeeds, but not by way of the impeachment-based procedures of Article I.

b. Former Officials?

The other major "who can be impeached" issue relates to timing: Can Congress act to impeach (and/or convict) only federal officials who remain in office at the time of the relevant proceedings, or can Congress also impeach (and/or convict) *former* federal officials as well? In one sense, this question might seem to be one of only academic interest, given the apparent redundancy of acting to

---

Blount, *The Senate Never Said That Senators Aren't Impeachable*, 33 QUINNIPIAC L. REV. 33, 36 (2014) (contending that "nowhere in the *Blount* proceedings did the Senate establish any rule or precedent that Senators cannot be impeached").

49 *See* GERHARDT, *supra* note 24, at 50 ("Ever since, the House and the Senate have regarded the Blount impeachment as standing for the proposition that senators are not impeachable because they are not 'civil officers of the United States.' "); *see also* Keith E. Whittington, *A Formidable Weapon of Faction? The Law and Politics of Impeachment*, 55 WAKE FOREST L. REV. 381, 394 (2020) (noting that "Congress currently takes the view that congressional members are not federal civil officers for the purposes of impeachment," while also noting that "there is nothing that prevents Congress from revisiting that conclusion"). Two lines of argument support the position attributed to the Senate in the Blount case. The first is based on the text: In particular, the Constitution uses the word "Officer" in several of its provisions, often in ways that would seem to exclude federal legislators from its scope. *See, e.g.*, U.S. CONST. art. I, § 6 (providing that "no Person holding any Office under the United States, shall be a Member of either House during his Continuance in Office" and thus drawing an implicit textual contrast between "hold[ing] any Office" and serving as a "Member of either House"); *see also* Akhil Reed Amar & Vikram David Amar, *Is the Presidential Succession Law Constitutional*, 48 STAN. L. REV. 113, 114–15 (1995) (highlighting additional clauses that use the term "Officer" in a manner that supports an "officer/legislator distinction"). The second argument relates to the sanction of *expulsion* the Senate already had imposed on Blount. In particular, that argument posits that, by explicitly authorizing each House of Congress to "punish its Members for disorderly Behaviour, and, with the Concurrence of two thirds, expel a Member," U.S. CONST. art. I, § 5; *see also supra* Section 14.B, the Constitution implicitly precludes Congress from relying on its impeachment provisions as a further or alternative method of punishment. *See* GERHARDT, *supra* note 24, at 79. *But see* 8 ANNALS OF CONG., *supra* note 47, at 2316–17 (noting an argument made by Robert Harper, one of the House managers in the Blount trial, that impeachment was necessary *in addition to expulsion* because impeachment alone permitted the remedy of disqualification from future office and therefore offered the only means of ensuring that "a great and wicked man" could never "return again, after being expelled").

remove from office a person who no longer holds it. In fact, however, the separate Article II remedy of disqualification from future office provides Congress with a freestanding reason for proceeding against former officials who might again seek to wield power in the future.[50]

The importance of this issue is not likely to be lost on anyone familiar with the tumultuous final months of Donald Trump's presidency. Having been defeated by Joseph Biden in the 2020 presidential election, the soon-to-be-ex-President vigorously resisted the transfer of power to his successor, falsely claiming he was the victim of a stolen election, pressuring state officials not to certify election results, urging state legislatures to appoint alternative slates of electors, supporting meritless legal challenges, and ultimately calling upon gathered supporters to march on the Capitol, where rioters then overwhelmed law enforcement officers and temporarily shut down Congress's formal counting of the electoral-college votes.[51] These actions (and particularly the last one) prompted the House to adopt—with just one week remaining in President Trump's term—an article of impeachment against the President on charges of "incitement of insurrection."[52] That article, however, was not taken up by the Senate until after President Trump's term had expired.

Emphasizing this fact, the former President's attorneys contended, and some commentators agreed, that the Senate lacked jurisdiction to move forward with his case.[53] A particularly high-profile endorsement of this view came from Michael Luttig, a former Fourth Circuit judge. In an op-ed piece published shortly before the House's impeachment vote, Judge Luttig maintained that "[t]he very

---

50 *See* U.S. CONST. art. I, § 3.

51 *See* Richard L. Hasen, *Identifying and Minimizing the Risk of Election Subversion and Stolen Elections in the Contemporary United States*, 135 HARV. L. REV. F. 265, 270 (2022) (describing in detail the various efforts underlying the President's "political and legal strategy aimed not just at sowing doubt but also at subverting the outcome of the presidential election").

52 H. RES. 24, 117th Cong. (2021).

53 As it happened, President Trump was not the first former official to have faced a Senate trial. Indeed, Senator Blount himself had been expelled from the upper chamber well before his trial, so that the Senate's decision to dismiss his case on grounds unrelated to his former-official status might suggest (albeit indirectly) that it did not regard his prior departure from office as presenting a jurisdictional problem. *See supra* Section 32.A.3.a. Even more on point is the 1876 case of Secretary of War William Belknap, who, having resigned just hours before a House impeachment vote, nonetheless found himself subject to trial by the Senate after it expressly rejected—pursuant to a majority vote—a motion to dismiss the case on jurisdictional grounds. *See* 3 ASHER C. HINDS, HINDS' PRECEDENTS OF THE HOUSE OF REPRESENTATIVES §§ 2466–67 (1907). Belknap, however, was ultimately acquitted by a narrow margin, thus muddying to some extent the precedential significance of his case. *See* GERHARDT, *supra* note 24, at 54 (noting that the "Senate vote to accept jurisdiction [in the Belknap case] provides . . . support for conducting a postresignation impeachment trial, even though the final Senate vote cuts the other way").

concept of constitutional impeachment presupposes the impeachment, conviction and removal of a president who is, *at the time of his impeachment*, an incumbent in the office from which he is removed."[54] This conclusion, Judge Luttig reasoned, found support in the "plain text of the Constitution's several Impeachment Clauses," including in particular Article II's stipulation that "[t]he President, Vice President and all civil officers of the United States, shall be *removed*" via impeachment, and in Article I's separate stipulation that "Judgment in Cases of Impeachment shall not extend further than to *removal* from Office, and disqualification."[55] These provisions together made clear, Judge Luttig asserted, that "[o]nce Trump's term ends on Jan. 20, Congress loses its constitutional authority to continue impeachment proceedings against him."[56]

A close examination, however, reveals some difficulties with this claim. To begin with, the argument relies in part on a question-begging assertion—namely, that "the very concept of constitutional impeachment presupposes" an active-duty defendant.[57] That is certainly one "concept" of impeachment, but there are other possibilities, too, including that the impeachment power exists not just, as Judge Luttig asserts, for the purpose of "remov[ing] from office a president or other 'civil offic[er]' before he could further harm the nation from the office he then occupies,"[58] but also for the purpose of averting future harms by securing the permanent disqualification of former officials who have revealed their unfitness for office.[59] In addition, the constitutional text may be less definitive on the issue than the no-former-Presidents argument suggests. Article II, section 4, for instance, states that persons convicted by the Senate "shall be removed" as a consequence of conviction—language that might be

---

54 J. Michael Luttig, *Opinion: Once Trump Leaves Office, the Senate Can't Hold an Impeachment Trial*, WASH. POST (Jan. 12, 2021), https://www.washingtonpost.com/opinions/2021/01/12/once-trump-leaves-office-senate-cant-hold-an-impeachment-trial/.

55 *Id.* (citing U.S. CONST. art. II, § 4 and *id.*, art. I, § 3) (emphasis added).

56 *Id.* Professor Philip Bobbitt also espoused a similar position. *See* Philip Bobbitt, *Why the Senate Shouldn't Hold a Late Impeachment Trial*, LAWFARE (Jan. 27, 2021), https://www.lawfareblog.com/why-senate-shouldnt-hold-late-impeachment-trial [hereinafter Bobbitt, *Late Impeachment*]; Philip Bobbitt, *The Constitutionality of Trying a Former President for Impeachment—A Reply to Frank Bowman*, LAWFARE (Feb. 12, 2021), https://www.lawfareblog.com/constitutionality-trying-former-president-impeachment%E2%80%93-reply-frank-bowman [hereinafter Bobbitt, *Reply*].

57 Luttig, *supra* note 54.

58 *Id.*

59 *See* Frank O. Bowman, III, *The Constitutionality of Trying a Former President Impeached While in Office*, LAWFARE (Feb. 3, 2021), https://www.lawfareblog.com/constitutionality-trying-former-president-impeached-while-office (contending that the impeachment-related clauses serve the "overall purpose of protecting [the] constitutional order against dangerous presidents").

read (as Judge Luttig contends) to require that any impeached official must be serving in office at the time the trial occurs. But the clause might instead signify only a prohibition on permitting any still-serving official from continuing to hold office upon an impeachment conviction, while saying nothing one way or the other about the Senate's ability to proceed against no-longer-serving officials.[60] In addition, Article I, section 3's specification that "Judgment in Cases of Impeachment shall not extend further than to removal . . . and disqualification" is also susceptible to an interpretation that does not bar former-official impeachment trials: What the provision says on its face, after all, is simply that the Senate "shall not" impose sanctions that reach "further than" removal and disqualification; its terms thus can be read as setting a ceiling (rather than a floor) on the remedies that the upper chamber can impose.[61] And because one of the two specified sanctions is a "disqualification" from holding office in the future, that clause by its own terms does not exclude—and perhaps even invites—the possibility of a former official's impeachment and conviction.[62]

Lurking in the background of this debate about the meaning of the constitutional text—text that the foregoing discussion shows is at least ambiguous in its treatment of former officeholders—are compelling practical concerns that provide commonsense support for permitting impeachment of former officeholders. Of greatest significance, if former officials are exempt from impeachment, Congress would become unable to hold them accountable for even the gravest forms of misconduct committed during the last days of their terms. Impeachment takes time, with a Senate trial in particular presenting opportunities for defendants (and their upper-chamber

---

[60] For an extensive examination of this provision's bearing on the former-officers debate, see Kalt, *supra* note 42, at 58–68; *see also id.* at 68 (arriving at the conclusion that the constitutional text alone "does not clearly and directly address the proper timing of impeachment" and that therefore "it is necessary to consult history, structure, and precedent to address the question of late impeachment"); *see also* BRIAN C. KALT, CONSTITUTIONAL CLIFFHANGERS 106–32 (2012).

[61] *See* Michael McConnell, Impeaching *Officials While They're in Office, But* Trying *Them After They Leave,* THE VOLOKH CONSPIRACY (Jan. 28, 2021), https://reason.com/volokh/2021/01/28/impeaching-officials-while-theyre-in-office-but-trying-them-after-they-leave/ (noting that "the clause does not say that both sanctions are required; it says that the judgment may not go beyond imposition of both sanctions").

[62] Relatedly, some commentators have argued that President Trump's second impeachment did not implicate hard questions regarding the impeachability of former officials because his *impeachment by the House* occurred while he was still serving as President. On this view, that is, the timing of the House vote, coupled with the constitutional text's proclamation that the Senate has the power to "try *all* Impeachments," *see* U.S. CONST. art. I, § 3 (emphasis added), eliminated any doubts regarding the validity of Trump's post-presidency impeachment trial. *See* McConnell, *supra* note 61 (suggesting the question whether "a former officer can be impeached" was "beside the point" in the Trump case because Trump himself had been impeached by the House while still serving as President).

political allies) to run out the clock as a term of office nears its end. Consequently, a rule that bars impeachment of former officials would enable currently-serving officials to flout their duties of office without consequence during the last few weeks or even months of their terms.[63] Relatedly, if only sitting officers are subject to conviction on impeachment charges, then already-impeached officers would be able to resign immediately prior to a judgment of conviction and thereby evade any judgment of disqualification that the Senate would otherwise issue.[64]

Ultimately, the Senate's weighing of these arguments following the House's post-Capitol-riot impeachment of President Trump produced a mixed result. On the one hand, fifty-five Senators voted against a resolution that would have deemed the case to fall outside the Senate's jurisdiction, an action signifying that a majority of the body was not prepared to declare that all former officers are *ipso facto* exempt from impeachment-based sanctions.[65] On the other hand, the necessary two-thirds majority for conviction never materialized, and several of the Senators who supported acquittal expressly attributed their votes, at least in part, to concerns about the Senate's power to proceed against former officials.[66] All things considered, then, former-President Trump's second impeachment trial failed to establish a clear precedent one way or the other regarding the

---

[63] The House managers pressed this claim throughout former-President Trump's Senate trial, contending that a rule that insulated former officers from impeachment would create a "January exception" for late-Term Presidents (and others) to exploit. *See* Trial Memorandum of the United States House of Representatives in the Impeachment Trial of President Donald J. Trump 48 (Feb. 2, 2021). One counterargument to this position focuses on the possibility that soon-to-be-former officers will be sufficiently deterred from engaging in acts of wrongdoing by the prospect of criminal liability, thus removing the need for the additional deterrent of a post-tenure impeachment proceeding. *Cf.* Bobbitt, *Reply*, *supra* note 56 (raising the possibility that former-President Trump might be criminally charged for his conduct leading up to the riot of January 6). One difficulty with this counterargument, however, is that it may prove too much: The threat of criminal sanctions, after all, exists throughout an official's tenure, but that fact has never been cited as a reason not to impeach currently serving officials. Why then (so the counter-counterargument goes) should it be any different when it comes to former officials? *See* KALT, *supra* note 60, at 120 (noting that "prosecutability doesn't protect sitting presidents from being impeached, so it should not preclude ex-presidents from being impeached either").

[64] *See* Kalt, *supra* note 42, at 75 (noting that under a no-former-officials rule, "a party by resigning, or a President by firing him, [could] flout any attempt by Congress to disqualify").

[65] *See* Nicholas Fandos, *Most G.O.P. Senators Vote Against Holding Impeachment Trial for Trump*, N.Y. TIMES (Jan. 26, 2021), https://www.nytimes.com/live/2021/01/26/us/biden-trump-impeachment.

[66] *See* Nicholas Fandos & Emily Cochrane, *Impeachment Trial: Trump Is Acquitted by the Senate*, N.Y. TIMES (Feb. 13, 2021), https://www.nytimes.com/live/2021/02/13/us/impeachment-trial. Senate Majority Leader Mitch McConnell, for instance, explained his vote by saying that "[w]hile a close call, I am persuaded that impeachments are a tool primarily of removal and we therefore lack jurisdiction." *See id.*

impeachability of no-longer-serving officials. The question thus remains open, just as it did before that trial began.

B. PRESIDENTIAL INABILITY AND SECTION 4 OF THE TWENTY-FIFTH AMENDMENT

In its original form, the Constitution provided that the "Powers and Duties" of the President "shall devolve on the Vice President" in the event of the President's "inability to discharge" them.[67] Later experience—especially during the presidencies of James Garfield, Woodrow Wilson, and Franklin Roosevelt—exposed gaps, ambiguities, and inadequacies in this provision's treatment of issues concerning inability-related transfers of power to the Vice-President.[68] Over the years, Congress made halting attempts to address these problems. But it was not until after the Kennedy assassination in 1963 that the House and Senate chose to tackle the subject head-on, resulting in the proposal and eventual ratification of the Twenty-fifth Amendment.[69]

The Amendment has four sections: Section 1 makes explicit what the original Constitution had made only implicit—namely that the "Vice President shall *become President*" (i.e., not just assume duties as Acting President) whenever a sitting President dies, resigns, or is removed from office.[70] Section 2 addresses the subject of *Vice Presidential* vacancies, providing that, the President "shall nominate" a replacement to fill any such vacancy, while also requiring "confirmation by a majority vote of both Houses of Congress."[71] Section 3 sets forth a process through which the President may voluntarily relinquish the "powers and duties of his office" for as long as "he is unable to discharge" them, as might be the case, for instance, when the President undergoes surgery, becomes mentally unstable, or is too distracted by private affairs to engage fully with his official responsibilities.[72] Finally, section 4 confronts the difficult problem of what to do about a President who is "unable

---

[67] *See* U.S. CONST. art. II, § 1.

[68] *See* BRIAN C. KALT, UNABLE: THE LAW POLITICS, AND LIMITS OF SECTION 4 OF THE TWENTY-FIFTH AMENDMENT 29–43 (2019).

[69] *Id.* at 43–48.

[70] *See* U.S. CONST. amend. 25, § 1.

[71] *Id.* amend. 25, § 2.

[72] *Id.* amend. 25, § 3. Notably, and in stark contrast to section 4 of the Twenty-fifth Amendment, section 3 provides that a President who has submitted a "written declaration that he is unable to discharge the powers and duties of his office" shall relinquish authority "until he transmits [to Congress] a written declaration to the contrary").

to discharge the powers and duties of his office" but either cannot or will not invoke section 3.[73]

Of these four provisions, section 4 carries the most explosive potential, as its successful invocation would involve divesting an unconsenting President of all executive authority. For that reason, the section itself is rife with procedural safeguards aimed at minimizing the risk of vice-presidential power grabs. The process, in a nutshell, works like this: The Vice President and a majority of the Cabinet (or of "such other body as Congress may by law provide")[74] may at any time "transmit" a declaration to the Speaker of the House and the President *pro tempore* of the Senate indicating that the President "is unable to discharge the powers and duties of his office."[75] Once that transmission occurs, the Vice President "shall immediately assume the powers and duties of the office as Acting President,"[76] while the now-sidelined President may contest, as promptly as desired, the declaration of inability by transmitting to the same congressional officers "his written declaration that no inability exists."[77] Once such a declaration is made, the President "shall resume the powers and duties of his office," unless the Vice President, along with the Cabinet (or the congressionally-designated alternative body), acts by "transmit[ting] within four days" a reaffirmation of the original inability declaration.[78] If the

---

[73] *Id.* amend. 25, § 4.

[74] Congress has not passed any law to this effect, but it could—at least in theory—invoke this provision under circumstances in which the President's Cabinet is unwilling to invoke section 4. *See* KALT, *supra* note 68, at 18. A section 4-resisting President, however, would likely veto any such measure, meaning that any such power-shifting law would likely require a supermajoritarian vote of support in each House in order to take effect. *See id.*

[75] U.S. CONST. amend. 25, § 4. Section 4 does not actually use the term "Cabinet" but rather speaks of "the principal officers of the executive departments." *Id.* The "executive departments" have been defined by statute to include fifteen executive-branch agencies: the Departments of State, Treasury, Defense, Justice, Interior, Agriculture, Commerce, Labor, Health and Human Services, Housing and Urban Development, Transportation, Energy, Education, Veterans Affairs, and Homeland Security. *See* 5 U.S.C. § 101. Thus, only the secretaries of *these Departments*—a group of individuals that might not perfectly map on to the President's "Cabinet" as the term is commonly understood—would be eligible to vote on an inability declaration. As used in the text, the term "Cabinet" is intended to capture in a shorthand way this most-of-the-Cabinet group of officials.

[76] U.S. CONST. amend. 25, § 4.

[77] *Id.*

[78] Although the text itself is not explicit on this point, the context and purpose of the Amendment make clear that the President does not immediately resume power upon submitting the "no inability" declaration but rather remains out of power unless and until Vice President and the Cabinet fail to reaffirm their initial declaration within the ensuing four-day period. *See* KALT, *supra* note 68, at 4 (noting that the idea that "the President can retake power instantly on his own say-so" is "wrong and very, very dangerous" and emphasizing that "[i]t is vital that this misreading be stamped out"); *see also* YALE LAW SCHOOL RULE OF LAW CLINIC, THE TWENTY-FIFTH AMENDMENT TO THE UNITED STATES CONSTITUTION: A READER'S GUIDE 47–50 (2018)

reaffirmation occurs, it then falls on Congress, within twenty-one days, to "determine[ ] by two-thirds vote of both Houses that the President is unable to discharge the powers and duties of his office" and that the Vice President should therefore remain as Acting President.[79] And if no such determination is made within that time period, the President "shall resume the powers and duties of his office."[80]

Although the processes of decisionmaking under section 4 are laid out in elaborate detail, the provision itself does not flesh out what it means, as a substantive matter, for the President to be "unable to discharge the powers and duties of his office," thus raising hard questions about the scope of its application. The phrase plainly encompasses situations in which the President is *physically unable* to act, as would be the case, for instance, if a coma renders a President unable to communicate and issue orders, and it likewise applies without difficulty to cases involving severe, judgment-distorting mental illness.[81] But how much farther does the Twenty-fifth Amendment reach? What about a President who is in an early stage of senility or who has experienced, for whatever reason, repeated and troubling episodes of forgetfulness? What if the President is contemplating catastrophically destructive actions—such as launching nuclear weapons in response to verbal criticisms leveled by a foreign leader—that no senior advisor views as plausibly justifiable? What if close advisors conclude that a President's personal interest or troubled emotional state threatens to distort key decisionmaking choices—for example, if a close family-member is being held hostage?[82] Given the Twenty-fifth Amendment's explicit vesting of the inability-declaring power in the Vice President and Cabinet, it is unlikely that the federal courts would ever weigh in on

---

[hereinafter "YALE REPORT"] (similar). Indeed, were it otherwise, the President could defeat any attempted invocation of section 4 by submitting a "no inability" declaration, reassuming power, and then immediately using that power to fire every member of the Cabinet, thus depriving the Vice President of the requisite "majority" of Cabinet officials needed to press on with the inability declaration. *See* KALT, *supra* note 68, at 133. It would for this reason (among others) make no sense to construe the provision as allowing for such an easy work-around of the protections it sets forth.

79 U.S. CONST. amend. 25, § 4. More specifically, Congress has twenty-one days to vote *if* it is in session when the transmission occurs. Otherwise, Congress shall "assembl[e] within forty-eight hours" and the 21-day clock starts running "after Congress is required to assemble." *Id.* Under the right circumstances, Congress thus could take up to 23 days to decide the issue. *See* KALT, *supra* note 68, at 23.

80 U.S. CONST. amend. 25, § 4.

81 *See, e.g.*, Mortimer Caplin, *Revisiting the Twenty-Fifth Amendment*, *in* 2 PAPERS ON PRESIDENTIAL DISABILITY AND THE TWENTY-FIFTH AMENDMENT BY SIX MEDICAL, LEGAL AND POLITICAL AUTHORITIES 9, 14 (Kenneth W. Thopmson, ed., 1991).

82 For a thorough exploration of these issues, see generally KALT, *supra* note 68, at 113–27.

these questions.[83] But judges are not the only government officers required to make constitutional determinations. And questions about whether the President in "unable" to discharge the duties of office within the meaning of the Twenty-fifth Amendment will inevitably arise in any case in which the Vice President, the Cabinet, and members of Congress find themselves grappling with whether to put that amendment to work.[84]

C. INSURRECTION AND INELIGIBILITY: SECTION 3 OF THE FOURTEENTH AMENDMENT

In contrast to section 4 of the Twenty-fifth Amendment, which creates a removal-like remedy for Presidents unable to discharge their duties, section 3 of the Fourteenth Amendment creates a disqualification-based prohibitory rule for persons who have "engaged in insurrection or rebellion against the United States" or who have "given aid or comfort to the enemies thereof."[85] In full, the provision states:

> No person shall be a Senator or Representative in Congress, or elector of President and Vice President, or hold any office, civil or military, under the United States, or under any State, who, having previously taken an oath, as a member of Congress, or as an officer of the United States, or as a member of any State legislature, or as an executive or judicial officer of any State, to support the Constitution of the United States, shall have engaged in insurrection or rebellion against the same, or given aid or comfort to the

[83] *See* YALE REPORT, *supra* note 78, at 64 (noting that "[t]he political question doctrine likely precludes any judicial review of the Vice President, Principal Officers, and Congress's substantive determination of presidential inability under Section 4").

[84] Indeed, just such a question was posed in the aftermath of the January 6 attack on the Capitol. Almost immediately after that event, the House passed a resolution calling on Vice President Mike Pence to "immediately use his powers under section 4 of the 25th Amendment to convene and mobilize the principal officers of the executive departments in the Cabinet to declare what is obvious to a horrified nation: That the President is unable to successfully discharge the duties and powers of his office." *See* H.R. Res. 21, 117th Cong. (2021). But the Vice President demurred, explaining that the Twenty-fifth Amendment "is not a means of punishment or usurpation" and that "[i]nvoking the 25th Amendment in such a manner would set a terrible precedent." Letter from Michael R. Pence, Vice President of the United States, to Nancy Pelosi, Speaker of the House of Representatives (Jan. 12, 2021). Vice President Pence's implicit suggestion was that, even if President Trump's conduct during the transition period reflected profoundly poor judgment, or even corrupt motivations, it did not demonstrate the sort of *incapacity* to exercise the powers and duties of the Presidency that the Twenty-fifth Amendment targets. *Accord* KALT, *supra* note 68, at 3 (maintaining that a section 4 invocation "would not be proper or effective" as a means of dealing with a President who "is doing deeply problematic things").

[85] U.S. CONST. amend. 14, § 3.

> enemies thereof. But Congress may by a vote of two-thirds of each House, remove such disability.[86]

The immediate purpose of this provision was to prevent former Confederate officials from gaining (or regaining) political power in the aftermath of the Civil War.[87] But it did not take long for influential leaders (including then-President Ulysses S. Grant) to begin wavering in their commitment to enforcing the section's terms. Indeed, in 1872, Congress enacted sweeping amnesty legislation that reestablished the opportunity to hold federal (and state) office for those who had only a decade earlier taken up arms against the United States.[88] To be sure, section 3 continued to bar some secessionists (including Jefferson Davis) from gaining access to government positions within the reconstituted Union.[89] But for the vast majority of ex-Confederates, Congress's decision to waive the operation of section 3 meant that it would have no exclusionary effect.

Following Reconstruction, section 3 fell into disuse.[90] But the events of January 6, 2021, sparked a renewed interest in the provision, as commentators raised the question whether President Trump and potentially others as well, by playing a key role in the events surrounding the attack on the U.S. Capitol, "engaged in insurrection" (or gave "aid or comfort" to "enemies" of the United States) within the meaning of section 3, thus disqualifying

---

86 *Id.*

87 *See* Gerard N. Magliocca, *Amnesty and Section Three of the Fourteenth Amendment*, 36 CONST. COMMENT. 87, 87 (2021).

88 Act of May 22, 1872, ch. 193, 17 Stat. 142 (1872).

89 Even these officials, moreover, would eventually see their eligibility restored. Of particular note, an 1885 opinion issued by Attorney General August Garland—himself a former member of the Confederate Congress—reached the dubious conclusion that the 1872 statute waived the section 3 disabilities of *all* officers who had received a presidential pardon. *See* Lawton's Case, 18 Op. Att'y Gen. 150 (1885). (This was a highly consequential reading, given that President Andrew Johnson had already pardoned "almost everyone in the Confederacy," including Garland himself. Magliocca, *supra* note 87, at 62.) Then, in 1898, Congress expanded its amnesty legislation to remove remaining disabilities under section 3 for all living ex-Confederates. *See* Act of June 6, 1898, ch. 389, 30 Stat. 432. Some seventy-five years later, Congress would again exercise its section 3 authority to effectuate posthumous disability waivers for Robert E. Lee and Jefferson Davis, who not been included within either the 1872 or 1898 acts. *See* S.J. Res. 23, 94th Cong. (1975) (Lee); S.J. Res. 16, 95th Cong. (1978) (Davis).

90 The one notable invocation of the provision occurred in 1919, when, in the midst of the Red Scare, the House of Representatives relied on section 3 as the basis for its refusal to seat Victor L. Berger, a Socialist Representative-Elect from Wisconsin who had been convicted on charges of violating the Espionage Act. *See* 6 CLARENCE CANNON, CANNON'S PRECEDENTS OF THE HOUSE OF REPRESENTATIVES OF THE UNITED STATES §§ 56–59 (1936). Berger's conviction was eventually overturned, *see* Berger v. United States, 295 U.S. 78 (1921), however, and he was permitted to take his seat after winning re-election in 1922. 65 Cong. Rec. 7 (1923).

themselves from holding office again.[91] That possibility brought into focus a congeries of questions about the section's operation, particularly with respect to issues of enforcement. Drawing on the example of the Enforcement Act of 1870, which had authorized federal prosecutors to seek *quo warranto* writs against state officials and judges holding office in violation of section 3,[92] members of Congress proposed post-January-6 legislation that would similarly authorize the Attorney General to bring disqualification actions against present-day insurrectionists.[93] But no such legislation has yet been enacted, thus giving rise to uncertainty about the current state of section 3's enforceability. A particularly important question is whether section 3 qualifies as a "self-executing" provision of the constitutional text, enforceable by the courts even in the absence of implementing legislation.

First appearances might well suggest that the provision is self-executing. After all, section 3 itself says nothing about the need for implementing legislation, and its opening phraseology ("no Person shall . . .") tracks the language of the Amendment's first section ("No state shall . . ."), which courts long have treated as unquestionably self-executing in character.[94] Even more important, section 3's express conferral on congressional supermajorities of the power to "remove" the disqualifications that the section otherwise imposes is difficult to reconcile with a non-self-executing reading of its terms. If, as the non-self-execution position insists, Congress must act affirmatively to disqualify insurrectionists from holding office under section 3, then it would seem both odd and superfluous to specify that Congress could remove such a disqualification only by way of a supermajority vote in each House—a result that, on the non-self-executing view of the clause, Congress could just as easily achieve by doing nothing at all.

On the other hand, one might challenge the pro-self-executing interpretation of section 3 on the ground that the Reconstruction Congress itself chose to enact implementing legislation not long after the Amendment's ratification, thus signifying (so the argument goes)

---

91 *See, e.g.*, Gerard Magliocca, *The 14th Amendment's Disqualification Provision and the Events of Jan. 6*, LAWFARE (Jan. 19, 2021), https://www.lawfareblog.com/14th-amendments-disqualification-provision-and-events-jan-6.

92 *See* First Ku Klux Klan Act, § 14, 16 Stat. 140 (1870). *Quo warranto* writs are judicial orders that explicitly disable named individuals from holding identified positions of power.

93 *See* H.R. 1405, § 1, 117th Cong. (2021).

94 *See* Magliocca, *supra* note 87, at 106; *see also* Myles S. Lynch, *Disloyalty & Disqualification: Reconstructing Section 3 of the Fourteenth Amendment*, 30 WM & MARY BILL RTS. J. 153, 206 (2021) ("It would be inherently inconsistent to interpret 'No state shall . . .' as self-executing but 'No person shall . . .' as requiring enacting legislation.").

its own understanding that that the provision accomplished nothing on its own.[95] An additional complication for the pro-self-executing position is posed by a Reconstruction-era opinion issued by Chief Justice Salmon Chase, who rejected a self-executing reading of section 3 on the ground that it would produce "great public and private mischief" by retroactively nullifying the official decisions rendered by officeholders who were eventually determined to fall within the provision's scope.[96] But Chief Justice Chase issued his opinion while riding circuit, and the full Supreme Court has never weighed in on the question.

So, what would the present-day Court do if a section 3-related case were to come before it—for example, in a challenge to the effort of an alleged participant in the Capitol riot to run for a House or Senate seat? Perhaps the Court would proceed to apply the provision directly,[97] offering its own, independent judgment as to whether the challenged individual's past conduct amounted to "engag[ing] in insurrection or rebellion" or "giv[ing] aid or comfort" to enemies. But if the Court were disinclined to weigh in on such issues, it might instead opt for the route taken by Chief Justice Chase some 150 years ago, deeming the federal courts powerless to enforce the provision's

---

[95] On the other hand, the Reconstruction Congress might have passed the law simply because it wanted to provide as much guidance as it could regarding section 3's application to former members of the Confederacy. *Accord* Magliocca, *supra* note 87, at 106 (noting that "[n]othing indicates that Congress saw Section Three as anything other than self-executing when the Fourteenth Amendment was drafted").

[96] *In re* Griffin, 11 F. Cas. 7, 26 (C.C.D. Va. 1869) (No. 5,815) (Chase, J.).

[97] It is perhaps worth noting in this respect that the Court often intervenes directly in election-related disputes, including in high-visibility and politically-charged contexts. *See, e.g.*, Bush v. Gore, 531 U.S. 98 (2000) (per curiam).

requirements unless and until Congress passed implementing legislation of its own.[98]

[98] Another possibility is that a *state* might adopt legislation that denies ballot access to candidates deemed ineligible for office under section 3. *See* Magliocca, *supra* note 87. Such a move would likely pose no difficulties as applied to candidates for state office. As for federal-office candidates, however, arguments of undue state-interference with national matters would be sure to surface. Even so, state-based enforcement of section 3 against federal office-seekers might draw support from the idea that, while states may not *add* to the constitutional qualifications for federal office, *see* U.S. Term Limits v. Thornton, 514 U.S. 779 (1995), they remain permitted to *enforce* with their own laws the qualifications that the Constitution itself sets forth—including the qualifications of section 3. *Cf. id.* at 787 n.2 (highlighting the possibility that section 3 poses a federal-office qualification enforceable by the states, while finding "no need to resolve that question today" (citing Powell v. McCormack, 395 U.S. 486, 520 n.41 (1969))). *See generally* Derek T. Muller, *Scrutinizing Federal Electoral Qualifications*, 90 IND. L.J. 559, 592–608 (2015) (considering, albeit outside the specific context of section 3 litigation, the extent to which states may refuse to place congressional and/or presidential candidates on their ballots on the ground that the state deems them to be ineligible for office). At the least, a state-based disqualification attempt might suffice to create a live case-or-controversy that tees up Section 3-related issues for merits-based resolution by the courts. *See* Gerard Magliocca, *State Law and Section Three of the Fourteenth Amendment*, PRAWFSBLAWG (Aug. 26, 2021), https://prawfsblawg.blogs.com/prawfsblawg/2021/08/state-law-and-section-three-of-the-fourteenth-amendment.html (raising this possibility).

Chapter 33

PRESIDENTIAL AND LEGISLATIVE IMMUNITIES FROM INVESTIGATION, LITIGATION, AND PROSECUTION

Analysis

The previous chapter considered key constitutional mechanisms—particularly the impeachment process—for dealing with claims of presidential misconduct. But these are far from the only mechanisms that might be put to work to address wrongdoing by the President or otherwise to embroil the President in burdensome legal processes. For example, Presidents (or presidential subordinates) might be on the receiving end of subpoenas or other evidentiary demands. A President might also be named as a defendant in a civil action in which a plaintiff seeks money damages or injunctive relief based on claims of unlawful official or unofficial actions. The President might even engage in conduct alleged to be a crime, thus raising the prospect of prosecution, conviction, and perhaps even imprisonment.

These and other possibilities have long given rise to the question whether the distinct constitutional status of Presidents should entitle them to protections not afforded to other individuals with respect to civil and criminal proceedings, as well as congressional investigations. That question is the primary focus of this chapter, which explores the topic from three distinct angles. First, it addresses cases in which Presidents have sought to resist judicial and legislative subpoenas, both by invoking an "executive privilege" that, they argue, permits them to withhold the information being sought and (when that privilege is unavailable) by contending that the investigations themselves exceed structural limits implied by the Constitution. Second, the discussion considers cases in which

Presidents named as defendants in civil actions have sought to assert: (1) an absolute immunity from damages liability and injunctive relief for actions taken in their official capacity; or (2) a temporary immunity from judicial process in suits based on claims of personal, rather than official, misconduct. Third, the discussion highlights the long-debated (but still unresolved) question whether the President (at least while in office) is immune from criminal prosecution and punishment.

Having considered these issues, the chapter turns to the separate but related topic of congressional immunity from judicial processes. The case law on this subject derives primarily from the Speech or Debate Clause of Article I,[1] which the Court has interpreted to shield from judicial inquiry all "legislative acts," but only "legislative acts," that members of Congress undertake.[2]

A. DEMANDS FOR PRESIDENTIAL INFORMATION

1. Executive Privilege

In general, the recipient of a duly issued subpoena must comply with its demands. The resulting duty to disclose information, however, is hemmed in by various common-law privileges that the recipient may invoke, including the attorney-client privilege, the doctor-patient privilege, the attorney work-product privilege, and the like.[3] The President, no less than any other individual, can assert privileges of this kind. But the President also has another arrow in the quiver that, in the right circumstances, can be used in countering demands for information about executive-branch activities: The President may assert an "executive privilege" that, the Court has held, is grounded directly in the Constitution itself.[4]

---

1 *See* U.S. CONST. art. 1, § 6.

2 United States v. Brewster, 408 U.S. 501 (1972). It merits emphasis that the Court also has developed specialized rules of immunity for judges and prosecutors, as well as for executive officials other than the President. Other legal treatises, particularly those concerning the law of constitutional torts, consider these immunities in detail. For a brief treatment of the subject, see *infra* notes 95–101 and accompanying text.

3 *See* FED. R. EVID. 501 (generally providing that "[t]he common law—as interpreted by United States courts in the light of reason and experience—governs a claim of privilege").

4 Unclear terminology has long bedeviled this area of the law. In particular, and as a leading treatise on the subject notes, some courts and commentators use the term "executive privilege" to refer broadly to a collection of different evidentiary protections—including, most significantly, the common-law "deliberative process" and "state secrets" privileges—that generally operate to shield executive-branch behavior from disclosure and review. *See* 26A CHARLES ALAN WRIGHT & KENNETH W. GRAHAM, FEDERAL PRACTICE AND PROCEDURE: EVIDENCE § 5673 (1st ed. Supp. 2021) [hereinafter WRIGHT & GRAHAM] (noting the tendency of some analysts to use the term

a. *Executive Privilege and the Criminal Process: The Nixon Tapes Case*

On July 16, 1973, a former White House assistant named Alexander Butterfield made a bombshell revelation before the Senate Select Committee on Presidential Campaign Activities: President Richard Nixon had installed recording devices in the Oval Office that had routinely captured conversations between the President and his advisors.[5] This revelation was of great interest to Justice Department officials, who promptly sought and eventually obtained a subpoena for recordings of key conversations regarding a suspected cover-up of criminal wrongdoing with respect to the Watergate scandal. In response, President Nixon moved to quash these subpoenas, contending that executive privilege negated any duty on the part of the President to turn over recordings of private conversations concerning public matters. A federal district court, however, denied the President's motion to quash, and the issue soon found its way to the Supreme Court. The Court heard argument in the case on July 8, 1974, and, only sixteen days later, issued its unanimous decision affirming the district court's ruling.[6]

The Court's decision in *United States v. Nixon*[7] marked the end of the road for President Nixon, who resigned from office less than one month later. But even though the decision was a decisive loss for Nixon, the opinion the Court issued offered more of a mixed verdict for the presidency as an institution.[8] On the one hand, and consistent with its affirmance of the district-court order, the Court flatly rejected the idea that there exists an "absolute, unqualified

---

as a single catch-all reference for "governmental privileges that are quite different in scope and function and deserve to be kept separate"). Throughout this chapter, and consistent with that treatise's approach, we use the term "executive privilege," to refer *only* to the *constitutionally* rooted privilege that may be invoked on the President's behalf—or what is sometimes separately known as the "presidential communications privilege." *Accord id.* (using this term "to refer only to the power of the President to withhold information from the courts and Congress").

5 Hearings Before the S. Select Comm. on Presidential Campaign Pracs., 93d Cong. 2073–2090 (1973) (statement of Alexander Butterfield, Administrator of Federal Aviation Administration).

6 For a detailed overview of the complex series of events leading up to the Court's decision, see Christopher H. Schroeder & Curtis A. Bradley, *The Story of United States v. Nixon: The President and the Tapes*, *in* PRESIDENTIAL POWER STORIES 343 (Christopher H. Schroeder & Curtis A. Bradley, eds., 2009).

7 418 U.S. 683 (1974).

8 For a suggestion that the Court in *Nixon* erred by moving too far in the direction of protecting presidential secrecy, see Eric Lane, Frederick A.O. Schwarz, Jr. & Emily Berman, *Too Big a Canon in the President's Arsenal: Another Look at* United States v. Nixon, 17 GEO. MASON L. REV. 737, 740 (2010) (maintaining that the Court failed to adequately weigh the costs of governmental secrecy, which "come from both the general degeneration of the democratic process and the specific damage that a policy cloaked in secrecy can cause").

Presidential privilege of immunity from judicial process under all circumstances,"[9] concluding instead that any such rule would "gravely impair the role of the courts under Art. III," while also threatening the constitutionally guaranteed fair-trial and due-process rights of criminal defendants.[10] On the other hand, the Court made clear that, under the right circumstances, claims of executive privilege could validly operate to shield the President and associated parties from otherwise binding investigative demands. Writing for the Court, Chief Justice Burger acknowledged that the constitutional text did not set forth this privilege in express terms.[11] He explained, however, that that privilege has "constitutional underpinnings" based on the "valid need" to avoid the result that Presidents and their key advisors would "temper candor with a concern for appearances and for their own interests to the detriment of the decisionmaking process."[12]

In short, the Court recognized a qualified executive privilege, the operation of which depended on the balancing of two competing imperatives: the need on the one hand of the judiciary to ensure the fairness and effectiveness of criminal proceedings, and the need on the other hand of Presidents and their subordinates to have significant assurances of confidentiality regarding their deliberative communications. But how was this balance to be struck? According to the Chief Justice, the proper approach was to begin with a "presumptive privilege for Presidential communications" and then to afford prosecutors the opportunity to rebut that claim of privilege on a case-by-case basis.[13] More specifically, "[i]f a President concludes

---

9 *Nixon*, 418 U.S. at 706.

10 *Id.* at 707 (internal quotation marks omitted). For example, criminal defendants might sometimes need access to presidential records or testimony in order to establish their innocence in a criminal trial, including by responding to the prosecution's evidence in an effective way. *Id.* at 711.

11 *See id.* at 705 n.16 (noting that "the silence of the Constitution on this score is not dispositive").

12 *Id.* at 705–06. In addition, the Court in *Nixon* found precedential support for its decision in various statements made by Chief Justice Marshall during the course of Aaron Burr's treason trial. *See* United States v. Burr, 25 F. Cas. 187 (C.C. Va. 1807) (No. 14,694) (opinion of Marshall, C.J.). Marshall, who was at the time riding circuit, found no constitutional difficulty in Burr's motion for a subpoena directed at President Thomas Jefferson, thus rejecting the prosecutor's claim that a sitting President was altogether exempt from judicial process. *See id.* at 191. But Marshall had also noted the special character of the presidential office and acknowledged that "[i]n no case of this kind would a court be required to proceed against the president as against an ordinary individual." *Id.* at 192, *quoted in Nixon*, 418 U.S. at 708. Marshall thus left open the possibility that some of the subpoenaed material, even if probative, might need to be withheld. *See* United States v. Burr, 25 F. Cas. 30, 34 (C.C. Va. 1807) (No. 14,692d) ("The guard, furnished to [the President] to protect him from being harassed by vexatious and unnecessary subpoenas, is to be looked for in the conduct of a court after those subpoenas have issued. . . ."), *quoted in Nixon*, 418 U.S. at 714.

13 *Nixon*, 418 U.S. at 708.

that compliance with a subpoena would be injurious to the public interest he may properly . . . invoke a claim of privilege on the return of the subpoena."[14] The burden would then shift to the prosecutor "to demonstrate that the Presidential material was essential to the justice of the pending criminal case."[15] Upon the making of such a showing, the district court would then proceed to conduct an "*in camera* examination of the subpoenaed material" so as to identify with precision the portions of that material that the prosecutor could secure.[16]

What sort of showing does a prosecutor need to make to overcome the presumption in favor of executive privilege? On this question, the Court's guidance proved to be elusive. Its overarching proclamation was that a claim of privilege based on the President's "generalized interest in confidentiality" had to "yield to the *demonstrated, specific need* for evidence in a pending criminal trial."[17] But Chief Justice Burger did not elaborate on what qualified as a "demonstrated, specific need," and he did not explain why the special prosecutor's demand for the Nixon tapes met this standard.[18] In a later case, the D.C. Circuit would offer its own gloss on the operative test, holding that a "demonstrated, specific need" exists where subpoenaed material contains "important evidence" that is "not available with due diligence elsewhere."[19] Under this formulation, then, the prosecutor must do more than show that the evidence meets the ordinarily applicable test of relevance.[20] Rather, to overcome the presumptive privilege in favor of executive-branch confidentiality, the prosecutor must demonstrate that the evidence

---

14 *Id.* at 713.

15 *Id.* (internal quotation omitted).

16 *Id.* at 714. The Court went on to explain that in conducting this *in camera* inspection, the District Court bore a "very heavy responsibility to see to it that Presidential conversations, which are either not relevant or not admissible, are accorded that high degree of respect due the President of the United States." *Id.* at 715. The D.C. Circuit has subsequently construed this language to mean that "[t]he court's task during its *in camera* review is simply to ensure that privileged materials that would not be of use to the subpoena proponent are not released." *See In re Sealed Case (Espy)*, 121 F.3d 729, 759 (D.C. Cir. 1997).

17 *Nixon*, 418 U.S. at 713 (emphasis added).

18 *See id.* at 714 (noting only that "[o]n the basis of our examination of the record we are unable to conclude that the District Court erred in ordering the inspection").

19 *See Espy*, 121 F.3d at 754.

20 *Id.* ("It would be strange indeed if *Nixon* required nothing more to overcome presidential privilege than the initial showing of relevancy, admissibility and specificity necessary to satisfy Rule 17(c) [of the Federal Rules of Criminal Procedure]. If this were true, the privilege would have no practical benefit."). The D.C. Circuit also made clear that the "demonstrated, specific need" standard, though originally applied to a claim of privilege asserted against a trial court's subpoena, also applies with full force to claims of privilege asserted in response to grand jury subpoenas. *See id.* at 756.

in question is both "important" to the case and not otherwise attainable through non-confidentiality-compromising means.[21]

---

[21] In the 1977 case of *Nixon v. Administrator of General Services* (*Nixon II*), 433 U.S. 425 (1977), the Court once again confronted a dispute concerning the Nixon tapes. Concerned about the possible destruction of the tapes and other historically significant records, Congress had enacted the Presidential Recordings and Materials Preservation Act (PRMPA), which directed an executive-branch official, the Administrator of General Services, to take custody of former-President Nixon's materials and to archive significant items for preservation and later public disclosure. Nixon, however, sought a judicial declaration that the statute contravened the separation of powers by, among other things, requiring him to disclose materials subject to executive privilege. In one sense, as Justice Brennan noted in an opinion for the Court, the underlying claim of executive privilege presented an "anomaly" insofar as it was being asserted by a former President "against the very Executive Branch in whose name the privilege is invoked." *Id.* at 447–48. Even so, Justice Brennan rejected the suggestion that former Presidents were *wholly* barred from invoking executive privilege, reasoning instead that a retained, post-presidency ability to assert the privilege might prove necessary to ensuring that advisors and assistance provide "full and frank submissions of facts and opinions upon which effective discharge of [the President's] duties depends." *Id.* at 449. At the same time, the Court made note of the fact that neither President Ford, who had signed the PRMPA into law, nor President Carter, who was then in office, had evinced any support for Nixon's position. *Id.* at 449. And because "it must be presumed that the incumbent President is vitally concerned with and in the best position to assess the present and future needs of the Executive Branch," President Carter's lack of support in particular served to "detract[ ] from the weight" of Nixon's claim. *Id.* at 449. The upshot of this discussion thus appeared to be that, while a former President retains the ability to assert a claim of executive privilege, an incumbent President could, by opposing the claim of privilege, reduce—perhaps greatly—the chances of that claim's success. *See* Daphna Renan, *The President's Two Bodies*, 120 COLUM. L. REV. 1119, 1190 (2020) (suggesting that "Justice Brennan's framework for assessing a former president's claim of executive privilege is analogous to the famous tripartite structure developed by Justice Jackson in the *Steel Seizure* case" in that "[a] claim of executive privilege is strongest when the former president and the incumbent act in concert" and is at "its lowest ebb" if "the former president's assertion of the privilege contravenes the incumbent's position"). Applying these principles, the Court rejected former-President Nixon's challenge to the PRMPA. For one thing, history made clear that "[t]he expectation of the confidentiality of executive communications . . . has always been limited and subject to erosion over time," as "[a]ll former Presidents from President Hoover to President Johnson ha[d] deposited their papers in Presidential libraries . . . for governmental preservation and eventual disclosure." *Nixon II*, 433 U.S. at 450–51. In addition, the act by its terms created only a "limited intrusion into executive confidentiality" because it included "safeguards . . . to prevent disclosure" of "the small fraction of the materials that implicate Presidential confidentiality, as well as personal and private materials." *Id.* at 452–54. Further supporting the statute's validity were "substantial public interests" in "establish[ing] regular procedures to deal with the perceived need to preserve the materials"—including to "facilitat[e] a full airing of the events leading to [Nixon's] resignation," to reveal "how . . . political processes had in fact operated in order to gauge the necessity for remedial legislation," and to ensure that the materials remained available to "shed light upon issues in civil or criminal litigation." *Id.* at 452–53. Thus, as far as the statute's facial validity was concerned, the separation-of-powers analysis came out decidedly in the government's favor. *See also* Trump v. Thompson, 20 F.4th 10, 32–33 (D.C. Cir. 2021) (rejecting an effort by former-President Trump to invoke executive privilege in an attempt to prevent the National Archives and Records Administration from turning over White House records to the House Select Committee to Investigate the January 6th Attack on the U.S. Capitol, while also suggesting that "the tests that courts have historically used to police document disputes between the Political Branches seem a poor fit when the Executive and Congress together have already determined that the demonstrated

b. *Executive Privilege and Civil Adjudication*

As *Nixon* itself involved a criminal prosecution, the Court could and did sidestep questions about how to balance "the President's generalized interest in confidentiality and the need for relevant evidence in civil litigation."[22] But it would subsequently, though somewhat obliquely, weigh in on the matter in *Cheney v. U.S. District Court for the District of Columbia*.[23] The procedural background of the case was highly complex, but by the time it arrived at the Court the central question had become whether Vice President Richard Cheney and other executive-branch officials could secure the pre-discovery dismissal of a case on the ground that the discovery process, if allowed to proceed, would result in the disclosure of sensitive communications involving the President.[24] The lower courts had said "no," concluding in effect that the executive branch was required, in keeping with *Nixon*, to make targeted assertions of privilege in response to specific evidentiary demands.[25] The Court, however, rejected that approach, and, in remanding the case for further proceedings, went out of its way to emphasize that the lower courts had "overlook[ed] fundamental differences" between *Nixon* and the case at hand.[26]

Among those fundamental differences was the *civil* rather than *criminal* nature of the case—a distinction that the Court viewed as cutting in favor of the White House's position. As stated by the Court, while "[t]he need for information for use in civil cases" is "far from negligible," civil discovery requests do not generally "share the urgency or significance of the criminal subpoena requests in *Nixon*,"[27]

---

and specific need for disclosure that former President Trump would require . . . has been met" (internal quotations and citations omitted)). *But cf.* Trump v. Thompson, 142 S. Ct. 680, 680 (2022) (declining to stay the D.C. Circuit's mandate but emphasizing, in light of that court's conclusion that "President Trump's claims would have failed even if he were the incumbent," that "any discussion of the Court of Appeals concerning President Trump's status as a former President must . . . be regarded as nonbinding dicta").

[22] *Nixon*, 418 U.S. at 712 n.19.

[23] 542 U.S. 367 (2004).

[24] *Id.* at 382–83.

[25] *Id.* at 376. More specifically, the district court had denied the defendants' motion to dismiss, *see* Jud. Watch, Inc. v. Nat'l Energy Pol'y Dev. Grp., 219 F. Supp. 2d 20, 54 (D.D.C. 2002), and the D.C. Circuit had refused to issue a writ of mandamus directing the district court to dismiss the claims against the Vice President, *see In re* Cheney, 334 F.3d 1096, 1098 (D.C. Cir. 2003). In support of its ruling, the D.C. Circuit reasoned that other avenues of relief remained available to the defendants—specifically, invocations of executive privilege in response to particular evidentiary demands. *Id.* at 1104.

[26] *Cheney*, 542 U.S. at 383.

[27] *Id.* at 384; *see id.* (noting that "our historical commitment to the rule of law is nowhere more profoundly manifest than in our view that the twofold aim of criminal

as those requests implicated the "primary constitutional duty of the Judicial Branch . . . to do justice in criminal prosecutions."[28] In addition, the Court worried that civil discovery requests were likely to impose just the sort of candor-curtailing pressures on the President and key advisors that the rule of executive privilege was designed to extirpate. While the criminal justice system included "various constraints, albeit imperfect, to filter out insubstantial legal claims,"[29] the civil discovery process lacked "analogous checks" and thus put the executive branch at a heightened risk of being overwhelmed by "meritless" discovery requests that would encroach on the President's ability to communicate openly with others.[30] Thus, while *Cheney*'s precise implications for the law of executive privilege are far from clear, the decision suggests, as one treatise on the subject has put it, "that the privilege is more robust in the civil setting than in the criminal setting, and that the information seeker in a civil case must make a stronger showing of need to overcome a privilege claim."[31]

c. *Executive Privilege and Congressional Investigations*

Congressional investigations also give rise to claims of executive privilege. Each House of Congress has the power of compulsory process, which derives from the Rules of Proceedings Clause, Congress's general lawmaking authority, and (in appropriate cases) the powers to impeach and convict federal officials.[32] Congress often invokes this power in the course of investigating executive-branch activities. And when it does so, the targets of its subpoenas often

---

justice is that guilt shall not escape or innocence suffer" (quoting *Nixon*, 418 U.S. at 708–09) (internal alterations omitted)).

[28] *Id.* at 384–85 (internal quotation marks and citations omitted). To be sure, the Court was somewhat ambiguous regarding the extent to which its reasoning on this score applied *generally* to all civil cases or *specifically* to the particular circumstances of the *Cheney* case. *Compare id.* at 384 (noting that "[t]he need for information for use in civil cases . . . does not share the urgency or significance of the criminal subpoena requests in *Nixon*"), *with id.* at 384–85 (noting that "the only consequence from respondents' inability to obtain the discovery they seek is that it would be more difficult for private complainants to vindicate Congress' policy objectives under [the Federal Advisory Committee Act]"). But even if some aspects of the Court's reasoning were tethered to the facts of *Cheney* itself, the opinion more generally left no doubt that, as the Court put it, "[t]he distinction *Nixon* drew between criminal and civil proceedings is not just a matter of formalism." *Id.* at 384.

[29] The Court noted, for instance, that criminal cases are brought by a "by a publicly accountable prosecutor subject to budgetary considerations and under an ethical obligation . . . to serve the cause of justice." *Id.* at 386.

[30] *Id.*

[31] 2 CHRISTOPHER B. MUELLER & LAIRD C. KIRKPATRICK, FEDERAL EVIDENCE § 5:61 (4th ed. Supp. 2021).

[32] *See, e.g.*, McGrain v. Daugherty, 273 U.S. 135, 174 (1927) ("[T]he power of inquiry—with process to enforce it—is an essential and appropriate auxiliary to the legislative function."); *see generally supra* Section 14.C.

claim executive privilege in response. The question thus arises as to how, if at all, the *Nixon* framework applies to those claims.

The Court in *Nixon* specifically declined to consider the impact of its ruling on "congressional demands for information."[33] Just a few months prior to *Nixon*, however, the D.C. Circuit in *Senate Select Committee on Presidential Campaign Activities v. Nixon*[34] issued a decision weighing in on a congressional effort to secure the Nixon tapes. In that case, the court rejected the idea of an *absolute* executive privilege regarding congressional subpoena requests, while at the same time subjecting such requests to a "presumption favoring confidentiality,"[35] rebuttable only upon a showing that "the subpoenaed evidence is *demonstrably critical* to the responsible fulfillment of [legislative-branch] functions."[36] Recently, the Supreme Court referenced the *Senate Select Committee* case in a way that seemed to evince approval of this "demonstrably critical" standard.[37] But neither the Court nor the D.C. Circuit has expounded on the precise relationship between the "demonstrably critical" standard and *Nixon*'s own "demonstrated, specific need" standard, thus rendering it unclear whether the two tests call for identical, or somewhat different, lines of judicial inquiry.

When it comes to legislative subpoenas, however, the details of judicial doctrine are likely to matter less than the extent to which Congress has a practical ability to enforce them. In theory, either House of Congress can attempt to compel compliance with its subpoenas by holding noncompliant officials in contempt and directing its Sergeant at Arms to take those officials into custody.[38] But that "inherent contempt" authority has not been used for decades,[39] and while alternative means of enforcement are available,

---

[33] *Nixon*, 418 U.S. at 712 n.19.

[34] 498 F.2d 725 (D.C. Cir. 1974) (en banc).

[35] *Id.* at 731.

[36] *Id.* (emphasis added). Applying that standard to the facts of the case, the court found that the Senate had failed to establish a "demonstrably critical" need. *Id.* This was so, according to the court, because the House Judiciary Committee had already received the tapes, thereby rendering the Senate's request "merely cumulative," and because the Senate already had transcripts of the tapes in question. *Id.* at 732–33.

[37] *See* Trump v. Mazars USA, LLP, 140 S. Ct. 2019, 2032 (2020).

[38] *See generally* Josh Chafetz, *Executive Branch Contempt of Congress*, 76 U. CHI. L. REV. 1083 (2009) (outlining both the history and mechanics of Congress's inherent contempt powers); *see also supra* Section 14.C.

[39] To be sure, Congress has issued contempt citations against executive branch officials on multiple occasions, *see id.* at 1140–41, but it has not attempted to *arrest* anyone on its own initiative since the 1930s. *See* TODD GARVEY, CONG. RSCH. SERV., R45653, CONGRESSIONAL SUBPOENAS: ENFORCING EXECUTIVE BRANCH COMPLIANCE (2019).

they too are subject to both legal and practical limitations.[40] Given this state of affairs, congressional officials have tended to respond to expansive claims of executive privilege not by throwing down the gauntlet and insisting on executive branch compliance, but instead by trying to negotiate a way around the impasse.[41] Congress's leverage during those negotiations, however, is necessarily limited by its own inability and/or unwillingness to utilize its enforcement-related powers, meaning that the executive branch will often hold the upper hand as deals are hammered out.[42] Indeed, the current imbalance in these standoffs may be so tilted in favor of the President as to render the *de facto* law in this area to be, as Professor Jonathan

---

[40] For example, a stonewalled House of Congress might make a criminal referral to the Justice Department, which might then attempt to prosecute the noncompliant official for contempt of Congress or some other statutory crime. But in part because the Attorney General is appointed by the President, such requests may sometimes go unheeded, particularly when the claim of privilege has at least some support in existing law. And even where the Justice Department brings criminal charges, the drawn-out nature of a criminal trial may lead to delay that effectively frustrates Congress's information-gathering efforts. In addition, Congress can challenge claims of privilege by bringing civil suits against the noncompliant officers, seeking (as it did in *Senate Select Committee*) a declaratory judgment that the noncomplying officer must honor the subpoena, 498 F.2d at 726, and/or seeking (as Congress has done on other occasions) an injunction requiring compliance with the subpoena, *see, e.g.*, Comm. on Jud. of U.S. House of Rep. v. McGahn, 968 F.3d 755, 762, 778 (D.C. Cir. 2020) (en banc) (finding that the House Judiciary Committee had Article III standing to bring such an action against former White House Counsel, Donald F. McGahn). Civil litigation, however, likewise takes time, thus creating the opportunity for executive-branch officials simply to run out that clock as new congressional elections approach. *See* Jonathan David Shaub, *The Executive's Privilege*, 70 DUKE L.J. 1, 9 (2020) (noting that "the judicial process takes too long to be effective in the context of congressional oversight"); *see also Breaking the Logjam: Principles and Practice of Congressional Oversight and Executive Privilege: Hearing on Oversight, Agency Action and Federal Rights Before the S. Subcomm. on Fed Cts.*, 117th Cong. 14 (2021) (testimony of Professor Kate Shaw) [hereinafter "Shaw Testimony"] (noting that "[i]n virtually every executive privilege dispute, the information or testimony sought is by definition in the possession of the executive branch; and in essentially all recent high-stakes disputes, the executive branch has been able to run out the clock until the end of the Congress that initiated the oversight effort, or of the administration Congress sought to investigate"). Other possible means of inducing executive-branch compliance with a congressional subpoena include threatening to withhold appropriations, placing holds on confirmation proceedings, or otherwise refusing to furnish forms of needed legislative assistance to the President until the claim of privilege is dropped. But these techniques also have only limited efficacy. *See, e.g.*, Shaub, *supra*, at 54 (noting that "[s]hutting down the government over what the executive branch would characterize as an assertion of a well-recognized, historically grounded constitutional authority may not, in reality, be a viable option").

[41] *See* Deborah Pearlstein, *The Executive Branch Anticanon*, 89 FORDHAM L. REV. 597, 625 (2020) (noting that congressional-executive information disputes "have been most commonly addressed through interbranch negotiations").

[42] *See* Chafetz, *supra* note 38, at 1155–56 (noting that "[a]s the executive continues to make expansive claims for its powers and privileges, and as courts continue to position themselves as the 'ultimate arbiters' of inter-branch conflicts, Congress has ceded ground to both").

Shaub has put it, "the doctrine of executive privilege as developed by the executive branch."[43]

d. *Related Doctrines: The Deliberative-Process Privilege and the State-Secrets Privilege*

The privilege recognized in *Nixon* does not supply the only ground on which the President and others might resist demands for information issued by courts or Congress. Other privileges might also be invoked, and two of them apply with special force to executive-branch actors.[44]

First, the *deliberative-process privilege* protects executive officials' "predecisional" communications made in the course of formulating official governmental policy.[45] The primary justification for this privilege mirrors the justification offered for the executive privilege recognized in *Nixon*, with courts defending the rule as necessary to safeguard "frank discussion between subordinate and chief concerning administrative action."[46] The deliberative-process privilege also resembles the privilege recognized in *Nixon* insofar as it may be overcome by a "sufficient showing of need."[47] But there are important differences between these two rules as well. Most important, the deliberative-process privilege enjoys only a common-law status and may be legislatively altered at any time.[48] In addition, the deliberative-process-privilege may be invoked on behalf of a wide

---

[43] Shaub, *supra* note 40, at 9; *see also* Shaw Testimony, *supra* note 40, at 13 (noting that the tools at Congress's disposal "were once understood to give it a comparative advantage in privilege disputes with the executive branch," while also suggesting that Congress has not recently made "active use" of them). For useful overviews of the body of OLC memos and other materials that set forth the executive-branch's (unsurprisingly capacious) view of executive privilege, see, for example, Shaub, *supra* note 40, at 55–70; Shaw Testimony, *supra* note 40, at 6–8.

[44] For additional such privileges, see generally MUELLER & KIRKPATRICK, *supra* note 31, §§ 5:53–5:64 (describing the confidential-informant privilege and the law-enforcement privilege).

[45] *See* U.S. Fish & Wildlife Serv. v. Sierra Club, Inc., 141 S. Ct. 777, 785–86 (2021) (noting the privilege "distinguishes between predecisional, deliberative documents, which are exempt from disclosure, and documents reflecting a final agency decision and the reasons supporting it, which are not").

[46] Kaiser Aluminum & Chem. Corp. v. United States, 157 F. Supp. 939, 946 (Ct. Cl. 1958) (citing Morgan v. United States, 304 U.S. 1, 18 (1938)). Courts have also justified the privilege as helping to "prevent[ ] public confusion from premature disclosure of agency opinions before the agency establishes final policy" and to "protect[ ] the integrity of an agency's decision" by ensuring that the public does "not judge officials based on information they considered prior to issuing their final decisions." Jud. Watch, Inc. v. Clinton, 880 F. Supp. 1, 12 (D.D.C. 1995).

[47] *See Espy*, 121 F.3d at 737.

[48] *See* Mila Sohoni, *The Power to Privilege*, 163 U. PA. L. REV. 487, 496 (2015) (noting that the deliberative-process privilege has been developed "[t]hrough common law decisionmaking").

array of executive officials, whereas the *Nixon* privilege is "specific to the President."[49]

Second, the *state-secrets privilege* operates to prevent disclosure of information that would compromise important national security or diplomatic interests.[50] In *Nixon* itself the Court alluded to the existence of this privilege, suggesting in particular that "a claim of need to protect military, diplomatic, or sensitive national security secrets" implicated an altogether different doctrinal analysis than the generalized candor-based privilege on which President Nixon relied.[51] The precise scope and status of this privilege remains uncertain,[52] but what is undoubtedly true is that the executive branch has relied on the privilege both frequently and aggressively in litigation concerning military and foreign affairs, particularly in the post-9/11 era.[53] Most invocations of the privilege have proven successful, thanks largely to the courts' longstanding reluctance to second guess the executive in dealing with matters of national security.[54]

---

49 Jud. Watch Inc. v. Dep't of Justice, 365 F.3d 1108, 1113–14 (D.C. Cir. 2004) ("Unlike the deliberative process privilege, which is a general privilege that applies to all executive branch officials, the presidential communications privilege is specific to the President . . . .").

50 *See Reynolds*, 345 U.S. at 10 (noting that a court must honor the state-secrets privilege if the government has established that there is "a reasonable danger that compulsion of the evidence will expose military matters which, in the interest of national security, should not be divulged").

51 *Nixon*, 418 U.S. at 706; *see also id.* at 707 (noting that the President must rely on "more than a generalized claim of the public interest in confidentiality of *nonmilitary and nondiplomatic discussions*" (emphasis added)). The Court's allusion to the state-secrets privilege in *Nixon* has raised questions about whether the privilege is merely a creature of the common law or is instead, like the *Nixon* privilege, rooted directly in separation-of-powers principles. *See* Sohoni, *supra* note 48, at 495 n.20, 527 (noting that the privilege "has a common law pedigree" but also that some commentators have understood the privilege to be constitutionally grounded).

52 For a recent effort to work through the doctrine's many complexities, see Laura K. Donohue, *The Shadow of State Secrets*, 159 U. PA. L. REV. 77 (2010).

53 *See, e.g.*, *id.* at 87 (noting that "the privilege played a significant role in the executive branch's national security litigation strategy" from January 2001 through January 2009); Timothy Bazzle, *Shutting the Courthouse Doors: Invoking the State Secrets Privilege To Thwart Judicial Review in the Age of Terror*, 23 GEO. MASON U. CIV. RTS. L.J. 29, 29–30 (2012) (noting that the Obama administration "assert[ed] the privilege with just as much fervor—if not as much regularity—as its predecessor" (internal footnote omitted)).

54 *See* Shirin Sinnar, *Rule of Law Tropes in National Security*, 129 HARV. L. REV. 1566, 1570–71(2016) (citing the state-secrets privilege as one of several areas of doctrine in which "[j]udges, whether because they believe they must or should, often defer to the executive branch on matters of national security"); *see also* Daniel R. Cassman, Note, *Keep It Secret, Keep It Safe: An Empirical Analysis of the State Secrets Doctrine*, 67 STAN. L. REV. 1173, 1188 (2015) (finding, based on a dataset of more than 300 cases concerning the state-secrets privilege, that invocations of the privilege were upheld in full 67% of the time and upheld in part 15% of the time).

2. Other Limits on Investigating the President: The Trump Cases

The protections of executive privilege cover only the President's *official* conduct and thus do not in themselves prohibit investigations of a sitting President's *personal conduct*. But personal-conduct investigations remain subject to other constitutional constraints, two of which figured prominently in a recent pair of cases involving investigations into former-President Trump's business and financial activities. First, in *Trump v. Vance*,[55] the Court articulated a set of *federalism-based* restrictions on the power of state-level actors to conduct criminal investigations of a sitting U.S. President. Second, in *Trump v. Mazars USA, LLP*,[56] the Court articulated a set of separation-of-powers-based limits on Congress's ability to issue subpoenas for information concerning the President's non-official conduct.

a. *Federalism-Based Limits on State-Based Investigations:* Trump v. Vance

Can a state prosecutor seek information about the affairs of the nation's President? Long a matter of mainly theoretical interest, the question became one of real-world urgency in 2019, when Manhattan District Attorney Cyrus Vance, Jr., served a subpoena on Donald Trump's accounting firm, Mazars USA.[57] The subpoena called for the delivery of records related to the President's personal business arrangements, and the President sued both Vance and Mazars in federal court in an effort to enjoin the subpoena's enforcement.[58] Notably, the President did not invoke executive privilege, presumably because the subpoenaed information did not relate to his official duties as President. Instead, he argued that Article II, the Supremacy Clause, and related structural principles gave sitting Presidents an absolute immunity from state criminal process—an immunity that was necessary to avoid making the leader of the federal government subject to the investigative whims of officials responsive to local, rather than national, interests.[59]

Writing for himself and four other Justices, Chief Justice Roberts rejected the President's claim of absolute immunity. This case, he acknowledged, was the first one in which the Court had squarely considered the legality of a state-level subpoena that

---

[55] 140 S. Ct. 2412 (2020).

[56] 140 S. Ct. 2019 (2020).

[57] *See Vance*, 140 S. Ct. at 2420.

[58] *Id.*

[59] *Id.* at 2425.

targeted the President.[60] Even so, he continued, the President's demand for absolute immunity was effectively foreclosed by the Court's prior decisions, which established that the mere potential for distracting, stigmatizing, or harassing litigation was not enough to support a categorical presidential protection against the rigors of the judicial process. In *Nixon* itself, the Chief Justice reasoned, the Court had made clear that the President lacked an absolute immunity from federal criminal subpoenas.[61] In addition, in *Clinton v. Jones*[62] (discussed in greater detail below) the Court had rejected the idea that the dangers of distraction, stigmatization, and harassment compelled an absolute immunity from civil suits against sitting Presidents.[63] To be sure, the Chief Justice acknowledged, the Court's precedents did afford the President an absolute immunity from damages liability for actions undertaken in his official capacity.[64] But that rule (also considered further below) was necessitated by the need to ensure that the President could "deal fearlessly and impartially with the duties of his office."[65] Here, by contrast, the subpoena concerned only the President's *unofficial* conduct and thus posed no risk of chilling or distorting the President's exercise of his Article II powers.

At the same time, the Chief Justice emphasized that the actions of local prosecutors would remain subject to meaningful review insofar as the President retained the ability to challenge state-level demands for information on a "subpoena-specific" basis.[66] For example, the President could raise the claim that a particular subpoena violated state-law prohibitions on overbroad or bad-faith investigative requests.[67] In addition, the President could direct targeted "*constitutional* challenges"[68] at subpoenas on the ground they ran afoul of the principle—first recognized in *McCulloch v. Maryland*—that states have "no power . . . to retard, impede, burden, or in any manner control the operations of the constitutional laws enacted by Congress."[69] From that principle, Chief Justice Roberts

60 *Id.* at 2420 (noting that "[t]his case involves—so far as we and the parties can tell—the first *state* criminal subpoena directed to a President").

61 *Id.* at 2425.

62 520 U.S. 681 (1997).

63 *See Vance*, 140 S. Ct. at 2428 (discussing *Jones*); *see also infra* Section 33.B.2 (describing the *Jones* opinion in greater detail).

64 *See Vance*, 140 S. Ct. at 2426 (citing Nixon v. Fitzgerald, 457 U.S. 731 (1982)).

65 *See id.* at 2426 (quoting *Fitzgerald*, 457 U.S. at 751–52); *see also infra* Section 33.B.1.a (discussing *Fitzgerald* in greater detail).

66 *Vance*, 140 S. Ct. at 2430.

67 *Id.*

68 *Id.* (emphasis added).

69 *Id.* at 2425 (quoting McCulloch v. Maryland, 17 U.S. (4 Wheat.) 159, 213 (1819)). On this point, the Court also noted that "federal law allows a President to

explained, it naturally followed that "States also lack the power to impede the President's execution of those laws,"[70] so that the courts were duty-bound to block subpoenas reflecting an "effort to manipulate a President's policy decisions,"[71] "to retaliate against a President for official acts,"[72] or otherwise "to influence the performance of [the President's] official duties."[73] Any such determination, however, would have to depend on the specifics of the subpoena in question, as the Court was unwilling to recognize an all-encompassing prohibition on state-level investigations into the potential illegality of the President's personal activities.[74]

---

challenge any allegedly unconstitutional influence *in a federal forum*, as the President has done here." *Id.* at 2426 (emphasis added) (citing 42 U.S.C. § 1983 and *Ex parte* Young, 209 U.S. 123 (1908)).

[70] *Id.* at 2425.

[71] *Id.* at 2428.

[72] *Id.* (internal quotations and alterations omitted).

[73] *Id.* at 2430; *see also id.* (noting that "[t]his avenue protects against local political machinations 'interposed as an obstacle to the effective operation of a federal constitutional power' " (quoting United States v. Belmont, 301 U.S. 324, 332 (1937))). To Justice Alito in dissent, these subpoena-specific safeguards were not enough to address the very real risk of state-level harassment of the President. As he saw things, the "enduring lesson" of *McCulloch* was that "a State may not block or interfere with the lawful work of the National Government." *Id.* at 2442 (Alito, J., dissenting). So understood, *McCulloch* warranted application of a stricter test that—while falling short of an absolute prohibition—would have served more effectively to "prevent interference with a President's discharge of the responsibilities of the office." *Id.* at 2448 (Alito, J., dissenting). Such a test, in Alito's view, would have placed the burden on the prosecutor "(1) to provide at least a general description of the possible offenses that are under investigation, (2) to outline how the subpoenaed records relate to those offenses, and (3) to explain why it is important that the records be produced and why it is necessary for production to occur while the President is still in office." *Id.* at 2449. Justice Thomas also dissented, maintaining that, while "the President has no absolute immunity from the issuance of a grand jury subpoena," he might still be able to contest the *enforcement* of a subpoena by arguing that he is "unable to comply because of his official duties." *Id.* at 2436 (Thomas, J., dissenting). Justice Kavanaugh, joined by Justice Gorsuch, issued an opinion concurring in the judgment, which, while expressing basic agreement with the majority's decision to remand for further consideration of the subpoena's validity, expressed disagreement with the majority's decision not to impose any burden on the prosecutor to make a heightened showing of need for the information being requested. In particular, Justice Kavanaugh would have instructed the lower courts to apply the "demonstrated, specific need" standard from *Nixon*, a "tried-and-true test that accommodates both the interests of the criminal process and the Article II interests of the Presidency." *Id.* at 2432 (Kavanaugh, J., concurring in the judgment) (internal quotations omitted). At the same time, Justice Kavanaugh suggested that the varying positions articulated by the Justices in *Vance* might not ultimately differ in any significant real-world sense, noting specifically that "[i]t will take future cases to determine precisely how much difference exists between (i) the various standards articulated by the majority opinion, (ii) the overarching *Nixon* 'demonstrated, specific need' standard that I would adopt, and (iii) Justice Thomas's and Justice Alito's other proposed standards." *Id.* at 2433.

[74] The Court itself did not consider whether Vance's subpoena request ran afoul of these principles, choosing instead to remand the case for further proceedings in light of its opinion. On remand, the President chose not to press any Supremacy Clause-based objection to the subpoena based on *McCulloch*, and the district court scuttled his claim that the subpoena was overbroad and issued in bad faith. *See* Trump v.

b. Separation of Powers-Based Limits on Congressional Investigations: **Trump v. Mazars USA, LLP**

On the same day that the Court decided *Vance* it also handed down its ruling in *Mazars*, which arose from two consolidated cases concerning another set of subpoenas for Trump-related financial information.[75] Unlike the subpoenas at issue in *Vance*, which had been issued at the behest of a local prosecutor, the subpoenas at issue in *Mazars* had been issued by three committees of the U.S. House of Representatives for the stated purpose of helping Congress evaluate existing statutory conflict-of-interest rules and other potential pieces of anti-corruption legislation.[76] As in *Vance*, these demands for information did not target President Trump himself; instead, their recipients were banks and accounting firms. Also as in *Vance*, the President did not invoke executive privilege. Instead, he contended that structural limits grounded in the separation of powers rendered the House subpoenas invalid on the theory that subpoenas themselves were not in furtherance of "a valid legislative aim."[77]

Chief Justice Roberts again wrote for a majority of the Court, and he again offered something of a middle-ground resolution of the question presented. He began by noting that Congress possesses a "broad" and "indispensable" "power to obtain information"[78] as "an essential and appropriate auxiliary to the legislative function."[79] In addition, under normal circumstances, that power sufficed to justify any and all subpoena requests that were "related to, and in furtherance of, a legitimate task of the Congress."[80] But the question here was whether Congress's investigative authorities were more limited in light of the "significant separation of powers issues raised

---

Vance, 480 F. Supp. 3d 460 (S.D.N.Y. 2020). After the Second Circuit affirmed, 977 F.3d 198 (2d Cir. 2020), President Trump sought a stay of the district court's judgment, but the Justices sat on the motion until his presidency had expired and then proceeded to deny the request. *See* Adam Liptak, William K. Rashbaum, Ben Protess & Benjamin Weiser, *Supreme Court Denies Trump's Final Bid to Block Release of Tax Returns*, N.Y. TIMES (Feb. 22, 2021), https://www.nytimes.com/2021/02/22/us/politics/supreme-court-trump-taxes-financial-records.html. Four days later, Mazars handed over to Vance the records he had sought. *See* Jonah E. Bromwich, *Manhattan D.A. Now Has Trump's Tax Returns*, N.Y. TIMES (Feb. 25, 2021), https://www.nytimes.com/2021/02/25/nyregion/trump-taxes-vance-supreme-court.html.

[75] 140 S. Ct. at 2028–29.

[76] *Id.* at 2027–28.

[77] *Id.* at 2026.

[78] *Id.* at 2031 (internal quotation marks omitted) (quoting Watkins v. United States, 354 U.S. 178, 187 (1957)).

[79] *Id.* (internal quotation marks omitted) (quoting McGrain v. Daugherty, 273 U.S. 135, 174 (1927)).

[80] *Id.* (quoting *Watkins*, 354 U.S. at 187); *see also id.* at 2032 (noting that "Congress may not issue a subpoena for the purpose of 'law enforcement' because 'those powers are assigned under our Constitution to the Executive and the Judiciary' " (quoting Quinn v. United States, 349 U.S. 155, 161 (1955))).

by congressional subpoenas for the President's information."[81] The President argued that they were and urged the Court to require a congressional showing both that there was a "demonstrated, specific need" for the information being sought and that the information itself was "demonstrably critical" to achieving a valid legislative goal.[82] The House, in response, argued against any departure from the Court's standard judicial approach for evaluating congressional subpoenas, maintaining that its committees needed to show only that the sought materials "relate to a valid legislative purpose or concern a subject on which legislation could be had."[83]

In the end, the Court embraced neither of these standards, instead appearing to split the difference by prescribing a "balanced approach" for "assessing whether a subpoena directed at the President's personal information is 'related to, and in furtherance of, a legitimate task of the Congress.' "[84] As formulated by the Chief Justice, this approach requires courts to attend to (at least) four "special considerations."[85] First, they must "carefully assess whether the asserted legislative purpose warrants the significant step of involving the President and his papers," especially in light of the possibility that "other sources could provide Congress the information it needs."[86] Second, courts should "insist on a subpoena no broader than reasonably necessary to support Congress's legislative objective," bearing in mind the risk that an overly broad subpoena could give rise to an "unnecessary intrusion into the operation of the Office of the President."[87] Third, courts should consider whether Congress has offered "detailed and substantial" evidence of a "valid legislative purpose" to which the subpoena relates.[88] Finally, courts must "carefully scrutinize[ ]" the "burdens imposed by a congressional subpoena," being mindful in particular that a "rival political branch" will sometimes have "incentives to use subpoenas for institutional advantage."[89] These four (and potentially other) avenues of inquiry, the Chief Justice claimed, would help to ensure that courts "take[ ] adequate account of the separation of

---

81 *Id.* at 2033.

82 *Id.* at 2032 (internal quotation marks omitted) (first quoting *Nixon*, 418 U.S. at 713; and then quoting *Senate Select Committee*, 498 F.2d at 731).

83 *Id.* at 2033 (internal quotations omitted).

84 *Id.* at 2035 (quoting *Watkins*, 345 U.S. at 187).

85 *Id.*

86 *Id.* at 2035–36.

87 *Id.* at 2036 (internal citations omitted).

88 *Id.*

89 *Id.*

powers principles at stake, including both the significant legislative interests of Congress and the 'unique position' of the President."[90]

One could be forgiven for wondering how "balanced" the Chief Justice's "balanced approach" really is. To be sure, the Court rejected President Trump's specific suggestion that Congress be required to show a "demonstrated, specific need" for any subpoena targeting the President's non-official papers because it feared that such a requirement "would risk seriously impeding Congress in carrying out its responsibilities."[91] The "balanced approach" it ultimately endorsed, however, seems likely to place similar obstacles in Congress's way, by requiring courts to conduct a "careful analysis" of the basis for, necessity of, and burdens imposed by any demand for the disclosure of non-official materials concerning the President.[92] The majority's multi-factor test assumes an even more pro-President cast when one recalls the practical difficulties of subpoena *enforcement* that Congress already confronts—difficulties that already add to the time-consuming and labor-intensive nature of Congress's information-seeking efforts.[93] With all this in mind, Presidents confronted with congressional subpoenas have good strategic reason to drag their heels by channeling underlying disputes into federal court, where the open-ended nature of the four-part inquiry is well-situated to yield a drawn-out tussle over the constitutionality of Congress's investigatory demands. In this sense, the Court's decision in *Mazars* can be seen as further strengthening the President's already-strong hand in contests over the

---

[90] *Id.* at 2035 (quoting *Jones*, 520 U.S. at 698). Looming over the entirety of this dispute was the specter of impeachment. Although President Trump had been impeached during the course of the *Mazars* litigation, none of the contested subpoenas had been issued in connection with that process. For Justice Thomas, who wrote in dissent, this fact should have made all the difference. According to him, Congress lacked the power "to issue a legislative subpoena for private, nonofficial documents" *unless* it was "proceed[ing] under the impeachment power." *Id.* at 2037 (Thomas, J., dissenting). The House committees, in his view, were seeking the President's financial information not for the actual purpose of helping them to develop prophylactic forms of conflict-of-interest legislation, but instead for the purpose of "engag[ing] in a nationwide inquisition" about alleged misconduct by the President of the United States. *Id.* at 2047 (Thomas, J., dissenting). The Constitution, however, designated a "special mechanism" for that endeavor—namely, the impeachment process—and that was the checking mechanism that Congress accordingly was required to use. *Id.* at 2045 (Thomas, J., dissenting). *But see* Trump v. Mazars, USA, LLP, 940 F.3d 710, 737–39 (D.C. Cir. 2019) (Tatel, J.) (noting that, on the impeachment-only view subsequently embraced by Justice Thomas, "Congress must either initiate the grave and weighty process of impeachment or forgo any investigation in support of potential legislation," meaning that "even a valid legislative purpose" would fail to justify an investigation of the President's potential misconduct), *vacated on other grounds*, 140 S. Ct. 2019.

[91] *Mazars*, 140 S. Ct. at 2033.

[92] *Id.* at 2035.

[93] *See supra* Section 33.A.1.c.

enforceability of congressional subpoenas aimed at getting information from or about the President.[94]

B. CIVIL LITIGATION AGAINST THE PRESIDENT

Presidents also have pointed to the unique nature of their office in seeking to exempt themselves, either permanently or temporarily, from civil litigation. In particular, they have done so in connection with two different types of civil lawsuits: (1) cases in which plaintiffs seek to secure a remedy, particularly in the form of money damages, from either active or former Presidents for injuries suffered as a result of the President's *official* acts; and (2) cases in which plaintiffs have sued sitting Presidents based on acts not involving the exercise of their official powers, including acts predating the President's inauguration. With respect to the first category of cases, the Court has recognized a robust immunity that absolutely prohibits plaintiffs from recovering damages for injuries caused by the President's "official" acts and that at least sometimes prohibits plaintiffs from securing injunctions against Presidents for ongoing official acts as well. With respect to the second category of cases by contrast, the Court has refused to recognize even a *temporary immunity* from suit, holding that a defendant's status as a sitting President affords no *ipso facto* constitutional exemption from the jurisdiction of a federal court.

1. Civil Suits Predicated on a President's Official Actions

a. Damages Liability

In evaluating private plaintiffs' efforts to recover damages for government officials' unlawful behavior, the Court has long recognized a variety of common-law-based "immunity" rules that these officials might invoke.[95] The most frequently litigated rule involves the "qualified immunity" defense, which insulates from liability a broad swath of executive officials at both the state and federal level, by providing that such officials need not pay damages

---

[94] The decision also had the related effect of elevating the judiciary's own role as chief arbiter of these disputes. *See* Josh Chafetz, *Nixon/Trump: Strategies of Judicial Aggrandizement*, 110 GEO. L.J. 125, 144 (2021) (noting that Chief Justice Roberts's opinions in *Vance* and *Mazars* offered "an exalted view of judicial process, coupled with a degraded view of congressional process," and contending that "[w]hether or not these cases are victories for the rule of law, they are certainly institutional victories for the judiciary").

[95] For a much more detailed investigation of these rules, see 2 SHELDON H. NAHMOD, CIVIL RIGHTS & CIVIL LIBERTIES LITIGATION: THE LAW OF SECTION 1983 §§ 7–8 (4th ed. Supp. 2021).

for conduct that, although unlawful when undertaken, did not at the time "violate clearly established statutory or constitutional rights of which a reasonable person would have known."[96] In addition, the Court long has held that some types of government officials enjoy an "absolute" immunity from damages liability for their official acts, even when they should have known of those actions' unlawfulness. For example, state legislators enjoy an absolute immunity from civil suits based on their legislative acts,[97] and judges likewise have an absolute immunity for any actions undertaken in their official judicial capacity.[98] Furthermore, the Court has bestowed on prosecutors an absolute immunity for acts "associated with the judicial phase of the criminal process,"[99] albeit while also suggesting that only a qualified immunity attaches to "those aspects of the prosecutor's responsibility that cast him in the role of an administrator or investigative officer rather than that of advocate."[100] All of these rules reflect the Court's concern that too much exposure to damages liability will deter individuals from serving in governmental positions and lead to overly guarded and hence ineffective exercises of their governmental powers.[101]

The Court's 1982 decision in *Nixon v. Fitzgerald*[102] added to this list of immunity doctrines a further rule that grants the President "absolute immunity from damages liability predicated on his official acts."[103] Writing for a five-Justice majority, Justice Powell defended this immunity as a "functionally mandated incident of the President's

---

[96] Harlow v. Fitzgerald, 457 U.S. 800, 818 (1982). For a general (and skeptical) overview of the courts' justifications for these rules, see William Baude, *Is Qualified Immunity Unlawful?*, 106 CAL. L. REV. 45, 49–79 (2018).

[97] Tenney v. Brandhove, 341 U.S. 367, 372 (1951). *But see* United States v. Gillock, 445 U.S. 360 (1980) (holding that this immunity does not extend to federal criminal prosecutions). The immunities of *federal* legislators are derived from the Constitution's Speech or Debate Clause, which is addressed later in this Chapter. *See infra* Section 33.D.

[98] *See* Pierson v. Ray, 386 U.S. 547, 554–55 (1967).

[99] *See* Imbler v. Pachtman, 424 U.S. 409, 430 (1976).

[100] *Id.* at 430–31.

[101] *See* Jennifer E. Laurin, *Rights Translation and Remedial Disequilibration in Constitutional Criminal Procedure*, 110 COLUM. L. REV. 1002, 1025 (2010) ("The rationale of both qualified and absolute immunity has been explained by the Court as embodying both individual fairness and societal benefit: Subjecting officials to the burdens and expense of litigation and liability for discretionary acts within the scope of their duties is unjust, risks deterring individuals from entering into government service, and encourages suboptimally cautious behavior in the exercise of official duties.").

[102] 457 U.S. 731.

[103] *Id.* at 749. A key question raised by this formulation is what, precisely, qualifies as an "official act" of the President. The Court in *Fitzgerald* did not give extensive attention to this issue, except that it noted that "the sphere of protected action" encompassed all "acts within the 'outer perimeter' of [the President's] official responsibility." *Id.* at 755–56 (quoting Barr v. Matteo, 360 U.S. 564, 575 (1959)).

unique office, rooted in the constitutional tradition of the separation of powers and supported by our history."[104] The rule was necessary, he explained, to ensure that Presidents—who "must make the most sensitive and far-reaching decisions entrusted to any official under our constitutional system"—could make those decisions "fearlessly and impartially," without the fear of lawsuits hanging over their heads.[105] Also supporting the rule was the unique "visibility of [the President's] office and the effect of his actions on countless people,"[106] which made the Chief Executive "an easily identifiable target for suits."[107]

The obvious downside to a rule of absolute presidential immunity is that it precludes judicial redress for even the most egregious abuses of presidential power. The majority in *Fitzgerald* acknowledged this concern, but it nonetheless predicted that a rule of absolute immunity from damages liability for official acts would not cause a rash of presidential wrongdoing in light of other "remedies and deterrents" built into the U.S. political system.[108] Foremost among these was the impeachment process, which opened the door to the removal from office of any President found to have committed high crimes and misdemeanors.[109] Also in the picture were such other checks as "[v]igilant oversight by Congress," "constant scrutiny by the press," and the President's "desire to earn reelection," all of which operated as additional "incentives to avoid misconduct."[110] Given these safeguards, Justice Powell reasoned, a rule of "absolute immunity [would] not place the President above the

---

104 *Fitzgerald*, 457 U.S. at 749. In characterizing the *Fitzgerald* rule as "rooted in the constitutional tradition of the separation of powers," Justice Powell appeared to suggest that, unlike other official immunities the Court has recognized, the presidential immunity might well be rooted in the Constitution itself and thus not subject to abrogation by Congress. *See also id.* at 760 (Burger, J., concurring) ("The Court today holds that the Constitution mandates such immunity and I agree."). In the end, however, the Court did not decide whether Congress could override this immunity by statutorily authorizing damages actions against the President, *id.* at 748 n.27, thus leading Justice White to perceive in the majority opinion a "serious ambiguity" on the issue, *id.* at 792 (White, J., dissenting). For now, at least, the question remains a hypothetical one, as Congress has not attempted to use its legislative powers in this way.

105 *Id.* at 752 (citations omitted).

106 *Id.* at 753.

107 *Id.* Such suits, Justice Powell continued, would likely cause worry and distraction to the President, which in turn would work "to the detriment of not only the President and his office but also the Nation that the Presidency was designed to serve." *Id.*

108 *Id.* at 758.

109 *Id.* at 757; *see also supra* Section 32.A.

110 *Fitzgerald*, 457 U.S. at 757. Interestingly (and perhaps tellingly), the Court did not reference the possibility of criminal sanctions, though as we will consider further below, most commentators believe that the President has at best only a temporary immunity from criminal prosecution while in office. *See infra* Section 33.C.

law."[111] Rather, it would "merely preclude[ ] a particular private remedy for alleged misconduct in order to advance compelling public ends."[112]

Two points might be offered in response to this line of analysis. First, it is by no means clear as an empirical matter that the "alternative remedies and deterrents" referenced in Justice Powell's opinion provide, without more, significant safeguards against presidential wrongdoing.[113] Second, even if one concedes that the deterrent force of damages liability is not necessary to keep the President in check, there still exists no substitute mechanism for achieving the additional—and, some would say, primary—goal of money damages suits: namely, the goal of providing compensation to the victim of a demonstrated legal wrong.[114] As Justice White put the point in his dissent in *Fitzgerald*, the majority—by absolutely immunizing the President against damages liability for official acts—made it impossible to "assure each individual that he, as an individual, has enforceable rights that he may pursue to achieve a peaceful redress of his legitimate grievances."[115]

b. Injunctive Relief

Fitzgerald establishes a rule of absolute immunity that blocks a plaintiff's recovery of damages from the President for official-capacity actions. But does a similarly absolute rule of immunity apply in actions brought against the President for injunctive relief? As it turns out, the Court confronted this question long before *Fitzgerald* in the 1866 case of *Mississippi v. Johnson*.[116] In that civil action, the state of Mississippi sought to enjoin President Andrew Johnson from enforcing the Reconstruction Acts.[117] The Court rejected Mississippi's request, reasoning that issuance of the requested injunction would run afoul of "general principles which forbid judicial interference with the exercise of Executive discretion."[118] At the same time, however, the Justices did not go so far as to recognize a categorical

---

111 *Fitzgerald*, 457 U.S. at 758 (internal quotation marks omitted).

112 *Id.*

113 For example, removal of the President by way of the impeachment process requires a level of bipartisan agreement that will only rarely, if ever, materialize. *See supra* Section 32.A. In addition, a President's "desire for reelection" comes into play only during that President's first term.

114 *Fitzgerald*, 457 U.S. at 797 (White J., dissenting).

115 *Id.*

116 71 U.S. (4 Wall.) 475 (1866).

117 *Id.* at 499.

118 *Id.* For an extended critique of the Court's reasoning in *Mississippi v. Johnson*, see Jonathan R. Siegel, *Suing the President: Nonstatutory Review Revisited*, 97 COLUM. L. REV. 1612, 1680–93 (1997) (noting that the Court's reasoning failed to "successfully distinguish the President from any other government official" and thus, in effect, ended up proving far too much).

prohibition on injunctions against the President, as they explicitly reserved judgment on the question whether the President might "be required . . . to perform a purely ministerial act under a positive law."[119] Nor has the Court in the 150-plus years since *Johnson* again squarely addressed these matters.[120] To be sure, the subpoena order that was upheld in the Nixon tapes case makes clear that Presidents are not immune from any and all forms of judicial process.[121] It remains an open question, however, whether the Court's decision in *Nixon* altered in any way the rules set forth in *Mississippi v. Johnson* with regard to injunctions directed against the President.[122]

In the end, the answer to this question may not matter much, at least in the lion's share of cases. The reason why is that plaintiffs can typically secure the relief they desire by challenging executive-branch policies without suing the President directly. Instead, such plaintiffs can sue *other* executive officials involved in the implementation of those policies and secure injunctions prohibiting those officials from carrying them out.[123] (In *Youngstown*, for example, the plaintiffs took this route by suing the Secretary of Commerce, who had been tasked by President Truman with implementing his order to seize the steel mills.)[124] Thus, while it

---

119 *Johnson*, 71 U.S. at 498.

120 *See* Franklin v. Massachusetts, 505 U.S. 788, 802 (1992) (opinion of O'Connor, J.) (noting that *Johnson* had "left open the question whether the President might be subject to a judicial injunction requiring the performance of a purely ministerial duty" (internal quotation and citation omitted)). In *Fitzgerald*, Justice Powell cited to *Mississippi v. Johnson* as reflective of a longstanding "tradition" of treating "the President's constitutional responsibilities and status as factors counseling judicial deference and restraint." *Fitzgerald*, 457 U.S. at 753. At no point, however, did he discuss how the courts might deal with the President's alleged failure to discharge "purely ministerial" duties, thus leaving (still) unresolved the question that *Johnson* had first teed up. *But see Franklin*, 505 U.S. at 828 (Scalia, J., concurring in part and concurring in the judgment) (noting that "injunctive or declaratory relief against the President is not mentioned" in *Fitzgerald* as one of the alternative "remedies and deterrents" against presidential wrongdoing, which thus perhaps implies that the Court in *Fitzgerald* viewed *Johnson* as setting forth an absolute rule against even injunctions targeting a President's ministerial duties (internal quotations and citations omitted)).

121 *See supra* Section 33.A.1.a; *see also Franklin*, 505 U.S. at 826 (Scalia, J., concurring in part and concurring in the judgment) (citing to *Nixon* and Chief Justice Marshall's statements during the *Burr* case, *see supra* note 12, as supportive of the proposition that "the President is not absolutely immune from judicial process").

122 *See id.* (seeking to reconcile the outcomes of *Nixon* and *Mississippi* by reference to the idea that the "order upheld [in *Nixon*] merely required the President to provide information relevant to an ongoing criminal prosecution, which is what any citizen might do" and that the order thus "did not require him to exercise the 'executive Power' in a judicially prescribed fashion").

123 *See* Siegel, *supra* note 118, at 1701 (noting that "in most cases, private rights violated by presidential action can be enforced via some other mechanism, such as a nonstatutory suit against some subordinate official").

124 *See* Youngstown Sheet & Tube Co. v. Sawyer, 343 U.S. 579 (1952). To take a more recent example, when a group of plaintiffs sought to prevent President Trump

remains uncertain whether plaintiffs might ever be permitted to secure injunctions directly against the President, the answer to that question has largely been mooted by the fact that executive-branch subordinates enjoy no immunity from court-ordered equitable remedies.[125]

2. Personal-Capacity Suits Against a Sitting President

Although much of the *Fitzgerald* litigation took place after Richard Nixon had left office, the timing of the case had no bearing on the Court's holding. The point of that decision's absolute-immunity rule, after all, was to remove unwanted chilling effects on the President's official behavior, and—because money is money—sitting Presidents have no less reason to worry about post-term damages awards than awards directed at them while they remain in office. Suppose, however, that a plaintiff sues a sitting President for conduct not undertaken in the President's official capacity—conduct, for instance, that predates the President's ascension to office or that, while engaged in during the President's term, fails to qualify as an "official act." The *Fitzgerald* rule would not bar recovery in such a lawsuit. But might the timing of the action nonetheless provide cause for concern? Litigation, after all, is a time-consuming and attention-draining ordeal. And, to say the least, the President already has much to do. Thus, the question arises: Might the President be entitled to at least a *temporary immunity* from personal-capacity litigation while in office—an immunity justified by the need to ensure that Presidents devote full attention to their critical official duties?

---

from blocking them from his Twitter account, they sued not just President Trump himself, but also other White House aides known to have access to the account. *See* Knight First Amendment Inst. at Columbia Univ. v. Trump, 302 F. Supp. 3d 541, 578–59 (S.D.N.Y. 2018), *aff'd*, 928 F. 3d 226 (2d Cir. 2019), *vacated as moot*, 141 S. Ct. 1220 (2021). In considering the case, the district court opined that the "intrusion on executive prerogative presented by an injunction directing the unblocking of the individual plaintiffs would be minimal" and that "the correction of an unconstitutional act" might well qualify as an injunction imposing a "mere ministerial duty" within the meaning of *Johnson* itself. *Id.* at 578. Even so, the court continued, it did not need to "ultimately resolve the question" because "injunctive relief" directed at Trump's aides might be issued instead. *Id.* at 579. In addition, the court noted that a declaratory judgment could be issued against all parties on the assumption that "it is substantially likely that the President and other executive officials would abide by an authoritative interpretation of a constitutional provision." *Id.* at 579 (alteration omitted) (quoting *Franklin*, 505 U.S. at 803).

[125] *But see* Siegel, *supra* note 118, at 1703 (noting that "[m]aintaining a personal immunity for the President . . . would cause genuine harm," not only because it would "expose plaintiffs to the danger of erroneous dismissals" but also because there might be "at least some cases in which the immunity would be likely to deny all relief to an injured plaintiff").

In *Clinton v. Jones*,[126] a damages suit brought against then-President Clinton based on allegations of sexual assault during his time as Governor of Arkansas, the Court answered this question in the negative. Writing for an eight-Justice majority, Justice Stevens emphasized that the "principal rationale" of *Fitzgerald*—namely, "to avoid rendering the President 'unduly cautious in the discharge of his official duties' "—was "inapplicable to unofficial conduct" and thus "provide[d] no support for" the sort of immunity that President Clinton had sought.[127] As for the President's claim that his "powers and responsibilities" were "so vast and important that the public interest demands that he devote his undivided time and attention to his public duties," the Court was similarly unmoved.[128] For one thing, the Court noted that during the "more than 200-year history of the Republic, only three sitting Presidents have been subjected to suits for their private actions"—a fact that, in its view, undercut the President's "predictive judgment" that private litigation against him would "hamper the performance of his official duties."[129] The Court also rejected the idea that all "interactions between the Judicial Branch and the Executive, even quite burdensome interactions, necessarily rise to the level of constitutionally forbidden impairment of the Executive's ability to perform its constitutionally mandated functions."[130] After all, according to Justice Stevens, it was well-accepted that the courts could review the lawfulness of presidential actions in cases properly subject to their jurisdiction (as happened, for instance, in the *Youngstown* case) and even to treat the President as "subject to judicial process in appropriate circumstances" (as had happened, for instance, in the Nixon tapes case).[131] These and other decisions thus made it clear that "[t]he fact that a federal court's exercise of its traditional Article III jurisdiction may significantly burden the time and attention of the Chief Executive is not sufficient to establish a violation of the Constitution."[132]

---

126 520 U.S. 681 (1997).

127 *Id.* at 692–94 (quoting *Fitzgerald*, 457 U.S. at 752 n.32). In a separate opinion, Justice Breyer resisted this conclusion, noting in particular that *Fitzgerald* had also made mention of the possibility "that civil lawsuits 'could distract a President from his public duties, to the detriment of not only the President and his office but also the Nation that the Presidency was designed to serve.' " *See id.* at 719–20 (Breyer, J., concurring in the judgment) (quoting *Fitzgerald*, 457 U.S. at 753). *But see id.* at 694 n.19 (majority opinion) (rejecting that reading of *Fitzgerald* because it was clear "[i]n context" that "our dominant concern was with the diversion of the President's attention during the decisionmaking process caused by needless worry as to the possibility of damages actions stemming from any particular official decision").

128 *Id.* at 697.

129 *Id.* at 702.

130 *Id.* at 701–02.

131 *Id.* at 703–04 (citing *Youngstown*, 343 U.S. at 579, and *Nixon*, 418 U.S. at 683).

132 *Id.* at 703.

To its basic holding, however, the Court added an important qualification: Even in the absence of a bright-line temporary-immunity rule, it remained "appropriate" for a district court to consider the "potential burdens on the President" in exercising the "broad discretion to stay proceedings as an incident to its power to control its own docket."[133] Thus, while sitting Presidents were not fully spared the burden of dealing with private-capacity suits, they remained able to seek special procedural treatment in the form of continuances and other adjustments, including with respect to "the timing and scope of discovery."[134] Moreover, in considering any such request for accommodation, district courts needed to take account of "[t]he high respect that is owed to the office of the Chief Executive."[135]

Put a bit differently, Justice Stevens rejected the President's request for a categorical protection from being drawn into civil

---

[133] *Id.* at 706–07.

[134] *Id.* at 707. Such discretion, of course, was not unlimited, and the Court itself illustrated this point by going on to hold that the district court in the *Jones* case had indeed abused its discretion by staying any trial until after Clinton's presidency had concluded. *See id.* at 707–08. That order, the Court explained, went too far, given that such a significant delay of the trial would "increase the danger of prejudice resulting from the loss of evidence" and that the decision had been "premature[ly]" made at a time when "there was no way to assess whether a stay of trial after the completion of discovery would be warranted." *Id.*

[135] *Id.* at 707. The Court's decision in *Jones* concerned a federal-court case, and it thus left open whether a sitting President could claim a temporary immunity from personal-capacity suits brought in state-court instead. *See id.* at 691 (noting that in state-court litigation the President "would presumably rely on federalism and comity concerns, as well as the interest in protecting federal officials from possible local prejudice" (internal footnote omitted)). This question took on real-world importance during Donald Trump's presidency, when he was sued in New York state court for making allegedly defamatory statements about the plaintiff, Summer Zervos, during the 2016 presidential campaign. *See* Zervos v. Trump, 171 A.D.3d 110 (N.Y. App. Div. 2019), *dismissed as moot*, 166 N.E. 3d 1059 (N.Y. 2021). President Trump moved to dismiss Zervos's complaint on immunity-based grounds, contending that *Jones* did not govern state-court suits and that the Supremacy Clause of Article VI prohibited state courts from in any way interfering with the day-to-day operations of a sitting President. *Id.* at 114. Ultimately, the trial court denied the motion, and an intermediate-level appellate court affirmed the denial, with both courts concluding that *Clinton v. Jones* did apply and the Supremacy Clause "does not deprive a state court of its power and authority to decide this case." *Id.* at 128. Was that the right result? As for the New York courts' reading of *Jones*, the bottom-line conclusion seems tenuous: True, the Supreme Court in *Jones* did not specifically decide whether the President might enjoy a more robust immunity in state-court litigation, but Justice Stevens's opinion not so subtly highlighted a few reasons why it might make sense to apply enhanced presidential protections in state-court proceedings. *See Jones*, 420 U.S. at 691. On the other hand, the Court's more recent decision in *Vance*, which rejected a categorical rule against state-level criminal investigations of the President's personal conduct, *see Vance*, 140 S. Ct. at 2425, might serve to validate (albeit after the fact) the New York courts' handling of the *Zervos* case. *See supra* Section 33.A.2.a. In particular, if concerns about stigmatization and time-consuming burdens are not enough to justify a categorical constitutional prohibition on state-level criminal investigations involving the President, then perhaps the same should be true when it comes to the generally less stigmatizing and arguably less burdensome business of a state-level civil lawsuit.

litigation for non-official actions while still serving in office by in effect putting to work a form of less-restrictive-alternatives analysis. In particular, he found that allowing private suits against a sitting President to proceed posed no great danger to the separation of powers because district courts already had, and could readily and adaptively exercise, authority to mitigate any distinct burdens that litigation might place on the executive branch.[136] Justice Breyer, who concurred only in the judgment, greeted this analysis with skepticism. "[P]redicting the future is difficult," he observed, and "ordinary case-management principles" might not be "sufficient to deal with private civil lawsuits for damages unless supplemented with a constitutionally based requirement."[137] Because individual district-court judges were not infallible, he reasoned, they might sometimes issue rulings that "pose[d] a significant threat to the President's official functions."[138] Justice Breyer thus would have established a rule offering broader protection to Presidents-turned-defendants, although he did not identify in detail just what that rule would be.[139]

C. CRIMINAL PROSECUTIONS AGAINST THE PRESIDENT

One last question looms over any inquiry into the checks-and-balances relationship between the President and the federal and state courts: Can a sitting President be made subject to a criminal prosecution?[140] No court has ever rendered a direct judgment on this issue, as no sitting President in U.S. history has ever been indicted on criminal charges. To be sure, a grand jury named President Nixon

---

136 Justice Stevens also made clear that Congress could confer on the President a statutory immunity from personal-capacity suits while in office. *Jones*, 420 U.S. at 709 (noting that the case's holding "raises no barrier to a statutory response").

137 *Id.* at 723–24 (Breyer, J., concurring in the judgment). Justice Breyer might here have added that forum-shopping plaintiffs would try to steer litigation to districts predominated by judges who liked to push cases forward, who might be disinclined to accommodate Presidents in general, or who might have an axe to grind with the particular President named as a defendant.

138 *Id.* at 723.

139 *Id.* at 710–11 (adverting to a "principle that forbids a federal judge . . . to interfere with the President's discharge of his public duties," while acknowledging that "this case does not require us now to apply the principle specifically, thereby delineating its contours").

140 Notably, this question remains open only with respect to the President specifically, and not with respect to executive officials more broadly, as these latter officials have never been understood to enjoy even a temporary immunity from criminal prosecution. *See* Memorandum from Randolph D. Moss, Assistant Attorney General, Office of Legal Counsel, *A Sitting President's Amenability to Indictment and Criminal Prosecution*, 24 OP. O.L.C. 222, 225 (2000) [hereinafter "Moss Memo"] (noting that "[t]he constitutional practice since the Founding . . . has been to prosecute and even imprison civil officers other than the President while they were still in office and prior to their impeachment").

as an unindicted co-conspirator in the Watergate case,[141] and the district attorney's subpoena in *Vance* came in the context of an ongoing criminal investigation connected up with the activities of a then-sitting President.[142] In neither case, however, was a President brought before a court on formal criminal charges.

In the face of this judicial silence, the U.S. Department of Justice has long espoused the position that it lacks the constitutional authority to secure the indictment of a sitting President. The rationale for this position was set forth most recently in a 2000 memorandum opinion issued by the department's Office of Legal Counsel, which concluded that a criminal indictment would " 'prevent the executive from accomplishing its constitutional functions' " and would not " 'be justified by an overriding need' to promote countervailing and legitimate government objectives."[143] More specifically, the memo highlighted three specific ways in which a criminal prosecution might interfere with the President's constitutional function: (1) it could result in a prison sentence, "which would make it physically impossible for the President to carry out his duties"; (2) it could impose a stigma that "compromise[s] the President's ability to fulfill his constitutionally contemplated leadership role"; and (3) it could create "mental and physical burdens," thus "severely hamper[ing] the President's performance of his official duties."[144] At the same time, the memo acknowledged the "important national interest in ensuring that no person—including the President—is above the law."[145] But it concluded that this

---

141 *See Nixon*, 418 U.S. at 687.

142 *See Vance*, 140 S. Ct. at 2420.

143 *See* Moss Memo, *supra* note 140, at 224 (quoting Memorandum from Robert G. Dixon, Jr., Assistant Attorney General, Office of Legal Counsel, *Amenability of the President, Vice President and Other Civil Officers to Federal Criminal Prosecution While in Office* (Sept. 24, 1973) [hereinafter "Dixon Memo"]). In setting forth this position, the OLC rejected a textual argument that has sometimes been made on behalf of a sitting President's immunity from criminal prosecution. That argument stems from the text of the Impeachment Clause of Article I, section 3, which provides that a party convicted in an impeachment proceeding "shall nevertheless be liable and subject to Indictment, Trial, Judgment and Punishment." U.S. CONST. art. I, § 3, cl. 7. That language might imply a temporary bar on criminal proceedings against the President by suggesting that such proceedings may take place *only after* the President has been impeached and removed for the relevant misconduct. *Cf. Vance*, 140 S. Ct. at 2444 (Alito, J., dissenting) (noting that the "plain implication" of this language "is that criminal prosecution, like removal from the Presidency and disqualification from other offices, is a consequence that can come about only after the Senate's judgment, not during or prior to the Senate trial"). The OLC, however, has declined to read the Impeachment Clause in this way, reasoning instead that its purpose was "to signify only that prior conviction in the Senate would not constitute a bar to subsequent prosecution" and "not that prosecution of a person subject to impeachment could occur only after conviction in the Senate." Moss Memo, *supra* note 140, at 224 (citing Dixon Memo, *supra*, at 2–3).

144 Moss Memo, *supra* note 140, at 246.

145 *Id.* at 255.

interest would be only partially disserved by a constitutional immunity rule, given that a prosecution for criminal misconduct could still occur "once the President's term is over or he is otherwise removed from office by resignation or impeachment."[146] To the obvious rebuttal that delaying prosecution could diminish the likelihood of conviction—because, for instance, a statute of limitations might run or because inculpatory evidence might disappear—the memo offered the response that these problems were manageable[147] and in any event involved risks worth accepting for the sake of avoiding the "overwhelming cost and substantial interference with the functioning of an entire branch of government."[148]

Not surprisingly, the OLC's analysis has triggered no small number of critiques.[149] For example, the OLC's stated concerns about

---

[146] *Id.*

[147] Courts, for instance, could recognize an equitable tolling of the statute-of-limitations period for a former-President defendant who was immune from suit while in office. *See id.* at 256 n.33. *But see* Kevin Foley, Comment, *Availability of Tolling in a Presidential Prosecution*, 168 U. PA. L. REV. 1789, 1828 (2020) (raising questions about courts' ability to "adopt a novel tolling rule" to address delayed presidential prosecutions and advocating for the use of sealed indictments and the enactment of explicit statutory tolling rules). As for the potential loss of evidence, that risk might be managed by allowing a grand jury to "continue to gather evidence throughout the period of immunity." *Id.* at 257 n.36; *see also id.* (noting that "the media and even Congress (through its own investigatory powers)" might manage to "pursue, collect and preserve evidence as well").

[148] Moss Memo, *supra* note 140, at 226. Although OLC's position is not binding on state prosecutors, the logic of the memo would seem to imply that the President should enjoy a similar immunity from indictment and prosecution in *state* courts. Indeed, given the special federalism-based concerns that state indictments/prosecutions might raise, even opponents of the OLC position might sensibly entertain something of a middle-ground position, according to which federal-court criminal indictments are permissible, but state-court criminal indictments are not, during the term of presidential service. Drawing such a strong distinction between federal and state prosecutions, however, might stand in tension with *Vance*, in which the Court refused to recognize a full-scale presidential immunity against state-based *investigative requests* (having earlier recognized no such immunity from such requests at the federal level) and instead suggested that federalism-based objections to these requests could be handled on a case-by-case basis. *Vance*, 140 S. Ct. at 2430.

[149] *See, e.g.*, Laurence Tribe, *Yes, the Constitution Allows Indictment of the President*, LAWFARE (Dec. 20, 2018), https://www.lawfareblog.com/yes-constitution-allows-indictment-president; Deborah Ramirez & Greer Clem, *Fortifying the Rule of Law: Filling the Gaps Revealed by the Mueller Report and Impeachment Proceedings*, 13 NE. U. L. REV. 1, 21–26 (2021); Ediberto Roman, Melissa Gonzales & Dianet Torres, *Collusion, Obstruction of Justice, and Impeachment*, 45 J. LEGIS. 9, 38–45 (2019); Daniel J. Hemel & Eric A. Posner, *Presidential Obstruction of Justice*, 106 CAL. L. REV. 1277, 1328–30 (2018) (noting that "the OLC opinions are open to question" in part because "[b]oth opinions were issued from the executive branch at a time that it was led by a president who was being threatened with impeachment or had recently been impeached"); Benjamin G. Davis, *United or Untied: On Confronting Presidential Criminality in the Savage Wars of Peace*, 84 TENN. L. REV. 671 (2017); *see also* Eric M. Freedman, *Achieving Political Adulthood*, 2 NEXUS J. OP. 67, 84 (1997) (arguing, albeit prior to publication of the 2000 OLC Memo, that Presidents are not immune from criminal prosecution). For general defenses of the position espoused by the OLC Memo

the stigmatizing effects of criminal prosecutions are not easy to reconcile with the Justice Department's longstanding practice of publicly investigating criminal conduct that places Presidents and their associates in a negative light.[150] In addition, the OLC's worries about the distracting effects of criminal proceedings stand in tension with the Court's willingness in *Jones* to expose sitting Presidents to the potentially distracting and time-consuming ordeal of confronting personal-conduct civil suits brought by private plaintiffs all over the country.[151] Finally, to the extent that the OLC's position derives from concerns about the absurd spectacle of a President overseeing the nation from a prison cell, that posited problem seems overstated. For one thing, a President might resign, be removed (via impeachment), or be declared unable to govern within the meaning of the Twenty-fifth Amendment,[152] thus allowing for the discontinuance of an incarcerated President's Article II authority.[153] In addition, courts themselves might sidestep the problem by recognizing a temporary immunity from *criminal punishment* during a President's term,

---

(but not necessarily the reasoning of the memo itself), see, for example, Akhil Reed Amar, *On Prosecuting Presidents*, 27 HOFSTRA L. REV. 671, 671 (1999); Keith King, *Indicting the President: Can A Sitting President Be Criminally Indicted?*, 30 SW. U. L. REV. 417, 418 (2001); and Philip Bobbit, *Indicting and Prosecuting a Sitting President*, LAWFARE (January 14, 2019), https://www.lawfareblog.com/indicting-and-prosecuting-sitting-president.

150 *Cf.* Bob Bauer, *What Tuesday's Post Story Reveals About the Absurd OLC Opinions Protecting a President from Indictment—and Mueller's Reading of His Authority*, LAWFARE (Apr. 5, 2018), https://www.lawfareblog.com/what-tuesdays-post-story-reveals-about-absurd-olc-opinions-protecting-president-indictmen-and (noting an inconsistency between (a) Special Counsel Robert Mueller's willingness to issue a report with stigmatizing information about President Trump and (b) the Justice Department's long-stated concern that a prosecution of a sitting President would have stigmatizing effects).

151 *See Jones*, 520 U.S. at 702 (casting doubt on the idea "that interactions between the Judicial Branch and the Executive, even quite burdensome interactions, necessarily rise to the level of constitutionally forbidden impairment of the Executive's ability to perform its constitutionally mandated functions"). To be sure, one might contend, along with the OLC memo, that the "burdens of responding to [criminal] charges are different in kind and far greater in degree than those of responding to civil litigation." Moss Memo, *supra* note 140, at 251. Even if true, however, it is by no means clear that the *cumulative* burden of responding to multiple civil suits around the country would not exceed in magnitude the burden of responding to a single, criminal prosecution already subject to heightened procedural safeguards. From that perspective, the Court's refusal to recognize an absolute immunity rule in *Jones* stands in tension with OLC's position that the distracting effects of a criminal prosecution militate in favor of a temporary presidential immunity from criminal prosecution.

152 *See supra* Section 32.B.

153 *See, e.g.*, Freedman, *supra* note 149, at 79–81 (raising the Twenty-fifth Amendment possibility). *But see* Akhil Reed Amar, *On Impeaching Presidents*, 28 HOFSTRA L. REV. 291, 295–96 (1999) ("If . . . we treated imprisonment as a 'disability' triggering vice-presidential succession under the Twenty-Fifth Amendment, how will we all feel if a later court invalidates the President's conviction on appeal?").

while nonetheless permitting an indictment and trial to move forward.[154]

There is also room to critique the OLC memo from the opposite direction, on the theory that the *temporary immunity* it recognizes is inconsistent with the Court's recognition in *Fitzgerald* of a *permanent* presidential immunity from damages liability for all official acts. In other words, if the Court in *Fitzgerald* was correct in recognizing a no-damages-ever rule as necessary to mitigate chilling effects on the President's decisionmaking processes, then a similarly categorical immunity from criminal process for in-office acts might seem to be likewise warranted. One potential response to this line of analysis would posit that the prospect of criminal liability is in fact less likely to distort the President's decisionmaking than the prospect of civil liability. (Civil actions, after all, can be brought by anyone, whereas federal criminal actions can be brought only by the Department of Justice, which works in a world of "settled legal standards," adheres to "the presumption of regularity in prosecutorial actions," and is subject to the " 'obvious political checks' against initiating a baseless investigation or prosecution of a former President."[155]) Another response, alluded to in the OLC memo itself, rests on the idea that the government interest in "seeking to redress an alleged crime against the public" is weightier than the interest of "a private person seeking compensation for a personal wrong."[156] And a final response might be to question the soundness of *Fitzgerald* itself: In other words, rather than ask whether the OLC's position underprotects the President in light of *Fitzgerald*, one might instead ask whether OLC's hesitance to recognize a permanent presidential immunity from criminal liability should prompt a rethinking, and abandonment, of the absolute and non-temporary civil immunity rule that the Court in *Fitzgerald* endorsed.[157]

---

[154] For example, Professor Laurence Tribe suggests that the President might arrange to have the criminal trial deferred on the condition that "he will not invoke the statute of limitations or accept a pardon to avoid trial and possible conviction once he is no longer in office." Tribe, *supra* note 149.

[155] 2 ROBERT S. MUELLER, III, U.S. DEP'T OF JUSTICE, OFFICE OF SPECIAL COUNSEL, REPORT ON THE INVESTIGATION INTO RUSSIAN INTERFERENCE IN THE 2016 PRESIDENTIAL ELECTION 178–80 (2019) (concluding that *Fitzgerald* did not bar an *investigation* into the question whether certain official acts undertaken by President Trump constituted obstruction of justice under federal criminal law).

[156] *See* Moss Memo, *supra* note 140, at 257.

[157] *Cf.* Akhil Reed Amar & Brian C. Kalt, *The Presidential Privilege Against Prosecution*, 2 NEXUS J. OP. 11, 16 (1997) ("This temporary privilege from prosecution is less of a threat to the rule of [ ] law than the immunity given to Presidents acting in their official capacities. President Nixon said that 'if the President does it, it's not illegal,' and the Supreme Court (in the case of *Nixon v. Fitzgerald*) essentially agreed with him.").

D. LEGISLATIVE IMMUNITY AND THE SPEECH OR DEBATE CLAUSE

While immunity-based protections for the President and other executive-branch officials lack explicit recognition in the constitutional text, a set of protections for *federal legislators* flows directly from the Speech or Debate Clause of Article I, section 6. That clause provides that members of Congress "shall not be questioned in any other Place" for "any Speech or Debate in either House,"[158] and it thus—as the Court put it in *United States v. Brewster*[159]—"protect[s] the integrity of the legislative process by insuring the independence of individual legislators."[160] With that overarching purpose in mind, the Court has held that the clause applies to more than just "words spoken in debate"[161] so as to shelter members of Congress from official investigations into any "legislative acts or the motivation for legislative acts."[162] The Court has further held that the clause guarantees an "absolute immunity from judicial interference" that cannot be overcome by even a compelling showing of prosecutorial need.[163] Hard questions loom, however, as to what sorts of actions qualify as "legislative acts" subject to Speech or Debate Clause protection and who in particular may invoke those protections during the course of judicial proceedings.

1. What Qualifies as a "Legislative Act"?

The Court has left no doubt that the "legislative act" label applies to votes on legislation, participation in floor debates, conduct during committee hearings, preparation of committee reports, and other "things generally done in a session of the House by one of its members in relation to the business before it."[164] On the other hand, the Court has declined to treat as "legislative" in nature "a wide range of legitimate 'errands' performed for constituents, the making of appointments with Government agencies, assistance in securing Government contracts, preparing so-called 'news letters' to constituents, news releases, and speeches delivered outside the

---

158 U.S. CONST. art. I, § 6, cl. 1. That provision further states that members of Congress "shall in all Cases, except Treason, Felony and Breach of the Peace, be privileged from Arrest during their Attendance at the Session of their respective Houses, and in going to and returning from the same." *Id.* For more on this "privilege from arrest," see, e.g., LAURENCE H. TRIBE, AMERICAN CONSTITUTIONAL LAW § 5–20, at 1012–13 (2000).

159 *See* 408 U.S. 501 (1972).

160 *Id.* at 507.

161 Gravel v. United States, 408 U.S. 606, 617 (1972).

162 *Brewster*, 408 U.S. at 512.

163 *See* Eastland v. U.S. Servicemen's Fund, 421 U.S. 491, 509 n.16 (1976).

164 Kilbourn v. Thompson, 103 U.S. 168, 204 (1880).

Congress."[165] Generally speaking, that is, the Court has held that speech-or-debate protections do not apply in connection with *all* actions that federal legislators undertake, including in their official capacities.[166] Rather, those protections cover only conduct that constitutes "an integral part of the deliberative and communicative processes by which Members participate in committee and House proceedings with respect to the consideration and passage or rejection of proposed legislation or with respect to other matters which the Constitution places within the jurisdiction of either House."[167]

Although this formulation has a functionalist quality, its on-the-ground application can yield seemingly formalist results.[168] Consider, for instance, the Court's ruling in *Gravel v. United States*,[169] which stemmed from a criminal investigation of Alaska Senator Mike Gravel's efforts to reveal the contents of the then-classified "Pentagon Papers." Gravel disclosed this classified material in two separate ways: first, by reading portions of it into the record during a Senate subcommittee hearing, and second, by having the same material turned over to a private publisher.[170] This conduct triggered a series of grand-jury subpoenas, which Senator Gravel sought to quash on Speech or Debate Clause grounds. The Court agreed with Gravel that the clause shielded his conduct at the subcommittee hearing.[171] It refused, however, to extend the same protection to his communications with the private publisher,[172] reasoning that those communications were not "part and parcel of the legislative process."[173] It may well have been true, as Justice Brennan observed in dissent, that Gravel's actions reflected the valid (if not vital) exercise of "the legislator's duty to inform the public about matters

---

[165] *Brewster*, 408 U.S. at 512.

[166] *See also* United States v. Helstoski, 442 U.S. 477, 489 (1979) (distinguishing between legislative acts, on the one hand, which are covered by the Speech or Debate Clause, and "[p]romises by a Member to perform [such acts] in the future," which are not).

[167] *Gravel*, 408 U.S. at 625.

[168] *See* James J. Brudney, *Congressional Accountability and Denial: Speech or Debate Clause and Conflict of Interest Challenges to Unionization of Congressional Employees*, 36 HARV. J. ON LEGIS. 1, 4 (1999) (noting that "the Supreme Court's precedents since 1970 have created a somewhat arbitrary but ultimately defensible distinction between legislating and important predicates or accompaniments to legislating").

[169] 408 U.S. 606 (1972).

[170] *Id.* at 609–10.

[171] *Id.* at 616 ("We have no doubt that Senator Gravel may not be made to answer—either in terms of questions or in terms of defending himself from prosecution—for the events that occurred at the subcommittee meeting.").

[172] *Id.* at 622.

[173] *Id.* at 625–26.

affecting the administration of government."[174] For the majority, however, that fact had no bearing on the outcome of the case because the Speech or Debate Clause's purpose was solely to promote the "due functioning of the legislative process" itself.[175]

A fine-grained distinction between legislative and non-legislative acts also drove the Court's decision in *Hutchinson v. Proxmire*.[176] Ronald Hutchinson, a research scientist, sued Senator William Proxmire for defamation, claiming that he had made false statements about Hutchinson's government-funded study of primate behavior. The allegedly defamatory comments—which focused on claimed problems of wasteful government spending—first appeared in a speech prepared by Senator Proxmire for delivery to the Senate, which later was published in the Congressional Record.[177] Senator Proxmire, however, did not stop there; he also reprinted the speech in a press release and in newsletters distributed by his office.[178] In rejecting Proxmire's attempt to dismiss Hutchinson's suit on speech-or-debate grounds, Chief Justice Burger, joined by seven of his colleagues, acknowledged that the clause would have protected the Senator if the allegedly defamatory statements had been submitted only to the Senate itself.[179] But, according to the Chief Justice, Proxmire's outside-the-Senate distribution of his speech was not "essential to the deliberations of the Senate" and thus fell beyond the reach of speech-and-debate immunity.[180] That was true, moreover, even if newsletters and press releases were generally more effective than Senate-floor soliloquys at drawing public attention to problems

---

[174] *Id.* at 649 (Brennan, J., dissenting).

[175] *Id.* at 625 (quoting United States v. Johnson, 383 U.S. 169, 172 (1966)). Similarly, in *United States v. Brewster*, 408 U.S. 501 (1972), the Court denied speech-or-debate immunity to a Senator charged with accepting a bribe in exchange for voting in favor of pending legislation. *Id.* at 503. Critical to that ruling was the Court's recognition that, while the vote itself was a "legislative act" entitled to speech-or-debate immunity, the criminal charges covered only the *acceptance* of the bribe and not "performance of the illegal promise." *Id.* at 526. In other words, the acceptance of a bribe was "obviously . . . no part of the legislative process or function," and therefore the government could bring charges based on that conduct. *Id.* at 526. The governing principle, according to the Court, is that the clause does "not prohibit inquiry into activities that are casually or incidentally related to legislative affairs but not a part of the legislative process itself." *Id.* at 528.

[176] 443 U.S. 111 (1979).

[177] It is not clear whether Proxmire ever delivered the speech, but it was uncontested that he put the speech into the Congressional Record, and the Court was, for purposes of the case, willing to "assume, without deciding, that a speech printed in the Congressional Record carries immunity under the Speech or Debate Clause as though delivered on the floor." *Id.* at 116 n.3.

[178] *Id.* at 116–17.

[179] *Id.* at 130 (noting that "[a] Speech by Proxmire in the Senate would be wholly immune").

[180] *Id.* at 130 (internal quotations omitted) (quoting *Gravel*, 408 U.S. at 625).

said to warrant a legislative response.[181] As "[v]aluable and desirable" as a lawmaker's public discussion of perceived government mismanagement might be, it was simply "not a part of the legislative function or the deliberations that make up the legislative process."[182]

2. Who May Invoke Speech-or-Debate Protections?

As for the question of *who* is shielded by clause's protections, the Court's opinion in *Gravel* again furnishes key guidance. In that case, government prosecutors argued that, whether or not the Speech or Debate Clause protected Senator Gravel himself, it did not bar the issuance of subpoenas to the Senator's legislative aides.[183] The Court, however, rejected this position. Emphasizing that "the complexities of the modern legislative process" make it "literally impossible" for "Members of Congress to perform their legislative tasks without the help of aides and assistants,"[184] the Court instead held that "a Member and his aide are to be 'treated as one' " for Speech or Debate Clause purposes.[185] That conclusion made sense, the Court continued, in light of "the central role of the Speech or Debate Clause," which is to "prevent intimidation of legislators by the Executive and accountability before a possibly hostile judiciary."[186]

---

181 *Id.* at 132.

182 *Id.* at 133. The Court has not rendered any major speech-or-debate decisions since *Hutchinson*, a result that Professor Michael Shenkman attributes to the "bright line regime" that decision helped to establish. Michael L. Shenkman, *Talking About Speech or Debate: Revisiting Legislative Immunity*, 32 YALE L. & POL'Y REV. 351, 383–84 (2014) (suggesting that the formalistic nature of the legislative/non-legislative distinction leaves "no room . . . for lower-court litigation to map out the borders of immunity on the basis of experience"). *But see* United States v. Menendez, 831 F.3d 155, 166–67 (3d Cir. 2016) (laying out a two-part test for determining whether an act qualifies as "legislative" under modern-day Speech or Debate Clause doctrine, according to which "manifestly legislative acts" enjoy full speech-or-debate protection, even if in pursuit of an "unworthy purpose," while "ambiguously legislative acts" may or may not qualify for speech-or-debate protection depending on their underlying "content, purpose, and motive").

183 *Gravel*, 408 U.S. at 616. The government contended that this result was dictated by the express terms of the clause because it specifies, and specifies only, that "Senators and Representatives" have immunity for their speech-or-debate-related activities. *Id.* (quoting U.S. CONST. art. I, § 6, cl. 1).

184 *Id.* at 616.

185 *Id.* (quoting United States v. Doe, 455 F.2d 753, 761 (1st Cir. 1972)).

186 *Id.* at 617. Reaching this result required the Court to distinguish away prior rulings in which it had denied speech-or-debate immunity to non-Members of Congress. *See, e.g.*, *Kilbourn*, 103 U.S. at 168 (holding that the Speech or Debate Clause did not bar the plaintiff from seeking damages from the House Sergeant-at-Arms for an arrest carried out pursuant to an allegedly unlawful legislative contempt order); Dombrowski v. Eastland, 387 U.S. 82, 84-85 (1967) (holding that the Speech or Debate Clause did not shield a lawyer for a Senate subcommittee from questioning about his collaboration with state officials to execute an allegedly unlawful seizure of records subject to a legislative subpoena); Powell v. McCormack, 395 U.S. 486, 501-06 (1969) (holding that the Speech or Debate Clause did not bar a judicial challenge to

That role of the clause, the Court insisted, would be severely compromised if government actors were free to throw the book at anyone who worked on Senators' and Representatives' behalf. The Court was thus willing to accommodate a modest departure from the clause's literal text in order to vindicate what it saw as the clause's key, overarching purpose.[187]

efforts by the Sergeant at Arms, the Clerk of the House, the Doorkeeper, and other legislative officials to enforce the House's unlawful order to prevent the seating of a Representative-elect). To do so, it emphasized that those earlier cases had turned not on any determination that "immunity was unavailable to congressional or committee employees because they were not Representatives or Senators," but rather on the conclusion that the underlying *conduct* was itself not entitled to speech-or-debate protection. *Gravel*, 408 U.S. at 620. Put differently, because those cases had involved matters other than the formulation of legislative acts, they posed no direct "threat to legislative independence" and therefore enjoyed no constitutional immunity from review by the other branches. *Id.* at 621.

[187] *See* U.S. CONST. art. I, § 6, cl. 1 (providing that "*Senators and Representatives* . . . shall not be questioned" for "any Speech or Debate in either House" (emphasis added)).

Chapter 34

THE POWER OF JUDICIAL REVIEW

Analysis

As defined by Article III, section 2, the "judicial power of the United States" includes the power to decide "all cases . . . arising under *this Constitution* . . . ."[1] This language leaves no doubt that the federal judiciary (and the Supreme Court in particular) has the authority to adjudicate disputes that raise questions of constitutional law. But what does that mean? Of particular significance, to what extent may the federal judiciary refuse to apply laws enacted by democratically elected legislatures, including acts of Congress, on the ground that those laws conflict with the judiciary's own understanding of the Constitution's commands? No one doubts that every government actor, including Congress, is duty-bound not to violate the Constitution. But recognizing this axiom gives rise to a question of foundational significance: *Who* gets to decide whether a constitutional violation has occurred? More specifically, if elected federal lawmakers deem their own enactment to comport with the Constitution's requirements, may unelected federal judges nonetheless cast that judgment aside and declare the enactment a nullity?

Whether courts have this power of "judicial review" is a matter of profound structural significance. After all, to the extent that judges—particularly members of the Supreme Court—can wield this power, they occupy a position in which their own constitutional views will take precedence over those of other institutional actors who are more directly accountable to the public at large. Two distinct features of the U.S. Constitution magnify the significance of this structural choice. First, the Constitution is full of vague and uncertain

---

1 U.S. CONST. art. III, § 2 (emphasis added).

terminology, thus giving rise to a range of value-laden interpretive questions on which reasonable people often disagree. (What is "due process of law"? When do government actions constitute "unreasonable searches and seizures"? What sorts of enactments qualify as "necessary and proper" to carry into execution Congress's powers? And so on.) Second, the supermajority voting requirements imposed by Article V make it nearly impossible for "We the People" to respond to unwanted rulings of the Court by way of the adoption of curative constitutional amendments.[2] As a result, a robust power of judicial review implies a largely—though, as we will see, not totally—unchecked judicial authority to dictate the substance of constitutional law, and to do so by applying a text that leaves open much room for discretionary judgment.

This chapter addresses the federal courts' power of judicial review. We begin with federal-court review of congressional enactments, giving special attention to: (1) the Marshall Court's foundational defense of the practice in *Marbury v. Madison*;[3] (2) the constitutional mechanisms through which the Court's power of judicial review is made subject to political control; and (3) the extent to which the federal judiciary's interpretations of the Constitution are binding on other government actors. We then turn to the federal courts' review-related powers over state-level decisions, focusing in particular on landmark rulings that established the Court's authority to exercise appellate jurisdiction over state courts' federal-law decisions.

A. *MARBURY* AND ITS LEGACY

1. *Marbury v. Madison*—Background Circumstances

Although the Constitution's drafters did not expressly endorse a power of judicial review, many of them anticipated that the federal courts would scrutinize the constitutionality of congressional acts.

---

[2] *Id.* art. V. In general, an amendment must secure the support of at least a two-thirds majority in each of House of Congress, plus ratification by at least three quarters of the states by way of (depending on Congress's choice) votes of the state legislatures or specially called state ratification conventions. *Id.* Alternatively, Article V requires Congress, "on the Application of the Legislatures of two thirds of the several States," to "call a Convention for proposing Amendments," while still requiring that any amendments proposed by such a convention receive the assent of at least three quarters of the states. *Id.* Given these rules, and in particular the three-fourths ratification requirement, it is not difficult to see why, as Professor Eric Posner has observed, "no serious political movements that seek constitutional amendment have existed in years." *See* Eric Posner, *The U.S. Constitution Is Impossible to Amend*, SLATE (May 5, 2014), https://slate.com/news-and-politics/2014/05/amending-the-constitution-is-much-too-hard-blame-the-founders.html.

[3] 5 U.S. (1 Cranch.) 137 (1803).

Several delegates at the Philadelphia Convention voiced this expectation,[4] and the notion received occasional public airings during the ratification debates as well.[5] Of particular prominence was (and still is) Alexander Hamilton's defense of the practice in *The Federalist No. 78*, which emphasized the intended role of the courts as "bulwarks of a limited constitution against legislative encroachments."[6] No less telling was the observation of the Antifederalist writer, Brutus, who posited that, under the system proposed by the Framers, "the judgment of the judicial [branch], on the constitution, will become the rule to guide the legislature in their construction of their powers."[7] These assertions, to be sure, provoked some opposition, and not all of the delegates spoke out in favor of a robust judicial review power.[8] Nevertheless, as Professor Michael Klarman has noted, while "the concept of judicial review was novel and controversial in 1787," the "practice became far less controversial during the 1790s,"[9] and several of the Court's earliest decisions seemed to take it for granted.[10] Despite these developments, it was

---

4 *See* Matthew P. Harrington, *Judicial Review Before John Marshall*, 72 GEO. WASH. L. REV. 51, 91 (2003) (noting that "most of those attending the Philadelphia Convention expected that some type of judicial review would be necessary to serve as a limit on legislative action").

5 *See* Mark A. Graber, *Establishing Judicial Review:* Marbury *and the Judicial Act of 1789*, 38 TULSA L. REV. 609, 633 (2003) (observing that "Federalists and anti-Federalists during the ratification debates agreed that federal courts were authorized to declare laws unconstitutional").

6 *See* THE FEDERALIST NO. 78 (Hamilton). The Constitution, Hamilton maintained, "must be regarded by the judges, as a fundamental law," and "[i]t therefore belongs to them to ascertain its meaning." *Id.* Accordingly, "whenever a particular statute contravenes the Constitution, it will be the duty of the judicial tribunals to adhere to the latter and disregard the former." *Id.*

7 Brutus XII, N.Y. J., Mar. 20, 1788, *reprinted in* 2 STORING, THE COMPLETE ANTI-FEDERALIST 423–24 (Herbert J. Storing, ed., 1981).

8 *See* Michael J. Klarman, *How Great Were the "Great" Marshall Court Decisions?*, 87 VA. L. REV. 1111, 1114–15 (2001) (noting that, at the Philadelphia Convention, "some delegates spoke in favor of judicial review, while others opposed it" and that James Madison, "who played the most critical role in Philadelphia, was genuinely ambivalent about judicial review").

9 *Id.*; *see also id.* at 1115–16 (noting other developments during this period, including certain decisions from lower federal courts that invalidated state-level debtor-relief statutes and the high-profile national debate over states' powers to nullify the Alien and Sedition Acts of 1798, during which all sides appeared to take for granted the baseline power of the judiciary to declare federal laws unconstitutional).

10 In *Hayburn's Case*, 2 U.S. (2 Dall.) 408 (1792), for example, several Supreme Court Justices had, while sitting in as circuit justices, declared unconstitutional the federal Invalid Pensions Act of 1792, but the Court itself never issued a formal decision or judgment in the case. In addition, an unreported decision from 1794 appeared to involve the Justices' refusal to sign off on certain official actions taken pursuant to that statute, possibly because of the Justices' earlier-expressed concerns about the statute's constitutionality. *See* United States v. Yale Todd (U.S. 1794), *reported in* United States v. Ferreira, 54 U.S. (13 How.) 40, 52–53 (1851); *see also* Keith E. Whittington, *Judicial Review of Congress Before the Civil War*, 97 GEO. L.J. 1257, 1274 (2009) (documenting judicial and scholarly disagreement on the question whether *Yale Todd* was decided on constitutional or statutory grounds). Even more to the point, the

not until its 1803 decision in *Marbury* that the Court offered a thoroughgoing defense of its authority to strike down acts of Congress on constitutional grounds.

The facts that gave rise to *Marbury* were packed with political tension. President John Adams and his Federalist party had suffered a major defeat in the election of 1800 to then-Vice President Thomas Jefferson and his fellow Jeffersonian Republicans.[11] Following the election but before Jefferson's inauguration, Adams and lame-duck Federalist majorities in both Houses of Congress moved to keep a foothold on power by installing political allies in judicial positions. The most brazen maneuver involved enactment of the Judiciary Act of 1801, which (among other things) established sixteen federal circuit-court judgeships for the soon-to-be-replaced President to fill.[12] The outgoing Federalists exploited other opportunities as well. Of the greatest enduring significance was the post-election appointment and confirmation of John Marshall, who was then serving as President Adams's Secretary of State, as Chief Justice of the United States.[13]

Of immediate relevance to *Marbury*, Congress in February 1801 authorized President Adams to nominate a slate of "justices of the peace" for the District of Columbia, with each appointed officer to

---

Court in 1796 upheld a federal carriage tax against constitutional attack, without voicing any doubt about its power to strike down federal statutes. *Hylton v. United States*, 3 U.S. (3 Dall.) 171 (1796); *see also* Klarman, *supra* note 8, at 1115 (noting that "several of the Justices [in *Hylton*] clearly assumed that they had the power to invalidate an unconstitutional federal statute"). Other cases from this time period evidenced a similar understanding. *See, e.g.*, Penhallow v. Doane's Administrators, 3 U.S. (3 Dall.) 54 (1795) (holding that the pre-constitutional Confederation Congress had acted within the scope of its powers under the Articles of Confederation in establishing a federal tribunal with jurisdiction to hear appeals from certain types of state-level admiralty proceedings); United States v. La Vengeance, 3 U.S. (3 Dall.) 297 (1796) (entertaining but rejecting an argument that the Sixth Amendment's jury-trial guarantee barred Congress from authorizing courts to exercise admiralty jurisdiction over certain types of forfeiture proceedings); Mossman v. Higginson, 4 U.S. (4 Dall.) 12 (1800) (refusing to allow an exercise of jurisdiction by a circuit court where the asserted jurisdiction was authorized by the Judiciary Act of 1789 but clearly precluded by the text of Article III).

[11] It was not in fact clear that Jefferson had prevailed over his supposed running mate, Aaron Burr, until months after the election. *See generally* EDWARD J. LARSON, A MAGNIFICENT CATASTROPHE: THE TUMULTUOUS ELECTION OF 1800, AMERICA'S FIRST PRESIDENTIAL CAMPAIGN (2007). But it was immediately apparent that, regardless of how that conflict would be resolved, the Federalists would soon be out of power.

[12] *See* Act. of Feb. 13, 1801, ch. 4, 2 Stat. 89. In a related move, Congress reduced the size of the Supreme Court, upon the next vacancy, from six Justices to five, thus depriving Jefferson of the likely future opportunity to replace Justice William Cushing, who was ill at the time and thus likely soon to leave the Court. *See* Act of Feb. 27, 1801, ch. 15, 2 Stat. 107; *see also* William W. Van Alstyne, *A Critical Guide to* Marbury v. Madison, 1969 DUKE L.J. 1, 4 (discussing this statutory reform).

[13] *See* Kathryn Turner, *The Appointment of Chief Justice Marshall*, 18 WM. & MARY Q. 143 (1960).

serve for five years.[14] The lame-duck Federalist Senate confirmed all of the nominees for these positions by March 3, 1801, the final full day of the Adams presidency. But a last-minute mix-up at the State Department prevented some of these appointments from taking effect. Under then-existing practice, the Secretary of State had the responsibility to deliver to each appointee a formal "commission" bearing the President's signature and the "Great Seal" of the United States. But not all the relevant commissions—even though they had been signed and sealed—made their way into the intended recipients' hands before Thomas Jefferson took the oath of office.[15] Normally, this lapse would have been easily correctible. But because it occurred on the literal eve of President Jefferson's inauguration, the misstep was fraught with consequence. By the time anyone realized what had happened, a new administration was in charge, and President Jefferson instructed his own Secretary of State, James Madison, to withhold a number of the undelivered commissions, thus blocking some justice-of-the-peace appointees—including William Marbury—from assuming their designated positions.[16]

Marbury turned to the Supreme Court for help.[17] Invoking the Court's original jurisdiction, he claimed that the signing and sealing of his commission entitled him to a "writ of mandamus" ordering Secretary Madison to finalize the document's delivery.[18] President Jefferson, however, wanted nothing to do with the suit, and even his administration's minimal participation in it "came grudgingly."[19] Most notably, Secretary Madison declined even to appear through counsel, and the Court thus never received any written or oral

---

14 *See* Act of Feb. 27, 1801, ch. 12, 2 Stat. 103.

15 Fault for the error likely lies with Marshall's brother James, who, though tasked with delivering all of the commissions, ended up leaving some of them behind. *See* Susan Low Bloch, *The* Marbury *Mystery: Why Did William Marbury Sue in the Supreme Court?*, 18 CONST. COMMENT. 607, 624 (2002). But (John) Marshall himself also bears some blame, given that he could have delivered (but ultimately failed to deliver) the commissions the following morning, as he himself would subsequently admit. *See* Letter from John Marshall to James M. Marshall (March 18, 1801), *in* LIBRARY OF CONGRESS: MARSHALL PAPERS ("I should . . . have sent out the commissions which had been signd & seald but for the extreme hurry of the time & the absence of Mr. Wagner who had been called on by the President to act as his private Secretary."), *quoted* in Bloch, *supra*, at 625; *see also id. at* 625–26 (raising the possibility that Marshall "knowingly withheld delivery of some commissions to set the stage for this profoundly important case").

16 *See* JOEL RICHARD PAUL, WITHOUT PRECEDENT: CHIEF JUSTICE JOHN MARSHALL AND HIS TIMES 244 (2018).

17 *See Marbury*, 5 U.S. at 137. Three other justice-of-the-peace appointees, who likewise had not received their commissions, joined in the suit as well. *See id.*

18 *See id.*

19 James M. O'Fallon, *Marbury*, 44 STAN. L. REV. 219, 242 (1992) (noting, among other things, the "reluctant and partial testimony of State Department officials" as well as "the Senate's refusal to provide a copy of its journal showing consent to [Marbury's] appointment").

argument in support of the administration's legal position in the case.[20] These events reflected more than partisan bickering. They pointed to the ominous possibility that Madison (at Jefferson's behest) would ignore any order the Justices might issue, thus provoking an interbranch showdown that the Court was almost certain to lose.[21] The Justices thus found themselves between a rock and a hard place. On the one hand, they could rule in favor of Secretary Madison, despite the administration's contemptuous flouting of the Court's processes, and thus publicly capitulate to Jefferson and his political allies. On the other hand, the Justices could take a firm stand against the administration, order delivery of the disputed commission, and then watch helplessly—again with no small measure of authority-diminishing embarrassment—as the Court's order was ignored.[22]

2. *Marbury v. Madison*—Preliminary Issues

Ultimately, the Court in *Marbury* managed to dodge this dilemma by crafting a resolution of the case that both avoided a direct conflict with the Jeffersonian Republicans and helped to lay the groundwork for later exercises of far-reaching judicial authority. The basic strategy was to dismiss Marbury's suit on jurisdictional grounds, thus avoiding the issuance of a judgment that the executive branch might choose to ignore.[23] On its way to making this jurisdictional ruling, however, the Court—in an opinion authored by Chief Justice Marshall—both faulted the Jefferson administration for its treatment of Marbury and asserted broad institutional authority for the federal judiciary. As for the first point, which concerned the merits of Marbury's claim (and which the Justices quite oddly chose to address given their bottom-line jurisdiction-based dismissal of the action),[24] the Court declared that Secretary

---

20 *See Marbury*, 5 U.S. at 153–54.

21 Madison's nonappearance in *Marbury* was not the only foreboding sign. In March of 1802, the Republican-controlled Congress had repealed the Judiciary Act of 1801, thereby effectively undoing many of Adams's "midnight" appointments. *See* Act of March 8, 1802, ch. 8, 2 Stat. 132; *see also* Van Alstyne, *supra* note 12, at 5. In addition, Congress had passed another law that canceled the Court's upcoming sitting, thus delaying the resolution of both *Marbury* and another case, *Stuart v. Laird*, in which the constitutionality of the 1802 Repeal Act was potentially at issue. *Id.* In short, by the time the Court reconvened to consider both *Marbury* and *Stuart*, several warning shots had already been fired across its bow.

22 *See* ROBERT G. MCCLOSKEY, THE AMERICAN SUPREME COURT 26 (Sanford Levinson rev. ed., 6th ed. 2016). *But see* Louise Weinberg, *Our* Marbury, 89 VA. L. REV. 1235, 1275–77 (2003) (questioning the conventional wisdom that Madison would not have complied with a writ of mandamus issued against him).

23 *See* Farah Peterson, *Expounding the Constitution*, 130 YALE L.J. 2, 49 (2020) (noting that, "as the opinion did not actually command or enjoin any action—as it failed to *do* anything—Jefferson was able to ignore it" (emphasis in original)).

24 *See, e.g.*, Steel Co. v. Citizens for a Better Env't, 523 U.S. 83, 101–02 (1998) ("For a court to pronounce upon the meaning or the constitutionality of a state or

Madison had indeed violated Marbury's "vested" legal rights by withholding delivery of a commission that had already been signed and sealed.[25] In addition, while conceding that the Court could never entertain questions that were "in their nature political, or which are, by the constitution and laws, submitted to the executive,"[26] the Chief Justice insisted that this case presented no such nonjusticiable question because Secretary Madison had breached "a specific duty . . . assigned by law."[27]

These aspects of the Court's opinion were important in and of themselves, particularly insofar as they opened a channel for the issuance of future judgments directed against high-ranking officers of a coordinate branch.[28] But the most enduringly significant aspect of *Marbury* came in the Court's ensuing discussion of the jurisdictional issue, which segued into its discussion of the power of judicial review. As the Court saw things, the jurisdictional problem was this: Section 13 of the Judiciary Act of 1789 (as construed by the Court) authorized original jurisdiction over all mandamus actions, including the one brought by Marbury.[29] But, according to the Court, the Constitution did not support this statutory grant because Article III, section 2 (again, as construed by the Court) limited the Court's original jurisdiction to "[c]ases affecting ambassadors, other public

---

federal law when it has no jurisdiction to do so is, by very definition, for a court to act ultra vires.").

[25] *Marbury*, 5 U.S. at 162.

[26] *Id.* at 170.

[27] *Id.* at 166. The Court also raised, but then rejected, the related suggestion that courts generally lack authority to issue orders against "heads of departments" who routinely deal with the President. According to the Chief Justice, even senior members of a President's administration enjoyed no immunity from suit in cases, like *Marbury*, that did not involve discretionary executive-branch choices or "secrets of the cabinet." *Id.* at 169–70.

[28] Indeed, the Court's suggestion that the executive branch enjoyed no general immunity from judicial process and court-ordered remedies was viewed by many at the time as a matter of even greater consequence than its ruling on the power of judicial review—a power that, as noted earlier, was already widely assumed to exist. *See* Klarman, *supra* note 8, at 1116–17 (noting that "it was these controversial separation-of-powers doctrines, not the pronouncement of the judicial review power, that aroused Jeffersonian anger at the decision and produced threats of retaliation against the Court").

[29] *Marbury*, 5 U.S. at 174. Critics have questioned the Court's construction of this statutory provision, which might alternatively have been read as making clear that the Court could issue the mandamus remedy in cases otherwise properly within its subject-matter jurisdiction. *See, e.g.*, Van Alstyne, *supra* note 4, at 14–16. That Chief Justice Marshall rejected this reading also suggests that, contrary to the modern-day practice of construing statutes to avoid constitutional questions, *see, e.g.*, Ashwander v. TVA, 297 U.S. 288, 345–46 (1936) (Brandeis, J., concurring), he was actively seeking to create a constitutional issue for the Court to decide. *See* Thomas Healy, *The Rise of Unnecessary Constitutional Rulings*, 83 N.C. L. REV. 847, 849 (2005) (noting that Marshall "gave no consideration to the possibility that a narrow construction of the Judiciary Act might have averted the issue of judicial review entirely").

ministers and consuls, and those in which a state shall be a party."[30] (Madison, it was widely agreed, did not qualify as a "public minister" within the meaning of that term, so that the Court's exercise of original jurisdiction could not be alternatively justified on that basis.) Consequently, to determine whether it could adjudicate the case, the Court needed to answer a question "not of an intricacy proportioned to its interest"—namely, "whether an act, repugnant to the constitution, can become the law of the land."[31] Deciding the jurisdictional issue thus boiled down to determining whether courts have the power of judicial review, and the Chief Justice devoted the remainder of his opinion to explaining why he believed that power to exist.

3. *Marbury v. Madison*—the Court's Defense of Judicial Review

Marshall offered no fewer than five different lines of argument in support of the conclusion that federal courts have the power of judicial review. First, the Chief Justice defended the power as flowing naturally from the supreme status of the Constitution.[32] More specifically, he reasoned that courts have no choice but to invalidate unconstitutional laws because the founding charter is the "fundamental and paramount law of the nation," thus rendering it "superior to any ordinary act of the Legislature."[33] Second, Marshall

---

[30] *Marbury*, 5 U.S. at 174 (quoting U.S. CONST. art. III, § 2). In this portion of his analysis, Marshall cited to Article III, section 2 as providing that "the supreme court shall have original jurisdiction in all cases affecting ambassadors, other public ministers and consuls, and those in which a state shall be a party," and that "[i]n all other cases, the supreme court shall have appellate jurisdiction." *Id.* In fact, however, and in language that Marshall would only later make reference to, the latter statement concludes with a potentially game-changing qualifier: "*with such Exceptions, and under such Regulations as the Congress shall make.*" U.S. CONST. art. III, § 2 (emphasis added); *see Marbury*, 5 U.S. at 175. One might thus have construed the text of Article III as establishing a floor for, but not a ceiling on, the Court's original jurisdiction, permitting Congress to add to but not take away from the three categories of original-jurisdiction cases that the Constitution sets forth. *See, e.g.*, Susan Low Bloch & Maeva Marcus, *John Marshall's Selective Use of History in* Marbury, 1986 WIS. L. REV. 301, 320 n.73 ("[T]he framers could have intended that the two specified categories were to be minimum definitions of the Court's original jurisdiction.").

[31] *Marbury*, 5 U.S. at 176.

[32] On this point, Marshall also noted that, "in declaring what shall be the supreme law of the land, the Constitution itself is first mentioned; and not the laws of the United States generally, but those only which shall be made in pursuance of the Constitution, have that rank." *Id.* at 180. That feature of the Constitution's "particular phraseology," he maintained, further supported "the principle . . . that a law repugnant to the Constitution is void; and that courts, as well as other departments, are bound by that instrument." *Id.*

[33] *Id.* at 177–78. Marshall sought to shore up this claim by pointing to absurd-seeming results that would follow from a lack of judicial authority to disregard obviously unconstitutional statutes. *See, e.g.*, *id.* at 179 (asking rhetorically whether courts must "condemn to death" persons prosecuted under an unconstitutional bill of attainder or *ex post facto* law and whether courts must enforce state tariffs that

pointed to the text of Article III, which, by vesting federal courts with the authority to decide "all cases . . . arising under this Constitution,"[34] implied a further power to apply the law of the Constitution to render statutes in opposition to it null and void.[35] Third, Marshall reasoned that federal judges' obligation under Article VI to swear an oath "to support this Constitution"[36] would be a "solemn mockery" if judges were to deem themselves free to ignore the document's terms by enforcing unconstitutional laws.[37] Fourth, Marshall defended judicial review as necessary to the sound operation of the government because Congress would have a "practical and real omnipotence" within the constitutional system if it could alone define the scope of its own power.[38] Finally, Marshall suggested that the power of constitutional review was an intrinsic component of the judicial power itself. It was, after all, "emphatically the province and duty of the judicial department to say what the law is," and "the law" of the Constitution was no less subject to this foundational proposition than any other legal material that the federal courts might happen to confront in processing cases that come before them.[39]

This multi-pronged defense of judicial review has drawn sustained scholarly criticism over the two-plus centuries of *Marbury*'s existence.[40] One recurring critique faults Marshall for failing to consider at all the problems that a system of judicial review creates. To be sure, as he suggested, judicial review might be advantageous insofar as it prevents Congress from transgressing constitutional limits on its own legislative powers. But, according to skeptics, this possible salutary effect comes at the expense of positioning judges to abuse their own powers by disregarding limits on their constitutional authority. Worse yet, whereas power-hungry members of Congress might be voted out of office, power-hungry members of the judiciary, with their Article III guarantees of life

---

obviously violate Article I's Import-Export Clause). As critics have noted, however, these examples at best help to justify a judicial power to invalidate *patently* unconstitutional legislative acts. *See* Klarman, *supra* note 8, at 1121 (suggesting that these examples merely reflected "the prevalent understanding that judicial review authorized invalidation of only obviously unconstitutional laws"). They thus provide little support for the more ambitious proposition that courts should be empowered to disregard Congress's reasonable, good-faith constructions of genuinely ambiguous constitutional language.

[34] U.S. CONST. art. III, § 2.

[35] *Marbury*, 5 U.S. at 178–79.

[36] U.S. CONST. art. VI.

[37] *Marbury*, 5 U.S. at 180.

[38] *Id.* at 178.

[39] *Id.* at 177.

[40] *See, e.g.*, Van Alstyne, *supra* note 12, at 16–29; Klarman, *supra* note 8, at 1117–20.

tenure, can largely avoid accountability for abuses of their authority.[41] When faced, then, with the dilemma of letting a democratically accountable legislature judge the constitutionality of its own statutes or instead letting a democratically unaccountable judiciary make judgments that trump the determinations of those elected officials, one might reasonably conclude, contrary to *Marbury*, that judicial review in fact poses the greater evil.

In addition, several of the Chief Justice's arguments were strikingly weak. His focus on the supremacy of constitutional law was beside the point in that it failed to address the key question of *who*, as between the courts and Congress, should decide whether a legislative act offends the governing principle of constitutional supremacy.[42] Likewise, the argument regarding judicial oath-taking failed to take account of the fact that members of Congress must take their own no-less-solemn oaths "to support this Constitution."[43] Chief Justice Marshall did more directly address the who-should-decide question with his claim about the federal courts' Article III authority to hear cases "arising under" the Constitution, but that argument failed to consider the possibility that the judiciary might have authority to assess the constitutionality of only some government actions—for example, as to whether discrete government searches by low-level executive officials violate the Fourth Amendment—without empowering the courts to second-guess the substantive constitutionality of federal legislation formally enacted by both chambers of Congress and signed by the President.[44] In similar fashion, while the Court had a point about the fox-guarding-the-

---

[41] For a canonical statement of this problem, memorably coined the "counter-majoritarian difficulty," see ALEXANDER M. BICKEL, THE LEAST DANGEROUS BRANCH: THE SUPREME COURT AT THE BAR OF POLITICS, 16–22 (1962).

[42] *See, e.g.*, R. George Wright, *The Distracting Debate Over Judicial Review*, 39 U. MEM. L. REV. 47, 53 (2008) (noting that "much of the argument [in *Marbury*] begs crucial questions regarding disputes among branches as to what the Constitution requires").

[43] *See* U.S. CONST. art. VI (noting that "[t]he Senators and Representatives before mentioned, and the Members of the several State Legislatures, and all executive and judicial Officers, both of the United States and of the several States, shall be bound by Oath or Affirmation, to support this Constitution"). The oath argument thus again sidestepped the key question of who, as between the oath-bound members of the judiciary and their oath-bound counterparts in the federal legislature, should have primacy in evaluating the constitutionality of laws that the legislature enacts. *See* Klarman, *supra* note 8, at 1118.

[44] *See also* Van Alstyne, *supra* note 12, at 27–28 (suggesting that the Article III provision might have been intended to cover constitutional cases "not in the least involv[ing] an Act of Congress," or to "contemplate a limited review of acts of Congress" that was "strictly limited to [the] *procedural* constitutionality of the congressional act"); Klarman, *supra* note 8, at 1118 ("[I]t is easy to think of reasons why the Framers might have created an 'arising under' jurisdiction that would not entail empowering federal courts to invalidate legislation. For example, the Framers might have wanted to license federal courts to check rogue executive officers, but not to invalidate statutes passed by the People's representatives in the legislature.").

henhouse-type dangers of letting Congress determine the scope of its own constitutional authority, the Chief Justice's opinion did not pause to address the flipside concern, noted above, that a Court empowered to invalidate federal laws might also proceed to fix the scope of its own authority in problematically power-aggrandizing ways.

Perhaps the strongest of the arguments in favor of judicial review stems from the idea that the practice inheres in the very nature of the judicial function. It is hard, after all, to disagree with Chief Justice Marshall's assertions that it is "emphatically the province and duty" of judges "to say what the law is" and that "[t]hose who apply the rule to particular cases, must of necessity expound and interpret that rule."[45] One might respond that the Constitution is not the sort of "law" that judges are best-equipped to expound.[46] But that rebuttal is undercut by the Constitution's reference to itself in the Supremacy Clause as a form of "law," as well as its treatment in that clause of "[t]his Constitution," alongside federal statutes and treaties, as kindred components of paramount federal law.[47] If, in short, courts *qua* courts have a distinctive institutional obligation to decide questions of "law," and if the Constitution is a form of "law," then the power of a court to ask whether a statute violates the Constitution should be no more controversial than is, say, its

---

45 *Marbury*, 5 U.S. at 177.

46 Such a rebuttal might indeed borrow from language that Marshall himself subsequently offered in *McCulloch v. Maryland*, 17 U.S. (4 Wheat.) 316, 407 (1819), when he maintained that a constitution's "nature . . . requires that only its great outlines should be marked" and that the document, in order to "be understood by the public," was consciously designed so as *not* to "partake of the prolixity of a legal code." *Id.* at 407; *see also id.* ("[W]e must never forget that it is a constitution we are expounding.").

47 As stated in the Supremacy Clause: "This Constitution, and the Laws of the United States which shall be made in Pursuance thereof; and all Treaties made, or which shall be made, under the Authority of the United States, shall be the supreme Law of the Land." U.S. CONST. art. VI. Article III's unitary commitment of jurisdiction to the federal courts in "all cases" arising under the "this Constitution, the laws of the United States, and Treaties" likewise suggests way that the Judiciary must interpret the Constitution in no different a manner than it interprets laws and treaties in the course of its work. *Id.* art. III, § 2. Incidentally, and in a provision not mentioned by Marshall in *Marbury*, Article VI stipulates that the "Judges in every State shall be bound" by the "supreme Law of the Land." *Id.* art. VI. That provision thus furnishes direct textual support for the authority—indeed, the duty—of *state court* judges to refuse application of unconstitutional laws. *See id.*; *see also* Klarman, *supra* note 8, at 1119–20 (noting that this language, though not mentioned by Marshall in *Marbury*, might support an analogous power of federal courts "to invalidate unconstitutional state laws," while adding that "[i]t is much more of a stretch to infer that either state or federal courts are empowered to invalidate federal legislation under the Constitution").

undisputed power to determine whether one statute supersedes another.[48]

This last argument goes a long way toward justifying the now widely accepted view that courts have a role to play in assessing the constitutional validity of federal statutes. It does not, however, speak to a separate question that continues to stir controversy to the present day. That question concerns the extent to which courts, when exercising the power of judicial review, should defer to the judgments of Congress and other institutional actors regarding the constitutionality of their own actions. In other words, there might well be near-universal agreement that courts can issue judgments about the constitutionality of federal legislation.[49] But there remains deep disagreement about the appropriate level of hesitancy and humility with which courts should undertake that task. Some analysts maintain that courts should exercise an aggressive and independent style of judicial review—one that pays little, if any, attention to a coordinate branch's opinions about the constitutionality of its own actions.[50] Others insist that courts should take a highly deferential approach in exercising the judicial-review power—thus acting to strike down only those government actions that plainly flout the unambiguous commands of the constitutional text.[51] Still others suggest that aggressive review is appropriate as courts assess some types of government actions (for instance, legislation that impairs the functioning of open political processes or laws that target "discrete and insular minorities"), while deferential review is appropriate for other sorts of actions (for instance, laws that

[48] Perhaps bolstering this conclusion is the thought that the Constitution embeds structures and values meant to endure over long stretches of time, including by establishing rights that bind government officials. Because elected politicians are (and should be) distinctly mindful of current voter preferences, the risk is great that they will sacrifice enduring values on the altar of passion and short-term interest. Against this backdrop, it might therefore make sense for federal courts, whose unelected judges are freer to take a long-term view of things, to have the power to determine "what the law is" as set forth in the Constitution.

[49] To be sure, many scholars have continued to challenge the fundamental wisdom and legitimacy of judicial review as an institutional practice. *See, e.g.*, LARRY D. KRAMER, THE PEOPLE THEMSELVES: POPULAR CONSTITUTIONALISM AND JUDICIAL REVIEW (2004); MARK TUSHNET, TAKING THE CONSTITUTION AWAY FROM THE COURTS (1999); Jeremy Waldron, *The Core of the Case Against Judicial Review*, 115 YALE L.J. 1346 (2006). But at least as a matter of black-letter constitutional doctrine, this question has long been settled.

[50] *See, e.g.*, RANDY E. BARNETT, RESTORING THE LOST CONSTITUTION: THE PRESUMPTION OF LIBERTY 226–54 (updated ed. 2013) (criticizing restraint-driven approaches to judicial review on the ground that they conflict with the original public meaning of the Constitution).

[51] *See, e.g.*, James B. Thayer, *The Origin and Scope of the American Doctrine of Constitutional Law*, 7 HARV. L. REV. 129, 144 (1893) (maintaining that courts should disregard an act of Congress only "when those who have the right to make laws have not merely made a mistake, but have made a very clear one,—so clear that it is not open to rational question").

embody substantive value judgments and that remain realistically subject to rejection or revision through the normal channels of political change).[52] *Marbury* did not address which of these approaches courts should take. And while the decision can fairly be credited with helping to solidify the legitimacy of the judicial review power itself, it left open these and other questions about the proper manner of its exercise—questions that today remain subject to serious debate.[53]

4. Post-*Marbury* Developments

The Court's decision in *Marbury* did not immediately solidify the federal judiciary's status as an institution capable of bending the other branches to its will. By dismissing Marbury's petition, the Court avoided a direct conflict with the executive branch,[54] and its constitutional ruling undid only a small part of a jurisdictional statute of little political salience.[55] Moreover, in the immediate wake of *Marbury*, the Court continued to steer clear of interbranch clashes, including by declining in *Stuart v. Laird*,[56] decided just six days after *Marbury*, to find any constitutional defects in the Judiciary Act of 1802, the Jeffersonians' own major piece of judiciary-reforming legislation. And while the Court in ensuing decades would occasionally declare that state laws and federal executive actions violated the Constitution,[57] it would not again invalidate an act of

---

[52] *See* United States v. Carolene Prods. Co., 304 U.S. 144, 152 n.4 (1938); *see also* JOHN HART ELY, DEMOCRACY AND DISTRUST: A THEORY OF JUDICIAL REVIEW (1980) (developing such a theory of "representation-reinforcement" judicial review).

[53] To say the least, that debate, which often bleeds over into broader debates about the proper methodologies of constitutional interpretation, is extremely important. It is also, however, a debate that lies beyond the scope of this book.

[54] *See* Peterson, *supra* note 23, at 51 (noting that *Marbury* reflected "diffidence in the face of extraordinary political pressure").

[55] *See* Richard K. Neumann Jr., *The Revival of Impeachment as a Partisan Political Weapon*, 34 HASTINGS CONST. L.Q. 162, 189 (2007) (noting that "[t]he statute struck down in *Marbury* was an obscure provision of the original Judiciary Act of 1789," and that the Court had not "held unconstitutional a statute enacted by a Jeffersonian-dominated Congress"). Relatedly, and as Professor Klarman has noted, the underlying constitutional issue in *Marbury* concerned federal subject-matter jurisdiction, a matter that fell "peculiarly within the province of courts," and the decision did not, in part for this reason, reflect an "expansion of judicial review beyond the narrow confines of what generally was accepted in 1803." Klarman, *supra* note 8, at 1122.

[56] 5 U.S. (1 Cranch) 299 (1803).

[57] *See, e.g.*, Fletcher v. Peck, 10 U.S. (6 Cranch) 87 (1810) (holding that a Georgia law nullifying a land grant earlier authorized via the state's Yazoo Land Act of 1795 violated the Contract Clause of Article I, section 10); Little v. Barreme, 6 U.S. (2 Cranch) 170 (1804) (holding that, where Congress had by statute authorized the seizure of certain ships, the President could not unilaterally order the seizure of additional ships not covered by the terms of the statute itself).

Congress until it issued its disastrous, pro-slavery decision in *Dred Scott v. Sandford* in 1857.[58]

Notwithstanding *Dred Scott*'s vivid illustration of the dangers of judicial review, the Court's invocation of the power accelerated during the late nineteenth and early twentieth centuries.[59] Indeed, by the time of the Great Depression, the power was so well-established that the Court did not hesitate to invoke it to strike down even key features of President Franklin Roosevelt's highly popular New Deal program.[60] In more recent times, the Court has not retreated from this pattern of active constitutional supervision.[61] Thus, from 2010 to 2020 the Court declared unconstitutional key parts of more than twenty different federal statutes,[62] including such high-profile enactments as the Bipartisan Campaign Reform Act,[63] the Voting Rights Act,[64] the Dodd-Frank Wall Street Reform and

---

[58] 60 U.S. (19 How.) 393 (1857). In particular, and among other things, the Court in *Dred Scott* invoked both the Due Process Clause of the Fifth Amendment and the Territories Clause of Article IV to hold that the Missouri Compromise of 1820 was unconstitutional insofar as it purported to abolish slavery in the territories. *See id.* at 406–07. For detailed and thought-provoking analyses of the decision, see, e.g., DON E. FEHRENBACHER, THE DRED SCOTT CASE: ITS SIGNIFICANCE IN AMERICAN LAW AND POLITICS (2001), and MARK A. GRABER, DRED SCOTT AND THE PROBLEM OF CONSTITUTIONAL EVIL (2006).

[59] *See* BARRY FRIEDMAN, THE WILL OF THE PEOPLE: HOW PUBLIC OPINION HAS INFLUENCED THE SUPREME COURT AND SHAPED THE MEANING OF THE CONSTITUTION 13 (2009) (noting that "[b]etween the end of Reconstruction and the Great Depression, the judiciary grew in power by offering its backing to corporate and commercial interests that exercised enormous authority throughout the country").

[60] *See supra* Chapter 2 (discussing the Court's controversial rulings following the election of President Franklin Roosevelt in 1932).

[61] *See* FRIEDMAN, *supra* note 59, at 13–14 (suggesting that the failure of President Roosevelt's 1937 Court-packing plan, discussed *infra* Section 34.B.1.c, "gave way to the seeming supremacy for which the Court is noted today"). For a quantitative historical overview of the Court's interventionism in responding to federal statutory enactments, see generally, KEITH E. WHITTINGTON, REPUGNANT LAWS: JUDICIAL REVIEW OF ACTS OF CONGRESS FROM THE FOUNDING TO THE PRESENT (2019) (demonstrating that: (a) prior to 1920, Supreme Court rulings that sustained constitutional challenges to federal laws averaged less than one per year; (b) from 1920 through 1932, this rate increased to approximately three laws per year; (c) that from 1933 through 1936 (during the height of the New Deal controversy), the rate increased to five per year; (d) that following the "switch in time" and up until 1954, the rate went back down to around one per year; and (e) that from 1954 through 2017 the rate has oscillated within a range of two to four rulings per year. *See id.* at 229 tab. 6–1, 297 tab. 7–1.

[62] *See* CONG. RSCH. SERV., TABLE OF LAWS HELD UNCONSTITUTIONAL IN WHOLE OR IN PART BY THE SUPREME COURT, U.S. CONSTITUTION ANNOTATED, https://constitution.congress.gov/resources/unconstitutional-laws/ (last visited Jan. 25, 2022).

[63] *See* Citizens United v. FEC, 558 U.S. 310, 372 (2010) (holding that a statutory limitation on corporate independent expenditures on political electioneering violated the First Amendment's free-speech guarantee).

[64] *See* Shelby County v. Holder, 570 U.S. 529, 535 (2013) (holding that the coverage formula of Section 4(b) of the Voting Rights Act violated "the principle that all States enjoy equal sovereignty" and thereby effectively nullifying the statute's requirement that covered jurisdictions receive federal "preclearance" for changes to

Consumer Protection Act,[65] and the Affordable Care Act.[66] These recurring interventions leave no doubt that the Court's *Marbury*-era hesitance to wield the power of judicial review is a long-gone thing of the past.

B. POLITICAL CONTROLS OVER THE JUDICIAL-REVIEW POWER

As the foregoing discussion shows, the authority of courts to overturn actions of both Congress and other governmental actors has evolved into a centerpiece of the constitutional scheme of separated powers. As that discussion also shows, however, the institution of judicial review remains subject to the criticism that it empowers politically unaccountable judges to affect citizens' lives in highly consequential (and often politically irreversible) ways.[67] Even so, it is wrong to assume that the courts, and particularly the Supreme Court, can and do act with no attention to public opinion. As *Marbury* itself illustrates, the Justices are likely to act in ways that support their institutional authority over time, which in turn may lead them to avoid alienating the public.[68] In addition, the Constitution itself

---

their voting rules); *see also supra* Section 11.B.5 (discussing this decision in greater detail).

65 *See* Seila Law LLC v. CFPB, 140 S. Ct. 2183, 2207 (2020) (holding that Congress lacked the power to insulate the director of the federal Consumer Financial Protection Bureau from at-will Presidential removal); *see also supra* Section 31.C.2 (discussing this decision in greater detail).

66 *See* Nat'l Fed. Ind. Bus. v. Sebelius, 567 U.S. 519, 549 (2012) (holding that the Medicaid expansion of the Affordable Care Act exceeded Congress's power under the Spending Clause); *see supra* Section 8.C (discussing this aspect of the decision in greater detail).

67 In this respect, the U.S. constitutional system differs from the systems of other nations that accord to legislative bodies the practical ability to overturn the decisions of their constitutional courts. To take one example, the "Notwithstanding Clause" of the Canadian Charter of Rights and Freedoms empowers both the federal legislature and provincial legislatures to override, through the enactment of ordinary legislation, several types of constitutional decisions rendered by the country's courts, including its Supreme Court. *See* Canadian Charter of Rights and Freedoms, Part I of the Constitution Act, 1982, being Schedule B to the Canada Act, 1982, c. 11, § 33 (U.K.).

68 This idea finds support in the observations of no less an authority than Chief Justice William Rehnquist. Early in his career, Rehnquist served as a clerk to Justice Robert Jackson during the time in which the Court handed down its ruling in the landmark Steel Seizure Case, *Youngstown Sheet & Tube v. Sawyer*, 343 U.S. 579 (1952). *See supra* Section 26.B.1. Reflecting back on the Justices' decisionmaking process in that case, Chief Justice Rehnquist wrote: "I think that this is one of those celebrated constitutional cases where what might be called the tide of public opinion suddenly began to run against the government, for a number of reasons, and that this tide of public opinion had a considerable influence on the Court." WILLIAM H. REHNQUIST, THE SUPREME COURT 189 (2d ed. 2001). He added: "No honorable judge would ever cast his vote in a particular case simply because he thought the majority of the public wanted him to vote that way, but that is quite a different thing from saying that no judge is ever influenced by the great tides of public opinion that run in a country such as ours. Judges are influenced by them, and I think that such influence

establishes mechanisms through which the political branches, acting as representatives of the people, can—if they so choose—act to influence and constrain the federal courts' decisionmaking authority. Indeed, the very existence of these mechanisms might sometimes help to mitigate the "counter-majoritarian difficulty" by pushing (or, at least, nudging) the courts away from decisions that depart from views widely held by the general public.

The ensuing discussion divides these court-influencing powers into two categories. The first category encompasses "personnel-influencing" powers—that is, powers that enable Congress and the President to exert influence on *who* serves on the federal courts. The second category encompasses "decision-influencing" powers—that is, powers through which the political branches try to influence *what* courts do as they confront (or steer clear of) particular types of constitutional cases.

1. Personnel-Influencing Powers

a. Appointment

The Appointments Clause of Article II, section 2 provides a key source of political influence over the judicial branch. That clause authorizes the President to appoint federal judges "by and with the Advice and Consent of the Senate,"[69] thus enabling political actors within both the executive and legislative branches to staff the federal judiciary with judges who share their legal and political ideologies. Because those political actors are themselves elected officials, who often run for office based on explicit promises to install particular types of judges, the Appointments Clause helps to produce, at least in certain circumstances, some alignment between the decisions of the courts and the views of the general public.

That alignment, however, is far from perfect. The most obvious complication stems from the life-tenure protection afforded to federal judges. Many judges serve for decades, so that the federal judiciary will at any moment in time consist largely (if not predominantly) of judges who were nominated by Presidents (and confirmed by Senators) who have long since departed from office.[70] Even in the near term, moreover, the judicial appointments process can produce serious departures from majoritarian sentiment. The vagaries of the electoral college system mean that judge-nominating Presidents can lack a political mandate from a majority, or even a plurality, of U.S.

---

played an appreciable part in causing the *Steel Seizure Case* to be decided the way it was." *Id.* at 192.

69 U.S. CONST. art. II, § 2; *see supra* Chapter 30.

70 *See* Corinna Barrett Lain, *Upside-Down Judicial Review*, 101 GEO. L.J. 113, 159 (2012) (noting this difficulty).

voters, and the two-members-per-state structure of the upper chamber means that judge-confirming Senate majorities sometimes represent far less than a majority of the nation's population.[71] In addition, by holding an effective veto power over judicial appointments, slim Senate majorities (again, not necessarily representing a majority of the U.S. population) can utilize their "advice and consent" function to deny to an opposite-party President the ability to fill a Supreme Court vacancy. (A telling example is provided by the Republican-controlled Senate's refusal even to hold hearings on President Obama's nomination of then-Judge Merrick Garland in 2016 to the seat formerly occupied by Justice Scalia.) To be sure, the appointments process may in some instances push the Court in the direction of majority public opinion, if only for a while.[72] In general, however, the appointments process—if viewed in isolation—offers only a crude means of aligning the views of the federal judiciary with the prevailing views of the citizenry.[73]

b. *Impeachment and Removal*

Elected representatives might seek to influence the judiciary's ideological composition not only by leveraging the appointments process, but also by removing (or threatening to remove) federal judges by way of the Article I impeachment mechanism.[74]

---

[71] *See* Joshua P. Zoffer & David Singh Grewal, *The Counter-Majoritarian Difficulty of a Minoritarian Judiciary*, 11 CAL. L. REV. ONLINE 437, 443 (2020) (noting, on the basis of various empirical measurements, that the Supreme Court currently has five Justices who were confirmed by Senate majorities representing less than half of the U.S. population and also noting that three of these Justices (Justices Gorsuch, Kavanaugh, and Barrett) were also appointed by a President who, in the preceding presidential election, had lost the popular vote).

[72] For example, President Roosevelt—who enjoyed the support of a large and persisting political coalition—was eventually able to push the Court in a direction that aligned more with majoritarian sentiments by making his own appointments to the Court. *See* William E. Forbath, *Caste, Class, and Equal Citizenship*, 98 MICH. L. REV. 1, 67–68 (1999) (noting that "[i]n the end, FDR and the New Dealers had to depend on neither the amendment process nor the court-packing plan to 'save the Constitution from the Court,' " and that "the appointments of New Dealers to the Court would turn acquiescence into assent toward the New Deal 'mandate' " (internal footnotes omitted)).

[73] Indeed, the appointments process may actually *exacerbate* the counter-majoritarian difficulty by enabling present-day legislative majorities to stack the courts with (oftentimes quite young) ideological allies who in turn can thwart the future legislative agendas of their partisan adversaries for decades on end. *See, e.g.*, Terri Peretti, *Democracy-Assisting Judicial Review and the Challenge of Partisan Polarization*, 2014 UTAH L. REV. 843, 849–50 (describing a "regime-theory" account of judicial review, according to which courts "craft[ ] legal doctrines that aid and advance the ideological commitments they share with their partisan allies in the other branches" and emphasizing that "[a]ny congruence with public opinion" in the Court's judgments "is incidental and a product of the Court's political dependence rather than its political independence").

[74] For a more detailed discussion of Congress's impeachment-related powers, see *supra* Section 32.A.

Jeffersonian Republicans in the House attempted such a maneuver in 1804, when they voted to impeach Justice Samuel Chase, a Federalist adversary.[75] The Senate, however, narrowly voted to acquit, establishing what some observers view as an important precedent against using the impeachment power to shape the ideological orientation of the courts.[76] Given the polarized conditions of today's politics and the two-thirds requirement for any senatorial vote to convict on any article of impeachment, a present-day legislative effort to remove an Article III judge on ideological grounds would almost certainly fail in any event. Even so, the impeachment mechanism provides at least a minimal constraint on the ability of federal judges to defy dominant public opinion.

c. *Court Packing*

A final personnel-related tool for dealing with the judiciary's frustration of widespread political preferences has its source in Congress's long-recognized authority to fix the number of seats on the Supreme Court—a power that legislative majorities might deploy to "pack" the Court with Justices sympathetic to the views of a political majority. The idea is straightforward: If the current Court is thwarting the legislative agenda of the party in power, that party can enact a statute that increases the size of the Court, thereby enabling the President to fill the new seats with ideological allies. (In similar fashion a lame-duck Congress, with the support of a lame-duck President, might *reduce* the size of the Court so as to eliminate looming vacancies that an incoming President would otherwise be able to fill.[77]) In fact, Congress enacted legislation that facilitated presidential Court packing both prior to and in the immediate wake of the Civil War.[78] Over the ensuing 150-plus years, however, federal legislators have not again put the power to use. A key turning point

---

[75] For a useful overview of the circumstances and aftermath of Chase's impeachment trial, see RICHARD E. ELLIS, THE JEFFERSONIAN CRISIS: COURT AND POLITICS IN THE YOUNG REPUBLIC 69–109 (1971); *see also* Neumann, *supra* note 55, at 187–213.

[76] *See, e.g.*, Adam A. Perlin, *The Impeachment of Samuel Chase: Redefining Judicial Independence*, 62 RUTGERS L. REV. 725, 788 (2010) (crediting Chase's acquittal with helping to establish "the idea of an independent judiciary"). *But see* Tuan Samahon, *Impeachment as Judicial Selection*, 18 WM. & MARY BILL RTS. J. 595, 604–07 (2010) (noting "[s]everal" post-Chase "episodes of impeachment as judicial selection," including President Richard Nixon's (successful) efforts to push Justice Abe Fortas off the bench with threats of impeachment in the House and the unsuccessful effort of both President Nixon and his successor Gerald Ford to secure the removal of Justice William O. Douglas).

[77] *See supra* note 12 (noting outgoing Federalists' use of this stratagem following the election of 1800).

[78] *See* Joshua Braver, *Court-Packing: An American Tradition?*, 61 B.C. L. REV. 2747 (2020) (recounting in detail the several past modifications to the size of the Court, with the last one occurring in 1869).

came in 1937, when President Franklin Roosevelt, frustrated with the Court's obstruction of his New Deal agenda, called on fellow Democrats in Congress to expand the size of the Court so as to enable him to make six additional appointments.[79] Roosevelt's effort, however, blew up in his face. A Senate committee report denounced the plan as an "invasion of judicial power," and prominent legislators voiced similar concerns about the threat the plan posed to judicial independence.[80] The episode is thus widely viewed as having created a strong legislative precedent against Court packing,[81] and no similar effort has since been made.[82] Even so, the *possibility* of Court-packing, like that of impeachment, might sometimes push the Court in the direction of aligning its actions with public opinion or at least in the direction of avoiding direct clashes with the political branches.

Indeed, conventional wisdom has long held that President Roosevelt's Court-packing effort was indirectly successful because it prompted the Court to assume a more deferential posture towards his New Deal program.[83] Modern scholars have refuted the most simplistic version of this narrative by pointing to evidence indicating that Justice Owen Roberts's famous vote in *West Coast Hotel Co. v. Parrish*[84] to uphold a Washington minimum wage law—the so-called

---

[79] For recent historical overviews of the conflict, see, e.g., JEFF SHESOL, SUPREME POWER: FRANKLIN ROOSEVELT VS. THE SUPREME COURT (2010), and MARIAN MCKENNA, FRANKLIN ROOSEVELT AND THE GREAT CONSTITUTIONAL WAR: THE COURT-PACKING CRISIS OF 1937 (2002).

[80] S. COMM. ON THE JUDICIARY, REORGANIZATION OF THE FEDERAL JUDICIARY, S. REP. NO. 75–711, at 11 (1937).

[81] *See, e.g.*, Tara Leigh Grove, *The Origins (and Fragility) of Judicial Independence*, 71 VAND. L. REV. 465, 506 (2018) ("Beginning in the late 1950s, government officials of both parties increasingly treated Roosevelt's 1937 Court-packing plan as a negative precedent—and used the label 'court packing' to condemn any judicial reform that they disliked. This repeated use of court packing as a political epithet . . . helps explain why the practice is off the table today."). *But see* AKHIL REED AMAR, AMERICA'S UNWRITTEN CONSTITUTION: THE PRECEDENTS AND PRINCIPLES WE LIVE BY 354–55 (2012) (contending that the episode does not support the idea that the Constitution precludes Congress from adjusting the size of the Court).

[82] Recently, some commentators have pushed Democrats in Congress to alter the size and structure of the Court in an effort to blunt the influence of its now well-entrenched conservative majority. *See, e.g.*, Michael Klarman, *The Democrats' Last Chance to Save Democracy*, THE ATLANTIC (Feb. 22, 2012), https://www.theatlantic.com/ideas/archive/2021/02/expanding-court-now-or-never/618063/. For a thoughtful catalogue (and defense of) potential reforms, see generally Daniel Epps & Ganesh Sitaraman, *How to Save the Supreme Court*, 129 YALE L.J. 148 (2019). For further discussion and debate, see Stephen E. Sachs, *Supreme Court as Superweapon: A Response to Epps & Sitaraman*, 129 YALE L.J.F. 93 (2019); Ryan Doerfler & Samuel Moyn, *Democratizing the Supreme Court*, 109 CAL. L. REV. 1703 (2021); Daniel Epps & Ganesh Sitaraman, *Supreme Court Reform and American Democracy*, 130 YALE L.J.F. 821 (2021).

[83] *See* Daniel E. Ho & Kevin M. Quinn, *Did a Switch in Time Save Nine?*, 2 J. LEGAL ANALYSIS 69, 70 (2010) (describing this as the "prevailing popular" account of the "switch in time," while noting the historical difficulties with that account).

[84] 300 U.S. 379 (1937).

"switch in time that saved nine"—had been cast prior to the announcement of the Court-packing plan and thus could not have been precipitated by the plan itself.[85] It remains true, however, that, beginning in 1937, the Court's pattern of rulings shifted significantly, and that the shift—even if not directly responsive to the Court-packing plan—may have been caused, at least to some degree, by the Justices' awareness of growing political disenchantment with their rulings.[86]

2. Decision-Influencing Powers

a. Jurisdiction Stripping

No one doubts that Congress has some amount of power to limit the subject matter jurisdiction of the federal courts. This authority emanates both implicitly from Congress's Article I power to "constitute Tribunals inferior to the Supreme Court"[87] and explicitly from its Article III power to make "Exceptions" to the Supreme Court's "appellate jurisdiction."[88] But how far does this jurisdiction-stripping power go? It is well accepted that Congress can narrow the federal judiciary's decisionmaking power by enacting generally applicable "housekeeping" measures, such as the rule that district courts lack diversity jurisdiction over cases in which $75,000 or less is at stake,[89] or the rule that the Supreme Court may not in civil cases grant certiorari petitions that are filed out of time.[90] What remains less clear is whether the power to fashion such limits permits Congress to preclude some or all of the federal courts from hearing whole categories of constitutional cases that federal legislators, for

---

85 *See, e.g.*, BARRY CUSHMAN, RETHINKING THE NEW DEAL COURT: THE STRUCTURE OF A CONSTITUTIONAL REVOLUTION 45–107 (1998) (attributing Justice Roberts's change of views in these cases to primarily "internalist" concerns, including concerns related to the doctrinal workability of the Court's existing liberty-of-contract and Commerce-Clause frameworks); *see also* Felix Frankfurter, *Mr. Justice Roberts*, 104 U. PA. L. REV. 311, 313 (1955) (denying the charge that Roberts's vote in *West Coast Hotel* reflected an effort to head off the court-packing plan).

86 *See, e.g.*, Laura Kalman, *The Constitution, the Supreme Court, and the New Deal*, 110 AM. HIST. REV. 1052, 1076 (2005) (suggesting that "the Court's anxiety about the possibility that Congress would try to curb it" played at least some causal role in prompting its doctrinal change in course, while attributing greater significance to the 1936 elections); *see also* Ho & Quinn, *supra* note 83, at 102–03 (concluding, on the basis of a quantitative assessment of Justice Roberts's rulings, that the 1936 elections played an important role, while also casting doubt on "naive accounts that Roberts's vote in *Parrish* was a direct result of the court-packing plan"). Also deserving of emphasis is the fact that these shifts in the Court's doctrinal approach were solidified by new appointments made by the President in the years immediately after the Court-packing plan was voted down—appointments that were themselves enabled by decisive electoral victories of the President and his party. *See supra* note 72.

87 *See* U.S. CONST. art. I, § 8, cl. 9.

88 *See id.* art. III, § 2.

89 *See* 28 U.S.C. § 1332.

90 *See* 28 U.S.C. §§ 1254, 1257, and 2101(c).

ideological reasons, do not want those courts (and especially the Supreme Court) to decide.

Over the years, Congress has considered many legislative proposals that would remove Supreme Court and/or lower-federal-court jurisdiction over constitutional cases involving abortion, school prayer, the Pledge of Allegiance, *Miranda* warnings, and other hot-button matters.[91] The goal of such legislation is to steer these cases away from federal judges (and Supreme Court Justices in particular), thus channeling them to state-court judges who might well prove less hospitable to litigants invoking controversial constitutional rights.[92] While almost all of these proposals have failed, debate over Congress's power to pass such laws continues to rage. The problem posed by such measures is clear: Constitutional rights may become substantially diluted if they are subject to vindication only by state-court judges "who, unlike their federal counterparts, almost universally serve limited terms and are subject to some sort of popular election."[93] In addition, from a separation-of-powers perspective, jurisdiction stripping creates no small tension with *Marbury*'s endorsement of the federal courts' power to "say what the law is,"[94] and it creates even greater tension with the Court's post-*Marbury* intimations—considered at greater length below[95]—that "the federal judiciary is *supreme* in the exposition of the law of the Constitution."[96] Finally, to the extent that jurisdiction-stripping statutes block the *Supreme Court* from deciding constitutional cases, those statutes undermine the goal of achieving "uniformity in the interpretation of the national laws,"[97] by inviting the creation of a cacophony of differing lower-court interpretations of key constitutional provisions. For these and other reasons, many commentators have argued for Article III-based limits on Congress's ability to constrict the ability of federal courts to hear certain categories of constitutional cases.[98]

---

[91] *See, e.g.*, Grove, *supra* note 81, at 522–27.

[92] *See, e.g.*, Brian T. Fitzpatrick, *The Constitutionality of Federal Jurisdiction-Stripping Legislation and the History of State Judicial Selection and Tenure*, 98 VA. L. REV. 839, 845–46 (2012).

[93] *Id.* at 846.

[94] *Marbury*, 5 U.S. at 177.

[95] *See infra* Section 34.C.2.

[96] Cooper v. Aaron, 358 U.S. 1, 18 (1958) (emphasis added).

[97] *See* THE FEDERALIST NO. 80 (Hamilton).

[98] For a small sampling of the voluminous literature that advocates for Article III-based limits on Congress's jurisdiction-limiting power, see Henry M. Hart, Jr., *The Power of Congress to Limit the Jurisdiction of Federal Courts: An Exercise in Dialectic*, 66 HARV. L. REV. 1362, 1364–65 (1953) (suggesting that Article III prohibits Congress from enacting jurisdiction-stripping statutes that are "such as will destroy the essential role of the Supreme Court in the constitutional plan"); Leonard G. Ratner, *Majoritarian Constraints on Judicial Review: Congressional Control of Supreme Court*

Jurisdiction, 27 VILL. L. REV. 929, 933 (1982) ("[Giving] Congress unlimited control over the appellate jurisdiction of the Court . . . is not consistent with the constitutional plan of judicial review . . . ."); Lawrence Gene Sager, *The Supreme Court, 1980 Term—Foreword: Constitutional Limitations on Congress' Authority to Regulate the Jurisdiction of the Federal Courts*, 95 HARV. L. REV. 17, 21 (1981) ("[I]f Congress stops speaking softly and actually swings its jurisdictional club, our basic institutional arrangements will be badly unsettled."); *cf. also* Paul M. Bator, *Congressional Power over the Jurisdiction of the Federal Courts*, 27 VILL. L. REV. 1030, 1039 (1982) (contending that "[a] statute depriving the Supreme Court of appellate jurisdiction over [an important category of] constitutional litigation would . . . violate the spirit of the Constitution, even if it would not violate its letter" (emphasis omitted)). For dissenting views, see, for example, Gerald Gunther, *Congressional Power to Curtail Federal Court Jurisdiction: An Opinionated Guide to the Ongoing Debate*, 36 STAN. L. REV. 895, 920 (1984) ("In my view, the basic structure of article III affords [jurisdiction stripping] power to Congress, and that power may even be exercised, as Herbert Wechsler argued years ago, to express disaffection with Court decisions."); Martin H. Redish, *Constitutional Limitations on Congressional Power to Control Federal Jurisdiction: A Reaction to Professor Sager*, 77 NW. L. REV. 143, 157 (1982) (concluding that, "when all is said and done, Congress has complete authority to have constitutional rights enforced exclusively in the state courts"). For an intermediate position, see Akhil Reed Amar, *A Neo-Federalist View of Article III: Separating the Two Tiers of Federal Jurisdiction*, 65 B.U. L. REV. 205, 229–30 (1985) (drawing on the text of Article III and Justice Story's opinion in *Martin v. Hunter's Lessee*, 14 U.S. (1 Wheat.) 304 (1816), to suggest that the Constitution requires Congress to vest at least one Article III court with subject matter jurisdiction over federal-question, admiralty, and public-ambassador cases, while leaving Congress free to decide whether to vest Article III courts with subject matter jurisdiction over cases belonging to the remaining jurisdictional categories). For a targeted treatment of Congress's ability to curtail lower-federal-court jurisdiction, even while leaving Supreme Court jurisdiction in place, see Christopher Jon Sprigman, *Congress's Article III Power and the Process of Constitutional Change*, 95 N.Y.U. L. REV. 1778, 1803–08 (2020). A separate question involves the extent to which "external" limits on Congress's jurisdiction-stripping power are "inferable from other provisions of the Constitution." Gunther, *supra*, at 900. Thus, for example, the Court has in the past suggested that Article I's specification that the privilege of the writ of habeas corpus cannot be "suspended" in the absence of a "rebellion" or "invasion" means that Congress cannot utilize its jurisdiction-stripping powers to make the privilege effectively unavailable to habeas petitioners in the absence of a valid exercise of the suspension authority. *See* Boumediene v. Bush, 553 U.S. 723, 771 (2008) (finding that a "statute stripping jurisdiction to issue the writ" violated the Suspension Clause because it failed to provide "adequate substitute procedures for habeas corpus"). *But see supra* Section 28.B.1.c (raising questions about the present-day Court's embrace of this principle). The Fifth Amendment's Due Process Clause similarly might sometimes prohibit forms of jurisdiction stripping that make it impossible for claimants to pursue pre- or post-deprivation redress for government-induced impairments of their life, liberty, or property. *See, e.g.*, Redish, *supra*, at 158–59 (suggesting that it would violate due process to prohibit federal courts from adjudicating constitutional claims against federal officials *unless* state courts remained available to hear such claims). Equal protection principles would preclude Congress from depriving the Court of jurisdiction to hear claims brought on behalf of certain categories of claimants, such as women or racial minorities. *See, e.g.*, Michael C. Dorf, *Congressional Power to Strip State Courts of Jurisdiction*, 97 TEX. L. REV. 1, 8 (2018). And perhaps certain substantive constitutional rights might of their own force prohibit Congress from removing Supreme Court (or all federal court) jurisdiction over cases involving those rights specifically. *See, e.g.*, Joseph Blocher, *Amending the Exceptions Clause*, 92 MINN. L. REV. 971, 1019 (2008) (suggesting, among other things, that "jurisdiction-stripping Acts attempt[ing] to limit First Amendment challenges to public prayer" are "themselves legislative acts of Congress subject to the First Amendment"). Thus, while much of the law within this area remains uncertain, there exists little doubt that even a jurisdiction-stripping power unfettered by the direct limits of Article III would

The Court itself, however, has yet to recognize any such restriction in express terms.[99] Indeed, with regard to limiting lower-federal-court jurisdiction, its rulings seem to recognize a broad congressional jurisdiction-confining power, although the case law on this point is both sparse and dated.[100] As for the appellate jurisdiction of the Supreme Court, the Justices' controversial ruling in *Ex parte McCardle*[101] seems at first glance to support an all-but-plenary congressional jurisdiction-stripping authority. But *McCardle* is subject to a narrow reading,[102] and the modern Court appears divided

---

remain subject to other important constitutional constraints. *See also* Patchak v. Zinke, 138 S. Ct. 897, 906 n.3 (2018) (opinion of Thomas, J.) (noting that "[j]urisdiction-stripping statutes can violate other provisions of the Constitution," even if they are not prohibited directly by Article III).

99 One limit about which the Court has long been steadfast involves Congress's power to control the outcomes of Article III proceedings over which the federal courts *do* have jurisdiction. Here, while the Court has long acknowledged that Congress may "change the law" that applies within a pending case, *see, e.g.*, *Patchak*, 138 S. Ct. at 921 (2018) (opinion of Thomas, J.), it may not go so far as to direct the courts to reach particular outcomes in particular cases, such as by passing "a statute that directs, in 'Smith v. Jones,' 'Smith wins.' " Bank Markazi v. Peterson, 136 S. Ct. 1310, 1326 (2016) (internal citations omitted); *see also* United States v. Klein, 80 U.S. (13 Wall.) 128, 146 (1872) (suggesting that a congressional statute was unconstitutional because, among other things, it impermissibly "prescribe[d] rules of decision to the Judicial Department of the government in cases pending before it"); Howard M. Wasserman, *The Irrepressible Myth of* Klein, 79 U. CIN. L. REV. 53 (2010) (elaborating further on *Klein*'s broader implications for modern-day jurisdiction-stripping debates).

100 *See, e.g.*, Lockerty v. Phillips, 319 U.S. 182, 187 (1943) ("The Congressional power to ordain and establish inferior courts includes the power of 'investing them with jurisdiction either limited, concurrent, or exclusive, and of withholding jurisdiction from them in the exact degrees and character which to Congress may seem proper for the public good.' " (quoting Cary v. Curtis, 44 U.S. (3 How.) 236, 245 (1845))); Sheldon v. Sill, 49 U.S. (8 How.) 441, 449 (1850) (holding that a lower-court jurisdiction-stripping statute "cannot be in conflict with the Constitution, unless it confers powers not enumerated therein").

101 74 U.S. (7 Wall.) 506 (1868).

102 *McCardle* arose from the efforts of a Reconstruction-era detainee to challenge his incarceration by seeking a writ of habeas corpus in the federal courts. A lower court rejected his claim, and the detainee then sought appellate review of that ruling in the Supreme Court, by invoking its appellate jurisdiction under the Habeas Corpus Act of 1867. *Id.* at 508. The then-sitting Republican-controlled Congress, fearing that the Court might "use the case to hold Reconstruction unconstitutional," repealed the jurisdictional grant of the 1867 Act while McCardle's appeal was pending before the Court. *See* Richard H. Fallon, Jr., *Jurisdiction-Stripping Reconsidered*, 96 VA. L. REV. 1043, 1068–69 (2010). The Court accordingly dismissed the case for lack of jurisdiction, reasoning that it was "not at liberty to inquire into the motives of the legislature" and that Congress's power to "make exceptions to the appellate jurisdiction of this court" was authorized by the "express words" of Article III. *McCardle*, 74 U.S. at 514. But the Court also observed that counsel for McCardle had erred by suggesting that Congress had taken away "the whole appellate power of the court, in cases of habeas corpus." *Id.* at 514. More specifically, and as the Court would soon thereafter make clear in *Ex parte Yerger*, 75 U.S. (8 Wall.) 85, 106 (1869), the "whole appellate power" had not been eliminated because Congress's repeal of the 1867 statute had not affected an alternative, pre-1867 procedural pathway to securing Supreme Court review of lower-court habeas denials. *Id.* at 106. Thus, the 1867 Repeal Act did not altogether foreclose Supreme Court review of a particular type of claim, and that fact may have played a decisive role in driving the Court's decision to sustain that law against constitutional

on the decision's bottom-line takeaway.[103] Thus, the scope of Congress's jurisdiction-stripping power remains, at least for now, fluid and unresolved,[104] and that fact in itself may help to strengthen Congress's hand when it comes to threatening jurisdiction-based retaliation for decisions with which it disagrees.

b. The Power of the Purse

In the *Federalist No. 78*, Alexander Hamilton famously argued for a robust conception of the power of federal judges because, among the three branches of the federal government, the judiciary is "the least dangerous."[105] One reason why, as he explained, is that Congress "commands the purse."[106] Thus, one lever that federal legislators can pull in their effort to control the substance of judicial decisions is to punish or reward federal judges in the budgeting process. This power, to be sure, is constrained in one key respect, as Article III expressly requires that that the salaries of federal judges "shall not be diminished during their Continuance in Office."[107] But the Article III courts require funding for much more than judges' take-home pay,[108] and Congress could, at least in theory, go so far as

---

attack. And if that is true, then it would follow that *McCardle* does not in fact stand for the proposition that Article III permits Congress's without limit to remove designated categories of cases from the Court's appellate jurisdiction.

[103] *Compare, e.g., Patchak*, 138 S. Ct. at 906–07 (opinion of Thomas, J.) (joined by Breyer, Alito, and Kagan, JJ.) (citing to *McCardle* for the proposition that "Congress generally does not violate Article III when it strips federal jurisdiction over a class of cases"), *with id.* at 921 (Roberts, J., dissenting) (joined by Kennedy and Gorsuch, JJ.) (indicating that *McCardle* might "support a more limited understanding of Congress's power to divest the courts of jurisdiction" insofar as the law that the Court there upheld was one that "did not foreclose all avenues for judicial review of McCardle's complaint").

[104] One reason why the constitutional status of jurisdiction-stripping statutes is so murky is that the Court has often applied what Professor Ernest Young calls a "super-strong clear statement" rule regarding the interpretation of jurisdiction-related statutes, Ernest A. Young, *Our Prescriptive Judicial Power: Constitutive and Entrenchment Effects of Historical Practice in Federal Courts Law*, 58 WM. & MARY L. REV. 535, 583 (2016), by bending over backwards to construe what seem to be jurisdiction-eliminating statutes as jurisdiction-preserving statutes instead. *See, e.g.*, Webster v. Doe, 486 U.S. 592, 601, 603 (1988); Bowen v. Mich. Acad. of Fam. Physicians, 476 U.S. 667, 681 n.12 (1986) (noting the "serious constitutional question" that would arise from a construction of a statute that would prohibit the courts from adjudicating certain constitutional claims arising out of an agency proceeding). To be sure, the Court's avoidance of constitutional questions about Congress's jurisdiction-stripping powers does not embody a rejection of even the broadest interpretation of *McCardle*. At the least, however, those rulings highlight the Justices' ongoing reluctance to embrace a no-holds-barred congressional authority to shield constitutional claims from federal-court review.

[105] THE FEDERALIST NO. 78 (Hamilton).

[106] *Id.*

[107] U.S. CONST. art. III, § 1.

[108] *See* Zachary S. Price, *Funding Restrictions and Separation of Powers*, 71 VAND. L. REV. 357, 388 (2018) (raising the possibility that Congress might cut or eliminate the salaries of the many administrators, assistants, law clerks, and others who help

to bring the courts' business to a grinding halt by refusing to fund their day-to-day operations.[109] As with Congress's jurisdiction-stripping authority, there may well be constitutional limits on the court-curtailing uses to which the spending power can be put.[110] But even a general power to wield the stick of threatened funding reductions (or to dangle the carrot of potential funding increases) furnishes Congress with a tool to use as it deals with a judiciary that has issued, or might in the future issue, politically unpopular decisions.

c. *Threatened Noncompliance*

The federal judiciary, as Hamilton famously put the point in *The Federalist No. 78*, has "neither Force nor Will, but merely judgment; and must ultimately depend upon the aid of the executive arm even for the efficacy of its judgments."[111] In other words, it is only with the support of the executive branch that federal-court rulings have a real-world effect. Thus, if the federal courts were to lose all support from the President, they also might well lose the practical authority to ensure compliance with their decisions. For this reason, the most potent inducement to judicial decisionmaking that aligns with the sentiments of the political branches is one that often goes unnoticed: A judiciary that too aggressively impedes elected officials from

---

the courts to operate on a day-to-day basis); Adrian Vermeule, *The Constitutional Law of Official Compensation*, 102 COLUM. L. REV. 501, 531 (2002) (noting that Congress might "curtail the judiciary's physical facilities and fringe benefits as it pleases"); *see also* G. Gregg Webb & Keith E. Whittington, *Judicial Independence, the Power of the Purse, and Inherent Judicial Powers*, 88 JUDICATURE 12, 13 (2004) (noting in light of these possibilities that the value of the Article III salary guarantee in safeguarding judicial independence is "fairly marginal").

109 *See, e.g.*, Todd D. Peterson, *Controlling the Federal Courts Through the Appropriations Process*, 1998 WIS. L. REV. 993, 994 (noting that Congress might use "the appropriations process to threaten subtly that certain actions or rulings by the courts may have adverse appropriations consequences"). Similarly, Congress might also enact measures that prohibit appropriated funds from being used to support work on particular types of cases. *Cf. id.* at 994 (noting that Congress might impose "direct restrictions on appropriations that prohibit the federal courts from spending any funds on certain projects"). In discussing this subject, Professor Peterson focuses on projects that do not directly involve the adjudication of Article III cases, *see, e.g.*, *id.* at 995–96 (noting past attempts by several members of Congress to secure an appropriations rider against "expenditures by the federal circuit judicial councils to support investigations into gender, race, and ethnic bias"), but it is not difficult to imagine how other such measures might more directly target adjudicative processes.

110 *See, e.g.*, *id.* at 997 (advocating for an outright prohibition on any funding decisions that would intrude upon the "the essential independence of the judicial branch"); Michael M. Baylson, Elizabeth Coyne, Martha Guarnieri & Samantha Weiss, *Judicial Independence Under Attack: A Theory of Necessity*, 168 U. PA. L. REV. ONLINE 1, 2 (2019) (maintaining that federal courts should be recognized as having an "inherent power," enforceable via mandamus and other extraordinary remedies, to "require the legislative and executive branches of government to provide reasonable and necessary funding").

111 THE FEDERALIST NO. 78 (Hamilton).

pursuing their political goals is a judiciary that might see its judgments go unenforced.

Given the judiciary's dependence on the executive branch for its bottom-line authority, it may be surprising that that branch has, in all but rare cases, honored the federal courts' constitutional judgments. One possible explanation is that political actors understand themselves to be bound by what has become an entrenched norm of official compliance with court judgments.[112] Strategic and self-interested calculations, particularly by politically powerful figures, may also help account for this deferential stance, particularly insofar as partisan actors see judicial review as a means of limiting the powers of future political majorities controlled by their adversaries.[113] But whatever forces might account for political authorities' present-day willingness to accept the court's judgments, that willingness might dissipate in the face of a judiciary that sustainedly and unswervingly stymies the achievement of prized political goals.[114] Aware of this reality, federal courts may well be incentivized not to steer constitutional doctrine too far away from the preferences of elected officials, particularly when those officials are backed by powerful political constituencies.[115]

---

[112] See *infra* Section 34.C.1 (discussing this point in terms of the real-world rejection of the view that government actors can defy formal judicial judgments).

[113] *See, e.g.*, Rosalind Dixon & Tom Ginsburg, *The Forms and Limits of Constitutions as Political Insurance*, 15 INT'L J. CONST. L. 988, 989 (2017) (suggesting that "political elites may use constitutions, and constitutional judicial review in particular, to provide a form of insurance against the risk that they will lose office and influence in future democratic elections"). Political elites may also value judicial review insofar as it empowers courts to pursue certain policy agendas that those elites personally support but that their constituents likely do not. *See, e.g.*, RON HIRSCHL, TOWARDS JURISTOCRACY, THE ORIGINS AND CONSEQUENCES OF THE NEW CONSTITUTIONALISM 16 (2004) (suggesting that "judicial empowerment through constitutionalization should be understood as part and parcel of a large-scale process whereby policy-making authority is increasingly transferred by hegemonic elites from majoritarian policy-making arenas to semiautonomous, professional policy-making bodies primarily in order to insulate their policy preferences from the vicissitudes of democratic politics"); Mark A. Graber, *The Countermajoritarian Difficulty: From Courts to Congress to Constitutional Order*, 4 ANN. REV. L. & SOC. SCI. 361, 364 (2008) (noting that, by exercising judicial review, courts can "enable elected officials to avoid taking firm stands on hotly contested political issues" and can "facilitate position taking by announcing policies that crucial elites support but cannot publicly endorse").

[114] *See* Lain, *supra* note 70, at 161 ("All other things being equal, one reason the Supreme Court issues majoritarian rulings is the difficulty of enforcing those rulings that are not.").

[115] *Cf.* United States v. Richardson, 418 U.S. 166, 188 (1974) (Powell, J., concurring) ("[R]epeated and essentially head-on confrontations between the life-tenured branch and the representative branches of government will not, in the long run, be beneficial to either. The public confidence essential to the former and the vitality critical to the latter may well erode if we do not exercise self-restraint in the utilization of our power to negative the actions of the other branches."). In seeking to avoid direct clashes with Congress or the President, the Justices can deploy a number of different strategies. One is simply to rule in favor of challenged legislation or

C. THE CONSTITUTION OUTSIDE THE COURTS

The power of judicial review gives federal courts sweeping authority to render judgments that reflect their own views of the Constitution's meaning. But does the power to interpret the Constitution belong *only* to the courts? If, for instance, a court declares a federal taxing statute to be unconstitutional, may executive officials nonetheless continue to collect taxes under the law if they view the court's decision to be misguided? If judicial precedent indicates that a proposed conditional-spending bill exceeds Congress's lawmaking power, may members of Congress who believe otherwise nonetheless vote in favor of its enactment? Can the President, in the face of a judicial pronouncement that a recently-enacted criminal statute is valid, still decline to apply it on the basis of an independent personal judgment that the law is unconstitutional?[116] These examples help to tee up the following, more general question: To what extent can nonjudicial government officers act upon interpretations of the Constitution that differ from

executive action, even where the Justices might in the abstract prefer to go the other way. *See, e.g.*, A.E. Dick Howard, *Out of Infancy: The Roberts Court at Seven*, 98 VA. L. REV. IN BRIEF 76, 89–90 (2012) (suggesting that Chief Justice Roberts's decision in *NFIB v. Sebelius* not to strike down the entirety of the Affordable Care Act, "a measure for which Roberts must surely have little sympathy," can best be understood "as a considered move to protect the Court's legitimacy and to enhance its capital in the country's affairs"). Another strategy is simply to draw upon the "passive virtues" of non-decision—by, for example, finding an absence of jurisdiction in a politically fraught case or by choosing not to review a lower-court ruling that, if reversed, would likely provoke a hostile political response. *See* BICKEL, *supra* note 41, at 111–99 (developing a typology of these strategies). A third strategy is to adjudicate the merits of politically controversial issues, but to do so in a manner that, as one of us has described it, effectively " 'remands' constitutionally controversial programs to the political branches—inviting a more studied consideration of the program than attended its initial adoption, and leaving open the possibility that the readopted program will be upheld against constitutional attack." Dan T. Coenen, *A Constitution of Collaboration: Protecting Fundamental Values with Second-Look Rules of Interbranch Dialogue*, 42 WM. & MARY L. REV. 1575, 1582 (2001) (cataloguing various types and examples of this sort of "semi-substantive review"); *see also* Dan T. Coenen, *The Rehnquist Court, Structural Due Process, and Semisubstantive Constitutional Review*, 75 S. CAL. L. REV. 1281 (2002). By thus engrafting into substantive constitutional doctrine self-restraining features that allow the political branches to displace constitutional rulings without resort to the constitutional amendment process (albeit with regard only to certain subjects), the Court might help to give life to constitutional values while also reducing friction with political decisionmakers. And, so the argument goes, by thus instigating and participating in an ongoing dialogue with the political branches about the requirements the Constitution imposes, the Court tends to check its own tendency to lock in rulings that drift too far away from strongly held popular opinions.

[116] Additional complexities regarding the President's own constitutional responsibilities are raised by the Take Care Clause of Article II, section 4, which we have elsewhere covered in greater detail. *See supra* Section 26.B.3.b.

those of the federal judiciary, particularly interpretations handed down by the Supreme Court?

In thinking about this question, it may be helpful to distinguish between two types of judicial actions: the *issuance of judgments*, on the one hand, and the *writing of opinions*, on the other. Judgments are judicial decrees that officially resolve the "case" or "controversy" involving the parties before the court, including in some cases by way of an order (or the appellate affirmance of an order) that party-defendants who are government actors must engage in specified conduct so as to comply with the Constitution.[117] In contrast, a judicial *opinion* serves—and serves only—to set forth the reasons behind the court's judgment.[118] Judgments, unlike opinions, thus bind the parties at whom they are directed, and they are directly enforceable by way of contempt-of-court sanctions for noncompliance. Opinions, unlike judgments, do not impose any enforceable duty on a party or anyone else. But opinions matter because they set forth holdings, rules, rationales, and analytical frameworks that subordinate courts must honor (and that the issuing court itself must, at least presumptively, also adhere to in then-pending and future cases).[119]

This foundational distinction between judgments and opinions suggests that nonjudicial actors might take any of three different approaches in responding to judicial decisions with which they disagree: (1) an approach that treats neither judgments nor opinions as binding on their constitutional decisionmaking (what might be called the "ignore-even-judgments approach"); (2) an approach that treats *both* judgments and opinions as binding (what might be called the "all-out-judicial-supremacy approach"); and (3) a middle-ground,

---

[117] *See* Howard M. Wasserman, *Precedent, Non-Universal Injunctions, and Judicial Departmentalism: A Model of Constitutional Adjudication*, 23 LEWIS & CLARK L. REV. 1077, 1080 (2020) (emphasizing that a judgment "controls the conduct of the defendant and those closely connected to the defendant" and "protects the rights-holders who are party to the specific case"). Thus, for instance, a judgment might come in the form of an injunction that prohibits a specific executive official, named as a party to the action, from enforcing a particular statute or an order that requires a particular state official or local government entity, named as party to the action, to pay damages for the harms caused by an unconstitutional act. On the other hand, a judgment might also resolve the case by taking the form of a declaration (often with res judicata effect) that the plaintiff is entitled to no relief.

[118] *See* Edward A. Hartnett, *A Matter of Judgment, Not a Matter of Opinion*, 74 NYU L. REV. 123, 126 (1999) (noting that "[t]he operative legal act performed by a court is the entry of a judgment; an opinion is simply an explanation of reasons for that judgment").

[119] *See* Wasserman, *supra* note 117, at 1081 (characterizing the opinion as "operat[ing] through the law of precedent and through its binding or persuasive effect on future courts resolving future cases or controversies raising similar legal issues among different parties").

"departmentalist" approach that treats judgments but not opinions as binding. We consider each in turn.

1. The Ignore-Even-Judgments Approach

Nonjudicial actors adhering to the ignore-even-judgments approach claim a wholesale power to render their own constitutional conclusions regarding their own official acts, leaving themselves free to disregard not only judicial opinions but also court-issued judgments that depart from their understanding of the Constitution's terms. It is sometimes said that President Abraham Lincoln embraced this position in the context of the interbranch showdown triggered by *Ex parte Merryman*.[120] In that case, as we have seen,[121] Chief Justice Taney (albeit acting only in his capacity as an individual judge) reached the conclusion that military officials were obligated to release a secessionist then being held pursuant to Lincoln's earlier suspension of the privilege of habeas corpus.[122] At Lincoln's behest, however, the military officers refused to release the prisoner.[123] In a later report to Congress, the President defended his actions by emphasizing his substantive disagreement with the constitutional rationale behind the Chief Justice's order. (Taney had reasoned that Lincoln lacked the power to suspend habeas corpus without congressional authorization, whereas Lincoln believed the President had such a power under emergency conditions, at least when Congress was not in session.) The precise nature of Lincoln's response to the *Merryman* decision remains a subject of scholarly

---

[120] *See* 17 F. Cas. 144 (C.C.D. Md. 1861) (No. 9,487).

[121] *See supra* Section 28.B.1.a.

[122] The Taney opinion did not directly call upon Lincoln to secure Merryman's release, but it did announce: (a) that Merryman's incarceration was unlawful; and (b) that the President had a duty "to determine what measures he will take to cause the civil process of the United States to be respected and enforced." *Merryman*, 17 F. Cas. at 153. Thus, the opinion has generally been understood as "directing Merryman's release," even if Taney never explicitly commanded it. *See* Richard H. Fallon, Jr., *Political Questions and the Ultra Vires Conundrum*, 87 U. CHI. L. REV. 1481, 1530 (2020); *see also* BRUCE A. RAGSDALE, *EX PARTE MERRYMAN* AND DEBATES ON CIVIL LIBERTIES DURING THE CIVIL WAR 12 (Federal Judicial Center 2007) (noting that Taney had issued an "oral opinion stating that Merryman was entitled to be freed" while never explicitly ordering his release). *But see* Seth Barrett Tillman, Ex Parte Merryman: *Myth, History, and Scholarship*, 224 MIL. L. REV. 481, 495 (2016) (emphasizing that "Taney never ordered anyone to release Merryman"). To the extent that Lincoln did tolerate defiance of a judgement in *Merryman*, he was arguably acting contrary to a position he himself had embraced in his First Inaugural Address, during which, in the context of discussing the *Dred Scott* opinion, he characterized the Court's decisions as "*binding in any case upon the parties*" while merely being "entitled to very high respect and consideration in all parallel cases by all other departments of the Government." First Inaugural Address of Abraham Lincoln (Mar. 4, 1861) (emphasis added), *available at* https://avalon.law.yale.edu/19th_century/lincoln1.asp.

[123] Fallon, *supra* note 122, at 1530.

disagreement.[124] Regardless, the *Merryman* episode illustrates the limited options at the disposal of a court whose judgment the President has chosen to ignore.

2. The All-out-Judicial-Supremacy Approach

The all-out-judicial-supremacy approach lies at the other end of the spectrum of possible ways in which to resolve clashes between judicial and nonjudicial constitutional interpretation. According to this approach, the political branches are bound not only by judgments issued directly against them, but also by constitutional interpretations set forth in judicial opinions, at least as announced by the Supreme Court. The Court itself came closest to endorsing this theory in *Cooper v. Aaron*,[125] where, in confronting ongoing southern-state resistance to its landmark desegregation decision in *Brown v. Board of Education*,[126] it unanimously declared itself to be "*supreme* in the *exposition* of the law of the Constitution" and added that "the interpretation of the Fourteenth Amendment enunciated by this Court in the *Brown* case is the supreme law of the land."[127] Taken for all it is worth,[128] this description of the judicial role suggests, as

---

124 The standard view is that Lincoln chose not to release Merryman because he disagreed with Taney's decision on the merits. *See, e.g.*, Michael Stokes Paulsen, *The* Merryman *Power and the Dilemma of Autonomous Executive Branch Interpretation of the Constitution*, 15 CARDOZO L. REV. 81, 95 (1997) (noting that Lincoln never "specifically discuss[ed] the question . . . whether, even if the President disagrees with the court's interpretation of the law on which a judgment is based, he must nonetheless enforce that judgment," but maintaining that "the plain implication of Lincoln's actions is that he believed the President need not enforce such a judgment"). Some scholars, however, contend that Lincoln's response to *Merryman* was driven more by his belief that Taney lacked jurisdiction to issue the decision in the first place. *See, e.g.*, William Baude, *The Judgment Power*, 96 GEO. L.J. 1807, 1853–61 (2008).

125 358 U.S. 1, 18 (1958).

126 347 U.S. 483 (1954).

127 *Cooper*, 358 U.S. at 18 (emphasis added). *Cooper* grew out of the lower courts' issuance of post-*Brown* orders requiring local officials to integrate the schools of Little Rock, Arkansas. As those officials moved to comply, Governor Orval Faubus—who was not a party to that proceeding—moved to block that effort, including by sending Arkansas National Guard troops to block the entry of Black students into Little Rock Central High School. In follow-on proceedings, the district court allowed a postponement of the Board's desegregation program, by pointing to the "chaos, bedlam, and turmoil" that engulfed the community in the wake of the Governor's actions. *Id.* at 13 (internal quotation marks omitted). The court of appeals, however, reversed this order, and the Supreme Court in *Cooper* emphatically affirmed that ruling. In particular, the Court not only rebuffed the school district's effort to delay desegregation, but also spoke to the constitutionality of the Governor's obstructionism. According to the Justices, the case raised "questions of the highest importance to the maintenance of our federal system of government" because it involved "actions by the Governor and Legislature of Arkansas upon the premise that they are not bound by our holding in [*Brown*]." *Id.* at 4. This premise, the Court continued, was not sustainable because *Marbury* had established that "the federal judiciary is *supreme* in the *exposition* of the law of the Constitution." *Id.* at 18 (emphasis added).

128 *Cooper*, to be sure, need not be read as reflecting an all-out embrace of the all-out-judicial-supremacy model. It may matter, for instance, that the case involved

Professors Larry Alexander and Frederick Schauer have written, "that the obligation of nonjudicial officials to obey the Constitution is an obligation to obey the Constitution as interpreted by the Supreme Court."[129] Thus, for example, if the Court asserts that a federal statute is unconstitutional when enjoining an executive official from enforcing it, then a legislator must not vote to reenact that same statute. And (so it would seem) if a circuit court holds that an agency's denial of benefits to a claimant is based on an unlawful regulation, then the agency must award benefits not only to that claimant but also to all other similarly situated non-party claimants within that circuit.[130] The idea, in short, is that nonjudicial actors should scrutinize questions of constitutional law not by asking what they themselves think the answer to these questions ought to be, but

---

state-level (as opposed to federal-level) officials, and indeed some language in *Cooper* itself might be read to imply that the opinion's broadest propositions about judicial supremacy were not intended to apply to the coordinate branches of the federal government. *See, e.g., id.* at 18 (noting that Article VI of the Constitution accords to the Court's holding in *Brown* "binding effect *on the States*" (emphasis added)). It may also be that *Cooper*'s rationale applies persuasively to the decisions of the Court itself, but less so to the decisions of lower federal courts, which, after all, are not even binding on other courts at the same level of the judicial hierarchy. *See, e.g.*, Samuel Estreicher & Richard L. Revesz, *Nonacquiescence by Federal Administrative Agencies*, 98 YALE L.J. 679, 723–32 (1989). Still, the Court in later years has cited *Cooper* in ways that lend support to the proposition that *all* nonjudicial actors must adhere to the Constitution *as interpreted by the courts. See* United States v. Morrison, 529 U.S. 598, 617 (2000) (characterizing it as a "permanent and indispensable feature of our constitutional system that 'the federal judiciary is supreme in the exposition of the law of the Constitution' " (internal quotation marks omitted) (quoting Miller v. Johnson, 515 U.S. 900, 922–23 (1995) (quoting *Cooper*, 358 U.S. at 18))). In addition, though not citing to *Cooper*, the Court again signaled its acceptance of the all-out-judicial-supremacy model in *City of Boerne v. Flores*, 521 U.S. 507 (1997), *see supra* Section 11.B.3, in which it held that Congress had exceeded its power to enforce the Fourteenth Amendment by attempting to enshrine by statute a gloss on the constitutional free-exercise guarantee that the Court had earlier rejected. *See City of Boerne*, 501 U.S. at 536 ("When the political branches of the Government act against the background of a judicial interpretation of the Constitution already issued, it must be understood that in later cases and controversies the Court will treat its precedents with the respect due them under settled principles, including *stare decisis*, and contrary expectations must be disappointed.").

129 Larry Alexander & Frederick Schauer, *On Extrajudicial Constitutional Interpretation*, 110 HARV. L. REV. 1359, 1359 (1997).

130 *See, e.g.*, Dan T. Coenen, *The Constitutional Case Against Intracircuit Nonacquiescence*, 75 MINN. L. REV. 1339, 1391–92 (1991) (characterizing agency departures from principles set forth in opinions issued by authoritative courts as inconsistent with the Court's holding in *Cooper*); Matthew Diller & Nancy Morawetz, *Intracircuit Nonacquiescence and the Breakdown of the Rule of Law: A Response to Estreicher and Revesz*, 99 YALE L.J. 801 (1990) (similar); Lopez v. Heckler, 713 F.2d 1432, 1441 (9th Cir. 1983) (Pregerson, J., concurring) (characterizing the practice as "flout[ing] . . . the tenet of judicial supremacy laid down in *Marbury*"). *But see* Estreicher & Revesz, *supra* note 128 (taking the contrary position).

instead by focusing only on what the courts have said about these questions in the past.[131]

3. The Departmentalist Approach

A final approach, sometimes described as "departmentalist," offers a middle-ground pathway for reconciling differing judicial and nonjudicial interpretations of the Constitution. According to this approach, nonjudicial actors must comply with constitutional *judgments* issued against them but need not adhere to propositions of law that merely appear in *judicial opinions*.[132] A well-known example of departmentalism in action involves President Andrew Jackson's decision to veto, on constitutional grounds, legislation that would have re-chartered the Bank of the United States—that is, the very same bank that the Court in *McCulloch v. Maryland* had found that Congress had the power to create.[133] Departmentalism also underlies the practice of "intracircuit nonacquiescence," pursuant to which executive branch agencies, while abiding by individual circuit-court judgments that prohibit them from enforcing their regulations against specified parties, nonetheless continue to enforce those same regulations against other parties who are located within that circuit but to whom those judgments do not apply.[134] The departmentalist approach also helps to explain Congress's continued enactment of so-called "legislative veto" provisions notwithstanding the Court's opinion in *INS v. Chadha*,[135] which characterized such laws as inconsistent with the constitutional requirements of bicameralism

---

131 Put another way, on this view, all nonjudicial interpreters of the Constitution—including the President and members of Congress—must strictly adhere to Supreme Court rulings in much the same way that subordinate courts must strictly adhere to those prior rulings under principles of vertical *stare decisis*.

132 For useful scholarly overviews of departmentalism, see, for example, Wasserman, *supra* note 117, and Kevin C. Walsh, *Judicial Departmentalism: An Introduction*, 58 WM. & MARY L. REV. 1713 (2017).

133 As Jackson himself put it in his veto message, "The opinion of the judges has no more authority over Congress than the opinion of Congress has over the judges, and on that point the President is independent of both." *See also* President Jackson's Veto Message Regarding the Bank of the United States (July 10, 1832), *available at* https://avalon.law.yale.edu/19th_century/ajveto01.asp; *see also* Wasserman, *supra* note 117, at 1117 (characterizing Jackson's bank veto as the "paradigm" example of a departmentalist decision).

134 *See* Joshua I. Schwartz, *Nonacquiescence,* Crowell v. Benson, *and Administrative Adjudication*, 77 GEO. L.J. 1815, 1829–30 (1989) (noting that "*Marbury* does not by itself establish the unlawfulness of nonacquiescence" insofar as that opinion means only that "the parties are obliged to abide by the court's judgment in a case presented to it for decision," while nonetheless questioning the lawfulness of intracircuit nonacquiescence on other grounds); *see also supra* note 130 (collecting other treatments of the subject).

135 462 U.S. 919 (1983).

and presentment.[136] In sum, under a departmentalist approach, as long as government officials avoid flouting judgments issued against them, they remain free to act based on their own understanding of the Constitution's meaning, even if that understanding is directly at odds with the pronouncements of the Supreme Court.[137]

4. Summing Things up

So, which of these approaches is the correct one? There is no clear blackletter-law answer to the question, and scholars have taken widely different views.[138] But four overarching points are worth highlighting. First, even if the ignore-even-judgments approach might be theoretically defensible in some instances,[139] it fails as a descriptive matter to capture real-world practice, which instead is marked by a widespread consensus that government officials are duty-bound to honor federal-court judgments issued directly against them.[140] Second, there exists a similar consensus view that the all-out-judicial-supremacy approach cannot possibly be controlling in all circumstances. (Few would argue, for instance, that President Jackson was constitutionally obligated to take the affirmative step of signing the Bank Bill simply because the Court in *McCulloch* had

[136] *See* Louis Fisher, *The Legislative Veto: Invalidated, It Survives*, 56 L. & CONTEMP. PROBS. 273, 288–91 (1993). For a detailed discussion of *Chadha*, see *supra* Section 29.D.2.

[137] While departmentalism differs sharply from the all-out-judicial-supremacy model as a matter of theory, these two approaches can often end up having similar on-the-ground effects. This is the case because a departmentalist official's refusal to abide by Supreme Court precedent will frequently result in subsequent, successful litigation involving that official, which in turn can (and usually will) produce a formal judgment that the official must honor even in keeping with the departmentalist model. *See* Larry Alexander & Lawrence B. Solum, *Popular? Constitutionalism?*, 118 HARV. L. REV. 1594, 1614–15 (2005) (reviewing LARRY D. KRAMER, THE PEOPLE THEMSELVES: POPULAR CONSTITUTIONALISM AND JUDICIAL REVIEW (2004)). Departmentalist prosecutors, for instance, might decline to bring charges under a statute that the Court has declared to be unconstitutional, not because those prosecutors see themselves as being formally "bound" by that ruling, but rather because they know that any later prosecution under the statute will trigger a motion to dismiss that, due to the Court's earlier opinion, the trial court will grant.

[138] To be sure, the Court spoke to these matters in *Cooper v. Aaron* in a manner substantially aligned with the all-out-judicial-supremacy approach, *see supra* Section 34.C.2, but the properly understood scope of that ruling is open to debate. *See supra* note 128.

[139] For a general defense of an executive power to ignore Supreme Court judgments, see Paulsen, *supra* note 124. For a more qualified defense, see Baude, *supra* note 124, at 1862 (contending that, while the executive must generally comply with a court's judgment, it need not do so where the court was without jurisdiction to issue the judgment in question).

[140] *See, e.g.*, Thomas W. Merrill, *Judicial Opinions as Binding Law and as Explanations for Judgments*, 15 CARDOZO L. REV. 43, 46 (1993) (citing "widespread agreement" on this point).

held, contrary to his own view, that the bank was constitutional.[141]) Third, the different approaches need not be seen as requiring a one-size-fits-all solution; rather, one or another approach may be warranted in some situations but not in others. (The ignore-even-judgments approach, for instance, might be viewed as presumptively impermissible but nonetheless available for use when the underlying federal court order is both: (a) legally indefensible; and (b) prohibitive of action that is necessary to confront an immediate threat to national security, public health, or some other value of paramount importance.)[142] Finally, to repeat a point developed in the prior section, practical limitations on the judiciary's power to compel official compliance with its decisions necessarily constrain its ability to dictate the degree to which other branches will incorporate the Court's views of the Constitution into their own decisionmaking processes.[143]

D. THE SUPREME COURT'S POWER TO REVIEW STATE-COURT JUDGMENTS

The cases thus far considered in this chapter have primarily concerned the federal judiciary's relationship to nonjudicial actors in the federal legislative and executive branches. In other cases, however, the Court has confronted another key relationship in the U.S. constitutional system—namely, the relationship between the federal judiciary and the state courts. The constitutional and statutory rules that govern this relationship are deeply complex and generally lie beyond the scope of this book.[144] Two early landmark cases, however, warrant close attention, as they establish basic principles that have guided the Court's work in this field of law over the centuries. Those cases set forth the bedrock proposition that the

---

[141] *See, e.g.*, Fallon, *supra* note 122, at 1544 (characterizing an "unalloyed embrace of judicial supremacy" as "untenable").

[142] In similar fashion, the argument for declaring intracircuit nonacquiescence to be unconstitutional, see *supra* note 130, accords more with the tenets of the all-out-judicial-supremacy approach than with those of the departmentalist approach. But that argument has its basis in both (1) specialized concerns about the potentially obstructionist and thinly justified character of this practice and (2) the particular obligations imposed on the executive branch by the Article II Take Care Clause. *See* Coenen, *supra* note 130, at 1389–1413. Those same concerns, however, might well not apply in the context of other executive-branch actions, such as a President's veto of a bill that the President objects to on constitutional grounds or a President's issuance of pardons to persons who, in the President's view, were the subject of unconstitutional criminal convictions.

[143] *See supra* Section 34.B.2.c.

[144] *See, e.g.*, 16B CHARLES ALAN WRIGHT & ARTHUR R. MILLER, FEDERAL PRACTICE AND PROCEDURE §§ 4006–4033 (3d ed. Supp. 2021) (canvassing the body of law governing the Supreme Court's appellate jurisdiction over state-court decisions); *see also id.* §§ 4201–4268.5 (canvassing various other aspects of the relationship between federal and state courts).

Supreme Court can exercise appellate jurisdiction to review the judgments of state judicial tribunals, thus facilitating the uniform, nationwide operation of federal constitutional and statutory law.

1. *Martin v. Hunter's Lessee*

In *Martin v. Hunter's Lessee*,[145] the Court first directly confronted the question whether it could exercise jurisdiction over appeals from state-court judgments involving the interpretation of federal law. Congress had authorized this form of appellate jurisdiction in section 25 of the Judiciary Act of 1789, which permitted the Court to "re-examine[ ]" some types of federal-law rulings rendered by each state's "highest court."[146] In an 1813 decision, however, the Virginia Court of Appeals (the state's highest court) announced its refusal to abide by an earlier decision that the Court had issued pursuant to section 25. According to the Virginia court, it could ignore that decision because section 25 itself amounted to an unconstitutional infringement on the state's sovereignty.[147] That proclamation provoked another appeal to the U.S. Supreme Court, which ruled in *Martin* that section 25 comported with the structural arrangements that the Constitution sets forth.

After Chief Justice Marshall recused himself from the case because of his family's involvement in the underlying land controversy, Justice Joseph Story took on the task of writing a unanimous opinion for the remaining Justices. He began his defense of section 25 by focusing on the text of Article III, which vests the Supreme Court with appellate jurisdiction over "all" federal-question cases (apart from original-jurisdiction cases), without making any reference to the "particular courts" from which the appeal had been taken.[148] On its own, this argument might have proved too much, because obviously Article III does not authorize the Court to hear direct appeals from foreign courts, private arbitration panels, or

---

145 14 U.S. (1 Wheat.) 304 (1816).

146 Judiciary Act of 1789, ch. 20, § 25, 1 Stat. 73, 85–87. In essence, the statute authorized appeals from decisions in which state courts had either sided with the challengers to a federal law (or other federal action) or ruled against parties seeking to challenge a state law (or other state action) as inconsistent with federal law. *Id.* The statute thus would not have authorized review of, say, a state-court determination that a federal statute comported with the U.S. Constitution or a state-court determination that a state-level statute was preempted by federal law. *See* Ann Woolhandler, *Power, Rights, and Section 25*, 86 NOTRE DAME L. REV. 1241, 1242 (2011) (noting that Section 25 "excluded some federal issues from Supreme Court review of state court judgments, particularly when the state court overvindicated a federal claim").

147 Hunter v. Martin, 18 Va. (4 Munf.) 1, 11, 31 (1815), *rev'd sub nom. Martin*, 14 U.S. 304.

148 *Martin*, 14 U.S. at 338.

various other bodies that might decide federal-law "cases."[149] But Justice Story cabined the scope of his textual point by recounting the underlying purposes of Article III. The Framers, he explained, had "foreseen that . . . state courts would incidentally take cognizance of cases arising under the constitution, the laws, and treaties of the United States," and, with that fact in mind, had opted in favor of Supreme Court review.[150] In addition, he continued, it was a "mistake" for the Virginia court to believe "that the constitution was not designed to operate upon states," as the document was "crowded with provisions which restrain or annul the sovereignty of the states in some of the highest branches of their prerogatives."[151] Thus, far from establishing an unstated sovereignty-based limitation on the Court's appellate jurisdiction, the Constitution did precisely the opposite, by making it clear in Article III that the state courts' pre-constitutional power to render unreviewable decisions about federal law under the Articles of Confederation was a form of authority to which they no longer could lay claim.[152]

Justice Story also advanced two policy arguments to support the Court's constitutional conclusion. First, a recognition of the Supreme Court's authority to review state-court judgments was of critical importance in ensuring a nationwide "*uniformity* of decisions" on federal-law issues.[153] In other words, if the Court lacked the power to review state-court interpretations of federal law, then each individual state supreme court could render and enforce its own preferred constructions of federal statutes, treaties, and constitutional provisions, thus giving geographically varied effect to what were meant to be nationwide rules.[154] Second, Justice Story raised the delicate point that state-court judges, unlike their federal compatriots, might not always interpret federal law in a properly dispassionate way. Disclaiming any personal lack of confidence in state-level jurists' "learning, integrity, and wisdom," Story nonetheless observed that the Constitution itself reflected the theory that "state attachments, state prejudices, state jealousies, and state interests, might some times obstruct, or control . . . the regular

---

149 *See* Peterson, *supra* note 23, at 53 (noting that Story's textual reading of Article III "would justify appellate jurisdiction over the courts of France or Spain").

150 *Martin*, 14 U.S. at 342.

151 *Id.* at 343.

152 On the other hand, as Professor Peterson has noted, Virginia could plausibly maintain in response that most of the Constitution's direct restrictions on state sovereignty had been set forth explicitly, rendering it unlikely that Article III would have sought to achieve "such a dramatic and unnecessary extension of federal power by implication." Peterson, *supra* note 23, at 53.

153 *Martin*, 14 U.S. at 347.

154 *Id.* at 346–47. For a thoughtful and somewhat skeptical reflection on these issues, see Amanda Frost, *Overvaluing Uniformity*, 94 VA. L. REV. 1567 (2008).

administration of justice" as state judges construe federal law.[155] In sum, a failure to recognize the Supreme Court's power to review state-court decisions interpreting federal law would generate a crazy quilt of conflicting rulings, issued by judges who, the Framers feared, would seek to curry favor with local constituents, local legislatures, and local executive officers. Thus, the Court reasoned, the appellate jurisdiction established by section 25 was not merely constitutionally authorized but also practically necessary to carrying out the overarching structural plan.

2. *Cohens v. Virginia*

Martin involved a civil proceeding in which the state was not a party. By contrast, *Cohens v. Virginia*,[156] which reached the Court a half decade after *Martin*, involved an appeal to the Court in a criminal case initiated by the state of Virginia itself. As a result, Virginia argued that *Martin* was distinguishable and that the Constitution barred the Court from hearing this appeal. The state's primary contention rested on Article III's grant of *original* Supreme Court jurisdiction over cases "in which a State shall be party"[157]—a grant that, Virginia argued, implicitly forbade the Court from exercising *appellate* jurisdiction over state-party cases, as it sought to do here.[158]

Writing for the Court, Chief Justice Marshall made short work of this claim.[159] The key point, he observed, was that *Cohens* was not only a case in which the state was a party but also a case that

---

155 *Martin*, 14 U.S. at 348–49. The question whether state courts are as institutionally well-situated as their federal-court counterparts to render high-quality federal-law decisions has long been the subject of scholarly debate. The canonical scholarly defense of the position set forth in *Martin* is Burt Neuborne, *The Myth of Parity*, 90 HARV. L. REV. 1105 (1977), which has prompted a raft of scholarly responses. *See, e.g.*, Paul M. Bator, *The State Courts and Federal Constitutional Litigation*, 22 WM. MARY L. REV. 605, 630–34 (1981); Sandra D. O'Connor, *Trends in the Relationship Between the Federal and State Courts from the Perspective of a State Court Judge*, 22 WM. & MARY L. REV. 801 (1981); Michael Wells, *Beyond the Parity Debate: The Decline of the Legal Process Tradition in the Law of Federal Courts*, 71 B.U. L. REV. 609, 610 (1991); William B. Rubenstein, *The Myth of Superiority*, 16 CONST. COMMENT. 599, 606–11 (1999); Michael E. Solimine, *The Future of Parity*, 46 WM. & MARY L. REV. 1457 (2005); *see also* Burt Neuborne, *Parity Revisited: The Uses of a Judicial Forum of Excellence*, 44 DEPAUL L. REV. 797 (1995).

156 19 U.S. (6 Wheat.) 264 (1821).

157 U.S. CONST. art. III, § 2.

158 *Cohens*, 19 U.S. at 392–93.

159 Notably, the Chief Justice also held that sovereign-immunity principles did not apply to this case because those principles concerned only suits that were "commence[d] or prosecute[d]" against a State without their consent. *Id.* at 412. Here, by contrast, Virginia itself had "commenced or prosecuted" the case by initiating criminal proceedings against the Cohens brothers. *Id.* at 412 (quoting U.S. CONST. amend. XI). *See generally supra* Section 5.C.1 (discussing the law of state sovereign immunity in greater detail).

qualified as "arising under" federal law, insofar as the defendants sought relief on the ground that their convictions had been based on an unconstitutional state law. And because Article III expressly gave the Court appellate jurisdiction over "all" such "arising under" cases, the state-party status of *Cohens* was irrelevant.[160] In shoring up this conclusion, the Chief Justice reiterated key points from Justice Story's opinion in *Martin* regarding (1) the "necessity of uniformity" in the application of federal law,[161] and (2) the "importance which th[e] Constitution attaches to the independence of judges"—an independence that state court judges, who "are dependent for office and for salary on the will of the legislature," might well lack.[162] *Cohens* thus drew on *Martin* in concluding that Article III gave the Court appellate jurisdiction over *all* state-court decisions on questions of federal law, "whoever may be the parties."[163]

In tandem, *Martin* and *Cohens* laid down bedrock constitutional principles that are now, but were not then, taken for granted. The key takeaway from both opinions is that Supreme Court can exercise appellate jurisdiction over the rulings of state courts and, in so doing, issue judgments that state-court judges must honor.[164] These

---

[160] *Cohens*, 19 U.S. at 397–98.

[161] *Id.* at 416.

[162] *Id.* at 386–87.

[163] *Id.* at 378.

[164] While *Martin* and *Cohens* establish that Article III generally permits the Court to review state-court decisions regarding federal-law issues, that does not mean the Court can hear every state court decision in which a federal question is in some way involved. For one thing, as Article III itself makes clear, Congress may choose to confer on the Court only a portion of the appellate jurisdiction that Article III describes, *see* U.S. CONST. art. III, § 2 (empowering Congress to make "exceptions" to the Court's appellate jurisdiction), and Congress has long exercised that authority to impose limits on the Court's jurisdiction to review state-court rulings. For example, 28 U.S.C. § 1257 today makes clear that the Court's appellate jurisdiction over state-court decisions encompasses only federal-question cases, with the statute altogether omitting reference to any cases not involving a federal-law issue of some sort. *See* 28 U.S.C. § 1257. (This arrangement accords with the Court's longstanding recognition that state supreme courts are the "ultimate expositors of state law" and that the federal courts—including the Supreme Court—are therefore bound by state-court judgments about the content of their own state's laws. Mullaney v. Wilbur, 421 U.S. 684, 691 (1975) (citing Murdock v. City of Memphis, 87 U.S. 590 (1874))). In addition, the jurisdiction conferred by section 1257 applies only to judgments rendered by the "*highest court of a State* in which a decision could be had," 28 U.S.C. § 1257 (emphasis added), meaning that adverse federal-law judgments from trial-level or intermediate-level state courts are not reviewable by the Court unless and until the parties have exhausted all available direct appeals within the state-court system. (The logic behind this requirement is that it preserves the Court's own resources by ensuring that higher-level state courts have an initial opportunity to "correct" any federal-law errors that might have been made in lower courts, while also promoting federal-state comity by eliminating the Court's ability to interfere with state-level litigation that has not yet played out.) Furthermore, section 1257 authorizes review of only "final judgments or decrees," meaning that, in general, the Court cannot hear appeals from interlocutory orders rendered in the course of ongoing state-court litigation. *But see* Cox Broad. Corp. v. Cohn, 420 U.S. 469, 477–87 (1975) (recognizing several important

principles, in turn, have continued to undergird a sweeping portion of the Court's work to the present day, as it routinely reviews the federal-law decisions of state courts in both criminal and civil cases.

---

exceptions to this basic rule). A further limitation on the Court's power to review state-court decisions applies to cases in which state courts' federal-law determinations have been reached in decisions that are also supported by "adequate and independent state grounds." Herb v. Pitcairn, 324 U.S. 117, 125 (1945). Thus, to take a simple example, if a state supreme court says that a defendant cannot be prosecuted for a state-law crime because (a) the (state-law) criminal statute does not cover defendant's conduct; and (b) the statute is in any event invalid under the (federal) Constitution, then the first, state-based conclusion would likely qualify as an "adequate and independent ground" for the state court's bottom-line decision and thus preclude Supreme Court review of state court's constitutional holding. This requirement has long been justified by reference to the Court's lack of constitutional authority to render advisory opinions. *See generally infra* Section 35.A. If, as Justice Robert Jackson once put it, the Court's only power "is to correct wrong judgments, not to revise opinions," it logically follows that the Court should not be in the business of correcting federal-law determinations that, due to the unreviewability of the state-law determination, will have no impact on the outcome of a case. *See Herb*, 324 U.S. at 126. At the same time, the Court has treated each of the twin conditions of *adequacy* and *independence* with some measure of flexibility. It has held, for instance, that the adequacy requirement enables it to exercise jurisdiction where the alleged state-law ground for the judgment below was so ad hoc, unreasonable, or otherwise unsupportable as to suggest a deliberate attempt to avoid Supreme Court review. *See, e.g.*, NAACP v. Alabama ex rel. Patterson, 357 U.S. 449, 456 (1958) (concluding that the Alabama Supreme Court had relied on an "inadequate" state-law ground in refusing to adjudicate the NAACP's First Amendment-based challenge to a contempt-of-court citation because the Alabama Supreme Court's decision could not be "reconcile[d]" with "its past unambiguous holdings"); *see also* Henry v. Mississippi, 379 U.S. 443, 447 (1965) (suggesting that some state law grounds for decision can qualify as inadequate if the underlying state-law rule fails to serve a "legitimate state interest"); Cynthia L. Fountaine, *Article III and the Adequate and Independent State Grounds Doctrine*, 48 AM. U. L. REV. 1053, 1065–66 (1999) (describing *Henry* in these terms). In similar fashion, it has held that the independence requirement does not preclude it from reviewing federal-law determinations in cases where the state-law grounds for decision that are so entangled with the federal-law grounds as to make it at least unclear whether a reversal on the federal-law issue would affect the ultimate disposition of the case. *See, e.g.*, Michigan v. Long, 463 U.S. 1032, 1040–41 (1983) ("[W]hen, as in this case, a state court decision fairly appears to rest primarily on federal law, or to be interwoven with the federal law, and when the adequacy and independence of any possible state law ground is not clear from the face of the opinion, we will accept as the most reasonable explanation that the state court decided the case the way it did because it believed that federal law required it to do so.").

Chapter 35

THE CASE-OR-CONTROVERSY REQUIREMENT OF ARTICLE III

Analysis

Article III uses the terms "cases" and "controversies" to describe the subjects to which the "judicial power of the United States" extends.[1] The Court has long pointed to this feature of the constitutional text as signaling the Framers' expectation that the newly created federal judiciary would exercise its powers for the limited purpose of resolving live, real-world conflicts.[2] The idea, in other words, is that Article III empowers courts to enunciate

---

1 U.S. CONST. art. III, § 2 (referencing, among other things, "*cases* . . . arising under [federal law]," "*cases* affecting ambassadors, other public Ministers and Consuls," "*controversies* between two or more states," and "*controversies* . . . between citizens of different states" (emphasis added)).

2 Notwithstanding these assertions, Professor James Pfander has recently suggested that the Court's modern-day gloss on the "case or controversy" requirement deviates in important ways from Founding-era understandings of Article III. *See generally* JAMES E. PFANDER, CASES WITHOUT CONTROVERSIES: UNCONTESTED ADJUDICATION IN ARTICLE III COURTS (2021). Drawing attention to the early writings of John Marshall and Joseph Story, Professor Pfander contends that the terms "cases" and "controversies," far from operating as synonymous descriptors of a single unitary concept, embodied separate meanings, with very different implications for the sorts of disputes that federal courts could decide. *Id.* at 5–6 (citing, among other sources, Osborn v. Bank of the U.S., 22 U.S. 738, 819 (1824) (Marshall, C.J.), and JOSEPH STORY, 3 COMMENTARIES ON THE CONSTITUTION 436 (Thomas M. Cooley ed., 4th ed. 1873)). According to this account, "controversies," as the Framers understood the term, could arise only "between specified opposing parties and were thought to require contestation." *Id.* at 5. The term "cases," however, encompassed a broader class of claims that, contrary to the teachings of modern-day justiciability doctrine, included "uncontested petitions to secure a right under federal law." *Id.* Thus, Pfander contends that, rather than give rise to a single, restrictive "case or controversy" requirement, Article III was in fact intended to establish: (a) a relatively lenient set of justiciability-based limits for "cases" (*e.g.*, federal-law disputes, admiralty and maritime disputes, and disputes involving ambassadors, public ministers, and consuls); and (b) a more demanding set of limits for "controversies" (*e.g.*, disputes involving interstate disagreements, the United States as a party, and parties with diverse citizenship). *Id.*

principles of law only in the process of umpiring actual and concrete disputes between parties. And the Court has over time given content to this idea by developing a collection of "justiciability" requirements that aim to capture the requisite elements of "cases" or "controversies" within the meaning Article III.

Although these requirements are commonly said to flow from Article III's case-or-controversy language,[3] the Court has also defended them as an important structural feature of the scheme of separated powers. Without these limitations in place, the argument goes, courts could (and probably would) too often meddle in the affairs of the coordinate branches—injecting themselves into congressional debates, operating as *de facto* supervisors of executive-branch operations, and otherwise acting as if they had a "roving commission to publicly opine on every legal question."[4] The limits imposed by the case-or-controversy requirement thus help to prevent power-seeking judges from aggrandizing their authority at the other branches' expense. Hence the Court's frequent suggestions that modern-day justiciability doctrine is animated by a "concern about the proper—and properly limited—role of the courts in a democratic society."[5]

While much of justiciability doctrine is said to derive from structural constitutional principles, the Court also has indicated that some aspects of that doctrine stem from *prudential* (and hence legislatively reversible) considerations about the proper use of the federal courts' powers. Making matters even more complex is the Court's occasional failure to make clear whether specific components

---

[3] *See, e.g.*, TransUnion LLC v. Ramirez, 141 S. Ct. 2190, 2203 (2021) (noting that "Article III confines the federal judicial power to the resolution of 'Cases' and 'Controversies'").

[4] *Id.*

[5] Allen v. Wright, 468 U.S. 737, 750 (1984) (quoting Warth v. Seldin, 422 U.S. 490, 498 (1975)). This may all make sense as an abstract matter, but skeptics have long wondered whether, practically speaking, the case-or-controversy requirement really does much to rein in the power of the federal courts and the Supreme Court in particular. One problem is that many aspects of modern-day justiciability doctrine have a malleable character, meaning that courts determined to reach the merits of legal issues often seem able to "find a way around" justiciability-based obstacles that lie in their path. In addition, legal advocates are often able to dodge the limits of Article III standing by overseeing the litigation of cases brought by parties they have recruited. *Cf.* Heather Elliott, *Associations and Cities as (Forbidden) Pure Private Attorneys General*, 61 WM. & MARY L. REV. 1329, 1334 (2020) (noting various ways in which modern standing doctrine permits organizations to "recruit new members who have an injury in fact"). Most important, once all the justiciability boxes have been checked, courts have broad discretion to shape substantive doctrine in ways that substantially limit the authority of other government actors. Indeed, to the extent one worries about judicial overreaching, the overall scope of the "case or controversy" requirement may matter far less than the scope of the courts' powers to review and remediate governmental actions in the cases or controversies that come before it—powers that the Court less often describes with the sort of restraint-heavy rhetoric that permeates its justiciability-related decisions.

of justiciability doctrine are constitutional or prudential in nature, thus creating uncertainty about which particular justiciability-related principles can be overridden by way of congressional legislation. Many aspects of justiciability law, to be sure, involve no such ambiguity, and it is clear that the constitutionally grounded aspects of justiciability law cannot be legislated away. As we soon will see, however, disaggregating the constitutional and prudential elements of the Court's justiciability jurisprudence is not always an easy task.

For these and other reasons, federal justiciability doctrine is vast and complex, and this single chapter can offer only a summary overview of key governing principles. (Far more extensive treatments appear in treatises that specifically address the law of federal courts.) We have organized our treatment of the subject as follows: At the outset, we consider the prohibition on judicial issuance of *advisory opinions*—a longstanding and foundational principle that informs the operation of every other major area of justiciability law. Next, we assess each of the four most prominent lines of justiciability doctrine. The first, concerning "ripeness," targets disputes as to which judicial intervention would be premature. The second, concerning "mootness," deals with one-time genuine conflicts that have gone away with the passage of time, thus rendering judicial intervention no longer necessary. The third, concerning "standing," focuses on questions about whether the party who seeks judicial relief has experienced the sort of remediable "personal injury" necessary to sustain a live case or controversy. The fourth, concerning "political questions," stems from the idea that some legal disputes, for various reasons, should be left for the political branches to work out without any input from the judiciary.

A. THE BAN ON ADVISORY OPINIONS

A core component of justiciability doctrine lies in the proposition that federal courts lack the power to issue "advisory opinions"—that is, simply to weigh in, at the request of others, on the legal permissibility of contemplated or ongoing actions. This rule finds its origins in the earliest days of the Republic, when President Washington's Secretary of State, Thomas Jefferson, sought the Justices' guidance on a list of legal issues raised by the President's proclamation of neutrality regarding various international conflicts stemming from the French Revolution.[6] The Justices responded to these questions by declining to answer them. As they explained in a letter addressed to the President, "the lines of Separation drawn by

---

6 *See* William R. Casto, *The Early Supreme Court Justices' Most Significant Opinion*, 29 OHIO N.U. L. REV. 173, 179–83 (2002).

the Constitution between the three Departments of Government, their being in certain Respects checks on each other, and our being judges of a court in the last Resort," militated "against the Propriety of our extrajudicially deciding the questions alluded to."[7] Much as the Justices "regret[ted] every Event that may cause Embarrassment to [the] administration," they refused to express any views on these legal questions, instead leaving it up to President Washington and his Cabinet to "discern what is right."[8]

Although this letter did not in explicit terms set forth an absolute prohibition on the federal judiciary's issuance of advisory opinions,[9] the Court has long understood it as doing just that.[10] As the Court put the point in *Flast v. Cohen*,[11] the advisory-opinion ban is "the oldest and most consistent thread in the federal law of justiciability."[12] Indeed, the ban is such a fundamental feature of

---

7 Letter from the Justices of the Supreme Court to George Washington (Aug. 8, 1793), *in* 6 DOCUMENTARY HISTORY OF THE SUPREME COURT OF THE UNITED STATES, 1789–1800 app., at 755 (Maeva Marcus et al. eds., 1998).

8 *Id.*

9 *See, e.g.*, Casto, *supra* note 6, at 191–92 (suggesting that "the Justices quite possibly wrote their opinion solely to address the narrow issue of Presidential authority to *compel* the rendering of an advisory opinion" and that "[n]othing in their letter expressly addresses the issue of whether the Justices had a discretionary power to render an advisory opinion" (emphasis added)); Christian R. Burset, *Advisory Opinions and the Problem of Legal Authority*, 74 VAND. L. REV. 621, 671 (2021) (emphasizing that the "Justices of 1793 meant to discourage the Washington Administration from seeking advisory opinions, but they did not declare them unconstitutional"). In addition, the letter's very existence somewhat undercuts the idea that Justices altogether lack the power to give advice. *See* Christopher L. Eisgruber, *Is the Supreme Court an Educative Institution?*, 67 N.Y.U. L. REV. 961, 1001 n.106 (1992) (noting that "the construction of the Constitution contained in the letter is itself an advisory opinion"). *But cf.* United States v. United Mine Workers, 330 U.S. 258, 292 n.57 (1946) (declaring that it is always the case that "a court has jurisdiction to determine its own jurisdiction" (internal quotations omitted)).

10 *See, e.g.*, Flast v. Cohen, 392 U.S. 83, 96 n.14 (1968) (tracing the "rule against advisory opinions" to the 1793 letter); Vieth v. Jubelirer, 541 U.S. 267, 302 (2004) (opinion of Scalia, J.) (characterizing the Justices as "saying [in the letter] that the giving of advisory opinions—not just advisory opinions on particular questions but *all* advisory opinions, presumably even those concerning legislation affecting the Judiciary—was beyond their power" (emphasis in original)).

11 392 U.S. 83 (1968).

12 *Id.* at 96 (quoting CHARLES ALAN WRIGHT, FEDERAL COURTS 34 (1963)). Another Founding-era precedent said to support the advisory-opinion ban is *Hayburn's Case*, 2 U.S. (2 Dall.) 408, 409–10 (1792), in which several members of the Court, while serving as circuit judges, questioned the constitutionality of the Invalid Pensions Act of 1792 on the ground that it called for the improper issuance of advisory opinions. *See* Maeva Marcus & Robert Teir, Hayburn's Case: *A Misinterpretation of Precedent*, 1988 WIS. L. REV. 527, 529–35. The Court did not render a decision in the case, *see Hayburn's Case*, 2 U.S. at 409–10 (noting that the Justices were "divided in opinion" on the question whether the Attorney General was authorized to request a writ of mandamus from the Court), but it has in the ensuing years cited to *Hayburn's Case* as supportive of the proposition that "[t]his Court is without power to give advisory opinions." Ala. State Fed'n of Labor, Local Union No. 103 v. McAdory, 325 U.S. 450, 461 (1945).

modern law that courts often defend justiciability-related rulings as supported by the need to avoid the *de facto* promulgation of advisory opinions.[13] The advisory-opinion rule thus operates not only as a freestanding limit on federal judicial authority but also as a fixed-star reference point that guides the application of other doctrines concerning the power of the federal courts.[14]

B. RIPENESS

Another strand of Article III justiciability law targets suits that are not yet ready for resolution. The contours of this "ripeness" doctrine are murky, in part because the Court has characterized it as grounded in an uncertain mix of constitutional and prudential principles,[15] and in part because ripeness-related rules overlap to some degree with the law of Article III "standing."[16] In some cases, however, ripeness doctrine does important work of its own, giving effect to the basic intuition that courts should steer clear of early-

---

[13] With respect to mootness doctrine, for example, the Court has suggested that only a "present, live controversy" can suffice to prevent the issuance of "advisory opinions on abstract propositions of law." Hall v. Beals, 396 U.S. 45, 48 (1969). Similarly, with respect to Article III standing, the Court has expressed concern that an unduly lenient application of standing-based requirements might "significantly weaken the longstanding legal doctrine preventing this Court from providing advisory opinions." Carney v. Adams, 141 S. Ct. 493, 501 (2020). In addition, as noted in an earlier chapter, the Court has pointed to the ban on advisory opinions as helping to justify its refusal to hear appeals from state-court decisions that, though involving questions of federal law, are also supported by "adequate and independent state grounds." Herb v. Pitcairn, 324 U.S. 117, 125 (1945); *see also supra* Section 34.D.2 n.164.

[14] As a real-world matter, the advisory-opinion ban does not always operate to prohibit Article III judges from offering non-binding "advice" to other nonjudicial actors. For example, the ban does not limit courts' ability to issue declaratory judgments in otherwise justiciable cases, *see, e.g.*, Aetna Life Ins. Co. v. Haworth, 300 U.S. 227, 242 (1937) (contending that, when issued in connection with a justiciable dispute, a request for a declaratory judgment does not call "for an advisory opinion upon a hypothetical basis, but for an adjudication of present right upon established facts"), even though such judgments simply describe rights and duties between parties and do not formally compel anyone to do anything. *But see* Samuel L. Bray, *The Myth of the Mild Declaratory Judgment*, 63 DUKE L.J. 1091, 1121 (2014) (noting that declaratory judgments are often in practical effect equivalent to injunctive relief and that, if that were not the case, they would be "impermissible advisory opinion[s]"). Of greater significance, the ban has long coexisted with the tendency of judges to inject wide-ranging dicta into their published opinions. Musings of this sort, made in the context of deciding true cases and controversies, may not technically qualify as advisory opinions. But they come close. *See* Burset, *supra* note 9, at 676 (observing that "[t]he law now treats dicta as a kind of loophole to the rule against advisory opinions").

[15] *See* Reno v. Catholic Soc. Servs., Inc., 509 U.S. 43, 57 n.18 (1993) (noting that ripeness doctrine is "drawn both from Article III limitations on judicial power and from prudential reasons for refusing to exercise jurisdiction").

[16] *See, e.g.*, Susan B. Anthony List v. Driehaus, 573 U.S. 149, 157 n.5 (2014) (noting that the "Article III standing and ripeness issues in this case 'boil down to the same question' " (quoting MedImmune, Inc. v. Genentech, Inc., 549 U.S. 118, 128 n.8 (2007))).

stage disputes that may never crystallize (or at least have not yet crystallized) into concrete clashes of competing interests.[17]

Ripeness-related issues often arise in connection with "pre-enforcement" challenges to statutes and regulations—that is, cases in which private-party plaintiffs seek declaratory and/or injunctive relief against the future enforcement of an allegedly unlawful rule that has not yet been applied to them. These challenges are susceptible to ripeness-based attack because they involve (at least usually) some speculation about whether, when, and how the plaintiffs will act to violate the rule and whether, when and, how anyone will seek to enforce the rule against them. The Court, however, has often declined to dismiss such cases on ripeness-related grounds, pointing to the unfairness that might otherwise arise from forcing plaintiffs to "bet the farm . . . by taking violative action" in order to test the problematic law's validity.[18]

---

17 *See, e.g.*, Texas v. United States, 523 U.S. 296, 300 (1998) ("A claim is not ripe for adjudication if it rests upon contingent future events that may not occur as anticipated, or indeed may not occur at all." (internal quotations omitted))). In resolving ripeness-related questions, courts often apply a test first set forth in *Abbott Labs. v. Gardner*, 387 U.S. 136 (1967), in which the Court characterized the ripeness inquiry as "best seen in a twofold aspect, requiring us to evaluate both the fitness of the issues for judicial decision and the hardship to the parties of withholding court consideration." *Id.* at 149. The first, "fitness," prong of this test goes to whether future events are likely to enrich the factual record in a way that makes the underlying issues easier for the reviewing court to decide, *id.*, whereas the second, "hardship," prong goes to whether a deferred ruling on the parties' legal rights and duties will prove burdensome and disruptive to them in the near-term future, thus giving the injury they claim a more concretized form. In short, if the issues are not yet fully fit for adjudication and if a delay would not impose hardship on the parties, then the test favors dismissal. *See, e.g.*, Toilet Goods Ass'n, Inc. v. Gardner, 387 U.S. 158, 162–66 (1967). If, by contrast, the issues are already well-defined and delay would pose hardship, the test favors adjudication. *See, e.g.*, *Abbott Labs.*, 387 U.S. at 149–53. Though useful in some cases, the *Abbott Labs* test has an uncertain status and scope of applicability: As originally formulated, the *Abbott Labs* was understood to set forth only a *prudential* ripeness principle associated more with courts' remedial discretion than with the "case or controversy" requirement itself. *See, e.g.*, Gene R. Nichol, Jr., *Ripeness and the Constitution*, 54 U. CHI. L. REV. 153, 175 (1987) (noting that the *Abbott Labs* test, as originally formulated "*assumes* the existence of concrete injury" sufficient to give rise to a justiciable case or controversy). But courts have more recently treated the rule of *Abbott Labs* as, at least in part, constitutionally derived. *See, e.g.*, Thomas v. Union Carbide Agric. Prods. Co., 473 U.S. 568, 579, 580–81 (1985) (drawing on the *Abbott Labs* formulation in the course of determining whether the underlying claims "demonstrate sufficient ripeness to establish a concrete case or controversy"); *see also* Nat'l Park Hosp. Ass'n v. Dep't of Interior, 538 U.S. 803, 807–08 (2003) (characterizing ripeness doctrine as rooted in both constitutional and prudential principles and then characterizing the *Abbott Labs* test as governing the question "whether administrative action is ripe for judicial review"); Simmonds v. INS, 326 F.3d 351, 359 (2d Cir. 2003) (noting that the *Abbott Labs* test can be "relevant to the constitutional ripeness determination").

18 *MedImmune*, 549 U.S. at 129. To be sure, the likelihood of government enforcement may sometimes be low enough to render a pre-enforcement action unripe, as might be the case when the challenged law has only rarely (if ever) been enforced against anyone over a long stretch of time. *See, e.g.*, Poe v. Ullman, 367 U.S. 497 (1961)

C. MOOTNESS

Whereas ripeness doctrine targets actions that are brought too soon, Article III mootness doctrine centers on actions that have been brought too late. The general idea is straightforward: If, either before or during the course of litigation, events have transpired that eliminate a plaintiff's "personal stake" in the case's outcome, then that case is no longer amenable to resolution by an Article III court.[19] For example, the repeal or replacement of a statute might moot an action founded on an effort to enjoin its future operation;[20] a government official's commitment not to enforce a law can moot a pre-enforcement challenge to the law's constitutionality;[21] acceptance of a settlement offer can moot a civil action for damages;[22] changed life circumstances can moot a request for an injunction or declaratory order;[23] and so forth.[24] In short, cases become moot when,

---

(declining to adjudicate a constitutional challenge to a state-law contraceptive ban that had never been enforced over the course of its 80-year existence). Ordinarily, however, it does not take much for persons predictably subject to a law's operation to clear the ripeness threshold in a pre-enforcement action. *See generally* 13 CHARLES ALAN WRIGHT & ARTHUR R. MILLER, FEDERAL PRACTICE AND PROCEDURE § 3532.5 (4th ed. Supp. 2021) (surveying the relevant case law and noting that "[t]here may be some movement toward relaxing the threat-of-enforcement requirement").

[19] Campbell-Ewald Co. v. Gomez, 577 U.S. 153, 160–61 (2016) (quoting Genesis Healthcare Corp. v. Symczyk, 569 U.S. 66, 72 (2013)); *see also* Arizonans for Official English v. Arizona, 520 U.S. 43, 67 (1997) (making clear that a justiciable case or controversy must remain "extant at all stages of review, not merely at the time the complaint is filed" (internal quotations omitted)).

[20] *See, e.g.*, N.Y. State Rifle & Pistol Ass'n, Inc. v. City of New York, 140 S. Ct. 1525, 1526 (2020); Ass'n of Am. Railroads v. U.S. Dep't of Transp., 896 F.3d 539, 550–551 (D.C. Cir. 2018) (treating as moot an Appointments Clause-based challenge to a statute after Congress amended the statute to remove the alleged constitutional defects); *see also* Schutz v. Thorne, 415 F.3d 1128, 1137–38 (10th Cir. 2005) (treating as moot a dormant Commerce Clause challenge to a Wyoming law after Congress enacted legislation that specifically authorized states to enact laws of that type).

[21] *See, e.g.*, Winsness v. Yocom, 433 F.3d 727, 736–37 (10th Cir. 2006) (finding that state officials had mooted a constitutional challenge to a Utah "flag-abuse statute" by explicitly disavowing any intention to enforce the statute).

[22] *See* U.S. Bancorp Mortg. Co. v. Bonner Mall P'ship, 513 U.S. 18, 20 (1994) (noting that the parties' agreement to settle had mooted the case). *But cf. Campbell-Ewald*, 577 U.S. at 162 (holding that an unaccepted offer of settlement is generally insufficient to moot a plaintiff's case).

[23] *See, e.g.*, DeFunis v. Odegaard, 416 U.S. 312 (1974) (holding that the plaintiff's challenge to a law school's admissions procedures was mooted by the plaintiff's subsequent enrollment in and imminent graduation from the school).

[24] At least as a matter of theory, it might be that the completion of a prison sentence should moot a defendant's appeal from a criminal conviction. In *Sibron v. New York*, 392 U.S. 40 (1968), however, the Court limited the applicability of the mootness rule in this context by adopting the rule that "a criminal case is moot only if it is shown that there is no possibility that any collateral legal consequences will be imposed on the basis of the challenged conviction," *id.* at 57; *see also* North Carolina v. Rice, 404 U.S. 244, 248 (1971) (holding that an appeal challenging only the legality of a *sentence*—and not the legality of the underlying conviction—is moot once the

for any reason, courts "can no longer provide a plaintiff with any effectual relief."[25]

The mootness rule does not apply with full force in every case, as the Court has long recognized significant exceptions to its basic operation. One exception applies when the apparent mooting of a case is attributable to the defendant's "voluntary cessation" of the challenged activity unaccompanied by a sufficiently definitive commitment not to resume that activity. This exception, the Court has explained, is necessary to foreclose what would otherwise be a readily available method of litigation-avoiding gamesmanship, whereby a defendant could "engage in unlawful conduct, stop when sued to have the case declared moot, then pick up where he left off, repeating this cycle until he achieves all his unlawful ends."[26] Under another exception, courts will not dismiss a case on mootness grounds when "(1) the challenged action is in its duration too short to be fully litigated prior to cessation or expiration, and (2) there is a reasonable expectation that the same complaining party will be subject to the same action again."[27] This "capable of repetition, yet evading review" exception,[28] the Court has explained, is necessary to give the judiciary an opportunity to adjudicate cases that otherwise would become subject to dismissal before a court (and especially an appellate court) had the opportunity to vindicate the legal interests

---

sentence has been served unless the challenged sentence itself gives rise to distinctive collateral consequences).

[25] Uzuegbunam v. Preczewski, 141 S. Ct. 792, 796 (2021); *see also* Chafin v. Chafin, 568 U.S. 165, 172 (2013) ("[A] case 'becomes moot only when it is impossible for a court to grant any effectual relief whatever to the prevailing party.' " (quoting Knox v. Serv. Emps. Int'l Union, Local 1000, 567 U.S. 298, 307 (2012))). This formulation of the requirement reveals its close connection to Article III standing doctrine and in particular that doctrine's "redressability" requirement. *See* Henry P. Monaghan, *Constitutional Adjudication: The Who and When*, 82 YALE L.J. 1363, 1384 (1973) ("Mootness is . . . the doctrine of standing set in a time frame: The requisite personal interest that must exist at the commencement of the litigation (standing) must continue throughout its existence (mootness)."). *See generally* Section *infra* 35.D.1.c (discussing the redressability rule).

[26] Already, LLC v. Nike, Inc., 568 U.S. 85, 91 (2013). Similarly, within the public-law sphere, the "voluntary cessation" exception helps to prevent government actors from proceeding to repeal a challenged law with plans to reenact it once the challenge gets dismissed. *See, e.g.*, City of Mesquite v. Aladdin's Castle, Inc., 455 U.S. 283, 289 & n.11 (1982) (refusing to conclude, on voluntary cessation grounds, that the removal of challenged language from a city ordinance had mooted the case in light of the city's "intention" to "reenact[ ] precisely the same provision if the District Court's judgment were vacated"). *But see, e.g.*, Citizen Ctr. v. Gessler, 770 F.3d 900, 908 (10th Cir. 2014) (noting that "a defendant's voluntary cessation moots a case when a challenged regulation is repealed and the government does not openly express intent to reenact it").

[27] Spencer v. Kemna, 523 U.S. 1, 17 (1998) (internal quotations and alterations omitted).

[28] S. Pac. Terminal Co. v. Interstate Commerce Comm'n, 219 U.S. 498, 515 (1911).

at stake.[29] A further limit applies in the class-action context, where the Court has declared that the mooting of a named plaintiff's claim need not always result in the mooting of the action as a whole.[30]

The Court's recognition of these exceptions gives rise to a puzzle regarding the relationship between the mootness doctrine and the constitutional demands of Article III. The problem arises because the Court has long characterized the mootness bar as a component of Article III's jurisdictional limits, on the theory that a mooted dispute, by virtue of the plaintiffs' lack of a continuing concrete stake in its resolution, cannot support a cognizable "case" or "controversy."[31] At the same time, however, the Court has founded its recognition of exceptions to the mootness rule on essentially pragmatic considerations—such as the need to conserve judicial resources, to deter bad behavior, and to ensure individual fairness—that, from all appearances, are insufficient to expand what is purported to be the

---

[29] For example, courts sometimes apply this principle to reach the merits of election-law disputes even after the relevant elections have concluded, because "[t]he inherently brief duration of an election is almost invariably too short to enable full litigation on the merits" and the complainant may well be subjected to the same rule during future election cycles. *See* Porter v. Jones, 319 F.3d 483, 489–90 (9th Cir. 2003); *see also* Republican Party of Pa. v. Degraffenreid, 141 S. Ct. 732, 737–38 (2021) (Alito, J., dissenting from denial of certiorari) (contending that an appeal from a Pennsylvania Supreme Court decision was not rendered moot by the conclusion of the 2020 presidential election because there was a "reasonable expectation" that the question presented "will evade future pre-election review, just as it did in these cases"). Similarly, the Court has applied this doctrine in the abortion context, because of (1) the limited duration of the human gestational period and (2) the possibility that the plaintiff may again become pregnant, and seek an abortion, in the future. *See, e.g.*, Roe v. Wade, 410 U.S. 113, 124–25 (1973); Singleton v. Wulff, 428 U.S. 106, 117 (1976) (noting that "[a] woman who is no longer pregnant may nonetheless retain the right to litigate the point" under the capable-of-repetition exception). Other disputes can also fall within the "capable of repetition yet evading review" category. *See, e.g.*, Honig v. Doe, 484 U.S. 305, 319–20 (1988) (applying the capable-of-repetition exception upon finding a "reasonable expectation" that a plaintiff suspended from school in alleged violation of a federal statute would be subject to the same action in the future, even though the plaintiff had moved out of the district and was currently attending a school not subject to the statutory requirement). *But see* WRIGHT & MILLER, *supra* note 18, § 3533.9 (noting that in *Honig* the "reasonable expectation" requirement was "relaxed to the point of virtual abolition" and highlighting other cases that "seem to dilute the requirement that an individual plaintiff will be affected by any future repetition of an activity that has abated for the moment").

[30] *See, e.g.*, Sosna v. Iowa, 419 U.S. 393, 402 n.11 (1975) (holding that a class action could proceed notwithstanding the mooting of the named plaintiff's claims, while not deciding whether a similar rule would apply if the named plaintiff's claim had become moot prior to class certification). For a general overview of the intersection of class litigation and the mootness rule, see WRIGHT & MILLER, *supra* note 18, § 3533.9.1.

[31] *See, e.g.*, Liner v. Jafco, Inc., 375 U.S. 301, 306 n.3 (1964) ("Our lack of jurisdiction to review moot cases derives from the requirement of Article III of the Constitution under which the exercise of judicial power depends upon the existence of a case or controversy.").

scope of the federal judicial power under Article III.[32] A question thus arises: How can the Court endorse pragmatically justified exceptions to the mootness rule if, as the Court has indicated, that rule states the non-pragmatic, and thus apparently non-displaceable, text-based minimum requirements for a "case" or "controversy" to exist?[33] If mootness means the absence of a case or controversy (as much of Supreme Court doctrine suggests), then moot disputes should always be dismissed, whether or not such dismissals produce untoward consequences. Yet pragmatically driven limits on the mootness rule *do* exist, thus suggesting, contrary to the Court's pronouncements, that the mootness rule is not jurisdictional after all.[34] There are, to be sure, some potential ways of squaring this circle.[35] But the Court itself has not yet grappled with the problem.

D. STANDING

Decisions about ripeness and mootness often veer into the vast territory of Article III "standing" law. This body of doctrine focuses on the sort of "injury" a plaintiff must suffer in relation to a defendant's challenged conduct in order to create a case or controversy cognizable in federal court. At a high level of generality, the purpose of standing doctrine is to prevent persons who lack an adequate connection to an actual or potential legal dispute from enlisting, whenever they might like, the federal judiciary to opine on questions of law. In keeping with this goal, the law of standing requires a plaintiff seeking judicial relief to demonstrate a personal

---

[32] *See* Matthew I. Hall, *The Partially Prudential Doctrine of Mootness*, 77 GEO. WASH. L. REV. 562, 563 (2009).

[33] *See Honig*, 484 U.S. at 330 (Rehnquist, C.J., concurring) ("If our mootness doctrine were forced upon us by the case or controversy requirement of [Article] III itself, we would have no more power to decide lawsuits which are 'moot' but which also raise questions which are capable of repetition but evading review than we would to decide cases which are 'moot' but raise no such questions."); *see also* Robert J. Pushaw, Jr., *Justiciability and Separation of Powers: A Neo-Federalist Approach*, 81 CORNELL L. REV. 393, 490 (1996) (characterizing the mootness exceptions as "incomprehensible if federal courts lack Article III jurisdiction to resolve moot cases at all").

[34] *See* Hall, *supra* note 32, at 575 (suggesting that modern-day mootness doctrine involves "a jurisdictional limitation imposed by the Constitution . . . made subordinate to judge-made common law exceptions").

[35] One possibility would be to recast *all* of mootness doctrine as grounded in prudential rather than constitutional requirements. *See, e.g.*, Evan Tsen Lee, *Deconstitutionalizing Justiciability: The Example of Mootness*, 105 HARV. L. REV. 603, 623–25 (1992). The opposite approach might be to recast the mootness exceptions in explicitly *constitutional* terms, such as by contending that voluntary-cessation and capable-of-repetition cases at all times remain fully "live" cases or controversies under Article III because they involve circumstances in which the threat of injury to the plaintiff never fully goes away. Finally, the Court might more systematically distinguish between different types of mootness claims, treating some as prudentially grounded (and thus subject to prudential exceptions) and others as constitutionally grounded (and thus not subject to any exceptions at all). *See* Hall, *supra* note 32, at 599–609 (developing such an approach).

stake in the case's outcome. More specifically, a plaintiff must demonstrate: (1) an "injury in fact"; (2) a "causal connection between the injury and the conduct complained of"; and (3) a sufficient likelihood that "the injury will be redressed by a favorable decision."[36] All three of these elements must be present for standing to exist; if any one of them is lacking, then "there is no case or controversy for the federal court to resolve."[37]

As we will see, the law of Article III standing is byzantine and opaque. Standing-related disputes arise with frequency and in cases involving every area of substantive law.[38] The decisions in these cases are not always easy to reconcile with one another, and each new piece of guidance from the Court is as likely to spawn new questions as it is to clear up prior points of confusion. In addition, and as in other areas of justiciability law, the Court has supplemented the "irreducible minimum"[39] standing requirements of Article III with an ill-defined set of "prudential standing" rules of its own creation. All of this adds up to an ever-shifting and inevitably confusing body of case law that resists easy synthesis and summary.

We begin our necessarily abbreviated treatment of standing doctrine by introducing each of its three core elements—that is, the injury-in-fact requirement, the causation requirement, and the redressability requirement. We then survey several specialized rules of Article III standing doctrine—namely, the rules of citizen standing, taxpayer standing, organizational standing, state standing, and legislative standing—that deal with recurring categories of plaintiffs asserting recurring theories of injury. Next, we consider the extent of Congress's power to create (or at least support) new theories of Article III standing by creating causes of action that permit individuals to bring suit to enforce statutory rights that Congress itself has established. Finally, we offer a brief overview

---

[36] Lujan v. Defenders of Wildlife, 504 U.S. 555, 560–61 (1992) (internal quotation omitted).

[37] *TransUnion LLC*, 141 S. Ct. at 2203 (internal quotations omitted). This requirement, moreover, is jurisdictional, meaning that it cannot be waived by the parties. *See, e.g.*, Va. House of Delegates v. Bethune-Hill, 139 S. Ct. 1945, 1953 n.3 (2019).

[38] The one major area in which Article III standing issues are not often litigated is the *criminal law*, as it has long been assumed that the United States has standing to bring prosecutions against persons alleged to have violated federal criminal law. *But see generally* Edward A. Hartnett, *The Standing of the United States: How Criminal Prosecutions Show That Standing Doctrine Is Looking for Answers in All the Wrong Places*, 97 MICH. L. REV. 2239, 2246–51 (1999) (maintaining that the United States does not in fact suffer a "particularized injury" in most criminal cases and that the Court's willingness to permit federal criminal prosecutions thus undercuts its long-stated position that Article III cases must always involve an injury in fact).

[39] *Lujan*, 504 U.S. at 560.

of the "prudential standing" rules that operate in some settings to supplement the core jurisdictional limits imposed by Article III.

1. The General Article III Standing Framework

a. The Injury-in-Fact Requirement

The "injury in fact" requirement operates to distinguish between a potential plaintiff's "generalized grievances" about an action's alleged unlawfulness and claims based on specifically identifiable harm caused to the plaintiff by that action.[40] To give purchase to this distinction, the Court has resisted recognition of "injuries" that amount to mere feelings of disappointment or demoralization about the existence of unlawful behavior. Instead, it has held that a plaintiff's alleged injury must be "concrete and particularized"—"concrete" in the sense of being "real, and not abstract,"[41] and "particularized" in the sense of "affect[ing] the plaintiff in a personal and individual way."[42] Thus, for instance, residents of Boston would not have standing to challenge a park closure in Boise based solely on their remorse about the destruction of green space in America. By contrast, residents of Boise would have standing to sue if they could show that they have visited the park in the past and would continue to do so were it to remain open.

In addition, Article III injuries must be "actual or imminent" as opposed to "conjectural or hypothetical."[43] The above-mentioned Bostonian plaintiffs, for instance, could not revive their challenge to the Boise park shutdown by announcing a vague, "some day"

---

40 *See Carney*, 141 S. Ct. at 498 (noting that "a grievance that amounts to nothing more than an abstract and generalized harm to a citizen's interest in the proper application of the law does not count as an 'injury in fact' ").

41 Spokeo, Inc. v. Robins, 578 U.S. 330, 340 (2016) (internal quotations omitted).

42 *Lujan*, 504 U.S. at 560. This particularity requirement does not function to disqualify any and all injuries that are in some sense "widely shared." FEC v. Akins, 524 U.S. 11, 24 (1998). Thus, for instance, if a large-scale disaster (such as a commercial airplane accident, a building explosion, etc.) were to cause physical injury to hundreds of people, each victim would still have standing to pursue redress in federal court. *Id.* at 25. Under such a scenario, the Court has suggested, albeit somewhat confusingly in light of its denial of standing to victims of generalized injuries in other settings, that the particularity requirement is satisfied because the defendant's wrongdoing affects each plaintiff "in a personal and individual way." *See Spokeo*, 578 U.S. at 339 & n.7 (quoting *Lujan*, 504 U.S. at 560 n.1).

43 *See Lujan*, 504 U.S. at 560; *see also* Clapper v. Amnesty Int'l USA, 568 U.S. 398, 410–11 (2013) (concluding that the plaintiffs had failed to allege an injury-in-fact in relation to a challenged federal surveillance program because their posited injury rested on a "speculative chain of possibilities" and was therefore not "certainly impending"); Los Angeles v. Lyons, 461 U.S. 95, 102–06 (1983) (concluding that the past victim of a challenged police-department "chokehold" policy did not have standing to pursue *prospective* relief against continued enforcement of the policy because of "the speculative nature of his claim that he will again experience injury as the result of that practice").

intention to visit the park in the future.[44] That claim of injury, though tethered to a harm more particularized than those plaintiffs' generalized frustration over greenspace loss, would nonetheless fail under governing Supreme Court precedent because of its dependence on the unduly speculative occurrence of future events.[45]

In applying the "injury-in-fact" requirement, the Court in recent years has placed an increased emphasis on "history and tradition" as a "meaningful guide" for standing-law analysis.[46] It has observed, for instance, that, when evaluating an injury's "concreteness," courts should "ask[ ] whether plaintiffs have identified a close historical or common-law analogue for their asserted injury,"[47] and it has more broadly suggested that theories of injury bearing a " 'close relationship' to harms traditionally recognized as providing a basis for lawsuits in American courts" will more likely pass muster under Article III than will newfangled theories of injury that courts have never before encountered.[48] Other factors, to be sure, continue to play a role in the injury-in-fact calculus, and—as we soon will see—things become especially complicated when Congress injects itself into the matter by enacting a statute that identifies an iffy injury as legally cognizable.[49] In general, however, recent decisions from the Roberts Court have tended to steer the injury-in-fact inquiry in a tradition-

---

44 *See Lujan*, 504 U.S. at 564 (holding that challengers of a government regulation that threatened certain habitats of endangered species could not allege an injury in fact by announcing " 'some day' intentions" to visit the jeopardized habitats, at least where those intentions were not supported by a "description of concrete plans, or indeed even any specification of *when* the some day will be").

45 A different question would arise if the Bostonians were to purchase plane tickets, prepare an itinerary, book a tour, and otherwise solidify their park-visiting plans, in which case their alleged injury might become sufficiently "actual or imminent" to meet constitutional requirements. Indeed, the Court in *Lujan* itself signaled that such a site-specific travel plan would almost certainly do the trick. *See id.*; *cf. also id.* at 92 (Blackmun, J., dissenting) (suggesting that, in demanding that the plaintiffs "purchas[e] plane tickets" to render their injuries non-speculative, the Court "demands what is likely an empty formality").

46 *TransUnion*, 141 S. Ct. at 2204 (quoting Sprint Commc'ns Co. v. APCC Servs., Inc., 554 U.S. 269, 274 (2008)).

47 *Id.*

48 *Id.* (citing *Spokeo*, 578 U.S. at 340–41). This is particularly so, the Court has suggested, when the alleged injury is "intangible," as opposed to "tangible," *see Spokeo*, 578 U.S. at 340 (noting that "tangible injuries are perhaps easier to recognize"). *See also* Rachel Bayefsky, *Constitutional Injury and Tangibility*, 59 WM. & MARY L. REV. 2285, 2291 (2018) (emphasizing that "the line between tangible and intangible harm is not a deep-seated or clear-cut feature of empirical reality, but a contextually sensitive boundary that reflects normative principles about which kinds of harm should count for standing purposes"). The Court has not clarified whether a historical analogue is necessary, sufficient, or simply relevant to the assessment of the concreteness of an injury (though it would not seem to be necessary if the concreteness of the injury is otherwise obvious, even if novel).

49 *See infra* Section 35.D.3.

focused direction, thereby making it more difficult for plaintiffs to vindicate interests lacking in deep common-law roots.[50]

b. Causation

The second, "causation," prong of the Article III standing test requires that a plaintiff's injury be "fairly traceable" to the defendant's challenged conduct. The underlying purpose of this requirement is to prevent would-be plaintiffs from leveraging the existence of a *bona fide* injury in fact to assert legal claims that are insufficiently related to the injury itself. Rather, to sustain a "case" or "controversy" the plaintiffs' legal claims must bear a sufficiently close causal connection to the injury being alleged. (A broken leg, for instance, may well confer standing to seek damages from the person who struck the leg with a baseball bat, but it would not likely confer standing to seek damages from the bat manufacturer on the theory that its industrial processes violate federal environmental law.) In other words, a concrete and particularized injury supports standing to challenge only those forms of conduct that relate to the injury in a not "too attenuated" way.[51]

In the public-law context, the Article III causation requirement contributes to a noteworthy asymmetry between judicial treatment of *regulated parties*, on the one hand, and *regulatory beneficiaries*, on the other. In general, when claimants allege injuries based on a government agency's exertion of coercive power against them, causation is easily shown. (A financial services firm, for example, will have no difficulty demonstrating that a government-imposed restriction on its services has directly caused it an injury in the form of lost profit-making opportunities.) In contrast, a party seeking to challenge an agency's *failure* to honor its regulatory obligations will have a "substantially more difficult" time establishing the requisite causal link.[52] (Clients of a financial firm, for instance, might struggle to persuade courts that the government's failure to police the firm's business practices caused them to suffer injury in the form of money

---

[50] *See* Louis J. Virelli III, *Constitutional Traditionalism in the Roberts Court*, 73 U. PITT L. REV. 1, 44–46 (2011).

[51] *Allen*, 468 U.S. at 752.

[52] *Id.* at 562 (quoting *Allen*, 468 U.S. at 752); *see, e.g.*, Linda R.S. v. Richard D., 410 U.S. 614, 618 (1973) (holding that the mother of a child lacked standing to challenge a district attorney's refusal to adequately enforce child-support obligations against the father; reasoning that, although the mother "no doubt suffered an injury" stemming from the father's nonpayment of child support, it remained "speculative" whether "prosecution will, at least in the future, result in payment of support"); Simon v. E. Ky. Welfare Rights Org., 426 U.S. 26, 42–43 (1976) (holding that plaintiffs seeking to challenge an IRS ruling concerning charitable hospitals' care for indigent patients lacked standing because it was unclear whether "the denial of access to hospital services in fact results from" the IRS's new ruling, as opposed to independent business decisions of the hospitals themselves).

lost to fraud.) Put another way, in these "regulatory beneficiary" cases, the government can often contend that third-party actors, including the bad actors whom the government failed to stop, have severed the causal link between the government's own inaction and the plaintiff's injury in fact.[53] This is not to say that such "regulatory beneficiary" cases can never clear the Article III bar.[54] Relative to

---

[53] *See Lujan*, 504 U.S. at 562 (noting that "much more is needed" when "a plaintiff's asserted injury arises from the government's allegedly unlawful regulation (or lack of regulation) of *someone else*," because, in those cases, "causation and redressability ordinarily hinge on the response of the regulated (or regulable) third party to the government action or inaction—and perhaps on the response of others as well" (emphasis in original)). In *Allen v. Wright*, for instance, the plaintiffs challenged the IRS's allegedly insufficient efforts to enforce legal prohibitions on tax-exempt status for racially discriminatory private schools. 468 U.S. at 739. That regulatory failure, the plaintiffs contended, had led to white flight out of the public-school system and thus imposed on their own children the Article III injury of a "diminished ability to receive an education in a racially integrated school." *Id.* at 756. The Court readily acknowledged that this form of injury was "judicially cognizable." *Id.* (noting that the injury was "beyond any doubt, not only judicially cognizable but, as shown by cases from *Brown v. Board of Education*, 347 U.S. 483 (1954) to *Bob Jones University v. United States*, 461 U.S. 574 (1983), one of the most serious injuries recognized in our legal system"). But it still rejected the theory of standing on the ground that "[t]he links in the chain of causation" were "far too weak." *Id.* at 759. Among other things, the Court suggested, it was "speculative . . . whether withdrawal of a tax exemption from any particular school would lead the school to change its policies." *Id.* at 758. And it was "just as speculative whether any given parent of a child attending such a private school would decide to transfer the child to public school as a result." *Id.* Notice, however, that in the counterfactual scenario of a private school (i.e., the regulated party) suing the IRS for alleged *over-enforcement* of the bar on tax-exempt status, Article III standing doctrine would likely have posed no problem for the plaintiff. The school would have claimed an injury based on its denied tax-exempt status, and that injury would have been "fairly traceable" to the IRS's decision to effectuate the denial. The Court's decision in *Allen* thus gave the IRS an incentive to err on the side of under-enforcing, rather than over-enforcing, statutory protections against race discrimination by private schools. If the IRS over-enforces, then it will almost certainly encounter federal-court review on the merits. If the IRS under-enforces, by contrast, a more likely outcome is an *Allen*-like dismissal for lack of Article III standing.

[54] A recent example of a successful "regulatory beneficiary" case is provided by *Massachusetts v. EPA*, 549 U.S. 497 (2007). The plaintiffs in that case were various states, local governments, and environmental organizations that sought to challenge as unlawful the EPA's refusal to regulate motor-vehicle greenhouse gas emissions. *Id.* They asserted an Article III injury by pointing to a feared loss of coastal land—an injury, they claimed, that stemmed in part from the EPA's regulatory laxness in dealing with the causes of climate change. *Id.* at 523. In response, the EPA contended, rather plausibly under then-existing doctrine, that the posited causal chain between its challenged inaction and the claimed injury involved too many links: (1) non-regulation by the EPA, leading to (2) higher greenhouse gas emissions from motor-vehicles, leading to (3) a rise in global temperatures, leading to (4) accelerated melting of the ice caps, leading to (5) the flooding of the plaintiffs' land. The Court, however, did not detect a jurisdiction-defeating causation problem. *Id.* at 523–24. Instead, it concluded, it was enough to observe that "U.S. motor-vehicle emissions make a meaningful contribution to greenhouse gas concentrations and hence . . . to global warming." *Id.* at 525. And that remained so even if the sought-after regulatory action would yield only a "small incremental step" toward mitigating the injury itself. *Id.* At least in comparison to prior causation decisions, *Massachusetts v. EPA* reflected an unusually "flexible and capacious view of standing law," Jody Freeman & Adrian Vermeule, Massachusetts v. EPA: *From Politics to Expertise*, 2007 SUP. CT. REV. 51,

their "regulated-party" counterparts, however, regulatory beneficiaries are more likely to see their cases founder on causation-related grounds.[55]

c. *Redressability*

The final prong of the standing test requires that the plaintiff's alleged injury—even if it is concrete and caused by the defendant's misconduct—must be "redressable" by a remedy that the court is authorized to issue. In practice, the redressability requirement tends to overlap with the causation requirement because harms not "fairly traceable" to a defendant's conduct are also not likely to be alleviated by any remedy issued against the defendant directly.[56] Even so, the Court has established a few principles of distinct relevance to the redressability requirement. It has indicated, for instance, that questions of Article III standing must be addressed on a *remedy-by-remedy* basis, meaning that a plaintiff's standing to pursue one remedy against a defendant does not automatically confer standing to pursue any other remedy as well.[57] In addition, the Court has made clear that the redressability inquiry does not depend on the merits of a plaintiffs' claim—that is, a defendant cannot put the cart before the horse by claiming that a plaintiff's injury is non-redressable because

---

65, leading many commentators to wonder what provoked it. The Court itself seemed to suggest that the result derived in part from the fact that the action had been brought by sovereign-state plaintiffs, *see Massachusetts*, 549 U.S. at 519–21, a point we consider in more detail below, *see infra* Section 35.D.2.d. Another possibility is that the Court's decision found some support in the majority's sympathy for the plaintiffs' claim on the merits. *See supra* note 5.

55 This doctrinal asymmetry may have significant consequences for federal policymaking. As Professor Richard Pierce has explained: "In a world in which agencies can predict with confidence that every decision unfavorable to regulated firms will be subjected to judicial review and that no decision unfavorable to unregulated firms is reviewable, they inevitably will begin to act in accordance with this new incentive structure." Richard J. Pierce, Lujan v. Defenders of Wildlife: *Standing as a Judicially Imposed Limit on Legislative Power*, 42 DUKE L.J. 1170, 1194–95 (1993). The upshot might be what Professor Heather Elliott has described as a " 'one-way ratchet' against regulation," with agencies choosing to "err on the side of under-enforcement" on the theory that a "lawsuit challenging such under-enforcement faces a much tougher standing hurdle." Heather Elliott, *Congress's Inability to Solve Standing Problems*, 91 B.U. L. REV. 159, 173 (2011) (quoting Cass R. Sunstein, *Reviewing Agency Inaction After* Heckler v. Chaney, 52 U. CHI. L. REV. 653, 666 (1985)).

56 *See* Luke Meier, *Using Tort Law to Understand the Causation Prong of Standing*, 80 FORDHAM L. REV. 1241, 1254 n.64 (2011) ("The redressability prong of standing has been understood to raise the same type of causal inquiry as the causation prong of standing analysis, except that redressability looks at the causal connection between the court's order (ordering the defendant to cease the illegal conduct) and the plaintiffs' requested relief.").

57 *See, e.g.*, *Lyons*, 461 U.S. 106–07 (holding that the plaintiff's "standing to claim damages against the individual officers" alleged to have subjected him to an illegal chokehold "does nothing to establish a real and immediate threat" of future harm necessary to support a request for injunctive relief).

the plaintiff will lose on the merits and thus lack any legal entitlement to the remedy being sought.[58] Finally, the Court has insisted that a plaintiff must show that it is "likely, as opposed to merely speculative, that the injury will be redressed" if the plaintiff can establish the defendant's wrongdoing.[59] In other words, the Court—in a manner that parallels its approach to the causation requirement—has distinguished between requested remedies that are only theoretically capable of alleviating a plaintiff's harm and those that are materially likely to do so.[60]

---

58 *See, e.g., Warth*, 422 U.S. at 500 (noting that "standing in no way depends on the merits of the plaintiff's contention that particular conduct is illegal"); *see also* Schlesinger v. Reservists Comm. to Stop the War, 418 U.S. 208, 226 (1974) (characterizing as "manifestly untenable" the "view that the inadequacy of the presentation on the merits would be an appropriate basis for denying standing"). The redressability question is also conceptually distinct (though sometimes difficult to disentangle) from the question whether the plaintiff has a cause of action to sue the defendant for the relief the plaintiff seeks. *See generally* WRIGHT & MILLER, *supra* note 18, § 3531.6 (discussing this relationship); *see also* John F. Preis, *How the Federal Cause of Action Relates to Rights, Remedies, and Jurisdiction*, 67 FLA. L. REV. 849, 862–63 (2016).

59 *Lujan*, 504 U.S. at 561 (internal quotations and citations omitted). Perhaps not surprisingly, the Court has wavered in its application of this requirement, sometimes finding standing in spite of speculative-seeming theories of redressability, and at other times finding no standing in spite of rather plausible theories of redressability. *Compare, e.g.*, Friends of the Earth, Inc. v. Laidlaw Envtl. Servs., Inc., 528 U.S. 167, 185–86 (2000) (finding that the defendant's payment of civil penalties to the government for past acts of water pollution would help to redress feared *future* harms suffered by plaintiffs exposed to the continued discharge of pollutants from the defendant's factory, on the theory that "a defendant once hit in its pocketbook will surely think twice before polluting again"), *with Linda R.S.*, 410 U.S. at 618–19 (concluding that it was "speculative" whether threatening a father with criminal prosecution for past nonpayment of child support would induce the father to pay child support in the future).

60 Sometimes, as Professor Cass Sunstein has noted, "to know whether the redressability requirements are met, it is necessary to know how to characterize the relevant injury." Cass R. Sunstein, *Standing for Animals (With Notes on Animal Rights)*, 47 UCLA L. REV. 1333, 1356 (2000). Consider in this respect the Court's decision in *Regents of the University of California v. Bakke*, 438 U.S. 265 (1978), a case in which a white student (Bakke) challenged the constitutionality of a race-conscious admissions program employed by the UC Davis Medical School. Bakke claimed that he suffered an injury based on the school's rejection of his application for admission, and he sought from the courts an injunction prohibiting continued use of the program for future admissions cycles. *Id.* at 278–79. The posture of this request prompted some amici to suggest that, insofar as Bakke's alleged injury was his "exclusion from the Medical School," he had failed to demonstrate redressability because he had not definitively shown that he would qualify for admission in the absence of the challenged program. *Id.* at 280 n.14. To at least five Justices, however, Bakke's underlying injury was not "exclusion from the Medical school," but rather an inability "to *compete* for all 100 places in the class" (an injury that, almost by definition, the injunction being sought would redress). *Id.* In reaching this conclusion, however, the Court did not attempt to reconcile its willingness to embrace an "equal opportunity"-type framing of Bakke's injury with its past unwillingness to do so in several earlier cases involving other merits-based issues. *See* Gene R. Nichol, Jr., *Rethinking Standing*, 72 CAL. L. REV. 68, 79–82 (1984) (noting that, under the reasoning utilized by several of the Court's pre-*Bakke* cases, "Bakke should have been made to prove that he would have gotten into medical school"); Michael Coenen, *Characterizing Constitutional Inputs*, 67

2. Specialized Applications of the Article III Test (a Non-Exhaustive Catalogue)

Judicial applications of the three-part Article III standing test have given rise to many doctrinal subrules that govern claims of injury asserted by specialized categories of plaintiffs. The ensuing discussion highlights several key subrules, each of which presents its own nettlesome problems of application.

a. Citizen Standing

Among the most well-established principles of Article III standing doctrine is the basic rule that citizens do not suffer an Article III injury simply because the government violates the law. In *Schlesinger v. Reservists Committee to Stop the War*,[61] the Court denied standing to a group of plaintiffs seeking a judicial declaration that the Incompatibility Clause of Article I, section 6 forbade members of Congress from holding military commissions during their time in office.[62] The problem these plaintiffs faced, the Court explained, was that their theory of standing relied on an "interest shared by all citizens"—namely, "the generalized interest . . . in constitutional governance."[63] And an affront to that interest could not alone constitute an Article III injury because, if it did, any citizen would have standing to sue any governmental official for any claimed constitutional violation.[64] Thus, the Court concluded—and continues

DUKE L.J. 743, 780–82 (2018) (noting that the "opportunity-based" characterization of the injury at issue in *Bakke* deviated from various "actuality-based" characterizations the Court had adopted in prior cases resulting in dismissals for lack of standing). To take one example, the Court in *Warth* held that the plaintiffs lacked standing to challenge a local government's exclusionary zoning policy based on their difficulty in obtaining local housing. That theory of standing foundered on causation and redressability grounds, the Court maintained, because it was not clear "whether petitioners' *inability to locate suitable housing* . . . reasonably can be said to have resulted, in any concretely demonstrable way, from respondents' alleged constitutional and statutory infractions." 422 U.S. at 504 (emphasis added). Thus, and in contrast to *Bakke*, the Court in *Warth* refused to characterize the plaintiffs' injury as something more abstract—*i.e.*, something like, say, an inability to compete with others for local housing on equal terms—and instead chose to frame it in a way that made the traceability and redressability requirements much more difficult to satisfy. *See, e.g.*, Nichol, *supra*, at 80 (noting that the *Warth* plaintiffs had an "interest in equal participation in a housing market not distorted by unconstitutional zoning practices," and suggesting that "[t]he denial of a meaningful opportunity to persuade others to construct low cost housing in [the city], for example, would have been redressed by a determination that the ordinance was unconstitutional").

61 418 U.S. 208 (1974).

62 *Id.* at 209. The Incompatibility Clause provides in relevant part that "no Person holding any Office under the United States, shall be a Member of either House during his Continuance in Office." U.S. CONST. art. I, § 6, cl.2.

63 *Schlesinger*, 418 U.S. at 227.

64 *Id.* ("The proposition that all constitutional provisions are enforceable by any citizen simply because citizens are the ultimate beneficiaries of those provisions has no boundaries.").

to assert today—that an unadorned interest in having others follow the law is not enough to support standing under Article III.[65]

b. Taxpayer Standing

In a limited set of cases, plaintiffs can sidestep the bar on "citizen standing" by invoking their status as taxpayers. The Court endorsed this proposition in its 1968 decision in *Flast v. Cohen*,[66] when it permitted a group of taxpayers to challenge under the First Amendment's Establishment Clause[67] a federal education law that made funds available to support instruction at religious and sectarian schools.[68] Backtracking on its earlier, seemingly categorical rejection of taxpayer suits in *Frothingham v. Mellon*,[69] the Court in *Flast* held that these federal taxpayers had standing to challenge "congressional action under the taxing and spending clause," on the theory that their "tax money is being extracted and spent in violation of specific constitutional protections"—here, protections put in place by the First Amendment.[70] Although the rhetoric of *Flast* seemed to signal a newfound judicial willingness to entertain a wide range of taxpayer-initiated constitutional challenges, the Court soon changed course, refusing to recognize taxpayer standing in other contexts,[71] including in a string of cases involving the Establishment Clause itself.[72] *Flast* thus stands today as a shell of its former self. Other

---

65 The Court in *Schlesinger* also held that it was of no relevance to the Article III inquiry that a failure to recognize the plaintiffs' theory of citizen standing might well leave the defendants' conduct effectively unreviewable by the courts. As Chief Justice Burger put it for the five-Justice majority, "[t]he assumption that if respondents have no standing to sue, no one would have standing, is not a reason to find standing." *Id.*

66 392 U.S. 83 (1968).

67 *See* U.S. CONST. amend. I ("Congress shall make no law respecting an establishment of religion . . . .").

68 *Flast*, 392 U.S. at 85–86.

69 262 U.S. 447 (1923); *see also* Doremus v. Bd. of Educ., 342 U.S. 429, 433 (1952) (holding that "the interests of a taxpayer in the moneys of the federal treasury are too indeterminable, remote, uncertain and indirect to furnish a basis for an appeal to the preventive powers of the Court over their manner of expenditure").

70 *Flast*, 392 U.S. at 106.

71 *See, e.g.*, United States v. Richardson, 418 U.S. 166 (1974) (refusing to recognize taxpayer standing to challenge the CIA's policy of withholding detailed information about its own expenditures of federal money, in alleged violation of the Accounts Clause of Article I, section 9); *Schlesinger*, 418 U.S. at 227–28 (refusing to recognize taxpayer standing to raise claims under the Incompatibility Clause of Article I, section 6); DaimlerChrysler Corp. v. Cuno, 547 U.S. 332, 348 (2006) (deeming *Flast* inapplicable to a taxpayer challenge based on the dormant Commerce Clause).

72 First, in *Valley Forge Christian College v. Americans United for Separation of Church and State*, 454 U.S. 464 (1982), the Court refused to apply *Flast* in connection with a taxpayer challenge to a federal agency's transfer of property to a religious institution, deeming the earlier ruling distinguishable because the case at hand involved neither (1) direct "congressional action" nor (2) an outright expenditure of money from the federal treasury. *Id.* at 479–89. Then, in *Hein v. Freedom from Religion Foundation, Inc.*, 551 U.S. 587 (2007), the Court blocked an effort by taxpayers to challenge, again under the Establishment Clause, an agency's channeling

than in a highly limited subset of Establishment Clause cases, the unlawful expenditure of tax-generated dollars does not inflict on even the most thereby-disgruntled taxpayer a cognizable Article III injury.

c. *Organizational Standing*

Collective entities such as trade associations, public interest groups, and other multimember organizations can establish Article III standing based on one of two theories. First, an organization can establish "representational" standing to sue on behalf of its members by demonstrating that: "(a) its members would otherwise have standing to sue in their own right; (b) the interests it seeks to protect are germane to the organization's purpose; and (c) neither the claim asserted nor the relief requested requires the participation of individual members in the lawsuit."[73] Alternatively, the organization can establish "direct" standing by demonstrating that the allegedly unlawful action has harmed the organization itself.[74] Exactly what qualifies as a sufficiently "direct" injury to a plaintiff organization remains a source of lower-court disagreement,[75] but it is well established that the organization cannot demonstrate direct standing simply by pointing to a conflict between the defendant's challenged conduct and the organization's general values, mission, or agenda.[76] Instead, it must show that the defendant's conduct has

---

of funds to a religious organization, with the Justices deeming *Flast* inapplicable because Congress had not "specifically authorized" the contested federal outlay. *Id.* at 595. Most recently, in *Arizona Christian School Tuition Organization v. Winn*, 563 U.S. 125 (2011)—a decision that Justice Kagan characterized as "ravaging *Flast*," *id.* at 168 (Kagan, J., dissenting)—the Court denied standing to taxpayers seeking to challenge an Arizona tax credit program, with a five-Justice majority insisting that the now-repeatedly-restricted 1968 ruling authorized taxpayer challenges to only the legislative "extract[ion]" of funds from a government treasury to directly channel money to a religious enterprise. *Id.* at 141–43 (majority opinion). The effect of this final decision, according to Justice Kagan, was to provide "a roadmap—more truly, just a one-step instruction—to any government that wishes to insulate its financing of religious activity from legal challenge," because so long as lawmakers simply repackage an outright spending program as a functionally equivalent tax-expenditure program, "[n]o taxpayer will have standing to object." *Id.* at 168 (Kagan, J., dissenting).

73 Hunt v. Wash. State Apple Advert. Comm'n, 432 U.S. 333, 343 (1977).

74 A leading case is *Havens Realty Corp. v. Coleman*, 455 U.S. 363 (1982), in which the Court held that a nonprofit fair-housing organization had standing to challenge a realtor's alleged use of racially discriminatory steering practices because the challenged conduct had "impaired [the organization's] ability to provide counseling and referral services for low-and moderate-income homeseekers" and produced a "consequent drain on the organization's resources." *Id.* at 379.

75 *Compare, e.g.*, Fair Hous. of Marin v. Combs, 285 F.3d 899, 904–05 (9th Cir. 2002) (requiring that an organization asserting direct standing demonstrate "both a diversion of its resources and frustration of its mission"), *with* Equal Rights Ctr. v. Equity Residential, 798 F. Supp. 2d 707, 720 n.6 (D. Md. 2011) (treating the "frustration of mission" and "diversion of resources" requirements as "one and the same for standing purposes").

76 *See, e.g.*, Abigail All. for Better Access to Developmental Drugs v. Eschenbach, 469 F.3d 129, 133 (D.C. Cir. 2006) (noting that organizations can establish standing

resulted in a "drain on the organization's resources" or otherwise inflicted on it some analogous form of concrete and particularized injury.[77]

d. *State Standing*

Another specialized body of Article III standing doctrine governs suits brought on behalf of state governments and similar public entities.[78] Claims of state standing, the Court has concluded, can be predicated on three different types of Article III injuries: (1) injuries to states' *proprietary* interests (such as interests in acquiring and disposing of real property, hiring workers and independent contractors, buying and selling goods and services, and otherwise participating in commercial markets);[79] (2) injuries to states' distinctly *sovereign* interests (such as interests in enforcing their laws or in maintaining their territorial boundaries);[80] and (3) injuries

---

by showing that "that their activities have been impeded" but not by showing that "their mission has been compromised"). For an overview (and critique) of the doctrine, see Ryan Baasch, *Reorganizing Organizational Standing*, 103 VA. L. REV. ONLINE 18 (2017).

[77] *Havens Realty*, 455 U.S. at 379. *But see, e.g.*, Am. Soc. For Prevention of Cruelty to Animals v. Feld Entm't, Inc., 659 F.3d 13, 25 (D.C. Cir. 2011) (noting that "an organization's diversion of resources to litigation or to investigation in anticipation of litigation is considered a 'self-inflicted' budgetary choice that cannot qualify as an injury in fact").

[78] Principles akin to those that govern state standing apply in particular to claims of standing asserted by U.S. territories, *see* Alfred L. Snapp & Son, Inc. v. Puerto Rico *ex rel.* Barez, 458 U.S. 592, 608 n.15 (1982), and Native nations, *see, e.g.*, WRIGHT & MILLER, *supra* note 18, § 3531.11.1 (noting that "states (and also Indian Tribes) have standing to protect proprietary and sovereign interests"); Seth Davis, *Tribal Rights of Action*, 45 COLUM. HUM. RTS. L. REV. 499, 537–38 (2014) ("Like other sovereigns, Tribes may also sue in a third-party capacity, as a *substitute* litigant advancing their members' rights rather than their own." (emphasis in original)). The Court, not surprisingly, has also recognized that the federal government has standing to bring suits in its own name, although such suits can present distinct Article III issues. *See generally* WRIGHT & MILLER, *supra* note 18, § 3531.11 (noting that suits brought by the United States and suits brought by state governments "present similar but often distinctive problems").

[79] *Alfred L. Snapp*, 458 U.S. at 601–02. The proprietary nature of these interests makes them analytically similar to the sorts of interests that "other associations and private parties" might assert on their own behalf. *See id; see also* Ann Woolhandler & Michael G. Collins, *State Standing*, 81 VA. L. REV. 387, 392–93 (1995) (contending as a general matter that prior to the twentieth century states could "pursue only their common-law interests" in federal-court suits).

[80] *Alfred L. Snapp*, 458 U.S. at 601–02. Thus, for instance, states' sovereign interest in enforcing their laws would likely give them standing to initiate a challenge to a federal statute that preempts a state law. *See* F. Andrew Hessick, *Quasi-Sovereign Standing*, 94 NOTRE DAME L. REV. 1927, 1931–32 (2019). Similarly, a state may rely on its sovereign interests as the basis for standing to challenge federal laws as unconstitutional encroachments on traditional areas of state regulation, *see, e.g.*, Missouri v. Holland, 252 U.S. 416, 431 (1920). In addition, the Court has long held that the special sovereign interests of states give them standing to *appeal* from lower-court decisions that invalidate their own laws on constitutional or other grounds. *See* Tara Leigh Grove, *When Can a State Sue the United States?*, 101 CORNELL L. REV. 851, 858 (2016). It has also been held that states may delegate to other official entities

to states' *quasi-sovereign* interest in ensuring "the health and well-being—both physical and economic—of [their] residents in general."[81] Each of these types of injury claims is subject to its own rules and limitations,[82] but they together furnish state officials with a significant degree of latitude to initiate federal-court litigation on their own states' behalf. Widening that latitude even more is the Court's recent proclamation in *Massachusetts v. EPA*,[83] that states

(including legislative bodies) the authority to bring such appeals on the state's behalf. *See Va. House of Delegates*, 139 S. Ct. at 1951 (noting that "if the State had designated the [Virginia House of Delegates] to represent its interests, and if the House had in fact carried out that mission, we would agree that the House could stand in for the State"); Hollingsworth v. Perry, 570 U.S. 693, 710 (2018) (noting that "a State must be able to designate agents to represent it in federal court"). At the same time, the Court has indicated that the state's power to authorize others to defend laws on its behalf is itself limited by Article III. Thus, in *Hollingsworth*, the proponents of Proposition 8—a voter referendum that purported to ban same-sex marriage in California—were found not to have standing to appeal from a district court decision striking down the referendum because, even though authorized to represent the state under California law, *see* Perry v. Brown, 265 P.3d 1002, 1007 (Cal. 2011), they lacked a "judicially cognizable interest" in defending Proposition 8 against constitutional attack, *see Hollingsworth*, 570 U.S. at 708 (quoting Diamond v. Charles, 476 U.S. 54, 71 (1986)). The Court's decision in *Hollingsworth* appeared to suggest that, while legislatures and other official governmental entities may have Article III standing to defend laws that the state itself has authorized them to defend, the same will not generally be true of private parties with "no 'direct stake' in the outcome" of the underlying case. *Id.* at 706 (quoting *Arizonans for Official English*, 520 U.S. at 64); *see also* Richard H. Fallon, Jr., *How to Make Sense of Supreme Court Standing Cases—A Plea for the Right Kind of Realism*, 23 WM. & MARY BILL RTS. J. 105, 112–14 (2014) (describing *Hollingsworth* in similar terms, while noting that the Court's reasoning and "struggle[ ] to distinguish" prior precedents led many observers to view the decision as "a manipulative device for disposing of a case that five Justices simply preferred not to decide on the merits").

81 *Alfred L. Snapp*, 458 U.S. at 601–02. Thus, for instance, in *Alfred L. Snapp* the Court held that the Commonwealth of Puerto Rico (treated as similar to a state for standing-related purposes) could challenge the hiring practices of several apple harvesters alleged to have discriminated against Puerto Rican migrant farmworkers in violation of the terms of a federal employment program. Puerto Rico, the Court explained, had a valid "state interest in securing residents from the harmful effects of discrimination" and thus could assert "*parens patriae* standing to pursue the interests of its residents in the Commonwealth's full and equal participation in the federal employment service scheme." *Id.* at 608–10. More recently, lower courts have held that states have standing to protect their quasi-sovereign interests in, among other things, protecting residents against the harms of air pollution, *see, e.g.*, New Jersey v. EPA, 989 F.3d 1038, 1045 (D.C. Cir. 2021), preserving natural resources for residents' use, Sierra Club v. Trump, 977 F.3d 853, 866 (9th Cir. 2020), *vacated on other grounds sub nom.* Biden v. Sierra Club, 142 S. Ct. 56 (2021), and securing economic opportunities for workers within their boundaries, Washington v. Geo Group, Inc., 283 F. Supp. 3d 967, 979 (W.D. Wash. 2017) (finding that a state had *parens patriae* standing to challenge various employers' failure to adhere to the state's own minimum wage law requirements).

82 For helpful doctrinal overviews, see, for example, Katherine Mims Crocker, Note, *Securing Sovereign State Standing*, 97 VA. L. REV. 2051, 2056–70 (2011); Seth Davis, *State Standing for Equality*, 79 LA. L. REV. 147, 154–55 (2018); Hessick, *supra* note 80, at 1929–35.

83 549 U.S. 497 (2007).

are entitled to "special solicitude in our standing analysis."[84] Neither the import of nor the rationale for that suggestion was made clear by the Court,[85] but state attorneys general have been quick to invoke this "special solicitude" language in support of claims of standing to bring a wide range of high-profile and politically-charged state-plaintiff lawsuits,[86] often in an effort to thwart the federal government's own policymaking efforts.[87]

---

84 *Id.* at 520. More specifically, the Court held that Massachusetts's ownership of coastal land gave it standing to challenge the EPA's failure to regulate motor-vehicle greenhouse gas emissions, which imposed an injury on the Commonwealth by exacerbating sea-level rise and thereby reducing the expanse of its coastal-area real property. *Id.* at 521–23.

85 The central difficulty with the Court's analysis stemmed from the apparent inconsistency between its suggestion that "Massachusetts' stake in protecting its *quasi-sovereign interests*" entitled it to "special solicitude in our standing analysis," *id.* at 520 (emphasis added), and its subsequent assertion that Massachusetts's *proprietary interests* in the integrity of its coastal properties underlay its Article III injury. *Id.* at 522 (noting that Massachusetts "has alleged a particularized injury in its capacity *as a landowner*" (emphasis added)); *see also* Connecticut v. Am. Elec. Power Co., Inc., 582 F.3d 309, 338 (2d Cir. 2009) (noting that the Court's analysis "appear[ed] to conflate, to an extent, state *parens patriae* standing and proprietary standing"), *rev'd on other grounds*, 564 U.S. 410 (2011); Johnathan Remy Nash, *Sovereign Preemption State Standing*, 112 NW. U. L. REV. 201, 206 (2017) (noting the existence of "profound confusion over whether the *Massachusetts v. EPA* opinion's invocation of the states' entitlement to 'special solicitude' meant that standing was based on economic or sovereignty-based injury"); *see also* Seth Davis, *The New Public Standing*, 71 STAN. L. REV. 1229, 1239–42 (2019) (summarizing the scholarly debate about the significance of the "special solicitude" language).

86 Thus, for instance, following the election of President Obama, state-initiated suits challenging federal immigration policies (often with Texas in the lead) soon sprang up. *See, e.g.*, Texas v. United States, 809 F.3d 134 (5th Cir. 2015), *aff'd by an equally divided Court*, 136 S. Ct. 2271 (2016). With the election of President Trump, another wave of state-initiated litigation rolled in, now with "blue states" filing actions that challenged (among other things) the President's "travel ban" involving citizens of Muslim-majority countries, *see, e.g.*, Trump v. Hawaii, 138 S. Ct. 2392 (2018), and the President's effort to build a wall along the U.S.-Mexico border, *see, e.g.* Washington v. Trump, 441 F. Supp. 3d 1101 (W.D. Wash. 2020) (finding standing based on a state's expected loss of revenue from the diversion of federal funding to support construction of the wall). With the installation of the Biden administration, this process has continued unabated, with "red states" once again pursuing federal-court challenges to a range of Biden administration policies. *See, e.g.*, Texas v. United States, 524 F. Supp. 3d 598, 619 (S.D. Tex. 2021) (finding that Texas had standing to challenge a temporary pause on deportations by reference to Texas's assertion that the policy would result in an injury to the state's "financial interests by requiring it to spend more than it had previously anticipated on State detention facilities and several public benefits and services"); *see also* Louisiana v. Becerra, ___ F. Supp. 3d ___, 2021 WL 5609846, at *4–*5 (W.D. La. Nov. 30, 2021) (finding that fourteen states had standing to challenge a COVID-19 vaccine mandate for healthcare workers at facilities participating in the federal Medicaid and Medicare programs "because the Government Defendants' actions harm Plaintiff States' sovereign, proprietary, and *parens patriae* interests"), *stay granted on other grounds*, Biden v. Missouri, 142 S. Ct. 647 (2022).

87 *See* Davis, *supra* note 85, at 1232 (noting that the Court in *Massachusetts v. EPA* "all but announced state governments as the new public interest litigants"); Tara Leigh Grove, *Foreword: Some Puzzles of State Standing*, 94 NOTRE DAME L. REV. 1883, 1884 (2019) ("There are likely multiple reasons for the recent explosion in state

e. *Legislative Standing*

Special standing problems also arise when legislators seek to assert their prerogatives as government officials by initiating litigation in federal court. The Court first dealt with so-called "legislative standing" in *Coleman v. Miller*,[88] holding that individual members of the Kansas state senate had standing to challenge that body's purported ratification of the proposed Child Labor Amendment to the U.S. Constitution.[89] According to the Court in *Coleman*, the plaintiff-senators could sue because they alleged that the votes they cast should have been "sufficient to defeat ratification" of the amendment and that they were therefore seeking to vindicate a "plain, direct and adequate interest in maintaining the effectiveness of their votes."[90] Several decades later, however, the Court in *Raines v. Byrd*[91] distinguished *Coleman* in rejecting a different sort of claim of legislative standing to sue.[92] *Coleman*, the Court in *Raines* made clear, stood "(at most) for the proposition that legislators whose votes would have been sufficient to defeat (or enact) a specific legislative Act have standing to sue . . . on the ground that their votes have been *completely* nullified."[93] That case accordingly did not support standing for legislators who complained that the federal Line Item Veto Act, which authorized the President to "cancel" individual spending items included in properly enacted appropriations legislation, would merely *diminish* their power in a general sense by enabling the President to cancel spending measures that they and others had voted into law.[94] This claimed injury, according to the Court, involved only the "abstract dilution of

---

lawsuits against the federal executive. But the *Massachusetts* decision appears to be one factor.").

[88] 307 U.S. 433 (1939).

[89] *Id.* at 438. The Court in the end declined to reach the merits of the dispute, holding that the underlying claim presented a nonjusticiable political question. *See id.* at 447–56.

[90] *Id.* at 438.

[91] 521 U.S. 811 (1997).

[92] *Id.* at 523–24.

[93] *Id.* at 823 (emphasis added) (internal citations omitted).

[94] The Court would subsequently address the Line Item Veto Act's constitutionality in another case, *Clinton v. City of New York*, 524 U.S. 417 (1998), that did not present Article III standing problems. *See supra* Section 26.B.2.g. More specifically, the plaintiffs in *Clinton* were several entities (including the City of New York) that could and did claim an Article III injury based on the President's invocation of the act to cancel several federal spending provisions that would have sent money their way. *Id.* at 429–36. The plaintiffs' theories of injury thus differed from the legislative injuries asserted in *Raines* "not only because the President's exercise of his cancellation authority has removed any concern about the ripeness of the dispute, but more importantly because the parties have alleged a 'personal stake' in having an actual injury redressed rather than an 'institutional injury' that is 'abstract and widely dispersed.' " *Id.* at 430 (quoting *Raines*, 521 U.S. at 829).

institutional legislative power" and thus did not suffice to support any individual legislator's standing to sue.[95]

3. Congress's Power to Create Article III Standing

An especially vexing line of standing jurisprudence concerns the power of Congress to confer standing on plaintiffs who otherwise would not have it.[96] For much of the Court's history, this power was broad. Indeed, until the 1970s, the Court routinely treated a plaintiff's standing to sue as coextensive with the plaintiff's legal right to seek redress for the defendant's alleged wrongs,[97] meaning that Congress could establish new forms of standing by giving plaintiffs statutory authority to enforce federal-law rules.[98] This understanding became unsettled, however, as the Court moved to the view that the "injury in fact" concept establishes a constitutional requirement that operates apart from the elements of any congressionally established cause of action.[99] The upshot was a major

---

[95] *Id.* at 826. In *Coleman* and *Raines*, the Court crafted rules concerning federal-court jurisdiction over cases brought by individual legislators. What if, however, the plaintiff is not an individual legislator, but instead a legislative body? In this context too, the Court has distinguished between injuries based on fully nullified powers and those based merely on diminished institutional strength. *Compare, e.g.*, Ariz. State Legis. v. Ariz. Indep. Redistricting Comm'n, 576 U.S. 787, 795–96, 803 (2015) (finding that the Arizona Legislature had standing to challenge passage of a state constitutional referendum that transferred redistricting authority to an independent commission because the effect of the referendum was to "completely nullify" future legislative votes about redistricting (internal quotation and alteration omitted)), *with Va. House of Delegates*, 139 S. Ct. at 1953 (holding that the Virginia House of Delegates (the lower house of the Virginia General Assembly) did not suffer an Article III injury on account of a district court's constitutional ruling regarding a districting plan because that ruling did not "alter the General Assembly's dominant initiating and ongoing role in redistricting"). In addition, courts have sometimes found that legislative bodies (or their committees) have standing to seek judicial enforcement of subpoenas they have issued. *See, e.g.*, Comm. on Judiciary of U.S. House of Reps. v. McGahn, 968 F.3d 755, 762–68 (D.C. Cir. 2020) (en banc) (holding that the House Judiciary Committee suffered a concrete and particularized injury when the target of one its subpoenas, former White House Counsel Donald McGahn, chose not to comply and thus deprived the committee of information that it sought); *see also id.* at 774 (finding that neither *Raines* nor *Arizona State Legislature* cut against the committee's theory of standing because those two cases "left open the possibility that some institutional injuries would be sufficient to confer a legislative body standing").

[96] *See* William Baude, *Standing in the Shadow of Congress*, 2016 SUP. CT. REV. 197, 212 (characterizing this area of the law as presenting "one of the hardest questions in modern federal courts doctrine").

[97] For a historical overview of these cases, see, e.g., Cass R. Sunstein, *What's Standing After* Lujan*?*, 91 MICH. L. REV. 163, 168–97 (1992).

[98] *See, e.g.*, *Linda R.S.*, 410 U.S. at 617 n.3 ("Congress may enact statutes creating legal rights, the invasion of which creates standing, even though no injury would exist without the statute.").

[99] Indeed, as Justice Thomas has noted, the Court's earlier "injury in fact" cases had actually operated to offer an "*additional* way to get into federal court" for plaintiffs who lacked an express cause of action under a federal statute. *See TransUnion LLC*, 141 S. Ct. at 2219 (Thomas, J., dissenting) (emphasis in original). But the injury-in-fact requirement was thereafter refashioned to operate as a limit on Congress's ability

shift in the relationship between the "case or controversy" requirement of Article III and Congress's legislative power to vest would-be beneficiaries of statutory enactments with standing to sue.

The modern Court's most prominent effort to synthesize this new approach came in its 1992 decision in *Lujan v. Defenders of Wildlife*.[100] That case concerned a provision of the Endangered Species Act (ESA) that generally required federal agencies to consult with designated federal officials, including the Secretary of the Interior, about the impact of their actions on jeopardized species. The plaintiffs challenged an executive-branch determination that the consultation requirement did not apply to actions undertaken by the federal government in foreign nations. And in claiming standing to sue, they relied heavily on the statute's "citizen suit" provision, which specifically authorized "any person" to bring suit against the government for alleged violations of the ESA.[101]

The lower court accepted this theory of standing, emphasizing Congress's clear intent "to bestow procedural rights upon environmental organizations."[102] But the Supreme Court reversed. The problem, as Justice Scalia explained for himself and five colleagues, was that this theory of "procedural injury" was not premised on any "separate concrete interest" of the plaintiffs that the alleged statutory violation had worked to "impair."[103] This point was decisive in Justice Scalia's view because even an incontestable violation of a congressionally conferred "procedural right" could not itself support standing under Article III.[104] More specifically, he reasoned that, if Congress could make any agency's failure to follow any statutory requirements the basis for anyone's standing to sue, then it would have the power to "convert the undifferentiated public interest in executive officers' compliance with the law into an 'individual right' vindicable in the courts."[105] And to allow that result would be to permit Congress to violate the separation of powers by "transfer[ring] from the President to the courts the Chief Executive's

---

to confer standing via newly created statutory causes of action. *Id.* at 2019–20 (Thomas, J., dissenting). For an early case that helped to trigger this doctrinal shift, see Ass'n of Data Processing Serv. Orgs., Inc. v. Camp, 397 U.S. 150, 153 (1970) (suggesting for the first time that the presence of an injury-in-fact was relevant to the federal courts' power to adjudicate a case, albeit in the context of the discussion not of Article III but of the scope of the statutory cause of action conferred by the federal Administrative Procedure Act).

100 504 U.S. 555 (1992).

101 *Id.* at 571–72.

102 Defenders of Wildlife v. Lujan, 911 F.2d 117, 121 (8th Cir. 1990), *rev'd*, 504 U.S. 555.

103 *Lujan*, 504 U.S. at 572.

104 *Id.* at 572 n.7.

105 *Id.* at 577.

most important constitutional duty, to 'take Care that the Laws be faithfully executed.' "[106]

Even while repudiating the *Lujan* plaintiffs' theory of a legislatively recognized procedural injury, the Court did acknowledge that Congress could in some ways augment Article III standing by way of statute. Indeed, Justice Scalia flagged three mechanisms through which Congress might manage to establish standing where it otherwise would not exist. First, in "unusual case[s]" Congress could "creat[e] a concrete private interest in the outcome of a suit against a private party for the government's benefit, by providing a cash bounty for the victorious plaintiff."[107] Second, although congressionally created "procedural rights" could not on their own establish Article III *injuries*, those rights could "at least" serve to relax "the normal standards for redressability and immediacy."[108] Finally, and most cryptically, Justice Scalia acknowledged that Congress retained a measure of power to "elevat[e] to the status of legally cognizable injuries concrete, *de facto* injuries that were previously inadequate in law."[109] Thus, while Congress could not go so far as to make "the public interest in proper administration of the laws" a source of Article III injury, it retained at least some authority, as Justice Kennedy explained in a separate concurrence joined by Justice Souter, to "define injuries and articulate chains of causation

[106] *Id.* Justice Scalia's analysis in *Lujan* tracked an analysis he had earlier set forth in a well-known 1983 law review article. *See* Antonin Scalia, *The Doctrine of Standing as an Essential Element of the Separation of Powers*, 17 SUFFOLK U. L. REV. 881 (1983).

[107] *Id.* at 573. This observation served the purpose of reconciling *Lujan* with the federal courts' longstanding willingness to entertain certain types of federal *qui tam* suits brought by individuals on the federal government's behalf. *See also* Vt. Agency of Nat. Res. v. United States *ex rel.* Stevens, 529 U.S. 765, 771, 773 (2000) (clarifying that an "adequate basis for the [qui tam] relator's suit for his bounty is to be found in the doctrine that the assignee of a claim has standing to assert the injury in fact suffered by the assignor" as well as in the "long tradition of *qui tam* actions in England and the American Colonies"). *See generally* Randy Beck, *Qui Tam Litigation Against Government Officials: Constitutional Implications of a Neglected History*, 93 NOTRE DAME L. REV. 1235, 1257 (2018).

[108] *Lujan*, 504 U.S. at 572 n.7. For example, as Justice Scalia suggested, a person "living adjacent to the site for proposed construction of a federally licensed dam" might—on account of a law authorizing suit to enforce compliance with the National Environmental Policy Act by such persons—have "standing to challenge the licensing agency's failure to prepare an environmental impact statement, even though he cannot establish with any certainty that the statement will cause the license to be withheld or altered." *Id.*

[109] *Id.* at 578. Justice Scalia went on to offer two examples: First, a statutory right might support standing for plaintiffs claiming injury based on a "personal interest in living in a racially integrated community." *Id.* (citing Trafficante v. Met. Life Ins. Co., 409 U.S. 205, 208–12 (1972)). Second, a statutory right might support standing for a company claiming injury based on an "interest in marketing its product free from competition" *Id.* (citing Hardin v. Ky. Utils. Co., 390 U.S. 1, 6 (1968)).

that will give rise to a case or controversy where none existed before."[110]

Lujan's separation-of-powers logic applies straightforwardly to instances in which Congress seeks to confer on everyday citizens a generalized and judicially enforceable "right" to have executive-branch agencies adhere to procedural rules.[111] In a particularly controversial set of follow-on decisions, however, the Court has broadened the reach of this holding in two important ways. First, whereas *Lujan* involved a suit brought directly against executive-branch officials, the Court now treats the decision as equally relevant to suits involving *private-party* defendants,[112] even though such suits do not implicate the specific separation-of-powers problem of converting the federal courts into "virtually continuing monitors of the wisdom and soundness of Executive action."[113] In the post-*Lujan* Court's view, however, such private-defendant actions pose their own serious threat to "the Executive Branch's Article II authority,"[114] on the theory that such suits, if unconstrained by the injury-in-fact requirement, give federal-court plaintiffs (and, by extension, federal judges) too much power to interfere with the President's choices about "how to prioritize and how aggressively to pursue legal actions against defendants who violate the law."[115]

Second, while the Court in *Lujan* faulted Congress for the "generalized" and "undifferentiated" nature of the "procedural

[110] *Id.* at 580 (Kennedy, J., concurring in part and concurring in the judgment), *quoted in Spokeo*, 578 U.S. at 341.

[111] This is not to say that the Court's separation-of-powers reasoning on this point is immune to criticism. One critique stems from the Court's failure to explain why the President's Article II authority would not similarly be encroached upon by a suit in which the plaintiff *did in fact* suffer an injury in fact, given the premise that it is the *President*'s job to see that the laws are faithfully executed. *See, e.g.*, Gene R. Nichol, Jr., *Justice Scalia, Standing, and Public Law Litigation*, 42 DUKE L.J. 1141, 1163–64 (1993) (noting that, on Justice Scalia's separation-of-powers logic, "a challenged legislative or judicial action either unconstitutionally abrogates executive power or it does not" and that "[i]t should make little difference what sort of plaintiff seeks to trigger the incursion"); *see also* Sunstein, *supra* note 97, at 213 ("If a plaintiff with a plane ticket can sue under the ESA without offense to Article II, then it makes no sense to say that Article II is violated if a plaintiff lacking such a ticket initiates a proceeding."). Another critique rests on the oddity of suggesting that the President's power "to take Care that the Laws be faithfully executed" is threatened by suits whose very object is to ensure executive *compliance* with the law. *See, e.g.*, *id.* at 212 (criticizing *Lujan* on the ground that "the Take Care Clause confers a duty insofar as it imposes on the President both a responsibility to be faithful to law and an obligation to enforce the law as it has been enacted, rather than as he would have wished it to be").

[112] *See Spokeo*, 578 U.S. at 337; *TransUnion*, 141 S. Ct. at 2203–04.

[113] *Lujan*, 504 U.S. at 577 (quoting *Allen*, 468 U.S. at 760 (quoting Laird v. Tatum, 408 U.S. 1, 15 (1972))).

[114] *TransUnion*, 141 S. Ct. at 2207.

[115] *Id.*

injury" it sought to recognize,[116] the Court has since made it clear that Congress likewise lacks the power to confer standing based on injuries that, though particularized to the plaintiff, nonetheless fail to qualify as "concrete."[117] As Justice Alito put the point for a five-Justice majority in *Spokeo v. Robins*,[118] while Congress remains "well positioned to identify intangible harms that meet minimum Article III requirements," it cannot simply dictate that "a plaintiff automatically satisfies the injury-in-fact requirement whenever a statute grants a person a statutory right and purports to authorize that person to sue to vindicate that right."[119] *Spokeo* itself involved a claim asserted under the Fair Credit Reporting Act (FCRA), which authorizes the recovery of statutorily specified damages of $100 to $1000 per violation from a credit-reporting agency that fails to follow "reasonable procedures" in compiling the plaintiff's credit report. Notwithstanding the statute's clear stipulation that plaintiffs could challenge only the preparation of *their own reports*, the Court concluded that Article III did not support standing insofar as a plaintiff alleged only a "bare procedural violation" that was "divorced from any concrete harm."[120] Instead, as another five-Justice majority made clear in *TransUnion LLC v. Ramirez*,[121] an FCRA plaintiff seeking damages for a past violation of the statute must demonstrate that the violation, in addition to being particularized to the individual claimant, actually caused that person a specialized form of harm—not just an error in the credit report itself, that is, but something like a lost job, a denied mortgage application, or a damaged image in the public eye.[122]

---

[116] *Lujan*, 504 U.S. at 575–77. *But see id.* at 573 (noting, albeit in passing, the "abstract" nature of the injury that the plaintiffs invoked).

[117] *Spokeo*, 578 U.S. at 339; *TransUnion*, 141 S. Ct. at 2200.

[118] 578 U.S. 330 (2016).

[119] *Id.* at 341; *see also* Bayefsky, *supra* note 48, at 2305–09, 2317–21 (discussing and critiquing *Spokeo*'s emphasis on "tangibility" as a variable of importance to the concreteness inquiry).

[120] *Spokeo*, 578 U.S. at 341.

[121] 141 S. Ct. 2190 (2021).

[122] *See TransUnion*, 141 S. Ct. at 2210 (rejecting the idea "that a material risk of future harm can satisfy the concrete-harm requirement" where the plaintiff seeks damages for an FCRA violation). *TransUnion* in this respect reflected a notable expansion of *Spokeo*, which had itself seemed to endorse the notion that FCRA plaintiffs would have standing to challenge violations that gave rise to a "*risk* of real harm." *Spokeo*, 578 U.S. at 341 (emphasis in original); *see also See* Jon Romberg, *Trust the Process: Understanding Procedural Standing Under* Spokeo, 72 OKLA. L. REV. 517, 525 (2020) (reading *Spokeo* as establishing that "Congress validly confers standing when denial of a procedure it mandates, though intangible, is concrete, and when the risk of harm resulting from that denial is real and not bare"). As the Court in *TransUnion* saw things, however, *Spokeo*'s "risk of real harm" language applied to only those cases in which plaintiffs sought *injunctive relief* against existing or feared future violations of the FCRA and not, as was the case in *TransUnion* itself, damages relief for a past violation of the FCRA. *See TransUnion*, 141 S. Ct. at 2210–11. But that was

These glosses on *Lujan* seem to leave Congress with little room to maneuver in its attempts to secure judicial enforcement of the statutory rights it confers, at least when violations of those rights would not otherwise result in the sorts of injuries deemed remediable at common law.[123] To be sure, the Court continues to say that Congress's views are "instructive" in guiding its own application of the Article III test.[124] The Court's actions, however, speak louder than its words, and its most recent standing-related rulings evidence little in the way of the "due respect" to Congress that the Court has purported to embrace.[125] In particular, in both *Spokeo* and *TransUnion*, the Court pushed aside Congress's focused determination that the careless compilation and dissemination of consumer credit reports works a real enough harm to the subjects of those very reports to give rise to a cognizable injury sufficient to support the award of monetary redress in federal court.[126] Moreover, in describing the sorts of injuries that would support Article III jurisdiction, the Court in those cases pointed only to harms whose concreteness seem in no way to depend on or to be bolstered by Congress's recognition of their existence.[127] To be sure, there may remain a set of injuries that Congress has the power to transform from generalized to concrete by creating focused statutory rights.[128] But if *Spokeo* and *TransUnion* are harbingers of things to come, that set of injuries may prove to be so limited as to border on the nonexistent.

4. Prudential Standing

We conclude this discussion with an overview of the "prudential" aspects of modern-day standing doctrine. Over the years, many

---

a dubious gloss on *Spokeo*, which nowhere purported to distinguish between past and future injuries for purposes of its Article III standing analysis. *See id.* at 2222–23 (Thomas, J., dissenting) (suggesting that the majority opinion's "reworking of *Spokeo* fails" in light of what the Court in *Spokeo* actually "said" and "did").

[123] *Lujan*, 504 U.S. at 580 (Kennedy, J., concurring in part and concurring in the judgment).

[124] *TransUnion*, 141 S. Ct. at 2204–05.

[125] *Id.* at 2204.

[126] *Id.* at 2221 (Thomas, J., dissenting) ("In the name of protecting the separation of powers, this Court has relieved the legislature of its power to create and define rights." (internal citations omitted)).

[127] *See, e.g.*, *id.* at 2208–09 (noting that a group of plaintiffs whose false credit reports were actually published had suffered a concrete injury because the resulting reputational harm they thereby suffered bore "a 'close relationship' to a harm traditionally recognized as providing a basis for a lawsuit in American courts—namely, the reputational harm associated with the tort of defamation" (quoting *Spokeo*, 578 U.S. at 341)).

[128] The one example alluded to in *Spokeo* was an injury caused by a government agency's unwillingness to disclose information to which the plaintiff was legally entitled. *See, e.g.*, *Spokeo*, 578 U.S. at 342 (citing FEC v. Akins, 524 U.S. 11, 20–25 (1998); and Pub. Citizen v. Dep't of Justice, 491 U.S. 440, 449 (1989)).

commentators have questioned both the legitimacy and the coherence of this line of cases,[129] and its influence may be waning.[130] Still, the Court continues to recognize at least two prudential standing limits of some practical importance.[131] The first is the rule regarding "third-party standing," which "normally bars litigants from asserting the rights or legal interests of others in order to obtain relief from injury to themselves."[132] This rule, however, is riddled with exceptions.[133] Among other things, for instance, the rule does not bar adjudication of cases in which "the party asserting the right has a 'close' relationship with the person who possesses the right" and "there is a 'hindrance' to the possessor's ability to protect his own interests."[134] The third-party standing rule also does not stand in the

---

[129] *See, e.g.*, William A. Fletcher, *The Structure of Standing*, 98 YALE L.J. 221, 243 (1988) (noting the "apparent lawlessness" of the doctrine).

[130] *See* Ernest A. Young, *Prudential Standing After* Lexmark International, Inc. v. Static Control Components, Inc., 10 DUKE J. CONST. L. & PUB. POL'Y 149, 151 (2014) (noting that the Court's decision in *Lexmark International, Inc. v. Static Control Components, Inc.*, 572 U.S. 118 (2014), reflected an "explicit shift away from the traditional rubric of prudential standing"); Fred O. Smith, Jr., *Undemocratic Restraint*, 70 VAND. L. REV. 845, 855–58 (2017) (noting the Court's recent movement to constitutionalize various aspects of prudential standing doctrine).

[131] Two other rules that were in the past characterized as a part of prudential standing doctrine are today more frequently treated as implicating other areas of doctrine. First, while the Court previously suggested that the doctrine encompassed a rule against the adjudication of "generalized grievances," *see, e.g.*, Elk Grove Unified Sch. Dist. v. Newdow, 542 U.S. 1, 12 (2004) (quoting *Allen*, 468 U.S. at 751), it has more recently asserted that this rule merely restates the Article III requirement that a plaintiff suffer a "concrete and particularized injury." *Lexmark*, 572 U.S. at 128 n.3 (emphasizing that suits raising generalized grievances are "barred for constitutional reasons, not 'prudential' ones"). Second, whereas the Court once suggested that prudential standing doctrine required that a "plaintiff's complaint fall within the zone of interests protected by the law invoked," *Elk Grove*, 542 U.S. at 12 (quoting *Allen* v, 468 U.S. at 751), it has subsequently made clear that the zone-of-interests requirement does not belong under the "prudential rubric" but instead concerns the question "whether a legislatively conferred cause of action encompasses a particular plaintiff's claim." *Lexmark*, 572 U.S. at 127 (internal quotations omitted).

[132] *Warth*, 422 U.S. at 509. In *Warth* itself, the Court held that even if a group of taxpayers had suffered an Article III injury as a result of an allegedly unlawful zoning practice, their suit was subject to dismissal because they sought to invoke legal rights that belonged not to them but instead to "persons of low and moderate income who are said to be excluded" from the locality. *Id.* at 509–10; *see also* Kowalski v. Tesmer, 543 U.S. 125, 127 (2004) (preventing a group of defense attorneys from challenging a law barring appointment of appellate counsel for some indigent defendants on the ground that, while the plaintiffs might have alleged an adequate Article III injury in the form of forgone fees that the state otherwise would have paid them, the rights at issue in the suit belonged to *criminal defendants* and not to the criminal attorneys themselves).

[133] *See generally* Brian Charles Lea, *The Merits of Third-Party Standing*, 24 WM. & MARY BILL RTS. J. 277, 296–302 (2015) (outlining these exceptions).

[134] *Kowalski*, 543 U.S. at 130. This idea has been invoked, for example, to permit *jus tertii* claims brought by doctors on behalf of patients, *see, e.g.*, Singleton v. Wulff, 428 U.S. 106, 113–18 (1976) (opinion of Blackmun, J.), parents on behalf of children, *see, e.g.*, Sessions v. Morales-Santana, 137 S. Ct. 1678, 1688–89 (2017), and even vendors on behalf of vendees, *see, e.g.*, Craig v. Boren, 429 U.S. 190, 193–97 (1976) (1976); *see also* Barrows v. Jackson, 346 U.S. 249, 257 (1953) (permitting various homeowners to challenge a racially discriminatory covenant as violating the rights of

way of First Amendment "overbreadth" claims, even though the litigants who press such claims are essentially challenging statutes on the ground that they abridge the free-speech rights of other persons.[135] And the Court has generally declined to invoke the third-party-standing rule to bar individual plaintiffs from raising claims that implicate the interests of government institutions such as Congress or the states, insisting instead that "[i]f the constitutional structure of our Government that protects individual liberty is compromised, individuals who suffer otherwise justiciable injury may object."[136] For these reasons, there is much accuracy in the observation of Professors Curtis Bradley and Ernest Young that the rule against third-party standing is one that "seems to be honored in the breach."[137]

A second prudential standing limit stems from the idea that the parties to an action must have clashing interests. Although the Court once indicated that this "adverseness" requirement flows from Article III,[138] its most recent proclamation on the subject suggests that this requirement—at least in some of its applications—is merely prudential in nature.[139] The doctrinal shift came in *United States v. Windsor*,[140] which involved section 3 of the Defense of Marriage Act (DOMA).[141] The United States, though nominally the defendant in

potential Black purchasers because "it would be difficult if not impossible for the persons whose rights are asserted to present their grievance before any court").

135 *See, e.g.*, Broadrick v. Oklahoma, 413 U.S. 601 (1973). For scholarly treatments of the overbreadth doctrine, see, for example, Michael C. Dorf, *Facial Challenges to State and Federal Statutes*, 46 STAN. L. REV. 235, 250–53 (1994), Richard H. Fallon, Jr., *Making Sense of Overbreadth*, 100 YALE L.J. 853, 859–62 (1991), and Henry Paul Monaghan, *Overbreadth*, 1981 SUP. CT. REV. 1. Though primarily associated with First Amendment-based free-speech doctrine, the Court has sometimes permitted overbreadth claims in other fields of rights-based law. *See, e.g.*, Dorf, *supra*, at 272 & n.158 (asserting that "*Roe v. Wade* exemplifies overbreadth analysis" and positing other examples as well (internal footnote omitted)).

136 Bond v. United States, 564 U.S. 211, 223 (2011). *See generally* Aziz Z. Huq, *Standing for the Structural Constitution*, 99 VA. L. REV. 1435, 1477 (2013) (noting that "[t]hird-party intermediation of the harm alleged to flow from structural constitutional wrongs occurs in many separation-of-powers cases").

137 Curtis A. Bradley & Ernest A. Young, *Unpacking Third-Party Standing*, 131 YALE L.J. 1, 3 (2021); *see also id.* at 5 (contending that "much of the . . . doctrine's incoherence stems from the attempt to capture, in a single principle, disparate scenarios raising distinct problems of both theory and practice").

138 *See, e.g.*, Richardson v. Ramirez, 418 U.S. 24, 36 (1974) (observing that Article III limits the Court to the "adjudication of actual disputes between adverse parties").

139 It is not altogether clear whether this adverseness requirement is more appropriately characterized as a prong of prudential standing doctrine or a separate prudential limit of its own. *See, e.g.*, Smith, *supra note* 130, at 858–59 (delineating adverseness as a prudential requirement that exists alongside, rather than within, the principles of prudential-standing doctrine).

140 570 U.S. 744 (2013).

141 *Id.* at 752. Section 3 codified the federal government's refusal to recognize as "married" within the meaning of federal law same-sex couples who had been validly

the suit, had chosen not to contest the plaintiff's position that section 3 unconstitutionally discriminated against same-sex couples, and the question thus arose whether the federal government had standing to appeal from a district court's ruling in line with that position.[142] In an opinion by Justice Kennedy, the Court said "yes": There was no Article III problem with the government's appeal, he explained, because the district court had ordered it to pay a tax refund to the plaintiff and had thus imposed on it a "real and immediate economic injury" that was unaffected by its agreement with the merits of the plaintiff's claim.[143] And while "the Executive's agreement with [the plaintiff's] legal argument" did to some degree deprive the case of the "concrete adverseness which sharpens the presentation of issues upon which the court so largely depends," this was ultimately only a "prudential" problem that the Court in this case was willing to overlook.[144] In particular, the Court noted that any problems posed by the government's non-adverse posture were mitigated by the involvement in the proceedings of another party, the Bipartisan Legal Advisory Group of the House of Representatives (BLAG), which had intervened to defend DOMA on Congress's behalf,[145] and whose continued participation in the litigation helped to ensure a "sharp adversarial presentation of the issues."[146] The Court also emphasized that a dismissal of *Windsor* for lack of adverseness would only cause "extensive litigation" about section 3 to "ensue," leaving the "[r]ights and privileges of hundreds of thousands of persons" hanging in the balance until the courts had finally found "a case in which all prudential concerns about justiciability are absent."[147] Under these "unusual and urgent circumstances," the Court concluded, the otherwise applicable prudential bar to hearing suits that lack a

---

married under state law, and it thus operated to deprive these couples of a wide array of federal benefits to which they would otherwise have been entitled. *Id.*

142 As for the strategic question of *why* the federal government chose to appeal from the district court's ruling, one possibility is that the President and his Attorney General anticipated a favorable ruling on the issue from the Court and accordingly sought to keep the case going so that the Justices would hear it. It was also the case that an appeal was already being taken by BLAG, *id.* at 754, and the government may have filed its own appeal simply to ensure for itself a continued active role in litigation that was going to move forward in any event.

143 *Id.* at 757–58.

144 *Id.* at 759–60 (quoting Baker v. Carr, 369 U.S. 185, 204 (1962)). In dissent, Justice Scalia vigorously contested the idea that adverseness operated as a merely a prudential limit on the federal judicial power. *See id.* at 784–85 (Scalia, J., dissenting) ("The question here is not whether, as the majority puts it, 'the United States retains a stake sufficient to support Article III jurisdiction[.]' [T]he question is whether there is any controversy (which requires *contradiction*) between the United States and Ms. Windsor. There is not." (internal citations omitted)).

145 *Id.* at 761 (majority opinion).

146 *Id.*

147 *Id.*

meaningful clash between adverse parties did not warrant dismissal.[148] At the same time, the Court cautioned that it was not endorsing this approach as "a common practice in ordinary cases," thus creating some uncertainty about how far its holding in *Windsor* might reach.[149] For now, at least, one can draw from the case little more than the conclusion that a lack of adverseness will often, but not always, provide a prudential basis for dismissal.

E. THE POLITICAL QUESTION DOCTRINE

Among the many points of law attributable to *Marbury v. Madison*[150] is the proposition that rulings on "[q]uestions, in their nature political, or which are, by the Constitution and laws, submitted to the Executive, can never be made in this court."[151] Though not deemed applicable to the facts of *Marbury* itself,[152] this limit on the judicial power has morphed over time into the now-established principle known as the "political question doctrine." In a nutshell, this doctrine dictates that disputes of an excessively "political" character do not qualify as the sort of judicially cognizable cases or controversies that support resolution by the Article III courts.[153] Instead, to the extent that such disputes give rise to constitutional or other legal issues, those issues must be resolved by the political branches themselves.

To say the least, the political question doctrine does not bar the adjudication of disputes simply because they raise politically controversial issues, are brought by (or against) prominent political figures, or carry important political ramifications—a truism underscored by such cases as *United States v. Nixon*,[154] *Clinton v.*

---

148 *Id.*

149 *Id.* at 762; *see also* Seila Law LLC v. Consumer Fin. Protection Bureau, 140 S. Ct. 2183, 1297 (2020) (noting that "as in *Windsor*, any prudential concerns with deciding an important legal question in this [non-adverse] posture can be addressed by 'the practice of entertaining arguments made by an *amicus* when the Solicitor General confesses error with respect to a judgment below' " (quoting *Windsor*, 570 U.S. at 760)).

150 5 U.S. (1 Cranch) 137 (1803).

151 *Id.* at 170.

152 *See supra* Section 34.A.2.

153 *See, e.g.*, Rucho v. Common Cause, 139 S. Ct. 2484, 2493–94 (2019) (treating the political question doctrine as rooted in the idea that "Article III of the Constitution limits federal courts to deciding 'Cases' and 'Controversies' ").

154 418 U.S. 683, 693 (1974) ("[T]he mere assertion of a claim of an 'intra-branch dispute,' without more, has never operated to defeat federal jurisdiction; justiciability does not depend on such a surface inquiry."). *See infra* Section 33.A.1.a.

Jones,[155] *Bush v. Gore*,[156] *Trump v. Mazars USA*,[157] and *Marbury* itself.[158] Rather, the Court applies the "political question" moniker to a narrower range of disputes that, for a more specific set of reasons, are deemed unsuitable for judicial resolution. As described by the Court in *Baker v. Carr*,[159] these disputes involve:

> a textually demonstrable constitutional commitment of the issue to a coordinate political department; or a lack of judicially discoverable and manageable standards for resolving it; or the impossibility of deciding without an initial policy determination of a kind clearly for nonjudicial discretion; or the impossibility of a court's undertaking independent resolution without expressing lack of the respect due coordinate branches of government; or an unusual need for unquestioning adherence to a political decision already made; or the potentiality of embarrassment from multifarious pronouncements by various departments on one question.[160]

Because this passage sets forth *six* distinct grounds for identifying cases subject to political-question-based dismissal, it might seem to indicate that cases implicating the political question

---

155 520 U.S. 681, 701 (1997) (noting that "in this case" the plaintiff "is merely asking the courts to exercise their core Article III jurisdiction to decide cases and controversies"). *See supra* Section 33.B.2.

156 531 U.S. 98, 111 (2000) ("When contending parties invoke the process of the courts . . ., it becomes our unsought responsibility to resolve the federal and constitutional issues the judicial system has been forced to confront.").

157 140 S. Ct. 2019, 2031 (2020) (noting that "the parties agree that this particular controversy is justiciable").

158 5 U.S. at 170 (noting that the case did not present a political question because it involved "the performance of a duty, not depending on executive discretion, but on particular acts of congress and the general principles of law"). *See generally* WRIGHT & MILLER, *supra* note 18, § 3534.1 (collecting additional such cases).

159 369 U.S. 186 (1962).

160 *Id.* at 217. The Court in *Baker* also reaffirmed the validity of what was then and likely remains among the most significant of its political question doctrine holdings—namely, its determination in *Luther v. Borden*, 48 U.S. 1 (1849), that issues related to a state's compliance with the Guarantee Clause of Article IV, *see supra* Section 15.A, are generally nonjusticiable. *See Baker*, 369 U.S. at 223–24 (affirming *Luther*'s holding that "the Guaranty Clause is not a repository of judicially manageable standards which a court could utilize independently in order to identify a State's lawful government" and noting further that the Court has since *Luther* "consistently held that a challenge to state action based on the Guaranty Clause presents no justiciable question"). Thus, the Court in *Baker* explained, to the extent that the constitutional challenge in that case—i.e., a challenge to a state's malapportioned legislative districts—rested on the Guarantee Clause itself, the underlying question was nonjusticiable. *Id.* at 227. Nevertheless, the Court continued, *Luther* did not require a political-question-based dismissal of *Baker* itself because the challengers in *Baker* had raised a separate claim under the Fourteenth Amendment's *Equal Protection Clause* and because that claim was "not so enmeshed with those political question elements which render Guaranty Clause claims nonjusticiable." *Id.* at 227.

doctrine frequently arise. In fact, however, the Court has only infrequently invoked the doctrine to divest itself of authority to decide contentious and high-profile cases.[161] Moreover, to the extent the Court has deemed the doctrine applicable, it has focused almost entirely on only two of the six prongs of the *Baker* test: (1) the prong that directs attention to "textually demonstrable constitutional commitments" of issues to the other branches; and (2) the prong that concerns the "lack of judicially discoverable and manageable standards for resolving" the underlying issue.[162] No less important, the Court has applied each of these prongs in a manner that suggests a substantial amount of overlap between the ostensibly justiciability-based determination as to whether a question qualifies as "political" and the essentially merits-based determination as to whether the plaintiff ought to prevail under governing substantive law (*e.g.*, because the Constitution grants to a political branch broad discretion to make the underlying decision). For this reason, it is not at all clear that the political question doctrine has *ever* operated to prevent the Court from vindicating a request for relief that it would otherwise have been inclined to grant. And this feature of the doctrine underlies the oft-stated criticism that, in the words of Professor Wayne McCormack, the doctrine offers "nothing other than a subterfuge for masking explicit review on the merits of particular claims that come before a court."[163]

Consider first the "textually demonstrable constitutional commitment" line of cases. Because the application of this criterion hinges directly on the commands of the Constitution itself, it blurs

---

[161] *See* Richard H. Fallon, Jr., *Political Questions and the Ultra Vires Conundrum*, 87 U. CHI. L. REV. 1481, 1483 (2020) (noting that, prior to its 2019 decision in *Rucho v. Common Cause*, 139 S. Ct. 2484 (2019), the Court had "only twice since the 1930s . . . ordered the dismissal of a case on political question grounds" (citing Gilligan v. Morgan, 413 U.S. 1 (1973) (barring on political-question grounds a suit seeking injunctive relief against National Guard officials); and Nixon v. United States, 506 U.S. 224 (1993) (discussed *supra* Section 32.A.1))). To be sure, and as Professor Fallon himself notes, invocations of the doctrine have surfaced more frequently in the lower courts, which do not have the luxury of denying certiorari in cases they would prefer not to hear. *See id.* at 1487 n.22. Thus, for instance, lower courts invoked the doctrine in turning away constitutional challenges to the U.S. government's involvement in the war in Vietnam and the later war in Nicaragua, *see* J. Peter Mulhern, *In Defense of the Political Question Doctrine*, 137 U. PA. L. REV. 97, 107 nn. 26–27 (1988); Stephen I. Vladeck, *War and Justiciability*, 49 SUFFOLK U.L. REV. 47, 48 (2017), and the doctrine has also occasionally been invoked in post-9/11 cases involving the global "War on Terror," *see* Stephen I. Vladeck, *The New National Security Canon*, 61 AM. U. L. REV. 1295, 1321–25 (2012); *see also* Samuel R. Howe, Note, *Congress's War Powers and the Political Question Doctrine After* Smith v. Obama, 68 DUKE L.J. 1231 (2019) (discussing recent developments).

[162] *See* Fallon, *supra* note 161, at 1494 (noting that the Court's modern cases "seem to focus almost exclusively" on these two prongs).

[163] Wayne McCormack, *The Political Question Doctrine—Jurisprudentially*, 70 U. DET. MERCY L. REV. 793, 822 (1993).

the boundary between justiciability and merits-based inquiries. For example, as explained in an earlier chapter, the Court in *Nixon v. United States*[164] read Article I, section 3, clause 6 of the Constitution, which grants to the Senate the "sole Power to try all Impeachments," as embodying a "textually demonstrable commitment" to the Senate of the power to determine the validity of its own impeachment-trial procedures.[165] In so doing, however, the Court came close to holding that the petitioner's own claim—based on his challenge to the validity of the procedures the Senate used in conducting his impeachment trial—was lacking in merit. Saying that the Constitution contained a "textually demonstrable commitment" to the Senate of the power to determine its own impeachment procedures, after all, was little different from saying that the Senate possessed an unreviewable discretion to structure its procedures in whatever manner it wanted.[166] And it is hard to see how recognizing this measure of senatorial discretion differed, in any functional sense, from holding on the merits that the Senate had not exceeded its powers in adopting the procedures that the plaintiff had challenged.[167]

The "judicially manageable standards" prong involves a similar, though subtler, connection between a political-question ruling and a court's view of a case's merits. Illustrative of the point is *Rucho v.*

---

164 506 U.S. 224 (1993); *see supra* Section 32.A.1.

165 *Nixon*, 506 U.S. at 229, 236.

166 *See* Mark Tushnet, *Law and Prudence in the Law of Justiciability: The Transformation and Disappearance of the Political Question Doctrine*, 80 N.C. L. REV. 1203, 1210–11 (2002) (suggesting that the Court's opinion in *Nixon* seemed to indicate at bottom that "the Senate was given wide latitude in specifying trial procedures").

167 The Court's decision in *Nixon* stands in contrast to its earlier decision in *Powell v. McCormack*, 395 U.S. 486 (1969). That case arose from a decision by the House of Representatives of the 90th Congress not to seat Adam Clayton Powell, Jr., a longtime Representative from New York, for reasons having to do with his alleged misappropriation of legislative funds. *Id.* at 553–55. Powell sought judicial review of this decision, contending that the House had exceeded the scope of its Article I authority to "be the Judge of the . . . Qualifications of its own Members" by excluding from the body someone who obviously satisfied the Constitution's specified age, citizenship, and residency-based qualifications for House membership. *See* U.S. CONST. art. I, § 5. In response, the defendants sought dismissal on political-question grounds, contending that that Article I, section 5 reflected a "textually demonstrable constitutional commitment" to each House of Congress of the power to "judge" for itself whether a given individual was entitled to serve in that body. But the Court disagreed. In its view, Article I, section 5 established "at most a 'textually demonstrable commitment' to Congress to judge only the qualifications *expressly set forth in the Constitution*," which in turn meant that the courts remained free to adjudicate Powell's claim that the House lacked authority to exclude him on other possible qualification-related grounds, such as his alleged past misconduct. *Id.* at 517 (emphasis added). With that determination reached, a holding on the merits naturally followed: Since Powell was "not ineligible to serve under any provision of the Constitution, the House was without power to exclude him from its membership." *Id.* at 550.

Common Cause,[168] in which the Court, in a 5–4 decision authored by Chief Justice Roberts, concluded that constitutional challenges to partisan gerrymandering are nonjusticiable because of "a lack of judicially discoverable and manageable standards for resolving" such cases.[169] On the surface, this conclusion did not communicate any position regarding the constitutional appropriateness of politically motivated redistricting efforts; rather, at least so it would seem, the Court simply left it up to other government actors to identify and to implement whatever constitutionally-rooted norm against partisan gerrymandering they might find to exist.[170] At a deeper level, however, the outcome in *Rucho* could not be fully disentangled from the majority's skepticism toward the idea that the Constitution enshrines a robust anti-gerrymandering norm.[171] For these reasons, the Court's ostensibly non-merits-related conclusion about the nonjusticiability of partisan-gerrymandering claims looked like a merits-based decision in disguise.[172] At the least, in disclaiming the existence of any "discoverable" or "manageable" standard against which to evaluate partisan-gerrymandering claims, the Court in effect endorsed a rule of constitutional law that permits legislative

---

168 139 S. Ct. 2484 (2019).

169 *Id.* at 2496.

170 Indeed, the Court went out of its way to signal that "our conclusion does not condone excessive partisan gerrymandering." *Id.* at 2507.

171 For example, the Court signaled its disagreement with the challengers' "instinct that groups with a certain level of political support should enjoy a commensurate level of political power and influence," while noting in particular that this "desire for proportional representation" was "based on a norm that does not exist in our electoral system." *Id.* at 2499 (internal quotation omitted). Similarly, in emphasizing the unworkability of any First Amendment-based rule against partisan gerrymandering, the Court rejected out of hand the suggestion that the amendment itself might categorically prohibit officials from relying on political considerations when drawing legislative maps. *Id.* at 2504–05. (To the contrary, Chief Justice Roberts suggested, some amount of "partisanship" in redistricting was inevitably "permissible," thus leaving courts with the near-impossible task of asking "how much is too much." *Id.* at 2501.) Finally, in rejecting the challengers' efforts to analogize their posited constitutional bar on *partisan gerrymandering* as analogous to the Court's long-recognized bar on *racial gerrymandering*, the Court made reference to "our Fourteenth Amendment jurisprudence, which always has reserved the strictest scrutiny for discrimination on the basis of race," *id.* at 2502, thus at least implying a belief that the Constitution did not require a similarly strict rule for discrimination on the basis of partisanship, *id.* at 2502. None of this, to be clear, is to suggest that these assessments were necessarily incorrect. It is to say, however, that the *Rucho* opinion is laden with conclusions about the meaning and import of underlying constitutional norms—and not merely conclusions about the "manageability" of a potential anti-gerrymandering rule.

172 Indeed, the Court's reliance on concerns about fashioning workable rules for vindicating constitutional values mirrored its not-uncommon reliance on that same concern in formulating merits-determinative constitutional doctrine. *See supra* Section 5.A.1 (highlighting the Court's reliance on workability-related concerns in *Garcia v. San Antonio Metropolitan Transit Authority*, 469 U.S. 528 (1985), to dispense with a posited external limit on the commerce power that it had earlier endorsed in *National League of Cities v. Usery*, 426 U.S. 833 (1976)).

officials to put in place even the most obviously partisan redistricting schemes.[173]

These and other cases have led commentators to wonder whether the political question doctrine carries any stand-alone significance as a jurisdictional rule.[174] To the extent the doctrine channels concerns about the other branches' superior institutional capacity to navigate certain types of issues, those concerns might more productively be dealt with by formulating issue-specific deference doctrines that require courts to deem valid (or treat as presumptively valid) certain types of determinations that other institutional actors have rendered.[175] In addition, courts might refashion some aspects of the political question doctrine as part of the law of remedies—in particular, as one aspect of the tradition that equity courts should hesitate to intervene if public policy considerations counsel caution in a particular case.[176] Finally, as suggested earlier, to the extent that the political question doctrine reflects the conclusion that some choices have been "textually . . . commit[ted]" by the Constitution to branches other than the judiciary, courts might do well to frame such rulings as merits-based assessments about the scope of other branches' decisionmaking powers.[177] These observations jibe with a question famously posed

---

[173] *See, e.g.*, RONALD D. ROTUNDA & JOHN E. NOWAK, 1 TREATISE ON CONSTITUTIONAL LAW—SUBSTANCE & PROCEDURE § 2.16(c)(viii)(1) (5th ed. May 2021 update) (characterizing *Rucho* as "essentially a ruling on the merits of a federal constitutional claim in this arena"). Notably, and in telling contrast to *Rucho*, the Court in *Baker* determined that voter-malapportionment claims under the Equal Protection Clause were in fact justiciable, 390 U.S. at 228–29, and shortly thereafter the Court vindicated such claims on the merits pursuant to the "one person, one vote" doctrine. *See, e.g.*, Reynolds v. Sims, 377 U.S. 533, 558 (1964).

[174] *See* Rachel E. Barkow, *More Supreme Than Court? The Fall of the Political Question Doctrine and the Rise of Judicial Supremacy*, 102 COLUM. L. REV. 237, 267 & nn.156–57 (2002) (noting, and collecting supportive citations for, the proposition that "the political question doctrine . . . has drawn scathing rebukes from scholars, with some calling for complete abandonment of the doctrine" (internal footnote omitted)).

[175] *Cf.* Louis Henkin, *Is There a "Political Question" Doctrine?*, 85 YALE L.J. 597, 601–07 (1976) (exploring the relationship between deference to the political branches and the dictates of the political-question doctrine). *But see* Barkow, *supra* note 174, at 330–31 (noting that "[t]he same institutional and structural concerns that support giving some deference to Congress's interpretative decisions also justify giving absolute deference to the political branches in certain circumstances" and suggesting that such "absolute deference" is properly effectuated by means of the political question doctrine).

[176] *See* Fallon, *supra* note 161, at 1525–26 (noting that "[i]t is hornbook law that courts of equity must balance public and private interests before issuing injunctions" and that "a number of the Supreme Court's political question holdings could be recast as decisions about the inappropriateness of requested equitable relief in light of the balance of public and private interests" (citing Henkin, *supra* note 175, at 617–22)).

[177] *See* Henkin, *supra* note 175, at 600 (asserting that many cases viewed as establishing the "political question" doctrine are actually cases in which the Court reached the straightforward conclusion that the challenged actions "were within the constitutional authority of [the] President or Congress" to pursue).

about the political question doctrine by Professor Louis Henkin some fifty years ago: "Would not the part of the courts in our system, the institution of judicial review, and their public and intellectual acceptance, fare better if we broke open that package, assigned its authentic components elsewhere, and threw the package away?"[178]

---

[178] *Id.* at 625.

Appendix

THE CONSTITUTION OF THE U.S.

PREAMBLE

We the People of the United States, in Order to form a more perfect Union, establish Justice, insure domestic Tranquility, provide for the common defence, promote the general Welfare, and secure the Blessings of Liberty to ourselves and our Posterity, do ordain and establish this Constitution for the United States of America.

ARTICLE I

Section 1. All legislative Powers herein granted shall be vested in a Congress of the United States, which shall consist of a Senate and House of Representatives.

Section 2. [1] The House of Representatives shall be composed of Members chosen every second Year by the People of the several States, and the Electors in each State shall have the Qualifications requisite for Electors of the most numerous Branch of the State Legislature.

[2] No Person shall be a Representative who shall not have attained to the Age of twenty five Years, and been seven Years a Citizen of the United States, and who shall not, when elected, be an Inhabitant of that State in which he shall be chosen.

[3] Representatives and direct Taxes shall be apportioned among the several States which may be included within this Union, according to their respective Numbers, which shall be determined by adding to the whole Number of free Persons, including those bound to Service for a Term of Years, and excluding Indians not taxed, three fifths of all other Persons. The actual Enumeration shall be made within three Years after the first Meeting of the Congress of the United States, and within every subsequent Term of ten Years, in such Manner as they shall by Law direct. The Number of Representatives shall not exceed one for every thirty Thousand, but each State shall have at Least one Representative; and until such enumeration shall be made, the State of New Hampshire shall be entitled to chuse three, Massachusetts eight, Rhode Island and Providence Plantations one, Connecticut five, New York six, New Jersey four, Pennsylvania eight, Delaware one, Maryland six,

Virginia ten, North Carolina five, South Carolina five, and Georgia three.

[4] When vacancies happen in the Representation from any State, the Executive Authority thereof shall issue Writs of Election to fill such Vacancies.

[5] The House of Representatives shall chuse their Speaker and other Officers; and shall have the sole Power of Impeachment.

Section 3. [1] The Senate of the United States shall be composed of two Senators from each State, chosen by the Legislature thereof, for six Years; and each Senator shall have one Vote.

[2] Immediately after they shall be assembled in Consequence of the first Election, they shall be divided as equally as may be into three Classes. The Seats of the Senators of the first Class shall be vacated at the Expiration of the Second Year, of the second Class at the Expiration of the fourth Year, and of the third Class at the Expiration of the sixth Year, so that one third may be chosen every second Year; and if Vacancies happen by Resignation, or otherwise, during the Recess of the Legislature of any State, the Executive thereof may make temporary Appointments until the next Meeting of the Legislature, which shall then fill such Vacancies.

[3] No Person shall be a Senator who shall not have attained to the Age of thirty Years, and been nine Years a Citizen of the United States, and who shall not, when elected, be an Inhabitant of that State for which he shall be chosen.

[4] The Vice President of the United States shall be President of the Senate, but shall have no Vote, unless they be equally divided.

[5] The Senate shall chuse their other Officers, and also a President pro tempore, in the Absence of the Vice President, or when he shall exercise the Office of President of the United States.

[6] The Senate shall have the sole Power to try all Impeachments. When sitting for that Purpose, they shall be on Oath or Affirmation. When the President of the United States is tried, the Chief Justice shall preside: And no Person shall be convicted without the Concurrence of two thirds of the Members present.

[7] Judgment in Cases of Impeachment shall not extend further than to removal from Office, and disqualification to hold and enjoy any Office of honor, Trust, or Profit under the United States: but the Party convicted shall nevertheless be liable and subject to Indictment, Trial, Judgment, and Punishment, according to Law.

Section 4. [1] The Times, Places and Manner of holding Elections for Senators and Representatives, shall be prescribed in each State by the Legislature thereof; but the Congress may at any time by Law make or alter such Regulations, except as to the Places of chusing Senators.

[2] The Congress shall assemble at least once in every Year, and such Meeting shall be on the first Monday in December, unless they shall by Law appoint a different Day.

Section 5. [1] Each House shall be the Judge of the Elections, Returns, and Qualifications of its own Members, and a Majority of each shall constitute a Quorum to do Business; but a smaller Number may adjourn from day to day, and may be authorized to compel the Attendance of absent Members, in such Manner, and under such Penalties as each House may provide.

[2] Each House may determine the Rules of its Proceedings, punish its Members for disorderly Behavior, and, with the Concurrence of two thirds, expel a Member.

[3] Each House shall keep a Journal of its Proceedings, and from time to time publish the same, excepting such Parts as may in their Judgment require Secrecy; and the Yeas and Nays of the Members of either House on any question shall, at the Desire of one fifth of those Present, be entered on the Journal.

[4] Neither House, during the Session of Congress, shall without the Consent of the other, adjourn for more than three days, nor to any other Place than that in which the two Houses shall be sitting.

Section 6. [1] The Senators and Representatives shall receive a Compensation for their Services, to be ascertained by Law, and paid out of the Treasury of the United States. They shall in all Cases, except Treason, Felony and Breach of the Peace, be privileged from Arrest during their Attendance at the Session of their respective Houses, and in going to and returning from the same; and for any Speech or Debate in either House, they shall not be questioned in any other Place.

[2] No Senator or Representative shall, during the Time for which he was elected, be appointed to any civil Office under the Authority of the United States, which shall have been created, or the Emoluments whereof shall have been increased during such time; and no Person holding any Office under the United States, shall be a Member of either House during his Continuance in Office.

Section 7. [1] All Bills for raising Revenue shall originate in the House of Representatives; but the Senate may propose or concur with Amendments as on other Bills.

[2] Every Bill which shall have passed the House of Representatives and the Senate, shall, before it become a Law, be presented to the President of the United States; If he approve he shall sign it, but if not he shall return it, with his Objections to that House in which it shall have originated, who shall enter the Objections at large on their Journal, and proceed to reconsider it. If after such Reconsideration two thirds of that House shall agree to pass the Bill, it shall be sent together with the Objections, to the other House, by which it shall likewise be reconsidered, and if approved by two thirds of that House, it shall become a Law. But in all such Cases the Votes of both Houses shall be determined by yeas and Nays, and the Names of the Persons voting for and against the Bill shall be entered on the Journal of each House respectively. If any Bill shall not be returned by the President within ten Days (Sundays excepted) after it shall have been presented to him, the Same shall be a Law, in like Manner as if he had signed it, unless the Congress by their Adjournment prevent its Return in which Case it shall not be a Law.

[3] Every Order, Resolution, or Vote, to Which the Concurrence of the Senate and House of Representatives may be necessary (except on a question of Adjournment) shall be presented to the President of the United States; and before the Same shall take Effect, shall be approved by him, or being disapproved by him, shall be repassed by two thirds of the Senate and House of Representatives, according to the Rules and Limitations prescribed in the Case of a Bill.

Section 8. [1] The Congress shall have Power To lay and collect Taxes, Duties, Imposts and Excises, to pay the Debts and provide for the common Defence and general Welfare of the United States; but all Duties, Imposts and Excises shall be uniform throughout the United States;

[2] To borrow money on the credit of the United States;

[3] To regulate Commerce with foreign Nations, and among the several States, and with the Indian Tribes;

[4] To establish an uniform Rule of Naturalization, and uniform Laws on the subject of Bankruptcies throughout the United States;

[5] To coin Money, regulate the Value thereof, and of foreign Coin, and fix the Standard of Weights and Measures;

[6] To provide for the Punishment of counterfeiting the Securities and current Coin of the United States;

[7] To Establish Post Offices and Post Roads;

[8] To promote the Progress of Science and useful Arts, by securing for limited Times to Authors and Inventors the exclusive Right to their respective Writings and Discoveries;

[9] To constitute Tribunals inferior to the supreme Court;

[10] To define and punish Piracies and Felonies committed on the high Seas, and Offenses against the Law of Nations;

[11] To declare War, grant Letters of Marque and Reprisal, and make Rules concerning Captures on Land and Water;

[12] To raise and support Armies, but no Appropriation of Money to that Use shall be for a longer Term than two Years;

[13] To provide and maintain a Navy;

[14] To make Rules for the Government and Regulation of the land and naval Forces;

[15] To provide for calling forth the Militia to execute the Laws of the Union, suppress Insurrections and repel Invasions;

[16] To provide for organizing, arming, and disciplining, the Militia, and for governing such Part of them as may be employed in the Service of the United States, reserving to the States respectively, the Appointment of the Officers, and the Authority of training the Militia according to the discipline prescribed by Congress;

[17] To exercise exclusive Legislation in all Cases whatsoever, over such District (not exceeding ten Miles square) as may, by Cession of particular States, and the Acceptance of Congress, become the Seat of the Government of the United States, and to exercise like Authority over all Places purchased by the Consent of the Legislature of the State in which the Same shall be, for the Erection of Forts, Magazines, Arsenals, dock-Yards, and other needful Buildings;—And

[18] To make all Laws which shall be necessary and proper for carrying into Execution the foregoing Powers, and all other Powers vested by this Constitution in the Government of the United States, or in any Department or Officer thereof.

Section 9. [1] The Migration or Importation of Such Persons as any of the States now existing shall think proper to admit, shall not be prohibited by the Congress prior to the Year one thousand eight hundred and eight, but a Tax or duty may be imposed on such Importation, not exceeding ten dollars for each Person.

[2] The privilege of the Writ of Habeas Corpus shall not be suspended, unless when in Cases of Rebellion or Invasion the public Safety may require it.

[3] No Bill of Attainder or ex post facto Law shall be passed.

[4] No Capitation, or other direct, Tax shall be laid, unless in Proportion to the Census or Enumeration herein before directed to be taken.

[5] No Tax or Duty shall be laid on Articles exported from any State.

[6] No Preference shall be given by any Regulation of Commerce or Revenue to the Ports of one State over those of another: nor shall Vessels bound to, or from, one State be obliged to enter, clear, or pay Duties in another.

[7] No money shall be drawn from the Treasury, but in Consequence of Appropriations made by Law; and a regular Statement and Account of the Receipts and Expenditures of all public Money shall be published from time to time.

[8] No Title of Nobility shall be granted by the United States: And no Person holding any Office of Profit or Trust under them, shall, without the Consent of the Congress, accept of any present, Emolument, Office, or Title, of any kind whatever, from any King, Prince, or foreign State.

Section 10. [1] No State shall enter into any Treaty, Alliance, or Confederation; grant Letters of Marque and Reprisal; coin Money; emit Bills of Credit; make any Thing but gold and silver Coin a Tender in Payment of Debts; pass any Bill of Attainder, ex post facto Law, or Law impairing the Obligation of Contracts, or grant any Title of Nobility.

[2] No State shall, without the Consent of the Congress, lay any Imposts or Duties on Imports or Exports, except what may be absolutely necessary for executing it's inspection Laws: and the net Produce of all Duties and Imposts, laid by any State on Imports or Exports, shall be for the Use of the Treasury of the United States; and all such Laws shall be subject to the Revision and Controul of the Congress.

[3] No State shall, without the Consent of Congress, lay any Duty of Tonnage, keep Troops, or Ships of War in time of Peace, enter into any Agreement or Compact with another State, or with a foreign Power, or engage in War, unless actually invaded, or in such imminent Danger as will not admit of delay.

ARTICLE II

Section 1. [1] The executive Power shall be vested in a President of the United States of America. He shall hold his Office during the Term of four Years, and, together with the Vice President, chosen for the same Term, be elected, as follows:

[2] Each State shall appoint, in such Manner as the Legislature thereof may direct, a Number of Electors, equal to the whole Number of Senators and Representatives to which the State may be entitled in the Congress; but no Senator or Representative, or Person holding an Office of Trust or Profit under the United States, shall be appointed an Elector.

[3] The Electors shall meet in their respective States, and vote by Ballot for two Persons, of whom one at least shall not be an Inhabitant of the same State with themselves. And they shall make a List of all the Persons voted for, and of the Number of Votes for each; which List they shall sign and certify, and transmit sealed to the Seat of the Government of the United States, directed to the President of the Senate. The President of the Senate shall, in the Presence of the Senate and House of Representatives, open all the Certificates, and the Votes shall then be counted. The Person having the greatest Number of Votes shall be the President, if such Number be a Majority of the whole Number of Electors appointed; and if there be more than one who have such Majority, and have an equal Number of Votes, then the House of Representatives shall immediately chuse by Ballot one of them for President; and if no Person have a Majority, then from the five highest on the List the said House shall in like Manner chuse the President. But in chusing the President, the Votes shall be taken by States the Representation from each State having one Vote; A quorum for this Purpose shall consist of a Member or Members from two thirds of the States, and a Majority of all the States shall be necessary to a Choice. In every Case, after the Choice of the President, the Person having the greatest Number of Votes of the Electors shall be the Vice President. But if there should remain two or more who have equal Votes, the Senate shall chuse from them by Ballot the Vice President.

[4] The Congress may determine the Time of chusing the Electors, and the Day on which they shall give their Votes; which Day shall be the same throughout the United States.

[5] No person except a natural born Citizen, or a Citizen of the United States, at the time of the Adoption of this Constitution, shall be eligible to the Office of President; neither shall any Person be eligible to that Office who shall not have attained to the Age of thirty five Years, and been fourteen Years a Resident within the United States.

[6] In case of the removal of the President from Office, or of his Death, Resignation or Inability to discharge the Powers and Duties of the said Office, the Same shall devolve on the Vice President, and the Congress may by Law provide for the Case of Removal, Death, Resignation or Inability, both of the President and Vice President,

declaring what Officer shall then act as President, and such Officer shall act accordingly, until the Disability be removed, or a President shall be elected.

[7] The President shall, at stated Times, receive for his Services, a Compensation, which shall neither be increased nor diminished during the Period for which he shall have been elected, and he shall not receive within that Period any other Emolument from the United States, or any of them.

[8] Before he enter on the Execution of his Office, he shall take the following Oath or Affirmation: "I do solemnly swear (or affirm) that I will faithfully execute the Office of President of the United States, and will to the best of my Ability, preserve, protect and defend the Constitution of the United States."

Section 2. [1] The President shall be Commander in Chief of the Army and Navy of the United States, and of the militia of the several States, when called into the actual Service of the United States; he may require the Opinion, in writing, of the principal Officer in each of the Executive Departments, upon any Subject relating to the Duties of their respective Offices, and he shall have Power to grant Reprieves and Pardons for Offenses against the United States, except in Cases of Impeachment.

[2] He shall have Power, by and with the Advice and Consent of the Senate to make Treaties, provided two thirds of the Senators present concur; and he shall nominate, and by and with the Advice and Consent of the Senate, shall appoint Ambassadors, other public Ministers and Consuls, Judges of the supreme Court, and all other Officers of the United States, whose Appointments are not herein otherwise provided for, and which shall be established by Law; but the Congress may by Law vest the Appointment of such inferior Officers, as they think proper, in the President alone, in the Courts of Law, or in the Heads of Departments.

[3] The President shall have Power to fill up all Vacancies that may happen during the Recess of the Senate, by granting Commissions which shall expire at the End of their next Session.

Section 3. He shall from time to time give to the Congress Information of the State of the Union, and recommend to their Consideration such Measures as he shall judge necessary and expedient; he may, on extraordinary Occasions, convene both Houses, or either of them, and in Case of Disagreement between them, with Respect to the Time of Adjournment, he may adjourn them to such Time as he shall think proper; he shall receive Ambassadors and other public Ministers; he shall take Care that the Laws be faithfully executed, and shall Commission all the Officers of the United States.

Section 4. The President, Vice President and all civil Officers of the United States, shall be removed from Office on Impeachment for, and Conviction of, Treason, Bribery, or other high Crimes and Misdemeanors.

ARTICLE III

Section 1. The judicial Power of the United States, shall be vested in one supreme Court, and in such inferior Courts as the Congress may from time to time ordain and establish. The Judges, both of the supreme and inferior Courts, shall hold their Offices during good Behaviour, and shall, at stated Times, receive for their Services a Compensation, which shall not be diminished during their Continuance in Office.

Section 2. [1] The judicial Power shall extend to all Cases, in Law and Equity, arising under this Constitution, the Laws of the United States, and Treaties made, or which shall be made, under their Authority;—to all Cases affecting Ambassadors, other public Ministers and Consuls;—to all Cases of admiralty and maritime Jurisdiction;—to Controversies to which the United States shall be a Party;—to Controversies between two or more States;—between a State and Citizens of another State;—between Citizens of different States;—between Citizens of the same State claiming Lands under the Grants of different States, and between a State, or the Citizens thereof, and foreign States, Citizens or Subjects.

[2] In all Cases affecting Ambassadors, other public Ministers and Consuls, and those in which a State shall be a Party, the supreme Court shall have original Jurisdiction. In all the other Cases before mentioned, the supreme Court shall have appellate Jurisdiction, both as to Law and Fact, with such Exceptions, and under such Regulations as the Congress shall make.

[3] The trial of all Crimes, except in Cases of Impeachment, shall be by Jury; and such Trial shall be held in the State where the said Crimes shall have been committed; but when not committed within any State, the Trial shall be at such Place or Places as the Congress may by Law have directed.

Section 3. [1] Treason against the United States, shall consist only in levying War against them, or, in adhering to their Enemies, giving them Aid and Comfort. No Person shall be convicted of Treason unless on the Testimony of two Witnesses to the same overt Act, or on Confession in open Court.

[2] The Congress shall have Power to declare the Punishment of Treason, but no Attainder of Treason shall work Corruption of Blood, or Forfeiture except during the Life of the Person attainted.

ARTICLE IV

Section 1. Full Faith and Credit shall be given in each State to the public Acts, Records, and judicial Proceedings of every other State. And the Congress may by general Laws prescribe the Manner in which such Acts, Records and Proceedings shall be proved, and the Effect thereof.

Section 2. [1] The Citizens of each State shall be entitled to all Privileges and Immunities of Citizens in the several States.

[2] A Person charged in any State with Treason, Felony, or other Crime, who shall flee from Justice, and be found in another State, shall on demand of the executive Authority of the State from which he fled, be delivered up, to be removed to the State having Jurisdiction of the Crime.

[3] No Person held to Service or Labour in one State, under the Laws thereof, escaping into another, shall, in Consequence of any Law or Regulation therein, be discharged from such Service or Labour, but shall be delivered up on Claim of the Party to whom such Service or Labour may be due.

Section 3. [1] New States may be admitted by the Congress into this Union; but no new State shall be formed or erected within the Jurisdiction of any other State; nor any State be formed by the Junction of two or more States, or Parts of States, without the Consent of the Legislatures of the States concerned as well as of the Congress.

[2] The Congress shall have Power to dispose of and make all needful Rules and Regulations respecting the Territory or other Property belonging to the United States; and nothing in this Constitution shall be so construed as to Prejudice any Claims of the United States, or of any particular State.

Section 4. The United States shall guarantee to every State in this Union a Republican Form of Government, and shall protect each of them against Invasion; and on Application of the Legislature, or of the Executive (when the Legislature cannot be convened) against domestic Violence.

ARTICLE V

The Congress, whenever two thirds of both Houses shall deem it necessary, shall propose Amendments to this Constitution, or, on the Application of the Legislatures of two thirds of the several States, shall call a Convention for proposing Amendments, which, in either Case, shall be valid to all Intents and Purposes, as part of this Constitution, when ratified by the Legislatures of three fourths of the several States, or by Conventions in three fourths thereof, as the one or the other Mode of Ratification may be proposed by the Congress; Provided that no Amendment which may be made prior to the Year One thousand eight hundred and eight shall in any Manner affect the first and fourth Clauses in the Ninth Section of the first Article; and that no State, without its Consent, shall be deprived of its equal Suffrage in the Senate.

ARTICLE VI

[1] All Debts contracted and Engagements entered into, before the Adoption of this Constitution shall be as valid against the United States under this Constitution, as under the Confederation.

[2] This Constitution, and the Laws of the United States which shall be made in Pursuance thereof; and all Treaties made, or which shall be made, under the Authority of the United States, shall be the supreme Law of the Land; and the Judges in every State shall be bound thereby, any Thing in the Constitution or Laws of any State to the Contrary notwithstanding.

[3] The Senators and Representatives before mentioned, and the Members of the several State Legislatures, and all executive and judicial Officers, both of the United States and of the several States, shall be bound by Oath or Affirmation, to support this Constitution; but no religious Test shall ever be required as a Qualification to any Office or public Trust under the United States.

ARTICLE VII

The Ratification of the Conventions of nine States shall be sufficient for the Establishment of this Constitution between the States so ratifying the Same.

AMENDMENTS OF THE CONSTITUTION OF THE UNITED STATES OF AMERICA, PROPOSED BY CONGRESS AND RATIFIED BY THE LEGISLATURES OF THE SEVERAL STATES PURSUANT TO THE FIFTH ARTICLE OF THE ORIGINAL CONSTITUTION.

AMENDMENT I [1791]

Congress shall make no law respecting an establishment of religion, or prohibiting the free exercise thereof; or abridging the freedom of speech, or of the press; or the right of the people peaceably to assemble, and to petition the Government for a redress of grievances.

AMENDMENT II [1791]

A well regulated Militia, being necessary to the security of a free State, the right of the people to keep and bear Arms, shall not be infringed.

AMENDMENT III [1791]

No Soldier shall, in time of peace be quartered in any house, without the consent of the Owner, nor in time of war, but in a manner to be prescribed by law.

AMENDMENT IV [1791]

The right of the people to be secure in their persons, houses, papers, and effects, against unreasonable searches and seizures, shall not be violated, and no Warrants shall issue, but upon probable cause, supported by Oath or affirmation and particularly describing the place to be searched, and the persons or things to be seized.

AMENDMENT V [1791]

No person shall be held to answer for a capital, or otherwise infamous crime, unless on a presentment or indictment of a Grand Jury, except in cases arising in the land or naval forces, or in the Militia, when in actual service in time of War or public danger; nor shall any person be subject for the same offence to be twice put in jeopardy of life or limb; nor shall be compelled in any criminal case to be a witness against himself, nor be deprived of life, liberty, or property, without due process of law; nor shall private property be taken for public use, without just compensation.

AMENDMENT VI [1791]

In all criminal prosecutions, the accused shall enjoy the right to a speedy and public trial, by an impartial jury of the State and district wherein the crime shall have been committed, which district shall have been previously ascertained by law, and to be informed of the nature and cause of the accusation; to be confronted with the witnesses against him; to have compulsory process for obtaining witnesses in his favor, and to have the Assistance of Counsel for his defence.

AMENDMENT VII [1791]

In Suits at common law, where the value in controversy shall exceed twenty dollars, the right of trial by jury shall be preserved, and no fact tried by a jury, shall be otherwise re-examined in any Court of the United States, than according to the rules of the common law.

AMENDMENT VIII [1791]

Excessive bail shall not be required, nor excessive fines imposed, nor cruel and unusual punishments inflicted.

AMENDMENT IX [1791]

The enumeration in the Constitution, of certain rights, shall not be construed to deny or disparage others retained by the people.

AMENDMENT X [1791]

The powers not delegated to the United States by the Constitution, nor prohibited by it to the States, are reserved to the States respectively, or to the people.

AMENDMENT XI [1798]

The Judicial power of the United States shall not be construed to extend to any suit in law or equity, commenced or prosecuted against one of the United States by Citizens of another State, or by Citizens or Subjects of any Foreign State.

AMENDMENT XII [1804]

The Electors shall meet in their respective states and vote by ballot for President and Vice-President, one of whom, at least, shall not be an inhabitant of the same state with themselves; they shall name in their ballots the person voted for as President, and in distinct ballots the person voted for as Vice-President, and they shall make distinct lists of all persons voted for as President, and of all persons voted for as Vice-President, and of the number of votes for each, which lists they shall sign and certify, and transmit sealed to the seat of the government of the United States, directed to the President of the Senate;—The President of the Senate shall, in the presence of the Senate and House of Representatives, open all the certificates and the votes shall then be counted;—The person having the greatest number of votes for President, shall be the President, if such number be a majority of the whole number of Electors appointed; and if no person have such majority, then from the persons having the highest numbers not exceeding three on the list of those voted for as President, the House of Representatives shall choose immediately, by ballot, the President. But in choosing the President, the votes shall be taken by states, the representation from each state having one vote; a quorum for this purpose shall consist of a member or members from two-thirds of the states, and a majority of all the states shall be necessary to a choice. And if the House of Representatives shall not choose a President whenever the right of choice shall devolve upon them before the fourth day of March next following, then the Vice-President shall act as President, as in the case of the death or other constitutional disability of the President.—The person having the greatest number of votes as Vice-President, shall be the Vice-President, if such number be a majority of the whole number of Electors appointed, and if no person have a majority, then from the two highest numbers on the list, the Senate shall choose the Vice-President; a quorum for the purpose shall consist of two-thirds of the whole number of Senators, and a majority of the whole number shall be necessary to a choice. But no person constitutionally ineligible to the office of President shall be eligible to that of Vice-President of the United States.

AMENDMENT XIII [1865]

Section 1. Neither slavery nor involuntary servitude, except as a punishment for crime whereof the party shall have been duly convicted, shall exist within the United States, or any place subject to their jurisdiction.

Section 2. Congress shall have power to enforce this article by appropriate legislation.

AMENDMENT XIV [1868]

Section 1. All persons born or naturalized in the United States, and subject to the jurisdiction thereof, are citizens of the United States and of the State wherein they reside. No State shall make or enforce any law which shall abridge the privileges or immunities of citizens of the United States; nor shall any State deprive any person of life, liberty, or property, without due process of law; nor deny to any person within its jurisdiction the equal protection of the laws.

Section 2. Representatives shall be apportioned among the several States according to their respective numbers, counting the whole number of persons in each State, excluding Indians not taxed. But when the right to vote at any election for the choice of electors for President and Vice President of the United States, Representatives in Congress, the Executive and Judicial officers of a State, or the members of the Legislature thereof, is denied to any of the male inhabitants of such State, being twenty-one years of age, and citizens of the United States, or in any way abridged, except for participation in rebellion, or other crime, the basis of representation therein shall be reduced in the proportion which the number of such male citizens shall bear to the whole number of male citizens twenty-one years of age in such State.

Section 3. No person shall be a Senator or Representative in Congress, or elector of President and Vice President, or hold any office, civil or military, under the United States, or under any State, who having previously taken an oath, as a member of Congress, or as an officer of the United States, or as a member of any State legislature, or as an executive or judicial officer of any State, to support the Constitution of the United States, shall have engaged in insurrection or rebellion against the same, or given aid or comfort to the enemies thereof. But Congress may by a vote of two-thirds of each House, remove such disability.

Section 4. The validity of the public debt of the United States, authorized by law, including debts incurred for payment of pensions and bounties for services in suppressing insurrection or rebellion, shall not be questioned. But neither the United States nor any State shall assume or pay any debt or obligation incurred in aid of insurrection or rebellion against the United States, or any claim for the loss or emancipation of any slave; but all such debts, obligations and claims shall be held illegal and void.

Section 5. The Congress shall have power to enforce, by appropriate legislation, the provisions of this article.

AMENDMENT XV [1870]

Section 1. The right of citizens of the United States to vote shall not be denied or abridged by the United States or by any State on account of race, color, or previous condition of servitude.

Section 2. The Congress shall have power to enforce this article by appropriate legislation.

AMENDMENT XVI [1913]

The Congress shall have power to lay and collect taxes on incomes, from whatever source derived, without apportionment among the several States, and without regard to any census or enumeration.

Amendment XVII [1913]

[1] The Senate of the United States shall be composed of two Senators from each State, elected by the people thereof, for six years; and each Senator shall have one vote. The electors in each State shall have the qualifications requisite for electors of the most numerous branch of the State legislatures.

[2] When vacancies happen in the representation of any State in the Senate, the executive authority of such State shall issue writs of election to fill such vacancies: *Provided,* That the legislature of any State may empower the executive thereof to make temporary appointments until the people fill the vacancies by election as the legislature may direct.

[3] This amendment shall not be so construed as to affect the election or term of any Senator chosen before it becomes valid as part of the Constitution.

AMENDMENT XVIII [1919]

Section 1. After one year from the ratification of this article the manufacture, sale, or transportation of intoxicating liquors within, the importation thereof into, or the exportation thereof from the United States and all territory subject to the jurisdiction thereof for beverage purposes is hereby prohibited.

Section 2. The Congress and the several States shall have concurrent power to enforce this article by appropriate legislation.

Section 3. This article shall be inoperative unless it shall have been ratified as an amendment to the Constitution by the legislatures of the several States, as provided in the Constitution, within seven years from the date of the submission hereof to the States by the Congress.

AMENDMENT XIX [1920]

[1] The right of citizens of the United States to vote shall not be denied or abridged by the United States or by any State on account of sex.

[2] Congress shall have power to enforce this article by appropriate legislation.

AMENDMENT XX [1933]

Section 1. The terms of the President and the Vice President shall end at noon on the 20th day of January, and the terms of Senators and Representatives at noon on the 3d day of January, of the years in which such terms would have ended if this article had not been ratified; and the terms of their successors shall then begin.

Section 2. The Congress shall assemble at least once in every year, and such meeting shall begin at noon on the 3d day of January, unless they shall by law appoint a different day.

Section 3. If, at the time fixed for the beginning of the term of the President, the President elect shall have died, the Vice President elect shall become President. If a President shall not have been chosen before the time fixed for the beginning of his term, or if the President elect shall have failed to qualify, then the Vice President elect shall act as President until a President shall have qualified; and the Congress may by law provide for the case wherein neither a President elect nor a Vice President elect shall have qualified, declaring who shall then act as President, or the manner in which one who is to act shall be selected, and such person shall act accordingly until a President or Vice President shall have qualified.

Section 4. The Congress may by law provide for the case of the death of any of the persons from whom the House of Representatives may choose a President whenever the right of choice shall have devolved upon them, and for the case of the death of any of the persons from whom the Senate may choose a Vice President whenever the right of choice shall have devolved upon them.

Section 5. Sections 1 and 2 shall take effect on the 15th day of October following the ratification of this article.

Section 6. This article shall be inoperative unless it shall have been ratified as an amendment to the Constitution by the legislatures of three-fourths of the several States within seven years from the date of its submission.

AMENDMENT XXI [1933]

Section 1. The eighteenth article of amendment to the Constitution of the United States is hereby repealed.

Section 2. The transportation or importation into any State, Territory, or possession of the United States for delivery or use therein of intoxicating liquors, in violation of the laws thereof, is hereby prohibited.

Section 3. This article shall be inoperative unless it shall have been ratified as an amendment to the Constitution by conventions in the several States, as provided in the Constitution, within seven years from the date of the submission hereof to the States by the Congress.

AMENDMENT XXII [1951]

Section 1. No person shall be elected to the office of the President more than twice, and no person who has held the office of President, or acted as President, for more than two years of a term to which some other person was elected President shall be elected to the office of President more than once. But this Article shall not apply to any person holding the office of President when this Article was proposed by the Congress, and shall not prevent any person who may be holding the office of President, or acting as President, during the term within which this Article becomes operative from holding the office of President or acting as President during the remainder of such term.

Section 2. This article shall be inoperative unless it shall have been ratified as an amendment to the Constitution by the legislatures of three-fourths of the several States within seven years from the date of its submission to the States by the Congress.

AMENDMENT XXIII [1961]

Section 1. The District constituting the seat of Government of the United States shall appoint in such manner as the Congress may direct:

A number of electors of President and Vice President equal to the whole number of Senators and Representatives in Congress to which the District would be entitled if it were a State, but in no event more than the least populous state; they shall be in addition to those appointed by the states, but they shall be considered, for the purposes of the election of President and Vice President, to be electors appointed by a state; and they shall meet in the District and perform such duties as provided by the twelfth article of amendment.

Section 2. The Congress shall have power to enforce this article by appropriate legislation.

AMENDMENT XXIV [1964]

Section 1. The right of citizens of the United States to vote in any primary or other election for President or Vice President, for electors for President or Vice President, or for Senator or Representative in Congress, shall not be denied or abridged by the United States or any State by reason of failure to pay any poll tax or other tax.

Section 2. The Congress shall have power to enforce this article by appropriate legislation.

AMENDMENT XXV [1967]

Section 1. In case of the removal of the President from office or of his death or resignation, the Vice President shall become President.

Section 2. Whenever there is a vacancy in the office of the Vice President, the President shall nominate a Vice President who shall take office upon confirmation by a majority vote of both Houses of Congress.

Section 3. Whenever the President transmits to the President pro tempore of the Senate and the Speaker of the House of Representatives his written declaration that he is unable to discharge the powers and duties of his office, and until he transmits to them a written declaration to the contrary, such powers and duties shall be discharged by the Vice President as Acting President.

Section 4. Whenever the Vice President and a majority of either the principal officers of the executive departments or of such other body as Congress may by law provide, transmit to the President pro tempore of the Senate and the Speaker of the House of

Representatives their written declaration that the President is unable to discharge the powers and duties of his office, the Vice President shall immediately assume the powers and duties of the office as Acting President.

Thereafter, when the President transmits to the President pro tempore of the Senate and the Speaker of the House of Representatives his written declaration that no inability exists, he shall resume the powers and duties of his office unless the Vice President and a majority of either the principal officers of the executive department or of such other body as Congress may by law provide, transmit within four days to the President pro tempore of the Senate and the Speaker of the House of Representatives their written declaration that the President is unable to discharge the powers and duties of his office. Thereupon Congress shall decide the issue, assembling within forty-eight hours for that purpose if not in session. If the Congress, within twenty-one days after receipt of the latter written declaration, or, if Congress is not in session, within twenty-one days after Congress is required to assemble, determines by two-thirds vote of both Houses that the President is unable to discharge the powers and duties of his office, the Vice President shall continue to discharge the same as Acting President; otherwise, the President shall resume the powers and duties of his office.

AMENDMENT XXVI [1971]

Section 1. The right of citizens of the United States, who are eighteen years of age or older, to vote shall not be denied or abridged by the United States or by any State on account of age.

Section 2. The Congress shall have power to enforce this article by appropriate legislation.

AMENDMENT XXVII [1992]

No law, varying the compensation for the services of the Senators and Representatives, shall take effect, until an election of Representatives shall have intervened.

Table of Cases

Index

References are to Pages